Annual Abstract of Statistics

2007 edition

No 143

Editor: Dave Sharp

Office for National Statistics

palgrave
macmillan

This publication is also available at the National Statistics website:
www.statistics.gov.uk

For any other use of this material please apply for a Click-Use Licence for core material at
www.opsi.gov.uk/click-use/system/online/pLogin.asp or by writing to:

Office of Public Sector Information
Information Policy Team
St Clements House
2–16 Colegate
Norwich NR3 1BQ
Fax: 01603 723000
E-mail: **hmsolicensing@cabinet-office.x.gsi.gov.uk**

First published 2007 by
PALGRAVE MACMILLAN

Houndmills, Basingstoke, Hampshire RG21 6XS and 175 Fifth Avenue, New York, NY 10010, USA

Companies and representatives throughout the world.

PALGRAVE MACMILLAN is the global academic imprint of the Palgrave Macmillan division of St. Martin's Press, LLC and of Palgrave Macmillan Ltd. Macmillan® is a registered trademark in the United States, United Kingdom and other countries. Palgrave is a registered trademark in the European Union and other countries.

ISBN 978–1–4039–9392–2

ISSN 0072–5730

This book is printed on paper suitable for recycling and made from fully managed and sustained forest sources.

A catalogue record for this book is available from the British Library.

10   9   8   7   6   5   4   3   2   1
15   14   13   12   11   10   09   08   07   06

Printed and bound in Great Britain by
Hobbs the Printers, Totton, Hampshire.

A National Statistics publication
National Statistics are produced to high professional standards set out in the National Statistics Code of Practice. They are produced free from political influence.

About the Office for National Statistics
The Office for National Statistics (ONS) is the government agency responsible for compiling, analysing and disseminating economic, social and demographic statistics about the United Kingdom. It also administers the statutory registration of births, marriages and deaths in England and Wales.

The Director of ONS is also the National Statistician and the Registrar General for England and Wales.

Contact points
For enquiries about this publication, contact Core Table Unit.
Tel: 01633 655851
E-mail: ctu@ons.gsi.gov.uk

For general enquiries, contact the National Statistics Customer Contact Centre.
Tel: 0845 601 3034
(minicom: 01633 812399)
E-mail: info@statistics.gsi.gov.uk
Fax: 01633 652747
Post: Room 1015, Government Buildings,
              Cardiff Road, Newport NP10 8XG

You can also find National Statistics on the Internet at:
www.statistics.gov.uk

Contents

Contents

Contents

Contents

Contents

Contents

Contents

Acknowledgements

The Editor would like to thank the following people for their help in producing this book:

Production team:	Anna Donabie
	Melanie Edwards
	Daniel Hern
	Ian Macrory
	Dilys Rosen

Contributors

The Editor also wishes to thank all his colleagues in ONS, the rest of the Government Statistical Service and all contributors in other organisations for their generous support and helpful comments, without whose help this publication would not be possible.

Typesetting by the **Desktop Publishing Unit**, ONS Titchfield.

Units of measurement

Length

1 millimetre (mm)		= 0.03937 inch
1 centimetre (cm)	= 10 millimetres	= 0.3937 inch
1 metre (m)	= 1,000 millimetres	= 1.094 yards
1 kilometre (km)	= 1,000 metres	= 0.6214 mile
1 inch (in.)		= 25.40 millimetres or 2.540 centimetres
1 foot (ft.)	= 12 inches	= 0.3048 metre
1 yard (yd.)	= 3 feet	= 0.9144 metre
1 mile	= 1,760 yards	= 1.609 kilometres

Area

1 square millimetre (mm²)		= 0.001550 square inch
1 square metre (m²)	= one million square millimetres	= 1.196 square yards
1 hectare (ha)	= 10,000 square metres	= 2.471 acres
1 square kilometre (km²)	= one million square metres	= 247.1 acres
1 square inch (sq. in.)		= 645.2 square millimetres or 6.452 square centimetres
1 square foot (sq. ft.)	= 144 square inches	= 0.09290 square metre or 929.0 square centimetres
1 square yard (sq. yd.)	= 9 square feet	= 0.8361 square metre
1 acre	= 4,840 square yards	4,046 square metres or 0.4047 hectare
1 square mile (sq. mile)	= 640 acres	= 2.590 square kilometres or 259.0 hectares

Volume

1 cubic centimetre (cm³)		= 0.06102 cubic inch
1 cubic decimetre (dm³)	= 1,000 cubic centimetres	= 0.03531 cubic foot
1 cubic metre (m³)	= one million cubic centimetres	= 1.308 cubic yards
1 cubic inch (cu.in.)		=16.39 cubic centimetres
1 cubic foot (cu. ft.)	= 1,728 cubic inches	= 0.02832 cubic metre or 28.32 cubic decimetres
1 cubic yard (cu. yd.)	= 27 cubic feet	= 0.7646 cubic metre

Capacity

1 litre (l)	= 1 cubic decimetre	= 0.2200 gallon
1 hectolitre (hl)	= 100 litres	= 22.00 gallons
1 pint		= 0.5682 litre
1 quart	= 2 pints	= 1.137 litres
1 gallon	= 8 pints	= 4.546 litres
1 bulk barrel	= 36 gallons (gal.)	= 1.637 hectolitres

Weight

1 gram (g)		= 0.03527 ounce avoirdupois
1 hectogram (hg)	= 100 grams	= 3.527 ounces or 0.2205 pound
1 kilogram (kg)	= 1,000 grams or 10 hectograms	= 2.205 pounds
1 tonne (t)	= 1,000 kilograms	= 1.102 short tons or 0.9842 long ton
1 ounce avoirdupois (oz.)	= 437.5 grains	= 28.35 grams
1 pound avoirdupois (lb.)	= 16 ounces	= 0.4536 kilogram
1 hundredweight (cwt.)	= 112 pounds	= 50.80 kilograms
1 short ton	= 2,000 pounds	= 907.2 kilograms or 0.9072 tonne
1 long ton (referred to as ton)	= 2,240 pounds	= 1,016 kilograms or 1.016 tonnes
1 ounce troy	= 480 grains	= 31.10 grams

Energy

British thermal unit (Btu)	= 0.2520 kilocalorie (kcal) = 1.055 kilojoule (kj)
Therm	= 10^5 British thermal units = 25,200 kcal = 105,506 kj
Megawatt hour (MWh)	= 10^6 watt hours (Wh)
Gigawatt hour (GWh)	= 10^6 kilowatt hours = 34,121 therms

Food and drink

Butter	23,310 litres milk	= 1 tonne butter (average)
Cheese	10,070 litres milk	= 1 tonne cheese
Condensed milk	2,550 litres milk	= 1 tonne full cream condensed milk
	2,953 litres skimmed milk	= 1 tonne skimmed condensed milk
Milk	1 million litres	= 1,030 tonnes
Milk powder	8,054 litres milk	= 1 tonne full cream milk powder
	10,740 litres skimmed milk	= 1 tonne skimmed milk powder
Eggs	17,126 eggs	= 1 tonne (approximate)
Sugar	100 tonnes sugar beet	= 92 tonnes refined sugar
	100 tonnes cane sugar	= 96 tonnes refined sugar

Shipping

Gross tonnage	= The total volume of all the enclosed spaces of a vessel, the unit of measurement being a 'ton' of 100 cubic feet.
Deadweight tonnage	= Deadweight tonnage is the total weight in tons of 2,240 lb. that a ship can legally carry, that is the total weight of cargo, bunkers, stores and crew.

Introduction

Welcome to the 2007 edition of the *Annual Abstract of Statistics*. This compendium draws together statistics from a wide range of official and other authoritative sources. Their help is gratefully acknowledged.

Regional information, supplementary to the national figures in *Annual Abstract*, appear in *Regional Trends*. The latest edition of *Regional Trends* is available electronically on the National Statistics Website free of charge. This can be accessed from the *Regional Trends* entry under the Compendia and Reference theme, or directly at: www.statistics.gov.uk/statbase/product. asp?vlnk=14356. Earlier editions are available via Palgrave Macmillan.

Current data for many of the series appearing in this Annual Abstract are contained in other ONS publications, such as *Economic & Labour Market Review, Monthly Digest of Statistics, Population Trends, Health Statistics Quarterly and Financial Statistics*. All are published by Palgrave Macmillan.

The name (and telephone number, where this is available) of the organisation providing the statistics are shown under each table. In addition, a list of Sources is given at the back of the book, which sets out the official publications or other sources to which further reference can be made.

Identification codes

The four-letter identification code at the top of each data column, or at the side of each row is the ONS reference for this series of data on our database. Please quote the relevant code if you contact us requiring any further information about the data. On some tables it is not possible to include these codes, so please quote the table number in these cases.

Definitions and Classification

Time Series
So far as possible annual totals are given throughout, but quarterly or monthly figures are given where these are more suitable to the type of series.

Explanatory notes
Most sections are preceded by explanatory notes which should be read in conjunction with the tables. Definitions and explanatory notes for many of the terms occurring in the *Annual Abstract* are also given in the *Annual Supplement to the Monthly Digest of Statistics*, published annually in the January edition. Detailed notes on items which appear in both the *Abstract* and *Financial Statistics* are given in an annual supplement to the latter entitled *Financial Statistics Explanatory Handbook*. The original sources listed in the Sources may also be consulted.

Standard Industrial Classification
A Standard Industrial Classification (SIC) was first introduced into the United Kingdom in 1948 for use in classifying business establishments and other statistical units by the type of economic activity in which they are engaged. The classification provides a framework for the collection, tabulation, presentation and analysis of data about economic activities. Its use promotes uniformity of data collected by various government departments and agencies. Since 1948 the classification has been revised in 1958, 1968, 1980, 1992, 2003 and 2007. One of the principal objectives of the 1980 revision was to eliminate differences from the activity classification issued by the Statistical Office of the European Communities (Eurostat) and entitled 'Nomenclature générale des activités économiques dans les Communautés Européennes', usually abbreviated to NACE. In 1990, the European Communities introduced a new statistical classification of economic activities (NACE Rev 1) by regulation. The regulation made it obligatory for the UK to introduce a new Standard Industrial Classification SIC(92), based on NACE Rev 1. UK SIC(92) was based exactly on NACE Rev 1 but, where it was thought necessary or helpful, a fifth digit was added to form subclasses of the NACE 1 four digit system. Classification systems need to be revised periodically because, over time, new products, processes and industries emerge. In January 2003, a minor revision of NACE Rev 1, known as NACE Rev 1.1, was published in the Official Journal of the European Communities.

Consequently, the UK was obliged to introduce a new Standard Industrial Classification, SIC(2003) consistent with NACE Rev 1.1. The UK took the opportunity of the 2003 revision also to update the national Subclasses. Full details are available in UK Standard Industrial Classification of Economic Activities 2003. Indexes to the UK Standard Industrial Classification of Economic Activities 2003. These are the most recent that are currently used. The most up to date version is the UK Standard Industrial Classification of Economic activities 2007 (SIC2007). However, this

Introduction

classification does not come into effect until 1 January 2008. For further information see http://www.statistics.gov.uk/methods_quality/sic/downloads/sic2007explanatorynotes.pdf

Revisions to contents

Some of the figures, particularly for the latest year, are provisional and may be revised in a subsequent issue of the *Annual Abstract*.

Symbols and conventions used

Change of basis

Where consecutive figures have been compiled on different bases and are not strictly comparable, a footnote is added indicating the nature of the difference.

Geographic coverage

Statistics relate mainly to the United Kingdom. Where figures relate to other areas this is indicated on the table.

Units of measurement

The various units of measurement used are listed following the Contents.

Rounding of figures

In tables where figures have been rounded to the nearest final digit, the constituent items may not add up exactly to the total.

Symbols

The following symbols have been used throughout:

.. = not available or not applicable (also information suppressed to avoid disclosure).

- = nil or less than half the final digit shown.

National Statistics Online: www.statistics.gov.uk

Web-based access to time series, cross sectional data and metadata from across the Government Statistical Service (GSS), is available using the site search and index functions from the homepage. Download many datasets, in whole or in part, or consult directory information for all GSS statistical resources, including censuses, surveys, periodicals and enquiry services. Information is posted as PDF electronic documents or in XLS and CSV formats, compatible with most spreadsheet packages.

Complete copies of this publication are available to download free of charge on the following web page:

www.statistics.gov.uk/statbase/product.asp?vlnk=94.

Contact point

The ONS welcomes any feedback on the content of the *Annual Abstract*, including comments on the format of the data and the selection of topics. Comments and requests for general information should be addressed to:

Core Table Unit

Social and Economic Micro-Analysis and Reporting Division
Room 2.101
Office for National Statistics
Government Buildings
Cardiff Road
Newport
South Wales NP10 8XG

or

Email: info@statistics.gov.uk
July 2007

Area

Chapter 1

Area

The United Kingdom (UK) comprises Great Britain and Northern Ireland. Great Britain comprises England, Wales and Scotland.

Physical Features

The United Kingdom (UK) constitutes the greater part of the British Isles. The largest of the islands is Great Britain. The next largest comprises Northern Ireland and the Irish Republic. Western Scotland is fringed by the large island chain known as the Hebrides, and to the north east of the Scottish mainland are the Orkney and Shetland Islands. All these, along with the Isle of Wight, Anglesey and the Isles of Scilly, form part of the UK, but the Isle of Man, in the Irish Sea and the Channel Islands, between Great Britain and France are largely self-governing and are not part of the UK. The UK is one of the 27 member states of the European Union following the accession of Bulgaria and Romania on 1 January 2007. With an area of about 243 000 sq km (about 94 000 sq miles), the UK is just under 1 000 km (about 600 miles) from the south coast to the extreme north of Scotland and just under 500 km (around 300 miles) across at the widest point.

- Highest mountain: Ben Nevis, in the highlands of Scotland, at 1 343 m (4 406 ft)

- Longest river: the Severn, 354 km (220 miles) long, which rises in central Wales and flows through Shrewsbury, Worcester and Gloucester in England to the Bristol Channel

- Largest lake: Lough Neagh, Northern Ireland, at 396 sqkm (153 sq miles)

- Deepest lake: Loch Morar in the Highlands of Scotland, 310 m (1 017 ft) deep

- Highest waterfall: Eas a'Chual Aluinn, from Glas Bheinn, in the highlands of Scotland, with a drop of 200 m (660 ft)

- Deepest cave: Ogof Ffynnon Ddu, Wales, at 308 m (1 010 ft) deep

- Most northerly point on the British mainland: Dunnet Head, north-east Scotland

- Most southerly point on the British mainland: Lizard Point, Cornwall

- Closest point to mainland continental Europe: Dover, Kent. The Channel Tunnel, which links England and France, is a little over 50 km (31 miles) long, of which nearly 38 km (24 miles) are actually under the Channel.

1.1 Area of the United Kingdom[1,2], 2005

	sq km		sq km
		Shropshire	3 197
		Staffordshire	2 620
United Kingdom	242 495	Warwickshire	1 975
		West Midlands (Met County)	902
Great Britain	228 945	Worcestershire	1 741
England and Wales	151 013	**East**	19 109
		Luton UA	43
		Peterborough UA	343
England	130 279	Southend-on-Sea UA	42
		Thurrock UA	163
North East	8 573		
		Bedfordshire	1 192
Darlington UA	197	Cambridgeshire	3 046
Hartlepool UA	94	Essex	3 465
Middlesbrough UA	54	Hertfordshire	1 643
Redcar and Cleveland UA	245	Norfolk	5 371
Stockton-on-Tees UA	204	Suffolk	3 800
Durham	2 226	**London**	1572
Northumberland	5 013		
Tyne and Wear (Met County)	540	Inner London	319
		Outer London	1 253
North West	14 106		
		South East	19 070
Blackburn with Darwen UA	137		
Blackpool UA	35	Bracknell Forest UA	109
Halton UA	79	Brighton and Hove UA	83
Warrington UA	181	Isle of Wight UA	380
		Medway UA	192
Cheshire	2 083	Milton Keynes UA	309
Cumbria	6 767	Portsmouth UA	40
Greater Manchester (Met County)	1 276	Reading UA	40
Lancashire	2 903	Slough UA	33
Merseyside (Met County)	645	Southampton UA	50
		West Berkshire UA	704
Yorkshire and The Humber	15 408	Windsor and Maidenhead UA	197
		Wokingham UA	179
East Riding of Yorkshire UA	2 408		
Kingston upon Hull, City of UA	71	Buckinghamshire	1 565
North East Lincolnshire UA	192	East Sussex	1 709
North Lincolnshire UA	846	Hampshire	3 679
York UA	272	Kent	3 544
		Oxfordshire	2 605
North Yorkshire	8 038	Surrey	1 662
South Yorkshire (Met County)	1 552	West Sussex	1 991
West Yorkshire (Met County)	2 029		
		South West	23 837
East Midlands	15 606		
		Bath and North East Somerset UA	346
Derby UA	78	Bournemouth UA	46
Leicester UA	73	Bristol, City of UA	110
Nottingham UA	75	North Somerset UA	374
Rutland UA	382	Plymouth UA	80
		Poole UA	65
Derbyshire	2 547	South Gloucestershire UA	497
Leicestershire	2 083	Swindon UA	230
Lincolnshire	5 921	Torbay UA	63
Northamptonshire	2 364		
Nottinghamshire	2 085	Cornwall and the Isles of Scilly	3 562
		Devon	6 564
West Midlands	12 998	Dorset	2 542
		Gloucestershire	2 653
Herefordshire, County of UA	2 180	Somerset	3 451
Stoke-on-Trent UA	93	Wiltshire	3 255
Telford and Wrekin UA	290		

1.1
continued

Area of the United Kingdom[1,2], 2005

	sq km		sq km
Wales	20 734	Dumfries & Galloway	6 426
		Dundee City	60
Blaenau Gwent	109	East Ayrshire	1 262
Bridgend	251	East Dunbartonshire	175
Caerphilly	277	East Lothian	679
Cardiff	140		
Carmarthenshire	2 371	East Renfrewshire	174
		Edinburgh, City of	263
Ceredigion	1 785	Eilean Siar[3]	3 055
Conwy	1 126	Falkirk	297
Denbighshire	837	Fife	1 325
Flintshire	438		
Gwynedd	2 535	Glasgow City	175
		Highland	25 684
Isle of Anglesey	711	Inverclyde	160
Merthyr Tydfil	111	Midlothian	354
Monmouthshire	849	Moray	2 238
Neath Port Talbot	441		
Newport	190	North Ayrshire	885
Pembrokeshire	1 619	North Lanarkshire	470
		Orkney Islands	990
Powys	5 181	Perth & Kinross	5 285
Rhondda, Cynon, Taff	424	Renfrewshire	262
Swansea	378	Scottish Borders	4 732
Torfaen	126		
The Vale of Glamorgan	331	Shetland Islands	1 467
Wrexham	504	South Ayrshire	1 222
		South Lanarkshire	1 772
		Stirling	2 187
Scotland	77 932	West Dunbartonshire	159
		West Lothian	428
Aberdeen City	186		
Aberdeenshire	6 313	**Northern Ireland**	13 576
Angus	2 182		
Argyll & Bute	6 908		
Clackmannanshire	159		

1 Figures relate to land area only.
2 The area measurements are a definitive set derived from boundaries maintained by Ordnance Survey and Ordnance Survey of Northern Ireland. The current measurements may differ from those published previously in tables, publications or other statistical outputs, even allowing for boundary changes or changes to the physical structure of the land because of improvements to the source of the data.
3 Formerly known as the Western Isles.

Source: Office for National Statistics

Parliamentary elections

2.1 Parliamentary elections[1]
United Kingdom

Thousands and percentages

		15 Oct 1964	31 Mar 1966	18 June 1970[1]	28 Feb 1974		10 Oct 1974	3 May 1979	9 June 1983	11 June 1987	9 April 1992	1 May 1997	7 June 2001	5 May 2005
United Kingdom														
Electorate	DZ5P	35 894	35 957	39 615	40 256	DZ6V	40 256	41 573	42 704	43 666	43 719	43 846	44 403	44 246
Average-electors per seat	DZ5T	57.0	57.1	62.9	63.4	DZ6R	63.4	65.5	66.7	67.2	67.2	66.5	67.4	68.5
Valid votes counted	DZ5X	27 657	27 265	28 345	31 340	DZ6N	29 189	31 221	30 671	32 530	33 614	31 286	26 367	27 149
As percentage of electorate	DZ63	77.1	75.8	71.5	77.9	DZ6J	72.5	75.1	71.8	74.5	76.7	71.4	59.4	61.4
England and Wales														
Electorate	DZ5Q	31 610	31 695	34 931	35 509	DZ6W	35 509	36 695	37 708	38 568	38 648	38 719	39 228	39 266
Average-electors per seat	DZ5U	57.8	57.9	63.9	64.3	DZ6S	64.3	66.5	67.2	68.8	68.8	68.0	68.9	69.0
Valid votes counted	DZ5Y	24 384	24 116	24 877	27 735	DZ6O	25 729	27 609	27 082	28 832	29 897	27 679	23 243	24 097
As percentage of electorate	DZ64	77.1	76.1	71.2	78.1	DZ6K	72.5	75.2	71.8	74.8	77.5	71.5	59.3	61.4
Scotland														
Electorate	DZ5R	3 393	3 360	3 659	3 705	DZ6X	3 705	3 837	3 934	3 995	3 929	3 949	3 984	3 840
Average-electors per seat	DZ5V	47.8	47.3	51.5	52.2	DZ6T	52.2	54.0	54.6	55.5	54.6	54.8	55.3	65.1
Valid votes counted	DZ5Z	2 635	2 553	2 688	2 887	DZ6P	2 758	2 917	2 825	2 968	2 931	2 817	2 313	2 334
As percentage of electorate	DZ65	77.6	76.0	73.5	77.9	DZ6L	74.5	76.0	71.8	74.3	74.2	71.3	58.1	60.8
Northern Ireland														
Electorate	DZ5S	891	902	1 025	1 027	DZ6Y	1 037	1 028	1 050	1 090	1 141	1 178	1 191	1 140
Average-electors per seat	DZ5W	74.2	75.2	85.4	85.6	DZ6U	86.4	85.6	61.8	64.1	67.1	65.4	66.2	63.3
Valid votes counted	DZ62	638	596	779	718	DZ6Q	702	696	765	730	785	791	810	718
As percentage of electorate	DZ66	71.7	66.1	76.0	69.9	DZ6M	67.7	67.7	72.9	67.0	68.8	67.1	68.0	62.9
Members of Parliament elected: (numbers)	DZV7	630	630	630	635	DZV8	635	635	650	650	651	659	659	646
Conservative	DZ67	303	253	330	296	DZ6D	276	339	396	375	336	165	166	198
Labour	DZ68	317	363	287	301	DZ6E	319	268	209	229	271	418	412	355
Liberal Democrat[2]	DZ69	9	12	6	14	DZ6F	13	11	23	22	20	46	52	62
Scottish National Party	DZ6A	–	–	1	7	DZ6G	11	2	2	3	3	6	5	6
Plaid Cymru	DZ6B	–	–	–	2	DZ6H	3	2	2	3	4	4	4	3
Other[3]	DZ6C	1	2	6	15	DZ6I	13	13	18	18	17	20	20	22

1 The Representation of the People Act 1969 lowered the minimum voting age from 21 to 18 years with effect from 16 February 1970.
2 Liberal before 1992. The figures for 1983 and 1987 include six and five MPs respectively who were elected for the Social Democratic Party.
3 Including the Speaker.

Source: University of Plymouth for the Electoral Commission: 01752 233205

2.2 Parliamentary by-elections
United Kingdom

	May 1997 - June 2001	General[1,2] Election May 1997	June 2001 - November 2004	General[1] Election June 2001	May 2005 - June 2006	General[1] Election May 2005
Numbers of by-elections	17		6		5	
Votes recorded						
By party (percentages)						
Conservative	27.0	25.1	17.7	21.2	21.1	28.0
Labour	29.7	40.1	40.8	58.3	23.2	26.8
Liberal Democrat	22.1	14.4	31.3	13.7	30.9	24.9
Scottish National Party	6.0	4.1	-	-	10.7	4.7
Plaid Cymru	2.5	2.3	2.7	2.1	1.1	0.5
Other	12.7	14.1	7.4	4.7	13.0	15.1
Total votes recorded (percentages)	100.0	100.0	100.0	100.0	100.0	100.0
(thousands)	435	723	140	205	158	171

1 Votes recorded in the same seats in the previous General Election.
2 Proportions of 'other' votes inflated by the fact that votes were cast for the retiring Speaker as 'The Speaker seeking re-election' and not as a party candidate.

Source: University of Plymouth for the Electoral Commission: 01752 233205

2.3 Devolved assembly elections
Wales and Scotland

Thousands and percentages

			6 May 1999	1 May 2003
Welsh Assembly				
Electorate	E28K		2 205	2 230
Average-electors per seat[1]	E28N		55.1	55.7
Valid votes counted	E28Q		1 023	850
As percentage of electorate	E28T		46.4	38.1
Members elected:[2] (numbers)	E2XI		60	60
Conservative	E2WG		9	11
Labour	E2WU		28	30
Liberal Democrat	E2WW		6	6
Plaid Cymru	E2X3		17	12
Other	E2WY		–	1
Scottish Parliament				
Electorate	E28L		4 024	3 879
Average-electors per seat[1]	E28O		55.1	53.1
Valid votes counted	E28R		2 342	1 916
As percentage of electorate	E28U		58.2	49.4
Members elected:[3] (numbers)	E2XJ		129	129
Conservative	E2WH		18	18
Labour	E2WV		56	50
Liberal Democrat	E2WX		17	17
Scottish National Party	E2X4		35	27
Other	E2WZ		3	17

1 This is the average in each first-past-the-post constituency. Additional members are then elected on the basis of a regional 'list' vote.
2 Comprising 40 from constituencies and 20 from the regional 'list'.
3 Comprising 73 from constituencies and 56 from the regional 'list'.

Source: University of Plymouth for the Electoral Commission: 01752 233205

2.4 Devolved assembly elections
Northern Ireland

Thousands and percentages

			25 June 1998	26 Nov 2003
Electorate	E28M		1 179	1 098
Average-electors per seat[1]	E28P		65.5	61.0
Valid votes counted	E28S		810	702
As percentage of electorate	E28V		68.7	64.0
Members elected: (numbers)	E2XK		108	108
Alliance Party	E2X5		6	6
SDLP	E2X6		24	18
Sinn Fein	E2X7		18	24
Democratic Unionist Party	E2X8		20	30
UK Unionist Party	E2X9		5	1
Ulster Unionist Party	E2XA		28	27
Other	E2X2		7	2

1 This is the average in each Westminster constituency. Six members are elected by single transferable vote (STV) in each constituency.

Source: University of Plymouth for the Electoral Commission: 01752 233205

International development

chapter 3

International development

Overseas development assistance

(Tables 3.1 and 3.2)

The Department for International Development (DFID) is the UK Government Department with lead responsibility for overseas development. DFID's aim is to eliminate poverty in poorer countries through achievement of the Millennium Development Goals (MDGs) by 2015, statistics relating to international development are published on a financial year basis and on a calendar year basis. Statistics on a calendar year basis allow comparisons of aid expenditure with other donor countries.

Aid flows can be measured before (gross) or after (net) deductions of repayments of principal on past loans. These tables show only the gross figures.

Aid is provided in two main ways: Bilateral funding is provided directly to partner countries while multilateral funding is provided through international organisations.

Funds can only be classified as multilateral if they are channelled through an organisation on a list in the OECD – Development Assistance Committee (DAC) Statistical Reporting Directives which identifies all multilateral organisations. This list also highlights some bodies that might appear to be multilateral but are actually bilateral (in particular this latter category includes some international non-governmental organisations such as the International Committee of the Red Cross and some Public-Private Partnerships such as the Global Alliance for Vaccines and Immunisation). The DAC list of multilaterals is updated annually based on members nominations; organisations must be engaged in development work to be classified as multilateral aid channels.[1]

While core funding to multilateral organisations is always classified as multilateral expenditure, additional funding channelled through multilaterals is often classified as bilateral expenditure. This would be the case in circumstances where a DFID country office transfers some money to a multilateral organisation (e.g. UN agency) for a particular programme in that country (or region). That is where DFID has control over what the money is being spent on and/or where it is being spent. Likewise, if DFID responds to an emergency appeal from an agency for a particular country or area, the funds will be

allocated as bilateral spend to that country or region. As a result, some organisations, such as UN agencies have some of their DFID funding classified as bilateral and some as multilateral.

DFID is planning to introduce a new activity reporting system from 2007. The new system will be more flexible and will allow more information to be gathered on aid flows, including details of how much of DFID's bilateral aid programme is channelled through multilateral organisations, and vice versa.

Table 3.1 shows the main groups of multilateral agencies, the International Development Association being the largest in the World Bank Group.

Bilateral assistance takes various forms:

Financial Aid – Poverty Reduction Budget Support (PRBS) – Funds provided to developing countries for them to spend in support of their expenditure programmes whose long-term objective is to reduce poverty; funds are spent using the overseas governments' own financial management, procurement and accountability systems to increase ownership and long term sustainability. This includes PRBS earmarked for a specific sector.

Other Financial Aid – Funding of projects and programmes such as Sector Wide Programmes not classified as PRBS. Financial aid in its broader sense covers all bilateral aid other than technical cooperation and administrative costs but in SID we separately categorise 'Grants and Other Aid in Kind', Humanitarian Assistance and DFID Debt Relief. Aid and Trade Provision which was previously identified in SID has now been merged into 'other financial aid' as it is a rapidly declining flow.

Technical Co-operation – Activities designed to enhance the knowledge, intellectual skills, technical expertise or the productive capability of people in recipient countries. It also covers funding of services which contribute to the design or implementation of development projects and programmes.

This assistance is mainly delivered through research and development, the use of consultants, training (generally overseas partners visiting the UK or elsewhere for a training programme) and employment of 'other Personnel' (non-DFID experts on fixed term contracts). This latter category is growing less significant over time as existing contracted staff reach the end of their assignments.

Grants and Other Aid in Kind – This category comprises support to the development work of UK and international Civil Society Organisations, (increasingly through partnership agreements with Civil Society Organisations) and grants to the British Council. It also covers equipment and supplies that the

---

[1] Money may be classified as bilateral while a case is being made for a new multilateral organisation to be recognised.

UK might provide (e.g. medical supplies) and funding under a Small Grant Scheme intended to allow Heads of Mission in a number of partner countries to fund eligible small projects of developmental value.

Humanitarian Assistance – Involves support to humanitarian organisations and the provision of material aid (including food, shelter and medical care) personnel and advice in emergency situations and their aftermath. Work of the conflict pools is also included.

DFID Debt Relief – This includes sums for debt relief on old DFID aid loans and cancellation of debt under the Commonwealth Debt Initiative (CDI). The non-CDI DFID debt relief is reported on the basis of the 'benefit to the recipient country'. This means that figures shown represent the money available to the country in the year in question that would otherwise have been spent on debt servicing. The CDI debt cancellation is reported on a 'lump sum' basis where all outstanding amounts on a loan are shown at the time the agreement to cancel is made. See Section 5 for more details on debt relief.

CDC Investments – CDC Group plc (or CDC) replaced the former Commonwealth Development Corporation in 1999. CDC was founded in 1948 and is now the UK government's instrument for investing in the private sector in developing economies (it does so through fund management companies). CDC has activities in more than 50 developing countries. CDC provides equities and concessional loans to companies in some aid-eligible countries, and these disbursements and repayments are included as UK flows. Although CDC no longer provides loans to governments, it did in the past and these existing loans can become eligible for debt relief.

Non-DFID Debt Relief – Comprises CDC Debt and ECGD Debt. CDC has a portfolio of loans to governments which can become eligible for debt relief under the HIPC (Heavily Indebted Poor Countries) or other debt relief deals. In 2005/06 £18 million of debts owed to CDC were reorganised.

ECGD is an agency of the Department of Trade and Industry which provides insurance for exporters against the main risks in selling overseas and guarantees to banks providing export finance. It also negotiates debt relief arrangements on commercial debt.

Other – This includes contributions from other Government Departments to CSO's, British Council and Global Conflict Pool, and small amounts of drug related assistance funded by the Home Office and FCO.

Further details on the UK's development assistance can be found in the Department for International Developments publication Statistics on International Development which can be found on the website www.dfid.gov.uk/pubs/files/sid2006/contents.asp. International Comparisons are available in the OECD Development Assistance Committee's annual report.

3.1 Gross public expenditure on aid (GPEX)[1]
United Kingdom

£ Thousand

		1997/98	1998/99	1999/00	2000/01	2001/02	2002/03	2003/04	2004/05	2005/06
Bilateral Assistance										
Department for International Development										
Poverty Reduction Budget Support	LUJS	–	20 000	26 000	263 998	268 218	208 185	313 474	421 902	524 687
Other Financial Aid	LUJW	181 216	241 207	289 348	205 998	264 202	304 167	367 876	283 411	361 096
Technical Co-operation Projects	LUOS	471 337	453 011	459 726	456 784	474 233	559 738	484 025	465 403	483 642
Grants and Other Aid in Kind	LUOT	185 039	212 527	219 198	242 124	294 233	407 971	469 827	589 712	684 909
Humanitarian Assistance	LUOU	94 680	113 711	224 210	221 931	192 576	294 974	310 125	336 225	410 616
DFID Debt Relief	LUOV	23 161	25 659	23 140	20 367	17 682	20 364	15 531	14 932	39 502
CDC Investments	LUOX	248 817	166 716	268 518	201 427	159 352	237 324	350 356	238 279	156 063
Debt Relief	EQ4B	..	..	..	82 150	251 741	408 063	175 544	618 390	1 588 235
Aid and Trade Provision	LUOW	60 711	56 898	37 790	..	..	..	..	..	..
Other	LUOY	170 171	87 147	100 721	66 978	67 795	79 459	111 197	143 460	152 989
Total	LUOZ	1 435 132	1 376 877	1 648 651	1 761 758	1 990 032	2 520 245	2 597 955	3 111 714	4 401 739
Multilateral Assistance										
European Community[2]	LUPA	557 287	754 549	752 473	727 685	756 885	901 059	1 085 594	1 210 392	1 172 547
World Bank Group	LUPB	189 851	175 254	167 297	242 965	219 616	221 939	382 594	206 455	272 226
IMF Poverty Reduction and Growth Facility	LUPC	20 000	18 000	17 000	..	11 147	11 434	9 417	1 767	23 728
Global Environmental Assistance	EQ4C	18 832	15 320	17 095	21 143	25 337	27 338	61 213	47 617	50 126
HIPC Trust Funds	EQ4D	..	..	..	27 518	23 400	17 855	19 949	42 123	11 094
UN Agencies	LUPD	141 300	133 983	175 730	245 299	226 069	192 169	211 368	221 617	324 209
Regional Development Banks	LUPE	60 411	66 295	67 178	54 803	75 382	90 647	80 391	82 165	77 746
Other	LUPF	12 014	15 037	15 355	15 539	16 649	16 515	15 783	27 038	24 907
Total	LUPG	999 695	1 178 438	1 212 128	1 334 952	1 354 485	1 478 956	1 866 309	1 839 174	1 956 583
Administrative costs	LUPH	91 436	98 645	104 601	138 507	132 214	153 348	249 414	226 844	253 936
Total Gross Public Expenditure on Aid	LUPI	2 526 263	2 653 960	2 965 380	3 235 217	3 476 732	4 152 550	4 713 678	5 177 732	6 612 258

1 See chapter text.
2 The institution, not the member states of the European Union.

Source: Department for International Development: 01355 843612

3.2 Total bilateral gross public expenditure on aid (GPEX): by main recipient countries and regions[1]
United Kingdom

£ Thousand

		1997/98	1998/99	1999/00	2000/01	2001/02	2002/03	2003/04	2004/05	2005/06
Main recipients										
Nigeria	C227	9 301	11 127	14 395	15 940	20 561	29 287	32 630	73 508	1 227 727
Iraq	C222	3 351	5 749	6 585	9 545	7 760	18 853	214 313	391 507	426 249
India	LUPJ	113 101	109 256	104 617	126 952	199 163	183 446	243 948	269 313	270 482
Bangladesh	LUPM	38 247	66 494	69 670	75 005	60 375	73 246	155 364	149 152	128 258
Afghanistan	C224	6 873	3 873	5 452	7 465	50 027	76 018	99 595	98 959	126 949
Sudan	EU5S	5 677	24 201	3 189	4 912	5 598	19 222	24 663	83 964	117 114
Tanzania	LUPK	51 363	77 904	74 709	111 743	205 493	98 348	162 372	129 977	114 138
Zambia	LUPO	46 583	33 537	46 657	93 345	59 203	45 138	32 267	163 507	101 514
Pakistan	LUPY	32 691	26 937	23 472	15 890	44 838	46 852	66 299	55 277	97 688
Ghana	LUPL	30 292	62 868	51 887	74 700	54 479	90 800	77 954	136 324	96 249
Uganda	LUPN	59 325	64 251	89 978	97 429	68 091	54 041	59 558	62 928	72 064
Rwanda	EU5T	6 166	13 568	14 279	32 451	26 818	34 986	26 910	45 053	70 427
Malawi	LUPP	30 355	52 572	49 058	55 144	49 563	52 211	57 344	56 429	68 803
Kenya	EU5W	29 985	42 027	32 665	62 601	33 875	63 005	28 454	37 824	65 084
Ethiopia	C225	11 867	9 793	7 299	16 484	12 088	44 224	43 665	73 044	62 562
South Africa	LUPT	28 372	35 110	47 838	36 766	44 178	57 186	93 332	49 141	62 485
Congo	C223	8 000	1 546	2 132	6 752	10 262	15 574	148 695	36 585	58 832
Indonesia	LUPZ	48 689	25 434	58 509	28 184	18 103	42 613	17 449	34 526	58 553
Vietnam	EU5V	4 329	4 698	4 981	5 633	15 810	18 508	23 264	40 425	57 510
Mozambique	LUPV	48 311	28 902	70 643	43 876	134 133	39 101	36 713	47 940	56 471
Total	LUQD	612 877	699 848	778 014	920 817	1 120 417	1 102 657	1 644 787	2 035 381	3 339 159
Total other countries	LUQE	822 255	677 029	870 637	840 941	869 615	1 417 589	953 169	1 076 332	1 062 579
Regional totals										
Africa	LUQF	448 830	573 350	628 017	776 030	871 199	896 464	1 060 942	1 270 918	2 405 795
America	LUQG	270 728	168 991	237 726	180 200	169 480	223 923	105 875	126 093	85 383
Asia	LUQH	390 164	348 004	376 137	413 324	535 412	610 007	969 302	1 243 777	1 356 165
Europe	LUQI	114 522	83 099	191 697	113 859	97 609	384 240	74 871	62 344	90 194
Pacific	LUQJ	26 888	20 249	7 248	5 029	6 885	5 362	4 484	3 272	3 823
World unallocated[2]	LUQK	183 999	183 184	207 827	273 316	309 447	400 249	382 481	405 310	460 378
Total Bilateral GPEX	LUQL	1 435 132	1 376 877	1 648 651	1 761 758	1 990 033	2 520 246	2 597 955	3 111 714	4 401 738

1 See chapter text.
2 Includes grants to Civil Society Organisations, Research Institutions and Commonwealth Organisations based in the UK.

Source: Department for International Development: 01355 843612

Defence

Chapter 4

Defence

This section includes figures on Defence expenditure, on the size and role of the Armed Forces and on related support activities.

Much of the material in this section can be found in *UK Defence Statistics 2006,* available from The Stationery Office.

Defence expenditure

(Table 4.1)

UK Defence Expenditure - the move from cash to resource accounting

Up until financial year 1998/99, Government expenditure was accounted for on a cash basis. In April 1999 the introduction of Resource Accounting and Budgeting (RAB) brought in an accruals-based accounting system, although Government departments were still controlled on a cash basis. This transitional accounting regime remained for two financial years. Government expenditure has been accounted for on a resource basis only since 2001/02.

The main difference arising from the adoption of RAB is that costs are accounted for as they are incurred (the principle of accruals), rather than when payment is made (the principle of cash). This gives rise to timing differences in accounting between the cash and RAB systems and also to the recognition of depreciation, which expends the cost of an asset over its useful economic life, and the cost of capital charge, equivalent to an interest charge on the net assets held on the Balance Sheet. At the time that RAB was introduced, the cost of capital charge was 6% of the net value of assets, although since 2003/04 this has reduced to 3.5%.

The change from cash based accounting to resource (accruals) based accounting, and the two-stage introduction of RAB (outlined below) has affected the time series comparability of the data.

Please refer to UK Defence Statistics 2006 Chapter 1 – Resource Accounting & Budgeting section for a summary of the key events leading to the introduction of RAB. Back copies of this publication are available at http://www.dasa.mod.uk/natstats/natstatsindex.html

Control Regime

Under Resource Accounting, Government Departments are accountable for their spending against Resource and Capital Departmental Expenditure Limits (DELs). Spending against the Resource DEL reflects resources consumed in year such as stock, maintenance of land and buildings, personnel costs, etc. Capital expenditure, whilst part of the overall DEL, reflects investment spending that will appear on the Department's balance sheet and be consumed over a number of years, net of the receipts from sale of assets. Departments are also responsible for Annually Managed Expenditure (AME). This spending is demand led (for example, payment of War Pensions) and therefore cannot be controlled by Departments in the same way.

For Stage 1 of RAB, which was introduced at the start of financial year 2001/02, non-cash costs such as depreciation and the cost of capital fell within Annually Managed Expenditure (AME) and were not controlled to the same degree as DELs. This allowed departments an interim period to gain experience of managing the new non-cash costs and to review their holdings of stocks and fixed assets, which impact the non-cash costs, prior to the charge impacting on the more tightly controlled DELs.

For Stage 2 of RAB, which was introduced at the start of the financial year 2003/04, non-cash costs (depreciation/impairments and the cost of capital charge) were moved from AME into the Resource DEL, and the cost of capital charge was reduced to 3.5% of the net value of assets.

The change in definition of the DELs combined with volatile non-cash costs over the Stage 1 period make time series comparisons over the period 2001/02 - 2003/04 complex. Additionally, the mix of cash and non-cash costs may be subject to change in future years.

Factors affecting Cash to RAB data consistency

- There are timing differences as to when payments are recognised.

- The movement of Non-Cash items of expenditure from AME into the Resource DEL from 2003/04 onwards has the 'apparent' effect of inflating the Resource DEL.

- In financial year 2003/04 the rate of interest used to calculate the cost of capital charge was reduced from 6 per cent to 3.5 per cent.

- The discount rate for provisions was changed from 3.5% real to 2.2% real with effect from 1 April 2005.

- The discount rate for pensions liabilities was changed from 3.5% real to 2.8% real with effect from 1 April 2005.

Resource DEL includes expenditure under the following headings:-

- *Equipment support*: internal and contracted out costs for equipment repair and maintenance.

- *Stock consumption*: consumption of armament, medical, dental, veterinary, oil, clothing, and general stores.

- *Property management*: estate and facilities management services and costs for building's maintenance.

- *Movements*: cost of transportation of freight and personnel.

- *Accommodation and utilities*: charges include rent, rates, gas, electricity, water and sewerage costs.

- *Professional fees*: includes legal and consultancy fees.

- *Fuel*: relates to fuel consumption by military vehicles, ships and aircraft.

- *Other Costs*: includes IT expenditure, Research and Development expenses and stock write off.

Expenditure on fixed asset categories in Capital DEL includes:-

- *Intangible assets*: comprise the development costs of major equipment projects and Intellectual Property Rights.

- *Fighting Equipment*: assets which only have a military use, such as tanks and fighter aircrafts. Items that also have a civilian use are recorded elsewhere.

- *Assets under Construction*: largely consist of major weapons platforms under construction in the Defence Procurement Agency (there is a smaller element of buildings under construction). Once construction is complete, those platforms will transfer to the relevant top-level budget holder as Fighting Equipment.

- *Capital spares*: from 2004/05, Capital Spares has been removed as a category, with the costs previously recorded here being incorporated into Transport Equipment or Fighting Equipment.

- *Redemption of QinetiQ preference shares*: refers to the proceeds received from the partial redemption of the redeemable preference shares during 2004/05.

Annual Managed Expenditure includes:

- *Other*: for 2001/02 and 2002/03, AME included depreciation and the cost of capital charge. Under Stage 2 of RAB, this category now contains only demand led payments, such as cash release and cost of capital credit on nuclear provisions and QinetiQ loan repayments.

In order to give a single measure of spending on public services under full resource budgeting, the Defence Spending line is presented as the sum of the resource and capital budgets, net of depreciation and impairments. This reflects the resources required plus the net investment in them, but avoids double counting the writing down of the existing capital stock and the cash outlay on new assets. Control is exercised separately on gross Capital and Resource DEL.

Service personnel

(Tables 4.2, 4.4, 4.5, 4.8 and 4.10)

The Regular Forces consist entirely of volunteer members serving on a whole-time basis, figures for which include both Trained and Untrained personnel and exclude Gurkhas, Full Time Reserve Service personnel, the Home Service battalions of the Royal Irish Regiment, mobilised reservists and Naval Activated Reservists.

Locally Entered Personnel are recruited outside the United Kingdom for whole-time service in special formations with special conditions of service and normally restricted locations. The Brigade of Gurkhas is an example.

The Regular Forces are supported by Reserves and Auxiliary Forces. There are both regular and volunteer Reserves. Regular Reserves consist of former Service personnel with a Reserve liability. Volunteer Reserves are open to both former Service personnel and civilians. The call out liabilities of the various reserve forces differ in accordance with their roles.

All three Services run cadet forces for young people and the Combined Cadet Force, which is found in certain schools where education is continued to the age of 17 or above, may operate sections for any or all of the Services.

Full-Time Reserve Service personnel represent reserves serving full-time in regular posts. This was made possible by the Reserve Forces Act 1996. None existed before 1998. FTRS figures include Full Commitment (FC), Home Commitment (HC) and Limited Commitment (LC) individuals.

Defence

Home Service battalions of the Royal Irish Regiment. Up until 1 July 1992, this was the Ulster Defence Regiment. The figures for the Territorial Army include Officer Training Corps and non-regular permanent staff.

The figures for cadet forces for each service include the Combined Cadet Force. Naval Service figures include officers and civilian instructors. The Army and Royal Air Force figures exclude officers and civilian instructors.

Intake of UK regular forces from civilian life: by service

(Table 4.2)

This table shows all intakes to UK Regular Forces including re-enlistments and rejoined reservists.

Formation of the armed forces

(Table 4.3)

This table shows the number of units which comprise the "teeth" elements of the Armed Forces and excludes supporting units.

Outflow of UK regular forces: by service

(Table 4.4)

This table does not include promotions to officer from other ranks and miscellaneous outflow.

Civilian personnel

(Table 4.6)

In previous years, the Ministry of Defence civilian workforce definition has reflected the historical requirement to understand the number of civil servants being directly funded. However with changes in employment legislation and the requirement to plan the future of the civilian workforce there was a need to change the definition to a more inclusive one better reflecting modern human resources methods and policies. In the longer term it will be used for skills planning, ensuring that the Ministry of Defence has a well-equipped workforce able to provide the best support to the UK Armed Forces.

In summary, the change over previous years is the addition of two further categories of individuals:

> *Casual staff* - those employed on a short-term casual contract;

Those not directly funded - staff who are employed by the Ministry of Defence, but whose salaries are paid for by another Department/Agency etc. This includes staff on loan to other government departments or working for NATO, as well as those on a career break or long term sickness absence.

These additions allow two levels of definition to be established:

Definition - Level 1 This includes permanent and casual personnel, Royal Fleet Auxiliaries, but excludes Trading Funds. This is generally used for internal reporting and planning.

Definition - Level 0 This contains all those at Level 1 plus Trading Funds and Locally Engaged Civilians. This is used for external reporting, including National Statistics publications CPS1 and UKDS, and Parliamentary business. For more information on the revised civilian workforce definition, visit: www.dasa.mod.uk/natstats/consultation/consultation.html

Prior to April 1995 all part-timers were counted as half of full time. From that date they are counted as the number of hours worked as a proportion of normal conditioned hours.

As from 1 April 2000 a new top level budget was formed in the Centre called Defence Logistics Organisation, replacing the top level budgets CinC Fleet Support, Quarter Master General and RAF Logistics Command.

The QinetiQ portion of the Defence Evaluation and Research Agency was established as a private company in July 2001. The War Pensions Agency transferred from the Department of Work & Pensions in 2001. The Clyde Dockyards were contractorised in 2002.

The 1993 to 1995 Royal Fleet Auxiliary (RFA) figures used in calculating the Level 1 measure are estimates. Data on manually paid staff before 1999 is not available, so estimates are used.

Totals and subtotals have been rounded separately and so may not appear to be the sums of their parts.

Family accommodation and defence land holdings

(Table 4.7)

In November 1996 most of the MOD's housing stock in England and Wales was sold to a private company, Annington Homes. The homes retained for use by Service families were leased back, with the condition that the MOD release a certain number of houses each year for disposal by Annington. The proceeds of the sale are being used to upgrade the housing stock.

The table also presents statistics of land and foreshore in the United Kingdom owned or leased by the Ministry of Defence or over which it has limited rights under grants or licences. Land declared as surplus to Defence requirements is also included.

Deployment of Service personnel

(Table 4.8)

The figures for Service personnel in England, Wales, Scotland and Northern Ireland are obtained from a different source from that used to compile the United Kingdom total. Consequently the sum of the national figures can differ from the United Kingdom total. The figures for Northern Ireland include all personnel who are serving on emergency tours of duty but exclude the former Ulster Defence Regiment, now the Home Services element of the Royal Irish Regiment. The figures for overseas countries include service personnel who are on loan to countries in the areas shown. Royal Navy and Royal Marines personnel on board ship are included in the United Kingdom figure if the ship was in home waters on the situation date or otherwise against the appropriate overseas area. All Defence Attaches and Advisers and their staffs are included under "Other Locations" and not identified within specific areas. From 2001 the grouping of overseas locations has been changed to give a more relevant overview.

UK regular forces - deaths

(Table 4.9)

Rates have been standardised to 2004 Tri-Service age and gender structure. In previous publications, deaths among the Brigade of Gurkhas were excluded, even though they belong to the regular Army, owing to the lack of reliable data on date of birth from which to calculate mortality rates. Gurkhas have been included in the number of deaths provided in Table 4.9. However they have been excluded from calculations for age and gender standardised rates.

Health

(Table 4.10)

The Services operate a number of hospitals in this country and in areas abroad where there is a significant British military presence. These hospitals take as patients, members of all three Services and their dependants; in addition, the hospitals in the United Kingdom take civilian patients under arrangements agreed with the National Health Service. Medical support is also supplied by Service medical staff at individual units, ships and stations.

Defence services and the civilian community

The Ministry of Defence helps the civil community in a variety of ways, for example by providing assistance in time of natural disasters or other emergencies and by undertaking community projects which are of training value to the Services. In some cases facilities established primarily for defence purposes also provide benefits to the general public.

Service assistance may be provided during an industrial dispute at the request of the civil ministries in order to maintain services essential to the life of the community (eg maintenance of emergency fire services).

(Table 4.11)

Search & Rescue (SAR)

This table covers incidents attended by military Search and Rescue units. The Royal Air Force and Royal Navy provide an essential service to the Search and Rescue (SAR) effort around the UK forming part of the national UK SAR coverage throughout the year for air, land and maritime operations. The military SAR teams' primary purpose is to recover aircrew from crashed military aircraft although, each year, over 90% of callouts are to civilian incidents. The SAR force currently consists of 6 x RAF and 2 x RN SAR Sea King helicopter units and 4 x RAF Mountain Rescue Teams operating from bases around the UK plus specially equipped RAF Nimrod aircraft based in RAF Kinloss in Scotland.

The table also includes urgent medical incidents in which the military SAR facilities gave assistance (eg inter-hospital transfers).

More than one SAR unit may be called to the same incident; consequently the number of callouts is likely to be greater than the number of incidents.

Persons moved involves moving people from a hostile environment to a safe environment or to a medical facility to receive urgent medical attention. People assisted by RAF Mountain Rescue Teams, but subsequently transported from the scene by helicopter, are recorded as having been rescued by the helicopter unit concerned.

Fisheries Protection

The Royal Navy Fishery Protection squadron operates within the British fishery limits under contract to the Department for Environment, Food and Rural Affairs. Boardings carried out by vessels of the Scottish Executive Environment and Rural Affairs Department and the Department of Agriculture for Northern Ireland are not included.

4.1 United Kingdom defence expenditure[1]

£ million[2]

		2001 /02	2002 /03	2003 /04	2004[3] /05	2005[4] /06
Defence Spending	C228	..	..	31 078	32 958	33 190
Departmental Expenditure Limits (DEL)	SNKJ	24 439	26 144	37 390	38 767	39 776
Resource DEL	E2XV	18 521	19 958	31 317	31 955	32 937
Expenditure on personnel	SNKK	9 456	9 969	10 435	10 995	11 255
Armed forces	SNKL	7 014	7 385	7 974	8 047	8 263
Civilians	SNKM	2 442	2 584	2 461	2 948	2 992
Depreciation/impairments	SNKN	..	..	6 313	5 808	6 587
Cost of capital	SNKO	..	..	3 000	3 025	3 106
Equipment support	SNKP	2 419	3 135	3 804	3 623	3 614
Stock consumption	SNKQ	1 294	1 222	1 060	1 079	1 039
Property management	SNKR	1 222	1 453	1 393	1 509	1 747
Movements	SNKS	718	505	491	710	821
Accommodation and utilities	SNKT	572	544	643	581	598
Professional fees	SNKU	559	468	549	565	553
Fuel	SNKV	160	185	161	239	369
Other	SNKW	2 121	2 477	3 468	3 821	3 247
Capital DEL	E2XW	5 918	6 185	6 073	6 812	6 840
Expenditure on fixed asset categories						
Intangible assets	SNKX	1 031	1 756	1 662	1 580	1 550
Land and buildings	SNKY	−163	−185	−211	388	31
Fighting equipment	SNKZ	34	320	348	435	402
Plant, machinery and vehicles	SNLA	99	132	66	124	64
IT and communications equipment	SNLB	85	94	37	134	180
Assets under construction	SNLC	4 479	3 601	3 594	4 335	4 879
Transport	E2XX	..	..	..	73	13
Capital spares	SNLD	353	467	581	..	..
Capital loan repayment	E2XY	..	..	−4	−25	−53
Redemption of QinetiQ	E2XZ	..	..	..	−49	−22
Capitalised provisions	GHF4	..	..	..	23	43
Proceeds of sales of fixed asset disposals	GHF5	..	..	..	−206	−253
Loans made to trading funds	GHF6	..	..	..	..	6
Annually Managed Expenditure (AME)	SNLF	14 962	19 293	1 011	908	890
War pensions	SNLG	1 238	1 166	1 116	1 110	1 067
Other	SNLH	13 724	18 127	−105	−202	−177

1 See chapter text.
2 Inclusive of non-recoverable VAT at current prices.
3 The 2004/05's Departmental Resource Accounts has been restated this year to reflect the transfer out of costs relating to the Nuclear Decommissioning Authority (NDA).
4 This is actual outturn data. Plans data are no longer shown.

Sources: Ministry of Defence/DASA (Economic Statistics);
0117 913 4530

4.2 Intake of United Kingdom regular forces from civilian life: by service[1]

Numbers

		1995 /96	1996 /97	1997[2] /98	1998 /99	1999 /00	2000 /01	2001 /02	2002 /03	2003 /04	2004 /05	2005 /06
All services:												
Male	KCJB	15 500	19 230	20 190	22 560	22 390	20 410	20 950	23 040	20 760	15 660	16 410
Female	KCJC	2 170	2 940	3 340	3 440	3 160	2 610	2 700	3 240	2 710	1 900	1 740
Total	KCJA	17 670	22 170	23 530	26 000	25 550	23 020	23 650	26 280	23 470	17 560	18 150
Naval service:												
Male	KCJE	1 990	3 400	3 970	4 110	4 250	3 990	4 270	4 420	3 530	3 240	3 480
Female	KCJF	350	560	630	660	700	630	740	800	580	460	460
Total	KCJD	2 340	3 960	4 600	4 770	4 950	4 620	5 010	5 220	4 120	3 690	3 940
Army:												
Male	KCJJ	11 530	13 580	13 390	15 010	14 750	13 450	13 620	15 060	13 930	10 780	11 740
Female	KCJK	1 380	1 940	2 010	1 980	1 750	1 320	1 240	1 550	1 260	910	990
Total	KCJI	12 910	15 520	15 400	16 990	16 500	14 770	14 850	16 610	15 190	11 690	12 730
Royal Air Force:												
Male	KCJM	1 980	2 250	2 830	3 450	3 380	2 980	3 070	3 550	3 290	1 640	1 190
Female	KCJN	450	430	700	800	710	660	720	890	870	530	290
Total	KCJL	2 420	2 680	3 530	4 250	4 100	3 630	3 780	4 450	4 160	2 180	1 480

1 See chapter text.
2 The definitions of intake used have been standardised from 1997/98 to give a more consistent picture across the three services.

Source: Ministry of Defence/DASA (Tri-Service): 020 7218 1470

4.3 Formation of the United Kingdom armed forces[1]

As at 1 April

Numbers

				1996	1997	1998	1999	2000	2001	2002	2003	2004	2005	2006
			Front Line Units											
Royal Navy[2]														
Submarines	KCGA		Vessels	15	15	15	15	16	16	16	16	15	15	14[3]
Carriers and assault ships	KCGB		"	5	5	5	6	6	6	4	4	5	6	5[4]
Destroyers and frigates	KCGC		"	36	35	35	35	32	32	32	31	31	28	25[5]
Mine counter-measure	KCGE		"	18	19	19	20	21	23	22	22	19	16	16
Patrol ships and craft	KCGF		"	32	34	28	24	23	23	23	22	26	26	22[6]
Fixed wing aircraft[7]	KCGG		Squadrons	3	3	3	3	1	1	1	1	1	1	1
Helicopters[8]	KCGH		"	15	15	12	12	9	9	8	8	5	6	6
Royal Marines	KCGI		Commandos	3	3	3	3	3	3	3	3	3	3	3
Regular Army														
Royal Armoured Corps[9]	KCGJ		Regiments	11	11	11	11	10	10	10	10	10	10	10
Royal Artillery	KCGK		"	16	15	15	15	15	15	15	15	14	14	14
Royal Engineers[10]	KCGL		"	10	10	10	10	11	11	11	11	11	11	11
Infantry	KCGM		Battalions	41	40	40	40	40	40	40	40	40	40	36
Special Air Service	KCGN		Regiments	1	1	1	1	..	..	..	..	..	..	..
Army Air Corps[8]	KCGO		"	5	5	5	5	..	..	..	..	..	..	..
Royal Air Force														
Strike/attack	KCGP		Squadrons	6	6	6	5	5	5	5	5	5	5)	
Offensive support[7]	KCGQ	ZIZM	"	5	5	5	5	2	2	2	2	2	1)	11[11]
Reconnaissance	KCGT		"	5	5	5	5	5	5	5	5	5	5)	
Air defence	KCGR		"	6	6	6	5	5	5	5	4	4	4	4
Maritime patrol	KCGS		"	3	3	3	3	3	3	3	3	3	3	2[12]
Airborne early warning[13]	KCGU		"	2	2	2	2	2	2	2	2	2	2	2
Air transport and tankers and helicopters[8]	KCGV		"	14	13	14	14	8	9	9	9	9	9	8
Search and rescue	KCGX		"	2	2	2	2	2	2	2	2	2	2	2
RAF FP Wg	GHN7		HQs	..	..	..	..	..	4	4	4	4	4	6
RAF Ground based air defence	GHN8		Squadrons	..	..	..	..	..	4	4	4	4	4	3
RAF Regiment Field[14]	GJ2F		"	..	..	..	..	..	6	6	6	6	6	6
Tactical Provost Wg	GJ2G		HQs	..	..	..	..	..	..	..	..	..	..	1
Tactical Provost	GJ2H		Squadrons	..	..	..	..	..	..	..	..	..	..	2
Joint Helicopter Command														
Royal Navy Helicopter	JUAT		"	..	..	..	..	4	4	4	4	4	4	4
Army Aviation	JUAU		Regiments	..	..	..	..	5	5	5	5	5	5	5
Royal Air Force Helicopter	JUAV		Squadrons	..	..	..	..	6	6	6	6	6	6	6
Joint Force Harrier														
Royal Navy	JUAW		"	..	..	..	..	3	3	3	3	2	1	1
Royal Air Force	JUAX		"	..	..	..	..	3	3	3	3	3	3	2
Joint Units														
Special Air Service	GL72		Regiments	..	..	..	..	1	1	1	1	1	1	1

1 See chapter text.
2 Only active vessels are shown.
3 HMS Spartan was withdrawn from service during the year
4 HMS Invincible went into Extended Readiness in late 2005
5 HMS Cardiff, HMS Marlborough and HMS Grafton were withdrawn from service
6 HMS Leeds Castle and the NI Squadron, consisting of HMS Brecon, HMS Cottesmore and HMS Dulverton, were withdrawn from service during the year.
7 From 2000 excludes aircraft transferred to the Joint Force Harrier squadron
8 From 2000 excludes helicopters transferred to the Joint Helicopter command.

9 From 2000 includes one Armoured Regiment which is committed to the new Joint Nuclear Biological and Chemical Regiment.
10 Figure for 2000 includes an additional Close Support Regiment formed as a result of the Stategic Defence Review.
11 From 2006, these squadrons are multi-roled.
12 206 Squadron was disbanded on 1 Apr 05.
13 Figure for 2001 includes an embedded Operational Conversion Unit at the Sentry Operation Establishments.
14 In UKDS editions 2003 and 2004, Ground Based Air Defence and Field Squadrons for years 2001 to 2004 were also included under Regular Air Force

Source: Ministry of Defence/DASA (Tri-Service): 020 7218 0390

4.4 Outflow of United Kingdom regular forces: by service[1]

Numbers

		1995 /96	1996 /97	1997[2] /98	1998 /99	1999 /00	2000 /01	2001 /02	2002 /03	2003 /04	2004 /05	2005 /06
All Services:												
Male	KDNA	25 750	29 320	21 860	24 500	23 870	22 520	22 360	21 770	21 200	21 330	21 290
Female	KDNB	3 120	3 680	2 490	2 970	2 750	2 430	2 350	2 340	2 200	2 100	1 980
Total	KDNC	28 860	33 000	24 350	27 470	26 620	24 950	24 710	24 100	23 400	23 430	23 260
Naval Service:												
Male	KDND	4 310	6 190	4 650	4 920	5 160	4 480	5 110	4 680	4 230	4 150	4 000
Female	KDNE	630	940	620	610	630	550	690	620	540	490	480
Total	KDNF	4 940	7 130	5 270	5 530	5 800	5 040	5 800	5 300	4 770	4 630	4 490
Army:												
Male	KDNI	13 940	13 760	13 190	15 320	14 620	13 900	13 290	13 420	13 500	13 990	13 240
Female	KDNJ	1 510	1 600	1 280	1 730	1 580	1 330	1 090	1 140	1 090	1 080	950
Total	KDNK	15 440	15 350	14 470	17 050	16 200	15 230	14 380	14 560	14 600	15 070	14 190
Royal Air Force:												
Male	KDNL	7 500	9 380	4 020	4 250	4 080	4 140	3 960	3 670	3 470	3 200	4 050
Female	KDNM	980	1 140	590	640	540	540	570	580	570	530	540
Total	KDNN	8 480	10 520	4 610	4 890	4 620	4 680	4 530	4 250	4 040	3 730	4 590

1 See chapter text. Comprises all those who left the Regular Forces and includes deaths.
2 The definitions of outflow used have been standardised from 1997/98 to give a more consistent picture across the three services.

Source: Ministry of Defence/DASA (Tri-Service): 020 7218 1470

4.5 United Kingdom Defence: service manpower strengths[1]
As at 1 April

Thousands

		1996	1997	1998	1999	2000	2001	2002	2003	2004	2005	2006
UK service personnel												
Full-time trained strength[2,3]	ZBTR	211.6	197.2	194.0	191.1	190.3	189.1	187.1	188.5	190.2	188.1	183.2
Trained Naval Service	ZBTS	45.6	41.7	40.5	39.3	38.9	38.5	37.5	37.6	37.5	36.4	35.6
UK regulars	ZBTT	45.6	41.7	40.4	39.1	38.5	38.0	36.8	36.6	36.4	35.5	34.9
Full-time reserve service	ZBTU	..	..	0.1	0.3	0.3	0.5	0.7	1.0	1.1	0.9	0.7
Trained Army[2,3]	ZBTV	103.6	101.4	100.9	99.8	100.2	100.4	100.4	102.0	103.6	102.4	100.6
UK regulars	ZBTW	99.5	97.8	97.5	96.3	96.5	96.3	96.0	97.6	99.4	98.5	96.8
Full-time reserve service[2,3]	ZBTX	..	..	..	0.2	0.5	0.7	0.9	1.0	0.7	0.4	0.5
Gurkhas	ZBTY	4.0	3.8	3.4	3.4	3.4	3.5	3.4	3.4	3.4	3.5	3.3
Trained Royal Air Force	ZBTZ	62.5	54.2	52.7	51.9	51.2	50.1	49.2	48.9	49.1	49.2	46.9
UK regulars	ZBUA	62.5	54.2	52.7	51.8	51.0	49.8	48.9	48.5	48.7	48.8	46.6
Full-time reserve service	ZBUB	..	..	..	0.1	0.2	0.3	0.3	0.4	0.4	0.4	0.3
Untrained UK regulars	ZBUC	14.3	17.2	19.7	21.5	21.6	21.5	23.0	24.2	22.5	18.3	17.5
Naval Service	ZBUD	2.8	3.5	4.1	4.6	4.3	4.4	4.9	5.0	4.5	4.4	4.5
Army	ZBUE	9.3	11.1	12.4	13.4	13.6	13.2	14.0	14.5	13.3	10.8	10.9
Royal Air Force	ZBUF	2.2	2.7	3.2	3.5	3.7	3.9	4.1	4.7	4.7	3.0	2.1
Locally Entered Personnel (excluding Gurkhas)	ZBUG	0.6	0.4	0.4	0.4	0.4	0.3	0.4	0.4	0.4	0.4	0.4
Royal Irish Regiment Home Service batallions	ZBUH	5.0	4.8	4.6	4.4	4.2	3.8	3.6	3.5	3.4	3.2	3.1
Reserve personnel	ZBUI	327.3	323.5	319.4	307.0	294.8	284.2	273.4	259.7	246.7	235.6	..
Regular Reserves	ZBUJ	264.6	259.4	254.9	247.6	241.6	234.9	224.9	212.6	201.4	191.5	..
Naval Services	ZBUK	23.9	24.1	24.8	24.7	24.2	23.5	23.5	23.2	22.8	22.2	..
Army	ZBUL	195.5	190.1	186.2	180.5	175.5	169.8	161.1	151.5	141.9	134.2	127.6
of which mobilised:	SNEO	..	..	0.2	0.1	0.3	0.2	0.3	0.4	0.1	0.2	0.3
Royal Air Force	ZBUM	45.2	45.3	43.9	42.4	41.9	41.5	40.2	37.7	36.4	35.0	34.4
of which mobilised:	SNEP	..	..	..	–	–	–	–	–	–	..	..
Volunteer Reserves	ZBUN	62.6	62.6	64.5	59.4	53.2	47.3	46.3	44.9	43.4	42.3	..
Royal Naval Reserve and Royal Marine Reserve[2]	ZBUO	3.5	4.3	4.4	4.5	4.8	4.8	5.0	4.9	4.5	4.4	..
of which mobilised:	SNEQ	..	..	..	..	..	..	..	0.4	0.1	..	..
Territorial Army	ZBUP	57.3	57.7	57.6	52.3	45.6	41.7	40.7	39.3	38.1	37.3	38.5
of which mobilised:	SNER	..	..	0.6	0.5	0.8	0.4	0.5	4.1	2.9	1.5	1.1
Royal Auxilliary Air Force	ZBUQ	1.9	1.4	2.5	2.6	2.7	1.6	1.5	1.5	1.4	1.4	1.4
of which mobilised:	SNES	..	..	..	–	–	–	0.1	0.8	–	..	0.1
Cadet Forces	ZBUR	152.1	151.0	150.2	151.0	154.5	151.0	152.3	155.6	155.6	153.1	..
Naval Service	ZBUS	26.9	26.3	25.9	24.5	24.1	23.8	23.8	23.2	22.6	21.9	..
Army	ZBUT	74.2	74.1	73.9	74.6	77.4	75.4	75.8	78.7	80.5	80.9	81.7
Royal Air Force	ZBUU	51.0	50.7	50.5	51.9	53.0	51.8	52.7	53.7	52.5	50.3	51.0

1 See chapter text.
2 Figures before 1997 do not include University Royal Navy Units.
3 Data between 1997 and 2005 have been revised due to re-examination of data.

Source: Ministry of Defence/DASA (Tri-Service): 020 7218 1470

4.6 United Kingdom defence: civilian manpower strengths[1]
As at 1 April

Thousands: Full-time Equivalent

		1996	1997	1998	1999	2000	2001	2002	2003	2004	2005	2006
Ministry of Defence civilians												
Centre												
Non-industrial	KDQE	21.8	22.9	22.2	21.5	19.7	19.1	20.0	21.2	22.7	24.0	24.6
Industrial	KDQF	0.9	1.2	1.1	1.0	0.9	0.9	0.8	0.7	0.6	0.7	0.8
Defence Logistics Organisation												
Non-industrial	ZBTJ	..	..	..	..	19.7	17.8	17.3	16.4	16.5	16.5	14.1
Industrial	ZBTK	..	..	..	..	11.5	8.4	6.3	4.4	4.3	4.1	3.9
Naval Service												
Non-industrial	KYCW	13.6	12.5	12.0	11.3	3.0	3.0	2.9	2.7	2.9	2.6	2.3
Industrial	KYCX	8.6	7.6	6.6	5.3	1.0	0.9	0.8	0.8	0.8	0.7	0.6
Royal Fleet Auxiliary	EQS9	2.2	2.2	2.4	2.4	2.4	2.4	2.4	2.5	2.3	2.3	2.3
Army												
Non-industrial	KDQK	22.9	22.4	21.7	21.6	16.3	16.4	16.0	16.0	14.7	14.5	13.4
Industrial	KDQL	14.4	13.8	12.1	10.6	5.8	5.7	5.5	5.4	5.6	5.5	5.2
Royal Air Force												
Non-industrial	KDQM	11.5	11.5	11.7	12.2	7.1	7.0	7.1	7.0	7.3	7.0	6.7
Industrial	KDQN	8.0	7.8	7.3	7.1	4.5	4.4	4.3	4.4	4.4	4.0	4.0
Level 1 Total	C7PE	103.8	101.9	97.1	94.1	91.9	86.0	83.6	81.5	82.2	82.0	78.1
Non-industrial	C7PF	69.7	69.4	67.6	66.6	65.8	63.4	63.4	63.3	64.1	64.7	61.3
Industrial	C7PG	31.9	30.3	27.1	25.1	23.7	20.2	17.8	15.7	15.7	15.0	14.5
Royal Fleet Auxiliary	EQT2	2.2	2.2	2.4	2.4	2.4	2.4	2.4	2.5	2.3	2.3	2.3
Locally engaged overseas	KDQA	17.1	15.9	15.2	14.9	14.8	13.3	14.1	13.8	15.4	15.7	15.1
Non-industrial	KDQT	7.1	7.0	6.7	6.7	6.7	6.3	6.5	6.5	7.3	..	..
Industrial	KDQU	10.0	8.9	8.4	8.1	8.2	7.0	7.6	7.4	8.1	..	..
Trading funds	GQHI	14.5	15.5	14.0	14.0	14.5	18.8	12.4	12.2	11.4	10.8	10.7
Level 0 Total	C7PH	135.4	133.3	126.3	123.0	121.3	118.2	110.1	107.6	109.0	108.5	103.9

1 See chapter text. Individuals on temporary and geographic (T&G) promotion are classed as non-industrial. From 2004, staff who cannot be correctly allocated to Top Level Budgets (TLBs) are included with the Centre figures. (numbering approx 200 in 2006).

Source: Ministry of Defence/DASA (Civilian): 020 7218 6019

4.7 Family accommodation and defence land holdings[1]
As at 1 April

Thousands and thousand hectares

		1996	1997	1998	1999	2000	2001	2002	2003	2004	2005	2006
Family accommodation (thousands)												
United Kingdom: Total	KDPA	72.1	68.6	67.3	65.5	64.8	59.2	55.8	53.8	52.8	51.9	51.8
Land holdings												
United Kingdom												
Land[2]	KDPF	222.6	221.0	220.0	220.2	219.9	224.3	222.4	221.4	221.3	222.1	222.0
Foreshore[2]	KDPH	18.5	18.6	18.6	18.6	18.6	18.6	18.6	18.6	18.6	18.6	18.6
Rights held	KDPJ	124.3	124.5	124.5	124.8	124.8	124.8	124.9	131.1	131.1	124.9	124.9
Defence land[3]												
Used for agricultural purposes	KDPL	107.4	96.2	103.5	114.5	92.2	98.6	91.8	103.0	100.5	106.3	..
Used for grazing only	KDPM	60.7	51.9	59.6	65.5	50.3	66.6	60.0	70.2	68.3	71.0	..
Full agricultural use	KDPN	46.7	44.3	43.9	49.0	41.9	32.0	31.8	32.8	32.2	35.3	..

1 See chapter text.
2 Freehold and leasehold.
3 Following changes in the tenancies of agricultural land, these data are no longer available. Alternative data are being sought.

Sources: Ministry of Defence/Defence Housing Executive: 020 7305 3051;
Ministry of Defence/Defence Estates: 0121 311 3818

4.8 Location of United Kingdom service personnel[1]
As at 1 July

Thousands

		1996	1997	1998	1999	2000	2001	2002	2003	2004	2005[2]	2006
UK Service personnel, Regular Forces:												
UK distribution[3,4]												
In United Kingdom[5]	KDOB	177.4	171.6	173.4	171.7	170.3	172.0	..	..	..	169.7	167.3
England	KDOC	146.6	142.6	144.6	144.3	143.0	144.1	..	..	..	145.0	142.1
Wales	KDOD	4.3	3.3	3.2	3.3	3.2	2.6	..	..	..	2.9	3.3
Scotland	KDOE	15.5	13.9	14.2	14.9	15.1	14.5	..	..	..	13.2	13.5
Northern Ireland	KDOF	10.5	11.5	11.0	9.0	8.4	9.4	..	..	..	7.0	6.8
Global location[3,4]												
United Kingdom	MKCN	172.0	167.5	165.0	161.0	163.1	162.8	..	..	..	169.7	167.3
Overseas	KDOG	48.5	42.6	43.1	47.1	43.0	40.9	..	..	..	29.2	28.5
Mainland European States[5,6]	KDOI	11.7	6.2	6.9	15.2	8.2	8.6	..	..	..	27.0	26.6
Germany[7]	KDOH	20.8	21.2	20.3	18.0	19.5	17.3	..	..	..	22.2	22.0
Balkans	MKCO	..	..	..	..	..	..	..	..	..	0.1	–
Mediterranean[8,9]	KDOM	0.5	0.3	1.2	1.3	1.1	2.3	..	..	..	..	..
Gibraltar	KDOJ	0.6	0.5	0.5	0.6	0.6	0.5	..	..	..	0.4	0.3
Cyprus	KDOL	4.0	3.9	3.6	3.6	3.5	3.5	..	..	..	3.2	3.0
Far East/Asia[10]	MKCT	1.2	1.5	0.3	0.3	1.0	0.3	..	..	..	0.3	0.3
Africa[11]	MKCP	..	..	..	..	..	–	..	..	..	0.6	0.6
North America	MKCQ	..	..	..	..	..	2.5	..	..	..	0.7	0.7
Central/South America	MKCR	..	..	..	..	..		..	..	..	0.1	0.1
Falkland Islands	MKCS	..	..	..	..	..	0.8	..	..	..	0.3	0.3
Other locations, including unallocated	KDOQ	9.8	9.0	10.4	8.2	9.1	5.1	..	..	..	1.1	1.0
Locally entered service personnel:[12]												
United Kingdom	KDOS	1.7	2.1	2.1	2.0	2.1	2.3	2.6	2.6	2.6	2.1	2.2
Gibraltar	KDOT	0.2	0.2	0.4	0.4	0.3	0.4	0.4	0.4	0.4	0.4	0.4
Hong Kong	KDOV	1.6	0.7	..	..	..	..	..	..	..	..	..
Brunei	KDOW	0.7	1.0	0.9	0.8	0.8	0.8	0.8	0.8	0.7	0.8	0.8
India/Nepal	KDOX	0.7	0.9	0.5	0.5	0.5	0.4	0.3	0.4	0.4	0.3	0.3
Total	KDOK	4.9	4.7	4.0	3.7	3.7	3.9	4.2	4.1	4.1	3.3	3.3

1 See chapter text.
2 Data from 2005 have been revised due to re-examination of data.
3 Figures for global deployment of service personnel are compiled using different methodologies to those for UK distribution. Comparison is therefore not possible between the two sets of UK personnel figures.
4 Includes personnel within the UK whose location is unknown on the 1st July.
5 Includes the Balkans until 2002.
6 Post 2002 Mainland European States figure includes Germany, Balkans, Mediterranean, Gibraltar and Cyprus.
7 Prior to 1996, figures for the Federal Republic of Germany and Mainland European States were combined.
8 Includes Med Near East and Middle East until 2002.
9 Post 2002 Mediterranean figure is not shown separately but is included in Mainland European States figure.
10 Prior to 1997 figures include personnel serving in Hong Kong.
11 Post 2002 Africa figure includes Middle East.
12 Including Gurkhas.

Source: Ministry of Defence/DASA (Tri-Service): 020 7218 1470

4.9 United Kingdom regular forces: deaths[1]

Numbers and rates per thousand

		1996	1997	1998	1999	2000	2001	2002	2003	2004	2005
Deaths											
Total	SNIA	144	164	165	141	147	142	147	173	169	158
Male	SNIB	142	155	157	138	143	139	138	166	163	150
Female	SNIC	2	9	8	3	4	3	9	7	6	8
Rates per thousand[2]											
Tri-service	SNIH	0.65	0.80	0.78	0.66	0.72	0.69	0.72	0.82	0.81	0.79
Navy	SNII	0.63	0.87	0.63	0.61	0.62	0.79	0.64	0.90	0.92	0.69
Army[3]	SNIJ	0.74	0.93	0.85	0.72	0.80	0.71	0.84	0.79	0.80	0.82
RAF	SNIK	0.45	0.49	0.64	0.48	0.62	0.49	0.52	0.74	0.60	0.71

1 See chapter text.
2 Rates age and gender standarised to 2004 Tri-Service strengths structure.
3 Excludes Gurkhas.

Source: Ministry of Defence/DASA (Health): 01225 467423

4.10 Strength of uniformed United Kingdom medical staff[1]
As at 1 April

Numbers

		1996	1997	1998	1999	2000	2001	2002	2003	2004	2005	2006
Qualified doctors:[2]												
Naval Service	KDMA	240	210	210	210	210	220	220	230	240	260	260
Army[3]	KDMB	430	430	440	450	460	470	490	550	600	610	650
Royal Air Force	KDMC	270	220	210	200	180	180	180	190	200	220	230
All Services	KDMD	940	870	850	860	860	870	890	970	1 040	1 090	1 140
Qualified dentists:[2]												
Naval Service	KDME	60	60	60	60	60	60	60	60	60	60	60
Army[3]	KDMF	140	140	140	140	140	150	140	150	150	150	140
Royal Air Force	KDMG	100	90	80	80	80	80	70	70	80	70	70
All Services	KDMH	310	290	280	290	280	290	280	270	290	280	270
Support staff:[4]												
Naval Service[5]	KDMI	1 290	1 020	990	970	1 000	1 030	1 010	1 060	1 110	1 110	1 120
Nursing services[5]	ZBTL	..	..	..	200	210	210	220	250	280	290	300
Support[5]	ZBTM	..	..	..	770	790	820	790	810	840	820	820
Army[3]	KDMJ	3 280	3 020	3 090	3 120	3 210	3 260	3 320	3 410	3 560	..	..
Nursing services[3,4,6]	ZBTN	..	..	..	520	570	610	650	710	770	770	800
Support[3]	ZBTO	..	..	..	2 600	2 640	2 650	2 670	2 700	2 800	..	..
Royal Air Force	KDMK	1 400	1 210	1 190	1 360	1 460	1 480	1 500	1 600	1 680	1 660	1 550
Nursing services	ZBTP	..	..	..	330	400	420	450	470	480	510	480
Support	ZBTQ	..	..	..	1 030	1 060	1 070	1 050	1 130	1 200	1 160	1 070
All Services	KDML	5 980	5 260	5 230	5 540	5 760	5 800	5 930	6 180	6 440	..	..

1 See chapter text. Includes staff employed at units (including ships) and in hospitals.
2 The Medical and Dental Officers are trained only and exclude Late Entry Personnel.
3 Due to a change in source data, Army figures prior to 2005 cannot be verified.

4 Includes all members of the Nursing Services/Nursing Corps. From 1999, figures for support staff have been split so that nurses are separate from other support staff.
5 Data between 1998 and 2005 have been revised due to re-examination of data.
6 The 2006 Nursing Services figure is trained and untrained Soldiers with Nursing trades in the QARANC and all trained Officers in QARANC.

Source: Ministry of Defence/DASA (Tri- Service): 020 7218 1470

4.11 United Kingdom defence services and the civilian community[1]

Numbers

		1996	1997	1998	1999	2000	2001	2002	2003	2004	2005	2006
Military Search and rescue operations at home												
Call outs: total	GPYC	2 164	1 941	1 898	1 912	1 941	1 763	1 684	1 714	1 638	1 702	1 875
Royal Navy helicopters	GPXO	512	495	463	499	499	502	436	424	453	478	497
Royal Air Force helicopters	GPXP	1 392	1 258	1 257	1 235	1 278	1 115	1 122	1 173	1 079	1 114	1 258
Contractorised and other helicopters	GPXQ	27	16	20	–	–	–	–	–	–	–	1
Royal Air Force Nimrod aircraft	GPXR	69	79	71	65	71	54	46	37	37	37	32
Other fixed wing aircraft[2]	GPXS	1	2	2	–	1	1	1	–	2	–	1
HM ships and auxilliary vessels[2]	KCMG	1	3	3	–	–	–	–	–	–	–	–
Royal Air Force mountain rescue teams	KCMH	162	88	82	113	92	91	79	80	67	73	86
Persons moved: total[3]	KCMI	1 550	1 226	1 243	1 204	1 316	1 182	1 224	1 273	1 412	1 384	1 463
Persons moved by rescue service												
Royal Navy helicopters	GPXT	356	328	283	355	360	386	314	320	416	380	479
Royal Air Force helicopters	GPXU	1 084	877	937	832	934	781	900	922	978	907	968
Royal Air Force mountain rescue teams	GPXV	100	15	12	17	22	15	10	31	17	97	16
Other	GPXW	10	6	11	–	–	–	–	–	1	–	–
Persons moved by type of assistance												
Rescue[4]	GPXX	307	219	317	307	276	281	343	280	494	119	102
Medrescue[5]	GPXY	921	721	667	640	713	629	654	779	672	670	736
Medevac[6]	GPXZ	275	224	209	216	241	228	201	174	195	141	175
Recovery[7]	GPYA	34	54	43	32	29	36	21	25	33	31	37
Airlift[8]	GPYB	13	8	7	9	57	8	5	15	18	22	23
Search and rescue incidents: total	KCMM	1 919	1 750	1 697	1 714	1 781	1 608	1 544	1 600	1 504	1 584	1 702

Source: Ministry of Defence/DASA (Logistics): 01225 67144/72112

		1996 /97	1997 /98	1998 /99	1999 /00	2000 /01	2001 /02	2002 /03	2003 /04	2004 /05	2005 /06
Fishery protection											
Vessels boarded	KCMO	1 884	1 715	1 879	1 716	1 603	1 464	1 375	1 710	1 748	1 371

Source: Fisheries Protection - Ministry of Defence

1 See chapter text.
2 Not permanently on stand-by.
3 Figures for 'Persons Moved' have been revised due to a recent change to the way data is recorded in the database to provide more accurate figures. The exercise included cleansing records from 2003.
4 Rescue: Moving an uninjured person from a hostile to a benign environment.
5 Medrescue: Moving an injured casualty from a hostile environment to a medical facility.

6 Medevac: Moving a sick person between medical facilities such as a hospital or occasionally to move transplant organs.
7 Recovery: Moving people declared dead on scene or confirmed dead on arrival by a qualified doctor.
8 Airlift: Moving military personnel, or their families, on compassionate grounds.

Population and vital statistics

Chapter 5

Population and vital statistics

This section begins with a summary of population figures for the United Kingdom (UK) and constituent countries for 1851 to 2026 and for Great Britain from 1801 (Table 5.1). Table 5.2 analyses the components of population change. Table 5.3 gives details of the national sex and age structures for years up to the present date, with projected figures up to the year 2026. Legal marital condition of the population is shown in Table 5.4. The distribution of population at regional and local levels is summarised in Table 5.5.

In the main, historical series relate to census information, while mid-year estimates, which make allowance for under-enumeration in the census, are given for the recent past and the present (from 1961 onwards).

Population

(Tables 5.1 - 5.3)

Figures shown in these tables relate to the population enumerated at successive censuses, (up to 1951), mid-year estimates (from 1961 to 2005) and population projections (up to 2026). Population estimates for 1992 to 2002 were revised in light of the local authority population studies. Further information can be found on the National Statistics website (www.statistics.gov.uk/popest).

Population projections are 2004-based and were published by the Government Actuary's Department on 20th October 2005. Further information can be found at www.gad.gov.uk/Population/index.asp

Definition of resident population

The estimated population of an area includes all those usually resident in the area, whatever their nationality. HM Forces serving abroad are excluded from, but non-UK Armed Forces stationed here are included within the estimates of resident population. Students are taken to be resident at their term-time addresses.

The projections of the resident population of the United Kingdom (UK) and constituent countries are prepared by the Government Actuary, in consultation with the Registrars General, as a common framework for use in national planning in a number of different fields. New projections are made every second year on assumptions regarding future fertility, mortality and migration which seem most appropriate on the basis of the statistical evidence available at the time. The population

projections in Tables 5.1 - 5.3 are based on the estimates of the population of the United Kingdom at mid-2001 made by the Registrars General.

Marital condition (de jure): estimated population

(Table 5.4)

This table shows population estimates by marital status. The mid-1991 to mid-2002 marital status estimates for England and Wales were revised in light of the local authority population studies.

Geographical distribution of the population

(Table 5.5)

The population enumerated in the censuses for 1911-1951, and the mid-year population estimates for later years, are provided for standard regions of the United Kingdom (UK), for metropolitan areas, for broad groupings of local authority (LA) districts by type within England and Wales, and for some of the larger cities. Projections of future sub-national population levels are prepared from time to time by the Registrar General, but are not shown in this publication.

Migration into and out of the United Kingdom

(Tables 5.7 - 5.9)

A migrant is defined as a person who changes his or her country of usual residence for a period of at least a year, so that the country of destination effectively becomes the country of usual residence.

The sources of international migration data are:

- migration data from the International Passenger Survey (IPS), which is a sample survey of passengers arriving at, and departing from, the main United Kingdom (UK) air and sea ports and the Channel Tunnel;

- visitor data from the IPS to estimate visitor switchers, who are those people who initially come to or leave the UK for a period of less than 12 months, but subsequently stay for a year or longer;

- Home Office data on asylum seekers and their dependants; and

- estimates of migration between the UK and the Irish Republic, which use information from the Irish Quarterly National Household Survey and the National Health Service Central Register, and are agreed between the Irish Central Statistics Office (CSO) and the Office for National Statistics (ONS).

The international migration estimates in Table 5.7 are derived from all these sources and represent Total International Migration. The estimates in Tables 5.8 and 5.9 are based on the International Passenger Survey (IPS) only (without the three adjustments outlined above).

Acceptances for settlement in the United Kingdom

(Table 5.10)

This table presents in geographic regions, the statistics of individual nationalities, arranged alphabetically within each region. The figures are on a different basis from those derived from the International Passenger Survey (IPS) (Tables 5.8 and 5.9) and relate only to people subject to immigration control. Persons accepted for settlement are allowed to stay indefinitely in the United Kingdom (UK). They exclude temporary migrants such as students and generally relate only to non-EEA nationals. Settlement can occur several years after entry to the country.

Applications received for asylum in the United Kingdom, excluding dependants

(Table 5.11)

This table shows statistics of applications for asylum in the United Kingdom (UK). Figures are shown for the main applicant nationalities by geographic region. The basis of assessing asylum applications, and hence of deciding whether to grant asylum in the UK, is the 1951 United Nations Convention on Refugees.

Marriages

(Table 5.12)

The figures in this table relate to marriages solemnised in the constituent countries of the United Kingdom (UK). They take no account of the growing trend towards marrying abroad.

Divorces

(Tables 5.13 and 5.14)

A marriage may be either *dissolved* following a petition for divorce and the granting of a decree absolute, or *annulled*, following a petition for nullity and the awarding of a decree of nullity. The first group of decrees are known as dissolutions of marriage and the second as annulments of marriage. In Table 5.13 the term 'divorce' includes both types of decrees, although strictly speaking, it should refer only to dissolutions.

Births

(Tables 5.15 –5.17)

For Scotland and Northern Ireland the number of births relate to those **registered** during the year. For England and Wales the figures up to and including 1930-32 are for those registered, while later figures relate to births **occurring** in each year.

All data for England and Wales and for Scotland include births occurring in those countries to mothers not usually resident in them. Data for Northern Ireland, and hence United Kingdom (UK), prior to 1981 include births occurring in Northern Ireland to non-resident mothers; from 1981, such births are excluded.

Deaths

(Tables 5.19 and 5.21)

The figures relate to the number of deaths registered during each calendar year. However, from 1993 onwards, the figures for England and Wales represent occurrences. This change has little effect on annual totals.

Infant and maternal mortality

(Table 5.20)

On 1 October 1992 the legal definition of a stillbirth was altered from a baby born dead after 28 completed weeks gestation or more, to one born after 24 completed weeks of gestation or more.

Life tables

(Table 5.22)

The current set of interim life tables are constructed from the estimated populations in 2003-2005 and the births, infant deaths and deaths by individual age occurring in those years for England & Wales and registered in those years for Scotland and Northern Ireland.

The estimates used in these interim life tables are the estimates, or revised estimates, published on the following dates:

Mid-year population estimates	England	Wales	Scotland	Northern Ireland
2003	September 2004	September 2004	April 2004	August 2004
2004	December 2005	August 2005	April 2005	July 2005
2005	August 2006	August 2006	April 2006	October 2006

Adoptions

(Tables 5.23)

The figures shown within these tables relate to the date the adoption was entered in the Adopted Children Register. Figures based on the date of court order are available for England and Wales in the volume *Marriage, divorce and adoption statistics 2004* (no. 32 in the FM2 series) available on the National Statistics website *www.statistics.gov.uk* or from the enquiry point in the ONS shown at the foot of the tables.

5.1 Population summary: by country and sex

Thousands

	United Kingdom			England and Wales			Wales	Scotland			Northern Ireland		
	Persons	Males	Females	Persons	Males	Females	Persons	Persons	Males	Females	Persons	Males	Females
Enumerated population: Census figures													
1801	..	..	..	8 893	4 255	4 638	587	1 608	739	869	..	..	..
1851	22 259	10 855	11 404	17 928	8 781	9 146	1 163	2 889	1 376	1 513	1 442	698	745
1901	38 237	18 492	19 745	32 528	15 729	16 799	2 013	4 472	2 174	2 298	1 237	590	647
1911	42 082	20 357	21 725	36 070	17 446	18 625	2 421	4 761	2 309	2 452	1 251	603	648
1921[1]	44 027	21 033	22 994	37 887	18 075	19 811	2 656	4 882	2 348	2 535	1 258	610	648
1931[1]	46 038	22 060	23 978	39 952	19 133	20 819	2 593	4 843	2 326	2 517	1 243	601	642
1951	50 225	24 118	26 107	43 758	21 016	22 742	2 599	5 096	2 434	2 662	1 371	668	703
1961	52 709	25 481	27 228	46 105	22 304	23 801	2 644	5 179	2 483	2 697	1 425	694	731
Resident population: mid-year estimates													
	DYAY	BBAB	BBAC	BBAD	BBAE	BBAF	KGJM	BBAG	BBAH	BBAI	BBAJ	BBAK	BBAL
1970	55 632	26 992	28 641	48 891	23 738	25 153	2 729	5 214	2 507	2 707	1 527	747	781
1971	55 928	27 167	28 761	49 152	23 897	25 255	2 740	5 236	2 516	2 720	1 540	755	786
1972	56 097	27 259	28 837	49 327	23 989	25 339	2 755	5 231	2 513	2 717	1 539	758	782
1973	56 223	27 332	28 891	49 459	24 061	25 399	2 773	5 234	2 515	2 719	1 530	756	774
1974	56 236	27 349	28 887	49 468	24 075	25 393	2 785	5 241	2 519	2 722	1 527	755	772
1975	56 226	27 361	28 865	49 470	24 091	25 378	2 795	5 232	2 516	2 716	1 524	753	770
1976	56 216	27 360	28 856	49 459	24 089	25 370	2 799	5 233	2 517	2 716	1 524	754	770
1977	56 190	27 345	28 845	49 440	24 076	25 364	2 801	5 226	2 515	2 711	1 523	754	769
1978	56 178	27 330	28 849	49 443	24 067	25 375	2 804	5 212	2 509	2 704	1 523	754	770
1979	56 240	27 373	28 867	49 508	24 113	25 395	2 810	5 204	2 505	2 699	1 528	755	773
1980	56 330	27 411	28 919	49 603	24 156	25 448	2 816	5 194	2 501	2 693	1 533	755	778
1981	56 357	27 412	28 946	49 634	24 160	25 474	2 813	5 180	2 495	2 685	1 543	757	786
1982	56 291	27 364	28 927	49 582	24 119	25 462	2 804	5 165	2 487	2 677	1 545	757	788
1983	56 316	27 371	28 944	49 617	24 133	25 484	2 803	5 148	2 479	2 669	1 551	759	792
1984	56 409	27 421	28 989	49 713	24 185	25 528	2 801	5 139	2 475	2 664	1 557	761	796
1985	56 554	27 489	29 065	49 861	24 254	25 606	2 803	5 128	2 470	2 658	1 565	765	800
1986	56 684	27 542	29 142	49 999	24 311	25 687	2 811	5 112	2 462	2 649	1 574	768	805
1987	56 804	27 599	29 205	50 123	24 371	25 752	2 823	5 099	2 455	2 644	1 582	773	809
1988	56 916	27 652	29 265	50 254	24 434	25 820	2 841	5 077	2 444	2 633	1 585	774	812
1989	57 076	27 729	29 348	50 408	24 510	25 898	2 855	5 078	2 443	2 635	1 590	776	814
1990	57 237	27 819	29 419	50 561	24 597	25 964	2 862	5 081	2 444	2 637	1 596	778	818
1991	57 439	27 909	29 530	50 748	24 681	26 067	2 873	5 083	2 445	2 639	1 607	783	824
1992	57 585	27 977	29 608	50 876	24 739	26 136	2 878	5 086	2 445	2 640	1 623	792	831
1993	57 714	28 039	29 675	50 986	24 793	26 193	2 884	5 092	2 448	2 644	1 636	798	837
1994	57 862	28 108	29 754	51 116	24 853	26 263	2 887	5 102	2 453	2 649	1 644	802	842
1995	58 025	28 204	29 821	51 272	24 946	26 326	2 889	5 104	2 453	2 650	1 649	804	845
1996	58 164	28 287	29 877	51 410	25 030	26 381	2 891	5 092	2 447	2 645	1 662	810	851
1997	58 314	28 371	29 943	51 560	25 113	26 446	2 895	5 083	2 442	2 641	1 671	816	856
1998	58 475	28 458	30 017	51 720	25 201	26 519	2 900	5 077	2 439	2 638	1 678	819	859
1999	58 684	28 578	30 106	51 933	25 323	26 610	2 901	5 072	2 437	2 635	1 679	818	861
2000	58 886	28 690	30 196	52 140	25 438	26 702	2 907	5 063	2 432	2 631	1 683	820	862
2001	59 113	28 832	30 281	52 360	25 574	26 786	2 910	5 064	2 434	2 630	1 689	824	865
2002	59 322	28 963	30 359	52 570	25 702	26 868	2 923	5 055	2 432	2 623	1 697	829	868
2003	59 554	29 108	30 446	52 794	25 841	26 953	2 938	5 057	2 435	2 623	1 703	833	870
2004	59 834	29 271	30 563	53 046	25 988	27 057	2 952	5 078	2 446	2 632	1 710	836	874
2005	60 209	29 479	30 730	53 390	26 179	27 211	2 959	5 095	2 456	2 639	1 724	844	880
Resident population: projections (mid-year)[2]													
	C59J	C59K	C59L	C59M	C59N	C59O	C59P	C59Q	C59R	C59S	C59T	C59U	C59V
2006	60 533	29 668	30 864	53 691	26 357	27 334	2 977	5 108	2 463	2 646	1 733	848	884
2011	61 892	30 438	31 454	55 005	27 100	27 904	3 037	5 120	2 470	2 649	1 767	868	900
2021	64 727	31 943	32 784	57 770	28 572	29 198	3 165	5 127	2 471	2 656	1 830	900	930
2026	66 002	32 579	33 423	59 042	29 212	29 831	3 219	5 109	2 457	2 652	1 851	911	940

1 Figures for Northern Ireland are estimated. The population at the Census of 1926 was 1 257 thousand (608 thousand males and 649 thousand females).
2 These projections are 2004-based. See chapter text for more detail.

Sources: *Office for National Statistics: 01329 813233;*
General Register Office for Scotland;
Northern Ireland Statistics and Research Agency;
Government Actuary's Department: 020 7211 2622

5.2 Population changes: by country

Thousands

	Population[1] at start of period	Average annual change				
		Overall annual change	Births	Deaths[2]	Natural change	Net migration and other changes
United Kingdom						
1901 - 1911	38 237	385	1 091	624	467	-82
1911 - 1921	42 082	195	975	689	286	-92
1921 - 1931	44 027	201	824	555	268	-67
1931 - 1951	46 038	213	793	603	190	22
1951 - 1961	50 225	258	839	593	246	12
1961 - 1971	52 807	312	962	638	324	-12
1971 - 1981	55 928	42	736	666	69	-27
1981 - 1991	56 357	108	757	655	103	5
1991 - 2001	57 439	161	731	631	100	61
2001 - 2005	59 113	274	692	600	92	182
2011 - 2021	61 892	284	716	578	139	145
England and Wales						
1901 - 1911	32 528	354	929	525	404	-50
1911 - 1921	36 070	182	828	584	244	-62
1921 - 1931	37 887	207	693	469	224	-17
1931 - 1951	39 952	193	673	518	155	38
1951 - 1961	43 758	244	714	516	197	47
1961 - 1971	46 196	296	832	560	272	23
1971 - 1981	49 152	48	638	585	53	-5
1981 - 1991	49 634	111	664	576	89	23
1991 - 2001	50 748	155	647	556	92	63
2001 - 2005	52 360	258	618	528	90	168
2011 - 2021	55 005	277	643	508	135	142
Scotland						
1901 - 1911	4 472	29	131	76	54	-25
1911 - 1921	4 761	12	118	82	36	-24
1921 - 1931	4 882	-4	100	65	35	-39
1931 - 1951	4 843	13	92	67	25	-12
1951 - 1961	5 096	9	95	62	34	-25
1961 - 1971	5 184	5	97	63	34	-30
1971 - 1981	5 236	-6	70	64	6	-11
1981 - 1991	5 180	-7	66	63	3	-10
1991 - 2001	5 083	-2	60	60	-1	-1
2001 - 2005	5 064	8	53	57	-5	12
2011 - 2021	5 120	1	51	55	-3	4
Northern Ireland						
1901 - 1911	1 237	1	31	23	8	-6
1911 - 1921	1 251	1	29	22	7	-6
1921 - 1931	1 258	-2	30	21	9	-11
1931 - 1951	1 243	6	28	18	10	-4
1951 - 1961	1 371	6	30	15	15	-9
1961 - 1971	1 427	11	33	16	17	-6
1971 - 1981	1 540	-	28	17	11	-11
1981 - 1991	1 543	6	27	16	12	-5
1991 - 2001	1 607	8	24	15	9	-
2001 - 2005	1 689	9	22	14	7	1
2011 - 2021	1 767	6	22	15	7	-1

1 Census enumerated population up to 1951; mid-year estimates of resident population from 1961 to 2001 and mid-2004-based projections of resident population thereafter.

2 Including deaths of non-civilians and merchant seamen who died outside the country. These numbered 577 000 in 1911-1921 and 240 000 in 1931-1951 for England and Wales; 74 000 in 1911-1921 and 34 000 in 1931-1951 for Scotland; and 10 000 in 1911-1926 for Northern Ireland.

Sources: Government Actuary's Department: 020 7211 2622;
Office for National Statistics: 01329 813233;
General Register Office for Scotland;
Northern Ireland Statistics and Research Agency

5.3 Age distribution of the resident population: by sex and country

Thousands

		United Kingdom															
		Population enumerated in Census					Estimated mid-year resident population						Projected mid-year resident population[1]				
		1901	1931	1951	1971	1981	1991[2]	2001[5]	2002	2003	2004	2005	2006	2011	2016	2021	2026
Persons: All ages	KGUA	38 237	46 038	50 225	55 928	56 357	57 439	59 114	59 322	59 554	59 834	60 209	60 533	61 892	63 304	64 727	66 002
Under 1	KGUK	938	712	773	899	730	790	663	661	679	705	716	707	698	714	722	713
1 - 4[3]	KABA	3 443	2 818	3 553	3 654	2 726	3 077	2 819	2 753	2 703	2 684	2 712	2 764	2 794	2 825	2 881	2 876
5 - 9	KGUN	4 106	3 897	3 689	4 684	3 677	3 657	3 735	3 689	3 650	3 608	3 560	3 503	3 488	3 509	3 557	3 620
10 - 14	KGUO	3 934	3 746	3 310	4 232	4 470	3 485	3 890	3 912	3 891	3 870	3 821	3 757	3 518	3 503	3 524	3 572
15 - 19	KGUP	3 826	3 989	3 175	3 862	4 735	3 719	3 678	3 761	3 855	3 920	3 965	3 986	3 823	3 584	3 569	3 591
20 - 29	KABB	6 982	7 865	7 154	7 968	8 113	9 138	7 499	7 401	7 379	7 458	7 641	7 807	8 428	8 530	8 130	7 880
30 - 44	KABC	7 493	9 717	11 125	9 797	10 956	12 125	13 405	13 499	13 519	13 471	13 408	13 299	12 587	12 299	12 821	13 265
45 - 59	KABD	4 639	7 979	9 558	10 202	9 540	9 500	11 168	11 316	11 424	11 517	11 624	11 757	12 310	13 090	12 945	12 268
60 - 64	KGUY	1 067	1 897	2 422	3 222	2 935	2 888	2 884	2 890	2 943	3 021	3 114	3 246	3 756	3 460	3 838	4 296
65 - 74	KBCP	1 278	2 461	3 689	4 764	5 195	5 067	4 947	4 969	5 005	5 033	5 048	5 052	5 550	6 404	6 610	6 742
75 - 84	KBCU	470	844	1 555	2 159	2 677	3 119	3 296	3 345	3 401	3 435	3 424	3 421	3 531	3 801	4 316	5 063
85 and over	KGVD	61	113	224	485	603	873	1 130	1 127	1 104	1 112	1 176	1 234	1 407	1 584	1 813	2 117
School ages (5-15)	KBWU	..	13 120	7 649	9 704	9 086	7 818	8 381	8 369	8 330	8 257	8 170	8 058	7 738	7 684	7 797	7 898
Under 18	KGUD	..	10 557	13 248	15 798	14 472	13 120	13 357	13 310	13 253	13 221	13 189	13 102	12 727	12 630	12 847	12 907
Pensionable ages[4]	KFIA	2 387	4 421	6 828	9 123	10 035	10 557	10 845	10 916	11 014	11 125	11 244	11 368	12 182	12 430	12 740	13 922
Males: All ages	KGWA	18 492	22 060	24 118	27 167	27 412	27 909	28 832	28 963	29 108	29 271	29 479	29 668	30 438	31 205	31 943	32 579
Under 1	KGWK	471	361	397	461	374	403	338	339	349	361	367	362	358	366	369	365
1 - 4[3]	KBCV	1 719	1 423	1 818	1 874	1 400	1 572	1 445	1 409	1 384	1 375	1 389	1 414	1 428	1 444	1 472	1 470
5 - 9	KGWN	2 052	1 967	1 885	2 401	1 889	1 871	1 913	1 890	1 869	1 848	1 823	1 792	1 780	1 789	1 813	1 845
10 - 14	KGWO	1 972	1 892	1 681	2 175	2 295	1 784	1 993	2 005	1 995	1 985	1 962	1 928	1 802	1 790	1 799	1 824
15 - 19	KGWP	1 898	1 987	1 564	1 976	2 424	1 905	1 879	1 930	1 983	2 017	2 038	2 052	1 970	1 845	1 833	1 842
20 - 29	KBCW	3 293	3 818	3 509	4 024	4 103	4 578	3 744	3 700	3 697	3 748	3 847	3 938	4 286	4 358	4 153	4 018
30 - 44	KBCX	3 597	4 495	5 461	4 938	5 513	6 045	6 645	6 690	6 701	6 675	6 645	6 598	6 255	6 136	6 436	6 695
45 - 59	KBUU	2 215	3 753	4 493	4 970	4 711	4 732	5 534	5 604	5 653	5 694	5 746	5 808	6 068	6 449	6 380	6 058
60 - 64	KGWY	490	894	1 061	1 507	1 376	1 390	1 412	1 414	1 439	1 476	1 519	1 585	1 830	1 682	1 863	2 083
65 - 74	KBWL	565	1 099	1 560	1 999	2 264	2 272	2 308	2 327	2 354	2 374	2 389	2 397	2 652	3 065	3 158	3 220
75 - 84	KBWM	196	335	617	716	922	1 146	1 308	1 339	1 371	1 394	1 403	1 417	1 533	1 700	1 956	2 306
85 and over	KGXD	23	36	70	126	141	212	312	316	313	323	352	378	475	581	708	852
School ages (5-15)	KBWV	..	6 711	3 895	4 982	4 666	4 001	4 294	4 289	4 269	4 233	4 190	4 130	3 959	3 923	3 979	4 031
Under 18	KGWD	..	3 630	6 753	8 108	7 430	6 711	6 845	6 822	6 794	6 780	6 765	6 717	6 516	6 457	6 564	6 595
Pensionable ages[4]	KFIB	785	1 471	2 247	2 841	3 327	3 630	3 928	3 982	4 038	4 091	4 143	4 192	4 660	5 346	5 822	6 378
Females: All ages	KGYA	19 745	23 978	26 107	28 761	28 946	29 530	30 281	30 359	30 446	30 563	30 730	30 864	31 454	32 099	32 784	33 423
Under 1	KGYK	466	351	376	437	356	387	324	323	331	343	349	345	341	349	352	348
1 - 4[3]	KBWN	1 724	1 397	1 735	1 779	1 327	1 505	1 375	1 344	1 319	1 309	1 323	1 349	1 366	1 381	1 409	1 406
5 - 9	KGYN	2 054	1 930	1 804	2 283	1 788	1 786	1 822	1 800	1 781	1 760	1 737	1 712	1 708	1 721	1 743	1 774
10 - 14	KGYO	1 962	1 854	1 629	2 057	2 175	1 701	1 897	1 907	1 896	1 884	1 859	1 829	1 716	1 712	1 725	1 748
15 - 19	KGYP	1 928	2 002	1 611	1 887	2 311	1 815	1 799	1 830	1 873	1 903	1 927	1 935	1 853	1 740	1 736	1 749
20 - 29	KBWO	3 690	4 047	3 644	3 945	4 009	4 560	3 755	3 701	3 682	3 710	3 794	3 869	4 142	4 172	3 977	3 862
30 - 44	KBWP	3 895	5 222	5 663	4 859	5 442	6 080	6 760	6 808	6 817	6 796	6 763	6 700	6 332	6 163	6 386	6 570
45 - 59	KBWR	2 424	4 226	5 065	5 231	4 829	4 769	5 634	5 713	5 771	5 823	5 878	5 949	6 241	6 640	6 564	6 210
60 - 64	KGYY	577	1 003	1 361	1 715	1 559	1 498	1 473	1 476	1 504	1 545	1 595	1 661	1 926	1 779	1 974	2 213
65 - 74	KBWS	713	1 361	2 127	2 765	2 931	2 795	2 640	2 641	2 651	2 659	2 659	2 655	2 898	3 339	3 452	3 522
75 - 84	KBWT	274	509	937	1 443	1 756	1 972	1 987	2 006	2 030	2 041	2 022	2 004	1 998	2 100	2 360	2 757
85 and over	KGZD	38	77	154	359	462	661	817	811	791	789	824	857	933	1 003	1 105	1 265
School ages (5-15)	KBWW	..	6 409	3 753	4 722	4 421	3 817	4 087	4 081	4 060	4 023	3 980	3 928	3 779	3 761	3 818	3 867
Under 18	KGYD	..	6 927	6 495	7 690	7 042	6 409	6 512	6 489	6 459	6 442	6 424	6 386	6 212	6 173	6 283	6 313
Pensionable ages[4]	KFIC	1 601	2 950	4 580	6 282	6 708	6 927	6 917	6 934	6 976	7 034	7 100	7 176	7 522	7 084	6 917	7 544

31

5.3 Age distribution of the resident population: by sex and country
continued

Thousands

		England Estimated mid-year resident population						England Projected population[1]				Wales Estimated mid-year resident population						Wales Projected population[1]	
		1991[2]	2001	2002	2003	2004	2005	2011	2026		1991[2]	2001	2002	2003	2004	2005	2011	2026
Persons: All ages	KCCI	47 875	49 450	49 647	49 856	50 093	50 432	51 967	55 823	KERY	2 873	2 910	2 923	2 938	2 952	2 959	3 037	3 219
Under 1	KCCJ	660	558	558	575	597	606	594	612	KFAC	38	32	30	31	32	32	32	32
1 - 4	KCCK	2 560	2 366	2 312	2 273	2 260	2 287	2 370	2 460	KFBX	153	136	132	129	127	127	130	133
5 - 9	KCCL	3 019	3 121	3 085	3 054	3 019	2 982	2 947	3 082	KFCA	186	185	183	181	178	175	164	172
10 - 14	KCCM	2 865	3 238	3 260	3 245	3 228	3 187	2 945	3 031	KFCB	177	196	197	197	195	193	176	174
15 - 19	KCCN	3 067	3 045	3 118	3 202	3 261	3 305	3 193	3 043	KFCC	187	186	191	196	199	200	195	175
20 - 29	KCEG	7 651	6 307	6 226	6 208	6 276	6 432	7 108	6 726	KFCD	415	336	334	336	342	348	394	357
30 - 44	KCEH	10 147	11 257	11 351	11 379	11 346	11 306	10 675	11 317	KFCE	583	608	611	611	608	601	557	609
45 - 59	KCEQ	7 920	9 327	9 448	9 533	9 600	9 682	10 259	10 377	KFCF	486	572	579	583	588	590	610	583
60 - 64	KCEW	2 399	2 395	2 397	2 438	2 503	2 586	3 127	3 586	KFCG	154	154	156	161	166	171	206	220
65 - 74	KCGD	4 222	4 113	4 130	4 159	4 181	4 191	4 613	5 583	KFCH	284	264	265	268	270	272	308	366
75 - 84	KCJG	2 626	2 764	2 804	2 852	2 879	2 870	2 948	4 231	KFCI	164	183	185	187	188	186	188	283
85 and over	KCKJ	739	959	956	936	943	997	1 189	1 775	KFCK	45	59	59	58	60	63	77	114
School ages (5-15)	KCWX	6 439	6 985	6 982	6 955	6 897	6 828	6 504	6 712	KFCL	397	420	419	417	413	408	377	381
Under 18	KCWY	10 840	11 146	11 118	11 082	11 065	11 048	10 718	10 988	KFCM	662	662	659	655	652	647	615	615
Pensionable ages[4]	KEAA	8 827	9 055	9 111	9 190	9 280	9 381	10 161	11 589	KFEB	573	584	589	596	602	609	666	762
Males: All ages	KEAB	23 291	24 166	24 288	24 415	24 554	24 741	25 615	27 630	KFEI	1 391	1 409	1 414	1 426	1 434	1 438	1 485	1 582
Under 1	KEAC	336	285	286	295	306	311	304	313	KFEJ	20	16	16	16	16	17	17	16
1 - 4	KEAD	1 307	1 212	1 183	1 164	1 158	1 171	1 211	1 258	KFEK	78	69	68	66	66	65	66	68
5 - 9	KEAE	1 545	1 599	1 580	1 564	1 546	1 526	1 504	1 572	KFEL	95	95	94	93	91	90	84	88
10 - 14	KEAF	1 467	1 658	1 671	1 664	1 657	1 638	1 508	1 548	KFFA	91	101	101	101	100	99	90	89
15 - 19	KECA	1 572	1 558	1 603	1 648	1 679	1 699	1 647	1 563	KFFN	95	94	97	100	102	103	100	90
20 - 29	KECB	3 835	3 155	3 117	3 113	3 156	3 240	3 614	3 428	KFHA	207	166	164	167	171	175	202	185
30 - 44	KECC	5 064	5 600	5 648	5 663	5 644	5 627	5 328	5 725	KFHB	289	297	297	297	295	291	270	308
45 - 59	KECD	3 957	4 624	4 682	4 721	4 752	4 792	5 074	5 155	KFHW	242	283	286	287	289	290	297	281
60 - 64	KECE	1 159	1 176	1 176	1 195	1 225	1 263	1 525	1 748	KFQO	74	75	77	79	82	84	101	106
65 - 74	KECF	1 900	1 928	1 944	1 965	1 981	1 992	2 209	2 674	KFQV	128	124	125	127	128	130	149	175
75 - 84	KECG	970	1 103	1 128	1 156	1 175	1 182	1 287	1 930	KFUK	60	73	74	75	76	77	83	130
85 and over	KECH	181	267	270	267	276	300	403	717	KFUL	11	16	16	16	17	19	26	46
School ages (5-15)	KECI	3 295	3 578	3 578	3 565	3 536	3 502	3 327	3 427	KFUV	204	215	215	214	212	209	194	195
Under 18	KECJ	5 545	5 712	5 698	5 681	5 674	5 667	5 488	5 615	KFVE	339	340	338	336	335	332	315	315
Pensionable ages[4]	KECK	3 050	3 298	3 342	3 388	3 431	3 474	3 900	5 322	KFVF	198	212	215	219	222	225	257	351
Females: All ages	KEJV	24 584	25 284	25 358	25 441	25 539	25 691	26 352	28 194	KFVL	1 482	1 502	1 509	1 512	1 518	1 521	1 552	1 637
Under 1	KEJW	324	273	272	280	291	296	290	298	KFYW	19	15	15	15	15	16	16	16
1 - 4	KEJX	1 253	1 154	1 129	1 109	1 103	1 116	1 159	1 203	KFZJ	75	66	65	63	62	61	63	65
5 - 9	KEKP	1 474	1 522	1 505	1 491	1 473	1 456	1 443	1 510	KGCK	91	90	89	88	87	85	80	84
10 - 14	KEKQ	1 399	1 580	1 589	1 581	1 571	1 550	1 436	1 483	KGCM	86	95	96	96	95	94	86	85
15 - 19	KEKR	1 495	1 487	1 516	1 554	1 582	1 606	1 546	1 481	KGCN	91	92	94	95	97	97	95	85
20 - 29	KEKS	3 816	3 152	3 108	3 095	3 120	3 192	3 493	3 298	KGCO	208	170	170	169	171	174	192	173
30 - 44	KENR	5 083	5 657	5 703	5 716	5 702	5 679	5 347	5 592	KGCP	294	312	314	314	312	310	286	302
45 - 59	KEOQ	3 964	4 702	4 766	4 812	4 849	4 890	5 186	5 222	KGGZ	244	289	293	296	299	300	313	302
60 - 64	KEOZ	1 239	1 219	1 220	1 243	1 278	1 322	1 603	1 839	KGIY	80	78	80	82	85	88	106	114
65 - 74	KEQJ	2 323	2 185	2 186	2 194	2 200	2 200	2 404	2 909	KGKR	156	141	140	141	142	142	159	191
75 - 84	KEQK	1 656	1 661	1 676	1 696	1 704	1 688	1 661	2 301	KGTQ	104	110	111	112	112	110	106	152
85 and over	KEQL	558	692	687	669	667	697	786	1 057	KGTZ	34	43	43	42	42	44	51	67
School ages (5-15)	KEQM	3 143	3 406	3 405	3 391	3 360	3 325	3 176	3 285	KGVG	194	204	204	203	201	199	184	186
Under 18	KEQN	5 295	5 434	5 420	5 401	5 391	5 381	5 230	5 372	KGVH	323	323	321	319	317	315	300	300
Pensionable ages[4]	KEQO	5 777	5 757	5 769	5 802	5 849	5 906	6 261	6 267	KGVK	375	372	374	377	380	384	409	411

5.3 Age distribution of the resident population: by sex and country
continued

Thousands

| | | Scotland | | | | | | | | | Northern Ireland | | | | | | | |
| | | Estimated mid-year resident population | | | | | | Projected population[1] | | | Estimated mid-year resident population | | | | | | Projected population[1] | |
		1991[2]	2001[5]	2002	2003	2004	2005	2011	2026		1991	2001[5]	2002	2003	2004	2005	2011	2026
Persons: All ages	KGVP	5 083	5 064	5 055	5 057	5 078	5 095	5 120	5 109	KIOY	1 607	1 689	1 697	1 703	1 710	1 724	1 767	1 851
Under 1	KHAQ	66	52	51	52	54	54	51	49	KIOZ	26	22	22	21	22	23	21	20
1 - 4	KHCT	258	224	217	212	210	211	208	199	KIPA	106	93	91	89	87	88	86	84
5 - 9	KHDN	320	306	299	294	290	285	267	256	KIPN	131	123	122	121	120	119	110	109
10 - 14	KHDQ	313	323	323	320	319	315	280	258	KIPP	129	132	131	129	128	126	117	109
15 - 19	KHDT	337	318	319	324	328	327	312	265	KIPQ	128	130	132	133	133	132	123	107
20 - 29	KHDU	820	630	619	614	617	630	672	579	KIPR	253	225	222	221	224	230	254	217
30 - 44	KHDV	1 080	1 163	1 158	1 150	1 140	1 124	1 003	966	KIPS	315	376	378	378	378	377	353	372
45 - 59	KHFK	853	979	993	1 008	1 025	1 042	1 098	967	KIPT	241	290	296	301	305	310	342	341
60 - 64	KHOZ	265	262	262	265	270	273	329	370	KIPU	70	74	75	78	81	84	93	119
65 - 74	KHTU	441	447	449	452	455	457	482	603	KIPV	120	123	125	126	127	128	147	190
75 - 84	KHUO	259	272	276	281	286	286	306	419	KIPW	69	77	79	81	82	83	89	130
85 and over	KHUQ	70	89	88	86	85	91	110	176	KIPX	19	23	24	24	24	25	32	53
School ages (5-15)	KHVV	697	694	687	679	672	664	606	567	KIPY	285	282	281	278	274	271	251	239
Under 18	KIMT	1 150	1 098	1 086	1 074	1 067	1 059	987	918	KIQL	467	451	447	443	437	435	407	386
Pensionable ages[4]	KIMU	912	944	950	958	968	975	1 047	1 198	KIQM	246	262	266	271	275	280	309	373
Males: All ages	KIMV	2 445	2 434	2 432	2 435	2 446	2 456	2 470	2 457	KIQN	783	824	829	833	836	844	868	911
Under 1	KIMW	34	26	26	26	28	28	26	25	KIQO	13	11	11	11	11	12	11	10
1 - 4	KIMX	132	115	111	108	107	107	106	102	KIQP	54	48	47	46	45	45	44	43
5 - 9	KIMY	164	156	153	151	149	146	136	130	KIQQ	67	63	63	62	62	61	56	55
10 - 14	KIMZ	161	166	165	164	163	161	143	131	KIQR	66	68	67	66	65	64	60	55
15 - 19	KINA	171	161	163	166	168	168	160	135	KIQS	66	66	68	68	68	68	63	55
20 - 29	KINB	410	311	308	306	309	317	340	293	KIQT	127	113	111	111	112	116	131	113
30 - 44	KINC	535	563	560	556	550	542	484	476	KIQU	156	185	186	186	186	185	173	187
45 - 59	KIND	415	483	490	496	503	511	530	458	KIQV	118	144	147	149	151	153	168	164
60 - 64	KINE	124	125	125	126	129	131	159	172	KIQW	32	35	36	38	39	41	45	57
65 - 74	KINR	192	200	202	204	207	208	225	281	KIRJ	53	56	56	57	58	59	69	91
75 - 84	KINS	91	103	106	108	111	112	126	187	KIRK	26	30	31	31	32	32	37	59
85 and over	KINT	16	23	23	23	23	25	35	68	KIRL	5	6	6	7	7	7	10	21
School ages (5-15)	KINU	357	356	352	348	344	340	309	288	KIRM	146	145	144	142	141	139	129	122
Under 18	KINV	588	562	556	550	546	543	504	467	KIRN	239	231	229	227	225	223	209	197
Pensionable ages[4]	KINW	299	327	331	336	341	345	386	535	KIRO	83	92	94	95	97	99	117	170
Females: All ages	KINX	2 639	2 630	2 623	2 623	2 632	2 639	2 649	2 652	KIRP	824	865	868	870	874	880	900	940
Under 1	KINY	32	26	25	25	26	26	25	24	KIRQ	13	10	11	10	11	11	10	10
1 - 4	KINZ	126	109	106	104	103	103	102	97	KIRR	52	45	44	43	42	43	42	41
5 - 9	KIOA	157	149	146	143	141	139	131	126	KIRS	64	60	59	59	58	58	54	53
10 - 14	KIOB	153	157	157	156	156	154	137	127	KIRT	63	65	64	63	62	62	57	53
15 - 19	KIOC	166	156	156	158	160	159	153	130	KIRU	62	64	65	65	65	64	59	52
20 - 29	KIOO	411	319	311	307	308	314	333	287	KISH	126	113	111	110	111	114	124	104
30 - 44	KIOP	545	600	598	595	590	583	518	491	KISI	159	191	192	193	192	192	181	185
45 - 59	KIOQ	437	496	504	512	521	531	568	509	KISJ	123	146	149	152	154	157	174	177
60 - 64	KIOR	141	137	137	139	141	142	170	197	KISK	38	38	39	40	42	43	48	62
65 - 74	KIOS	249	246	247	248	248	249	258	323	KISL	67	68	68	68	69	69	77	99
75 - 84	KIOT	168	169	171	173	175	174	180	232	KISM	44	47	48	49	50	50	52	71
85 and over	KIOU	54	66	65	63	62	65	74	108	KISN	14	17	17	17	17	18	22	32
School ages (5-15)	KIOV	340	339	335	331	328	324	297	279	KISO	139	138	137	135	134	132	122	117
Under 18	KIOW	562	536	530	524	520	516	483	451	KISP	228	220	218	215	213	212	199	189
Pensionable ages[4]	KIOX	612	617	619	622	627	630	660	663	KISQ	163	170	173	175	178	181	192	203

1 2004-based projections are made as described in the chapter text.
2 Data for mid 1991 for UK, England and Wales and Scotland are revised in light of the 2001 Census.
3 1961 estimates are for ages 0 - 4.
4 The pensionable age population is that over state retirement age. The 2011 figures take account of planned changes in retirement age from 65 for men and 60 for women at present to 65 for both sexes. This change will be phased in between April 2010 and March 2020.
5 The mid-2001 estimates for Scotland and Northern Ireland are based on the 2001 census.

Sources: Office for National Statistics: 01329 813233;
General Register Office for Scotland;
General Register Office for Northern Ireland;
Government Actuary's Department: 020 7211 2622

5.4 Marital condition (*de jure*): estimated population: by age and sex
England and Wales

Thousands

		Males							Females					
		1991[1]	2001[2]	2002[2]	2003	2004	2005		1991[1]	2001[2]	2002[2]	2003	2004	2005
All ages:														
	Single	KRPL	11 131	12 270	12 422	12 582	12 756	12 959	KUBS	9 824	10 917	11 051	11 188	11 338	11 528
	Married	KRPM	11 636	11 090	11 015	10 940	10 863	10 800	KVCC	11 833	11 150	11 073	11 000	10 935	10 880
	Widowed	KRPN	727	733	731	728	726	723	KVCD	2 951	2 745	2 709	2 668	2 628	2 588
	Divorced	KRPO	1 187	1 482	1 535	1 590	1 644	1 695	KVCE	1 459	1 975	2 035	2 096	2 156	2 215
Age groups:														
0 - 14:	Single	KRPP	4 939	5 036	4 999	4 963	4 940	4 916	KVCF	4 720	4 796	4 760	4 722	4 697	4 673
15 - 19:	Single	KRPQ	1 659	1 645	1 694	1 743	1 777	1 800	KVCG	1 554	1 560	1 595	1 637	1 668	1 694
	Married	KRPR	8	5	4	4	3	2	KVCH	32	16	13	12	11	9
	Widowed	KRPS	–	1	1	1	–	–	KVCI	–	1	1	1	–	–
	Divorced	KRPT	–	1	1	1	–	–	KVCJ	–	1	1	–	–	–
20 - 24:	Single	KRPU	1 717	1 501	1 534	1 573	1 621	1 682	KVCK	1 421	1 390	1 428	1 466	1 499	1 545
	Married	KRPV	242	74	69	69	67	65	KVCL	490	178	166	161	156	149
	Widowed	KRPW	–	1	1	1	1	1	KVCM	1	1	1	1	2	2
	Divorced	KRPX	12	3	3	3	3	3	KVCN	29	8	8	8	8	8
25 - 34:	Single	KRPY	1 652	2 227	2 238	2 253	2 279	2 331	KVCO	1 135	1 770	1 795	1 820	1 857	1 921
	Married	KRPZ	2 028	1 391	1 293	1 206	1 129	1 063	KVCP	2 488	1 768	1 662	1 566	1 481	1 415
	Widowed	KRQA	2	3	3	3	3	3	KVCQ	8	10	9	8	8	7
	Divorced	KRQB	237	136	131	126	121	115	KVCR	312	231	219	208	196	185
35 - 44:	Single	KRQC	477	963	1 031	1 089	1 142	1 195	KVEH	280	692	751	805	858	911
	Married	KRQD	2 632	2 494	2 489	2 471	2 445	2 415	KVEI	2 760	2 649	2 650	2 634	2 614	2 584
	Widowed	KRQE	11	12	12	12	11	11	KVEJ	34	36	35	34	32	31
	Divorced	KRQF	384	411	424	435	444	449	KVEK	444	558	571	583	593	597
45 - 54:	Single	KRQG	251	419	433	451	474	502	KVEL	144	256	271	289	311	336
	Married	KUAR	2 347	2 511	2 433	2 379	2 348	2 335	KVEM	2 322	2 548	2 475	2 427	2 400	2 388
	Widowed	KUBA	31	37	35	34	33	32	KVEN	118	111	105	99	96	93
	Divorced	KUBB	290	448	455	466	481	499	KVEO	332	557	566	578	594	614
55 - 59:	Single	KUBC	101	128	141	151	158	165	KVEP	69	74	81	87	92	97
	Married	KUBD	1 050	1 156	1 240	1 280	1 287	1 281	KVEQ	982	1 125	1 211	1 258	1 272	1 272
	Widowed	KUBE	34	34	36	37	37	37	KVER	136	112	115	114	112	109
	Divorced	KUBF	95	174	195	210	222	232	KVES	107	210	235	256	271	283
60 - 64:	Single	KUBG	104	97	97	100	103	108	KVET	80	62	61	62	63	65
	Married	KUBH	997	980	976	989	1 009	1 034	KVEU	908	906	909	928	956	990
	Widowed	KUBI	63	50	49	48	47	48	KVEV	250	178	172	167	163	160
	Divorced	KUBJ	70	125	131	138	147	157	KVEW	82	151	158	168	180	194
65 - 74:	Single	KUBK	150	155	154	154	153	152	KMGN	176	130	126	123	120	117
	Married	KUBL	1 574	1 569	1 582	1 600	1 612	1 619	KMGO	1 317	1 322	1 336	1 354	1 371	1 384
	Widowed	KUBM	229	188	184	179	176	172	KMGP	879	697	675	654	633	609
	Divorced	KUBN	74	139	149	159	169	180	KMGQ	107	177	190	204	218	231
75 and over:	Single	KUBO	81	99	101	104	107	110	KMGR	246	188	182	178	173	169
	Married	KUBP	759	909	928	945	963	986	KMGS	536	639	651	661	673	690
	Widowed	KUBQ	357	407	411	415	418	421	KMGT	1 526	1 598	1 597	1 590	1 583	1 577
	Divorced	KUBR	25	44	48	52	56	61	KMGU	46	81	86	91	96	103

1 Mid-1991 marital status estimates are revised in light of the 2001 Census
2 Mid-2001 and Mid-2002 marital status estimates were revised in light of the
  Local Authority Population Studies

Source: Office for National Statistics: 01329 813233

5.5 Geographical distribution of the population

Thousands

		Population enumerated in Census			Mid-year population estimates							
		1911	1931	1951	1971	1981	1991	2001	2002	2003	2004	2005
United Kingdom	KIUR	42 082	46 074	50 225	55 928	56 357	57 439	59 113	59 322	59 554	59 834	60 209
Great Britain	KISR	40 831	44 795	48 854	54 388	54 815	55 831	57 424	57 625	57 851	58 124	58 485
England	KKOJ	33 650	37 359	41 159	46 412	46 821	47 875	49 450	49 647	49 856	50 093	50 432
Standard Regions												
North	KKNA	2 729	2 938	3 009	3 152	3 117	3 073	3 028	3 026	3 029	3 040	3 057
Yorkshire and Humberside	KKNB	3 896	4 319	4 567	4 902	4 918	4 936	4 977	4 993	5 009	5 039	5 064
East Midlands	KKNC	2 467	2 732	3 118	3 652	3 853	4 011	4 190	4 223	4 252	4 280	4 306
East Anglia	KKND	1 191	1 231	1 381	1 688	1 894	2 068	2 181	2 192	2 219	2 238	2 265
South East	KKNE	11 613	13 349	14 877	17 125	17 011	17 511	18 566	18 645	18 712	18 792	18 959
South West	KKNF	2 818	2 984	3 479	4 112	4 381	4 688	4 943	4 968	4 999	5 038	5 068
West Midlands	KKNG	3 277	3 743	4 423	5 146	5 187	5 230	5 281	5 304	5 320	5 334	5 365
North West	KKNH	5 659	6 062	6 305	6 634	6 459	6 357	6 285	6 296	6 315	6 332	6 347
Government Office Regions												
North East	JZBU	..	–	–	2 679	2 636	2 587	2 540	2 538	2 539	2 545	2 558
North West (including Merseyside)	JZBW	..	–	–	7 108	6 940	6 843	6 773	6 783	6 805	6 827	6 846
Yorkshire and The Humber	JZBX	..	–	–	4 902	4 918	4 936	4 977	4 993	5 009	5 039	5 064
East Midlands	JZBY	..	–	–	3 652	3 853	4 011	4 190	4 223	4 252	4 280	4 306
West Midlands	JZBZ	..	–	–	5 146	5 187	5 230	5 281	5 304	5 320	5 334	5 365
South West	JZCA	..	–	–	4 112	4 381	4 688	4 943	4 968	4 999	5 038	5 068
East of England	JZCB	..	–	–	4 454	4 854	5 121	5 400	5 422	5 463	5 491	5 542
London	JZCC	..	–	–	7 529	6 806	6 829	7 322	7 371	7 388	7 429	7 518
South East	JZCD	..	–	–	6 830	7 245	7 629	8 023	8 044	8 080	8 110	8 164
Wales	KKNI	2 421	2 593	2 599	2 740	2 813	2 873	2 910	2 923	2 938	2 952	2 959
Scotland	KGJB	4 761	4 843	5 096	5 236	5 180	5 083	5 064	5 055	5 057	5 078	5 095
Northern Ireland[3]	KGJC	1 251	1 280	1 371	1 540	1 543	1 607	1 689	1 697	1 703	1 710	1 724
Greater London	KKNJ	7 161	8 110	8 197	7 529	6 806	6 829	7 322	7 371	7 388	7 429	7 518
Inner London[1]	KISS	4 998	4 893	3 679	3 060	2 550	2 599	2 859	2 892	2 905	2 931	2 986
Outer London[1]	KITF	2 162	3 217	4 518	4 470	4 255	4 230	4 463	4 479	4 483	4 498	4 532
Metropolitan areas of England and Wales	KITG	9 716	10 770	11 365	11 862	11 353	11 085	10 888	10 908	10 925	10 956	11 005
Tyne and Wear	KGJN	1 105	1 201	1 201	1 218	1 155	1 124	1 087	1 084	1 083	1 086	1 095
West Yorkshire	KGJP	1 852	1 939	1 985	2 090	2 067	2 062	2 083	2 091	2 096	2 108	2 119
South Yorkshire	KGJO	963	1 173	1 253	1 331	1 317	1 289	1 266	1 269	1 273	1 278	1 286
West Midlands	KGJQ	1 780	2 143	2 547	2 811	2 673	2 619	2 568	2 576	2 578	2 579	2 591
Greater Manchester	KGJR	2 638	2 727	2 716	2 750	2 619	2 554	2 516	2 522	2 531	2 539	2 548
Merseyside	KGJS	1 378	1 587	1 663	1 662	1 522	1 438	1 368	1 365	1 364	1 366	1 367
Principal Metropolitan Cities[1]	KITH	3 154	3 906	3 915	3 910	3 550	3 415	3 344	3 355	3 361	3 379	3 410
Newcastle	KGJT	267	286	292	312	284	275	266	266	267	269	276
Leeds	KGJX	446	483	505	749	718	707	716	716	715	720	723
Sheffield	KGJV	455	512	513	579	548	520	513	513	513	516	521
Birmingham	KGKF	526	1 003	1 113	1 107	1 021	1 005	985	990	992	992	1 001
Manchester	KGKJ	714	766	703	554	463	433	423	429	432	437	441
Liverpool	KGKM	746	856	789	610	517	476	442	442	442	444	447
Other metropolitan districts[1]	KITI	6 562	6 864	7 450	7 952	7 803	7 670	7 544	7 552	7 565	7 577	7 596
Non-metropolitan districts of England and Wales	KITJ	19 194	21 072	24 196	29 761	31 475	32 834	31 239	31 368	31 543	31 708	31 908
Non-metropolitan cities[1,2]	KITK	..	–	–	4 715	4 617	–	–	–	–	–	–
Incl. Kingston-upon-Hull	KKNZ	278	314	299	288	274	263	250	248	248	249	249
Leicester	KKOA	227	239	285	285	283	281	283	284	284	285	288
Nottingham	KKNX	260	269	308	302	278	279	269	271	274	275	279
Bristol	KKNV	357	397	443	433	401	392	390	390	392	394	398
Plymouth	KITL	207	215	225	249	253	251	241	241	241	244	246
Stoke-on-Trent	KKOD	235	277	275	265	252	249	240	239	238	238	238
Cardiff	KKOB	182	224	244	291	281	297	310	313	315	317	320
Industrial districts[1,2]	KITM	..	–	–	6 486	6 713	..	–	–	–	–	–
New Towns[1,2]	KITN	..	–	–	1 895	2 194	..	–	–	–	–	–
Resort, port and retirement districts[1,2]	KITO	..	–	–	3 184	3 368	–	–	–	–	–	–
Urban and mixed urban/rural districts[1,2]	KITP	..	–	–	8 821	9 446	–	–	–	–	–	–
Remoter, mainly rural districts[1,2]	KITQ	..	–	–	4 661	5 137	–	–	–	–	–	–
City of Edinburgh local government district	KGKU	320	439	467	478	446	436	449	448	448	455	458
City of Glasgow local government district	KGKT	784	1 088	1 090	983	774	629	579	577	577	578	579
Belfast[3]	KGKV	387	438	444	–	316	293	277	274	272	269	–

1 Details of the classification by broad area type are given in recent issues of the ONS annual reference volume *Key Population and Vital Statistics; local and health authority areas* (Series VS). The ten broad area types include all local authorities in England and Wales.

2 The breakdown of non-metropolitan districts by area type has not been provided from mid-2001 onwards. This is because the effect of boundary changes due to the major local government reorganisation on 1 April 1995 and 1 April 1996 (particularly in Wales) make the comparison of 2001 data with data for earlier years invalid.

3 1931 figures shown for Northern Ireland and the City of Belfast relate to the 1937 Census.

Sources: Office for National Statistics: 01329 813318; General Register Office for Scotland; Northern Ireland Statistics and Research Agency

5.6 Population: by ethnic group and age, January - December 2005
United Kingdom

Percentages and thousands

	0 to 4	5 to 9	10 to 14	15 to 19	20 to 24	25 to 29	30 to 34	35 to 44	45 to 59	60 to 74	75 and over	All ages (=100%) (thousands)
White												
British	5	6	6	6	6	5	6	15	21	15	8	48 973
Other	4	4	4	4	8	11	10	17	18	14	7	2 570
Mixed												
White and Black Caribbean	17	19	17	15	9	6	4	6	4	1	0	211
White and Black African	19	17	12	11	11	7	2	10	8	1	1	76
White and Asian	19	15	16	11	7	6	5	12	5	3	0	151
Other Mixed	16	13	13	9	12	8	5	11	11	2	1	135
Asian												
Indian	7	6	7	7	9	11	9	16	18	8	2	1 081
Pakistani	11	11	10	10	10	8	9	13	12	4	1	829
Bangladeshi	13	12	11	10	10	9	8	12	10	5	1	334
Other Asian	9	7	6	6	7	10	14	18	16	6	1	380
Black												
Black Caribbean	6	7	7	7	6	6	6	22	15	12	5	583
Black African	12	10	8	8	7	10	11	18	11	3	1	653
Black Other	9	11	11	10	9	7	8	14	13	6	1	60
Chinese	5	4	5	7	20	13	8	14	18	5	2	228
Other	7	8	6	7	8	13	12	19	15	4	1	700
All[1]	6	6	7	7	6	6	7	15	20	14	7	58 692

1 Includes those who did not state their ethnic origin.

Source: Office for National Statistics, Annual Population Survey

5.7 Total international migration estimates:[1] citizenship
United Kingdom

Thousands

	All citizenships	British	Non-British	European Union[2]	Commonwealth Old[3]	Commonwealth New[4]	Other foreign[5]
Inflow							
	C58E	C58H	C58K	C58N	C58Q	C58T	C58W
1997	326.1	88.9	237.2	71.5	31.2	58.7	75.7
1998	390.3	103.1	287.3	81.8	53.9	51.0	100.5
1999	453.8	116.4	337.4	66.6	54.4	66.5	149.9
2000	483.4	104.1	379.3	63.1	57.2	90.9	168.1
2001	479.6	106.3	373.3	60.4	67.4	83.9	161.6
2002	512.8	94.6	418.2	62.8	65.6	92.9	196.8
2003	512.6	105.8	406.8	64.0	62.7	103.1	177.0
2004	582.1	88.0	494.1	117.3	76.2	143.0	157.7
2005	565.0	91.0	474.0	145.0	68.0	121.0	140.0
Outflow							
	C58F	C58I	C58L	C58O	C58R	C58U	C58X
1997	279.2	148.7	130.6	53.2	20.1	19.8	37.5
1998	251.5	125.8	125.7	48.9	19.7	13.2	44.0
1999	290.8	139.2	151.6	58.6	28.8	12.3	51.9
2000	320.7	161.1	159.6	57.0	32.2	14.9	55.5
2001	307.7	159.2	148.5	49.1	32.1	18.6	48.6
2002	359.4	185.7	173.7	51.7	42.3	15.8	63.9
2003	361.5	190.9	170.6	49.9	41.9	16.6	62.2
2004	359.5	207.6	151.9	43.1	35.1	20.0	53.6
2005	380.0	198.0	181.0	56.0	39.0	24.0	62.0
Balance							
	C58G	C58J	C58M	C58P	C58S	C58V	C58Y
1997	46.8	−59.8	106.6	18.3	11.2	38.9	38.2
1998	138.8	−22.7	161.6	33.0	34.2	37.9	56.6
1999	163.0	−22.8	185.8	8.0	25.6	54.2	98.0
2000	162.8	−57.0	219.7	6.1	25.0	76.0	112.6
2001	171.8	−53.0	224.8	11.2	35.2	65.4	113.0
2002	153.4	−91.1	244.5	11.1	23.4	77.1	132.9
2003	151.0	−85.2	236.2	14.2	20.8	86.5	114.8
2004	222.6	−119.6	342.2	74.1	41.1	123.0	104.0
2005	185.0	−107.0	292.0	89.0	29.0	97.0	78.0

1 Based mainly on data from the International Passenger Survey. Includes adjustments for (1) those whose intended length of stay changes so that their migrant status changes; (2) asylum seekers and their dependants not identified by the IPS; and (3) flows between the UK and the Republic of Ireland.
2 Up to and including 2003, estimates are shown for the EU15 (UK, Austria, Belgium, Denmark, Finland, France, Germany, Greece, the Irish Republic, Italy, Luxembourg, Netherlands, Portugal, Spain and Sweden). From 2004 onwards, the estimates are for the EU25 (EU15 plus the 10 countries of Cyprus, the Czech Republic, Estonia, Hungary, Latvia, Lithuania, Malta, Poland, Slovakia and Slovenia). These countries are included in the definition for the whole of 2004, whether migration occurred before or after 1 May.
3 Figures for all years include South Africa in the Old Commonwealth.
4 Figures for all years include Pakistan in the New Commonwealth. From 2004 onwards, the New Commonwealth excludes Malta and Cyprus.
5 Figures for all years include Hong Kong.

Source: Office for National Statistics: 01329 813255

5.8 Estimates of migration into and out of the United Kingdom by usual occupation[1,2] and sex

Thousands

	Total			Professional and managerial			Manual and clerical			Not gainfully employed[3]		
	Persons	Males	Females	Persons	Males	Females	Persons	Males	Females	Persons	Males	Females
Inflow												
	KGOA	KGOB	KGOC	KGOD	KGOE	KGOF	KGOG	KGOH	KGOI	KGOJ	KGOK	KGOL
1997	273	137	136	89	57	33	42	23	19	141	57	84
1998	318	160	158	112	65	47	71	35	35	136	60	76
1999	354	181	173	131	77	54	77	41	36	146	63	83
2000	364	191	173	163	98	65	64	34	30	137	60	77
2001	372	187	185	142	78	63	77	38	39	154	71	82
2002	386	200	186	142	78	64	83	44	39	161	77	83
2003	431	212	220	144	77	67	98	46	52	189	89	100
2004	518	261	257	175	102	72	131	66	66	212	92	120
2005	496	273	223	170	100	70	143	86	57	184	87	96
Outflow												
	KGPA	KGPB	KGPC	KGPD	KGPE	KGPF	KGPG	KGPH	KGPI	KGPJ	KGPK	KGPL
1997	232	125	107	88	59	29	50	23	26	94	43	51
1998	206	103	103	82	48	34	42	22	21	82	33	48
1999	245	132	114	97	60	38	69	32	37	79	41	39
2000	278	154	124	128	80	48	59	36	23	90	37	53
2001	251	136	115	104	67	37	60	30	30	88	39	49
2002	306	162	144	124	79	45	80	41	40	102	42	59
2003	314	165	149	108	60	49	103	59	44	103	46	57
2004	310	152	158	114	65	49	73	40	33	123	47	76
2005	328	187	141	137	88	50	83	47	37	108	53	55
Balance												
	KGRA	KGRB	KGRC	KGRD	KGRE	KGRF	KGRG	KGRH	KGRI	KGRJ	KGRK	KGRL
1997	40	12	29	1	−2	3	−7	−1	−7	47	14	33
1998	113	57	55	30	17	13	28	13	15	54	27	27
1999	109	49	60	33	17	16	8	9	−2	67	22	45
2000	87	38	49	35	18	17	5	−2	8	47	22	24
2001	121	51	69	38	11	26	17	8	10	66	33	34
2002	80	38	42	18	−1	19	3	4	−1	59	35	24
2003	118	47	71	36	17	18	−5	−14	9	87	43	44
2004	208	109	99	61	37	23	58	26	32	89	46	43
2005	168	86	82	33	12	21	60	39	20	76	35	41

1 See chapter text.
2 Refers to regular occupation before migration.
3 Includes housewives, students, children and retired persons.

Source: Office for National Statistics: 01329 813255

5.9 Estimates of migration into and out of the United Kingdom by citizenship and country of last or next residence

Thousands

| | All migrants | British citizens | | | | | | European Union citizens[1] (excluding British) | | | |
| | | | Country of last/next residence | | | | | | Country of last/next residence | | |
	Total	Total	European[1] Union	Old[2] Common-wealth	New[3] Common-wealth	United States of America	Other countries	Total	European[1] Union	Other Europe	Other countries
Inflow											
	KEZR	KGLA	KGLB	KGLC	KGLD	KGLE	KGLF	KGLG	KGLH	KGLI	KGLJ
1997	273	90	36	20	10	7	17	62	56	–	6
1998	318	104	29	29	14	16	16	70	62	–	7
1999	354	117	32	38	16	11	20	60	55	–	5
2000	364	104	34	29	14	8	19	59	53	–	6
2001	372	106	26	31	17	10	22	57	54	–	3
2002	386	94	29	22	10	9	24	59	53	3	3
2003	431	106	40	29	12	10	15	61	54	1	6
2004	518	85	23	24	15	9	16	108	100	..	7
2005	496	89	36	23	12	8	11	125	117	2	6
Outflow											
	KEZS	KGMA	KGMB	KGMC	KGMD	KGME	KGMF	KGMG	KGMH	KGMI	KGMJ
1997	232	135	41	38	13	16	27	32	27	1	4
1998	206	114	37	36	8	15	19	26	21	1	4
1999	245	115	37	41	8	14	14	47	41	–	6
2000	278	141	41	48	9	19	24	46	39	1	6
2001	251	134	43	47	7	15	22	40	34	1	5
2002	306	165	69	44	10	18	24	42	38	..	4
2003	314	170	71	55	9	13	22	42	33	3	5
2004	310	184	68	62	12	16	27	34	30	1	3
2005	328	174	74	62	6	10	22	47	42	1	4
Balance											
	KEZT	KGNA	KGNB	KGNC	KGND	KGNE	KGNF	KGNG	KGNH	KGNI	KGNJ
1997	40	−45	−5	−18	−2	−9	−10	30	29	−1	2
1998	113	−10	−8	−7	7	1	−3	44	41	−1	4
1999	109	2	−6	−3	7	−3	6	13	14	–	−2
2000	87	−37	−8	−19	6	−12	−4	13	14	−1	–
2001	121	−28	−17	−15	10	−6	..	17	20	−1	−1
2002	80	−70	−40	−21	..	−9	−1	17	15	3	−1
2003	118	−64	−31	−26	3	−3	−7	19	21	−3	1
2004	208	−99	−46	−38	3	−7	−11	74	70	−1	4
2005	168	−85	−38	−39	5	−2	−11	78	74	1	3

5.9 Estimates of migration into and out of the United Kingdom by citizenship and country of last or next residence

continued

Thousands

| | Commonwealth[4] citizens | | | | | | | | | | Other foreign citizens[1] | | | | |
| | Country of last/next residence | | | | | | | | | | Country of last/next residence | | | | |
	Total	Aust-ralia	Canada	New Zealand	South Africa	Bangl-adesh, India, Sri Lanka	Pakistan	Other African Common-wealth	Carib-bean Common-wealth	Other[5] count-ries	Total	Euro-[1]pean Union	Other Europe	United States of America	Other coun-tries
Inflow															
	KGLK	KGLL	KGLM	KGLN	KTDK	KGLO	KGLP	KGLQ	KGLR	KGLT	KGLU	KGLV	KGLW	KGLX	KGLY
1997	75	14	5	7	5	15	5	6	1	18	45	–	7	11	27
1998	88	24	5	13	11	10	4	10	1	11	56	4	7	18	27
1999	98	26	2	12	12	14	6	14	3	9	79	3	19	15	42
2000	114	23	6	11	14	21	9	13	1	16	87	2	11	13	61
2001	123	32	4	10	12	21	9	18	2	14	87	1	12	12	61
2002	124	22	5	9	20	27	6	23	2	9	109	2	11	16	81
2003	141	20	6	8	20	37	8	23	3	16	124	2	23	16	82
2004	205	26	5	8	29	55	21	39	4	17	120	1	11	14	95
2005	172	24	4	11	23	59	14	24	1	12	110	4	13	14	79
Outflow															
	KGMK	KGML	KGMM	KGMN	KTDL	KGMO	KGMP	KGMQ	KGMR	KGMT	KGMU	KGMV	KGMW	KGMX	KGMY
1997	36	7	1	5	5	2	2	2	1	12	29	2	5	9	13
1998	30	9	1	3	4	2	1	2	–	6	35	2	7	9	18
1999	38	11	2	6	4	1	–	1	–	11	45	–	9	14	21
2000	43	12	3	8	5	2	2	2	1	8	48	3	11	9	24
2001	44	15	3	6	5	3	1	2	1	7	33	1	9	7	16
2002	52	18	6	9	5	3	2	2	–	7	47	2	12	16	18
2003	53	19	2	8	9	4	1	2	–	8	48	2	12	8	26
2004	50	17	4	5	7	3	1	3	–	11	42	5	2	8	28
2005	59	15	4	8	9	8	6	2	..	6	49	1	7	14	28
Balance															
	KGNK	KGNL	KGNM	KGNN	KTDM	KGNO	KGNP	KGNQ	KGNR	KGNT	KGNU	KGNV	KGNW	KGNX	KGNY
1997	39	7	4	2	1	13	3	4	–	7	16	–2	2	3	14
1998	59	15	3	10	7	7	3	8	1	5	21	2	–	9	9
1999	60	15	–	6	8	13	6	12	3	–2	34	3	10	2	20
2000	71	11	3	3	9	19	8	10	–	7	40	–1	–	4	36
2001	79	17	..	4	7	18	9	16	1	7	53	..	3	5	45
2002	72	4	–1	..	15	24	4	21	2	2	61	..	–2	..	63
2003	87	1	3	..	11	33	7	21	3	8	75	..	11	8	56
2004	154	9	1	4	22	52	20	36	4	6	79	–4	9	6	67
2005	114	9	1	3	14	52	9	22	1	5	61	3	7	1	51

1 Up to and including 2003, estimates are shown for the EU15 (UK, Austria, Belgium, Denmark, Finland, France, Germany, Greece, the Irish Republic, Italy, Luxembourg, Netherlands, Portugal, Spain and Sweden). From 2004 onwards, the estimates are for the EU25 (EU15 plus the 10 countries of Cyprus, the Czech Republic, Estonia, Hungary, Latvia, Lithuania, Malta, Po-land, Slovakia and Slovenia). These countries are included in the definition for the whole of 2004, whether migration occurred before or after 1 May.

2 Figures for all years include South Africa in the Old Commonwealth.

3 Figures for all years include Pakistan in the New Commonwealth. From 2004 onwards, the New Commonwealth excludes Malta and Cyprus.

4 Figures for all years include South Africa and Pakinstan in the Commonwealth. From 2004 onwards, the Commonwealth excludes Malta and Cyprus.

5 From 2004 onwards, Other countries includes Malta and Cyprus.

Source: Office for National Statistics: 01329 813255

5.10 Acceptances for settlement by nationality[1,2]
United Kingdom

Number of persons

Geographical region and nationality		2003	2004[3,4]	2005[5]	Geographical region and nationality		2003	2004[3,4]	2005[5]
All nationalities	KGFA	139 280	139 210	179 120	**Africa (continued)**				
					Somalia	KGHG	6 305	3 825	8 255
Europe[1]					South Africa	KGHH	8 805	7 560	9 385
					Sudan	KGHI	665	745	730
Accession States					Tanzania	KGHJ	510	570	700
Cyprus	KGFN	565	160	..	Tunisia	KGHK	220	115	135
Czech Republic	LQLS	515	520	..	Uganda	KGHL	830	960	1 065
Estonia	LQLU	75	165	..	Zambia	KGHM	560	500	830
Hungary	KGFZ	325	100	..	Zimbabwe	KGHN	3 675	3 765	4 520
Latvia	LQLV	125	210	..	Other Africa	KOSU	3 080	3 585	5 600
Lithuania	LQLW	325	610	..					
Malta	KGFP	95	25	..	Africa	KGHO	44 860	39 430	54 080
Poland	KGGA	1 290	1 220	..					
Slovakia	LQLT	425	255	..	**Asia**				
Slovenia	LQMB	20	5	..	Indian sub-continent				
					Bangladesh	KGHP	5 590	3 115	3 085
Accession States	EL2O	3 755	3 275	..	India	KGHQ	10 955	11 100	16 720
					Pakistan	KGHR	12 945	10 020	9 185
Remainder of Europe									
Bulgaria	KGFW	750	625	1 225	Indian sub-continent	KGHS	29 490	24 235	28 990
Croatia	LQMA	280	985	625	Middle East				
Romania	KGGB	565	560	955	Iran	KGHT	1 585	1 725	2 055
Russia	LQLX	2 160	1 620	1 795	Iraq	KGHU	1 440	1 725	4 675
Serbia & Montenegro	LQMC	1 165	9 590	6 805	Israel	KGHV	500	505	590
Turkey	KGFT	4 365	6 060	5 330	Jordan	KGHW	180	250	310
Ukraine	LQLY	805	1 050	1 195	Kuwait	KGHX	75	90	70
Other former USSR	LQLZ	625	830	1 015	Lebanon	KGHY	310	490	535
Other former Yugoslavia	LQMD	510	285	385	Saudi Arabia	KGHZ	75	60	70
Other Europe	KOSO	315	1 700	1 485	Syria	KGIA	280	255	295
					Yemen	KOSV	405	420	410
Remainder of Europe	EL2P	11 540	23 310	20 810	Other Middle East	KOSW	170	525	380
Europe[1]	KOSP	15 295	26 585	20 810	Middle East	KGIB	5 020	6 045	9 395
Americas					**Remainder of Asia**				
Argentina	KGGF	155	95	145	China	KGIC	2 540	2 310	3 985
Barbados	KGGG	160	145	120	Hong Kong[7]	KOSX	725	540	805
Brazil	KGGH	695	565	645	Indonesia	KGID	315	195	300
Canada	KGGI	1 710	1 225	1 215	Japan	KGIE	1 850	1 360	1 540
Chile	KGGJ	120	65	50	Malaysia	KGIF	1 150	955	1 945
Colombia	KGGK	1 000	1 745	1 555	Philippines	KGIG	3 810	8 200	14 710
Guyana	KGGM	275	170	235	Singapore	KGIH	265	305	290
Jamaica	KGGN	4 500	2 930	2 780	South Korea	KOTE	735	570	815
Mexico	KGGO	245	130	140	Sri Lanka	KGII	2 555	4 870	5 475
Peru	KGGP	180	110	220	Taiwan	KOSY	255	205	230
Trinidad and Tobago	KGGQ	655	565	505	Thailand	KGIJ	2 020	985	1 945
USA	KGGR	5 620	4 120	4 350	Other Asia	KOSZ	4 215	2 320	13 315
Venezuela	KGGT	120	85	155					
Other Americas	KOSR	1 025	2 175	1 790	Remainder of Asia	KGIL	20 435	22 815	45 355
Americas	KGGU	16 465	14 130	13 905	Asia	KGIM	54 945	53 095	83 740
Africa					**Oceania**				
Algeria	KGGV	945	1 005	940	Australia	KGIN	4 120	3 240	3 740
Angola	KOSS	620	1 090	1 695	New Zealand	KGIO	2 920	2 370	2 505
Congo (Dem. Rep.)[6]	KOST	1 475	2 410	2 960	Other Oceania	KOTA	85	85	90
Egypt	KGGW	615	485	615					
Ethiopia	KGGX	285	520	735	Oceania	KGIP	7 125	5 690	6 335
Ghana	KGGY	4 015	2 305	2 880					
Kenya	KGHA	1 585	2 255	2 690	British Overseas citizens	KGIQ	265	75	95
Libya	KGHB	380	465	360	Nationality unknown	KGIS	330	205	160
Mauritius	KGHC	695	530	860					
Morocco	KGHD	660	305	390	**All nationalities**	KGFA	139 280	139 210	179 120
Nigeria	KGHE	7 570	4 620	5 310					
Sierra Leone	KGHF	1 375	1 805	3 420					

1 Excluding European Economic Area and Swiss nationals throughout the period covered.
2 Data from 2003 also excludes dependants of EEA and Swiss nationals in confirmed relationships granted permanant residence.
3 Includes nationals of the Czech Republic, Cyprus, Estonia, Hungary, Latvia, Luthuania, Malta, Poland, Slovakia and Slovenia before 1 May, but excludes them from this date.
4 Revised.
5 Provisional.
6 Formerly known as Zaire.
7 Hong Kong (Special Administrative Region of China) includes British overseas territories citizens and stateless persons from Hong Kong and British Nationals (overseas).

Source: Home Office: 020 8760 8289

5.11 Applications[1] received for asylum in the United Kingdom, excluding dependants, by nationality

Number of principal applicants

		1997	1998	1999[2]	2000[2]	2001	2002	2003	2004	2005[3]
Europe										
Albania	LQME	445	560	1 310	1 490	1 065	1 150	595	295	175
Macedonia	PTDW	20	50	90	65	755	310	60	15	5
Moldova	VQHP	20	25	180	235	425	820	380	170	115
Romania	KEAV	605	1 015	1 985	2 160	1 400	1 210	550	295	115
Russia	ZAEQ	180	185	685	1 000	450	295	280	190	130
Serbia & Montenegro	ZAFA	1 865	7 395	11 465	6 070	3 230	2 265	815	290	155
Turkey	KEAW	1 445	2 015	2 850	3 990	3 695	2 835	2 390	1 230	755
Ukraine	ZAER	490	370	775	770	445	365	300	120	55
E U Accession States	GH5T	2 785	4 975	5 350	3 745	2 025	3 200	310	75	10
Other Former USSR	ZAES	155	300	875	1 050	485	615	520	315	265
Europe Other	ZAEU	1 135	855	2 715	2 310	245	175	85	35	35
Total	KEAZ	9 145	17 745	28 280	22 880	14 215	13 235	6 295	3 025	1 810
Americas										
Colombia	KEBZ	1 330	425	1 000	505	365	420	220	120	70
Ecuador	KYDB	1 205	280	610	445	255	315	150	35	10
Jamaica	PTDX	130	105	180	310	525	1 310	965	455	325
Americas Other	PTDY	165	165	240	155	170	240	230	130	100
Total	KECT	2 825	975	2 025	1 420	1 315	2 290	1 560	740	505
Africa										
Algeria	KOTB	715	1 260	1 385	1 635	1 140	1 060	550	490	255
Angola	KECU	195	150	545	800	1 015	1 420	850	400	145
Burundi	PTDZ	85	215	780	620	610	700	650	265	90
Cameroon	VQHU	175	95	245	355	380	615	505	360	290
Congo	PTEA	90	150	450	485	540	600	320	150	65
Dem. Rep. Congo	KEEH	690	660	1 240	1 030	1 370	2 215	1 540	1 475	1 080
Eritrea	PTEC	125	345	565	505	620	1 180	950	1 105	1 760
Ethiopia	KECW	145	345	455	415	610	700	640	540	385
Gambia	DMMA	125	45	30	50	65	130	95	100	90
Ghana	KECX	350	225	195	285	190	275	325	355	230
Ivory Coast	DMLZ	70	95	190	445	275	315	390	280	210
Kenya	KOTC	605	885	485	455	305	350	220	145	100
Liberia	C53K	205	70	65	55	115	450	740	405	175
Nigeria	KECY	1 480	1 380	945	835	810	1 125	1 010	1 090	1 025
Rwanda	ZAEV	90	280	820	760	530	655	260	75	40
Sierra Leone	KOTD	815	565	1 125	1 330	1 940	1 155	380	230	135
Somalia	KECZ	2 730	4 685	7 495	5 020	6 420	6 540	5 090	2 585	1 760
Sudan	KEEE	230	250	280	415	390	655	930	1 305	885
Tanzania	DMMC	90	80	80	60	80	40	30	20	20
Uganda	KEEG	220	210	420	740	480	715	705	405	205
Zimbabwe	GRFS	60	80	230	1 010	2 140	7 655	3 295	2 065	1 075
Africa Other	PTEB	220	305	400	615	555	845	895	910	615
Total	KEEJ	9 515	12 380	18 435	17 920	20 590	29 390	20 370	14 745	10 640
Middle East										
Iran	KEEK	585	745	1 320	5 610	3 420	2 630	2 875	3 455	3 150
Iraq	KEEL	1 075	1 295	1 800	7 475	6 680	14 570	4 015	1 695	1 415
Libya	GH5U	100	115	115	155	140	200	145	160	125
Syria	GH5V	50	65	95	140	110	70	110	350	330
Middle East Other	ZAEX	525	565	835	1 035	915	850	825	870	715
Total	KEGY	2 335	2 785	4 165	14 415	11 265	18 315	7 970	6 525	5 730
Asia										
Afghanistan	DMLY	1 085	2 395	3 975	5 555	8 920	7 205	2 280	1 395	1 580
Bangladesh	ZAEY	545	460	530	795	510	720	735	510	425
China	KEGZ	1 945	1 925	2 625	4 000	2 390	3 675	3 450	2 365	1 730
India	KEIL	1 285	1 030	1 365	2 120	1 850	1 865	2 290	1 405	940
Pakistan	KEIM	1 615	1 975	2 615	3 165	2 860	2 405	1 915	1 710	1 145
Sri Lanka	KEIN	1 830	3 505	5 130	6 395	5 510	3 130	705	330	395
Vietnam	VQIB	10	35	105	180	400	840	1 125	755	380
Asia Other	PTEE	255	615	1 120	1 025	1 040	915	655	375	320
Total	KEJO	8 570	11 940	17 465	23 230	23 480	20 755	13 155	8 850	6 915
Nationality not known	KEJP	105	190	785	450	160	145	55	70	105
Grand Total	KEJQ	32 500	46 015	71 160	80 315	71 025	84 130	49 405	33 960	25 710

1 Figures rounded to the nearest 5.
2 May exclude some cases lodged at Local Enforcement Offices between
   January 1999 and March 2000.
3 Provisional figures.

Source: Home Office: 020 8760 8274

41

5.12 Marriages: by previous marital status, sex, age and country

Numbers

		1995	1996	1997	1998	1999	2000	2001	2002	2003	2004	2005
United Kingdom[1,2]												
Marriages	KKAA	322 251	317 514	310 218	304 797	301 083	305 912	286 129	293 021	308 623	313 551	283 731
Persons marrying per 1,000 resident population	KKAB	11.1	10.9	10.6	10.4	10.3	10.4	9.7	9.9	10.4	10.4	9.4
Previous marital status												
Single men[3]	KKAC	227 717	221 826	216 237	214 005	211 820	213 777	202 690	206 196	217 534	221 477	199 268
Divorced men	KKAD	85 743	87 113	85 625	82 977	81 750	84 771	76 852	80 040	84 011	85 210	77 995
Widowers	KKAE	8 791	8 575	8 356	7 815	7 513	7 364	6 587	6 785	7 078	6 864	6 468
Single women[3]	KKAF	228 462	221 697	216 776	215 399	213 246	215 865	205 048	208 385	219 828	224 344	202 994
Divorced women	KKAG	85 396	87 618	85 648	82 016	80 816	83 166	74 807	78 182	82 181	82 559	14 555
Widows	KKAH	8 393	8 199	7 794	7 382	7 021	6 881	6 274	6 454	6 614	6 648	66 182
First marriage for both partners	KMGH	192 078	185 293	181 135	180 404	178 759	180 020	171 912	174 374	184 661	188 517	170 838
First marriage for one partner	KMGI	72 023	72 937	70 743	68 596	67 548	69 602	63 914	65 833	68 040	68 787	60 566
Remarriage for both partners	KMGJ	58 150	59 284	58 340	55 797	54 776	56 290	50 303	52 814	55 922	56 247	52 317
Males												
Under 21 years	KKAI	6 302	5 497	5 126	5 173	5 234	5 019	4 625	4 396	4 340	4 233	3 179
21-24	KKAJ	49 432	42 488	36 875	32 723	29 390	28 467	25 840	26 293	27 155	27 223	22 105
25-29	KKAK	105 218	101 647	97 345	94 696	90 412	85 870	78 687	74 858	75 580	74 873	67 177
30-34	KKAL	68 245	69 867	70 904	71 096	72 129	73 809	70 657	72 592	75 892	75 705	67 623
35-44	KKAM	53 350	56 513	58 292	59 838	62 114	68 019	65 242	69 747	75 695	79 510	73 559
45-54	KKAN	24 786	26 252	26 472	26 118	26 581	28 791	26 122	27 801	30 387	31 851	30 518
55 and over	KKAO	14 918	15 250	15 204	15 153	15 223	15 937	14 956	17 334	19 574	20 156	19 580
Females												
Under 21 years	KKAP	20 643	18 485	17 254	16 793	16 082	15 938	13 874	13 194	13 510	12 878	8 941
21-24	KKAQ	75 071	66 191	59 549	54 645	50 350	48 578	45 687	45 789	47 400	46 891	39 067
25-29	KKAR	100 644	99 651	97 932	97 181	94 703	92 753	85 647	82 892	84 066	84 714	78 647
30-34	KKAS	54 819	57 752	58 589	59 349	60 446	62 478	59 859	62 279	65 979	66 508	60 298
35-44	KKAT	43 115	45 969	47 267	47 721	50 136	54 697	52 209	56 997	61 682	65 007	60 401
45-54	KKAU	19 720	21 025	21 038	20 708	20 822	22 621	20 459	22 187	24 721	25 846	24 811
55 and over	KKAV	8 239	8 441	8 589	8 400	8 544	8 847	8 394	9 683	11 265	11 707	11 566
England and Wales[1]												
Marriages	KKBA	283 012	278 975	272 536	267 303	263 515	267 961	249 227	255 596	270 109	273 069	244 710
Persons marrying per 1,000 resident population	KKBB	11.0	10.9	10.6	10.3	10.1	10.3	9.5	9.7	10.2	10.3	9.2
Previous marital status												
Single men[3]	KKBC	198 208	193 306	188 268	186 329	184 266	186 113	175 721	179 121	189 470	191 956	170 890
Divorced men	KKBD	76 967	78 003	76 839	74 029	72 617	75 378	67 678	70 506	74 397	75 129	68 130
Widowers	KKBE	7 837	7 666	7 429	6 945	6 632	6 470	5 828	5 969	6 242	5 984	5 690
Single women[3]	KKBF	198 603	192 707	188 457	187 391	185 328	187 717	177 506	180 675	191 170	194 348	173 930
Divorced women	KKBG	76 869	78 939	77 098	73 330	71 971	74 092	66 120	69 234	73 071	72 875	5 350
Widows	KKBH	7 540	7 329	6 981	6 582	6 216	6 152	5 601	5 687	5 868	5 846	65 430
First marriage for both partners	KMGK	166 418	160 680	156 907	156 539	155 027	156 140	148 642	151 014	160 283	163 007	146 120
First marriage for one partner	KMGL	63 975	64 653	62 911	60 642	59 540	61 550	55 943	57 768	60 074	60 290	52 560
Remarriage for both partners	KMGM	52 619	53 642	52 718	50 122	48 948	50 271	44 642	46 814	49 752	49 772	46 020
Males												
Under 21 years	KKBI	5 520	4 877	4 574	4 608	4 629	4 536	4 160	3 952	3 885	3 803	2 800
21-24	KKBJ	42 711	36 713	31 907	28 389	25 424	24 764	22 436	22 961	23 802	23 873	19 180
25-29	KKBK	91 607	88 338	84 644	82 135	78 364	74 367	67 934	64 619	65 568	64 701	57 300
30-34	KKBL	60 014	61 582	62 265	62 323	63 212	64 611	61 409	62 998	66 060	65 510	58 000
35-44	KKBM	47 330	50 038	51 654	52 812	54 528	59 834	56 872	61 196	66 364	69 364	63 610
45-54	KKBN	22 349	23 661	23 688	23 385	23 676	25 470	22 949	24 336	26 785	27 830	26 460
55 and over	KKBO	13 481	13 766	13 804	13 651	13 682	14 379	13 467	15 534	17 645	17 988	17 370
Females												
Under 21 years	KKBP	18 343	16 510	15 439	15 065	14 379	14 421	12 467	11 916	12 270	11 667	8 010
21-24	KKBQ	65 126	57 296	51 766	47 446	43 691	42 265	39 746	39 968	41 567	40 962	33 770
25-29	KKBR	87 680	86 838	85 352	84 399	82 250	80 312	73 799	71 540	72 790	73 072	67 130
30-34	KKBS	48 216	50 799	51 405	51 982	52 721	54 649	51 865	53 970	57 348	57 592	51 620
35-44	KKBT	38 367	40 889	41 838	42 245	44 199	48 245	45 672	49 984	54 103	56 660	52 190
45-54	KKBU	17 791	18 992	18 938	18 575	18 572	20 083	18 071	19 535	21 858	22 648	21 640
55 and over	KKBV	7 489	7 651	7 798	7 591	7 703	7 986	7 607	8 683	10 173	10 468	10 350

5.12 Marriages: by previous marital status, sex, age and country
continued

Numbers

		1995	1996	1997	1998	1999	2000	2001	2002	2003	2004	2005
Scotland												
Marriages	KKCA	30 663	30 242	29 611	29 668	29 940	30 367	29 621	29 826	30 757	32 154	30 881
Persons marrying per 1,000 resident population	KKCB	12.0	11.9	11.7	11.7	11.8	12.0	11.7	11.8	12.2	12.7	12.1
Previous marital status												
Single men[3]	KKCC	22 126	21 454	20 994	20 987	21 052	21 201	20 737	20 671	21 477	22 526	21 421
Divorced men	KKCD	7 741	8 048	7 845	7 934	8 142	8 427	8 238	8 475	8 574	8 930	8 796
Widowers	KKCE	796	740	772	747	746	739	646	680	706	698	664
Single women[3]	KKCF	22 410	21 799	21 303	21 241	21 308	21 608	21 223	21 180	21 974	22 884	21 991
Divorced women	KKCG	7 542	7 718	7 621	7 754	7 949	8 141	7 825	8 008	8 157	8 622	8 244
Widows	KKCH	711	725	687	673	683	618	573	638	626	648	646
First marriage for both partners	KEZV	18 822	18 071	17 751	17 677	17 680	17 864	17 468	17 426	18 232	19 039	18 221
First marriage for one partner	KEZW	6 892	7 111	6 795	6 874	7 000	7 081	7 024	6 999	6 987	7 332	6 970
Remarriage for both partners	KEZX	4 949	5 060	5 065	5 117	5 260	5 422	5 129	5 401	5 538	5 783	5 690
Males												
Under 21 years	KKCI	577	452	406	421	490	364	371	367	361	336	304
21-24	KKCJ	4 915	4 191	3 494	3 147	2 853	2 720	2 489	2 395	2 507	2 501	2 120
25-29	KKCK	10 209	10 056	9 495	9 439	9 031	8 536	7 949	7 468	7 219	7 365	6 981
30-34	KKCL	6 574	6 574	6 911	6 988	7 179	7 419	7 464	7 692	7 752	7 992	7 516
35-44	KKCM	5 021	5 412	5 649	5 945	6 470	7 018	7 215	7 328	8 007	8 553	8 390
45-54	KKCN	2 124	2 288	2 459	2 412	2 575	2 960	2 816	3 033	3 213	3 503	3 588
55 and over	KKCO	1 243	1 269	1 197	1 316	1 342	1 350	1 317	1 543	1 698	1 904	1 982
Females												
Under 21 years	KKCP	1 728	1 423	1 302	1 289	1 322	1 171	1 111	996	1 007	954	724
21-24	KKCQ	7 264	6 474	5 568	5 248	4 778	4 581	4 343	4 171	4 199	4 358	3 772
25-29	KKCR	9 904	9 818	9 574	9 764	9 539	9 495	8 994	8 520	8 321	8 528	8 339
30-34	KKCS	5 401	5 675	5 927	6 036	6 433	6 463	6 618	6 832	7 110	7 235	7 016
35-44	KKCT	4 025	4 378	4 722	4 726	5 150	5 633	5 712	6 115	6 583	7 163	7 083
45-54	KKCU	1 689	1 794	1 844	1 900	1 994	2 279	2 147	2 322	2 589	2 821	2 862
55 and over	KKCV	652	680	674	705	724	745	696	870	948	1 095	1 085
Northern Ireland[2]												
Marriages	KKDA	8 576	8 297	8 071	7 826	7 628	7 584	7 281	7 599	7 757	8 328	8 140
Persons marrying per 1,000 resident population	KKDB	10.4	10.0	9.7	9.3	9.1	9.0	8.6	9.0	9.1	9.7	9.4
Previous marital status												
Single men[3]	KKDC	7 383	7 066	6 975	6 689	6 502	6 463	6 232	6 404	6 587	6 995	6 957
Divorced men	KKDD	1 035	1 062	941	1 014	991	966	936	1 059	1 040	1 151	1 069
Widowers	KKDE	158	169	155	123	135	155	113	136	130	182	114
Single women[3]	KKDF	7 449	7 191	7 016	6 767	6 610	6 540	6 319	6 530	6 684	7 112	7 073
Divorced women	KKDG	985	961	929	932	896	933	862	940	953	1 062	961
Widows	KKDH	142	145	126	127	122	111	100	129	120	154	106
First marriage for both partners	KEZY	6 838	6 542	6 477	6 188	6 052	6 016	5 802	5 934	6 146	6 471	6 497
First marriage for one partner	KEZZ	1 156	1 173	1 037	1 080	1 008	971	947	1 066	979	1 165	1 036
Remarriage for both partners	KFBI	582	582	557	558	568	597	532	599	632	692	607
Males												
Under 21 years	KKDI	205	168	146	144	115	119	94	77	94	94	75
21-24	KKDJ	1 806	1 584	1 474	1 187	1 113	983	915	937	846	849	805
25-29	KKDK	3 402	3 253	3 206	3 122	3 017	2 967	2 804	2 771	2 793	2 807	2 896
30-34	KKDL	1 657	1 711	1 728	1 785	1 738	1 779	1 784	1 902	2 080	2 203	2 107
35-44	KKDM	999	1 063	989	1 081	1 116	1 167	1 155	1 223	1 324	1 593	1 559
45-54	KKDN	313	303	325	321	330	361	357	432	389	518	470
55 and over	KKDO	194	215	203	186	199	208	172	257	231	264	228
Females												
Under 21 years	KKDP	572	552	513	439	381	346	296	282	233	257	207
21-24	KKDQ	2 681	2 421	2 215	1 951	1 881	1 732	1 598	1 650	1 634	1 571	1 525
25-29	KKDR	3 060	2 995	3 006	3 018	2 914	2 946	2 854	2 832	2 955	3 114	3 178
30-34	KKDS	1 202	1 278	1 257	1 331	1 292	1 366	1 376	1 477	1 521	1 681	1 662
35-44	KKDT	723	702	707	750	787	819	825	898	996	1 184	1 128
45-54	KKDU	240	239	256	233	256	259	241	330	274	377	309
55 and over	KKDV	98	110	117	104	117	116	91	130	144	144	131

1 Figures for 2005 are provisional. These may not add precisely due to rounding.

2 From 2004 data onwards, single men and single women include a small number of persons who "previously went through a form of marriage".

3 Single men and single women are those who have never been married.

Sources: Office for National Statistics: 01329 813758;
General Register Office for Scotland;
Northern Ireland Statistics and Research Agency

43

5.13 Divorce: by duration of marriage, age of wife and country

Numbers

		1995	1996	1997	1998	1999	2000	2001	2002	2003	2004	2005
United Kingdom												
Decrees absolute granted[1,2,5]:												
Number	ZBRL	170 050	171 729	161 087	160 057	158 746	154 628	156 814	160 726	166 737	167 138	155 052
Duration of marriage:												
0-4 years	ZBRM	36 594	37 016	33 719	33 087	31 047	28 933	28 306	28 591	28 781	28 746	26 549
5-9 years	ZBRN	48 309	48 670	45 040	44 243	43 357	41 621	42 360	42 924	43 558	42 855	39 070
10-14 years	ZBRO	30 257	30 159	29 085	29 706	30 270	30 166	30 849	31 257	32 564	31 775	29 007
15-19 years	ZBRP	21 040	21 379	20 211	20 078	20 147	19 902	20 568	21 881	23 119	23 898	22 593
20 years and over	ZBRQ	33 840	34 487	33 020	32 935	33 916	34 000	34 729	36 073	38 713	39 844	37 824
Not stated	ZBRR	10	18	12	8	9	6	2	–	2	20	9
Age of wife at marriage:												
16-19 years	ZBRS	35 145	33 590	28 987	27 627	25 440	23 505	22 558	22 107	22 367	20 948	18 507
20-24 years	ZBRT	78 341	78 075	72 971	71 416	69 509	66 215	66 282	66 264	67 070	65 671	58 829
25-29 years	ZBRU	31 611	33 634	33 452	34 195	35 585	36 009	37 418	39 116	41 464	42 544	40 143
30-34 years	ZBRV	12 322	13 122	12 968	13 719	14 420	14 892	15 842	17 374	18 658	19 729	19 366
35-39 years	ZBRW	6 172	6 470	6 155	6 571	6 848	6 993	7 417	8 070	8 742	9 456	9 275
40-44 years	ZBRX	3 335	3 507	3 375	3 360	3 557	3 568	3 778	4 104	4 404	4 550	4 703
45 years and over	ZBRY	3 052	3 239	3 094	3 086	3 291	3 352	3 429	3 572	3 917	4 093	4 042
Not stated	ZBRZ	72	92	85	83	96	94	90	119	115	147	187
Age of wife at divorce:												
16-24 years	ZBSA	10 517	9 298	7 371	6 758	5 671	5 115	4 874	4 998	5 092	4 885	4 388
25-29 years	ZBSB	33 354	32 808	28 814	26 968	24 120	21 280	19 635	18 340	17 633	16 972	14 870
30-34 years	ZBSC	38 839	39 497	37 257	36 795	36 052	34 356	34 194	33 555	32 774	30 754	26 431
35-39 years	ZBSD	30 280	31 497	30 641	31 688	32 605	32 588	33 997	35 050	36 465	35 894	32 722
40-44 years	ZBSE	22 791	22 843	22 246	22 810	23 614	23 879	25 579	27 564	30 154	31 372	30 359
45 years and over	ZBSF	34 187	35 684	34 662	34 947	36 578	37 311	38 442	41 102	44 498	47 108	46 085
Not stated	ZBSG	82	102	96	91	106	99	93	117	121	153	197
Divorces in which there were[3,4]:												
No children aged under 16	ZBSH	78 844	..	..	..	..	..	..	..	..	..	..
One or more children aged under 16	ZBSI	91 206	..	..	..	..	..	..	..	..	..	..
England and Wales												
Decrees absolute granted[1,2]:												
Number	KKEA	155 499	157 107	146 689	145 214	144 556	141 135	143 818	147 735	153 490	153 399	141 750
Rate per 1,000 married couples	KKEB	13.6	13.8	13.0	12.9	12.9	12.7	12.9	13.4	14.0	14.1	13.0
Duration of marriage:												
0-4 years	KKEC	34 507	34 924	31 767	31 136	29 307	27 474	26 987	27 344	27 511	27 389	25 345
5-9 years	KKED	44 304	44 609	41 260	40 239	39 676	38 206	39 079	39 730	40 599	39 779	36 161
10-14 years	KKEE	27 365	27 332	26 215	26 698	27 384	27 459	28 176	28 592	29 831	29 086	26 394
15-19 years	KKEF	18 943	19 321	18 027	17 934	18 072	17 870	18 603	19 784	20 923	21 591	20 363
20 years and over	KKEG	30 370	30 912	29 408	29 199	30 108	30 120	30 971	32 285	34 624	35 554	33 478
Not stated	KKEH	10	9	12	8	9	6	2	–	2	–	9
Age of wife at marriage:												
16-19 years	KKEI	31 322	29 927	25 579	24 276	22 486	20 930	20 218	19 828	20 063	18 709	16 519
20-24 years	KKEJ	71 360	71 123	66 167	64 453	62 853	59 874	60 211	60 353	61 057	59 548	53 041
25-29 years	KKEK	29 441	31 396	31 022	31 533	32 867	33 282	34 759	36 387	38 722	39 575	37 103
30-34 years	KKEL	11 585	12 335	12 094	12 788	13 507	13 972	14 890	16 339	17 567	18 545	18 138
35-39 years	KKEM	5 800	6 051	5 767	6 153	6 432	6 562	6 956	7 623	8 249	8 912	8 755
40-44 years	KKEN	3 121	3 254	3 156	3 135	3 331	3 378	3 559	3 841	4 154	4 274	4 421
45 years and over	KKEO	2 870	3 021	2 904	2 876	3 080	3 137	3 225	3 364	3 678	3 836	3 773
Age of wife at divorce:												
16-24 years	KKEP	9 783	8 615	6 871	6 298	5 318	4 839	4 643	4 808	4 867	4 658	4 216
25-29 years	KKEQ	30 563	30 075	26 435	24 586	22 173	19 650	18 231	17 227	16 539	15 867	13 905
30-34 years	KKER	35 538	36 274	33 967	33 446	32 837	31 420	31 489	30 982	30 345	28 368	24 381
35-39 years	KKES	27 550	28 727	27 715	28 605	29 663	29 820	31 164	32 282	33 519	33 013	29 864
40-44 years	KKET	20 739	20 774	20 125	20 521	21 325	21 469	23 190	25 017	27 610	28 558	27 570
45 years and over	KKEU	31 316	32 633	31 564	31 750	33 231	33 931	35 099	37 419	40 608	42 935	41 805
Not stated	KKEV	10	9	12	8	9	6	2	–	2	–	9
Divorces in which there were[3]:												
No children aged under 16	ZBSJ	69 632	70 174	66 019	64 738	65 258	64 359	64 541	66 738	69 681	71 382	88 349
One or more children aged under 16	ZBSK	85 867	86 933	80 670	80 476	79 298	76 776	79 277	80 997	83 809	82 017	75 340

5.13 Divorce: by duration of marriage, age of wife and country

continued

Numbers

		1995	1996	1997	1998	1999	2000	2001	2002	2003	2004	2005
Scotland												
Decrees absolute granted[2]												
Number	KKFA	12 249	12 308	12 222	12 384	11 864	11 143	10 631	10 826	10 928	11 227	10 940
Rate per 1,000 married couples	KKFB	10.8	10.9	11.0	11.3	10.9	10.3	9.7	10.0	10.2	10.5	10.3
Duration of marriage:												
0-4 years	KKFC	1 908	1 914	1 793	1 766	1 588	1 304	1 159	1 128	1 141	1 204	1 089
5-9 years	KKFD	3 399	3 432	3 224	3 360	3 095	2 890	2 721	2 689	2 450	2 536	2 403
10-14 years	KKFE	2 407	2 310	2 385	2 456	2 368	2 168	2 163	2 183	2 222	2 173	2 113
15-19 years	KKFF	1 698	1 709	1 804	1 729	1 686	1 622	1 562	1 705	1 773	1 810	1 789
20 years and over	KKFG	2 837	2 934	3 016	3 073	3 127	3 159	3 026	3 121	3 342	3 504	3 546
Not stated	ZBSL	–	9	–	–	–	–	–	–	–	–	–
Age of wife at marriage:												
16-19 years	ZBSM	3 091	2 939	2 749	2 654	2 374	2 043	1 839	1 845	1 816	1 753	1 557
20-24 years	ZBSN	5 845	5 822	5 714	5 744	5 453	5 142	4 873	4 823	4 869	4 892	4 721
25-29 years	KKFJ	1 887	1 933	2 151	2 314	2 333	2 318	2 233	2 316	2 307	2 462	2 515
30-34 years	KKFK	654	697	791	824	829	805	827	895	958	1 025	1 065
35-39 years	KKFL	338	393	360	382	379	378	401	407	432	489	455
40-44 years	KKFM	196	234	199	198	208	193	170	193	235	219	252
45 years and over	KKFN	166	198	173	185	192	193	175	186	212	221	232
Not stated	KKFO	72	92	85	83	96	94	90	119	115	133	143
Age of wife at divorce:												
16-24 years	KKFP	622	583	426	377	301	232	182	180	191	192	148
25-29 years	KKFQ	2 353	2 269	2 021	1 957	1 597	1 330	1 109	974	884	869	777
30-34 years	KKFR	2 747	2 708	2 736	2 767	2 642	2 381	2 215	2 174	1 943	1 918	1 641
35-39 years	KKFS	2 290	2 307	2 469	2 562	2 450	2 298	2 311	2 281	2 388	2 278	2 304
40-44 years	KKFT	1 734	1 761	1 819	1 951	1 929	1 999	1 963	2 110	2 106	2 341	2 330
45 years and over	KKFU	2 431	2 587	2 667	2 687	2 848	2 810	2 760	2 990	3 297	3 496	3 596
Not stated	KKFV	72	93	84	83	97	93	91	117	119	133	144
Divorces in which there were[3,4]:												
No children aged under 16	KKFW	7 515	..	..	..	..	..	..	..	..	..	..
One or more children under 16	KKFX	4 734	..	..	..	..	..	..	..	..	..	..
Northern Ireland												
Decrees absolute granted:[2,5]												
Number	ZBSO	2 302	2 314	2 176	2 459	2 326	2 350	2 365	2 165	2 319	2 512	2 362
Duration of marriage:												
0-4 years	ZBSP	179	178	159	185	152	155	160	119	129	153	115
5-9 years	ZBSQ	606	629	556	644	586	525	560	505	509	540	506
10-14 years	ZBSR	485	517	485	552	518	539	510	482	511	516	500
15-19 years	ZBSS	399	349	380	415	389	410	403	392	423	497	441
20 years and over	ZBST	633	641	596	663	681	721	732	667	747	786	800
Not stated[5]	EK8B	–	–	–	–	–	–	–	–	–	20	–
Age of wife at marriage:												
16-19 years	ZBSU	732	724	659	697	580	532	501	434	488	486	431
20-24 years	ZBSV	1 136	1 130	1 090	1 219	1 203	1 199	1 198	1 088	1 144	1 231	1 067
25-29 years	ZBSW	283	305	279	348	385	409	426	413	435	507	525
30-34 years	ZBSX	83	90	83	107	84	115	125	140	133	159	163
35-39 years	ZBSY	34	26	28	36	37	53	60	40	61	55	65
40-44 years	ZBSZ	18	19	20	27	18	20	26	28	31	24	30
45 years and over	ZBTA	16	20	17	25	19	22	29	22	27	36	37
Not stated[5]	EK8C	–	–	–	–	–	–	–	–	–	14	44
Age of wife at divorce:												
16-24 years	ZBTB	112	100	74	83	52	44	49	10	34	35	24
25-29 years	ZBTC	438	464	358	425	350	300	295	139	210	236	188
30-34 years	ZBTD	554	515	554	582	573	555	490	399	486	468	409
35-39 years	ZBTE	440	463	457	521	492	470	522	487	558	603	554
40-44 years	ZBTF	318	308	302	338	360	411	426	437	438	473	459
45 years and over	ZBTG	440	464	431	510	499	570	583	693	593	677	684
Not stated[5]	EK8D	–	–	–	–	–	–	–	–	–	20	44
Divorces in which there were[3]:												
No children aged under 16	ZBTH	1 697	1 676	1 573	1 807	1 649	1 051	1 054	972	1 050	1 218	982
One or more children aged under 16	ZBTI	605	638	603	652	677	1 299	1 311	1 193	1 269	1 282	1 380
Not stated[5]	EK8E	–	–	–	–	–	–	–	–	–	12	–

1 Data for 2005 are provisional.
2 Includes decrees of nullities.
3 Children of the family as defined by the Matrimonial Causes Act 1973.
4 Data not available in Scotland.
5 Marital estimates are not available for Northern Ireland - no divorce rate for
  UK/Northern Ireland.

Sources: Office for National Statistics: 01329 813758;
General Register Office for Scotland;
Northern Ireland Statistics and Research Agency

5.14 Divorce proceedings: by country

Numbers

		1995	1996	1997	1998	1999	2000	2001	2002	2003	2004	2005
United Kingdom												
Dissolution of marriage[1],[4]												
Decree absolute/decree granted	ZBXR	169 621	171 309	160 733	159 688	158 418	154 273	156 562	160 528	166 536	166 937	154 879
On grounds of:												
Adultery	ZBXS	41 313	41 127	38 652	37 302	35 545	34 082	33 452	33 389	33 844	32 586	28 433
Behaviour	ZBXT	71 733	72 581	68 546	68 685	67 851	65 687	66 818	68 499	70 866	70 879	66 944
Desertion	ZBXU	1 196	1 101	956	828	748	722	718	727	697	675	612
Separation (2 years and consent)	ZBXV	41 969	42 265	39 398	39 627	40 368	39 763	40 699	42 579	44 012	44 819	41 433
Separation(5 years)	ZBXW	12 699	13 547	12 552	12 697	13 389	13 653	14 575	15 076	16 831	17 714	17 101
Combination of more than one ground and other	ZBXX	711	688	629	549	517	366	300	259	286	264	356
Decree absolute/decree granted to:												
the wife	ZBXY	118 869	119 570	111 912	111 556	109 828	106 958	107 345	108 106	114 665	113 971	105 009
the husband	ZBXZ	50 268	51 247	48 393	47 764	48 236	47 069	49 015	52 251	51 691	52 793	49 725
both	ZBYA	490	493	430	369	358	247	202	173	181	174	146
Nullity of marriage[2]												
Decree absolute/decree granted	ZBYB	429	420	354	369	328	355	252	198	201	201	173
England and Wales												
Dissolution of marriage[4]												
Petitions filed[3]	KKGA	173 966	177 970	163 769	165 870	162 137	157 809	172 341	177 223	173 240	167 193	151 654
Decree nisi granted[3]	KKGM	155 739	157 588	148 310	144 231	143 446	143 729	163 146	170 996	167 992	166 042	150 668
Decree absolute granted	KKGN	155 076	156 692	146 339	144 851	144 233	140 783	143 568	147 538	153 294	153 199	141 583
On grounds of:												
Adultery	KKGB	40 178	40 012	37 592	36 319	34 584	33 310	32 839	32 829	33 331	32 035	28 014
Behaviour	KKGC	68 168	68 986	65 047	65 257	64 816	63 182	64 768	66 480	68 944	68 859	65 289
Desertion	KKGD	1 108	1 030	912	790	713	680	689	681	665	654	593
Separation (2 years and consent)	KKGE	35 030	35 422	32 638	32 394	33 482	32 820	33 703	35 476	36 931	37 543	34 388
Separation(5 years)	KKGF	9 930	10 626	9 592	9 616	10 193	10 498	11 355	11 896	13 239	13 933	13 196
Combination of more than one ground and other	ZBYC	662	616	558	475	445	293	214	176	184	175	103
Decree absolute granted to[2]:												
the wife	ZBYD	108 764	109 489	102 173	101 583	100 469	98 227	98 992	102 676	106 208	105 381	96 855
the husband	ZBYE	45 823	46 712	43 739	42 902	43 413	42 311	44 378	44 694	46 915	47 651	44 583
both	ZBYF	489	491	427	366	351	245	198	168	171	167	145
Nullity of marriage												
Petitions filed[3]	KKGO	881	702	485	505	549	452	492	443	463	492	436
Decree nisi granted[3]	KKGR	425	332	248	281	495	274	297	216	204	308	257
Decree absolute granted	KKGS	423	415	350	363	323	352	250	197	196	200	167
Judicial separation												
Petitions filed[3]	KKGT	1 694	1 584	1 078	916	882	650	1 078	1 001	826	742	692
Decrees granted[3]	KKGW	1 543	1 199	589	519	696	540	925	560	467	419	387

5.14 Divorce proceedings: by country

continued

Numbers

		1995	1996	1997	1998	1999	2000	2001	2002	2003	2004	2005
Scotland												
Dissolution of marriage[1]												
Decree granted	ZBYG	12 243	12 307	12 220	12 383	11 860	11 142	10 631	10 825	10 927	11 226	10 939
On grounds of:												
Adultery	ZBYH	956	943	909	832	770	610	473	428	401	413	327
Behaviour	ZBYI	3 203	3 184	3 081	3 005	2 611	2 099	1 639	1 656	1 537	1 546	1 344
Desertion	ZBYJ	72	61	33	28	18	34	24	42	23	15	17
Separation (2 years and consent)	ZBYK	5 846	5 835	5 773	6 121	5 908	5 878	5 943	6 101	6 016	6 122	5 989
Separation(5 years)	ZBYL	2 166	2 284	2 424	2 397	2 553	2 521	2 552	2 598	2 950	3 130	3 262
Decree granted to[2]												
the wife	ZBYM	8 545	8 559	8 266	8 329	7 774	7 191	6 775	4 025	6 927	6 939	6 654
the husband	ZBYN	3 704	3 749	3 956	4 055	4 090	3 952	3 856	6 801	4 001	4 288	4 286
Nullity of marriage												
Decree granted	ZBYO	6	1	2	1	4	1	–	1	1	1	1
Northern Ireland												
Dissolution of marriage												
Petitions filed	ZBYP	2 875	2 695	2 808	2 760	2 414	3 005	2 869	2 929	3 192	2 808	3 299
Decree nisi granted	ZBYQ	2 535	2 419	2 532	2 904	2 393	2 456	2 615	2 454	2 616	2 697	2 594
Decree absolute granted	ZBYR	2 302	2 310	2 174	2 454	2 325	2 348	2 363	2 165	2 315	2 512	2 357
On grounds of:												
Adultery	ZBYS	179	172	151	151	191	162	140	132	112	138	92
Behaviour	ZBYT	362	411	418	423	424	406	411	363	385	474	311
Desertion	ZBYU	16	10	11	10	17	8	5	3	9	6	2
Separation (2 years and consent)	ZBYV	1 093	1 010	991	1 112	978	1 065	1 053	1 002	1 065	1 154	1 056
Separation(5 years)	ZBYW	603	637	536	684	643	634	668	582	642	651	643
Combination of more than one ground and other	ZBYX	49	70	67	74	72	73	86	83	102	89	253
Decree absolute granted to:												
the wife	ZBYY	1 560	1 522	1 473	1 644	1 585	1 540	1 578	1 405	1 530	1 651	1 500
the husband	ZBYZ	741	786	698	807	733	806	781	755	775	854	856
both	ZBZA	1	2	3	3	7	2	4	5	10	7	1
Nullity of marriage												
Petitions filed	ZBZB	5	5	7	5	1	2	1	5	4	8	9
Decree nisi granted	ZBZC	5	5	2	6	2	5	2	2	5	3	3
Decree absolute granted	ZBZD	–	4	2	5	1	2	2	–	4	–	5
Judicial separation												
Petitions filed	ZBZE	84	63	70	64	50	54	40	27	35	18	3
Decrees granted	ZBZF	30	22	34	40	31	23	25	15	22	12	4

1 The terms petition filed, decree nisi granted, decree absolute and judicial separation are not used in Scotland. Decree absolute granted to 'both' and 'Combination of more than one ground and other' are not procedures used in Scotland.

2 Information on Decree granted for the wife or husband for Scotland includes nullities (these are identified separately under 'Nullity of marriage'); figures excluding nullities are not available.

3 Data supplied by Her Majesty's Court Service (30 January 2007) with the introduction of Management Information System Data. The information contained in this publication has been produced using the Management Information System (MIS), a new data warehousing facility drawing directly from court-based information systems. The new facility enables the Department access to more complete data than was previously possible. In some instances this has meant that previously published figures will have changed, since the new facility. This has also enabled the Department to include late data and also to revise erroneous data included in previous publications.

4 2005 data are provisional.

Sources: Office for National Statistics: 01329 813758;
General Register Office for Scotland;
Northern Ireland Statistics and Research Agency;
Her Majesty's Court Service;
Scottish Courts Administration;
Northern Ireland Courts Administration

5.15 Births:[1] by country and sex

Thousands

| | Live births | | | | Rates | | | | |
	Total	Male	Female	Sex ratio[2]	Crude birth rate[3]	General fertility rate[4]	TFR[5]	Still-births[6]	Still-birth rate[6]
United Kingdom[7]									
1900 - 02	1 095	558	537	1 037	28.6	115.1	..	..	..
1910 - 12	1 037	528	508	1 039	24.6	99.4	..	..	..
1920 - 22	1 018	522	496	1 052	23.1	93.0	..	..	..
1930 - 32	750	383	367	1 046	16.3	66.5	..	..	..
1940 - 42	723	372	351	1 062	15.0	..	1.89	..	..
1950 - 52	803	413	390	1 061	16.0	73.7	2.21	..	..
1960 - 62	946	487	459	1 063	17.9	90.3	2.80	18.6	19.2
1970 - 72	880	453	427	1 064	15.8	82.5	2.36	11.3	12.7
1980 - 82	735	377	358	1 053	13.0	62.5	1.83	5.0	6.8
1990 - 92	790	405	385	1 051	13.8	63.7	1.81	3.6	4.6
2000 - 02	672	345	328	1 052	11.4	54.7	1.64	3.6	5.4
	BBCA	KBCZ	KBCY	KMFW	KBCT	KBCS	KBCR	KBCQ	KMFX
1995	732	375	357	1 052	12.6	60.1	1.71	4.1	5.6
1996	733	376	357	1 055	12.6	60.2	1.73	4.1	5.5
1997	727	372	354	1 051	12.6	59.6	1.72	3.9	5.3
1998	717	367	350	1 052	12.3	58.8	1.71	3.9	5.4
1999	700	359	341	1 056	11.9	57.3	1.69	3.7	5.3
2000	679	348	331	1 051	11.5	55.4	1.64	3.6	5.3
2001	669	343	326	1 050	11.3	54.3	1.63	3.6	5.3
2002	669	343	326	1 054	11.3	54.2	1.64	3.8	5.6
2003	696	357	339	1 052	11.7	56.2	1.72	4.0	5.7
2004	716	368	348	1 055	12.0	57.7	1.77	4.0	5.7
2005	723	370	353	1 050	12.0	57.9	1.79	4.0	5.3
England and Wales									
1900 - 02	932	475	458	1 037	28.6	114.7	..	..	..
1910 - 12	884	450	433	1 040	24.5	98.6	..	..	..
1920 - 22	862	442	420	1 051	22.8	91.1	..	..	..
1930 - 32	632	323	309	1 047	15.8	64.4	..	27.0	..
1940 - 42	607	312	295	1 057	15.6	61.3	1.81	22.0	..
1950 - 52	683	351	332	1 058	15.6	72.1	2.16	16.0	..
1960 - 62	812	418	394	1 061	17.6	88.9	2.77	15.6	18.9
1970 - 72	764	394	371	1 061	15.6	81.4	2.31	9.7	12.5
1980 - 82	639	328	311	1 053	12.9	61.8	1.81	4.3	6.7
1990 - 92	698	358	340	1 051	13.8	63.8	1.82	3.2	4.5
2000 - 02	598	307	292	1 052	11.4	55.2	1.65	3.2	5.4
	BBCB	KMFY	KMFZ	KMGA	KMGB	KMGC	KMGD	KMGE	KMGF
1995	648	332	316	1 051	12.6	60.5	1.72	3.6	5.5
1996	649	333	316	1 055	12.6	60.6	1.74	3.5	5.4
1997	643	330	314	1 051	12.5	60.0	1.73	3.4	5.3
1998	636	326	310	1 051	12.3	59.2	1.72	3.4	5.3
1999	622	319	303	1 055	12.0	57.8	1.70	3.3	5.3
2000	604	310	295	1 050	11.6	55.9	1.65	3.2	5.3
2001	595	305	290	1 050	11.4	54.7	1.63	3.2	5.3
2002	596	306	290	1 055	11.3	54.7	1.65	3.4	5.6
2003	621	318	303	1 051	11.8	56.8	1.73	3.6	5.8
2004	640	328	311	1 054	12.1	58.2	1.78	3.5	5.7
2005	646	331	315	1 049	12.1	58.4	1.80	3.5	5.4

5.15 Births:[1] by country and sex
continued

Thousands

| | Live births | | | | Rates | | | | |
	Total	Male	Female	Sex ratio[2]	Crude birth rate[3]	General fertility rate[4]	TFR[5]	Still-births[6]	Still-birth rate[6]
Scotland									
1900 - 02	132	67	65	1 046	29.5	120.6	..	..	..
1910 - 12	123	63	60	1 044	25.9	107.4	..	..	..
1920 - 22	125	64	61	1 046	25.6	105.9	..	..	..
1930 - 32	93	47	45	1 040	19.1	78.8	..	..	..
1940 - 42	89	46	43	1 051	18.5	73.7	..	4.0	..
1950 - 52	91	47	44	1 060	17.9	81.4	2.41	2.0	..
1960 - 62	102	53	50	1 060	19.7	97.8	2.98	2.2	20.8
1970 - 72	84	43	41	1 057	16.1	83.3	2.46	1.1	13.5
1980 - 82	68	35	33	1 051	13.1	62.2	1.80	0.4	6.3
1990 - 92	66	34	32	1 052	13.0	59.2	1.68	0.4	5.7
2000 - 02	52	27	26	1 046	10.3	48.6	1.48	0.3	5.6
	BBCD	KMEU	KMEV	KMEW	KMEX	KMEY	KMEZ	KMFM	KMFN
1995	60	31	29	1 043	11.8	54.6	1.55	0.4	6.6
1996	59	31	29	1 061	11.6	54.1	1.56	0.4	6.4
1997	59	31	29	1 055	11.7	54.4	1.58	0.3	5.3
1998	57	29	28	1 060	11.3	52.7	1.55	0.4	6.1
1999	55	28	27	1 050	10.9	50.9	1.51	0.3	5.2
2000	53	27	26	1 051	10.5	49.2	1.48	0.3	5.6
2001	53	27	26	1 041	10.4	48.8	1.49	0.3	5.7
2002	51	26	25	1 047	10.1	48.1	1.48	0.3	5.4
2003	52	27	26	1 054	10.4	49.4	1.54	0.3	5.6
2004	54	28	26	1 060	10.6	51.0	1.60	0.3	5.8
2005	54	28	26	1 068	10.7	51.5	1.62	0.3	5.3
Northern Ireland[7]									
1900 - 02	..	..	..	..	..	..	..	..	..
1910 - 12	..	..	..	..	..	..	..	..	..
1920 - 22	31	16	15	1 048	24.2	105.9	..	..	..
1930 - 32	26	13	12	1 047	20.5	78.8	..	..	..
1940 - 42	27	14	13	1 078	20.8	73.7	..	..	..
1950 - 52	29	15	14	1 066	20.9	81.4	..	..	..
1960 - 62	31	16	15	1 068	22.5	111.5	3.47	0.7	22.0
1970 - 72	31	16	15	1 074	20.4	105.7	3.13	0.5	14.3
1980 - 82	28	14	13	1 048	18.0	87.5	2.59	0.2	8.4
1990 - 92	26	13	13	1 051	16.1	74.8	2.15	0.1	4.6
2000 - 02	22	11	11	1 054	12.8	58.8	1.78	0.1	5.0
	BBCE	KMFO	KMFP	KMFQ	KMFR	KMFS	KMFT	KMFU	KMFV
1995	24	12	11	1 078	14.4	66.6	1.91	0.1	6.1
1996	24	12	12	1 032	14.7	67.8	1.95	0.2	6.2
1997	24	12	12	1 048	14.4	66.4	1.93	0.1	5.4
1998	24	12	12	1 039	14.1	65.0	1.90	0.1	5.1
1999	23	12	11	1 084	13.7	62.9	1.86	0.1	5.7
2000	22	11	10	1 070	12.8	58.7	1.75	0.1	4.3
2001	22	11	11	1 058	13.0	59.7	1.80	0.1	5.1
2002	21	11	11	1 035	12.6	58.1	1.77	0.1	5.7
2003	22	11	10	1 081	12.7	59.0	1.81	0.1	5.0
2004	22	11	11	1 059	13.0	60.6	1.87	0.1	5.0
2005	22	11	11	1 032	12.9	60.4	1.87	0.1	4.0

1 See chapter text.
2 Males per 1,000 females (calculated using whole numbers).
3 Rate per 1,000 population (calculated using whole numbers).
4 Rate per 1,000 women aged 15 - 44.
5 Total fertility rate is the average number of children which would be born to a woman if she experienced the age-specific fertility rates of the period in question throughout her child-bearing life span. UK figures for the years 1970-72 and earlier are estimates.
6 On 1 October 1992 the legal definition of a stillbirth was changed from a baby born dead after 28 completed weeks gestation or more to one born

dead after 24 completed weeks gestation or more. Between 1 October and 31 December 1992 in the UK there were 258 babies born dead between 24 and 27 completed weeks gestation (216 in England and Wales, 35 in Scotland and 7 in Northern Ireland). If these babies were included in the stillbirth figures given, the stillbirth rate would be 4.7 for the UK and England and Wales, while Scotland and Northern Ireland stillbirth rate would remain as stated.
7 From 1981, data for the United Kingdom and Northern Ireland have been revised to exclude births in Northern Ireland to non-residents of Northern Ireland.

Sources: Office for National Statistics: 01329 813758;
General Register Office for Scotland;
Northern Ireland Statistics and Research Agency

5.16 Birth occurrence inside and outside marriage by age of mother

Thousands

	Inside marriage						Outside marriage					
	All ages	Under 20	20 - 24	25 - 29	Over 30	Mean[1] age (Years)	All ages	Under 20	20 - 24	25 - 29	Over 30	Mean[1] age (Years)
United Kingdom[2]												
	KKEY	KKEZ	KKFY	KKFZ	KKGX	KKGY	KKGZ	KKIC	KKID	KKIE	KKIF	KKIG
1961	890	55	273	280	282	27.7	54	13	17	10	13	25.5
1971	828	70	301	271	185	26.4	74	24	25	13	12	23.8
1981	640	36	193	231	180	27.3	91	30	33	16	13	23.4
1987	598	18	153	235	192	28.1	178	48	68	37	26	23.9
1988	589	16	144	234	195	28.2	198	51	76	42	29	24.1
1989	570	14	130	228	198	28.4	207	49	79	46	32	24.3
1990	576	13	121	233	209	28.6	223	51	83	53	37	24.5
1991	556	10	109	224	213	28.9	236	50	87	58	41	24.8
1992	540	9	98	216	218	29.1	241	46	86	62	46	25.1
1993	520	8	87	204	221	29.3	242	44	84	64	50	25.4
1994	510	7	78	194	231	29.6	240	41	80	65	55	25.7
1995	486	6	69	180	232	29.8	246	42	79	66	60	25.9
1996	473	6	61	170	237	30.1	260	45	80	69	66	26.0
1997	460	6	55	159	240	30.3	267	47	79	71	71	26.1
1998	447	6	51	149	243	30.5	270	49	77	70	74	26.2
1999	428	6	47	136	239	30.7	272	49	77	68	77	26.3
2000	411	5	44	126	237	30.9	268	47	77	66	78	26.4
2001	401	5	44	116	236	30.9	268	45	77	64	82	26.7
2002	397	5	44	109	239	31.1	272	44	80	62	85	26.7
2003	407	5	44	110	249	31.2	288	45	86	65	92	26.8
2004	413	4	44	110	255	31.3	303	47	90	69	97	26.9
2005	412	4	43	111	254	31.4	310	47	93	72	98	26.9
Great Britain												
	KKIH	KKII	KKIJ	KKIK	KKIL	KKIM	KKIN	KKIO	KKIP	KKIQ	KKIR	KKIS
1961	859	53	264	270	272	27.7	53	13	17	10	13	25.5
1971	797	68	293	261	176	26.4	73	24	25	13	12	23.8
1981	614	34	186	223	171	27.2	89	29	32	16	13	23.3
1987	574	17	147	227	184	28.0	174	46	66	36	25	23.4
1988	566	16	138	226	186	28.2	194	49	74	42	29	23.6
1989	549	13	125	220	190	28.4	202	48	77	45	32	24.2
1990	554	12	116	225	201	28.6	218	49	81	52	36	24.6
1991	535	10	105	216	205	28.9	231	48	85	57	41	24.8
1992	520	9	94	208	210	29.1	235	45	84	61	46	25.1
1993	500	7	84	196	213	29.3	236	42	82	62	49	25.4
1994	492	7	75	188	222	29.6	235	41	78	63	53	25.7
1995	468	6	66	173	223	29.8	240	40	77	65	59	25.9
1996	455	6	59	163	227	30.1	254	44	78	68	65	26.0
1997	442	6	53	152	231	30.3	261	46	76	69	69	26.2
1998	430	6	49	143	233	30.5	263	48	74	68	73	26.3
1999	412	6	46	131	230	30.7	265	48	74	67	76	26.4
2000	396	5	43	121	228	30.9	261	46	74	65	77	26.5
2001	386	5	43	112	227	30.9	261	44	75	62	80	26.6
2002	383	5	43	105	230	31.1	265	43	77	61	84	26.7
2003	393	4	43	106	239	31.2	281	44	83	64	90	26.9
2004	399	4	43	106	245	31.3	295	45	88	67	95	26.9
2005	398	4	42	107	245	31.4	302	45	90	70	97	26.9

1 The mean ages presented in this table are unstandardised and therefore take no account of the age structure of the population.
2 From 1981, data for the United Kingdom have been revised to exclude births in Northern Ireland to non-residents of Northern Ireland.

Sources: Office for National Statistics: 01329 813758; General Register Office for Scotland; Northern Ireland Statistics and Research Agency

5.17 Live births: by age of mother and country

Numbers

	Under 20	20 - 24	25 - 29	30 - 34	35 - 39	40 - 44	45 and over	All ages
United Kingdom								
All live births[1,2]								
	KMDV	KMDW	KMDX	KMDY	KMDZ	KMES	KMET	KMBZ
1995	47 646	147 056	246 017	204 601	73 945	12 008	585	731 882
1996	50 793	141 090	238 857	210 490	78 335	12 832	638	733 163
1997	52 851	133 257	229 429	212 162	84 508	13 731	618	726 622
1998	54 822	127 230	218 072	212 876	88 729	14 453	640	716 888
1999	54 921	124 036	204 808	208 986	91 272	15 210	695	699 976
2000	52 059	120 305	191 583	202 893	95 400	16 032	708	679 029
2001	50 157	121 664	179 776	202 017	97 379	17 271	831	669 123
2002	49 165	123 844	171 852	203 261	101 379	18 273	968	668 777
2003	49 874	129 867	175 473	210 071	109 038	20 233	933	695 549
2004	50 752	134 614	179 050	213 620	114 852	22 107	975	715 996
2005	50 396	135 891	183 513	211 076	116 902	23 518	1 176	722 549
Age-specific fertility rates[3]								
	KMBR	KMBS	KMBT	KMBU	KMBV	KMBW	KMBX	KMBY
1995	28.2	75.4	108.4	88.1	36.1	6.4	0.3	60.1
1996	29.6	75.7	106.6	89.6	37.2	6.8	0.3	60.2
1997	30.2	74.9	104.2	89.8	39.1	7.1	0.3	59.6
1998	30.8	73.6	101.4	90.4	40.0	7.4	0.3	58.8
1999	30.7	71.8	98.0	89.4	40.2	7.6	0.4	57.3
2000	29.2	68.7	93.9	87.7	41.0	7.8	0.4	55.4
2001	27.9	68.0	91.5	88.0	41.3	8.2	0.4	54.3
2002	26.9	68.1	91.3	89.7	42.6	8.4	0.5	54.2
2003	26.6	70.1	95.9	94.5	45.9	9.1	0.5	56.2
2004	26.7	71.5	98.0	99.1	48.6	9.7	0.5	57.7
2005	26.2	70.5	98.3	100.7	50.0	10.1	0.6	57.9
England and Wales								
All live births								
	KGSA	KGSB	KGSC	KGSD	KGSE	KGSF	KGSG	KGSH
1995	41 938	130 744	217 418	181 202	65 517	10 779	540	648 138
1996	44 667	125 732	211 103	186 377	69 503	11 516	587	649 485
1997	46 372	118 589	202 792	187 528	74 900	12 332	582	643 095
1998	48 285	113 537	193 144	188 499	78 881	12 980	575	635 901
1999	48 375	110 722	181 931	185 311	81 281	13 617	635	621 872
2000	45 846	107 741	170 701	180 113	84 974	14 403	663	604 441
2001	44 189	108 844	159 926	178 920	86 495	15 499	761	594 634
2002	43 467	110 959	153 379	180 532	90 449	16 441	895	596 122
2003	44 236	116 622	156 931	187 214	97 386	18 205	875	621 469
2004	45 094	121 072	159 984	190 550	102 228	19 884	909	639 721
2005	44 830	122 145	164 348	188 153	104 113	21 155	1 091	645 835
Age-specific fertility rates[3]								
	KGSI	KGSJ	KGSK	KGSL	KGSM	KGSN	KGSO	KGSP
1995	28.5	76.4	108.4	88.3	36.3	6.5	0.3	60.5
1996	29.7	77.0	106.6	89.8	37.5	6.9	0.3	60.6
1997	30.2	76.0	104.3	89.8	39.4	7.3	0.3	60.0
1998	30.9	74.9	101.5	90.6	40.4	7.5	0.3	59.2
1999	30.9	73.0	98.3	89.6	40.6	7.7	0.4	57.8
2000	29.3	70.0	94.3	87.9	41.4	8.0	0.4	55.9
2001	28.0	69.0	91.7	88.0	41.5	8.4	0.5	54.7
2002	27.0	69.2	91.6	89.8	43.0	8.6	0.5	54.7
2003	26.8	71.2	96.4	94.8	46.4	9.3	0.5	56.8
2004	26.9	72.7	98.4	99.4	48.9	9.9	0.5	58.2
2005	26.3	71.7	98.8	100.9	50.3	10.3	0.6	58.4

5.17 Live births: by age of mother and country
continued

Numbers

	Under 20	20 - 24	25 - 29	30 - 34	35 - 39	40 - 44	45 and over	All ages
Scotland								
All live births[1]								
	KGTA	KGTB	KGTC	KGTD	KGTE	KGTF	KGTG	KGTH
1995	4 280	11 913	20 395	16 803	5 799	811	26	60 051
1996	4 544	11 026	19 511	17 038	6 126	891	32	59 296
1997	4 835	10 607	18 782	17 455	6 740	936	19	59 440
1998	4 802	9 804	17 477	17 207	6 893	1 027	43	57 319
1999	4 755	9 440	16 011	16 722	7 034	1 096	41	55 147
2000	4 599	8 962	14 676	16 233	7 395	1 133	29	53 076
2001	4 444	9 121	13 763	16 206	7 701	1 224	40	52 527
2002	4 195	9 267	12 694	16 038	7 727	1 267	47	51 270
2003	4 155	9 626	12 725	16 085	8 310	1 432	39	52 432
2004	4 172	9 950	13 131	16 085	8 912	1 631	50	53 957
2005	4 171	10 008	13 229	15 962	9 179	1 694	66	54 386
Age-specific fertility rates[3]								
	KGTI	KGTJ	KGTK	KGTL	KGTM	KGTN	KGTO	KGTP
1995	28.2	66.6	101.3	80.6	30.4	4.8	0.1	54.6
1996	29.7	64.5	98.5	81.9	31.4	5.2	0.2	54.1
1997	31.0	65.5	97.4	83.9	34.0	5.3	0.1	54.4
1998	30.6	62.8	94.3	83.2	34.1	5.7	0.3	52.7
1999	30.3	61.0	90.4	82.0	34.3	5.9	0.2	50.9
2000	29.3	57.6	86.5	81.3	35.6	6.0	0.2	49.2
2001	28.4	57.8	85.1	82.2	36.9	6.3	0.2	48.8
2002	26.8	58.3	83.3	83.6	37.1	6.4	0.3	48.1
2003	26.3	60.1	86.5	86.8	40.0	7.1	0.2	49.4
2004	26.1	61.8	89.4	90.3	43.3	7.9	0.3	51.0
2005	26.2	60.9	88.6	93.2	45.4	8.1	0.3	51.5
Northern Ireland								
All live births[2]								
	KMDF	KMDG	KMDH	KMDI	KMDJ	KMDK	KMDL	KMDM
1995	1 428	4 399	8 204	6 596	2 629	418	19	23 693
1996	1 582	4 332	8 243	7 075	2 706	425	19	24 382
1997	1 644	4 061	7 855	7 179	2 868	463	17	24 087
1998	1 735	3 889	7 451	7 170	2 955	446	22	23 668
1999	1 791	3 874	6 866	6 953	2 957	497	19	22 957
2000	1 614	3 602	6 206	6 547	3 031	496	16	21 512
2001	1 524	3 699	6 087	6 891	3 183	548	30	21 962
2002	1 502	3 619	5 779	6 691	3 203	565	26	21 385
2003	1 483	3 619	5 817	6 772	3 342	596	19	21 648
2004	1 486	3 592	5 935	6 985	3 712	592	16	22 318
2005	1 395	3 738	5 936	6 961	3 610	669	19	22 328
Age-specific fertility rates[2,3]								
	KMDN	KMDO	KMDP	KMDQ	KMDR	KMDS	KMDT	KMDU
1995	23.4	73.5	129.1	102.7	45.5	8.4	0.4	66.6
1996	25.7	73.8	129.4	108.3	45.4	8.4	0.4	67.8
1997	26.4	71.1	124.2	109.2	46.6	8.8	0.3	66.4
1998	27.8	69.6	119.0	108.4	47.2	8.2	0.4	65.0
1999	28.6	70.6	112.3	105.6	46.1	8.9	0.4	62.9
2000	25.6	66.0	103.9	100.4	46.2	8.5	0.3	58.7
2001	23.9	67.5	105.1	106.0	48.0	9.1	0.6	59.7
2002	23.3	66.0	102.9	104.2	48.2	9.2	0.5	58.1
2003	22.8	65.5	106.8	107.0	50.2	9.8	0.3	59.0
2004	23.0	62.8	109.8	112.6	56.1	9.5	0.3	60.6
2005	21.7	63.2	108.6	114.8	55.0	10.2	0.3	60.4

1 The 'All ages' figure for Scotland includes births to mothers whose age was not known. There were 24 such births in 1995, 128 in 1996, 66 in 1997, 66 in 1998, 48 in 1999, 49 in 2000, 28 in 2001, 35 in 2002, 60 in 2003, 26 in 2004 and 77 in 2005.

2 From 1981 data for the United Kingdom and Northern Ireland have been revised to exclude births in Northern Ireland to non residents in Northern Ireland.

3 The rates for women of all ages, under 20, and 45 and over are based upon the populations of women aged 15-44, 15-19 and 45 respectively.

Sources: Office for National Statistics: 01329 813758; General Register Office for Scotland; Northern Ireland Statistics and Research Agency

5.18 Legal abortions[1]: by age for residents

Numbers

	All ages	Under 15	15	16 - 19	20 - 24	25 - 29	30 - 34	35 - 39	40 - 44	45 and over	Not stated
England and Wales											
	C53Z	C542	C543	C544	C545	C546	C547	C548	C549	C54A	C54B
1986	147 619	924	2 970	33 819	45 316	28 656	18 005	12 977	4 521	409	22
1987	156 191	907	2 858	35 167	49 256	31 243	18 960	12 639	4 757	390	14
1988	168 298	859	2 709	37 928	54 067	34 584	20 000	12 681	5 047	412	11
1989	170 463	803	2 580	36 182	54 880	36 604	21 284	12 713	5 020	388	9
1990	173 900	873	2 549	35 520	55 281	38 770	22 431	12 956	5 104	404	12
1991	167 376	886	2 272	31 130	52 678	38 611	23 445	13 035	4 901	408	10
1992	160 501	905	2 095	27 589	49 052	38 430	23 870	13 252	4 844	452	12
1993	157 846	964	2 119	25 806	46 846	38 139	24 690	13 885	4 889	494	14
1994	156 539	1 080	2 166	25 223	44 871	38 081	25 507	14 156	5 008	440	7
1995	154 315	946	2 324	24 945	43 394	37 254	25 759	14 352	4 868	457	16
1996	167 916	1 098	2 547	28 790	46 356	39 311	28 228	16 118	5 027	428	13
1997	170 145	1 020	2 414	29 947	44 960	40 159	28 892	16 858	5 413	482	..
1998	177 871	1 103	2 656	33 236	45 766	40 366	30 449	18 174	5 576	511	34
1999	173 701	1 066	2 537	32 807	45 004	38 492	29 139	18 341	5 755	502	58
2000	175 542	1 048	2 700	33 218	47 099	37 852	28 735	18 589	5 794	459	48
2001	176 364	1 066	2 592	33 431	48 267	36 506	28 782	19 146	6 094	456	24
2002	175 932	1 075	2 658	32 985	48 359	35 795	28 503	19 450	6 531	457	119
2003	181 582	1 171	2 796	34 247	51 201[2]	36 018	28 749	19 868	7 032	500	–
2004	185 415	1 034	2 722	35 386	52 701[2]	37 759	28 064	19 820	7 422	507	–
2005	186 416	1 083	2 703	35 313	53 342[2]	38 330	27 836	19 782	7 459	568	–
Scotland											
	C54C	C54D	C54E	C54F	C54G	C54H	C54I	C54J	C54K	C54L	EVH4
1986	9 628	74	236	2 529	2 985	1 744	1 081	708	249	22	–
1987	9 460	70	210	2 417	2 996	1 729	1 082	697	242	17	–
1988	10 128	65	218	2 529	3 304	1 970	1 107	663	257	15	–
1989	10 209	53	209	2 561	3 202	1 968	1 229	706	266	15	–
1990	10 219	54	186	2 539	3 242	2 063	1 161	700	253	21	–
1991	11 068	77	203	2 571	3 486	2 253	1 445	743	262	28	–
1992	10 818	73	174	2 377	3 389	2 291	1 444	799	254	17	–
1993	11 076	92	193	2 300	3 368	2 447	1 492	891	264	29	–
1994	11 392	78	215	2 312	3 486	2 431	1 648	877	315	30	–
1995	11 143	79	233	2 169	3 399	2 438	1 609	887	296	33	–
1996	11 978	87	236	2 362	3 571	2 603	1 801	960	331	27	–
1997	12 109	85	204	2 431	3 444	2 651	1 854	1 093	322	25	–
1998	12 485	73	213	2 707	3 426	2 749	1 807	1 149	339	22	–
1999	12 168	69	182	2 635	3 354	2 554	1 810	1 180	361	23	–
2000	11 997	93	181	2 610	3 355	2 403	1 769	1 177	381	28	–
2001	12 128	66	210	2 722	3 462	2 322	1 818	1 127	378	23	–
2002	11 870	79	194	2 653	3 453	2 172	1 736	1 171	382	29	1
2003[3]	12 306	71	243	2 789	3 690	2 233	1 726	1 113	413	28	–
2004[3]	12 461	102	207	2 909	3 703	2 269	1 666	1 186	385	32	2
2005	12 603	93	248	2 963	3 761	2 329	1 684	1 101	398	26	–

1 Refers to therapeutic abortions notified in accordance with the Abortion Act
1967.
2 Records with missing ages were assigned to the 20 - 24 age group.
3 Revised.

Sources: Department of Health;
Information Services Division

5.19 Deaths: by sex and age[1]

Numbers

	All ages[2]	Under 1 year	1-4	5-9	10-14	15-19	20-24	25-34	35-44	45-54	55-64	65-74	75-84	85 and over
United Kingdom														
Males														
1900 - 02	340 664	87 242	37 834	8 429	4 696	7 047	8 766	19 154	24 739	30 488	37 610	39 765	28 320	6 563
1910 - 12	303 703	63 885	29 452	7 091	4 095	5 873	6 817	16 141	21 813	28 981	37 721	45 140	29 397	7 283
1920 - 22	284 876	48 044	19 008	6 052	3 953	5 906	6 572	13 663	19 702	29 256	40 583	49 398	34 937	7 801
1930 - 32	284 249	28 840	11 276	4 580	2 890	5 076	6 495	12 327	16 326	29 376	47 989	63 804	45 247	10 022
1940 - 42	314 643	24 624	6 949	3 400	2 474	4 653	4 246	11 506	17 296	30 082	57 076	79 652	59 733	12 900
1950 - 52	307 312	14 105	2 585	1 317	919	1 498	2 289	5 862	11 074	27 637	53 691	86 435	79 768	20 131
1960 - 62	318 850	12 234	1 733	971	871	1 718	1 857	3 842	8 753	26 422	63 009	87 542	83 291	26 605
1970 - 72	335 166	9 158	1 485	1 019	802	1 778	2 104	3 590	7 733	24 608	64 898	105 058	82 905	30 027
1980 - 82	330 495	4 829	774	527	652	1 999	1 943	3 736	6 568	19 728	54 159	105 155	98 488	31 936
1990 - 92	312 521	3 315	623	372	396	1 349	2 059	4 334	6 979	15 412	40 424	87 849	106 376	43 032
2000 - 02	288 261	2 065	365	233	326	1 032	1 502	4 270	7 181	15 370	32 328	66 808	98 363	58 419
	KHUA	KHUB	KHUC	KHUD	KHUE	KHUF	KHUG	KHUH	KHUI	KHUJ	KHUK	KHUL	KHUM	KHUN
1994	303 333	2 660	497	319	400	1 041	1 829	4 741	6 661	14 983	36 469	86 896	98 982	47 855
1995	310 722	2 595	447	314	388	1 115	1 810	4 748	6 754	15 644	36 068	85 459	103 324	52 056
1996	305 323	2 562	489	267	352	1 104	1 693	4 746	6 789	15 796	35 033	81 333	102 090	53 069
1997	300 414	2 391	456	300	364	1 111	1 712	4 583	6 667	15 689	33 707	77 870	101 365	54 199
1998	300 160	2 327	463	283	343	1 058	1 539	4 684	6 902	15 825	33 778	75 718	101 468	55 772
1999	300 368	2 318	456	257	319	1 085	1 553	4 516	6 946	15 849	33 338	73 736	101 795	58 200
2000	290 186	2 120	380	253	326	1 042	1 491	4 397	7 081	15 470	32 556	69 499	98 075	57 496
2001	286 760	2 042	347	223	330	1 061	1 508	4 262	7 156	15 515	32 005	66 111	97 816	58 384
2002	287 837	2 032	368	223	321	992	1 508	4 150	7 305	15 126	32 423	64 814	99 198	59 377
2003	288 604	2 029	351	214	289	969	1 467	3 823	7 408	14 689	32 825	63 574	100 933	60 033
2004	277 840	2 017	329	202	286	917	1 373	3 642	7 285	14 342	31 583	60 587	98 365	56 912
2005	276 803	2 109	324	185	286	915	1 345	3 402	7 235	14 167	31 621	58 819	95 763	60 632
Females														
1900 - 02	322 058	68 770	36 164	8 757	5 034	6 818	8 264	18 702	21 887	25 679	34 521	42 456	34 907	10 099
1910 - 12	289 608	49 865	27 817	7 113	4 355	5 683	6 531	15 676	19 647	24 481	32 813	46 453	37 353	11 828
1920 - 22	274 772	35 356	17 323	5 808	4 133	5 729	6 753	14 878	18 121	24 347	34 026	48 573	45 521	14 203
1930 - 32	275 336	21 072	9 995	3 990	2 734	4 721	5 931	12 699	15 373	24 695	39 471	59 520	56 250	18 886
1940 - 42	296 646	17 936	5 952	2 743	2 068	4 180	5 028	11 261	14 255	23 629	42 651	70 907	71 377	24 658
1950 - 52	291 597	10 293	2 098	880	625	1 115	1 717	5 018	8 989	18 875	37 075	75 220	92 848	36 844
1960 - 62	304 871	8 887	1 334	627	522	684	811	2 504	6 513	16 720	36 078	73 118	105 956	51 117
1970 - 72	322 968	6 666	1 183	654	459	718	900	2 110	5 345	15 594	36 177	75 599	109 539	68 024
1980 - 82	330 269	3 561	585	355	425	733	772	2 099	4 360	12 206	32 052	72 618	117 760	82 743
1990 - 92	328 218	2 431	485	259	255	520	714	1 989	4 340	9 707	25 105	61 951	115 467	104 994
2000 - 02	317 356	1 586	283	188	208	446	536	1 877	4 426	10 270	20 549	47 324	101 650	128 012
	KIUA	KIUB	KIUC	KIUD	KIUE	KIUF	KIUG	KIUH	KIUI	KIUJ	KIUK	KIUL	KIUM	KIUN
1994	324 303	1 989	410	205	232	406	626	2 053	4 285	10 081	22 401	62 069	106 816	112 730
1995	334 771	1 931	370	224	250	449	592	2 140	4 203	10 389	22 093	60 988	110 247	120 895
1996	330 701	1 904	355	214	224	493	589	2 140	4 215	10 301	21 406	57 889	109 578	121 393
1997	329 332	1 862	333	215	239	487	574	1 960	4 323	10 412	20 999	55 687	108 276	123 965
1998	329 012	1 752	347	213	215	486	568	1 971	4 289	10 430	20 874	54 200	107 135	126 532
1999	331 694	1 727	338	195	240	473	553	1 924	4 372	10 430	21 045	52 240	106 841	131 316
2000	318 180	1 671	277	177	203	449	535	1 961	4 509	10 459	20 533	48 994	101 711	126 701
2001	315 508	1 622	297	208	207	439	552	1 821	4 385	10 287	20 481	46 964	100 907	127 338
2002	318 379	1 465	276	180	214	449	521	1 849	4 385	10 063	20 633	46 013	102 333	129 998
2003	322 584	1 657	312	176	221	424	539	1 802	4 482	9 830	20 962	45 364	105 158	131 657
2004	305 242	1 590	257	153	191	445	533	1 715	4 425	9 438	20 452	43 005	100 640	122 398
2005	305 860	1 574	253	150	202	439	536	1 620	4 354	9 466	20 658	41 899	98 441	126 268

5.19 Deaths: by sex and age[1]

continued

	All ages[2]	Under 1 year	1-4	5-9	10-14	15-19	20-24	25-34	35-44	45-54	55-64	65-74	75-84	85 and over
England and Wales														
Males														
1900 - 02	288 886	76 095	32 051	7 066	3 818	5 611	7 028	15 869	21 135	26 065	31 600	33 568	23 835	5 144
1910 - 12	257 253	54 678	24 676	5 907	3 348	4 765	5 596	13 603	18 665	24 820	32 217	38 016	24 928	6 036
1920 - 22	240 605	39 796	15 565	5 151	3 314	4 901	5 447	11 551	17 004	25 073	34 639	42 025	29 685	6 455
1930 - 32	243 147	23 331	9 099	3 844	2 435	4 354	5 580	10 600	14 041	25 657	41 581	54 910	39 091	8 624
1940 - 42	268 876	19 393	5 616	2 834	2 051	3 832	3 156	9 484	14 744	25 983	50 058	68 791	51 779	11 158
1950 - 52	266 879	11 498	2 131	1 087	778	1 248	1 947	4 990	9 489	23 815	46 948	75 774	69 496	17 677
1960 - 62	278 369	10 157	1 444	812	742	1 523	1 624	3 278	7 524	22 813	54 908	77 000	73 180	23 364
1970 - 72	293 934	7 818	1 259	860	677	1 524	1 788	3 079	6 637	21 348	56 667	92 389	73 365	26 522
1980 - 82	290 352	4 168	657	452	555	1 716	1 619	3 169	5 590	16 909	47 144	92 485	87 338	28 551
1990 - 92	275 550	2 926	545	325	338	1 157	1 757	3 717	6 057	13 258	34 977	77 063	94 672	38 757
2000 - 02	253 706	1 836	323	200	282	862	1 244	3 619	6 104	13 184	27 696	58 114	87 481	52 761
	KHVA	KHVB	KHVC	KHVD	KHVE	KHVF	KHVG	KHVH	KHVI	KHVJ	KHVK	KHVL	KHVM	KHVN
1994	267 555	2 367	432	278	331	843	1 550	4 065	5 769	12 923	31 320	76 270	88 230	43 177
1995	274 449	2 305	391	269	340	910	1 533	4 043	5 880	13 487	30 973	74 970	92 291	47 057
1996	268 682	2 272	441	236	291	925	1 409	4 064	5 843	13 565	30 066	71 046	90 708	47 816
1997	264 865	2 137	412	267	325	947	1 442	3 940	5 707	13 484	28 907	68 024	90 207	49 066
1998	264 707	2 070	413	240	291	875	1 292	4 013	5 895	13 595	29 052	66 099	90 450	50 422
1999	264 299	2 075	405	218	275	902	1 270	3 847	5 934	13 620	28 689	64 296	90 431	52 337
2000	255 547	1 886	335	217	284	872	1 224	3 755	6 048	13 367	27 898	60 593	87 126	51 942
2001	252 426	1 808	318	185	281	882	1 266	3 633	6 065	13 271	27 469	57 492	87 013	52 743
2002	253 144	1 813	315	197	280	833	1 243	3 470	6 198	12 915	27 721	56 258	88 304	53 597
2003	253 852	1 809	305	189	244	808	1 229	3 260	6 318	12 694	28 221	55 118	89 629	54 028
2004	244 130	1 792	287	170	257	775	1 146	3 092	6 191	12 249	27 040	52 536	87 266	51 329
2005	243 324	1 869	282	157	246	749	1 113	2 888	6 143	12 084	27 268	51 010	84 783	54 732
Females														
1900 - 02	269 432	60 090	30 674	7 278	4 010	5 265	6 497	15 065	18 253	21 474	28 424	35 307	29 118	7 977
1910 - 12	242 079	42 642	23 335	5 883	3 519	4 522	5 256	12 742	16 363	20 611	27 571	38 489	31 363	9 782
1920 - 22	229 908	29 178	14 174	4 928	3 456	4 719	5 533	12 244	15 142	20 580	28 633	41 010	38 439	11 871
1930 - 32	233 915	16 929	8 013	3 338	2 293	3 969	4 198	10 716	13 022	21 190	33 798	50 844	48 531	16 234
1940 - 42	253 702	14 174	4 726	2 265	1 695	3 426	4 198	9 470	12 093	20 413	36 814	60 987	61 891	21 550
1950 - 52	252 176	8 367	1 727	732	520	893	1 365	4 131	7 586	16 161	31 875	65 087	81 154	32 579
1960 - 62	266 849	7 409	1 103	527	444	591	700	2 147	5 576	14 389	31 083	63 543	93 548	45 789
1970 - 72	284 181	5 677	1 020	562	396	620	806	1 814	4 585	13 417	31 222	65 817	96 952	61 293
1980 - 82	290 026	3 064	511	301	365	635	670	1 821	3 740	10 420	27 606	63 023	103 676	74 194
1990 - 92	288 851	2 161	420	227	217	455	625	1 718	3 765	8 347	21 466	53 783	101 752	93 914
2000 - 02	279 482	1 412	251	168	182	382	455	1 629	3 805	8 893	17 659	40 734	89 387	114 525
	KIVA	KIVB	KIVC	KIVD	KIVE	KIVF	KIVG	KIVH	KIVI	KIVJ	KIVK	KIVL	KIVM	KIVN
1994	285 639	1 753	364	187	204	357	535	1 771	3 669	8 688	19 039	53 921	94 197	100 954
1995	295 234	1 677	333	196	210	382	502	1 859	3 644	9 001	18 891	52 987	97 162	108 390
1996	291 453	1 687	320	175	196	430	507	1 852	3 658	8 852	18 244	50 195	96 679	108 658
1997	290 416	1 663	297	177	209	426	490	1 718	3 737	9 016	17 949	48 293	95 508	110 933
1998	290 308	1 555	309	177	189	407	480	1 724	3 678	9 066	17 927	46 894	94 713	113 189
1999	291 819	1 546	300	168	215	385	470	1 668	3 786	9 029	18 031	45 100	93 878	117 243
2000	280 117	1 491	246	156	179	384	466	1 688	3 874	9 090	17 635	42 174	89 310	113 424
2001	277 947	1 432	270	188	178	378	467	1 591	3 768	8 917	17 610	40 465	88 808	113 875
2002	280 383	1 314	236	159	189	384	432	1 608	3 772	8 672	17 733	39 564	90 043	116 277
2003	284 402	1 497	281	153	193	353	461	1 569	3 860	8 514	17 989	38 991	92 670	117 871
2004	268 411	1 426	229	133	163	375	455	1 486	3 794	8 114	17 601	36 928	88 269	109 438
2005	269 368	1 390	219	131	175	368	457	1 417	3 727	8 149	17 800	35 973	86 412	113 150

5.19 Deaths: by sex and age[1]
continued

Numbers

	All ages[2]	Under 1 year	1-4	5-9	10-14	15-19	20-24	25-34	35-44	45-54	55-64	65-74	75-84	85 and over
Scotland														
Males														
1900 - 02	40 224	9 189	4 798	1 083	672	1 069	1 292	2 506	2 935	3 591	4 597	4 531	3 117	834
1910 - 12	35 981	7 510	3 935	962	595	826	910	1 969	2 469	3 325	4 356	5 113	3 182	813
1920 - 22	34 649	6 757	2 847	710	489	747	791	1 616	2 128	3 314	4 785	5 624	3 928	911
1930 - 32	32 476	4 426	1 771	610	365	568	706	1 352	1 848	2 979	5 095	6 906	4 839	1 010
1940 - 42	36 384	3 973	1 011	449	321	668	888	1 643	2 090	3 348	5 728	8 556	6 317	1 337
1950 - 52	32 236	1 949	349	175	105	200	265	693	1 267	3 151	5 574	8 544	8 094	1 871
1960 - 62	32 401	1 578	222	121	102	146	185	456	1 013	2 986	6 682	8 505	7 980	2 425
1970 - 72	32 446	944	168	119	93	178	233	396	875	2 617	6 641	10 176	7 383	2 624
1980 - 82	31 723	451	80	56	71	206	233	423	776	2 280	5 601	10 152	8 804	2 591
1990 - 92	29 421	287	57	34	40	137	230	485	744	1 730	4 402	8 611	9 311	3 353
2000 - 02	27 526	165	30	23	30	119	196	523	882	1 775	3 781	7 038	8 535	4 430
	KHWA	KHWB	KHWC	KHWD	KHWE	KHWF	KHWG	KHWH	KHWI	KHWJ	KHWK	KHWL	KHWM	KHWN
1994	28 416	212	42	27	48	133	212	538	715	1 684	4 114	8 575	8 446	3 670
1995	28 791	197	37	30	30	152	195	563	698	1 746	4 144	8 449	8 604	3 946
1996	29 223	206	41	23	46	139	212	556	755	1 845	4 087	8 259	8 926	4 128
1997	28 305	186	32	22	27	114	208	521	788	1 794	3 876	7 909	8 791	4 037
1998	28 132	183	37	34	39	134	200	524	843	1 796	3 828	7 746	8 585	4 183
1999	28 605	161	31	23	33	138	215	545	818	1 820	3 773	7 569	8 908	4 571
2000	27 511	173	33	24	28	115	198	512	842	1 716	3 789	7 224	8 523	4 334
2001	27 324	155	22	27	35	131	179	510	902	1 820	3 751	6 950	8 433	4 409
2002	27 743	167	34	17	27	111	211	546	901	1 789	3 804	6 940	8 648	4 548
2003	27 832	146	35	15	31	122	186	469	893	1 634	3 787	6 797	8 994	4 723
2004	26 775	160	29	21	23	105	181	449	889	1 676	3 629	6 507	8 733	4 373
2005	26 522	159	33	19	30	106	150	385	882	1 654	3 478	6 352	8 691	4 583
Females														
1900 - 02	39 891	7 143	4 477	1 162	747	1 058	1 246	2 625	2 732	3 130	4 485	5 273	4 305	1 508
1910 - 12	36 132	5 854	3 674	981	618	836	910	2 149	2 473	2 909	3 960	5 636	4 588	1 552
1920 - 22	34 449	5 029	2 602	687	489	711	889	1 947	2 266	2 828	4 157	5 587	5 443	1 814
1930 - 32	32 377	3 319	1 602	527	339	568	666	1 508	1 812	2 731	4 380	6 630	6 178	2 117
1940 - 42	33 715	2 852	921	373	283	595	656	1 382	1 672	2 528	4 430	7 674	7 613	2 536
1950 - 52	31 525	1 432	284	115	84	185	293	714	1 127	2 188	4 204	8 157	9 310	3 431
1960 - 62	30 559	1 107	170	80	63	72	87	287	762	1 897	4 115	7 752	9 991	4 177
1970 - 72	30 978	694	118	69	46	73	74	231	608	1 769	4 036	7 823	10 112	5 324
1980 - 82	32 326	337	49	37	44	74	73	213	493	1 456	3 565	7 781	11 333	6 871
1990 - 92	31 747	190	45	20	29	49	72	218	458	1 093	2 966	6 630	11 079	8 898
2000 - 02	30 235	123	24	14	21	50	64	199	493	1 110	2 341	5 326	9 785	10 685
	KIWA	KIWB	KIWC	KIWD	KIWE	KIWF	KIWG	KIWH	KIWI	KIWJ	KIWK	KIWL	KIWM	KIWN
1994	30 912	170	29	11	19	33	74	229	495	1 102	2 723	6 617	10 008	9 402
1995	31 709	178	26	16	26	50	70	231	435	1 100	2 601	6 449	10 452	10 075
1996	31 448	159	24	31	21	49	67	218	453	1 172	2 573	6 206	10 256	10 219
1997	31 189	130	23	28	21	43	71	199	496	1 128	2 480	5 985	10 164	10 421
1998	31 032	137	26	28	19	55	68	198	485	1 106	2 416	5 955	9 913	10 626
1999	31 676	115	26	20	17	65	58	201	467	1 128	2 431	5 837	10 198	11 113
2000	30 288	132	20	10	21	46	56	222	510	1 086	2 324	5 512	9 875	10 474
2001	30 058	135	20	16	21	47	71	189	480	1 111	2 361	5 235	9 695	10 677
2002	30 360	103	32	15	20	58	65	185	489	1 134	2 339	5 232	9 784	10 904
2003	30 640	119	24	18	20	57	64	181	489	1 062	2 446	5 194	9 977	10 989
2004	29 412	106	19	15	22	52	62	179	492	1 065	2 291	4 924	9 924	10 261
2005	29 225	125	27	11	18	55	58	163	506	1 073	2 316	4 841	9 620	10 412

5.19 Deaths: by sex and age[1]

continued

Numbers

	All ages[2]	Under 1 year	1-4	5-9	10-14	15-19	20-24	25-34	35-44	45-54	55-64	65-74	75-84	85 and over
Northern Ireland														
Males														
1900 - 02	11 554	1 958	985	280	206	367	446	779	669	832	1 413	1 666	1 368	585
1910 - 12	10 469	1 697	841	222	152	282	311	569	679	836	1 148	2 011	1 287	434
1920 - 22	9 622	1 491	596	191	150	258	334	496	570	869	1 159	1 749	1 324	435
1930 - 32	8 626	1 083	406	126	90	154	209	375	437	740	1 313	1 988	1 317	388
1940 - 42	9 383	1 258	322	117	102	153	202	379	462	751	1 290	2 305	1 637	405
1950 - 52	8 197	658	105	55	36	50	77	179	318	671	1 169	2 117	2 178	583
1960 - 62	8 080	499	67	38	27	49	48	108	216	623	1 419	2 037	2 131	816
1970 - 72	8 786	396	58	40	32	76	83	115	221	643	1 590	2 493	2 157	881
1980 - 82	8 420	211	37	20	26	77	92	144	202	539	1 414	2 518	2 346	795
1990 - 92	7 550	102	21	13	18	55	73	132	178	423	1 044	2 175	2 393	922
2000 - 02	7 029	64	13	11	14	50	62	128	195	411	851	1 656	2 347	1228
	KHXA	KHXB	KHXC	KHXD	KHXE	KHXF	KHXG	KHXH	KHXI	KHXJ	KHXK	KHXL	KHXM	KHXN
1994	7 362	81	23	14	21	65	67	138	177	376	1 035	2 051	2 306	1 008
1995	7 482	93	19	15	18	53	82	142	176	411	951	2 040	2 429	1 053
1996	7 418	84	7	8	15	40	72	126	191	386	880	2 028	2 456	1 125
1997	7 244	68	12	11	12	50	62	122	172	411	924	1 937	2 367	1 096
1998	7 321	74	13	9	13	49	47	147	164	434	898	1 873	2 433	1 167
1999	7 464	82	20	16	11	45	68	124	194	409	876	1 871	2 456	1 292
2000	7 128	61	12	12	14	55	69	130	191	387	869	1 682	2 426	1 220
2001	7 010	79	7	11	14	48	63	119	189	424	785	1 669	2 370	1 232
2002	6 950	52	19	9	14	48	54	134	206	422	898	1 616	2 246	1 232
2003	6 920	74	11	10	14	39	52	94	197	361	817	1 659	2 310	1 282
2004	6 935	64	13	11	7	37	46	101	205	417	914	1 544	2 366	1 210
2005	6 957	81	9	9	10	60	82	129	210	429	875	1 457	2 289	1 317
Females														
1900 - 02	12 735	1 537	1 013	317	277	495	521	1 012	902	1 075	1 612	1 876	1 484	614
1910 - 12	11 397	1 369	808	249	218	325	365	785	811	961	1 282	2 328	1 402	494
1920 - 22	10 415	1 149	547	193	188	299	331	687	713	939	1 236	1 976	1 639	518
1930 - 32	9 044	824	380	125	102	184	226	475	539	774	1 293	2 046	1 541	535
1940 - 42	9 229	910	305	105	90	159	174	409	490	688	1 207	2 246	1 873	572
1950 - 52	7 896	494	87	33	21	37	59	173	276	526	996	1 976	2 384	834
1960 - 62	7 463	371	61	20	15	21	24	70	175	434	880	1 823	2 417	1 151
1970 - 72	7 809	295	45	23	17	25	20	65	152	408	919	1 959	2 475	1 407
1980 - 82	7 917	160	26	17	17	23	29	65	127	329	881	1 813	2 752	1 678
1990 - 92	7 620	80	20	12	9	16	17	53	117	267	672	1 538	2 636	2 182
2000 - 02	7 638	50	9	7	5	13	17	49	129	266	548	1 263	2 479	2 802
	KIXA	KIXB	KIXC	KIXD	KIXE	KIXF	KIXG	KIXH	KIXI	KIXJ	KIXK	KIXL	KIXM	KIXN
1994	7 752	66	17	7	9	16	17	53	121	291	639	1 531	2 611	2 374
1995	7 828	76	11	12	14	17	20	50	124	288	601	1 552	2 633	2 430
1996	7 800	58	11	8	7	14	15	70	104	277	589	1 488	2 643	2 516
1997	7 727	69	13	10	9	18	13	43	90	268	570	1 409	2 604	2 611
1998	7 672	60	12	8	7	24	20	49	126	258	531	1 351	2 509	2 717
1999	8 199	66	12	7	8	23	25	55	119	273	583	1 303	2 765	2 960
2000	7 775	48	11	11	3	19	13	51	125	283	574	1 308	2 526	2 803
2001	7 503	55	7	4	8	14	14	41	137	259	510	1 264	2 404	2 786
2002	7 636	48	8	6	5	7	24	56	124	257	561	1 217	2 506	2 817
2003	7 542	41	7	5	8	14	14	52	133	254	527	1 179	2 511	2 797
2004	7 419	58	9	5	6	18	16	50	139	259	560	1 153	2 447	2 699
2005	7 267	59	7	8	9	16	21	40	121	244	542	1 085	2 409	2 706

1 See chapter text.
2 In some years the totals include a small number of persons whose age was not stated.

Sources: Office for National Statistics: 020 7533 5249;
General Register Office for Scotland;
Northern Ireland Statistics and Research Agency

5.20 Infant and maternal mortality[1]
(i) - By country. (ii) - Infant mortality by country, type of death and sex

| | Deaths of Infants under 1 year of age per thousand live births | | | | | | | | | | | | Maternal deaths per thousand live births[3] | | | |
| | United Kingdom | | | England and Wales[2] | | | Scotland | | | Northern Ireland | | | United Kingdom | England and Wales | Scotland | Northern Ireland |
	Total	Males	Females	Total	Males	Females	Total	Males	Females	Total	Males	Females				
1900 - 02	142	156	128	146	160	131	124	136	111	113	123	103	4.71	4.67	4.74	6.03
1910 - 12	110	121	98	110	121	98	109	120	97	101	110	92	3.95	3.67	5.65	5.28
1920 - 22	82	92	71	80	90	69	94	106	82	86	95	77	4.37	4.03	6.36	5.62
1930 - 32	67	75	58	64	72	55	84	94	73	75	83	66	4.54	4.24	6.40	5.24
1940 - 42	59	66	51	55	62	48	77	87	66	80	89	70	3.29	2.74	4.50	3.79
1950 - 52	30	34	26	29	33	25	37	42	32	40	45	36	0.88	0.79	1.09	1.09
1960 - 62	22	25	19	22	24	19	26	30	22	27	30	24	0.36	0.36	0.37	0.43
1970 - 72	18	20	16	18	20	15	19	22	17	22	24	20	0.17	0.17	0.17	0.12
1980 - 82	12	13	10	11	13	10	12	13	10	13	15	12	0.09	0.09	0.14	0.06
1990 - 92	7	8	6	7	8	6	7	8	6	7	8	6	0.07	0.07	0.10	-
2000 - 02	5	6	5	5	6	5	5	6	5	5	6	5	0.07	0.06	0.12	0.05
	KKAW	KKAX	KKAY	KKAZ	KKBW	KKBX	KKBY	KKBZ	KKCW	KKCX	KKCY	KKCZ	KKDW	KKDX	KKDY	KKDZ
1994	6.2	6.9	5.4	6.2	6.9	5.4	6.2	6.8	5.6	6.1	6.5	5.6	0.08	0.08	0.15	–
1995	6.2	6.9	5.4	6.1	6.9	5.3	6.2	6.4	6.1	7.1	7.5	6.6	0.07	0.07	0.10	–
1996	6.1	6.8	5.4	6.1	6.9	5.4	6.2	6.7	5.5	5.8	6.7	4.8	0.07	0.07	0.10	0.04
1997	5.8	6.4	5.3	5.9	6.5	5.3	5.3	6.1	4.5	5.6	5.5	5.8	0.06	0.06	0.07	–
1998	5.7	6.3	5.0	5.7	6.4	5.0	5.6	6.2	4.9	5.6	6.1	5.1	0.07	0.07	0.09	0.04
1999	5.8	6.4	5.1	5.8	6.5	5.1	5.0	5.7	4.3	6.4	6.8	5.9	0.05	0.05	0.13	–
2000	5.6	6.1	5.0	5.6	6.1	5.1	5.7	6.4	5.1	5.1	5.5	4.6	0.07	0.06	0.15	–
2001	5.5	6.0	5.0	5.4	5.9	4.9	5.5	5.8	5.2	6.1	7.0	5.2	0.07	0.07	0.11	0.09
2002	5.2	5.9	4.5	5.2	5.9	4.5	5.3	6.4	4.1	4.7	4.8	4.6	0.06	0.06	0.10	0.05
2003	5.3	5.7	4.9	5.3	5.7	4.9	5.1	5.4	4.7	5.2	6.5	3.9	0.10	0.07	0.10	0.14
2004	5.0	5.5	4.6	5.0	5.5	4.6	4.9	5.8	4.0	5.3	5.4	5.2	0.07	0.07	0.11	0.04
2005	5.1	5.7	4.5	5.0	5.7	4.4	5.2	5.7	4.8	6.1	7.0	5.3	0.06	0.06	0.07	0.04

5.20

Infant and maternal mortality[1]
(i) - By country. (ii) - Infant mortality by country, type of death and sex

continued

Deaths per thousand live births

		1995	1996	1997	1998	1999	2000	2001	2002	2003	2004	2005
Total												
United Kingdom:												
Stillbirths[4]	KHNQ	5.6	5.5	5.3	5.4	5.3	5.3	5.3	5.6	5.7	5.7	5.3
Perinatal[4]	KHNR	8.9	8.7	8.3	8.3	8.2	8.1	8.0	8.3	8.5	8.3	8.0
Neonatal	KHNS	4.2	4.1	3.9	3.8	3.9	3.9	3.6	3.5	3.6	3.4	3.5
Post neonatal	KHNT	2.0	2.0	2.0	1.9	1.9	1.7	1.8	1.7	1.7	1.6	1.6
England and Wales:												
Stillbirths[4]	KHNU	5.5	5.4	5.3	5.3	5.3	5.3	5.3	5.6	5.7	5.7	5.4
Perinatal[4]	KHNV	8.7	8.6	8.3	8.2	8.2	8.2	8.0	8.3	8.5	8.4	8.0
Neonatal	KHNW	4.1	4.1	3.9	3.8	3.9	3.9	3.6	3.6	3.6	3.5	3.4
Post neonatal	KHNX	2.0	2.0	2.0	1.9	1.9	1.7	1.9	1.7	1.7	1.6	1.6
Scotland:												
Stillbirths[4]	KHNY	6.6	6.4	5.3	6.1	5.2	5.6	5.7	5.4	5.6	5.8	5.3
Perinatal[4]	KHNZ	9.6	9.2	7.8	8.7	7.6	8.4	8.5	7.6	8.0	8.1	7.7
Neonatal	KHOA	4.0	3.9	3.2	3.6	3.3	4.0	3.8	3.2	3.4	3.1	3.5
Post neonatal	KHOB	2.2	2.2	2.1	2.0	1.7	1.8	1.7	2.1	1.7	1.9	1.7
Northern Ireland:												
Stillbirths[4]	KHOC	6.1	6.3	5.4	5.1	5.7	4.3	5.1	5.7	4.9	5.0	4.0
Perinatal[4]	KHOD	10.4	9.4	8.2	8.1	10.0	7.3	8.5	8.9	8.0	8.0	8.1
Neonatal	KHOE	5.5	3.7	4.2	3.9	4.8	3.8	4.5	3.5	3.9	3.6	4.9
Post neonatal	KHOF	1.6	2.0	1.4	1.7	1.6	1.3	1.6	1.2	1.3	1.7	1.3
Males												
United Kingdom:												
Perinatal[4]	KHOG	9.4	9.1	8.7	8.8	8.7	8.7	8.6	8.9	8.8	8.8	8.3
Neonatal	KHOH	4.6	4.6	4.2	4.2	4.3	4.2	4.0	4.0	3.9	3.8	3.9
Infant mortality	KHOI	6.9	6.8	6.4	6.3	6.4	6.1	6.0	5.9	5.7	5.5	5.7
England and Wales:												
Perinatal[4]	KHOK	9.3	9.0	8.7	8.8	8.6	8.7	8.5	8.9	8.9	8.8	8.4
Neonatal	KHOL	4.6	4.6	4.2	4.3	4.3	4.2	3.9	4.0	3.8	3.8	3.8
Infant mortality	KHOM	6.9	6.9	6.5	6.4	6.5	6.1	5.9	5.9	5.7	5.5	5.7
Scotland:												
Perinatal[4]	KHOO	10.1	10.0	8.1	9.6	8.4	9.5	9.2	7.9	8.4	8.8	7.6
Neonatal	KHOP	4.1	4.3	3.4	4.0	3.8	4.5	4.0	3.7	3.6	3.6	3.8
Infant mortality	KHOQ	6.4	6.7	6.1	6.2	5.7	6.4	5.8	6.4	5.4	5.8	5.7
Northern Ireland:												
Perinatal[4]	KHOS	10.4	10.1	8.5	8.9	10.5	8.0	9.8	10.0	8.2	8.2	9.2
Neonatal	KHOT	5.7	4.3	4.3	4.4	5.5	4.2	5.3	3.8	4.6	3.7	5.5
Infant mortality	KHOU	7.5	6.7	5.5	6.1	6.8	5.5	7.0	4.8	6.5	5.4	7.0
Females												
United Kingdom:												
Perinatal[4]	KHOW	8.3	8.2	7.9	7.7	7.8	7.5	7.4	7.7	8.2	7.9	7.6
Neonatal	KHOX	3.7	3.6	3.5	3.3	3.4	3.5	3.3	3.1	3.4	3.1	3.1
Infant mortality	KHOY	5.4	5.4	5.3	5.0	5.1	5.0	5.0	4.5	4.9	4.6	4.5
England and Wales:												
Perinatal[4]	KHPA	8.1	8.2	7.9	7.7	7.8	7.6	7.3	7.7	8.2	8.0	7.6
Neonatal	KHPB	3.6	3.6	3.6	3.3	3.5	3.5	3.2	3.1	3.4	3.1	3.0
Infant mortality	KHPC	5.3	5.4	5.3	5.0	5.1	5.1	4.9	4.5	4.9	4.6	4.4
Scotland:												
Perinatal[4]	KHPE	9.2	8.4	7.5	7.9	6.7	7.2	7.8	7.2	7.7	7.3	7.9
Neonatal	KHPF	3.9	3.5	2.9	3.2	2.8	3.5	3.5	2.6	3.1	2.5	3.2
Infant mortality	KHPG	6.1	5.5	4.5	4.9	4.3	5.1	5.2	4.1	4.7	4.0	4.8
Northern Ireland:												
Perinatal[4]	KHPI	10.5	8.6	8.0	7.3	9.5	6.5	7.0	7.8	7.8	7.8	6.9
Neonatal	KHPJ	5.2	3.1	4.0	3.4	4.1	3.4	3.6	3.1	3.2	3.5	4.2
Infant mortality	KHPK	6.6	4.8	5.8	5.1	5.9	4.6	5.2	4.6	3.9	5.2	5.3

1 See chapter text.
2 From 1937 to 1956 death rates are based on the births to which they relate
  in the current and preceding years.
3 Deaths in pregnancy and childbirth.
4 Deaths per 1,000 live and stillbirths. See chapter introduction.

Sources: General Register Office for Scotland;
General Register Office (Northern Ireland)

5.21

Death rates by sex and age
United Kingdom

Rates per 1,000 population

	All ages	0-4	5-9	10-14	15-19	20-24	25-34	35-44	45-54	55-64	65-74	75-84	85 and over
Males													
1900 - 02	18.4	57.0	4.1	2.4	3.7	5.0	6.6	11.0	18.6	35.0	69.9	143.6	289.6
1910 - 12	14.9	40.5	3.3	2.0	3.0	3.9	5.0	8.0	14.9	29.8	62.1	133.8	261.5
1920 - 22	13.5	33.4	2.9	1.8	2.9	3.9	4.5	6.9	11.9	25.3	57.8	131.8	259.1
1930 - 32	12.9	22.3	2.3	1.5	2.6	3.3	3.5	5.7	11.3	23.7	57.9	134.2	277.0
1940 - 42	..	..	..	..	..	..	..	..	..	..	..	..	..
1950 - 52	12.6	7.7	0.7	0.5	0.9	1.4	1.6	3.0	8.5	23.2	55.2	127.6	272.0
1960 - 62	12.5	6.4	0.5	0.4	0.9	1.1	1.1	2.5	7.4	22.2	54.4	123.4	251.0
1970 - 72	12.4	4.6	0.4	0.4	0.9	1.0	1.0	2.4	7.3	20.9	52.9	116.3	246.1
1980 - 82	12.1	3.2	0.3	0.3	0.8	0.9	0.9	1.9	6.3	18.2	46.7	107.1	224.9
1990 - 92	11.2	2.0	0.2	0.2	0.7	0.9	1.0	1.8	4.6	14.2	38.6	93.0	201.4
2000 - 02	10.0	1.4	0.1	0.2	0.5	0.8	1.0	1.6	4.0	10.4	28.9	75.2	187.7
	KHZA	KHZB	KHZC	KHZD	KHZE	KHZF	KHZG	KHZH	KHZJ	KHZK	KHZL	KHZM	KHZN
1994	10.8	1.6	0.2	0.2	0.6	0.9	1.0	1.7	4.1	12.8	36.8	90.3	194.8
1995	11.0	1.6	0.2	0.2	0.6	0.9	1.0	1.7	4.2	12.6	36.7	90.0	202.1
1996	10.8	1.6	0.1	0.2	0.6	0.9	1.0	1.7	4.2	12.3	35.2	86.0	199.6
1997	10.6	1.5	0.2	0.2	0.6	1.0	1.0	1.7	4.1	11.8	33.9	83.2	196.7
1998	10.5	1.5	0.1	0.2	0.6	0.9	1.1	1.7	4.1	11.6	33.0	81.8	193.6
1999	10.5	1.5	0.1	0.2	0.6	0.9	1.0	1.7	4.1	11.2	32.2	80.9	195.7
2000	10.1	1.4	0.1	0.2	0.6	0.8	1.0	1.6	4.0	10.7	30.3	76.8	187.9
2001	9.9	1.3	0.1	0.2	0.6	0.8	1.0	1.6	4.0	10.4	28.6	74.8	186.9
2002	9.9	1.4	0.1	0.2	0.5	0.8	1.0	1.6	4.0	10.1	27.8	74.1	188.2
2003	9.9	1.4	0.1	0.1	0.5	0.8	1.0	1.6	3.9	9.9	27.0	73.6	191.7
2004	9.5	1.4	0.1	0.1	0.5	0.7	0.9	1.6	3.8	9.3	25.5	70.6	176.3
2005	9.4	1.4	0.1	0.1	0.4	0.7	0.9	1.6	3.7	9.2	24.6	68.3	172.4
Females													
1900 - 02	16.3	47.9	4.3	2.6	3.5	4.3	5.8	9.0	14.4	27.9	59.3	127.0	262.6
1910 - 12	13.3	34.0	3.3	2.1	2.9	3.4	4.4	6.7	11.5	23.1	50.7	113.7	234.0
1920 - 22	11.9	26.9	2.8	1.9	2.8	3.4	4.1	5.6	9.3	19.2	45.6	111.5	232.4
1930 - 32	11.5	17.7	2.1	1.5	2.4	2.9	3.3	4.6	8.3	17.6	43.7	110.1	246.3
1940 - 42	..	..	..	..	..	..	..	..	..	..	..	..	..
1950 - 52	11.2	6.0	0.5	0.4	0.7	1.0	1.4	2.3	5.3	12.9	35.5	98.4	228.8
1960 - 62	11.2	4.9	0.3	0.3	0.4	0.5	0.8	1.8	4.5	11.0	30.8	87.3	218.5
1970 - 72	11.3	3.6	0.3	0.2	0.4	0.4	0.6	1.6	4.5	10.5	27.5	76.7	196.1
1980 - 82	11.4	2.3	0.2	0.2	0.3	0.4	0.5	1.3	3.9	9.9	24.8	67.2	179.5
1990 - 92	11.1	1.5	0.1	0.2	0.3	0.3	0.4	1.1	2.9	8.4	22.1	58.7	157.2
2000 - 02	10.5	1.1	0.1	0.1	0.2	0.3	0.4	1.0	2.6	6.4	17.9	51.1	157.3
	KHZO	KHZP	KHZQ	KHZR	KHZS	KHZT	KHZU	KHZV	KHZW	KHZX	KHZY	KHZZ	KHZI
1994	10.9	1.3	0.1	0.1	0.2	0.3	0.4	1.1	2.8	7.6	21.7	57.5	154.8
1995	11.2	1.2	0.1	0.1	0.3	0.3	0.5	1.1	2.8	7.5	21.7	57.8	161.4
1996	11.1	1.2	0.1	0.1	0.3	0.3	0.5	1.1	2.7	7.3	21.0	56.4	159.4
1997	11.0	1.2	0.1	0.1	0.3	0.3	0.4	1.1	2.7	7.1	20.5	55.2	160.3
1998	11.0	1.2	0.1	0.1	0.3	0.3	0.4	1.0	2.7	7.0	20.2	54.4	159.8
1999	11.0	1.2	0.1	0.1	0.3	0.3	0.4	1.0	2.7	6.9	19.6	54.2	163.7
2000	10.5	1.1	0.1	0.1	0.3	0.3	0.5	1.0	2.7	6.6	18.5	51.6	155.8
2001	10.4	1.1	0.1	0.1	0.2	0.3	0.4	1.0	2.6	6.4	17.8	50.8	155.8
2002	10.5	1.0	0.1	0.1	0.2	0.3	0.4	1.0	2.6	6.2	17.4	51.0	160.3
2003	10.6	1.2	0.1	0.1	0.2	0.3	0.4	1.0	2.6	6.1	17.1	51.8	166.4
2004	10.0	1.1	0.1	0.1	0.2	0.3	0.4	1.0	2.4	5.8	16.2	49.3	155.2
2005	10.0	1.1	0.1	0.1	0.2	0.3	0.4	0.9	2.4	5.8	15.8	48.7	153.2

Sources: Office for National Statistics;
General Register Office for Scotland;
Northern Ireland Statistics and Research Agency

5.22 Interim life tables, 2003-05

	United Kingdom				England and Wales			
	Males		Females		Males		Females	
	l_x	e^0_x	l_x	e^0_x	l_x	e^0_x	l_x	e^0_x
Age(x)								
0 years	100 000	76.6	100 000	81.0	100 000	76.9	100 000	81.1
5 years	99 340	72.1	99 452	76.4	99 344	72.4	99 452	76.6
10 years	99 286	67.2	99 407	71.4	99 292	67.4	99 408	71.6
15 years	99 214	62.2	99 353	66.5	99 222	62.5	99 355	66.7
20 years	98 984	57.4	99 239	61.5	99 005	57.6	99 246	61.7
25 years	98 625	52.5	99 098	56.6	98 666	52.8	99 111	56.8
30 years	98 232	47.8	98 922	51.7	98 292	48.0	98 938	51.9
35 years	97 738	43.0	98 681	46.8	97 821	43.2	98 702	47.0
40 years	97 091	38.2	98 319	42.0	97 205	38.5	98 352	42.2
45 years	96 171	33.6	97 738	37.2	96 318	33.8	97 784	37.4
50 years	94 754	29.0	96 789	32.6	94 946	29.2	96 857	32.7
55 years	92 552	24.7	95 325	28.0	92 796	24.9	95 424	28.2
60 years	89 248	20.5	93 118	23.6	89 583	20.6	93 273	23.8
65 years	83 858	16.6	89 672	19.4	84 346	16.8	89 920	19.6
70 years	75 948	13.1	84 301	15.5	76 588	13.2	84 682	15.6
75 years	64 337	10.0	75 948	11.9	65 128	10.0	76 470	12.0
80 years	48 415	7.4	62 946	8.8	49 235	7.4	63 582	8.9
85 years	30 205	5.4	45 275	6.3	30 865	5.4	45 912	6.3
90 years	13 809	3.8	24 949	4.3	14 206	3.8	25 396	4.4

	Scotland				Northern Ireland			
	Males		Females		Males		Females	
	l_x	e^0_x	l_x	e^0_x	l_x	e^0_x	l_x	e^0_x
Age(x)								
0 years	100 000	74.2	100 000	79.3	100 000	76.0	100 000	80.8
5 years	99 317	69.7	99 461	74.7	99 260	71.6	99 438	76.3
10 years	99 256	64.8	99 409	69.7	99 179	66.6	99 387	71.3
15 years	99 171	59.8	99 345	64.8	99 101	61.7	99 326	66.4
20 years	98 843	55.0	99 175	59.9	98 773	56.9	99 204	61.4
25 years	98 328	50.3	98 987	55.0	98 277	52.2	99 058	56.5
30 years	97 739	45.6	98 778	50.1	97 837	47.4	98 888	51.6
35 years	96 979	40.9	98 470	45.3	97 350	42.6	98 659	46.7
40 years	96 007	36.3	97 987	40.5	96 671	37.9	98 287	41.9
45 years	94 760	31.8	97 288	35.7	95 768	33.2	97 664	37.2
50 years	92 918	27.3	96 120	31.1	94 290	28.7	96 779	32.5
55 years	90 213	23.1	94 355	26.7	92 101	24.3	95 311	27.9
60 years	86 070	19.1	91 587	22.4	88 563	20.2	93 058	23.5
65 years	79 265	15.5	87 262	18.4	82 994	16.4	89 617	19.3
70 years	69 946	12.2	80 719	14.7	75 121	12.8	84 190	15.4
75 years	57 121	9.3	71 155	11.3	62 936	9.7	75 737	11.8
80 years	41 075	7.0	57 096	8.4	46 609	7.3	62 819	8.7
85 years	24 252	5.1	39 381	6.0	28 875	5.2	45 068	6.2
90 years	10 288	3.7	20 803	4.2	12 717	3.7	24 809	4.2

Note Column l_x shows the number who would survive to exact **age**(x), out of 100,000 born, who were subject throughout their lives to the death rates experienced in the three-year period indicated. Column e^0_x is 'the expectation of life', that is, the average future lifetime which would be lived by a person aged exactly x if likewise subject to the death rates experienced in the three-year period indicated. See introductory notes.

Source: Government Actuary's Department: 020 7211 2622

5.23 Adoptions by date of entry in Adopted Children Register: by sex, age and country

	All ages		Under 1		1-4		5-9		10-14		15-17	
	Numbers	Percentages	Numbers	Percentages	Numbers	Percentages	Numbers	Percentages	Numbers	Percentages	Numbers	Percentages
United Kingdom **Persons**												
	VOXI	VOXJ	VOXK	VOXL	VOXM	VOXN	VOXO	VOXP	VOXQ	VOXR	VOXS	VOXT
2000	5 503	100	283	5	2 203	40	1 745	32	1 025	19	247	4
2001[1,3]	6 588	100	272	4	2 874	44	2 047	31	1 103	17	292	4
2002	6 240	100	314	5	2 737	44	1 937	31	999	16	253	4
2003[6]	5 426	100	212	4	2 481	46	1 716	32	789	15	228	4
2004	6 125	100	279	5	2 847	46	1 857	30	873	14	269	4
2005	6 161	100	247	4	3 130	51	1 761	29	795	13	228	4
Males												
	VOXU	VOXV	VOXW	VOXX	VOXY	VOXZ	VOYA	VOYB	VOYC	VOYD	VOYE	VOYF
2000	2 740	100	144	5	1 115	41	867	32	491	18	123	4
2001[2,4]	3 314	100	138	4	1 483	45	1 006	30	547	17	140	4
2002	3 140	100	176	6	1 425	45	935	30	488	16	116	4
2003[7]	2 634	100	104	4	1 224	46	844	32	351	13	111	4
2004	3 056	100	146	5	1 429	47	938	31	417	14	126	4
2005	3 082	100	123	4	1 571	51	913	30	369	12	106	3
Females												
	VOYG	VOYH	VOYI	VOYJ	VOYK	VOYL	VOYM	VOYN	VOYO	VOYP	VOYQ	VOYR
2000	2 763	100	139	5	1 088	39	878	32	534	19	124	4
2001[2,5]	3 274	100	134	4	1 391	42	1 041	32	556	17	152	5
2002	3 100	100	138	4	1 312	42	1 002	32	511	16	137	4
2003[8]	2 792	100	108	4	1 257	45	872	31	438	16	117	4
2004	3 069	100	133	4	1 418	46	919	30	456	15	143	5
2005	3 079	100	124	4	1 559	51	848	28	426	14	122	4
England and Wales **Persons**												
	GQTP	GQTQ	GQTR	GQTS	GQTT	GQTU	GQTV	GQTW	GQTX	GQTY	GQTZ	GQUA
2000	4 940	100	251	5	2 019	41	1 549	31	906	18	215	4
2001[1]	5 981	100	246	4	2 648	44	1 845	31	983	16	257	4
2002	5 680	100	287	5	2 532	45	1 748	31	900	16	213	4
2003	4 818	100	183	4	2 260	47	1 503	31	683	14	189	4
2004	5 571	100	254	5	2 633	47	1 653	30	786	14	245	4
2005	5 582	100	223	4	2 915	52	1 561	28	684	12	199	4
Males												
	GQUB	GQUC	GQUD	GQUE	GQUF	GQUG	GQUH	GQUI	GQUJ	GQUK	GQUL	GQUM
2000	2 452	100	127	5	1 022	42	759	31	434	18	110	4
2001[2]	3 011	100	124	4	1 370	45	904	30	494	16	118	4
2002	2 871	100	160	6	1 324	46	846	29	443	15	98	3
2003	2 339	100	91	4	1 115	48	737	32	301	13	95	4
2004	2 782	100	132	5	1 330	48	833	30	373	13	114	4
2005	2 804	100	112	4	1 468	52	813	29	321	11	90	3
Females												
	GQUN	GQUO	GQUP	GQUQ	GQUR	GQUS	GQUT	GQUU	GQUV	GQUW	GQUX	GQUY
2000	2 488	100	124	5	997	40	790	32	472	19	105	4
2001[2]	2 970	100	122	4	1 278	43	941	32	489	16	140	5
2002	2 809	100	127	5	1 208	43	902	32	457	16	115	4
2003	2 479	100	92	4	1 145	46	766	31	382	15	94	4
2004	2 789	100	122	4	1 303	47	820	29	413	15	131	5
2005	2 778	100	111	4	1 447	52	748	27	363	13	109	4

5.23
continued

Adoptions by date of entry in Adopted Children Register: by sex, age and country

	All ages		Under 1		1-4		5-9		10-14		15-17	
	Numbers	Percentages	Numbers	Percentages	Numbers	Percentages	Numbers	Percentages	Numbers	Percentages	Numbers	Percentages
Scotland												
Persons												
	GQUZ	GQVA	GQVB	GQVC	GQVD	GQVE	GQVF	GQVG	GQVH	GQVI	GQVJ	GQVK
2000	391	100	24	6	140	36	123	31	85	22	19	5
2001[3]	468	100	18	4	176	38	161	34	92	20	21	4
2002	385	100	13	3	143	37	130	34	73	19	26	7
2003[6]	468	100	25	5	153	33	170	36	88	19	32	7
2004	393	100	21	5	144	37	143	36	67	17	18	5
2005	439	100	18	4	162	37	155	35	81	18	23	5
Males												
	GQVL	GQVM	GQVN	GQVO	GQVP	GQVQ	GQVR	GQVS	GQVT	GQVU	GQVV	GQVW
2000	210	100	13	6	75	36	71	34	43	20	8	4
2001[4]	241	100	11	5	93	39	83	34	40	17	14	6
2002	193	100	8	4	75	39	60	31	37	19	13	7
2003[7]	228	100	11	5	78	34	85	37	43	19	11	5
2004	200	100	13	7	67	34	77	39	34	17	9	5
2005	217	100	9	4	80	37	79	36	36	17	13	6
Females												
	GQVX	GQVY	GQVZ	GQWA	GRFK	GRFL	GRFM	GRFN	GRFO	GRFP	GRFQ	GRFR
2000	181	100	11	6	65	36	52	29	42	23	11	6
2001[5]	227	100	7	3	83	37	78	34	52	23	7	3
2002	192	100	5	3	68	35	70	36	36	19	13	7
2003[8]	240	100	14	6	75	31	85	35	45	19	21	9
2004	193	100	8	4	77	40	66	34	33	17	9	5
2005	222	100	9	4	82	37	76	34	45	20	10	5
Northern Ireland												
Persons												
	VOYS	VOYT	VOYU	VOYV	VOYW	VOYX	VOYY	VOYZ	VOZA	VOZB	VOZC	VOZD
2000	172	100	8	5	44	26	73	42	34	20	13	8
2001	139	100	8	6	50	36	41	29	28	20	12	9
2002	174	100	13	7	62	36	59	34	26	15	14	8
2003	140	100	4	3	68	49	43	31	18	13	7	5
2004	161	100	4	2	70	43	61	38	20	12	6	4
2005	140	100	6	4	53	38	45	32	30	21	6	4
Males												
	VOZE	VOZF	VOZG	VOZH	VOZI	VOZJ	VOZK	VOZL	VOZM	VOZN	VOZO	VOZP
2000	78	100	4	5	18	23	37	47	14	18	5	6
2001	62	100	3	5	20	32	19	31	13	21	7	11
2002	76	100	8	11	26	34	29	38	8	11	5	7
2003	67	100	2	3	31	46	22	33	7	10	5	7
2004	74	100	1	1	32	43	28	38	10	14	3	4
2005	61	100	2	3	23	38	21	34	12	20	3	5
Females												
	VOZQ	VOZR	VOZS	VOZT	VOZU	VOZV	VOZW	VOZX	VOZY	VOZZ	VPAA	VPVD
2000	94	100	4	4	26	28	36	38	20	21	8	9
2001	77	100	5	6	30	39	22	29	15	19	5	6
2002	98	100	5	5	36	37	30	31	18	18	9	9
2003	73	100	2	3	37	51	21	29	11	15	2	3
2004	87	100	3	3	38	44	33	38	10	11	3	3
2005	79	100	4	5	30	38	24	30	18	23	3	4

1 Includes two cases where age was greater than 17 - these have been included in the '15-17' age group.
2 Includes one case where age was greater than 17 - these have been included in the '15-17' age group.
3 Includes four adoptions where age was greater than 17 - these have been included in the '15-17' age group.
4 Includes one adoptions where age was greater than 17 - this has been included in the '15-17' age group.
5 Includes three adoptions where age was greater than 17 - these have been included in the '15-17' age group.

6 Includes three adoptions where age was greater than 17 - these have been included in the '15-17' age group.
7 Includes two adoptions where age was greater than 17 - these have been included in the '15-17' age group.
8 Includes one adoption where age was greater than 17 - this has been included in the '15-17' age group.

Sources: Office for National Statistics: 01329 813758;
General Register Office for Scotland;
Northern Ireland Statistics and Research Agency

Education

Chapter 6

Education

Educational establishments in the United Kingdom (UK) are administered and financed in several ways. Most schools are controlled by local authorities (LAs), which are part of the structure of local government, but some are 'assisted', receiving grants direct from central government sources and being controlled by governing bodies which have a substantial degree of autonomy. Completely outside the public sector are non-maintained schools run by individuals, companies or charitable institutions.

For the purposes of UK education statistics, schools fall under the following broad categories:

Mainstream state schools

(Grant-aided mainstream schools in Northern Ireland)

These schools work in partnership with other schools and local education authorities and they receive funding from LAs. Since 1 September 1999, the categories (typically in England) are:

Community - schools formerly known as 'county' plus some former Grant-maintained (GM) schools;

Foundation - most former GM schools;

Voluntary Aided - schools formerly known as 'aided' and some former GM schools;

Voluntary Controlled - schools formerly known as 'controlled'.

Non-maintained mainstream schools consisting of

(a) Independent schools

Schools which charge fees and may also be financed by individuals, companies or charitable institutions. These include Direct Grant schools, where the governing bodies are assisted by Departmental grants and a proportion of the pupils attending them do so free or under an arrangement by which local authorities meet tuition fees. City technology colleges and Academies (applicable in England only) are also included as independent schools.

(b) Non-maintained schools

Run by voluntary bodies who may receive some grant from central government for capital work and for equipment, but their current expenditure is met primarily from the fees charged to the LAs for pupils placed in schools.

Special schools

Provide education for children with special educational needs (SEN) (Record of Needs, in Scotland) who cannot be educated satisfactorily in an ordinary school. Maintained special schools are run by LAs, while non-maintained special schools are financed as shown at (b) above.

Pupil Referral Units

Pupil Referral Units (PRUs) operate in England and Wales and provide education outside of a mainstream or special school setting, to meet the needs of difficult or disruptive children.

Schools in Scotland are categorised as Education Authority, Grant-Aided, Opted-out/Self-governing (these three being grouped together as 'Publicly funded' schools), Independent schools and Partnership schools.

The home Government Departments dealing with education statistics are:

Department for Education and Skills (DfES);

Welsh Assembly Government (WAG);

Scottish Executive (SE);

Northern Ireland Department of Education (DENI);

Northern Ireland Department for Employment and Learning (DELNI).

Each of the home Education Departments in Great Britain, along with the Northern Ireland Department of Education, have overall responsibility for funding the schools sectors in their own country.

Up to March 2001, further education (FE) courses in FE sector colleges in England and in Wales were largely funded through grants from the respective Further Education Funding Councils. In April 2001, however, the Learning and Skills Council (LSC) took over the responsibility for funding the FE sector in England, and the National Council for Education and Training for Wales (part of Education and Learning Wales – ELWa) did so for Wales. The LSC in England is also responsible for funding provision for FE and some non-prescribed higher education in FE sector colleges; it also funds some FE provided by LA maintained and other institutions referred to as 'external institutions'. In Wales, the National Council – ELWa, funds FE provision made by FE institutions via a third party or sponsored arrangements. The Scottish Further Education Funding Council (SFEFC) funds FE colleges in Scotland, while the Department for

Employment and Learning funds FE colleges in Northern Ireland.

Higher Education (HE) courses in HE establishments are largely publicly funded through block grants from the HE funding councils in England and Scotland, the Higher Education Council – ELWa in Wales, and the Department of Employment and Learning in Northern Ireland. In addition, some designated HE (mainly HND/HNC Diplomas and Certificates of HE) is also funded by these sources. The FE sources mentioned above fund the remainder.

Statistics for the separate systems obtained in England, Wales, Scotland and Northern Ireland are collected and processed separately in accordance with the particular needs of the responsible Departments. Since 1994/95 the Higher Education Statistics Agency (HESA) has undertaken the data collection for all Higher Education Institutions (HEIs) in the UK. This includes the former Universities Funding Council (UFC) which funded UK universities previously collected by the Universities Statistical Record. There are some structural differences in the information collected for schools, further and higher education in each of the four home countries and in some tables the GB/UK data presented are amalgamations from sources that are not entirely comparable.

Stages of education

There are five stages of education: foundation, primary, secondary, Further and Higher Education (FE and HE). Education is compulsory for all children between the ages of five (four in Northern Ireland) and sixteen. The non-compulsory fourth stage, FE, covers non-advanced education, which can be taken at both further (including tertiary) education colleges, Higher Education Institutions (HEI's) and increasingly in secondary schools. The fifth stage, HE, is study beyond A levels and their equivalent which, for most full-time students, takes place in universities and other HEI's.

Foundation education

In recent years there has been a major expansion of pre-school education and in England, the National Curriculum has been extended to include the Foundation stage and covers children's education from the age of three to the end of reception year, when most are just five and some almost six years old. Children under five attend a variety of settings including state nursery schools, nursery classes within primary schools and in England and Wales, reception classes within primary schools, as well as settings outside the state sector such as voluntary pre-schools or privately run nurseries.

Primary education

The primary stage covers three age ranges: nursery (under 5), infant (5 to 7 or 8) and junior (up to 11 or 12) but in Scotland and Northern Ireland there is generally no distinction between infant and junior schools. Most public sector primary schools take both boys and girls in mixed classes. It is usual to transfer straight to secondary school at age 11 (in England, Wales and Northern Ireland) or 12 (in Scotland), but in England some children make the transition via middle schools catering for various age ranges between 8 and 14. Depending on their individual age ranges, middle schools are classified as either primary or secondary.

Secondary education

Public provision of secondary education in an area may consist of a combination of different types of school, the pattern reflecting historical circumstance and the policy adopted by the local education authority. Comprehensive schools largely admit pupils without reference to ability or aptitude and cater for all the children in a neighbourhood, but in some areas they co-exist with grammar, secondary modern or technical schools. In 2005/06, 88 per cent of secondary pupils in England attended comprehensive schools while all secondary schools in Wales are comprehensive schools. The majority of education authority secondary schools in Scotland are comprehensive in character and offer six years of secondary education; however, in remote areas there are several two-year and four-year secondary schools. In Northern Ireland, post primary education is provided by grammar schools and non-selective secondary schools. In England, the Specialist Schools Programme helps schools, in partnership with private sector sponsors and supported by additional Government funding, to establish distinctive identities through their chosen specialisms and achieve their targets to raise standards. Specialist schools have a special focus on their chosen subject area but must meet the National Curriculum requirements and deliver a broad and balanced education to all pupils. Any maintained secondary school in England can apply to be designated as a specialist school in one of ten specialist areas: arts, business & enterprise, engineering, humanities, languages, mathematics & computing, music, science, sports and technology. Schools can also combine any two specialisms.

Special schools

Special schools (day or boarding) provide education for children who require specialist support to complete their education, for example, because they have physical or other difficulties. Many pupils with special educational needs are educated in main-stream schools. All children attending special schools are offered a curriculum designed to overcome their learning difficulties and to enable them to become self-reliant. Since December 2005, special schools have also been able to apply for the Special Educational Needs (SEN) specialism, under the Specialist Schools Programme.

Further education

The term Further Education (FE) may be used in a general sense to cover all non-advanced courses taken after the period of compulsory education, but more commonly it excludes those staying on at secondary school and those in higher education (HE), i.e. courses in universities and colleges leading to qualifications above GCE A Level, SCE H Grade, GNVQ/NVQ level 3 and their equivalents. Since 1 April 1993 sixth form colleges in England and Wales have been included in the FE sector.

Higher education

Higher Education (HE) is defined as courses that are of a standard that is higher than GCE A level, the Higher Grade of the Scottish Certificate of Education, GNVQ/NVQ level 3 or the Edexcel (formerly BTEC) or SQA National Certificate/ Diploma. There are three main levels of HE course:

(i) postgraduate courses leading to higher degrees, diplomas and certificates (including postgraduate certificates of education and professional qualifications) which usually require a first degree as entry qualification;
(ii) first degrees which includes first degrees, first degrees with qualified teacher status, enhanced first degrees, first degrees obtained concurrently with a diploma, and intercalated first degrees;
(iii) other undergraduate courses which includes all other HE courses, for example HND's and Diplomas in HE. As a result of the 1992 Further and Higher Education Act, former polytechnics and some other Higher Education Institutions (HEI's) were designated as universities in 1992/93. Students normally attend HE courses at HEI's, but some attend at Further Education (FE) colleges. Some also attend institutions which do not receive public grant (such as the University of Buckingham) and these numbers are excluded from the tables, however, the University of Buckingham is included in Table 6.10.

6.1 Number of schools by type and establishments of further and higher education
Academic years

Numbers

		1990/91	1995[1]/96	2001[1]/02	2002[1]/03	2003[1]/04	2004[1]/05	2005/06
United Kingdom:								
Public sector mainstream								
Nursery[2,3]	KBFK	1 364	1 486	3 227	3 394	3 438	3 425	3 347
Primary[4]	KBFA	24 135	23 441	22 800	22 638	22 509	22 343	22 156
Secondary[5]	KBFF	4 790	4 463	4 306	4 284	4 255	4 230	4 206
of which 6th form colleges	KPGM	116	..	..	..	..	..	..
Non-maintained mainstream	KBFU	2 508	2 500	2 407	2 380	2 524	2 476	2 493
Special - all	KBFP	1 830	1 560	1 483	1 473	1 465	1 436	1 416
maintained	KPVX	..	1 456	1 387	1 369	1 362	1 329	1 311
non maintained	KPGO	..	104	96	104	103	107	105
Pupil referral units	KXEP	..	315	340	390	457	478	481
Universities (including Open University)[6,7,8]	KAHG	48	96	97	96	114	119	123
All other further and higher education institutions	KJPQ	588	609	541	520	520	527	519
Higher education institutions	KPVY	..	66	58	54	55	47	43
Further education institutions	KSNY	..	543	483	466	465	480	476
of which 6th form colleges	KPGP	..	110	101	103	102	102	102
England:								
Public sector mainstream								
Nursery	KBAK	566	547	494	475	468	456	453
Primary	KBAA	19 047	18 480	17 985	17 861	17 762	17 642	17 504
Secondary[5]	KBAF	3 897	3 594	3 457	3 436	3 409	3 385	3 367
of which 6th form colleges	KPGS	114	..	..	..	..	..	..
Non-maintained	KBAU	2 289	2 266	2 206	2 180	2 330	2 283	2 301
Special - all	KBAP	1 380	1 263	1 161	1 160	1 148	1 122	1 105
maintained	KPGT	..	1 191	1 098	1 088	1 078	1 049	1 033
non maintained	KPGU	..	72	63	72	70	73	72
Pupil referral units	KXEQ	..	291	312	360	426	447	449
Universities (including Open University)[6,7]	KAHM	37	72	73	72	90	96	100
All other further and higher education institutions	KJPR	460	503	441	422	422	414	422
Higher education institutions	KPXA	..	50	45	41	42	34	31
Further education institutions	KPWC	..	453	396	381	380	395	391
of which 6th form colleges	KPGV	..	110	101	103	102	102	102
Wales:								
Public sector mainstream								
Nursery	KBBK	54	52	40	37	34	34	33
Primary	KBBA	1 717	1 681	1 624	1 602	1 588	1 572	1 555
Secondary[5]	KBBF	230	228	227	227	227	227	224
of which 6th form colleges	KPGY	2	..	..	..	..	..	..
Non-maintained	KBBU	71	62	56	59	60	58	56
Special (Maintained)	KBBP	61	54	44	43	43	43	43
Pupil referral units	KZBF	..	24	28	30	31	31	32
Universities[6,8]	KAHS	1	9	9	9	9	8	8
All other further and higher education institutions	KJQP	38	31	28	27	27	27	27
Higher education institutions	KSNZ	..	5	4	4	4	4	4
Further education institutions	KPGZ	..	26	24	23	23	23	23
Scotland:								
Public sector mainstream								
Nursery[2]	KBDK	659	796	2 597	2 782	2 836	2 836	2 761
Primary	KBDA	2 372	2 332	2 271	2 258	2 248	2 217	2 194
Secondary	KBDF	424	405	387	386	386	386	385
Non-maintained	KBDU	131	151	120	119	117	118	117
Special - all	KBDP	343	196	230	223	227	226	223
maintained	KYCZ	343	164	197	191	194	192	190
non-maintained	KYDA	..	32	33	32	33	34	33
Universities[6]	KAHX	8	13	13	13	13	13	13
All other further and higher education institutions	KJRA	64	56	53	53	53	53	52
Higher education institutions	KPWE	..	9	7	7	7	7	6
Further education institutions	KPHB	..	47	46	46	46	46	46
Northern Ireland:								
Grant aided mainstream								
Nursery[3]	KBEK	85	91	96	100	100	99	100
Primary[4]	KBEA	999	948	920	917	911	912	903
Secondary	KBEF	239	236	235	235	233	232	230
Non-maintained	KBEU	17	21	25	22	17	17	19
Special (Maintained)	KBEP	46	47	48	47	47	45	45
Universities	KIAD	2	2	2	2	2	2	2
Colleges of education	KIAE	2	2	2	2	2	2	2
Further education colleges	KIAG	24	17	17	16	16	16	16

1 Includes revised data.
2 Nursery schools figures for Scotland prior to 1998/99 only include data for Local Authority pre-schools. Data thereafter include partnership pre-schools. From 2005/06, figures exclude pre-school education centres not in partnership with the Local Aurhority.
3 Excludes voluntary and private pre-school education centres in Northern Ireland (366 in total in 2005/06).
4 From 1995/96 includes Preparatory Departments in Northern Ireland Grammer Schools (17 in total in 2005/06).
5 From 1993/94, excludes sixth form colleges in England and Wales which were reclassified as further education colleges on 1 April 1993.
6 From 1993/94, includes former polytechnics and colleges which became universities as a result of the Further and Higher Education Act 1992.
7 From 2003/04, universities includes the members of the University of London separately. For earlier years, its member institutions are counted as one institution.
8 From 1995/96, universities includes the members of the University of Wales separately. For 1990/91, its member institutions are counted as one institution.

Source: Education Departments: 01325 392754

6.2 Full-time and part-time pupils in school[1] by age and gender[2,3]
United Kingdom
All schools at January[4]

Thousands

		1996	1997	1998	1999	2000	2001	2002	2003	2004	2005	2006[5]
Age at previous 31 August[6]												
Number (thousands)												
England[7]	KBIA	8 110	8 195	8 261	8 310	8 346	8 374	8 369	8 367	8 335	8 274	8 216
Wales	KBIB	508	510	513	513	512	512	511	509	506	501	495
Scotland[2]	KBIC	846	848	850	844	874	882	876	874	866	851	850
Northern Ireland[3]	KBID	353	354	352	352	349	348	346	345	341	337	333
United Kingdom	KBIE	9 816	9 907	9 975	10 020	10 081	10 116	10 102	10 095	10 048	9 963	9 894
Boys and girls												
2 - 4[8]	KBIF	1 146	1 148	1 149	1 154	1 184	1 187	1 180	1 189	1 145	1 138	1 135
5 - 10	KBIG	4 583	4 628	4 668	4 661	4 629	4 597	4 537	4 489	4 403	4 378	4 317
11	KBIH	717	744	746	762	783	771	783	791	784	758	756
12 - 14	KBII	2 157	2 151	2 182	2 211	2 256	2 297	2 320	2 343	2 355	2 369	2 344
15	KBIK	722	716	701	706	705	732	737	751	775	764	777
16	KBIL	279	289	288	283	285	287	298	290	314	304	304
17	KBIM	191	206	217	218	213	219	223	217	238	226	235
18 and over	KBIN	22	22	24	25	27	27	23	24	32	27	26
Boys												
14	KBIO	370	365	368	367	381	384	391	401	394	402	407
15	KBIP	368	365	358	361	359	374	377	384	394	390	397
16	KBIQ	137	141	140	137	138	139	145	140	150	146	146
17	KBIR	92	100	104	104	101	105	107	104	112	107	111
18 and over	KBIS	12	12	13	13	14	15	13	13	17	14	15
Girls												
14	KBIT	355	349	350	352	364	365	373	384	378	384	388
15	KBIU	354	351	343	345	346	358	360	368	379	375	380
16	KBIV	143	148	149	146	147	148	153	150	161	159	159
17	KBIW	99	107	113	114	111	114	116	113	124	119	123
18 and over	KBIX	10	10	11	11	13	12	11	11	15	12	12

1 From 1 April 1993 excludes 6th form colleges in England and Wales which were reclassified as further education colleges.
2 Figures for Scotland are estimates using the stage rolls.
3 In Northern Ireland, a gender split is not collected by age but is available by year group and so this is used as a proxy.
4 In Scotland, as at the previous September.
5 Provisional.
6 1 July for Northern Ireland and 31 December for Scotland.
7 From 1992, figures for independent schools in England include pupils aged less than 2.
8 Includes the so-called "rising 5s" (i.e. those pupils who become 5 during the autumn term).

Source: Education Departments: 01325 392754

6.3 Number of pupils and teachers, and pupil:teacher ratios:[1] by school type
United Kingdom
At January[2]

Numbers

		2001	2002	2003	2004	2005[3,4]	2006[4,5]
All schools or departments							
Total							
Pupils (thousands)							
Full-time and full-time equivalent of part-time	KBCA	9 856.3	9 858.1	9 852.2	9 812.6	9 686.7	9 613.9
Teachers[6] (thousands)	KBCB	553.1	558.3	561.6	561.4	562.6	568.6
Pupils per teacher[6]:							
United Kingdom[6]	KBCC	17.9	17.7	17.6	17.6	17.3	17.0
England	KBCD	18.1	18.0	17.9	17.8	17.5	17.2
Wales	KBCE	18.4	18.1	18.0	18.0	18.0	17.6
Scotland	KBCF	15.4	15.4	14.9	15.0	14.3	13.8
Northern Ireland	KBCG	16.6	16.4	16.3	16.5	16.5	16.7
Public sector mainstream schools or departments							
Nursery							
Pupils (thousands)							
Full-time equivalent of part-time	KBFM	77.5	85.6	84.8	83.9	29.1	29.1
Teachers[6] (thousands)	KBFN	3.4	3.6	3.6	3.5	1.7	1.7
Pupils per teacher[6]	KBFO	23.1	23.6	23.6	23.7	17.6	17.3
Primary[7]							
Pupils (thousands)							
Full-time and full-time equivalent of part-time	KBFB	5 130.5	5 083.4	5 021.9	4 953.9	4 896.6	4 831.9
Teachers[6] (thousands)	KBFD	229.6	231.5	228.9	224.9	224.2	226.6
Pupils per teacher[6]	KBFE	22.3	22.0	21.9	22.0	21.8	21.3
Secondary[8]							
Pupils (thousands)							
Full-time and full-time equivalent of part-time	KBFG	3 915.5	3 948.0	3 994.0	4 014.1	4 001.9	3 987.1
Teachers[6] (thousands)	KBFH	237.0	241.2	243.3	243.8	246.6	248.5
Pupils per teacher[6]	KBFI	16.5	16.4	16.4	16.5	16.2	16.0
Special schools							
Pupils (thousands)							
Full-time and full-time equivalent of part-time	KPGE	106.5	105.4	104.5	102.2	100.4	99.5
Teachers[6] (thousands)	KPGG	17.0	17.0	17.0	16.9	16.8	17.0
Pupils per teacher[6]	KPGI	6.3	6.2	6.1	6.1	6.0	5.9

1 'All schools' pupil:teacher ratios exclude Pupil Referral Units and non-maintained special schools.
2 In Scotland, as at the previous September.
3 Includes revised data.
4 Excluding nursery school figures for Scotland as FTE pupil numbers are not available.
5 Provisional
6 Figures of teachers and of pupil/teacher ratios take account of the full-time equivalent of part-time teachers.

7 Includes preparatory departments attached to grammer schools in Northern Ireland.
8 Includes voluntary grammar schools in Northern Ireland.

Source: Education Departments: 01325 392754

6.4 Full-time and part-time pupils with special educational needs (SEN)[1], 2005/06[2]
United Kingdom
By type of school

Thousands and percentages

	United Kingdom	England[3]	Wales	Scotland	Northern Ireland
All schools					
Total pupils	9 898.6	8 215.7	494.5	849.4	339.0
SEN pupils with statements[4]	278.3	236.7	15.8	13.8	12.0
Incidence (%)[5]	*2.8*	*2.9*	*3.2*	*1.6*	*3.5*
Maintained schools[6]					
Nursery[7]					
Total pupils[8]	156.5	37.0	1.8	105.8	11.8
SEN pupils with statements[4]	0.4	0.3	-	..	-
Incidence (%)[5]	*0.2*	*0.9*	*0.8*	*..*	*0.4*
Placement (%)[9]	*0.1*	*0.1*	*0.1*	*..*	*0.4*
Primary[10]					
Total pupils	4 974.9	4 149.0	265.7	390.3	169.9
SEN pupils without statements	793.7	716.8	49.6	..	27.3
SEN pupils with statements	78.1	64.9	5.5	3.6	4.2
Pupils with statements -incidence (%)[5]	*1.6*	*1.6*	*2.1*	*0.9*	*2.5*
Pupils with statements - placement (%)[9]	*28.1*	*27.4*	*34.6*	*26.1*	*35.2*
Secondary					
Total pupils	3 987.5	3 306.8	213.0	315.8	151.8
SEN pupils without statements	550.9	506.6	31.1	..	13.2
SEN pupils with statements	87.8	73.8	5.9	4.5	3.6
Pupils with statements - incidence (%)[5]	*2.2*	*2.2*	*2.8*	*1.4*	*2.4*
Pupils with statements - placement (%)[9]	*31.6*	*31.2*	*37.7*	*32.3*	*29.9*
Special[11,12]					
Total pupils	100.3	84.6	3.9	7.1	4.6
SEN pupils with statements	96.0	82.6	3.9	5.4	4.1
Incidence (%)[5]	*95.7*	*97.6*	*100.0*	*75.2*	*89.7*
Placement (%)[9]	*34.5*	*34.9*	*25.0*	*38.9*	*34.5*
Pupil referral units[11,13]					
Total pupils	15.6	15.2	0.4	..	..
SEN pupils with statements	2.4	2.3	0.1	..	..
Incidence (%)[5]	*15.4*	*15.0*	*30.6*	*..*	*..*
Placement (%)[9]	*0.9*	*1.0*	*0.7*	*..*	*..*
Other schools					
Independent					
Total pupils	658.0	618.3	9.6	29.2	0.8
SEN pupils with statements	8.5	8.2	0.3	-	..
Incidence (%)[5]	*1.3*	*1.3*	*3.1*	*0.1*	*..*
Placement (%)[9]	*3.1*	*3.5*	*1.9*	*0.2*	*..*
Non-maintained special[11]					
Total pupils	5.9	4.8	..	1.1	..
SEN pupils with statements	5.0	4.7	..	0.3	..
Incidence (%)[5]	*84.8*	*97.7*	*..*	*30.4*	*..*
Placement (%)[9]	*1.8*	*2.0*	*..*	*2.5*	*..*

1 For Scotland, pupils with a Record of Needs including some who had an Individualised Educational Programme.

2 Provisional.

3 Includes new codes for recording SEN status following the introduction of a new SEN Code of Practice from January 2002. Data are therefore not directly comparable prior to 2001/02.

4 Excluding nursery schools in Scotland as SEN pupils with statements data are not available for 2005/06.

5 Incidence of pupils - the number of pupils with statements within each school type expressed as a proportion of the total number of pupils on roll in each school type.

6 Grant-Aided schools in Northern Ireland.

7 Includes pupils in Voluntary and Private Pre-School Centres in Northern Ireland funded under the Pre-School Expansion Programme which began in 1998/99.

8 In Scotland, on pupils in centres providing pre-school education as a Local Authority centre or in partnership with the Local Authority only. Children are counted once for each centre they are registered with.

9 Placement of pupils - the number of pupils with statements within each school type expressed as a proportion of the number of pupils with statements in all schools.

10 Includes nursery classes (except for Scotland, where they are included with Nursery schools) and reception classes in Primary schools.

11 England and Wales figures exclude dually registered pupils.

12 Including general and hospital special schools.

13 England and Wales only.

Source: Education Departments: 01325 392754

6.5 GCE, GCSE and SCE/NQ[1] and vocational qualifications obtained by pupils and students

United Kingdom

Percentages and thousands

	Pupils in their last year of compulsory education[2]					Pupils/students in education[3]			
						% achieving GCE A Levels and equivalent[4,5]			Population aged 17[4] (thousands)
	5 or more grades A*-C[6]	1-4 grades A*-C[6]	Grades D-G[7] only	No graded results	Total (=100%) (Thousands)	1 pass[8]	2 or more passes[9]	3 or more passes	
2000/01[10]									
All	51.0	24.1	19.4	5.5	729.7	4.9	37.4	..	717.9
Males	45.7	24.6	23.1	6.5	372.1	4.7	33.4	..	366.6
Females	56.5	23.6	15.5	4.4	357.6	5.1	41.6	..	351.3
2001/02[10]									
All	52.5	23.7	18.4	5.4	732.5	4.7	37.4	..	739.0
Males	47.2	24.4	22.0	6.4	374.0	4.5	33.0	..	379.8
Females	58.0	23.1	14.6	4.3	358.5	4.9	42.0	..	359.2
2002/03[10]									
All	53.5	23.1	18.2	5.2	750.2	3.8	38.4	..	771.2
Males	48.3	23.6	21.8	6.3	382.7	3.8	33.9	..	397.2
Females	58.8	22.7	14.4	4.1	367.6	3.8	43.2	..	374.0
2003/04[10]									
All	54.2	22.7	18.8	4.4	772.0	3.2	39.2	..	769.5
Males	49.2	23.1	22.4	5.3	392.6	3.2	34.7	..	395.8
Females	59.3	22.2	15.0	3.4	379.4	3.2	44.0	..	373.7
2004/05[11]									
All	57.0	22.1	17.9	3.0	759.1	2.1	36.9	30.4	722.7
Males	52.1	22.8	21.4	3.7	385.5	2.1	32.6	26.4	371.4
Females	62.1	21.4	14.2	2.3	373.5	2.0	41.4	34.7	351.3

1 From 1999/00 National Qualifications (NQ) were introduced in Scotland but are not all shown until 2001/01. NQs include Standard Grades, Intermediate 1 & 2 and Higher Grades. The figures for Higher Grades combine the new NQ Higher and the old SCE Higher and include Advanced Highers, and are included in the table up to 2003/04.

2 Pupils aged 15 at the start of the acadamic year, pupils in Year S4 in Scotland. For 2004/05, pupils at the end of Key Stage 4 in England.

3 Pupils in schools and students in further education institutions generally aged 16-18 at the start of the academic year in England, Wales and Northern Ireland as a percentage of the 17 year old population. Data from 2002/03 for Wales and Northern Ireland however, relate to schools only. Pupils in Scotland generally sit Highers one year earlier than their A level counterparts and the figures relate to the results of pupils in Year S5/S6.

4 The GCE A level and equivalent, and age 17 population figures, for 2004/05, exclude Scotland.

5 Includes Vocational Certificates of Education (VCE) and, previously, Advanced level GNVQ/GSVQ which is equivalent to 2 GCE A levels or AS equivalents/3 SCE/NQ Higher grades.

6 Standard Grades 1-3/Intermediate 2 A-C/Intermediate 1 A in Scotland.

7 Grades D-G at GCSE and Scottish Standard Grades 4-6/Intermediate 1 B and C/Access 3 (pass).

8 2 AS levels or 2 Highers/1 Advanced Higher or 1 each in Scotland, count as 1 A level pass. Includes those with 1.5 A level passes.

9 3 or more SCE/NQ Higher Grades/2 or more Advanced Highers/1 Advanced Higher with 2 or more Higher Passes in Scotland.

10 Includes revised data.

11 Provisional.

Source: Source: Education Departments: 01325 392754

6.6 Students in further[1] education: by country, mode of study,[2] sex and age,[3] during 2004/05[4]

United Kingdom (home and overseas students)

Thousands

	United Kingdom		England[5]		Wales		Scotland[6]		Northern Ireland[7]	
	Full-time	Part-time	Full-time	Part-time	Full-time	Part-time	Full-time	Part-time	Full-time	Part-time
All										
Age under 16	5.7	67.2	3.2	26.1	0.6	4.9	1.7	28.4	0.1	7.9
16	300.9	77.2	268.9	50.7	13.7	3.0	9.7	13.4	8.7	10.1
17	246.2	84.8	217.8	59.1	10.6	3.6	9.7	14.7	8.2	7.5
18	117.6	88.9	100.1	68.9	5.3	3.8	6.9	11.0	5.3	5.3
19	48.6	85.0	40.9	68.7	2.2	3.7	3.4	8.8	2.1	3.8
20	27.2	80.3	23.3	67.2	1.1	3.3	2.0	6.9	0.8	2.8
21	20.8	83.7	18.2	71.8	0.8	3.5	1.4	5.7	0.5	2.7
22	18.3	88.2	16.3	76.2	0.6	3.8	1.2	5.5	0.3	2.6
23	17.0	91.8	15.2	80.0	0.5	3.7	1.0	5.5	0.2	2.6
24	16.2	95.1	14.7	83.1	0.5	3.8	0.9	5.6	0.2	2.6
25	14.2	91.7	12.9	80.4	0.4	3.7	0.8	5.3	0.1	2.3
26	12.7	85.1	11.6	74.6	0.3	3.4	0.7	4.9	0.1	2.2
27	11.6	82.3	10.7	72.1	0.3	3.5	0.5	4.7	0.1	2.1
28	11.6	82.7	10.7	72.5	0.3	3.5	0.5	4.7	0.1	2.0
29	11.2	83.0	10.3	72.9	0.3	3.4	0.5	4.8	0.1	1.9
30+	203.5	2 692.6	192.3	2 342.6	3.8	135.2	6.4	164.7	0.9	50.3
Unknown	0.1	4.1	0.1	0.4	0.1	3.5	-	-	-	0.1
All ages	1 083.5	3 963.7	967.3	3 367.2	41.4	193.4	47.3	294.4	27.5	108.7
Males										
Age under 16	3.3	33.6	1.8	11.2	0.4	2.6	1.0	15.0	0.1	4.9
16	146.2	38.0	129.0	25.7	6.8	1.5	5.5	6.1	5.0	4.7
17	118.9	42.3	104.2	29.5	5.1	1.9	5.0	7.4	4.6	3.4
18	59.9	43.6	50.8	32.4	2.7	2.0	3.4	6.6	3.0	2.5
19	26.3	40.0	22.0	31.0	1.2	1.9	1.7	5.3	1.3	1.8
20	14.3	35.8	12.3	29.0	0.6	1.6	1.0	3.9	0.5	1.3
21	10.5	35.0	9.1	29.5	0.4	1.6	0.6	2.8	0.3	1.2
22	9.0	35.7	8.1	30.8	0.3	1.5	0.5	2.4	0.1	1.0
23	8.1	36.8	7.4	31.9	0.2	1.6	0.4	2.3	0.1	0.9
24	7.8	38.1	7.1	33.3	0.2	1.6	0.4	2.2	0.1	0.9
25	6.6	36.4	6.1	31.9	0.1	1.5	0.3	2.2	-	0.8
26	6.0	33.9	5.5	29.8	0.1	1.4	0.3	1.9	-	0.8
27	5.6	33.0	5.2	29.0	0.1	1.4	0.2	1.8	-	0.8
28	5.6	33.3	5.2	29.3	0.1	1.4	0.2	1.8	-	0.7
29	5.4	33.3	5.0	29.2	0.1	1.4	0.2	1.9	-	0.8
30+	98.6	983.8	95.1	856.1	1.1	50.5	2.2	59.9	0.2	17.3
Unknown	0.1	1.7	-	0.2	-	1.4	-	-	-	0.1
All ages	532.0	1 534.3	474.2	1 289.8	19.6	76.8	22.9	123.6	15.3	44.0
Females										
Age under 16	2.4	33.6	1.4	15.0	0.2	2.3	0.7	13.4	0.1	2.9
16	154.7	39.2	139.9	25.0	6.9	1.6	4.2	7.2	3.7	5.4
17	127.3	42.5	113.6	29.5	5.5	1.6	4.7	7.3	3.5	4.0
18	57.7	45.3	49.3	36.4	2.6	1.8	3.4	4.4	2.3	2.8
19	22.3	44.9	18.9	37.7	1.0	1.8	1.7	3.5	0.8	1.9
20	12.9	44.5	11.1	38.2	0.5	1.7	1.0	3.1	0.4	1.5
21	10.4	48.7	9.1	42.3	0.4	1.9	0.7	2.9	0.2	1.5
22	9.3	52.5	8.2	45.4	0.3	2.3	0.7	3.1	0.1	1.6
23	8.9	55.0	7.8	48.0	0.3	2.2	0.6	3.2	0.1	1.6
24	8.5	57.0	7.5	49.8	0.3	2.2	0.5	3.3	0.1	1.7
25	7.6	55.3	6.8	48.5	0.2	2.2	0.5	3.1	0.1	1.5
26	6.8	51.2	6.1	44.8	0.2	2.1	0.4	3.0	-	1.4
27	6.0	49.3	5.5	43.1	0.2	2.1	0.3	2.8	-	1.3
28	6.0	49.4	5.5	43.1	0.2	2.1	0.3	2.9	-	1.3
29	5.8	49.7	5.3	43.7	0.2	2.0	0.3	2.9	-	1.2
30+	104.9	1 708.8	97.2	1 486.5	2.7	84.6	4.3	104.7	0.7	32.9
Unknown	0.1	2.4	-	0.2	-	2.1	-	-	-	0.1
All ages	551.5	2 429.4	493.1	2 077.4	21.8	116.5	24.4	170.8	12.2	64.7

1 Further education (FE) institution figures are whole year counts. Higher education (HE) institution figures are based on the HESA 'standard registration' count and are not directly comparable with previous years prior to 2001/02.

2 Full-time includes sandwich. Part-time comprises both day and evening, including block release and open/distance learning.

3 Ages as at 31 August 2004 (1 July in Northern Ireland and 31 December in Scotland).

4 Provisional. Figures in table 6.6 are calculated on a different basis to those in table 6.7.

5 Further education institution figures for England include LSC funded students only and are not therefore directly comparable with previous years prior to 2002/03.

6 Figures for Scotland further education colleges are vocational course enrolments rather than headcounts.

7 FE institution figures for Northern Ireland are whole year counts and are not directly comparable with snapshot figures used in earlier years.

Source: Education Departments: 01325 392754

6.7 Students in further education:[1] by country, mode of study,[2] sex and area of learning,[3] 2004/05[4]

United Kingdom - Home and overseas students

Thousands

	United Kingdom		England[5]		Wales		Scotland[6]		Northern Ireland[7]	
	Full-time	Part-time	Full-time	Part-time	Full-time	Part-time	Full-time	Part-time	Full-time	Part-time
All persons										
Business Administration, Management & Professional	67.1	371.2	60.6	316.6	-	-	3.4	26.5	3.1	28.0
Construction	47.6	94.3	37.1	72.3	-	-	5.2	14.8	5.3	7.1
Engineering, Technology and Manufacturing	54.6	140.0	46.5	117.2	-	0.1	5.3	18.3	2.7	4.4
English, Languages and Communications	43.1	239.8	40.2	214.0	-	0.2	2.9	25.7	-	-
Foundation programmes	109.5	507.2	109.0	503.0	-	-	0.5	4.2	-	-
Hairdressing and Beauty Therapy	55.9	77.1	49.5	65.6	-	-	4.1	7.4	2.3	4.2
Health, Social Care and Public Services	179.8	575.0	167.7	507.5	-	-	8.7	58.6	3.4	8.9
Hospitality, Sports, Leisure and Travel	76.1	309.7	68.8	269.1	-	-	4.7	33.2	2.7	7.4
Humanities	69.3	88.6	66.8	78.5	-	-	2.5	10.1	-	-
Information & Communication Technology	72.9	756.2	68.1	682.8	-	-	3.0	54.4	1.8	19.0
Land-based provision	21.0	51.1	19.6	42.5	-	-	1.3	8.3	0.1	0.3
Retailing, Customer Service and Transportation	7.0	63.9	6.8	55.7	-	-	0.1	5.5	0.1	2.7
Science and Mathematics	55.8	113.6	51.4	96.2	-	-	1.0	5.4	3.5	12.0
Visual and Performaing Arts & Media	114.6	210.4	107.5	173.7	-	-	4.6	22.0	2.5	14.7
Other Subjects[8]	23.9	89.2	23.5	82.2	0.4	6.9	-	0.1	-	-
Unknown	85.3	276.5	44.3	90.4	41.0	186.1	-	-	-	-
All subjects	1 083.5	3 963.7	967.2	3 367.3	41.4	193.4	47.3	294.4	27.5	108.7
Males										
Business Administration, Management & Professional	32.0	128.2	29.8	107.7	-	-	0.9	8.9	1.3	11.6
Construction	45.8	88.2	35.6	68.1	-	-	4.9	13.6	5.3	6.5
Engineering, Technology and Manufacturing	51.7	117.8	44.0	97.6	-	0.1	5.1	15.9	2.7	4.2
English, Languages and Communications	16.4	88.0	15.0	77.9	-	-	1.4	10.1	-	-
Foundation programmes	52.4	206.8	52.1	204.9	-	-	0.3	1.9	-	-
Hairdressing and Beauty Therapy	1.9	7.2	1.7	6.7	-	-	0.1	0.3	0.1	0.2
Health, Social Care and Public Services	71.7	182.0	70.1	160.9	-	-	1.3	19.8	0.3	1.3
Hospitality, Sports, Leisure and Travel	43.6	112.4	39.5	98.1	-	-	2.7	11.6	1.4	2.8
Humanities	24.7	25.1	23.8	22.1	-	-	0.9	3.1	-	-
Information & Communication Technology	49.2	283.8	45.8	257.3	-	-	2.0	19.6	1.4	6.9
Land-based provision	9.2	22.5	8.4	17.3	-	-	0.8	5.1	-	0.1
Retailing, Customer Service and Transportation	4.1	29.1	4.0	24.0	-	-	0.1	4.2	-	0.8
Science and Mathematics	28.3	36.5	26.3	30.2	-	-	0.4	2.1	1.6	4.3
Visual and Performaing Arts & Media	51.5	59.3	48.1	46.5	-	-	2.2	7.3	1.3	5.5
Other Subjects[8]	8.6	36.3	8.5	33.9	0.1	2.4	-	-	-	-
Unknown	40.9	111.0	21.4	36.7	19.5	74.3	-	-	-	-
All subjects	532.0	1 534.3	474.2	1 289.8	19.6	76.8	22.9	123.6	15.3	44.0
Females										
Business Administration, Management & Professional	35.1	243.0	30.8	208.9	-	-	2.5	17.6	1.8	16.5
Construction	1.8	6.1	1.5	4.3	-	-	0.3	1.2	0.1	0.6
Engineering, Technology and Manufacturing	2.8	22.2	2.5	19.5	-	-	0.2	2.4	0.1	0.2
English, Languages and Communications	26.7	151.8	25.1	136.1	-	0.1	1.5	15.6	-	-
Foundation programmes	57.1	300.4	56.9	298.1	-	-	0.2	2.3	-	-
Hairdressing and Beauty Therapy	54.0	69.9	47.8	58.9	-	-	4.0	7.0	2.2	4.0
Health, Social Care and Public Services	108.1	393.0	97.6	346.6	-	-	7.4	38.8	3.2	7.6
Hospitality, Sports, Leisure and Travel	32.5	197.3	29.2	171.1	-	-	2.1	21.6	1.2	4.6
Humanities	44.6	63.4	43.0	56.4	-	-	1.6	7.0	-	-
Information & Communication Technology	23.7	472.4	22.3	425.5	-	-	0.9	34.7	0.4	12.2
Land-based provision	11.8	28.7	11.1	25.2	-	-	0.6	3.2	0.1	0.2
Retailing, Customer Service and Transportation	2.9	34.8	2.8	31.7	-	-	0.1	1.3	0.1	1.9
Science and Mathematics	27.5	77.1	25.1	66.1	-	-	0.6	3.3	1.9	7.7
Visual and Performaing Arts & Media	63.1	151.1	59.4	127.2	-	-	2.4	14.7	1.3	9.2
Other Subjects[8]	15.3	52.9	15.1	48.3	0.2	4.6	-	0.1	-	-
Unknown	44.4	165.5	22.9	53.7	21.6	111.8	-	-	-	-
All subjects	551.5	2 429.5	493.1	2 077.4	21.8	116.5	24.4	170.8	12.2	64.7

1 Further education (FE) institution figures are whole year counts. Higher education (HE) institution figures are based on the HESA 'standard registration' count and are not directly comparable with previous years prior to 2001/02.

2 Full-time includes sandwich. Part-time comprises both day and evening including block release.

3 Data are shown by area of learning and are not directly comparable with subject groups previously shown, prior to 2002/03.

4 Provisional. Figures in table 6.7 are calculated on a different basis to those in table 6.6.

5 Further education institution figures for England include LSC funded students only and are not therefore directly comparable with previous years prior to 2002/03.

6 Figures for Scotland further education colleges are vocational course enrolments rather than headcounts.

7 FE institution figures for Northern Ireland are whole year counts and are not directly comparable with snapshot figures used in earlier years.

8 For UK higher education institutions, includes the previous subject groups not allocated to specific areas of learning, ie: medicine & dentistry, subjects allied to medicine, biological, veterinary, physical, mathematical, computing & social (inc law) sciences, creative arts & design and education.

Source: Education Departments: 01325 392754

6.8 Students in higher[1] education by level, mode of study,[2] sex and age,[3] 2004/05[4,5,6]
United Kingdom (home and overseas students)

Thousands

	Postgraduate level						First degree		Other undergraduate		Total higher education[7]	
	PhD and equivalent		Masters and others		Total Postgraduate							
	Full-time	Part-time	Full-time	Part-time	Full-time	Part-time	Full-time	Part-time	Full-time	Part-time	Full-time	Part-time
All												
Age under 16	-	-	-	-	-	-	-	-	-	0.6	-	0.6
16	-	-	-	-	-	-	0.3	-	0.6	3.5	1.0	3.6
17	-	-	-	-	-	-	9.8	0.1	4.5	2.3	14.3	2.5
18	-	-	-	-	-	-	165.3	1.2	20.1	6.4	185.5	7.6
19	-	-	0.1	-	0.1	-	226.8	3.7	25.4	10.3	252.4	14.0
20	-	-	1.3	0.3	1.3	0.3	231.3	5.8	20.0	12.2	252.7	18.3
21	0.6	-	15.9	1.8	16.5	1.8	155.0	8.3	14.3	12.3	185.8	22.4
22	2.9	0.1	27.1	5.8	30.0	6.0	74.6	9.1	10.3	13.2	115.0	28.2
23	5.1	0.3	26.0	9.9	31.1	10.1	39.7	8.4	8.2	14.6	79.0	33.3
24	6.3	1.1	20.9	11.7	27.2	12.8	24.9	7.9	7.0	15.9	59.1	36.6
25	5.3	2.6	15.7	12.0	21.0	14.6	16.9	7.3	5.6	15.6	43.5	37.5
26	3.9	2.7	11.6	11.2	15.5	13.9	12.0	6.4	4.6	14.3	32.1	34.6
27	3.4	2.4	9.0	10.5	12.4	13.0	9.2	5.9	3.9	13.7	25.5	32.6
28	2.7	2.2	7.3	10.3	10.0	12.5	7.8	5.9	3.8	13.4	21.6	31.8
29	2.3	2.1	5.9	10.0	8.2	12.2	6.5	5.7	3.5	13.0	18.2	30.9
30+	14.5	31.1	38.8	181.2	53.4	212.3	68.9	129.0	48.1	350.6	170.4	692.2
Unknown	-	0.1	0.1	2.0	0.2	2.1	0.2	0.2	0.1	8.6	0.5	11.0
All ages	47.0	44.7	179.9	266.8	226.9	311.5	1 049.3	204.9	180.1	520.5	1 456.7	1 037.6
Males												
Age under 16	-	-	-	-	-	-	-	-	-	0.2	-	0.2
16	-	-	-	-	-	-	0.2	-	0.3	1.6	0.4	1.6
17	-	-	-	-	-	-	4.4	0.1	2.0	1.0	6.4	1.1
18	-	-	-	-	-	-	73.4	0.5	8.9	3.7	82.3	4.2
19	-	-	-	-	-	-	102.6	1.8	11.7	5.8	114.3	7.6
20	-	-	0.6	0.1	0.6	0.1	105.4	2.9	8.9	6.4	115.0	9.4
21	0.3	-	6.5	0.6	6.8	0.6	75.3	4.2	6.2	6.0	88.4	10.7
22	1.6	0.1	11.6	2.3	13.2	2.3	38.7	4.5	4.3	5.5	56.3	12.4
23	2.9	0.1	11.8	3.9	14.7	4.0	20.6	3.8	3.3	5.5	38.6	13.4
24	3.6	0.6	10.0	4.6	13.6	5.2	12.7	3.3	2.6	5.7	28.8	14.2
25	2.9	1.5	7.7	4.8	10.6	6.3	8.4	2.9	2.1	5.6	21.0	14.9
26	2.1	1.6	5.9	4.5	8.0	6.1	5.7	2.5	1.6	5.1	15.3	13.7
27	1.8	1.3	4.6	4.3	6.5	5.6	4.3	2.3	1.3	4.7	12.0	12.7
28	1.5	1.2	3.8	4.3	5.3	5.4	3.6	2.2	1.2	4.6	10.1	12.3
29	1.3	1.1	3.1	4.4	4.4	5.6	2.9	2.2	1.2	4.6	8.5	12.3
30+	8.3	17.1	20.6	79.8	28.9	96.9	23.1	47.4	12.2	117.4	64.2	261.7
Unknown	-	-	0.1	0.9	0.1	0.9	0.1	0.1	-	3.0	0.2	4.0
All ages	26.5	24.6	86.3	114.5	112.8	139.2	481.3	80.7	67.7	186.4	661.9	406.5
Females												
Age under 16	-	-	-	-	-	-	-	-	-	0.3	-	0.4
16	-	-	-	-	-	-	0.2	-	0.4	1.9	0.5	2.0
17	-	-	-	-	-	-	5.4	0.1	2.5	1.3	7.9	1.4
18	-	-	-	-	-	-	92.0	0.7	11.2	2.7	103.2	3.4
19	-	-	0.1	-	0.1	-	124.3	1.9	13.8	4.5	138.1	6.4
20	-	-	0.7	0.2	0.7	0.2	125.9	2.9	11.1	5.8	137.7	8.9
21	0.3	-	9.4	1.2	9.7	1.2	79.7	4.1	8.0	6.3	97.4	11.6
22	1.2	0.1	15.6	3.6	16.8	3.6	35.9	4.6	6.0	7.6	58.7	15.9
23	2.2	0.2	14.3	6.0	16.4	6.1	19.0	4.6	4.9	9.1	40.4	19.8
24	2.6	0.5	11.0	7.0	13.6	7.6	12.2	4.7	4.4	10.2	30.2	22.4
25	2.4	1.1	8.0	7.2	10.4	8.3	8.5	4.3	3.6	10.0	22.5	22.6
26	1.8	1.1	5.7	6.7	7.5	7.9	6.3	3.9	3.0	9.2	16.8	20.9
27	1.5	1.1	4.4	6.3	5.9	7.4	4.9	3.6	2.6	9.0	13.5	20.0
28	1.2	1.0	3.5	6.0	4.7	7.0	4.2	3.6	2.6	8.8	11.5	19.5
29	1.0	1.0	2.8	5.6	3.8	6.6	3.6	3.6	2.4	8.4	9.8	18.6
30+	6.2	14.0	18.3	101.4	24.5	115.3	45.8	81.6	35.9	233.3	106.2	430.4
Unknown	-	-	-	1.1	0.1	1.2	0.1	0.2	0.1	5.6	0.3	6.9
All ages	20.5	20.0	93.6	152.3	114.2	172.3	568.0	124.3	112.4	334.1	794.8	631.0

1 Includes Open University students. Part-time figures include dormant modes, those writing up at home and on sabbaticals.
2 Full-time includes sandwich. Part-time comprises both day and evening, including block release and open/distance learning.
3 Ages as at 31 August 2004 (1 July in Northern Ireland and 31 December in Scotland).
4 Provisional. Figures in table 6.8 are calculated on a different basis to those in table 6.9.
5 Figures for higher education (HE) institutions are based on the HESA 'standard registration' count and are not directly comparable with previous years prior to 2001/02. Figures for further education (FE)

institutions in Wales and Northern Ireland are snapshots counted at a particular point in the year (November for FE institutions in Northern Ireland, and December for FE institutions in Wales). Students starting courses after these dates will not therefore be counted. Figures for Scotland and England, however, are whole year (not shapshot) enrolments (rather than headcounts).
6 FE institution figures for England include Learning and Skills Council (LSC) funded students only.
7 Includes data for higher education students in further education institutions in Wales which cannot be split by level.

Source: Education Departments: 01325 392754

6.9 Students in higher[1] education by level, mode of study[2], sex and subject group[3], 2004/05[4,5,6]

United Kingdom - Home and overseas students

Thousands

	Postgraduate level						First degree		Other undergraduate		Total higher education[7]	
	PhD and equivalent		Masters and others		Total Postgraduate							
	Full-time	Part-time	Full-time	Part-time	Full-time	Part-time	Full-time	Part-time	Full-time	Part-time	Full-time	Part-time
All persons												
Medicine & Dentistry	3.2	4.1	3.0	7.1	6.2	11.2	38.1	0.1	0.3	0.1	44.6	11.5
Subjects Allied to Medicine	2.2	3.0	6.1	32.1	8.4	35.1	77.3	32.8	70.2	79.1	155.8	147.0
Biological Sciences	7.3	4.8	6.9	9.2	14.3	14.1	97.0	14.6	3.4	6.5	114.6	35.2
Vet. Science, Agriculture & related	0.8	0.6	1.4	1.3	2.2	1.9	11.0	0.5	4.0	3.6	17.3	6.0
Physical Sciences	6.8	3.4	5.5	3.8	12.4	7.2	47.2	6.8	0.9	4.3	60.5	18.4
Mathematical and Computing Sciences	3.8	2.4	13.0	11.2	16.8	13.6	86.3	16.8	10.2	25.0	113.3	55.4
Engineering & Technology	7.3	4.4	14.3	14.2	21.5	18.5	70.4	10.7	10.3	24.0	102.3	53.2
Architecture, Building & Planning	0.8	0.7	4.9	7.6	5.6	8.3	22.0	6.3	3.0	11.9	30.7	26.6
Social Sciences (inc Law)	5.0	5.1	29.8	27.6	34.8	32.7	148.1	28.7	8.7	37.4	191.6	98.9
Business & Administrative Studies	1.9	3.0	37.5	64.2	39.4	67.2	139.1	18.8	24.9	100.8	203.5	186.7
Mass Communication & Documentation	0.3	0.4	4.8	4.0	5.1	4.4	32.4	1.7	5.5	6.6	43.0	12.7
Languages	2.7	2.8	6.6	5.3	9.2	8.0	72.3	8.3	2.4	36.8	84.0	53.1
Historical and Philosophical Studies	2.8	3.6	4.6	7.3	7.4	10.9	50.3	14.1	0.9	20.3	58.6	45.3
Creative Arts & Design	1.0	1.4	7.9	5.3	8.9	6.7	107.4	4.3	15.1	14.1	131.4	25.0
Education[8]	1.0	4.9	33.4	64.0	34.4	68.9	38.1	8.9	3.3	49.8	75.8	127.6
Other subjects[9]	-	0.1	0.1	2.5	0.2	2.6	12.2	31.6	16.8	100.1	29.2	134.3
Unknown[7]	-	-	-	-	-	-	-	-	0.1	-	0.4	0.6
All subjects	47.0	44.7	179.9	266.8	226.9	311.5	1 049.3	204.9	180.1	520.5	1 456.7	1 037.6
of which overseas students	21.6	15.1	91.6	37.7	113.2	52.7	115.7	8.6	14.6	18.7	243.6	80.0
Males												
Medicine and Dentistry	1.3	2.2	1.2	3.3	2.5	5.5	15.6	-	-	-	18.2	5.5
Subjects Allied to Medicine	0.9	1.2	1.9	8.3	2.8	9.5	16.5	4.5	9.1	9.9	28.4	23.8
Biological Sciences	2.9	2.1	2.5	2.9	5.5	5.0	35.4	3.8	1.8	2.3	42.6	11.1
Vet. Science, Agriculture & related	0.4	0.3	0.7	0.6	1.1	1.0	3.3	0.2	1.5	1.6	5.9	2.8
Physical Sciences	4.4	2.2	3.1	2.1	7.5	4.4	28.0	3.8	0.5	2.3	36.0	10.5
Mathematical and Computing Sciences	2.9	1.9	9.9	8.2	12.8	10.1	66.5	12.2	8.5	13.5	87.8	35.8
Engineering & Technology	5.8	3.6	11.5	11.6	17.2	15.2	59.8	9.7	9.2	22.0	86.2	46.9
Architecture, Building & Planning	0.5	0.5	3.0	4.7	3.5	5.2	15.5	5.0	2.4	9.4	21.4	19.6
Social Sciences (inc Law)	2.6	2.7	13.1	10.9	15.7	13.6	60.2	10.0	2.4	9.5	78.2	33.2
Business & Administrative Studies	1.1	1.9	20.0	33.3	21.1	35.2	69.7	8.0	11.6	35.5	102.5	78.7
Mass Communication & Documentation	0.1	0.2	1.6	1.3	1.8	1.5	13.7	0.7	3.9	4.1	19.4	6.3
Languages	1.1	1.1	2.0	1.6	3.1	2.7	20.6	2.0	1.2	14.3	24.9	19.1
Historical and Philosophical Studies	1.6	2.1	2.3	3.5	3.8	5.6	23.3	5.5	0.4	6.9	27.5	18.0
Creative Arts & Design	0.5	0.7	3.2	2.2	3.7	2.9	41.9	1.4	6.5	4.5	52.1	8.8
Education[8]	0.3	2.0	10.1	18.7	10.5	20.7	6.5	1.3	0.8	13.5	17.8	35.5
Other subjects[9]	-	-	0.1	1.2	0.1	1.3	4.7	12.3	7.9	37.1	12.7	50.7
Unknown[7]	-	-	-	-	-	-	-	-	0.1	-	0.2	0.3
All subjects	26.5	24.6	86.3	114.5	112.8	139.2	481.3	80.7	67.7	186.4	661.9	406.5
of which overseas students	12.9	8.9	48.9	21.0	61.9	30.0	59.2	4.4	7.4	8.2	128.5	42.6
Females												
Medicine & Dentistry	1.9	1.9	1.8	3.9	3.6	5.8	22.4	0.1	0.3	0.1	26.4	5.9
Subjects Allied to Medicine	1.3	1.8	4.2	23.8	5.6	25.7	60.7	28.3	61.1	69.2	127.4	123.2
Biological Sciences	4.4	2.8	4.4	6.3	8.8	9.1	61.6	10.8	1.6	4.2	72.0	24.1
Vet. Science, Agriculture & related	0.4	0.3	0.7	0.6	1.1	0.9	7.7	0.3	2.5	2.0	11.4	3.3
Physical Sciences	2.4	1.2	2.4	1.7	4.8	2.9	19.2	3.1	0.5	2.0	24.5	7.9
Mathematical and Computing Sciences	0.9	0.6	3.1	3.0	4.0	3.6	19.8	4.6	1.7	11.5	25.5	19.6
Engineering & Technology	1.5	0.8	2.8	2.6	4.3	3.4	10.7	1.0	1.1	2.0	16.1	6.3
Architecture, Building & Planning	0.3	0.2	1.9	2.9	2.2	3.1	6.6	1.4	0.6	2.5	9.4	7.0
Social Sciences (inc Law)	2.4	2.4	16.7	16.7	19.2	19.1	87.9	18.6	6.3	27.9	113.4	65.6
Business & Administrative Studies	0.8	1.1	17.5	31.0	18.3	32.1	69.4	10.7	13.3	65.3	101.0	108.1
Mass Communication & Documentation	0.2	0.2	3.1	2.7	3.4	2.9	18.7	0.9	1.5	2.6	23.6	6.4
Languages	1.6	1.6	4.5	3.6	6.1	5.3	51.7	6.2	1.2	22.5	59.0	34.0
Historical and Philosophical Studies	1.2	1.5	2.4	3.8	3.5	5.3	27.0	8.6	0.6	13.4	31.1	27.3
Creative Arts & Design	0.5	0.6	4.7	3.1	5.2	3.8	65.5	2.8	8.6	9.6	79.3	16.2
Education[8]	0.6	2.8	23.2	45.4	23.9	48.2	31.6	7.6	2.5	36.3	58.0	92.1
Other subjects[9]	-	-	0.1	1.3	0.1	1.3	7.5	19.3	8.9	63.1	16.5	83.6
Unknown[7]	-	-	-	-	-	-	-	-	-	-	0.2	0.3
All subjects	20.5	20.0	93.6	152.3	114.2	172.3	568.0	124.3	112.4	334.1	794.8	631.0
of which overseas students	8.7	6.1	42.7	16.6	51.4	22.8	56.5	4.2	7.2	10.4	115.1	37.4

1 Higher Education Statistics Agency (HESA) higher education institutions include Open University students. Part-time figures include dormant modes, those writing up at home and on sabbaticals.

2 Full-time includes sandwich. Part-time comprises both day and evening, including block release and open/distance learning.

3 For HE students in further education institutions in England, includes those areas of learning which cannot be allocated to specific subject groups shown.

4 Provisional. Figures in table 6.9 are calculated on a different basis to those in table 6.8.

5 FE institution figures for England include Learning and Skills Council (LSC) funded students only.

6 Figures for further education (FE) institutions in Wales and Northern Ireland are snapshots counted at a particular point in the year [November in Northern Ireland and December in Wales]. Students starting courses after these dates will not therefore be counted. Figures for Scotland and England, however, are whole year (not snapshot) enrolments (rather than headcounts).

7 Includes data for higher education students in further education institutions in Wales which cannot be split by level.

8 Including ITT and INSET.

9 Includes Combined and general categories.

Source: Education Departments: 01325 392754

6.10 Students[1,2] obtaining higher education qualifications:[3,4] by level, sex and subject group, 2004/05

United Kingdom

Thousands

			Postgraduate			
	Sub-degree[3]	First degree	PhD and equivalent	Other	Total	Total higher education

All persons

Subject group

	Sub-degree[3]	First degree	PhD and equivalent	Other	Total	Total higher education
Medicine & Dentistry	0.1	7.4	1.6	3.0	4.5	12.1
Subjects Allied to Medicine	43.9	27.9	0.9	9.3	10.2	82.0
Biological Sciences	3.1	27.2	2.5	5.9	8.4	38.7
Vet. Science, Agriculture & related	1.3	2.9	0.3	1.1	1.4	5.7
Physical Sciences	2.5	12.5	2.3	3.8	6.2	21.2
Mathematical & Computer Sciences	9.4	25.4	1.0	10.0	11.0	45.8
Engineering & Technology	5.2	19.6	2.0	10.6	12.6	37.4
Architecture, Building & Planning	2.4	6.6	0.2	4.9	5.1	14.1
Social Sciences (inc Law)	19.5	42.6	1.5	26.9	28.4	90.5
Business & Administrative Studies	15.1	42.2	0.6	39.6	40.1	97.4
Mass Communication & Documentation	1.7	8.9	0.1	4.4	4.4	15.0
Languages	4.2	20.0	0.9	5.1	6.0	30.2
Historical and Philosophical Studies	4.2	15.5	0.9	4.3	5.2	24.9
Creative Arts & Design	5.6	30.6	0.3	6.0	6.2	42.4
Education[5]	14.8	10.6	0.7	41.3	41.9	67.4
Combined, general	1.7	6.5	-	0.1	0.1	8.3
All subjects	134.9	306.4	15.8	176.0	191.8	633.0

Males

Subject group

	Sub-degree[3]	First degree	PhD and equivalent	Other	Total	Total higher education
Medicine and Dentistry	-	3.2	0.7	1.3	2.0	5.2
Subjects Allied to Medicine	5.4	4.9	0.4	2.3	2.7	13.0
Biological Sciences	1.3	9.4	1.0	1.9	2.9	13.7
Vet. Science, Agriculture & related	0.6	0.9	0.2	0.6	0.7	2.2
Physical Sciences	1.3	7.1	1.5	2.1	3.6	12.0
Mathematical & Computer Sciences	6.8	18.9	0.7	7.3	8.0	33.7
Engineering & Technology	4.7	16.7	1.6	8.4	10.0	31.4
Architecture, Building & Planning	1.7	4.7	0.2	3.0	3.1	9.6
Social Sciences (inc Law)	5.3	16.7	0.8	11.5	12.3	34.3
Business & Administrative Studies	6.7	19.3	0.4	20.7	21.1	47.1
Mass Communication & Documentation	0.9	3.4	-	1.4	1.5	5.8
Languages	1.5	5.3	0.4	1.5	1.9	8.7
Historical and Philosophical Studies	1.5	6.8	0.6	2.0	2.6	10.8
Creative Arts & Design	2.5	11.8	0.1	2.3	2.5	16.8
Education[5]	3.7	1.8	0.3	12.0	12.2	17.7
Combined, general	0.7	2.9	-	-	-	3.6
All subjects	44.4	133.9	8.9	78.3	87.3	265.6

Females

Subject group

	Sub-degree[3]	First degree	PhD and equivalent	Other	Total	Total higher education
Medicine & Dentistry	0.1	4.2	0.8	1.7	2.5	6.9
Subjects Allied to Medicine	38.5	23.0	0.5	7.0	7.5	69.0
Biological Sciences	1.8	17.8	1.5	4.0	5.5	25.1
Vet. Science, Agriculture & related	0.7	2.0	0.2	0.6	0.7	3.4
Physical Sciences	1.2	5.4	0.8	1.8	2.5	9.2
Mathematical & Computer Sciences	2.6	6.5	0.2	2.7	2.9	12.1
Engineering & Technology	0.5	2.9	0.4	2.2	2.6	6.0
Architecture, Building & Planning	0.7	1.8	0.1	1.9	2.0	4.5
Social Sciences (inc Law)	14.3	25.8	0.7	15.3	16.0	56.2
Business & Administrative Studies	8.4	22.9	0.2	18.8	19.0	50.3
Mass Communication & Documentation	0.8	5.5	-	2.9	3.0	9.2
Languages	2.7	14.8	0.5	3.6	4.1	21.5
Historical and Philosophical Studies	2.7	8.7	0.4	2.3	2.6	14.0
Creative Arts & Design	3.1	18.8	0.1	3.6	3.8	25.6
Education[5]	11.2	8.8	0.4	29.3	29.7	49.7
Combined, general	1.0	3.6	-	0.1	0.1	4.7
All subjects	90.4	172.5	6.8	97.7	104.6	367.5

1 Includes students on Open University courses.
2 Includes students qualifying on all modes of study.
3 Includes higher education in higher education institutions in the UK only. Excludes qualifications from the private sector, except for the University of Buckingham who returned data to HESA in 2004/05, and higher education qualifications in further education institutions (approximately 8% of the total number of students).

4 Excludes students who successfully completed courses for which formal qualifications are not awarded.
5 Includes ITT and INSET.

Source: Education Departments: 01325 392754

6.11 Qualified teachers: by type of school and sex[1]

Thousands

	Public sector mainstream schools		Non-maintained mainstream schools	All special schools	Total[3]
	Nursery and primary	Secondary[2]			
All full-time teachers					
United Kingdom					
1990/91[4]	208.8	233.1	44.9	19.0	505.7
1995/96[4,5]	211.8	222.1	48.6	17.2	499.7
2000/01[6,7,8]	211.2	225.7	52.3	16.5	505.7
2001/02[8]	211.2	227.1	52.8	16.3	507.3
2002/03[8,9]	210.5	229.7	53.6	19.8	513.6
2003/04[8]	205.7	233.4	55.8	17.2	512.1
2004/05[10]	208.5	232.5	56.3	19.9	517.2
of which:					
England and Wales[1]	179.0	199.3	53.7	17.2	449.1
Scotland	21.6	23.2	2.5	2.1	49.4
Northern Ireland	7.9	10.0	0.1	0.7	18.7
Full-time male teachers					
United Kingdom					
1990/91[4]	37.7	120.7	20.6	5.9	184.9
1995/96[4,5]	35.5	107.9	21.1	5.4	169.8
2000/01[6,7,8]	32.1	102.9	21.3	5.0	161.3
2001/02	31.8	102.6	21.5	4.9	160.8
2002/03[8,9]	31.7	101.6	21.6	5.9	160.8
2003/04[8]	30.7	102.2	22.7	5.0	160.7
2004/05[10]	31.2	101.5	22.9	5.9	161.5
of which:					
England and Wales[1]	28.2	87.3	21.9	5.3	142.6
Scotland	1.6	10.3	1.0	0.5	13.3
Northern Ireland	1.4	4.0	-	0.1	5.6
Full-time female teachers					
United Kingdom					
1990/91[4]	171.1	112.3	24.3	13.1	320.8
1995/96[4,5]	176.3	114.2	27.4	11.8	329.9
2000/01[6,7,8]	179.1	122.8	30.9	11.6	344.4
2001/02	179.4	124.5	31.2	11.4	346.5
2002/03[8,9]	178.8	128.2	32.0	13.9	352.8
2003/04[8]	175.0	131.3	33.0	12.1	351.5
2004/05[10]	177.3	131.0	33.4	14.0	355.7
of which:					
England and Wales[1]	150.8	112.0	31.8	11.9	306.5
Scotland	20.1	12.9	1.5	1.6	36.1
Northern Ireland	6.5	6.1	0.1	0.6	13.1
All full time equivalents (FTE) of part-time teachers					
United Kingdom					
1990/91	..	..	..	..	30.0
1995/96[4,5]	19.1	17.7	8.9	1.5	47.2
2000/01[6,7,8]	21.9	16.7	10.2	1.6	50.4
2001/02	23.4	17.4	10.4	1.8	53.0
2002/03[8,9]	23.8	17.8	11.1	1.7	54.4
2003/04[8]	25.3	18.8	11.4	1.9	57.4
2004/05[10]	26.3	19.8	11.4	1.9	59.4

1 Public sector teachers numbers in England & Wales have been provided from the 618G survey and gender split has been calculated by using the proportions from the Database of Teacher Records (DTR).
2 From 1993/94 excludes sixth form colleges in England and Wales which were reclassified as further education colleges on 1 April 1993.
3 Excludes Pupil Referral Units (PRUs).
4 Figures for non-maintained mainstream schools refer to Great Britain.
5 Includes 1994/95 data for Northern Ireland.
6 Includes 1999/00 pre-school data for Scotland.
7 Includes 2001/02 data for Northern Ireland.
8 Includes revised data.
9 Includes 2001/02 pre-school and 2003/04 school data for Scotland.
10 Provisional.

Source: Education Departments: 01325 392754

Labour market

Chapter 7

Labour market

Labour Force Survey

(Tables 7.1 to 7.3, 7.6, 7.9, 7.10, 7.11, 7.13 and 7.16 to 7.18)

The impact of Census 2001 on LFS data

(Tables 7.1 to 7.3, 7.6, 7.9, 7.10 to 7.11, 7.16 to 7.18)

The first results of the 2001 Census, published on 30 September 2002, showed that previous estimates of the total UK population were about 1 million too high. Please see the introduction for more details. Estimates of employment and unemployment levels from the LFS released before 30 October 2002 are therefore too high, with rates also affected. This has led to the Labour Force Survey (LFS) needing to reweight their estimates to the new population figures.

ONS has published interim reweighted LFS estimates for the UK, which have been used in this chapter. The interim reweighted figures only cover top-level seasonally adjusted series published in the Labour Market Statistics First Release. The non-seasonally adjusted series, used in previous editions of the Annual Abstract, were not available in time for this publication.

Future editions of the Annual Abstract will continue to show seasonally adjusted data for these tables, in line with other headline publications. These figures are not directly comparable to the non-seasonally adjusted figures previously published in the Annual Abstract.

Background

The LFS is the largest regular household survey in the United Kingdom. LFS interviews are conducted continuously throughout the year. In any 3-month period, a nationally representative sample of approximately 102,000 people aged 16 or over in around 57,000 households are interviewed. Each household is interviewed five times, at 3 monthly intervals. The initial interview is done face-to-face by an interviewer visiting the address. The other interviews are done by telephone wherever possible. The survey asks a series of questions about respondents' personal circumstances and their labour market activity. Most questions refer to activity in the week before the interview.

The concepts and definitions used in the LFS are agreed by the International Labour Organisation (ILO) - an agency of the United Nations. The definitions are used by European Union member countries and members of the Organisation for Economic Co-operation and Development (OECD).

The Labour Force Survey was carried out every two years from 1973 to 1983. The ILO definition was first used in 1984. This was also the first year in which the survey was conducted on an annual basis with results available for every spring quarter (representing an average of the period from March to May). The survey moved to a continuous basis in spring 1992 in Great Britain and in winter 1994/5 in Northern Ireland, with average quarterly results published 4 times a year for seasonal quarters: spring (March to May), summer (June to August), autumn (September to November) and winter (December to February). From April 1998, results are published 12 times a year for the average of 3 consecutive months.

The LFS collects information on a sample of the population. To convert this information to give estimates for the population the data must be grossed. This is achieved by calculating weighting factors (often referred to simply as weights) which can be applied to each sampled individual in such a way that the weighted-up results match estimates or projections of the total population in terms of age distribution, sex, and region of residence.

Strengths and limitations of the LFS

The LFS produces coherent labour market information on the basis of internationally standard concepts and definitions. It is a rich source of data on a wide variety of labour market and personal characteristics. It is the most suitable source for making comparisons between countries. The LFS is designed so that households interviewed in each three month period constitute a representative sample of UK households. The survey covers those living in private households and nurses in National Health Service accommodation. Students living in halls of residence have been included since 1992 as information about them is collected at their parents' address.

However the LFS has its limitations. It is a sample survey and is therefore subject to sampling variability. The survey does not include people living in institutions such as hostels or residential homes. 'Proxy' reporting (when members of the household are not present at the interview, another member of the household answers the questions on their behalf) can affect the quality of information on topics such as earnings, hours worked, benefit receipt and qualifications. Around one third of interviews are conducted 'by proxy', usually by a spouse or partner but sometimes by a parent or other near relation.

Sampling Variability

Survey estimates are prone to sampling variability. The easiest way to explain this concept is by example. In the September to

November 1997 period, ILO unemployment in Great Britain (seasonally adjusted) stood at 1,847,000. If we drew another sample for the same period we could get a different result, perhaps 1,900,000 or 1,820,000.

In theory, we could draw many samples, and each would give a different result. This is because each sample would be made up of different people who would give different answers to the questions. The spread of these results is the sampling variability. Sampling variability is determined by a number of factors including the sample size, the variability of the population from which the sample is drawn and the sample design. Once we know the sampling variability we can calculate a range of values about the sample estimate that represents the expected variation with a given level of assurance. This is called a confidence interval. For a 95% confidence interval we expect that in 95% of the samples (19 times out of 20) the confidence interval will contain the true value that would be obtained by surveying the entire population. For the example given above, we can be 95% confident that the true value was in the range 1,791,000 to 1,903,000.

Unreliable estimates

Very small estimates have relatively wide confidence intervals making them unreliable. For this reason, the ONS does not publish LFS estimates below 10,000.

Non-Response

Non-response can introduce bias to a survey, particularly if the people not responding have characteristics that are different from those who do respond. The LFS has a response rate of around 80 per cent to the first interview, and over 90 per cent of those who are interviewed once go on to complete all five interviews. These are relatively high levels for a household survey. Any bias from non-response is minimised by *weighting* the results.

Weighting (or grossing) converts sample data to represent the full population. In the LFS, the data are weighted separately by age, sex and area of residence to population estimates based on the Census. Weighting also adjusts for people not in the survey and thus minimises non-response bias.

Labour Force Survey Concepts and Definitions

Discouraged workers - a sub-group of the economically inactive population, defined as those neither in employment nor unemployed (on the ILO measure) who said they would like a job and whose main reason for not seeking work was because they believed there were no jobs available.

Economically active - people aged 16 and over who are either in employment or ILO unemployed.

Economic activity rate - the percentage of people aged 16 and over who are economically active.

Economically inactive - people who are neither in employment nor unemployed. This group includes, for example, all those who were looking after a home or retired.

Employment - people aged 16 or over who did at least one hour of paid work in the reference week (whether as an employee or self-employed); those who had a job that they were temporarily away from (on holiday, for example); those on Government-supported training and employment programmes (from spring 1983); and those doing unpaid family work (from spring 1992).

Employees - the division between employees and self-employed is based on survey respondents' own assessment of their employment status.

Full Time - the classification of employees, self-employed and unpaid family workers in their main job as full-time or part-time is on the basis of self-assessment. Up until autumn 1995, people who were on government work-related training programmes are classified as full-time or part-time according to whether their usual hours of work per week were over 30 or 30 and under; from winter 1995/96 onwards, the full-time/part-time classification for this group has been changed to self-assessment, in line with the other groups outlined above. People on Government-supported training and employment programmes who are at college in the survey reference week are classified, by convention, as part-time.

Government-supported training and employment programmes - comprise all people aged 16 and over participating in one of the Government's employment and training programmes (Youth Training, Training for Work and Community Action), together with those on similar programmes administered by Training and Enterprise Councils in England and Wales, or Local Enterprise Companies in Scotland.

Hours worked - respondents to the LFS are asked a series of questions enabling the identification of both their usual hours and their actual hours. Total hours include overtime (paid and unpaid) and exclude lunchbreaks.

Unemployment – Unemployment figures from the Labour Force Survey (LFS), which are based upon the International

Labour Organisation (ILO) definition, were re-labelled 'unemployment' rather than 'ILO unemployment' in January 2003. This emphasises that the LFS figures provide the official and only internationally comparable measure of unemployment in the UK. For more details see the National Statistics website at www.statistics.gov.uk/ cci/nugget. asp?id=251

The International Labour Office (ILO) measure of unemployment used throughout this supplement refers to people without a job who were available to start work in the two weeks following their LFS interview and who had either looked for work in the four weeks prior to interview or were waiting to start a job they had already obtained. This definition of unemployment is in accordance with that adopted by the 13th International Conference of Labour Statisticians, further clarified at the 14th ICLS, and promulgated by the ILO in its publications.

Unemployment (rate) - the percentage of economically active people who are unemployed on the ILO measure.

Unemployment (duration) - defined as the shorter of the following two periods: (a) duration of active search for work; and (b) length of time since employment.

Part-Time - see full-time

Second jobs - jobs which LFS respondents hold in addition to a main full-time or part -time job.

Self-employment - See Employees

Temporary employees - in the LFS these are defined as those employees who say that their main job is non permanent in one of the following ways: fixed period contract; agency temping; casual work; seasonal work; other temporary work.

Unpaid Family Workers - the separate identification from spring 1992 of this group in the LFS is in accordance with international recommendations. The group comprises persons doing unpaid work for a business they own or for a business that a relative owns.

Distribution of workforce

(Table 7.4)

Claimant unemployed - those people who were claiming unemployment-related benefits (contributions or income related Jobseeker's Allowance and/or National Insurance credits) at Jobcentre Plus local offices on the day of the monthly count. The seasonally adjusted claimant

unemployment series allows for all relevant changes which, unless adjusted for, would distort comparisons over time.

Workforce jobs (formerly workforce in employment) - comprises employee jobs, self-employment jobs (from the Labour Force Survey), HM Forces and government supported trainees.

HM Forces (provided by Ministry of Defence) – represent the total number of UK service personnel, male and female, in HM Regular Forces, wherever serving and including those on leave. Full Time Reserve personnel, mobilised reservists, the Ghurkhas and the Home Service battalions of the Royal Irish Regiment, wherever serving and including those on leave.

Self-employed jobs - estimates are based on the results of the Labour Force Survey. The Northern Ireland estimates are not seasonally adjusted.

Government-supported trainees - include all participants on government training and employment programmes who are receiving some work experience on their placement but who do not have a contract of employment (those with a contract are included in the employee jobs series). The numbers are not subject to seasonal adjustment.

Civil Service employment

(Table 7.8)

There have been definition changes effective from Q3 2005 which has seen an upward and downward movement of staff in departments. The largest contributor to this has been the Department for Work and Pensions (DWP) who reported an additional 680 employees. Overall these definition changes resulted in an increase of 350 employees.

There has also been a number of changes to departments since Q3 2005 through transfers and the merging of departments, these include:

- The Government Car and Despatch Agency which has transferred from the Cabinet Office to the Department of Transport from November 2005,

- The Office of the Chief of the House of Commons and the Chief Whip of the House of Lords transferred to the Privy Council Office on 1 February 2006,

- The Government Social Research Unit transferred to HM Treasury on 13 February 2006,

- HM Customs and Excise and Inland Revenue merged on 18April 2005 to form HM Revenue and Customs (HMRC). At the same time the Valuation Office transferred from Chancellor's other departments to HMRC,

- The Magistrates' Court Service transferred from local government to HM Court Services on 1 April 2005,

- The Marine Fisheries Agency and the Government Decontamination Service were established as Executive Agencies of DEFRA on 1 October 2005,

- HMRC figures include 1127 employment (FTE) transferred to the Serious Organised Crime Agency (SOCA) on 1 April 2006,

- The Forensic Science Service became a Government Owned Company on 5 December and transferred out of the Home Office.

Persons employed in local authorities

(Table 7.9)

The full-time equivalents for local authorities are derived by applying factors to the numbers of part-time workers in three groups based on average hours worked in each group nationally.

Jobseekers allowance claimant count

(Tables 7.14 and 7.15)

This is a count of all those people who are claiming Jobseeker's Allowance (JSA) at Jobcentre Plus local offices. People claiming JSA must declare that they are out of work capable of, available for and actively seeking work during the week in which the claim is made. All people claiming Jobseeker's Allowance (JSA) on the day of the monthly count are included in the claimant count, irrespective of whether they are actually receiving benefits.

Labour disputes

(Table 7.19)

These figures exclude details of stoppages involving fewer than ten workers or lasting less than one day except any in which the aggregate number of working days lost is 100 or more. There may be some under-recording of small or short stoppages; this would have much more effect on the total of stoppages than of working days lost. Some stoppages which affected more than one industry group have been counted under each of the industries but only once in the totals. Stoppages have been classified using *Standard Industrial Classification (SIC) 1992*.

The figures for working days lost and workers involved have been rounded and consequently the sum of the constituent items may not agree with the totals. Classifications by size are based on the full duration of stoppages where these continue

into the following year. Working days lost per thousand employees are based on the latest available mid-year (June) estimates of employee jobs.

Earnings

(Tables 7.20 to 7.25)

The total gross remuneration employees receive before any statutory deductions (tax, national insurance). Income in kind and pension funds are excluded.

Annual Survey of Hours and Earnings

(Tables 7.20, 7.21, 7.24 and 7.25)

The Annual Survey of Hours and Earnings (ASHE) is a new survey that has been developed to replace the New Earnings Survey (NES). The ASHE includes improvements to the coverage of employees and to the weighting of earnings estimates. The data variables collected remain broadly the same, although an improved questionnaire will be introduced for the 2005 survey. The change in methodology means that statistics on pay and hours published from the ASHE, including the calculation of ONS's low pay statistics, are discontinuous with previous NES surveys.

To improve coverage and make the survey more representative, supplementary information was collected for the 2004 ASHE survey on businesses not registered for VAT and for people who changed or started new jobs between sample selection and the survey reference period. The 2004 ASHE results are therefore discontinuous with the results for 2003, for which no supplementary information was collected. However, for 2004 two sets of results are available; the headline results that include supplementary information and results that exclude this information. These second set of results are given solely for comparison to earlier results.

The ASHE methodology includes imputation and weighting, the main impact of these changes when applied to existing NES data for 1997 to 2003 are:

- To increase the estimates of the level of average weekly pay over estimates published from the NES.

- For males the increase in estimates of earnings is more than the increase for females. In particular this affects hourly pay excluding overtime, which is used in the calculation of the ONS' preferred measure of the gender pay gap. The estimate of hourly pay for males is increased more then the estimate for females, which widens the estimate of the gap between male and female hourly pay.

Labour market

- Estimates of the level of earnings for people working in London are increased more than estimates for other regions. This widens the estimate of the difference in pay between London and other regions of the UK.

Average earnings index

(Tables 7.22 and 7.23)

The Average Earnings Index (AEI) is designed to measure changes in the level of earnings, i.e. wage inflation in Great Britain. Average earnings are calculated as the total wages and salaries paid by firms, divided by the number of employees paid. Like all indices, changes are measured against a base year, whose index value is set to 100. The current base year is 2000 for Tables 7.22 and 7.23.

Users should note that the data contained in table 7.23 of the Annual Abstract since 2003 are not comparable with that published up until 2002. Table 7.23 now shows the set of 20 industry sectors. That better reflect the current state of the economy, and supersedes the previous set of 26 industry sectors. The new series are available in the format of excluding bonus index, including bonus index, and an annual percentage change for including and excluding bonuses. An article covering the reasons for the change can be found on our website www.statistics.gov.uk/labour.

The AEI is published monthly in the Labour Market Statistics First Release. The main indicator of growth, the headline rate, is based on the annual change in the seasonally adjusted index values for the latest 3 months compared with the same period a year ago. The use of a 3-month average reduces the level of volatility seen in the data on a month-on-month basis.

Strengths of the AEI

The AEI, based on monthly survey data, is a timely indicator of changes in the level of earnings.

Limitations of the AEI

The index is not adjusted for any changes in the composition of the workforce such as changes in the share of full-time and part-time workers, or in the share of skilled and unskilled workers. Similarly, the index does not account for changes in the number of hours worked, or any temporary factors that affect earnings.

The sample of the Monthly Wages and Salaries Survey on which the AEI is based is not designed to provide information on the level of earnings. The sample is not completely representative of the economy as firms with fewer than 20 employees are excluded, as are the earnings of self employed persons.

The AEI only covers earnings in Great Britain as earnings information is not collected for Northern Ireland and regional data are not available.

Trade unions

(Table 7.26)

The statistics relate to all organisations of employees known to Certification Officer with head offices in the United Kingdom that fall within the appropriate definition of a trade union in the 1992 Trade Union and Labour Relations Act. Included in the data are home and overseas membership figures of contributory and non-contributory members. Employment status of members is not provided and the figures may therefore include some people who are self-employed, unemployed or retired.

The membership part of this table was revised in 2001, so that statistics presented here are on a consistent basis with the GB table produced by the Certification Officer in his Annual Report and with tables produced in the annual Labour Market Trends Trade Union article. There is a break in the time series for the figures in this table between the years 1988 (contained within previous publications) and 1989. GB data for 1989-95 are DTI analyses of annual returns, with 1996-1999 as published in the Certification Officer's Annual Report. Data for Northern Ireland for 1989-1991 are DTI analyses of annual returns, with 1992-1999 from the Certification Officer's Annual Report.

7.1 Labour force summary:[1] by sex
United Kingdom
At Quarter 2 each year[2]. Seasonally adjusted

Thousands and percentages

	All aged 16 and over					Percentages			
	Total[3]	Total economically active	Total in employment	Total unemployed	Economically inactive	Economic activity rate 16-59/64[4]	Employment rate all aged 16 and over[5]	Employment rate 16-59/64[6]	Unemployment rate[7]
All Persons									
	MGSL	MGSF	MGRZ	MGSC	MGSI	MGSO	MGSR	MGSU	MGSX
1996	45 355	28 345	26 009	2 336	17 010	78.4	57.3	71.8	8.2
1997	45 509	28 561	26 513	2 048	16 949	78.6	58.3	72.9	7.2
1998	45 675	28 509	26 721	1 788	17 166	78.3	58.5	73.3	6.3
1999	45 880	28 833	27 090	1 743	17 047	78.7	59.0	73.9	6.0
2000	46 128	29 061	27 461	1 599	17 067	78.8	59.5	74.4	5.5
2001	46 440	29 167	27 694	1 472	17 274	78.6	59.6	74.5	5.0
2002	46 727	29 420	27 905	1 515	17 306	78.6	59.7	74.5	5.2
2003	47 020	29 655	28 192	1 464	17 365	78.7	60.0	74.8	4.9
2004	47 352	29 844	28 412	1 433	17 508	78.5	60.0	74.7	4.8
2005	47 753	30 126	28 693	1 433	17 628	78.5	60.1	74.7	4.8
2006	48 131	30 613	28 930	1 683	17 518	79.0	60.1	74.6	5.5
Male									
	MGSM	MGSG	MGSA	MGSD	MGSJ	MGSP	MGSS	MGSV	MGSY
1996	21 801	15 682	14 166	1 517	6 119	84.9	65.0	76.6	9.7
1997	21 883	15 707	14 442	1 265	6 175	84.8	66.0	77.9	8.1
1998	21 968	15 650	14 576	1 074	6 318	84.1	66.4	78.3	6.9
1999	22 081	15 790	14 731	1 059	6 291	84.5	66.7	78.7	6.7
2000	22 213	15 854	14 897	957	6 359	84.4	67.1	79.2	6.0
2001	22 393	15 875	14 994	882	6 518	83.9	67.0	79.2	5.6
2002	22 564	15 978	15 068	910	6 586	83.8	66.8	79.0	5.7
2003	22 738	16 179	15 294	886	6 558	84.2	67.3	79.5	5.5
2004	22 926	16 199	15 358	841	6 727	83.6	67.0	79.2	5.2
2005	23 146	16 314	15 480	833	6 832	83.4	66.9	79.1	5.1
2006	23 353	16 553	15 578	975	6 800	83.7	66.7	78.7	5.9
Female									
	MGSN	MGSH	MGSB	MGSE	MGSK	MGSQ	MGST	MGSW	MGSZ
1996	23 553	12 663	11 843	820	10 890	71.5	50.3	66.7	6.5
1997	23 627	12 853	12 071	783	10 773	72.0	51.1	67.5	6.1
1998	23 707	12 859	12 144	715	10 847	72.0	51.2	67.9	5.6
1999	23 799	13 043	12 359	684	10 756	72.6	51.9	68.7	5.2
2000	23 915	13 207	12 565	642	10 708	72.9	52.5	69.3	4.9
2001	24 047	13 291	12 701	591	10 756	72.9	52.8	69.5	4.4
2002	24 163	13 443	12 837	606	10 720	73.1	53.1	69.7	4.5
2003	24 283	13 476	12 898	578	10 807	72.9	53.1	69.7	4.3
2004	24 427	13 646	13 054	592	10 781	73.1	53.4	69.8	4.3
2005	24 607	13 812	13 212	599	10 796	73.3	53.7	70.0	4.3
2006	24 778	14 061	13 352	708	10 717	74.0	53.9	70.1	5.0

1 See chapter text. In August 2006, ONS published the mid-year population estimates for 2005. These estimates have now been incorporated into the LFS estimates from Autumn 2004. Further details can be found at http://www.statistics.gov.uk/cci/article.asp?id=1647

2 The Labour Force Survey has now moved to calendar quarters from May 2006. More information can be found on page 5 of the Concepts and Definitions.pdf by following this link:- www.statistics.gov.uk/downloads/theme_labour/Concepts_Definitions_HQS.pdf

3 Population aged 16 and over in private households and student halls of residence.

4 Economically active of working age as a percentage of all persons of working age (men 16-64, women 16-59).

5 Total employed as a percentage of all persons aged 16 and over.

6 Total employed of working age as a percentage of all persons of working age (men 16-64, women 16-59).

7 Total unemployed as a percentage of all economically active.

Sources: Labour Force Survey, Office for National Statistics;
Helpline: 020-7533 6094

7.2 Employment status: full-time, part-time and temporary employees[1]
United Kingdom
At Quarter 2 each year[2]. Seasonally adjusted

Thousands

	All in employment[3]					Total employment[3]		Employees[3]		Self-employed[3]			
	Total	Employees	Self employed	Unpaid family workers	Government supported training and employment programmes[4]	Full-time	Part-time	Full-time	Part-time	Full-time	Part-time	Workers with second jobs[5]	Temporary employees

All Persons

	MGRZ	MGRN	MGRQ	MGRT	MGRW	YCBE	YCBH	YCBK	YCBN	YCBQ	YCBT	YCBW	YCBZ
1996	26 009	22 145	3 501	120	242	19 499	6 510	16 538	5 607	2 794	707	1 274	1 648
1997	26 513	22 709	3 470	115	218	19 832	6 680	16 948	5 761	2 730	740	1 242	1 787
1998	26 721	23 088	3 368	100	164	20 000	6 721	17 261	5 827	2 616	752	1 197	1 711
1999	27 090	23 509	3 324	100	156	20 288	6 802	17 593	5 916	2 590	735	1 299	1 673
2000	27 461	23 948	3 255	113	146	20 524	6 937	17 897	6 051	2 519	736	1 167	1 705
2001	27 694	24 177	3 276	96	145	20 718	6 977	18 037	6 141	2 579	697	1 185	1 717
2002	27 905	24 365	3 336	97	106	20 777	7 128	18 146	6 220	2 561	775	1 133	1 590
2003	28 192	24 453	3 559	88	92	20 918	7 274	18 134	6 319	2 721	837	1 110	1 489
2004	28 412	24 514	3 676	98	123	21 052	7 360	18 145	6 368	2 826	850	1 072	1 503
2005	28 693	24 848	3 630	101	114	21 365	7 327	18 473	6 376	2 811	819	1 076	1 441
2006	28 930	25 023	3 719	93	94	21 588	7 342	18 674	6 349	2 852	867	1 047	1 454

Male

	MGSA	MGRO	MGRR	MGRU	MGRX	YCBF	YCBI	YCBL	YCBO	YCBR	YCBU	YCBX	YCCA
1996	14 166	11 391	2 588	38	148	12 952	1 213	10 522	869	2 340	248	545	736
1997	14 442	11 734	2 538	35	135	13 164	1 278	10 794	940	2 275	263	536	810
1998	14 576	11 984	2 456	30	107	13 282	1 294	11 030	953	2 173	283	511	765
1999	14 731	12 154	2 439	34	103	13 373	1 358	11 143	1 012	2 165	273	550	775
2000	14 897	12 413	2 360	37	87	13 529	1 368	11 389	1 025	2 076	284	489	775
2001	14 994	12 458	2 404	34	97	13 622	1 371	11 411	1 048	2 142	262	485	769
2002	15 068	12 535	2 442	31	61	13 591	1 478	11 425	1 110	2 125	317	473	742
2003	15 294	12 603	2 607	32	52	13 704	1 589	11 408	1 195	2 256	350	455	682
2004	15 358	12 545	2 700	40	72	13 732	1 626	11 340	1 206	2 341	359	450	696
2005	15 480	12 705	2 668	37	70	13 841	1 639	11 456	1 249	2 332	336	462	685
2006	15 578	12 783	2 704	36	54	13 911	1 667	11 524	1 259	2 350	354	449	647

Female

	MGSB	MGRP	MGRS	MGRV	MGRY	YCBG	YCBJ	YCBM	YCBP	YCBS	YCBV	YCBY	YCCB
1996	11 843	10 754	912	83	94	6 547	5 296	6 016	4 738	454	458	730	912
1997	12 071	10 975	932	80	84	6 668	5 403	6 154	4 821	455	478	706	976
1998	12 144	11 105	912	71	58	6 718	5 426	6 231	4 873	443	469	685	945
1999	12 359	11 355	886	66	53	6 915	5 444	6 451	4 904	424	461	749	897
2000	12 565	11 534	895	76	60	6 995	5 569	6 508	5 026	443	452	679	930
2001	12 701	11 719	872	62	48	7 096	5 605	6 626	5 093	438	434	700	948
2002	12 837	11 831	895	65	45	7 187	5 650	6 721	5 110	436	459	660	848
2003	12 898	11 850	952	57	39	7 213	5 685	6 726	5 124	465	487	655	806
2004	13 054	11 969	976	58	51	7 320	5 734	6 806	5 163	485	491	622	808
2005	13 212	12 144	961	64	44	7 524	5 688	7 017	5 127	479	483	614	756
2006	13 352	12 240	1 015	57	41	7 677	5 675	7 151	5 090	502	513	598	806

1 See chapter text. In August 2006, ONS published the mid-year population estimates for 2005. These estimates have now been incorporated into the LFS estimates from Autumn 2004. Further details can be found at http://www.statistics.gov.uk/cci/article.asp?id=1647

2 The Labour Force Survey has now moved to calendar quarters from May 2006. More information can be found on page 5 of the Concepts and Definitions.pdf by following this link:- www.statistics.gov.uk/downloads/theme_labour/Concepts_Definitions_HQS.pdf

3 People whose main job is full or part-time and based on respondents' self assessment.

4 Those on employment and training programmes are classified as in employment. Some of those on programmes may consider themselves to be employees or self employed so appear in other categories.

5 Second jobs reported in LFS in addition to person's main full or part-time job.

Sources: Labour Force Survey, Office for National Statistics;
Helpline: 020-7533 6094

7.3 Employment: by sex and age[1]
United Kingdom
At Quarter 2 each year[2]. Seasonally adjusted

Thousands and percentages

	All aged 16 and over	16-59/64	16-17	18-24	25-34	35-49	50-64 (m) 50-59 (f)	65+ (m) 60+ (f)
Thousands								
All Persons								
	MGRZ	YBSE	YBTO	YBTR	YBTU	YBTX	MGUW	MGUZ
2000	27 461	26 630	673	3 246	6 876	10 071	5 763	832
2001	27 694	26 863	669	3 321	6 738	10 212	5 924	831
2002	27 905	27 024	648	3 386	6 537	10 427	6 026	881
2003	28 192	27 263	651	3 381	6 387	10 590	6 254	929
2004	28 412	27 401	632	3 503	6 296	10 695	6 275	1 011
2005	28 693	27 633	628	3 508	6 280	10 853	6 363	1 060
2006	28 930	27 775	563	3 565	6 260	10 940	6 446	1 155
Male								
	MGSA	YBSF	YBTP	YBTS	YBTV	YBTY	MGUX	MGVA
2000	14 897	14 618	330	1 706	3 759	5 395	3 428	279
2001	14 994	14 720	330	1 746	3 684	5 441	3 520	273
2002	15 068	14 776	323	1 763	3 578	5 551	3 561	292
2003	15 294	14 963	319	1 785	3 505	5 648	3 707	331
2004	15 358	15 017	306	1 857	3 418	5 716	3 720	341
2005	15 480	15 125	305	1 856	3 420	5 772	3 772	355
2006	15 578	15 186	263	1 867	3 408	5 819	3 830	392
Female								
	MGSB	YBSG	YBTQ	YBTT	YBTW	YBTZ	MGUY	MGVB
2000	12 565	12 012	342	1 541	3 117	4 677	2 336	553
2001	12 701	12 143	339	1 575	3 053	4 771	2 404	558
2002	12 837	12 248	325	1 623	2 960	4 875	2 465	589
2003	12 898	12 300	332	1 596	2 882	4 942	2 548	598
2004	13 054	12 384	326	1 645	2 878	4 979	2 555	670
2005	13 212	12 508	323	1 652	2 861	5 081	2 590	705
2006	13 352	12 589	300	1 699	2 853	5 121	2 616	763
Percentages[3]								
All Persons								
	MGSR	MGSU	YBUA	YBUD	YBUG	YBUJ	YBUM	YBUP
2000	59.5	74.4	46.9	67.2	80.1	81.8	66.9	8.0
2001	59.6	74.5	45.4	67.9	80.0	81.7	67.7	8.0
2002	59.7	74.5	42.9	68.0	79.6	82.1	68.0	8.4
2003	60.0	74.8	42.7	66.2	79.6	82.2	70.0	8.8
2004	60.0	74.7	40.6	67.0	79.9	82.0	69.8	9.5
2005	60.1	74.7	39.9	65.6	80.3	82.3	70.4	9.8
2006	60.1	74.6	35.7	65.1	80.5	82.2	70.8	10.6
Male								
	MGSS	MGSV	YBUB	YBUE	YBUH	YBUK	YBUN	YBUQ
2000	67.1	79.2	45.2	70.9	88.6	88.6	68.9	7.4
2001	67.0	79.2	43.8	71.6	88.4	88.0	69.8	7.2
2002	66.8	79.0	41.8	70.8	88.0	88.4	70.0	7.6
2003	67.3	79.5	40.8	69.6	88.2	88.7	72.2	8.4
2004	67.0	79.2	38.4	70.6	87.5	88.7	71.9	8.6
2005	66.9	79.1	37.8	68.7	88.2	88.6	72.2	8.8
2006	66.7	78.7	32.5	67.3	88.4	88.4	72.6	9.7
Female								
	MGST	MGSW	YBUC	YBUF	YBUI	YBUL	YBUO	YBUR
2000	52.5	69.3	48.7	63.6	71.8	75.1	64.1	8.4
2001	52.8	69.5	47.1	64.2	71.8	75.5	64.7	8.5
2002	53.1	69.7	44.2	65.2	71.4	75.9	65.4	8.9
2003	53.1	69.7	44.5	62.7	71.2	75.9	67.1	9.0
2004	53.4	69.8	42.9	63.4	72.4	75.5	67.0	10.0
2005	53.7	70.0	42.1	62.4	72.5	76.2	67.8	10.4
2006	53.9	70.1	39.0	62.8	72.7	76.0	68.4	11.2

1 See chapter text. In August 2006, ONS published the mid-year population estimates for 2005. These estimates have now been incorporated into the LFS estimates from Autumn 2004. Further details can be found at http://www.statistics.gov.uk/cci/article.asp?id=1647

2 The Labour Force Survey has now moved to calendar quarters from May 2006. More information can be found on page 5 of the Concepts and Definitions.pdf by following this link:- www.statistics.gov.uk/downloads/theme_labour/Concepts_Definitions_HQS.pdf

3 Total in employment as a percentage of all persons in the relevant group.

Sources: Labour Force Survey, Office for National Statistics;
Helpline: 020-7533 6094

7.4 Distribution of the workforce:[1,2] by sex
At mid-June each year. Seasonally adjusted

Thousands

		1996	1997	1998	1999	2000	2001	2002	2003	2004	2005	2006
United Kingdom												
Claimant count	BCJD	2 087.5	1 584.5	1 347.8	1 248.1	1 088.4	969.9	946.6	933.0	853.5	861.8	944.1
Males	DPAE	1 593.1	1 214.9	1 029.4	955.0	831.6	739.6	717.1	700.3	636.4	639.8	696.9
Females	DPAF	494.4	369.6	318.4	293.1	256.8	230.3	229.6	232.8	217.1	222.0	247.2
Workforce jobs	DYDC	28 222	28 698	28 831	29 159	29 603	29 918	30 071	30 366	30 690	31 042	31 409
Males	KAMS	14 787	15 142	15 335	15 675	15 793	15 995	15 996	16 248	16 373	16 493	16 738
Females	KAMT	13 436	13 556	13 497	13 484	13 810	13 923	14 075	14 118	14 317	14 549	14 671
HM Forces	KAMU	230	220	219	218	217	214	214	223	218	209	204
Males	KAMV	214	204	203	201	199	196	197	203	199	191	185
Females	KAMW	16	16	17	17	18	18	18	19	19	18	18
Self-employment jobs	DYZN	3 894	3 843	3 691	3 682	3 577	3 597	3 664	3 882	3 974	3 957	4 073
Males	KAMZ	2 832	2 745	2 642	2 639	2 552	2 588	2 631	2 785	2 874	2 851	2 893
Females	KANA	1 062	1 098	1 049	1 043	1 025	1 009	1 033	1 097	1 100	1 106	1 179
Employees jobs	BCAJ	23 905	24 464	24 790	25 129	25 690	26 008	26 102	26 169	26 389	26 779	27 067
Males	KANC	11 622	12 088	12 414	12 755	12 969	13 149	13 113	13 204	13 234	13 393	13 620
Females	KAND	12 283	12 376	12 376	12 374	12 721	12 859	12 989	12 965	13 155	13 386	13 447
of whom												
Total, production and construction industries	KANF	5 292	5 398	5 525	5 382	5 349	5 194	4 951	4 747	4 592	4 469	4 453
Total, all manufacturing industries	KANG	4 138	4 190	4 208	4 059	3 959	3 805	3 599	3 410	3 246	3 101	2 999
Government-supported trainees	KANH	194	171	131	131	119	99	91	92	109	97	66
Males	KANI	119	105	76	81	73	62	55	55	65	58	39
Females	KANJ	75	66	55	50	46	38	36	37	44	38	27
Great Britain												
Claimant count	DPAG	2 003.7	1 521.1	1 290.3	1 197.3	1 046.3	930.5	910.2	898.5	822.7	833.2	916.2
Males	ZSDP	1 528.2	1 165.0	984.6	915.7	799.6	709.7	689.3	673.9	613.0	618.1	676.0
Females	ZSDQ	475.5	356.1	305.7	281.6	246.8	220.8	220.9	224.6	209.8	215.1	240.3
Workforce jobs	KANQ	27 542	27 994	28 116	28 436	28 858	29 164	29 310	29 586	29 891	30 219	30 576
Males	KANR	14 420	14 762	14 947	15 287	15 390	15 590	15 592	15 835	15 946	16 055	16 294
Females	KANS	13 122	13 232	13 168	13 149	13 468	13 574	13 718	13 751	13 944	14 165	14 283
HM Forces	BCAH	230	220	219	218	217	214	214	223	218	209	204
Males	KANU	214	204	203	201	199	196	197	203	199	191	185
Females	KANV	16	16	17	17	18	18	18	19	19	18	18
Self-employment jobs	KANW	3 809	3 752	3 603	3 596	3 484	3 502	3 575	3 783	3 863	3 837	3 949
Males	KANX	2 760	2 672	2 569	2 569	2 474	2 509	2 557	2 705	2 784	2 753	2 794
Females	KANY	1 048	1 080	1 035	1 026	1 010	993	1 018	1 078	1 079	1 083	1 155
Employee jobs	KANZ	23 325	23 866	24 176	24 503	25 048	25 357	25 437	25 494	25 707	26 083	26 365
Males	KAOA	11 337	11 791	12 110	12 444	12 651	12 829	12 788	12 876	12 903	13 056	13 281
Females	KAOB	11 989	12 075	12 067	12 059	12 397	12 528	12 649	12 618	12 804	13 026	13 084
of whom												
Total, production and construction industries	KAOC	5 158	5 256	5 382	5 239	5 205	5 051	4 813	4 614	4 461	4 339	4 324
Total, all manufacturing industries	KAOD	4 034	4 083	4 101	3 954	3 855	3 703	3 501	3 318	3 157	3 013	2 913
Government-supported trainees	KAOE	178	157	117	120	110	92	84	86	102	90	59
Males	KAOF	109	96	67	73	67	57	50	51	60	54	34
Females	KAOG	69	61	50	47	43	35	34	35	42	36	25

Note. Because the figures have been rounded independently totals may differ from the sum of the components. Also the totals may include some employees whose industrial classification could not be ascertained.

1 The data in this table have not been adjusted to reflect the 2001 Census population data. See chapter text.

2 All figures have been revised. For further information see: http://www.statistics.gov.uk/cci/article.asp?id=1340

Source: Earnings and Employment Division, Office for National Statistics: 01633 812318

7.5 Employee jobs: by industry[1,2]
Standard Industrial Classification 1992
At June each year. Not seasonally adjusted

Thousands

		SIC 1992	United Kingdom							Great Britain					
			2001	2002	2003	2004	2005	2006		2001	2002	2003	2004	2005	2006
All sections	KAOH	A - O	25 984	26 081	26 146	26 358	26 747	27 035	LMAB	25 334	25 417	25 473	25 678	26 053	26 335
Index of production and construction industries	KAOI	C - F	5 185	4 943	4 738	4 583	4 460	4 445	LMAH	5 042	4 805	4 606	4 452	4 331	4 315
Index of production industries	KAOJ	C - E	4 009	3 797	3 594	3 413	3 255	3 157	LMAF	3 902	3 694	3 497	3 320	3 163	3 066
of which, manufacturing industries	KAOK	D	3 802	3 597	3 409	3 245	3 100	2 999	KAPQ	3 700	3 499	3 317	3 156	3 013	2 913
Service industries	KAOL	G - O	20 521	20 882	21 179	21 550	22 048	22 364	LMAJ	20 028	20 371	20 654	21 014	21 497	21 805
Agriculture, hunting and forestry and fishing	KAOM	A/B	279	256	228	226	239	227	KAPS	264	242	213	211	226	215
Agriculture hunting and forestry	KPHI	A	270	246	221	219	233	220	KOVW	255	231	207	204	220	208
Agriculture hunting & related activities	KPHJ	01	259	235	210	209	223	211	KOVX	245	221	196	195	210	199
Fishing	KPHK	B	9	10	7	7	5	7	KOVY	9	10	7	7	5	7
Mining and quarrying	KPHL	C	72	68	62	58	57	58	KOVZ	70	66	60	56	55	56
Mining and quarrying of energy producing materials	KPHM	CA	43	41	38	35	34	36	KOWA	43	41	37	35	34	36
Mining	KAPG	10/12	..	..	..	..	..	..	KOWB	13	12	10	9	7	7
Extraction of crude petroleum	KPHN	11	..	..	..	..	..	..	KOWC	30	29	27	25	27	29
Mining and quarrying except of energy producing materials	KPHO	CB(13/14)	29	27	24	23	23	22	KOWD	28	25	23	22	21	20
Energy and water supply industries	KAOO	C/E	207	200	185	168	154	158	LMAM	202	195	180	163	149	153
Manufacturing	KPHP	D	3 802	3 597	3 409	3 245	3 100	2 999	LMAD	3 700	3 499	3 317	3 156	3 013	2 913
Manufacture of food products Beverages and tobacco	KPHQ	DA	478	464	456	443	429	421	LMAN	459	445	437	424	410	402
Of food	KPHR	151 to 158	..	..	..	..	..	..	KOWH	406	393	387	375	365	358
Of beverages and tobacco	KPHS	159/16	..	..	..	..	..	..	KOWI	53	52	50	48	45	44
Manufacture of textiles and textile products	KPHT	DB	224	193	163	142	124	114	KOWJ	210	181	154	135	119	110
Of textiles	KPHU	17	135	119	106	95	84	78	KOWK	127	113	101	90	81	76
Of made-up textile articles except apparel	KPHV	174	..	..	..	..	..	..	KOWL	34	33	31	29	27	27
Of textiles excluding made-up textile	KPHW	Rest of 17	..	..	..	..	..	..	KOWM	93	80	70	61	54	49
Of wearing apparel,dressing and dyeing of fur	KPHX	18	89	74	57	47	39	36	KOWN	83	69	54	45	38	35
Manufacture of leather and leather products including footwear	KPHY	DC	21	18	14	12	11	9	KOWO	20	18	14	12	11	9
Of leather and leather goods	KPHZ	191/192	..	..	..	..	..	..	KOWP	9	8	6	6	5	5
Of footwear	KPIA	193	..	..	..	..	..	..	KOWQ	11	10	8	6	5	4
Manufacture of wood and wood products	KPIB	DD(20)	82	83	83	83	81	80	LMAP	78	80	79	79	77	76
Manufacture of pulp paper and paper products, publishing and printing	KPIC	DE	451	440	426	412	400	386	LMAQ	445	434	420	406	394	380
Of pulp paper and paper products	KPID	21	95	89	87	82	77	73	KOWT	93	87	85	80	76	71
Publishing printing and reproduction of recorded media	KPIE	22	356	351	339	330	322	313	KOWU	352	346	335	326	318	309
Manufacture of coke refined petroleum products and nuclear fuel	KPIF	DF(23)	28	26	25	24	21	19	KOWV	27	26	25	23	21	19
Manufacture of chemicals, chemical products and man-made fibres	KPIG	DG(24)	234	233	226	210	198	191	LMAR	230	229	222	207	195	188
Manufacture of rubber and plastics	KPIH	DH(25)	228	221	214	212	203	191	LMAS	221	214	206	205	196	184
Manufacture of other non-metallic mineral products	KPII	DI(26)	134	127	121	118	111	106	KOWZ	129	121	115	112	105	100
Manufacture of basic metals and fabricated metal products	KPIJ	DJ	491	462	443	417	398	392	KOXA	484	455	436	409	391	384
Of basic metals	KPIK	27	108	98	92	81	74	74	KOXB	108	97	91	81	73	73
except machinery	KPIL	28	383	364	351	335	324	318	KOXC	377	358	344	328	317	311

7.5

Employee jobs: by industry[1,2]
Standard Industrial Classification 1992
At June each year. Not seasonally adjusted

Thousands

		SIC 1992	United Kingdom						Great Britain					
			2001	2002	2003	2004	2005	2006	2001	2002	2003	2004	2005	2006
Manufacture of Machinery and Equipment not elsewhere classified	KPIM	DK(29)	348	326	301	285	280	273 LMAU	341	320	294	279	273	266
Manufacture of electrical and optical equipment	KPIN	DL	481	426	380	351	333	318 LMAV	468	415	370	341	324	309
Of office machinery and computers	KPIO	30	50	42	37	33	30	28 KOXF	48	40	34	30	28	25
Of electrical machinery and apparatus	KPIP	31	169	153	138	127	122	116 KOXG	166	150	135	123	118	113
Of electric motors etc control apparatus and insulated cable	KPIQ	311 to 313	..	..	..	..	..	.. KOXH	96	86	74	66	63	61
Of accumulators, primary cells, batteries, lamps and electrical equipment	KPIR	314 to 316	..	..	..	..	..	.. KOXI	70	64	61	58	56	52
Radio television and communication equipment	KPIS	32	126	99	81	74	66	59 KOXJ	120	95	79	72	64	57
Of electronic components	KPIT	321	..	..	..	..	..	.. KOXK	40	33	29	29	27	24
Of radio TV and telephone apparatus, sound and video recorders	KPIU	322/323	..	..	..	..	..	.. KOXL	80	62	49	42	37	33
Of medical precision and optical equipment, watches	KPIV	33	135	131	124	118	115	115 KOXM	134	130	122	116	114	114
Manufacture of transport equipment	KPIW	DM	388	371	356	343	330	323 LMAW	375	358	345	333	320	314
Of motor vehicles and trailers	KPIX	34	212	210	205	196	184	177 KOXO	207	206	200	193	180	174
Of other transport equipment	KPIY	35	176	160	151	146	146	146 KOXP	168	153	145	140	140	139
Manufacturing not elsewhere classified	KPIZ	DN(36/37)	215	207	203	197	182	177 KOXQ	211	203	199	193	178	173
Electricity gas and water supply	KPJA	E	135	132	123	110	98	100 KOXR	132	129	120	107	95	97
Electricity gas steam and hot water supply	KPJB	40	..	..	..	..	..	.. KOXT	97	95	90	82	71	74
Collection purification and distribution of water	KPJC	41	..	..	..	..	..	.. KOXU	35	33	30	25	23	23
Construction	KPJD	F(45)	1 176	1 147	1 145	1 169	1 206	1 288 LMAY	1 140	1 110	1 109	1 133	1 168	1 249
Services	KPJE	G - O	20 521	20 882	21 179	21 550	22 048	22 364 KOXX	20 028	20 371	20 654	21 014	21 497	21 805
Wholesale and retail trade; Repair of motor vehicles, motorcycles and personal household goods	KPJF	G (50 - 52)	4 485	4 536	4 535	4 562	4 597	4 598 LMAZ	4 379	4 424	4 422	4 445	4 478	4 477
Sale maintenance and repair of motor vehicles, retail of automotive fuel	KPJG	50	565	572	563	561	565	569 KOXZ	550	557	548	546	550	554
Sale of motor vehicles, motorcycles and parts, motorcycle repair and sale of automotive fuel	KPJH	501/503 - 505	..	..	..	..	..	.. KOYA	333	338	329	327	331	331
Maintenance and repair of motor vehicles	KPJI	502	..	..	..	..	..	.. KOYB	165	166	167	168	170	175
Wholesale trade and commission trade except motor vehicles	KPJJ	51	1 159	1 134	1 127	1 119	1 133	1 141 KOYC	1 136	1 111	1 104	1 095	1 110	1 117
Wholesale on a fee of contract basis	KPJK	511	..	..	..	..	..	.. KOYD	60	56	59	60	62	66
Wholesale agricultural raw materials and live animals	KPJL	512	..	..	..	..	..	.. KPLD	24	23	23	23	22	20
Wholesale food beverages & tobacco	KPJM	513	..	..	..	..	..	.. KPLE	192	189	190	188	190	194
Wholesale household goods	KPJN	514	..	..	..	..	..	.. KPLF	270	266	264	267	274	273
Wholesale of non-agricultural intermediate products waste & scrap	KPJO	515	..	..	..	..	..	.. KPLG	233	235	232	232	232	231
Wholesale machinery eqpt. & supplies	KPJP	516	..	..	..	..	..	.. KPLH	251	243	238	230	239	241
Other wholesale	KPJQ	517	..	..	..	..	..	.. KPLI	106	100	98	95	91	91
Retail trade except of motor vehicles and motorcycles;repair of personal and household goods	KPJR	52	2 762	2 829	2 845	2 882	2 899	2 888 KPLJ	2 692	2 756	2 770	2 804	2 819	2 807
Non-specialised stores selling mainly food beverages & tobacco	KPJS	5211/5221-4,5227	..	..	..	..	..	.. KPLK	1 083	1 144	1 143	1 120	1 138	1 130
Other non-specialised stores second hand shops & sales not in stores	KPJT	5212/525-526	..	..	..	..	..	.. KPLL	379	367	365	360	353	351

7.5 Employee jobs: by industry[1,2]
Standard Industrial Classification 1992
continued At June each year. Not seasonally adjusted

Thousands

		SIC 1992	United Kingdom							Great Britain					
			2001	2002	2003	2004	2005	2006		2001	2002	2003	2004	2005	2006
Alcoholic & other beverages, tobacco	KPJU	5225 to 5226	..	..	..	..	..	..	KPLM	68	64	56	54	49	46
Pharmaceutical & medical goods cosmetics & toilet articles	KPJV	523	..	..	..	..	..	..	KPLN	92	96	93	99	103	107
Clothing footwear & leather goods	KPJW	5242/5243	..	..	..	..	..	..	KPLO	355	340	369	409	415	425
Textile furniture lighting equipment electrical household appliances radio and TV paints glass hardware and household goods not elsewhere classified	KPJX	5241/5244-46	..	..	..	..	..	..	KPLP	291	303	296	304	299	295
Books newspapers and stationery, other retail in specialised stores	KPJY	5247/5248	..	..	..	..	..	..	KPLQ	400	416	421	432	435	430
Repair of personal and household goods	KPJZ	527	..	..	..	..	..	..	KPLR	24	26	27	26	26	22
Hotels and restaurants	KPKA	H	1 698	1 749	1 792	1 839	1 855	1 839	LMBA	1 660	1 708	1 751	1 798	1 814	1 796
Hotels camp sites short-stay accom.	KPKB	551/552	..	..	..	..	..	..	KPLT	370	365	369	379	387	378
Restaurants	KPKC	553	..	..	..	..	..	..	KPLU	509	547	575	594	614	617
Bars	KPKD	554	..	..	..	..	..	..	KPLV	525	531	540	558	552	549
Canteens and catering	KPKE	555	..	..	..	..	..	..	KPLW	256	265	267	267	261	252
Transport, storage and communication	KPKF	I	1 589	1 581	1 587	1 570	1 597	1 601	KPLX	1 562	1 553	1 559	1 542	1 567	1 572
Land transport, transport via pipelines	KPKG	60	522	518	518	519	534	550	KPLY	510	506	505	505	521	536
Transport via railways	KPKH	601	..	..	..	..	..	..	KPLZ	50	49	49	50	53	52
Other land transport and via pipelines	KPKI	602/603	..	..	..	..	..	..	KPMA	461	457	457	456	468	484
Water transport	KPKJ	61	17	18	17	17	19	20	KPMB	17	17	16	17	18	19
Air transport	KPKK	62	93	88	90	85	90	91	KPMC	92	87	90	85	89	90
Supporting and auxiliary transport activities, activities of travel agents	KPKL	63	403	403	412	440	453	448	KPMD	398	398	406	435	447	442
Travel agencies and tour operators	KPKM	633	..	..	..	..	..	..	KPME	132	128	124	133	120	106
Post and telecommunications	KPKN	64	555	554	551	509	500	494	LMBC	545	545	542	500	491	484
National post and courier activities	KPKO	641	..	..	..	..	..	..	KPMG	300	295	297	275	275	267
Telecommunications	KPKR	6420	..	..	..	..	..	..	KPMJ	246	249	245	225	216	218
Financial intermediation	KPKS	J	1 088	1 112	1 104	1 073	1 067	1 068	LMBD	1 072	1 095	1 087	1 056	1 049	1 050
Financial intermediation except insurance and pension funding	KPKT	65	616	638	639	621	616	610	KPML	605	627	627	609	603	597
Insurance and pension funding except compulsory social security	KPKU	66	228	223	215	197	183	179	KPMM	226	221	213	196	181	176
Activities auxiliary to financial intermediation	KPKV	67	244	251	249	255	268	280	KPMN	241	248	246	252	265	276
Except insurance and pension funding	KPKW	671	..	..	..	..	..	..	KPMO	107	111	113	123	136	144
Auxiliary to insurance and pension funding	KPKX	672	..	..	..	..	..	..	KPMP	134	137	133	129	129	133
Real estate renting & business activities	KPKY	K	3 933	3 956	3 996	4 129	4 338	4 507	KPMQ	3 881	3 901	3 938	4 065	4 270	4 439
Real estate activities	KPKZ	70	364	369	381	409	450	492	LMBE	360	365	378	402	443	484
Activities with own property, letting of own property	KPLA	701/702	..	..	..	..	..	..	KPMS	219	218	224	236	252	273
Activities on a fee or contract basis	KPLB	703	..	..	..	..	..	..	KPMT	141	147	154	166	190	211

7.5 Employee jobs: by industry[1,2]
Standard Industrial Classification 1992
continued   At June each year. Not seasonally adjusted

Thousand

	SIC 1992	United Kingdom							Great Britain					
		2001	2002	2003	2004	2005	2006		2001	2002	2003	2004	2005	2006
Renting of machinery and equipment without operator & of personal & household goods KPLC	71	156	157	151	153	157	157	KPMU	154	155	149	150	155	154
Construction and civil engineering machinery KOUU	7132	..	..	..	..	..	..	KPMV	45	45	42	41	42	43
All other goods and equipment KOUV	Rest of 71	..	..	..	..	..	..	KPMW	109	110	107	109	113	111
Computer and related equipment KOUW	72	503	494	501	488	493	514	KPMX	497	489	495	482	487	507
Research and development KOUX	73	104	108	106	101	104	107	KPMY	102	106	105	100	103	105
Other business activities KOUY	74	2 806	2 828	2 857	2 978	3 134	3 238	KPMZ	2 767	2 786	2 811	2 930	3 083	3 188
Legal, accounting, book-keeping & auditing activities KOUZ	741	..	..	..	..	..	..	KPNA	..	..	..	840	890	938
Legal activities KOVA	7411	..	..	..	..	..	..	KPNB	240	248	250	254	260	273
Accounting, book-keeping auditing, tax consultancy KOVB	7412	..	..	..	..	..	..	KPNC	207	195	191	194	203	219
Market research business and consultancy activities KOVC	7413/7414	..	..	..	..	..	..	KPND	246	270	272	291	317	337
Management activities of holding companies[3] KOVD	7415	..	..	..	..	..	..	KPNE	..	..	..	101	110	108
Architectural engineering activities and related technical consultancy, technical testing KOVE	742/743	..	..	..	..	..	..	KPNF	331	332	332	340	347	360
Advertising KOVF	744	..	..	..	..	..	..	KPNG	93	87	83	80	84	81
Industrial cleaning KOVG	747	..	..	..	..	..	..	KPNH	425	418	418	414	436	448
Public administration and defence, compulsory social security KOVH	L(75)	1 379	1 416	1 469	1 496	1 520	1 519	LMBG	1 320	1 356	1 406	1 435	1 460	1 459
Education KOVI	M(80)	2 104	2 151	2 233	2 311	2 359	2 414	LMBH	2 038	2 083	2 164	2 242	2 286	2 340
Health and social work KOVJ	N	2 896	2 989	3 081	3 182	3 298	3 365	LOJV	2 799	2 889	2 976	3 074	3 188	3 253
Human health, veterinary activities KOVK	851/852	..	..	..	..	..	..	KPNL	1 805	1 890	1 965	2 027	2 101	2 129
Social work activities KOVL	853	..	..	..	..	..	..	KPNM	994	999	1 011	1 047	1 087	1 124
Other community social and personal service activities, private households with employed persons, extra-territorial organisations and bodies KOVM	O	1 348	1 392	1 383	1 388	1 417	1 451	LMBK	1 319	1 362	1 351	1 357	1 385	1 420
Sewage and refuse disposal; sanitation KOVN	90	109	105	96	100	104	108	KPNO	106	103	93	97	101	105
Activities of membership organisations KOVO	91	215	226	224	212	215	220	KPNP	207	218	216	204	206	212
Recreational cultural and sporting activities KOVP	92	705	730	741	762	779	798	KPNQ	690	715	725	747	764	783
Motion picture video radio TV news agencies and entertainment activities KOVQ	921 to 924	..	..	..	..	..	..	KPNR	215	226	220	224	222	232
Libraries, museums, cultural and recreational activities GL7E	925 to 927	..	..	..	..	..	..	GL7F	476	489	506	522	542	551
Other service activities, private households with employed persons, extra territorial organisations KOVT	93/95/99	319	330	322	314	318	325	KPNU	315	325	317	309	313	320
Washing, dry cleaning of textile and fur products KOVU	9301	..	..	..	..	..	..	KPNV	48	46	46	42	40	42
Hairdressing, other beauty treatment, physical and well-being activities KOVV	9302/9304	..	..	..	..	..	..	KPNW	100	102	104	105	114	119

Note. Because the figures have been rounded independently totals may differ from the sum of the components. Also the totals may include some employees whose industrial classification could not be ascertained.

1 See chapter text. The data in this table have not been adjusted to reflect the 2001 Census population data.

2 All figures have been revised. For further information see: http://www.statistics.gov.uk/cci/article.asp?id=1340

3 Head office and holding company local units were reclassified to Class 74.15 (within Section K) from December 2003 as a result of the SIC 2003 update.

Source: Earnings and Employment Division, ONS: 01633 812318

7.6 Weekly hours worked: by sex[1,2]
United Kingdom
At Quarter 2 each year[3]. Seasonally adjusted

Hours

| | All workers' weekly hours[4,5] | | Average actual weekly hours of work[5] | | |
	Total (millions)	Average	Full-time employment[4,6]	Part-time employment[6]	Second jobs[7]
All Persons					
	YBUS	YBUV	YBUY	YBVB	YBVE
1996	863.9	33.3	38.8	15.1	8.9
1997	877.2	33.2	38.6	15.2	9.4
1998	884.5	33.2	38.6	15.2	9.2
1999	890.3	32.9	38.2	15.3	9.0
2000	895.2	32.7	38.0	15.4	9.0
2001	906.0	32.8	38.0	15.7	9.3
2002	897.8	32.2	37.4	15.5	9.4
2003	908.0	32.2	37.5	15.6	9.2
2004	908.1	32.0	37.3	15.6	8.8
2005	918.2	32.0	37.2	15.7	9.6
2006	926.3	32.1	37.2	15.6	9.5
Male					
	YBUT	YBUW	YBUZ	YBVC	YBVF
1996	551.6	39.1	40.9	14.9	10.0
1997	558.7	38.8	40.6	15.0	10.6
1998	563.0	38.7	40.6	14.8	9.8
1999	562.2	38.3	40.2	15.1	9.8
2000	564.7	38.0	39.9	15.1	9.7
2001	568.7	38.0	39.9	15.5	10.2
2002	558.8	37.1	39.2	15.0	10.3
2003	567.0	37.1	39.2	15.5	10.2
2004	566.2	36.9	39.1	15.4	9.7
2005	569.6	36.8	39.0	15.6	10.6
2006	571.6	36.7	38.9	15.4	10.2
Female					
	YBUU	YBUX	YBVA	YBVD	YBVG
1996	312.3	26.4	34.7	15.1	8.2
1997	318.5	26.4	34.5	15.3	8.4
1998	321.4	26.5	34.6	15.3	8.8
1999	328.1	26.6	34.5	15.4	8.5
2000	330.5	26.3	34.2	15.5	8.5
2001	337.3	26.6	34.3	15.7	8.7
2002	339.1	26.4	34.1	15.7	8.7
2003	341.0	26.5	34.2	15.7	8.6
2004	341.9	26.2	33.8	15.7	8.1
2005	348.6	26.4	33.8	15.7	8.8
2006	354.8	26.6	34.0	15.7	8.9

1 See chapter text. In August 2006, ONS published the mid-year population estimates for 2005. These estimates have now been incorporated into the LFS estimates from Autumn 2004. Further details can be found at http://www.statistics.gov.uk/cci/article.asp?id=1647

2 Average hours actually worked in the reference week which includes hours worked in second jobs.

3 The Labour Force Survey has now moved to calendar quarters from May 2006. More information can be found on page 5 of the Concepts and Definitions.pdf by following this link:- www.statistics.gov.uk/downloads/theme_labour/Concepts_Definitions_HQS.pdf

4 Main and second job.

5 Includes both paid and unpaid overtime.

6 People whose main job is full-time or part-time and based on respondents' self assessment.

7 Second jobs reported in the LFS in addition to persons' main full time job.

Sources: Labour Force Survey, Office for National Statistics;
Helpline: 020-7533 6094

7.7 Civil Service staff: by ministerial responsibility[1,2]
At 1 April each year

Full-time equivalents (thousands)[3]

		1994	1995	1996	1997	1998	1999	2000	2001	2002	2003	2004
Agriculture, Fisheries and Food	BCDA	11.0	10.6	10.8	10.1	10.8	11.7	10.8	11.4	..	..	..
Cabinet Office	BBGD	12	12	12	8	8	8	7	7	7	7	7
Chancellor of the Exchequer's Departments:												
Customs and Excise	BCDC	25.0	24.1	23.2	23.1	23.4	22.5	21.9	21.7	21.8	22.2	22.6
Inland Revenue	BCDD	64.0	59.1	56.5	54.4	53.4	61.3	66.3	66.9	68.2	75.6	80.1
Department for National Savings	BCDE	6.0	5.4	4.7	4.3	4.1	0.1	0.1	0.1	0.1	0.1	0.1
Treasury and others	BCDF	5.0	4.3	6.0	5.1	5.1	5.0	5.5	5.5	5.6	5.8	6.1
Total	BCDB	99.0	92.9	90.3	86.8	86.0	89.0	93.8	94.2	95.7	103.7	108.9
Culture, Media and Sport	DMTC	..	..	..	..	1	1	1	1	1	1	1
Education	BCDG	2.0	2.5	..	..	..	..	..	..	..	..	..
Education and Employment	BBFT	..	..	40.8	34.1	33.6	34.6	36.5	38.3	..	..	..
Education and Skills	LNFW	..	..	..	..	..	..	..	..	7	8	8
Environment	BCDJ	10.0	9.4	10.9	9.6	..	..	..	..	..	..	..
Environment, Food and Rural Affairs	LNFX	..	..	..	..	..	..	..	..	15	15	15
Environment, Transport and the Regions	CKUZ	..	..	..	..	21.2	21.8	23.2	25.4	..	..	..
Foreign and Commonwealth	BCDK	8	8	7	7	5	6	6	6	6	6	6
Health	BAKR	7	6	5	5	5	5	7	7	5	5	4
Home	BCDL	51	51	51	50	51	50	54	60	61	66	70
International Development	DMUA	..	..	..	..	1	1	1	1	2	2	2
Legal Departments	BBGE	29.0	28.7	27.8	26.3	25.4	25.5	24.9	25.0	26.9	28.2	28.8
National Heritage	BBGF	1.0	1.0	1.0	1.0	..	..	..	..	..	..	..
Northern Ireland	BBGG	..	–	–	–	–	–	–	–	–	–	–
Office of the Deputy Prime Minister	YEGA	..	..	..	..	..	..	..	..	..	5	5
Scotland	BCDN	13.0	12.1	11.7	11.8	12.0	12.5	13.6	13.7	14.3	14.8	15.3
Social Security	BAKS	90.0	89.2	91.5	93.1	87.2	81.6	83.5	81.9	..	..	..
Trade and Industry	BCDQ	11	11	11	10	10	11	11	11	12	12	12
Transport	BCDR	14	13	11	11	..	..	..	..	..	21	16
Transport, Local Government and the Regions	LNFZ	..	..	..	..	..	..	..	..	23.9	..	..
Welsh Office	BCDS	2.0	2.2	2.1	2.2	2.1	2.3	2.7	3.2	3.5	3.7	4.4
Work and Pensions	LNGA	..	..	..	..	..	..	..	..	122	124	129
Total civil departments	BCDU	418.0	400.8	384.6	366.3	359.1	359.1	375.1	384.4	401.2	420.0	432.2
Defence	BCDW	122	116	110	109	104	101	100	98	89	91	91
Total all departments	BCDX	540	517	495	476	463	460	475	483	490	511	524
of which												
Non-industrial staff	BCDY	494.0	474.1	458.7	439.6	430.5	429.2	446.0	453.8	462.9	490.2	503.6
Industrial staff	BCDZ	46.0	42.0	35.9	36.0	32.8	30.8	29.4	28.9	27.3	21.1	20.0

1 The figures include non-industrial and industrial staff but exclude casual or seasonal staff and employees of the Northern Ireland Civil Service.
2 A comprehensive list of Machinery of Government changes is listed on the Cabinet Office's web site at: *www.civil-service.gov.uk/statistics*
3 Figures included are measured as 'full-time equivalent' staff. Part-time staff are recorded as a proportion of full-time employees according to the proportion of a full week that they work.

Source: Cabinet Office: 020 7276 1532

7.8 Civil Service employment by department[1,2]
As at 31 March each year

Full-time equivalents, Great Britain, not seasonally adjusted

		2005	2006
Attorney General's Departments	GB3F	9 150	9 340
Cabinet Office	BBGD	1 990	1 740
Other Cabinet Office Agencies	GB3G	720	750
HM Treasury	GB3H	1 140	1 190
Chancellor's other departments	GB3I	10 830	5 510
Charity Commission	GB3J	560	500
Communities and Local Government	YEGA	6 090	5 710
Constitutional Affairs	GB3K	21 670	22 000
Culture, Media and Sport	DMTC	660	640
Defence	BCDW	91 930	87 900
Education and Skills	LNFW	4 750	4 320
Environment, Food and Rural Affairs	LNFX	13 750	13 370
Export Credits Guarantee Department	GB3L	330	280
Foreign and Commonwealth	BCDK	6 420	6 190
Health	BAKR	6 150	6 350
HM Revenue and Customs	GB3M	97 820	98 840
Home Office	BCDL	73 490	72 140
International Development	DMUA	1 890	1 800
Northern Ireland Office	BBGG	160	140
Office for Standards in Education	GB3N	2 450	2 450
Security and Intelligence Services	GB3O	4 780	4 880
Trade and Industry	BCDQ	11 380	10 830
Transport	BCDR	17 350	18 560
Work and Pensions	LNGA	124 190	118 710
Central Governments Departments Total	GB3P	509 650	494 150
Scottish Executive	GB3Q	15 950	15 850
Welsh Assembly	GB3R	4 130	4 040
TOTAL	BCDX	529 730	514 030
HM Court Service (former Magistrates Service)	GO36	–	10 990
Central Government Departments Total (including former Magistrates Service)	GO37	509 650	505 140
TOTAL (including former Magistrates Service)	GO38	529 730	525 020

1 Numbers are rounded to the nearest ten.
2 See chapter text.

Source: Office for National Statistics

7.9 Unemployment: number by sex and age group[1]
United Kingdom
At Quarter 2 each year[2]. Seasonally adjusted

Thousands

	All aged 16 and over	16-59/64	16-17	18-24	25-34	35-49	50-64 (m) 50-59 (w)	65+ (m) 60+ (w)
All Persons								
	MGSC	YBSH	YBVH	YBVN	YCGM	YCGS	MGVL	MGVO
2000	1 599	1 582	165	388	366	407	255	18
2001	1 472	1 458	152	377	340	387	202	14
2002	1 515	1 493	161	386	341	385	220	22
2003	1 464	1 446	176	400	310	345	215	18
2004	1 433	1 416	173	403	290	353	197	17
2005	1 433	1 416	176	436	276	335	193	17
2006	1 683	1 656	179	520	331	415	211	27
Male								
	MGSD	YBSI	YBVI	YBVO	YCGN	YCGT	MGVM	MGVP
2000	957	951	90	234	212	233	183	..
2001	882	875	91	221	203	213	147	..
2002	910	900	92	242	192	225	149	10
2003	886	876	98	243	174	213	147	..
2004	841	832	98	231	177	187	139	..
2005	833	826	100	262	153	183	127	..
2006	975	963	104	313	182	228	137	11
Female								
	MGSE	YBSJ	YBVJ	YBVP	YCGO	YCGU	MGVN	MGVQ
2000	642	631	76	154	155	175	73	11
2001	591	584	62	156	138	174	55	..
2002	606	593	69	145	149	160	70	13
2003	578	569	78	157	135	131	68	..
2004	592	583	74	172	113	166	58	..
2005	599	590	76	173	124	151	66	..
2006	708	692	74	207	149	187	74	16

1 See chapter text. In August 2006, ONS published the mid-year population estimates for 2005. These estimates have now been incorporated into the LFS estimates from Autumn 2004. Further details can be found at http://www.statistics.gov.uk/cci/article.asp?id=1647
2 The LFS has now moved to calendar quarters from May 2006. More

information is on page 5 of the Concepts and Definitions.pdf : www.statistics.gov.uk/downloads/theme_labour/Concepts_Definitions_HQS.pdf
Source: LFS, Office for National Statistics; Helpline: 020-7533 6094

7.10 Unemployment: percentage by sex and age group[1,2]
United Kingdom
At Quarter 2 each year[3]. Seasonally adjusted

Percentages

	All aged 16 and over	16-59/64	16-17	18-24	25-34	35-49	50-64 (m) 50-59 (w)	65+ (m) 60+ (w)
All Persons								
	MGSX	YBTI	YBVK	YBVQ	YCGP	YCGV	MGXE	MGXH
2000	5.5	5.6	19.7	10.7	5.1	3.9	4.2	2.1
2001	5.0	5.1	18.5	10.2	4.8	3.7	3.3	1.6
2002	5.2	5.2	19.9	10.2	5.0	3.6	3.5	2.4
2003	4.9	5.0	21.3	10.6	4.6	3.2	3.3	1.9
2004	4.8	4.9	21.5	10.3	4.4	3.2	3.0	1.7
2005	4.8	4.9	21.9	11.0	4.2	3.0	2.9	1.6
2006	5.5	5.6	24.1	12.7	5.0	3.7	3.2	2.3
Male								
	MGSY	YBTJ	YBVL	YBVR	YCGQ	YCGW	MGXF	MGXI
2000	6.0	6.1	21.3	12.1	5.3	4.1	5.1	..
2001	5.6	5.6	21.6	11.2	5.2	3.8	4.0	..
2002	5.7	5.7	22.2	12.0	5.1	3.9	4.0	3.2
2003	5.5	5.5	23.5	12.0	4.7	3.6	3.8	..
2004	5.2	5.3	24.3	11.1	4.9	3.2	3.6	..
2005	5.1	5.2	24.7	12.4	4.3	3.1	3.3	..
2006	5.9	6.0	28.4	14.4	5.1	3.8	3.4	2.8
Female								
	MGSZ	YBTK	YBVM	YBVS	YCGR	YCGX	MGXG	MGXJ
2000	4.9	5.0	18.1	9.1	4.7	3.6	3.0	1.9
2001	4.4	4.6	15.4	9.0	4.3	3.5	2.2	..
2002	4.5	4.6	17.6	8.2	4.8	3.2	2.8	2.1
2003	4.3	4.4	19.0	8.9	4.5	2.6	2.6	..
2004	4.3	4.5	18.6	9.5	3.8	3.2	2.2	..
2005	4.3	4.5	19.1	9.5	4.1	2.9	2.5	..
2006	5.0	5.2	19.9	10.9	5.0	3.5	2.8	2.1

Note: Where figure denoted as .. it is not shown as it is based on a small sample size and is subject to a margin of uncertainty.

1 See chapter text. In August 2006, ONS published the mid-year population estimates for 2005. These estimates have now been incorporated into the LFS estimates from Autumn 2004. Further details can be found at http://www.statistics.gov.uk/cci/article.asp?id=1647

2 Total unemployment as a percentage of all economically active persons in the relevant age group.

3 The Labour Force Survey has now moved to calendar quarters from May 2006. More information can be found on page 5 of the Concepts and Definitions.pdf by following this link:- www.statistics.gov.uk/downloads/theme_labour/Concepts_Definitions_HQS.pdf

Sources: Labour Force Survey, Office for National Statistics;
Helpline: 020-7533 6094

7.11 Duration of unemployment: by sex[1,2]
United Kingdom
At Quarter 2 each year[3]. Seasonally adjusted

Thousands

		1996	1997	1998	1999	2000	2001	2002	2003	2004	2005	2006
All Persons												
All unemployed[4]	MGSC	2 336	2 048	1 788	1 743	1 599	1 472	1 515	1 464	1 433	1 433	1 683
Duration of unemployment												
Less than 6 months	YBWF	1 049	1 009	980	986	920	878	977	947	922	911	1 024
6 months & less than 1 year	YBWG	388	298	252	268	240	219	218	205	227	215	303
1 year or more	YBWH	899	741	556	490	439	376	320	312	284	307	356
1 year or more as % of total	YBWI	38.5	36.2	31.1	28.1	27.5	25.5	21.1	21.3	19.8	21.5	21.2
Male												
All unemployed[4]	MGSD	1 517	1 265	1 074	1 059	957	882	910	886	841	833	975
Duration of unemployment												
Less than 6 months	MGYK	591	550	518	536	500	481	536	537	503	487	546
6 months & less than 1 year	MGYM	246	178	160	165	140	131	147	131	141	137	177
1 year or more	MGYO	680	538	396	359	317	269	227	218	197	209	252
1 year or more as % of total	YBWJ	44.8	42.5	36.9	33.9	33.1	30.5	24.9	24.6	23.5	25.1	25.8
Female												
All unemployed[4]	MGSE	820	783	715	684	642	591	606	578	592	599	708
Duration of unemployment												
Less than 6 months	MGYL	458	459	462	450	420	396	441	410	419	424	477
6 months & less than 1 year	MGYN	143	121	93	102	100	87	71	74	86	77	126
1 year or more	MGYP	220	203	160	131	122	107	94	94	86	98	105
1 year or more as % of total	YBWK	26.8	26.0	22.4	19.2	19.0	18.1	15.4	16.3	14.6	16.3	14.8

1 All aged 16 and over. See chapter text.
2 In August 2006, ONS published the mid-year population estimates for 2005. These estimates have now been incorporated into the LFS estimates from Autumn 2004. Further details can be found at http://www.statistics.gov.uk/cci/article.asp?id=1647
3 The Labour Force Survey has now moved to calendar quarters from May 2006. More information can be found on page 5 of the Concepts and Definitions.pdf by following this link:- www.statistics.gov.uk/downloads/theme_labour/Concepts_Definitions_HQS.pdf
4 Totals include people who did not state their duration of unemployment.

Sources: Labour Force Survey, Office for National Statistics;
Helpline: 020-7533 6094

7.12 Claimant count:[1] by age and duration
Computerised claims only
United Kingdom. Seasonally adjusted

Thousands

		2000	2001	2002	2003	2004	2005	2006
Annual averages								
Males								
All ages								
All durations	AGNG	826.1	733.6	708.3	693.0	630.9	635.1	693.6
Up to 6 months	AGXK	481.4	449.4	457.4	451.2	408.9	423.4	438.5
Over 6 and up to 12 months	ELNP	142.7	125.4	124.2	127.1	113.7	113.3	136.3
All over 12 months	ELON	202.0	158.8	126.7	114.7	108.3	98.3	118.8
All over 24 months	IKBS	102.4	77.5	50.7	37.6	34.6	33.1	34.4
Aged 18 to 24								
All durations	JLGC	182.3	167.9	168.1	171.9	161.8	174.6	195.5
Up to 6 months	JLGD	149.6	141.4	141.0	143.8	134.3	143.6	155.0
Over 6 and up to 12 months	JLGE	28.3	23.4	23.8	24.5	23.3	25.9	33.0
All over 12 months	JLGF	4.4	3.1	3.3	3.6	4.2	5.0	7.5
All over 24 months	JLGH	0.5	0.3	0.3	0.4	0.5	0.6	0.9
Aged 25 to 49								
All durations	AGMA	506.1	445.9	421.8	404.8	362.4	357.6	387.1
Up to 6 months	JLHG	266.8	248.2	254.9	248.0	221.3	226.0	228.8
Over 6 and up to 12 months	JLHH	92.8	83.1	80.9	82.9	72.9	70.4	83.3
All over 12 months	JLHI	146.5	114.7	86.1	73.8	68.2	61.2	75.0
All over 24 months	JLHK	70.5	52.4	29.2	17.0	14.2	14.2	15.2
Aged 50 and over								
All durations	JLHL	137.7	119.8	118.4	116.3	106.7	103.0	111.0
Up to 6 months	JLHM	65.0	59.9	61.6	59.4	53.2	53.8	54.7
Over 6 and up to 12 months	JLHN	21.6	18.9	19.6	19.7	17.5	17.0	20.0
All over 12 months	JLHO	51.1	41.0	37.3	37.2	35.9	32.1	36.3
All over 24 months	JLHQ	31.5	24.8	21.1	20.2	19.9	18.3	18.4
Females								
All ages								
All durations	JLGI	254.8	227.9	226.8	230.1	214.7	220.0	245.7
Up to 6 months	JLGK	172.5	160.4	163.6	166.3	153.1	159.3	171.3
Over 6 and up to 12 months	JLGJ	40.9	35.1	35.5	37.2	34.9	35.6	43.6
All over 12 months	JLGL	41.4	32.5	27.6	26.5	26.7	25.1	30.8
All over 24 months	JLGN	18.2	13.9	9.7	8.1	8.0	7.9	8.4
Aged 18 to 24								
All durations	JLGO	79.3	73.4	75.0	77.3	73.9	79.0	90.1
Up to 6 months	JLGP	65.7	62.1	62.9	64.9	61.4	65.3	72.2
Over 6 and up to 12 months	JLGQ	11.7	9.8	10.4	10.6	10.5	11.4	14.6
All over 12 months	JLGR	1.9	1.4	1.8	1.8	2.1	2.3	3.3
All over 24 months	JLGT	0.2	0.2	0.2	0.3	0.3	0.4	0.5
Aged 25 to 49								
All durations	JLHR	128.0	113.3	111.4	112.1	102.1	101.8	111.8
Up to 6 months	JLHS	80.8	74.4	76.7	77.3	69.0	70.4	73.6
Over 6 and up to 12 months	JLHT	21.3	18.6	18.5	19.9	18.2	17.7	21.2
All over 12 months	JLHU	25.9	20.4	16.2	14.9	14.9	13.7	16.9
All over 24 months	JLHW	10.9	8.2	4.7	3.1	2.9	3.0	3.3
Aged 50 and over								
All durations	JLHX	47.5	41.3	40.4	40.7	38.7	39.1	43.9
Up to 6 months	JLHY	26.0	23.9	24.1	24.1	22.7	23.6	25.5
Over 6 and up to 12 months	JLHZ	7.9	6.7	6.6	6.8	6.3	6.5	7.8
All over 12 months	JLIA	13.6	10.7	9.7	9.8	9.7	9.1	10.6
All over 24 months	JLIC	7.1	5.5	4.8	4.7	4.8	4.5	4.7

1 Count of claimants of unemployment-related benefits.

Source: Office for National Statistics: 020 7533 6094

7.13 Unemployment rates: by region[1,2,3]
At Quarter 2 each year[4]. Seasonally adjusted[5]

Percentages

		1996	1997	1998	1999	2000	2001	2002	2003	2004	2005	2006
North East	YCNC	10.3	9.8	8.3	9.6	8.9	7.4	6.5	6.1	5.5	6.8	6.1
North West	YCND	8.4	7.1	6.9	6.3	5.3	5.3	5.5	5.0	4.4	4.4	5.3
Yorkshire and The Humber	YCNE	8.4	7.5	7.3	6.3	6.1	5.5	5.3	5.1	4.6	4.8	5.7
East Midlands	YCNF	7.3	5.9	4.9	5.4	4.8	5.0	4.6	4.3	4.2	4.2	5.4
West Midlands	YCNG	9.4	6.8	5.9	6.9	6.1	5.5	5.7	5.6	5.5	4.7	5.7
East	YCNH	6.4	6.3	4.9	4.3	3.7	3.6	3.7	3.9	3.8	3.9	5.0
London	YCNI	11.6	9.3	8.6	7.5	7.4	6.2	6.8	7.2	7.0	7.2	7.9
South East	YCNJ	6.1	5.3	4.4	4.0	3.3	3.2	3.8	3.9	3.7	3.8	4.7
South West	YCNK	6.2	5.8	4.8	4.5	4.3	3.6	3.7	3.4	3.7	3.2	3.7
Wales	YCNM	8.3	8.3	7.0	7.5	6.1	6.1	5.7	4.5	4.2	4.6	5.7
Scotland	YCNN	8.5	8.6	7.4	7.1	7.1	6.3	6.3	5.3	6.0	5.4	5.4
Northern Ireland	ZSFB	10.6	8.1	6.9	7.6	6.7	6.1	5.6	5.2	5.1	4.9	4.2

1 Total unemployed as a percentage of all economically active persons.
2 All aged 16 and over. See chapter text.
3 In August 2006, ONS published the mid-year population estimates for 2005. These estimates have now been incorporated into the LFS estimates from Autumn 2004. Further details can be found at http://www.statistics.gov.uk/cci/article.asp?id=1647
4 The Labour Force Survey has now moved to calendar quarters from May 2006. More information can be found on page 5 of the Concepts and Definitions.pdf by following this link:- www.statistics.gov.uk/downloads/theme_labour/Concepts_Definitions_HQS.pdf
5 Previously not seasonally adjusted data was shown.

Sources: Labour Force Survey, Office for National Statistics;
Helpline: 020-7533 6094

7.14 Claimant count rates: by region[1]
Seasonally adjusted annual averages

Percentages

		1996	1997	1998	1999	2000	2001	2002	2003	2004	2005	2006
United Kingdom	BCJE	6.9	5.3	4.5	4.1	3.6	3.2	3.1	3.0	2.7	2.7	3.0
North East	DPDM	9.7	7.9	7.0	6.9	6.2	5.6	5.0	4.5	4.0	3.9	4.4
North West	IBWC	7.3	5.7	5.0	4.6	4.1	3.7	3.5	3.2	2.8	2.9	3.3
Yorkshire and the Humber	DPBI	7.4	6.0	5.4	5.0	4.3	3.9	3.6	3.3	2.8	2.9	3.4
East Midlands	DPBJ	6.4	4.6	3.9	3.6	3.3	3.1	2.9	2.8	2.5	2.5	3.0
West Midlands	DPBN	6.8	5.2	4.5	4.5	4.0	3.7	3.5	3.5	3.3	3.4	4.0
East	DPDP	5.7	4.0	3.2	2.9	2.4	2.0	2.1	2.1	2.0	2.1	2.3
London	DPDQ	8.3	6.3	5.1	4.5	3.7	3.3	3.6	3.6	3.5	3.4	3.6
South East	DPDR	4.9	3.3	2.6	2.3	1.9	1.6	1.6	1.7	1.6	1.6	1.9
South West	DPBM	5.9	4.2	3.4	3.0	2.5	2.1	1.9	1.9	1.6	1.6	1.8
England	VASQ	6.8	5.1	4.3	3.9	3.4	3.0	2.9	2.9	2.6	2.6	3.0
Wales	DPBP	7.7	6.1	5.4	5.0	4.4	3.9	3.6	3.3	3.0	3.0	3.3
Scotland	DPBQ	7.1	6.0	5.3	5.0	4.5	3.9	3.8	3.7	3.5	3.2	3.3
Northern Ireland	DPBR	10.6	8.0	7.3	6.3	5.3	4.9	4.4	4.1	3.6	3.3	3.3
Great Britain	DPAJ	6.8	5.2	4.4	4.1	3.5	3.1	3.0	3.0	2.7	2.7	3.0

1 The number of unemployment-related benefit claimants as a percentage of the estimated total workforce (the sum of claimants, employee jobs, self-employed, participants on work-related government training programmes and HM Forces) at mid-year. Excluded are claimants under 18, consistent with current coverage. See chapter text.

Source: Office for National Statistics: 020 7533 6094

7.15 Claimant count:[1] by region
Seasonally adjusted

Thousands

	North East	North West	Yorkshire and the Humber	East Midlands	West Midlands	East	London	South East	South West	England	Wales	Scotland	Great Britain	Northern Ireland	United Kingdom
	DPDG	IBWA	DPAX	DPAY	DPBC	DPDJ	DPDK	DPDL	DPBB	IBWK	DPBE	DPBF	DPAG	DPBG	BCJD
1991 Jan	116.7	261.8	176.4	113.1	171.0	112.5	255.8	149.7	122.2	1 478.8	95.0	200.9	1 775.1	96.0	1 871.1
Apr	126.2	285.9	197.5	132.0	203.5	138.5	303.2	190.5	146.9	1 723.9	108.8	212.7	2 045.7	97.9	2 143.6
Jul	130.5	305.4	211.9	145.5	225.4	158.9	342.3	221.3	165.7	1 906.8	115.5	220.1	2 242.5	98.8	2 341.3
Oct	133.2	318.2	219.6	154.5	240.0	172.4	368.9	240.9	178.6	2 025.9	119.3	224.0	2 369.6	100.5	2 470.1
1992 Jan	133.9	325.4	222.7	160.4	250.6	183.3	389.8	258.4	188.4	2 112.6	121.3	228.0	2 462.2	102.2	2 564.4
Apr	135.7	332.8	227.6	168.0	260.0	196.0	409.6	277.7	199.0	2 205.5	123.4	231.8	2 561.6	103.4	2 665.0
Jul	136.7	335.2	232.4	172.1	266.1	205.1	426.2	288.9	206.6	2 268.9	124.1	235.2	2 628.6	104.6	2 733.2
Oct	141.4	343.6	240.2	178.8	277.4	218.6	448.0	308.4	215.3	2 371.1	129.2	242.4	2 743.3	105.1	2 848.4
1993 Jan	146.2	348.3	247.5	185.2	286.2	229.5	464.6	325.2	222.6	2 454.4	131.4	245.3	2 832.0	105.5	2 937.5
Apr	148.0	345.2	246.5	183.6	285.1	228.2	469.5	321.4	220.0	2 446.6	130.3	243.2	2 821.0	104.5	2 925.5
Jul	148.5	338.0	240.9	180.8	278.7	223.5	466.3	314.0	214.4	2 404.4	129.3	241.2	2 775.6	102.5	2 878.1
Oct	147.5	331.1	237.8	177.8	271.5	216.6	460.4	306.6	208.4	2 356.8	127.8	236.6	2 722.1	101.8	2 823.9
1994 Jan	145.6	325.1	233.7	174.7	262.3	210.0	451.4	296.7	203.6	2 302.3	126.7	236.0	2 665.8	100.2	2 766.0
Apr	141.6	314.5	227.4	170.7	252.0	200.4	440.4	280.9	194.5	2 221.7	123.3	231.7	2 577.4	98.9	2 676.3
Jul	139.1	304.2	222.7	166.3	242.3	191.0	428.1	268.1	188.1	2 148.8	119.0	227.4	2 496.3	97.2	2 593.5
Oct	136.0	291.7	215.9	160.1	230.5	180.5	415.4	251.1	178.9	2 059.0	112.9	218.1	2 391.1	93.8	2 484.9
1995 Jan	133.0	280.1	210.6	153.2	218.5	172.3	401.4	237.9	171.4	1 977.5	108.3	209.3	2 296.0	91.3	2 387.3
Apr	130.0	270.8	206.8	148.1	211.0	167.1	395.0	229.7	166.0	1 923.8	106.2	200.3	2 231.0	88.6	2 319.6
Jul	128.2	266.1	204.6	145.3	206.9	165.0	390.2	225.1	162.5	1 892.8	106.7	195.3	2 195.9	87.6	2 283.5
Oct	126.4	260.9	200.7	142.3	201.3	160.7	383.2	219.1	159.4	1 852.7	105.4	193.5	2 152.9	85.8	2 238.7
1996 Jan	123.1	255.8	197.0	140.0	196.5	157.2	376.8	213.3	155.6	1 814.6	104.0	193.2	2 112.5	85.9	2 198.4
Apr	121.7	254.9	195.7	137.7	194.2	153.5	367.9	207.6	152.3	1 785.1	104.6	194.9	2 085.0	86.1	2 171.1
Jul	116.9	248.2	188.8	131.8	187.6	146.8	357.5	198.9	146.8	1 722.5	101.8	191.9	2 017.0	86.4	2 103.4
Oct	110.5	238.4	181.1	124.9	177.8	138.5	341.6	185.5	137.9	1 635.0	98.2	186.3	1 920.7	81.7	2 002.4
1997 Jan	101.0	218.5	166.4	111.8	160.1	123.5	312.6	163.3	126.0	1 483.2	90.3	173.8	1 747.3	71.1	1 818.4
Apr	95.2	201.3	154.7	102.4	147.3	110.6	284.9	144.4	112.1	1 352.9	82.5	162.2	1 597.6	65.0	1 662.6
Jul	92.4	188.9	148.2	95.0	138.0	102.5	264.3	131.0	100.7	1 261.0	78.1	153.6	1 492.7	61.4	1 554.1
Oct	90.4	177.6	142.0	87.6	131.7	94.3	246.4	120.4	93.0	1 183.4	73.6	146.5	1 403.5	60.6	1 464.1
1998 Jan	87.6	170.6	137.2	82.8	126.1	88.5	234.3	112.3	88.7	1 128.1	70.9	141.6	1 340.6	59.9	1 400.5
Apr	84.1	165.4	134.1	79.9	122.3	85.2	229.4	108.0	85.1	1 093.5	69.3	138.7	1 301.5	57.9	1 359.4
Jul	81.8	163.7	133.3	80.0	121.4	83.7	225.2	105.5	84.1	1 078.7	68.6	139.4	1 286.7	57.3	1 344.0
Oct	82.1	160.9	130.9	79.9	121.4	82.0	219.3	102.5	81.8	1 060.8	68.1	136.9	1 265.8	56.1	1 321.9
1999 Jan	82.6	159.5	129.5	79.0	122.6	80.3	214.5	101.2	81.2	1 050.4	67.8	135.6	1 253.8	55.9	1 309.7
Apr	82.5	157.2	127.0	78.2	123.1	79.1	207.8	98.8	78.4	1 032.1	67.1	133.9	1 233.1	55.0	1 288.1
Jul	80.3	153.8	122.4	75.9	120.2	76.6	202.2	94.4	74.9	1 000.7	63.8	130.2	1 194.7	50.0	1 244.7
Oct	76.7	150.0	118.3	73.6	115.9	73.6	196.5	91.1	71.4	967.1	61.0	126.1	1 154.2	46.5	1 200.7
2000 Jan	75.7	145.7	114.6	73.2	112.1	70.3	189.4	87.2	68.0	936.2	59.3	123.2	1 118.7	44.2	1 162.9
Apr	73.6	139.9	108.9	70.0	108.1	66.9	181.6	81.3	63.8	894.1	57.8	119.0	1 070.9	42.4	1 113.3
Jul	72.0	135.4	104.9	68.7	107.2	62.5	172.0	77.5	61.1	861.3	57.1	115.1	1 033.5	41.2	1 074.7
Oct	69.5	131.0	102.5	67.7	106.5	60.7	165.0	74.3	58.1	835.3	56.4	111.7	1 003.4	41.3	1 044.7
2001 Jan	66.2	127.4	99.9	66.6	104.0	57.2	158.2	69.7	54.9	804.1	54.9	108.8	967.8	40.8	1 008.6
Apr	63.2	124.9	97.6	65.1	100.8	54.8	151.8	66.1	53.6	777.9	52.4	105.3	935.6	39.9	975.5
Jul	61.4	121.5	95.1	63.0	97.4	53.7	151.0	65.1	52.1	760.3	49.8	102.4	912.5	39.3	951.8
Oct	61.5	121.4	93.2	61.6	95.7	54.3	156.3	65.9	51.1	761.0	49.2	104.2	914.4	38.6	953.0
2002 Jan	60.9	121.3	91.4	60.6	95.4	55.4	163.1	68.6	51.1	767.8	48.1	104.3	920.2	38.0	958.2
Apr	59.2	119.4	89.4	59.4	93.6	56.4	166.2	71.0	50.9	765.5	47.5	104.4	917.4	37.5	954.9
Jul	58.5	118.1	89.1	58.6	93.4	57.5	167.3	72.3	50.1	764.9	46.8	101.9	913.6	36.4	950.0
Oct	55.9	116.1	87.6	57.9	93.7	57.2	167.6	72.3	49.3	757.6	46.7	100.1	904.4	35.1	939.5
2003 Jan	54.8	115.9	87.0	58.0	94.3	57.4	168.6	72.9	48.9	757.8	46.3	100.2	904.3	35.0	939.3
Apr	53.5	112.7	84.1	58.8	94.7	58.5	171.3	75.6	48.6	757.8	45.2	99.1	902.1	34.0	936.1
Jul	52.6	112.5	84.2	59.9	94.9	58.7	171.7	76.4	49.1	760.0	45.0	100.6	905.6	34.6	940.2
Oct	51.1	108.7	81.6	58.8	94.2	57.3	170.2	76.0	47.4	745.3	43.1	98.9	887.3	34.7	922.0
2004 Jan	49.6	104.2	78.1	56.1	92.9	56.6	167.8	74.8	45.0	725.1	41.9	96.7	863.7	33.5	897.2
Apr	47.4	101.3	75.4	53.9	90.0	56.2	165.0	71.9	42.9	704.0	41.7	94.4	840.1	31.8	871.9
Jul	45.4	96.7	71.7	51.1	86.8	54.4	162.2	68.8	40.5	677.6	39.5	90.2	807.3	29.8	837.1
Oct	45.4	97.0	71.4	51.1	85.9	55.1	159.3	69.6	40.7	675.5	39.2	89.8	804.5	29.7	834.2
2005 Jan	43.4	94.0	69.6	50.6	85.3	55.0	158.6	68.0	40.5	665.0	38.7	86.8	790.5	29.1	819.6
Apr	44.9	97.7	73.0	52.0	88.0	56.4	161.5	69.5	41.5	684.5	39.8	86.1	810.4	28.8	839.2
Jul	46.3	102.0	76.3	54.4	96.6	58.6	162.5	72.0	42.7	711.4	41.6	84.9	837.9	28.2	866.1
Oct	47.6	106.5	80.1	56.7	99.4	60.3	166.4	74.1	43.1	734.2	43.0	85.8	863.0	28.2	891.2
2006 Jan	46.5	108.3	83.4	58.4	102.0	61.9	167.8	77.6	43.5	749.4	43.4	84.1	876.9	28.2	905.1
Apr	49.8	114.9	86.8	61.9	108.6	65.1	167.1	81.3	48.0	783.5	45.3	88.0	916.8	28.3	945.1
Jul	50.4	116.5	88.6	62.9	109.3	65.1	167.8	83.7	49.2	793.5	44.3	88.6	926.4	27.6	954.0
Oct	51.3	118.2	89.0	63.2	110.1	67.7	166.2	82.6	49.1	797.4	43.9	87.4	928.7	27.8	956.5

1 The figures are based on the number of claimants receiving unemployment related benefits and are adjusted for seasonality and discontinuities to be consistent with current coverage. See chapter text.

The latest national and regional seasonally adjusted claimant count figures are provisional and subject to revision in the following month.

Source: Office for National Statistics: 020 7533 6094

7.16 Economic activity: by sex and age[1]
United Kingdom
At Quarter 2 each year[2]. Seasonally adjusted

Thousands and percentages

	All aged 16 and over	16-59/64	16-17	18-24	25-34	35-49	50-64 (m) 50-59 (w)	65+ (m) 60+ (w)
Thousands								
All Persons								
	MGSF	YBSK	YBZL	YBZO	YBZR	YBZU	YBZX	YCAD
2000	29 061	28 212	838	3 634	7 243	10 479	6 018	849
2001	29 167	28 322	821	3 698	7 078	10 599	6 126	845
2002	29 420	28 517	809	3 773	6 878	10 812	6 246	903
2003	29 655	28 709	827	3 781	6 697	10 934	6 470	946
2004	29 844	28 816	805	3 905	6 586	11 048	6 472	1 028
2005	30 126	29 049	805	3 944	6 557	11 188	6 555	1 076
2006	30 613	29 430	741	4 085	6 591	11 356	6 657	1 183
Male								
	MGSG	YBSL	YBZM	YBZP	YBZS	YBZV	YBZY	YCAE
2000	15 854	15 568	420	1 939	3 971	5 628	3 610	286
2001	15 875	15 595	421	1 966	3 887	5 654	3 667	280
2002	15 978	15 676	415	2 005	3 769	5 777	3 710	302
2003	16 179	15 839	417	2 028	3 679	5 861	3 854	340
2004	16 199	15 849	404	2 088	3 595	5 902	3 860	349
2005	16 314	15 951	405	2 119	3 572	5 955	3 899	363
2006	16 553	16 149	367	2 179	3 589	6 047	3 967	404
Female								
	MGSH	YBSM	YBZN	YBZQ	YBZT	YBZW	YBZZ	YCAF
2000	13 207	12 643	418	1 695	3 271	4 851	2 408	563
2001	13 291	12 727	401	1 731	3 191	4 945	2 459	565
2002	13 443	12 841	394	1 768	3 109	5 035	2 536	601
2003	13 476	12 870	410	1 753	3 018	5 074	2 615	606
2004	13 646	12 967	400	1 817	2 991	5 146	2 613	679
2005	13 812	13 098	399	1 825	2 984	5 233	2 656	714
2006	14 061	13 281	374	1 906	3 002	5 309	2 690	779
Percentages[3]								
All Persons								
	MGWG	MGSO	YCAG	YCAJ	YCAM	YCAP	MGWP	MGWS
2000	63.0	78.8	58.4	75.3	84.3	85.1	69.8	8.2
2001	62.8	78.6	55.8	75.6	84.1	84.8	70.0	8.1
2002	63.0	78.6	53.6	75.7	83.8	85.1	70.5	8.6
2003	63.1	78.7	54.2	74.0	83.5	84.9	72.4	9.0
2004	63.0	78.5	51.7	74.7	83.6	84.7	72.0	9.6
2005	63.1	78.5	51.1	73.7	83.8	84.8	72.5	10.0
2006	63.6	79.0	47.0	74.6	84.7	85.3	73.1	10.9
Male								
	MGWH	MGSP	YCAH	YCAK	YCAN	YCAQ	MGWQ	MGWT
2000	71.4	84.4	57.5	80.6	93.6	92.4	72.5	7.6
2001	70.9	83.9	55.8	80.7	93.3	91.5	72.8	7.3
2002	70.8	83.8	53.7	80.5	92.7	92.0	72.9	7.8
2003	71.2	84.2	53.4	79.1	92.6	92.1	75.1	8.7
2004	70.7	83.6	50.7	79.3	92.0	91.6	74.6	8.8
2005	70.5	83.4	50.2	78.4	92.1	91.4	74.7	9.0
2006	70.9	83.7	45.4	78.6	93.1	91.9	75.1	9.9
Female								
	MGWI	MGSQ	YCAI	YCAL	YCAO	YCAR	MGWR	MGWU
2000	55.2	72.9	59.4	70.0	75.3	77.9	66.1	8.6
2001	55.3	72.9	55.7	70.6	75.0	78.2	66.2	8.6
2002	55.6	73.1	53.6	71.0	75.0	78.4	67.2	9.1
2003	55.5	72.9	55.0	68.9	74.6	77.9	68.9	9.1
2004	55.9	73.1	52.7	70.0	75.3	78.0	68.5	10.1
2005	56.1	73.3	52.0	68.9	75.6	78.4	69.5	10.6
2006	56.7	74.0	48.7	70.5	76.5	78.8	70.3	11.4

1 See chapter text. In August 2006, ONS published the mid-year population estimates for 2005. These estimates have now been incorporated into the LFS estimates from Autumn 2004. Further details can be found at http://www.statistics.gov.uk/cci/article.asp?id=1647

2 The Labour Force Survey has now moved to calendar quarters from May 2006. More information can be found on page 5 of the Concepts and Definitions.pdf by following this link:- www.statistics.gov.uk/downloads/theme_labour/Concepts_Definitions_HQS.pdf

3 Total economically active as a percentage of all persons in the relevant age group.

Sources: Labour Force Survey, Office for National Statistics;
Helpline: 020-7533 6094

7.17 Economically inactive: by sex and age[1]
United Kingdom
At Quarter 2 each year[2]. Seasonally adjusted

Thousands and percentages

	All aged 16 and over	16-59/64	16-17	18-24	25-34	35-49	50-64 (m) 50-59 (w)	65+ (m) 60+ (w)
Thousands								
All Persons								
	MGSI	YBSN	YCAS	YCAV	YCAY	YCBB	MGWA	MGWD
2000	17 067	7 571	596	1 195	1 344	1 835	2 602	9 496
2001	17 274	7 717	652	1 192	1 342	1 901	2 629	9 557
2002	17 306	7 744	700	1 208	1 332	1 888	2 615	9 562
2003	17 365	7 757	699	1 328	1 325	1 944	2 462	9 607
2004	17 508	7 878	752	1 323	1 295	1 989	2 518	9 630
2005	17 628	7 933	770	1 407	1 268	2 001	2 487	9 694
2006	17 518	7 822	836	1 390	1 189	1 961	2 446	9 696
Male								
	MGSJ	YBSO	YCAT	YCAW	YCAZ	YCBC	MGWB	MGWE
2000	6 359	2 878	311	467	272	461	1 367	3 481
2001	6 518	2 983	333	471	280	526	1 373	3 535
2002	6 586	3 022	358	486	295	502	1 380	3 564
2003	6 558	2 979	364	535	295	505	1 280	3 579
2004	6 727	3 106	393	544	312	539	1 317	3 621
2005	6 832	3 174	402	582	306	561	1 322	3 658
2006	6 800	3 145	442	592	267	532	1 312	3 656
Female								
	MGSK	YBSP	YCAU	YCAX	YCBA	YCBD	MGWC	MGWF
2000	10 708	4 694	285	728	1 072	1 374	1 235	6 015
2001	10 756	4 734	319	721	1 062	1 375	1 256	6 022
2002	10 720	4 722	342	723	1 037	1 386	1 235	5 998
2003	10 807	4 778	335	793	1 030	1 438	1 183	6 028
2004	10 781	4 772	359	779	983	1 450	1 201	6 009
2005	10 796	4 759	369	824	962	1 440	1 165	6 036
2006	10 717	4 677	394	798	922	1 429	1 134	6 040
Percentages[3]								
All Persons								
	YBTC	YBTL	LWEX	LWFA	LWFD	LWFG	LWFJ	LWFM
2000	37.0	21.2	41.6	24.7	15.7	14.9	30.2	91.8
2001	37.2	21.4	44.2	24.4	15.9	15.2	30.0	91.9
2002	37.0	21.4	46.4	24.3	16.2	14.9	29.5	91.4
2003	36.9	21.3	45.8	26.0	16.5	15.1	27.6	91.0
2004	37.0	21.5	48.3	25.3	16.4	15.3	28.0	90.4
2005	36.9	21.5	48.9	26.3	16.2	15.2	27.5	90.0
2006	36.4	21.0	53.0	25.4	15.3	14.7	26.9	89.1
Male								
	YBTD	YBTM	LWEY	LWFB	LWFE	LWFH	LWFK	LWFN
2000	28.6	15.6	42.5	19.4	6.4	7.6	27.5	92.4
2001	29.1	16.1	44.2	19.3	6.7	8.5	27.2	92.7
2002	29.2	16.2	46.3	19.5	7.3	8.0	27.1	92.2
2003	28.8	15.8	46.6	20.9	7.4	7.9	24.9	91.3
2004	29.3	16.4	49.3	20.7	8.0	8.4	25.4	91.2
2005	29.5	16.6	49.8	21.6	7.9	8.6	25.3	91.0
2006	29.1	16.3	54.6	21.4	6.9	8.1	24.9	90.1
Female								
	YBTE	YBTN	LWEZ	LWFC	LWFF	LWFI	LWFL	LWFO
2000	44.8	27.1	40.6	30.0	24.7	22.1	33.9	91.4
2001	44.7	27.1	44.3	29.4	25.0	21.8	33.8	91.4
2002	44.4	26.9	46.4	29.0	25.0	21.6	32.8	90.9
2003	44.5	27.1	45.0	31.1	25.4	22.1	31.1	90.9
2004	44.1	26.9	47.3	30.0	24.7	22.0	31.5	89.9
2005	43.9	26.7	48.0	31.1	24.4	21.6	30.5	89.4
2006	43.3	26.0	51.3	29.5	23.5	21.2	29.7	88.6

1 See chapter text. In August 2006, ONS published the mid-year population estimates for 2005. These estimates have now been incorporated into the LFS estimates from Autumn 2004. Further details can be found at http://www.statistics.gov.uk/cci/article.asp?id=1647

2 The Labour Force Survey has now moved to calendar quarters from May 2006. More information can be found on page 5 of the Concepts and Definitions.pdf by following this link:- www.statistics.gov.uk/downloads/theme_labour/Concepts_Definitions_HQS.pdf

3 Total economically inactive as a percentage of all persons in the relevant age group.

Sources: Labour Force Survey, Office for National Statistics;
Helpline: 020-7533 6094

7.18 Economically inactive:[1,2] by reason and sex
United Kingdom
At Quarter 2 each year[3]. Seasonally adjusted

Thousands and percentages

		Economic inactivity by reason:						by:		All economically inactive
	Student	Looking after family/home	Temporary sick	Long-term sick	Discouraged workers[4]	Retired	Other	Does not want a job	Wants a job	

Thousands

All Persons

	BEDZ	BEEC	BEBK	BEBN	YCFO	BEEI	BEEL	YBVZ	YBWC	YBSN
1999	1 437	2 453	173	2 184	66	520	744	5 285	2 292	7 577
2000	1 433	2 371	187	2 149	69	553	810	5 258	2 314	7 571
2001	1 505	2 392	192	2 212	33	594	790	5 526	2 191	7 717
2002	1 519	2 384	177	2 228	32	584	819	5 495	2 248	7 744
2003	1 646	2 401	193	2 110	38	569	801	5 614	2 143	7 757
2004	1 697	2 342	191	2 170	35	598	845	5 857	2 021	7 878
2005	1 785	2 334	189	2 149	33	623	821	5 855	2 078	7 933
2006	1 807	2 305	188	2 085	36	591	810	5 748	2 074	7 822

Male

	BEEX	BEAQ	BEDI	BEDL	YCFP	BEDR	BEDU	YBWA	YBWD	YBSO
1999	694	174	77	1 235	39	354	277	1 928	922	2 851
2000	705	163	88	1 202	38	383	299	1 939	939	2 878
2001	731	180	91	1 242	21	405	313	2 078	905	2 983
2002	750	182	87	1 242	21	396	343	2 086	936	3 022
2003	819	181	88	1 150	20	389	333	2 064	915	2 979
2004	857	188	93	1 184	23	410	350	2 250	856	3 106
2005	886	193	100	1 190	21	427	357	2 332	842	3 174
2006	896	197	94	1 141	26	437	354	2 251	894	3 145

Female

	BEBL	BEBO	BEEG	BEEJ	YCFQ	BEEP	BEES	YBWB	YBWE	YBSP
1999	743	2 278	97	948	27	167	467	3 357	1 370	4 727
2000	729	2 207	99	947	31	170	511	3 319	1 375	4 694
2001	774	2 212	101	970	13	188	477	3 449	1 285	4 734
2002	769	2 203	90	986	11	188	476	3 410	1 312	4 722
2003	827	2 220	105	960	18	181	468	3 550	1 228	4 778
2004	840	2 154	97	986	12	188	495	3 607	1 165	4 772
2005	899	2 141	89	959	12	196	464	3 523	1 237	4 759
2006	911	2 108	94	944	10	154	457	3 497	1 180	4 677

Percentages[5]

All Persons

	BEDJ	BEDM	BEDP	BEDS	BEDV	BEDY	BEEB	BEEE	BEBM	BEAR
1999	19.0	32.4	2.3	28.8	0.9	6.9	9.8	69.8	30.2	100.0
2000	18.9	31.3	2.5	28.4	0.9	7.3	10.7	69.4	30.6	100.0
2001	19.5	31.0	2.5	28.7	0.4	7.7	10.2	71.6	28.4	100.0
2002	19.6	30.8	2.3	28.8	0.4	7.5	10.6	71.0	29.0	100.0
2003	21.2	30.9	2.5	27.2	0.5	7.3	10.3	72.4	27.6	100.0
2004	21.5	29.7	2.4	27.6	0.4	7.6	10.7	74.3	25.7	100.0
2005	22.5	29.4	2.4	27.1	0.4	7.9	10.3	73.8	26.2	100.0
2006	23.1	29.5	2.4	26.7	0.5	7.6	10.4	73.5	26.5	100.0

Male

	BEEH	BEEK	BEEN	BEEQ	BEET	BEEW	BEEZ	BEAS	BEGT	BEBP
1999	24.3	6.1	2.7	43.3	1.4	12.4	9.7	67.6	32.4	100.0
2000	24.5	5.7	3.0	41.8	1.3	13.3	10.4	67.4	32.6	100.0
2001	24.5	6.0	3.1	41.6	0.7	13.6	10.5	69.7	30.3	100.0
2002	24.8	6.0	2.9	41.1	0.7	13.1	11.3	69.0	31.0	100.0
2003	27.5	6.1	3.0	38.6	0.7	13.0	11.2	69.3	30.7	100.0
2004	27.6	6.1	3.0	38.1	0.7	13.2	11.3	72.4	27.6	100.0
2005	27.9	6.1	3.2	37.5	0.7	13.4	11.2	73.5	26.5	100.0
2006	28.5	6.3	3.0	36.3	0.8	13.9	11.2	71.6	28.4	100.0

Female

	BEGZ	BEHC	BEHF	BEHI	BEHL	BEHO	BEBQ	BEHR	BEHU	BEGW
1999	15.7	48.2	2.0	20.1	0.6	3.5	9.9	71.0	29.0	100.0
2000	15.5	47.0	2.1	20.2	0.7	3.6	10.9	70.7	29.3	100.0
2001	16.4	46.7	2.1	20.5	0.3	4.0	10.1	72.8	27.2	100.0
2002	16.3	46.7	1.9	20.9	0.2	4.0	10.1	72.2	27.8	100.0
2003	17.3	46.5	2.2	20.1	0.4	3.8	9.8	74.3	25.7	100.0
2004	17.6	45.1	2.0	20.7	0.3	3.9	10.4	75.6	24.4	100.0
2005	18.9	45.0	1.9	20.2	0.3	4.1	9.8	74.0	26.0	100.0
2006	19.5	45.1	2.0	20.2	0.2	3.3	9.8	74.8	25.2	100.0

1 All persons aged 16-59(women)/ 64 (men). See chapter text.

2 In August 2006, ONS published the mid-year population estimates for 2005. These estimates have now been incorporated into the LFS estimates from Autumn 2004. Further details can be found at http://www.statistics.gov.uk/cci/article.asp?id=1647

3 The Labour Force Survey has now moved to calendar quarters from May 2006. More information can be found on page 5 of the Concepts and Definitions.pdf by following this link:- www.statistics.gov.uk/downloads/theme_labour/Concepts_Definitions_HQS.pdf

4 People whose reason for not seeking work was that they believed no jobs were available.

5 Reasons for inactivity as a percentage of all economically inactive.

Sources: Labour Force Survey, Office for National Statistics; Helpline: 020-7533 6094

7.19 Labour disputes: by industry[1]
United Kingdom
Standard Industrial Classification 1992

Thousands and numbers

		1999	2000	2001	2002	2003	2004	2005
Working days lost through all stoppages in progress (thousands)	KBBZ	242	499	525	1 323	499	905	157
Analysis by industry								
Mining, quarrying, electricity, gas and water	DMME	–	3	25	–	–	5	6
Manufacturing	BBFX	57	52	43	21	63	31	16
Construction	DMMG	49	49	10	17	14	–	2
Transport, storage and communication	BBFY	50	97	107	96	126	44	33
Public administration and defence	BBFZ	35	50	216	488	138	437	23
Education	BBGA	25	50	43	376	131	379	43
Health and social work	BBGB	5	122	73	148	15	4	–
Other community, social and personal services	DMML	7	36	4	107	10	4	6
All other industries and services	DMMM	12	40	4	70	2	2	29
Analysis by number of working days lost in each stoppage								
Under 250 days	KBFC	11	12	9	7	6	7	5
250 and under 500 days	KBFJ	13	9	11	8	6	5	4
500 and under 1,000 days	KBFL	16	21	15	15	13	12	7
1,000 and under 5,000 days	KBFY	69	71	59	47	69	51	78
5,000 and under 25,000 days	KBFZ	133	85	140	104	46	59	63
25,000 and under 50,000 days	KBGS	–	–	72	122	112	–	–
50,000 days and over	KBGT	–	301	220	1 021	248	770	–
Working days lost per 1 000 employees all industries and services	KBHA	10	20	20	51	19	34	6
Workers directly and indirectly involved (thousands)	KBHB	141	183	180	943	151	293	93
Analysis by industry								
Mining, quarrying, electricity, gas and water	DMMN	–	1	3	–	–	1	6
Manufacturing	DMMO	31	28	17	10	18	14	3
Construction	DMMP	18	16	3	17	2	–	1
Transport, storage and communications	DMMQ	42	39	69	33	52	12	13
Public administration and defence	DMMR	17	29	46	171	56	207	15
Education	DMMS	28	17	34	388	15	55	43
Health and social work	DMMT	–	28	6	144	3	1	–
Other community, social and personal services	DMMU	2	13	1	103	3	3	6
All other industries and services	DMMV	2	12	1	76	1	1	5
Analysis by duration of stoppage								
Not more than 5 days	KBHM	129	82	98	828	78	222	89
Over 5 but not more than 10 days	KBHN	8	9	43	57	23	47	3
Over 10 but not more than 20 days	KBJQ	3	8	4	3	31	1	1
Over 20 but not more than 30 days	KBJR	–	–	–	1	–	3	–
Over 30 but not more than 50 days	KBJS	–	83	6	1	–	–	1
Over 50 days	KBJT	–	1	30	55	20	20	–
Numbers of stoppages in progress: total	KBLG	205	212	194	146	133	130	116
Analysis by industry								
Mining, quarrying, electricity, gas and water	DMMW	–	3	3	2	1	3	2
Manufacturing	DMMX	37	38	32	33	43	30	19
Construction	DMMY	20	16	9	3	4	1	3
Transport, storage and communications	DMMZ	91	116	94	51	45	46	42
Public administration and defence	DMNA	17	7	22	20	12	19	13
Education	DMNB	21	18	16	16	15	16	22
Health and social work	DMNC	4	10	12	14	7	4	1
Other community, social and personal services	DMND	8	13	10	11	9	12	5
All other industries and services	DMNE	8	5	9	12	4	4	10
Analysis of number of stoppages by duration								
Not more than 5 days	KBNH	179	187	162	118	113	111	102
Over 5 but not more than 10 days	KBNI	8	14	15	16	10	10	8
Over 10 but not more than 20 days	KBNJ	9	5	7	3	5	4	3
Over 20 but not more than 30 days	KBNK	4	1	1	3	1	2	–
Over 30 but not more than 50 days	KBNL	3	3	4	1	1	1	3
Over 50 days	KBNM	2	2	5	5	3	2	–

1 See chapter text.

Source: Labour Market Statistics, Office for National Statistics: 01633 819205

7.20 Average earnings and hours of full-time employees by industry division:[1] by sex
United Kingdom
At April. Standard Industrial Classification 1992

	Agriculture, Hunting and Forestry	Fishing	Mining and Quarrying	Manufacturing	Electricity, Gas and Water Supply	Construction	Wholesale and Retail Trade; repair of motor vehicles, cycles, personal and household goods
All employees							
Weekly earnings							
	C9EG	C9EI	C9EK	C9EM	C9EO	C9EP	C9EQ
2002	336.1	350.7	591.7	455.6	543.0	466.4	403.6
2003	340.5	392.7	657.0	476.5	561.5	489.8	414.6
2004[2]	355.8	415.7	617.1	485.0	579.2	505.1	421.3
	362.5	419.0	633.5	493.1	591.9	509.4	433.3
2005	364.7	440.6	657.9	508.0	612.2	524.6	425.2
2006	386.6	466.8	782.0	528.4	632.7	548.0	447.4
Total hours worked							
	C5TJ	C5TK	C5TL	C5TV	C5TW	C5TX	C5U3
2002	44.7	43.4	43.2	41.0	39.9	43.4	40.5
2003	44.9	42.9	45.3	40.9	39.6	43.4	40.4
2004[2]	44.5	43.8	43.2	41.0	40.0	43.2	40.4
		43.5	43.4			43.1	
2005	43.7	43.1	43.5	40.6	39.3	43.0	40.3
2006	44.1	42.4	42.8	40.8	40.4	43.1	40.4
Hourly earnings excluding overtime							
	C9HV	C9HX	C9HZ	C9I3	C9I5	C9I7	C9IA
2002	7.42	7.93	14.01	11.09	13.41	10.73	9.97
2003	7.44	9.09	14.99	11.62	13.99	11.22	10.26
2004[2]	7.87	9.41	14.60	11.80	14.29	11.68	10.44
	8.03	9.57	14.97	12.01	14.61	11.81	10.74
2005	8.27	10.14	15.56	12.50	15.33	12.15	10.57
2006	8.68	11.10	18.86	12.97	15.37	12.66	11.10
Males employees							
Weekly earnings							
	C9FZ	C9F4	C9F6	C9F8	C9FA	C9FC	C9FE
2002	350.5	353.4	608.8	482.9	584.7	478.5	453.7
2003	356.2	391.4	671.2	503.2	595.7	503.8	464.4
2004[2]	369.1	426.6	637.1	511.2	607.9	517.8	470.3
	375.4	433.2	653.7	519.4	626.1	521.5	483.2
2005	384.3	445.7	675.4	533.8	647.3	537.6	469.5
2006	..	450.4	804.2	554.9	669.1	563.3	493.6
Total hours worked							
	C5W8	C5WE	C5WH	C5WK	C5WN	C5WQ	C5WT
2002	45.8	44.1	44.1	41.6	40.6	44.0	41.5
2003	46.1	43.4	46.5	41.5	40.1	44.0	41.5
2004[2]	45.6	45.5	44.2	41.6	40.5	43.8	41.4
		45.4	44.4			43.7	
2005	44.7	43.4	44.4	41.2	39.9	43.5	41.2
2006	45.0	43.5	43.7	41.3	41.1	43.7	41.3
Hourly earnings excluding overtime							
	C9IS	C9IU	C9IW	C9IY	C9J2	C9J4	C9J6
2002	7.56	7.84	14.19	11.62	14.22	10.87	10.97
2003	7.57	8.95	14.97	12.12	14.70	11.39	11.21
2004[2]	7.96	9.26	14.80	12.28	14.82	11.83	11.38
	8.11	9.47	15.16	12.49	15.29	11.95	11.71
2005	8.46	10.13	15.72	12.98	15.96	12.30	11.42
2006	8.86	10.38	19.03	13.46	15.94	12.85	11.99
Female employees							
Weekly earnings							
	C9G6	C9G8	C9GA	C9GC	C9GE	C9GG	C9GI
2002	272.3	–	478.6	350.8	405.1	356.9	310.1
2003	270.8	–	566.5	372.8	426.0	370.8	321.6
2004[2]	290.9	–	496.3	380.8	464.8	392.8	330.9
	297.5		511.0	388.1	453.0	403.8	339.3
2005	287.6	–	552.5	404.3	490.2	411.5	343.2
2006	321.7	–	668.8	422.6	505.9	416.8	363.1
Total hours worked							
	C7NN	C7NP	C7NR	C7NT	C7NV	C7OA	C7OC
2002	39.8	40.0	37.8	38.8	37.7	38.2	38.7
2003	39.6	39.8	37.6	38.7	37.9	38.3	38.3
2004[2]	39.2	36.5	37.3	38.7	38.1	38.3	38.5
			37.2			38.2	
2005	39.0	42.2	38.1	38.4	37.3	38.0	38.5
2006	40.6	–	37.7	38.6	37.8	38.5	38.8
Hourly earnings excluding overtime							
	C9JO	C9JQ	C9JS	C9JU	C9JW	C9JY	C9K2
2002	6.80	–	12.76	9.03	10.69	9.33	8.02
2003	6.81	–	15.17	9.62	11.17	9.69	8.38
2004[2]	7.38	–	13.31	9.84	12.17	10.25	8.60
	7.55		13.73	10.02	11.83	10.55	8.82
2005	7.35	–	14.54	10.51	13.13	10.82	8.92
2006	7.91	–	17.95	10.97	13.37	10.83	9.40

7.20
continued

Average earnings and hours of full-time employees by industry division:[1] by sex
United Kingdom
At April. Standard Industrial Classification 1992

	Hotels and restaurants	Transport, Storage and Communication	Financial Inter-mediation	Real Estate, Renting and Business	Public Administration and Defence; compulsory social security	Educa-tion	Health and Social work	Other community, social and personal service activities
All employees								
Weekly earnings								
	C9ER	C9ES	C9ET	C9EU	C9EV	C9EW	C9EX	C9EY
2002	295.9	462.3	671.0	564.4	456.7	459.6	427.7	468.4
2003	311.3	476.3	660.6	568.5	469.9	481.6	446.8	486.8
2004[2]	319.1	494.4	667.5	573.9	497.6	495.9	478.9	499.5
	323.8	504.3	696.3	590.6	496.6	493.6	474.9	515.4
2005	323.5	508.0	701.3	589.3	525.0	518.6	503.2	503.8
2006	333.4	527.6	720.2	616.6	544.3	533.7	516.7	527.1
Total hours worked								
	C5U4	C5U5	C5U6	C5U7	C5U8	C5V5	C5V8	C5VU
2002	40.7	42.7	36.3	39.3	38.5	35.5	38.5	39.6
2003	40.7	43.0	36.1	39.3	39.1	35.6	38.5	39.4
2004[2]	41.2	42.7	36.3	39.3	39.2	35.6	38.6	39.8
	41.1	42.6						
2005	40.9	42.9	36.0	39.1	39.1	35.5	38.7	40.0
2006	41.0	42.3	36.1	39.4	..	35.6	38.6	39.9
Hourly earnings excluding overtime								
	C9IC	C9IE	C9IG	C9II	C9IK	C9IM	C9IO	C9IQ
2002	7.27	10.93	18.56	14.45	11.77	12.98	11.07	11.89
2003	7.63	11.20	18.32	14.54	11.88	13.55	11.57	12.38
2004[2]	7.74	11.73	18.44	14.67	12.62	13.96	12.39	12.60
	7.86	11.99	19.25	15.10	12.57	13.90	12.29	13.02
2005	7.93	11.89	19.54	15.14	13.28	14.64	12.99	12.65
2006	8.13	12.57	20.00	15.73	13.80	15.06	13.41	13.29
Males employees								
Weekly earnings								
	C9FO	C9FQ	C9FS	C9FU	C9FW	C9FY	C9G2	C9G4
2002	332.9	480.4	855.9	635.3	506.0	504.3	549.9	536.3
2003	351.9	493.5	832.1	636.7	522.5	528.8	581.1	562.2
2004[2]	345.9	514.0	829.8	635.3	549.0	542.2	624.3	572.8
	352.5	522.0	869.2	652.5	547.9	539.3	614.8	593.1
2005	357.2	527.7	872.4	654.9	583.6	568.4	669.5	563.6
2006	365.3	545.0	881.9	685.5	599.4	586.7	693.0	585.4
Total hours worked								
	C5WW	C5WZ	C7MU	C7MW	C7NF	C7NH	C7NJ	C7NL
2002	41.7	43.7	36.4	40.2	39.1	36.6	39.8	40.7
2003	41.8	44.0	36.3	40.1	40.0	36.7	39.4	40.4
2004[2]	42.1	43.6	36.4	40.2	40.0	36.6	39.5	40.9
		43.5			40.1			
2005	41.8	43.8	36.2	39.9	40.1	36.5	39.7	41.1
2006	41.8	43.3	36.3	40.3	40.0	36.7	39.4	40.8
Hourly earnings excluding overtime								
	C9J8	C9JA	C9JC	C9JE	C9JG	C9JI	C9JK	C9JM
2002	8.00	11.12	23.66	15.97	12.86	13.87	13.83	13.30
2003	8.40	11.37	23.01	15.99	12.91	14.48	14.73	14.00
2004[2]	8.23	11.97	22.88	15.94	13.62	14.88	15.82	14.14
	8.38	12.20	23.99	16.39	13.56	14.79	15.57	14.68
2005	8.56	12.12	24.19	16.52	14.43	15.64	16.91	13.83
2006	8.74	12.70	24.37	17.16	14.90	16.14	17.58	14.48
Female employees								
Weekly earnings								
	C9GK	C9GM	C9HJ	C9HL	C9HN	C9HP	C9HR	C9HT
2002	249.8	402.9	463.7	436.3	377.6	425.7	380.1	375.7
2003	262.2	410.0	463.7	446.4	390.9	445.9	394.0	379.1
2004[2]	283.8	423.1	474.1	461.0	420.8	461.8	419.7	398.4
	287.2	439.0	492.5	474.5	418.9	460.2	417.9	405.7
2005	282.4	432.8	500.0	472.8	440.2	484.0	440.3	417.9
2006	293.8	464.4	526.3	492.7	463.4	498.3	451.1	441.3
Total hours worked								
	C7OE	C7OG	C7OI	C7OK	C7OM	C7OO	C7OQ	C7OS
2002	39.5	39.2	36.2	37.8	37.6	34.7	38.1	38.2
2003	39.4	39.1	35.9	37.7	37.8	34.8	38.1	38.0
2004[2]	40.0	39.4	36.1	37.7	37.9	34.9	38.2	38.3
	39.9	39.3	36.2					38.2
2005	39.7	39.3	35.7	37.6	37.9	34.8	38.4	38.4
2006	40.1	38.7	35.8	37.8	38.2	34.9	38.3	38.7
Hourly earnings excluding overtime								
	C9K4	C9K6	C9K8	C9KG	C9KI	C9KK	C9KS	C9KU
2002	6.31	10.28	12.80	11.57	9.99	12.28	9.98	9.87
2003	6.64	10.51	12.88	11.83	10.28	12.83	10.30	9.98
2004[2]	7.07	10.80	13.10	12.22	11.07	13.26	10.97	10.39
	7.16	11.22	13.62	12.58	11.01	13.22	10.93	10.60
2005	7.12	10.99	14.00	12.59	11.57	13.92	11.49	10.90
2006	7.33	12.06	14.69	13.06	12.13	14.32	11.82	11.48

1 See chapter text. Employees on adult rates whose pay for the survey pay-period was not affected by absence.

2 For 2004, two sets of figures are shown. The first does not include supplementary information and therefore is comparable with earlier years. The second includes supplementary information and so is discontinuous with previous years (where the two figures are equal, only one appears).

Sources: Annual Survey of Hours and Earnings; Office for National Statistics: 01633 819024

7.21 Average earnings and hours of full-time employees:[1] by sex
United Kingdom
At April

£ and numbers

	All Industries				Manufacturing industries			
	Average weekly earnings	Total hours worked (numbers)	Average hourly earnings		Average weekly earnings	Total hours worked (numbers)	Average hourly earnings	
			including overtime	excluding overtime			including overtime	excluding overtime
All employees								
	C7Q5	C7QX	C7Q7	C7Q9	C7PU	C7QL	C7PV	C7PW
2001	449.8	39.7	11.33	11.36	439.9	41.3	10.66	10.62
2002	472.2	39.6	11.94	11.98	455.6	41.0	11.12	11.09
2003	487.1	39.5	12.32	12.34	476.5	40.9	11.65	11.62
2004[2]	498.2	39.5	12.60	12.63	485.0	41.0	11.83	11.80
	506.1		12.80	12.84	493.1		12.03	12.01
2005	516.5	39.4	13.11	13.15	508.0	40.6	12.51	12.50
2006	537.4	37.5	13.62	13.67	528.4	40.8	12.96	12.97
Male employees								
	C7QA	C7QZ	C7QC	C7QE	C7PX	C7QT	C7PY	C7PZ
2001	498.6	41.0	12.16	12.24	469.5	41.9	11.21	11.19
2002	523.4	40.8	12.83	12.92	482.9	41.6	11.62	11.62
2003	539.3	40.8	13.21	13.28	503.2	41.5	12.13	12.12
2004[2]	548.1	40.8	13.44	13.51	511.2	41.6	12.30	12.28
	557.4		13.67	13.76	519.4		12.50	12.49
2005	568.1	40.6	13.98	14.05	533.8	41.2	12.97	12.98
2006	591.6	40.7	14.54	14.62	554.9	41.3	13.43	13.46
Female employees								
	C7QF	C7SA	C7QH	C7QJ	C7Q2	C7QV	C7Q3	C7Q4
2001	367.1	37.5	9.79	9.79	332.2	39.0	8.52	8.50
2002	386.8	37.5	10.32	10.32	350.8	38.8	9.04	9.03
2003	400.7	37.4	10.71	10.70	372.8	38.7	9.64	9.62
2004[2]	416.8	37.5	11.11	11.12	380.8	38.7	9.83	9.84
	422.1		11.26	11.27	388.1		10.02	10.02
2005	435.7	37.4	11.64	11.65	404.3	38.4	10.52	10.51
2006	453.6	37.6	12.08	12.11	422.6	38.6	10.94	10.97

1 See chapter text. Employees on adult rates whose pay for the survey period was not affected by absence.
2 For 2004, two sets of figures are shown. The first does not include supplementary information and therefore is comparable with earlier years. The second includes supplementary information and so is discontinuous with previous years (where the two figures are equal only one appears).

Sources: Annual Survey of Hours and Earnings;
Office for National Statistics: 01633 819024

7.22 Average earnings index:[1] all employees by main industrial sectors
Great Britain
Analyses by industry based on Standard Industrial Classification 1992

Indices (2000=100)

	Annual averages	Jan-uary	Feb-ruary	March	April	May	June	July	August	Sept-ember	Oct-ober	Nov-ember	Dec-ember
						Not seasonally adjusted							
Whole economy (Divisions 01 - 93)													
	LNMM												
2004	116.7	118.2	118.1	122.2	115.0	114.8	116.1	115.4	114.8	114.9	115.7	116.2	119.5
2005	121.4	123.3	124.9	127.5	119.9	119.2	120.4	120.5	119.0	118.8	119.1	119.9	124.6
2006	126.4	127.2	131.6	133.2	124.1	124.5	126.4	125.2	123.5	123.7	123.9	124.6	129.4
Manufacturing industries (Divisions 15 - 37)													
	LNMN												
2004	115.9	112.8	114.9	122.1	115.6	115.5	114.9	116.1	113.6	114.2	115.4	115.7	119.8
2005	120.1	116.3	119.2	126.6	120.0	117.5	118.2	119.9	118.1	119.2	120.4	120.5	125.1
2006	126.2	121.9	125.5	133.0	126.8	124.1	125.2	125.5	124.4	125.6	126.5	126.1	130.0
Production industries (Divisions 10 - 41)													
	LNMO												
2004	115.8	112.6	115.1	122.1	115.9	115.2	115.3	115.7	113.4	113.9	115.4	115.6	119.5
2005	120.0	116.3	119.6	126.6	120.2	117.4	118.5	119.6	117.9	118.9	120.1	120.1	125.3
2006	126.0	121.7	125.2	133.0	126.9	124.1	125.6	125.3	124.0	125.2	126.0	125.9	129.4
Service industries (Divisions 50 - 93)													
	LNMP												
2004	116.8	119.8	119.0	122.0	114.7	114.4	116.1	115.1	115.0	114.8	115.6	115.7	119.1
2005	121.6	125.0	126.4	127.6	119.8	119.4	120.7	120.5	119.2	118.3	118.5	119.4	123.8
2006	126.5	128.6	133.4	133.5	123.5	124.6	126.6	125.1	123.5	123.3	123.4	124.2	129.1
Private sector services (Divisions 50-99)													
	JJGF												
2004	115.5	121.0	119.7	123.7	113.1	112.6	114.0	113.1	112.3	112.2	113.5	113.6	117.6
2005	120.1	125.9	127.8	129.1	117.9	116.3	118.7	118.8	116.7	115.7	115.9	116.9	122.1
2006	125.2	129.2	135.1	135.3	121.5	121.6	125.1	123.0	121.0	120.8	121.0	121.7	127.3
						Seasonally adjusted							
Whole economy (Divisions 01 - 93)													
	LNMQ												
2004	116.8	116.3	113.6	115.4	115.7	115.9	116.2	116.4	117.3	117.8	118.6	119.0	119.0
2005	121.5	120.9	119.8	120.0	120.6	120.6	120.6	121.7	122.1	122.3	122.5	123.3	124.1
2006	126.5	124.1	125.8	125.3	124.8	125.9	126.6	126.5	126.8	127.3	127.6	128.2	128.9
Manufacturing industries (Divisions 15 - 37)													
	LNMR												
2004	116.0	114.3	114.3	114.7	115.3	116.4	116.1	116.2	116.1	116.4	116.9	117.3	117.9
2005	120.2	117.8	118.4	119.2	119.0	118.7	119.4	120.3	121.0	121.5	122.0	122.3	123.1
2006	126.4	123.8	124.5	124.9	126.0	125.5	126.4	126.1	127.4	128.0	128.2	128.0	127.9
Production industries (Divisions 10 - 41)													
	LNMS												
2004	115.8	114.1	114.2	114.5	115.2	116.1	115.9	116.0	115.9	116.2	116.8	117.0	117.5
2005	120.0	117.7	118.4	118.6	118.8	118.5	119.1	120.0	120.7	121.2	121.7	121.7	123.4
2006	126.0	123.6	123.9	124.4	125.7	125.4	126.1	125.9	127.0	127.6	127.7	127.6	127.4
Service industries (Divisions 50 - 93)													
	LNMT												
2004	116.8	116.1	113.2	115.5	115.5	115.7	116.1	116.3	117.4	118.0	118.9	119.2	119.3
2005	121.7	120.9	120.1	120.2	120.8	121.0	120.9	122.0	122.2	122.2	122.4	123.4	124.1
2006	126.6	123.5	126.2	125.5	124.7	126.1	126.7	126.6	126.7	127.3	127.7	128.4	129.2
Private sector services (Divisions 50-93)													
	JJGH												
2004	115.7	116.4	111.5	114.4	114.5	114.8	114.9	114.9	116.1	116.9	117.9	118.1	118.2
2005	120.4	120.7	118.8	119.0	119.5	119.2	119.5	120.8	121.0	120.9	120.9	122.0	122.8
2006	125.5	122.7	125.2	124.4	123.4	124.8	125.8	125.3	125.6	126.3	126.7	127.4	128.3

1 See chapter text.

Source: Office for National Statistics: 01633 819024

7.23 Average earnings index:[1] all employee jobs: by industry
Great Britain
Not seasonally adjusted

Indices (2000=100)

	Agriculture, forestry and fishing	Mining and quarrying	Food products, beverages and tobacco	Textiles, leather and clothing	Chemicals and man-made fibres	Basic metals and metal products	Engineering and allied industries	Other manufacturing	Electricity, gas and water supply	Construction
Excluding bonuses										
SIC 1992	(A,B)	(C)	(DA)	(DB,DC)	(DG)	(DJ)	(DK, DL,DM)	(DD,DE,DF, DH,DI,DN)	(E)	(F)
	JVUZ	JVVA	JVVB	JVVC	JVVD	JVVE	JVVF	JVVG	JVVH	JVVI
2005	125.3	123.1	121.9	119.3	120.0	120.9	121.6	120.2	114.1	124.0
2006	134.5	129.1	127.6	122.5	122.8	127.4	126.6	126.5	116.0	127.9
2004 Jun	123.9	116.2	117.6	117.6	119.5	115.5	117.1	116.0	113.3	119.5
Jul	122.5	116.1	117.8	119.6	119.0	117.3	118.3	116.3	111.4	120.4
Aug	120.5	114.6	118.0	117.2	118.9	116.7	117.5	115.2	110.9	119.7
Sep	123.4	115.9	117.4	118.4	118.1	116.7	117.2	115.9	109.5	120.7
Oct	122.5	127.3	118.1	118.5	120.4	117.6	118.6	116.2	111.3	121.4
Nov	127.2	122.5	119.6	118.5	120.2	117.1	119.0	116.8	110.9	121.9
Dec	128.2	121.3	121.9	119.4	121.2	116.3	119.3	117.2	111.1	122.2
2005 Jan	125.1	120.4	119.4	118.1	120.9	118.5	119.0	116.2	111.2	121.8
Feb	121.5	123.6	118.3	116.1	121.0	119.1	119.5	117.3	111.6	120.4
Mar	124.8	120.4	121.8	118.3	122.0	118.4	120.0	117.5	110.9	121.7
Apr	124.3	123.1	120.7	119.0	118.8	120.9	121.2	118.8	113.4	122.3
May	120.9	123.3	121.8	118.1	118.3	120.0	121.3	119.3	113.4	123.1
Jun	125.9	122.4	120.7	121.0	119.4	121.4	121.3	120.4	115.6	124.4
Jul	122.2	122.1	121.2	119.1	118.5	122.2	122.7	120.3	115.3	125.1
Aug	122.5	122.5	122.0	117.0	119.7	122.2	121.7	121.0	115.2	123.3
Sep	131.7	123.5	122.6	118.9	119.2	123.2	122.5	122.1	113.7	125.7
Oct	130.3	125.2	123.1	121.6	119.4	122.9	123.6	122.3	115.2	126.2
Nov	126.8	125.6	125.2	121.9	121.1	122.1	123.1	122.9	116.1	128.1
Dec	127.6	125.1	126.2	122.4	121.3	120.0	123.6	124.2	117.8	126.4
2006 Jan	129.0	127.4	125.0	122.1	121.3	124.0	123.0	124.1	115.7	126.6
Feb	132.0	124.9	124.3	123.1	121.6	124.5	124.7	124.7	116.3	127.6
Mar	133.0	126.1	125.2	121.4	121.1	125.7	125.2	125.1	115.2	127.0
Apr	141.3	127.6	129.4	122.5	122.1	125.2	126.4	125.2	114.2	126.6
May	140.2	128.1	128.4	123.2	122.0	126.9	126.3	125.9	118.3	127.2
Jun	141.4	128.4	127.8	124.0	123.0	129.5	126.5	126.9	118.2	127.9
Jul	137.2	128.7	128.3	122.8	121.6	128.4	126.4	126.5	118.7	128.2
Aug	139.9	129.0	128.2	120.1	122.5	127.9	126.2	127.1	116.2	126.7
Sep	135.7	131.0	128.1	122.1	124.3	129.3	127.7	127.7	114.6	128.5
Oct	130.3	131.3	128.2	122.0	125.1	129.2	128.8	127.8	113.0	129.5
Nov	123.8	131.7	127.7	122.4	123.9	129.9	129.1	128.8	116.6	130.0
Dec	130.5	134.7	130.0	124.4	125.2	127.9	128.6	128.6	114.9	129.3
2007 Jan	129.5	133.0	126.9	123.4	122.9	128.2	129.6	128.4	114.3	130.7
Percentage change on the year										
	JVVT	JVVU	JVVV	JVVW	JVVX	JVVY	JVVZ	JVWA	JVWB	JVWC
2005 Jun	1.6	5.4	2.7	2.9	−0.1	5.2	3.6	3.7	2.0	4.1
Jul	−0.2	5.2	2.9	−0.4	−0.4	4.2	3.8	3.5	3.6	3.9
Aug	1.6	6.9	3.4	−0.2	0.7	4.7	3.6	5.0	3.9	3.1
Sep	6.8	6.5	4.5	0.4	0.9	5.5	4.5	5.3	3.9	4.1
Oct	6.4	−1.7	4.3	2.6	−0.8	4.5	4.2	5.3	3.5	3.9
Nov	−0.3	2.6	4.7	2.8	0.8	4.3	3.5	5.2	4.7	5.1
Dec	−0.4	3.2	3.5	2.5	−	3.2	3.6	6.0	6.0	3.4
2006 Jan	3.1	5.8	4.7	3.3	0.3	4.7	3.4	6.7	4.1	3.9
Feb	8.6	1.0	5.0	6.1	0.6	4.5	4.3	6.4	4.2	6.0
Mar	6.6	4.7	2.8	2.6	−0.7	6.2	4.3	6.5	3.9	4.4
Apr	13.7	3.6	7.2	2.9	2.8	3.6	4.2	5.4	0.7	3.4
May	16.0	4.0	5.5	4.4	3.1	5.8	4.1	5.5	4.4	3.3
Jun	12.3	4.8	5.9	2.5	3.0	6.7	4.2	5.4	2.3	2.8
Jul	12.2	5.5	5.8	3.1	2.6	5.1	3.0	5.1	2.9	2.4
Aug	14.2	5.3	5.1	2.7	2.3	4.7	3.7	5.1	0.8	2.8
Sep	3.0	6.1	4.5	2.7	4.3	5.0	4.2	4.6	0.8	2.2
Oct	−	4.9	4.1	0.4	4.9	5.1	4.3	4.5	−1.9	2.7
Nov	−2.4	4.8	2.0	0.4	2.3	6.4	4.9	4.8	0.4	1.5
Dec	2.2	7.6	3.0	1.6	3.2	6.6	4.0	3.5	−2.4	2.3
2007 Jan	0.4	4.4	1.5	1.1	1.3	3.4	5.3	3.5	−1.2	3.2

7.23 Average earnings index:[1] all employee jobs: by industry
Great Britain

continued   Not seasonally adjusted   Indices (2000=100)

	Wholesale trade	Retail trade and repairs	Hotels and restaurants	Transport, storage and communication	Financial interm- ediation	Real estate renting and business activities	Public admini- stration	Education	Health and social work	Other services
Excluding bonuses										
SIC 1992	(G:51)	(G:50,52)	(H)	(I)	(J)	(K)	(L)	(M)	(N)	(O)
	JVVJ	JVVK	JVVL	JVVM	JVVN	JVVO	JVVP	JVVQ	JVVR	JVVS
2005	117.6	116.4	126.6	123.6	120.6	122.6	124.2	124.1	132.4	117.3
2006	121.9	118.8	133.2	126.8	125.3	127.8	128.3	128.7	137.5	121.8
2004 Jun	112.9	114.7	121.9	119.7	115.1	117.5	118.1	119.0	130.2	111.9
Jul	112.8	114.8	123.5	119.1	114.9	118.4	118.2	119.5	128.3	114.1
Aug	113.0	115.4	124.2	119.8	115.2	118.2	119.7	123.2	128.1	114.3
Sep	113.7	115.1	122.7	120.3	115.1	118.2	121.7	123.3	128.6	113.2
Oct	113.5	114.4	124.9	121.5	116.5	118.3	120.7	121.6	128.7	112.8
Nov	114.0	113.2	123.9	120.8	116.7	118.9	122.1	120.6	129.2	115.0
Dec	115.6	114.7	128.4	120.6	117.3	120.1	121.7	121.9	129.2	113.9
2005 Jan	115.6	117.3	122.8	121.4	117.7	120.5	120.5	122.0	129.2	114.7
Feb	115.2	115.5	123.7	120.7	118.3	121.0	121.9	120.8	128.8	114.5
Mar	116.9	115.7	126.8	121.0	121.6	120.7	125.9	120.7	128.9	116.7
Apr	117.3	117.9	125.9	122.4	120.9	122.1	124.3	124.0	132.9	115.3
May	117.6	116.3	126.3	123.3	121.3	122.1	123.0	123.5	132.9	116.8
Jun	117.3	116.0	126.8	125.2	119.2	122.3	123.0	124.0	133.9	119.2
Jul	118.0	117.8	127.1	123.9	121.8	123.5	124.3	124.5	133.0	121.3
Aug	118.1	118.3	127.3	123.4	121.1	123.0	124.7	126.1	132.9	118.8
Sep	118.0	115.8	126.2	125.8	119.5	123.2	125.3	126.8	132.9	118.6
Oct	119.1	116.0	126.7	124.9	121.0	123.7	125.4	126.3	133.2	115.4
Nov	119.1	115.2	127.4	125.2	121.3	124.3	125.7	124.9	135.0	116.8
Dec	119.3	115.4	132.5	126.4	123.3	124.7	126.9	125.4	134.7	119.8
2006 Jan	119.8	117.9	127.2	124.9	123.9	126.3	126.0	124.8	135.3	120.0
Feb	119.8	115.8	127.8	124.6	123.1	125.4	129.5	125.0	135.9	118.8
Mar	119.8	116.6	130.9	125.3	123.9	126.2	127.5	125.8	136.2	120.2
Apr	120.9	117.9	131.8	127.2	126.4	127.3	127.9	127.8	136.5	122.0
May	120.9	120.0	133.1	127.5	126.5	127.3	127.9	127.1	137.2	122.3
Jun	122.1	118.5	132.1	127.9	125.7	128.0	128.4	127.6	138.7	124.6
Jul	122.0	119.2	134.0	126.8	125.8	128.0	128.5	128.8	138.7	123.0
Aug	122.1	120.1	134.1	126.8	125.6	128.1	127.2	131.6	137.7	122.7
Sep	122.4	120.5	134.7	128.3	124.9	128.3	128.4	132.2	137.7	121.4
Oct	123.6	120.5	136.2	127.0	126.3	129.3	128.2	131.3	137.8	121.2
Nov	124.4	118.7	136.1	127.4	125.8	129.4	128.8	130.9	139.4	122.3
Dec	125.3	119.7	139.8	128.0	125.8	130.1	131.4	131.4	139.2	123.3
2007 Jan	124.7	121.5	136.5	128.0	127.1	131.1	129.3	130.3	139.7	124.0
Percentage change on the year										
	JVWD	JVWE	JVWF	JVYJ	JVYK	JVYL	JVYM	JVYN	JVYO	JVYP
2005 Jun	3.9	1.2	4.0	4.5	3.5	4.1	4.1	4.2	2.9	6.5
Jul	4.6	2.6	2.9	4.0	6.0	4.3	5.1	4.2	3.7	6.4
Aug	4.5	2.5	2.5	3.0	5.1	4.1	4.2	2.4	3.8	4.0
Sep	3.8	0.7	2.9	4.6	3.9	4.2	2.9	2.9	3.4	4.8
Oct	4.9	1.4	1.5	2.8	3.9	4.6	3.9	3.9	3.5	2.3
Nov	4.5	1.7	2.9	3.6	3.9	4.5	3.0	3.5	4.5	1.6
Dec	3.2	0.6	3.2	4.9	5.1	3.8	4.3	2.9	4.3	5.2
2006 Jan	3.7	0.6	3.6	2.9	5.3	4.8	4.6	2.3	4.7	4.6
Feb	4.0	0.3	3.3	3.3	4.0	3.7	6.2	3.4	5.5	3.8
Mar	2.5	0.8	3.3	3.6	1.9	4.6	1.3	4.3	5.7	3.0
Apr	3.0	–	4.6	3.9	4.5	4.3	2.9	3.0	2.7	5.8
May	2.8	3.1	5.4	3.4	4.2	4.2	4.0	2.9	3.3	4.8
Jun	4.1	2.2	4.2	2.2	5.4	4.7	4.3	3.0	3.6	4.5
Jul	3.3	1.2	5.4	2.4	3.3	3.7	3.4	3.5	4.3	1.3
Aug	3.4	1.5	5.4	2.8	3.8	4.1	2.0	4.3	3.6	3.3
Sep	3.7	4.0	6.8	1.9	4.5	4.2	2.5	4.3	3.6	2.4
Oct	3.8	3.9	7.5	1.7	4.4	4.5	2.3	3.9	3.4	5.0
Nov	4.4	3.1	6.8	1.8	3.7	4.1	2.4	4.8	3.3	4.6
Dec	5.0	3.7	5.5	1.3	2.0	4.4	3.5	4.7	3.3	2.9
2007 Jan	4.0	3.0	7.3	2.5	2.6	3.8	2.7	4.4	3.3	3.4

7.23
continued

Average earnings index:[1] all employee jobs: by industry
Great Britain
Not seasonally adjusted

Indices (2000=100)

Including bonuses

SIC 1992	Agriculture, forestry and fishing	Mining and quarrying	Food products, beverages and tobacco	Textiles, leather and clothing	Chemicals and man-made fibres	Basic metals and metal products	Engineering and allied industries (DK, DL,DM)	Other manufacturing (DD,DE,DF, DH,DI,DN)	Electricity, gas and water supply	Construction
	(A,B)	(C)	(DA)	(DB,DC)	(DG)	(DJ)	(DK, DL,DM)	(DD,DE,DF, DH,DI,DN)	(E)	(F)
	JVUF	JVUG	JVUH	JVUI	JVUJ	JVUK	JVUL	JVUM	JVUN	JVUO
2005	124.5	127.2	117.3	119.5	120.4	124.2	122.2	116.8	115.5	124.3
2006	132.7	134.9	123.2	124.9	119.7	132.5	129.0	123.3	117.6	125.8
2004 Jun	123.9	116.1	112.4	114.4	117.3	115.1	117.5	112.1	123.1	117.7
Jul	122.2	114.8	112.9	116.9	117.6	120.5	118.1	112.4	109.1	119.5
Aug	118.8	114.2	111.2	113.6	115.0	115.4	116.8	109.7	108.8	116.4
Sep	122.7	118.2	113.4	114.4	113.1	115.4	117.0	110.9	106.5	118.2
Oct	121.4	127.5	110.5	115.4	116.5	120.2	118.1	111.7	108.6	119.0
Nov	126.3	123.8	112.0	114.8	114.1	117.4	119.6	112.4	108.1	124.0
Dec	125.8	125.6	120.5	120.1	121.7	120.5	122.7	115.1	108.4	124.7
2005 Jan	123.4	128.8	112.3	117.0	117.9	122.6	118.7	111.8	110.0	121.3
Feb	119.5	137.2	114.2	116.7	121.6	122.3	124.4	113.5	117.3	119.8
Mar	126.0	148.9	129.2	117.2	150.3	125.0	126.2	120.3	112.0	128.8
Apr	122.0	137.9	116.9	117.1	122.5	126.3	123.4	114.2	113.6	120.5
May	118.0	119.2	114.6	116.0	115.7	119.9	119.9	115.4	114.6	122.6
Jun	122.7	120.5	113.3	120.2	116.5	121.5	121.0	115.5	124.9	123.0
Jul	119.4	117.8	117.8	120.0	115.5	126.9	121.7	116.8	115.0	124.4
Aug	120.1	120.1	116.6	117.2	115.6	122.8	119.3	115.8	112.7	120.9
Sep	143.4	125.6	118.0	118.1	115.8	125.2	120.3	116.7	110.2	124.3
Oct	127.5	121.8	115.3	126.6	115.1	128.8	121.8	118.1	112.7	124.9
Nov	125.6	123.5	116.2	121.3	116.1	124.9	122.5	119.0	111.4	127.6
Dec	125.9	124.6	122.9	126.6	122.0	124.5	126.9	124.2	130.8	132.9
2006 Jan	126.1	130.8	117.0	123.7	117.4	127.8	123.4	120.4	113.7	123.9
Feb	129.2	131.0	120.8	123.6	121.2	125.4	132.1	121.0	115.7	125.2
Mar	130.5	160.6	132.4	125.5	146.2	130.5	135.4	127.2	118.8	130.3
Apr	138.9	150.4	127.2	124.4	121.1	132.3	130.4	121.8	116.9	122.8
May	137.3	130.3	122.0	124.4	112.9	130.2	126.7	122.3	121.3	123.0
Jun	139.0	128.8	122.5	125.6	115.4	131.8	127.0	124.1	129.6	125.8
Jul	134.5	126.8	122.5	125.4	114.8	135.2	127.4	123.6	119.2	125.1
Aug	137.2	126.6	120.4	121.8	114.7	130.4	126.3	124.0	115.6	121.6
Sep	133.0	130.6	125.1	122.7	117.8	135.6	127.6	121.9	114.4	125.1
Oct	127.6	130.2	121.6	125.1	116.5	139.6	129.6	122.6	114.3	125.1
Nov	121.2	136.8	121.4	125.5	114.5	133.2	130.5	123.4	116.5	127.8
Dec	138.2	135.7	125.7	131.2	123.5	138.2	132.3	127.3	115.1	133.8
2007 Jan	127.6	138.4	117.5	123.6	115.6	131.3	130.3	123.6	114.3	126.9

Percentage change on the year

	JVYQ	JVYR	JVYS	JVYT	JVYU	JVYV	JVYW	JVYX	JVYY	JVYZ
2005 Jun	−1.0	3.8	0.8	5.1	−0.6	5.6	3.0	3.1	1.5	4.5
Jul	−2.3	2.6	4.4	2.6	−1.8	5.3	3.0	4.0	5.4	4.1
Aug	1.1	5.2	4.8	3.2	0.6	6.5	2.2	5.6	3.6	3.9
Sep	16.9	6.2	4.1	3.3	2.4	8.5	2.8	5.3	3.5	5.2
Oct	5.1	−4.5	4.4	9.7	−1.2	7.1	3.1	5.7	3.8	5.0
Nov	−0.5	−0.2	3.8	5.6	1.8	6.4	2.4	5.8	3.0	2.9
Dec	0.1	−0.8	2.0	5.4	0.2	3.4	3.5	7.9	20.7	6.5
2006 Jan	2.2	1.5	4.2	5.7	−0.4	4.2	4.0	7.7	3.4	2.1
Feb	8.1	−4.6	5.7	5.9	−0.3	2.5	6.3	6.6	−1.4	4.6
Mar	3.6	7.9	2.5	7.1	−2.8	4.4	7.3	5.8	6.0	1.2
Apr	13.8	9.1	8.8	6.2	−1.2	4.8	5.7	6.6	2.9	1.9
May	16.4	9.3	6.5	7.2	−2.4	8.6	5.7	6.0	5.9	0.3
Jun	13.3	6.9	8.1	4.5	−0.9	8.4	5.0	7.4	3.8	2.3
Jul	12.6	7.7	4.0	4.5	−0.6	6.5	4.7	5.8	3.6	0.6
Aug	14.2	5.4	3.3	3.9	−0.8	6.2	5.8	7.1	2.5	0.6
Sep	−7.3	4.0	6.0	3.9	1.7	8.3	6.0	4.5	3.8	0.6
Oct	0.1	6.9	5.4	−1.2	1.2	8.4	6.4	3.7	1.4	0.2
Nov	−3.5	10.7	4.4	3.5	−1.4	6.6	6.5	3.7	4.6	0.1
Dec	9.8	8.9	2.3	3.7	1.2	10.9	4.3	2.4	−12.1	0.7
2007 Jan	1.2	5.9	0.4	−	−1.5	2.8	5.6	2.6	0.5	2.4

7.23 continued

Average earnings index:[1] all employee jobs: by industry
Great Britain
Not seasonally adjusted

Indices (2000=100)

	Wholesale trade	Retail trade and repairs	Hotels and restaurants	Transport, storage and communication	Financial interm-ediation	Real estate renting and business activities	Public admini-stration	Education	Health and social work	Other services
Including bonuses										
SIC 1992	(G:51)	(G:50,52)	(H)	(I)	(J)	(K)	(L)	(M)	(N)	(O)
	JVUP	JVUQ	JVUR	JVUS	JVUT	JVUU	JVUV	JVUW	JVUX	JVUY
2005	119.3	116.6	131.5	124.6	114.4	118.4	124.1	123.8	132.5	120.3
2006	124.0	119.4	137.1	127.5	123.9	123.8	129.1	128.4	137.5	123.2
2004 Jun	114.7	115.1	124.0	126.1	93.3	113.4	117.3	118.7	130.1	120.9
Jul	114.1	114.0	126.2	117.0	92.1	114.8	117.5	119.3	128.3	116.4
Aug	113.2	114.1	126.6	116.8	90.9	112.7	121.2	123.0	128.0	115.3
Sep	113.9	114.6	125.6	117.3	90.5	111.5	121.1	122.9	128.5	115.6
Oct	114.1	113.8	128.5	118.3	96.3	112.5	120.1	121.3	128.7	116.2
Nov	116.5	112.4	127.8	118.8	93.2	113.4	121.4	120.5	129.2	120.0
Dec	123.7	114.8	135.6	121.0	101.7	117.7	122.3	121.6	129.3	119.1
2005 Jan	117.0	117.0	128.6	118.2	163.7	117.7	119.6	121.7	129.1	119.5
Feb	118.9	117.5	132.0	121.6	173.7	117.3	121.1	120.7	129.2	116.0
Mar	126.3	118.7	134.5	121.7	156.0	124.5	125.3	120.4	129.3	123.7
Apr	120.8	119.0	129.4	122.6	101.0	117.3	123.6	123.9	133.0	118.3
May	116.6	115.9	131.5	131.6	96.2	116.9	122.3	123.2	132.9	120.2
Jun	118.1	116.9	129.9	133.3	96.9	118.3	122.2	123.6	134.0	127.8
Jul	118.7	117.2	130.2	125.5	97.0	120.7	124.2	124.3	133.0	122.2
Aug	115.3	116.9	130.9	121.4	96.1	117.1	126.4	125.9	133.0	120.3
Sep	115.5	114.1	128.5	122.8	94.8	115.3	124.6	126.5	132.8	119.7
Oct	119.9	115.6	129.8	122.0	93.1	116.0	125.2	126.0	133.4	116.3
Nov	121.3	114.3	131.7	123.6	96.4	117.1	125.6	124.5	134.9	117.2
Dec	123.8	116.1	140.5	130.4	108.1	122.8	129.0	125.1	134.8	122.8
2006 Jan	121.1	118.0	129.9	123.6	168.7	120.9	125.5	124.4	135.2	121.1
Feb	121.4	115.6	134.7	124.1	209.8	121.1	129.1	124.8	135.9	121.1
Mar	129.6	122.2	136.5	125.7	175.6	129.8	127.5	125.5	137.1	123.3
Apr	121.0	119.3	134.5	124.3	105.4	122.9	127.9	127.4	136.4	123.2
May	120.2	119.7	138.4	139.0	103.4	122.3	127.7	126.8	137.0	125.4
Jun	123.0	120.8	134.7	138.2	113.2	124.7	129.1	127.3	138.5	124.9
Jul	123.9	121.3	136.5	127.5	103.4	124.9	131.2	128.7	138.5	123.9
Aug	121.3	119.0	136.9	124.6	99.3	122.2	130.1	131.3	137.4	123.2
Sep	121.9	119.6	137.6	124.6	96.7	122.3	128.6	131.9	137.4	121.6
Oct	124.6	120.2	139.4	122.9	97.7	122.6	128.6	130.9	137.6	120.6
Nov	126.6	118.0	140.7	124.4	100.4	122.7	129.1	130.7	139.2	123.5
Dec	133.9	118.9	145.5	130.8	113.5	129.5	134.7	131.2	139.2	126.7
2007 Jan	129.1	120.1	140.0	125.4	195.4	125.9	129.0	130.0	139.8	126.9
Percentage change on the year										
	JVZA	JVZB	JVZC	JVZD	JVZE	JVZF	JVZG	JVZH	JVZI	JVZJ
2005 Jun	2.9	1.6	4.8	5.7	3.9	4.3	4.1	4.1	2.9	5.7
Jul	4.0	2.8	3.2	7.3	5.3	5.1	5.6	4.2	3.7	5.0
Aug	1.8	2.4	3.4	4.0	5.8	3.9	4.3	2.3	3.9	4.3
Sep	1.5	−0.4	2.3	4.6	4.8	3.4	2.9	3.0	3.3	3.5
Oct	5.1	1.5	1.0	3.1	−3.3	3.1	4.3	3.9	3.7	0.1
Nov	4.1	1.7	3.1	4.0	3.4	3.3	3.4	3.4	4.4	−2.3
Dec	0.1	1.2	3.6	7.7	6.3	4.3	5.5	2.9	4.3	3.1
2006 Jan	3.5	0.9	1.0	4.6	3.1	2.8	4.9	2.3	4.7	1.3
Feb	2.1	−1.6	2.0	2.0	20.8	3.2	6.6	3.4	5.2	4.4
Mar	2.6	2.9	1.5	3.3	12.6	4.3	1.7	4.2	6.1	−0.3
Apr	0.2	0.2	4.0	1.4	4.3	4.8	3.5	2.9	2.6	4.2
May	3.1	3.3	5.2	5.6	7.6	4.6	4.4	3.0	3.1	4.3
Jun	4.2	3.3	3.7	3.7	16.7	5.4	5.6	3.0	3.4	−2.2
Jul	4.3	3.5	4.9	1.6	6.6	3.5	5.7	3.5	4.1	1.4
Aug	5.2	1.8	4.6	2.6	3.3	4.3	2.9	4.3	3.3	2.4
Sep	5.5	4.8	7.0	1.5	2.0	6.1	3.1	4.2	3.5	1.6
Oct	3.9	4.0	7.4	0.7	4.9	5.8	2.7	3.9	3.2	3.8
Nov	4.4	3.3	6.9	0.6	4.2	4.8	2.8	5.0	3.2	5.4
Dec	8.1	2.3	3.6	0.3	5.0	5.4	4.5	4.8	3.2	3.1
2007 Jan	6.6	1.8	7.7	1.5	15.8	4.1	2.8	4.5	3.4	4.7

1 See chapter text.

Source: Office for National Statistics: 01633 819024

7.24 Gross weekly and hourly earnings of full-time employees:[1] by sex
United Kingdom
At April

£

	Gross weekly earnings					Gross hourly earnings				
	Lowest decile	Lower quartile	Median	Upper quartile	Highest decile	Lowest decile	Lower quartile	Median	Upper quartile	Highest decile
All employees										
	C5U9	C5UC	C5UF	C5UI	C5UL	C5UO	C5UR	C5UU	C5V2	C5UX
2001	205.0	268.2	375.9	527.8	731.1	5.20	6.67	9.32	13.73	19.60
2002	214.4	279.1	390.9	551.8	767.8	5.44	6.97	9.74	14.36	20.60
2003	222.7	288.0	404.0	572.6	794.2	5.68	7.23	10.07	14.82	21.27
2004[2]	231.9	301.3	422.8	595.0	827.3	5.91	7.54	10.56	15.41	22.18
	230.3	298.0	419.2	590.6	814.4	5.84	7.45	10.44	15.32	21.83
2005	235.4	305.3	431.2	611.6	850.5	6.00	7.68	10.77	15.91	22.86
2006	244.1	316.3	447.1	632.9	886.1	6.24	7.96	11.21	16.50	23.71
Male employees										
	C5UA	C5UD	C5UG	C5UJ	C5UM	C5UP	C5US	C5UV	C5V3	C5UY
2001	229.5	299.6	415.7	575.8	813.3	5.52	7.13	9.99	14.62	21.43
2002	239.0	310.2	430.1	599.9	857.5	5.78	7.41	10.40	15.32	22.56
2003	246.6	320.3	444.6	622.8	881.9	6.00	7.68	10.75	15.83	23.17
2004[2]	254.5	333.3	463.0	647.8	916.8	6.21	7.99	11.23	16.42	24.08
	250.0	329.4	460.0	640.5	900.7	6.13	7.89	11.10	16.25	23.67
2005	255.6	335.4	471.0	666.0	939.1	6.27	8.08	11.42	16.88	24.74
2006	264.9	347.2	487.4	689.9	985.3	6.50	8.39	11.83	17.53	25.82
Female employees										
	C5UB	C5UE	C5UH	C5UK	C5UN	C5UQ	C5UT	C5UW	C5V4	C5UZ
2001	183.1	231.3	314.3	449.4	585.5	4.82	6.07	8.28	12.15	16.77
2002	192.1	241.8	330.7	474.0	623.7	5.04	6.35	8.70	12.80	17.66
2003	201.3	251.6	343.0	490.2	645.7	5.30	6.63	9.07	13.28	18.33
2004[2]	210.8	265.3	360.8	515.5	678.8	5.53	6.96	9.57	13.96	19.19
	209.3	262.3	356.7	510.0	673.9	5.50	6.91	9.42	13.82	18.96
2005	217.5	271.6	371.4	532.8	704.7	5.71	7.16	9.85	14.45	20.01
2006	226.8	283.1	386.8	555.6	728.9	5.98	7.44	10.26	15.12	20.60

1 See chapter text. Employees on adult rates whose pay for the survey period was not affected by absence.
2 For 2004, two sets of figures are shown. The first does not include supplementary information and therefore is comparable with earlier years. The second includes supplementary informaion and so is discontinuous with previous years.

Sources: Annual Survey of Hours and Earnings;
Office for National Statistics: 01633 819024

7.25 Average earnings by age group of full-time employees:[1,2] by sex, 2006
United Kingdom
At April

£ and numbers

	Average gross weekly pay excluding overtime	Average gross weekly overtime	Average weekly hours (numbers)		Average gross hourly earnings excluding overtime
			Total	Overtime	
All employees					
16 to 17	172.0	..	39.0	..	4.57
18 to 21	243.3	25.7	38.9	3.3	6.30
22 to 29	364.1	38.9	37.5	3.5	9.54
30 to 39	477.7	54.2	37.5	4.3	12.51
40 to 49	479.9	60.7	37.5	4.7	12.63
50 to 59	441.8	55.5	37.5	4.6	11.56
60+	377.4	52.2	38.4	5.0	9.73
All ages	423.5	50.5	37.5	4.3	11.12
Male employees					
16 to 17	171.1	..	39.8	..	4.44
18 to 21	250.4	30.5	40.0	4.0	6.36
22 to 29	371.4	46.7	39.0	4.1	9.53
30 to 39	498.1	64.2	39.0	5.0	12.85
40 to 49	525.3	74.2	39.0	5.5	13.59
50 to 59	477.3	69.0	38.9	5.7	12.32
60+	390.0	58.3	39.5	5.5	9.94
All ages	455.0	62.1	39.0	5.0	11.71
Female employees					
16 to 17	175.3	..	37.5	..	5.00
18 to 21	237.3	19.5	37.5	2.3	6.23
22 to 29	355.7	27.7	37.5	2.5	9.55
30 to 39	440.8	35.1	37.0	2.9	12.00
40 to 49	404.8	33.6	37.0	3.0	11.10
50 to 59	382.3	28.0	37.0	2.8	10.36
60+	339.6	29.2	37.0	2.7	9.22
All ages	378.7	29.8	37.0	2.8	10.24

1 See chapter text. Employees on adult rates whose pay for the survey period was not affected by absence.
2 All averages in the table are medians.

Sources: Annual Survey of Hours and Earnings, Office for National Statistics;
01633 819024

7.26 Trade unions[1]
United Kingdom
Year ending 31st March[2]

Percentages

		1997/98	1998/99	1999/00	2000/01	2001/02	2002/03	2003/04	2004/05
Number of trade unions	KCLB	252	238	237	226	216	210	206	193
Analysis by number of members:									
Under 100 members	KCLC	15.5	16.4	18.6	22.1	19.0	19.5	19.9	17.6
100 and under 500	KCLD	22.6	21.8	20.7	18.1	18.5	19.0	17.5	20.7
500 and under 1,000	KCLE	12.3	10.9	9.3	9.3	11.6	10.5	10.7	9.3
1,000 and under 2,500	KCLF	14.7	13.0	14.3	12.4	10.2	11.0	11.7	13.0
2,500 and under 5,000	KCLG	7.9	9.7	9.7	9.3	11.6	11.0	10.7	10.9
5,000 and under 10,000	KCLH	5.6	5.9	5.1	5.3	4.2	4.8	5.3	5.7
10,000 and under 15,000	KCLI	2.8	2.1	1.7	1.8	2.8	3.3	2.4	2.1
15,000 and under 25,000	KCLJ	2.4	2.9	4.2	5.3	6.0	4.3	4.9	4.1
25,000 and under 50,000	KCLK	7.1	8.0	7.6	6.6	6.5	7.1	7.3	7.8
50,000 and under 100,000	KCLL	2.4	2.5	2.1	2.7	2.3	1.9	2.4	1.6
100,000 and under 250,000	KCLM	3.2	2.5	2.1	2.2	2.3	2.9	2.4	2.6
250,000 and over	KCLN	3.6	4.2	4.6	4.9	5.1	4.8	4.9	4.7
All sizes	KCLP	100	100	100	100	100	100	100	100
Membership									
Analysis by size of union:									
Under 100 members	KCLQ	–	–	–	–	–	–	–	–
100 and under 500	KCLR	0.2	0.2	0.2	0.2	0.2	0.2	0.1	0.1
500 and under 1,000	KCLS	0.3	0.2	0.2	0.2	0.2	0.2	0.2	0.2
1,000 and under 2,500	KCLT	0.8	0.7	0.7	0.6	0.5	0.5	0.5	0.6
2,500 and under 5,000	KCLU	0.9	1.1	1.1	1.0	1.2	1.1	1.0	1.0
5,000 and under 10,000	KCLV	1.3	1.3	1.2	1.1	0.9	0.9	1.1	1.2
10,000 and under 15,000	KCLW	1.2	0.9	0.7	0.6	0.9	1.1	0.8	0.6
15,000 and under 25,000	KCLX	1.3	1.6	2.3	2.9	3.3	2.2	2.5	1.9
25,000 and under 50,000	KCLY	7.7	8.0	7.8	6.6	6.3	6.7	6.9	7.1
50,000 and under 100,000	KCLZ	4.5	4.5	3.8	4.6	4.0	3.1	4.4	2.6
100,000 and under 250,000	KCMA	15.4	12.0	10.0	9.8	9.6	10.2	9.0	10.6
250,000 and over	KCMB	66.5	69.5	72.1	72.4	73.0	73.9	73.3	74.1
All sizes	KCMC	100	100	100	100	100	100	100	100
Total membership (thousands)	KCMD	7 801 000	7 851 904	7 897 519	7 779 393	7 750 990	7 735 983	7 559 062	7 473 000

1 See chapter text.
2 Data derived from trade union annual returns with periods which ended between October and September each year. The majority, however, ended in December. In the case of year 2004/05, for example, the data derived from annual returns with periods which ended between October 2004 and September 2005 - approximately 73% ended in December.

Source: Certification Office

Personal income, expenditure and wealth

Chapter 8

Personal income, expenditure and wealth

Distribution of total incomes

(Table 8.1)

The information shown in Table 8.1 comes from the Survey of Personal Incomes for the financial years 2001/02, 2002/03, 2003/04 and 2004/05. This is an annual survey that covers approximately 520,000 individuals across the whole of the United Kingdom (UK). It is based on administrative data held by HMRC Offices on individuals who could be liable to tax.

The table relates only to those individuals who are taxpayers. The distributions cover only incomes as computed for tax purposes and above a level which for each year corresponds approximately to the single person's allowance. Incomes below these levels are not shown because the information about them is incomplete.

Investment income from which tax has been deducted at source is not always known to local tax offices. Estimates of missing bank and building society interest and dividends from UK companies are included in these tables. The missing investment income is distributed, in a manner consistent with information from the Expenditure and Food Survey and the National Accounts, to individuals for whom there is no investment income already reported by the tax office.

Superannuation contributions are estimated and included in total income. They have been distributed among earners in the Survey of Personal Incomes sample by a method consistent with information about the number of employees who are contracted in or out of the State Earnings Related Pension Scheme and the proportion of their earnings contributed.

When comparing results of these surveys across years, it should be noted that the Survey of Personal Incomes is not a longitudinal survey. However, sample sizes have increased in recent years to increase precision.

Average incomes of households

(Table 8.2)

Original income is the total income in cash of all the members of the household before receipt of state benefits or the deduction of taxes. It includes income from employment, self-

employment, investment income and occupational pensions. Gross income is original income plus cash benefits received from government (retirement pensions, child benefit, etc). Disposal income is the income available for consumption. It is equal to gross income less direct taxes which include income tax, national insurance contributions, and council tax. By further allowing for taxes paid on goods and services purchased, such as VAT, an estimate of post-tax income is derived. These income figures are derived from estimates made by the Office for National Statistics, based largely on information from the Expenditure and Food Survey (EFS), and published each year in *Economic Trends*, and available on the National Statistics website.

For the purposes of table 8.2, a retired household is defined as one where the combined income of retired members amounts to at least half the total gross income of the household, where a retired person is defined as anyone who describes themselves as "retired" or anyone over the minimum NI pension age describing themselves as "unoccupied" or "sick or injured but not intending to seek work."

Children are defined as persons aged under 16 or aged between 16 and 18, unmarried and receiving full-time non-advanced further education.

Expenditure and Food Survey

(Tables 8.3 - 8.5)

The Expenditure and Food Survey (formerly the Family Expenditure Survey) is a sample survey of around 6,800 private households in the UK. The sample is representative of all regions of the UK and of different types of households. The survey is continuous with interviews spread evenly over the year to ensure that estimates are not biased by seasonal variation. The survey results show how households spend their money; how much goes on food, clothing and so on; and how spending patterns vary depending upon income, household composition, and regional location of households.

One of the main purposes of the EFS is to define the 'basket of goods' for the Retail Price Index (RPI) and the Consumer Price Index (CPI). The RPI has a vital role in the uprating of state pensions and welfare benefits, while the CPI is a key instrument of the government's monetary policy. Information from the survey is also a major source for estimates of Household Expenditure in the UK National Accounts. In addition, many other government departments use EFS data as a basis for policy making, for example in the areas of housing and transport. The Department for Environment, Food and Rural Affairs (DEFRA) uses EFS data to report on trends in food consumption and nutrient intake within the UK. Users of the EFS outside government include independent research institutes, academic researcher and business and market researchers.

Like all surveys based on a sample of the population, its results are subject to sampling variability and potentially to some bias due to non-response.

The results of the survey are published in an annual report, the latest being 'Family Spending 2005-2006'. The report includes a list of definitions used in the survey, items on which information is collected and a brief account of the fieldwork procedure.

8.1 Distribution of total income before and after tax
United Kingdom
Years ending 5 April

| | 2001/2002 Annual Survey | | | | | 2002/03 Annual Survey | | | |
| | | £ million | | | | | £ million | | |
Lower limit of range of income	Number of individuals (Thousands)	Total income before tax	Total tax	Total income after tax	Lower limit of range of income	Number of individuals (Thousands)	Total income before tax	Total tax	Total income after tax
All incomes[1]	28 600	611 600	107 000	504 700	All incomes[1]	28 900	624 000	108 800	515 200
Income before tax (£)					**Income before tax (£)**				
4 535	525	2 500	12	2 490	4 615	439	2 110	8	2 100
5 000	1 070	5 890	98	5 790	5 000	1 050	5 760	88	5 670
6 000	2 890	20 200	696	19 500	6 000	2 860	20 100	652	19 400
8 000	2 800	25 200	1 670	23 500	8 000	2 840	25 600	1 630	23 900
10 000	2 650	29 100	2 600	26 500	10 000	2 660	29 200	2 550	26 600
12 000	2 580	33 400	3 600	29 800	12 000	2 520	32 600	3 470	29 200
14 000	2 340	35 100	4 220	30 900	14 000	2 310	34 600	4 130	30 500
16 000	2 040	34 600	4 490	30 100	16 000	2 060	34 900	4 510	30 400
18 000	1 700	32 200	4 440	27 700	18 000	1 740	33 100	4 540	28 600
20 000	5 510	134 300	20 500	113 800	20 000	5 700	138 900	21 200	117 700
30 000	3 160	116 900	21 500	95 400	30 000	3 300	122 400	22 500	100 000
50 000	1 050	69 800	18 500	51 300	50 000	1 090	72 100	19 100	53 000
100 000	237	31 500	10 000	21 500	100 000	249	33 100	10 600	22 500
200 000 and over	91	41 000	14 600	26 500	200 000 and over	91	39 500	13 900	25 700
Income after tax (£)					**Income after tax (£)**				
4 535	577	2 770	14	2 750	4 615	488	2 350	10	2 340
5 000	1 190	6 680	121	6 560	5 000	1 160	6 510	109	6 400
6 000	3 440	25 100	1 060	24 100	6 000	3 390	24 800	983	23 800
8 000	3 400	33 100	2 570	30 600	8 000	3 440	33 400	2 490	30 900
10 000	3 310	40 500	4 130	36 300	10 000	3 280	40 000	4 000	36 000
12 000	2 940	43 400	5 180	38 200	12 000	2 930	43 100	5 090	38 000
14 000	2 500	43 000	5 640	37 400	14 000	2 500	43 000	5 600	37 400
16 000	2 020	39 800	5 570	34 200	16 000	2 110	41 600	5 580	35 800
18 000	1 670	37 100	5 490	31 600	18 000	1 720	38 200	5 620	32 500
20 000	4 730	136 000	21 830	114 200	20 000	4 900	140 900	22 600	118 300
30 000	2 140	100 000	21 880	78 100	30 000	2 270	105 700	23 000	82 600
50 000	560	52 200	15 390	36 800	50 000	578	53 800	16 000	37 900
100 000	111	22 500	7 560	14 900	100 000	113	22 800	7 690	15 100
200 000 and over	44	29 400	10 520	18 900	200 000 and over	43	27 900	9 840	18 100

8.1
continued

Distribution of total income before and after tax
United Kingdom
Years ending 5 April

| | 2003/04 Annual Survey | | | | | 2004/05 Annual Survey | | | |
| | Number of individuals (Thousands) | £ million | | | | Number of individuals (Thousands) | £ million | | |
		Total income before tax	Total tax	Total income after tax			Total income before tax	Total tax	Total income after tax
Lower limit of range of income					**Lower limit of range of income**				
All incomes[1]	28 500	624 900	110 600	514 300	All incomes[1]	30 300	691 000	123 000	568 000
Income before tax (£)					Income before tax (£)				
4 615	498	2 390	8	2 380	4 745	329	1 600	4	1 600
5 000	1 090	6 000	93	5 900	5 000	1 110	6 090	80	6 010
6 000	2 710	19 100	636	18 400	6 000	2 760	19 500	600	18 900
8 000	2 660	23 900	1 570	22 300	8 000	2 950	26 500	1 600	24 900
10 000	2 570	28 300	2 500	25 800	10 000	2 760	30 300	2 580	27 700
12 000	2 430	31 600	3 400	28 200	12 000	2 470	32 100	3 350	28 700
14 000	2 270	33 900	4 130	29 800	14 000	2 280	34 200	4 080	30 100
16 000	1 990	33 700	4 450	29 300	16 000	2 050	34 800	4 520	30 300
18 000	1 730	32 900	4 610	28 300	18 000	1 790	34 100	4 720	29 300
20 000	5 710	139 400	21 800	117 500	20 000	6 000	146 000	22 700	124 000
30 000	3 360	124 500	22 800	101 700	30 000	4 090	152 000	27 300	125 000
50 000	1 110	73 600	19 300	54 200	50 000	1 270	83 700	21 600	62 100
100 000	256	34 000	10 800	23 200	100 000	300	40 000	12 600	27 400
200 000 and over	95	41 600	14 400	27 200	200 000 and over	111	49 500	17 300	32 200
Income after tax (£)					Income after tax (£)				
4 615	545	2 620	10	2 610	4 745	364	1 770	5	1 770
5 000	1 220	6 820	116	6 710	5 000	1 220	6 830	98	6 730
6 000	3 190	23 500	955	22 500	6 000	3 270	24 100	902	23 200
8 000	3 270	31 900	2 470	29 400	8 000	3 600	34 800	2 510	32 300
10 000	3 160	38 600	3 920	34 700	10 000	3 280	40 000	3 920	36 000
12 000	2 890	42 600	5 120	37 500	12 000	2 920	43 000	5 050	37 900
14 000	2 460	42 400	5 660	36 800	14 000	2 540	43 700	5 730	38 000
16 000	2 090	41 300	5 910	35 400	16 000	2 180	43 200	6 090	37 100
18 000	1 720	38 400	5 840	32 600	18 000	1 850	41 400	6 210	35 200
20 000	4 900	141 600	23 300	118 300	20 000	5 320	154 000	25 100	129 000
30 000	2 280	106 000	22 800	83 200	30 000	2 840	131 000	27 100	104 000
50 000	601	55 700	16 300	39 400	50 000	681	63 200	18 300	44 800
100 000	119	23 800	7 930	15 800	100 000	143	28 400	9 420	19 000
200 000 and over	45	29 600	10 200	19 300	200 000 and over	53	35 500	12 500	23 000

1 See chapter text. All figures have been independently rounded.

Sources: Survey of Personal Incomes;
Board of HM Revenue & Customs:020 7147 2917

8.2 Average incomes of households before and after taxes and benefits,[1] 2004/05
United Kingdom

	Retired households		Non-retired households								
	1 adult	2 or more adults	1 adult	2 adults	3 or more adults	1 adult with children	2 adults with 1 child	2 adults with 2 children	2 adults with 3 or more children	3 or more adults with children	All house-holds
Number of households in the population (thousands)	3 476	3 069	3 291	5 221	2 275	1 322	1 751	2 168	949	910	24 431
Average per household (£ per year)											
Original income	4 203	10 990	18 352	38 903	48 494	10 274	39 878	41 576	37 379	46 549	27 569
Gross income	10 951	20 197	20 502	40 841	51 173	18 040	42 407	44 416	42 739	51 471	31 884
Disposable income	9 830	17 624	15 898	31 229	40 270	16 232	32 856	34 904	33 886	41 253	25 360
Post-tax income	8 181	13 946	12 980	25 580	32 686	12 888	27 058	28 403	27 248	33 202	20 627

1 See chapter text. Figures taken from the article "Effects of taxes and bene-fits on household income, 2004/05", published on the National Statistics website *www.statistics.gov.uk/taxesbenefits* and in the May 2006 edition of *Economic Trends*.

Source: Office for National Statistics: 020 7533 5770

8.3 Sources of gross household income[1]
United Kingdom
Financial Years

		1995 /96	1996 /97	1997 /98	1998[2] /99	1999 /00	2000 /01	2001[3] /02	2002 /03	2003 /04	2004 /05	2005 /06
Weighted number of households (thousands)	GH92	24 130	24 310	24 560	24 660	25 330	25 030	24 450	24 350	24 670	24 430	24 800
Number of households supplying data	KPDA	6 797	6 415	6 409	6 630	7 097	6 637	7 473	6 927	7 048	6 798	6 785
Average weekly household income by source (£)												
Wages and salaries	KPCB	245.00	256.30	280.20	309.20	315.40	336.70	369.30	373.90	383.90	409.70	414.80
Self-employment	KPCC	32.90	37.50	32.90	37.20	46.00	44.50	43.10	44.50	49.80	49.00	50.80
Investments	KPCD	18.10	17.70	18.70	18.80	21.80	20.00	20.00	18.80	16.70	16.50	19.50
Annuities and pensions (other than social security benefits)	KPCE	26.00	26.00	28.90	30.30	32.80	35.00	37.00	39.90	40.90	41.70	45.50
Social security benefits[4]	KPCF	52.40	54.10	55.00	55.80	58.00	60.10	64.50	68.50	72.50	76.90	78.00
Other sources	KPCH	6.60	5.30	5.20	5.70	5.90	6.20	6.70	6.70	6.40	6.90	7.40
Total[5]	KPCI	380.90	396.90	420.80	457.00	479.90	502.50	540.60	552.30	570.30	600.70	615.90
Sources of household income as a percentage of total household income												
Wages and salaries	KPCJ	64	65	67	68	66	67	68	68	67	68	67
Self-employment	KPCK	9	9	8	8	10	9	8	8	9	8	8
Investments	KPCL	5	4	4	4	5	4	4	3	3	3	3
Annuities and pensions (other than social security benefits)	KPCM	7	7	7	7	7	7	7	7	7	7	7
Social security benefits[4]	KPCN	14	14	13	12	12	12	12	12	13	13	13
Other sources	KPCP	2	1	1	1	1	1	1	1	1	1	1
Total[5]	KPCQ	100	100	100	100	100	100	100	100	100	100	100

1 See chapter text.
2 Based on weighted data from 1998/99.
3 From 2001/02 onwards, weighting is based on the population estimates from the 2001 census.
4 Excluding housing benefit and council tax benefit (rates rebate in Northern Ireland) and their predecessors in earlier years.
5 Does not include imputed income from owner-occupied and rent-free occupancy.

Sources: Expenditure and Food Survey and Family Expenditure Survey;
Office for National Statistics

8.4 Household expenditure based on FES classification[1]
United Kingdom
Financial Years

		1995 /96	1996 /97	1997 /98	1998[2] /99	1999 /00	2000 /01	2001[3] /02	2002 /03	2003 /04	2004 /05	2005 /06
Weighted number of households (thousands)	GH92	24 130	24 310	24 560	24 660	25 330	25 030	24 450	24 350	24 670	24 430	24 800
Number of households supplying data	KPDA	6 797	6 415	6 409	6 630	7 097	6 637	7 473	6 927	7 048	6 798	6 785

Average weekly household expenditure on commodities and services (£)

		1995 /96	1996 /97	1997 /98	1998[2] /99	1999 /00	2000 /01	2001[3] /02	2002 /03	2003 /04	2004 /05	2005 /06
Housing (NET)	KPEV	48.30	49.10	51.50	57.20	57.00	63.90	65.90	66.70	69.90	76.70	80.90
Fuel and power	KPEW	12.90	13.40	12.70	11.70	11.30	11.90	11.70	11.70	12.00	12.50	13.90
Food and non-alcoholic drinks	KPEX	52.90	55.20	55.90	58.90	59.60	61.90	61.90	64.30	64.90	67.30	67.90
Alcoholic drink	KPEY	11.40	12.40	13.30	14.00	15.30	15.00	14.30	14.80	14.70	14.80	14.80
Tobacco	KPEZ	5.80	6.10	6.10	5.80	6.00	6.10	5.50	5.40	5.50	5.00	4.50
Clothing and footwear	KCWC	17.20	18.30	20.00	21.70	21.00	22.00	22.30	22.00	22.40	23.50	22.40
Household goods	KCWH	23.50	26.70	26.90	29.60	30.70	32.60	33.00	33.80	35.10	35.60	33.50
Household services	KCWI	15.10	16.40	17.90	18.90	18.90	22.00	23.60	23.30	24.90	26.30	27.10
Personal goods and services	KCWJ	11.60	11.60	12.50	13.30	13.90	14.70	14.90	15.20	16.20	16.00	16.90
Motoring	KCWK	37.00	41.20	46.60	51.70	52.60	55.10	57.90	61.70	62.40	62.60	63.80
Fares and other travel costs	KCWL	6.20	7.50	8.10	8.30	9.20	9.50	9.30	9.70	9.60	9.50	11.10
Leisure goods	KCWM	13.20	15.20	16.40	17.80	18.50	19.70	19.60	20.50	21.40	21.40	19.40
Leisure services	KCWN	32.10	34.00	38.80	41.90	43.90	50.60	51.90	53.60	55.00	59.60	63.00
Miscellaneous	KCWO	2.40	2.20	2.00	1.20	1.40	0.70	1.90	2.00	1.90	2.00	2.20
Total	KCWP	289.90	309.10	328.80	352.20	359.40	385.70	393.90	404.70	415.70	432.90	441.40

Expenditure on commodity or service as a percentage of total expenditure

		1995 /96	1996 /97	1997 /98	1998[2] /99	1999 /00	2000 /01	2001[3] /02	2002 /03	2003 /04	2004 /05	2005 /06
Housing (NET)	KPFH	17	16	16	16	16	17	17	16	17	18	18
Fuel and power	KPFI	4	4	4	3	3	3	3	3	3	3	3
Food and non-alcoholic drinks	KPFJ	18	18	17	17	17	16	16	16	16	16	15
Alcoholic drink	KPFK	4	4	4	4	4	4	4	4	4	3	3
Tobacco	KPFL	2	2	2	2	2	2	1	1	1	1	1
Clothing and footwear	KPFM	6	6	6	6	6	6	6	5	5	5	5
Household goods	KCWQ	8	9	8	8	9	8	8	8	8	8	8
Household services	KCWR	5	5	5	5	5	6	6	6	6	6	6
Personal goods and services	KCWS	4	4	4	4	4	4	4	4	4	4	4
Motoring	KCWT	13	13	14	15	15	14	15	15	15	14	14
Fares and other travel costs	KCWU	2	2	2	2	3	2	2	2	2	2	3
Leisure goods	KCWV	5	5	5	5	5	5	5	5	5	5	4
Leisure services	KCWW	11	11	12	12	12	13	13	13	13	14	14
Miscellaneous	KPFR	1	1	1	–	–	–	–	–	–	–	–
Total	KPFS	100	100	100	100	100	100	100	100	100	100	100

1 Data are based on the Family Expenditure Survey (FES) classification and not the Expenditure and Food Survey (EFS) standard classification: Classification of Individual Consumption by Purpose (COICOP). This has been done to preserve an historical time-series, as COICOP data are only available from 2001/02.

2 From 1998-99 figures shown are based on weighted data, including children's expenditure.

3 From 2001/02 onwards, weighting is based on population estimates from the 2001 census.

Sources: Expenditure and Food Survey and Family Expenditure Survey; Office for National Statistics

8.5 Percentage of households with certain durable goods
United Kingdom
Financial Years

Percentages

		1995 /96	1996 /97	1997 /98	1998[1] /99	1999 /00	2000 /01	2001[2] /02	2002 /03	2003 /04	2004 /05	2005 /06
Weighted number of households (thousands)	GH92	24 130	24 310	24 560	24 660	25 330	25 030	24 450	24 350	24 670	24 430	24 800
Number of households supplying data	KPDA	6 797	6 415	6 409	6 630	7 097	6 637	7 473	6 927	7 048	6 798	6 785
Car	KPDB	70	69	70	72	71	72	74	74	75	75	74
One	KPDC	47	43	44	44	43	44	44	44	44	42	46
Two	KPDD	19	22	21	23	21	22	23	25	25	27	23
Three or more	KPDE	4	5	5	5	6	6	6	6	6	6	5
Central heating, full or partial	KPDF	85	87	89	89	90	91	92	93	94	95	94
Washing machine	KPDG	91	91	91	92	91	92	93	94	94	95	95
Fridge/freezer or deep freezer	KPDI	87	91	90	92	91	94	95	96	96	96	97
Dishwasher	GPTL	20	20	22	23	23	25	27	29	31	33	35
Telephone	KPDL	92	93	94	95	95	93	94	94	92	93	92
Mobile phone	GH96	..	16	20	27	44	47	64	70	76	78	79
Home computer	KPDM	..	27	29	33	38	44	49	55	58	62	65
Video recorder	KPDN	79	82	84	85	86	87	90	90	90	88	86
Digital television service[3]	GH97	..	19	26	28	32	40	43	45	49	58	65
Internet connection	ZBUZ	..	..	..	10	19	32	39	45	49	53	55

1 Based on weighted data from 1998/99.
2 From 2001/02 onwards, weighting is based on the population estimates from the 2001 census.
3 Includes digital, satelite and cable receivers.

Sources: Expenditure and Food Survey and Family Expenditure Survey; Office for National Statistics

Health

Chapter 9

Health

Hospital and family health services

(Table 9.1)

The courses of treatment are for the General Dental Services (GDS). A course of treatment is complete when the treatment that is required – or such of it that the patient is willing to undergo – has been carried out. A dentist in accepting a patient for continuing care (adults) or capitation (children), undertakes to provide the care and treatment necessary to secure and maintain oral health.

Deaths: analysed by cause

(Table 9.6)

All figures in this table for England and Wales represent the number of deaths occurring in each calendar year. All data for Scotland and Northern Ireland relate to the number of deaths registered during each calendar year. From 2001, all three constituent countries of the United Kingdom are coding their causes of death using the latest, tenth, revision of the International Statistical Classification of Diseases and Related Health Problems (ICD-10). All cause of death information from 2001 (also for 2000 for Scotland) presented in this table is based on the revised classification.

To assist users in assessing any discontinuities arising from the introduction of the revised classification, bridge- coding exercises were carried out on all deaths registered in 1999 in England and Wales and also in Scotland. For further information about ICD-10 and the bridge-coding carried out by The Office for National Statistics, see the ONS Report: Results of the ICD-10 bridge-coding study, England and Wales, 1999. Health Statistics Quarterly 14 (2002), pages 75-83 or log on to the National Statistics website at: www.statistics.gov.uk. For information on the Scottish bridge-coding exercise, consult the Annual Report of the General Register Office for Scotland or log on to their website at: www.gro- scotland.gov.uk. No bridge-coding exercise was conducted for Northern Ireland.

Neonatal deaths and homicide and assault

For England and Wales, neonatal deaths (those at age under 28 days) are included in the number of total deaths but excluded from the cause figures. This has particular impact on the totals shown for the chapters covered by the ranges P and Q, 'Conditions originating in the perinatal period' and 'Congenital malformations, deformations and chromosomal abnormalities'. These are considerably lower than the actual number of deaths because it is not possible to assign an underlying cause of death from the neonatal death certificate used in England and Wales. Also, for England and Wales only, the total number shown for Homicide and assault, X85-Y09, will not be a true representation because the registration of these deaths is often delayed by adjourned inquests.

Occupational ill health

(Tables 9.8 and 9.9)

There are a number of sources of data on the extent of occupational or work-related ill health in Great Britain. For some potentially severe lung diseases caused by exposures which are highly unlikely to be found in a non-occupational setting, it is useful to count the number of death certificates issued each year. This is also true for mesothelioma, a cancer affecting the lining of the lungs and stomach, for which the number of cases with non-occupational causes is likely to be larger (although 122 still a minority). **Table 9.9** shows the number of deaths for mesothelioma and asbestosis (linked to exposure to asbestos), pneumoconiosis (linked to coal dust or silica), byssinosis (linked to cotton dust) and some forms of allergic alveolitis (including farmer's lung). For asbestos-related diseases the figures are derived from a special register maintained by HSE.

Most conditions which can be caused or made worse by work can also arise from other factors. The remaining sources of data on work-related ill health rely on attribution of individual cases of illness to work causes. In The Health and Occupation Reporting Network (THOR), this is done by specialist doctors - either occupational physicians or those working in particular disease specialisms (covering musculoskeletal, psychological, respiratory, skin, audiological and infectious disease). **Table 9.8** presents data from THOR for the last three years. It should be noted that not all cases of occupational disease will be seen by participating specialists; for example, the number of deaths due to mesothelioma (shown in Table 9.9) is known to be greater than the number of cases reported to THOR.

Injuries at work

(Table 9.10)

The appropriate 'responsible person' is required to report injuries arising from workplace activities to HSE or the local authority under the Reporting of Injuries, Diseases and Dangerous Occurrences Regulations 1995 (RIDDOR 95). This includes fatal injuries, nonfatal major injuries, as defined by the Regulations, and other injuries causing incapacity for work for more than 3 days. As of 1 April 2001, reports are to be made to an Incident Centre (ICC), based at Caerphilly.

HSE gets to know about virtually all workplace fatalities. However, it is known that employers and others do not report all non-fatal reportable injuries. To estimate the level of under-reporting by employers, HSE place questions each year with the Labour Force Survey (LFS), asking respondents if they have suffered a workplace injury in the past year.

The results from the latest LFS show that in Great Britain employers report around 49 per cent of reportable injuries (2004/05). When compared to the previous year, these results also indicate a drop of in the non-fatal injury rate of10.0%. The self-employed report between 5 and 10% of reportable non-fatal injuries.

9.1 Hospital and family health services
England and Wales

			England						Wales				
			2001	2002	2003	2004	2005		2001	2002	2003	2004	2005
Hospital services[1]													
Average daily number of available beds	KNMY	Thousands	185	184	184	181	176	KNHY	14	14	14	14	14
Average daily occupation of beds:													
All departments	KNMX	"	157	157	158	154	149	KNHX	12	12	12	12	11
Psychiatric departments	KNMW	"	..	..	..	..	..	KNGZ	2	2	2	2	2
Persons waiting for admission at 31 March[2]	KNMV	"	1 035	992	906	822	809	KNGY	71	75	75	66	69
Finished consultant episodes[3]													
Day case admissions	KNLY	"	3 588	3 703	3 757	3 848	4 113	KNBZ	131	107	109	109	111
Ordinary admissions	KIBS	"	8 750	9 012	9 417	9 859	10 310	KNEO	570	564	593	600	611
Out-patients													
New cases	KNLX	"	12 613	12 879	13 431	13 370	..	KNBY	697	737	739	741	776
Total attendances	KNLW	"	43 675	43 765	45 120	44 768	..	KNBX	2 762	2 843	2 868	2 804	2 882
Accident and Emergency:													
New cases	KOTH	"	12 853	12 945	15 313	16 712	17 775	KTCO	878	889	916	937	942
Total attendances	KOTI	"	14 044	14 046	16 517	17 837	18 759	KTCP	1 010	1 005	1 036	1 059	1 061
Ward attendances	KOTJ	"	1 089	1 179	..	..	..	KTCQ	..	..	..	..	..
Family health services[4]													
Medical services:													
Doctors on the list[5]	KNKX	Numbers	..	..	..	..	..	KNBR	1 807	1 808	1 822	1 816	1 849
Number of GPs (exc. Retainers and Registrars)[6]	LQZZ	"	28 802	29 202	30 358	31 523	32 738	ZCMA	1 807	1 808	1 822	1 816	1 849
Number of patients per GP (exc. Retainers and Registrars)	KNKW	"	1 780	1 764	1 736	1 666	1 613	KNBQ	1 665	1 679	1 659	1 674	1 650
Paid to doctors[7]	KNKV	£ million	..	..	..	..	..	KNBP	222	241	269	..	..
Pharmaceutical services:[8,9]													
Number of prescription forms	KWUK	Millions	315	326	..	..	366	VQEU	..	..	..	..	..
Number of prescription items	KWUL	"	587	617	650	686	733	KNBO	46	49	51	54	57
Total cost	KWUM	£ million	6 488	7 162	..	..	8 542	KNBN	472	..	..	..	..
Average total cost per prescription	KWUN	£	11.0	12.0	..	..	12.0	KNBK	10.0	..	..	..	..
Income from patients	KWUO	£ million	408	423	..	..	368	KNBM	23	23	23	..	..
General Dental Services (GDS) and Personal Dental Services (PDS):													
Dentists as at 30 September[10]	KIAZ	Numbers	18 821	19 056	19 339	19 722	20 890	KIBG	931	927	919	927	928
Number of adult courses of treatment[11]	KIBA	Thousands	26 571	26 637	26 726	27 032	26 488	KIBH	1 564	1 886	1 629	1 689	..
Number of adults registered[12]	KIBB	"	17 280	17 281	17 064	17 374	17 237	KIBI	1 063	1 065	1 079	1 050	1 023
Number of children registered[12]	KIBC	"	7 001	6 982	6 841	6 964	6 891	KIBJ	403	400	397	384	389
Gross expenditure[13]	KIBD	£ million	–	–	..	..	..	KIBK	95	99	104	107	..
Paid by patients[13]	KIBE	"	–	–	..	..	..	KIBL	25	25	27	26	..
Paid out of public funds[13]	KIBF	"	–	–	..	..	..	KIBM	71	74	76	82	..
General ophthalmic services:													
Sight tests[14]	KNJL	Thousands	9 807	9 662	9 845	10 149	10 355	KNBD	668	647	646	656	674
Pairs of spectacles for which NHS vouchers redeemed	KNJK	"	3 607	3 472	3 520	3 624	3 678	KNBC	273	252	252	251	252
Cost of services (gross)[13]	KNJJ	£ million	311	304	..	..	..	KNBA	22	22	22	23	..
Paid out of public funds:[13]													
For sight testing	KNJH	"	167	166	..	..	..	KMZZ	11	11	11	11	..
For cost of vouchers[12]	WMPC	"	143	137	..	..	..	KMZX	10	9	9	10	..

1 Data shown reflect data for the financial year commencing the year in the heading (for example, the figures under 2001 reflects 2001/2002 data). Out-patient figures do not include accident and emergency figures or ward attenders which are given separately. Information on general practitioner maternity clinics is not collected separately in England but is included for Wales.

2 People awaiting elective admission at NHS Trusts in England and Wales, as an inpatient or a day case.

3 Finished Consultant Episode (FCE). An FCE is defined as a period of admitted patient care under one consultant within one healthcare provider. Please note that the figures do not represent the number of patients, as a person may have more than one episode of care within the year.

4 Welsh FHS expenditure and income is based upon cash payments and receipts in each financial year, as accrued gross expenditure is not available in a common format for all years shown in this series. Welsh Dental Services data excludes refunds of dental charges.

5 For Wales, all practitioners (excluding GP registrars and GP retainers) at 30 September.

6 GP's includes Contracted GP's, GMS Others and PMS Others. English GP data are at 30 September.

7 For Wales, includes PFMA but excludes GPFH drugs and payments to providers.

8 Welsh data are based on pricing bureau totals of prescriptions dispensed in a calendar year and paid during the financial year. Data shown reflects data for the year commencing the year in the heading (for example, the figures under 2001 reflects 2001/2002 data). Financial year is from 1 April to 31 March.

9 The data cover all prescription items dispensed by community pharmacists and appliance contractors, dispensing doctors and prescriptions submitted by prescribing doctors for items personally administered. Total cost refers to the cost of the drug less discounts and includes on cost allowance, dispensing fees, container allowance, oxygen payments and VAT. Income from patients relates to financial years and from 2001/2002 is taken from HA annual accounts. Previous years taken from the Appropriation Account. Income includes charges retained by pharmacists & dispensing doctors, sales of pre-payment certificates and recoveries from patients.

10 Dentis consist of principals, assistants and trainees. Information on NHS dentistry in the community dental services, in hospitals and prisons are excluded.

11 Data shown reflect data for the financial year ending in the year in the heading (i.e. data under 2001 represent data for the year ending 31 March 2001).

12 Personal Dental Services (PDS) schemes had varying registrations periods. To ensure comparibility with corresponding General Dental Services (GDS) data, PDS registrations are estimated using "proxy registrations", namely the number of patients seen by PDS practices in the previous 15 months. PDS proxy registrations were not estimated for the periods before September 2003 - actual registrations were used before this date.

13 Figures for England are based on provisional outturn figures, with gross expenditure and patient figures having been adjusted from previous publications to include refunds of dental charges. For Wales, figures are for the financial year and based on the Appropriation account.

14 Number of NHS sight tests paid for by FHSAs/HAs in the period.

Sources: Department of Health;
The Information Centre for health and social care;
NHS Business Services Authority;
Welsh Assembly Government

9.2 Hospital and primary care services
Scotland

			1995	1996	1997	1998	1999	2000	2001	2002	2003	2004	2005
Hospital and community services													
In-patients:[1,2]													
Average available staffed beds	KDEA	Thousands	42.4	40.6	38.4	36.8	35.2	33.5	32.1	30.9	29.8	28.9	28.1
Average occupied beds:													
All departments	KDEB	"	34.3	32.8	30.9	29.5	28.2	26.9	25.8	25.1	24.2	23.2	22.5
Psychiatric and learning disability	KDEC	"	12.6	11.7	10.8	10.0	9.1	8.3	7.6	7.0	6.4	5.9	5.5
Discharges or deaths[3]	KDED	"	960	973	965	978	977	965	957	952	939	968	1 003
Outpatients:[2,4]													
New cases	KDEE	"	2 577	2 666	2 675	2 715	2 734	2 766	2 748	2 728	2 730	2 748	2 720
Total attendances	KDEF	"	6 241	6 338	6 272	6 331	6 424	6 451	6 381	6 254	6 192	6 144	5 990
Medical and dental staff:[5]	JYXO	Numbers	8 451	8 699	9 018	9 081	9 273	9 325	9 644	10 256	10 407	10 658	10 871
Whole-time	KDEG	"	6 402	6 729	7 024	7 057	7 185	7 216	7 530	8 115	8 349	8 612	8 796
Part-time	KDEH	"	1 494	1 461	1 510	1 550	1 632	1 648	1 681	1 697	1 636	1 630	1 670
Honorary	JYXN	"	578	534	521	506	495	495	468	468	437	431	418
Professional and technical staff:[6]													
Whole-time	KDEI	"	10 452	10 584	10 740	10 884	11 261	11 261	11 705	12 265	12 942	13 258	13 750
Part-time	KDEJ	"	4 075	4 370	4 738	4 928	5 218	5 483	5 852	6 273	6 708	6 968	7 440
Nursing and midwifery staff:[7]													
Whole-time	KDEK	"	32 693	32 560	32 218	32 156	32 356	32 401	33 334	34 294	34 939	35 338	36 093
Part-time	KDEL	"	30 580	29 917	29 736	29 178	29 242	29 131	29 004	29 015	29 354	29 484	29 688
Administrative and clerical staff:[8]													
Whole-time	KDEM	"	15 815	15 155	14 707	14 564	14 541	14 710	15 361	16 200	17 260	17 806	18 434
Part-time	KDEN	"	7 005	6 986	7 174	7 265	7 456	7 677	8 075	8 630	9 307	9 943	10 707
Domestic, transport, etc, staff:[9]													
Whole-time	KDEO	"	9 037	8 596	8 187	8 090	7 972	7 848	7 625	7 768	8 234	8 305	8 516
Part-time	KDEP	"	14 105	13 554	13 082	12 716	12 424	12 272	11 522	11 915	12 588	12 324	12 545
Cost of services (gross)[10]	KDEQ	£ million	3 269.5	3 430.6	3 610.3	3 856.0	4 309.7	4 862.6	5 378.6	5 919.5	..	..	..
Payments by patients[10]	KDER	"	0.02	0.01	0.01	0.01	0.01	0.01	–	..	..	..	..
Payments out of public funds[10]	KDES	"	3 269.5	3 430.6	3 610.3	3 855.9	4 309.7	4 862.6	5 378.6	5 919.5	..	..	..
Primary care services													
Medical services													
Doctors on the list:[11]													
Principals[12]	KDET	Numbers	3 524	3 573	3 625	3 660	3 698	3 707	3 756	3 765	3 801	3 782	3 807
Assistants	KDEU	"	28	22	22	27	19	25	39	37	47	..	..
Average number of patients per principal doctor[13]	KDEV	"	1 506	1 488	1 468	1 450	1 441	1 425	1 409	1 392	1 381	1 421	1 416
Payments to doctor[14]	KDEW	£ million	311.9	333.2	356.4	365.9	377.5	404.7	429.6	467.5	..	..	..
Pharmaceutical services[15]													
Prescriptions dispensed	KDEX	Millions	51.08	54.62	56.64	58.52	60.36	62.34	65.56	69.13	71.83	74.66	76.74
Payments to pharmacists (gross)	KDEY	£ million	474.2	543.4	588.4	627.2	693.7	731.0	788.6	868.9	946.3	988.0	993.7
Average gross cost per prescription	KDEZ	£	9.3	10.0	10.4	10.7	11.5	11.7	12.0	12.6	13.2	13.2	12.9
Dental services													
Dentists on list[16]	KDFA	Numbers	1 691	1 709	1 710	1 739	1 786	1 808	1 808	1 844	1 869	1 882	1 900
Number of courses of treatment completed	KDFB	Thousands	2 723	2 711	2 825	3 406	3 349	3 406	3 395	3 390	3 433	3 370	3 375
Payments to dentists (gross)	KDFC	£ million	136.1	137.3	139.2	154.9	157.5	160.6	162.9	165.1	172.3	170.4	173.5
Payments by patients	KDFD	"	42.2	41.7	41.4	45.9	47.4	48.8	50.6	52.3	54.7	53.3	53.9
Payments out of public funds	KDFE	"	93.9	95.6	97.8	109.0	110.1	111.8	112.3	112.9	117.6	117.1	119.6
Average gross cost per course	KDFF	£	38.0	38.0	40.1	36.5	38.0	38.0	37.0	38.0	40.0	40.0	40.0
General ophthalmic services													
Number of sight tests given[17]	KDFG	Thousands	614	618	635	656	657	850	861	877	907	920	935
Number of pairs of glasses supplied[18]	KDFH	"	473	461	474	488	485	494	439	463	458	450	457
Payments out of public funds for sight testing and dispensing	KDFK	£ million	25.8	27.7	29.1	29.8	32.0	33.1	..	..	34.9	35.5	37.8

1 Excludes joint user and contractual hospitals.
2 In year to 31 March.
3 Includes transfers out and emergency inpatients treated in day bed units.
4 Including attendances at accident and emergency consultant clinics.
5 As at 30 September. Figures exclude officers holding honorary locum appointments. Part-time includes maximum part-time appointments. There is an element of double counting of "heads" in this table as doctors can hold more than one contract. For example, they may hold contracts of different type, eg part time and honorary. Doctors holding two or more contracts of the same type, eg part time, are not double counted. Doctors, whose sum of contracts amounts to whole time, are classed as such. Figures have been revised due to coding changes.
6 As at 30 September. Comprises Therapeutic, Healthcare science, Technical and Pharmacy staff.
7 As at 30 September. Includes Health Care Assistants. Figures post 2003 have been ammended due to a coding error resulting in some staff previously in this group have been moved to the admin and clerical group.
8 As at 30 September. Comprises Senior Management and Administrative and Clerical staff. Figures from 2003 onwards have been ammended due to the inclusion of some staff previously in the nursing and midwifery staff group

9 As at 30 September. Comprises Ambulance, Works, Ancillary and Trades.
10 These figures are for Health Boards only and do not include the 2 NHS Trusts in 1995 and 47 in 1995/96. Estimated from financial years.
11 At 1 October.
12 Unrestricted principals in post.
13 Unrestricted principals: establishment.
14 Data relate to financial year, eg 1997 data are for year ending 31 March 1998. As 1994/95 data are unavailable for Dumfries & Galloway Health Board, 1993/94 data have been substituted for that board only.
15 For prescriptions dispensed in calendar year by all community pharmacists (including stock orders), dispensing doctors and appliance suppliers.
16 Comprises principals only.
17 This figure represents sight tests paid for by health boards, hospital eye service referrals and GOS(s) ST (v) claimants. From 1995, data refers to financial year (eg 1995 data is for year ending 31 March 1995). 1994 calander year data is missing.
18 Does not include hospital eye service.

Sources: NHS National Services Scotland and The Scottish Executive.;
0131 551 8899

9.3 Hospital and general health services
Northern Ireland

			1996	1997	1998	1999	2000	2001	2002	2003	2004	2005
Hospital services[1]												
In-patients:												
Beds available[2]	KDGA	Numbers	9 464	9 006	8 818	8 639	8 571	8 419	8 301	8 347	8 323	8 238
Average daily occupation of beds	KDGB	Percentages	*78.9*	*80.8*	*81.9*	*81.5*	*82.0*	*83.3*	*84.3*	*84.1*	*84.2*	*83.6*
Discharges or deaths[3]	KDGC	Thousands	300	305	335	332	333	328	327	332	337	343
Out-patients:[4]												
New cases	KDGD	"	933	952	962	984	994	997	992	1 014	1 027	1 043
Total attendances	KDGE	"	2 070	2 084	2 091	2 111	2 114	2 131	2 122	2 161	2 175	2 221
General health services												
Medical services[1]												
Doctors (principals) on the list[5,6]	KDGF	Numbers	1 028	1 039	1 042	1 054	1 066	1 073	1 076	1 076	1 078	1 084
Number of patients per doctor	KDGG	"	1 698	1 690	1 693	1 678	1 661	1 651	1 652	1 658	1 663	1 655
GrossPayments to doctors[7]	KDGH	£ thousand	67 872	69 889	71 385	78 604	82 471	84 664	88 194	96 894	..	..
Pharmaceutical services[8]												
Prescription forms dispensed	KDGI	Thousands	12 802	13 246	13 489	13 454	13 666	14 277	14 622	15 158	15 283	15 860
Number of prescriptions	KDGJ	"	21 203	22 047	22 754	23 249	23 985	24 705	25 501	26 656	27 401	28 417
Gross Cost[9]	KDGK	£ thousand	219 978	236 746	248 845	266 535	278 405	303 489	327 045	362 401	382 789	390 763
Charges[10]	KDGL	"	6 224	6 784	7 007	8 183	8 499	9 074	9 597	9 798	10 262	10 676
Net Cost[9]	KDGM	"	213 950	229 962	241 837	258 353	269 906	294 415	317 448	352 602	372 527	380 087
Average gross cost per prescription[9]	KDGN	£	10.38	10.74	10.94	11.46	11.61	12.28	12.82	13.60	13.97	13.75
Dental services[8,11]												
Dentists on the list[5]	KDGO	Numbers	584	592	612	632	661	673	689	696	720	726
Number of courses of paid treatment	KDGP	Thousands	928	1 053	1 088	1 086	1 113	1 126	1 123	1 107	1 086	1 084
Gross cost	KDGQ	£ thousand	51 512	53 735	56 835	58 712	61 237	64 454	66 201	66 910	67 294	69 480
Patients	KDGR	Thousands	11 870	12 433	13 686	14 358	15 302	16 041	930	919	907	910
Contributions (Net cost)	KDGS	£ thousand	39 642	41 303	43 149	44 354	46 152	48 413	49 376	50 282	50 498	52 308
Average gross cost per paid treatment	KDGT	£	56	50	52	54	55	57	59	60	62	64
Ophthalmic services[8]												
Number of sight tests given[12]	KDGU	Thousands	212	227	236	305	307	326	334	346	347	360
Number of optical appliances supplied[13]	KDGV	"	153	159	179	178	181	187	190	192	189	194
Cost of service (gross)[14]	KDGW	£ thousand	9 555	10 271	10 303	11 509	12 035	12 738	13 473	13 981	14 444	15 496
Health and social services[15]												
Medical and dental staff:												
Whole-time	KDGZ	Numbers	2 107	2 156	2 196	2 231	2 224	2 281	2 411	2 607	2 749	2 948
Part-time	KDHA	"	1 094	1 041	1 009	1 014	580	597	626	620	627	562
Nursing and midwifery staff:												
Whole-time	KDHB	"	10 578	10 114	10 117	10 135	9 926	9 828	10 248	10 729	11 137	11 416
Part-time	KDHC	"	8 943	9 015	8 287	8 813	7 591	7 814	8 395	8 706	8 887	9 047
Administrative and clerical staff:												
Whole-time	KDHD	"	7 055	6 915	7 019	7 230	7 373	7 536	7 966	8 370	8 846	9 047
Part-time	KDHE	"	2 518	2 708	2 776	2 910	2 972	3 136	3 372	3 609	3 858	4 190
Professional and technical staff:												
Whole-time	KDHF	"	2 939	2 933	3 014	3 177	3 642	3 762	3 975	4 163	4 528	4 695
Part-time	KDHG	"	985	1 060	1 146	1 226	1 283	1 369	1 499	1 616	1 731	1 827
Social services staff(excluding casual home helps):												
Whole-time	KDHH	"	3 441	3 349	3 262	3 319	3 017	3 127	3 284	3 461	3 716	3 777
Part-time	KDHI	"	2 250	2 394	2 241	2 358	868	911	986	1 105	1 207	1 297
Ancillary and other staff:												
Whole-time	KDHJ	"	3 812	3 569	3 423	3 426	3 506	3 472	3 426	3 418	3 470	2 308
Part-time	KDHK	"	3 558	3 482	3 558	3 913	4 508	4 925	5 125	5 420	5 588	5 472
Cost of services (gross)[14]	KDHL	£ thousand	1 120 563	1 153 741	1 292 348	1 422 920	1 576 657	1 639 283	1 868 538	2 113 453	..	..
Payments by recipients	KDHM	Thousands	40 725	49 498	59 484	65 533	71 411	78 478	88 860	87 999	..	..
Payments out of public funds	KDHN	£ thousand	1 079 838	1 104 243	1 232 864	1 357 387	1 505 246	1 560 805	1 779 678	2 025 454	..	..

1 Financial Year.
2 Average available beds in wards open overnight during the year.
3 Includes transfers to other hospitals.
4 Includes consultant outpatient clinics and Accident and Emergency departments.
5 At beginning of period for Dentists. Doctors numbers at 2002 (Oct), 2003 (Nov), 2004 & 2005 (Oct).
6 From 2003 onwards (UPE's).
7 These costs refer to the majority of non-cash limited services: further expenditure under GMS is allocated through HSS Boards on a cash limited basis. Change between 2002 and 2003 is due to advance payments being made in relation to the new GMS contract introduced in April 2004.
8 From 1995 onwards figures are taken from financial year.
9 Gross cost is defined as net ingredient costs plus on-cost, fees and other payments.
10 Excludes amount paid by patients for pre-payment certificates.
11 Due to changes in the Dental Contract which came into force in October 1990 dentists are paid under a combination of headings relating to Capitation and Continuing Care patients. Prior to this, payment was simply on an item of service basis.

12 Excluding sight tests given in hospitals and under the school health service and in the home.
13 Relates to the number of vouchers supplied and excludes repair/replace spectacles.
14 Figures relate to the costs of the hospital, community health and personal social services, and have been estimated from financial year data.
15 Workforce figures until 1999 refer to 31st December and are taken from the Trust and Board payroll system. Figures from 2000 onwards are at 30th September and are taken from the Trust and Board Human Resource Management Systems. Figures for 2000 onwards exclude all home helps and all agency/bank staff but include Ambulance and Works staff in the Ancillary & Other Staff category. As a result, backward comparison of the workforce is not advisable as definitions differ. Some figures for 2000 have been revised.

Sources: Central Services Agency Northern Ireland: 028 9032 4431;
Dept of Health, Social Services & Public Safety Northern Ireland: 028 9052 2509;
(Figures on Hospital Services: 028 9052 2800)

9.4 Health services: workforce summary[1,2]
Great Britain
As at 30 September

Whole-time equivalent

		1996	1997	1998	1999	2000	2001	2002	2003	2004	2005
Health service staff and practitioners											
Medical staff: total	KDBC	62 176	64 316	67 408	69 089	70 939	73 206	78 024	82 294	89 450	93 532
Hospital medical staff: total[3]	KDBD	59 592	61 937	65 088	66 812	68 767	71 107	76 122	80 537	87 641	13 452
Consultant	KDBE	21 066	21 699	23 139	24 250	25 067	26 106	27 951	29 566	31 628	33 844
Staff grade	KADJ	2 440	2 785	3 458	3 868	4 423	4 720	5 409	5 462	5 648	5 576
Associate specialist	KDBF	1 223	1 340	1 439	1 527	1 572	1 609	1 780	1 993	2 263	2 485
Registrar group[4]	KWUG	11 898	12 435	12 863	13 299	13 372	13 826	14 530	15 580	17 890	19 337
Senior registrar	KDBG	..	..	..	..	..	..	..	..	..	..
Registrar	KDBH	..	..	..	..	..	..	..	..	..	..
Senior house officer	KDBI	16 616	17 353	17 760	17 518	17 945	18 377	19 850	21 525	23 567	24 702
House officer	KADK	4 025	4 163	4 287	4 364	4 518	4 560	4 944	4 985	5 276	5 637
Hospital practitioner[5]	KDBL	212	198	220	230	231	223	248	247	256	211
Clinical assistant[5]	KDBM	2 094	1 924	1 907	1 744	1 638	1 684	1 407	1 179	1 064	765
Other staff[6]	KDBK	18	38	16	11	1	1	3	–	50	542
Public health medicine and community health services medical staff[3]	KDBN	2 584	2 379	2 320	2 278	2 172	2 100	1 902	1 756	1 809	434
Dental staff: total	KDBO	3 127	3 078	3 193	3 147	3 107	3 152	3 357	3 429	3 571	3 680
Hospital dental staff: total[3]	KDBP	1 737	1 696	1 807	1 816	1 781	1 816	1 944	1 981	2 021	357
Consultant	KDBQ	556	524	570	581	580	578	610	664	689	726
Staff grade	KADL	67	86	99	113	118	135	154	158	163	181
Associate specialist	KDBR	65	62	68	70	73	74	75	79	93	97
Registrar group[4]	LQMZ	..	..	309	314	295	311	339	329	344	388
Senior registrar	KDBS	138	169	..	..	..	..	..	..	..	..
Registrar	KDBT	183	125	..	..	..	..	..	..	..	..
Senior house officer	KDBU	490	491	531	496	497	513	572	584	580	616
Dental house officer	KDBV	68	58	59	68	60	61	60	38	31	28
Hospital practitioner[7]	KDBX	23	22	21	23	21	18	20	20	22	17
Clinical assistant[7]	KDBY	145	152	144	146	136	126	112	108	98	89
Other staff[6]	KDBW	3	6	5	6	–	–	1	–	1	1 137
Community health dental staff[3]	KDBZ	1 390	1 382	1 386	1 331	1 326	1 336	1 413	1 448	1 550	401
Non-medical staff: total	KWUH	856 732	849 426	855 305	870 921	890 282	927 831	974 390	1 022 837	1 061 640	1 093 439
Nursing and midwifery staff:[8,9,10] (excluding agency): total	KDCA	410 693	407 760	409 045	415 786	423 737	437 417	455 361	474 263	485 180	492 391
of which:											
qualified	KSBR	300 371	298 483	299 654	303 644	309 682	320 685	335 313	349 701	360 910	368 276
unqualified[10]	KSBS	106 181	106 313	106 773	109 687	111 931	114 532	117 582	121 896	121 194	121 129
learners	KSBT	2 804	2 356	2 178	1 961	2 054	2 201	2 387	2 591	3 076	2 985
All Professional and Technical staff (excluding works)[11,12]	KSBM	118 403	120 439	123 902	128 116	131 943	138 348	146 804	155 507	164 419	171 326
Health care assistants	KWUI	18 025	19 268	22 026	22 746	24 919	30 047	33 301	36 027	37 829	39 272
Support staff	KWUJ	75 836	72 608	71 043	69 883	68 449	69 245	69 628	69 553	69 749	73 457
Ancillary, Works & Maintainance[13]	KSBN	27 603	26 037	25 131	24 468	23 962	23 013	23 430	23 820	24 708	23 438
Administrative and Estates staff	KSBO	183 049	183 112	184 711	190 421	197 327	209 004	224 490	241 634	256 412	269 131
Ambulance staff	KSBP	18 655	18 751	18 382	18 552	19 209	19 888	20 864	21 449	22 753	23 888
Others	KSBQ	4 159	1 079	906	780	746	711	512	584	590	535

1 Whote-time equivalent. Figures exclude locums and occasional seasonal staff.
2 Medical and dental data (1996-2004) have been revised for comparability purposes. Since 2005, data can no longer be split by sector (hospital and community).
3 Does not include Enagland data as hospital and community staff are no longer split.
4 Includes Specialist Registrar (SpR), Senior Registrar and Registrar. The SpR grade was introduced formally on 1 April 1996.
5 Scottish figures not available 2005.
6 Includes Senior clinical medical officiers, clinical medical officers, GDP/GMP grades (including Clinical Assistant (Para. 94 and Para. 107 appointments), Hospital Practitioner and Limited Specialist. Staff in these grades may also hold General Medical services, or General Dental Service appointments), Medical Adviser, Assistant Prescribing Adviser, Dental Adviser, Dental Officer, Senior Dental Officer, Assistant/ Chief Administrative Dental Officers, Clinical Director/Assistant Clinical Director.
7 Excludes bank nurses for Wales & Scotland.
8 Nursing total includes qualified, unqualified and others only. England & Wales.
9 Nursing total includes Registered and Unregistered nurses and midwives only. Scotland.
10 Excludes health care assistants.
11 GP Registrars were formally referred to as Trainees.
12 Include Therapeutic, Healthcare Science, Technical & Pharmacy staff.
13 Welsh figures not available 2005.

Sources: Information Centre for Health and Social Care;
Welsh Assembly Government.;
NHS ISD Scotland;
Scottish Health Service Common Services Agency

9.5 Health and personal social services: workforce summary
Great Britain

Numbers

		1996	1997	1998	1999[3]	2000	2001	2002	2003	2004	2005
Family Health services:											
General medical practitioners[1]											
All practitioners: total[2,3]	GPYL	..	..	..	36 954	37 583	38 172	38 656	40 021	41 322	42 531
All practitioners (excluding GP Retainees)	LQZN	34 825	35 204	35 618	35 957	36 233	36 761	37 283	38 769	40 273	41 650
GP Registrars[4]	LQZU	1 605	1 677	1 830	1 902	2 028	2 278	2 386	2 626	2 959	2 973
GP Retainees[5]	GPYM	–	–	–	997	1 350	1 411	1 373	1 252	1 049	903
General dental practitioners: total[6]	KDCQ	19 139	19 598	20 216	20 833	21 316	21 929	22 194	22 507	22 997	24 123
General Dental Service	GPYN	19 139	19 598	20 216	20 750	21 124	21 462	21 538	21 701	20 826	17 943
Personal Dental Service	GPYO	..	..	..	83	192	467	656	806	2 171	5 149
Ophthalmic medical practitioners [7]	KDCT	799	833	863	827	819	754	686	644	614	498
Ophthalmic opticians [7]	KDCU	7 582	7 790	8 024	8 423	8 742	8 650	8 761	9 123	9 349	9 599
Personal Social Services staff: total[8]	KDDE	233 700	229 400	223 500	221 700	217 500	212 000	209 700	211 600	213 300	216 500
of which:											
Home help service	KSBU	55 400	53 600	50 500	47 200	42 900	40 200	37 800	34 900	34 400	38 200
Field Social Workers	KSBX	32 100	33 000	33 400	33 900	34 700	35 200	35 900	37 100	37 800	40 800
Day care establishments staff	KADV	31 600	30 800	30 300	30 800	30 800	29 500	29 500	28 800	28 600	30 600
Residential care staff	KADW	68 000	65 400	62 100	59 200	56 600	53 800	51 500	51 300	49 000	52 200

NoteScotland GPs figures included in this table will be slightly different to GPs 'headcount' figures published on the ISD Scotland website as GPs holding more than one contract will be counted in this table by the 'number of contracts held' in each year rather than the 'headcount' of GPs.

1 All GP data as at 1 October except England and Wales as at 30 September from 2000 and Scotland from 2005.

2 The 'All practitioners' totals do not add up to the sum of their parts, having been adjusted in respect of some Scotish GPs who have posts in two separate categories.

3 All Practitioners data for 1999 does not include Scotland retainees as these were first collected in April 2000.

4 GP Registrars were formerly referred to as Trainees. From 2004 GP Registrars are known as Performer Registrars in Scotland and these data include Performer Registrars working in 2C practices.

5 From 2004 GP Retainees are known as Performer Retainees in Scotland and these data include Performer Retainees working in 2C practices.

6 Includes principals, assistants and trainees. Prison contracts and salaried dentists are excluded. A small proportion of dentists work in both the GDS and PDS. These dentists have been counted only within GDS figures to avoid double counting.

7 Figures for Scotland are as at 31 March, and figures for England and Wales are as at 31 December, of that year. Count of OMPs and OOs holding contracts with FHSAs/HA's/LHBs and/ or Scottish NHS Boards to carry out NHS Sight Tests. Practitioners with contracts in both England and Scotland are counted twice for these statistics. The OMP figure for 2003 (644) includes an estimate of 22 OMP's for Scotland, the OMP figure for Scotland being unavailable for 2003.

8 Figures for 2005 England and Wales only.

Sources: The Information Centre for health and social care;
Dental Practice Board;
Welsh Assembly Government;
Scottish Health Service Common Services Agency

9.6 Deaths: by cause
International Statistical Classification of Diseases, Injuries and Causes of Death[1]
Tenth Revision 2001

Numbers

		England and Wales				
	ICD-10 code	2001	2002	2003	2004	2005
Total deaths		530 373	533 527	538 254	512 541	512 692
Deaths from natural causes	A00-R99	511 667	515 262	519 297	493 835	494 054
Certain infectious and parasitic diseases	A00-B99	4 253	4 330	4 763	5 009	6 141
Intestinal infectious diseases	A00-A09	777	847	1 063	1 382	2 221
Respiratory and other tuberculosis including late effects	A15-A19,B90	446	443	451	388	406
Meningococcal infection	A39	201	115	118	72	86
Viral hepatitis	B15-B19	196	170	209	197	205
AIDS (HIV - disease)	B20-B24	180	198	224	209	230
Neoplasms	C00-D48	139 135	140 174	139 360	138 062	138 454
Malignant neoplasms	C00-97	135 839	136 777	135 955	134 856	135 252
Malignant neoplasm of oesophagus	C15	6 107	6 330	6 427	6 298	6 490
Malignant neoplasm of stomach	C16	5 606	5 588	5 285	5 098	4 927
Malignant neoplasm of colon	C18	9 436	9 504	9 152	9 130	9 076
Malignant neoplasm of rectum and anus	C20-C21	3 927	3 907	3 982	3 917	3 995
Malignant neoplasm of pancreas	C25	6 011	6 142	6 242	6 294	6 509
Malignant neoplasm of trachea, bronchus and lung	C33-C34	28 728	28 806	28 765	28 328	28 792
Malignant neoplasm of skin	C43	1 470	1 480	1 585	1 597	1 622
Malignant neoplasm of breast	C50	11 638	11 557	11 276	11 031	11 121
Malignant neoplasm of cervix uteri	C53	1 039	1 001	951	957	911
Malignant neoplasm of prostate	C61	8 912	8 973	9 166	9 169	9 042
Leukaemia	C91-C95	3 781	3 911	3 916	3 828	3 910
Diseases of the blood and blood-forming organs and certain disorders involving the immune mechanism	D50-D89	1 000	1 086	1 065	1 014	1 096
Endocrine, nutritional and metabolic diseases	E00-E90	7 711	7 897	8 016	7 519	7 433
Diabetes mellitus	E10-E14	6 119	6 192	6 316	5 837	5 677
Mental and behavioural disorders	F00-F99	14 143	14 444	14 846	14 299	14 563
Vascular and unspecified dementia	F01,F03	12 572	12 753	13 401	12 756	12 995
Alcohol abuse (inc. alcoholic psychosis)	F10	477	435	469	538	523
Drug dependence and non-dependent abuse of drugs	F11-F16,F18-F19	798	882	655	718	762
Diseases of the nervous system and sense organs	G00-H95	14 372	14 796	15 793	14 645	15 253
Meningitis (including meningococcal)	G00-G03	189	173	229	182	187
Alzheimer's disease	G30	4 579	4 771	5 055	4 821	4 914
Diseases of the circulatory system	I00-I99	211 842	209 433	205 508	190 603	183 997
Ischaemic heart diseases	I20-I25	105 895	102 833	99 790	92 528	88 271
Cerebrovascular diseases	I60-I69	58 517	59 068	57 808	52 899	50 772
Diseases of the respiratory system	J00-J99	67 391	69 900	75 138	69 213	72 517
Influenza	J10-J11	38	38	77	25	44
Pneumonia	J12-J18	31 636	32 631	34 400	30 649	31 443
Bronchitis, emphysema and other chronic obstructive pulmonary diseases	J40-J44	23 700	24 159	25 765	23 204	24 230
Asthma	J45-J46	1 268	1 264	1 284	1 243	1 186
Diseases of the digestive system	K00-K93	23 386	24 124	24 948	24 912	25 213
Gastric and duodenal ulcer	K25-K27	3 802	3 746	3 678	3 495	3 266
Chronic liver disease	K70,K73-K74	5 234	5 376	5 844	5 824	5 873
Diseases of the skin and subcutaneous tissue	L00-L99	1 291	1 470	1 661	1 670	1 788
Diseases of the musculo-skeletal system and connective tissue	M00-M99	4 588	4 647	4 634	4 393	4 378
Rheumatoid arthritis and juvenile arthritis	M05-M06,M08	970	966	907	794	835
Osteoporosis	M80-M81	1 542	1 605	1 583	1 478	1 416
Diseases of the genito-urinary system	N00-N99	7 682	8 452	9 120	9 397	10 231
Diseases of the kidney and ureter	N00-N29	3 848	4 072	4 135	4 024	3 967
Complications of pregnancy, childbirth and the puerperium	O00-O99	42	34	45	46	36
Certain conditions originating in the perinatal period (excluding neonatals)[1]	P00-P96	200	208	207	213	205
Congenital malformations, deformations and chromosomal abnormalities (excluding neonatals)[1]	Q00-Q99	1 280	1 233	1 299	1 274	1 292
Congenital malformations of the nervous system	Q00-Q07	119	127	142	116	123
Congenital malformations of the circulatory system	Q20-Q28	592	541	540	527	535
Symptoms, signs and abnormal clinical and laboratory findings not elsewhere classified	R00-R99	13 351	13 034	12 894	11 566	11 457
Senility without mention of psychosis (old age)	R54	11 900	11 645	11 394	9 905	9 785
Sudden infant death syndrome	R95	195	137	136	148	164
Deaths from external causes	V01-Y89	16 569	16 139	16 693	16 497	16 411
All accidents	V01-X59,Y85,Y86	10 733	10 382	10 979	10 735	11 053
Land transport accidents	V01-V89	2 949	2 929	2 943	2 693	2 697
Accidental falls	W00-W19	2 617	2 509	2 732	2 915	3 006
Accidental poisonings	X40-X49	1 037	814	835	927	910
Suicide and intentional self-harm	X60-X84,Y87.0	3 264	3 269	3 270	3 306	3 172
Homicide and assault[1]	X85-Y09,Y87.1	386	373	318	363	326
Event of undetermined intent	Y10-Y34, Y87.2	1 803	1 754	1 776	1 685	1486

9.6
continued

Deaths: by cause
International Statistical Classification of Diseases, Injuries and Causes of Death[1]
Tenth Revision 2001

Numbers

	ICD-10 code	Scotland				
		2001	2002	2003	2004	2005
Total deaths		57 382	58 103	58 472	56 187	55 747
Deaths from natural causes	A00-R99	54 961	55 689	56 161	53 759	53 535
Certain infectious and parasitic diseases	A00-B99	558	651	660	688	719
Intestinal infectious diseases	A00-A09	65	96	85	104	99
Respiratory and other tuberculosis including late effects	A15-A19,B90	54	52	59	52	49
Meningococcal infection	A39	12	13	5	8	4
Viral hepatitis	B15-B19	6	13	23	20	16
AIDS (HIV - disease)	B20-B24	33	33	33	16	31
Neoplasms	C00-D48	15 475	15 391	15 412	15 336	15 408
Malignant neoplasms	C00-C97	15 196	15 051	15 116	15 047	15 135
Malignant neoplasm of oesophagus	C15	752	763	776	801	798
Malignant neoplasm of stomach	C16	678	621	579	615	590
Malignant neoplasm of colon	C18	1 062	975	966	917	966
Malignant neoplasm of rectum and anus	C20-21	405	384	368	383	367
Malignant neoplasm of pancreas	C25	595	562	641	615	603
Malignant neoplasm of trachea, bronchus and lung	C33-34	3 915	4 039	3 893	3 923	4 009
Malignant neoplasm of skin	C43	145	132	146	151	158
Malignant neoplasm of breast	C50	1 150	1 110	1 149	1 093	1 151
Malignant neoplasm of cervix uteri	C53	113	100	120	102	127
Malignant neoplasm of prostate	C61	777	775	786	802	765
Leukaemia	C91-C95	350	330	367	352	351
Diseases of the blood and blood-forming organs and certain disorders involving the immune mechanism	D50-D89	124	122	148	111	118
Endocrine, nutritional and metabolic diseases	E00-E90	891	902	958	972	988
Diabetes mellitus	E10-E14	695	676	709	760	745
Mental and behavioural disorders	F00-F99	2 425	2 446	2 637	2 670	2 454
Vascular and unspecified dementia	F01,F03	1 809	1 763	1 997	1 955	1 835
Alcohol abuse (inc. alcoholic psychosis)	F10	341	339	356	421	343
Drug dependence and non-dependent abuse of drugs	F11-F16,F18-F19	238	294	228	238	217
Diseases of the nervous system and sense organs	G00-H95	1 243	1 317	1 303	1 254	1 306
Meningitis (including meningococcal)	G00-G03	16	6	19	25	18
Alzheimer's disease	G30	324	388	354	399	415
Diseases of the circulatory system	I00-I99	22 666	22 688	22 102	20 837	20 060
Ischaemic heart diseases	I20-I25	11 914	11 692	11 441	10 778	10 331
Cerebrovascular diseases	I60-I69	6 621	6 722	6 497	6 155	5 789
Diseases of the respiratory system	J00-J99	6 435	6 806	7 454	6 743	7 093
Influenza	J10-J11	5	6	15	3	11
Pneumonia	J12-J18	2 370	2 466	2 859	2 399	2 483
Bronchitis, emphysema and other chronic obstructive pulmonary diseases	J40-J44	2 836	2 840	3 014	2 752	2 857
Asthma	J45-J46	101	131	98	94	100
Diseases of the digestive system	K00-K93	3 063	3 153	3 215	3 065	3 221
Gastric and duodenal ulcer	K25-K27	308	350	316	305	230
Chronic liver disease	K70,K73-K74	1 061	1 128	1 170	1 044	1 152
Diseases of the skin and subcutaneous tissue	L00-L99	90	118	131	131	127
Diseases of the musculo-skeletal system and connective tissue	M00-M99	357	384	369	350	326
Rheumatoid arthritis and juvenile arthritis	M05-M06,M08	125	133	103	107	109
Osteoporosis	M80-M81	56	59	70	52	47
Diseases of the genito-urinary system	N00-N99	969	1 013	1 056	965	1 063
Diseases of the kidney and ureter	N00-N29	638	627	670	574	617
Complications of pregnancy, childbirth and the puerperium	O00-O99	6	5	7	6	4
Certain conditions originating in the perinatal period	P00-P96	167	155	149	151	164
Congenital malformations, deformations and chromasomal abnormalities	Q00-Q99	172	168	172	134	159
Congenital malformations of the nervous system	Q00-Q07	16	31	23	21	15
Congenital malformations of the circulatory system	Q20-Q28	65	60	63	53	58
Symptoms, signs and abnormal clinical and laboratory findings not elsewhere classified	R00-R99	320	370	388	346	325
Senility without mention of psychosis (old age)	R54	172	191	236	193	210
Sudden infant death syndrome	R95	32	32	43	28	20
Deaths from external causes	V01-Y89	2 421	2 414	2 311	2 428	2 212
All accidents	V01-X59,Y85,Y86	1 350	1 315	1 326	1 390	1 284
Land transport accidents	V01-V89	367	321	357	325	293
Accidental falls	W00-W19	626	668	668	690	676
Accidental poisonings	X40-X49	50	37	30	57	48
Suicide and intentional self-harm	X60-X84,Y87.0	609	636	560	606	547
Homicide and assault	X85-Y09,Y87.1	92	118	101	121	80
Event of undetermined intent	Y10-Y34, Y87.2	278	263	234	229	216

9.6
Deaths: by cause
International Statistical Classification of Diseases, Injuries and Causes of Death[1]

Tenth Revision 2001

Numbers

		Northern Ireland				
	ICD-10 code	2001	2002	2003	2004	2005
Total deaths		14 513	14 586	14 462	14 354	14 224
Deaths from natural causes	A00-R99	13 968	13 949	13 912	13 711	13 463
Certain infectious and parasitic diseases	A00-B99	117	134	157	149	162
Intestinal infectious diseases	A00-A09	7	11	13	16	16
Respiratory and other tuberculosis including late effects	A15-A19,B90	6	10	11	13	4
Meningococcal infection	A39	4	7	4	5	1
Viral hepatitis	B15-B19	-	-	-	1	2
AIDS (HIV - disease)	B20-B24	-	3	2	-	5
Neoplasms	C00-D48	3 802	3 766	3 882	3 835	3 826
Malignant neoplasms	C00-C97	3 696	3 652	3 757	3 757	3 735
Malignant neoplasm of oesophagus	C15	155	163	154	138	162
Malignant neoplasm of stomach	C16	174	164	165	180	161
Malignant neoplasm of colon	C18	271	270	313	286	293
Malignant neoplasm of rectum and anus	C20-C21	100	90	103	94	99
Malignant neoplasm of pancreas	C25	176	194	173	152	173
Malignant neoplasm of trachea, bronchus and lung	C33-C34	782	802	810	837	824
Malignant neoplasm of skin	C43	37	38	40	36	43
Malignant neoplasm of breast	C50	316	278	291	320	307
Malignant neoplasm of cervix uteri	C53	24	25	31	37	20
Malignant neoplasm of prostate	C61	214	193	217	241	222
Leukaemia	C91-C95	87	93	85	95	92
Diseases of the blood and blood-forming organs and certain disorders involving the immune mechanism	D50-D89	32	24	37	34	36
Endocrine, nutritional and metabolic diseases	E00-E90	200	238	246	248	302
Diabetes mellitus	E10-E14	145	187	190	189	224
Mental and behavioural disorders	F00-F99	381	411	341	370	408
Vascular and unspecified dementia	F01,F03	298	329	284	298	316
Alcohol abuse (inc. alcoholic psychosis)	F10	75	74	52	68	86
Drug dependence and non-dependent abuse of drugs	F11-F16,F18-F19	2	6	3	2	2
Diseases of the nervous system and sense organs	G00-H95	467	531	481	487	484
Meningitis (including meningococcal)	G00-G03	9	5	3	1	2
Alzheimer's disease	G30	211	246	224	251	207
Diseases of the circulatory system	I00-I99	5 829	5 729	5 448	5 272	5 002
Ischaemic heart diseases	I20-I25	3 148	2 948	2 843	2 775	2 708
Cerebrovascular diseases	I60-I69	1 531	1 573	1 531	1 435	1 307
Diseases of the respiratory system	J00-J99	1 975	1 883	2 082	1 950	1 921
Influenza	J10-J11	-	1	4	1	-
Pneumonia	J12-J18	1 028	951	1 025	909	895
Bronchitis, emphysema and other chronic obstructive pulmonary diseases	J40-J44	584	553	660	609	596
Asthma	J45-J46	38	36	32	44	32
Diseases of the digestive system	K00-K93	556	581	587	691	584
Gastric and duodenal ulcer	K25-K27	76	62	77	70	60
Chronic liver disease	K70,K73-K74	133	166	156	189	150
Diseases of the skin and subcutaneous tissue	L00-L99	24	21	15	19	20
Diseases of the musculo-skeletal system and connective tissue	M00-M99	94	90	93	66	95
Rheumatoid arthritis and juvenile arthritis	M05-M06,M08	31	21	26	15	28
Osteoporosis	M80-M81	12	19	16	10	12
Diseases of the genito-urinary system	N00-N99	278	333	327	364	351
Diseases of the kidney and ureter	N00-N29	192	246	225	252	210
Complications of pregnancy, childbirth and the puerperium	O00-O99	2	1	3	1	1
Certain conditions originating in the perinatal period	P00-P96	63	62	62	64	81
Congenital malformations, deformations and chromasomal abnormalities	Q00-Q99	83	53	69	61	82
Congenital malformations of the nervous system	Q00-Q07	16	7	12	10	10
Congenital malformations of the circulatory system	Q20-Q28	24	17	16	17	20
Symptoms, signs and abnormal clinical and laboratory findings not elsewhere classified	R00-R99	65	92	82	100	108
Senility without mention of psychosis (old age)	R54	37	63	63	70	71
Sudden infant death syndrome	R95	2	0	-	-	2
Deaths from external causes	V01-Y89	545	637	550	643	761
All accidents	V01-X59,Y85,Y86	361	424	364	448	492
Land transport accidents	V01-V89	148	144	120	161	175
Accidental falls	W00-W19	52	60	44	63	99
Accidental poisonings	X40-X49	13	30	30	17	40
Suicide and intentional self-harm	X60-X84,Y87.0	141	162	132	128	186
Homicide and assault	X85-Y09,Y87.1	20	27	30	32	32
Event of undetermined intent	Y10-Y34, Y87.2	17	21	12	18	27

1 See chapter text

Sources: Office for National Statistics;
General Register Office, Scotland;
Northern Ireland Statistics and Research Agency

9.7 Notifications of infectious diseases: by country

Numbers

		1995	1996	1997	1998	1999	2000	2001	2002	2003	2004	2005
United Kingdom[1]												
Measles	KHQD	9 017	6 866	4 844	4 540	2 951	2 865	2 661	3 675	2 726	2 703	2 326
Mumps	KWNN	2 400	2 182	2 264	1 917	2 000	3 367	3 433	2 333	4 565	20 742	66 541
Rubella	KWNO	7 674	11 720	4 205	4 064	2 575	2 064	1 782	2 002	1 525	1 548	1 327
Whooping cough	KHQE	2 399	2 721	3 669	1 902	1 461	866	1 059	1 051	509	619	679
Scarlet fever	KHQC	6 863	6 101	4 639	4 708	2 956	2 544	2 320	2 749	3 252	2 642	2 075
Dysentery	KHQG	5 498	2 643	2 427	1 934	1 630	1 613	1 495	1 167	1 144	1 301	1 346
Food poisoning	KHQH	92 604	94 923	105 579	105 060	96 866	98 076	95 752	81 562	79 073	78 812	78 959
Typhoid and Paratyphoid fevers	KHQB	386	291	249	252	278	205	254	183	277	282	300
Hepatitis	KWNP	3 823	2 876	3 601	3 781	4 365	4 530	4 419	5 035	5 203	5 054	5 246
Tuberculosis	KHQI	6 176	6 238	6 367	6 605	6 701	7 100	7 204	7 239	6 978	7 259	8 017
Malaria	KWNQ	1 363	1 743	1 549	1 163	1 038	1 166	1 118	866	820	634	700
England and Wales[2]												
Measles	KHRD	7 447	5 614	3 962	3 728	2 438	2 378	2 250	3 187	2 488	2 356	2 089
Mumps	KWNR	1 936	1 747	1 914	1 587	1 691	2 162	2 741	1 997	4 204	16 367	56 256
Rubella	KWNS	6 196	9 081	3 260	3 208	1 954	1 653	1 483	1 660	1 361	1 287	1 155
Whooping cough	KHRE	1 869	2 387	2 989	1 577	1 139	712	888	883	409	504	594
Scarlet fever	KHRC	5 296	4 873	3 569	3 339	2 086	1 933	1 756	2 159	2 553	2 201	1 678
Dysentery	KHRG	4 651	2 312	2 274	1 813	1 538	1 494	1 388	1 087	1 047	1 203	1 237
Food poisoning	KHRH	82 041	83 233	93 901	93 932	86 316	86 528	85 468	72 649	70 895	70 311	70 407
Typhoid and Paratyphoid fevers	KHRB	370	276	241	243	276	204	250	175	275	280	298
Viral hepatitis	KWNT	3 296	2 437	3 186	3 183	3 424	3 541	3 388	3 859	4 004	3 932	4 109
Tuberculosis[3]	KHRJ	5 608	5 654	5 859	6 087	6 144	6 572	6 714	6 753	6 518	6 723	7 628
Malaria	KWNU	1 300	1 659	1 476	1 110	1 005	1 128	1 081	847	791	609	679
Total meningitis	KHRO	2 285	2 686	2 345	2 072	2 094	2 432	2 623	1 545	1 472	1 267	1 381
Meningococcal meningitis	KHRP	1 146	1 164	1 220	1 152	1 145	1 164	1 020	706	646	554	579
Meningococcal septicaemia	KWNV	707	1 129	1 440	1 509	1 822	1 614	1 238	842	732	691	721
Ophthalmia neonatorum	KHRI	245	246	224	198	163	176	115	91	102	85	87
Scotland[1]												
Measles	KHSE	1 307	1 055	762	700	434	395	315	399	181	257	181
Mumps	KWNW	371	368	282	251	216	199	155	259	181	3 595	5 729
Rubella	KWNX	1 258	2 449	818	745	548	349	234	292	130	222	141
Whooping cough	KHSF	399	186	545	225	214	93	106	99	60	87	57
Scarlet fever	KHSD	1 065	750	645	883	438	301	281	376	395	213	211
Dysentery	KHSH	575	176	124	103	82	95	85	73	83	90	102
Food poisoning[4]	KHSI	9 297	10 234	10 144	9 186	8 517	9 263	8 640	7 693	6 910	6 835	7 143
Typhoid and Paratyphoid fevers	KHSB	16	14	6	6	2	1	3	4	2	2	1
Viral hepatitis	KWNY	405	360	359	490	863	943	1 008	1 165	1 159	1 063	1 063
Tuberculosis[5]	KHSL	478	509	433	457	496	469	442	418	422	463	321
Malaria	KWUC	58	70	57	30	20	27	24	17	28	20	19
Meningococcal infection	KWUD	190	201	271	313	329	301	256	175	117	147	149
Erysipelas	KHSC	125	84	95	66	64	41	39	41	28	28	17
Northern Ireland												
Measles	KHTD	263	197	120	112	79	92	96	89	57	90	56
Mumps	KHTR	93	67	68	79	93	1 006	537	77	180	780	4 556
Rubella	KHTQ	220	190	127	111	73	62	65	50	34	39	31
Whooping cough	KHTE	131	148	135	100	108	61	65	69	40	28	28
Scarlet fever	KHTC	502	478	425	486	432	310	283	214	304	228	186
Dysentery	KHTG	272	155	29	18	10	24	22	7	14	8	7
Food poisoning	KHTH	1 266	1 456	1 534	1 942	2 033	2 285	1 644	1 220	1 268	1 666	1 409
Typhoid and Paratyphoid fevers	KHTB	–	1	2	3	–	–	1	4	–	–	1
Infective hepatitis	KHTO	122	79	56	108	78	46	23	11	40	59	74
Tuberculosis	KHTI	90	75	75	61	61	59	48	68	38	73	68
Malaria	KWUE	5	14	16	23	13	11	13	2	1	5	2
Acute encephalitis/meningitis	KHTM	116	105	91	64	99	130	97	98	78	64	66
Meningococcal septicaemia	KWUF	42	67	56	87	145	123	90	98	76	82	66
Gastro-enteritis (children under 2 years)	KHTP	1 072	745	896	1 371	1 121	1 205	1 106	882	867	697	736

1 Scotland data for the latest period are provisional, therefore United Kingdom for latest period includes provisional Scottish data.

2 The figures show the corrected number of notifications, incorporating revisions of diagnosis, either by the notifying medical practitioner or by the medical superintendent of the infectious diseases hospital. Cases notified in Port Health Authorities are included.

3 Formal notifications of new cases only. The figures exclude chemoprophylaxis.

4 Scotland's food poisoning includes 'otherwise ascertained' for the first time in 1995.

5 Figures include cases of tuberculosis not notified before death.

Sources: Information and Statistics Division, NHS in Scotland;
Communicable Disease Surveillance Centre (Northern Ireland);
Health Protection Agency, Centre for Infections, IM&T Dept: 020 8200 6868

9.8 Estimated number of cases of work-related disease reported by specialist physicians to THOR[1]

Great Britain

Numbers

	All physicians			Disease specialist			Occupational physicians		
	2003	2004	2005	2003	2004	2005	2003	2004	2005
Musculoskeletal disorders									
					MOSS			OPRA	
Upper limb	3 359	4 189	3 530	1 477	1 534	1 412	1 882	2 655	2 118
Spine/ back	1 997	2 028	1 712	501	394	411	1 496	1 634	1 301
Lower limb	352	580	441	40	175	122	312	405	319
Other	176	252	209	68	29	33	108	223	176
Total number of diagnoses	5 981	7 161	6 020	2 123	2 181	2 059	3 858	4 980	3 961
Total number of individuals[2]	5 804	6 879	5 760	2 066	2 063	1 931	3 738	4 816	3 829
Mental ill health									
					SOSMI			OPRA	
Stress/ anxiety/ depression	6 529	6 440	6 027	1 705	1 804	1 739	4 824	4 636	4 288
Other	880	869	912	604	663	702	276	206	210
Total number of diagnoses	7 409	7 309	6 939	2 309	2 467	2 441	5 100	4 842	4 498
Total number of individuals[2]	6 747	6 801	6 360	2 175	2 282	2 211	4 572	4 519	4 149
Respiratory disease									
					SWORD			OPRA	
Asthma	667	555	492	351	386	374	316	169	118
Malignant mesothelioma	875	830	762	869	819	754	6	11	8
Benign pleural disease	1 094	1 132	1 493	1 082	1 120	1 478	12	12	15
Other	820	825	893	549	567	619	271	258	274
Total number of diagnoses	3 456	3 342	3 640	2 851	2 892	3 225	605	450	415
Total number of individuals[2]	3 357	3 237	3 593	2 764	2 799	3 203	593	438	390
Skin disease									
					EPIDERM			OPRA	
Contact dermatitis	2 617	2 374	2 230	1 668	1 750	1 643	949	624	587
Skin neoplasia	361	616	434	361	615	434	-	1	-
Other	419	325	361	220	215	176	199	110	185
Total number of diagnoses	3 397	3 315	3 025	2 249	2 580	2 253	1 148	735	772
Total number of individuals[2]	3 331	3 281	2 990	2 183	2 546	2 220	1 148	735	770
Audiological disease									
					OSSA			OPRA	
Sensorineural hearing loss	488	291	303	212	33	53	276	258	250
Other	170	41	48	146	12	22	24	29	26
Total number of diagnoses	658	332	351	358	45	75	300	287	276
Total number of individuals[2]	529	321	328	229	34	54	300	287	274
Infections									
					SIDAW			OPRA	
Diarrhoeal diseases	962	916	1 429	959	915	1 396	3	1	33
Other	181	192	149	106	123	121	75	69	28
Total number of diagnoses	1 143	1 108	1 578	1 065	1 038	1 517	78	70	61
Total number of individuals[2]	1 143	1 108	1 578	1 065	1 038	1 517	78	70	61

1 THOR: The Health and Occupation Reporting Network (formerly know as ODIN) comprises of the following schemes: MOSS: Musculoskeletal Occupation Surveillance Scheme; SOSMI: Surveillance of Occupational Stress and Mental Illness; SWORD: Surveillance or Work-related and Occupational Respiratory Disease; EPIDERM: Occupational Skin Disease Surveillance by Dermatologists; OSSA: Occupational Surveillance Scheme for Audiologists; SIDAW: Surveillance of Infectious Disease at Work.

2 Individuals may have more than one diagnosis.

Source: Health and Safety Executive: 0151 951 3479/4355

9.9 Deaths due to occupationally related lung disease
Great Britain

Numbers

		1994	1995	1996	1997	1998	1999	2000	2001	2002	2003	2004
Asbestosis (without mesothelioma)[1]	KADY	174	166	196	191	165	171	186	233	234	235	266
Mesothelioma	KADZ	1 246	1 317	1 322	1 367	1 541	1 615	1 633	1 862	1 867	1 885	1 969
Pneumoconiosis (other than asbestosis)	KAEA	276	287	223	230	268	321	279	240	271	231	214
Byssinosis	KAEB	7	6	3	5	5	6	4	2	–	3	4
Farmer's lung and other occupational allergic alveolitis	KAEC	10	10	1	5	8	9	7	7	6	7	5
Total	KAED	1 713	1 786	1 745	1 798	1 987	2 122	2 109	2 344	2 377	2 349	2 458

1 By definition every case of asbestosis is due to asbestos; the association with mesothelioma is also very strong, though there is thought to be a low natural background incidence.

Sources: Office for National Statistics; Health and Safety Executive: 0151 951 3479/4355

9.10 Injuries to workers:[1] by industry and severity of injury
Great Britain
As reported to all enforcing authorities

Numbers

				Fatal			Major			Over 3 Days[2]		
		Section	SIC (92)	2002 /03	2003 /04	2004 /05	2002 /03	2003 /04	2004 /05	2002 /03	2003 /04	2004 /05
Agriculture, hunting, forestry and fishing[3]	KSYS	A,B	01,02,05	36	44	42 KSZN	642	574	586 KTAZ	1 320	1 007	933
Energy and water supply industries	KSYT	C,E	10-14,40/41	3	10	2 KSZO	443	408	411 KTBH	1 890	1 827	1 565
Mining and quarrying	KSYU	C	10-14	1	8	2 KSZP	276	207	235 KTBI	1 086	943	722
Mining and quarrying of energy producing materials	KSON	CA	10-12	..	5	1 KSZQ	163	124	141 KTBJ	751	641	484
Mining and quarrying except energy producing materials	KSOO	CB	13/14	1	3	1 KSZR	113	83	94 KTBK	335	302	238
Electricity, gas and water supply	KSOP	E	40/41	2	2	– KSZS	167	201	176 KTBL	804	884	843
Manufacturing	KSOQ	D	15-37	43	30	43 KSZT	6 789	6 449	6 201 KTBM	33 195	30 042	26 408
of food products; beverages and tobacco	KSOR	DA	15/16	3	2	3 KSZU	1 308	1 209	1 133 KTBN	8 685	7 896	6 523
of textile and textile products	KSOS	DB	17/18	1	1	1 KSZV	177	195	157 KTBO	903	828	618
of leather and leather products	KSOT	DC	19	..	..	– KSZW	21	20	13 KTBP	112	52	38
of wood and wood products	KSOU	DD	20	2	2	3 KSZX	343	300	288 KTBQ	1 139	795	678
of pulp, paper and paper products; publishing and printing	KSOV	DE	21/22	..	2	2 KSZY	459	388	398 KTBR	2 105	1 793	1 600
of coke, refined petroleum products and nuclear fuel	KSOW	DF	23	1	..	– KSZZ	18	23	16 KTBS	79	79	40
of chemicals, chemical products and man-made fibres	KSOX	DG	24	2	..	3 KTAE	407	361	327 KTBT	1 569	1 501	1 230
of rubber and plastic products	KSOY	DH	25	4	..	9 KTAF	557	450	444 KTBU	3 021	2 093	1 959
of other non-metallic mineral products	KSOZ	DI	26	4	4	4 KTAG	383	338	331 KTBV	1 827	1 469	1 349
of basic metals and fabricated metal products	KSYV	DJ	27/28	13	9	7 KTAH	1 285	1 218	1 301 KTBW	4 731	4 247	4 122
of machinery and equipment not elsewhere classified	KSYW	DK	29	4	2	3 KTAI	544	392	332 KTBX	2 468	1 795	1 604
of electrical and optical equipment	KSYX	DL	30-33	3	1	1 KTAJ	356	262	221 KTBY	1 774	1 196	1 180
of transport equipment	KSYY	DM	34/35	3	1	5 KTAK	538	594	534 KTBZ	3 171	3 144	2 725
Manufacturing not elsewhere classified	KSYZ	DN	36/37	3	6	2 KTAL	393	699	706 KTCA	1 611	3 154	2 742
Construction	KSZA	F	45	70	71	69 KTAM	4 721	4 728	4 496 KTCB	9 578	8 995	8 288
Total service industries	KSZB	G-Q	50-99	75	81	67 KTAN	16 597	19 813	20 008 KTCC	83 152	90 260	85 728
Wholesale and retail trade, and repairs	KSZC	G	50-52	19	16	11 KTAO	3 618	4 045	3 967 KTCD	15 379	15 818	15 355
Hotel and restaurants	KSZD	H	55	1	5	3 KTAP	997	1 197	1 256 KTCE	3 367	3 900	4 001
Transport, storage and communication[4]	KSZE	I	60-64	28	33	22 KTAQ	3 237	3 729	3 782 KTCF	23 340	24 148	22 303
Financial intermediation	KSZF	J	65-67	2	..	– KTAR	252	269	326 KTCG	919	960	895
Real estate, renting and business activities	KSZG	K	70-74	9	11	8 KTAS	1 645	2 806	2 694 KTCH	5 206	7 899	7 248
Public administration and defence	KSZH	L	75	5	4	9 KTAT	2 362	3 409	3 280 KTCI	13 941	18 308	16 951
Education	KSZI	M	80	..	1	1 KTAU	1 338	1 064	1 042 KTCJ	4 290	2 732	2 625
Health and social work	KSZJ	N	85	..	4	– KTAV	1 877	2 113	2 339 KTCK	12 576	13 450	13 266
Other community, social and personal services activities	KSZK	O-Q	90-99	11	7	13 KTAW	1 271	1 181	1 322 KTCL	4 134	3 045	3 084
All industries	KSZM			227	236	223 KTAY	29 192	31 972	31 702 KTCN	129 135	132 131	122 922

1 See chapter text.
2 Injuries causing incapacity for normal work for more than 3 days.
3 Excludes sea fishing.

4 Injuries arising from shore based services only. Excludes incidents reported under merchant shipping legislation.

Source: Health and Safety Executive (HSE): 0151 951 4355/3479

Social protection

Chapter 10

Social protection

Social security

(Tables 10.2 to 10.11, 10.13 and 10.15 to 10.19)

Tables 10.2 to 10.6, 10.9 - 10.11 and 10.13 to 10.19 give details of contributors and beneficiaries under the National Insurance and Industrial Injury Acts, supplementary benefits and war pensions.

There are four classes of National Insurance Contributions (NICs):

Class 1   Earnings-related contributions paid on earnings from employment. Employees pay primary Class 1 contributions and employers pay secondary Class 1 contributions.   Payment of Class 1 contributions builds up entitlement to contributory benefits which include Basic State Pension; Additional State Pension (State Earnings Related Pension Scheme SERPS and from April 2002, State Second Pension, S2P); Contribution Based Jobseeker's Allowance; Bereavement Benefits; Incapacity Benefit.

Primary class 1 contributions stop at State Pension age, but not Class 1 secondary contributions paid by employers.

There are reduced contribution rates where the employee contracts out of S2P (previously SERPS). They still receive a Basic State Pension but an Occupational or Personal Pension instead of the Additional State Second Pension.

Class 2   Flat rate contributions paid by the self-employed whose profits are above the small earnings exception. Payment of Class 2 contributions builds up entitlement to the contributory benefits which include Basic State Pension; Bereavement Benefits; Maternity Allowance and Incapacity Benefit. But not Additional State Second Pension or Contribution Based Jobseeker's Allowance

Class 2 contributions stop at State Pension age.

Class 3   Flat rate voluntary contributions, which can be paid by someone whose contribution record is insufficient. Payment of Class 3 contributions builds up entitlement to contributory benefits which include Basic State Pension; Bereavement Benefits.

Class 4   Profit-related contributions paid by the self-employed in addition to Class 2 contributions. Class 4 contributions stop at State Pension age.

Under some circumstances people who are not in employment do not have to make voluntary contributions to accrue a qualifying year for Basic State Pension.

Home Responsibilities Protection

Home Responsibilities Protection (HRP) helps to protect the basic State Pension of those precluded from regular employment because they are caring for children or a sick or disabled person at home. To be entitled to HRP, a person must have been precluded from regular employment for a full tax year. HRP reduces the amount of qualifying years a person would otherwise need for a Basic State Pension.

National Insurance Credits

In addition to paying, or being treated as having paid contributions, a person can be credited with National Insurance. Contribution credits help to protect people's rights to State Retirement Pension and other Social Security Benefits.

A person is likely to be entitled to contributions credits if they are; a student in full time education or training, in receipt of Jobseekers Allowance, unable to work due to sickness or disability, entitled to Statutory Maternity Pay or Statutory Adoption Pay, or they have received Carers Allowance.

Credits are automatically awarded for men aged 60 to 65 provided they are not liable to pay Class 1 or 2 NICs and to young people for the tax years containing their 16th, 17th and 18th birthdays.

Jobseeker's Allowance

(Table 10.6)

Jobseeker's Allowance (JSA) replaced Unemployment Benefit and Income Support for unemployed claimants on 7 October 1996. It is a unified benefit with two routes of entry: contribution-based which depends mainly upon national insurance contributions and income-based which depends mainly upon a means test. Some claimants can qualify by either route. In practice they receive income-based JSA but have an underlying entitlement to the contribution-based element.

Sickness Benefit, Invalidity Benefit and Incapacity Benefit (Tables 10.7 and 10.8)

Incapacity Benefit replaced Sickness Benefit and Invalidity Benefit from 13 April 1995. The first condition for entitlement to these contributory benefits is that the claimants are incapable of work because of illness or disablement. Secondly, that they satisfy the contribution conditions which depend on contributions paid as an employed (Class 1) or self-employed person (Class 2). Under Sickness and Invalidity Benefits the contribution conditions were automatically treated as satisfied if a person was incapable of work because of an industrial accident or prescribed disease. Under Incapacity Benefit those who do not satisfy the contribution conditions in this case do not have them treated as satisfied. Class 1A contributions paid by employers are in respect of the benefit of cars provided for the private use of employees, and the free fuel provided for private use. These contributions do not provide any type of benefit cover.

Since 6 April 1983, most people working for an employer and paying National Insurance contributions as employed persons, receive Statutory Sick Pay (SSP) from their employer when they are off work sick. SSP was payable for a maximum of 8 weeks until 5 April 1986, and 28 weeks thereafter. People who do not work for an employer, and employees who are excluded from the SSP scheme, or those who have run out of SSP before reaching the maximum of 28 weeks and are still sick can claim benefit. Any period of SSP is excluded from the tables.

Spells of incapacity of 3 days or less do not count as periods of interruption of employment, and are excluded from the tables. Exceptions are where people are receiving regular weekly treatment by dialysis, or treatment by radiotherapy, chemotherapy or plasmapheresis where 2 days in any 6 consecutive days make up a period of interruption of employment, and those whose incapacity for work ends within 3 days of the end of SSP entitlement.

At the beginning of a period of incapacity, benefit is subject to 3 waiting days, except where there was an earlier spell of incapacity of more than 3 days in the previous 8 weeks. Employees entitled to SSP for less than 28 weeks and who are still sick can get Sickness Benefit or Incapacity Benefit Short Term (Low) until they reach a total of 28 weeks provided they satisfy the conditions. After 28 weeks SSP and/or Sickness Benefit (SB), Invalidity Benefit (IVB) was payable up to pension age for as long as the incapacity lasts. From pension age Invalidity Benefit was paid at the person's State Pension rate, until entitlement ceases when SP is paid or at deemed pension age (70 for a man, 65 for a woman). For people on Incapacity Benefit under State pension age there are two short-term rates: the lower rate is paid for the first 28 weeks of sickness and the higher rate for weeks 29 to 52. From week 53 the Long Term rate Incapacity Benefit is payable. The Short Term rate Incapacity Benefit is based on State Pension entitlement for people over State Pension age and is paid for up to a year if incapacity began before pension age.

The long-term rate of Incapacity Benefit applies to people under State Pension age who have been sick for more than a year. People with a terminal illness or who are receiving the higher rate care component of Disability Living Allowance will get the Long Term rate. The Long Term rate is not paid for people over pension age.

Under Incapacity Benefit, for the first 28 weeks of incapacity, people previously in work will be assessed on the 'own occupation' test - the claimant's ability to do their own job. Otherwise, incapacity will be based on a personal capability assessment, which will assess ability to carry out a range of work-related activities. The test will apply after 28 weeks of incapacity or from the start of the claim for people who did not previously have a job. Certain people will be exempted from this test.

The tables exclude all men aged over 65 and women aged over 60 who are in receipt of State Pension, and all people over deemed pension age (70 for a man and 65 for a woman), members of the Armed Forces, mariners while at sea, and married women and certain widows who have chosen not to be insured for sickness benefit. The tables include a number of individuals who were unemployed prior to incapacity.

The Short Term (Higher) and Long Term rates of Incapacity Benefit are treated as taxable income.

There were transitional provisions for people who were on Sickness or Invalidity Benefit on 12 April 1995. They were automatically transferred to Incapacity Benefit, payable on the same basis as before. Former IVB recipients continue to get Additional Pension entitlement, but frozen at 1994 levels. Also their IVB is not subject to tax. If they were over State Pension age on 12 April 1995 they may get Incapacity Benefit for up to 5 years beyond pension age.

Child Benefits

(Table 10.9)

Child Benefit (CB) is paid to those responsible for children (aged under 16) or qualifying young people. The latter includes:

a) a person under age 19 in full-time non-advanced education or (from April 2006) on certain approved vocational training programmes;

b) a person who is aged 19 who began their course of full-time non-advanced education or approved training before reaching age 19; (Note: those reaching 19 up to 9 April 2006 ceased to qualify on their 19th birthdays)

c) a person who has reached age 16 until the 31 August following their 16th birthday.

Social protection

d) a person aged 16 or 17 who has left education and training who is registered with the Careers service or with Connexions and is awaiting a placement in employment or training for the limited period of up to 20 weeks from the date they left education or training.

Entitlement for a qualifying young person continues until the terminal date following the date they leave full-time education or approved training. The terminal dates are at the end of August, November, February and May (there is a slight variation for Scotland). Entitlement is also maintained for a person who is entered for external examinations connected with their course throughout the period between a person leaving education or training and completing those examinations.

Entitlement in all cases ceases when a person reaches age 20.

Guardian's Allowance is an additional allowance for people bringing up a child because one or both of their parents has died. They must be getting CB for the child.

The table show the number of families in the United Kingdom in receipt of CB. The numbers shown in the table are estimates based on a random 5 per cent sample of awards current at 31 August and are therefore subject to sampling error. The figures take no account of new claims, or revisions to claims that were received or processed after 31 August even if they are backdated to start before 31 August.

Family Credit/ Working Families' Tax Credit

(Table 10.10)

Working Families' Tax Credit (WFTC) replaced Family Credit from 5 October 1999.

Family Credit was, and Working Families' Tax Credit is, available to families with at least one adult in remunerative work for at least 16 hours per week and who is responsible for at least one child under 16 (under 19 if in full time education up to A-level or equivalent standard). The rate of payment of WFTC depends on the number of such children and expenditure incurred on eligible childcare. It is also higher if the worker works for at least 30 hours per week, or if there are disabled children or severely disabled adults in the family. It is tapered away above an income threshold. Further details can be obtained from the Inland Revenue.

Child and Working Tax Credits (New Tax Credits)

(Table 10.11)

Child and Working Tax Credits (NTC's) replaced Working Families' Tax Credit (WFTC) from 6th April 2003.

CTC and WTC are claimed by individuals, or jointly by couples, whether or not they have children.

Child Tax Credit (CTC) provides support to families for the children (up to the 31 August after their 16th birthdays) and the "qualifying" young people (in full-time non-advanced education until their 19th birthdays) for which they are responsible. It is paid in addition to Child Benefit.

Working Tax Credit (WTC) tops up the earnings of families on low or moderate incomes. People working for at least 16 hours a week can claim it if they (a) are responsible for at least one child or qualifying young person, (b) have a disability which puts them at a disadvantage in getting a job, or (c) in the first year of work, having returned to work aged at least 50 after a period of at least six months receiving out-of-work benefits. Other adults also qualify if they are aged at least 25 and work for at least 30 hours a week.

Widow's Benefit and Bereavement Benefit

(Table 10.12 and 10.13)

Widow's Benefit is payable to women widowed on or after 11 April 1988 and up to and including 8 April 2001. There are three types of widow's benefits: Widow's Payment, Widowed Mother's Allowance and Widow's Pension. Women widowed before 11 April 1988 continue to receive Widow's Benefit based on the rules that existed before that date. Bereavement Benefit was introduced on 9 April 2001 as a replacement of Widows Benefit, payable to both men and women widowed on or after 9 April 2001. There are three types of Bereavement Benefits available: Bereavement Payment, Widowed Parent's Allowance and Bereavement Allowance.

Government expenditure on social services and housing

(Table 10.20 to 10.25)

The tables of general government expenditure on social services and housing in the United Kingdom comprise a summary table followed by separate tables for each of the social services and housing categories. The definition of government expenditure used in the tables is consistent with Table 5.2.4S & Table 11.2 of the Blue Book 2006 Edition, and covers both current and capital expenditure of central government (including the National Insurance Fund) and local authorities.

The figures in the tables have been compiled based on the United Nations Classification of the Functions of Government (COFOG) and are consistent with the European System of Accounts 1995 (ESA95). The format of the tables has been revised since last published. As such they may not be comparable with earlier editions of the Annual Abstract of Statistics, which were based on data information supplied directly by government departments. This information from government departments is generally no longer available, as such the tables are compiled under the categories of National Accounts.

Useful links

National Accounts Blue Book   http://www.statistics.gov.uk/statbase/Product.asp?vlnk=1143

UN CoFoG classification   http://unstats.un.org/unsd/cr/registry/regcst.asp?Cl=4

The main categories of expenditure now used are:

Final Consumption Expenditure– The expenditure on goods and services that are used for the direct satisfaction of individual needs or the collective needs of members of the community as distinct from their purchase for use in the productive process. It may be contrasted with Actual final consumption, which is the value of goods consumed but not necessarily purchased by that sector.

Compensation of Employees – Total remuneration payable to employees in cash or in kind. Includes the value of social contributions payable by the employer

Net Procurement – current expenditure less receipts for sales and charges.

Gross Capital Formation – Acquisition less disposals of fixed assets and the improvement of land.

Subsidies – Current unrequited payments made by general government or the European Union to enterprises. Those made on the basis of a quantity or value of goods or services are classified as 'subsidies on products' . Other subsidies based on levels of productive activity (e.g. numbers employed) are designated Other subsidies on production.

Capital Transfers – Transfers which are related to the acquisition or disposal of assets by the recipient or payer. They may be in cash or kind, and may be imputed to reflect the assumption or forgiveness of debt.

Non-produced financial or non financial assets – assets produced either through production or otherwise of a non-financial nature.

Non-market capital consumption – Output of own account production of goods and services provided free or at prices that are not economically significant. Non-market output is produced mainly by the general government and NPISH sectors.

Education

(Table 10.21)

Table 10.21 includes expenditure by the Education Departments, local education authorities and the University Grants Committee on education in schools, training colleges, technical institutions and universities. Compensation of employees figures are based on revenue outturn returns produced by Department for Communities and Local Government, National Assembly for Wales and the Scottish Executive.

National Health Service

(Table 10.22)

Table 10.22 includes expenditure by central government on hospital and community health, family practitioner and other health services. The figures are based on Departmental expenditure reported to HM Treasury.

Welfare services

(Table 10.23)

Personal social services: This table covers local authority and central government expenditure, on such things as the aged, handicapped, homeless, child care, care of mothers and young children, mental health, domestic help, etc.

Social security

(Table 10.24)

Table 10.24 comprises both benefits under the Social Security schemes and non-contributory benefits and allowances, administered by the Department for Work and Pensions. Benefits paid overseas are also included, as are unfunded social benefits such as voluntary employer social contributions. The analysis by type of Income Support is not exact; the estimates are derived from average numbers in receipt of benefit and average amounts paid. War pensions which are now administered by the Ministry of Defence are included in this table. Child and Working Tax Credits (NTC's) replaced Working Families' Tax Credit (WFTC) from 6 April 2003 and are administered by the Inland Revenue.

Housing

(Table 10.25)

The table shows government expenditure on housing. It includes expenditure made by the central and local government sectors, but excludes expenditure by public corporations. The Housing Revenue Account is classified as a quasi-public corporation, so that most of its current and capital expenditure and income is included in the corporate rather than government sector. All overhead and administration expenses are included in final current expenditure. Non-capitalised support for public corporations and other market bodies relating to housing is recorded as subsidies. Capital transfers are paid mainly by local government to individuals for repair and improvement of privately owned housing. Current transfers paid include insurance premiums. Gross capital formation includes that of the council houses administered by the Housing Revenue Account. This is net of any sales of housing either through Right to Buy or Large Scale Voluntary Transfers. Housing benefit in the form of rent rebates and rent allowances is not included in the table, as they are regarded as forms of social security.

10.1 National Insurance Fund
(Great Britain and Northern Ireland)
Years ended 31 March

£ million

		1997/98	1998/99	1999/00	2000/01	2001/02	2002/03	2003/04	2004/05	2005/06
Receipts										
Opening balance	KJFB	7 869	9 763	12 625	14 909	19 868	24 177	27 267	27 816	29 804
Contributions	JXVM	46 755	50 023	51 852	55 627	58 050	59 658	59 827	62 863	67 786
State Scheme Premiums[1]	C59W	..	..	..	..	..	194	147	115	117
Grant from Consolidated Fund	KOTF	966	3	2	..	..	..	..	..	..
Compensation for SSP/SMP	KJQM	601	576	625	688	710	775	1 346	1 470	1 392
Transfers from Great Britian	KOTG	150	315	230	200	110	350	260	270	185
Income from investments	KJFE	474	667	724	884	1 146	1 457	1 292	1 288	1 399
Other receipts	KJFF	97	92	127	112	67	80	82	72	66
Redundancy receipts	KIBQ	25	21	21	23	22	24	28	32	38
Total	JYJO	56 937	61 462	66 206	72 442	79 972	86 716	90 249	93 926	100 787
Expenditure										
Total benefits	JYJP	45 321	46 822	50 026	50 960	54 550	54 201	56 255	58 572	61 304
Jobseeker's Allowance (Contributory)	LUQW	489	489	475	449	478	519	512	455	497
Incapacity	JYXL	7 739	7 574	7 206	6 982	7 074	7 104	7 116	6 910	7 028
Maternity	KETY	37	39	40	46	57	70	128	153	128
Widows' pensions	KEWU	1 021	1 008	1 020	1 008	1 132	1 142	1 033	946	903
Guardian's allowances and Child's special allowance[2]	KJFK	2	2	2	2	2	2	2	1	2
Retirement pensions[3]	JYJV	36 396	38 072	41 157	42 350	45 677	45 240	47 339	49 979	52 578
Pensioners' lump sum payments	KAAW	126	128	126	123	131	124	125	128	168
Other payments	KAAZ	19	18	19	21	29	27	34	30	33
Administration	KABE	1 073	1 053	847	1 197	873	1 280	1 794	1 521	1 464
Transfers to Northern Ireland	KABF	150	315	230	200	110	350	260	270	185
Redundancy payments	KIBR	120	140	174	195	232	255	243	222	295
Personal Pensions	C59X	..	..	..	..	..	3 336	3 847	3 508	2 566
Total	JYJU	47 173	48 837	51 297	52 574	55 795	59 449	62 433	64 123	65 847
Accumulated funds	KABH	9 763	12 625	14 909	19 868	24 177	27 267	27 816	29 804	34 940

1 State Scheme Premiums are payable in respect of employed persons who cease to be covered, in certain circumstances, by a contracted out pension scheme.
2 Includes Child's special allowance for Northern Ireland
3 Includes personal pensions up to 2001/02.

Source: HM Revenue and Customs: 020 7438 7370

10.2 Persons who paid National Insurance contributions[1] in a tax year:[2] by sex
United Kingdom

Millions

		Total				Men				Women		
		2002/03	2003/04	2004/05		2002/03	2003/04	2004/05		2002/03	2003/04	2004/05
Total[3]	KABI	28.96	29.22	28.30	KEYF	16.06	16.16	15.68	KEYP	12.90	13.06	12.62
Class 1	KABJ	25.89	26.10	25.18	KEYG	13.80	13.89	13.41	KEYQ	12.08	12.22	11.78
Not contracted out[4]	KABK	16.69	17.12	17.12	KEYH	9.31	9.57	9.57	KEYR	7.38	7.55	7.55
Contracted out	KABL	7.58	7.48	6.84	KEYI	3.80	3.69	3.32	KEYS	3.77	3.79	3.52
Mixed contracted in/out[5]	KABM	1.52	1.43	1.17	KEYJ	0.69	0.63	0.51	KEYT	0.83	0.80	0.66
Class 1 Reduced rate (including standard rate)	KABO	0.10	0.08	0.05	KEYL	..	..	..	KEYV	0.10	0.08	0.05
Class 2 exclusively	KABP	2.27	2.28	2.35	KEYM	1.75	1.74	1.78	KEYW	0.53	0.54	0.57
Mixed Class 1 and Class 2	KABQ	0.60	0.66	0.65	KEYN	0.42	0.45	0.44	KEYX	0.19	0.21	0.21
Class 3 exclusively[6]	KABR	0.19	0.17	0.11	KEYO	0.09	0.08	0.05	KEYY	0.10	0.09	0.06

1 Estimates obtained from a 3% sample of the National Insurance Recording System (NIRS2) taken at November 2006.
2 See chapter text. The tax year commences on 6 April and ends on 5 April of the following year.
3 Components may not sum to totals as a result of rounding.
4 Includes those persons with an Appropriate Personal Pension (such persons pay contributions at the not contracted out rate but then receive a rebate).
5 Not included in the above rows.
6 Persons who paid a mixture of Class 3 contributions and others are not included in this category.

Source: Department for Work and Pensions: 020 7122 2444

10.3 National Insurance contributions
United Kingdom

	Employee's standard contibutions[1]		Employer's standard contributions[1]	
	not contracted-out rate	contracted-out rate[2]	not contracted-out rate	contracted-out rate[3]
Class 1				
Weekly earnings				
2000/01				
Below 67.00 (LEL)	-	-	-	-
67.00-75.99 (PT)	-	See note 4	-	See note 5
76.00-83.99 (ST)	10.0%	8.4%	-	
84.00-535.00 (UEL)	10.0%	8.4%	12.2%	9.2%
Above 535.00 (UEL)	£45.90	£38.41	12.2%	12.2%
2001/02				
Below 72.00 (LEL)	-	-	-	-
72.00-86.99 (PT/ST)	-	See note 4	-	See note 5
87.00-575.00 (UEL)	10.0%	8.4%	11.9%	8.9%
Above 575.00 (UEL)	£48.80	£40.75	11.9%	11.9%
2002/03				
Below 75.00 (LEL)	-	-	-	-
75.00-88.99 (PT/ST)	-	See note 4	-	See note 6
89.00-585.00 (UEL)	10.0%	8.4%	11.8%	8.3%
Above 585.00 (UEL)	£49.60	£41.44	11.8%	11.8%
2003/04				
Below 77.00 (LEL)	-	-	-	-
77.00-88.99 (PT/ST)	-	See note 4	-	See note 6
89.00-595.00 (UEL)	11.0%	9.4%	12.8%	9.3%
	£55.66	£47.37		
Above 595.00 (UEL)	1%	1%	12.8%	12.8%
2004/05				
Below 79.00 (LEL)	-	-	-	-
79.00-90.99 (PT/ST)	-	See note 4	-	See note 6
91.00-610.00 (UEL)	11.0%	9.4%	12.8%	9.3%
	£57.09	£48.59		
Above 610.00 (UEL)	1.0%	1.0%	12.8%	12.8%
2005/06				
Below 82.00 (LEL)	-	-	-	-
82.00-93.99 (PT/ST)	-	See note 4	-	See note 6
94.00-630.00 (UEL)	11.0%	9.4%	12.8%	9.3%
	£58.96	£50.38		
Above 630.00 (UEL)	1.0%	1.0%	12.8%	12.8%
2006/07				
Below 84.00 (LEL)	-	-	-	-
84.00-96.99 (PT/ST)	-	See note 4	-	See note 6
97.00-644.99 (UEL)	11.0%	9.4%	12.8%	9.3%
	£60.28	£51.51		
Above 645.00 (UEL)	1.0%	1.0%	12.8%	12.8%

	2000/01	2001/02	2002/03	2003/04	2004/05	2005/06	2006/07
Class 2							
Flat rate weekly	£2.00	£2.00	£2.00	£2.00	£2.05	£2.10	£2.10
Small earnings exception[7] (per annum)	£3,825	£3,955	£4,025	£4,095	£4,215	£4,345	£4,465
Class 3							
Flat-rate voluntary weekly contributions	£6.55	£6.75	£6.85	£6.95	£7.15	£7.35	£7.55
Class 4 (Self-employed; profit-related)							
Rate on profits between LPL and UPL	7.0%	7.0%	7.0%	8.0%	8.0%	8.0%	8.0%
Rate on profits above UPL	..	..	..	1.0%	1.0%	1.0%	1.0%
Lower profits limit (LPL)	£4,385	£4,535	£4,615	£4,615	£4,745	£4,895	£5,035
Upper profits limit (UPL)	£27,820	£29,900	£30,420	£30,940	£31,720	£32,760	£33,540

Note: LEL: Lower Earnings Limit; UEL: Upper Earnings Limit. PT: Primary Threshold; ST: Secondary Threshold.

1 Married women opting to pay contributions at the reduced rate at 3.85% before 2003-04 and 4.85% from 2003-04 earn no entitlement to contributory National Insurance benefits as a result of these contributions. No women have been allowed to exercise this option since 1977, but around 70,000 women who have been continually married or widowed and in the labour market since that time have retained their right to pay the reduced rate.

2 The contracted-out rebate for employees' contributions is applied only between LEL and UEL. Earnings below LEL are charged at the appropriate not contracted-out rate (which depends on total earnings). Earnings above the UEL are not subject to employee NICs before 2003-04.

3 The rates shown only apply to Contracted-Out Salary Related schemes. (COSR). Earnings below the LEL and above the UEL are charged at the appropriate not-contracted out rate. The employers' contracted-out rate applies only between the LEL and the UEL.

4 The contracted-out rebate for primary contributions is 1.6 per cent of earnings between the LEL and the UEL for all forms of contracting-out.

5 The contracted-out rebate for secondary contributions is 3.0 per cent of earnings between the LEL and the UEL.

6 The contracted-out rebate for secondary contributions is 3.5 per cent of earnings between the LEL and the UEL.

7 If earnings from self-employment are below this annual limit and the contributor applies for and is granted a small earnings exception Class 2 contributions need not be paid. Class 2 or 3 contributions may be paid voluntarily.

Source: HM Revenue and Customs: 020 7147 3082

10.4 Weekly rates of principal social security benefits[1]
Great Britain
At April

£

		1996	1997	1998	1999	2000	2001	2002	2003	2004	2005	2006
Unemployment Benefit:[2,3]												
Men and women	KJNA	48.25	..	..	..	..	..	..	..	..	..	..
Jobseeker's Allowance:[3]												
Personal allowances												
Single												
Aged under 18	KXDH	..	29.60	30.30	30.95	31.45	31.95	32.50	32.90	33.50	33.85	34.60
Aged 18 - 24	KXDJ	..	38.90	39.85	40.70	41.35	42.00	42.70	43.25	44.05	44.50	45.50
Aged 25 or over	KXDK	..	49.15	50.35	51.40	52.20	53.05	53.95	54.65	55.65	56.20	57.45
Lone parent												
Aged under 18 - usual rate	F92E	..	..	..	..	31.45	31.95	32.50	32.90	33.50	33.85	34.60
Aged under 18 - higher rate payable in specific circumstances	F92F	..	..	..	..	41.35	42.00	42.70	43.25	44.05	44.50	45.50
Aged 18 or over	F92G	..	..	..	..	52.20	53.05	53.95	54.65	55.65	56.20	57.45
Couple												
Both aged under 18[4]	KXDL	..	58.70	30.30	30.95	31.45	31.95	32.50	32.90	33.50	33.85	34.60
Both under 18, one disabled	KXDI	..	38.90	39.85	40.70	41.35	42.00	42.70	43.25	44.05	44.50	45.50
Both under 18, with a child	F92H	..	..	..	..	62.35	63.35	64.45	65.30	66.50	67.15	68.65
One under 18, one 18 - 24	KXDI	..	38.90	39.85	40.70	41.35	42.00	42.70	43.25	44.05	44.50	45.50
One under 18, one 25+	F92I	..	..	..	..	52.20	53.05	53.95	54.65	55.65	56.20	57.45
Both aged 18 or over	KXDM	..	77.15	79.00	80.65	81.95	83.25	84.65	85.75	87.30	88.15	90.10
Dependant children and young people												
Aged under 11 - 16	KXDN	..	16.90	17.30	20.20	26.60	31.45	33.50	38.50	42.27	43.88	45.58
Aged 16 - 18	KXDP	..	29.60	30.30	30.95	31.75	32.25	34.30	38.50	42.27	43.88	45.58
Invalidity allowance[5]												
High rate	KJND	12.90	13.15	13.60	14.05	14.20	14.65	14.90	15.15	15.55	16.05	16.50
Middle rate	KJNE	8.10	8.30	8.60	8.90	9.00	9.30	9.50	9.70	10.00	10.30	10.60
Low rate	KJNF	4.05	4.15	4.30	4.45	4.50	4.65	4.75	4.85	5.00	5.15	5.30
Increase for dependants[5]												
Adult	KJNG	36.60	37.35	38.70	39.95	40.40	41.75	42.45	43.15	44.35	45.70	46.95
Each child[6]	KJNH	11.15	11.20	11.30	11.35	11.35	11.35	11.35	11.35	11.35	11.35	11.35
Incapacity Benefit:[5]												
Short term (Lower) Under pension age	KOSB	46.15	47.10	48.80	50.35	50.90	52.60	53.50	54.40	55.90	57.65	59.20
Increase for adult dependant	KOSC	28.55	29.15	30.20	31.15	31.50	32.55	33.10	33.65	34.60	35.65	36.60
Short term (Lower) Over pension age	KOSD	58.65	59.90	62.05	64.05	64.75	66.90	68.05	69.20	71.15	73.35	75.35
Increase for adult dependant	KOSE	35.15	35.90	37.20	38.40	38.80	40.10	42.45	41.50	42.65	43.95	45.15
Short term (Higher)	KOSF	54.55	55.70	57.70	59.55	60.20	62.20	63.25	64.35	66.15	68.20	70.05
Increase for dependants:												
Adult	KOSG	28.55	29.15	30.20	31.15	31.50	32.55	33.10	33.65	34.60	35.65	36.60
Child[6]	KOSH	11.15	11.20	11.30	11.35	11.35	11.35	11.35	11.35	11.35	11.35	11.35
Long term	KOSI	61.15	62.45	64.70	66.75	67.50	69.75	70.95	72.15	74.15	76.45	78.50
Increase for dependants:												
Adult	KOSJ	36.60	37.35	38.70	39.95	40.40	41.75	42.45	43.15	44.35	45.70	46.95
Child[6]	KOSK	11.15	11.20	11.30	11.35	11.35	11.35	11.35	11.35	11.35	11.35	11.35
Incapacity age addition:[7]												
Higher rate	KOSL	12.90	13.15	13.60	14.05	14.20	14.65	14.90	15.15	15.55	16.05	16.50
Lower rate	KOSM	6.45	6.60	6.80	7.05	7.10	7.35	7.45	7.60	7.80	8.05	8.25
Attendance Allowance:												
Higher rate	KJNI	48.50	49.50	51.30	52.95	53.55	55.30	56.25	57.20	58.80	60.60	62.25
Lower rate	KJNJ	32.40	33.10	34.30	35.40	35.80	37.00	37.65	38.30	39.35	40.55	41.65
Disability Living Allowance:												
Care component												
Higher rate	KXDC	48.50	49.50	51.30	52.95	53.55	55.30	56.25	57.20	58.80	60.60	62.25
Middle rate	KXDD	32.40	33.10	34.30	35.40	35.80	37.00	37.65	38.30	39.35	40.55	41.65
Lower rate	KXDE	12.90	13.15	13.60	14.05	14.20	14.65	14.90	15.15	15.55	16.05	16.50
Mobility component												
Higher rate	KXDF	33.90	34.60	35.85	37.00	37.40	38.65	39.30	39.95	41.05	42.30	43.45
Lower rate	KXDG	12.90	13.15	13.60	14.05	14.20	14.65	14.90	15.15	15.55	16.05	16.50

10.4
Weekly rates of principal social security benefits[1]
Great Britain
continued At April

£

		1996	1997	1998	1999	2000	2001	2002	2003	2004	2005	2006
Maternity Benefit:												
Maternity allowances for insured women[8]												
Higher rate	KOSN	54.55	55.70	57.70	59.55	60.20	..	..	..	..	..	..
Lower rate[9]	KJNL	47.35	48.35	50.10	51.70	52.25	..	..	..	..	..	..
Standard rate[10]	GPTJ	..	..	..	..	..	62.20	75.00	100.00	102.80	106.00	108.85
Threshold[11]	GPTK	..	..	..	..	..	30.00	30.00	30.00	30.00	30.00	30.00
Guardian's Allowance	KJNN	11.15	11.20	11.30	11.35	11.35	11.35	11.35	11.55	11.85	12.20	12.50
Widow's Benefit:												
Widow's pension	KJNO	61.15	62.45	64.70	66.75	67.50	72.50	75.50	77.45	79.60	82.05	84.25
Widowed mother's allowance	KJNP	61.15	62.45	64.70	66.75	67.50	72.50	75.50	77.45	79.60	82.05	84.25
Addition for each child	KJNQ	11.15	11.20	11.30	11.35	11.35	11.35	11.35	11.35	11.35	11.35	11.35
Bereavement Benefit:												
Bereavement allowance	WMPF	..	..	..	..	..	72.50	75.50	77.45	79.60	82.05	84.25
Widowed parent's allowance	WMOZ	..	..	..	..	..	72.50	72.50	77.45	79.60	82.05	84.25
Addition for each child	WMPA	..	..	..	..	..	11.35	11.35	11.35	11.35	11.35	11.35
State Pension contributory:[12]												
Single person	KJNR	61.15	62.45	64.70	66.75	67.50	72.50	75.50	77.45	79.60	82.05	84.25
Married couple	KJNS	97.75	99.80	103.40	106.70	107.90	115.90	120.70	122.80	127.25	131.20	134.75
State Pension non contributory:												
Man or woman	KJNT	36.60	37.35	38.70	39.95	40.40	43.40	45.20	45.45	47.65	49.15	50.50
Married woman	KJNU	21.90	22.35	23.15	23.90	24.15	24.95	27.00	27.70	28.50	29.40	30.20
Industrial Injuries Benefit:												
Disablement pension at 100 per cent rate	KJNW	99.00	101.10	104.70	108.10	109.30	112.90	114.80	116.80	120.10	123.80	127.10
Widow's or widower's pension	KJNX	61.15	62.45	..	..	..	..	..	..	..	..	..
Increase for dependants:[13]												
Adult	KJNY	29.75	..	..	..	..	..	..	..	..	..	..
Child Benefit:												
First child	KJOA	10.80	11.05	11.45	14.40	15.00	15.50	15.75	16.05	16.50	17.00	17.45
Subsequent children	KETZ	8.80	9.00	9.30	9.60	10.00	10.35	10.55	10.75	11.05	11.40	11.70
Family Credit[14]												
(maximum awards payable):[15]												
Families with 1 child												
Birth to September following 11th birthday	KJOB	58.20	59.70	61.15	64.95	..	..	..	..	..	..	..
From September following 11th birthday to September following 16th birthday	KJOC	65.90	67.60	69.25	70.70	..	..	..	..	..	..	..
From September following 16th birthday to day before 19th birthday	KJOD	70.60	72.45	74.20	75.95	..	..	..	..	..	..	..
Increase for each additional child												
Birth to September following 11th birthday	KJOF	11.75	12.05	12.35	15.15	..	..	..	..	..	..	..
From September following 11th birthday to September following 16th birthday	KJOG	19.45	19.95	20.45	20.90	..	..	..	..	..	..	..
From September following 16th birthday to day before 19th birthday	KJOH	24.15	24.80	25.40	25.95	..	..	..	..	..	..	..
War pension:												
Ex-private (100 per cent assessment)	KJOJ	105.00	107.20	111.10	114.70	116.00	119.80	121.80	127.38	130.16	123.90	133.63
War widow	KJOK	79.35	81.00	83.90	86.60	87.55	90.45	92.00	92.69	95.27	98.08	100.76

10.4 continued

Weekly rates of principal social security benefits[1]
Great Britain
At April

£

		1996	1997	1998	1999	2000	2001	2002	2003	2004	2005	2006
Income Support:												
Personal allowances[16]												
Single												
aged 16-17 usual rate	KJOW	28.85	29.60	30.30	30.95	31.45	31.95	32.50	32.90	33.50	33.85	34.60
aged 16-17 higher rate in specific circumstances	KABS	37.90	38.90	39.85	40.70	41.35	42.00	42.70	43.25	44.05	44.50	45.50
aged 18-24	KJOX	37.90	38.90	39.85	40.70	41.35	42.00	42.70	43.25	44.05	44.50	45.50
aged 25 or over	KJOY	47.90	49.15	50.35	51.40	52.20	53.05	53.95	54.65	55.65	56.20	57.45
Couple												
both aged under 18[4]	KJOZ	..	..	..	..	31.45	31.95	32.50	32.90	33.50	33.85	34.60
both aged under 18, one disabled	F92J	..	..	..	..	41.35	42.00	42.70	43.25	44.05	44.50	45.50
both aged under 18, with a child	F92K	..	..	..	..	62.35	63.35	64.45	65.30	66.50	67.15	68.65
One aged under 18, one 18-24	F92L	..	..	..	..	41.35	42.00	42.70	43.25	44.05	44.50	45.50
One aged under 18, one 25+	F92M	..	..	..	..	52.20	53.05	53.95	54.65	55.65	56.20	57.45
Both aged 18 or over	KJPA	75.20	77.15	79.00	80.65	81.95	83.25	84.65	85.75	87.30	88.15	90.10
Lone parent												
aged 16-17 usual rate	KJPB	28.85	29.60	30.30	30.95	31.45	31.95	32.50	32.90	33.50	33.85	34.60
aged 16-17 higher rate in specific circumstances	KABT	37.90	38.90	39.85	40.70	41.35	42.00	42.70	43.25	44.05	44.50	45.50
aged 18 or over	KJPC	47.90	49.15	50.35	51.40	52.20	53.05	53.95	54.65	55.65	56.20	57.45
Dependant children and young people[16]												
1994 to 1996												
aged under 11	KJPD	16.45	..	..	..	..	..	..	..	..	..	..
aged 11-15	KJPE	24.10	..	..	..	..	..	..	..	..	..	..
aged 16-17	KJPF	28.85	..	..	..	..	..	..	..	..	..	..
aged 18	KABU	37.90	..	..	..	..	..	..	..	..	..	..
From 1997 to 1999												
Birth to September following												
11th birthday	KXDQ	..	16.90	17.30	20.20	..	..	..	..	..	..	..
From September following												
11th birthday to September following 16th	KXDR	..	24.75	25.35	25.90	..	..	..	..	..	..	..
From September following												
16th birthday to day before 19th	KXDS	..	29.60	30.30	30.95	..	..	..	..	..	..	..
Dependant children and young people - from 2000												
Birth to September following 16th birthday	WMOD	..	..	..	..	26.60	31.45	33.50	38.50	42.27	43.88	45.58
From September following 16th birthday to day before 19th	WMOP	..	..	..	..	31.75	32.25	34.30	38.50	42.27	43.88	45.58
Pension Credit[17]												
Standard minimum guarantee:												
single	C59Y	..	..	..	..	..	..	..	102.10	105.45	109.45	114.05
couple	C59Z	..	..	..	..	..	..	..	155.80	160.95	167.05	174.05
Additional amount for severe disability												
single	C5A2	..	..	..	..	..	..	..	42.95	44.15	45.50	46.75
couple (one qualifies)	C5A3	..	..	..	..	..	..	..	42.95	44.15	45.50	46.75
couple (both qualifies)	C5A4	..	..	..	..	..	..	..	85.90	88.30	91.00	93.50
Additional amount for carers	C5A8	..	..	..	..	..	..	..	25.10	25.55	25.80	26.35
savings credit												
threshold single	C5A9	..	..	..	..	..	..	..	77.45	79.60	82.05	84.25
threshold couple	C5AA	..	..	..	..	..	..	..	123.80	127.25	131.20	134.75
maximum single	C5AB	..	..	..	..	..	..	..	14.79	15.51	16.44	17.88
maximum couple	C5AC	..	..	..	..	..	..	..	19.20	20.22	21.51	23.58

1 See chapter text
2 Persons under the age of 18 are entitled to the appropriate adult rate.
3 Jobseeker's Allowance, introduced 7 October 1996, replaced Unemployment Benefit and Income Support for the unemployed.
4 From 12 April 1999 the personal allowance for couples where both members are not yet 18 or one of the couples is aged 18 or over depends on the couple's circumstances. They may be entitled to a couple allowance or a single person's allowance dependant on certain criteria.
5 Incapacity benefit introduced from 13 April 1995, has replaced sickness benefit and invalidity benefit.
6 For the first child only the Child Dependency increase is reduced by £1.30 to £9.90 because of child benefit.
7 The rate of age addition depends on age at date of onset of incapacity: higher rate for under age 35 and lower rate for age 35-44.
8 Following a EU Directive, employee's maternity benefit is aligned with the state benefit they would receive if off work sick.
9 Women who were either not employed or self-employed received the lower rate.

10 New Standard rate introduced from April 2000.
11 MA Earnings Threshold introduced April 2000.
12 Retirement pensioners over 80 receive 25p addition.
13 An allowance for one adult dependent was payable, where appropriate, with unemployment benefit, sickness benefit, retirement pension, injury benefit and maternity allowance.
14 Family credit was replaced by In-work Families with Child or Working Child Tax Credit awards. Some children have protected rights. Further information is available from the Department for Work and Pensions.
15 Maximum award does not include the 30 hour credit.
16 In addition to personal allowances, a claimant may also be entitled to premiums. The types of premiums are family, lone parent, pensioner, higher pensioner, disability, severe disability and disabled child.
17 Pension Credit replaced Minimum Income Guarantee (MIG) for Income Support for those aged 60 and over on 6th Ocotober 2003.

Sources: Department for Work and Pensions;
Information and Analysis Directorate : 0191 225 7373;
HM Revenue and Customs: 020 7438 7370;
Ministry of Defence/DASA (Pay & Pensions): 020 7218 4271

Social protection

10.5 Social Security Acts: number of persons receiving benefit[1]
Great Britain
At any one time

Thousands

Persons receiving:		1996	1997	1998	1999	2000	2001	2002	2003	2004	2005	2006
Unemployment Benefit[2]	KJHA	397.8	..	..	..	..	..	..	..	..	..	..
Jobseeker's Allowance[2,3]	JYXM	..	1 406.30	1 181.20	1 105.80	1 060.40	936.40	906.10	914.50	806.40	830.10	930.90
Incapacity benefit[5]	KXDT	1 812.80	1 749.20	1 671.20	1 557.10	2 352.50	2 420.90	2 471.10	2 494.90	2 508.80	2 490.90	2 450.00
Attendance Allowance[6,15]	KXDU	1 120.60	1 183.20	1 225.60	1 243.80	1 556.10	1 570.90	1 579.40	1 566.00	1 543.40	1 506.30	1 460.10
Disability Living Allowance[6]	KXDW	1 729.20	1 886.50	1 995.90	2 061.30	2 193.10	2 306.40	2 424.40	2 547.10	2 644.30	2 729.70	2 799.20
Widows' Benefits[7]	KJHF	308.90	296.40	278.70	267.60	265.10	255.00	223.40	191.50	163.40	139.00	117.70
Bereavement Benefits[7]	VQAA	..	..	..	..	..	..	41.50	47.70	51.20	55.20	57.70
National Insurance												
State pension contributory[4]:												
Males[8]	KJHH	3 688.20	3 786.50	3 880.40	3 956.30	4 039.40	4 083.90	4 149.20	4 211.40	4 275.70	4 336.80	4 374.20
Females[8]	KJHL	6 733.50	6 783.20	6 850.70	6 886.30	6 928.00	6 959.70	6 972.20	7 037.20	7 117.80	7 197.90	7 245.70
Total[8]	KJHG	10 421.70	10 569.70	10 731.10	10 842.60	10 967.40	11 043.60	11 121.40	11 248.50	11 393.50	11 534.70	11 619.90
State pension non contributory[4]:												
Males[7]	KJHI	5.70	5.60	5.50	5.10	5.20	5.10	5.30	5.40	5.40	5.30	5.40
Females[7]	KJHJ	22.30	20.90	19.80	18.80	18.00	18.20	18.10	17.70	17.30	16.70	16.60
Total[7]	KJHK	28.00	26.50	25.20	23.90	23.20	23.30	23.30	23.10	22.70	22.10	21.90
Industrial Injuries Disablement												
Pensions assessments[8,9]	KJHN	249.20	257.80	269.10	278.20	280.80	280.40	264.80	267.10	266.50	266.60	265.70
Reduced Earnings Allowance/												
Retirement Allowance assessments[8,9]	KEYC	154.90	155.60	152.80	153.50	153.50	152.30	144.30	143.00	140.00	136.90	133.60
Family Credit[10]	ZCGF	693.0	748.0	767.5	791.2	–	..	..	..	..	..	..
Income Support (Excluding MIG)[2,11]	KABV	5 545.80	3 958.00	3 853.10	3 814.40	2 237.10	2 260.60	2 238.80	2 236.40	2 192.60	2 139.80	2 114.80
Pension Credit[11]	C5AP	..	..	..	..	..	..	..	..	2 490.8	2 682.7	2 717.4
Housing Benefit and Council Tax Benefit												
Housing Benefit Total[12]	EW3X	4 775.90	4 639.40	4 474.70	4 313.10	4 033.30	3 874.40	3 812.60	3 796.40	3 879.40	3 957.10	3 990.00
Social Landlord[13]	KABY	2 898.30	2 792.30	2 664.10	2 518.50	3 218.40	3 131.10	3 093.80	3 081.70	3 135.50	3 166.80	3 152.30
Private Landlord	KABZ	1 877.60	1 847.10	1 810.60	1 794.60	815.00	743.30	718.80	714.80	743.90	790.30	837.80
Council tax benefit[14]	KJPO	5 611.20	5 498.30	5 325.70	5 166.10	4 830.10	4 673.40	4 601.70	4 627.80	4 800.20	4 959.60	5 050.00
War pensions[4]	KADG	323.74	324.64	317.65	306.06	295.67	284.33	272.78	260.79	247.59	235.30	223.85

1 See chapter text. Caseload counts at a specific date in the year which varies from benefit to benefit.

2 Figures are given at May each year and based on 100% Work and Pensions Longitudinal Study (WPLS) data.

3 Jobseeker's Allowance introduced 7 October 1996, replacing Unemployment Benefit and Income Support for the unemployed.

4 Includes overseas cases. As at end of March.

5 Incapacity Benefit replaced Sickness Benefit and Invalidity Benefit from 13 April 1995. Figures are taken at the last day in February from 100% data.

6 AA and DLA figures based on WPLS data from 2002. Prior to 2002 a consistent series for caseload, based on WPLS levels, has been created by combining older information, available from the previously published 5% sample data, with the WPLS data.

7 Includes overseas cases up to 2002.

8 A person may be in receipt of either IIDB or REA or both. The figure for 2002 has been amended.

9 Figures from 2000 to 2001 are based on 10% data at March, 2002 and 2003 are at March from 100%, from 2004 are as at May.

10 Family Credit was replaced by Working Families' Tax Credit from October.

11 Pension Credit replaced MIG on 6th October 2003 and extended Income Support entitlement to customers aged 60+. MIG claimants have been excluded from the IS figures in order to keep the series consistent.

12 Housing Benefit figures excludes any Extended Payment cases.

13 Social landlord figures include registered social landlord tenants.

14 Figure excludes Second Adult Rebate Claims.

15 Figures are cases with an underlying entitlement including suspended cases.

Sources: Department for Work and Pensions;
Information and Analysis Directorate : 0191 225 7373;
HM Revenue and Customs: 020 7438 7370;
Ministry of Defence/DASA (Pay & Pensions): 020 7218 4271

10.6 Jobseeker's Allowance[1,2,3,4] claimants: by benefit entitlement
Great Britain

As at May

Thousands

		2000	2001	2002	2003	2004	2005	2006
All Persons								
All with benefit - total	KXDX	966.4	843.2	816.2	823.8	725.7	755.1	843.7
Contribution-based JSA only	KXDY	147.3	146.1	160.4	165.6	135.9	144.6	139.8
Contribution based JSA & income-based JSA	KXDZ	18.8	18.1	19.1	18.7	14.0	14.0	13.5
Income-based JSA only payment	KXEA	800.3	679.0	636.7	639.5	575.8	596.4	690.4
No benefit in payment	KXEB	94.0	93.2	89.8	90.7	80.7	75.0	87.1
Total	KXEC	1 060.4	936.4	906.1	914.5	806.3	830.1	930.9
Males								
All with benefit - total	KXED	750.1	655.4	626.0	625.3	546.9	565.4	630.4
Contribution-based JSA only	KXEE	103.5	103.8	114.4	117.8	97.3	103.1	99.6
Contribution based JSA & income-based JSA	KXEF	17.1	16.6	17.3	16.4	12.7	13.1	12.4
Income-based JSA only payment	KXEG	629.5	534.9	494.3	491.1	436.8	449.2	518.4
No benefit in payment	KXEH	63.0	61.5	61.4	62.3	54.7	51.6	58.8
Total	KXEI	813.1	716.9	687.4	687.6	601.6	617.0	689.3
Females								
All with benefit - total	KXEJ	216.3	187.8	190.3	198.5	178.8	189.7	213.3
Contribution-based JSA only	KXEK	43.7	42.3	46.0	47.8	38.6	41.5	40.3
Contribution based JSA & income-based JSA	KXEL	1.7	1.5	1.8	2.3	1.3	0.9	1.0
Income-based JSA only payment	KXEM	170.8	144.0	142.4	148.4	139.0	147.3	172.0
No benefit in payment	KXEN	31.0	31.7	28.4	28.5	26.0	23.4	28.3
Total	KXEO	247.3	219.5	218.6	227.0	204.8	213.1	241.6

1 See chapter text. Jobseeker's Allowance (JSA) has two routes of entry: contribution-based which depends mainly upon national insurance contributions and income-based which depends mainly on a means test. Some claimants can qualify by either route. In practice they receive income-based JSA but have an underlying entitlement to the contribution-based element.
2 Figures are given at May each year and have been derived by applying 5% proportions to 100% totals taken from the DWP 100% Work and Pensions Longitudinal Study (WPLS).
3 Figures are rounded to the nearest hundred and quoted in thousands.
4 Totals may not sum due to rounding.

Sources: Department for Work and Pensions;
Information and Analysis Directorate: 0191 225 7373

10.7 Sickness Benefit, Invalidity Benefit and Incapacity Benefit[1],[2] claimants: by sex, age and duration of spell

Great Britain. At end of May

Thousands

		2001	2002	2003	2004	2005	2006
Males							
All durations: All ages	KJJA	1 512.24	1 526.17	1 525.02	1 517.62	1 492.38	1 455.52
Under 20	KJJB	11.33	21.79	21.81	22.04	21.45	19.95
20-29	KJJC	129.02	133.83	138.54	142.68	143.24	141.80
30-39	KJJD	245.71	250.79	254.30	253.32	245.61	233.70
40-49	KJJE	298.04	304.47	311.85	318.04	320.77	319.77
50-59	KJJF	482.18	478.01	472.03	463.37	451.93	439.54
60-64	KJJG	345.87	337.22	326.45	318.12	309.36	300.73
65 and over	KJJH	0.09	0.05	0.05	0.05	0.04	0.02
Over six months: All ages	KJJI	1 338.11	1 346.80	1 359.53	1 359.08	1 347.43	1 323.20
Under 20	KJJJ	3.52	6.91	13.40	13.78	13.51	12.85
20-29	KJJK	94.86	96.61	105.72	110.85	114.57	115.21
30-39	KJJL	207.75	213.19	217.05	217.81	213.91	205.36
40-49	KJJM	264.41	271.25	278.53	285.90	290.72	291.36
50-59	KJJN	439.78	438.55	434.04	427.06	418.60	409.46
60-64	KJJO	327.73	320.26	310.75	303.64	296.10	288.93
65 and over	KJJP	0.06	0.03	0.03	0.04	0.02	0.02
Females							
All durations: All ages	KJJQ	908.03	944.44	969.44	990.84	998.20	994.33
Under 20	KJJR	13.68	21.51	21.49	21.48	20.51	18.92
20-29	KJJS	92.79	96.66	100.78	105.02	108.61	109.73
30-39	KJJT	172.04	175.37	177.70	177.91	173.45	167.36
40-49	KJJU	243.27	252.82	262.20	270.90	276.62	279.32
50-59	KJJV	386.21	398.06	407.24	415.52	418.99	418.99
60 and over	KJJW	0.04	0.03	0.03	0.02	0.02	0.02
Over six months: All ages	KJJX	795.67	825.25	858.03	880.52	894.57	896.33
Under 20	KJJY	4.74	7.41	12.35	12.40	12.10	11.13
20-29	KJJZ	70.88	72.32	79.63	84.02	88.98	90.99
30-39	KJKA	148.19	151.59	154.19	154.95	152.48	148.00
40-49	KJKB	216.19	225.65	234.71	243.52	250.11	253.50
50-59	KJKC	355.64	368.25	377.12	385.61	390.88	392.69
60 and over	KJKD	0.04	0.03	0.03	0.02	0.02	0.02
Unknown Gender							
All durations	EW44	0.62	0.54	0.44	0.31	0.26	0.15
Over 6 months	EW45	0.28	0.29	0.21	0.16	0.13	0.10

1 See chapter text. Figures are given at May each year and are based on 100% Work and Pensions Longitudinal Study (WPLS) data.
2 Figures will Include a small number of overseas cases.

Sources: Department for Work and Pensions;
Information and Analysis Directorate: 0191 225 7373

10.8 Sickness, Invalidity and Incapacity Benefit: days of certified incapacity

Great Britain analysis by age at end of period[1]

Years starting on first Monday in April[2]

Millions

		1992 /93	1993 /94	1994[3] /95	1995 /96	1996 /97	1997 /98	1998 /99	1999 /00	2000 /01	2001 /02	2002 /03
Age at 31 March[4]												
Males: All ages	KJKH	445.5	468.8	507.9	596.2	576.3	563.5	538.6	526.7	531.7	536.1	540.3
Under 20	KJKI	1.5	1.6	1.8	3.4	3.1	3.5	3.7	3.3	2.6	3.5	5.4
20 - 29	KJKJ	24.5	27.0	30.4	43.7	42.4	43.2	41.7	38.3	38.9	40.4	44.3
30 - 39	KJKK	41.4	46.6	56.0	72.3	73.9	77.7	78.2	75.8	81.3	84.0	85.1
40 - 49	KJKL	64.6	72.7	78.9	98.5	98.5	97.7	97.6	98.0	103.9	106.0	106.8
50 - 59	KJKM	121.7	129.8	141.4	172.0	170.7	172.2	170.0	161.9	165.9	168.5	168.1
60 - 64	KJKN	102.4	107.3	112.6	127.9	127.8	126.7	124.3	126.0	125.8	120.2	116.3
65 and over	KJKO	80.4	83.9	86.8	78.4	59.9	41.7	23.0	23.4	13.3	13.4	14.4
Females: All ages	KJKP	190.7	211.4	237.5	279.5	285.8	292.8	294.8	315.0	325.1	338.7	344.6
Under 20	KJKQ	2.1	2.4	2.6	4.8	4.1	4.4	4.5	4.0	3.5	3.9	5.4
20 - 29	KJKR	22.1	22.1	23.9	31.9	32.0	32.1	31.3	30.7	30.3	32.3	34.4
30 - 39	KJKS	28.5	32.7	37.6	48.0	49.8	51.4	53.4	54.9	58.9	59.9	61.3
40 - 49	KJKT	46.6	51.5	58.9	72.1	74.0	75.8	77.1	79.1	82.8	88.9	89.8
50 - 59	KJKU	71.3	79.1	88.4	101.0	107.5	115.3	120.0	134.3	142.2	145.9	146.0
60 and over	KJKV	20.1	23.6	26.1	21.7	18.4	13.8	8.4	12.0	7.3	7.9	7.7

1 See chapter text. The end of the statistical year up to 1993/94 was the Saturday before the first Monday in April.
2 Up to and including 1994/95 years start first Monday in April. The 1995/96 year started 13 April and ended 31 March. From 1996/97 years start 1 April.
3 The statistical year for 1994/95 was extended to 12 April 1995, the day before the introduction of the new Incapacity Benefit which replaced Sickness and Invalidity Benefit.
4 Until 1995/96 then at 1 March.

Sources: Department for Work and Pensions;
Taken from 1% extract;
Information and Analysis Directorate: 0191 225 7373

10.9 Child benefits[1]

Thousands

		Great Britain As at 31 December					United Kingdom As at 31 August						
		1996	1997[2]	1998[2]	1999		2000	2001	2002	2003	2004	2005	2006
Families receiving allowances:													
Total	KJMU	7 024	6 956	6 976	7 102	VOWX	7 340	7 335	7 336	7 342	7 353	7 375	7 441
With 1 child	KJMV	2 983	..	..	3 015	VOWY	3 128	3 143	3 162	3 189	3 219	3 260	3 329
2 children	KJMW	2 794	..	..	2 822	VOWZ	2 898	2 891	2 894	2 890	2 885	2 882	2 884
3 children	KJMX	929	..	..	943	VOXA	977	970	954	942	931	920	917
4 children	KJMY	236	..	..	241	VOXB	251	247	242	239	235	233	231
5 or more children	KJMZ	82	..	..	82	VOXC	86	84	83	82	82	80	80
Families receiving Guardian's Allowance	VOXG	2.2	2.3	2.3	2.3	VOXH	2.5	2.3	2.5	2.6	2.9	2.8	3.2

1 See chapter text.
2 Figures provided by Child Benefit Centre Management Information Statistics
  as a new scan was being developed.

Source: HM Revenue and Customs: 020 7147 3021

10.10 Family Credit/ Working Families' Tax Credit[1,2]

Thousands

		Great Britain As at 31 December						United Kingdom As at 30 November			
		1994	1995	1996	1997	1998		1999	2000	2001	2002
Families in receipt:											
Total	KJTO	578.0	646.5	716.7	751.4	779.7	ZCMK	965.3	1 167.8	1 293.7	1 377.3
Two-parent families: total	KJTP	324.6	356.9	390.2	388.0	383.4	ZCML	467.6	565.9	617.2	639.8
With 1 child	KJTQ	80.1	89.7	98.6	96.6	95.4	ZCMM	116.8	144.8	151.6	159.0
2 children	KJTR	122.4	135.1	146.1	144.4	141.7	ZCMN	178.4	220.1	243.5	252.7
3 children	KJTS	76.4	83.4	91.1	91.4	89.1	ZCMO	107.8	129.2	142.9	147.3
4 children or more children	ZIYM	45.8	48.6	54.4	55.6	57.3	ZCMP	64.6	71.8	79.2	80.8
One-parent families: total	KJTW	253.4	289.6	326.5	363.4	396.3	ZIYI	497.8	601.8	676.5	737.6
With 1 child	KJTX	133.8	152.2	170.4	189.3	203.4	ZIYJ	259.6	313.7	349.5	381.2
2 children	KJTY	86.0	99.1	111.2	121.8	136.1	ZIYK	169.6	207.6	238.7	261.6
3 or more children	KJTZ	33.5	38.3	45.0	52.3	56.9	ZIYL	68.6	80.5	88.3	94.8

1 See chapter text. Family Credit was replaced by Working Families Tax
  Credit (WFTC) in October 1999. The WFTC figures for December 1999 include Family Credit awards made before October 1999 and still current
  (both FC and WFTC awards last for 26 weeks).
2 WFTC was replaced by Child Credit and Working Tax Credit on 6th April
  2003. See table 10.11.

Sources: Board of Inland Revenue: 020 7438 7370;
Department for Work and Pensions;
Information and Analysis Directorate: 0191 225 7373

10.11 In-work families with Child Tax Credit or Working Tax Credit awards
United Kingdom
As at December

Thousands

		2003[1]	2004[2]	2005[3]	2006[4]
In-work families with award:	C5PF	4 640	4 948	5 167	5 340
With children	C5PG	4 259.0	4 364.0	4 362.0	4 382.0
Receiving Working Tax Credit and Child Tax Credit	C5PH	1 548.0	1 492.0	1 497.0	1 596.0
Receiving Child Tax Credit only	C5PI	2 660.0	2 769.0	2 721.0	2 608.0
Without children	C5PK	381.0	585.0	805.0	958.0
Receiving Working Tax Credit	C5PL	215.0	258.0	320.0	323.0

1 Child and Working Tax Credits replaced Working Families' Tax Credit on
  6th April 2003. Figures for 2003 are based on awards current at 5th January
  2004. See chapter text.
2 Figures for 2004 are based on awards current at 3rd December 2004.
3 Figures for 2005 are based on awards current at 5th December 2005.

4 Figures for 2006 are based on awards current at 2nd December 2006.

Source: HM Revenue and Customs: 020 7147 3083

10.12 Widows' Benefit (excluding bereavement payment[1,2]): by type of benefit
Great Britain

Number in receipt of windows benefit as at May 2006

Thousands

		2001	2002	2003	2004	2005	2006
All Widows' Benefit (excluding bereavement allowance)							
All ages	KJGA	255.0	223.4	191.5	163.4	139.0	117.7
Unknown Age	EW4O	0.2	0.2	0.1	–	–	–
18 - 24	EW4P	0.1	0.1	–	–	–	..
25 - 29	EW4Q	0.8	0.5	0.3	0.2	0.1	0.1
30 - 34	EW4R	3.2	2.3	1.7	1.2	0.8	0.5
35 - 39	EW4S	7.8	6.4	5.1	3.9	2.9	2.1
40 - 44	EW4T	12.7	10.8	9.1	7.5	6.1	4.9
45 - 49	EW4U	24.6	20.1	16.3	13.2	11.0	9.1
50 - 54	EW4V	62.6	50.2	40.6	33.3	26.9	21.8
55 - 59	EW4W	113.7	103.4	90.9	77.7	66.9	57.3
60 - 64	EW4X	29.3	29.5	27.4	26.4	24.3	21.8
Widowed parents' allowance - with dependant children							
All ages	KJGG	47.6	40.7	34.2	28.2	23.2	19.0
Unknown Age	EW4Y	0.1	0.1	0.1	–	–	..
18 - 24	EW4Z	0.1	0.1	–	–	–	..
25 - 29	EW52	0.8	0.5	0.3	0.2	0.1	0.1
30 - 34	EW53	3.1	2.3	1.6	1.1	0.8	0.5
35 - 39	EW54	7.5	6.2	4.9	3.8	2.8	2.1
40 - 44	EW55	11.7	10.0	8.4	7.0	5.7	4.6
45 - 49	EW56	12.3	10.8	9.3	7.8	6.7	5.6
50 - 54	EW57	8.8	7.6	6.6	5.7	4.8	4.1
55 - 59	EW58	3.1	3.0	2.7	2.3	2.0	1.8
60 - 64	EW59	0.2	0.2	0.3	0.3	0.3	0.2
Widowed parents' allowance - without dependant children							
All ages	KJGM	2.7	2.3	1.8	1.4	1.1	0.8
Unknown Age	EW5A	–	–	–	–	–	..
18 - 24	EW5B	0.1	–	–	–	–	..
25 - 29	EW5C	–	–	–	–	–	..
30 - 34	EW5D	0.1	0.1	–	–	–	–
35 - 39	EW5E	0.3	0.2	0.2	0.1	0.1	0.1
40 - 44	EW5F	0.6	0.5	0.4	0.3	0.2	0.2
45 - 49	EW5G	0.7	0.6	0.5	0.4	0.3	0.2
50 - 54	EW5H	0.7	0.6	0.5	0.3	0.3	0.2
55 - 59	EW5I	0.4	0.4	0.3	0.2	0.2	0.1
60 - 64	EW5J	0.1	0.1	0.1	–	–	–
Age -related bereavement allowance							
All ages	KJGS	150.9	138.7	124.3	110.1	96.6	84.0
Unknown Age	EW5K	–	–	–	–	–	–
18 - 24	EW5L	–	–	–	–	–	..
25 - 29	EW5M	–	–	–	–	–	..
30 - 34	EW5N	–	–	–	–	–	..
35 - 39	EW5O	–	–	–	–	–	..
40 - 44	EW5P	0.4	0.3	0.2	0.2	0.2	0.1
45 - 49	EW5Q	11.7	8.7	6.6	5.1	4.0	3.3
50 - 54	EW5R	51.8	41.0	32.8	26.7	21.4	17.2
55 - 59	EW5S	77.5	77.7	73.5	66.3	59.0	50.9
60 - 64	EW5T	9.6	11.0	11.2	11.9	12.0	12.5
Bereavement allowance (Not age related)[3]							
All ages	KJGW	53.7	41.7	31.3	23.7	18.1	13.9
Unknown Age	EW5U	0.1	–	–	–	–	..
18 - 24	EW5V	–	–	–	–	–	..
25 - 29	EW5W	–	–	–	–	–	..
30 - 34	EW5X	–	–	–	–	–	..
35 - 39	EW5Y	–	–	–	–	–	..
40 - 44	EW5Z	–	–	–	–	–	..
45 - 49	EW62	–	–	–	–	–	..
50 - 54	EW63	1.5	1.1	0.8	0.6	0.5	0.3
55 - 59	EW64	32.7	22.4	14.4	8.8	5.6	4.4
60 - 64	EW65	19.5	18.2	16.0	14.2	12.0	9.1

1 Definitions and Conventions: "-" Nil or Negligible; "." Not applicable; Caseload figures are rounded to the nearest hundred and displayed in thousands.

2 Caseload (Thousands) All Claimants of Widows Benefit are female. No new claims for WB have been accepted since April 2001 when it was replaced by Bereavement Benefit.

3 Figures include overseas cases.

Sources: DWP Information Directorate: Work and Pensions Longitudinal Study 100% data; Information and Analysis Directorate: 0191 225 7373

10.13 Bereavement Benefit[1] (excluding bereavement payment): by sex, type of benefit and age of widow/er

Great Britain. Number in payment at March

Thousands

		Males				Females		
		2004	2005	2006		2004	2005	2006
All Bereavement Benefit (excluding bereavement allowance)								
All ages	WLSX	16.8	17.6	18.0	WLTC	34.3	37.6	39.7
18 - 24	EVW9	..	..	..	EVY2	0.1	0.1	0.1
25 - 29	EVX2	0.1	0.1	0.1	EVY3	0.4	0.5	0.5
30 - 34	EVX3	0.4	0.4	0.3	EVY4	1.4	1.6	1.7
35 - 39	EVX4	1.2	1.2	1.2	EVY5	3.0	3.5	3.8
40 - 44	EVX5	2.4	2.5	2.6	EVY6	4.7	5.7	6.5
45 - 49	EVX6	3.2	3.3	3.5	EVY7	6.3	7.4	8.1
50 - 54	EVX7	3.2	3.4	3.4	EVY8	7.7	8.0	8.3
55 - 59	EVX8	3.5	3.6	3.7	EVY9	10.8	11.0	10.7
60 - 64	EVX9	2.8	3.2	3.2	EVZ2	–	–	..
Widowed parents' allowance - with dependant children								
All ages	WLUD	10.2	10.7	11.1	WLUH	17.5	21.4	24.4
18 - 24	EVZ3	–	–	..	EW24	0.1	0.1	0.1
25 - 29	EVZ4	0.1	0.1	0.1	EW25	0.4	0.5	0.5
30 - 34	EVZ5	0.4	0.4	0.3	EW26	1.4	1.6	1.7
35 - 39	EVZ6	1.2	1.2	1.2	EW27	2.9	3.4	3.8
40 - 44	EVZ7	2.3	2.5	2.6	EW28	4.6	5.6	6.4
45 - 49	EVZ8	2.7	2.8	2.9	EW29	4.3	5.4	6.3
50 - 54	EVZ9	2.0	2.1	2.3	EW2A	2.7	3.4	4.0
55 - 59	EW22	1.2	1.2	1.2	EW2B	1.1	1.5	1.7
60 - 64	EW23	0.4	0.4	0.5	EW2C	–	–	..
Widowed parents' allowance - without dependant children								
All ages	WLVK	0.1	0.1	0.1	WMMR	0.4	0.4	0.4
18 - 24	EW2D	–	–	..	EW2M	–	–	..
25 - 29	EW2E	–	–	..	EW2N	–	–	–
30 - 34	EW2F	–	–	..	EW2O	–	–	–
35 - 39	EW2G	–	–	–	EW2P	0.1	0.1	0.1
40 - 44	EW2H	–	–	–	EW2Q	0.1	0.1	0.1
45 - 49	EW2I	–	–	–	EW2R	0.1	0.1	0.1
50 - 54	EW2J	–	–	–	EW2S	0.1	0.1	0.1
55 - 59	EW2K	–	–	..	EW2T	–	0.1	–
60 - 64	EW2L	–	–	..	EW2U	–	–	..
Age-related bereavement allowance								
All ages	WMOB	1.9	1.9	1.9	WMOC	7.5	7.1	6.6
18 - 24	EW2V	–	–	..	EW36	–	–	..
25 - 29	EW2W	–	–	..	EW37	–	–	..
30 - 34	EW2X	–	–	..	EW38	–	–	..
35 - 39	EW2Y	–	–	..	EW39	–	–	..
40 - 44	EW2Z	–	–	..	EW3A	–	–	..
45 - 49	EW32	0.5	0.5	0.5	EW3B	1.9	1.9	1.8
50 - 54	EW33	1.2	1.2	1.2	EW3C	4.9	4.5	4.2
55 - 59	EW34	0.2	0.2	0.2	EW3D	0.7	0.7	0.6
60 - 64	EW35	–	–	..	EW3E	–	–	..
Bereavement allowance (not age related)								
All ages	WMOX	4.7	5.0	5.0	WMOY	8.9	8.8	8.3
18 - 24	EW3F	–	–	..	EW3O	–	–	..
25 - 29	EW3G	–	–	..	EW3P	–	–	..
30 - 34	EW3H	–	–	..	EW3Q	–	–	..
35 - 39	EW3I	–	–	..	EW3R	–	–	..
40 - 44	EW3J	–	–	..	EW3S	–	–	..
45 - 49	EW3K	–	–	..	EW3T	–	–	..
50 - 54	EW3L	–	–	..	EW3U	–	–	..
55 - 59	EW3M	2.2	2.3	2.2	EW3V	8.9	8.8	8.3
60 - 64	EW3N	2.5	2.7	2.7	EW3W	–	–	..

1 Bereavement Benefit replaced Widow's Benefit and is payable to both men and women widowed on or after 9 April 2001. Figures include overseas cases.

Source: Work and Pensions longitudinal study (WPLS) 100%: 0191 225 7874

10.14 Contributory and non-contributory retirement pensions:[1] by sex and age of claimant

Great Britain. Numbers in payment at end of May

Thousands and percentages

		2002	2003	2004	2005	2006
Men:						
Age-groups:						
65-69	KJSB	1 308.6	1 330.2	1 354.3	1 364.1	1 341.5
Percentage	KJSC	*31.5*	*31.5*	*31.6*	*31.4*	*30.6*
70-74	KJSD	1 129.3	1 136.6	1 140.3	1 150.0	1 160.1
Percentage	KJSE	*27.2*	*27.0*	*26.6*	*26.5*	*26.5*
75-79	KJSF	864.1	867.1	875.0	887.1	903.0
Percentage	KJSG	*20.8*	*20.6*	*20.4*	*20.4*	*20.6*
80-84	KJSH	531.9	565.3	593.7	593.3	596.9
Percentage	KJSI	*12.8*	*13.4*	*13.9*	*13.7*	*13.6*
85-89	KJSJ	233.3	225.9	221.4	246.4	273.1
Percentage	KJSK	*5.6*	*5.4*	*5.2*	*5.7*	*6.2*
90 and over	KJSL	85.9	90.6	95.5	100.2	103.6
Percentage	KJSM	*2.1*	*2.1*	*2.2*	*2.3*	*2.4*
Unknown age	EW3Y	1.2	1.0	0.8	1.1	1.2
Percentage	EW3Z	–	–	–	–	–
Total all ages	KJSA	4 154.4	4 216.7	4 281.1	4 342.2	4 379.5
Women:						
Age-groups:						
60-64	KJSO	1 371.7	1 402.7	1 451.3	1 498.7	1 524.0
Percentage	KJSP	*19.6*	*19.9*	*20.3*	*20.8*	*21.0*
65-69	KJSQ	1 410.0	1 429.7	1 452.7	1 464.2	1 453.1
Percentage	KJSR	*20.2*	*20.3*	*20.4*	*20.3*	*20.0*
70-74	KJSS	1 333.6	1 329.1	1 319.2	1 314.5	1 312.7
Percentage	KJST	*19.1*	*18.8*	*18.5*	*18.2*	*18.1*
75-79	KJSU	1 175.2	1 161.9	1 156.7	1 158.6	1 165.5
Percentage	KJSV	*16.8*	*16.5*	*16.2*	*16.1*	*16.0*
80-84	KJSW	893.1	939.4	973.9	951.6	933.3
Percentage	KJSX	*12.8*	*13.3*	*13.6*	*13.2*	*12.9*
85-89	KJSY	514.2	491.3	473.1	511.0	552.7
Percentage	KJSZ	*7.4*	*7.0*	*6.6*	*7.1*	*7.6*
90 and over	KJTA	289.1	298.8	307.2	314.9	319.4
Percentage	KJTB	*4.1*	*4.2*	*4.3*	*4.4*	*4.4*
Unknown age	EW42	3.4	2.0	1.1	1.3	1.5
Percentage	EW43	–	–	–	–	–
Total all ages	KJSN	6 990.3	7 054.9	7 135.1	7 214.7	7 262.3

1 See chapter text. Including pensions payable to persons residing overseas.

Sources: Department for Work and Pensions;
Work and Pensions Longitudinal Study (WPLS);
Information and Analysis Directorate: 0191 225 7373

10.15 War pensions: estimated number of pensioners[1]
Great Britain

At 31 March each year   Thousands

		1996	1997	1998	1999	2000	2001	2002[2]	2003[2]	2004[2]	2005[2]	2006[3]
Disablement	KADH	265.37	264.59	259.16	248.93	240.76	231.62	221.80	212.18	201.55	191.75	182.80
Widows and dependants	KADI	58.37	60.05	58.49	55.85	54.92	52.71	50.98	48.61	46.04	43.55	41.05
Total	KADG	323.74	324.64	317.65	306.06	295.67	284.33	272.78	260.79	247.59	235.30	223.85

1 See chapter text. From 1914 war, 1939 war and later service.
2 Data from 2002 have been revised due to changes in methodology.
3 The discontinuity between 2005 and 2006 is due to improvements in data processing.

Source: Ministry of Defence/DASA (Pay & Pensions): 020 7218 0031

10.16 Income support[1] (excluding MIG)[2] by statistical group[3]:number of claimants
Great Britain

Thousands[4]

		2001	2002	2003	2004	2005	2006
All income support claimants (excluding MIG)[5]	F8YY	2 260.6	2 238.8	2 236.4	2 192.6	2 139.8	2 114.8
Incapacity Benefits	F8YZ	1 182.8	1 197.9	1 215.1	1 205.2	1 193.8	1 183.2
Lone Parent	F8Z2	895.5	865.9	853.3	823.3	789.3	774.9
Carer	F8Z3	73.2	75.7	77.5	78.4	79.0	80.2
Others on Income Related Benefits	F8Z4	109.2	99.3	90.5	85.9	77.7	76.5

1 Figures are given at May each year and are taken from the DWP 100% Work and Pensions Longitudinal Study (WPLS).
2 Figures exclude MIG claimants. Pension Credit replaced MIG on 6th October 2003 and extended Income Support entitlements to customers aged 60 and over.
3 Statistical groups are defined as follows:
  Incapacity Benefits- claimants aged under 60 on Incapacity Benefit or Severe Disablement Allowance;
  Lone Parent - single claimants aged under 60 with dependants not in receipt of IB/SDA;
  Carer- claimants aged under 60 entitled to Carer's Allowance;
  Other Income Related Benefit- claimants not in one of the above categories.
4 Figures are rounded to the nearest hundred and quoted in thousands.
5 Totals may not sum due to rounding.

Sources: Department for Work and Pensions;
Information and Analysis Directorate: 0191 225 7373

10.17 MIG/Pension Credit[1,2]:number of claimants
Great Britain

End of May   Thousands[3]

		2001[4]	2002[4]	2003[4]	2004[5]	2005[5]	2006[5]
All Pension Credit	F8Z5	..	..	..	2 490.8	2 682.7	2 717.4
Guarantee Credit Only	F8Z6	..	..	..	735.0	767.3	775.6
Guarantee Credit Only and Savings Credit	F8Z7	..	..	..	1 269.5	1 321.7	1 343.2
Savings Credit	F8Z8	..	..	..	486.0	593.7	598.6
(Residual)[6] MIG Case	F8Z9	1 714.4	1 737.5	1 777.8	0.3	–	–

1 Source Data: Work and Pensions Longitudinal Data in each May from 2000 - 2005.
2 Pension Credit was introduced on 6th October 2003 and replaced Monthly Income Guarantee (Income Support for people aged 60 or over). The vast majority of people who were in receipt of MIG transferred to PC in October 2003.
3 Figures are rounded to the nearest hundred and expressed in thousands.
4 Columns 2001 - 2003 represent MIG caseloads.
5 Columns 2004 onwards represent Pension Credit Caseloads.
6 When MIG was replaced by Pension Credit in October 2003 some cases continued to be MIG cases. These were cases where the partner aged under 60 continued as the claimant. These cases are minimal and are reducing each quarter.

Sources: Department for Work and Pensions;
Information and Analysis Directorate: 0191 225 7373

10.18 Income support: average weekly amounts of benefit[1,2]
Great Britain
As at May

£ per week

		2001	2002	2003	2004	2005	2006
All income support claimants (excluding MIG)[3]	F8ZF	84.34	84.83	91.07	91.14	85.81	83.41
Incapacity benefits[4]	F8ZG	74.25	72.32	76.10	77.70	76.93	78.12
Lone Parent[4]	F8ZH	101.36	105.85	116.52	114.96	102.85	94.88
Carer[4]	F8ZI	69.33	71.50	76.63	76.78	72.42	70.40
Others on income related benefits[4]	F8ZJ	64.09	62.45	64.43	64.25	62.69	62.62

1 Figures are given at May each year and are taken from the DWP Work and Pensions Longitudinal Study (WPLS).
2 Average amounts are rounded to the nearest penny.
3 Figures exclude MIG claimants. Pension Credit replaced MIG on 6 October 2003 and extended Income Support entitlement to customers aged 60 and over.
4 Statistical groups are defined as follows:
Incapacity Benefits- claimants under 60 on incapacity benefit or Severe Disablement Allowance;
Lone Parent- single claimants aged under 60 with dependants not in receipt of IB/SDA;
Carer- claimants aged under 60 entitled to Carer's Allowance;
Other Income Related Benefit- claimants not in one of the above categories.

Sources: Department for Work and Pensions; Information and Analysis Directorate: 0191 225 7373

10.19 MIG/Pension Credit: average weekly amounts of benefit[1,2]
Great Britain
As at May

£ per week[3]

		2001[4]	2002[4]	2003[4]	2004[5]	2005[5]	2006[5]
All Pension Credit	F8ZA	..	..	..	42.30	43.62	46.75
Guarantee Credit Only	F8ZB	..	..	..	71.91	75.43	79.56
Guarantee Credit and Savings Credit	F8ZC	..	..	..	37.51	39.87	43.11
Savings Credit only	F8ZD	..	..	..	10.03	10.83	12.39
(Residual) MIG Case[6]	F8ZE	50.00	49.45	50.37	47.49	68.89	110.60

1 Figures are given in each May from 2000 - 2005 and are taken from the DWP Work and Pensions Longitudinal Study (WPLS).
2 Pension Credit was introduced on 6th October 2003 and replaced Minimum Income Guarantee (Income Support for people aged 60 or over).
3 Average amounts are shown as pounds per week and rounded to the nearest penny.
4 Columns 2001-2003 represent MIG average amounts.
5 Colums 2004 onwards represent Pension Credit Average amounts.
6 When MIG replaced pension credit in October 2003 some cases continued to be MIG cases. These were cases where the partner aged under 60 continued as the claimant. These cases are minimal and are reducing each quarter.

Sources: Department for Work and Pensions; Information and Analysis Directorate: 0191 225 7373

10.20 Summary of government expenditure on social services and housing[1]
Years ended 31 March

£ million

		1998/99	1999/00	2000/01	2001/02	2002/03	2003/04	2004/05	2005/06
Final Consumption Expenditure									
Education	QYWZ	38 500	43 044	46 933	52 752	57 475	61 983	65 653	68 536
Health	QYXA	48 595	52 901	57 362	62 727	69 065	75 585	83 989	91 497
Personal social services	GB7F	11 476	12 659	13 717	15 033	17 232	19 930	21 922	23 401
Social benefits	GG5O	106 143	106 998	110 417	121 098	126 345	135 571	141 612	148 543
Housing	QYXD	6 524	6 168	6 387	6 590	7 236	10 802	11 222	12 129
Total government expenditure	GH2K	211 238	221 770	234 816	258 200	277 353	303 871	324 398	344 106
Total government expenditure on social services and housing as a percentage of GDP	GGN7	24.4	24.1	24.4	25.6	26.1	27.0	27.2	27.8

1 See chapter text.

Source: Office for National Statistics: 020 7533 5985

10.21 Summary of Government expenditure on education[1]
Years ended 31 March

£ million

		1998 /99	1999 /00	2000 /01	2001 /02	2002 /03	2003 /04	2004 /05	2005 /06
Education									
Final consumption expenditure									
Current expenditure									
Compensation of employees									
Local Authorities[2]									
Nursery and primary schools	G8ZX	7 685	8 396	9 092	10 079	10 740	11 955	13 132	13 867
Secondary schools	G8ZY	7 314	7 991	8 652	9 592	10 356	11 570	13 115	13 849
Special schools	G8ZZ	785	858	929	1 030	1 164	1 145	1 362	1 438
Central Government									
Northern Ireland wages and salaries	HMPM	633	666	709	769	841	928	959	995
Other wages and salaries[3]	GB7H	1 459	275	297	463	529	610	661	729
Total Central Government expenditure	MMTF	2 092	941	1 006	1 232	1 370	1 538	1 620	1 724
Tertiary Education & Other Education[4]	G922	1 776	3 284	3 569	3 840	4 127	3 728	2 553	2 682
Total Compensation of employees	QYSA	19 652	21 470	23 248	25 773	27 757	29 936	31 782	33 446
Net procurement									
Local Government Net procurement[5]	QTKJ	5 959	5 839	6 154	6 407	7 620	7 785	8 418	8 902
Central Government Net procurement[6]	QTLN	1 576	1 560	1 737	1 623	1 787	1 933	2 020	1 768
Nursery/Primary schools									
secondary schools									
Tertiary education									
Total	QYSB	7 535	7 399	7 891	8 030	9 407	9 718	10 438	10 670
Non-market capital consumption	QYSD	1 077	1 108	1 142	1 200	1 248	1 305	1 409	1 568
Total final consumption expenditure	QYSE	28 264	29 977	32 281	35 003	38 412	40 959	43 629	45 684
Other current transfers	QZNU	8 409	11 061	12 123	14 315	15 407	17 050	17 862	17 321
Gross capital formation	QYVD	1 690	1 843	2 188	2 863	2 753	2 936	3 094	3 853
Non-produced non-financial assets	QYWM	−182	−167	−151	−187	−191	−206	−217	−229
Capital transfers	QZKJ	319	330	492	758	1 094	1 244	1 285	1 907
Total Central Government Expediture	G924	13 919	15 584	17 411	20 623	22 239	24 519	25 690	25 351
Total Local Government Expediture	G925	24 581	27 460	29 522	32 129	35 236	37 464	39 963	43 185
Total government expenditure	QYWZ	38 500	43 044	46 933	52 752	57 475	61 983	65 653	68 536
Total government education expenditure as a percentage of GDP	GGN8	4.4	4.7	4.9	5.2	5.4	5.5	5.5	5.6

1 See chapter text.
2 Based on pay figures published by Dept for Communities and Local Government , Scottish Executive and National Assembly for Wales.
3 Includes wages/salaries for Scotland, Wales and Non-Departmental Public Bodies (NDPBs).
4 Includes Higher, Further, Adult and Continuing education.
5 Net of VAT.
6 Includes Central Government Net Procurement on NDPBs, Scotland, Wales, Northern Ireland and Education in Healthcare.

Sources: Department for Education and Skills;
Office for National Statistics: 020 7533 5985

10.22 Summary of Government expenditure on Health[1]
Years ended 31 March

£ million

		1998/99	1999/00	2000/01	2001/02	2002/03	2003/04	2004/05	2005/06
Final Consumption expenditure[2]									
Current expenditure[3]									
Compensation of employees	QWWQ	25 211	26 560	28 794	31 470	34 954	38 140	42 574	44 301
non-market capital consumption	QYOB	1 396	1 492	1 593	1 574	1 680	1 787	1 884	2 113
other	QTLP	20 332	22 413	23 954	26 155	28 407	31 218	34 446	40 712
Total Final consumption expenditure	QYOT	46 939	50 465	54 341	59 199	65 041	71 145	78 904	87 126
Subsidies	CBRA	–	–	28	34	33	21	21	21
other current transfers	QZMR	198	931	1 277	1 312	1 171	1 220	1 248	1 424
Grosss capital formation	QYVE	1 387	1 440	1 643	2 067	2 581	3 049	3 727	2 757
Non produced non financial assets	QYWN	–	–	–	–	–	–	–	–
Capital transfers	HMSF	71	65	73	115	239	150	89	169
total outlays	QYXA	48 595	52 901	57 362	62 727	69 065	75 585	83 989	91 497
Total NHS expenditure as a percentage of GDP	GGN9	5.6	5.8	5.9	6.2	6.5	6.7	7.1	7.4

1 See chapter text.
2 Figures are based on Departmental Expenditure reported to HM Treasury Statistics database.
3 Includes expenditure by Dept. of Health, NHS Trusts, Scottish Executive, National Assembly for Wales and Northern Ireland Executive.

Source: Office for National Statistics: 020 7533 5985

10.23 Summary of Government expenditure on personal social services[1]
Years ended 31 March

£ million

		1998/99	1999/00	2000/01	2001/02	2002/03	2003/04	2004/05	2005/06
Personal social services									
Central government Current Expenditure									
Compensation of employees	ADQ7	254	282	318	331	376	462	482	519
Net Procurement	ADR2	182	252	311	343	532	489	667	634
Total	GB7D	436	534	629	674	908	951	1 149	1 153
Local Authorities Current Expenditure									
Compensation of employees	CFCR	5 453	5 735	5 760	5 936	6 385	6 960	7 506	7 925
Net Procurement	QWSB	5 522	6 326	7 259	8 349	9 859	11 934	13 165	14 205
Total	GB7E	10 975	12 061	13 019	14 285	16 244	18 894	20 671	22 130
Capital Expenditure	GDZU	65	64	69	74	80	85	102	118
Total Final Consumption Expenditure	GB7F	11 476	12 659	13 717	15 033	17 232	19 930	21 922	23 401
Total government expenditure as a percentage of GDP	GGO2	1.3	1.4	1.4	1.5	1.6	1.8	1.8	1.9

1 See chapter text.

Source: Office for National Statistics: 020 7533 5985

10.24 Summary of Government expenditure on social security benefits[1] and administration

Years ended 31 March

£ million

		1998/99	1999/00	2000/01	2001/02	2002/03	2003/04	2004/05	2005/06
Social benefits									
Social security benefits in cash									
National Insurance fund									
Retirement pensions	CSDG	35 885	37 965	38 923	42 157	44 590	46 701	48 969	51 549
Widows and Guardians allowances	CSDH	973	989	980	1 099	1 093	1 006	923	886
Unemployment Benefit	CSDI	–	–1	–1	–	–2	–	–	–3
Jobseeker's Allowance[2]	CJTJ	474	462	435	470	520	506	445	488
Sickness Benefit[3]	CSDJ	–	–	–	–	–	–	–	–
Invalidity Benefit[3]	CSDK	–	–	–	–	–	–	–	–
Incapacity Benefit[3]	CUNL	7 295	6 896	6 677	6 678	6 839	6 801	6 754	6 726
Maternity Benefit	CSDL	39	41	45	56	69	124	152	165
Statutory sick pay	CSDQ	28	28	32	32	32	76	75	80
Statutory maternity pay	GTKZ	552	604	645	676	736	1 088	1 339	1 295
Payment in lieu of benefits foregone	GTKV	–	–	–	–	–	–	–	–
Total national insurance fund benefits	ACHH	45 263	47 034	47 807	51 188	53 931	56 187	58 657	61 186
Redundancy fund benefit	GTKN	116	148	156	194	230	229	186	248
Maternity fund benefit	GTKO	–	–	–	–	–	–	–	–
Social fund benefit	GTLQ	360	1 024	1 784	1 883	1 925	2 159	2 200	2 256
Benefits paid to overseas residents	FJVZ	1 101	1 112	1 176	1 262	1 357	1 445	1 522	1 607
Total social security benefits in cash	QYRJ	46 823	49 241	50 851	54 497	57 426	60 315	62 565	65 297
Total unfunded social benefits[4]:	QYJT	11 369	12 394	13 108	13 979	14 558	16 532	16 816	17 271
Social assistance benefits in cash									
War pensions and allowances[5]	CSDD	1 262	1 254	1 201	1 200	1 186	1 100	1 114	1 020
Income Support	CSDE	11 793	12 227	13 076	14 100	14 584	15 028	16 356	15 883
Income tax credits and reliefs	RYCQ	1 878	2 623	4 654	5 745	6 711	9 485	11 566	12 938
Child benefit	EKY3	9 757	10 167	8 532	8 795	8 955	9 414	9 565	9 978
Non-contributory job seekers allowance	EKY4	3 079	2 813	2 442	2 124	2 118	2 062	1 780	1 809
Care allowances	EKY5	2 681	2 834	2 955	5 096	5 214	5 445	5 714	5 992
Disability benefits	EKY6	5 319	5 653	6 021	7 310	7 863	8 389	8 900	9 432
Other benefits	EKY7	8 616	4 242	4 360	4 387	3 924	4 473	4 554	5 612
Benefits paid to overseas residents	RNNF	71	59	54	55	48	48	48	48
Total social assistance benefits in cash	NZGO	44 457	41 872	43 295	48 812	50 546	55 522	59 597	62 599
Total social benefits	NMDR	102 649	103 261	106 591	117 037	122 511	131 799	137 787	146 315
Administration[6]	KJEE	4 349	3 737	3 826	4 061	3 834	3 772	3 774	3 376
Total benefits and administration	GG5O	106 143	106 998	110 417	121 098	126 345	135 571	141 612	148 543
Total government benefit expenditure as a percentage of GDP	GGO3	12.3	11.7	11.5	11.2	11.9	12.0	11.9	12.0

1 See chapter text. Figures are based on table 5.2.4s of the Blue Book 2006. They are not fully comparable with earlier editions of the Annual Abstract.
2 Jobseeker's allowance was introduced in October 1996 to replace Unemployment benefit and Income Support for the unemployed.
3 Sickness benefit and Invalidity benefit were replaced by a single incapacity benefit in 1995.
4 Includes Civil & Defence, voluntary employer social contributions, teachers & NHS inflationary pensions increase payments.
5 From 2002/03 War Pensions are administered by the Ministry of Defence.
6 Figures published by HM Treasury in Public Expenditure Statistical Analyses.

Sources: Office for National Statistics: 020 7533 5985; Department for Work and Pensions; HM Treasury

10.25 Summary of Government expenditure on social services and housing[1]
Years ended 31 March

£ million

		1998 /99	1999 /00	2000 /01	2001 /02	2002 /03	2003 /04	2004 /05	2005 /06
Housing									
Final consumption expenditure									
Compensation of employees	QYSV	870	748	776	851	985	1 077	1 172	1 198
Other current expenditure on goods and services	QYSW	999	709	935	1 068	1 295	3 023	2 940	3 631
Capital consumption	QYSY	1 015	1 117	1 181	1 301	1 407	1 454	1 632	1 564
Total	QYSZ	2 884	2 574	2 892	3 220	3 687	5 554	5 744	6 393
Subsidies	QYVP	941	798	759	613	611	495	302	478
Other current transfers	QZNY	40	30	42	129	93	539	119	227
Gross Fixed Capital Formation	QYVH	331	312	434	497	552	1 184	1 408	1 458
Non-produced financial assets	QYWQ	–	–	–	–	–	–	–	–
Capital transfers	GVFX	2 328	2 454	2 260	2 131	2 293	3 030	3 649	3 573
Total government expenditure	QYXD	6 524	6 168	6 387	6 590	7 236	10 802	11 222	12 129
Total public sector housing expenditure as a percentage of GDP	GGO4	0.8	0.7	0.7	0.7	0.7	1.0	1.0	1.0

1 See chapter text.

Source: Office for National Statistics: 020 7533 5985

Crime and justice

Chapter 11

Crime and justice

There are differences in the legal and judicial systems of England and Wales, Scotland and Northern Ireland which make it impossible to provide tables covering the United Kingdom as a whole in this section. These differences concern the classification of offences, the meaning of certain terms used in the statistics, the effects of the several Criminal Justice Acts and recording practices.

Recorded crime statistics

(Table 11.2)

Crimes recorded by the police provide a measure of the amount of crime committed. The statistics are based on counting rules, revised with effect from 1 April 1998, which are standard for all the police forces in England, Wales and Northern Ireland and now include all indictable and triable-either-way offences together with a few summary offences which are closely linked to these offences. The new rules have changed the emphasis of measurement more towards one crime per victim, and have also increased the coverage of offences. These changes have particularly impacted on the offence groups of violence against the person, fraud and forgery, drugs offences and other offences.

For a variety of reasons many offences are either not reported to the police or not recorded by them. The changes in the number of offences recorded do not necessarily provide an accurate reflection of changes in the amount of crime committed.

In order to further improve the consistency of recorded crime statistics and to take a more victim oriented approach to crime recording, the National Crime Recording Standard (NCRS) was introduced in England, Wales and Northern Ireland from 1 April 2002. Some police forces implemented the principles of NCRS in advance of its implementation across all forces in April 2002. The NCRS had the effect of increasing the number of offences recorded by the police.

Similarly, the Scottish Crime Recording Standard (SCRS) was introduced by the 8 Scottish police forces with effect from 1 April 2004. This means that no corroborative evidence is required initially to record a crime related incident as a crime if so perceived by the victim. Again, the introduction of this new recording standard was expected to increase the numbers of minor crimes recorded by the police, such as minor crimes of vandalism and minor thefts and offences of petty assault and

breach of the peace. However, it was expected that the SCRS would not have much impact on the figures for the more serious crimes such as serious assault, sexual assault, robbery or housebreaking.

The Sexual Offences Act 2003 introduced in May 2004 altered the definition and coverage of sexual offences. In particular, it redefined indecent exposure as a sexual offence which is likely to account for much of the increase in sexual offences.

Further information is available from the Home Office: Crime in England and Wales 2002/2003, ed: Jon Simmons and Tricia Dodd.

Court proceedings and police cautions

(Tables 11.3 - 11.7, 11.13 - 11.17, 11.20 - 11.22)

The statistical basis of the tables of court proceedings is broadly similar in England and Wales, Scotland and Northern Ireland; the tables show the number of persons found guilty, recording a person under the heading of the principal offence of which he is found guilty, excluding additional findings of guilt at the same proceedings. A person found guilty at a number of separate court proceedings is included more than once.

The statistics on offenders cautioned in England and Wales cover only those who, on admission of guilt, were given a formal caution by, or on the instructions of, a senior police officer as an alternative to prosecution. Written warnings by the police for motor offences and persons paying fixed penalties for certain motoring offences are excluded. Formal cautions are not issued in Scotland. There are no statistics on cautioning available for Northern Ireland.

The Crime and Disorder Act 1998 created provisions in relation to reprimands and final warnings, new offences and orders which have been implemented nationally since 1 June 2000. They replace the system of cautioning for offenders aged under 18. Reprimands can be given to first-time offenders for minor offences. Any further offending results in either a final warning or a charge.

For persons proceeded against in Scotland, the statistics relate to the High Court of Justiciary, the Sheriff Court and the District Court. The High Court deals with serious solemn (ie Jury) cases and has unlimited sentencing power. The Sheriff Court is limited to imprisonment of 3 years for solemn cases, or 3 months (6 months when specified in legislation for second or subsequent offences and 12 months for certain statutory offences) for summary (ie non-Jury) cases. The District Court deals only with summary cases and is limited to 60 days imprisonment and level 4 fines. Stipendiary Magistrates sit in

Glasgow District Court and have the summary sentencing powers of a Sheriff.

In England and Wales, indictable offences are offences which are:

(a) Triable only on indictment. These offences are the most serious breaches of the criminal law and must be tried at the Crown Court. 'Indictable-only' offences include murder, manslaughter, rape and robbery.

(b) Triable either way. These offences may be tried at the Crown Court or Magistrates' Court.

The Criminal Justice Act 1991 led to the following main changes in the sentences available to the courts in England and Wales:

(a) introduction of combination orders,

(b) introduction of the "unit fine scheme" at Magistrates' courts,

(c) abolishing the sentence of detention in a young offender institution for 14 year old boys and changing the minimum and maximum sentence lengths for 15 to 17 year olds to 10 and 12 months respectively, and

(d) abolishing partly suspended sentences of imprisonment and restricting the use of a fully suspended sentence.

The Criminal Justice Act 1993 abolished the "Unit Fine Scheme" in Magistrates' courts which had been introduced under the Criminal Justice Act 1991.

A charging standard for assault was introduced in England and Wales on 31 August 1994 with the aim to promote consistency between the police and prosecution on the appropriate level of charge to be brought.

The Criminal Justice and Public Order Act 1994 created several new offences in England and Wales, mainly in the area of Public Order, but also including male rape (there is no statutory offence of 'male rape' in Scotland, although such a crime may be charged as serious assault). The Act also:

(a) extended the provisions of section 53 of the Children and Young Persons Act 1993 for 10 to 13 year olds,

(b) increased the maximum sentence length for 15 to 17 year olds to 2 years,

(c) increased the upper limit from £2,000 to £5,000 for offences of criminal damage proceeded against as if triable only summarily,

(d) introduced provisions for the reduction of sentences for early guilty pleas, and

(e) increased the maximum sentence length for certain firearm offences.

Provisions within the Crime (Sentences) Act 1997 (as amended by the Powers of Criminal Courts Sentencing Act 2000), in England and Wales, and the Crime and Punishment (Scotland) Act 1997, in Scotland, included:

(a) an automatic life sentence for a second serious violent or sexual offence unless there are exceptional circumstances (this provision has not been enacted in Scotland),

(b) a minimum sentence of seven years for an offender convicted for a third time of a class A drug trafficking offence unless the court considers this to be unjust in all the circumstances, and in England and Wales,

(c) the new section 38A of the Magistrates' Courts' Act 1980 extending the circumstances in which a magistrates' court may commit a person convicted of an offence triable either way to the Crown Court for sentence - it was implemented in conjunction with section 49 of the Criminal Procedure and Investigations Act 1996, which involves the magistrates' courts in asking defendants to indicate plea before the mode of trial decision is taken and compels the court to sentence or commit for sentence any defendant who indicates a guilty plea.

Under the Criminal Justice and Court Service Act 2000 new terms were introduced for certain orders. Community rehabilitation order is the new name for a probation order. A community service order is now known as a community punishment order. Finally, the new term for a combination order is community punishment and rehabilitation order. In April 2000 the secure training order was replaced by the detention and training order. Section 53 of the Children and Young Persons Act 1993 was repealed on 25 August 2000 and its provisions were transferred to Sections 90-92 of the Powers of Criminal Courts (Sentencing) Act 2000. Reparation and Action plan order were implemented nationally from 1 June 2000. Drug treatment and testing order was implemented in England, Scotland and Wales from October 2000. Referral order was implemented in England, Scotland and Wales from April 2000. These changes are now reflected in Table 11.7.

The system of Magistrates' courts and Crown Courts in Northern Ireland operates in a similar way to that in England and Wales. A particularly significant statutory development, however, has been the Criminal Justice (NI) Order 1996 which introduces a new sentencing regime into Northern Ireland, largely replicating that which was introduced into England and Wales by the Criminal Justice Acts of 1991 and 1993. The order makes many changes to both community and custodial sentences, while introducing new orders such as the combination order, the custody probation order and orders for release on licence of sexual offenders.

Previous convictions of prisoners

(Tables 11.8 and 11.9)

Technical Note

Criminal Histories – Data sources

Information on previous convictions of prisoners published prior to 1995 was based upon Prison Service records. However, details of a prisoner's previous convictions were often not recorded (eg. this information was missing for 44 per cent of the 1990 male receptions under sentence). To overcome this problem the Home Office Offenders Index (a computerised database containing details of convictions for standard list offences) was used to provide information on prisoners' previous convictions in previous publications.

The Offenders Index (OI) is populated from court records and contains details of all convictions for standard list offences since 1963. Standard list offences cover all indictable offences and some of the more serious summary offences. Previous convictions refer to a court appearance at which there was a finding of guilt in respect of one or more offences.

The criminal histories of prisoners are now obtained from the Home Office copy of the Police National Computer (HOPNC). This marks another change in the data source for criminal histories as previous publications were based on the Offenders Index (OI) or Prison Service records. The HOPNC became operational in the Home Office in early 2005 and holds the criminal histories of all people convicted of any recordable offence (indictable and summary) in England and Wales.

The HOPNC is a more comprehensive data source than the Offenders Index data in two ways:

1. The HOPNC covers a wider range of offences. OI data was restricted to the more serious 'standard list' offences; indictable only, triable either way offences, and some of the more serious summary offences. Because the HOPNC covers a wider range of offences, previous convictions for more minor offences are included in HOPNC figures. This has the effect of increasing the number of previous convictions.

2. The HOPNC also provides information on cautions. Offences for which a caution was given are included only in the figures presented in Tables 11.8 and 11.9

The main effect of including cautions is to reduce the proportion of offenders with no previous conviction and increase the proportion of offenders with a larger number of previous convictions, in particular the 7-10 and 11+ categories. This is understandable given that the inclusion of cautions will lead to the proportion of first time offenders being depressed as we can expect that some individuals will have been cautioned before appearing at court.

The process for matching prisoners to the HOPNC is more stringent than the matching process used previously for the OI. For example, matching an offender to the PNC requires that the conviction date on the PNC is within 7 days either side of the sentence date in the probation or prison data.

Expenditure on penal establishments in Scotland

(Table 11.19)

The results shown in this table are reported on a cash basis for financial years 1995-96 to 2000-01 in line with funding arrangements. Financial year 2001-02 is reported on a resource accounting basis in line with the introduction of Resource Budgeting. Capital Charges were introduced with Resource Accounting and Budgeting.

11.1 Police force strength: by country and sex
End of year

Numbers

		1996[1]	1997[1]	1998[1]	1999[1]	2000[1]	2001[1]	2002[1]	2003[1]	2004[1]	2005[1]	2006
England and Wales												
Regular Police(FTE)												
Strength:												
Men	KERB	106 756	106 271	105 145	103 956	101 801	102 321	104 483	106 996	110 150	110 597	109 327
Women	KERC	18 087	18 780	19 611	19 885	20 155	21 155	22 784	24 430	26 956	28 898	30 307
Seconded:[2]												
Men	KERD	1 859	1 882	1 836	2 017	2 077	1 914	2 031	1 689	1 811	1 514	1 545
Women	KERE	198	225	222	238	307	292	305	251	284	222	203
Additional Officers:[3]												
Men	KERF	111	200	267	324	361	493	567	375	394	522	676
Women	KERG	57	158	514	582	519	509	564	709	969	1 042	1 213
Special constables												
Strength:												
Men	KERH	12 838	12 886	11 977	10 860	9 623	8 630	8 014	7 718	7 645	8 074	8 829
Women	KERI	6 937	6 988	6 279	5 624	4 724	4 108	3 584	3 319	3 343	3 844	4 350
Scotland												
Regular police												
Strength:[4,6]												
Men	KERK	12 627	12 752	12 753	12 545	12 374	12 547	12 513	12 590	12 685	12 798	12 820
Women	KERL	1 885	2 037	2 227	2 265	2 325	2 602	2 738	2 897	2 898	3 203	3 401
Central service:[4,5]												
Men	KERM	94	85	85	88	95	87	116	131	166	195	171
Women	KERN	8	4	6	9	13	10	12	17	29	29	25
Seconded:[6]												
Men	KERO	105	101	101	85	130	140	133	166	192	216	200
Women	KERP	16	13	10	12	18	14	18	24	30	31	30
Additional regular police:												
Men	HFVM	81	71	88	85	80	83	80	79	88	79	85
Women	HFVN	5	1	9	6	4	5	12	10	13	21	15
Special constables												
Strength:												
Men	KERS	1 411	1 336	1 286	1 229	981	924	812	711	773	718	888
Women	KERT	467	450	437	422	355	336	307	280	328	437	432
Northern Ireland												
Regular police[7,9]												
Strength:[7]												
Men	KERU	7 526	7 562	7 523	7 406	6 844	6 227	6 057	6 171	6 108	6 016	5 992
Women	KERV	897	923	933	987	966	1 009	1 080	1 266	1 418	1 547	1 534
Reserve[8]												
Strength:[7]												
Men	KERW	3 727	3 587	3 469	3 199	2 962	2 629	2 223	1 983	1 824	1 431	1 424
Women	KERX	675	719	705	641	607	556	510	453	485	410	402

1 Figures for England and Wales are as 31 March and are based on full-time equivalent strength excluding those on career breaks or maternity/ parternity leave. Figures for Scotland are as at 31 December until 1994 and from 1995 onwards as at 31 March. From 1999, figures for Northern Ireland reflect the position at the end of the financial year, i.e. 1999 and 2000 figures are as at 31 March 2000 and 31 March 2001 respectively. Prior to this figures were as at 31 December.

2 Figures exclude secondments outside the police service in England and Wales (eg to the private sector or to law enforcement agencies overseas).

3 Figures include those officers on career breaks or maternity/paternity leave. Prior to 2003, these figures were not collected centrally.

4 'Strength' includes central service and seconded police.

5 Instructors at Training Establishments, etc, formerly shown as secondments.

6 Scottish Drug Enforcement Agency, officers on courses, etc.

7 Does not include officers on secondment.

8 Includes part-time reserve and full-time reserve, FTR - 1011 as at 31 March 2006 (931 males and 80 females). PTR - 815 as at 31 March 2006 (493 males and 322 females).

9 Also includes student officers.

Sources: Home Office: 020 7035 0289;
The Scottish Executive Justice Department: 0131 244 2148;
The Police Service of Northern Ireland: 028 9065 0222 ext 24070

11.2 Recorded crime statistics: by offence group[1]
England and Wales

Thousands

		1995	1996	1997	1998[2,3] /99	1998[3] /99	1999 /00	2000 /01	2001[4] /02	2002[4,5] /03	2003 /04	2004 /05	2005 /06
Violence against the person	BEAB	212.6	239.3	250.8	230.8 LQMP	502.8	581.0	600.9	650.3	845.1	967.2	1 048.2	1 059.9
Sexual offences[6]	BEAC	30.3	31.4	33.2	34.9 LQMQ	36.2	37.8	37.3	41.4	49.2	52.7	62.1	62.1
Burglary	BEAD	1 239.5	1 164.6	1 015.1	951.9 LQMR	953.2	906.5	836.0	878.5	890.1	820.0	681.1	645.1
Robbery	BEAE	68.1	74.0	63.1	66.2 LQMS	66.8	84.3	95.2	121.4	110.3	103.7	90.7	98.2
Theft and handling stolen goods	BEAF	2 452.1	2 383.9	2 165.0	2 126.7 LQMT	2 191.4	2 223.6	2 145.4	2 267.0	2 411.6	2 312.9	2 069.4	2 019.3
Fraud and forgery	BEAG	133.0	136.2	134.4	173.7 LQMU	279.5	334.8	319.3	314.9	331.1	319.6	280.5	233.0
Criminal damage	BEAH	914.0	951.3	877.0	834.4 LQMV	879.6	945.7	960.1	1 064.5	1 120.6	1 218.5	1 198.2	1 184.7
Drug offences[5]	LQMO	..	..	..	21.3 LQYT	135.9	121.9	113.5	121.4	143.3	143.5	145.5	178.5
Other offences[5]	BEAI	29.4	33.6	36.6	42.0 LQYU	63.6	65.7	63.2	65.7	73.7	75.5	64.9	75.7
Total	BEAA	5 100.2	5 036.6	4 598.3	4 481.8 LQYV	5 109.1	5 301.2	5 170.8	5 525.0	5 975.0	6 013.8	5 640.6	5 556.5

1 See chapter text.
2 Estimates.
3 The counting rules were revised on 1 April 1998
4 The National Crime Recording Standard (NCRS) was introduced in England and Wales from 1 April 2002. For more details about the inflationary effects of the NCRS on the 2001/02 and 2002/03 figures see chapter text.
5 Includes the British Transport Police (BTP) from 2002/03 onwards.

6 See chapter text.
7 Prior to 1 April 1998 the offence of drug trafficking was included in the 'Other offences' group. From 1 April 1999, under the new counting rules, drug trafficking became part of a new 'Drug offences' group which, now includes possession and other drug offences. For 1998/99 under the old counting rules, drug trafficking has been separated out and listed under drugs offences.

Source: Home Office: 020 7035 0307

167

11.3 Offenders found guilty: by offence group[1,5,6]
England and Wales
Magistrates' courts and the Crown Court

Thousands

		1994	1995	1996	1997	1998	1999	2000	2001	2002	2003	2004
All ages[2]												
Indictable offences												
Violence against the person:	KJEJ	37.6	29.1	30.0	34.6	35.7	34.4	34.0	35.3	37.7	38.0	39.1
Murder	KESB	0.2	0.2	0.3	0.3	0.3	0.3	0.3	0.3	0.3	0.3	0.4
Manslaughter	KESC	0.2	0.2	0.3	0.3	0.3	0.3	0.3	0.3	0.3	0.2	0.3
Wounding	KESD	36.1	27.4	28.3	32.7	35.2	33.9	33.5	33.5	35.7	35.9	35.0
Other offences of violence against the person	KESE	1.0	1.2	1.2	1.3	1.3	1.3	1.3	1.2	1.4	1.5	1.9
Sexual offences	KESF	4.5	4.7	4.4	4.5	4.6	4.3	3.9	3.8	4.4	4.4	4.8
Burglary	KESG	38.0	35.3	32.2	31.7	30.8	29.3	26.2	24.8	26.7	25.7	24.3
Robbery	KESH	4.9	5.2	5.9	5.6	5.5	5.6	6.0	6.8	7.7	7.3	7.5
Theft and handling stolen goods	KESI	121.6	116.1	114.5	118.4	125.7	131.2	128.0	127.0	127.3	119.1	110.6
Fraud and forgery	KESJ	18.4	17.2	16.3	17.0	19.8	20.3	19.2	18.3	18.1	18.0	18.1
Criminal damage	KESK	10.0	9.6	9.8	10.5	10.9	10.9	10.2	10.7	11.0	11.2	11.7
Drugs	KBWX	27.8	31.6	34.1	40.7	48.8	48.7	44.6	45.6	49.0	51.2	54.5
Other offences (excluding motoring)	KESL	39.4	42.2	43.5	47.6	49.6	47.9	44.5	44.2	48.0	51.4	54.7
Motoring offences	KESM	12.0	11.2	9.9	9.5	9.0	8.1	7.6	7.7	8.2	8.7	8.0
Total	KESA	314.1	302.2	300.6	320.1	341.7	342.0	325.5	324.2	338.3	335.1	317.8
Summary offences[3]												
Assaults	KESO	21.9	29.3	30.0	32.0	35.3	37.5	37.4	37.7	40.7	45.6	53.4
Betting and gaming	KESP	–	–	–	–	–	–	–	–	–	–	–
Offences with pedal cycles	KBWY	1.0	1.1	1.3	1.5	2.1	1.3	0.8	0.6	0.5	0.6	0.7
Other Highways Acts offences	KBWZ	3.4	2.6	2.8	3.2	3.1	2.9	2.7	2.4	2.2	1.9	1.8
Breach of local or other regulations	KESQ	9.4	6.7	5.9	6.4	5.8	6.5	5.0	4.3	3.9	3.4	3.1
Intoxicating Liquor Laws:												
Drunkenness	KESR	20.2	19.8	24.2	28.8	30.8	28.7	27.2	26.2	26.9	27.7	21.1
Other offences	KESS	0.7	0.7	0.5	0.6	0.6	0.5	0.4	0.3	0.4	0.7	0.8
Education Acts	KEST	2.8	3.1	3.5	3.7	5.0	5.1	5.1	5.6	5.8	5.8	6.5
Game Laws	KESU	0.6	0.4	0.4	0.3	0.4	0.3	0.2	0.2	0.3	0.2	0.2
Labour Laws	KESV	0.1	0.1	–	0.1	0.1	0.1	0.1	–	–	0.1	–
Summary offences of criminal damage and malicious damage	KESW	22.7	22.6	23.4	24.7	26.5	27.9	28.0	26.9	28.3	29.8	31.5
Offences by prostitutes	KESX	7.7	6.8	6.6	6.6	6.0	4.0	4.1	3.7	4.2	3.9	2.9
Railway offences	KESY	5.6	6.2	9.1	11.4	12.6	15.2	17.4	22.6	29.4	34.8	35.0
Revenue Laws[3]	KESZ	126.2	123.8	139.1	143.5	174.7	165.8	175.0	146.9	167.8	172.5	175.5
Vagrancy Acts	KETB	1.9	1.6	2.0	2.0	2.2	2.7	3.3	3.2	3.8	3.8	2.9
Wireless Telegraphy Acts[3]	KETC	162.9	113.8	164.9	77.0	76.6	55.8	105.7	83.8	96.6	79.9	89.3
Other summary offences	KETD	67.8	71.5	74.7	74.7	80.9	79.3	78.1	77.8	76.4	82.9	97.9
Motoring offences (summary)[3]	KETA	638.7	642.4	649.0	649.3	665.2	632.9	607.5	583.3	595.8	662.6	707.9
Total	KESN	1 093.5	1 052.4	1 137.4	1 065.8	1 128.0	1 066.5	1 098.2	1 025.5	1 083.0	1 156.1	1 230.7
Persons aged 10 to under 18[3,4]												
Indictable offences												
Violence against the person:	KETF	5.8	4.7	5.3	5.9	5.9	6.2	6.4	6.9	6.9	6.6	6.9
Murder	KBXA	–	–	–	–	–	–	–	–	–	–	–
Manslaughter	KBXB	–	–	–	–	–	0.2	–	–	–	–	–
Wounding	KBXC	5.7	4.7	5.3	5.8	5.9	5.9	6.3	6.8	6.8	6.5	6.5
Other offences of violence against the person	KCAA	–	–	–	0.1	0.1	–	0.1	0.1	0.1	0.1	0.3
Sexual offences	KETG	0.4	0.4	0.4	0.5	0.5	0.5	0.5	0.5	0.6	0.4	0.6
Burglary	KETH	8.9	9.1	8.6	8.6	8.5	7.8	6.8	6.3	6.4	5.8	5.9
Robbery	KETI	1.7	2.0	2.4	2.3	2.2	2.0	2.2	2.8	2.8	2.6	3.0
Theft and handling stolen goods	KETJ	14.4	18.2	19.0	19.6	21.9	22.7	21.0	20.6	18.4	16.5	16.8
Fraud and forgery	KETK	0.5	0.6	0.7	0.8	1.0	1.1	1.0	1.0	1.2	0.8	0.8
Criminal damage	KETL	2.0	2.1	2.2	2.3	2.3	2.7	2.6	2.9	2.9	2.9	3.2
Drugs	KCAB	1.1	1.3	1.6	1.8	2.7	3.1	3.7	4.3	5.0	5.1	4.5
Other offences (excluding motoring)	KETM	2.8	3.3	3.8	4.2	4.2	4.3	4.4	4.4	4.4	4.3	4.6
Motoring	KETN	0.3	0.4	0.4	0.4	0.4	0.4	0.6	0.7	0.8	0.8	0.7
Total	KETE	37.9	42.2	44.4	46.4	49.7	50.6	49.2	50.3	49.1	46.0	47.0
Summary offences[3]												
Offences with pedal cycles	KETP	0.1	0.2	0.2	0.2	0.3	0.3	0.2	0.2	0.2	0.2	0.2
Breach of local or other regulations	KETR	0.1	0.2	0.3	0.2	0.2	0.2	0.2	0.2	0.1	0.1	0.1
Summary offences of criminal damage and malicious damage	KETS	2.9	3.4	3.9	4.4	5.2	6.1	6.7	6.9	7.0	7.2	8.3
Railway offences	KETT	0.3	0.4	0.4	0.5	0.5	0.5	0.4	0.4	0.4	0.3	0.4
Other summary offences	KETU	9.7	7.2	8.8	10.1	12.1	11.7	11.3	11.6	11.7	10.3	11.0
Motoring offences (summary)[3]	KCAC	8.6	9.3	10.8	10.8	11.3	12.6	14.5	16.7	17.1	17.8	17.0
Total	KETO	21.7	25.6	30.3	22.0	36.8	39.6	42.2	45.2	45.4	46.6	49.2

1 See chapter text.
2 Includes 'Companies', etc.
3 It is estimated that in 1995 there was a shortfall of 75,100 offenders found guilty for certain summary offences.
4 Figures for persons aged 10 to under 18 are included in the totals above.
5 These data are on the principal offence basis.

6 Every effort is made to ensure that the figures presented are accurate and complete. However, it is important to note that these data have been extracted from large administrative data systems generated by the courts and police forces. As a consequence, care should be taken to ensure data collection processes and their inevitable limitations are taken into account when those data are used.

Source: Home Office:020 8760 1404

11.4 Offenders cautioned: by offence group[1,4,5]
England and Wales

Thousands

		1994	1995	1996	1997	1998	1999	2000	2001	2002	2003	2004
All ages[2]												
Indictable offences												
Violence against the person	KELB	21.8	20.4	21.8	23.6	23.5	21.2	19.9	19.5	23.6	28.8	36.6
Murder	KCAD	–	–	–	–	–	–	–	–	–	–	–
Manslaughter	KCAE	–	–	–	–	–	–	–	–	–	–	–
Wounding	KCAF	21.4	20.1	21.4	23.3	22.9	20.6	19.3	18.9	22.9	27.9	35.0
Other violence against the person	KCAG	0.4	0.3	0.4	0.4	0.6	0.6	0.6	0.6	0.7	0.9	1.2
Sexual offences	KELC	2.0	2.3	2.0	1.9	1.7	1.5	1.3	1.2	1.1	1.4	1.6
Burglary	KELD	10.2	10.5	10.2	9.4	8.4	7.7	6.6	6.4	5.8	5.6	5.6
Robbery	KELE	0.6	0.6	0.6	0.7	0.6	0.6	0.6	0.5	0.4	0.4	0.5
Theft and handling stolen goods	KELF	93.6	104.9	93.6	82.8	83.6	75.4	67.6	63.5	54.2	54.5	61.9
Fraud and forgery	KELG	7.5	7.9	7.5	7.2	7.4	7.2	6.2	5.8	5.3	5.5	6.0
Criminal damage	KELH	3.1	3.8	3.1	2.8	2.7	3.0	3.2	3.4	3.1	3.7	5.5
Drug offences	KCAI	47.5	48.2	47.5	56.0	58.7	49.4	41.1	39.4	44.9	45.7	32.6
Other offences	KELI	4.4	4.0	4.4	5.0	5.0	4.6	4.4	4.2	4.4	5.3	6.0
All offenders cautioned	KELA	190.8	202.6	190.8	189.4	191.7	170.6	150.9	143.9	142.9	150.7	156.3
Summary offences												
Assaults	KELK	4.2	8.1	9.1	9.1	..	17.0	17.2	18.2	17.3	19.8	26.1
Betting and gaming	KELL	–	–	–	–	–	–	–	–	–	–	–
Offences with pedal cycles	KCAK	0.8	0.8	0.9	0.9	0.8	0.6	0.3	0.2	0.1	0.1	0.3
Other Highways Acts offences	KCAL	0.9	0.9	0.8	0.8	0.8	0.7	0.4	0.3	0.2	0.3	0.3
Breach of local or other regulations	KELM	1.1	0.9	0.8	0.9	0.9	0.7	0.5	0.3	0.3	0.2	0.3
Intoxicating Liquor Laws:												
Drunkenness	KELN	37.7	22.9	25.9	25.7	22.8	20.3	18.1	16.6	16.2	18.1	13.5
Other offences	KELO	1.0	1.0	0.9	0.9	0.7	0.4	0.2	0.3	0.3	0.3	0.3
Education Acts	KELP	–	–	–	–	–	–	–	–	–	0.1	0.1
Game Laws	KELQ	0.1	0.1	0.1	0.1	0.1	0.1	–	–	–	–	–
Labour Laws	KELR	–	–	–	–	–	–	–	–	–	–	–
Summary offences of criminal damage and malicious damage	KELS	23.1	25.1	27.7	27.6	28.3	28.7	26.8	26.7	24.7	27.6	33.3
Offences by prostitutes	KELT	3.6	3.3	3.5	3.5	3.5	2.1	1.3	1.0	1.8	1.3	1.6
Railway offences	KELU	0.2	0.3	0.2	0.1	–	–	–	–	–	–	–
Revenue Laws	KELV	0.2	0.2	0.1	0.1	0.1	0.1	–	–	–	–	–
Vagrancy Acts	KELX	1.0	1.0	0.6	0.6	1.2	0.8	0.4	0.3	0.3	0.3	0.2
Wireless Telegraphy Acts[4]	KELY	–	–	–	–	–	–	–	–	–	–	–
Other summary offences	KELZ	24.6	24.2	24.7	22.3	37.0	24.1	22.5	21.9	21.0	22.9	23.5
All offenders cautioned	KELJ	98.7	88.7	95.4	92.7	96.2	95.6	88.1	85.9	82.4	91.1	99.5
Persons aged 10 to under 18[3]												
Indictable offences												
Violence against the person	KEMB	9.4	9.4	9.4	9.6	9.5	8.5	8.3	8.7	9.3	11.0	13.6
Murder	KCAN	–	–	–	–	–	–	–	–	–	–	–
Manslaughter	KCAO	–	–	–	–	–	–	–	–	–	–	–
Wounding	KCAP	9.4	9.4	9.4	9.6	9.4	8.4	8.2	8.6	9.2	10.9	13.5
Other violence against the person	KCCE	–	–	–	–	0.1	0.1	0.1	0.1	0.1	0.1	0.1
Sexual offences	KEMC	0.7	0.8	0.7	0.7	0.6	0.6	0.5	0.5	0.4	0.5	0.5
Burglary	KEMD	8.2	8.5	8.2	7.5	6.7	6.1	5.4	5.3	4.6	4.4	4.2
Robbery	KEME	0.6	0.5	0.6	0.6	0.5	0.5	0.5	0.5	0.4	0.4	0.4
Theft and handling stolen goods	KEMF	48.2	57.4	48.2	40.9	44.0	39.6	36.9	35.2	28.1	28.3	33.1
Fraud and forgery	KEMG	1.5	1.6	1.5	1.4	1.6	1.7	1.5	1.3	1.1	1.0	1.0
Criminal damage	KEMH	2.0	2.4	2.0	1.8	1.7	1.9	2.1	2.3	1.9	2.3	3.1
Drug offences	KCCF	7.9	8.7	7.9	9.7	11.0	9.6	7.9	8.5	9.5	9.6	8.3
Other offences	KEMI	1.3	1.3	1.3	1.5	1.5	1.4	1.3	1.3	1.3	1.4	1.6
All offenders cautioned	KEMA	79.9	90.6	79.9	73.7	77.2	69.8	64.3	63.5	56.6	58.7	65.9
Summary offences												
Offences with pedal cycles	KEMK	0.5	0.4	0.5	0.5	0.4	0.3	0.2	0.1	0.1	0.1	0.2
Breach of local or other regulations	KEMM	0.4	0.3	0.3	0.3	0.3	0.2	0.2	0.1	0.1	0.1	0.1
Summary offences of criminal damage and malicious damage	KEMN	12.5	12.8	13.8	13.5	14.2	14.7	14.4	15.2	12.6	14.3	17.1
Railway offences	KEMO	0.1	0.1	0.1	0.1	–	–	–	–	–	–	–
Other summary offences	KEMP	15.6	10.3	10.8	9.1	13.8	9.9	9.2	9.5	8.5	9.2	10.1
All offenders cautioned	KEMJ	29.2	30.0	33.2	30.8	32.5	34.2	33.2	34.5	29.9	33.3	39.1

1 See chapter text.
2 Includes 'Companies', etc.
3 Figures for persons aged 10 to under 18 are included in the totals above.
4 These data are on the principal offence basis.
5 Every effort is made to ensure that the figures presented are accurate and complete. However, it is important to note that these data have been extracted from large administrative data systems generated by police forces. As a consequence, care should be taken to ensure data collection processes and their inevitable limitations are taken into account when those data are used.

Source: Office for Criminal Justice Reform:020 8760 1404

11.5 Offenders found guilty of offences: by age and sex[1,3,4]
England and Wales
Magistrates' courts and the Crown Court

Thousands

		1994	1995	1996	1997	1998	1999	2000	2001	2002	2003	2004
Males												
Indictable offences												
All ages	KEFA	273.2	263.2	261.1	276.5	292.9	291.7	276.5	275.5	287.1	283.4	268.4
10 and under 15 years	KEFB	6.9	7.1	6.6	7.1	8.1	8.9	8.7	9.0	8.8	8.0	8.5
15 and under 18 years	KEFC	28.7	30.2	32.5	33.6	35.2	35.1	33.8	34.4	33.7	31.4	31.8
18 and under 21 years	KEFD	50.3	47.4	46.3	48.4	51.8	52.6	49.9	48.2	46.6	43.8	39.9
21 years and over	KEFE	187.4	178.6	175.6	187.3	197.9	195.0	184.0	183.9	198.0	200.2	188.2
Summary offences[2]												
All ages	KEFF	871.0	862.0	903.6	880.9	929.0	886.6	881.0	826.6	866.4	937.1	990.0
10 and under 15 years	KEFG	2.3	2.9	2.8	3.0	3.9	5.1	5.8	6.2	6.1	6.1	6.7
15 and under 18 years	KEFH	17.7	20.5	24.6	25.9	28.5	30.3	32.2	34.5	34.6	35.3	36.5
18 and under 21 years	KEFI	82.9	84.0	88.4	91.0	96.3	94.8	93.0	92.2	94.7	99.9	98.2
21 years and over	KEFJ	768.2	754.6	787.9	761.0	800.3	756.5	750.0	693.6	731.0	795.8	848.8
Females												
Indictable offences												
All ages	KEFK	39.5	37.5	38.0	42.2	47.3	49.0	47.7	47.4	50.0	50.2	48.4
10 and under 15 years	KEFL	1.0	1.0	1.0	1.0	1.4	1.4	1.5	1.6	1.6	1.6	1.7
15 and under 18 years	KEFM	3.8	4.0	4.2	4.6	5.1	5.2	5.2	5.3	5.1	4.9	5.0
18 and under 21 years	KEFN	6.2	5.7	5.7	6.3	7.1	7.6	7.5	7.0	6.9	6.2	5.7
21 years and over	KEFO	28.6	26.8	27.2	30.4	33.7	34.7	33.5	33.5	36.5	37.5	35.9
Summary offences[2]												
All ages	KEFP	211.5	180.5	222.9	174.9	188.3	171.0	208.3	190.2	208.7	210.5	231.2
10 and under 15 years	KEFQ	0.2	0.4	0.4	0.5	0.6	0.8	0.9	0.9	1.1	1.2	1.5
15 and under 18 years	KEFR	1.5	1.8	2.6	3.4	3.8	3.4	3.3	3.6	3.6	4.0	4.6
18 and under 21 years	KEFS	9.6	10.4	12.1	11.1	12.1	10.8	11.8	11.1	11.6	12.6	13.0
21 years and over	KEFT	200.2	167.9	207.9	160.0	171.7	155.4	192.3	174.7	192.4	192.7	212.2
Companies, etc												
Indictable offences	KEFU	1.4	1.5	1.5	1.3	1.5	1.3	1.3	1.3	1.2	1.4	1.1
Summary offences[2]	KEFV	10.9	9.9	10.9	10.0	10.7	8.9	8.8	8.6	7.9	8.6	1.9

1 See chapter text.
2 It is estimated that in 1995 there was a shortfall of 75,100 offenders found guilty for certain summary offences.
3 These data are on the principal offence basis.
4 Every effort is made to ensure that the figures presented are accurate and complete. However, it is important to note that these data have been extracted from large administrative data systems generated by the courts and police forces. As a consequence, care should be taken to ensure data collection processes and their inevitable limitations are taken into account when those data are used.

Source: Office for Criminal Justice Reform: 020 8760 1404

11.6 Persons cautioned by the police: by age and sex[1,3,4]
England and Wales

Thousands

		1994	1995	1996	1997	1998	1999	2000	2001	2002	2003	2004
Males												
Indictable offences												
All ages	KEGA	153.6	149.3	142.6	143.3	142.9	126.1	109.7	103.8	104.4	109.8	110.0
10 and under 15 years[2]	KEGB	32.3	29.2	25.1	22.9	23.7	22.0	20.3	19.7	16.7	16.9	18.7
15 and under 18 years[2]	KEGC	35.5	35.3	33.0	32.0	32.0	28.7	25.0	24.5	23.3	24.1	25.9
18 and under 21 years	KEGD	25.0	24.8	24.3	25.2	25.7	22.7	20.1	18.5	18.9	19.4	16.7
21 years and over	KEGE	60.7	60.0	60.2	63.2	61.5	52.7	44.3	41.2	45.6	49.4	48.7
Summary offences												
All ages	KEGF	83.6	73.8	79.2	75.7	76.9	76.1	69.6	68.0	63.8	70.9	76.0
10 and under 15 years[2]	KEGG	10.5	10.1	10.3	9.9	10.6	11.7	12.0	12.7	10.3	10.9	12.6
15 and under 18 years[2]	KEGH	14.7	15.4	18.0	16.1	16.1	16.1	14.9	15.2	13.3	15.1	17.2
18 and under 21 years	KEGI	11.3	11.1	13.0	12.9	13.2	13.0	11.9	11.0	11.0	12.4	12.3
21 years and over	KEGJ	47.0	37.1	37.9	36.9	37.0	35.3	30.9	29.0	29.2	32.5	33.9
Females												
Indictable offences												
All ages	KEGK	56.2	53.3	48.2	46.0	48.8	44.5	41.2	40.1	38.5	41.0	46.3
10 and under 15 years[2]	KEGL	15.2	14.0	10.8	9.2	11.1	9.8	10.0	10.1	8.4	8.6	10.6
15 and under 18 years[2]	KEGM	12.4	12.2	10.9	9.5	10.3	9.3	9.0	9.3	8.3	9.1	10.7
18 and under 21 years	KEGN	6.1	6.0	5.6	5.7	5.9	5.7	5.2	4.9	4.8	4.9	5.2
21 years and over	KEGO	22.4	21.1	20.9	21.5	21.4	19.6	17.0	15.9	17.0	18.4	19.9
Summary offences												
All ages	KEGP	15.1	14.8	16.2	17.0	19.2	9.4	18.5	18.0	18.6	20.2	23.5
10 and under 15 years[2]	KEGQ	1.5	1.7	1.8	1.7	2.1	2.5	2.8	2.9	2.7	3.0	3.9
15 and under 18 years[2]	KEGR	2.5	2.7	3.2	3.2	3.7	3.9	3.7	3.8	3.6	4.3	5.4
18 and under 21 years	KEGS	1.9	1.9	2.1	2.3	2.6	2.7	2.5	2.3	2.4	2.7	2.9
21 years and over	KEGT	9.2	8.6	9.1	9.9	10.8	10.3	9.6	9.0	9.8	10.2	11.3

1 See chapter text.
2 From 1 June 2000 the Crime and Disorder Act 1998 came into force nationally and removed the use of cautions for persons under 18 and replaced them with reprimands and final warnings.
3 These data are on the principal offence basis.
4 Every effort is made to ensure that the figures presented are accurate and complete. However, it is important to note that these data have been extracted from large administrative data systems generated by police forces. As a consequence, care should be taken to ensure data collection processes and their inevitable limitations are taken into account when those data are used.

Source: Office for Criminal Justice Reform:020 8760 1404

11.7 Sentence or order passed on persons sentenced for indictable offences: by sex[1]
England and Wales
Magistrates' courts and the Crown Court

Percentages and thousands

		1994	1995	1996	1997	1998	1999	2000	2001	2002	2003	2004
Males												
Sentence or order												
Absolute discharge	KEJB	0.8	0.8	0.8	0.7	0.7	0.6	0.6	0.6	0.8	0.9	0.8
Conditional discharge	KEJC	17.4	16.2	15.6	15.5	15.3	15.0	14.1	13.4	12.4	13.0	12.2
Fine	KEJF	31.8	30.0	28.6	28.2	28.4	27.7	25.7	24.5	23.9	24.0	20.9
Community rehabilitation order	KEJD	10.2	10.0	9.9	10.0	10.0	10.1	10.1	10.7	10.6	10.1	9.5
Supervision order	KEJE	2.4	2.7	2.9	2.7	2.7	2.7	2.4	2.3	2.1	1.8	2.0
Community punishment order	KEJG	11.1	10.6	9.9	9.5	9.3	9.3	9.5	9.0	8.6	8.3	8.8
Attendance centre order	KEJH	2.0	2.0	1.9	1.8	1.7	1.8	1.5	1.2	0.7	0.6	0.6
Community punishment and rehabilitation order	KIJW	2.7	3.0	3.5	3.7	3.8	3.7	3.6	2.6	2.6	2.6	2.8
Curfew order	LUJP	..	..	0.1	0.1	0.2	0.3	0.5	0.7	1.1	1.6	2.7
Reparation order	SNFI	..	..	..	..	..	..	0.7	1.3	0.8	0.4	0.4
Action plan order	SNFJ	..	..	..	..	..	..	0.9	1.7	1.1	0.7	0.8
Drug treatment and testing order	SNFK	..	..	..	..	..	..	0.1	1.2	1.4	1.9	2.3
Referral order	SNFL	..	..	..	..	..	..	..	..	3.0	4.0	4.4
Community order[2]	GN7P	..	..	..	..	..	..	..	..	..	..	..
Suspended sentence order	KEJL	0.7	0.7	0.8	0.8	0.7	0.6	0.7	0.6	0.5	0.5	0.6
Imprisonment												
Sec 90-92	LUJQ	0.1	0.1	0.2	0.3	0.2	0.2	0.2	0.2	0.2	0.2	0.2
Detention and training order	LUJR	..	..	..	..	..	..	1.4	1.9	1.8	1.5	1.6
Young offender institution	KEJK	4.9	5.6	6.1	6.1	6.0	6.2	5.2	4.5	4.2	3.6	3.8
Unsuspended imprisonment	KEJM	13.6	16.0	17.2	17.9	18.2	18.7	19.9	20.0	20.9	20.6	21.5
Other sentence or order	KEJN	2.3	2.2	2.4	3.0	2.6	3.1	3.1	3.4	3.3	3.5	4.1
Total number of males (thousands) = 100 per cent	KEJA	272.6	262.9	260.8	275.4	292.4	291.3	277.1	274.6	285.6	282.3	267.5
Females												
Sentence or order												
Absolute discharge	KEKB	0.9	0.8	0.9	0.8	0.7	0.7	0.6	0.6	0.9	1.0	0.8
Conditional discharge	KEKC	34.4	32.4	30.6	29.4	28.7	26.9	24.9	23.9	22.0	22.5	21.8
Fine	KEKF	25.6	24.1	22.5	21.8	21.3	20.8	20.1	18.6	17.9	18.5	16.7
Community rehabilitation order	KEKD	17.5	18.0	19.0	19.1	19.1	19.4	19.6	19.1	19.2	17.0	15.4
Supervision order	KEKE	2.4	2.7	2.9	2.9	3.1	2.9	2.8	2.7	2.1	2.1	2.1
Community punishment order	KEKG	6.4	6.6	6.5	6.5	6.5	7.1	7.5	7.3	6.8	6.6	7.6
Attendance centre order	KEKH	0.8	1.0	1.0	1.0	0.9	0.9	0.8	0.6	0.4	0.3	0.3
Community punishment and rehabilitation order	KIJX	2.1	2.4	3.0	3.2	3.4	3.3	3.0	2.1	2.1	1.8	1.9
Curfew order	LUJT	..	..	–	0.1	0.1	0.3	0.4	0.6	0.8	1.4	2.2
Reparation order	SNFX	..	..	..	..	..	..	0.8	1.6	0.8	0.4	0.5
Action plan order	SNFZ	..	..	..	..	..	..	1.0	2.0	1.2	0.8	0.8
Drug treatment and testing order	SNGA	..	..	..	..	..	..	0.1	1.4	1.7	2.4	3.2
Referral order	SNGB	..	..	..	..	..	..	..	..	3.9	5.1	5.6
Community order[2]	GN7Q	..	..	..	..	..	..	..	..	..	..	..
Suspended sentence order	KEKL	1.1	1.4	1.5	1.6	1.5	1.3	1.3	1.2	1.1	1.0	1.3
Imprisonment												
Sec 90-92	LUJU	–	0.1	0.1	0.1	..	0.1	0.1	0.1	0.1	0.1	0.1
Detention and training order	LUJV	..	..	..	..	..	..	0.6	0.8	0.8	0.7	0.7
Young offender institution	KEKK	1.1	1.5	1.8	1.9	2.2	2.4	2.2	2.0	1.9	1.7	1.4
Unsuspended imprisonment	KEKM	5.9	7.4	8.4	9.4	10.0	11.0	11.5	12.1	12.7	12.8	13.2
Other sentence or order	KEKN	1.7	1.8	2.0	2.2	2.5	3.0	2.9	3.5	3.4	3.8	4.3
Total number of females (thousands) = 100 per cent	KEKA	39.5	37.5	38.0	42.1	47.2	49.0	47.8	47.3	49.9	50.2	48.3

1 See chapter text. Every effort is made to ensure that the figures presented are accurate and complete. However, it is important to note that these data have been extracted from large administrative data systems generated by the courts and police forces. As a consequence, care should be taken to ensure data collection processes and their inevitable limitations are taken into account when those data are used.
2 The community order was introduced on 4 April 2005 and applies to offences committed on or after that date.

Source: Office for Criminal Justice Reform: 020 8760 1404

11.8 Adult[1] offenders sentenced to immediate custody for recordable offences[2]: by sex and number of previous convictions or cautions[3]

England and Wales

Percentages[4] and numbers[5]

	Previous convictions or cautions					Number sentenced to custody in Quarter 1, all offences
	Nil	1 - 2	3 - 6	7 - 10	11 and over	
Year and sex						
2000						
Males	7	10	20	19	44	23 236
Females	14	12	22	18	35	1 954
Total	8	10	20	19	43	25 190
2001						
Males	8	9	19	18	46	22 178
Females	18	11	21	18	33	1 874
Total	9	10	19	18	45	24 052
2002						
Males	7	8	17	18	49	24 221
Females	17	10	18	18	37	2 140
Total	8	8	17	18	48	26 361
2003						
Males	7	8	16	17	53	24 114
Females	11	9	19	18	43	2 279
Total	8	8	16	17	52	26 393
2004						
Males	7	8	15	16	54	26, 305
Females	13	9	16	18	44	2 617
Total	8	8	15	16	53	28 922
2005						
Males	7	8	15	15	54	23 387
Females	15	8	15	15	46	2 193
Total	8	8	15	15	53	25 580

1 Aged 18 or over.
2 See 'technical note' in chapter text.
3 Criminal histories presented here are taken from the Home Office copy of the Police National Compter(HOPNC). The HOPNC covers all recordable offences and includes information on cautions as well as convictions. Previous convictions or cautions are a count of the number of distinct occasions where an offender received at least one conviction or caution for a recordable offence. Offences for which a caution was given are therefore included in this analysis.
4 Percentages are rounded and therefore may not add to 100.
5 The figures in this table are based on samples comprising all offenders sentenced to custody for a recordable offence in the first quarter of each year.

Source: Home Office: 0207 035 8385

11.9 Population in Prison Service establishments under sentence[1]: by sex and number of previous convictions or cautions[2,3]

England and Wales, on 30 June each year:

Percentages[4] and numbers

	Previous convictions not found[5]	Nil	1 - 2	3 - 6	7 - 10	11 and over	Number of prisoners
Year and sex							
2002							
Males	9	12	10	15	15	40	52 204
Females	13	27	13	15	12	20	3 250
Total	9	12	11	17	15	36	55 455
2003							
Males	9	11	10	16	15	39	54 451
Females	11	24	12	16	13	25	3 426
Total	9	12	10	16	15	38	57 877
2004							
Males	8	11	10	16	14	40	56 109
Females	11	22	13	15	12	27	3 450
Total	9	11	10	16	14	39	59 560

1 See 'technical note' in chapter text.
2 Some prisoners are not included, such as offenders on remand and juveniles.
3 Criminal histories presented here are taken from the Home Office copy of the Police National Computer(HOPNC). The HOPNC covers all recordable offences and includes information on cautions as well as convictions. Previous convictions or cautions are a count of the number of distinct occasions where an offender received at least one conviction or caution for a recordable offence. Offences for which a caution was given are therefore included in this analysis.
4 Percentages are rounded and therefore may not add to 100.
5 This comprises offenders in prison establishments who were not found on the HOPNC.

Source: Home Office: 0207 035 8385

11.10 Receptions and average population in custody
England and Wales

Numbers[1]

		1995	1996	1997	1998	1999	2000	2001	2002	2003	2004	2005
Receptions												
Type of inmate:												
Untried	KEDA	55 287	58 888	62 066	64 697	64 572	54 892	53 467	58 708	58 696	54 556	55 455
Convicted, unsentenced	KEDB	32 039	34 987	36 424	43 387	45 893	43 889	46 851	53 301	53 246	50 115	49 104
Sentenced	KEDE	89 173	82 861	87 168	91 282	93 965	93 671	91 978	94 807	93 495	95 161	92 452
Immediate custodial sentence	KEDF	69 016	74 306	80 832	85 908	90 238	91 195	90 523	93 615	92 245	93 326	90 414
Young offenders	KEDG	16 244	17 593	18 743	19 599	21 020	21 333	20 969	20 236	18 179	18 264	17 819
Up to 12 months	KEDH	11 308	11 285	11 867	12 942	14 330	14 639	14 234	12 891	11 850	11 855	11 610
12 months up to 4 years	KEDJ	4 393	5 497	5 949	5 921	5 904	5 877	5 856	6 355	5 412	5 426	5 243
4 years up to and including life	KEDL	543	811	927	736	786	817	879	990	917	983	966
Adults	KFBO	52 772	56 713	62 089	66 309	69 218	69 862	69 554	73 379	74 066	75 062	72 595
Up to 12 months	KEDV	33 053	34 864	38 702	42 513	45 662	46 759	46 146	47 870	48 962	49 814	48 190
12 months up to 4 years	KEDW	15 328	16 560	17 546	18 100	17 751	17 290	17 116	18 313	17 968	17 988	17 397
4 years up to and including life	KEDX	4 391	5 289	5 841	5 696	5 805	5 813	6 292	7 196	7 136	7 260	7 008
Committed in default of payment												
of a fine	KEDY	20 157	8 555	6 336	5 374	3 727	2 476	1 455	1 192	1 250	1 835	1 876
Young offenders	KEEA	2 846	885	555	568	366	216	138	110	116	155	162
Adults	KAFQ	17 311	7 670	5 781	4 806	3 361	2 260	1 317	1 082	1 134	1 680	1 714
Non-criminal prisoners	KEDM	3 789	3 128	3 204	3 290	3 271	3 153	4 630	2 674	3 142	3 669	3 668
Immigration Act 1971	KEDN	1 825	1 857	2 122	2 348	2 443	2 455	4 035	2 093	2 457	3 041	3 093
Others	KEDO	1 964	1 271	1 082	942	828	698	595	581	685	628	575
Average population												
Total in custody	KEDP	51 047	55 281	61 114	65 298	64 771	64 602	66 301	70 861	73 038	74 657	75 979
Total in prison service establishments	KFBQ	50 962	55 281	61 114	65 298	64 771	64 602	66 301	70 778	73 038	74 657	75 979
Police cells[2]	KFBN	85	–	–	–	–	–	–	83	–	–	–
Untried	KEDQ	8 352	8 374	8 453	8 157	7 947	7 098	6 924	7 727	7 862	7 735	8 088
Convicted, unsentenced	KEDR	2 954	3 238	3 678	4 411	4 571	4 177	4 314	5 064	5 060	4 750	4 806
Remanded for medical examination	KEDS	9	6	8	9	8	..	40	..	..	–	–
Others	KEDT	2 945	3 232	3 670	4 402	4 563	..	4 274	..	..	–	–
Sentenced	KEDU	39 040	43 043	48 413	52 176	51 691	52 685	54 051	57 222	59 007	61 071	61 991
Immediate custodial sentence	KFBR	38 636	42 863	48 272	52 045	51 596	52 620	54 006	57 184	58 959	61 012	61 925
Young offenders	KFBS	5 752	6 700	7 821	8 490	8 335	8 435	8 559	8 777	8 422	8 290	8 236
Up to 12 months	KFBU	1 721	1 788	1 820	1 964	1 997	2 414	2 330	2 051	1 899	1 942	1 943
12 months up to 4 years	KFBV	2 987	3 748	4 466	4 795	4 674	4 517	4 562	4 867	4 525	4 294	4 281
4 years up to and including life	KFBW	1 042	1 164	1 534	1 730	1 665	1 504	1 667	1 860	1 997	2 053	2 012
Adults	KFCO	32 902	36 162	40 451	43 555	43 261	44 186	45 447	48 408	50 536	52 721	53 684
Up to 12 months	KFCP	4 930	5 136	5 428	5 898	5 635	6 053	5 904	5 755	6 000	6 238	6 142
12 months up to 4 years	KFCQ	11 976	13 383	15 073	16 079	15 048	15 161	15 525	16 845	16 664	17 054	17 216
4 years up to and including life	KFCR	15 998	17 644	19 950	21 580	22 578	22 971	24 021	25 808	27 871	29 428	30 326
Committed in default of payment												
of a fine	KFCS	403	180	141	131	95	64	45	37	48	59	71
Young offenders	KFEW	54	22	13	15	9	4	6	2	3	4	3
Adults	KFEX	349	158	128	116	86	60	39	35	45	55	68
Non-criminal prisoners	KEEB	615	626	571	554	558	641	1 012	847	1 107	1 100	1 087
Immigration Act 1971	KEEC	483	516	485	476	485	576	955	777	995	1 032	1 022
Others	KEED	132	111	87	78	73	63	57	70	112	68	65

1 The components do not always add up to the totals as they have been rounded independently.
2 Mostly untried prisoners.

Source: Home Office: 020 7217 5567

173

11.11 Prison population serving sentences: by age and offence[1,2]
England and Wales

Numbers

	15 - 17	18 - 20	21 - 24	25 - 29	30 - 39	40 - 49	50 - 59	60 and over	Total
					Age in years				
At 30 June 2000									
Offences									
Males									
Total	1 788	5 911	8 691	10 060	14 454	5 720	2 749	1 140	50 514
Violence against the person	256	1 092	1 658	1 964	3 440	1 480	690	226	10 807
Sexual offences	58	139	261	460	1 424	1 157	937	635	5 070
Burglary	453	1 426	2 165	2 291	2 040	359	77	13	8 824
Robbery	399	1 087	1 343	1 315	1 556	387	57	14	6 158
Theft, handling, fraud and forgery	312	798	1 006	1 118	1 419	483	233	53	5 422
Drugs offences	43	405	949	1 591	2 765	1 188	480	106	7 526
Other offences	225	818	1 180	1 161	1 616	598	236	76	5 909
Offences not known	43	148	131	160	194	67	38	16	797
Females									
Total	65	266	457	563	863	335	102	15	2 666
Violence against the person	22	46	56	71	122	62	26	6	410
Sexual offences	-	1	1	1	7	5	2	2	20
Burglary	10	24	33	45	40	5	1	-	158
Robbery	13	43	39	39	50	10	1	-	195
Theft, handling, fraud and forgery	7	61	117	154	196	74	24	4	638
Drugs offences	6	58	151	200	354	141	34	2	947
Other offences	5	26	47	40	70	31	9	1	229
Offences not known	2	7	13	12	23	7	5		69
At 30 June 2001									
Offences									
Males									
Total	1 918	5 864	9 051	9 964	14 538	6 044	2 723	1 211	51 313
Violence against the person	343	1 180	1 810	1 997	3 432	1 631	702	252	11 347
Sexual offences	53	145	265	406	1 368	1 172	953	686	5 048
Burglary	383	1 176	2 039	2 190	2 158	389	61	15	8 410
Robbery	429	1191	1 436	1 309	1 652	360	60	12	6 449
Theft, handling, fraud and forgery	318	742	1 086	1 080	1 362	510	217	55	5 370
Drugs offences	47	423	1 126	1 686	2 828	1 278	479	113	7 980
Other offences	285	840	1 146	1 163	1 541	616	213	66	5 868
Offences not known	61	165	143	133	196	90	40	13	841
Females									
Total	63	305	493	589	906	406	119	18	2 899
Violence against the person	18	63	55	72	123	81	24	6	441
Sexual offences	-	2	1	1	7	10	2	2	25
Burglary	9	29	44	29	36	5	2	-	153
Robbery	10	53	63	54	55	13	1	-	248
Theft, handling, fraud and forgery	12	53	100	155	178	64	29	4	594
Drugs offences	3	72	183	215	411	193	49	4	1130
Other offences	8	27	40	50	82	32	9	2	249
Offences not known	3	7	8	14	14	9	4	-	59
At 30 June 2002									
Offences									
Males									
Total	1 986	5 821	9 722	10 196	15 415	6 630	2 832	1 365	53 967
Violence against the person	336	1 187	1 942	1 937	3 490	1 769	749	267	11 678
Sexual offences	58	167	262	406	1 347	1 241	996	794	5 270
Burglary	396	1 130	2 159	2 331	2 379	448	58	15	8 917
Robbery	503	1 285	1 647	1 390	1 865	443	66	10	7 208
Theft, handling, fraud and forgery	302	570	1 055	1 105	1 416	480	213	62	5 203
Drugs offences	43	431	1 255	1 763	3 142	1 496	495	129	8 754
Other offences	275	875	1 195	1 103	1 555	640	205	73	5 921
Offences not known	72	174	207	162	222	113	50	15	1 016
Females									
Total	103	356	596	662	1 030	439	134	19	3 339
Violence against the person	27	67	73	85	163	84	33	6	538
Sexual offences	0	1	0	1	11	6	3	1	23
Burglary	9	37	58	54	68	12	1	0	239
Robbery	19	63	89	65	60	14	3	1	314
Theft, handling, fraud and forgery	22	56	103	139	168	68	20	4	581
Drugs offences	8	94	206	256	474	216	60	6	1 319
Other offences	12	32	52	50	73	34	9	1	262
Offences not known	6	7	16	13	13	5	4	0	63

11.11
continued

Prison population serving sentences: by age and offence[1],[2]
England and Wales

Numbers

				Age in years					
	15 - 17	18 - 20	21 - 24	25 - 29	30 - 39	40 - 49	50 - 59	60 and over	Total
At 30 June 2003									
Offences									
Males									
Total	1 724	5 740	10 112	10 441	16 304	7 252	2 975	1 413	55 962
Violence against the person	310	1 257	2 112	2 068	3 733	1 932	780	290	12 482
Sexual offences	42	183	310	390	1 376	1 353	1 023	838	5 514
Burglary	289	919	2 003	2 204	2 555	527	71	11	8 579
Robbery	436	1 370	1 910	1 546	2 022	514	69	12	7 879
Theft, handling, fraud and forgery	291	543	1 020	1 060	1 437	472	201	45	5 069
Drugs offences	43	452	1 256	1 791	3 215	1 579	528	127	8 993
Other offences	271	884	1 329	1 218	1 760	787	263	69	6 581
Offences not known	42	133	172	164	205	89	40	21	865
Females									
Total	57	305	670	702	1 100	492	123	28	3 477
Violence against the person	10	61	91	66	155	82	32	7	506
Sexual offences	0	0	2	1	11	7	3	2	26
Burglary	1	24	64	60	77	12	2	0	240
Robbery	21	60	105	100	93	24	4	0	407
Theft, handling, fraud and forgery	10	56	117	128	199	70	18	11	609
Drugs offences	6	73	226	271	453	253	54	8	1 343
Other offences	7	27	58	66	108	39	6	0	311
Offences not known	2	3	8	10	5	4	4	0	36
At 30 June 2004									
Offences									
Males									
Total	1 706	5 585	10 095	10 738	17 021	7 858	3 013	1 508	57 523
Violence against the person	326	1 353	2 247	2 272	3 965	2 107	799	304	13 373
Sexual offences	55	193	329	424	1 433	1 416	1 030	865	5 747
Burglary	242	855	1 807	2 141	2 662	608	71	11	8 397
Robbery	449	1 254	1 865	1 691	2 127	583	70	17	8 056
Theft, handling, fraud and forgery	272	502	903	1 045	1 479	573	180	63	5 017
Drugs offences	51	471	1 383	1 789	3 258	1 615	537	150	9 256
Other offences	286	848	1 390	1 249	1 895	868	284	87	6 908
Offences not known	25	108	171	126	202	87	41	10	769
Females									
Total	58	300	632	727	1 056	507	152	20	3 453
Violence against the person	15	70	98	89	192	95	36	9	603
Sexual offences	-	-	3	3	8	7	4	2	27
Burglary	6	19	59	83	56	22	3	-	247
Robbery	8	65	93	90	114	20	2	-	392
Theft, handling, fraud and forgery	11	28	100	140	171	67	25	1	543
Drugs offences	6	78	197	245	392	246	65	6	1 235
Other offences	11	37	75	72	108	44	13	2	361
Offences not known	2	3	8	7	15	7	4	-	46
At 30 June 2005									
Offences									
Males									
Total	1 782	5 597	9 950	10 982	16 866	8 745	3 263	1 598	58 784
Violence against the person	366	1 493	2 553	2 553	4 017	2 403	840	319	14 544
Sexual offences	65	186	397	505	1 436	1 553	1 084	922	6 148
Burglary	285	719	1 559	1 947	2 570	669	78	17	7 844
Robbery	422	1 307	1 819	1 705	2 035	649	83	15	8 035
Theft, handling, fraud and forgery	240	434	860	1 075	1 450	652	238	56	5 005
Drugs offences	76	491	1 332	1 835	3 265	1 744	545	149	9 437
Other offences	310	871	1 312	1 250	1 911	989	365	101	7 110
Offences not known	18	96	118	112	181	86	30	19	661
Females									
Total	55	269	614	680	1 073	585	179	24	3 480
Violence against the person	23	68	109	85	190	114	40	9	638
Sexual offences	-	2	3	4	12	8	7	3	39
Burglary	4	18	50	62	79	23	3	-	239
Robbery	16	59	61	82	102	20	3	-	343
Theft, handling, fraud and forgery	4	35	105	119	202	88	27	3	583
Drugs offences	3	54	195	255	366	268	84	9	1 234
Other offences	5	30	84	68	117	56	14	-	374
Offences not known	-	3	7	5	5	8	1	-	30[3]

1 The data presented in this table are drawn from administrative IT systems. Where figures in the table have been rounded to the nearest whole number, the rounded components do not always add to the totals, which are calculated and rounded independently. Reconciliation exercises with published Home Office figures may demonstrate differences due to rounded components. A programme of work is currently being undertaken to audit the quality of the data and to identify priorities for improvements.
2 Includes persons committed in default of payment of a fine.
3 Includes one adult female fine defaulter whose age is not known.

Source: Home Office: 020 7035 3437

175

11.12 Expenditure on prisons
England and Wales
Operating cost and total capital employed, years ending 31 March

£ thousand

		1999 /00	2000 /01	2001 /02	2002 /03	2003 /04	2004 /05	2005 /06
Expenditure								
Staff costs	KWUV	1 044 700	1 094 500	1 138 400	1 259 500	1 364 200	1 439 900	1 498 400
Accommodation costs	KXCO	149 300	153 700	193 100	200 000	194 000	185 400	150 300
Other operating costs	KXCP	584 300	654 200	706 100	756 200	653 000	694 600	528 500
Depreciation	KXCQ	115 700	117 200	128 100	132 600	129 600	143 800	8 000
Cost of capital	KXCR	254 900	259 900	284 900	292 700	164 400	170 300	300
Total expenditure	KXCS	2 148 900	2 279 500	2 450 600	2 641 000	2 505 200	2 634 000	2 185 500
Income								
Contributions from industries	KXCT	−10 400	−10 600	−11 600	−10 100	−11 000	−10 600	−11 200
Other operating income	KXCU	−9 600	−10 300	−13 100	−15 500	−21 000	−38 400	−41 300
Income from Other Government Departments[1]	GDPM	−	−123 900	−180 600	−210 200	−368 000	−381 500	−302 500
Total income	KXCV	−20 000	−144 800	−205 300	−235 800	−400 000	−430 500	−355 000
Net operating costs	KXCW	2 128 900	2 134 700	2 245 300	2 405 200	2 105 200	2 203 500	1 830 500
Total capital employed	KXCX	4 382 600	4 726 200	4 859 600	4 821 500	5 228 600	5 116 700	5 700

1 Income from the Youth Justice Board (a non-departmental public body of the
Home Office) for the provision of juvenile custody within the Prison Service,
Department for Education and Skills for the provision of education services
and Department and Health and PCTs for the provision of healthcare.

Source: Home Office: 020 7217 5567

11.13 Crimes and offences recorded by the police: by crime group[1]
Scotland

Thousands

		1996/97	1997/98	1998/99	1999/00	2000/01	2001/02	2002/03	2003/04	2004[4]/05	2005/06
Non-sexual crimes of violence against the person	BEBC	14.2	13.4	14.7	15.8	14.8	15.7	16.1	15.2	14.7	13.7
Serious assault, etc	KAFS	6.6	6.2	6.7	7.3	6.9	7.5	7.6	7.5	7.8	7.2
Robbery	KAFU	5.1	4.6	5.0	4.9	4.3	4.6	4.6	4.2	3.7	3.6
Other	KAFV	2.5	2.6	3.0	3.6	3.6	3.5	3.8	3.5	3.2	3.0
Crimes involving indecency	BEBD	5.9	7.4	7.1	5.9	5.7	6.0	6.6	6.8	7.3	6.6
Rape and attempted rape[2]	OXBQ	0.6	0.8	0.8	0.8	0.7	0.8	0.9	1.0	1.1	1.2
Indecent assault[2]	OXBR	1.1	1.3	1.3	1.1	1.0	1.2	1.4	1.4	1.5	1.5
Lewd and indecent behaviour	KAFY	2.5	3.0	2.9	2.3	2.4	2.4	2.8	2.6	2.8	2.7
Other	KAFZ	1.7	2.4	2.1	1.7	1.6	1.6	1.6	1.7	1.9	1.2
Crimes involving dishonesty	BEBE	285.8	266.9	277.0	275.6	253.3	242.9	224.8	211.0	210.4	187.8
Housebreaking	KAGB	61.6	55.6	55.8	52.9	47.7	45.5	40.6	36.4	35.0	31.3
Theft by opening lockfast places	KAGC	8.4	10.5	12.1	11.6	10.6	8.2	7.8	7.4	7.9	8.3
Theft from a motor vehicle (OLP)	EPI4	48.9	39.8	39.5	38.0	32.0	32.7	30.4	26.8	20.4	16.5
Theft of a motor vehicle	KAGD	32.5	27.9	29.3	28.9	25.6	23.1	20.9	17.6	15.6	14.0
Shoplifting	KAGE	26.2	27.0	30.8	32.1	32.3	31.6	28.3	27.9	28.5	28.2
Other theft	KAGF	81.7	80.0	80.1	81.2	76.6	76.0	73.2	72.5	77.6	72.1
Fraud	KAGG	15.8	16.2	18.4	20.6	20.0	17.4	15.8	15.3	18.3	11.1
Other	KAGH	10.7	9.9	11.1	10.3	8.4	8.4	7.9	7.0	7.1	6.3
Fire-raising, vandalism, etc	BEBF	86.0	81.0	77.6	81.2	85.8	94.9	97.6	103.7	128.6	127.9
Fire-raising	KAGJ	3.2	2.7	2.5	2.3	2.4	2.9	3.8	4.2	4.7	4.9
Vandalism, etc	KAGK	82.8	78.3	75.2	78.9	83.4	92.0	93.8	99.6	123.9	123.0
Other crimes	BEBG	48.7	52.3	57.7	57.0	58.9	66.8	73.2	77.5	77.1	81.8
Crimes against public justice	KAGM	16.3	16.6	17.7	18.4	18.6	20.9	22.7	25.8	25.6	27.7
Handling offensive weapons[3]	KAFT	6.5	6.2	7.1	8.1	8.1	9.0	9.4	9.3	9.5	9.6
Drugs	KAGN	25.8	29.4	32.8	30.4	32.1	36.8	40.9	42.3	41.8	44.2
Other	KAGO	0.1	0.1	0.1	0.1	0.1	0.1	0.2	0.2	0.2	0.3
Total crimes	KAGQ	440.7	421.0	434.1	435.5	418.5	426.2	418.3	414.2	438.1	417.8
Miscellaneous offences	BEBH	149.3	156.6	153.3	151.9	154.9	163.5	169.6	181.0	214.3	219.5
Petty assault	KAGS	48.3	50.2	51.6	54.6	54.1	55.4	55.0	57.4	73.7	72.3
Breach of the peace	KAGT	71.5	73.3	71.7	71.3	70.2	72.7	74.7	77.9	90.0	89.6
Drunkenness	KAGU	9.8	9.6	8.4	7.6	7.8	7.8	7.3	7.5	7.2	7.0
Other	KAGV	19.8	23.4	21.6	18.4	22.8	27.6	32.6	38.2	43.4	50.6
Motor vehicle offences	BEBI	311.1	339.6	367.2	347.5	340.1	362.6	348.0	426.7	418.7	374.3
Dangerous and careless driving	KAGX	17.1	16.2	15.8	13.2	12.0	12.2	12.7	12.0	13.1	13.0
Drunk driving	KAGY	11.8	11.1	10.6	10.9	10.8	11.5	11.8	11.6	11.1	11.3
Speeding	KAGZ	85.6	95.6	119.7	123.4	113.9	126.8	117.2	199.2	210.1	167.7
Unlawful use of a motor vehicle	KAHA	78.3	77.3	76.0	80.7	83.3	88.7	92.9	91.3	71.1	69.0
Vehicle defect offences	KAHB	56.9	62.3	63.8	48.0	46.8	45.5	46.5	37.2	27.0	23.9
Other	KAHC	61.4	77.0	81.3	71.2	73.3	77.9	66.9	75.4	86.3	89.4
Total offences	KAHD	460.4	496.2	520.5	499.4	495.0	526.1	517.5	607.6	633.0	593.8
Total crimes and offences	BEBB	901.1	917.2	954.6	934.9	913.5	952.3	935.8	1 021.8	1 071.1	1 011.6

1 See chapter text.
2 The category of 'sexual assault' was split into 'rape and attempted rape' and 'indecent assault' with effect from 2001.
3 'Handling offensive weapons' used to be included in the group 'non-sexual crimes of violence'.
4 The introduction of the Scottish Crime Recording Standard on 1 April 2004 has increased the number of minor crimes recorded, such as minor crimes of theft, vandalism, petty assault and breach of the peace.

Source: The Scottish Executive Justice Department: 0131 244 2226

11.14 Persons with a charge proved: by crime group[1,2]
Scotland

Numbers

		1994/95	1995/96	1996/97	1997/98	1998/99	1999/00	2000/01	2001/02	2002/03	2003/04	2004[4]/05
Non-sexual crimes of violence	KEHC	1 859	1 812	2 002	2 039	2 000	2 003	1 976	2 082	2 372	2 531	2 337
Homicide	KEHD	97	125	119	104	92	105	100	99	97	116	113
Serious assault, etc	KEHE	820	847	954	1 039	1 036	1 053	1 089	1 167	1 359	1 445	1 338
Robbery	KEHG	754	640	720	666	652	659	603	625	677	669	591
Other violence	KEHH	188	200	209	230	220	186	184	191	239	301	295
Crimes of indecency	KEHI	1 395	1 259	938	1 329	1 280	790	633	612	559	660	787
Rape and attempted rape	HFVU	49	56	57	55	58	48	52	66	53	54	62
Indecent assault	KEHJ	88	73	67	91	83	84	60	48	65	93	88
Lewd and libidinous practices	KEHK	320	300	292	343	320	302	256	297	272	296	315
Other indecency	KEHL	938	830	522	840	819	356	265	201	169	217	322
Crimes of dishonesty	KEHM	29 560	27 626	26 779	25 272	24 726	22 652	20 571	21 536	21 699	19 887	19 605
Housebreaking	KEHN	4 885	4 249	3 736	3 174	3 071	2 860	2 676	2 672	2 752	2 508	2 373
Theft by opening lockfast places	KEHO	2 716	2 394	2 362	1 940	1 770	1 614	1 504	1 478	1 448	1 288	1 193
Theft of motor vehicle	KEHP	2 494	2 402	2 313	2 006	1 882	1 536	1 426	1 386	1 486	1 268	1 097
Shoplifting	KEHQ	6 522	6 648	7 197	7 313	7 559	7 753	7 345	8 366	8 825	8 123	8 396
Other theft	KEHR	6 375	6 177	6 031	5 866	5 796	5 026	4 303	4 234	3 783	3 521	3 531
Fraud	KEHS	2 528	2 215	1 956	1 992	1 920	1 595	1 448	1 479	1 459	1 444	1 352
Other dishonesty	KEHT	4 040	3 541	3 184	2 981	2 728	2 268	1 869	1 921	1 946	1 735	1 663
Fire-raising, vandalism, etc	KEHU	4 731	4 870	5 211	4 871	4 591	3 979	3 941	4 051	4 212	4 756	5 004
Fire-raising	KEHV	165	132	146	112	125	102	108	125	147	167	191
Vandalism, etc	KEHW	4 566	4 738	5 065	4 759	4 466	3 877	3 833	3 926	4 065	4 589	4 813
Other crime	KEHX	13 921	15 172	15 061	14 551	13 698	12 887	12 556	13 819	13 938	15 439	16 703
Crime against public justice	KFBK	6 998	7 362	6 553	5 096	4 776	4 589	4 929	5 257	5 048	5 289	5 756
Handling offensive weapons	KEHF	1 529	1 867	2 309	2 173	2 033	2 118	2 340	2 633	2 771	2 875	3 444
Drugs offences	KFBL	5 373	5 912	6 162	7 236	6 861	6 157	5 277	5 910	6 095	7 246	7 472
Other	KFBM	21	31	37	46	28	23	10	19	24	29	31
Total crimes	KEHB	51 466	50 739	49 991	48 062	46 295	42 311	39 677	42 100	42 780	43 273	44 436
Miscellaneous offences	KEHZ	44 442	46 305	45 599	45 816	39 241	34 189	33 262	34 659	37 004	39 623	42 612
Common assault	KEIA	11 526	11 926	12 387	12 441	11 677	10 749	10 270	10 821	11 743	12 313	13 530
Breach of the peace	KEIB	17 078	18 451	19 292	19 355	17 156	14 023	13 031	13 950	14 383	15 048	16 089
Drunkenness	KEIC	1 384	1 270	1 028	937	626	454	430	374	370	418	308
Breach of social work orders	HFVT	2 605	2 842	3 260	3 765	4 217	4 684	4 611	4 509	4 945	5 093	5 291
Other miscellaneous offences	KEID	11 849	11 816	9 632	9 318	5 565	4 279	4 920	5 005	5 563	6 751	7 394
Motor vehicle offences	KEIE	64 170	57 987	55 975	55 456	51 638	51 603	40 264	44 821	47 956	50 621	47 411
Dangerous and careless driving	KEIF	4 926	4 847	4 825	4 577	3 764	3 431	2 561	3 319	3 628	4 117	3 806
Drunk driving	KEIG	7 526	7 578	8 367	8 173	7 290	7 366	6 265	6 538	9 508	8 158	7 999
Speeding[3]	KEIH	16 696	14 546	12 141	12 220	12 971	15 293	9 427	9 988	9 832	12 700	13 513
Unlawful use of vehicle	KEII	22 067	19 609	19 870	20 052	18 662	16 950	15 987	18 553	19 192	19 563	16 659
Vehicle defect offences	KEIJ	3 344	3 259	3 221	3 198	2 470	2 075	1 302	1 252	1 510	1 859	1 788
Other motor vehicle offences	KEIK	9 611	8 148	7 551	7 236	6 481	6 488	4 722	5 171	4 286	4 224	3 646
Total offences	KEHY	108 612	104 292	101 574	101 272	90 879	85 792	73 526	79 480	84 960	90 244	90 023
Total crimes and offences	KEHA	160 078	155 031	151 565	149 334	137 174	128 103	113 203	121 580	127 740	133 517	134 459

1 See chapter text. Data as at 12 February 2007.
2 All figures are now reported as financial years.
3 Includes motorway and clearway offences.
4 Figures for 2004-05 for some categories dealt with by the High Court - including homicide, rape and major drug cases - may be underestimated slightly due to late recording of disposals on SCRO.

Source: Scottish Executive Justice Department: 0131 244 2229

11.15 Persons with a charge proved: by court procedure[1,2]
Scotland

Numbers

		1994/95	1995/96	1996/97	1997/98	1998/99	1999/00	2000/01	2001/02	2002/03	2003/04	2004/05
Court procedure												
High Court[3]	KEIQ	1 001	1 093	1 086	1 126	1 062	1 182	1 096	1 124	1 173	1 131	795
Sheriff Court	KEIU	84 969	84 327	84 973	82 150	78 362	74 913	70 043	76 244	84 835	85 043	85 972
District Court[4]	KEIV	63 905	60 188	56 803	57 500	50 953	46 228	38 580	38 665	41 732	47 340	47 692
Stipendiary Magistrate Court[4]	KEIW	10 199	9 420	8 703	8 556	6 797	5 779	3 482	5 543	..	..	..
Total called to court[5]	KEIZ	160 078	155 031	151 565	149 334	137 174	128 103	113 203	121 580	127 740	133 517	134 459

1 See chapter text.
2 All figures are now reported as financial years.
3 Including cases remitted to the High Court from the Sheriff Court. Figure for 2004/05 may be an underestimate due to late recording of disposals on SCRO.
4 District Court figures from 2002/03 include the Stipendiary Magistrates Court.
5 Includes court type not known.

Source: Scottish Executive Justice Department: 0131 244 2229

11.16 Persons with charge proved: by main penalty[1,2]
Scotland

Numbers

Main penalty		1994/95	1995/96	1996/97	1997/98	1998/99	1999/00	2000/01	2001/02	2002/03	2003/04	2004/05
Restriction of liberty order[3]	ZBRE	..	..	..	..	125	230	189	193	743	1 048	1 310
Supervised attendance order[4]	ZBRF	..	..	11	93	78	97	64	58	54	38	42
Drug treatment and testing order[5]	OEWA	..	..	..	..	..	5	147	327	428	695	784
Absolute discharge	KEXA	895	927	1 045	1 046	914	991	978	1 055	1 020	1 102	1 195
Admonition or caution	KEXB	16 030	15 972	15 582	14 707	13 841	12 647	11 648	12 175	12 828	13 439	14 205
Probation	KEXC	5 959	6 176	6 604	6 817	7 464	7 258	7 343	8 496	9 437	8 898	9 393
Remit to children's hearing	KEXD	145	189	194	208	176	120	116	159	230	196	220
Community service order	KEXE	5 290	5 399	5 705	5 605	5 254	4 776	4 744	4 726	5 279	4 878	5 423
Fine	KEXF	113 719	108 525	103 969	103 091	91 904	84 778	71 104	76 641	78 957	84 797	83 541
Compensation order	KEXG	1 570	1 494	1 367	1 308	1 261	1 171	1 087	1 164	1 362	1 789	1 712
Insanity, hospital, guardianship order	KYAN	127	143	151	160	130	136	128	103	105	130	90
Prison	KEXI	11 812	11 593	12 070	11 754	11 456	11 518	11 389	12 402	13 533	13 082	13 342
Young offenders' institution	KEXJ	4 484	4 576	4 823	4 521	4 547	4 363	4 253	4 067	3 738	3 396	3 169
Detention of child	KEXM	47	37	44	24	24	13	13	14	25	25	20
Total persons with charge proved[6]	KEXO	160 078	155 031	151 565	149 334	137 174	128 103	113 203	121 580	127 740	133 517	134 459

1 See chapter text.
2 All figures are now reported as financial years.
3 A community sentence introduced by Section 5 of the Crime and Punishment (Scotland) Act 1995 and available on a pilot basis to 3 Scottish sheriff courts since August 1998. This sentence was made available to High Court, Sheriff Courts and Stipendiary Magistrates court from 1 May 2002.
4 The pilot scheme under the Crime and Punishment (S) Act 1995, where fines for 16 & 17 year olds were replaced by supervised attendance orders, was discontinued in December 1999. The majority of supervised attendance orders recorded from the year 2000-01 onwards were disposals relating to the breach of an existing order.
5 Drug treatment and testing orders are new measures made available on a pilot basis to the High Court and to Sheriff Courts for residents in Glasgow (from October 1999), Fife (from July 2000) and Aberdeen/Aberdeenshire (from December 2001).
6 Totals from 2002/03 include a small number of cases where penalty is unknown.

Source: Scottish Executive Justice Department: 0131 244 2229

11.17 Persons with charge proved[1]: by age and sex[2]
Scotland

Numbers

		1994/95	1995/96	1996/97	1997/98	1998/99	1999/00	2000/01	2001/02	2002/03	2003/04	2004/05
Males	KEWA	137 509	131 710	130 331	128 079	118 583	110 741	96 914	104 767	108 427	112 198	112 494
Under 16	KEWB	171	180	149	138	135	75	55	76	125	96	107
16 to 20	KEWC	30 708	30 113	31 704	31 319	29 317	26 949	24 362	25 170	24 769	24 706	24 438
21 to 30	KEWD	56 519	54 184	52 218	50 714	46 149	41 716	38 585	39 813	40 892	41 122	41 231
Over 30	KEWE	47 788	47 648	45 799	46 299	44 061	40 831	37 596	38 340	40 338	44 041	46 713
Age not known	KEWF	1 347	1 205	1 091	1 049	868	871	745	425	43	4	5
Females	KEWG	21 544	22 413	20 452	20 535	17 923	16 784	15 915	16 469	18 958	20 851	21 468
Under 16	KEWH	9	16	12	14	2	5	10	4	5	18	16
16 to 20	KEWI	2 924	3 104	3 358	3 426	3 401	3 278	2 952	2 906	3 013	3 044	3 004
21 to 30	KEWJ	8 997	9 297	8 090	8 183	7 121	6 506	6 155	6 528	7 307	7 938	8 043
Over 30	KEWK	9 055	9 405	8 394	8 497	7 091	6 734	6 555	6 960	8 629	9 849	10 405
Age not known	KEWL	559	591	598	415	308	261	243	71	4	2	–
Males and Females	KEWM	158 183	155 742	152 269	149 765	139 200	126 990	117 717	119 972	124 674	130 180	133 979
Under 16	KEWN	179	197	161	149	140	81	64	81	128	112	123
16 to 20	KEWO	33 647	33 211	35 006	34 743	32 678	30 224	27 414	28 088	27 800	27 724	27 442
21 to 30	KEWP	65 709	63 468	60 679	58 809	53 607	48 212	44 870	46 196	48 078	48 785	49 279
Over 30	KEWQ	56 790	57 087	54 693	54 565	51 593	47 330	44 365	45 065	48 615	53 554	57 130
Age not known	KEWR	1 858	1 779	1 730	1 499	1 182	1 143	1 004	542	53	5	5
Companies	KEWS	1 021	905	772	718	659	562	316	320	343	451	480
Total persons with charge proved[3]	KEWT	159 178	156 707	153 087	150 508	139 877	127 560	118 152	120 325	125 029	130 606	134 459

1 See chapter text.
2 All figures are now reported as financial years.
3 Includes sex unknown.

Source: Scottish Executive Justice Department: 0131 244 2229

11.18 Penal establishments: average daily population and receptions
Scotland[1]

Numbers

		1997 /98	1998 /99	1999 /00	2000 /01	2001 /02	2002 /03	2003 /04	2004 /05	2005 /06
Average daily population										
Male	KEPB	5 874	5 830	5 765	5 676	5 929	6 193	6 307	6 447	6 523
Female	KEPC	186	199	210	207	257	282	314	332	334
Total	KEPA	6 059	6 029	5 975	5 883	6 186	6 475	6 621	6 779	6 857
Analysis by type of custody										
Remand	KEPD	927	971	976	881	1 019	1 247	1 246	1 216	1 242
Persons under sentence: total	KEPE	5 129	5 056	4 997	5 001	5 165	5 226	5 375	5 561	5 614
Adult prisoners	KEPF	4 357	4 347	4 317	4 346	4 537	4 624	4 802	5 001	4 989
Young offenders	KEPI	773	708	679	655	628	601	573	560	625
Persons recalled from supervision/licence[2]	KEPN	51	78	100	145	202	250	310	356	400
Others[2]	KEPO	18	21	28	36	37	6	6	5	1
Persons sentenced by court martial[2]	KEPP	1	–	2	–	–	–	–	1	–
Civil prisoners[2]	KEPQ	2	1	1	1	1	2	–	1	1
Receptions to penal establishments										
Remand	KEPR	14 685	15 713	14 626	14 062	15 725	19 198	18 963	18 892	19 593
Male	KEPS	13 677	14 527	13 450	13 042	14 402	17 455	17 111	17 085	17 796
Female	KEPT	1 008	1 186	1 176	1 020	1 323	1 743	1 852	1 807	1 797
Persons under sentence: total	KEPU	21 910	22 376	20 336	19 136	18 953	20 084	19 357	18 584	19 477
Male	KEPV	20 698	20 952	19 125	17 953	17 755	18 779	18 013	17 272	18 161
Female	KEPW	1 212	1 424	1 211	1 183	1 198	1 305	1 344	1 312	1 316
Imprisoned: Adults:										
directly	KEPX	9 697	9 887	9 217	8 943	9 470	10 571	10 255	10 299	10 746
in default of fine[3]	KEPY	7 650	7 907	7 030	6 450	5 882	6 081	6 063	5 404	5 442
Sentenced to young offenders' institution:										
directly	KEQA	2 811	2 824	2 582	2 436	2 312	2 207	1 949	1 908	2 170
in default of fine[3]	KEQB	1 695	1 606	1 328	1 116	1 109	1 016	825	694	771
Persons recalled from supervision/licence[4]	JYYD	57	152	179	191	180	209	265	279	348
Persons sentenced by court martial	KEQH	6	2	3	2	2	3	1	5	–
Civil prisoners[3]	KEQI	22	10	17	10	8	11	10	7	4

1 All figures are now reported as financial years, as Scotland is now publishing all figures on a financial year basis.
2 Persons recalled from supervision/licence and others are included in persons under sentence. Persons sentenced by court martial and civil prisoners are not included in persons under sentence.

3 Includes in default of compensation orders.
4 Now covers all recalls from supervised release orders.

Source: The Scottish Executive Justice Department: 0131 244 2225

11.19 Expenditure on penal establishments[1]
Scotland

Years ended 31 March

£ thousand

		1995 /96	1996 /97	1997 /98	1998 /99	1999 /00	2000 /01	2001 /02	2002 /03	2003 /04	2004 /05	2005 /06
Departmental Expenditure												
Manpower and Associated Services	KPHC	135 941	143 107	137 890	144 660	170 347	160 242	172 490	168 593	169 784	181 931	200 742
Prisoner and Associated Costs	KPHD	12 373	13 377	16 313	18 891	22 930	23 501	24 652	23 363	51 070	42 767	28 582
Capital Expenditure	KPHE	15 377	22 577	22 136	23 697	28 918	24 283	24 955	36 519	34 617	72 812	70 406
Gross Expenditure	KPHF	163 691	179 061	176 339	187 248	222 195	208 026	222 097	228 475	255 471	297 510	299 730
Less Receipts	KPHG	2 800	2 600	2 810	8 160	6 668	8 380	8 194	3 485	3 298	3 312	2 872
Net Departmental Expenditure	KPHH	160 891	176 461	173 529	179 088	215 527	199 646	213 903	224 990	252 173	294 198	296 858
Plus Annually Managed Expenditure Capital Charges	DSJI	..	..	..	..	..	..	31 341	40 432	41 728	48 497	52 840
Total Net Expenditure	DSNX	160 891	176 461	173 529	179 088	215 527	199 646	245 244	265 422	293 901	342 695	349 698

1 See chapter text.

Source: The Scottish Executive Justice Department: 0131 244 2225

11.20 Recorded crime statistics: by offence group[1]
Northern Ireland

Thousands

		Old counting rules					New counting rules							
		1995	1996	1997	1998/99		1998/99	1999/00	2000/01	2001/02	2002/03	2003/04	2004/05	2005/06
Violence against the person	RVCP	5.2	5.6	5.2	6.6	RVCQ	18.5	21.4	21.4	26.1	28.5	29.0	29.3	31.0
Sexual offences	RVCR	1.7	1.7	1.4	1.5	RVCS	1.6	1.3	1.2	1.4	1.5	1.8	1.7	1.7
Burglary	RVCT	16.5	16.1	14.3	15.5	RVCU	15.5	16.1	15.8	17.1	18.7	16.4	13.4	12.8
Robbery	RVCV	1.5	1.7	1.7	1.4	RVCW	1.4	1.4	1.8	2.2	2.5	2.0	1.5	1.7
Theft	RVCX	33.5	32.8	29.5	34.6	RVCY	35.4	37.0	36.9	41.7	41.9	35.7	31.1	29.5
Fraud and forgery	RVCZ	4.9	4.1	3.8	5.3	RVDA	6.8	7.9	8.0	8.6	8.8	6.3	5.2	5.1
Criminal damage	RVDB	3.8	4.8	4.7	9.8	RVDC	27.7	31.2	32.3	40.0	36.6	32.4	31.4	34.8
Offences against the state	RVDD	0.3	0.4	0.5	0.5	RVDE	0.6	0.7	0.8	1.2	1.8	1.3	1.2	1.3
Other notifiable offences	RVDF	1.5	1.2	1.1	1.5	RVDG	1.7	2.1	1.7	1.4	2.4	3.2	3.3	5.3
of which drug offences	RVDH	1.4	1.1	1.0	1.4	RVDI	1.4	1.7	1.5	1.1	1.9	2.6	2.6	2.9
Total	RVDR	68.8	68.5	62.2	76.6	RVDS	109.1	119.1	119.9	139.8	142.5	128.0	118.1	123.2

1 See chapter text.

Source: The Police Service of Northern Ireland

11.21 Persons found guilty at all courts: by offence group[1]
Northern Ireland

Numbers

		1994	1995	1996	1997	1998	1999	2000	2001	2002	2003	2004
Violence against the person	KYCT	1 498	1 685	1 597	1 594	1 596	1 699	1 858	1 621	1 790	1 965	2 012
Sexual offences	KEVG	148	182	184	130	128	90	130	112	84	108	137
Burglary	KYBW	979	951	801	715	647	703	703	496	595	602	620
Robbery	KYBX	168	195	161	166	134	129	122	121	152	192	159
Theft	KYBY	3 044	3 128	2 765	2 596	2 342	1 995	2 111	1 831	1 695	1 803	1 819
Fraud and forgery	KYBZ	568	533	467	491	426	476	403	398	362	314	359
Criminal damage	KYCA	1 134	1 008	1 076	1 163	1 043	931	1 060	917	957	1 034	1 094
Offences against the state	KYCB	137	166	147	165	198	178	174	158	215	274	252
Other indictable[2]	KYCC	669	863	899	739	936	943	700	495	453	527	636
Total indictable[3]	KYCD	8 345	8 711	8 097	7 759	7 450	7 144	7 261	6 149	6 303	6 819	7 088
Summary[4]	KYCE	4 369	4 137	4 402	4 435	4 062	3 598	3 967	3 735	3 453	3 514	3 622
Motoring[5]	KYCF	21 502	20 124	18 177	18 770	15 369	15 782	15 390	14 466	14 344	16 342	17 215
All offences	KYCG	34 216	32 972	30 676	30 964	26 881	26 524	26 618	24 350	24 100	26 675	27 925

1 See chapter text.
2 1998 and 1999 figures include 'dangerous driving' (a triable-either-way offence).
3 From 2000, includes 'indictable-only' motoring offences.
4 Excludes motoring offences.
5 Prior to 2000, includes all motoring offences (except for note 2 above). From 2000, includes summary and triable-either-way motoring offences.

Source: Northern Ireland Office: 028 9052 7157

11.22 Juveniles found guilty at all courts:[1] by offence group
Northern Ireland

Numbers

		1994	1995	1996	1997	1998	1999	2000	2001	2002	2003	2004
Violence against the person	KYCH	49	51	75	49	97	73	77	66	82	75	78
Sexual offences	KAHF	8	7	4	8	12	12	4	1	6	5	7
Burglary	KYCI	180	170	137	124	108	117	125	73	77	89	66
Robbery	KYCJ	9	22	13	18	4	7	15	8	14	10	6
Theft	KYCK	283	345	338	334	304	227	254	244	212	173	183
Fraud and forgery	KYCL	14	21	14	11	4	10	2	9	3	7	2
Criminal damage	KYCM	117	116	121	136	139	102	143	152	132	162	129
Offences against the state	KYCN	8	9	6	10	11	12	8	10	20	26	18
Other indictable[2]	KYCO	6	14	24	10	20	17	10	12	7	19	22
Total indictable[3]	KYCP	674	755	732	700	699	577	638	575	553	566	511
Summary[4]	KYCQ	131	180	182	198	187	163	180	203	194	174	135
Motoring[5]	KYCR	74	74	58	57	98	97	82	102	89	94	76
All offences	KYCS	879	1 009	972	955	984	837	900	880	836	834	722

1 See chapter text. Juveniles are aged 10 - 16 years inclusive.
2 1998 and 1999 figures include 'dangerous driving'.
3 From 2000, includes 'indictable-only' motoring offences.
4 Excludes motoring offences.
5 Prior to 2000 includes all motoring offences (except for note 2 above). From 2000, includes summary and triable-either-way motoring offences.

Source: Northern Ireland Office: 028 9052 7157

11.23 Disposals given to those convicted by court
Northern Ireland

Numbers

		1994	1995	1996	1997	1998	1999	2000	2001	2002	2003	2004
Magistrates court - all offences												
Prison[1]	KYAO	945	1 046	1 003	989	996	1 278	1 356	1 048	1 107	1 133	1 101
Custody Probation Order[1]	EOG9	..	..	..	..	..	..	..	..	..	7	7
Young offenders centre	KYAP	499	483	443	430	326	243	191	209	288	395	456
Training school[2]	KYAQ	193	169	147	148	136	13	..	..	..	..	..
Juvenile Justice Centre order[2]	OEUX	..	..	..	..	..	22	78	72	58	48	50
Total immediate custody	KYAR	1 637	1 698	1 593	1 567	1 458	1 556	1 625	1 329	1 453	1 583	1 614
Prison suspended	KYAS	1 558	1 674	1 722	1 506	1 025	1 080	1 247	1 215	1 278	1 407	1 469
YOC suspended	KYAT	447	385	444	461	139	104	93	77	100	201	372
Attendance centre	KYAU	89	101	91	66	55	14	20	37	84	91	108
Probation/supervision[3]	KYAV	1 017	1 137	1 134	1 155	1 473	1 246	1 096	1 070	1 005	974	991
Community service order	KYAW	551	547	591	561	622	678	726	587	643	623	647
Combination order	OEUZ	..	..	..	..	38	7	48	24	36	96	78
Fine[4]	KYAX	24 390	22 726	20 614	21 313	17 956	18 076	17 716	16 439	15 968	17 546	18 520
Recognizance	KYAY	961	1 001	1 203	1 267	1 134	1 089	1 357	810	912	1 091	913
Conditional discharge	KYAZ	1 830	1 928	1 679	1 597	1 538	1 439	1 286	1 559	1 497	1 526	1 524
Absolute discharge	KYBA	661	608	509	424	303	223	242	209	163	201	183
Youth conference order[5]	GGL8	..	..	..	..	..	..	..	..	..	..	21
Community responsibility order	GGL9	..	..	..	..	..	..	..	..	..	..	1
Other	KYBC	17	10	15	8	123	221	57	61	104	215	190
Total	KYBD	33 158	31 815	29 595	29 925	25 864	25 733	25 513	23 417	23 243	25 554	26 631
Crown court - all offences												
Prison[1]	KYBE	471	533	469	475	520	386	521	407	410	238	259
Custody Probation Order[1]	EOH2	..	..	..	..	..	..	..	..	..	331	332
Young offenders centre	KYBF	87	76	106	111	63	67	32	42	23	51	47
Training school[2]	KYBG	5	6	–	4	2	–	..	..	..	..	..
Juvenile Justice Centre order[2]	VQEV	..	..	..	..	–	–	–	–	2	–	–
Total immediate custody	KYBH	563	615	575	590	585	453	553	449	435	620	638
Prison suspended	KYBI	277	265	253	220	199	185	313	262	220	240	262
YOC suspended	KYBJ	43	63	71	60	49	41	48	37	35	50	72
Attendance centre	KYBK	1	–	–	–	–	–	–	–	1	–	–
Probation/supervision[3]	KYBL	58	60	49	47	70	43	68	48	49	63	93
Community service order	KYBM	59	60	54	37	33	24	29	45	25	27	33
Combination order	ZAEP	..	..	..	..	13	6	7	5	18	34	33
Fine[4]	KYBN	23	27	39	40	25	20	40	38	32	49	108
Recognizance	KYBO	16	–	7	10	7	–	4	11	12	8	6
Conditional discharge	KYBR	15	64	30	31	23	17	38	36	20	24	45
Absolute discharge	KYBS	2	1	–	1	6	–	3	–	6	1	1
Youth conference order[5]	GGM2	..	..	..	..	..	..	..	..	..	..	–
Community responsibility order	GGM3	..	..	..	..	..	..	..	..	..	..	–
Other	KYBU	1	2	3	3	7	2	2	2	4	5	3
Total	KYBV	1 058	1 157	1 081	1 039	1 017	791	1 105	933	857	1 121	1 294

1 Custody Probation Orders cannot be separately identified from 'prison' sentences from 1998 to 2002. Thus during this timeframe, figures for prison include custody probation orders.

2 The Juvenile Justice Centre order replaced the training school order from 31st January 1999.

3 Supervision orders were abolished with the introduction of the Criminal Justice (Children) Northern Ireland Order 1998.

4 From 2000, fine incorporates 'fine plus disqualification' and 'fine plus penalty points'.

5 Refers to the number of youth conference orders completed.

Source: Northern Ireland Office: 028 9052 7157

11.24 Prisons and Young Offenders Centres
Northern Ireland
Receptions and average population

Numbers

		1995	1996	1997	1998	1999	2000	2001	2002	2003	2004	2005
Receptions:												
Reception of untried prisoners	KEOA	2 003	2 292	2 188	2 284	2 497	2 197	1 922	2 337	2 439	2 440	2 776
Reception of sentenced prisoners:												
Imprisonment under sentence of immediate custody[1]	KEOB	1 070	1 070	1 062	949	963	1 001	791	916	1 032	975	966
Imprisonment in default of payment of a fine	KEOC	1 248	1 374	1 513	1 530	1 423	1 261	1 090	990	1 140	1 296	1 437
Total	KEOD	2 318	2 444	2 575	2 479	2 386	2 262	1 881	1 906	2 172	2 271	2 403
Reception into Young Offender Centres:												
Detention under sentence of immediate custody	KEOE	371	362	331	347	346	282	252	315	268	287	222
Detention in default of payment of a fine	KEOF	351	373	366	385	417	389	303	250	313	351	377
Total	KEOG	722	735	697	732	763	671	555	565	581	638	599
Other receptions[2]	KEOL	45	27	42	70	38	56	58	57	117	106	134
Daily average population:												
Unconvicted[3]	KEON	322	337	376	383	377	317	272	347	393	456	450
Convicted[4]	KEOP	1 440	1 302	1 256	1 124	867	751	638	679	767	818	851
Total	KEOM	1 762	1 639	1 632	1 507	1 244	1 068	910	1 026	1 160	1 274	1 301

1 Includes those detained under Section 73 of the Children and Young Persons (NI) Act 1968.
2 Non-criminal prisoners including those imprisoned for non-payment of maintenance, non-payment of debt, contempt of court or are being held under the terms of an Immigration Act.
3 Prisoners on remand or awaiting trial and prisoners committed by civil process.
4 Includes those sentenced to immediate custody and fine defaulters.

Source: Northern Ireland Office: 028 9052 7534

Lifestyles

Chapter 12

Lifestyles

Expenditure by the Department for Culture, Media and Sport

(Table 12.1)

The figures in this table are taken from the Department's Annual Report and are outturn figures for each of the headings shown (later figures are the estimated outturn). The Department's planned expenditure for future years is also shown.

Cinema statistics

(Table 12.4)

This table now includes data from CAA/Gallup/Nielsen EDI which replaces the previous ONS Inquiry data which are no longer collected.

Domestic tourism

(Table 12.6)

The figures in this table are compiled using data from the United Kingdom Tourism Survey (UKTS) and represent trips of one or more nights away from home. The UKTS changed survey methodology in 2000 and 2005. Data from 1995 to 1999 were reworked to allow comparisons to be made with 2000-2004 data. 2004 data should be used and interpreted with caution. 2005 data is not comparable with previous years.

International tourism and Holidays abroad

(Tables 12.7 and 12.8)

The figures in these tables are compiled using data from the International Passenger Survey. A holiday abroad is a visit made for holiday purposes. Business trips and visits to friends and relatives are excluded.

Attendances at leisure and cultural activities

(Table 12.9)

The definitions used in this table differ from those normally used to define regular attendees by the Department for Culture, Media and Sport.

Gambling

(Table 12.10)

The National Lottery figures in this table are the latest figures at the time of going to press which have been released by The National Lottery Commission, and represent ticket sales (money staked) for each of the games which comprise the lottery. The figures have been adjusted to real terms using the Retail Prices Index.

The National Lottery commenced on the 19 November 1994, with the first instant ticket being sold in March 1995. Various other games have been started since, the latest shown in the table being the Euromillions game. The sum of the individual games may not agree exactly with the figures for total sales. Total sales also includes the Easy Play games which commenced in 1998, but were dropped in 1999.

The other gambling figures in this table are obtained from the Gaming Board and H.M. Revenue and Customs. The figures have been adjusted to real terms using the Retail Prices Index.

The money staked at bingo clubs refers to licensed clubs only. Prior to 1994-95 the figures for bingo clubs relate to the year ending August.

12.1 Expenditure by the Department for Culture, Media and Sport[1]

£ million

	Museums, galleries and libraries[2]	The arts (England)	Sports (UK)	Architecture and the Historic Environment (England)	The Royal Parks (UK)	Tourism (UK)	Broadcasting and media (UK)	Administration and research	Gambling and the National Lottery	Commemorative services (Queen's Golden Jubilee)	Regional Cultural Consortiums	Unallocated Provision	Total Resource Budget
	GQIF	KWFP	KWFQ	KWFR	LQYY	KWFS	KWFT	GQIG	SNKA	SNKB	GLZ8	GLZ9	GM22
2000/01	407	239	52	137	24	48	2 490	29	801	–	–	–	4 228
2001/02	302	254	67	133	42	68	2 700	33	944	–	–	–	4 544
2002/03	406	286	126	143	26	75	3 019	38	683	6	–	–	4 807
2003/04	764	329	67	348	26	52	2 965	42	719	–	–	–	5 311
2004/05	450	367	109	162	27	50	3 036	42	706	–	2	–	4 952
2005/06[3]	403	417	148	170	20	101	3 170	52	825	–	2	9	5 317
2006/07[4]	545	418	146	158	26	51	3 322	50	765	–	2	13	5 496
2007/08[4]	549	419	171	159	26	54	3 423	48	670	–	2	20	5 541

1 See chapter text.
2 Includes museums and galleries (England), libraries (UK) and museums library archives (UK).
3 Data is an estimate.
4 Data are forecasts.
NOTE: Prior year figures have been amended from last year's reports as a result of: - a reclassification of capital Grants from Resource DEL to Capital DEL in accordance with guidance received from HM Treasury - this affects all years in the table above;

- the ONS announcement in 2005 that the licence fee income of the BBC was not a charge for a service but a tax. The impact of this is that the BBC is now classed as a Central Government body and consumption of its Sector.

Source: Department for Culture, Media and Sport: 020 7211 6121

12.2 Employment in tourism
United Kingdom

Non seasonally adjusted. At June each year

Thousands

	Hotels and other tourist accommodation	Restaurants, bars and canteens	Transport	Travel agents, tour operators	Recreation services	Rest of the economy	All tourism related industries		
								Of which:	
							All	Employee jobs	Self-employment jobs
	EUR7	EUR8	EUR9	EUS2	EUS3	EUS4	EUS5	EUS6	EUS7
2000	230.0	556.1	132.2	135.2	73.2	205.2	1 331.9	1 214.4	117.5
2001	226.8	567.2	134.5	144.5	72.6	207.5	1 353.0	1 231.1	121.9
2002	222.0	586.8	133.4	138.8	78.4	208.2	1 367.4	1 247.1	120.3
2003	226.4	610.4	133.8	137.5	79.6	210.0	1 397.7	1 270.9	126.8
2004	229.6	618.2	131.5	146.8	82.7	211.1	1 419.9	1 293.8	126.1

Sources: Department for Culture, Media and Sport: 020 7211 6121; using data from Labour Force Survey, Office for National Statistics

12.3 Employment in creative industries
Great Britain

Thousands

	Advertising	Architecture	Crafts	Design and designer fashion[1]	Film, video and photography[1]	Music and the visual and performing arts	Publishing	Software computer games and electronic publishing	Television and radio	Art/antiques	All
	EUS8	EUS9	EUT2	EUT3	EUT4	EUT5	EUT6	EUT7	EUT8	EUT9	EUU2
1997	201.0	95.8	95.0	80.7	64.2	226.3	308.5	379.4	97.6	20.2	1 568.7
1998	204.2	101.5	119.8	88.8	64.1	217.8	317.1	426.0	101.5	19.8	1 660.7
1999	200.9	101.5	96.8	93.5	61.9	255.7	317.0	488.6	92.5	20.8	1 729.3
2000	206.0	102.6	111.3	98.5	67.5	224.3	283.9	544.6	109.8	20.9	1 769.4
2001	220.5	103.4	115.1	103.0	75.5	224.6	293.3	567.7	104.1	20.9	1 828.1
2002	215.4	102.9	114.1	115.0	68.9	240.8	286.8	556.7	108.8	21.4	1 830.7
2003	213.8	103.1	108.7	113.2	74.3	245.8	305.2	581.2	110.9	22.5	1 878.8
2004	200.0	102.6	112.9	110.4	65.5	232.3	274.3	593.9	110.6	22.5	1 825.0
2005	223.4	108.2	95.5	115.5	63.8	236.3	253.3	596.8	108.7	22.9	1 824.4

1 Revisions due to minor amendments in the classifications.

Sources: Creative Industries Economic Estimates Statistical Bulletin;
Department for Culture, Media and Sport

12.4 Cinema statistics[1,2]
United Kingdom

	Sites (numbers)	Screens (numbers)	Total number of admissions[3] (millions)	Gross box office takings (£ million)	Revenue per admission[3] (£)	Revenue per screen (£ thousand)
	JMHX	JMHY	JMHZ	JMIA	JMIB	JMIC
1998	761	2 638	135.2	504.9	3.73	191.4
1999	751	2 825	139.1	549.7	3.95	194.6
2000	754	3 017	142.5	572.8	4.02	189.9
2001	766	3 248	155.9	645.0	4.14	198.6
2002	775	3 402	175.9	755.3	4.29	222.0
2003	776	3 433	167.3	742.0	4.44	216.1
2004	773	3 475	171.3	769.6	4.49	221.4
2005	771	3 486	164.7	770.3	4.68	221.0
2006	783	3 569	156.6	762.1	4.87	213.5

1 See chapter text.
2 Includes Isle of Man and the Channel Islands.
3 Admissions are based on all cinemas taking advertising.

Source: CAA/Gallup/Nielsen EDI

12.5 Films
United Kingdom

Numbers and £ million

	Production of UK films		Expenditure on feature films (Current prices)				
	Films produced in the UK (numbers)	Production costs (1998 prices)	UK box office	Video rental	Video retail[1]	Subscriptions to movie channels	Box office, video, subscription channels
	KWGD	KWGE	KWHU	KWHV	KWHW	KWHX	KWHY
1995	78	421.0	385	351	789	721	2 246
1996	128	726.0	411	382	733	1 319	2 930
1997	116	558.0	489	369	784	..	1 733
1998	88	487.0	547	437	896	..	1 892
1999	100	570.0	563	408	878	..	1 896
2000	98	793.0	583	444	1 100	..	2 176
2001	96	..	645	465	1 417	..	..
2002	119	550.0	755	476	1 895	..	..
2003	173	1 158.0	742	450	2 244	..	..
2004	133	812.0	770	461	2 478	..	..
2005	124	569.0	770	404	2 317	..	..

1 In 2005 the British Video Association changed its methodology for producing
market value which has necessitated a change to historical figures quoted.

Source: UK Film Council

12.6 Domestic tourism[1]
United Kingdom

	Number of trips (millions)	Number of nights spent (millions)	Expenditure at current prices (£ million)	Average nights spent (numbers)	Average expenditure per trip (£)
	GQGY	GQGZ	GQHA	GQHB	GQHC
1996	154.2	532.8	22 041	3.5	142.9
1997	162.2	555.3	24 137	3.4	148.8
1998	148.8	516.0	22 814	3.5	153.3
1999	173.1	568.6	25 635	3.3	148.1
2000	175.4	576.4	26 133	3.3	149.0
2001	163.1	529.6	26 094	3.2	160.0
2002	167.3	531.9	26 699	3.2	159.6
2003	151.0	490.5	26 482	3.2	175.4
2004[2]	126.6	408.9	24 357	3.2	192.4
2005[3]	138.7	442.3	22 667	3.2	163.4

1 See chapter text.
2 There were concerns that data for 2004 was not truly representative of the United Kingdom population. Data for 2004 should be used and interpreted with caution.

3 The UKTS underwent a methodological change in 2005 and results should not be compared with previous years. The survey did not run between Jan-April 2005, as a result full-year estimates were made using Jan-April 2003 data.

Source: United Kingdom Tourism Survey, VisitBritain: 020 8563 3317

12.7 International tourism[1]

Thousands and £ million

	Visits to the UK by overseas residents (thousands)	Spending in the UK by overseas residents		Visits overseas by UK residents (thousands)	Spending overseas by UK residents	
		Current prices	Constant 1995 prices		Current prices	Constant 1995 prices
	GMAA	GMAK	CQPR	GMAF	GMAM	CQPS
1996	25 163	12 290	11 954	42 050	16 223	15 897
1997	25 515	12 244	11 542	45 957	16 931	18 652
1998	25 745	12 671	11 573	50 872	19 489	21 847
1999	25 394	12 498	11 133	53 881	22 020	24 676
2000	25 209	12 805	11 102	56 837	24 251	27 281
2001	22 835	11 306	9 528	58 281	25 332	27 710
2002	24 180	11 737	9 641	59 377	26 962	29 311
2003	24 715	11 855	9 451	61 424	28 550	28 677
2004	27 755	13 047	10 146	64 194	30 285	31 459
2005	29 970	14 248	10 714	66 441	32 154	33 630
2006	32 135	14 357	10 718	68 547	32 401	32 997

1 See chapter text.

Sources: International Passenger Survey, Office for National Statistics;
020 7533 5765

12.8 Holidays abroad:[1] by destination

Percentages

		1971	1981	1991	1999	2000	2001	2002	2003	2004	2005	2006
Spain[2]	JTKC	34.30	29.80	21.30	27.20	27.80	27.90	28.50	29.80	28.40	27.20	27.80
France	JTKD	15.90	18.10	25.80	19.70	18.30	18.30	19.00	18.10	17.30	16.60	15.90
Greece	JTKF	4.50	6.60	7.60	6.50	6.80	7.80	7.00	6.60	5.70	5.10	5.00
United States	JTKE	1.00	5.50	6.80	7.50	7.30	6.30	5.40	5.50	6.10	6.00	5.10
Italy	JTKG	9.20	5.00	3.50	4.10	4.20	4.30	4.60	5.00	5.00	5.40	5.40
Ireland	JTKI	–	3.70	3.00	5.50	4.60	4.10	4.10	3.70	3.80	3.80	4.00
Portugal	JTKH	2.60	4.00	4.80	3.70	3.90	3.60	4.00	4.00	3.50	3.60	3.70
Cyprus	JTKL	1.00	2.70	2.40	2.40	3.30	3.50	3.00	2.70	2.60	2.80	2.40
Netherlands	JTKK	3.60	2.60	3.50	2.40	2.20	2.60	2.80	2.60	2.60	2.50	2.70
Turkey	JTKJ	–	2.30	0.70	2.10	1.80	2.00	2.20	2.30	2.30	2.70	2.70
Belgium	JTKM	–	2.20	2.10	1.90	1.80	2.10	2.00	2.20	1.80	1.90	2.00
Germany	JTKN	3.40	1.20	2.70	1.60	1.70	1.40	1.50	1.20	1.60	1.70	1.70
Austria	JTKP	5.50	1.10	2.40	1.00	1.00	1.10	1.40	1.10	1.40	1.30	1.20
Malta	JTKO	–	1.00	1.70	1.00	1.10	1.00	1.00	1.00	1.00	1.10	1.00
Other countries	JTKQ	19.00	14.20	11.80	13.30	14.10	13.80	13.60	14.20	16.80	18.40	19.70

1 See chapter text.
2 Excludes the Canary Islands prior to 1981.

Sources: International Passenger Survey, Office for National Statistics;
020 7533 5765

12.9 Attendance at leisure and cultural activities[1]
Great Britain
At Spring

Percentages

		1995 /96	1996 /97	1997 /98	1998 /99	1999 /00	2000 /01	2001 /02	2002 /03	2003 /04	2004 /05	2005 /06
Attendance by men at:												
Cinema	JSPR	53	55	55	57	58	57	58	62	59	65	59
Plays	JSPS	21	21	20	20	21	20	21	22	23	22	25
Art galleries and exhibitions	JSPT	22	22	20	20	21	21	22	23	24	24	27
Classical music	JSPU	12	12	11	10	11	12	12	12	13	12	15
Ballet	JSPV	4	4	4	4	4	4	4	5	5	5	5
Opera	JSPW	6	6	6	5	6	6	6	6	6	7	7
Contemporary dance	JSPX	3	3	4	3	3	3	3	4	5	4	4
Taking part in sporting events - regularly[2]	EU5X	..	..	..	..	50	48	49	50	52	54	65
Watching sporting events	JSPY	88	87	87	86	85	85	78	76	73	76	72
Pop/rock concerts	C3Q8	..	..	..	..	..	..	..	25	26	26	29
Attendance by women at:												
Cinema	JSQA	50	52	54	57	54	54	57	60	62	65	61
Plays	JSQB	25	26	25	23	25	25	26	27	27	27	33
Art galleries and exhibitions	JSQC	22	23	22	22	22	22	23	25	24	25	30
Classical music	JSQD	13	12	13	12	12	12	13	13	14	14	17
Ballet	JSQE	9	9	8	8	9	8	8	9	10	10	12
Opera	JSQF	7	7	7	7	7	7	7	8	8	8	10
Contemporary dance	JSQG	5	5	5	5	5	5	6	6	7	7	9
Taking part in sporting events - regularly[2]	EU5Y	..	..	..	..	42	40	40	44	42	42	54
Watching sporting events	JSQH	72	69	67	66	65	65	56	58	55	60	58
Pop/rock concerts	C3Q9	..	..	..	..	..	..	..	21	23	24	26
Attendance by all persons at:												
Cinema	JSQJ	51	54	55	57	56	55	57	61	61	65	60
Plays	JSQK	23	24	22	22	23	23	24	24	25	25	29
Art galleries and exhibitions	JSQL	22	22	21	21	22	21	22	24	24	24	29
Classical music	JSQM	12	12	12	11	12	12	12	13	13	13	16
Ballet	JSQN	7	7	6	6	6	6	6	7	8	8	9
Opera	JSQO	6	7	6	6	6	6	6	7	8	7	9
Contemporary dance	JSQP	4	4	5	4	4	4	5	5	6	6	7
Taking part in sporting events - regularly[2]	EU5Z	..	..	..	..	46	44	45	47	47	48	59
Watching sporting events	JSQQ	80	78	78	76	75	75	67	68	63	68	68
Pop/rock concerts	C3QA	..	..	..	..	..	..	..	23	25	25	27

1 Percentage of resident population aged 15 and over attending 'these days'. See chapter text.
2 From 2002 the question asked to the respondent was changed.

Source: Target Group Index, BMRB International: 020 8433 4125

12.10 Gambling[1]
United Kingdom

£ million at 2005/06 prices[2]

		1995 /96	1996 /97	1997 /98	1998 /99	1999 /00	2000 /01	2001 /02	2002 /03	2003 /04	2004 /05	2005 /06
Money staked on gambling												
National Lottery - Total[3]	C229	6 404	5 603	6 325	5 809	5 450	5 315	5 029	4 670	4 614	4 757	5 000
Lotto including on-line	C3PU	4 526	4 564	5 408	5 064	4 641	4 416	4 038	3 479	3 225	3 225	3 021
Instants[4]	C3PV	1 878	1 039	917	744	612	590	606	592	641	729	804
Thunderball	C3PW	..	..	..	..	197	257	254	287	351	343	355
Lottery Extra	C3PX	..	..	..	..	..	51	131	90	78	77	57
HotPicks	C3PY	..	..	..	..	..	..	..	222	244	219	228
Christmas draw	C3PZ	..	..	..	..	..	..	..	..	15	..	..
Euromillions	C3Q2	..	..	..	..	..	..	..	..	15	104	427
Daily Play	C3Q3	..	..	..	..	..	..	..	..	45	59	54
Lotteries (excluding the National Lottery)[5]	C3Q4	96	136	144	179	114	114	114	134	127	141	139
Bingo clubs	C3Q5	1 101	1 148	1 170	1 159	1 179	1 190	1 221	1 256	1 381	1 783	1 826
Football pools	C3Q6	727	548	400	286	221	185	151	124	112	109	90
Off-course betting[6]	C3Q7	7 671	7 972	7 869	7 916	7 996	7 689	9 969	17 985	32 265	44 971	44 437

1 See chapter text.
2 Adjusted to real terms using the Retail Prices Index.
3 Includes Easy Play tickets which are not shown separately.
4 From 2003/04 includes Inter-active games.
5 From 2002/03 includes Hotspot lotteries.
6 From 2001/02 includes Fixed Odds Betting Terminals.

Sources: National Lottery Commission;
Gaming Board for Great Britain: 020 7306 6253;
Department for Culture, Media and Sport: 020 7211 6451

Environment

Chapter 13

Environment

Air emissions

(Table 13.1 to 13.7)

Emissions of air pollutants arise from a wide variety of sources. The National Atmospheric Emissions Inventory (NAEI) is prepared annually for the Government and the devolved administrations by AEA Energy and Environment, with the work being co-ordinated by Defra. Information is available for a range of point sources, including the most significant polluters. However, a different approach has to be taken for diffuse sources such as transport and domestic emissions where this type of information is not available and estimates for these are derived from statistical information and from research on emission factors for stationary and mobile sources. Although for any given year considerable uncertainties surround the emission estimates for each pollutant, trends over time are likely to be more reliable.

UK national emission estimates are updated annually and any developments in methodology are applied retrospectively to earlier years. Adjustments in the methodology are made to accommodate new technical information and to improve international comparability.

Three different classification systems are used in the tables presented here: a National Accounts basis (Table 13.1); the format required by the Inter-governmental Panel on Climate Change (IPCC) (Table 13.2); and the EMEP format used by the United Nations Economic Commission for Europe (UNECE) (Tables 13.3-13.7).

The EMEP source categories are detailed below, together with details of the main sources of these emissions:

Energy industries: Public electricity and heat production, petroleum refining, manufacture of solid fuels and other energy industries.

Manufacturing industries and construction: Iron and steel, autogenerators, foundries, sinter production, other industrial fuel combustion including ammonia, fletton brick and cement production.

Road transport: Passenger cars, light duty vehicles, buses, HGVs, mopeds, motorcycles; gasoline evaporation from vehicles, tyre and brake wear.

Other transport: Civil aviation (domestic cruise, take off and landing cycles), railway locomotives, national navigation, fishing vessels, and other mobile sources including agricultural machinery; gardening, construction and aircraft support equipment and mobile industrial equipment powered by diesel or petrol engines.

Commercial and institutional: Public sector industrial and commercial combustion, and railways stationary combustion.

Residential: Residential plant, household and gardening (mobile).

Agriculture and forestry fuel use: Stationary, off road vehicles and other machinery.

Military aircraft and shipping: Military aircraft and naval vessels and military machinery (military road vehicles are included in road transport).

Fugitive emissions from fuels: Solid fuel transformation, exploration production, transport, venting and flaring.

Industrial processes: Emissions from industrial processes other than fuel combustion including road paving, chemical industry and metal production.

Solvent and other product use: Paint application, degreasing and dry cleaning, chemical products, manufacture and processing wood impregnation and tyre manufacture.

Agriculture: Culture with and without fertilisers; enteric fermentation and manure management of animals and field burning of agricultural waste.

Land-use change and forestry: Emissions from managed and unmanaged forests, and forest and grassland conversion.

Waste treatment and disposal: Treatment of domestic, industrial and other waste, including landfill and waste incineration.

In tables 13.3 and 13.5, the figures on emissions from individual large combustion plants (LCPs) for 1991 onwards are totals of those reported by the Environment Agency to Defra. For 1970–1990, estimates are made assuming all power station emissions from coal, fuel oil and orimulsion stations are included, plus 79 per cent of refineries' emissions, 12 per cent of iron and steel emissions and 38 per cent of other (Table 13.3), and 88 per cent of refineries' emissions, 11 per cent of iron and steel emissions and 40 per cent of other industrial combustions in fuel extraction and transformation (Table 13.5). It is not possible to calculate LCP figures from the categories presented in these tables as refineries and other industrial combustion are both included in more than one category.

Estimated atmospheric emissions on a National Accounts basis

(Table 13.1)

The National Accounts figures in Table 13.1 differ from those on an IPCC basis in that they include estimated emissions from fuels purchased by UK residents either at home or abroad, including emissions from UK international shipping and aircraft operators and exclude emissions in the UK resulting from the activities of non-residents.

Greenhouse gases include carbon dioxide, methane, nitrous oxide, hydro-fluorocarbons, perfluorocarbons and sulphur hexafluoride which are expressed in thousand tonnes of carbon dioxide equivalent.

Acid rain precursors include sulphur dioxide, nitrogen oxides and ammonia which are expressed as thousand tonnes of sulphur dioxide equivalent.

PM10 are carbon particles in the air arising from incomplete combustion.

Estimated total emissions of greenhouse gases on an IPCC basis

(Table 13.2)

The IPCC classification is used to report greenhouse gas emissions under the Framework Convention on Climate Change and includes land use change and all emissions from domestic aviation and shipping, but excludes international marine and aviation bunker fuels. Estimates of the relative contribution to global warming of the main greenhouse gases, or classes of gases, is presented weighted by their global warming potential.

Emissions of PM[10]

(Table 13.4)

Emissions of PM[10] includes particles which pass through a size selective inlet with a 50 per cent efficiency cut-off at 10μm aerodynamics diameter.

Emissions of nitrogen oxides

(Table 13.5)

Most of the figures in this table are based on a single NO_x emission factor for each fuel which is held constant over time. Emissions are expressed as nitrogen dioxide equivalent.

Emissions of carbon monoxide

(Table 13.6)

Most of the figures in this table are based on a single carbon monoxide emission factor for each fuel held constant over time.

Emissions of volatile organic compounds

(Table 13.7)

Most of the figures in this table are based on a single volatile organic compound emission factor for each source held constant over time.

Biological and chemical quality of rivers and canals

(Table 13.9)

The chemical quality of river and canal waters is monitored in a series of separate national surveys in England and Wales and Northern Ireland. The General Quality Assessment (GQA) Scheme used in the surveys provides a rigorous and objective method for assessing the basic chemical quality of rivers and canals based on three determinants – dissolved oxygen, biochemical oxygen demand (BOD), and ammoniacal nitrogen. The GQA grades river stretches into six categories (A–F) of chemical quality and these in turn have been grouped into four broader groups – good (classes A and B), fair (C and D), poor (E) and bad (F).

To provide a more comprehensive picture of the health of rivers and canals, biological testing has also been carried out. The biological grading is based on the monitoring of tiny animals (invertebrates) which live in or on the bed of the river. Research has shown that there is a relationship between species composition and water quality. Using a procedure known as the River Invertebrate Prediction and Classification System (RIVPACS), species groups recorded at a site were compared with those which would be expected to be present in the absence of pollution, allowing for the different environmental characteristics in different parts of the country. Two different summary statistics (known as ecological quality indices (EQI)) were calculated and then the biological quality was assigned to one of six bands based on a combination of these two statistics.

River length stretches were allocated to Government Office Regions using a 1995 digitised map. This provides consistently smaller total river lengths for local areas than the equivalent Environment Agency figures. This is because of differences between stretch lengths used by the Environment Agency and those calculated using the map, and because it was not possible to link all stretch codes to the map, so some stretches were excluded. It should be noted that the monitoring network only covers stretches the Environment Agency are required to monitor, that is rivers and streams with a flow greater than 1m³/second. On this basis 40,000km of river network are monitored in England and Wales out of an estimated total river length of 150,000km. No canals are classified in Northern Ireland. The figures in table 13.9 are rounded to the nearest 10km and may not sum to totals.

Water quality of rivers and canals

(Table 13.10)

In Scotland, river and canal water quality is based upon the Scottish River Classification Scheme of 20 June 1997 which combines chemical, biological, nutrient and aesthetic quality using the following classes: excellent (A1), good (A2), fair (B), poor (C) and seriously polluted (D). The figures in the table are also rounded to the nearest 10km and may not sum to totals.

During 2000 a new digitised river network (DRN) was developed, based on 1:50,000 ordnance survey data digitised by the Institute of Hydrology. The new network ensures consistency between all SEPA areas and includes the Scottish Islands which were not previously covered. Data based on this network are published for the first time in the 2004 edition of Annual Abstract and are not consistent with data which have previously been published. The DRN includes:

all mainland and islands rivers with a catchment area of 10 km² or more. This is known as the "baseline network".

mainland and islands stream stretches with a catchment of less than 10 km² which are classified as fair, poor or seriously polluted and have been monitored. These are added to the baseline network to give a "classification network".

It is intended that future emphasis will be placed on the baseline network, which is likely to be reportable for the purposes of the EC Water Framework Directive. Efforts to improve the quality of the downgraded smaller streams will continue, but once this has been sustainably achieved, their monitoring may be reduced. Many of these streams are the subject of current attention because of their influence on the quality of larger classification network rivers.

Using the DRN scheme, data for every routine sampling point are automatically applied to an identified river stretch of predetermined length. The loss in total river length in moving to the DRN (i.e. despite the first time inclusion of islands rivers) arises mainly from the exclusion from classification of thousands of small remote headwater streams which were never monitored, but assumed to be of excellent quality. The smaller reduction in length of downgraded waters arises mainly from using 1:50,000 maps for the DRN; in the former system lengths were hand measured from 1:10,000 maps, so more minor channel bends were included.

Water industry expenditure

(Table 13.12)

The table is informed by the annual and regulatory accounts of water and sewerage companies and water companies of England and Wales. The elements which make up operating expenditure are as follows: manpower costs, other costs of employment, power, agencies, associated companies, Environment Agency charges, bulk supply imports, general and support, customer services, scientific services, other business activities, local authority rates, water charges, local authority sewerage agencies, materials and consumables, hired and contracted services, charge for bad and doubtful debts, depreciation, infrastructure renewals expenditure, infrastructure renewals accrual, exceptional items and other operating costs. Capital expenditure figures are the addition to tangible fixed assets including management and general expenditure but excluding infrastructure renewals expenditure. Adopted assets at nil cost are also included.

Water pollution incidents

(Table 13.13)

The Environment Agency responds to complaints and reported incidents of pollution in England and Wales. Each incident is then logged and categorised according to its severity. The category describes the impact of each incident on our water, land and air. The impact of an incident on each medium is considered and reported separately. If no impact has occurred for a particular medium, the incident is reported as a Category 4. Before 1999, the reporting system was used only for water pollution incidents, thus the total number of substantiated incidents was lower as it did not include incidents not relating to the water environment.

Bathing waters

(Table 13.14)

Under the EC Bathing Water Directive 76/160/EEC, eleven physical, chemical and microbiological parameters are measured including total and faecal coliforms which are generally considered to be the most important indicators of the extent to which water is contaminated by sewage. The mandatory value for total coliforms is 10,000 per 100 ml, and for faecal coliforms 2,000 per 100 ml. For a bathing water to comply with the coliform standards, the Directive requires that at least 95 per cent of samples taken for each of these parameters over the bathing season are less than or equal to the mandatory values. In the UK a minimum of 20 samples are normally taken at each site. In practice this means that where 20 samples are taken, a maximum of only one sample may exceed the mandatory value for the bathing water to comply, and where less than 20 samples are taken none may exceed the mandatory value for the bathing water to comply.

The bathing water season is from mid-May to end-September in England and Wales, but shorter in Scotland and Northern Ireland. Bathing waters which are closed for the season are excluded for that year.

The table shows Environment Agency (EA) regions for England and Wales. The boundaries of which are based on river catchment areas and not county borders. In particular, the figures shown for Wales are the EA Welsh Region, the boundary of which does not coincide with the boundary of Wales.

Surface and groundwater abstractions

(Table 13.15)

Significant changes in the way data is collected and/or reported were made in 1991 (due to Water Resources Act 1991) and 1999 (commission of National Abstraction Licensing Database). Figures are therefore not strictly comparable with those in previous/intervening years. From 1999 data has been stored and retrieved from one system nationally and is therefore more accurate and reliable. Some regions report licensed and actual abstracts for financial rather than calendar years. As figures represent an average for the whole year expressed as daily amounts, differences between amounts reported for financial and calendar years are small.

The following changes have occurred in the classification of individual sources:-

Spray irrigation: This category includes small amounts of non-agricultural spray irrigation.

Mineral washing: From 1999 was not reported as a separate category, licences for mineral washing are now contained in 'Other industry'.

Private water supply: was shown as separate category from 1992 and includes private abstractions for domestic use and individual households.

Fish farming, cress growing, amenity ponds: Includes amenity ponds, but excludes miscellaneous from 1991.

Radioactive wastes

(Table 13.16)

Solid radioactive wastes are not discharged to the environment but stored and conditioned by processes such as supercompaction, cementation or turning into glass. Such wastes cover a wide range of materials and can be classified,

according to the nature and quantity of radioactivity associated with them, as high level wastes (HLW), intermediate level wastes (ILW) or low level wastes (LLW). HLW result from the reprocessing of irradiated nuclear fuel and are intensely radioactive. They contain over 90 per cent of all the radioactivity in wastes from nuclear establishments. HLWs are of relatively small in volume, but have a high heat output as a result of the energy from radioactive decay. ILW include the irradiated metal cladding for nuclear reactor fuel, reactor components, and chemical process residues and filters. They have a lower radioactivity and heat output than HLW but their radioactivity content exceeds the upper limits for LLW. LLW includes concrete, rubble and soil from building demolition, discarded protective clothing and worn out or damaged plant and equipment. LLW do not normally require shielding against radiation emissions during handling and transport.

The table shows recent trends in the volume of radioactive waste stocks for particular groups of nuclear sites. Data are presented in the physical state "as stored". "As stored" is the form in which the waste is currently stored. For the majority of LLW, storage is short term prior to disposal.

Annual waste arisings

(Table 13.17)

Agriculture: The estimates are derived from the Environment Agency's survey of agricultural waste and relate to the United Kingdom (UK). These data exclude manure, slurry and straw as these are not considered wastes.

Mining and quarrying: The UK minerals waste estimates are based on Defra ratios of waste to product. Product figures come from the British Geological Society.

Sewage sludge: The estimate of sewage sludge arisings comes from Water UK figures. The data are measured as dry weight.

Dredged material: The data for dredged material are for all UK sea waters and come from CEFAS. These data exclude river dredging waste, which however, only accounts for a very small proportion of total dredging waste.

Municipal waste: The UK data on municipal waste is based on returns made by local authorities in England, Wales, Scotland and Northern Ireland.

Commercial and industrial: UK totals are estimated from figures for England and Wales, based on a 2002/03 survey by the Environment Agency.

Demolition and construction: The UK total is estimated from figures for England and Wales, based on survey by Communities and Local Government (DCLG) in 2003.

Environment

Noise complaints

(Table 13.19)

The table shows trends in the number of complaints received by local authority Environmental Health Officers (EHOs). The figures are from those authorities making returns and are calculated per million people based on the population of the authorities making returns.

Most complaints about traffic noise are usually addressed to highways authorities or Department for Transport (DfT) Regional Directors, and will not necessarily be included in the figures. Similarly, complaints about noise from civil aircraft are generally received by aircraft operators, the airport companies, the DfT or Civil Aviation Authority. Complaints about military flying are dealt with either by Station Commanding Officers or by Ministry of Defence headquarters. It is also true that railway noise will be reported elsewhere. Thus the figures in this table will not necessarily include these complaints and are likely to be considerably understated. Therefore the information reported to the EHOs is considered to give, at best, only a very approximate indication of the trend in noise complaints from these sources.

Over time some of the categories shown in this table have changed. These have included:- Up until 1996/97 Section 62 of the Control of Pollution Act 1974 covered noise in the streets - it primarily included the chimes of ice-cream vendors and the use of loudspeakers other than for strictly defined purposes. From 1997/98 all complaints about noise in the street are included with 'vehicles machinery and equipment in streets'. From 1997/98 complaints about road works are included with 'vehicles machinery and equipment in streets'. The use of the category "Other" was discontinued in England and Wales from 1997/98. It included some complaints not covered by the other specified sources, but also those where the source was not certain or was due to more than one source. From 1997/98 in England and Wales more vigorous procedures have allocated complaints to the most appropriate source.

Material flows

(Table 13.20)

Economy-wide material flow accounts record the total mass of natural resources and products that are used by the UK economy, either directly in the production and distribution of products and services, or indirectly through the movement of materials which are displaced in order for production to take place.

The direct movement of materials into the economy derives primarily from domestic extraction, that is from biomass (agricultural harvest, timber, fish and animal grazing), fossil fuel extraction (such as coal, crude oil and natural gas) and mineral extraction (metal ores, industrial minerals such as pottery clay, and construction material such as crushed rock, sand and gravel). This domestic extraction is supplemented by the imports of products, which may be of raw materials such as unprocessed agricultural products, but can also be semi-manufactured or finished products. In a similar way the UK produces exports of raw materials, semi-manufactured and finished goods which can be viewed as inputs to the production and consumption of overseas economies.

Indirect flows of natural resources consist of the unused material resulting from domestic extraction such as mining and quarrying overburden and the soil removed during construction and dredging activities. They also include the movement of used and unused material overseas which is associated with the production and delivery of imports. Water – except for that included directly in products – is excluded from the accounts.

There are three main indicators used to measure inputs. The Direct Material Input (DMI) measures the input of used materials into the economy, that is all materials which are of economic value and are used in production and consumption activities (including the production of exports). Domestic material consumption (DMC) measures the total amount of material directly used in the economy, ie it includes imports but excludes exports. The Total Material Requirement (TMR) measures the total material basis of the economy, that is the total primary resource requirements of all the production and consumption activities. It includes not only the direct use of resources for producing exports, but also indirect flows from the production of imports and the indirect flows associated with domestic extraction. Although TMR is widely favoured as a resource use indicator, the estimates of indirect flows are less reliable than those for materials directly used by the economy, and the indicator therefore needs to be considered alongside other indicators.

Designated areas

(Table 13.21)

National Parks, Areas of Outstanding Natural Beauty (AONB's) in England, Wales and Northern Ireland and National Scenic Areas in Scotland are the major areas which have been designated to protect their landscape importance. National Scenic Areas in Scotland are the equivalent of AONB's in England, Wales and Northern Ireland.

Some areas may be in more than one category. All areas shown in the table are at March 2005, except for Green Belt land which relates to 1 January 1997.

The area for Green Belt land is based on a new methodology in which the extent of Green Belt land is captured in digital form.

This approach provides much more reliable figures than those previously published in earlier years.

Further details regarding tables 13.2 to 13.7, 13.9, 13.13 to 13.18 and 13.21 can be found in *Defra's e-Digest of Environmental Statistics* (on the Defra website at: www.defra. gov.uk/environment/statistics/index.htm). If you would like to discuss the tables, Adrian Redfern can be contacted at Defra on 020 7082 8608.

13.1 Estimated atmospheric emissions on a National Accounts basis,[1] 2004
United Kingdom

Thousand tonnes

	Greenhouse gases[2]	Acid rain precursors[3]	PM_{10}	Carbon monoxide	Volatile organic compounds[4]	Benzene	Butadiene	Lead (Tonnes)	Cadmium (Tonnes)	Mercury (Tonnes)
					Emissions affecting air quality					
Agriculture	52 069	597.60	23.06	42.36	83.83	0.09	0.29	0.42	0.031	0.032
Mining and quarrying	29 915	78.48	10.53	39.30	108.49	0.36	0.03	0.24	0.063	0.020
Manufacturing	132 885	504.74	42.89	822.62	373.24	3.16	1.09	98.02	3.886	3.587
Electricity, gas and water supply	185 803	733.68	9.39	69.73	50.73	0.53	0.00	22.17	0.596	1.709
Construction	7 453	20.30	6.00	31.67	58.27	0.08	0.05	4.59	0.043	0.011
Wholesale and retail trade	16 596	43.65	4.86	45.81	65.71	0.19	0.15	0.16	0.031	0.004
Transport and communication	97 961	916.37	18.01	150.52	45.57	3.50	0.76	4.75	3.662	0.207
Financial intermediation	6 318	11.95	1.72	44.75	4.24	0.09	0.04	0.10	0.047	0.003
Public administration	8 993	35.38	1.04	29.83	2.39	0.15	0.02	0.29	0.023	0.022
Education, health and social work	10 736	13.40	0.64	6.87	1.70	0.04	-	0.20	0.013	0.019
Other services	20 861	41.79	1.31	34.04	15.42	1.00	0.04	0.35	0.028	4.638
Domestic	162 325	310.22	43.74	1 689.24	300.88	8.47	0.97	7.08	0.453	0.221
Total	731 915	3 307.56	163.19	3 006.74	1 110.48	17.68	3.45	138.38	8.876	10.473
Of which, emissions from road transport	127 639	450.63	36.01	1 385.74	146.60	3.48	1.93	2.03	0.415	0.004

1 See chapter text.
2 Thousand tonnes of carbon dioxide equivalent.
3 Thousand tonnes of sulphur dioxide equivalent.
4 Excluding methane, but including benzene and 1,3-butadiene.

Sources: National Environmental Technology Centre;
Office for National Statistics: 020 7533 5904

13.2 Estimated emissions[1] of greenhouse gases on an IPCC basis[2]: 1990 to 2005
United Kingdom[3]

Million tonnes (Carbon dioxide equivalent[4])

		1990	1994	1995	1996	1997	1998	1999	2000	2001	2002	2003	2004	2005
Net CO_2 emissions/removals	JZCK	592.1	559.2	549.6	571.3	548.4	550.1	540.8	548.8	559.6	543.2	555.1	554.6	554.2
Methane(CH_4)	GXDO	103.4	91.0	90.1	87.7	82.8	78.2	72.9	68.4	62.4	59.4	53.4	51.6	49.3
Nitrous oxide(N_2O)	GXDP	63.6	54.1	52.8	53.2	54.6	54.3	44.0	43.5	41.4	39.9	39.6	40.4	39.6
Hydrofluorocarbons(HFCs)	JZCN	11.4	14.0	15.5	16.7	19.2	17.3	10.9	9.1	9.7	9.9	10.2	8.9	9.2
Perfluorocarbons(PFCs)	JZCO	1.4	0.5	0.5	0.5	0.4	0.4	0.4	0.5	0.4	0.3	0.3	0.3	0.4
Sulphur hexafluoride(SF_6)	JZCP	1.0	1.2	1.2	1.3	1.2	1.3	1.4	1.8	1.4	1.5	1.3	1.1	1.1
Kyoto greenhouse gas basket[5]	F92X	770.3	719.3	709.0	730.1	706.4	701.9	670.9	672.8	675.9	655.8	661.5	659.3	656.2
1990 Baseline[6]	GXJK	775.2	..	..	..	..	..	..	..	..	..	..	..	..
Percentage change for basket from 1990 baseline	GXDR	−0.6	−7.2	−8.5	−5.8	−8.9	−9.5	−13.4	−13.2	−12.8	−15.4	−14.7	−15.0	−15.3

1 Net emissions weighted by global warming potential. Emissions inventories based on the methodology developed by the Intergovernmental Panel on Climate Change (IPCC) are used to report UK emissions to the Climate Change Convention.
2 See chapter text.
3 Figures shown include Crown Dependancies but exclude overseas territories except for the Kyoto Basket.
4 12 tonnes of carbon is equivalent to 44 tonnes of carbon dioxide.
5 Kyoto basket total differs slightly from sum of individual pollutants above as the basket uses a narrower definition for the Land Use Change and Forestry sector, and includes emissions from UK Overseas Territories.

6 The base year used for the Kyoto Protocol consists of 1990 emissions of CO_2 (without LUCF), CH_4 and N_2O and 1995 emissions of HFCs, PFCs and SF_6. In addition there is a small allowance (equal to 0.1 million tonnes carbon for net emissions from deforestation in 1990, as allowed under Article 3.7 of the Kyoto Protocol). It is used as the baseline against which progress is measured, to meet the UK commitment of a 12.5 per cent reduction in greenhouse gas emissions, required by the Kyoto Protocol.

Sources: AEA Energy & Environment;
for Department for Environment, Food and Rural Affairs 020 7082 8608

13.3 Estimated emissions of sulphur dioxide (SO_2): by source[1]
United Kingdom

Thousand tonnes

By source category (UNECE/EMEP)		Percentage of total in 2005	1970	1980	1990	1995	1996	1997	1998	1999	2000	2001	2002	2003	2004	2005
Energy industries	EU62	65	3 307	3 230	2 873	1 715	1 440	1 147	1 188	871	905	823	751	746	583	462
Manufacturing industries and construction	EU63	20	1 858	911	426	320	258	252	224	182	173	172	153	146	146	141
Road transport	EU64	0	46	43	64	52	38	28	23	14	7	4	4	4	4	3
Other transport	EU65	6	42	31	30	31	32	30	27	24	23	19	17	27	34	40
Commercial and institutional	EU66	1	413	193	80	50	48	40	27	21	14	16	9	6	6	6
Residential	EU67	3	521	226	113	71	76	68	57	54	47	41	33	29	27	21
Agriculture and forestry fuel use	EU68	1	45	27	11	10	10	8	7	7	4	4	4	4	4	4
Military aircraft and shipping	EU69	1	9	9	9	8	8	8	6	6	6	6	5	4	5	5
Fugitive emissions from fuels	EU6A	1	62	39	28	17	19	19	17	10	9	10	7	9	10	9
Industrial processes	EU6B	2	59	59	46	43	42	41	41	36	26	23	19	16	15	14
Waste treatment and disposal	EU6C	0	8	8	7	4	3	1	1	1	1	2	1	1	1	1
Total	EU6D	100	6 370	4 775	3 687	2 322	1 973	1 641	1 619	1 227	1 215	1 119	1 002	991	836	706
Emissions from large combustion plants																
Large combustion plants	EU6E		3 732	3 457	2 934	1 756	1 468	1 107	1 208	881	873	762	658	715	539	370
Index (1980=100)	ZBZL		108	100	85	51	42	32	35	25	25	22	19	21	16	11

1 See chapter text.

Sources: AEA Energy & Environment; Environment Agency;
for Department for Environment, Food and Rural Affairs: 020 7082 8608

13.4 Estimated emissions of PM_{10}[1]: by source
United Kingdom

Thousand tonnes

By source category (UNECE/EMEP)		Percentage of total in 2005	1970	1980	1990	1995	1996	1997	1998	1999	2000	2001	2002	2003	2004	2005
Energy industries	EVH5	8	83	83	74	43	40	27	29	23	25	20	11	11	11	12
Manufacturing industries and construction	EVH6	14	72	41	37	34	32	32	31	28	25	25	23	23	22	21
Road transport	EVH7	22	42	51	60	54	51	47	45	43	39	38	37	36	36	34
Other transport	EVH8	5	6	5	6	6	6	6	6	5	5	4	4	5	6	7
Commercial and institutional	EVH9	1	18	8	5	3	3	3	2	2	2	2	1	1	1	1
Residential	EVI2	14	209	94	50	33	35	33	35	35	29	27	24	22	22	21
Agriculture and forestry fuel use	EVI3	5	11	10	11	11	11	11	11	10	10	10	9	9	8	8
Military aircraft and shipping	EVI4	1	2	2	2	1	1	1	1	1	1	1	1	1	1	1
Fugitive emissions from fuels	EVI5	1	1	3	2	2	2	2	2	2	1	1	1	1	1	1
Industrial processes	EVI6	12	27	23	28	26	25	24	22	20	20	19	19	19	19	19
Solvent and other product use	EVI7	4	7	7	8	6	6	6	6	6	6	5	5	5	5	6
Agriculture	EVI8	9	11	12	13	12	13	15	14	14	14	14	14	14	14	13
Waste treatment and disposal	EVI9	4	8	8	8	7	7	6	6	6	6	10	6	6	6	6
Other	EVJ2	1	1	1	1	1	1	1	1	1	1	1	1	1	1	1
Total	EVJ3	100	499	349	305	238	233	214	209	197	184	178	155	155	154	150

1 See chapter text.

Sources: AEA Energy & Environment; Environment Agency;
for Department for Environment, Food and Rural Affairs: 020 7082 8608

13.5 Estimated emissions of nitrogen oxides (NO$_x$): by source[1]
United Kingdom

Thousand tonnes

By source category (UNECE/EMEP)		Percentage of total in 2005	1970	1980	1990	1995	1996	1997	1998	1999	2000	2001	2002	2003	2004	2005
Energy industries	EVJ6	28	1 333	936	852	555	510	436	431	392	421	444	440	467	454	462
Manufacturing industries and construction	EVJ7	16	605	433	377	352	328	326	324	314	304	292	268	273	266	267
Road transport	EVJ8	34	765	989	1 324	1 098	1 068	1 014	960	900	818	749	692	636	597	549
Other transport	EVJ9	8	96	105	116	107	115	113	110	104	103	91	84	120	120	134
Commercial and institutional	EVK2	1	66	44	35	36	38	35	34	34	31	32	27	31	22	22
Residential	EVK3	7	121	109	104	104	119	109	112	111	112	115	111	112	115	109
Agriculture and forestry fuel use	EVK4	3	72	74	76	77	77	78	76	75	72	70	67	63	58	53
Military aircraft and shipping	EVK5	1	39	39	42	33	33	34	26	27	26	25	24	18	24	22
Fugitive emissions from fuels	EVK6	0	2	8	14	14	11	5	4	5	4	4	4	3	3	3
Industrial processes	EVK7	0	13	14	11	5	4	5	4	4	4	3	2	3	3	2
Agriculture	EVK8	0	10	15	9	–	–	–	–	–	–	–	–	–	–	–
Land-use change and forestry	EVK9	0	..	..	–	–	–	–	–	–	–	–	–	–	–	–
Waste treatment and disposal	EVL2	0	8	8	7	5	5	2	2	2	2	3	2	2	2	2
Total	EVL3	100	3 130	2 772	2 966	2 384	2 309	2 157	2 083	1 969	1 897	1 828	1 721	1 728	1 664	1 627

Emissions from large combustion plants

Large combustion plants	EVL4		939	955	848	524	471	371	369	320	343	359	316	368	355	339
Index (1980=100)	ZBZN		98	100	89	55	49	39	39	34	36	38	33	39	37	35

1 See chapter text.

Sources: AEA Energy & Environment; Environment Agency; for Department for Environment, Food and Rural Affairs: 020 7082 8608

13.6 Estimated emissions of carbon monoxide (CO):[1] by source
United Kingdom

Thousand tonnes

By source category (UNECE/EMEP)		Percentage of total in 2005	1970	1980	1990	1995	1996	1997	1998	1999	2000	2001	2002	2003	2004	2005
Energy industries	EVL5	4	171	139	131	123	122	63	77	70	82	81	77	85	85	98
Manufacturing industries and construction	EVL6	21	1 315	598	723	724	730	720	693	709	614	654	595	489	509	516
Road transport	EVL7	47	5 353	5 390	5 480	4 180	3 999	3 664	3 337	3 003	2 500	2 128	1 853	1 594	1 366	1 124
Other transport	EVL8	3	91	58	46	45	49	54	54	61	68	72	62	61	68	74
Commercial and institutional	EVL9	0	56	28	15	9	10	10	8	8	7	7	6	6	6	6
Residential	EVM2	15	4 498	2 145	1 191	851	871	800	758	760	644	626	522	458	431	361
Agriculture and forestry fuel use	EVM3	1	38	38	39	39	39	39	39	39	38	38	37	37	37	36
Military aircraft and shipping	EVM4	0	11	11	13	10	10	9	8	8	7	7	8	7	7	7
Fugitive emissions from fuels	EVM5	1	93	87	60	55	54	49	48	41	39	28	21	23	19	19
Industrial processes	EVM6	6	162	158	225	223	225	230	208	201	197	184	132	143	140	133
Agriculture	EVM7	0	288	449	266	–	–	–	–	–	–	–	–	–	–	–
Land-use change and forestry	EVM8	0	..	..	5	4	5	5	5	7	9	10	9	9	8	8
Waste treatment and disposal	EVM9	1	28	28	29	28	28	27	28	29	28	50	28	29	28	28
Other	EVN2	0	6	6	6	6	6	6	6	6	6	6	6	6	6	6
Total	EVN3	100	12 108	9 137	8 229	6 296	6 147	5 674	5 269	4 940	4 239	3 891	3 356	2 947	2 711	2 417

1 See chapter text.

Sources: AEA Energy & Environment; Environment Agency; for Department for Environment, Food and Rural Affairs: 020 7082 8608

13.7

Estimated emissions of volatile organic compounds (VOCs)[1]: by source
United Kingdom

Thousand tonnes

By source category (UNECE/EMEP)		Percentage of total in 2005	1970	1980	1990	1995	1996	1997	1998	1999	2000	2001	2002	2003	2004	2005
Energy industries	EVN4	1	8	9	8	8	9	9	6	8	8	7	8	7	7	6
Manufacturing industries and construction	EVN5	3	36	31	31	31	31	31	31	30	30	30	29	28	28	29
Road transport	EVN6	12	524	652	867	634	560	506	436	376	303	249	210	175	144	119
Other transport	EVN7	1	8	8	8	7	8	8	8	8	8	7	7	8	9	9
Commercial and institutional	EVN8	0	1	1	1	1	1	1	1	1	1	1	1	1	1	1
Residential	EVN9	4	318	153	91	66	68	65	66	67	58	54	50	48	46	43
Agriculture and forestry fuel use	EVO2	1	11	12	12	12	12	13	12	12	12	12	11	11	10	10
Military aircraft and shipping	EVO3	0	3	3	3	2	2	2	2	2	2	2	2	1	2	2
Fugitive emissions from fuels	EVO4	21	173	356	381	358	342	370	331	303	306	291	275	223	202	201
Industrial processes	EVO5	15	194	220	256	239	233	215	195	165	155	147	143	142	144	143
Solvent and other product use	EVO6	41	590	577	670	539	527	513	497	463	433	416	404	400	399	398
Agriculture	EVO7	0	31	46	26	–	–	–	–	–	–	–	–	–	–	–
Waste treatment and disposal	EVO8	2	25	28	32	30	29	27	26	24	23	21	20	19	18	18
Total	EVO9	100	1 923	2 097	2 386	1 928	1 823	1 759	1 610	1 459	1 338	1 237	1 159	1 064	1 009	977

1 See chapter text.

Sources: AEA Energy & Environment; Environment Agency;
for Department for Environment, Food and Rural Affairs: 020 7082 8608

13.8

Annual rainfall: by region
United Kingdom

Millimetres and percentages

			Annual rainfall as a percentage of the 1961-1990 average										
			1996	1997	1998	1999	2000	2001	2002	2003	2004	2005	2006[3]
Region[1]		1961 - 1990 rainfall average (= 100%) millimetres											
United Kingdom	JSJB	1 080	85	95	117	115	124	97	119	83	112	100	109
North West	JSJC	1 201	78	90	115	109	129	92	118	84	113	94	113
Northumbria	JSJD	853	81	93	120	103	129	104	122	79	117	108	101
Severn Trent	JSJE	754	80	96	116	121	133	105	120	82	111	93	104
Yorkshire	JSJF	821	83	92	114	109	135	99	124	81	113	95	111
Anglian	JSJG	596	78	95	120	115	130	125	120	87	117	90	103
Thames	JSLK	688	78	89	119	112	140	118	130	82	104	80	108
Southern	JSLL	778	82	99	111	107	149	115	131	86	98	80	104
Wessex	JSLM	839	90	101	119	121	140	103	136	86	101	92	103
South West	JSLN	1 173	94	100	121	116	131	94	124	80	101	92	91
England	JSLO	823	81	94	116	112	133	105	122	82	108	91	103
Wales[2]	JSLP	1 355	86	94	122	117	135	100	120	84	110	96	106
Scotland	JSLQ	1 436	85	95	117	116	113	91	113	84	117	110	114
Northern Ireland	JSLR	1 059	103	98	119	117	115	85	133	88	103	101	109

1 The regions of England shown in this table correspond to the original nine English regions of the National Rivers Authority (NRA); the NRA became part of the Environment Agency upon its creation in April 1996.
2 The figures in this table relate to the country of Wales, not the Environment Agency Welsh Region.

3 Data from October 2006 are provisional and subject to revision.

Sources: The Met Office;
Centre for Ecology and Hydrology, Wallingford: 01491 838800

13.9 Biological[1] and chemical[2] water quality of rivers and canals[3]
England, Wales and Northern Ireland

Length surveyed (Kilometres)[5] and percentages

| | | Length surveyed | | | | | | | Percentage of total | |
| | | Good | | Fair | | | | | | |
	Years	A	B	C	D	Poor E	Bad F	Total	Good or fair	Poor or bad
Biological quality										
North East	1990	590	770	300	160	140	30	1 990	91	9
	2005	940	740	190	160	50	10	2 080	97	3
North West	1990	450	1 200	630	340	700	460	3 770	69	31
	2005	920	1 670	990	630	450	50	4 710	89	11
Yorkshire and the Humber	1990	800	500	340	250	210	220	2 330	81	19
	2005	1 360	940	580	390	240	80	3 590	91	9
East Midlands	1990	340	790	1 140	320	160	40	2 800	93	7
	2005	850	1 330	810	260	110	-	3 360	97	3
West Midlands	1990	440	580	560	350	120	80	2 130	91	9
	2005	940	1240	770	400	300	120	3 750	89	11
East	1990	620	1 130	930	240	100	20	3 040	96	4
	2005	1 350	1 250	600	150	70	10	3 430	98	2
London	1990	-	30	80	80	80	20	290	65	35
	2005	20	80	120	100	40	10	360	87	13
South East	1990	1 020	1 180	700	240	130	30	3 290	95	5
	2005	1 830	1 480	660	190	70	-	4 240	98	2
South West	1990	2 380	2 300	720	220	120	60	5 800	97	3
	2005	3 720	1 810	550	120	50	30	6 260	99	1
England[4]	1990	6 980	9 010	5 640	2 300	1 850	990	26 770	89	11
	2005	12 650	11 420	5 610	2 500	1 410	300	33 890	95	5
Wales	1990	1 190	1 310	450	170	50	10	3 190	98	2
	2005	1 220	2 250	730	110	40	-	4 350	99	1
Northern Ireland	1991	710	950	410	100	10	-	2 190	100	-
	2005	830	2 220	1 650	660	100	10	5 460	98	2
Chemical quality										
North East	1990	230	560	170	70	70	30	1 130	92	8
	2005	860	870	200	70	60	-	2 060	97	3
North West	1990	660	590	520	450	610	200	3 030	73	27
	2005	1 980	1 420	1 020	580	350	80	5 430	92	8
Yorkshire and the Humber	1990	590	1 060	400	370	610	160	3 180	76	24
	2005	1 140	1 390	850	300	330	20	4 030	91	9
East Midlands	1990	50	570	1 120	700	550	80	3 060	79	21
	2005	530	1 580	870	360	180	30	3 550	94	6
West Midlands	1990	190	1 150	850	610	540	80	3 420	82	18
	2005	950	1 370	940	360	280	40	3 940	92	8
East	1990	50	690	1 350	790	570	70	3 510	82	18
	2005	270	1 380	1 040	470	420	10	3 590	88	12
London	1990	-	50	120	110	110	10	390	71	29
	2005	-	150	90	90	90	10	420	78	22
South East	1990	330	1 380	1 350	550	610	60	4 290	84	16
	2005	820	1 900	1 020	400	290	10	4 440	93	7
South West	1990	1 590	2 320	1 280	720	380	60	6 360	93	7
	2005	2 700	2 490	870	300	180	10	6 550	97	3
England[4]	1990	4 200	9 160	7 670	4 640	4 300	770	30 740	84	16
	2005	9 790	13 300	7 210	3 110	2 340	200	35 960	93	7
Wales	1990	1 850	1 120	230	130	50	20	3 410	98	2
	2005	3 420	840	140	30	70	10	4 490	98	2
Northern Ireland	1991	100	640	680	170	60	20	1 680	95	5
	2005	690	2 420	1 150	440	190	30	4 910	96	4

1 Based on the River Invertebrate Prediction and Classification System (RIVPACS).
2 Based on the General Quality Assessment (GQA) Scheme.
3 See chapter text.
4 Figures for the English regions will not add to the national figure for England because a small amount of river lengths which are located along the border between England and Wales are counted in both the national figures for England and Wales.
5 Figures may not sum to totals as data has been rounded to the nearest 10km.

Sources: Environment Agency;
Environment and Heritage Service

13.10 Chemical and biological water quality of rivers and canals[1]
Scotland

Kilometres and percentages

	Length surveyed							Percentage of total	
	Excellent A1	Good A2	Unclassified assumed good	Fair B	Poor C	Seriously polluted D	Total	Good or fair[2]	Poor or seriously polluted

Scottish Environment Protection Agency Regions

North

	DYO4	DYO5	DYO6	DYO7	DYO8	DYO9	DYP2	DYP3	DYP4
2000	960	1 650	8 260	390	140	10	11 400	99	1
2001	1 420	1 560	7 950	380	90	20	11 420	99	1
2002	2 020	3 480	5 140	660	90	10	11 400	99	1
2003	2 610	4 310	3 950	430	90	10	11 390	99	1
2004	3 330	5 010	2 570	370	110	10	11 390	99	1
2005	3 130	6 270	1 360	540	90	–	11 390	99	1

South East Scotland

	DYP5	DYP6	DYP7	DYP8	DYP9	DYQ2	DYQ3	DYQ4	DYQ5
2000	1 430	2 270	2 120	920	390	20	7 160	94	6
2001	1 520	2 450	1 670	1 000	520	20	7 170	93	7
2002	2 260	2 800	610	980	510	10	7 160	93	7
2003	2 570	2 810	430	990	360	10	7 160	95	5
2004	2 550	2 810	300	1 170	310	20	7 160	95	5
2005	2 830	2 760	260	950	340	10	7 160	95	5

South West Scotland

	DYQ6	DYQ7	DYQ8	DYQ9	DYR2	DYR3	DYR4	DYR5	DYR6
2000	780	2 170	2 440	1 150	320	30	6 900	95	5
2001	930	2 320	2 340	960	320	40	6 920	95	5
2002	1 000	2 370	2 230	930	310	40	6 880	95	5
2003	1 630	2 430	1 530	960	300	40	6 880	95	5
2004	1 780	2 790	940	1 050	300	30	6 880	95	5
2005	2 040	3 020	510	980	290	40	6 880	95	5

Scotland

	DZ38	DZ39	DZ3A	DZ3B	DZ3C	DZ3D	DZ3E	DZ3F	DZ3G
2000	3 170	6 090	12 820	2 450	850	70	25 450	96	4
2001	3 870	6 320	11 960	2 340	930	80	25 510	96	4
2002	5 280	8 660	7 990	2 560	900	60	25 440	96	4
2003	6 820	9 540	5 900	2 370	750	50	25 440	97	3
2004	7 660	10 610	3 810	2 590	720	50	25 430	97	3
2005	8 000	12 050	2 130	2 470	720	50	25 430	97	3

1 See chapter text.
2 Classes A1, A2, B and unclassified.

Source: Scottish Environmental Protection Agency: 01786 457700

13.11 Water reservoir stocks:[1] by month
England and Wales

Percentages

		1996	1997	1998	1999	2000	2001	2002	2003	2004	2005	2006
January	JTAS	61.2	79.1	90.5	95.8	95.8	94.8	86.5	95.1	79.9	91.2	85.9
February	JTAT	71.3	75.6	93.1	97.0	95.9	94.4	93.7	95.0	93.8	92.3	88.7
March	JTAU	81.8	91.6	92.3	96.5	97.4	95.0	95.5	92.1	92.1	92.1	91.2
April	JTAV	84.9	92.3	96.9	96.9	95.2	95.5	94.5	92.3	94.4	93.6	96.2
May	JTAW	86.2	87.1	97.0	97.0	97.0	96.7	91.9	88.6	94.7	95.0	93.4
June	JTAX	88.1	87.7	93.9	95.4	95.7	91.9	97.0	93.1	90.5	93.0	94.4
July	JTAY	82.2	87.8	95.1	92.0	93.8	85.1	94.9	87.0	84.8	85.6	88.4
August	JTAZ	73.4	81.3	93.5	82.6	88.5	80.7	91.1	81.1	78.5	77.9	77.2
September	JTBA	63.0	73.8	88.3	76.9	83.2	77.9	85.9	69.9	82.4	71.5	70.7
October	JTBB	54.6	70.6	86.6	79.7	88.0	77.0	77.3	60.4	84.2	67.4	67.8
November	JTBC	63.3	69.1	93.3	81.7	95.2	85.5	82.9	53.0	87.5	77.2	80.0
December	JTBD	77.3	76.4	93.1	84.9	96.7	87.9	91.8	60.9	86.2	83.8	89.8

1 Reservoir stocks are the percentage of useable capacity based on a representative selection of reservoirs; the percentages relate to the beginning of each month.

Sources: Water PLCs;
Environment Agency;
Centre for Ecology and Hydrology, Wallingford: 01491 838800

13.12 Water industry expenditure[1]
England and Wales

£ million

		1995 /96	1996 /97	1997 /98	1998 /99	1999 /00	2000 /01	2001 /02	2002 /03	2003 /04	2004 /05	2005 /06
Operating expenditure												
Water supply	KQQX	2 319.6	2 314.9	2 339.3	2 386.1	2 448.1	2 391.0	2 426.9	2 544.2	2 676.5	2 690.7	2 942.7
Sewerage services	KQQY	1 738.4	1 780.7	1 854.6	1 971.3	2 069.8	2 087.1	2 167.6	2 265.2	2 319.4	2 499.3	2 708.1
Capital expenditure												
Water supply	KQSX	1 074.5	1 314.3	1 467.2	1 294.1	1 290.0	935.0	1 132.5	1 347.1	1 346.4	1 309.0	1 282.5
Sewerage	KQSY	375.6	479.9	455.2	507.5	488.5	352.0	362.4	507.2	617.6	601.4	476.1
Sewage treatment and disposal	KQSZ	773.0	959.4	1 296.3	1 374.5	1 440.8	1 040.9	996.0	1 066.2	1 235.6	1 185.6	1 046.2

1 See chapter text.

Source: Office of Water Services: 0121 625 1300

13.13 Water pollution incidents[1]
United Kingdom

Numbers

		1993	1994	1995	1996	1997	1998		2001[2]	2002[2]	2003	2004	2005
Categories 1 to 3													
Environment Agency Regions													
North West	JZIA	3 656	3 532	3 717	2 818	2 160	2 201	MKDB	1 734	1 805	1 534	1 091	1 056
North East	JZIB	3 642	3 243	2 576	2 143	2 404	1 993	MKDC	1 952	1 789	1 971	1 692	1 448
Midlands	JZKR	4 876	4 895	4 259	4 305	4 411	4 061	MKDD	2 862	2 843	2 464	1 955	1 890
Anglian	JZKS	2 625	2 819	2 156	2 417	2 411	2 163	MKDE	1 606	1 716	1 616	1 418	1 290
Thames	JZKT	2 071	2 006	1 972	1 959	1 917	1 819	MKDF	1 510	1 630	1 447	1 211	1 203
Southern	JZKU	1 355	1 316	1 235	1 189	1 174	1 138	MKDG	1 585	1 511	1 543	1 218	955
South West	JZKV	4 129	4 340	4 558	3 042	2 847	2 603	MKDH	2 292	1 929	1 882	1 689	1 744
Welsh	JZKW	2 945	3 264	2 990	2 285	2 247	1 885	MKDI	1 475	1 287	1 356	1 309	1 260
England and Wales	JZKX	25 299	25 415	23 463	20 158	19 571	17 863	MKDJ	15 016	14 510	13 813	11 583	10 846
Scotland[3]	JZKY	3 081	3 170	2 752	2 878	3 356	2 329	MKDK	1 829	1 409	1 708	1 480	1 377
Northern Ireland	JZKZ	..	..	..	2 087	1 826	1 644	MKDL	1 546	1 510	1 551	1 227	1 174
By category in England and Wales													
Category 1	MKCW	331	229	199	156	194	128	MKDM	118	82	94	114	99
Category 2	MKCX	6 768	6 567	2 194	1 510	1 354	1 238	MKDN	860	784	685	594	562
Category 3	MKCY	18 200	18 619	21 070	18 492	18 023	16 497	MKDO	14 038	13 644	13 034	10 875	10 185
Category 4[2,4]	MKCZ	..	..	..	..	..	..	MKDP	18 706	15 370	15 813	13 613	12 658
Total substantiated incidents[4]	MKDA	25 299	25 415	23 463	20 158	19 571	17 863	MKDQ	33 722	29 880	29 626	25 196	23 504

1 See chapter text. Substantiated incidents to water, unless otherwise specified.
2 From 1999, categories 1-3 do not include all substantiated incidents to water. An additional category (Category 4) was introduced which includes all incidents which were substantiated, but which had no impact on the water environment. Therefore, data are not comparable to previous years.

3 Data for all years refer to financial years.
4 Category 4 and Total substantiated incidents include incidents to other media (air, land), which did not involve the water environment.

Sources: Environment Agency;
Scottish Environment Protection Agency;
Environment and Heritage Service

13.14
Bathing water:[1] by region
United Kingdom

Numbers and percentages

Compliance with EC Bathing Water Directive coliform standards during the bathing season

		Identified bathing waters (numbers)						Numbers complying						Percentage complying
		2002	2003	2004	2005	2006		2002	2003	2004	2005	2006		2006
Coastal bathing waters														
Environment Agency Regions														
United Kingdom	GPKA	547	554	556	559	561	GPKN	535	545	543	550	559	GPLA	100
North East	GPKB	56	55	55	55	55	GPKO	55	53	53	53	54	GPLB	98
North West	GPKC	34	34	34	34	33	GPKP	33	33	33	32	33	GPLC	100
Anglian	GPKE	38	38	38	39	39	GPKR	38	38	38	39	39	GPLE	100
Thames	GPKF	5	8	8	8	8	GPKS	5	8	8	8	8	GPLF	100
Southern	GPKG	79	79	79	79	78	GPKT	78	79	78	79	78	GPLG	100
South West	GPKH	186	188	190	190	191	GPKU	183	186	187	189	191	GPLH	100
England	GPKI	398	402	404	405	404	GPKV	392	397	397	400	403	GPLI	100
Wales	GPKJ	75	78	78	80	80	GPKW	75	77	78	80	79	GPLJ	99
Scotland	GPKL	58	58	58	58	61	GPKY	53	55	54	55	61	GPLL	100
Northern Ireland	GPKM	16	16	16	16	16	GPKZ	15	16	14	15	16	GPLM	100
Inland bathing waters														
United Kingdom	JTIG	11	11	11	11	11	JTIH	11	11	11	11	10	JTII	91

1 See chapter text.

Sources: Environment Agency;
Scottish Environment Protection Agency;
Environment and Heritage Service, Northern Ireland

13.15
Estimated abstractions from all surface and groundwater sources: by purpose[1]
England and Wales

Megalitres per day

		1994	1995	1996	1997	1998	1999	2000	2001	2002	2003	2004
Public water supply	JZLA	16 735	17 346	17 453	16 820	16 765	16 255	16 990	16 231	16 938	16 920	17 210
Spray irrigation	JZLB	283	352	369	292	282	325	291	259	248	315	225
Agriculture (excl spray irrigation)	JZLC	115	103	136	108	111	142	152	108	120	132	122
Electricity supply industry[2]	JZLD	27 732	29 510	31 294	33 307	34 587	29 490	31 546	32 263	35 447	31 378	30 568
Other industry[3]	JZLE	4 292	3 808	4 960	4 352	4 964	5 428	5 433	4 772	4 883	6 623	6 585
Mineral washing	JZLF	222	262	250	297	223	..	..	..	..	..	..
Fish farming, cress growing, amenity ponds	JYXG	3 985	4 268	4 338	4 211	5 495	4 867	4 709	4 657	3 215	3 077	4 068
Private water supply	JZLG	82	98	171	162	175	91	102	92	54	61	30
Other	JZLH	194	223	531	408	289	526	559	108	77	86	77
Total	JZLI	53 640	55 970	59 503	59 957	62 891	57 123	59 782	58 489	60 981	58 593	58 885

1 See chapter text.
2 Increased electricity supply abstraction from 2002 due to increased production from power station in Anglian Region and two new licences issued in Southern Region.

3 Three abstraction licences re-assigned to other industry from electricty supply in Midlands Region (2003).

Source: Environment Agency

13.16 Radioactive waste stocks and arisings[1,2,3]
Great Britain

Stocks in cubic metres

		1986	1987	1988	1989	1991	1994	1998	2001	2004
High level waste										
As stored	JTCG	1 350	1 430	1 460	1 580	1 690	1 640	1 800	1 960	1 890
Sellafield	JTBE	1 200	1 250	1 250	1 320	1 420	1 480	1 580	1 770	1 890
Dounreay[4]	JTBF	150	180	210	260	270	160	230	200	–
Intermediate level waste										
As stored	JTCI	41 890	43 600	47 780	45 310	51 560	61 490	70 950	75 300	82 460
Sellafield	JTBI	28 200	29 000	32 900	30 500	33 100	40 000	47 620	51 910	57 520
Dounreay	JTBJ	1 620	1 740	1 810	1 900	2 280	3 320	3 640	3 560	3 770
Other BNFL sites[5]	JTBK	80	80	70	70	90	60	60	60	80
Other UKAEA[6]	JTBL	2 340	2 620	2 680	2 630	3 000	3 120	3 370	2 810	3 010
Power stations[7]	JTBM	9 520	9 780	9 920	9 820	10 760	11 940	12 580	12 620	13 410
GE Healthcare	JTBN	130	380	400	390	380	290	290	360	450
URENCO[8]	JTBO	–	–	–	–	–	30	–	–	–
Ministry of Defence	JTBP	..	..	..	..	1 950	2 750	3 390	4 090	4 210
Low level waste										
As stored	JTCK	2 430	2 340	1 000	13 750	6 250	7 880	7 980	14 580	20 850
Sellafield	JTBY	120	540	520	600	420	1 630	1 910	1 580	4 000
Dounreay	JTBZ	–	–	–	12 000	2 690	–	1 090	5 640	5 890
Other BNFL sites[5]	JTCA	830	670	150	260	1 040	2 830	2 050	3 470	5 010
Other UKAEA[6]	JTCB	810	830	90	230	390	560	230	490	1 750
Power stations[7]	JTCC	670	300	240	660	450	780	940	1 680	1 930
GE Healthcare	JTCD	–	–	–	–	60	10	–	–	50
URENCO[8]	JTCE	–	–	–	–	–	–	80	70	20
Ministry of Defence	JTCF	..	..	..	..	1 200	2 080	1 700	1 650	2 200

1 See chapter text.
2 Up to 1991 as at 1st January and from 1994 as at 1st April.
3 Excludes waste from defence establishments before 1991.
4 The fall between 1991 and 1994 is due to increased evaporation of liquid waste and its planned vitrification. Since the 2004 Inventory Dounreay has not declared any waste as HLW, this decision was taken following a Public consultation exercise.
5 Includes Calder Hall, Chapelcross, Capenhurst and Springfields.
6 UKAEA (United Kingdom Atomic Energy Authority) includes wastes from minor producers. Some of this is stored at Harwell, while low level waste suitable for disposal goes to Drigg.
7 Includes all BNFL Magnox stations (except Calder Hall and Chapelcross), British Energy power stations and Berkeley Centre.
8 In 1993, BNFL's enrichment business at Capenhurst was transferred to the newly formed URENCO (Capenhurst) Ltd.

Sources: Poyry for;
Department for Environment, Food and Rural Affairs 020 7082 8608

13.17 Estimated total annual waste arisings: by sector
United Kingdom

Million tonnes

| Sector | | Status[2] | \multicolumn{5}{c}{Annual arisings} | | Percentage of total arisings |
			2000	2001	2002	2003	2004		2002[1]
Agriculture[3]	JSNA	C	..	..	..	0.4	0.4	JSNP	–
Minerals (Mining and quarrying)[4]									
colliery	JSNB	NC	9	9	8	8	6	JSNU	2
coal	JSNC	NC	7	7	7	6	6	JSNV	2
china clay	JSND	NC	21	20	19	19	18	JSNW	6
clay	JSNE	NC	13	12	12	12	13	JSNX	4
slate	JSNF	NC	10	11	15	18	20	JSNY	5
quarrying	JSNG	NC	36	37	34	34	33	JSNZ	10
Sewage sludge[5,6]	JSNH	C	..	..	1	1	1	JSOA	–
Dredged material[7]	JSNI	C	..	..	17	..	16	JSOB	5
Municipal waste[8]	JSNJ	C	34	35	36	35	36	JSOC	..
of which household	JSNK	C	30	31	31	31	31	JSOD	9
Commercial[9]	JSNL	C	..	..	35	..	..	JSOE	11
Industrial[9]	JSNM	C	..	..	45	..	..	JSOF	14
Demolition and construction[10]	JSNN	C	..	105	..	109	..	JSOG	33
Total (latest available year)	JSNO	C	..	..	333	..	..	JSOH	100

1 2003 figures used if 2002 not available.
2 NC = Not classed as a controlled waste under the terms of the Environmental Protection Act (Controlled Waste Regulations) 1992. C = controlled wastes under the terms of the Environmental Protection Act (Controlled Waste Regulations) 1992.
3 Estimate is for United Kingdom, derived from a survey of agricultural waste commissioned by Environmental Agency/Defra. Agricultural waste is currently excluded from national waste legislation but new regulations were introduced from September 2005 to introduce similar controls that already exist for other forms of waste under the Waste Framework Directive.

4 Minerals waste is not subject to control by the EU Waste Framework Directive.
5 Dry weight arisings.
6 Water UK (formerly Water Services Association and Water Companies Association).
7 The data are for all UK waters.
8 UK estimates based on survey returns made by local authorities in England, Wales, Scotland and Northern Ireland.
9 Estimates from EA survey based on England and Wales.
10 Estimates from DCLG/EA survey based on England and Wales.

Sources: Department for Environment, Food and Rural Affairs 020 7082 8608;
Environment Agency;
Water UK

13.18 Recycling[1] of selected materials
United Kingdom

Scrap reused as a percentage of consumption

		1993	1994	1995	1996	1997	1998	1999[2]	2000	2001	2002	2003
Aluminium packaging	C4VH	..	..	..	..	..	..	..	..	24	25	26
Copper	JYWS	35	32	34	36	37	38	47	45	46	..	..
Ferrous	JYWQ	42	42	40	44	45	35	35	34	31	29	33
Glass	JYWW	22	22	22	22	21	22	27	33	34	34	35
Lead	JYWT	67	74	71	73	69	66	64	67	64	60	60
Paper and board	JYWV	32	34	37	38	38	38	38	38	37	38	38
Plastics	C22N	2	3	3	3	3	3	5	6	6	8	10
Waste paper used in newsprint	C22O	31	33	35	44	47	52	55	60	64	65	68
Zinc	JYWU	21	20	20	19	19	18	18	17	16	14	..

1 The ratios shown reflect the amount of secondary material used (scrap collected less exported scrap plus imported scrap) in the UK in a year as a proportion of consumption in that year.
2 Ferrous recycling level for 1999 is estimated.

Sources: Department for Environment, Food and Rural Affairs 020 7082 8608;
Alupro;
World Bureau of Metal Statistics;
HM Revenue & Customs;
Corus;
British Glass Manufacturers Confederation;
Environment Agency;
British Paper & Board Industry Federation;
British Plastics Federation;
The Paper Federation of Great Britain

13.19 Noise complaints received by Environmental Health Officers[1]
England and Wales

Number per million people

		1998/99	1999/00	2000/01	2001/02	2002/03	2003/04	2004/05
Not controlled by the Environmental Protection Act 1990:								
Road traffic	JZLJ	39	38	44	37	36	32	..
Aircraft	JZLK	109	121	26	101	104	120	..
Railway	JTHH	14	17	16	12	18	21	..
Total	JUZR	162	176	86	150	158	173	..
Controlled by the Environmental Protection Act 1990:								
Industrial/commercial premises	JZLN	1 280	1 368	1 381	1 273	1 315	1 480	1 260
Industrial	EAC3	..	..	..	..	301	284	219
Commercial/leisure[2]	EAC4	..	..	..	..	1 014	1 196	1 041
Construction/Demolition sites	SNLE	248	292	325	347	325	335	343
Domestic premises	JZLP	4 330	5 149	5 001	5 540	5 573	5 973	5 903
Vehicles, machinery and equipment in streets	JZLQ	252	269	365	372	377	346	330
Miscellaneous[3]	EAC2	..	..	..	..	..	..	433
Total	JZLR	6 110	7 078	7 072	7 532	7 590	8 134	8 269

1 See chapter text.
2 Includes railway noise and airports (non aircraft).
3 From 2004/05 includes 'traffic' which consists of commercial vehicles, cars
  motorbikes, fixed-wing aircraft in flight and helicopters in flight.

Source: The Chartered Institute of Environmental Health

13.20 Material flows[1]
United Kingdom

Million tonnes

		1970	1975	1980	1985	1990	1995	2000	2001	2002	2003	2004	2005
Domestic extraction													
Biomass													
Agricultural harvest	JKUN	42	38	47	47	46	47	51	45	51	48	48	47
Timber	JKUO	3	3	4	5	6	8	8	8	8	8	8	8
Animal grazing	JKUP	49	49	49	48	47	45	43	43	43	43	43	43
Fish	JKUQ	1	1	1	1	1	1	1	1	1	1	1	1
Total	JKUR	96	92	101	100	101	100	102	97	102	100	101	99
Minerals													
Ores	JKUS	12	5	1	1	–	–	–	–	–	–	–	–
Clay	JKUT	38	33	25	23	21	18	15	14	14	14	15	13
Other industrial minerals	JKUU	14	11	11	11	11	10	8	9	8	9	8	8
Sand and gravel	JKUV	122	131	110	112	128	106	106	105	98	95	102	100
Crushed stone	JKUW	156	169	150	160	212	200	176	183	173	170	175	169
Total	JKUX	342	349	298	307	373	334	305	311	293	288	300	291
Fossil fuels													
Coal	JKUY	149	129	130	94	94	53	31	32	30	28	25	21
Natural gas	JKUZ	11	37	39	37	43	71	111	109	106	106	96	88
Crude oil	JKVA	–	2	80	128	92	130	126	117	116	106	95	85
Total	JKVB	161	168	249	259	229	254	268	257	252	240	217	193
Total domestic extraction	JKVC	598	608	648	666	702	688	676	665	648	628	618	583
Imports													
Biomass	JKVD	38	33	30	31	38	40	42	46	47	49	50	50
Minerals	JKVE	30	32	24	34	41	50	51	54	55	55	60	58
Fossil fuels	JKVF	123	111	74	76	89	73	83	99	95	102	127	137
Other products	JKVG	6	7	14	15	19	23	34	34	32	34	36	35
Total	JKVH	197	184	141	157	187	188	210	232	228	240	273	280
Exports													
Biomass	JKVI	3	5	8	11	13	15	17	13	15	19	18	19
Minerals	JKVJ	17	20	26	22	25	39	44	43	42	44	48	48
Fossil fuels	JKVK	23	19	60	102	67	103	115	118	120	104	98	88
Other products	JKVL	5	7	8	11	12	17	21	21	20	21	21	21
Total	JKVM	47	51	101	146	117	173	198	194	197	189	185	177
Indirect flows													
From domestic extraction,[2] excluding soil erosion	JKVN	576	575	633	627	693	634	567	573	564	549	547	518
Of which:													
Unused biomass	JKVO	25	23	32	35	37	37	40	35	40	38	39	37
Fossil fuels	JKVP	169	202	287	274	309	276	231	241	225	209	204	178
Minerals and ores	JKVQ	185	155	120	120	144	116	97	95	101	100	104	101
Soil excavation and dredging	JKVR	197	195	195	199	203	204	199	202	199	202	201	203
From production of imports	JKVS	394	395	368	423	457	527	614	711	648	671	692	752
Summary aggregates													
Physical Trade Balance (export - imports)[3]	F8YL	−150	−133	−40	−11	−70	−14	−13	−38	−32	−52	−88	−103
Direct material input (Domestic extraction + imports)	JKVT	796	792	789	822	889	876	886	898	876	869	891	864
Domestic material consumption (Domestic extraction + imports - exports)	JKVU	748	741	688	677	772	703	689	704	679	680	706	686
of which													
Biomass	G9A8	131	119	123	120	125	126	127	130	134	130	133	130
Minerals	G9A9	355	361	296	319	389	346	312	322	307	298	312	300
Fossil fuels	G9AA	261	260	263	233	250	224	236	238	227	239	246	242
Total material requirement (Direct material input + indirect flows)	JKVV	1 765	1 762	1 790	1 872	2 039	2 036	2 067	2 182	2 089	2 089	2 130	2 134

1 See chapter text. Components may not sum to totals due to rounding.
2 Indirect flows from domestic extraction relate to unused material which is moved during extraction, such as overburden from mining and quarrying.
3 A negative physical trade balance indicates a net import of material into the UK.

Source: Office for National Statistics: 020 7533 5904

13.21 Designated areas:[1] by region, 2005[2]

	National Parks		Areas of Outstanding Natural Beauty[3]		Green Belt Land		Defined Heritage Coasts length (km)
	Area (thousand hectares)	*Percentage of total area in region*	Area (thousand hectares)	*Percentage of total area in region*	Area (thousand hectares)	*Percentage of total area in region*	
United Kingdom	2 026	*8*	3 406	*14*	2 032	*8*	1 568
North East	111	*13*	146	*17*	53	*6*	138
North West	262	*18*	157	*11*	252	*18*	6
Yorkshire and the Humber	315	*20*	92	*6*	264	*17*	80
East Midlands	89	*6*	52	*3*	80	*5*	-
West Midlands	20	*2*	128	*10*	267	*21*	..
East	30	*2*	112	*6*	237	*12*	121
London	-	*-*	..	*..*	36	*22*	..
South East	54	*3*	636	*33*	356	*19*	74
South West	167	*7*	712	*29*	106	*4*	638
England	1 048	*8*	2 035	*15*	1 650	*13*	1 057
Wales	410	*20*	84	*4*	..	*..*	511
Scotland	568	*9*	1 002	*13*	155	*2*	..
Northern Ireland	-	*-*	285	*20*	227	*16*	..

1 See chapter text.
2 At March 2005, except for Green Belt land which relates to 1 January 1997.
3 National Scenic Area in Scotland. The South East includes London.

Source: Department for Environment, Food and Rural Affairs 020 7082 8608

Housing

Chapter 14

Housing

Permanent dwellings

(Table 14.1, 14.3)

Local housing authorities include the Commission for the New Towns and New Towns Development Corporations, Communities Scotland and the Northern Ireland Housing Executive. The figures shown for housing associations include dwellings provided by housing associations other than the Communities Scotland and the Northern Ireland Housing Executive and provided or authorised by government departments for the families of police, prison staff, the Armed Forces and certain other services.

Households in Temporary Accommodation under homelessness provisions

(Table 14.9)

Comprises households in accommodation arranged by local authorities pending enquiries or after being accepted as owed a main homeless duty under the 1996 Act (includes residual cases awaiting re-housing under the 1985 Act). Excludes "homeless at home" cases.

14.1 Stock of dwellings:[1] by tenure and country

Thousands

		1995	1996	1997	1998	1999	2000	2001	2002	2003	2004	2005
England												
Owner occupied	JUTY	13 700	13 865	14 041	14 237	14 433	14 635	14 818	14 956	15 110	15 261	15 352
Rented	JUUC	6 606	6 603	6 582	6 541	6 495	6 440	6 388	6 381	6 371	6 375	6 452
Local Authority	JUTZ	3 565	3 470	3 401	3 309	3 178	3 012	2 812	2 706	2 457	2 335	2 166
Privately	JUUA	2 184	2 191	2 196	2 192	2 171	2 155	2 152	2 208	2 293	2 375	2 469
Registered Social Landlords	JUUB	857	942	985	1 040	1 146	1 273	1 424	1 467	1 621	1 665	1 817
All dwellings	JUUD	20 305	20 468	20 622	20 778	20 927	21 075	21 207	21 337	21 481	21 636	21 804
Wales												
Owner occupied	JUUE	870	878	885	894	902	911	920	930	942	955	967
Rented	JUUI	354	355	357	357	357	356	354	352	347	341	338
Local Authority	JUUF	210	207	204	201	197	193	188	183	177	162	158
Privately	JUUG	102	104	105	106	108	109	111	112	113	115	115
Registered Social Landlords	JUUH	42	45	48	50	52	54	55	57	57	64	65
All dwellings	JUUJ	1 224	1 233	1 243	1 251	1 259	1 267	1 274	1 282	1 289	1 297	1 306
Scotland												
Owner occupied	JUUK	1 293	1 327	1 366	1 400	1 435	1 472	1 468	1 496	1 548	1 580	1 614
Rented	JUUO	938	921	899	883	869	849	855	847	814	805	793
Local Authority	JUUL	692	668	630	608	583	557	535	514	388	377	363
Privately	JUUM	155	154	154	154	155	155	176	175	177	178	178
Registered Social Landlords	JUUN	91	99	115	121	131	137	144	158	249	250	252
All dwellings	JUUP	2 230	2 248	2 266	2 283	2 303	2 322	2 323	2 343	2 363	2 385	2 407
Northern Ireland[2]												
Owner occupied	JUUQ	409	422	434	446	455	489	–	491	507	525	503
Rented	JUUU	188	186	183	180	180	184	–	172	166	154	192
Local Authority	JUUR	152	148	142	137	131	130	–	117	109	95	102
Privately	JUUS	22	23	26	27	32	34	–	34	35	37	68
Registered Social Landlords	JUUT	14	15	15	16	17	20	–	21	22	22	22
All dwellings	JUUV	597	608	618	626	636	674	–	663	673	679	695
United Kingdom[3]												
Owner occupied	JUVY	16 272	16 492	16 726	16 977	17 225	17 507	17 206	17 873	18 107	18 321	18 436
Rented	JUWC	8 086	8 065	8 021	7 961	7 901	7 829	7 597	7 752	7 698	7 675	7 775
Local Authority	JUVZ	4 619	4 493	4 377	4 255	4 089	3 892	3 535	3 520	3 131	2 969	2 789
Privately	JUWA	2 463	2 472	2 481	2 479	2 466	2 453	2 439	2 529	2 618	2 705	2 830
Registered Social Landlords	JUWB	1 004	1 101	1 163	1 227	1 346	1 484	1 623	1 703	1 949	2 001	2 156
All dwellings	JUWD	24 356	24 557	24 749	24 938	25 125	25 338	24 804	25 625	25 806	25 997	26 212

1 At 31 March for England and Wales and at 31 December for Scotland. At 31 March for Northern Ireland, but data prior to 2002 are at 31 December.
2 To include estimates for vacants in the tenure figures the total dwelling stock figures in Northern Ireland have been apportioned according to the % of occupied dwellings.
3 Calculated from data for England, Wales and Northern Ireland for the current year with Scotland data for the previous year, except for 2001 and earlier where Northern Ireland data for the previous year are used.

Sources: Communities and Local Government;
Welsh Assembly Government;
Scottish Executive;
Department for Social Development (Northern Ireland)

14.2 Type of accommodation by Tenure, 2005[1,2]
Great Britain

Weighted Percentages

	House or bungalow			Flat or maisonette		
	Detached	Semi-detached	Terraced	Purpose-built	Other[3]	All dwellings[4]
Owner-occupied						
Owned outright	34	35	21	7	2	100
Owned with mortgage	26	34	30	7	2	100
All owner-occupied	30	35	26	7	2	100
Rented from social sector						
Council[5]	1	26	28	42	2	100
Housing association	1	19	34	41	5	100
All rented from social sector	1	24	30	42	3	100
Rented privately[4]						
Furnished	5	14	30	30	20	100
Unfurnished[6]	14	20	33	18	15	100
All rented privately	11	19	32	22	16	100
All tenures	22	31	28	16	4	100

1 2005 data includes last quarter of 2004/05 data due to survey change from financial year to calendar year.
2 Data now at Household level to fall in-line with GHS survey.
3 Includes other type of accommodation, such as mobile homes.
4 Includes rent free accommodation. Tenants whose accommodation goes with the job of someone in the household who has been allocated to 'rented privately'. Squatters are also included.
5 Council includes local authorities and Scottish Homes.
6 Includes partly furnished.

Source: General Household Survey, Office for National Statistics

14.3 Permanent dwellings completed:[1] by tenure and country

Numbers

	United Kingdom				England and Wales			
	All dwellings	Local authorities[2]	Private enterprise	Registered Social Landlords[3]	All dwellings	Local authorities[2]	Private enterprise	Registered Social Landlords[3]
	KAAD	KAAE	KAAF	KAAG	KAAH	KAAI	KAAJ	KAAK
1980	242 017	88 534	131 989	21 494	214 934	78 539	116 179	20 216
1981	206 915	68 554	118 647	19 714	180 147	58 633	104 069	17 445
1982	181 894	40 091	128 088	13 715	159 407	33 544	113 893	11 970
1983	207 496	39 161	151 638	16 697	181 391	31 625	134 901	14 865
1984	220 414	37 573	165 555	17 286	191 112	31 338	145 263	14 511
1985	205 938	30 420	161 828	13 690	178 284	24 359	142 020	11 905
1986	214 471	25 377	175 905	13 189	187 710	20 496	156 056	11 158
1987	226 167	21 833	191 250	13 084	198 732	17 435	169 895	11 402
1988	242 233	21 448	207 423	13 362	214 156	16 921	185 733	11 502
1989	221 494	19 323	187 542	14 629	190 990	15 332	163 344	12 314
1990/91	198 060	16 550	162 182	19 328	171 031	13 425	141 166	16 440
1991/92	191 849	10 027	160 664	21 158	165 553	7 447	139 583	18 523
1992/93	178 872	4 433	144 367	30 072	152 452	2 706	123 045	26 701
1993/94	185 960	3 611	145 914	36 435	157 813	1 726	122 779	33 308
1994/95	197 169	2 970	156 547	37 652	168 301	997	133 002	34 302
1995/96	198 212	3 045	156 696	38 471	164 581	954	130 891	32 736
1996/97	185 654	1 538	153 165	30 951	156 334	474	128 682	27 178
1997/98	190 748	1 519	160 675	28 554	157 987	325	134 327	23 335
1998/99	178 700	865	154 968	22 867	148 445	207	128 084	20 154
1999/00	185 315	317	160 685	24 313	150 752	58	132 576	18 118
2000/01	156 957	291	134 916	21 750	141 851	226	124 293	17 332
2001/02	173 585	221	151 771	21 593	138 265	131	123 321	14 813
2002/03	183 061	390	162 796	19 875	146 287	205	132 217	13 865
2003/04	190 340	199	170 935	19 206	152 254	207	137 959	14 088
2004/05	205 327	116	182 821	22 390	164 385	131	147 118	17 136
2005/06	212 246	330	187 349	24 567	171 655	326	152 820	18 509

	Scotland				Northern Ireland			
	All dwellings	Local authorities[2]	Private enterprise	Registered Social Landlords[3]	All dwellings	Local authorities[2]	Private enterprise	Registered Social Landlords[3]
	BLFI	BAEZ	BLFK	BLFO	BLGI	BAFA	BLGK	BLGO
1979	23 782	4 755	15 175	3 852	7 312	3 507	3 574	231
1980	20 611	7 488	12 242	881	6 474	2 563	3 568	343
1981	20 011	7 062	11 021	1 928	6 757	3 082	3 557	118
1982	16 423	3 733	11 523	1 167	6 074	3 032	2 672	370
1983	17 929	3 492	13 166	1 271	8 176	4 093	3 571	512
1984	18 838	2 647	14 115	2 076	8 937	3 594	4 610	733
1985	18 411	2 828	14 435	1 148	8 697	3 235	4 837	625
1986	18 637	2 301	14 870	1 466	10 130	2 580	7 082	468
1987	17 707	2 634	13 904	1 169	9 669	1 764	7 451	454
1988	18 272	2 815	14 179	1 278	9 962	1 715	7 511	736
1989	20 190	2 283	16 287	1 620	10 304	1 708	7 911	685
1990/91	19 457	1 801	15 305	2 351	7 572	1 324	5 711	537
1991/92	18 956	1 619	15 528	1 809	7 340	961	5 553	826
1992/93	18 902	778	15 563	2 561	7 518	949	5 759	810
1993/94	20 985	997	17 407	2 581	7 162	888	5 728	546
1994/95	22 136	1 095	18 195	2 846	6 732	878	5 350	504
1995/96	24 381	729	18 955	4 697	9 250	1 362	6 850	1 038
1996/97	20 414	241	17 210	2 963	8 906	823	7 273	810
1997/98	22 580	114	17 977	4 489	10 181	1 080	8 371	730
1998/99	20 637	120	18 764	1 753	9 618	538	8 120	960
1999/00	24 209	69	19 037	5 103	10 349	190	9 067	1 092
2000/01	23 465	112	18 035	5 318	11 670	46	10 512	1 112
2001/02	23 610	65	18 066	5 479	13 487	29	12 072	1 386
2002/03	23 361	94	18 572	4 695	14 415	2	13 387	1 026
2003/04	23 662	–	19 935	3 727	14 511	–	13 951	560
2004/05	26 408	–	21 656	4 752	15 768	–	14 940	828
2005/06	24 482	–	19 380	5 102	17 410	–	16 628	782

1 See chapter text.
2 Including the Commission for the New Towns Development Corporations, Communities Scotland, the Northern Ireland Housing Executive.
3 Dwellings provided by housing associations other than Communities Scotland and the Northern Ireland Housing Trust and provided or authorised by government departments for families of police, prison staff, the armed forces and certain other services.

Sources: Communities and Local Government;
Scottish Executive;
Welsh Assembly Government;
Department for Social Development, Northern Ireland

14.4 Stock of dwellings: Estimated annual gains and losses
England

Thousands of dwellings

		1994 /95	1995 /96	1996 /97	1997 /98	1998 /99	1999 /00	2000[2] /01	2001 /02	2002 /03	2003 /04	2004 /05
Dwelling stock at start of financial year	GRWM	20 139	20 305	20 468	20 622	20 778	20 927	21 075	21 207	21 337	21 481	21 636
Gains to dwelling stock:												
Housebuilding completions	GRWN	158.0	154.6	146.2	149.6	138.6	141.4	133.1	129.8	137.7	143.6	154.5
Conversions (net gain)[1]	GRWO	9.9	8.9	8.6	2.8	4.2	3.5	2.8	..	..	..	..
Change of use	GRWP	..	..	..	11.6	15.9	13.9	10.1	..	..	..	..
Non-permanent dwellings additions	GRWQ	..	..	..	0.2	0.2	0.3	0.3	..	..	..	..
Losses from dwelling stock:												
Slum clearance (non LA owned dwelling demolished)	GRWR	3.0	2.7	2.9	1.3	1.3	1.4	1.7	..	..	..	..
Other demolitions[1]	GRWS	5.8	4.8	4.1	12.8	13.2	15.8	18.3	..	..	..	..
Change of use	GRWT	..	..	..	0.7	1.4	0.8	0.7	..	..	..	..
Non-permanent dwelling losses	GRWU	..	..	..	0.1	0.2	0.1	0.3	..	..	..	..
New gain in year	GRWV	159.0	156.0	147.8	149.3	143.0	140.9	125.3	130.5	143.7	154.8	167.9
Adjustment[3]	VQDN	6.6	6.6	6.6	6.6	6.6	6.6	6.6	..	..	..	..
Dwelling stock at end of financial year	GRWW	20 305	20 468	20 622	20 778	20 927	21 075	21 207	21 337	21 481	21 636	21 804

1 Figures prior to 1997/98 include change of use, and zero for net non-permanent dwellings.

2 Figures for 2000/01 conversions, change of use and non permanent dwellings are based on reported figures and do not include estimates for missing returns.

3 Series has been adjusted so that the 2000/01 estimates matches the 2001 Census.

Source: Communities and Local Government

14.5 Housebuilding completions: by number of bedrooms

Percentages

		1995 /96	1996 /97	1997 /98	1998 /99	1999 /00	2000 /01	2001 /02	2002 /03	2003 /04	2004 /05	2005 /06
England												
1 bedroom	JUWJ	11	8	7	7	7	7	7	6	8	10	10
2 bedrooms	JUWK	32	29	27	27	26	27	25	29	33	38	42
3 bedrooms	JUWL	35	36	38	36	35	34	31	30	29	29	27
4 or more bedrooms	JUWM	23	26	28	30	32	32	37	34	30	23	21
All houses and flats	JUWN	100	100	100	100	100	100	100	100	100	100	100
Wales												
1 bedroom	JUWO	8	5	4	3	5	5	4	6	6	7	9
2 bedrooms	JUWP	30	27	24	21	19	18	19	18	20	21	27
3 bedrooms	JUWQ	44	47	46	46	43	42	39	35	37	35	35
4 or more bedrooms	JUWR	18	21	26	31	34	34	38	41	37	37	30
All houses and flats	JUWS	100	100	100	100	100	100	100	100	100	100	100

Sources: Communities and Local Government;
Welsh Assembly Government

14.6 Mortgages
United Kingdom

		1995	1996	1997	1998	1999	2000	2001	2002	2003	2004	2005
Mortgages[1] (Thousands)	JUTH	10 512	10 637	10 738	10 821	10 982	11 173	11 270	11 364	11 452	11 512	11 596
Arrears and repossessions[1] (Thousands)												
Loans in arrears at end-period												
By 6-12 months	JUTI	127	101	74	74	57	48	41	34	29	27	35
By over 12 months	JUTJ	85	67	45	35	30	21	18	16	13	11	14
Properties repossessed in period	JUTK	49	43	33	34	30	23	17	12	8	6	10
Type of mortgage for house purchase[2] (Percentages)												
Standard repayment	JUTL	33.8	38.6	39.6	42.6	46.1	60.1	72.0	83.1	81.7	79.0	71.5
Endowment	JUTM	52.0	38.2	36.0	33.7	27.1	17.5	9.7	5.4	4.3	4.5	3.8
Other[3]	JUTN	14.2	23.2	24.4	23.7	26.8	22.5	18.3	11.4	14.0	16.5	24.7

1 Estimates cover only members of the Council of Mortgage Lenders; these account for 98 per cent of all mortgages outstanding.

2 Includes new mortgages advanced by building societies, banks and other major lenders. Includes sitting tenants.

3 Includes interest only, PEP/ISA and pension.

Source: Council of Mortgage Lenders

14.7 County Court mortgage possession actions:[1,2] by region

Thousands

		1996	1997	1998	1999	2000	2001	2002	2003	2004	2005	2006
Claims issued[3]												
England and Wales	JURS	79.8	67.0	84.8	82.6	73.0	67.4	61.7	67.0	77.9	115.4	131.7
North East	JURT	3.5	3.0	4.3	4.6	4.0	3.5	3.1	3.0	3.5	5.6	7.1
North West	JURU	12.6	10.9	14.2	13.8	12.4	12.4	10.7	10.2	10.7	15.3	19.3
Yorkshire and the Humber	JURV	7.6	6.9	8.2	8.7	7.8	7.2	6.2	6.0	6.6	10.2	12.0
East Midlands	JURW	5.9	4.9	6.4	6.8	5.7	5.3	4.7	4.9	5.8	8.7	10.2
West Midlands	JURX	7.6	6.7	8.1	9.5	9.8	7.8	6.3	7.4	8.6	12.2	14.8
East	JURY	8.3	6.7	8.5	7.3	6.2	5.7	5.4	6.4	7.9	11.3	12.1
London	JURZ	11.4	9.2	11.4	10.0	8.1	7.7	8.7	10.7	13.5	21.2	21.9
South East	JUSA	11.6	9.1	11.2	9.4	8.6	8.6	8.0	9.5	11.5	16.6	17.5
South West	JUSB	6.3	5.7	7.3	7.0	5.2	4.5	4.1	4.6	5.4	7.9	8.5
England	JUSC	74.9	63.1	79.6	77.1	67.7	62.7	57.1	62.6	73.7	108.8	123.4
Wales	JUSD	4.9	3.9	5.4	5.5	5.3	4.7	4.7	4.4	4.2	6.6	8.3
Northern Ireland[4]	JUSE	..	..	..	1.9	1.7	1.6	1.6	1.7	2.2	2.6	2.5
Suspended orders												
England and Wales	JUSF	43.4	34.6	40.8	37.1	31.7	29.1	23.5	23.9	26.1	37.7	44.5
North East	JUSG	2.0	1.6	2.3	2.5	1.9	1.7	1.2	1.2	1.2	1.8	2.6
North West	JUSH	7.6	5.5	6.4	6.0	5.7	5.5	4.5	3.9	3.7	5.0	6.7
Yorkshire and the Humber	JUSI	3.9	3.5	4.3	4.3	3.7	3.4	2.5	2.2	2.4	3.5	4.3
East Midlands	JUSJ	3.0	2.6	3.1	2.8	2.4	2.4	1.8	1.8	2.1	2.8	3.4
West Midlands	JUSK	3.9	3.4	3.8	4.1	3.7	3.6	2.5	2.8	3.1	4.2	5.2
East	JUSL	4.0	3.0	3.9	3.5	2.5	2.3	2.0	2.2	2.6	3.8	4.0
London	JUSM	6.4	4.7	5.3	4.5	3.1	2.7	2.7	3.2	3.9	6.4	6.9
South East	JUSN	6.6	5.4	5.8	4.4	3.9	3.4	2.9	3.2	3.8	5.4	5.9
South West	JUSO	3.3	2.7	3.0	2.8	2.3	1.9	1.7	1.6	1.8	2.7	2.9
England	JUSP	40.7	32.2	37.9	34.9	29.1	27.0	21.7	22.2	24.6	35.6	41.7
Wales	JUSQ	2.7	2.4	2.8	2.2	2.6	2.1	1.9	1.7	1.5	2.1	2.7
Northern Ireland[4]	JUSR	..	..	..	0.3	0.2	0.2	0.2	0.3	0.5	0.5	0.4
Orders made												
England and Wales	JUSS	27.8	22.5	25.3	23.6	20.4	18.7	16.2	16.7	20.3	33.1	46.7
North East	JUST	1.1	1.0	1.2	1.1	1.1	1.2	0.8	0.8	0.9	1.4	2.5
North West	JUSU	4.0	3.3	3.7	3.7	3.7	3.8	3.0	2.8	2.7	4.1	6.6
Yorkshire and the Humber	JUSV	2.6	2.3	3.1	3.0	2.4	2.3	1.7	1.6	1.7	2.9	4.2
East Midlands	JUSW	2.0	1.7	1.7	1.8	1.6	1.6	1.4	1.2	1.6	2.7	3.8
West Midlands	JUSX	2.1	2.0	2.4	2.3	2.3	2.2	1.7	1.8	2.2	3.4	5.1
East	JUSY	3.4	2.5	2.6	2.2	1.6	1.4	1.3	1.5	2.0	3.3	4.5
London	JUSZ	4.8	3.4	3.5	3.4	2.1	1.8	2.3	2.8	3.8	6.7	8.4
South East	JUTA	4.0	3.1	3.4	2.7	2.6	1.9	1.8	2.2	2.9	4.7	5.8
South West	JUTB	2.4	1.9	2.1	2.0	1.3	1.1	1.0	1.0	1.4	2.3	2.9
England	JUTC	26.4	21.2	23.7	22.2	18.7	17.3	15.0	15.6	19.2	31.3	43.9
Wales	JUTD	1.4	1.3	1.7	1.5	1.6	1.4	1.2	1.1	1.1	1.8	2.8
Northern Ireland[4]	JUTE	..	..	..	0.7	0.6	0.7	0.5	0.6	1.2	1.6	1.7

Note In 2001 the data extraction method changed. From 2001 the data are collected electronically from Caseman, the main administrative system in the county courts. Previously they were collected from Stats Module, a manual form completed monthly by all county courts.

1 Local authority and private.
2 County Court mortgage possession orders for Northern Ireland
3 Actions entered for Northern Ireland.
4 Mortgage possession actions are heard in Chancery Division of Northern Ireland High Court.

Sources: HM Court Service: 020 7210 1752;
Northern Ireland Court Service: 028 9032 8594

14.8 Sales and transfers of local authority dwellings
Great Britain

Thousands

		1995	1996	1997	1998	1999	2000	2001	2002	2003	2004	2005
Right to buy sales	JUQV	49.6	45.0	58.1	56.0	66.8	71.3	66.6	78.5	94.1	74.7	41.6
Large scale voluntary transfers[1]	JUQW	47.7	29.9	21.1	36.9	88.7	111.4	100.8	102.5	104.6	67.9	81.7
Other sales and transfers[2]	JUQX	3.2	3.0	3.4	2.7	3.3	2.4	1.6	1.4	0.6	0.5	0.3
Total sales and transfers	JUQY	100.5	77.9	82.6	95.5	158.8	185.2	168.9	182.4	199.4	143.1	123.6

1 Except for 2003 large scale and voluntary transfers are included in other sales and transfers for Wales.
2 Excludes new town and Scottish Homes sales and transfers.

Sources: Communities and Local Government;
Welsh Assembly Government;
Scottish Executive

14.9 Households in Temporary Accommodation[1]
Great Britain

As at 31st March of each year

Households

		1996 /97	1997 /98	1998 /99	1999 /00	2000 /01	2001 /02	2002 /03	2003 /04	2004 /05	2005 /06
Bed and breakfast hotels	JUWF	4 501	5 269	7 062	9 254	11 436	13 404	13 654	8 985	9 100	7 288
Hostels/women's refuges	JUWG	11 420	11 356	11 567	12 068	12 273	11 128	11 707	12 753	12 205	10 979
Social sector accommodation[2]	JXVN	11 409	16 077	20 686	23 510	27 826	30 310	31 719	31 821	31 295	27 758
Private sector accommodation and other[3]	JXVO	18 140	19 282	21 934	25 067	28 533	30 391	38 715	52 456	58 129	61 086
All accommodation[4]	JUWI	45 470	52 070	61 393	70 100	80 334	85 665	96 015	107 146	111 960	108 092

1 Households in temporary accommodation arranged by the local authority pending enquiries, or after being accepted as owed a main duty under homelessness legislation. Excludes 'homeless at home' cases who have remained in their existing accommodation after acceptance but have the same rights to suitable alternative housing as those in accommodation arranged directly by authorities.
2 Local authorities' and Registered Social Landlords' own stock.
3 Includes private sector properties leased by social sector landlords, households placed directly with a private sector landlord and other accommodation. From 2002 some self-contained B&B Annexe-style units, previously recorded under B&B have been more appropriately attributed to private sector accommodation.
4 Includes 'homeless at home' for Wales.

Sources: Communities and Local Government;
Welsh Assembly Government;
Scottish Executive

Transport and communication

Chapter 15

Transport and communication

Road data

(Tables 15.4, 15.5, 15.6 and 15.7)

The Department of Transport has undertaken significant development work over the last two years to improve its traffic estimates and measurement of traffic flow on particular stretches of the road network. This work has previously been outlined in a number of publications (Road Traffic Statistics: 2001 SB(02)23, Traffic in Great Britain Q4 2002 Data SB(03)5 and Traffic in Great Britain Q1 2003 SB(03)6).

The main point to note is that figures for 1993 to 2004 have been calculated on a different basis from years prior to 1993. Therefore, figures prior to 1993 are not directly comparable with estimates for later years. Estimates on the new basis for 1993 and subsequent years were first published by the Department on 8th May 2003 in Traffic in Great Britain Q1 2003 SB(03)6.

A summary of the main methodological changes to take place over the last couple of years appears below:

Traffic estimates are now disaggregated for roads in urban and rural areas rather than between built-up and non built-up roads. Built-up roads were defined as those with a speed limit of 40mph or lower. This created difficulties in producing meaningful disaggregated traffic estimates because an increasing number of clearly rural roads were subject to a 40mph speed limit for safety reasons. The urban/rural split of roads is largely determined by whether roads lie within the boundaries of urban areas with a population of 10,000 or more with adjustments in some cases for major roads at the boundary.

Traffic estimates are based on the results of many 12-hour manual counts in every year which are grossed up to estimates of annual average daily flows using expansion factors based on data from automatic traffic counters on similar roads. These averages are needed so that traffic in off-peak times, at weekends and in the summer and winter months (when only special counts are undertaken) can be taken into account when assessing the traffic at each site. For this purpose roads are now sorted into 22 groupings (previously there were only 7) and this allows a better match of manual count sites with our automatic count sites. These groupings are based on a detailed analyses of the results from all the individual automatic count sites and take into account regional groupings, road category (i.e. both the urban/rural classification of the road and the road class) and traffic flow levels. The groupings range from lightly-trafficked, rural minor roads in holiday areas such as Cornwall and Devon, to major roads in Central London.

With the increasing interest in sub-regional statistics, we have undertaken a detailed study of traffic counts on minor roads carried out in the last ten years. This has been done in conjunction with a Geographic Information System to enable us to establish general patterns of minor road traffic in each local authority. As a result of this, we have been able to produce more reliable estimate of traffic levels in each authority in our base year of 1999. This in turn has enabled us to produce better estimates of traffic levels back to 1993, as well as more reliable estimates for 1999 onwards.

The Department created a database for major roads based on a Geographic Information System and Ordnance Survey data. This was checked by local authorities and discussed with Government Regional Offices and the Highways Agency to ensure that good local knowledge supplemented the available technical data.

Road class

(Tables 15.5 and 15.6)

Urban major and minor roads, from 1993 onwards are defined as being within an urban area with a population of more than 10,000 people, these are based on the 2001 urban settlements. The definition for 'urban settlement' is 'Urban and rural area definitions: a user guide which can be found on the ODPM web site at: http://www.odpm.gov.uk/stellent/groups/odpm_planning/documents/page/odpm_plan_609188.hcsp.

Rural major and minor roads, from 1993 onwards, are defined as being outside an urban settlement.

New vehicle registrations

(Table 15.9)

Special concession group

Various revisions to the vehicle taxation system were introduced on 1 July 1995 and on 29 November 1995. Separate taxation classes for farmers' goods vehicles were abolished on 1 July 1995; after this date new vehicles of this type were registered as HGVs. The total includes 5,900 vehicles registered between 1 January and 30 June in the (now abolished) agricultural and special machines group in classes which were not eligible to register in the special concession group. The old agricultural and special machines taxation group was abolished at end June 1995. The group includes agricultural and mowing machines, snow ploughs and gritting vehicles. Electric vehicles are also included in this group and are no longer exempt from VED. Steam propelled vehicles were added to this group from November 1995.

Other licensed vehicles

Includes three wheelers, pedestrian controlled vehicles, general haulage and showmen's tractors and recovery vehicles. Recovery vehicle tax class introduced January 1988.

Special vehicles group

The special vehicles group was created on 1 July 1995 and consists of various vehicle types over 3.5 tonnes gross weight but not required to pay VED as heavy goods vehicles. The group includes mobile cranes, works trucks, digging machines, road rollers and vehicles previously taxed as showman's goods and haulage. Figure shown for 1995 covers period from 1 July to 31 December only.

National Travel Survey data

(Tables 15.1, 15.11)

The National Travel Survey (NTS) is designed to provide a databank of personal travel information for Great Britain. It has been conducted as a continuous survey since July 1988, following ad hoc surveys since the mid-1960s. The survey is designed to identify long-term trends and is not suitable for monitoring short-term trends.

For the first time, the 2005 NTS results were based on weighted data, and data from 1995 onwards have now been weighted. The weighting methodology adjusts for non-response bias and also adjusts for the drop-off in the number of trips recorded by respondents during the course of the travel week. All results now published for 1995 onwards are based on weighted data, and direct comparisons cannot be made to earlier years or previous publications.

During 2005, over 8,400 households provided details of their personal travel by filling in travel diaries over the course of a week. The drawn sample size from 2002 was nearly trebled compared with previous years following recommendations in a National Statistics Review of the NTS. This enables most results to be presented on a single year basis from 2002

Travel included in the NTS covers all trips by British residents within Great Britain for personal reasons, including travel in the course of work.

A trip is defined as a one-way course of travel having a single main purpose. It is the basic unit of personal travel defined in the survey. A round trip is split into two trips, with the first ending at a convenient point about half-way round as a notional stopping point for the outward destination and return origin. A stage is that portion of a trip defined by the use of a specific method of transport or of a specific ticket (a new stage being defined if either the mode or ticket changes). The main mode of a trip is that used for the longest stage of the trip. With stages of equal length the mode of the latest stage is used. Walks of less than 50 yards are excluded.

Travel details provided by respondents include trip purpose, method of travel, time of day and trip length. The households also provided personal information, such as their age, sex, working status, and driving licence holding, and details of the cars available for their use.

Because estimates made from a sample survey depend upon the particular sample chosen they generally differ from the true values of the population. This is not usually a problem when considering large samples (such as all car trips in Great Britain), but may give misleading information when considering data from small samples even after weighting.

The most recent editions of all NTS publications are available on the DfT website at www.dft.gov.uk/transtat/personaltravel. Bulletins of key results are published annually. The most recent bulletin is National Travel Survey: 2005.

Households with regular use of cars

(Table 15.12)

The mid-year estimates of the percentage of households with regular use of a car or van are based on combined unweighted data from the National Travel Survey (NTS), the Expenditure and Food Survey (EFS) (previously the Family Expenditure Survey) and the General Household Survey (GHS), where available. Data by area type are based on weighted data from the NTS only.

Continuing Survey of Road Goods Transport (CSRGT)

(Tables 15.3, 15.18, 15.19)

The estimates are derived from the Continuing Survey of Road Goods Transport (CSRGT) which in 2005 was based on an average weekly returned sample of some 330 heavy goods vehicles. The samples are drawn from the computerised vehicle licence records held by the Driver and Vehicle Licensing Agency

Transport and communication

(DVLA). Questionnaires are sent to the registered keepers of the sampled vehicles asking for a description of the vehicle and its activity during the survey week. The estimates are grossed to the vehicle population and at the overall national level have a two per cent margin of error (at 95 per cent confidence level). Further details and results are published in Road Freight Statistics 2005 and previously in Transport of Goods by Road in Great Britain.

Methodological changes

A key component of National Statistics outputs is a programme of quality reviews carried out at least every five years to ensure that such statistics are fit for purpose and that their quality and value continue to improve. A quality review of the Department for Transport's road freight surveys, including the CSRGT, was carried out in 2003. A copy of the report can be accessed at

http://www.statistics.gov.uk/nsbase/methods_quality/quality_review/downloads/NSQR30FinalReport.doc

The quality review made a number of recommendations about the CSRGT. The main methodological recommendation was that, to improve the accuracy of survey estimates, the sample strata should be amended to reflect current trends in vehicle type, weight and legislative groups. These new strata are described more fully in Appendix C of the survey report. For practical and administrative reasons, changes were also made to the sample selection methodology (see Appendix B of the report). These changes have resulted in figures from 2004 not being fully comparable with those for 2003 and earlier years. Detailed comparisons should therefore be made with caution.

Railways: permanent way and rolling stock

(Table 15.22)

1. Locomotives - locos owned by Northern Ireland Railways (NIR), does not include those from the Republic of Ireland Railway System (IE).

2. Diesel electric etc rail motor vehicles - powered passenger carrying vehicles, includes diesel electric (DE) power cars and all Construcciones y Auxiliar de Ferocarriles (CAF) vehicles. (But note only 16 of the CAF sets were delivered to NIR at the time).

3. Loco hauled coaches - NIR owned De Dietrich plus Gatwick but not including gen van.

4. Rail car trailers - 80 class and 450 class trailers. Not CAF, they are all powered.

5. Rolling stock for maintenance and repair - a 'stand alone' figure - may or may not be included in the above totals.

Anything listed as 'repair' or 'workshop' in the Motive Power Sheets is included. Also those CAF vehicles not yet delivered at the time.

6. The information is a 'snapshot' taken from the motive power sheets at end of March, together with any other known information.

Activity at civil aerodromes

(Table 15.28)

Figures exclude Channel Island airports. 'Other' covers local pleasure flights, scheduled service, positioning flights and non-transport charter flights for reward (for example: aerial survey work, crop dusting and delivery of empty aircraft) and 'Non-commercial' covers test and training flights, private, aeroclub, military and official flights, and Business Aviation etc.

Roll-on/roll-off Enquiry

(Table 15.30)

Statistics on the number of lorries and unaccompanied trailers travelling from Great Britain to mainland Europe and Ireland are compiled from quarterly returns provided by roll-on/roll-off ferry operators and Eurotunnel. (Unaccompanied trailers are not carried on the Eurotunnel freight service.) The results are broken down by country of vehicle registration, by country of disembarkation and by GB port group. Separate figures are given for powered vehicles and unaccompanied trailers. The statistics presented in Table 15.30 refer to vehicles travelling to mainland Europe only and exclude those to Ireland.

Powered vehicles comprise rigid vehicles, lorries with semi-trailers (articulated units) and lorries with drawbar trailers. (Some vehicles under 3.5 tonnes gross vehicle weight are also included.) Unaccompanied trailers are trailers and semi-trailers not accompanied on the ferry by a powered unit. Up to 1978 inward traffic was also recorded, but because it was similar to outward traffic the data requirement was discontinued to save respondent effort.

More detailed analyses are provided in the Department's quarterly publication Road Goods Vehicles Travelling to Mainland Europe, available on the Department's website.

Postal services and television licences

(Table 15.31)

Letters posted category includes printed papers, newspapers, postcards and sample packets. Where airmail includes letters without special charge for air transport. Business reply and freepost is now known as Response Services.

15.1 Trips per person per year: by sex, main mode[1] and trip purpose, 2005
Great Britain

Numbers

	Males					
	Car	Walk	Bus and coach	Rail[2]	Other[3]	All modes
Social/entertainment	159	47	11	5	13	236
Shopping	116	47	11	1	6	182
Other escort	84	8	1	-	1	94
Other personal business	70	24	6	1	4	105
Commuting	133	15	12	14	14	187
Education	22	30	10	1	6	70
Escort education	17	9	1	-	-	27
Business	41	4	1	2	2	49
Holiday/day trip	28	3	2	1	6	40
Other, including just walk	-	40	-	-	-	40
All purpose (=100%) (number)	671	228	55	27	51	1031
Base						
Unweighted Base(Trips)	117,445	41,608	8,982	3,976	8,688	180,699

	Females					
	Car	Walk	Bus and coach	Rail[2]	Other[3]	All modes
Social/entertainment	170	45	12	4	9	241
Shopping	145	54	23	2	5	230
Other escort	86	11	2	-	1	100
Other personal business	74	28	8	1	3	113
Communting	90	19	14	8	4	135
Education	20	27	9	2	4	62
Escort education	37	28	2	-	-	67
Business	20	3	1	1	1	26
Holiday/day trip	29	3	2	1	3	38
Other, including just walk	1	43	-	-	-	44
All purposes (numbers)	671	261	72	20	32	1056
Bases						
Unweighted Base(Trips)	124,689	51,635	13,096	3,188	6,008	198,616

	All persons					
	Car	Walk	Bus and coach	Rail[2]	Other[3]	All modes
Social/entertainment	165	46	12	5	11	239
Shopping	131	51	17	2	5	206
Other escort	85	10	2	-	1	97
Other personal business	72	26	7	1	4	109
Commuting	111	17	13	11	9	161
Education	21	29	10	2	5	66
Escort education	27	19	1	-	-	48
Business	30	3	1	2	2	37
Holiday/daytrip	29	3	2	1	4	39
Other, including just walk	1	41	-	-	-	42
All purposes (numbers)	671	245	64	23	41	1044
Bases						
Unweighted Base(Trips)	242,134	93,243	22,078	7,164	14,696	379,315

1 Main mode is that used for the longest part of the trip.
2 Includes London Underground.
3 Includes bicycles, two-wheeled motor vehicles, motorcaravans, taxis/ mini-cabs, domestic air travel and other private and public transport.

Source: National Travel Survey, Department for Transport 020 7944 3097

15.2 Retail Prices Index: transport components: 1995 - 2005
Great Britain

Indices (1995=100)

		Motor vehicles							Fares & other
	All items	Purchase	Maintenance	Petrol and oil	Tax and insurance	All motoring	Rail fares	Bus fares	travel costs
	ENX3	ENX4	ENX5	ZCFV	ENX6	ZCFW	ZCFX	ENX7	ENX8
1995	100.0	100.0	100.0	100.0	100.0	100.0	100.0	100.0	100.0
1996	102.4	103.3	104.5	105.0	96.7	103.0	103.7	103.7	103.0
1997	105.6	105.8	110.2	115.5	100.7	108.5	106.2	107.4	106.5
1998	109.3	104.6	114.7	121.2	109.5	111.9	110.5	111.0	108.8
1999	110.9	100.1	119.2	131.4	118.5	114.6	114.6	115.0	112.2
2000	114.2	94.8	124.2	148.7	131.1	119.0	116.5	119.6	115.9
2001	116.2	93.4	130.2	141.1	138.0	118.3	121.0	124.7	119.6
2002	118.2	91.5	137.0	136.7	140.1	117.4	123.8	128.5	123.0
2003	121.6	89.0	145.2	141.6	146.2	118.9	125.9	133.9	131.6
2004	125.2	86.2	154.0	149.5	146.9	120.1	130.7	140.7	136.2
2005	128.8	81.7	163.3	162.6	144.9	120.9	136.0	150.0	141.8

Source: Consumer Prices and Inflation Division, ONS: 020 7533 5874

15.3 Domestic freight transport: by mode
Great Britain

		1995	1996	1997	1998	1999	2000	2001	2002	2003	2004	2005
Goods moved (billion tonnes kilometres)												
Petroleum products												
Road[1]	ZBZP	5.7	6.1	5.8	5.2	5.0	6.4	5.8	5.2	5.5	5.7	5.5
Rail[2]	ZBZQ	1.8	..	..	1.6	1.5	1.4	1.2	1.2	1.2	1.2	1.3
Water[3]	ZBZR	42.5	45.9	38.3	45.2	48.6	52.7	43.5	51.7	46.9	46.9	47.2
of which: coastwise	ZBZS	31.4	38.7	33.8	36.4	33.3	26.0	23.1	24.2	23.3	26.6	30.3
Pipeline	ZBZT	11.1	11.6	11.2	11.7	11.6	11.4	11.5	10.9	10.5	10.7	10.8
All modes	ZBZU	61.1	63.6[4]	55.3[4]	63.7	66.7	71.9	62.0	69.0	64.1	64.5	64.8
Coal and coke												
Road[1]	ZBZV	2.7	2.5	2.7	2.0	2.2	1.5	2.1	1.5	1.5	1.2	1.5
Rail[2]	ZBZW	3.6	3.8	4.4	4.5	4.8	4.8	6.2	5.7	5.8	7.0	8.6
Water[3]	ZBZX	2.3	0.6	0.6	0.5	0.5	0.2	0.5	0.3	0.5	0.3	0.4
All modes	ZBZY	8.6	6.9	7.7	7.0	7.5	6.5	8.8	7.5	7.9	8.5	10.5
Other traffic												
Road[1]	ZBZZ	141.2	145.3	148.9	153.1	150.5	151.5	150.6	152.7	154.7	155.6	156.4
Rail[2]	ZCAA	7.9	11.3	12.5	11.2	11.9	11.9	12.0	11.7	11.9	12.4	12.3
Water[3]	ZCAB	8.3	8.7	9.2	11.2	9.6	14.6	14.8	15.2	13.5	12.3	13.3
All modes	ZCAC	157.4	165.3	170.6	175.5	172.0	178.0	177.4	179.6	180.0	180.3	182.0
All traffic												
Road[1,5]	KCTA	149.6	153.9	157.4	160.3	157.7	159.4	158.5	159.4	161.7	165.5	163.4
Rail[2]	KCTB	13.3	15.1	16.9	17.3	18.2	18.1	19.4	18.5	18.9	20.6	22.1
Water[3]	KCTAD	53.1	55.3	48.1	56.9	58.7	67.4	58.8	67.2	60.9	59.4	60.9
Pipeline	KCTE	11.1	11.6	11.2	11.7	11.6	11.4	11.5	10.9	10.5	10.7	10.8
All modes	KCTF	227.1	235.9	233.6	246.2	246.2	256.3	248.2	256.0	252.0	253.2	257.3
Percentage of all traffic												
Road[1]	ZCAE	66	65	67	65	64	62	64	62	64	64	64
Rail[2]	ZCAF	6	6	7	7	7	7	8	7	7	8	9
Water[3]	ZCAG	23	23	21	23	24	26	24	26	24	23	24
Pipeline	ZCAH	5	5	5	5	5	4	5	4	4	4	4
All modes	ZCAI	100	100	100	100	100	100	100	100	100	100	100
Goods lifted (million tonnes)												
Petroleum products												
Road[1]	ZCAJ	71	75	73	61	61	75	74	59	64	67	70
Rail[2]	ZCAK	6	..	..	..	..	..	..	..	..	..	..
Water[3]	ZCAL	72	71	69	76	72	72	60	67	64	63	66
of which: coastwise	ZCAM	47	54	52	55	52	40	34	36	35	38	42
Pipeline	ZCAN	168	157	148	153	155	151	151	146	141	158	168
All modes	ZCAO	317	303[4]	290[4]	290[4]	288[4]	298[4]	285[4]	272[4]	269[4]	288[4]	..
Coal and coke												
Road[1]	ZCAP	34	32	37	26	28	22	21	17	22	14	21
Rail[2,6]	ZCAQ	45	52	50	45	44	46	46	41	42	52	55
Water[3]	ZCAR	4	3	4	3	3	3	3	2	2	1	2
All modes	ZCAS	83	87	91	70	75	71	70	60	66	67	..
Other traffic												
Road[1]	ZCAT	1 596	1 623	1 630	1 640	1 575	1 596	1 587	1 658	1 667	1 782	1 777
Rail[2,6]	ZCAU	50	50	55	57	48	50	48	46	47	50	49
Water[3]	ZCAV	67	67	69	70	70	62	68	70	67	63	65
All modes	ZCAW	1 713	1 740	1 754	1 767	1 693	1 708	1 703	1 774	1 781	1 895	..
All traffic												
Road[1,5]	KCTG	1 701	1 730	1 740	1 727	1 664	1 693	1 682	1 734	1 753	1 863	1 868
Rail[2,6]	KCTH	101	102	105	102	92	95	94	87	89	102	104
Water[3]	ZCAX	143	142	142	149	144	137	131	139	133	127	133
Pipeline	KCTK	168	157	148	153	155	151	151	146	141	158	168
All modes	KCTL	2 113	2 131	2 135	2 131	2 055	2 076	2 058	2 106	2 116	2 250	..
Percentage of all traffic												
Road[1]	ZCAY	80	81	81	81	81	82	82	82	83	83	..
Rail[2]	ZCAZ	5	5	5	5	4	5	5	4	4	5	..
Water[3]	ZCBA	7	7	7	7	7	7	6	7	6	6	..
Pipeline	ZCBB	8	7	7	7	8	7	7	7	7	7	..
All modes	ZCBC	100	100	100	100	100	100	100	100	100	100	..

1 All goods vehicles, including those up to 3.5 tonnes gross vehicle weight.
2 Figures for rail are for financial years e.g 1995/96 etc
3 Figures for water are for UK traffic.
4 Excludes rail.
5 Figures for 2004 and 2005 are not fully comparable with those for 2003 and
earlier years. Detailed comparisons should therefore be made with caution.
6 Figures for 2004 are not fully comparable with those for 2003 and earlier
years. Detailed comparisons should therefore be made with caution.

Sources: Department for Transport;
Rail: 020 7944 4977;
Road & pipeline: 020 7944 4261;
Water: 020 7944 4131

15.4 Passenger transport:[1] by mode
Great Britain

		1995	1996	1997	1998	1999	2000	2001	2002	2003	2004	2005[4]
Billion passenger kilometres												
Road												
Buses and coaches	GRXK	43	43	44	45	46	47	47	47	47	48	48
Cars, vans and taxis	GRXG	618	622	632	636	642	640	654	677	673	678	678
Motor cycles	GRXH	4	4	4	4	5	5	5	5	6	6	6
Pedal cycles	GRXI	4	4	4	4	4	4	4	4	5	4	4
All road	GRXJ	669	674	685	689	697	695	710	733	731	736	735
Rail[2]	KCTN	37	39	42	44	46	47	47	48	49	50	52
Air	KCTM	6	6	7	7	7	8	8	9	9	10	10
All modes[3]	GRXM	712	719	733	740	751	749	765	790	789	796	797
Percentages												
Road												
Buses and coaches	GRXN	6	6	6	6	6	6	6	6	6	6	6
Cars, vans and taxis	GRXO	87	87	86	86	86	85	85	86	85	85	85
Motor cycles	GRXP	1	1	1	1	1	1	1	1	1	1	1
Pedal cycles	GRXQ	1	1	1	1	1	1	1	1	1	–	1
All road	GRXR	94	94	93	93	93	93	93	93	93	92	92
Rail[2]	ZCBJ	5	5	6	6	6	6	6	6	6	6	6
Air	ZCBK	1	1	1	1	1	1	1	1	1	1	1
All modes[3]	GRXU	100	100	100	100	100	100	100	100	100	100	100

1 See chapter text.
2 Financial years. National rail, urban metros & modern trams.
3 Excluding travel by water within the United Kingdom (including the Channel Islands), estimated at 0.7 billion passenger kilometres in 2000.
4 Data are provisional.

Sources: Department for Transport;
Bus & coach: 020 7944 3076;
Car, m/cycle & pedal cycle: 020 7944 3097;
Rail: 020 7944 3076;
Air: 020 7944 3088

15.5 Motor vehicle traffic[1]: by road class
Great Britain

Billion vehicle kilometres

		1995	1996	1997	1998	1999	2000[2]	2001[3]	2002	2003	2004	2005
Motorways	JSZV	73.9	78.3	82.1	85.7	87.8	88.4	90.8	92.6	93.0	96.6	97.0
Rural 'A' roads[4]												
Trunk[5]	JSZW	57.9	60.4	62.5	63.3	64.7	64.2	65.9	64.6	61.5	59.7	58.0
Principal[5]	JSZX	61.6	63.1	64.1	65.4	66.0	65.8	67.4	71.8	77.7	81.6	83.3
All rural 'A' roads	JSZY	119.5	123.5	126.6	128.7	130.7	130.0	133.3	136.4	139.3	141.3	141.3
Urban 'A' roads[6]												
Trunk[5]	JSZZ	13.8	13.9	13.8	13.8	14.0	14.0	7.6	7.4	6.7	6.0	5.5
Principal[5]	JTAA	66.2	67.0	67.1	67.5	67.9	67.7	74.2	74.8	75.1	76.8	76.2
All urban 'A' roads	JTAB	80.1	80.9	80.9	81.3	81.9	81.7	81.8	82.2	81.7	82.8	81.7
Minor roads												
Minor rural roads	JTAC	57.8	58.9	60.0	60.4	61.3	61.5	61.6	64.5	64.4	65.9	66.8
Minor urban roads	JTAD	98.5	99.6	100.7	102.4	105.3	105.5	106.9	110.8	111.9	112.0	112.5
All minor roads	JTAE	156.2	158.5	160.7	162.8	166.6	167.0	168.5	175.3	176.4	177.9	179.3
All roads	JTAF	429.7	441.1	450.3	458.5	467.0	467.1	474.4	486.5	490.4	498.6	499.4

1 See chapter text.
2 The decline in the use of cars and taxis in 2000 was due to the fuel dispute.
3 Figures affected by the impact of Foot and Mouth disease during 2001.
4 Rural roads; Major and minor roads, from 1993 onwards, are defined as being outside an urban area.
5 Figures for trunk and principal 'A' roads in England, from 2001 onwards, are affected by the detrunking programme.

6 Urban roads; Major and minor roads, from 1993 onwards, are defined as within an urban area with a population of 10,000 or more. These are based on the 2001 urban settlements.

Source: Department for Transport: 020 7944 3095

15.6
Public road length:[1] by road type
Great Britain

Kilometres

		1995	1996	1997	1998	1999	2000	2001	2002	2003	2004	2005
Trunk motorway	JSZD	3 197	3 253	3 333	3 376	3 404	3 422	3 431	3 433	3 432	3 478	3 466
Principal motorway	JSZE	72	45	45	44	45	45	45	45	46	46	54
Rural 'A' roads[2]:												
Trunk[3]	JSZF	10 510	10 598	10 690	10 585	10 611	10 627	10 607	9 973	9 027	8 641	8 239
Principal[3]	JSZG	24 759	24 592	24 636	24 783	24 852	24 866	24 915	25 559	26 498	26 889	27 312
All rural 'A' roads	JSZH	35 269	35 190	35 326	35 369	35 463	35 493	35 522	35 532	35 525	35 530	35 550
Urban 'A' roads[4]:												
Trunk[3]	JSZI	1 133	1 117	1 108	1 096	1 087	1 074	762	705	587	506	444
Principal[3]	JSZJ	9 902	9 885	9 923	9 931	10 019	10 040	10 370	10 436	10 539	10 632	10 663
All urban 'A' roads	JSZK	11 035	11 002	11 031	11 027	11 106	11 114	11 132	11 141	11 127	11 138	11 107
Minor rural roads[5]:												
B roads	JSZL	24 610	24 603	24 594	24 586	24 579	24 570	24 562	24 554	24 547	24 640	24 639
C roads	JSZM	73 124	73 218	73 312	73 405	73 500	73 593	73 688	73 783	73 878	73 363	73 581
Unclassified	JSZN	110 481	110 698	110 915	111 132	111 350	111 568	111 787	112 006	112 231	109 561	109 426
All minor rural roads	JSZO	208 215	208 518	208 820	209 123	209 429	209 731	210 037	210 343	210 656	207 565	207 646
Minor urban roads[5]:												
B roads	JSZP	5 611	5 615	5 618	5 622	5 626	5 630	5 633	5 638	5 641	5 538	5 550
C roads	JSZQ	10 922	10 943	10 966	10 986	11 009	11 031	11 054	11 076	11 098	10 859	10 878
Unclassified	JSZR	112 081	112 417	112 754	113 093	113 432	113 772	114 114	114 456	114 816	113 520	113 757
All minor urban roads	JSZS	128 614	128 975	129 338	129 702	130 068	130 432	130 802	131 169	131 556	129 917	130 186
All major roads	GG5B	49 572	49 490	49 735	49 816	50 018	50 074	50 130	50 152	50 130	50 192	50 176
All minor roads[5]	JSZT	336 828	337 494	338 158	338 825	339 496	340 163	340 838	341 512	342 212	337 482	337 832
All roads	JSZU	386 401	386 983	387 893	388 641	389 515	390 237	390 969	391 663	392 342	387 674	388 008

1 See chapter text. A number of minor revisions have been made to the lengths of major roads for all years.
2 Rural roads: Major and minor roads, from 1993 onwards, are defined as being outside an urban area.
3 Figures for trunk and principal 'A' roads in England, from 2001 onwards, are affected by the detrunking programme.

4 Urban roads: Major and minor roads, from 1993 onwards, are defined as within an urban area with a population of 10,000 or more. These are based on the 2001 urban settlements.
5 New information has enabled better estimates of minor road lengths to be made from 2004.

Sources: National Road Traffic Survey;
Department for Transport 020 7944 3095

15.7
Road traffic:[1] by type of vehicle
Great Britain

Billion vehicle kilometres

		1995	1996	1997	1998	1999	2000[2]	2001[3]	2002	2003	2004	2005
Cars and taxis	JTAH	351.1	359.9	365.8	370.6	377.4	376.8	382.8	392.9	393.1	398.1	397.2
Motor cycles etc.	JTAI	3.7	3.8	4.0	4.1	4.5	4.6	4.8	5.1	5.6	5.2	5.4
Larger buses and coaches	JTAJ	4.9	5.0	5.2	5.2	5.3	5.2	5.2	5.2	5.4	5.2	5.2
Light vans[4]	JTAK	44.5	46.2	48.6	50.8	51.6	52.3	53.7	55.0	57.9	60.8	62.6
Goods vehicles[5]:												
2 axles rigid	JTAL	10.7	10.9	11.0	11.1	11.6	11.7	11.5	11.6	11.7	11.7	11.5
3 axles rigid	JTAM	1.6	1.6	1.6	1.9	1.7	1.7	1.8	1.8	1.8	1.9	1.9
4 or more axles rigid	JTAN	1.5	1.5	1.5	1.6	1.5	1.5	1.5	1.5	1.6	1.6	1.7
3 and 4 axles artic	JTAO	3.3	3.3	3.2	3.0	3.0	2.7	2.5	2.3	2.2	2.2	2.0
5 axles artic	JTAP	6.4	6.6	7.1	7.3	7.2	6.7	6.4	6.4	6.2	6.5	6.4
6 or more axles artic	JTAQ	2.0	2.3	2.5	2.9	3.3	4.1	4.5	4.8	5.0	5.4	5.5
All	JTAR	25.4	26.2	26.9	27.7	28.1	28.2	28.1	28.3	28.5	29.4	29.0
All motor vehicles	JURA	429.7	441.1	450.3	458.5	467.0	467.1	474.4	486.5	490.4	498.6	499.4
Pedal cycles[6]	JURB	4.1	4.1	4.1	4.0	4.1	4.2	4.2	4.4	4.5	4.2	4.4

1 See chapter text.
2 The decline in the use of cars and taxis in 2000 was due to the fuel dispute.
3 Figures affected by the impact of Foot and Mouth disease during 2001.
4 Not exceeding 3,500 kgs gross vehicle weight.
5 Over 3,500 kgs gross vehicle weight.

6 Refinements to the minor roads pedal cycle methodology have been made; these improvements have resulted in revisions to 2004 and onwards pedal cycle estimates.

Sources: National Road Traffic Survey;
Department for Transport 020 7944 3095

15.8 Motor vehicles currently licenced
Great Britain
At end of year

Thousands

	Private and light goods										Body type cars	
	Private cars	Other vehicles	Motor cycles, scooters and mopeds	Public transport vehicles[1]	Goods vehicles	Special machines/ special conces- sionary	Other vehicles	Crown and exempt vehicles[3]	Special vehicles group	All vehicles[4]	All	Percent- age of company cars
	BMBJ	BMBK	BMBB	BMBE	BMBD	KSBY	BMBF	BMBL	KSBZ	BMBI	ZCGR	ZCGS
1995[2]	20 505	2 217	594	74	421	274	44	1 169	28	25 369	21 394	10.4
1996	21 172	2 267	609	77	413	254	40	1 424	48	26 302	22 238	10.3
1997	21 681	2 317	626	79	414	249	38	1 522	48	26 974	22 832	10.5
1998	22 115	2 362	684	80	412	243	37	1 558	47	27 538	23 293	10.4
1999	22 785	2 427	760	84	415	241	36	1 573	47	28 368	23 975	10.0
2000	23 196	2 469	825	86	418	233	34	1 590	46	28 898	24 406	10.3
2001	23 899	2 544	882	89	422	233	33	1 602	45	29 747	25 126	9.7
2002	24 543	2 622	941	92	425	243	32	1 855	46	30 557	25 782	9.0
2003	24 985	2 730	1 005	96	426	258	32	1 887	47	31 207	26 240	8.4
2004	25 754	2 900	1 060	100	434	–	32	1 929	50	32 259	27 028	8.5
2005	26 208	3 019	1 075	103	433	–	31	1 978	51	32 897	27 520	8.8

1 Taxation group now restricted to only vehicles with 9 or more seats.
2 The vehicle taxation system was subject to substantial revision from 1 July 1995.

3 Vehicles in this taxation class are exempt from duty and form part of the crown and exempt class with effect from January 2002.
4 Contains 44,000 vehicles still taxed in classes abolished from 1 July 1995.

Source: Department for Transport 020 7944 3077

15.9 New vehicle registrations by taxation class
Great Britain

Thousands

		1995	1996	1997	1998	1999	2000	2001	2002	2003	2004	2005
Total	BBKD	2 306.5	2 410.1	2 597.7	2 740.3	2 765.8	2 870.9	3 137.7	3 229.4	3 231.9	3 185.4	3 021.4
Private and light goods												
Private cars	BMAA	1 828.3	1 888.4	2 015.9	2 123.5	2 100.4	2 174.9	2 431.8	2 528.8	2 497.1	2 437.4	2 266.3
Other vehicles	BMAE	195.7	205.0	228.4	244.5	241.6	254.9	277.9	286.8	323.5	347.3	337.2
Total	BMAK	2 024.0	2 093.4	2 244.3	2 368.0	2 342.0	2 429.8	2 709.7	2 815.6	2 820.7	2 784.7	2 603.5
Motor cycles, etc:												
Up to 50 c.c.	KCUH	6.3	8.9	14.2	22.6	36.2	49.4	45.6	35.6	34.9	27.2	24.0
Other	KCUI	62.6	80.7	107.1	120.7	132.2	133.5	131.5	126.6	122.4	106.5	108.3
Total	BMAL	68.9	89.6	121.3	143.3	168.4	182.9	177.1	162.2	157.3	133.7	132.3
Public road passenger vehicles												
Buses, coaches, taxis, etc												
Not over 8 seats[1]	KCUJ	..	..	..	..	..	..	..	..	..	..	..
Over 8 seats	KCUK	5.2	6.5	6.6	7.4	8.0	7.5	6.8	7.8	8.4	8.3	8.9
Total	BBJZ	5.2	6.5	6.6	7.4	8.0	7.5	6.8	7.8	8.4	8.3	8.9
Heavy general goods and farmers[2]												
Goods vehicles: by weight	BBJY	48.0	45.5	41.8	49.1	48.3	50.4	48.6	44.9	48.4	48.0	51.2
Special concession group[3]	BBKA	33.3	25.7	21.7	15.2	17.3	16.9	19.8	23.1	24.1	25.0	23.4
Other licensed vehicles[4]	KCUM	1.0	1.0	1.5	1.4	1.5	1.2	1.2	1.3	1.2	0.7	0.9
Special vehicles group[5]	DMNR	3.3	8.1	8.6	7.6	7.6	6.5	7.0	7.2	8.1	7.6	8.0
Exempt from licence duty												
Crown vehicles	KCUN	3.3	1.2	0.7	1.1	1.1	1.0	1.0	1.4	1.4	1.4	1.3
All other exempt vehicles[2,6]	KCUO	118.1	139.1	150.7	146.6	170.4	173.9	166.5	166.1	162.1	175.8	191.7
Total	KCUP	121.4	140.3	151.4	147.7	171.6	174.9	167.5	167.5	163.5	177.2	193.1

1 From 1 July 1995 separate taxation of public transport vehicles with 8 or fewer seats was abolished. After this date new vehicles of this type were registered as PLG.
2 From 1st July 1995 separate taxation group for Farmers and Showman were abolished.
3 Various revisions to the vehicle taxation system were introduced on 1 July 1995 and on 29 November 1995. Separate taxation classes for farmers goods vehicles were abolished on 1 July 1995; after this date new vehicles of this type were registered as HGV's. The total includes 5,900 vehicles registered between 1 January and 30 June in the (now abolished) agricultural special machine group in classes which were not eligable to register in the special concession group. The old agricultural and special machines taxation group was abolished at end of June 1995. The group includes agricultural and mowing machines, snow ploughs and gritting

vehicles. Electric vehicles are also included in this group and are no longer exempt from VED. Steam propelled vehicles were added to this group from November 1995.
4 Includes three wheelers, pedestrian controlled vehicles, general haulage and showmen's tractors and recovery vehicles. Recovery vehicle tax class introduced January 1988.
5 The special vehicle group was created on 1 July 1995 and consists of various vehicle types over 3.5 tonnes gross weight but not required to pay VED as heavy goods vehicles. The group includes mobile cranes, works trucks, digging machines, road rollers and vehicles previously taxed as showman's goods and haulage. Figure shown for 1995 covers period from 1 July to 31 December only.
6 From 1 July 1995 electric vehicles pay VED as part of the special concession group.

Source: Department for Transport: 020 7944 3077

15.10
Driving test pass rates: by sex and type of vehicle licence
Great Britain

Percentages

		1989 /90	1991 /92	1998 /99	1999 /00	2000 /01	2001 /02	2002 /03	2003 /04	2004 /05	2005 /06
Males											
Motorcycle	JTRB	72	69	69	67	68	67	66	67	66	66
Car	JTRC	58	57	51	48	48	47	47	46	46	46
Bus	JTTG	–	–	48	49	47	46	44	46	43	44
Lorry	JTTH	–	–	52	53	53	50	50	49	47	45
All males	JTTI	–	–	–	51	51	50	49	48	47	47
Females											
Motorcycle	JTTJ	68	63	63	55	56	55	54	53	53	52
Car	JTTK	47	46	42	40	40	40	40	40	39	40
Bus	JTTL	–	–	47	46	45	40	40	45	46	47
Lorry	JTTM	–	–	50	49	53	47	46	48	45	44
All females	JTTN	–	–	–	40	41	41	40	40	40	40
All											
Motorcycle	JTTO	–	–	68	66	66	66	65	65	64	64
Car	JTTP	–	–	46	44	44	43	43	43	42	43
Bus	JTTQ	–	–	48	49	48	45	44	46	44	45
Lorry	JTTR	–	–	52	53	54	56	49	49	46	45
All persons	JTTS	–	–	–	46	46	46	45	44	43	44

Source: Driving Standards Agency - info.rsis@dsa.gov.uk

15.11
Full car driving licence holders by sex and age[1]
Great Britain

Percentages and millions

	All aged 17+	17-20	21-29	30-39	40-49	50-59	60-69	70 and over	Estimated number of licence holders (millions)
All adults									
1975/76	48	28	59	67	60	50	35	15	19.4
1985/86	57	33	63	74	71	60	47	27	24.3
1989/91	64	43	72	77	78	67	54	32	27.8
1992/94	67	48	75	82	79	72	57	33	29.3
1995/97[2]	69	43	74	81	81	75	63	38	30.3
1998/00	71	41	75	84	83	77	67	39	31.4
	GB9O	C98J	C98K	C98L	C98M	C98N	C98O	C98P	C98Q
2002	70	33	67	82	84	81	70	44	31.9
2003	70	29	67	82	83	80	72	44	32.1
2004	70	27	65	82	83	80	72	46	32.2
2005	72	32	66	82	84	82	74	51	33.3
Males									
1975/76	69	36	78	85	83	75	58	32	13.4
1985/86	74	37	73	86	87	81	72	51	15.1
1989/91	80	52	82	88	89	85	78	58	16.7
1992/94	81	54	83	91	88	88	81	59	17.0
1995/97[2]	81	50	80	88	89	89	83	65	17.2
1998/00	82	44	80	89	91	88	83	65	17.4
	GB9P	C98R	C98S	C98T	C98U	C98V	C98W	C98X	C98Y
2002	80	35	71	88	90	89	85	68	17.5
2003	81	33	73	87	90	91	87	69	17.8
2004	79	30	68	87	89	90	86	72	17.7
2005	81	37	69	86	90	90	88	73	18.1
Females									
1975/76	29	20	43	48	37	24	15	4	6.0
1985/86	41	29	54	62	56	41	24	11	9.2
1989/91	49	35	64	67	66	49	33	15	11.1
1992/94	54	42	68	73	70	57	37	16	12.2
1995/97[2]	57	36	67	74	73	62	45	21	13.1
1998/00	60	38	69	78	76	67	53	22	14.0
	GB9Q	C98Z	C992	C993	C994	C995	C996	C997	C998
2002	61	31	62	76	78	73	55	27	14.4
2003	61	25	62	77	77	70	58	26	14.3
2004	61	24	62	77	77	71	58	28	14.5
2005	63	27	62	77	79	73	61	35	15.2

1 See chapter text.
2 Figures for 1995 onwards are based on weighted data.

Source: National Travel Survey, DfT

15.12 Households with regular use of cars[1]
Great Britain

Percentages and millions

	No car	One car	Two cars	Three or more cars	Total (millions)
	ZCGA	ZCGB	ZCGC	ZCGD	ZCGE
1994	32	45	20	4	23.5
1995	30	45	21	4	23.7
1996	30	45	21	4	23.9
1997	30	45	21	5	24.1
1998	28	44	23	5	24.3
1999	28	44	22	5	24.5
2000	27	45	23	5	24.6
2001	26	45	23	5	24.8
2002	26	44	24	5	24.9
2003	26	44	25	5	24.1
2004	25	44	25	5	25.3

	No car	One car	Two or more cars	Total
Government Office Regions, 2004				
Great Britain	25	44	30	100
North East	35	42	24	100
North West	26	44	30	100
Yorkshire and The Humber	27	46	27	100
East Midlands	22	46	32	100
West Midlands	24	44	33	100
East	17	45	37	100
London	39	43	18	100
South East	18	43	39	100
South West	16	47	37	100
England	25	44	31	100
Wales	25	44	31	100
Scotland	31	43	25	100

	No car	One car	Two or more cars	Total
Area type, 2005				
Great Britain	25	43	32	100
London	39	43	18	100
Metropolitan areas	32	41	27	100
Other urban areas with population:				
Over 250,000	23	45	32	100
25,000 - 250,000	25	43	31	100
10,000 - 25,000	23	47	30	100
3,000 - 10,000	20	43	37	100
Rural areas	11	37	52	100

1 Includes cars and light vans normally available to the household.

Sources: Office for National Statistics; Department for Transport 020 7944 3097

15.13 Vehicles with current licences[1]
Northern Ireland

Numbers

		1995	1996[4]	1997	1998	1999	2000	2001[5]	2002	2003	2004	2005
Private cars, etc	KNKA	521 610	540 083	575 923	584 706	608 316	615 180	644 968	666 731	711 913	737 198	765 061
Cycles and tricycles	KNKB	8 775	8 775	8 775	8 775	8 775	8 775	8 775	8 775	8 775	8 775	8 775
Public road passenger vehicles:												
Taxis up to 4 seats	KNKD	739	..	..	..	..	..	..	..	..	–	..
Buses, coaches, over 4 seats	KNKE	1 353	2 090	2 144	2 175	2 204	2 266	2 315	2 322	2 353	2 378	2 566
Total	KNKC	2 092	2 090	2 144	2 175	2 204	2 266	2 315	2 322	2 353	2 378	2 566
General (HGV) goods vehicles:	KNKF	16 338	17 401	18 172	18 312	17 075	17 864	19 415	20 244	22 100	23 062	23 517
Agricultural tractors and engines, etc[2]	KNKM	9 074	5 911	6 378	5 906	5 505	5 048	4 901	5 731	7 503	8 674	9 584
Other	KNKN	1 257	1 019	1 188	1 193	1 446	1 287	1 366	1 347	1 588	1 708	1 669
Vehicles exempt from duty:												
Government owned	KNKP	3 872	3 753	3 705	3 785	4 032	3 822	6 427	6 383	6 172	6 116	6 367
Other:												
Ambulances	KNKQ	250	371	389	425	417	452	318	299	325	355	355
Fire engines	KNKR	301	292	291	285	286	290	181	174	170	178	179
Other exempt[3]	KNKS	47 626	58 340	64 447	66 981	68 277	70 405	72 209	73 648	76 715	78 973	81 874
Total	KNKO	52 049	62 756	68 832	71 476	73 012	74 969	79 135	80 504	83 382	85 622	88 755
Total	KNKT	611 562	639 286	683 569	695 431	720 645	730 730	767 305	794 477	852 742	883 261	917 399

1 Licences current at any time during the quarter ended December.
2 Owned by a farmer and available for hauling produce and requisites for his farm.
3 Changes in the Mobility Allowance (DWP) have contributed to the increase in Other exempt.

4 Due to a revision of taxation classes, 1996 data are not directly comparable with previous years.
5 Taxation classes have been revised.

Source: Driver and Vehicle Licensing, Northern Ireland: 028 7034 6903

15.14 New vehicle registrations
Northern Ireland

Numbers

		1995	1996	1997	1998	1999	2000	2001	2002	2003	2004	2005
Private cars, etc	KNLA	73 718	77 817	83 968	91 141	89 078	84 973	88 592	83 402	87 506	85 190	86 366
Cycles and tricycles	KNLB	2 362	2 803	3 376	4 307	5 310	6 010	5 591	5 596	6 804	4 601	4 648
Public road passenger vehicles	KNLC	622	724	714	486	568	565	451	439	609	467	621
Goods vehicles:												
General haulage vehicles:												
Under 3.5 tonnes	KNLH	7 357	7 232	8 468	10 107	11 054	12 617	13 274	12 007	10 716	11 090	12 300
3.5 tonnes and over	KNLJ	2 935	3 492	3 521	3 572	3 697	3 502	4 534	3 669	3 776	3 987	3 768
Agricultural tractors[1]	KNLM	1 619	1 292	1 364	971	987	1 313	301	1	9	2	2
Vehicles exempt from duty	KNLR	8 333	10 520	10 885	10 718	11 083	10 789	12 126	12 515	11 907	12 881	13 987
General haulage and special types	JTAG	..	..	..	..	..	..	..	15	12	11	16
Total	KNLS	96 946	103 880	112 296	121 302	121 777	119 769	124 869	117 644	121 339	118 229	121 708

1 Agricultural tractors driven on public roads. From April 2001 tractors were exempt.

Source: Driver and Vehicle Licensing, Northern Ireland: 028 7034 6903

15.15 Local bus services: passenger journeys by area: 1995/96-2005/06[1]

Millions

		1995 /96	1996 /97	1997 /98	1998 /99	1999 /00	2000 /01	2001 /02	2002 /03	2003 /04	2004 /05	2005 /06
Great Britain	ZCET	4 489	4 455	4 430	4 350	4 376	4 420	4 455	4 550	4 681	4 718	4 719
London	KILS	1 193	1 230	1 281	1 266	1 294	1 347	1 422	1 527	1 692	1 777	1 810
English Metropolitan Counties	KILT	1 358	1 310	1 292	1 256	1 213	1 203	1 196	1 182	1 162	1 131	1 117
English other areas	KILU	1 303	1 304	1 286	1 286	1 297	1 292	1 263	1 255	1 233	1 213	1 198
All outside London	ZCES	3 296	3 225	3 149	3 084	3 082	3 073	3 033	3 023	2 989	2 941	2 909
England	ZCER	3 853	3 844	3 859	3 808	3 804	3 842	3 881	3 964	4 087	4 121	4 125
Scotland	KILV	506	478	449	424	455	458	466	471	478	479	477
Wales	KILW	130	133	122	118	117	119	108	115	116	118	118

1 Previous years figures have been revised.

Source: Department for Transport 020 7944 3076

15.16 Local bus services: fare indices: by area
Current prices

Indices (1995=100)

		1995 /96	1996 /97	1997 /98	1998 /99	1999 /00	2000 /01	2001 /02	2002 /03	2003 /04	2004 /05	2005 /06
Great Britain	KNEU	101.2	106.3	112.0	117.1	122.0	126.4	130.6	134.5	139.1	145.7	156.3
London	KNEP	101.1	105.4	109.3	113.7	117.2	117.2	115.5	114.8	116.9	126.8	139.7
English Metropolitan Counties	KILD	101.5	106.9	113.3	118.7	124.6	129.9	137.4	142.7	148.0	154.2	167.0
English other areas	KILE	101.1	106.0	111.5	116.7	122.0	128.6	135.1	141.7	148.5	155.7	165.9
All outside London	ZCEQ	101.2	106.6	112.8	118.2	123.4	129.2	135.3	140.8	146.3	152.5	162.4
England	ZCEP	101.2	106.1	111.4	116.5	121.5	125.9	130.3	134.2	139.1	146.2	159.2
Scotland	KILF	100.8	108.0	116.5	121.8	125.3	129.9	131.8	134.5	136.8	140.4	144.6
Wales	KILG	100.7	104.4	110.1	116.3	122.2	127.5	133.5	139.5	145.5	152.4	160.2
Retail Prices Index (1995=100)	KNEV	100.7	103.1	106.5	109.9	111.6	114.9	116.6	119.1	122.4	126.2	129.6

Source: Department for Transport 020 7944 3076

15.17 Road accident casualties: by road user type and severity
Great Britain

Numbers

		1995	1996	1997	1998	1999	2000	2001	2002	2003	2004	2005
Child pedestrians[1]:												
Killed	ZCDH	132	131	138	103	107	107	107	79	74	77	63
Killed or seriously injured	KIJS	4 400	4 132	3 954	3 737	3 457	3 226	3 144	2 828	2 381	2 339	2 134
All severities	ZCDI	18 590	18 510	18 407	17 971	16 876	16 184	15 819	14 231	12 544	12 234	11 250
Adult pedestrians[2]:												
Killed	ZCDJ	897	858	835	803	760	750	712	688	695	589	604
Killed or seriously injured	KIJT	7 716	7 300	6 925	6 592	6 221	6 112	5 745	5 644	5 422	5 005	4 847
All severities	ZCDK	27 178	26 827	26 223	25 827	24 806	24 481	23 463	23 258	22 531	21 404	20 725
Child pedal cyclists[1]:												
Killed	ZCDL	48	54	33	32	36	27	25	22	18	25	20
Killed or seriously injured	KIJU	1 249	1 231	1 016	915	950	758	674	594	595	577	527
All severities	ZCDM	8 133	8 217	7 899	6 930	7 290	6 260	5 451	4 809	4 769	4 682	4 286
Adult pedal cyclists[2]:												
Killed	ZCDN	164	148	150	126	135	98	111	107	95	109	127
Killed or seriously injured	KIJV	2 673	2 517	2 542	2 345	2 172	1 954	1 951	1 801	1 776	1 697	1 787
All severities	ZCDO	16 140	15 778	16 181	15 326	14 834	13 630	12 974	11 712	11 643	11 366	11 637
Motorcyclists[3] and passengers:												
Killed	ZCDP	445	440	509	498	547	605	583	609	693	585	569
Killed or seriously injured	ZCDQ	6 615	6 208	6 446	6 442	6 908	7 374	7 305	7 500	7 652	6 648	6 508
All severities	BMDH	23 524	23 133	24 492	24 610	26 192	28 212	28 810	28 353	28 411	25 641	24 824
Car drivers and passengers:												
Killed	ZCDS	1 749	1 806	1 795	1 696	1 687	1 665	1 749	1 747	1 769	1 671	1 675
Killed or seriously injured	ZCDT	23 461	24 048	23 191	21 676	20 368	19 719	19 424	18 728	17 291	16 144	14 617
All severities	ZCDU	194 027	205 336	211 448	210 474	205 735	206 799	202 802	197 425	188 342	183 858	178 302
Bus/coach drivers and passengers:												
Killed	ZCDV	35	11	14	18	11	15	14	19	11	20	9
Killed or seriously injured	KCUZ	836	695	601	631	611	578	562	551	500	488	363
All severities	ZCDW	9 278	9 345	9 439	9 839	10 252	10 088	9 884	9 005	9 068	8 820	7 920
LGV drivers and passengers:												
Killed	ZCDX	69	61	64	67	65	66	64	70	72	62	54
Killed or seriously injured	ZCDY	1 106	989	928	949	867	813	811	780	765	631	587
All severities	ZCDZ	7 200	7 215	7 476	7 672	7 124	7 007	7 304	7 007	6 897	6 166	6 048
HGV drivers and passengers:												
Killed	ZCEA	57	63	45	60	52	55	54	63	44	47	55
Killed or seriously injured	ZCEB	635	555	573	560	540	571	500	524	429	406	395
All severities	ZCEC	3 331	3 245	3 302	3 444	3 484	3 597	3 388	3 178	3 061	2 883	2 843
All road users[4]:												
Killed	BMDC	3 621	3 598	3 599	3 421	3 423	3 409	3 450	3 431	3 508	3 221	3 201
Killed or seriously injured	ZCEE	49 154	48 097	46 583	44 255	42 545	41 564	40 560	39 407	37 215	34 351	32 155
All severities	BMDA	310 687	320 578	327 803	325 212	320 310	320 283	313 309	302 605	290 607	280 840	271 017

1 Casualities aged 0 - 15.
2 Casualities aged 16 and over.
3 Includes mopeds and scooters.
4 Includes other motor or non-motor vehicle users, and unknown road user
  type and casualty age.

Source: Department for Transport 020 7944 3078

233

15.18 Freight transport by road: goods moved by goods vehicles over 3.5 tonnes[1]
Great Britain

Billion tonne kilometres

		1995	1996	1997	1998	1999	2000	2001	2002	2003	2004[2]	2005[2]
By mode of working												
Mainly public haulage	KNND	106.5	109.1	112.2	114.3	110.9	113.0	114.7	110.6	114.3	110.8	109.7
Mainly own account	KNNC	37.2	37.7	37.4	37.6	38.3	37.5	34.7	39.2	37.4	41.4	43.0
All modes	KNNB	143.7	146.8	149.6	151.9	149.2	150.5	149.4	149.8	151.7	152.2	152.7
By gross weight of vehicle												
Rigid vehicles:												
3.5-17 tonnes	ZCIL	18.7	19.5	19.2	17.8	17.9	15.8	13.1	11.9	10.1	9.1	8.1
17-25 tonnes	ZCIM	5.6	5.3	4.7	4.2	4.3	4.8	5.7	6.3	6.8	7.9	8.3
25 tonnes and over	ZCIN	13.3	13.5	14.3	14.7	15.3	15.4	15.6	17.3	18.3	18.9	20.3
All rigids	ZCIO	37.5	38.3	38.1	36.6	37.5	36.0	34.5	35.6	35.2	35.9	36.7
Articulated vehicles:												
3.5-33 tonnes	ZCIP	15.9	15.9	14.3	14.4	14.0	14.0	12.8	9.9	8.8	7.0	6.3
33 tonnes and over	ZCIQ	90.2	92.6	97.1	100.9	97.7	100.4	102.1	104.4	107.7	109.4	109.7
All articulated vehicles	ZCIR	106.1	108.5	111.4	115.3	111.7	114.4	114.9	114.3	116.5	116.4	116.0
All vehicles												
3.5-25 tonnes	ZCIS	24.7	25.3	24.3	22.5	22.7	21.3	19.3	18.7	17.3	17.3	16.7
25 tonnes and over	KNNG	119.0	121.5	125.2	129.4	126.5	129.2	130.1	131.1	134.4	134.9	136.0
All weights	ZCIT	143.7	146.8	149.6	151.9	149.2	150.5	149.4	149.8	151.7	152.2	152.7
By commodity												
Food, drink and tobacco	ZCIU	37.5	39.3	40.8	42.5	41.5	44.3	41.4	43.1	42.2	41.7	40.6
Wood, timber and cork	ZCIV	3.2	3.8	3.5	3.6	3.8	3.7	3.9	3.8	4.1	4.5	4.7
Fertiliser	ZCIW	1.4	1.5	1.3	1.2	1.4	1.2	1.2	1.2	1.2	0.8	1.1
Crude minerals	ZCIX	13.5	13.5	13.6	13.3	12.7	12.4	13.0	13.9	13.8	14.1	14.8
Ores	ZCIY	1.5	1.3	1.7	1.1	1.3	1.2	1.2	1.1	1.2	1.4	1.7
Crude materials	ZCIZ	1.9	2.1	2.1	2.6	2.6	2.6	2.3	2.7	2.3	3.3	2.4
Coal and coke	ZCJA	2.7	2.5	2.7	2.0	2.2	1.5	2.1	1.5	1.5	1.2	1.5
Petrol and petroleum products	ZCJB	5.7	6.1	5.8	5.2	5.0	6.4	5.8	5.2	5.5	5.7	5.5
Chemicals	ZCJC	7.4	7.7	8.2	7.9	7.4	6.8	7.2	6.5	6.8	6.3	7.6
Building materials	ZCJD	10.7	9.6	11.1	10.7	10.6	10.6	11.7	10.9	12.0	12.1	10.9
Iron and steel products	ZCJE	7.8	7.2	7.9	7.7	6.8	6.8	5.7	5.3	5.4	5.4	5.2
Other metal products	ZCJF	1.7	1.7	1.5	1.7	1.7	1.7	1.4	1.5	1.5	1.9	2.1
Machinery and transport equipment	ZCJG	7.4	7.7	8.4	9.1	8.7	9.1	8.9	8.5	8.7	8.9	9.3
Miscellaneous manufactures	ZCJH	13.3	14.2	14.2	15.9	15.7	15.1	15.4	16.2	15.8	16.3	15.5
Miscellaneous transactions	ZCJI	27.8	28.4	26.8	27.5	27.9	27.1	28.2	28.4	29.5	28.8	29.8
All commodities	ZCJJ	143.7	146.8	149.6	151.9	149.2	150.5	149.4	149.8	151.7	152.2	152.7

1 Rigid vehicles or articulated vehicles (tractive unit and trailer) with gross vehicle weight over 3.5 tonnes.

2 Figures for 2004 and 2005 are not fully comparable with those for 2003 and earlier years. Detailed comparisons should therefore be made with caution.

Source: Department for Transport 020 7944 3093

15.19

Freight transport by road: goods lifted by goods vehicles over 3.5 tonnes[1]
Great Britain

Million tonnes

		1995	1996	1997	1998	1999	2000	2001	2002	2003	2004[2]	2005[2]
By mode of working												
Mainly public haulage	ZCJK	987	1 011	1 044	1 041	991	1 038	1 052	1 019	1 053	1 101	1 079
Mainly own account	ZCJL	622	618	599	589	576	556	529	608	590	643	667
All modes	ZCJM	1 609	1 628	1 643	1 630	1 567	1 593	1 581	1 627	1 643	1 744	1 746
By gross weight of vehicle												
Rigid vehicles:												
3.5-17 tonnes	ZCJN	298	306	294	268	254	229	203	188	159	160	135
17-25 tonnes	ZCJO	162	133	120	106	86	87	86	90	100	113	118
25 tonnes and over	ZCJP	373	371	380	401	408	424	443	491	506	539	559
All rigids	ZCJQ	833	811	793	776	748	741	733	768	765	812	812
Articulated vehicles:												
3.5-33 tonnes	ZCJR	139	138	124	125	113	107	97	81	69	60	51
33 tonnes and over	ZCJS	637	679	726	729	706	746	751	778	809	872	883
All articulated vehicles	ZCJT	776	817	850	854	819	852	848	859	878	932	934
All vehicles												
3.5-25 tonnes	ZCJU	467	447	419	382	346	325	294	283	265	277	257
25 tonnes and over	ZCJV	1 142	1 181	1 224	1 248	1 221	1 268	1 287	1 343	1 378	1 467	1 489
All weights	ZCJW	1 609	1 628	1 643	1 630	1 567	1 593	1 581	1 627	1 643	1 744	1 746
By commodity												
Food, drink and tobacco	ZCJX	308	326	342	346	333	346	321	339	333	351	339
Wood, timber and cork	ZCJY	24	27	26	27	28	26	28	28	32	42	36
Fertiliser	ZCJZ	11	13	10	9	11	10	9	11	12	7	14
Crude minerals	ZCKA	319	320	329	327	297	308	298	333	327	364	370
Ores	ZCKB	18	18	25	18	20	16	16	17	21	22	23
Crude materials	ZCKC	16	18	17	20	20	18	20	21	19	25	22
Coal and coke	ZCKD	34	32	37	26	28	22	21	17	22	14	21
Petrol and petroleum products	ZCKE	71	75	73	61	61	75	74	59	64	67	70
Chemicals	ZCKF	50	51	53	53	47	49	50	41	47	46	53
Building materials	ZCKG	161	142	156	161	159	165	165	167	165	185	169
Iron and steel products	ZCKH	54	52	55	54	48	49	44	39	41	43	42
Other metal products	ZCKI	17	15	16	18	17	16	14	14	16	19	19
Machinery and transport equipment	ZCKJ	61	59	71	73	67	69	70	68	66	70	76
Miscellaneous manufactures	ZCKK	85	88	90	96	91	97	97	105	98	111	109
Miscellaneous transactions	ZCKL	379	393	343	342	340	328	353	367	379	378	384
All commodities	ZCKM	1 609	1 628	1 643	1 630	1 567	1 593	1 581	1 627	1 643	1 744	1 746

1 Rigid vehicles or articulated vehicles (tractive unit and trailer) with gross vehicle weight over 3.5 tonnes.

2 Figures for 2004 and 2005 are not fully comparable with those for 2003 and earlier years. Detailed comparisons should therefore be made with caution.

Source: Department for Transport 020 7944 3093

15.20 Rail systems summary

		1995/96	1996/97	1997/98	1998/99	1999/00	2000/01	2001/02	2002/03	2003/04	2004/05	2005/06
Passenger journeys (millions)												
National Rail network[1]	ZCKN	761	801	846	892	931	957	960	976	1 012	1 045	1 082
London Underground	KNOE	784	772	832	866	927	970	953	942	948	976	970
Docklands Light Railway	ZCKO	14	17	21	28	31	38	41	46	48	50	52
Glasgow Underground	ZCKP	14	14	14	15	15	14	14	13	13	13	13
Tyne and Wear Metro[2]	ZCKQ	36	35	35	34	33	33	33	37	38	37	36
Blackpool trams[3]	EL9L	5	5	5	4	4	4	5	4	4	4	4
Manchester Metrolink[4]	ZCKS	13	13	14	13	14	17	18	19	19	20	20
Midland Metro[5]	ZCKR	–	–	–	–	5	5	5	5	5	5	5
Croydon Tramlink[6]	GEOE	–	–	–	–	–	15	18	19	20	22	23
Sheffield Supertram	ZCKT	5	8	9	10	11	11	11	12	12	13	13
Nottingham NET[7]	C3MI	–	–	–	–	–	–	–	–	–	8	10
All rail	ZCKU	1 632	1 665	1 776	1 862	1 971	2 065	2 059	2 072	2 119	2 193	2 227
All light rail	GENZ	87	92	98	104	113	138	146	154	160	172	175
Passenger revenue (£ million at current prices)												
National Rail network	KNDL	2 379	2 573	2 821	3 089	3 368	3 413	3 548	3 663	3 901	4 158	4 493
London Underground	KNOA	765	797	899	977	1 058	1 129	1 151	1 138	1 161	1 241	1 309
Docklands Light Railway	ZCKV	9	12	14	20	22	29	32	36	37	40	46
Glasgow Underground	ZCKW	8	8	9	9	10	10	10	10	10	11	11
Tyne and Wear Metro	ZCKX	20	21	22	23	24	24	25	29	31	33	34
Blackpool trams	EL9M	5	4	5	4	4	4	5	5	4	4	4
Manchester Metrolink	ZCKZ	11	13	14	..	..	18	20	20	21	22	23
Midland Metro	ZCKY	–	–	–	–	..	3	4	5	5	6	6
Croydon Tramlink	GEOF	–	–	–	–	–	12	13	15	16	18	19
Sheffield Supertram	ZCLA	4	5	6	6	7	7	8	10	9	11	10
Nottingham NET	C3MJ	–	–	–	–	–	–	–	–	..	6	7
All rail	ZCLB	3 200	3 433	3 790	4 128	4 493	4 650	4 815	4 931	5 197	5 550	5 963
All light rail	GEOA	56	63	70	62	68	108	117	130	135	151	161
Passenger kilometres (millions)												
National Rail network	KNDZ	30 000	32 100	34 700	36 280	38 472	38 179	39 141	39 678	40 937	41 762	43 211
London Underground	KNOI	6 337	6 153	6 479	6 716	7 171	7 470	7 451	7 367	7 340	7 606	7 586
Docklands Light Railway	ZCLC	70	86	103	144	172	200	207	232	235	245	257
Glasgow Underground	ZCLD	41	40	45	47	47	46	44	43	43	43	42
Tyne and Wear Metro	ZCLE	261	254	249	238	230	229	238	275	284	283	279
Blackpool trams	EL9N	..	..	..	..	13	13	15	14	11	12	11
Manchester Metrolink	ZCLG	81	86	88	117	126	152	161	167	169	204	206
Midland Metro	ZCLF	–	–	–	–	50	56	50	50	54	52	54
Croydon Tramlink	GEOG	–	–	–	–	–	96	99	100	105	112	117
Sheffield Supertram	ZCLH	20	29	34	35	37	38	39	40	42	44	44
Nottingham NET	C3MK	–	–	–	–	–	–	–	–	2	37	42
All rail	ZCLI	36 810	38 748	41 698	43 577	46 318	46 479	47 446	47 965	49 222	50 401	51 849
All light rail	GEOB	473	495	519	581	675	830	854	920	945	1 033	1 052
Route kilometres open for passenger traffic (numbers)												
National Rail network[8]	ZCLJ	15 002	15 034	15 024	15 038	15 038	15 042	15 042	15 042	14 883	14 328	14 356
London Underground	ZCLK	392	392	392	392	408	408	408	408	408	408	408
Docklands Light Railway	ZCLM	22	22	22	22	26	26	26	26	26	26	30
Glasgow Underground	ZCLN	11	11	11	11	11	11	11	11	11	11	10
Tyne and Wear Metro	ZCLO	59	59	59	59	59	59	78	78	78	78	78
Blackpool trams	EL9O	18	18	18	18	18	18	18	18	18	18	18
Manchester Metrolink	ZCLQ	31	31	31	31	39	39	39	39	39	39	39
Midland Metro	ZCLP	–	–	–	–	20	20	20	20	20	20	20
Croydon Tramlink	GEOH	–	–	–	–	–	28	28	28	28	28	28
Sheffield Supertram	ZCLR	29	29	29	29	29	29	29	29	29	29	29
Nottingham NET	C3ML	–	–	–	–	–	–	–	–	14	14	15
All rail	ZCLS	15 564	15 596	15 586	15 600	15 648	15 680	15 699	15 699	15 554	14 999	15 032
All light rail	GEOC	170	170	170	170	202	230	249	249	263	263	268
Stations served (numbers)												
National Rail network	ZCLT	2 497	2 498	2 495	2 499	2 503	2 508	2 508	2 508	2 507	2 508	2 510
London Underground	KNOO	245	245	245	246	253	253	253	253	253	253	253
Docklands Light Railway	ZCLU	28	28	29	29	34	34	34	34	34	34	38
Glasgow Underground	ZCLV	15	15	15	15	15	15	15	15	15	15	15
Tyne and Wear Metro	ZCLW	46	46	46	46	46	46	58	58	58	58	59
Blackpool trams	EL9P	124	124	124	124	124	124	124	124	124	124	124
Manchester Metrolink	ZCLY	26	26	26	26	36	36	36	37	37	37	37
Midland Metro	ZCLX	–	–	–	–	23	23	23	23	23	23	23
Croydon Tramlink	GEOI	–	–	–	–	–	38	38	38	38	38	39
Manchester Metrolink	ZCLY	26	26	26	26	36	36	36	37	37	37	37
Sheffield Supertram	ZCLZ	45	45	46	47	47	47	48	48	48	48	48
Nottingham NET	C3MM	–	–	–	–	–	–	–	–	23	23	23
All rail	ZCLL	3 026	3 027	3 026	3 032	3 081	3 124	3 137	3 138	3 160	3 161	3 169
All light rail	GSOC	284	284	286	287	325	363	376	377	400	400	406

1 Franchised train operating companies from Feb 1996 after privatisation.
2 Tyne & Wear Metro extension to Sunderland opened in March 2002.
3 Blackpool Trams shown as a self-contained system.
4 Transfer of 20 stations from the rail network to Manchester Metrolink.
5 Midland Metro opened in 1999.
6 Croydon Tramlink opened in 2000.
7 Nottingham Express Transit opened in March 2004.
8 Break in series due to change in methodology.

Sources: Department for Transport: 020 7944 3076; Network Rail, former Railtrack, SRA, TfL, light rail operators and PTEs

15.21

National railways freight
Great Britain

Billion tonne kilometres

		1995 /96	1996[2] /97	1997 /98	1998 /99	1999 /00	2000 /01	2001 /02	2002 /03	2003 /04	2004 /05	2005 /06
Freight moved by commodity[1]												
Coal	ZCGG	3.6	3.9	4.4	4.5	4.8	4.8	6.2	5.7	5.8	7.0	8.6
Metals	ZCGH	1.7	..	..	2.1	2.2	2.1	2.4	2.7	2.4	2.6	2.2
Construction	ZCGI	2.3	..	..	2.1	2.0	2.4	2.8	2.5	2.7	2.8	3.0
Oil and petroleum	ZCGJ	1.8	..	..	1.6	1.5	1.4	1.2	1.2	1.2	1.2	1.3
Other traffic	ZCGK	3.9	11.2	12.5	7.1	7.6	7.4	6.7	6.6	6.8	7.0	7.1
All traffic	VOXD	13.3	15.1	16.9	17.3	18.2	18.1	19.4	18.5	18.9	20.6	22.1
Freight lifted by commodity[3]												
Coal	ZCGL	45.2	52.2	50.3	45.3	44.3	45.7	46.1	40.7	42.0	51.7[4]	54.5
Metals	ZCGM	15.1	..	..	..	..	..	..	..	..	..	..
Construction	ZCGN	11.5	..	..	..	..	..	..	..	..	..	..
Oil and petroleum	ZCGO	6.3	..	..	..	..	..	..	..	..	..	..
Other traffic	ZCGP	22.6	49.6	55.1	56.8	47.6	49.7	48.3	46.4	46.9	50.2[4]	49.4
All traffic	VOXE	100.7	101.8	105.4	102.1	91.9	95.4	94.4	87.0	88.9	101.9[4]	103.9

1 Revised series on new basis from 1998/99.
2 Owing to changes in the way freight traffic has been estimated following privatisation, data since 1996/97 are not comparable to those for previous years. Freight excludes parcels and materials carried for rail infrastructure.
3 Break in series from 1999/2000.
4 Break in series, increase largely due to changes in coverage.

Source: Department for Transport: 020 7944 4977

15.22

Railways: permanent way and rolling stock
Northern Ireland

At end of year

Numbers

		1995	1996	1997	1998	1999	2000	2001	2002	2003	2004	2005
Length of road open for traffic[1] (Km)	KNRA	333	335	335	335	335	356	334	334	334	299	299
Length of track open for traffic (Km)												
Total	KNRB	506	506	505	526	526	547	480	480	480	445	445
Running lines	KNRC	464	464	464	484	484	505	464	464	464	427	427
Sidings (as single track)	KNRD	42	42	42	42	42	42	16	16	16	18	18
Locomotives[2]												
Diesel-electrics	KNRE	11	8	6	5	6	6	6	6	5	6	5
Passenger carrying vehicles[2]												
Total	KNRF	112	112	112	120	108	108	106	106	100	108	130
Rail motor vehicles:												
Diesel-electric, etc	KNRG	30	30	30	28	30	30	29	28	28	28	70
Trailer carriages:												
Total locomotive hauled	KNRH	28	28	28	38	21	21	25	22	22	22	22
Ordinary coaches	KNRI	26	26	26	36	19	19	23	20	20	20	20
Restaurant cars	KNRJ	2	2	2	2	2	2	2	2	2	2	2
Rail car trailers	KNRK	54	54	54	54	54	54	52	50	50	52	32
Rolling stock for maintenance and repair	KNRT	41	41	41	26	18	18	18	18	39	46	48

1 The total length of railroad open for traffic irrespective of the number of tracks comprising the road.
2 See chapter text.

Sources: Department for Regional Development; Northern Ireland: 028 9054 0801

15.23 Operating statistics of railways
Northern Ireland

		Unit	1995	1996	1997	1998	1999	2000	2001	2002	2003	2004	2005
Maintenance of way and works													
Material used:													
Ballast	KNSA	Thousand m^2	22.5	27.0	51.3	38.5	40.0	47.0	80.0	40.0	130.0	70.0	90.0
Rails	KNSB	Thousand tonnes	1.8	2.1	0.4	2.5	3.0	3.5	2.5	1.0	4.5	1.0	3.2
Sleepers	KNSC	Thousands	22.9	27.5	5.1	32.0	30.0	40.0	50.0	5.0	40.0	28.0	45.0
Track renewed	KNSD	Km	16.0	20.0	2.4	22.5	7.0	29.0	15.0	5.0	25.8	2.0	29.0
New Track laid	KPGD	Km	2.5	–	–	–	–	21.0	–	–	–	–	–
Engine kilometres													
Total[1]	KNSE	Thousand Km	4 000	4 100	4 100	4 100	4 100	4 100	4 056	4 056	4 170	4 110	3 610
Train kilometres:													
Total	KNSF	"	3 570	3 670	3 670	3 670	3 670	3 670	3 626	3 626	3 704	3 610	3 610
Coaching	KNSG	"	3 566	3 666	3 666	3 666	3 666	3 666	3 622	3 622	3 700	3 610	3 610
Freight	KNSH	"	4	4	4	4	4	4	4	4	4	–	–

1 Including shunting, assisting, light, departmental, maintenance and repair.

Sources: Department for Regional Development; Northern Ireland: 028 9054 0801

15.24 Main output of United Kingdom airlines

Available tonne kilometres (millions)

		1995	1996	1997	1998	1999	2000	2001	2002	2003	2004	2005
All services	KNTA	29 904	32 210	35 538	40 021	42 002	43 379	42 370	40 550	42 784	43 883	48 186
Percentage growth on previous year	KNTB	*7.4*	*7.7*	*10.3*	*12.5*	*5.0*	*3.6*	*-2.4*	*-4.3*	*5.5*	*2.6*	*9.8*
Scheduled services	KNTC	22 016	23 793	26 504	29 756	31 815	32 938	31 866	30 433	31 513	32 422	36 937
Percentage growth on previous year	KNTD	*8.1*	*8.1*	*11.4*	*12.3*	*6.9*	*3.5*	*-3.3*	*-4.5*	*3.6*	*2.9*	*13.9*
Non-scheduled services	KNTE	7 695	8 044	9 034	10 265	10 186	10 440	10 505	10 117	11 271	11 461	11 249
Percentage growth on previous year	KNTF	*5.9*	*4.5*	*7.3*	*13.3*	*-0.7*	*4.1*	*0.6*	*-3.7*	*11.4*	*1.7*	*-1.8*

Source: Civil Aviation Authority: 020 7453 6246

15.25 Air traffic between the United Kingdom and abroad[1]

Thousands

		1995	1996	1997	1998	1999	2000	2001	2002	2003	2004	2005
Flights												
United Kingdom airlines												
Scheduled services	KNUA	342.1	373.0	410.3	443.7	480.9	520.3	536.7	531.3	517.7	546.5	584.2
Non-scheduled services	KNUB	204.8	198.0	208.2	218.7	212.6	216.2	208.5	218.6	211.0	198.6	200.6
Overseas airlines[2]												
Scheduled services	KNUC	363.3	390.0	399.6	426.4	467.6	467.6	496.8	487.5	487.0	544.2	584.5
Non-scheduled services	KNUD	31.5	31.3	32.5	34.8	31.7	31.7	26.0	36.7	27.1	28.8	33.7
Total	KNUE	941.7	992.3	1 050.6	1 123.6	1 192.8	1 235.8	1 268.0	1 274.1	1 242.8	1 318.1	1 403.0
Passengers carried												
United Kingdom airlines												
Scheduled services	KNUF	34 934.7	37 902.2	41 854.7	46 747.7	50 148.5	54 522.8	53 591.7	54 360.0	56 476.7	63 216.1	69 106.2
Non-scheduled services	KNUG	20 484.5	26 304.4	28 699.5	31 616.6	32 603.8	33 185.9	34 009.1	33 935.7	33 385.6	32 195.7	30 179.4
Overseas airlines[2]												
Scheduled services	KNUH	34 568.5	36 992.1	39 900.7	42 554.5	46 628.0	46 627.9	51 107.8	51 317.6	54 504.0	60 278.0	67 634.9
Non-scheduled services	KNUI	4 244.2	4 416.3	4 413.0	4 569.7	4 156.5	4 156.5	3 966.1	3 956.3	3 947.1	4 068.3	4 169.1
Total	KNUJ	94 231.9	105 615.0	114 867.9	125 488.5	133 536.8	138 493.1	142 674.7	143 569.6	148 313.4	159 758.1	171 089.6

1 Excludes travel to and from the Channel Islands.
2 Includes airlines of overseas UK Territories.

Source: Civil Aviation Authority: 020 7453 6246

15.26

Operations and traffic on scheduled services: revenue traffic
United Kingdom airlines[1]

		Unit	1995	1996	1997	1998	1999	2000	2001	2002	2003	2004	2005
All services													
Aircraft stage flights:													
Number	KNFA	Numbers	658 958	702 492	749 806	797 682	835 031	878 582	921 556	911 518	895 095	926 498	1 016 354
Average length	KNFB	Kilometres	1 032	1 047	1 079	1 111	1 134	1 156	1 138	1 149	1 215	1 227	1 304
Aircraft-kilometres flown	KNFC	Millions	680	735	809	886	947	1 016	1 049	1 047	1 088	1 137	1 325
Passengers uplifted	KNFD	"	48	51	56	62	65	70	70	72	76	83	94
Seat-kilometres used	KNFE	"	115 347	124 847	136 388	151 969	160 336	170 469	158 651	156 494	164 806	173 722	200 460
Cargo uplifted:[2]	KNFF	Tonnes	643 181	690 806	782 855	831 436	860 291	897 184	742 705	768 736	800 645	842 912	921 412
Tonne-kilometres used:		Millions											
Passenger	KNFH	"	11 172	12 190	13 287	14 755	15 518	16 507	15 258	15 035	15 419	15 580	15 044
Freight	KNFI	"	3 567	3 832	4 454	4 663	4 925	5 160	4 548	4 941	5 187	5 297	5 998
Mail	KNFJ	"	151	176	172	178	153	179	102	57	55	75	90
Total	KNFG	"	14 890	16 198	17 913	19 596	20 596	21 846	19 908	20 032	20 660	20 952	21 133
Domestic services													
Aircraft stage flights:													
Number	KNFK	Numbers	318 884	331 109	336 218	352 936	354 864	353 525	365 881	359 400	345 954	373 858	394 069
Average length	KNFL	Kilometres	317	320	330	333	337	344	350	350	357	360	374
Aircraft-kilometres flown	KNFM	Millions	101	106	111	118	120	121	128	126	123	135	147
Passengers uplifted	KNFN	"	14	15	16	17	17	18	18	20	21	22	23
Seat-kilometres used	KNFO	"	5 754	6 204	6 646	6 948	7 184	7 542	7 645	8 322	8 904	9 263	9 795
Cargo uplifted:[2]	KNFP	Tonnes	33 659	35 432	30 679	31 879	25 964	24 644	19 498	16 755	17 248	14 862	10 015
Tonne-kilometres used:		Millions											
Passenger	KNFR	"	485	528	569	593	610	640	649	703	738	757	784
Freight	KNFS	"	7	7	6	6	6	6	4	4	3	3	3
Mail	KNFT	"	7	6	6	6	4	4	4	3	3	3	–
Total	KNFQ	"	499	542	581	605	620	650	656	709	744	762	787
International services													
Aircraft stage flights:													
Number	KNFU	Numbers	339 714	371 400	413 588	444 746	480 167	525 057	555 675	552 118	549 141	552 640	622 285
Average length	KNFV	Kilometres	1 703	1 695	1 688	1 729	1 723	1 704	1 656	1 670	1 758	2 148	1 893
Aircraft-kilometres flown	KNFW	Millions	579	630	698	769	827	895	921	921	965	1 002	1 178
Passengers uplifted	KNFX	"	34	36	40	45	48	52	52	52	56	61	71
Seat-kilometres used	KNFY	"	109 593	118 642	129 743	145 022	153 153	162 927	151 006	148 172	155 903	164 459	190 666
Cargo uplifted:[2]	KNFZ	Tonnes	609 522	655 374	752 176	799 557	834 327	872 540	723 206	751 975	783 397	828 051	911 398
Tonne-kilometres used:		Millions											
Passenger	KNJX	"	10 686	11 662	12 718	14 162	14 908	15 867	14 610	14 332	14 681	14 824	14 260
Freight	KNJY	"	3 560	3 825	4 448	4 657	4 919	5 154	4 544	4 937	5 184	5 294	5 995
Mail	KNJZ	"	144	170	166	172	149	176	98	54	51	72	90
Total	KNJW	"	14 391	15 656	17 333	18 991	19 976	21 197	19 252	19 322	19 916	20 190	20 345

1 Includes services of British Airways and other UK private companies.
2 Cargo has re-defined as freight and mail.

Source: Civil Aviation Authority: 020 7453 6246

15.27 Accidents on scheduled fixed wing passenger-carrying services[1]
United Kingdom airlines

	Number of fatal accidents	Passenger casualties		Crew casualties		Thousand aircraft stage flights per fatal accident	Million aircraft-kms. flown per fatal accident	Thousand passengers carried per passenger killed	Million passenger kms. flown per passenger killed	Fatal accidents		Passengers killed per hundred million passenger-kms.
		Killed	Seriously injured	Killed	Seriously injured					per 100 000 aircraft stage flights	per hundred million aircraft-kms.	
1950-54	7	194	9	28	4	107.4	61.8	46.1	50.1	0.93	1.62	2.00
1955-59	7	123	28	29	8	158.3	92.1	155.2	158.5	0.63	1.09	0.63
1960-64	5	104	35	21	6	303.7	182.2	373.4	390.6	0.33	0.55	0.26
1965-69	6	273	2	32	2	282.7	194.9	222.2	255.2	0.35	0.51	0.39
1970-74	2	167	5	14	2	889.5	737.1	464.3	657.7	0.11	0.14	0.15
1975-79	1	54	6	9	-	1 773.0	1 523.5	1 688.2	3 239.9	0.06	0.07	0.03
1980-84	-	-	4	-	1	-	-	-	-	-	-	-
1985-89	2	47	79	1	8	1 220.0	1 014.5	3031.0	6 262.9	0.08	0.10	0.02
1990-94	-	-	1	-	9	-	-	-	-	-	-	-
1995-99	1	9	1	3	3	3 699.9	4 026.0	31 265.6	76 539.4	0.03	0.02	0.001
	KCVN	KCVO	KCVP	KCVQ	KCVR							
2000	-	-	1	-	-	-	-	-	-	-	-	-
2001	-	-	-	-	-	-	-	-	-	-	-	-
2002	-	-	-	-	3	-	-	-	-	-	-	-
2003	-	-	1	-	1	-	-	-	-	-	-	-
2004	-	-	2	-	-	-	-	-	-	-	-	-
2005	-	-	-	-	-	-	-	-	-	-	-	-

1 Excluding accidents involving the deaths of third parties only.

Source: Civil Aviation Authority: 01293 573446

15.28 Activity at civil aerodromes
United Kingdom[1]

Thousands and tonnes

		1997	1998	1999	2000	2001	2002	2003	2004	2005	2006
Movement of civil aircraft (thousands)											
Commercial											
Transport	KNQC	1 764	1 871	1 959	2 045	2 095	2 094	2 160	2 277	2 406	2 451
Other[2]	KNQD	143	162	159	159	150	120	117	116	120	129
Total	KNQB	1 907	2 033	2 118	2 204	2 245	2 214	2 277	2 393	2 526	2 580
Non-commercial[3]	KNQE	1 330	1 343	1 263	1 186	1 207	1 100	1 186	1 135	1 129	1 059
Total	KNQA	3 237	3 376	3 381	3 390	3 452	3 314	3 463	3 528	3 655	3 639
Passengers handled											
Terminal	KNQG	146 657	158 856	168 363	179 885	181 231	188 761	199 950	215 681	228 214	235 139
Transit	KNQH	1 405	1 226	1 156	1 167	1 087	1 054	990	950	984	1 016
Total	KNQF	148 062	160 082	169 519	181 052	182 318	189 815	200 940	216 631	229 198	236 155
Commercial freight handled[4] (tonnes)											
Set down	KNQJ	981 861	1 072 127	1 135 065	1 174 635	1 093 142	1 124 026	1 172 552	1 267 411	1 282 724	1 277 177
Picked up	KNQK	960 859	1 008 358	1 053 902	1 139 292	1 052 379	1 071 407	1 035 680	1 103 539	1 080 620	1 038 261
Total	KNQI	1 942 720	2 080 485	2 188 967	2 313 927	2 145 521	2 195 433	2 208 232	2 370 950	2 363 344	2 315 438
Mail handled											
Set down	KNQM	88 366	88 766	92 974	101 743	98 690	90 738	86 415	108 481	102 344	91 535
Picked up	KNQN	115 066	113 993	114 752	123 352	117 389	99 747	93 096	112 424	110 576	98 391
Total	KNQL	203 432	202 759	207 726	225 095	216 079	190 485	179 511	220 905	212 920	189 926

1 Figures exclude Channel Island Airports.
2 Local pleasure flights, charter service positioning flights, and non- transport charter flights for reward (for example; aerial survey work, crop dusting and delivery of empty aircraft).
3 Test and training flights, other flights by Air Transport Operators, private, aero-club and official flights & business aviation etc,.

4 With effect from 2001, passengers, freight and mail handled exclude traffic carried on air taxi operations.

Source: Civil Aviation Authority: 020 7453 6258

15.29 United Kingdom ports: foreign, coastwise and one-port traffic

Thousand tonnes

		1995	1996	1997	1998	1999	2000	2001	2002	2003	2004	2005
Foreign												
Liquid bulk traffic												
Imports	EL9Q	58 512	59 309	61 060	61 346	56 528	70 788	74 495	62 811	66 447	75 897	76 988
Exports	EL9R	111 651	106 169	104 654	106 041	110 591	118 509	110 321	107 516	100 772	95 974	87 995
All	EL9S	170 164	165 478	165 714	167 387	167 120	189 297	184 816	170 327	167 218	171 871	164 983
Dry bulk traffic												
Imports	EL9T	62 121	63 905	68 208	68 333	65 219	65 652	77 360	67 575	72 644	76 625	87 546
Exports	EL9U	19 632	19 549	19 596	20 840	18 905	19 739	17 206	18 026	20 559	18 098	18 409
All	EL9V	81 753	83 454	87 805	89 173	84 124	85 391	94 565	85 600	93 203	94 722	105 955
Container and roll-on traffic												
Imports	EL9W	51 668	52 008	58 822	61 191	64 272	64 753	65 721	68 371	69 199	75 520	77 431
Exports	EL9X	41 694	43 711	48 805	49 029	49 616	49 323	47 334	47 313	47 291	49 869	51 045
All	EL9Y	93 362	95 719	107 628	110 220	113 889	114 076	113 054	115 685	116 490	125 390	128 476
Semi-bulk traffic												
Imports	EL9Z	16 445	15 987	16 097	16 878	15 967	17 174	17 059	18 523	17 284	18 413	16 766
Exports	ELA2	4 891	5 267	5 142	4 897	4 519	4 411	3 737	3 613	3 848	4 342	5 287
All	ELA3	21 337	21 253	21 239	21 775	20 486	21 584	20 796	22 136	21 131	22 755	22 054
Conventional traffic												
Imports	ELA4	1 555	1 493	1 506	1 531	1 595	2 500	3 730	3 645	3 699	3 990	3 529
Exports	ELA5	932	1 094	1 100	854	735	1 145	1 786	1 705	1 535	1 314	1 393
All	ELA6	2 487	2 587	2 607	2 385	2 330	3 645	5 515	5 349	5 234	5 304	4 922
All foreign traffic												
Imports	ELA7	190 302	192 702	205 694	209 279	203 581	220 866	238 364	220 924	229 273	250 445	262 261
Exports	ELA8	178 801	175 790	179 298	181 661	184 367	193 127	180 383	178 173	174 003	169 597	164 129
All	ELA9	369 103	368 492	384 992	390 940	387 948	413 993	418 747	399 097	403 276	420 042	426 390
Coastwise traffic												
Liquid bulk traffic												
Inwards	ELB2	48 393	52 354	49 981	51 514	48 164	36 677	37 008	38 694	36 973	39 236	41 308
Outwards	ELB3	51 459	57 146	53 753	52 622	51 966	41 696	36 049	37 535	35 371	38 788	42 477
All	ELB4	99 852	109 501	103 734	104 136	100 131	78 373	73 058	76 229	72 344	78 024	83 786
Dry bulk traffic												
Inwards	ELB5	9 352	7 613	6 678	7 599	6 792	8 243	8 032	7 245	7 956	6 453	6 716
Outwards	ELB6	9 968	7 942	6 963	7 882	7 229	8 201	7 112	7 785	8 438	7 814	8 730
All	ELB7	19 319	15 555	13 642	15 480	14 021	16 444	15 144	15 030	16 395	14 268	15 446
Container and roll-on traffic												
Inwards	ELB8	9 820	9 623	10 522	11 236	11 542	12 186	11 797	11 854	11 788	12 510	13 241
Outwards	ELB9	10 205	9 716	10 786	10 660	11 396	11 506	11 064	11 341	11 426	12 026	12 995
All	ELC2	20 025	19 339	21 307	21 895	22 938	23 692	22 861	23 195	23 214	24 537	26 236
Semi-bulk traffic												
Inwards	ELC3	172	187	166	176	203	247	364	324	373	320	217
Outwards	ELC4	266	251	188	477	221	311	570	546	544	519	565
All	ELC5	437	438	354	653	424	558	934	870	917	838	783
Conventional traffic												
Inwards	ELL6	161	139	161	212	274	96	74	99	194	73	278
Outwards	ELM5	238	261	314	306	285	139	131	124	368	518	451
All	ELN2	399	400	475	518	559	236	206	223	562	591	729
All coastwise traffic												
Inwards	ELN3	67 898	69 917	67 508	70 736	66 975	57 448	57 276	58 215	57 285	58 592	61 761
Outwards	ELN4	72 134	75 316	72 004	71 946	71 098	61 853	54 926	57 331	56 147	59 665	65 218
All	ELN5	140 032	145 233	139 512	142 682	138 073	119 302	112 202	115 546	113 432	118 257	126 979

15.29 United Kingdom ports: foreign, coastwise and one-port traffic

continued

Thousand tonnes

		1995	1996	1997	1998	1999	2000	2001	2002	2003	2004	2005
One-port traffic												
Liquid bulk traffic												
Inwards	ELN6	10 848	10 861	6 871	10 587	20 220	24 937	18 245	25 886	22 328	19 152	16 169
Outwards	ELN7	8 882	8 847	8 560	4 365	126	485	647	693	563	361	421
All	ELN8	19 731	19 708	15 431	14 951	20 346	25 422	18 892	26 579	22 892	19 513	16 590
Dry bulk traffic												
Inwards	ELN9	14 964	13 260	14 123	14 436	15 051	12 503	14 362	15 197	14 389	13 821	13 476
Outwards	ELO2	105	98	106	98	41	41	68	67	70	28	52
All	ELO3	15 069	13 357	14 229	14 534	15 092	12 544	14 430	15 264	14 460	13 849	13 529
Non-oil traffic with UK off-shore installations												
Inwards	ELO4	914	984	851	1 063	1 136	589	643	606	490	414	724
Outwards	ELO5	3 382	3 468	3 515	4 332	3 019	1 199	1 452	1 234	1 112	995	1 470
All	ELO6	4 296	4 453	4 366	5 394	4 155	1 789	2 095	1 840	1 602	1 409	2 194
All one-port traffic												
Inwards	ELO7	26 726	25 105	21 844	26 085	36 407	38 030	33 250	41 688	37 208	33 388	30 369
Outwards	ELO8	12 369	12 413	12 181	8 794	3 186	1 725	2 167	1 994	1 745	1 383	1 944
All	ELO9	39 095	37 518	34 026	34 880	39 593	39 755	35 417	43 682	38 953	34 771	32 313
Foreign and domestic traffic												
Liquid bulk traffic												
Inwards	ELP2	117 754	122 524	117 912	123 446	124 913	132 402	129 748	127 391	125 748	134 285	134 465
Outwards	ELP3	171 992	172 163	166 967	163 028	162 684	160 690	147 017	145 744	136 706	135 123	130 894
All	ELP4	289 746	294 687	284 879	286 474	287 597	293 092	276 765	273 134	262 454	269 408	265 359
Dry bulk traffic												
Inwards	ELP5	86 437	84 778	89 009	90 367	87 062	86 398	99 754	90 016	94 990	96 899	107 739
Outwards	ELP6	29 705	27 588	26 666	28 820	26 175	27 981	24 386	25 878	29 067	25 940	27 191
All	ELP7	116 141	112 366	115 675	119 187	113 237	114 379	124 140	115 894	124 057	122 839	134 930
Container and roll-on traffic												
Inwards	ELP8	61 487	61 631	69 344	72 427	75 814	76 939	77 518	80 225	80 987	88 030	90 672
Outwards	ELP9	51 899	53 427	59 591	59 689	61 013	60 829	58 398	58 654	58 717	61 896	64 040
All	ELQ2	113 387	115 058	128 935	132 115	136 827	137 768	135 915	138 879	139 704	149 926	154 712
Semi-bulk traffic												
Inwards	ELQ3	16 617	16 174	16 263	17 054	16 170	17 421	17 423	18 847	17 657	18 733	16 984
Outwards	ELQ4	5 157	5 518	5 330	5 374	4 740	4 721	4 307	4 159	4 392	4 860	5 853
All	ELQ5	21 774	21 692	21 593	22 428	20 910	22 142	21 730	23 006	22 049	23 593	22 836
Conventional traffic												
Inwards	ELQ6	1 716	1 632	1 667	1 744	1 869	2 596	3 804	3 744	3 893	4 063	3 807
Outwards	ELQ7	1 170	1 355	1 414	1 159	1 020	1 284	1 917	1 828	1 903	1 832	1 843
All	ELQ8	2 886	2 987	3 082	2 903	2 889	3 880	5 721	5 572	5 796	5 895	5 651
Non-oil traffic with UK off-shore installations												
Inwards	ELQ9	914	984	851	1 063	1 136	589	643	606	490	414	724
Outwards	ELR2	3 382	3 468	3 515	4 332	3 019	1 199	1 452	1 234	1 112	995	1 470
All	ELR3	4 296	4 453	4 366	5 394	4 155	1 789	2 095	1 840	1 602	1 409	2 194
All foreign and domestic traffic												
Inwards	ELR4	284 926	287 724	295 046	306 100	306 963	316 344	328 890	320 828	323 766	342 425	354 391
Outwards	ELR5	263 304	263 519	263 484	262 402	258 651	256 706	237 477	237 497	231 896	230 645	231 291
All	ELR6	548 230	551 243	558 530	568 502	565 614	573 050	566 366	558 325	555 662	573 070	585 682

Source: Department for Transport; 020 7944 3087

15.30 Roll-on/roll-off ferry and Channel Tunnel traffic; road goods vehicles outward to mainland Europe: by country of registration

Thousands

		1995	1996	1997	1998	1999	2000	2001	2002	2003	2004	2005
Powered vehicles:												
United Kingdom	ZCGT	486.0	531.1	543.2	544.3	562.7	544.8	517.6	493.3	473.9	493.1	517.4
Austria	ZCGU	9.7	8.6	5.4	10.2	14.9	17.0	42.0	45.8	42.9	30.0	27.0
Belgium/Luxembourg	ZCGV	45.7	41.0	53.6	74.5	96.7	114.1	119.3	121.4	104.3	112.4	112.4
Denmark	ZCGW	4.5	4.6	5.5	7.3	8.7	9.5	12.0	16.9	13.7	17.1	17.7
Finland	ZCGX	0.3	0.2	0.1	0.6	0.7	0.9	3.1	2.0	1.1	0.1	0.2
Germany	ZCGY	28.0	30.4	39.3	52.4	73.1	111.5	132.0	148.2	155.7	164.7	168.3
France	ZCGZ	154.9	181.7	234.2	272.4	319.1	338.8	352.4	363.1	363.2	388.0	361.4
Greece	ZCHA	1.8	2.1	2.6	1.9	2.6	2.9	2.6	2.8	3.6	4.0	3.6
Irish Republic	ZCHB	31.0	30.1	32.3	38.8	44.7	48.5	46.6	44.6	30.8	27.6	31.9
Italy	ZCHC	29.3	28.8	30.4	35.3	45.8	67.8	91.1	127.8	132.4	120.1	96.9
Netherlands	ZCHD	84.6	87.2	107.0	125.4	153.3	185.1	187.5	186.3	210.2	252.1	253.2
Spain	ZCHE	38.4	39.4	45.1	56.3	67.7	81.8	93.9	102.2	105.9	109.8	105.1
Sweden	ZCHF	0.7	0.9	8.9	10.3	1.0	1.4	1.8	1.8	1.4	1.4	1.3
Portugal	ZCHG	3.4	3.1	5.1	6.7	9.2	10.7	10.2	11.0	9.4	8.9	9.5
EU15 (excluding UK)	ZCHH	432.2	458.1	569.5	692.1	837.3	990.0	1 094.5	1 173.9	1 174.6	1 236.2	1 188.5
Cyprus[1]	GG5P	..	..	..	..	0.1	0.2	0.1	0.2	0.2	0.2	0.1
Czech Republic[1]	GG5Q	..	..	..	..	5.4	5.2	6.8	7.8	13.1	25.0	40.6
Estonia[1]	GG5R	..	..	..	..	–	0.1	0.2	0.3	0.3	0.8	1.6
Hungary[1]	GG5S	..	..	..	..	6.9	8.0	11.1	12.4	12.7	24.6	38.0
Latvia[1]	GG5T	..	..	..	..	0.3	0.3	0.1	0.2	0.2	0.2	1.3
Lithuania[1]	GG5U	..	..	..	..	0.9	1.4	1.0	0.7	1.6	2.9	7.5
Malta[1]	GG5V	..	..	..	..	0.2	0.3	0.3	0.3	0.2	0.1	0.1
Poland[1]	GG5W	..	..	..	..	7.0	10.4	12.5	12.0	14.2	31.0	54.5
Slovakia[1]	GG5X	..	..	..	..	0.2	0.2	0.4	1.0	2.4	8.0	12.7
Slovenia[1]	GG5Y	..	..	..	..	1.5	1.9	3.5	4.7	4.7	10.0	10.8
NMS10[1]	GG5Z	..	..	..	..	22.5	28.0	36.2	39.5	49.5	102.9	167.2
Non-European Union	ZCHI	29.0	26.3	28.0	33.3	24.9	24.9	43.2	76.7	97.6	107.6	116.5
Unknown	ZCHJ	3.0	2.2	5.7	4.8	6.3	17.7	20.5	18.1	19.1	17.0	31.8
All countries	ZCHK	950.2	1 017.7	1 146.4	1 274.8	1 453.7	1 605.4	1 711.9	1 801.5	1 814.7	1 956.8	2 021.4
Unaccompanied trailers	ZCHL	677.4	626.4	740.0	737.5	737.8	712.9	686.4	726.0	780.4	782.2	756.0
Powered vehicles and unaccompanied trailers	ZCHM	1 627.6	1 644.1	1 886.4	2 012.3	2 191.4	2 318.3	2 398.3	2 527.5	2 595.1	2 739.0	2 777.4

1 New Member State countries that joined the EU on 1st May 2004. There is no individual breakdown available before 1999 for these countries.

Source: Department for Transport; 0117 372 8484

15.31 Postal services and television licences[1]
United Kingdom

Millions and thousands

		1996	1997	1998	1999	2000	2001	2002	2003	2004	2005	2006
Letters, etc posted (millions)	KMRA	18 322	18 101	18 350	18 878	19 711	20 076	20 648	21 979	22 837	24 341	24 880
of which:												
Registered and insured	KMRB	23.5	25.6	28.7	31.6	30.2	32.3	36.1	38.5	41.4	45.3	45.3
Airmail (Commonwealth and foreign)	KMRC	655.1	684.5	658.4	693.2	672.3	659.2	600.7	541.6	512.0	457.9	502.2
Business reply and freepost items	KMRD	493.1	505.8	524.7	503.6	475.3	487.4	486.2	434.4	397.7	401.1	402.3
Postal orders Total issued (thousands)[2]	KMRH	35 542	33 404	31 907	30 289	30 153	30 931	29 150	28 666	28 888	29 344	20 489
Television licences (thousands) In force on 31 March	KMQL	21 105	21 305	21 723	22 240	22 625	22 839	23 157	23 486	23 899	24 162	24 419
of which: Colour	KMQM	20 505	20 849	21 344	21 944	22 413	22 684	23 040	23 392	23 824	24 103	24 370

1 See chapter text.
2 Excluding those issued on HM ships, in many British possessions and in other places abroad. Up to 1998 includes Postal Orders issued Overseas and by Ministry of Defence.

Sources: Royal Mail: 0207 2502890;
Capita Business Services Limited: 0117 3021003;
Post Office Limited: 0207 3207424

National accounts

Chapter 16

National accounts

National accounts

(Tables 16.1 to 16.22)

The tables which follow are based on those in the *Blue Book* 2006 Edition. Some of the figures are provisional and may be revised later; this applies particularly to the figures for 2004 and 2005.

The accounts are based on the European System of Accounts 1995 (ESA95). The *Blue Book* contains an introduction to the system of the UK accounts outlining some of the main concepts and principles of measurement used. It explains how key economic indicators are derived from the sequence of accounts and how the figures describing the whole economy are broken down by sector and by industry. A detailed description of the structure for the accounts is provided in a separate ONS publication *United Kingdom National Accounts*: *Concepts, Sources and Methods* (TSO 1998). Further information on the financial accounts is given in the *Financial Statistics Explanatory Handbook*.

In the tables in this chapter on national income, analyses by industry are based, as far as possible, on the Standard Industrial Classification Revised 1992. The principal aggregate measured in these tables is the Gross domestic product (GDP). This is a concept of the value of the total economic activity taking place in UK territory. It can be viewed as incomes earned, as expenditures incurred, or as production. Adding all primary incomes received from the rest of the world and deducting all primary incomes payable to non-residents produces Gross national income (previously known as gross national product). This is a concept of the value of all incomes earned by UK residents.

ESA95, the internationally compatible accounting framework, provides a systematic and detailed description of the UK economy. It includes the sector accounts which provide, by institutional sector, a description of the different stages of the economic process from production through income generation, distribution and use of income to capital accumulation and financing; and the input-output framework, which describes the production process in more detail. It contains all the elements required to compile such aggregate measures as GDP, gross national income (GNI) and saving.

Gross domestic product and national income

(Tables 16.1, 16.2, 16.3)

Table 16.1 shows the main national accounts aggregates, both at current prices and chained volume measures.

Table 16.2 shows the various money flows which generate the gross domestic product and gross national income. The output approach to GDP shows the total output of goods and services, the use of goods and services in the production process (intermediate consumption) and taxes and subsidies on products. The expenditure approach to GDP shows consumption expenditure by households and government, gross capital formation and expenditure on UK exports by overseas purchasers. The sum of these items overstates the amount of income generated in the United Kingdom by the value of imports of goods and services; this item is therefore subtracted to produce gross domestic product at market prices. The income approach to GDP shows gross operating surplus, mixed income and compensation of employees (previously known as income from employment). Taxes are added and subsidies are deducted to produce the total of the income-based components at market prices.

Table 16.2 also shows the primary incomes received from the rest of the world, which are added to GDP and primary incomes payable to non-residents, which are deducted from GDP, to arrive at Gross national income. Primary income comprises compensation of employees, taxes less subsidies on production and property and entrepreneurial income.

Table 16.3 shows the expenditure approach to the chained volume measure of GDP. When looking at the change in the economy over time the main concern is usually whether more goods and services are actually being produced now than at some time in the past. Over time changes in current price GDP show changes in the monetary value of the components of GDP and, as these changes in value can reflect changes in both price and volume, it is difficult to establish how much of an increase in the series is due either to increased activity in the economy or to an increase in the price level. As a result, when looking at the real growth in the economy over time it is useful to look at volume estimates of GDP. In chained volume series, volume measures for each year are produced in prices of the previous year. These volume measures are then 'chain-linked' together to produce a continuous time series.

Industrial analysis

(Tables 16.4, 16.5)

The analysis of gross value added by industry at current prices shown in Table 16.4 reflects the estimates based on the Standard Industrial Classification, revised 1992 (SIC92). The table is based on current price data reconciled through the input-output process for 1992 to 2004. The estimates are valued at basic prices, that is, the only taxes included in the price will be taxes paid as part of the production process, such as business rates, and not any taxes specifically levied on the production of a unit of output, for example VAT.

Table 16.5 shows chained volume measures of gross value added at basic prices by industry. Chained volume measures of gross value added (output approach) provides the lead indicator of economic change in the short term. The output analysis of gross value added is estimated in terms of change and expressed in index number form. It is therefore inappropriate to show as a statistical adjustment any divergence of an output measure of GDP derived from it from other measures of GDP. Such an adjustment does, however, exist implicitly.

Sector analysis – Distribution of income accounts and capital account

(Tables 16.6 to 16.13)

The National Accounts accounting framework includes the sector accounts which provide, by institutional sector, a description of the different stages of the economic process from production through income generation, distribution and use of income to capital accumulation and financing.

Tables 16.6 to 16.12 show the allocation of primary income account and the secondary distribution of income account for the non-financial corporations, financial corporations, government and households sectors. Additionally, Table 16.12 shows the use of income account for the households sector and Table 16.13 provides a summary of the capital account. The full sequence of accounts is shown in the *Blue Book*.

The allocation of primary income account shows the resident units and institutional sectors as recipients rather than producers of primary income. It demonstrates the extent to which operating surpluses are distributed to the owners of the enterprises. The resources side of the allocation of primary income accounts includes the components of the income approach to measurement of GDP. The balance of this account is the gross balance of primary income (B.5g) for each sector, and if the gross balance is aggregated across all sectors of the economy the result is *Gross national income*.

The secondary distribution of income account describes how the balance of income for each sector is allocated by redistribution; through transfers such as taxes on income, social contributions and benefits and other current transfers. The balancing item of this account is gross disposable income (B.6g). For the households sector, the chained volume measure of gross disposable income is shown as real household disposable income.

Table 16.12 shows, for the households sector, the use of disposable income where the balancing item is saving (B.8g). For the non-financial corporations sector the balancing item of the secondary distribution of income account, gross disposable income (B.6g) is equal to saving (B.8g).

The summary capital account (Table 16.13) brings together the saving and investment of the several sectors of the economy. It shows saving, capital transfers, gross capital formation and net acquisition of non-financial assets for each of the four sectors.

Household and non-profit institutions serving households (NPISH) consumption expenditure at current market prices and chained volume measures

(Tables 16.14 to 16.17)

Household and NPISH consumption expenditure is a major component of the expenditure measure of gross domestic product both at current prices (Table 16.2) and chained volume measures (Table 16.3).

Household final consumption expenditure includes the value of income-in-kind and imputed rent of owner-occupied dwellings but excludes business expenditure allowed as deductions in computing income for tax purposes. It includes expenditure on durable goods, for instance motor cars, which from the point of view of the individual might more appropriately be treated as capital expenditure. The only exceptions are the purchase of land and dwellings and costs incurred in connection with the transfer of their ownership and expenditure on major improvements by occupiers, which are treated as personal capital expenditure.

The estimates of household consumption expenditure include purchases of second-hand as well as new goods, *less* the proceeds of sales of used goods.

The most detailed figures are published quarterly in *Consumer Trends* (available as a web-only publication on the National Statistics website www.statistics.gov.uk).

Change in inventories (previously known as value of physical increase in stocks and work in progress)

(Table 16.18)

This table gives a broad analysis by industry, and, for manufacturing industry, by asset, of the value of entries less withdrawals and losses of inventories (stocks).

Gross fixed capital formation

(Table16.19 to 16.22)

Gross fixed capital formation comprises expenditure on the replacement of, and additions to, fixed capital assets located in the United Kingdom, including all ships and aircraft of UK ownership.

16.1 United Kingdom national and domestic product[1]
Main aggregates
At current prices and chained volume measures, reference year 2003

Indices (2003=100) and £ million

		1998	1999	2000	2001	2002	2003	2004	2005	2006
INDICES (2003=100)										
VALUES AT CURRENT PRICES										
Gross domestic product at current market prices ("money GDP")	YBEU	77.5	81.7	85.9	89.8	94.5	100.0	106.0	110.4	116.2
Gross value added at current basic prices	YBEX	77.5	81.2	85.3	89.6	94.4	100.0	105.9	110.4	116.2
CHAINED VOLUME MEASURES										
Gross domestic product at market prices	YBEZ	87.2	89.8	93.2	95.4	97.4	100.0	103.3	105.3	108.2
Gross national disposable income at market prices	YBFP	85.9	87.7	90.8	93.8	97.2	100.0	103.4	104.5	106.6
Gross value added at basic prices	CGCE	87.6	90.3	93.7	95.7	97.4	100.0	103.3	105.3	108.2
PRICES										
Implied deflator of GDP at market prices	YBGB	88.9	90.9	92.1	94.1	97.0	100.0	102.6	104.9	107.4
VALUES AT CURRENT PRICES (£ million)										
Gross measures (before deduction of fixed capital consumption) at current market prices										
Gross Domestic Product ("money GDP")	YBHA	860 796	906 567	953 227	996 987	1 048 767	1 110 296	1 176 527	1 225 978	1 289 989
Employment, property and entrepreneurial income from the rest of the world (receipts *less* payments)	YBGG	12 320	1 270	4 540	11 664	23 443	24 646	26 596	29 871	..
Subsidies (receipts) *less* taxes (payments) on products from/to the rest of the world	-QZOZ	−3 651	−3 438	−4 098	−3 920	−2 890	−2 596	−1 640	−4 243	..
Other subsidies on production from/to the rest of the world	-IBJL	246	309	292	298	519	..	..	..	..
Gross National Income (GNI)	ABMX	869 706	904 737	954 004	1 005 313	1 069 839	1 132 938	1 202 075	1 252 406	1 311 753
Current transfers from the rest of the world (receipts *less* payments)	-YBGF	−4 966	−4 435	−6 253	−3 426	−6 711	−8 130	−9 920	−11 219	..
Gross National Disposable Income	NQCO	864 740	900 302	947 751	1 001 887	1 063 128	1 124 808	1 192 155	1 241 220	1 300 668
Adjustment to current basic prices										
Gross Domestic Product (at current market prices)	YBHA	860 796	906 567	953 227	996 987	1 048 767	1 110 296	1 176 527	1 225 978	1 289 989
Adjustment to current basic prices (*less* taxes *plus* subsidies on products)	-NQBU	−97 116	−105 956	−112 248	−114 234	−118 470	−124 738	−132 362	−137 472	−144 822
Gross Value Added (at current basic prices)	ABML	763 680	800 611	840 979	882 753	930 297	985 558	1 044 165	1 088 506	1 145 167
Net measures (after deduction of fixed capital consumption) at current market prices	-NQAE	−95 051	−101 055	−106 372	−110 434	−116 007	−119 239	−128 427	−131 093	..
Net domestic product	NHRK	765 745	805 512	846 855	886 553	932 760	991 057	1 048 100	1 093 622	..
Net national income	NSRX	774 655	803 682	847 632	894 879	953 832	1 013 699	1 073 648	1 122 468	..
Net national disposable income	NQCP	769 689	799 247	841 379	891 453	947 121	1 005 569	1 063 728	1 111 249	..
CHAINED VOLUME MEASURES (Reference year 2003, £ million)										
Gross measures (before deduction of fixed capital consumption) at market prices										
Gross Domestic Product	ABMI	968 040	997 295	1 035 295	1 059 648	1 081 469	1 110 296	1 146 523	1 168 674	1 200 960
Terms of trade effect ("Trading gain or loss")	YBGJ	−7 260	−5 466	−8 013	−9 971	−2 937	−	1 226	−5 946	..
Real gross domestic income	YBGL	960 780	991 829	1 027 282	1 049 677	1 078 532	1 110 296	1 147 749	1 161 846	..
Real employment, property and entrepreneurial income from the rest of the world (receipts *less* payments)	YBGI	13 712	1 386	4 880	12 256	24 093	24 646	25 969	28 360	..
Subsidies (receipts) *less* taxes (payments) on production from/to the rest of the world	-QZPB	−2 848	−2 701	−3 686	−3 393	−2 624	−2 596	−1 762	−2 155	..
Other subsidies on production from/to the rest of the world	-IBJN	215	298	305	590	707	592	661	660	..
Gross National Income (GNI)	YBGM	971 737	990 758	1 028 387	1 058 873	1 100 663	1 132 938	1 172 617	1 188 711	..
Real current transfers from the rest of the world (receipts *less* payments)	-YBGP	−5 527	−4 841	−6 721	−3 600	−6 897	−8 130	−9 686	−10 652	..
Gross National Disposable Income	YBGO	966 211	985 921	1 021 664	1 055 282	1 093 767	1 124 808	1 162 931	1 175 725	1 199 205
Adjustment to basic prices										
Gross Domestic Product (at market prices)	ABMI	968 040	997 295	1 035 295	1 059 648	1 081 469	1 110 296	1 146 523	1 168 674	1 200 960
Adjustment to basic prices (*less* taxes *plus* subsidies on products)	-NTAQ	−105 165	−107 873	−112 020	−116 584	−121 657	−124 738	−128 660	−130 607	..
Gross Value Added (at basic prices)	ABMM	863 147	889 722	923 583	943 186	959 811	985 558	1 017 863	1 038 113	1 066 594
Net measures (after deduction of fixed capital consumption) at market prices	-CIHA	−101 125	−105 781	−109 621	−112 575	−117 430	−119 239	−126 566	−126 926	..
Net national income at market prices	YBET	873 745	887 078	920 088	946 908	983 179	1 013 699	1 046 052	1 061 786	..
Net national disposable income at market prices	YBEY	868 217	882 247	913 358	943 332	976 285	1 005 569	1 036 366	1 051 134	..

1 See chapter text.

Source: Office for National Statistics: 020 7533 6045

16.2 United Kingdom gross domestic product and national income[1]
Current prices

£ million

		1998	1999	2000	2001	2002	2003	2004	2005	2006
Gross domestic product: Output										
Gross value added, at basic prices										
Output of goods and services	NQAF	1 592 209	1 676 034	1 772 646	1 853 342	1 937 482	2 038 942	2 151 833	..	..
less intermediate consumption	-NQAJ	−828 529	−875 423	−931 667	−970 589	−1 007 185	−1 053 384	−1 107 668	..	..
Total Gross Value Added	ABML	763 680	800 611	840 979	882 753	930 297	985 558	1 044 165	1 088 506	1 145 167
Value added taxes (VAT) on products	QYRC	56 702	61 719	64 464	67 549	71 374	77 665	81 747	..	..
Other taxes on products	NSUI	46 999	50 512	54 086	52 845	53 945	54 813	58 102	59 053	..
less subsidies on products	-NZHC	−6 424	−6 068	−6 027	−5 708	−6 534	−7 410	−7 280	−4 646	..
Gross Domestic Product at market prices	YBHA	860 796	906 567	953 227	996 987	1 048 767	1 110 296	1 176 527	1 225 978	1 289 989
Gross domestic product: Expenditure										
Final consumption expenditure										
Actual individual consumption										
Household final consumption expenditure	ABPB	534 153	567 994	600 826	632 496	664 562	697 160	732 531	760 032	793 322
Final consumption expenditure of NPISH	ABNV	20 837	21 874	23 169	24 720	25 968	27 185	28 953	31 588	33 312
Individual government final consumption expenditure	NNAQ	94 783	102 742	109 297	118 458	130 816	143 954	155 811	166 699	178 838
Total actual individual consumption	NQEO	649 773	692 610	733 292	775 674	821 346	868 299	917 295	958 319	1 005 472
Collective government final consumption expenditure	NQEP	61 626	66 778	72 554	76 045	81 648	88 745	94 897	102 792	108 797
Total final consumption expenditure	ABKW	711 399	759 388	805 846	851 719	902 994	957 044	1 012 192	1 061 111	1 114 269
Households and NPISH	NSSG	554 990	589 868	623 995	657 216	690 530	724 345	761 484	791 620	826 634
Central government	NMBJ	97 145	103 580	110 807	118 762	130 326	142 639	152 325	163 173	176 059
Local government	NMMT	59 264	65 940	71 044	75 741	82 138	90 060	98 383	106 318	111 576
Gross capital formation										
Gross fixed capital formation	NPQX	151 083	156 344	161 468	165 472	173 525	178 751	194 491	205 891	223 682
Changes in inventories	ABMP	5 026	6 060	5 271	6 189	2 909	3 983	4 856	4 071	5 510
Acquisitions less disposals of valuables	NPJO	429	229	3	396	214	−37	−37	−377	45
Total gross capital formation	NQFM	156 538	162 633	166 742	172 057	176 648	182 697	199 310	209 585	229 237
Exports of goods and services	KTMW	232 034	239 782	267 602	273 140	276 511	285 397	298 694	325 946	370 103
less imports of goods and services	-KTMX	−239 175	−255 236	−286 963	−299 929	−307 386	−314 842	−333 669	−370 420	−424 189
External balance of goods and services	KTMY	−7 141	−15 454	−19 361	−26 789	−30 875	−29 445	−34 975	−44 474	−54 086
Statistical discrepancy between expenditure components and GDP	RVFD	−	−	−	−	−	−	−	−244	569
Gross Domestic Product at market prices	YBHA	860 796	906 567	953 227	996 987	1 048 767	1 110 296	1 176 527	1 225 978	1 289 989
Gross domestic product: Income										
Operating surplus, gross										
Non-financial corporations										
Public non-financial corporations	NRJT	7 754	7 678	7 188	6 892	6 657	7 265	6 653	7 833	8 339
Private non-financial corporations	NRJK	174 846	178 939	185 198	185 942	189 906	202 479	219 738	228 054	241 966
Financial corporations	NQNV	18 430	15 976	12 398	12 052	32 230	39 936	46 020	37 512	42 179
Adjustment for financial services	-NSRV	−27 658	−29 468	−33 465	−33 648	−41 136	−45 370	−50 165	−51 846	−56 310
General government	NMXV	8 999	9 262	9 542	9 796	10 289	10 807	11 681	12 605	13 650
Households and non-profit institutions serving households	QWLS	47 642	51 195	53 960	59 083	62 544	67 935	72 709	77 680	82 269
Total operating surplus, gross	ABNF	230 013	233 582	234 821	240 117	260 490	283 052	306 636	311 838	332 093
Mixed income	QWLT	52 823	55 734	57 805	62 121	65 771	69 122	71 958	76 112	78 866
Compensation of employees	HAEA	466 080	495 793	532 179	564 194	587 396	616 893	648 717	685 345	717 665
Taxes on production and imports	NZGX	119 450	128 713	135 597	137 870	143 086	150 430	158 104	..	..
less subsidies	-AAXJ	−7 475	−7 069	−6 936	−6 952	−8 007	−9 436	−9 371	−9 391	..
Statistical discrepancy between income components and GDP	RVFC	−	−	−	−	−	−	−	77	273
Gross Domestic Product at market prices	YBHA	860 796	906 567	953 227	996 987	1 048 767	1 110 296	1 176 527	1 225 978	1 289 989

16.2 United Kingdom gross domestic product and national income[1]
Current prices
continued

		1998	1999	2000	2001	2002	2003	2004	2005	2006
Gross Domestic Product at market prices	YBHA	860 796	906 567	953 227	996 987	1 048 767	1 110 296	1 176 527	1 225 978	1 289 989
Compensation of employees										
receipts from the rest of the world	KTMN	840	960	1 032	1 087	1 121	1 116	1 171	1 211	1 249
less payments to the rest of the world	-KTMO	−850	−759	−882	−1 021	−1 054	−1 057	−1 100	−1 146	−1 191
Total	KTMP	−10	201	150	66	67	59	71	65	58
less Taxes on products paid to the rest of the world										
plus Subsidies received from the rest of the world	-QZOZ	−3 651	−3 438	−4 098	−3 920	−2 890	−2 596	−1 640	−4 243	..
Other subsidies on production	-IBJL	246	309	292	298	519	..	..	..	..
Property and entrepreneurial income										
receipts from the rest of the world	HMBN	103 388	101 952	134 114	139 848	123 505	124 881	141 030	186 219	241 564
less payments to the rest of the world	-HMBO	−91 058	−100 883	−129 724	−128 250	−100 129	−100 294	−114 505	−158 868	−218 821
Total	HMBM	12 330	1 069	4 390	11 598	23 376	24 587	26 525	27 351	22 743
Gross National Income at market prices	ABMX	869 706	904 737	954 004	1 005 313	1 069 839	1 132 938	1 202 075	1 252 406	1 311 753

1 See chapter text.

Source: Office for National Statistics: 020 7533 6046

16.3 United Kingdom gross domestic product[1]
Chained volume measures, reference year 2003

£ million

		1998	1999	2000	2001	2002	2003	2004	2005	2006
Gross domestic product: expenditure approach										
Final consumption expenditure										
Actual individual consumption										
Household final consumption expenditure	ABPF	579 342	606 648	633 662	653 326	676 833	697 160	721 434	731 274	744 933
Final consumption expenditure of non-profit institutions serving households	ABNU	25 092	25 023	27 177	27 155	27 130	27 185	27 327	28 119	29 883
Individual government final consumption expenditure	NSZK	107 339	109 554	111 763	114 159	117 238	120 288	..	..	..
Total actual individual consumption	YBIO	729 353	760 171	792 076	815 286	843 504	868 299	897 055	910 300	..
Collective government final consumption expenditure	NSZL	72 925	76 926	80 829	82 502	85 331	88 745	91 835	95 552	..
Total final consumption expenditure	ABKX	802 340	837 119	872 899	897 801	928 849	957 044	988 890	1 005 852	..
Gross capital formation										
Gross fixed capital formation	NPQR	158 525	163 039	167 486	171 639	178 066	178 751	189 492	195 107	207 704
Changes in inventories	ABMQ	4 291	5 803	4 648	5 577	2 289	3 982	4 597	3 611	5 501
Acquisitions less disposals of valuables	NPJP	30	–	−28	342	183	−37	−42	−354	66
Total gross capital formation	NPQU	163 325	169 032	172 430	177 892	180 731	182 697	194 047	198 026	..
Gross domestic final expenditure	YBIK	965 970	1 006 378	1 045 373	1 075 760	1 109 596	1 139 741	1 182 937	1 205 170	1 241 320
Exports of goods and services	KTMZ	238 344	247 289	269 830	277 694	280 593	285 397	299 289	322 869	360 440
Gross final expenditure	ABME	1 203 987	1 253 258	1 315 374	1 353 632	1 390 217	1 425 138	1 482 225	1 528 039	1 601 760
less imports of goods and services	-KTNB	−238 834	−257 809	−281 081	−294 449	−308 706	−314 842	−335 703	−359 132	−401 331
Statistical discrepancy between expenditure components and GDP	GIXS	–	–	–	–	–	–	–	−233	529
Gross Domestic Product at market prices	ABMI	968 040	997 295	1 035 295	1 059 648	1 081 469	1 110 296	1 146 523	1 168 674	1 200 960
of which External balance of goods and services	KTNC	−490	−10 520	−11 251	−16 755	−28 113	−29 445	−36 414	−36 263	−40 891

1 See chapter text.

Source: Office for National Statistics: 020 7533 6045

16.4 Gross value added at current basic prices: by industry[1,2]
United Kingdom

£ million

		1998	1999	2000	2001	2002	2003	2004	2005	2006
Agriculture, hunting, forestry and fishing	EWSH	9 457	9 270	8 789	8 566	9 218	10 031	10 323	..	..
Production										
Mining and quarrying										
Mining and quarrying of energy producing materials										
Mining of coal	QTOQ	817	642	611	548	534	468	385	..	..
Extraction of mineral oil and natural gas	QTOR	13 054	14 694	22 283	20 940	20 006	19 542	19 845	..	..
Other mining and quarrying	QTOS	1 645	1 716	1 795	1 760	1 474	1 524	1 646	..	..
Total mining and quarrying	EWSL	15 516	17 053	24 689	23 251	22 012	21 534	21 876	..	..
Manufacturing										
Food; beverages and tobacco	QTOU	20 047	20 220	20 261	20 914	21 052	21 654	22 288	..	..
Textiles and textile products	QTOV	6 803	6 270	5 863	5 390	4 857	4 318	3 823	..	..
Leather and leather products	QTOW	822	808	750	650	594	463	347	..	..
Wood and wood products	QTOX	2 329	2 248	2 336	2 369	2 516	2 694	2 904	..	..
Pulp, paper and paper products; publishing and printing	QTOY	18 781	19 619	20 207	20 155	19 988	19 698	20 157	..	..
Coke, petroleum products and nuclear fuel	QTOZ	2 524	2 569	2 361	2 493	2 433	2 358	2 420	..	..
Chemicals, chemical products and man-made fibres	QTPA	14 873	15 136	14 982	15 979	15 984	15 980	16 233	..	..
Rubber and plastic products	QTPB	8 026	7 794	7 692	7 730	7 627	7 569	7 824	..	..
Other non-metal mineral products	QTPC	5 028	4 952	5 013	5 084	5 333	5 452	5 686	..	..
Basic metals and fabricated metal products	QTPD	17 633	16 675	16 023	15 637	14 957	14 807	15 097	..	..
Machinery and equipment not elsewhere classified	QTPE	13 591	12 731	12 343	12 265	12 056	12 071	12 198	..	..
Electrical and optical equipment	QTPF	19 826	20 442	20 414	18 382	16 501	15 529	15 625	..	..
Transport equipment	QTPG	16 179	16 064	16 016	16 100	16 136	15 801	16 318	..	..
Manufacturing not elsewhere classified	QTPH	6 282	6 422	6 555	6 704	6 588	6 438	6 548	..	..
Total manufacturing	EWSP	152 744	151 951	150 819	149 852	146 621	144 830	147 468	..	..
Electricity, gas and water supply	EWST	15 887	15 784	15 942	15 826	16 084	16 482	17 103	..	..
Total production	QTPK	184 147	184 787	191 449	188 929	184 717	182 846	186 446	..	..
Construction	EWSX	39 970	42 511	45 975	50 903	55 020	59 855	64 747	..	..
Service industries										
Wholesale and retail trade (including motor trade); repair of motor vehicles, personal and household goods	QTPM	93 572	99 981	103 910	110 658	113 988	120 605	127 520	..	..
Hotels and restaurants	QTPN	22 547	24 476	26 004	27 384	29 023	30 509	33 074	..	..
Transport, storage and communication										
Transport and storage	QTPO	40 072	41 138	42 648	43 360	44 633	47 108	49 516	..	..
Communication	QTPP	22 297	23 935	26 652	27 142	28 346	29 376	29 762	..	..
Total	EWTF	62 369	65 073	69 299	70 502	72 980	76 485	79 279	..	..
Financial intermediation	QTPR	46 952	46 229	46 093	46 956	68 120	77 852	86 145	..	..
Adjustment for financial services (FISIM)	-NSRV	−27 658	−29 468	−33 465	−33 648	−41 136	−45 370	−50 165	−51 846	−56 310
Real estate, renting and business activities										
Letting of dwellings including imputed rent of owner occupiers	QTPS	56 741	60 501	63 176	68 802	72 531	77 913	83 037	..	..
Other real estate, renting and business activities	QTPT	108 523	119 892	131 348	142 806	150 399	162 851	175 333	..	..
Total	QTPU	165 264	180 393	194 525	211 608	222 930	240 765	258 370	..	..
Public administration and defence (PAD)[3]	EWTN	39 561	40 909	42 712	45 025	47 528	51 302	55 280	..	..
Education[3]	QTPW	41 687	44 879	48 069	51 616	55 025	58 246	61 786	..	..
Health and social work	QTPX	48 800	51 688	55 390	59 623	64 552	70 630	75 817	..	..
Other social and personal services, private households with employees and extra-territorial organisations	EWTV	37 011	39 881	42 228	44 629	48 331	51 802	55 543	..	..
Total service industries	QTPZ	530 106	564 043	594 765	634 354	681 342	732 825	782 647	..	..
All industries	ABML	763 680	800 611	840 979	882 753	930 297	985 558	1 044 165	1 088 506	1 145 167

1 See chapter text. Components may not sum to totals as a result of rounding.
2 Because of differences in the annual and monthly production inquiries, estimates of current price output and value added by industry derived from the current price input-output supply-use balances are not consistent with the equivalent measures of constant price growth given in Table 16.5. These differences do not affect GDP totals. For further information see "Experimental Constant Price Input-Output Supply-Use Balances: An approach to improving the quality of the national accounts" Nadim Ahmad, *Economic Trends*, July 1999 (No. 548).

3 Central government expenditure on education is included in PAD in 1995. For 1996 onwards it is included in Education.

Source: Office for National Statistics: 020 7533 6045

16.5 Gross value added at basic prices: by industry[1,2,3,4]
Chained volume indices
United Kingdom

Indices (2003=100)

	Weight per 1000[1]		1998	1999	2000	2001	2002	2003	2004	2005	2006
	2003										
Agriculture, hunting, forestry and fishing	9.9	GDQA	97.9	101.1	100.3	90.9	102.1	100.0	99.0	101.4	99.6
Production											
Mining and quarrying											
Mining and quarrying of energy producing materials											
Mining of coal	0.6	CKZP	149.5	132.5	113.1	112.6	105.9	100.0	85.8	66.9	63.7
Extraction of mineral oil and natural gas	25.1	CKZO	112.4	117.7	113.6	107.3	105.9	100.0	91.6	81.7	74.5
Other mining and quarrying	2.0	CKZQ	76.8	82.6	85.8	80.4	98.7	100.0	101.4	110.1	109.9
Total mining and quarrying	27.7	CKYX	110.2	114.8	111.1	105.0	105.4	100.0	92.1	83.4	76.8
Manufacturing											
Food; beverages and tobacco	23.8	CKZA	97.6	97.5	96.7	98.0	100.0	100.0	101.6	102.3	102.1
Textiles and textile products	6.3	CKZB	135.0	125.3	122.4	107.2	99.7	100.0	91.8	90.2	86.8
Leather and leather products	0.7	CKZC	165.3	156.2	137.7	140.0	122.5	100.0	74.6	68.9	69.8
Wood and wood products	2.7	CKZD	98.2	94.1	96.5	96.6	99.2	100.0	101.8	97.4	94.9
Pulp, paper and paper products; publishing and printing	23.2	CKZE	100.9	101.1	101.5	101.3	101.4	100.0	99.1	94.0	91.7
Coke, petroleum products and nuclear fuel	2.9	CKZF	118.9	107.2	112.9	106.9	108.3	100.0	105.8	109.9	105.2
Chemicals, chemical products and man-made fibres	18.4	CKZG	85.8	88.9	93.6	99.3	99.1	100.0	103.4	104.3	107.9
Rubber and plastic products	9.0	CKZH	107.4	107.0	107.0	103.2	99.2	100.0	98.5	94.9	98.0
Other non-metallic mineral products	5.8	CKZI	93.0	92.8	95.6	96.0	94.5	100.0	105.8	105.5	107.5
Basic metals and fabricated metal products	17.8	CKZJ	103.9	101.4	103.5	101.4	102.4	100.0	103.1	103.2	104.6
Machinery and equipment not elsewhere classified	13.9	CKZK	108.8	102.4	102.3	104.2	98.3	100.0	105.8	109.0	114.0
Electrical and optical equipment	21.3	CKZL	101.0	111.5	128.2	118.7	102.6	100.0	101.8	96.9	98.2
Transport equipment	18.1	CKZM	100.1	103.8	99.7	97.9	94.8	100.0	105.8	105.3	111.4
Manufacturing not elsewhere classified	7.6	CKZN	98.7	101.6	100.4	99.9	100.5	100.0	99.3	99.8	100.7
Total manufacturing	171.6	CKYY	100.5	101.4	103.8	102.5	99.8	100.0	102.0	101.0	102.5
Electricity, gas and water supply	18.2	CKYZ	88.8	92.1	95.0	98.0	98.4	100.0	101.1	100.9	98.1
Total production	217.6	CKYW	100.5	101.9	103.8	102.3	100.3	100.0	100.8	98.9	99.0
Construction	56.7	GDQB	89.7	89.8	90.2	92.2	95.5	100.0	104.0	105.6	106.8
Service industries											
Wholesale and retail trade (including motor trade); repair of motor vehicles, personal and household goods	125.5	GDQC	83.3	85.9	89.0	92.3	96.9	100.0	105.3	106.5	109.1
Hotels and restaurants	33.3	GDQD	84.6	88.3	89.4	91.3	94.4	100.0	104.5	106.0	112.9
Transport, storage and communication											
Transport and storage	49.8	GDQF	87.2	90.5	95.6	97.7	99.2	100.0	103.4	107.9	112.1
Communication	31.3	GDQG	61.2	73.4	88.8	96.0	96.5	100.0	101.2	105.5	107.3
Total	81.0	GDQH	76.2	83.4	92.9	97.0	98.2	100.0	102.5	107.0	110.3
Financial intermediation	48.5	GDQI	79.9	82.0	87.1	90.2	93.7	100.0	107.6	113.9	123.6
Adjustment for financial services (FISIM)	−38.1	GDQJ	72.0	73.7	81.7	86.3	89.2	100.0	113.0	123.3	138.3
Real estate, renting and business activities											
Letting of dwellings, including imputed rent of owner occupiers	77.8	GDQL	92.2	93.3	95.2	96.5	97.7	100.0	101.5	102.9	105.2
Other real estate, renting and business activities	160.4	GDQK	74.4	80.6	87.6	92.9	94.7	100.0	107.7	114.5	122.8
Total	238.3	GDQM	79.8	84.5	89.9	94.0	95.7	100.0	105.7	110.7	117.1
Public administration and defence (PAD)[4]	55.6	GDQO	91.2	91.4	91.9	93.0	95.3	100.0	101.9	102.8	103.5
Education[4]	58.7	GDQP	94.4	95.7	96.9	97.6	99.3	100.0	100.4	102.0	103.1
Health and social work[4]	62.3	GDQQ	84.2	86.3	89.6	92.8	96.3	100.0	103.9	107.4	110.7
Other social and personal services, private households with employees and extra-territorial organisations	51.0	GDQR	91.9	91.5	94.7	98.5	100.1	100.0	101.3	103.1	105.9
Total service industries	715.8	GDQS	83.8	87.2	91.3	94.5	96.9	100.0	103.9	106.9	110.8
All industries	1 000.0	CGCE	87.6	90.3	93.7	95.7	97.4	100.0	103.3	105.3	108.2

1 See chapter text. The weights are in proportion to total gross value added (GVA) in 2003 and are used to combine the industry output indices to calculate the totals for 2004 and 2005. For 2003 and earlier, totals are calculated using the equivalent weight for the previous year (eg totals for 2002 use 2001 weights).

2 As GVA is expressed in index number form, it is inappropriate to show as a statistical adjustment any divergence from the other measures of GDP. Such an adjustment does, however, exist implicitly.

3 See footnote 2 to Table 16.4.

4 The GVA for PAD, education and Health and social work in this table follows the SIC(92) and differs from that used in Table 2.3 in *United Kingdom National Accounts* (the *Blue Book*) which is based on Input-Output groups. The administration costs of the NHS are included in PAD in this table but are included in Health and social work in Table 2.3. Central government expenditure on teachers is included in this table but, for 1995 only, are included in PAD in Table 16.4.

Source: Office for National Statistics: 020 7533 6045

16.6 Non-financial corporations[1]
Allocation of primary income account[2]
United Kingdom. ESA95 sector S.11

£ million

		1998	1999	2000	2001	2002	2003	2004	2005	2006
Resources										
Operating surplus, gross	NQBE	182 600	186 617	192 386	192 834	196 563	209 744	226 391	235 887	250 305
Property income, received										
Interest	EABC	14 015	10 794	14 427	12 860	9 338	9 032	11 428	16 046	..
Distributed income of corporations	EABD	25 086	21 501	26 631	36 868	32 210	..	..	..	..
Reinvested earnings on direct foreign investment	HDVR	10 979	16 214	20 118	22 950	26 893	12 492	24 181	31 877	43 340
Attributed property income of insurance policy-holders	FAOF	463	338	489	280	302	..	..	..	..
Rent	FAOG	118	117	117	117	118	..	..	..	..
Total	FAKY	50 663	48 935	61 471	73 796	67 240	72 370	80 188	95 614	108 296
Total resources	FBXJ	233 263	235 552	253 857	266 630	263 803	282 114	306 579	331 501	358 601
Uses										
Property income, paid										
Interest	EABG	32 046	31 857	38 389	40 056	37 134	36 445	42 002	50 263	..
Distributed income of corporations	NVCS	78 299	87 100	83 202	100 810	91 868	..	..	..	..
Reinvested earnings on direct foreign investment	HDVB	3 117	2 776	7 348	1 699	1 614	3 955	6 729	5 044	15 593
Rent	FBXO	584	564	1 319	1 896	1 853	..	..	..	..
Total	FBXK	115 392	123 593	133 583	149 517	130 849	140 764	149 298	164 791	182 980
Balance of primary incomes, gross	NQBG	117 871	111 959	120 274	117 113	132 954	141 350	157 281	166 710	175 621
Total uses	FBXJ	233 263	235 552	253 857	266 630	263 803	282 114	306 579	331 501	358 601
After deduction of fixed capital consumption	-DBGF	−57 625	−60 263	−62 465	−64 028	−65 775	−67 438	−69 979	−71 335	−72 737
Balance of primary incomes, net	FBXQ	60 246	51 696	57 809	53 085	67 179	73 912	87 302	93 950	..

1 See chapter text.
2 Before deduction of fixed capital formation.

Source: Office for National Statistics: 020 7533 5498

16.7 Non-financial corporations[1]
Secondary distribution of income account
United Kingdom. ESA95 sector S.11

£ million

		1998	1999	2000	2001	2002	2003	2004	2005	2006
Resources										
Balance of primary incomes, gross	NQBG	117 871	111 959	120 274	117 113	132 954	141 350	157 281	166 710	175 621
Social contributions										
Imputed social contributions	NSTJ	3 454	3 845	4 175	4 357	4 575	4 229	3 864	3 612	3 490
Current transfers other than taxes, social contributions and benefits										
Non-life insurance claims	FCBP	4 849	4 151	4 456	4 565	7 789	..	..	..	..
Miscellaneous transfers	NRJY	595	611	622	619	616	..	..	..	..
Total	NRJB	4 978	4 260	6 008	5 122	5 599	6 595	6 619	7 539	8 300
Total resources	FCBR	126 303	120 064	130 457	126 592	143 128	152 174	167 764	177 861	187 411
Uses										
Current taxes on income, wealth etc.										
Taxes on income	FCBS	27 256	22 948	24 497	23 177	24 038	23 702	27 348	33 790	38 819
Social benefits other than social transfers in kind	NSTJ	3 454	3 845	4 175	4 357	4 575	4 229	3 864	3 612	3 490
Current transfers other than taxes, social contributions and benefits										
Net non-life insurance premiums	FCBY	4 849	4 151	4 456	4 565	7 789	..	..	..	..
Miscellaneous current transfers	FDBI	444	569	413	411	422	434	446	..	..
Total, other current transfers	FCBX	5 475	4 860	6 476	5 506	5 932	6 933	7 042	8 027	8 777
Gross Disposable Income	NRJD	90 118	88 411	95 309	93 552	108 583	117 310	129 510	132 432	136 325
Total uses	FCBR	126 303	120 064	130 457	126 592	143 128	152 174	167 764	177 861	187 411
After deduction of fixed capital consumption	-DBGF	−57 625	−60 263	−62 465	−64 028	−65 775	−67 438	−69 979	−71 335	−72 737
Disposable income, net	FCCF	32 493	28 148	32 844	29 524	42 808	49 872	59 531	59 957	..

1 See chapter text.

Source: Office for National Statistics: 020 7533 5498

16.8 General government[1]
Allocation of primary income account
United Kingdom. ESA95 sector S.13 Unconsolidated

£ million

		1998	1999	2000	2001	2002	2003	2004	2005	2006
Resources										
Operating surplus, gross	NMXV	8 999	9 262	9 542	9 796	10 289	10 807	11 681	12 605	13 650
Taxes on production and imports, received										
Taxes on products										
Value added tax (VAT)	NZGF	52 293	57 701	59 985	63 522	68 251	74 595	79 751	81 445	85 569
Taxes and duties on imports excluding VAT										
Import duties	NMXZ	–	–	–	–	–	–	–	–	–
Taxes on imports excluding VAT and import duties	NMBT	–	–	–	–	–	–	–	..	..
Taxes on products excluding VAT and import duties	NMYB	44 881	48 442	51 956	50 745	52 001	52 858	55 932	56 814	60 240
Total taxes on products	NVCC	97 194	106 143	111 941	114 267	120 252	127 453	135 683	138 259	145 809
Other taxes on production	NMYD	15 815	16 503	17 083	17 565	18 113	18 517	18 945	19 805	21 148
Total taxes on production and imports, received	NMYE	113 009	122 646	129 024	131 832	138 365	145 970	154 628	158 064	166 957
less Subsidies, paid										
Subsidies on products	-NMYF	−3 729	−3 625	−3 791	−3 953	−4 672	−5 311	−4 961	−5 047	−5 483
Other subsidies on production	-LIUF	−810	−663	−574	−662	−954	−1 434	−1 499	−1 399	−1 420
Total	-NMRL	−4 539	−4 288	−4 365	−4 615	−5 626	−6 745	−6 460	−6 446	−6 903
Property income, received										
Total Interest	NMYL	7 912	7 335	7 340	7 332	6 624	7 053	6 280	6 313	6 908
Distributed income of corporations	NMYM	7 514	7 303	7 777	6 910	6 156	8 073	7 869	4 508	3 507
Property income attributed to insurance policy holders	NMYO	48	33	54	24	22	19	17	27	25
Rent										
from sectors other than general government	NMYR	547	529	1 289	1 919	1 901	1 565	1 422	1 352	1 210
Total	NMYU	16 021	15 200	16 460	16 185	14 703	16 710	15 588	12 200	11 650
Total resources	NMYV	133 490	142 820	150 661	153 198	157 731	166 742	175 437	176 423	185 354
Uses										
Property income, paid										
Total interest	NRKB	34 861	30 699	30 639	27 965	25 463	26 955	27 050	29 489	..
Total	NMYY	34 861	30 699	30 639	27 965	25 463	26 955	27 050	29 448	30 413
Balance of primary incomes, gross	NMZH	98 629	112 121	120 022	125 233	132 268	139 787	148 387	146 975	154 941
Total uses	NMYV	133 490	142 820	150 661	153 198	157 731	166 742	175 437	176 423	185 354
After deduction of fixed capital consumption	-NMXO	−8 999	−9 262	−9 542	−9 796	−10 289	−10 807	−11 681	−12 605	−13 650
Balance of primary incomes, net	NMZI	89 630	102 859	110 480	115 437	121 979	128 980	136 706	135 873	..

1 See chapter text.

Source: Office for National Statistics: 020 7533 5985

16.9 General government[1]
Secondary distribution of income account
United Kingdom. ESA95 sector S.13 Unconsolidated

£ million

		1998	1999	2000	2001	2002	2003	2004	2005	2006
Resources										
Balance of primary incomes, gross	NMZH	98 629	112 121	120 022	125 233	132 268	139 787	148 387	146 975	154 941
Current taxes on income, wealth etc.										
Taxes on income	NMZJ	123 683	129 553	140 002	147 264	142 842	144 234	154 717	173 246	192 748
Other current taxes	NVCM	18 120	19 519	20 287	22 068	23 664	26 016	27 718	29 054	30 476
Total	NMZL	141 803	149 072	160 289	169 332	166 506	170 250	182 435	202 300	223 224
Social contributions										
Actual social contributions										
Employers' actual social contributions	NMZM	30 593	33 401	36 397	38 460	38 780	45 067	49 602	52 821	55 081
Employees' social contributions	NMZN	25 234	26 645	27 293	28 725	29 568	34 376	38 150	41 472	43 250
Social contributions by self- and non-employed persons	NMZO	1 729	1 883	2 049	2 183	2 318	2 595	2 727	2 825	2 913
Total	NMZP	57 556	61 929	65 739	69 368	70 666	82 038	90 479	97 118	101 244
Imputed social contributions	NMZQ	6 981	6 927	7 395	7 577	8 348	6 456	5 928	7 282	7 158
Total	NMZR	64 537	68 856	73 134	76 945	79 014	88 494	96 407	104 400	108 402
Other current transfers										
Non-life insurance claims	NMZS	499	410	403	353	400	296	285	341	372
Current transfers within general government	NMZT	60 367	64 446	66 187	72 522	77 592	85 224	91 910	100 215	109 614
Current international cooperation	NMZU	1 384	3 176	2 084	4 568	3 112	3 570	3 604	3 668	3 594
Miscellaneous current transfers										
from sectors other than general government	NMZX	498	392	447	460	502	562	610	627	601
Other current transfers	NNAA	62 748	68 424	69 121	77 903	81 606	89 652	96 409	104 851	114 181
Total resources	NNAB	367 717	398 473	422 566	449 413	459 394	488 183	523 638	558 526	600 748
Uses										
Social benefits other than social transfers in kind	NNAD	117 668	117 685	120 163	129 591	136 801	146 066	154 216	162 488	167 976
Other current transfers										
Net non-life insurance premiums	NNAE	499	410	403	353	400	296	285	341	372
Current transfers within general government	NNAF	60 367	64 446	66 187	72 522	77 592	85 224	91 910	100 215	109 614
Current international cooperation	NNAG	1 705	1 667	2 418	2 434	2 573	2 720	3 180	3 174	3 770
Miscellaneous current transfers										
to sectors other than general government	NNAI	14 829	18 466	20 913	22 131	27 351	30 275	32 550	34 336	34 091
Of which: GNP based fourth own resource	NMFH	3 920	4 632	4 379	3 858	5 335	6 772	7 549	8 732	8 521
Other current transfers	NNAN	77 400	84 989	89 921	97 440	107 916	118 515	127 925	138 066	147 847
Gross Disposable Income	NNAO	171 819	194 938	211 622	221 480	213 801	222 760	240 660	257 146	284 067
Total uses	NNAB	367 717	398 473	422 566	449 413	459 394	488 183	523 638	558 526	600 748
After deduction of fixed capital consumption	-NMXO	−8 999	−9 262	−9 542	−9 796	−10 289	−10 807	−11 681	−12 605	−13 650
Disposable income, net	NNAP	162 820	185 676	202 080	211 684	203 512	211 953	228 979	248 402	..

1 See chapter text.

Source: Office for National Statistics: 020 7533 5985

16.10 Households and non-profit institutions serving households[1]
Allocation of primary income account
United Kingdom. ESA95 sectors S.14 and S.15

£ million

		1998	1999	2000	2001	2002	2003	2004	2005	2006
Resources										
Operating surplus, gross	QWLS	47 642	51 195	53 960	59 083	62 544	67 935	72 709	77 680	82 269
Mixed income, gross	QWLT	52 823	55 734	57 805	62 121	65 771	69 122	71 958	76 112	78 866
Compensation of employees										
Wages and salaries	QWLW	406 548	431 795	462 505	491 044	508 681	527 689	550 654	577 048	603 203
Employers' social contributions	QWLX	59 522	64 199	69 824	73 216	78 782	89 263	98 134	108 362	114 520
Total	QWLY	466 070	495 994	532 329	564 260	587 463	616 952	648 788	685 410	717 723
Property income										
Interest	QWLZ	29 867	24 147	28 239	26 823	20 878	20 966	26 242	31 424	33 186
Distributed income of corporations	QWMA	38 649	40 411	44 408	49 881	43 695	44 843	46 239	51 247	51 556
Attributed property income of insurance policy holders	QWMC	56 242	56 303	56 048	56 109	55 057	54 997	54 589	63 725	68 145
Rent	QWMD	105	105	105	105	106	108	110	110	112
Total	QWME	124 863	120 966	128 800	132 918	119 736	120 914	127 180	146 506	152 999
Total resources	QWMF	691 398	723 889	772 894	818 382	835 514	874 923	920 635	985 708	1 031 857
Uses										
Property income										
Interest	QWMG	51 219	47 434	52 875	52 141	51 513	53 576	62 677	71 091	75 053
Rent	QWMH	216	215	215	215	216	220	224	224	224
Total	QWMI	51 435	47 649	53 090	52 356	51 729	53 796	62 901	71 315	75 277
Balance of primary incomes, gross	QWMJ	639 963	676 240	719 804	766 026	783 785	821 127	857 734	914 393	956 580
Total uses	QWMF	691 398	723 889	772 894	818 382	835 514	874 923	920 635	985 708	1 031 857
After deduction of										
fixed capital consumption	-QWLL	−25 053	−27 976	−30 517	−32 909	−36 043	−36 903	−42 366	−42 623	..
Balance of primary incomes, net	QWMK	614 910	648 264	689 287	733 117	747 742	784 224	815 368	868 981	..

1 See chapter text.

Source: Office for National Statistics: 020 7533 6058

16.11 Households and non-profit institutions serving households[1]
Secondary distribution of income account
United Kingdom. ESA95 sectors S.14 and S.15

£ million

		1998	1999	2000	2001	2002	2003	2004	2005	2006
Resources										
Balance of primary incomes, gross	QWMJ	639 963	676 240	719 804	766 026	783 785	821 127	857 734	914 393	956 580
Imputed social contributions	RVFH	478	450	476	502	530	505	495	500	508
Social benefits other than social transfers in kind	QWML	154 438	157 647	162 833	171 814	182 673	193 596	202 074	214 367	223 341
Other current transfers										
Non-life insurance claims	QWMM	15 224	13 762	16 150	15 607	17 177	14 824	15 494	17 863	19 486
Miscellaneous current transfers	QWMN	21 181	24 392	27 520	29 080	33 041	34 687	36 284	37 878	38 204
Total	QWMO	36 405	38 154	43 670	44 687	50 218	49 511	51 778	55 741	57 690
Total resources	QWMP	831 284	872 491	926 783	983 029	1 017 206	1 064 739	1 112 081	1 185 001	1 238 119
Uses										
Current taxes on income, wealth etc										
Taxes on income	QWMQ	89 276	96 528	105 299	111 888	112 171	113 087	120 253	131 194	140 215
Other current taxes	NVCO	17 290	18 658	19 427	21 166	22 788	25 174	26 881	28 228	29 618
Total	QWMS	106 566	115 186	124 726	133 054	134 959	138 261	147 134	159 422	169 833
Social contributions										
Actual social contributions										
Employers' actual social contributions	QWMT	48 138	52 529	57 288	60 296	64 805	77 571	87 347	96 464	102 856
Employees' social contributions	QWMU	54 761	57 434	58 806	60 599	62 458	66 490	69 576	77 417	82 843
Social contributions by self and non-employed	QWMV	1 729	1 883	2 049	2 183	2 318	2 595	2 727	2 825	2 913
Total	QWMW	104 628	111 846	118 143	123 078	129 581	146 656	159 650	176 281	..
Imputed social contributions	QWMX	11 384	11 670	12 536	12 920	13 977	11 692	10 787	11 898	11 664
Total	QWMY	116 012	123 516	130 679	135 998	143 558	158 348	170 437	187 600	..
Social benefits other than social transfers in kind	QWMZ	950	922	948	977	1 006	987	984	994	1 004
Other current transfers										
Net non-life insurance premiums	QWNA	15 224	13 762	16 150	15 607	17 177	14 824	15 494	17 863	19 486
Miscellaneous current transfers	QWNB	9 742	10 117	10 865	11 081	11 458	11 930	12 349	13 340	13 280
Total	QWNC	24 966	23 879	27 015	26 688	28 635	26 754	27 843	31 203	32 766
Gross Disposable Income[2]	QWND	582 790	608 988	643 415	686 312	709 048	740 389	765 683	804 778	834 240
Total uses	QWMP	831 284	872 491	926 783	983 029	1 017 206	1 064 739	1 112 081	1 185 001	1 238 119
After deduction of fixed capital consumption	-QWLL	−25 053	−27 976	−30 517	−32 909	−36 043	−36 903	−42 366	−42 623	..
Disposable income, net	QWNE	557 737	581 012	612 898	653 403	673 005	703 486	723 317	758 292	..

1 See chapter text.
2 Gross household disposable income revalued by the implied households and NPISH's final consumption expenditure deflator. For more details see table 6.1.4 on page 217 in *United Kingdom National Accounts* (the *Blue book*).

Source: Office for National Statistics: 020 7533 6031

16.12 Households and non-profit institutions serving households[1]
Use of disposable income account
United Kingdom. ESA95 sectors S.14 and S.15

£ million and percentages

		1998	1999	2000	2001	2002	2003	2004	2005	2006
Resources										
Disposable income, gross	QWND	582 790	608 988	643 415	686 312	709 048	740 389	765 683	804 778	834 240
Adjustment for the change in net equity of households in pension funds	NSSE	14 044	14 016	14 164	16 041	17 783	21 377	25 108	31 210	35 307
Total resources	NSSF	596 834	623 004	657 579	702 353	726 831	761 766	790 791	835 988	869 547
Uses										
Final consumption expenditure										
Individual consumption expenditure	NSSG	554 990	589 868	623 995	657 216	690 530	724 345	761 484	791 620	826 634
Saving, gross	NSSH	41 844	33 136	33 584	45 137	36 301	37 421	29 307	44 368	42 913
Total uses	NSSF	596 834	623 004	657 579	702 353	726 831	761 766	790 791	835 988	869 547
Saving ratio (percentages)	RVGL	7.0	5.3	5.1	6.4	5.0	4.9	3.7	5.3	4.9

1 See chapter text.

Source: Office for National Statistics: 020 7533 6058

16.13 The sector accounts: key economic indicators[1]
United Kingdom

£ million and indices (2003=100)

		1998	1999	2000	2001	2002	2003	2004	2005	2006
Net lending/borrowing by:										
Non-financial corporations	EABO	−6 930	−13 157	−7 541	−10 509	6 529	18 181	26 255	18 290	17 770
Financial corporations	NHCQ	−5 086	−14 185	−27 457	−22 800	7 018	19 335	26 479	10 099	3 916
General government	NNBK	868	11 105	16 636	11 327	−16 613	−35 027	−36 827	−39 071	−36 818
Households and NPISH's	NSSZ	8 765	−4 112	−4 205	2 938	−11 841	−14 687	−32 241	−17 313	−27 247
Rest of the world	NHRB	2 706	20 970	23 130	20 566	15 581	13 455	17 265	27 674	42 675
Private non-financial corporations										
Gross trading profits										
Continental shelf profits	CAGJ	11 696	13 864	21 458	20 397	18 742	..	..	..	..
Others	CAED	152 774	156 399	155 606	154 014	161 426	174 873	192 807	196 624	205 352
Rental of buildings	FCBW	9 767	10 821	11 747	12 394	12 904	13 891	14 864	15 404	16 004
less Holding gains of inventories	-DLQZ	754	−1 800	−2 941	438	−2 856	−4 266	−6 158	−6 619	−5 085
Gross operating surplus	NRJK	174 846	178 939	185 198	185 942	189 906	202 479	219 738	228 054	241 966
Households and NPISH										
Household gross disposable income	QWND	582 790	608 988	643 415	686 312	709 048	740 389	765 683	804 778	834 240
Implied deflator of household and NPISH individual consumption expenditure indicies (2003=100)	YBFS	91.8	93.4	94.4	96.6	98.1	100.0	101.7	104.2	106.7
Real household disposable income:										
Chained volume measures (Reference year 2003)	RVGK	634 508	652 060	681 249	710 531	722 823	740 389	752 890	772 016	781 945
Indices (2003=100)	OSXR	85.7	88.1	92.0	96.0	97.6	100.0	101.7	104.3	105.6
Gross saving	NSSH	41 844	33 136	33 584	45 137	36 301	37 421	29 307	44 368	42 913
Households total resources	NSSJ	691 617	725 746	766 876	820 811	857 647	905 720	946 602	1 002 687	1 048 385
Saving ratio (percentages)	RVGL	*7.0*	*5.3*	*5.1*	*6.4*	*5.0*	*4.9*	*3.7*	*5.3*	*4.9*

1 See chapter text.

Source: Office for National Statistics: 020 7533 6045

16.14 Household final consumption expenditure: by purpose[1]
Current market prices

United Kingdom

£ million

		1998	1999	2000	2001	2002	2003	2004	2005	2006
Durable goods										
Furnishings, household equipment and routine maintenance of the house	LLIJ	15 873	16 566	18 006	19 275	20 470	21 595	22 363	22 335	22 938
Health	LLIK	1 717	1 881	1 997	2 109	2 411	2 604	2 727	2 710	3 076
Transport	LLIL	30 851	31 888	33 291	35 864	36 574	38 016	38 792	38 319	38 646
Communication	LLIM	440	512	601	636	644	810	859	958	937
Recreation and culture	LLIN	12 953	14 262	14 878	15 970	16 471	17 752	19 373	19 593	20 285
Miscellaneous goods and services	LLIO	3 320	3 398	3 403	3 750	4 204	4 284	4 539	4 307	4 545
Total durable goods	UTIA	65 154	68 507	72 176	77 604	80 774	85 061	88 653	88 222	90 427
Semi-durable goods										
Clothing and footwear	LLJL	31 249	32 661	34 759	36 092	38 351	40 389	42 006	42 970	45 051
Furnishings, household equipment and routine maintenance of the house	LLJM	9 751	10 577	11 677	12 400	13 361	13 932	14 462	13 641	14 273
Transport	LLJN	2 925	3 018	2 772	2 783	3 112	3 423	3 381	3 537	3 784
Recreation and culture	LLJO	17 292	19 049	20 405	21 606	23 910	26 009	28 228	28 692	29 832
Miscellaneous goods and services	LLJP	1 816	1 926	2 018	2 427	2 886	3 356	3 754	3 432	3 306
Total semi-durable goods	UTIQ	63 033	67 231	71 631	75 308	81 620	87 109	91 831	92 272	96 246
Non-durable goods										
Food & drink	ABZV	55 162	57 040	58 628	59 804	61 310	63 174	65 521	67 539	70 809
Alcohol & tobacco	ADFL	22 459	24 458	24 617	25 158	25 966	27 297	27 713	28 009	28 522
Housing, water, electricity, gas and other fuels	LLIX	22 094	21 800	22 265	23 076	23 444	24 241	27 011	28 305	32 866
Furnishings, household equipment and routine maintenance of the house	LLIY	2 505	2 657	2 786	2 972	3 169	3 338	3 391	3 456	3 679
Health	LLIZ	2 975	3 111	3 268	3 613	3 855	3 938	4 023	3 715	3 735
Transport	LLJA	16 615	18 210	19 987	19 391	19 129	20 072	21 873	23 689	23 918
Recreation and culture	LLJB	12 136	12 665	12 959	13 107	13 392	13 507	13 650	13 831	14 173
Miscellaneous goods and services	LLJC	8 727	9 121	9 463	9 884	11 272	12 602	13 486	14 108	14 338
Total non-durable goods	UTII	142 673	149 062	153 973	157 005	161 537	168 169	176 668	182 652	192 040
Total goods	UTIE	270 860	284 800	297 780	309 917	323 931	340 339	357 152	363 146	378 713
Services										
Clothing and footwear	LLJD	698	714	720	730	741	766	786	843	896
Housing, water, electricity, gas and other fuels	LLJE	76 020	81 393	85 785	92 829	97 794	104 810	111 029	118 358	125 873
Furnishings, household equipment and routine maintenance of the house	LLJF	2 873	3 046	3 206	3 327	3 448	3 601	3 813	4 013	4 171
Health	LLJG	3 614	3 783	3 943	4 254	4 512	4 793	5 182	5 578	5 690
Transport	LLJH	32 115	34 121	37 002	38 397	41 332	43 058	45 167	47 393	50 157
Communication	LLJI	10 462	11 493	12 755	13 521	14 031	14 844	15 589	15 842	15 974
Recreation and culture	LLJJ	20 865	21 505	21 912	22 769	25 349	27 118	29 806	32 002	33 478
Education	ADIE	7 814	8 943	9 534	9 409	9 381	9 610	9 990	10 409	10 998
Restaurants and hotels	ADIF	61 807	64 387	68 557	71 620	76 426	78 902	83 595	88 937	91 918
Miscellaneous goods and services	LLJK	44 656	48 431	52 691	56 199	57 054	57 161	58 381	61 462	63 592
Total services	UTIM	260 924	277 816	296 105	313 055	330 068	344 663	363 338	384 837	402 747
Final consumption expenditure in the UK by resident and non-resident households (domestic concept)	ABQI	531 784	562 616	593 885	622 972	653 999	685 002	720 490	747 983	781 460
Final consumption expenditure outside the UK by UK resident households	ABTA	16 913	19 690	21 654	22 907	24 435	26 314	27 739	29 209	30 338
less Final consumption expenditure in the UK by households resident in the rest of the world	CDFD	−14 544	−14 312	−14 713	−13 383	−13 872	−14 156	−15 698	−17 160	−18 476
Final consumption expenditure by UK resident households in the UK and abroad (national concept)	ABPB	534 153	567 994	600 826	632 496	664 562	697 160	732 531	760 032	793 322

1 See chapter text. Additional detail is published in *Consumer Trends* and table A7 of *UK Economic Accounts*, available from the National Statistics website *www.statistics.gov.uk/statbase/Product.asp?vlnk=1904.*

Source: Office for National Statistics: 020 7533 6058

16.15

Household final consumption expenditure: by purpose[1]
Chained volume measures, reference year 2003

United Kingdom

£ million

		1998	1999	2000	2001	2002	2003	2004	2005	2006
Durable goods										
Furnishings, household equipment and routine maintenance of the house	LLME	16 112	16 764	18 442	19 542	20 603	21 595	22 030	21 705	21 994
Health	LLMF	2 749	2 585	2 455	2 337	2 421	2 604	2 612	2 562	2 924
Transport	LLMG	27 974	29 455	31 680	35 100	36 057	38 016	39 107	39 571	40 362
Communication	LLMH	322	428	536	582	640	810	883	1 082	1 136
Recreation and culture	LLMI	7 644	9 657	11 243	13 344	14 911	17 752	21 381	24 910	28 960
Miscellaneous goods and services	LLMJ	3 632	3 656	3 618	3 932	4 360	4 284	4 445	4 178	4 150
Total durable goods	UTIC	56 607	61 603	67 366	74 551	78 825	85 061	90 458	94 008	99 526
Semi-durable goods										
Clothing and footwear	LLNG	25 971	27 921	30 969	33 712	37 727	40 389	43 327	45 424	48 105
Furnishings, household equipment and routine maintenance of the house	LLNH	9 321	10 177	11 473	12 221	13 215	13 932	14 426	13 861	14 616
Transport	LLNI	3 089	3 136	2 856	2 880	3 172	3 423	3 313	3 369	3 484
Recreation and culture	LLNJ	15 150	17 229	19 175	20 339	23 040	26 009	29 115	30 179	31 897
Miscellaneous goods and services	LLNK	1 814	1 932	2 053	2 438	2 920	3 356	3 771	3 354	3 181
Total semi-durable goods	UTIS	55 217	60 277	66 478	71 563	80 058	87 109	93 952	96 187	101 283
Non-durable goods										
Food & drink	ADIP	58 058	59 904	61 944	61 048	62 143	63 174	65 181	66 230	67 861
Alcohol & tobacco	ADIS	26 829	27 623	26 704	26 497	26 884	27 297	27 444	27 258	27 007
Housing, water, electricity, gas and other fuels	LLMS	22 897	22 594	23 189	23 958	23 881	24 241	25 723	24 615	24 471
Furnishings, household equipment and routine maintenance of the house	LLMT	2 401	2 492	2 666	2 878	3 101	3 338	3 519	3 582	3 685
Health	LLMU	3 242	3 314	3 397	3 686	3 895	3 938	4 043	3 728	3 740
Transport	LLMV	19 538	19 691	19 114	19 550	19 825	20 072	20 731	20 718	19 874
Recreation and culture	LLMW	13 410	13 713	13 657	13 537	13 681	13 507	13 463	13 571	13 565
Miscellaneous goods and services	LLMX	8 456	8 669	9 248	9 586	11 124	12 602	13 631	14 399	15 135
Total non-durable goods	UTIK	154 422	157 573	159 677	160 597	164 482	168 169	173 735	174 101	175 338
Total goods	UTIG	263 426	277 468	292 390	306 198	323 179	340 339	358 145	364 296	376 147
Services										
Clothing and footwear	LLMY	834	819	805	790	775	766	760	773	785
Housing, water, electricity, gas and other fuels	LLMZ	100 061	101 184	102 168	102 778	104 106	104 810	105 767	107 025	109 116
Furnishings, household equipment and routine maintenance of the house	LLNA	3 834	3 874	3 821	3 718	3 646	3 601	3 602	3 595	3 573
Health	LLNB	4 595	4 531	4 612	4 683	4 665	4 793	4 954	5 244	5 158
Transport	LLNC	39 140	41 413	43 153	40 971	42 611	43 058	43 459	43 647	44 121
Communication	LLND	9 341	10 527	12 167	13 877	14 158	14 844	15 478	16 068	16 203
Recreation and culture	LLNE	24 555	24 795	25 101	25 960	26 216	27 118	28 930	29 934	29 830
Education	ADMJ	10 530	11 394	11 489	10 692	10 091	9 610	9 541	9 475	9 480
Restaurants and hotels	ADMK	73 811	74 191	76 252	76 434	78 303	78 902	81 796	83 882	83 560
Miscellaneous goods and services	LLNF	51 249	53 735	55 696	57 368	57 336	57 161	56 232	55 742	55 651
Total services	UTIO	316 510	325 416	334 699	337 218	341 883	344 663	350 519	355 385	357 477
Final consumption expenditure in the UK by resident and non-resident households (domestic concept)	ABQJ	576 994	600 627	625 437	642 595	664 790	685 002	708 664	719 681	733 624
Final consumption expenditure outside the UK by UK resident households	ABTC	18 787	21 899	24 189	24 897	26 376	26 314	28 068	27 745	28 155
less Final consumption expenditure in the UK by households resident in the rest of the world	CCHX	−16 713	−16 031	−16 038	−14 164	−14 292	−14 156	−15 298	−16 152	−16 846
Final consumption expenditure by UK resident households in the UK and abroad (national concept)	ABPF	579 342	606 648	633 662	653 326	676 833	697 160	721 434	731 274	744 933

1 See chapter text. Additional detail is published in *Consumer Trends* and table A7 of *UK Economic Accounts*, available from the National Statistics website *www.statistics.gov.uk/statbase/Product.asp?vlnk=1904*.

Source: Office for National Statistics: 020 7533 6058

16.16 Individual consumption expenditure: by households, NPISHs and general government[1] Current market prices

United Kingdom. Classified by function (COICOP/COPNI/COFOG)[2]

£ million

		1998	1999	2000	2001	2002	2003	2004	2005	2006
FINAL CONSUMPTION EXPENDITURE OF HOUSEHOLDS										
Food and non-alcoholic beverages	ABZV	55 162	57 040	58 628	59 804	61 310	63 174	65 521	67 539	70 809
Food	ABZW	49 104	50 685	51 905	52 742	53 984	55 507	57 357	59 366	61 697
Non-alcoholic beverages	ADFK	6 058	6 355	6 723	7 062	7 326	7 667	8 164	8 173	9 112
Alcoholic beverages and tobacco	ADFL	22 459	24 458	24 617	25 158	25 966	27 297	27 713	28 009	28 522
Alcoholic beverages	ADFM	9 096	10 166	10 395	10 700	11 344	12 027	12 213	12 280	12 394
Tobacco	ADFN	13 363	14 292	14 222	14 458	14 622	15 270	15 500	15 729	16 128
Clothing and footwear	ADFP	31 947	33 375	35 479	36 822	39 092	41 155	42 792	43 813	45 947
Clothing	ADFQ	27 508	28 932	31 048	32 103	33 927	35 689	37 112	38 151	40 210
Footwear	ADFR	4 439	4 443	4 431	4 719	5 165	5 466	5 680	5 662	5 737
Housing, water, electricity, gas and other fuels	ADFS	98 114	103 193	108 050	115 905	121 238	129 051	138 040	146 663	158 739
Actual rentals for housing	ADFT	21 155	22 584	23 595	25 302	25 828	27 610	28 784	30 244	32 539
Imputed rentals for housing	ADFU	47 689	51 401	54 378	59 581	63 279	68 458	73 160	78 383	82 586
Maintenance and repair of the dwelling	ADFV	9 960	10 234	10 512	11 340	12 306	12 615	13 379	13 340	13 856
Water supply and miscellaneous dwelling services	ADFW	4 961	5 201	5 033	5 059	5 222	5 438	5 698	6 388	7 032
Electricity, gas and other fuels	ADFX	14 349	13 773	14 532	14 623	14 603	14 930	17 019	18 308	22 726
Furnishings, household equipment and routine maintenance of the house	ADFY	31 002	32 846	35 675	37 974	40 448	42 466	44 029	43 445	45 061
Furniture, furnishings, carpets and other floor coverings	ADFZ	11 667	12 437	13 758	14 362	15 591	16 789	17 645	17 416	18 108
Household textiles	ADGG	3 676	3 972	4 465	4 636	5 086	5 452	5 680	5 326	5 405
Household appliances	ADGL	5 080	5 038	5 156	5 758	5 715	5 578	5 563	5 560	5 799
Glassware, tableware and household utensils	ADGM	3 410	3 722	4 231	4 609	4 710	4 701	4 635	4 591	4 767
Tools and equipment for house and garden	ADGN	2 332	2 586	2 722	2 977	3 355	3 589	3 919	3 670	3 677
Goods and services for routine household maintenance	ADGO	4 837	5 091	5 343	5 632	5 991	6 357	6 587	6 882	7 305
Health	ADGP	8 306	8 775	9 208	9 976	10 778	11 335	11 932	12 003	12 501
Medical products, appliances and equipment	ADGQ	4 692	4 992	5 265	5 722	6 266	6 542	6 750	6 425	6 811
Out-patient services	ADGR	2 010	2 107	2 178	2 344	2 422	2 553	2 752	3 007	2 990
Hospital services	ADGS	1 604	1 676	1 765	1 910	2 090	2 240	2 430	2 571	2 700
Transport	ADGT	82 506	87 237	93 052	96 435	100 147	104 569	109 213	112 938	116 505
Purchase of vehicles	ADGU	30 851	31 888	33 291	35 864	36 574	38 016	38 792	38 319	38 646
Operation of personal transport equipment	ADGV	32 045	34 450	37 059	37 028	38 816	40 507	42 915	45 683	47 354
Transport services	ADGW	19 610	20 899	22 702	23 543	24 757	26 046	27 506	28 936	30 505
Communication	ADGX	10 902	12 005	13 356	14 157	14 675	15 654	16 448	16 800	16 911
Postal services	CDEF	919	899	873	870	878	890	892	926	895
Telephone & telefax equipment	ADWO	440	512	601	636	644	810	859	958	937
Telephone & telefax services	ADWP	9 543	10 594	11 882	12 651	13 153	13 954	14 697	14 916	15 079
Recreation and culture	ADGY	63 246	67 481	70 154	73 452	79 122	84 386	91 057	94 118	97 768
Audio-visual, photographic and information processing equipment	ADGZ	15 132	16 312	17 034	17 580	18 051	19 408	21 820	21 586	21 738
Other major durables for recreation and culture	ADHL	3 089	3 582	3 944	4 325	4 672	5 126	5 428	5 737	6 268
Other recreational items and equipment; flowers, garden and pets	ADHZ	16 237	17 655	18 636	20 216	22 475	23 894	25 041	25 605	26 996
Recreational and cultural services	ADIA	19 255	19 876	20 272	21 034	23 555	25 278	27 772	29 887	31 275
Newspapers, books and stationery	ADIC	9 533	10 056	10 268	10 297	10 369	10 680	10 996	11 303	11 491
Package holidays[3]	ADID	–	–	–	–	–	–	–	–	–
Education										
Education services	ADIE	7 814	8 943	9 534	9 409	9 381	9 610	9 990	10 409	10 998
Restaurants and hotels	ADIF	61 807	64 387	68 557	71 620	76 426	78 902	83 595	88 937	91 918
Catering services	ADIG	52 671	55 164	59 019	62 449	66 701	68 839	72 837	77 050	78 919
Accommodation services	ADIH	9 136	9 223	9 538	9 171	9 725	10 063	10 758	11 887	12 999
Miscellaneous goods and services	ADII	58 519	62 876	67 575	72 260	75 416	77 403	80 160	83 309	85 781
Personal care	ADIJ	12 574	13 229	13 883	14 626	16 444	18 181	19 558	20 328	20 629
Personal effects not elsewhere classified	ADIK	4 490	4 673	4 748	5 455	6 140	6 462	6 866	6 531	6 826
Social protection	ADIL	8 332	8 446	8 643	8 963	9 219	9 501	9 821	10 124	10 282
Insurance	ADIM	17 911	20 257	22 238	25 423	25 456	24 373	23 178	24 393	24 279
Financial services not elsewhere classified	ADIN	8 742	10 009	11 974	11 708	11 982	12 529	14 208	15 174	16 980
Other services not elsewhere classified	ADIO	6 470	6 262	6 089	6 085	6 175	6 357	6 529	6 759	6 785
Final consumption expenditure in the UK by resident and non-resident households (domestic concept)	ABQI	531 784	562 616	593 885	622 972	653 999	685 002	720 490	747 983	781 460
Final consumption expenditure outside the UK by UK resident households	ABTA	16 913	19 690	21 654	22 907	24 435	26 314	27 739	29 209	30 338
less Final consumption expenditure in the UK by households resident in the rest of the world	CDFD	−14 544	−14 312	−14 713	−13 383	−13 872	−14 156	−15 698	−17 160	−18 476
Final consumption expenditure by UK resident households in the UK and abroad (national concept)	ABPB	534 153	567 994	600 826	632 496	664 562	697 160	732 531	760 032	793 322

16.16
continued

Individual consumption expenditure: by households, NPISHs and general government[1] Current market prices
United Kingdom. Classified by function (COICOP/COPNI/COFOG)[2]

£ million

		1998	1999	2000	2001	2002	2003	2004	2005	2006
FINAL CONSUMPTION EXPENDITURE OF UK RESIDENT HOUSEHOLDS										
Final consumption expenditure of UK resident households in the UK and abroad	ABPB	534 153	567 994	600 826	632 496	664 562	697 160	732 531	760 032	793 322
FINAL INDIVIDUAL CONSUMPTION EXPENDITURE OF NPISH										
Final individual consumption expenditure of NPISH	ABNV	20 837	21 874	23 169	24 720	25 968	27 185	28 953	31 588	33 312
FINAL INDIVIDUAL CONSUMPTION EXPENDITURE OF OF GENERAL GOVERNMENT										
Health	QYOT	45 843	49 739	52 537	57 962	63 272	69 791	75 722	83 579	..
Recreation and culture	QYSU	3 465	3 736	3 898	4 049	4 335	4 513	4 272	..	..
Education	QYSE	27 878	29 484	31 521	33 900	37 535	39 876	42 727	..	..
Social protection	QYSP	15 520	16 843	18 055	19 441	22 464	25 517	28 028	..	..
Housing	QYXO	–	–	–	–	–	..	..	..	..
Final individual consumption expenditure of general government	NNAQ	94 783	102 742	109 297	118 458	130 816	143 954	155 811	166 699	178 838
Total, individual consumption expenditure/ actual individual consumption	NQEO	649 773	692 610	733 292	775 674	821 346	868 299	917 295	958 319	1 005 472

1 See chapter text.
2 "Purpose" or "function" classifications are designed to indicate the "socioeconomic objectives" that institutional units aim to achieve through various kinds of outlays. COICOP is the Classification of Individual Consumption by Purpose and applies to households. COPNI is the Classification of the Purposes of Non-Profit Institutions Serving Households and COFOG the Classification of the Functions of Government. The introduction of ESA95 coincides with the redefinition of these classifications and data will be available on a consistent basis for all European Union member states.
3 Package holidays data are dispersed between components (transport etc).

Source: Office for National Statistics: 020 7533 6058

16.17 Individual consumption expenditure: by households, NPISHs and general government[1] Chained volume measures, reference year 2003

United Kingdom. Classified by function (COICOP/COPNI/COFOG)[2]

£ million

		1998	1999	2000	2001	2002	2003	2004	2005	2006
FINAL CONSUMPTION EXPENDITURE OF HOUSEHOLDS										
Food and non-alcoholic beverages	ADIP	58 058	59 904	61 944	61 048	62 143	63 174	65 181	66 230	67 861
Food	ADIQ	52 174	53 697	55 255	53 992	54 835	55 507	56 946	57 996	59 014
Non-alcoholic beverages	ADIR	5 945	6 260	6 725	7 063	7 312	7 667	8 235	8 234	8 847
Alcoholic beverages and tobacco	ADIS	26 829	27 623	26 704	26 497	26 884	27 297	27 444	27 258	27 007
Alcoholic beverages	ADIT	9 290	10 309	10 476	10 831	11 516	12 027	12 369	12 523	12 559
Tobacco	ADIU	17 988	17 541	16 341	15 716	15 380	15 270	15 075	14 735	14 448
Clothing and footwear	ADIW	26 736	28 689	31 744	34 485	38 499	41 155	44 087	46 197	48 890
Clothing	ADIX	22 562	24 424	27 394	29 827	33 315	35 689	38 407	40 393	42 922
Footwear	ADIY	4 264	4 324	4 360	4 660	5 185	5 466	5 680	5 804	5 968
Housing, water, electricity, gas and other fuels	ADIZ	122 959	123 662	125 299	126 749	127 979	129 051	131 490	131 640	133 587
Actual rentals for housing	ADJA	27 333	27 366	27 345	27 418	27 084	27 610	27 555	27 779	28 928
Imputed rentals for housing	ADJB	63 624	64 980	65 704	66 495	67 872	68 458	69 617	70 635	71 179
Maintenance and repair of the dwelling	ADJC	11 784	11 791	11 675	12 139	12 702	12 615	13 007	12 586	12 669
Water supply and miscellaneous dwelling services	ADJD	5 218	5 228	5 386	5 379	5 424	5 438	5 412	5 522	5 692
Electricity, gas and other fuels	ADJE	14 877	14 363	15 149	15 277	14 891	14 930	15 899	15 118	15 119
Furnishings, household equipment and routine maintenance of the house	ADJF	31 443	33 130	36 305	38 310	40 552	42 466	43 577	42 743	43 868
Furniture, furnishings, carpets and other floor coverings	ADJG	12 452	13 120	14 514	14 860	15 896	16 789	17 206	16 525	16 790
Household textiles	ADJH	3 448	3 743	4 361	4 534	5 043	5 452	5 604	5 375	5 573
Household appliances	ADJI	4 613	4 648	4 922	5 549	5 566	5 578	5 649	5 734	6 153
Glassware, tableware and household utensils	ADJJ	3 383	3 699	4 266	4 655	4 717	4 701	4 620	4 674	4 861
Tools and equipment for house and garden	ADJK	2 167	2 435	2 590	2 856	3 238	3 589	3 972	3 799	3 726
Goods and services for routine household maintenance	ADJL	5 468	5 556	5 708	5 859	6 092	6 357	6 526	6 636	6 765
Health	ADJM	10 472	10 362	10 421	10 697	10 980	11 335	11 609	11 534	11 822
Medical products, appliances and equipment	ADJN	5 885	5 839	5 819	6 020	6 315	6 542	6 655	6 290	6 664
Out-patient services	ADJO	2 624	2 556	2 528	2 560	2 492	2 553	2 685	2 903	2 773
Hospital services	ADJP	1 974	1 976	2 082	2 122	2 173	2 240	2 269	2 341	2 385
Transport	ADJQ	89 008	92 969	96 209	98 485	101 621	104 569	106 610	107 305	107 841
Purchase of vehicles	ADJR	27 974	29 455	31 680	35 100	36 057	38 016	39 107	39 571	40 362
Operation of personal transport equipment	ADJS	39 196	39 617	39 124	39 225	40 668	40 507	40 578	40 223	39 519
Transport services	ADJT	22 700	24 661	25 913	24 214	24 965	26 046	26 925	27 511	27 960
Communication	ADJU	9 644	10 948	12 698	14 452	14 796	15 654	16 361	17 150	17 339
Postal services	CCGZ	980	960	916	901	906	890	866	941	996
Telephone & telefax equipment	ADQF	322	428	536	582	640	810	883	1 082	1 136
Telephone & telefax services	ADQG	8 416	9 604	11 264	12 978	13 254	13 954	14 612	15 127	15 207
Recreation and culture	ADJV	57 871	63 601	68 038	72 552	77 597	84 386	92 889	98 594	104 252
Audio-visual, photographic and information processing equipment	ADJW	9 019	11 178	13 022	14 690	16 301	19 408	24 316	27 665	31 285
Other major durables for recreation and culture	ADJX	3 330	3 798	4 182	4 560	4 817	5 126	5 261	5 490	5 976
Other recreational items and equipment; flowers, gardens and pets	ADJY	14 621	16 190	17 455	18 980	21 642	23 894	25 585	26 490	28 383
Recreational and cultural services	ADJZ	22 533	22 827	23 206	24 049	24 333	25 278	26 993	28 011	27 907
Newspapers, books and stationery	ADKM	10 998	11 242	11 181	10 910	10 756	10 680	10 734	10 938	10 701
Package holidays[3]	ADMI	–	–	–	–	–	–	–	–	–
Education										
Education services	ADMJ	10 530	11 394	11 489	10 692	10 091	9 610	9 541	9 475	9 480
Restaurants and Hotels	ADMK	73 811	74 191	76 252	76 434	78 303	78 902	81 796	83 882	83 560
Catering services	ADML	62 710	63 354	65 644	66 815	68 462	68 839	71 244	72 803	72 014
Accommodation services	ADMM	11 123	10 851	10 610	9 620	9 843	10 063	10 552	11 079	11 546
Miscellaneous goods and services	ADMN	65 059	67 867	70 524	73 239	75 715	77 403	78 079	77 673	78 117
Personal care	ADMO	13 192	13 497	14 251	14 719	16 526	18 181	19 482	20 113	20 713
Personal effects not elsewhere classified	ADMP	4 741	4 871	4 922	5 607	6 289	6 462	6 791	6 379	6 378
Social protection	ADMQ	11 178	10 778	10 357	10 058	9 760	9 501	9 306	9 033	8 634
Insurance	ADMR	20 780	22 511	23 526	25 453	24 880	24 373	22 776	22 399	21 926
Financial services not elsewhere classified	ADMS	7 776	8 966	10 421	10 694	11 733	12 529	13 678	13 819	14 824
Other services not elsewhere classified	ADMT	8 524	7 937	7 336	6 827	6 536	6 357	6 046	5 930	5 642
Final consumption expenditure in the UK by resident and non-resident households (domestic concept)	ABQJ	576 994	600 627	625 437	642 595	664 790	685 002	708 664	719 681	733 624
Final consumption expenditure outside the UK by UK resident households	ABTC	18 787	21 899	24 189	24 897	26 376	26 314	28 068	27 745	28 155
less Final consumption expenditure in the UK by households resident in the rest of the world	CCHX	−16 713	−16 031	−16 038	−14 164	−14 292	−14 156	−15 298	−16 152	−16 846
Final consumption expenditure by UK resident households in the UK and abroad (national concept)	ABPF	579 342	606 648	633 662	653 326	676 833	697 160	721 434	731 274	744 933

16.17
continued

Individual consumption expenditure: by households, NPISHs and general government[1] Chained volume measures, reference year 2003
United Kingdom. Classified by function (COICOP/COPNI/COFOG)[2]

£ million

		1998	1999	2000	2001	2002	2003	2004	2005	2006
FINAL CONSUMPTION EXPENDITURE OF UK RESIDENT HOUSEHOLDS										
Final consumption expenditure of UK resident households in the UK and abroad	ABPF	579 342	606 648	633 662	653 326	676 833	697 160	721 434	731 274	744 933
FINAL INDIVIDUAL CONSUMPTION EXPENDITURE OF NPISH										
Final individual consumption expenditure of NPISH	ABNU	25 092	25 023	27 177	27 155	27 130	27 185	27 327	28 119	29 883
FINAL INDIVIDUAL CONSUMPTION EXPENDITURE OF GENERAL GOVERNMENT										
Health	EMOA	55 065	56 805	58 517	61 019	63 272	65 611	68 758	..	..
Recreation and culture	QYXK	3 716	3 930	4 051	3 968	4 470	4 717	..	..	..
Education	EMOB	35 939	36 520	36 876	37 100	37 535	37 732	37 944	..	..
Social protection	QYXM	23 369	23 359	23 454	23 645	24 864	25 843	26 811	27 099	..
Housing	QYXN	–	–	–	–	–	–	..	..	..
Final individual consumption expenditure of general government	NSZK	107 339	109 554	111 763	114 159	117 238	120 288	..	..	..
Total, individual consumption expenditure/ actual individual consumption	YBIO	729 353	760 171	792 076	815 286	843 504	868 299	897 055	910 300	..

Source: Office for National Statistics: 020 7533 6058

1 See chapter text.
2 "Purpose" or "function" classifications are designed to indicate the "socio-economic objectives" that institutional units aim to achieve through various kinds of outlays. COICOP is the Classification of Individual Consumption by Purpose and applies to households. COPNI is the Classification of the Purposes of Non-Profit Institutions Serving Households (NPISH) and COFOG the Classification of the Functions of Government. The introduction of ESA95 coincides with the redefinition of these classifications and data will be available on a consistent basis for all European Union member states.
3 Package holidays data are dispersed between components (transport etc).

16.18

Change in inventories[1,2]
Chained volume measures, reference year 2003
United Kingdom

Reference year 2003, £ million

	Mining and quarrying	Manufacturing industries				Electricity, gas and water supply	Distributive trades		Other industries[4]	Change in inventories
		Materials and fuel	Work in progress	Finished goods	Total		Wholesale[3]	Retail[3]		
	FADO	FBID	FBIE	FBIF	DHBH	FADP	FAJM	FBYH	DLWV	ABMQ
1997	72	254	−1 413	295	−864	54	1 703	979	1 713	3 394
1998	367	537	−703	317	151	−163	666	1 186	2 636	4 291
1999	−325	503	−259	−430	−186	−167	1 743	1 722	3 464	5 803
2000	−263	543	358	418	1 319	202	1 939	1 480	−283	4 648
2001	87	−513	369	160	16	16	887	1 113	3 458	5 577
2002	−37	−496	−149	−372	−1 017	−132	788	1 716	971	2 289
2003	−66	−198	−650	−138	−986	−13	407	1 241	3 399	3 982
2004	−46	7	−614	−296	−903	8	304	1 000	4 234	4 597
2005	−47	−179	863	56	740	586	978	−412	1 766	3 611
2006	−74	−362	742	−147	233	197	340	470	4 333	5 501

1 See chapter text. Estimates are given to the nearest £ million but cannot be regarded as accurate to this degree.
2 Components may not sum to totals due to rounding.
3 Wholesaling and retailing estimates exclude the motor trades.
4 Quarterly alignment adjustment included in this series.

Source: Office for National Statistics 020 7533 5934

16.19 Gross fixed capital formation at current purchasers' prices: by broad sector and type of asset[1,2]

United Kingdom. Total economy

£ million

		1998	1999	2000	2001	2002	2003	2004	2005	2006
Private sector										
New dwellings, excluding land	DFDF	23 317	23 921	25 604	27 085	31 455	34 804	40 927	44 618	51 914
Other buildings and structures	EQBU	29 364	31 828	31 966	32 730	33 580	35 366	36 994	39 577	..
Transport equipment	EQBV	15 242	13 919	12 859	13 897	15 637	14 708	13 735	14 101	..
Other machinery and equipment and cultivated assets	EQBW	56 892	57 957	61 236	58 062	53 498	50 228	52 359	52 848	..
Intangible fixed assets	EQBX	3 555	3 624	4 048	4 285	4 674	4 894	5 258	5 594	..
Costs associated with the transfer of ownership of non-produced assets	EQBY	7 504	9 784	11 174	12 697	15 399	16 385	20 752	20 625	21 209
Total	EQBZ	135 874	141 033	146 887	148 756	154 243	156 385	170 025	177 123	..
Public non-financial corporations										
New dwellings, excluding land	DEER	1 632	1 529	1 421	2 387	2 837	3 509	3 235	3 574	4 117
Other buildings and structures	DEES	1 608	1 692	1 775	1 854	2 304	2 236	1 493	1 656	..
Transport equipment	DEEP	179	155	178	171	110	126	193	335	..
Other machinery and equipment and cultivated assets	DEEQ	437	617	600	628	787	1 037	1 042	921	..
Intangible fixed assets	DLXJ	605	625	551	397	556	623	737	754	..
Costs associated with the transfer of ownership of non-produced assets	DLXQ	−1 162	−1 906	−2 171	−2 254	−2 764	−5 674	−5 440	−2 675	−2 562
Total	FCCJ	3 299	2 712	2 354	3 183	3 830	1 857	1 260	20 742	5 702
General government										
New dwellings, excluding land	DFHW	273	250	369	334	207	149	137	181	..
Other buildings and structures	EQCH	9 302	9 414	9 434	10 348	11 678	14 693	15 866	18 533	..
Transport equipment	EQCI	692	609	540	588	567	758	1 011	915	..
Other machinery and equipment and cultivated assets	EQCJ	1 586	2 096	1 699	2 239	2 867	3 176	3 652	3 526	..
Intangible fixed assets	EQCK	387	396	367	334	358	384	400	409	..
Costs associated with the transfer of ownership of non-produced assets	EQCL	−330	−166	−182	−310	−225	1 349	2 140	2 063	..
Total	NNBF	11 910	12 599	12 227	13 533	15 452	20 509	23 206	7 661	24 054
Total gross fixed capital formation	NPQX	151 083	156 344	161 468	165 472	173 525	178 751	194 491	205 891	223 682

1 See chapter text.
2 Components may not sum to totals due to rounding.

Source: Office for National Statistics: 020 7533 5934

16.20 Gross fixed capital formation at current purchasers' prices: by type of asset[1,2]

United Kingdom. Total economy

£ million

		1998	1999	2000	2001	2002	2003	2004	2005	2006
Tangible fixed assets										
New dwellings, excluding land	DFDK	25 222	25 700	27 394	29 806	34 499	38 462	44 299	48 263	56 037
Other buildings and structures	DLWS	39 041	41 680	43 878	45 381	47 308	52 036	..	..	..
Transport equipment	DLWZ	16 113	14 683	13 577	14 656	16 314	15 592	14 939	14 948	15 494
Other machinery and equipment and cultivated assets	DLXI	58 915	60 670	63 535	60 929	57 152	54 441	57 053	57 036	59 815
Total	EQCQ	140 524	143 987	147 681	150 323	155 527	160 790	170 644	180 946	..
Intangible fixed assets	DLXP	4 547	4 645	4 966	5 016	5 588	5 901	6 395	6 775	7 303
Costs associated with the transfer of ownership of non-produced assets	DFBH	6 012	7 712	8 821	10 133	12 410	12 060	17 452	18 140	..
Total gross fixed capital formation	NPQX	151 083	156 344	161 468	165 472	173 525	178 751	194 491	205 891	223 682

1 See chapter text.
2 Components may not sum to totals due to rounding.

Source: Office for National Statistics: 020 7533 5934

16.21 Gross fixed capital formation: by broad sector and type of asset[1,2,3]
Chained volume measures, reference year 2003

United Kingdom. Total economy   £ million

		1998	1999	2000	2001	2002	2003	2004	2005	2006
Private sector										
New dwellings, excluding land	DFDP	31 971	30 928	31 041	31 318	33 748	34 804	38 245	39 102	42 081
Other buildings and structures	EQCU	32 821	33 931	33 206	33 251	33 406	35 366	35 786	38 157	..
Transport equipment	EQCV	15 334	13 778	12 713	13 863	15 708	14 708	13 704	13 901	..
Other machinery and equipment and cultivated assets	EQCW	46 556	49 522	53 869	54 140	52 405	50 228	53 997	54 467	..
Intangible fixed assets	EQCX	4 124	4 090	4 461	4 637	5 024	4 894	4 880	5 105	..
Costs associated with the transfer of ownership of non-produced assets	EQCY	15 614	16 821	16 293	16 173	17 369	16 385	19 616	18 043	17 392
Total	EQCZ	145 434	148 498	152 120	154 006	157 670	156 385	166 228	168 604	..
Public non-financial corporations										
New dwellings, excluding land	DEEW	1 974	1 747	1 552	2 521	2 898	3 509	3 161	3 423	3 876
Other buildings and structures	DEEX	1 852	1 890	1 939	1 961	2 342	2 236	1 426	1 499	..
Transport equipment	DEEU	193	164	186	180	114	126	193	333	..
Other machinery and equipment and cultivated assets	DEEV	332	504	516	588	765	1 037	1 063	941	..
Intangible fixed assets	EQDE	672	684	586	415	572	623	716	713	..
Costs associated with the transfer of ownership of non-produced assets	EQDF	−2 284	−3 141	−3 093	−2 825	−3 092	−5 674	−5 561	−2 896	−2 147
Total	EQDG	2 030	1 796	1 695	2 424	3 019	1 857	998	2 800	..
General government										
New dwellings, excluding land	DFID	333	286	404	354	213	149	135	174	..
Other buildings and structures	EQDI	10 936	10 792	10 513	11 107	12 115	14 693	14 877	16 423	..
Transport equipment	EQDJ	773	676	606	672	586	758	809	797	..
Other machinery and equipment and cultivated assets	EQDK	1 115	1 632	1 424	2 063	2 801	3 176	3 757	3 754	..
Intangible fixed assets	EQDL	245	241	219	196	211	384	698	738	..
Costs associated with the transfer of ownership of non-produced assets	EQDM	32 408	−1 728	−542	−548	−261	1 349	1 991	1 827	..
Total	EQDN	12 218	13 059	12 665	13 980	15 740	20 509	22 266	6 495	21 737
Total gross fixed capital formation	NPQR	158 525	163 039	167 486	171 639	178 066	178 751	189 492	195 107	207 704

1 See chapter text.
2 For the years before 2003, the total differs from the sum of their components.
3 Components may not sum to totals due to rounding.

Source: Office for National Statistics: 020 7533 6031

16.22 Gross fixed capital formation: by type of asset[1,2,3]
Chained volume measures, reference year 2003

United Kingdom. Total economy   £ million

		1998	1999	2000	2001	2002	2003	2004	2005	2006
Tangible fixed assets										
New dwellings, excluding land	DFDV	34 201	32 863	32 888	34 172	36 839	38 462	41 541	42 594	45 963
Other buildings and structures	EQDP	45 712	46 738	45 780	46 413	47 913	52 295	52 089	56 079	..
Transport equipment	DLWJ	16 279	14 602	13 489	14 698	16 414	15 592	14 706	14 899	15 459
Other machinery and equipment and cultivated assets	DLWM	47 919	51 650	55 766	56 779	55 968	54 441	58 817	58 867	63 310
Total	EQDS	142 732	145 621	148 509	152 571	157 257	160 790	167 152	173 126	..
Intangible fixed assets	EQDT	4 982	4 956	5 172	5 129	5 676	5 901	6 294	6 573	6 991
Costs associated with the transfer of ownership of non-produced assets	DFDW	12 098	13 088	12 810	12 960	14 097	12 060	16 046	15 436	..
Total gross fixed capital formation	NPQR	158 525	163 039	167 486	171 639	178 066	178 751	189 492	195 107	207 704

1 See chapter text.
2 For the years before 2003, the total differs from the sum of their components.
3 Components may not sum to totals due to rounding.

Source: Office for National Statistics: 020 7533 6031

Prices

Chapter 17

Prices

Producer price index numbers

(Tables 17.1 and 17.2)

The producer price indices were published for the first time in August 1983, replacing the former wholesale price indices. Full details of the differences between the two indices were given in an article published in British Business, 15 April 1983. The producer price indices are calculated using the same general methodology as that used by the wholesale price indices.

The high level index numbers in Tables 17.1 and 17.2 are constructed on a net sector basis. That is to say, they are intended to measure only transactions between the sector concerned and other sectors. Within sector transactions are excluded. Index numbers for the whole of manufacturing are thus not weighted averages of sector index numbers.

The index numbers for selected industries in Tables 17.1 and 17.2 are constructed on a gross sector basis i.e. all transactions are included in deriving the weighting patterns, including sales within the same industry.

All the index numbers are compiled exclusive of value-added tax. Excise duties on cigarettes, manufactured tobacco and alcoholic liquor are included, as is the duty on hydrocarbon oils.

The indices relate to the average prices for a year. The movement in these prices are weighted to reflect the relative importance of the composite products in a chosen year (known as the base year), currently 2000.

Since July 1995, PPIs have been published fully reclassified to the 1992 version of the Standard Industrial Classification (SIC).

Further details are available from the National Statistics website: www.statistics.gov.uk/ppi.

Purchasing power of the pound

(Table 17.3)

Changes in the internal purchasing power of a currency may be defined as the 'inverse' of changes in the levels of prices; when prices go up, the amount which can be purchased with a given sum of money goes down. Movements in the internal purchasing power of the pound are based on the consumers' expenditure deflator (CED) prior to 1962 and on the General index of retail prices (RPI) from January 1962 onwards. The CED shows the movement in prices implied by the national

accounts estimates of consumers' expenditure valued at current and at constant prices, whilst the RPI is constructed directly by weighting together monthly movements in prices according to a given pattern of household expenditure derived from the Expenditure and Food Survey. If the purchasing power of the pound is taken to be 100p in a particular month (quarter, year), the comparable purchasing power in a subsequent month (quarter, year) is:

$$100 \quad x \quad \frac{\text{earlier period price index}}{\text{later period price index}}$$

where the price index used is the CED for years 1946–1961 and the RPI for periods after 1961.

Consumer prices index

(Table 17.4)

The consumer prices index (CPI) is the main United Kingdom domestic measure of inflation for macro-economic purposes. Like the RPI (see below) it measures the average change from month to month in the prices of consumer goods and services purchased in the UK, but there are differences in coverage and methodology. A detailed description of these differences is given in the paper entitled "The New Inflation Target: the Statistical Perspective". This paper is available on the National Statistics website:www.statistics.gov.uk/StatBase/Product. asp?vlnk=10913.

Since 10 December 2003, the Government inflation target for the UK has been defined in terms of the CPI measure of inflation. Prior to that the CPI had been published in the UK as the harmonised index of consumer prices (HICP); the two shall remain one and the same index.

The HICPs are calculated in each Member State of the European Union (EU), according to rules specified in a series of European Regulations developed by the EU statistical office in conjunction with the EU Member States. The HICPs are used to compare inflation rate across the EU. Since January 1999 it has also been used by the European Central Bank (ECB) as the measure of price stability across the euro area. Additional information on HICPs is available from the National Statistics website: www.statistics.gov.uk/hicp

CPI inflation rates prior to 1997 and index levels prior to 1996 are estimated. See article on National Statistics website:www. statistics.gov.uk/cci/article.asp?ID=31 Also the coverage of CPI categories for health, education and miscellaneous goods and services have been extended between 2000 and 2002. Details are given in articles available on the website: www.statistics. gov.uk/cci/searchres2.asp?ct=6&term=HICP

Further details on the CPI are available from the National Statistics website: www.statistics.gov.uk/cpi

Retail prices index

(Table 17.5)

The retail prices index (RPI) is the most familiar general purpose measure of inflation in the UK, measuring the percentage changes month by month in the average level of prices of the goods and services purchased by the great majority of households in the United Kingdom. The uses of the RPI include indexation of pensions, state benefits and index-linked gilts. The expenditure pattern on which the index is based is revised each year using information from the Expenditure and Food Survey. The expenditure of certain higher income households and households of retired people dependent mainly on social security benefits is excluded.

The index covers a large and representative selection of more than 650 separate goods and services, for which price movements are regularly measured in around 150 locations throughout the country. Around 120,000 separate price quotations are used in compiling the index.

Further details are available from the National Statistics website: www.statistics.gov.uk/rpi

Tax and price index (TPI)

(Table 17.6)

The purpose and methodology of the TPI were described in an article in the August 1979 issue (No 310) of Economic Trends (The Stationery Office). The TPI measures the change in gross taxable income needed for taxpayers to maintain their purchasing power, allowing for changes in retail prices. The TPI thus takes account of the changes to direct taxes (and employees' National Insurance contributions) facing representative cross-section of taxpayers as well as changes in the retail prices index (RPI).

When direct taxation or employees' National Insurance contributions change, the TPI will rise by less than or more than the RPI according to the type of changes made. Between Budgets, the monthly increase in the TPI is normally slightly larger than that in the RPI, since all the extra income needed to offset any rise in retail prices is fully taxed.

Index numbers of agricultural prices

(Tables 17.7 and 17.8)

The Indices of producer prices of agricultural products are currently based on the calendar year 2000. They are designed to provide short-term and medium-term indications of movements in these prices. All annual series are base-weighted Laspeyres type, using value weights derived from the Economic Accounts for Agriculture prepared for the Statistical Office of the European Union. Prices are measured exclusive of VAT. For table 17.7, it has generally been necessary to measure the prices of materials (inputs) ex-supplier. For table 17.8, it has generally been necessary to measure the prices received by producers (outputs) at the first marketing stage. The construction of the indices enables them to be combined with similar indices for other member countries of the European Union to provide an overall indication of trends within the Union which appears in the Union's Eurostat series of publications.

Index numbers at a more detailed level and for earlier based series are available from the Department for Environment and Rural Affairs, Food Chain Analysis Division, SSP, Room 133a Foss House, Kingspool 1-2 Peasholme Green, York, YO1 7PX Tel 01904 455249

17.1 Producer price index of materials and fuels purchased: by all manufacturing and selected industries SIC(92)[1]

United Kingdom: Annual averages

Indices (2000=100)

			1999	2000	2001	2002	2003	2004	2005	2006
Net sector										
Materials and fuel purchased by manufacturing industry[2]	RNNK	6292000050	93.1	100.0	98.8	94.4	95.7	99.5	111.1	121.8
Materials	PLKX	6292000010	92.3	100.0	98.1	93.7	95.2	98.7	108.1	116.1
Fuels[2]	RNNL	6292000060	103.6	100.0	107.1	103.4	102.1	109.9	152.1	198.7
Materials and fuels purchased by manufacturing industry-seasonally adjusted[2]	RNPE	6292008950	93.1	100.0	98.8	94.4	95.7	99.5	111.1	121.7
Materials and fuels purchased by manufacturing industry other than food, beverages, petroleum and tobacco[2]	RNNQ	6292990050	96.4	100.0	98.7	94.0	93.7	95.4	103.0	111.1
Materials	RWCJ	6292990010	95.8	100.0	98.1	93.2	93.0	94.2	98.9	103.8
Fuel[2]	RNNS	6292990060	103.7	100.0	106.8	103.1	101.8	109.6	151.6	198.3
Materials and fuels purchased by manufacturing industries other than food, beverages, petroleum and tobacco-seasonally adjusted[2]	RNPF	6292998950	96.4	100.0	98.7	94.0	93.7	95.4	103.0	111.1
Gross sector[3]										
All manufacturing	RBBO	6192000000	96.3	100.0	99.3	97.1	98.4	102.1	109.7	116.9
Other mining and quarrying products[4]	RABE	6112140000	90.2	100.0	96.9	92.3	93.1	96.0	107.6	114.5
Manufacture of food products	RBBQ	6192151600	102.3	100.0	103.2	102.3	105.2	108.5	109.3	113.6
Food products and beverages	RABF	6112150000	102.3	100.0	103.3	102.3	105.2	108.6	109.3	113.6
Tobacco products	RABG	6112160000	100.8	100.0	100.0	101.2	106.9	107.0	107.9	110.9
Manufacture of textiles	RBBR	6192171800	98.7	100.0	100.5	98.4	99.2	99.6	103.3	106.4
Textiles	RABH	6112170000	98.7	100.0	100.5	98.6	99.8	100.0	105.4	109.3
Wearing apparel	RABI	6112180000	98.5	100.0	100.4	97.8	98.0	98.7	99.8	101.4
Manufacture of leather	RBBS	6192190000	97.9	100.0	101.9	100.0	101.1	102.0	105.7	109.5
Manufacture of wood and wood products	RBBT	6192200000	100.2	100.0	99.2	96.5	96.8	99.5	104.1	109.2
Manufacture of pulp, paper, publishing and printing	RBBU	6192212200	97.0	100.0	100.9	99.2	99.4	100.4	103.8	108.0
Pulp and paper products	RABL	6112210000	96.0	100.0	100.7	97.5	96.5	96.9	100.7	106.5
Printed matter and recording material	RABM	6112220000	97.4	100.0	101.0	100.0	100.8	102.2	105.3	108.8
Manufacture of coke	RBBV	6192230000	65.4	100.0	92.0	89.2	95.4	109.1	150.9	175.6
Manufacture of chemical products	RBBW	6192240000	96.1	100.0	101.1	99.4	103.0	105.5	114.4	120.6
Manufacture of rubber products	RBBX	6192250000	96.6	100.0	99.1	97.7	99.5	102.6	110.8	116.2
Manufacture of other non-metallic mineral products	RBBY	6192260000	97.4	100.0	100.5	99.6	100.7	103.0	111.8	120.0
Manufacture of basic metals	RBBZ	6192272800	94.8	100.0	98.5	96.6	99.8	111.8	123.0	137.3
Basic metals	RABV	6112270000	93.4	100.0	98.6	96.8	101.3	115.7	127.0	144.8
Fabricated metal products	RABW	6112280000	96.1	100.0	98.4	96.4	98.6	108.4	119.5	130.9
Manufacture of machinery and equipment not elsewhere classified	RBCA	6192290000	97.8	100.0	98.9	97.1	97.8	102.4	109.3	116.7
Manufacture of electrical and optical equipment	RBCB	6192303300	99.8	100.0	97.2	92.5	88.8	87.7	90.1	93.9
Office machinery and computers	RABY	6112300000	99.5	100.0	95.5	87.4	80.7	78.5	79.3	81.1
Electrical machinery and apparatus not elsewhere classified	RACB	6112310000	98.1	100.0	98.5	95.8	94.5	96.1	101.5	108.8
Radio, television and communication equipment	RACC	6112320000	99.0	100.0	98.1	94.5	92.1	92.4	96.6	103.5
Medical, precision, optical instruments and clocks	RACD	6112330000	99.0	100.0	98.2	95.2	92.3	90.6	93.3	97.0
Manufacture of transport equipment	RBCC	6192343500	99.6	100.0	99.1	97.3	98.1	100.1	105.3	110.4
Motor vehicles, trailers and semi-trailers	RACE	6112340000	100.3	100.0	99.3	98.1	99.3	101.5	106.8	111.6
Other transport equipment	RACF	6112350000	97.8	100.0	98.7	95.4	95.5	97.0	102.0	107.7
Manufacturing not elsewhere classified	RBCD	6192363700	97.8	100.0	99.1	97.8	99.9	104.4	109.9	116.4
Electricity including Climate Change Levy	RCVR	7167850000	107.5	100.0	96.2	92.5	89.3	95.2	127.5	173.2
Gas including Climate Change Levy	RCVW	7167860000	91.9	100.0	140.7	136.5	141.3	155.5	231.8	286.9
Collected and purified water	PQNB	7167870000	102.4	100.0	101.6	103.4	107.0	113.9	131.1	144.5

1 See chapter text.
2 These indices include the Climate Change Levy which was introduced in April 2001.
3 The Climate Change Levy is excluded from the detailed industry input index.
4 These indices include the Aggregates Levy which was introduced in April 2002.

Source: Office for National Statistics: 01633 815783

17.2 Producer price index of output: by all manufacturing and selected industries SIC(92)[1]

United Kingdom: Annual averages

Indices (2000=100)

			1999	2000	2001	2002	2003	2004	2005	2006
Net sector										
Output of manufactured products	PLLU	7209200000	98.5	100.0	99.7	99.8	101.3	103.8	106.7	109.3
All manufacturing excluding duty	PVNP	7209200010	99.0	100.0	99.7	99.7	101.2	103.7	106.8	109.7
All manufacturing excluding duty - seasonally adjusted	PVNQ	7209200890	99.0	100.0	99.7	99.8	101.2	103.7	106.8	109.7
Products of manufacturing industries other than the food, beverages, petroleum and tobacco manufacturing industries - not seasonally adjusted	PLLV	7209299000	100.2	100.0	99.4	99.3	100.6	102.5	104.7	107.1
All manufacturing excluding food, beverages, tobacco and petroleum - seasonally adjusted	PLLW	7209299890	100.2	100.0	99.4	99.3	100.6	102.5	104.7	107.1
Gross sector										
Manufactured products excluding duty	POKE	7109200000	97.8	100.0	99.4	99.1	100.8	104.0	108.8	112.6
Manufactured products excluding food, drink, tobacco and petroleum	POKF	7109299000	100.1	100.0	99.4	99.3	100.5	103.0	106.2	109.2
Other mining and quarrying products[2]	ROFV	7112148000	96.2	100.0	104.4	120.3	126.9	129.1	129.9	133.4
Food products, beverages and tobacco excluding duty	POKH	7111151600	100.5	100.0	101.9	103.3	104.6	106.9	108.4	110.7
Food products, beverages and tobacco including duty	RBGA	7111151680	99.1	100.0	102.0	103.3	104.7	107.3	108.9	111.2
Food products and beverages including duty	RPUN	7112150080	100.4	100.0	101.5	102.6	103.6	105.9	107.1	109.0
Food products excluding beverages	RBGD	7112159900	100.9	100.0	101.7	102.7	103.7	106.0	107.1	108.8
Alcoholic beverages including duty	RPUX	7113159080	98.7	100.0	101.6	103.1	103.7	106.8	108.2	110.2
Tobacco products including duty	RPUS	7112160080	91.6	100.0	105.0	107.8	111.2	115.3	119.8	124.7
Textiles and textile products	POKI	7111171800	99.9	100.0	99.2	98.8	98.7	98.5	100.0	101.2
Textiles	POKZ	7112170000	100.2	100.0	99.4	99.2	99.4	99.2	101.2	102.7
Wearing apparel: Furs	POLA	7112180000	99.2	100.0	99.0	97.9	97.2	97.0	97.4	98.0
Leather and leather products	POKJ	7111190000	99.2	100.0	102.5	102.7	102.9	102.9	104.5	106.5
Wood and wood products	POKK	7111200000	101.5	100.0	99.9	100.0	101.8	105.2	110.0	113.0
Pulp, paper and paper products, recorded media and printing services	POKL	7111212200	98.2	100.0	101.5	102.1	104.0	106.0	108.6	110.7
Pulp, paper and paper products	POLD	7112210000	96.8	100.0	101.0	100.3	100.1	99.7	99.0	100.8
Printed matter and recorded media	POLE	7112220000	98.8	100.0	101.7	102.7	105.5	108.4	112.2	114.3
Chemicals, chemical, products and manmade fibres	POKN	7111240000	97.2	100.0	100.2	100.5	103.9	106.7	111.5	115.8
Rubber and plastic products	POKO	7111250000	100.4	100.0	100.3	100.4	100.5	101.5	106.3	109.8
Other non-metallic mineral products	POKP	7111260000	99.3	100.0	101.9	105.0	107.8	109.6	113.9	118.3
Base metals and fabricated metal products	POKQ	7111272800	98.7	100.0	99.9	99.5	101.3	108.8	118.4	125.4
Base metals	POLJ	7112270000	94.7	100.0	98.4	96.0	99.2	113.1	126.6	141.5
Fabricated metal products, except machinery and equipment	POLK	7112280000	100.6	100.0	100.6	101.1	102.3	106.8	114.5	118.0
Machinery and equipment not elsewhere classified	POKR	7111290000	99.1	100.0	100.9	101.8	101.9	103.3	106.5	109.2
Electrical and optical equipment	POKS	7111343500	106.2	100.0	94.7	90.0	87.5	86.6	85.9	86.8
Office machinery and computers	POLM	7112300000	124.1	100.0	75.2	64.6	57.1	52.2	46.7	44.3
Electrical machinery and apparatus not elsewhere classified	POLN	7112310000	101.3	100.0	99.9	100.4	100.6	102.8	106.2	111.5
Radio, television and communication equipment and apparatus	POLO	7112320000	104.2	100.0	97.3	88.0	84.3	82.1	80.1	79.3
Medical precision and optical instruments, watches and clocks	POLP	7112330000	99.2	100.0	101.1	102.4	103.3	103.6	104.1	104.8
Transport equipment	POKT	7111343500	100.9	100.0	98.4	98.8	99.2	100.3	102.4	103.9
Motor vehicles, trailers and semi-trailers	POLQ	7112340000	102.3	100.0	96.6	96.3	96.1	97.2	98.6	99.5
Other transport	POLR	7112350000	98.0	100.0	102.3	103.8	105.8	107.0	110.5	113.2
Furniture: other manufactured goods not elsewhere classified	POLS	7112360000	100.9	100.0	100.3	100.9	103.8	104.4	104.5	105.7

1 See chapter text.
2 These indices include the Aggregates Levy which was introduced in April 2002. These indices do not feed into Net Sector output (PLLU).

Source: Office for National Statistics: 01633 815783

273

17.3 Internal purchasing power of the pound[1,2]
United Kingdom

Pence

	Year in which purchasing power was 100p																			
	1987	1988	1989	1990	1991	1992	1993	1994	1995	1996	1997	1998	1999	2000	2001	2002	2003	2004	2005	2006
	BAMT	BAMU	BAMV	BAMW	BASX	CZVM	CBXX	DOFX	DOHR	DOLM	DTUL	CDQG	JKZZ	ZMHO	IKHI	FAUI	SEZH	C687	E9AO	GB4Y
1987	100	105	113	124	131	136	138	141	146	150	155	160	162	167	170	173	178	183	188	194
1988	95	100	108	118	125	130	132	135	139	143	147	152	155	159	162	165	170	175	180	185
1989	88	93	100	109	116	120	122	125	129	133	137	141	144	148	150	153	157	162	167	172
1990	81	85	91	100	106	110	112	114	118	121	125	129	131	135	137	140	144	148	152	157
1991	76	80	86	94	100	104	105	108	112	114	118	122	124	128	130	132	136	140	144	148
1992	74	77	83	91	96	100	102	104	108	110	114	118	119	123	125	127	131	135	139	143
1993	72	76	82	90	95	98	100	102	106	109	112	116	118	121	123	125	129	133	136	141
1994	71	74	80	88	93	96	98	100	103	106	109	113	115	118	120	122	126	130	133	137
1995	68	72	77	85	90	93	94	97	100	102	106	109	111	114	116	118	122	125	129	133
1996	67	70	75	83	87	91	92	94	98	100	103	107	108	112	113	115	119	122	126	130
1997	65	68	73	80	85	88	89	92	95	97	100	103	105	108	110	112	115	119	122	126
1998	63	66	71	77	82	85	86	88	92	94	97	100	102	105	106	108	111	115	118	122
1999	62	65	70	76	81	84	85	87	90	92	95	98	100	103	105	107	110	113	116	120
2000	60	63	68	74	78	81	83	85	88	90	92	96	97	100	102	103	106	110	113	116
2001	59	62	66	73	77	80	81	83	86	88	91	94	95	98	100	102	105	108	111	114
2002	58	61	65	72	76	79	80	82	85	87	89	92	94	97	98	100	103	106	109	112
2003	56	59	64	70	74	76	78	79	82	84	87	90	91	94	96	97	100	103	106	109
2004	55	57	62	68	72	74	75	77	80	82	84	87	89	91	93	94	97	100	103	106
2005	53	56	60	66	70	72	73	75	78	80	82	85	86	89	90	92	94	97	100	103
2006	51	54	58	64	67	70	71	73	75	77	80	82	83	86	87	89	92	94	97	100

1 See chapter text. These figures are calculated by taking the inverse ratio of the respective annual averages of the Retail Prices Index (RPI).
2 To find the purchasing power of the pound in 1995, given that it was 100 pence in 1990, select the column headed 1990 and look at the 1995 row. The result is 85 pence.

Source: Office for National Statistics: 020 7533 5874

17.4 Consumer Prices Index:[1] detailed figures by division
United Kingdom

Indices (2005=100)

	Food and non-alcoholic beverages	Alcoholic beverages and tobacco	Clothing and footwear	Housing, water, electricity, gas & other fuels	Furniture, household equipment & routine maintenance	Health	Transport	Communication	Recreation and culture	Education	Restaurants and hotels	Miscellaneous goods and services	CPI (overall index)
COICOP Division	01	02	03	04	05	06	07	08	09	10	11	12	
Weights 2006	102	44	65	108	73	24	155	25	147	17	134	106	1000
	D7BU	D7BV	D7BW	D7BX	D7BY	D7BZ	D7C2	D7C3	D7C4	D7C5	D7C6	D7C7	D7BT
2004 Nov	98.4	98.2	105.9	96.0	100.4	98.2	96.4	100.8	101.0	98.7	97.8	97.3	98.6
Dec	99.0	97.8	104.5	96.6	102.7	98.0	98.0	100.5	101.2	98.7	98.0	97.4	99.1
2005 Jan	99.2	98.8	100.7	97.2	98.6	98.7	96.4	100.3	100.7	98.7	98.2	98.5	98.6
Feb	99.9	99.2	100.5	97.4	99.0	98.8	97.3	100.5	100.2	98.7	98.4	98.6	98.8
Mar	100.8	98.7	101.3	97.7	100.7	98.9	98.0	100.4	100.2	98.7	98.7	98.8	99.3
Apr	99.9	99.8	100.9	99.6	99.3	99.5	98.5	100.5	100.7	98.7	99.5	99.3	99.7
May	100.6	100.2	101.0	99.8	100.1	99.7	99.5	100.1	100.4	98.7	99.8	99.4	100.0
Jun	100.6	100.3	100.6	100.0	100.4	99.8	99.6	100.3	100.3	98.7	99.9	99.6	100.0
Jul	99.4	100.6	96.5	100.4	99.4	100.6	102.1	99.5	99.8	98.7	100.3	100.4	100.1
Aug	99.6	100.5	98.2	100.4	99.6	100.8	103.3	99.9	99.3	98.7	100.6	100.6	100.4
Sep	99.7	100.3	99.9	100.7	100.2	100.7	102.2	99.8	99.6	100.8	100.8	100.8	100.6
Oct	99.5	100.7	99.9	101.7	99.4	101.0	102.0	99.5	99.7	103.3	101.2	101.2	100.7
Nov	100.1	100.7	100.5	102.3	100.5	101.0	100.4	99.6	99.5	103.3	101.2	101.4	100.7
Dec	100.7	100.2	100.1	102.8	102.8	100.3	100.7	99.4	99.5	103.3	101.4	101.5	101.0
2006 Jan	100.4	101.0	96.0	103.3	97.8	101.0	101.2	100.9	98.6	103.3	101.5	102.0	100.5
Feb	101.0	100.8	95.9	103.6	98.5	101.1	101.4	101.0	99.4	103.3	101.9	102.1	100.9
Mar	100.4	101.1	96.5	104.5	100.3	101.0	101.4	100.9	98.9	103.3	102.2	102.4	101.1
Apr	100.2	102.3	96.5	107.3	98.5	102.2	102.9	100.9	99.1	103.3	102.5	103.3	101.7
May	101.7	102.5	97.2	108.8	99.3	102.6	103.5	99.7	98.9	103.3	103.0	103.4	102.2
Jun	102.4	103.6	96.7	109.7	100.2	102.5	103.5	100.0	98.7	103.3	103.1	103.9	102.5
Jul	102.6	103.4	92.2	110.5	98.1	103.0	105.5	99.8	98.4	103.3	103.5	104.0	102.5
Aug	103.0	103.8	94.4	110.9	99.1	103.4	105.8	99.2	98.4	103.3	103.6	104.5	102.9
Sep	103.6	103.7	96.4	111.5	100.6	103.6	102.9	99.6	98.6	107.9	103.8	104.7	103.0
Oct	104.2	103.9	96.6	112.7	99.0	104.2	101.5	100.4	98.6	117.8	104.2	105.0	103.2
Nov	105.1	103.4	97.2	113.7	100.0	104.1	101.1	100.3	98.7	117.8	104.5	105.0	103.4
Dec	105.4	103.0	96.0	114.5	103.3	104.2	102.8	99.9	99.2	117.8	104.7	104.9	104.0
2007 Jan	104.4	104.5	92.0	114.9	98.3	104.8	102.1	99.0	98.3	117.8	104.9	105.1	103.2
Feb	105.4	105.1	91.9	115.1	99.6	104.9	102.8	98.1	98.4	117.8	105.2	105.8	103.7

Percentage change on a year earlier

	D7G8	D7G9	D7GA	D7GB	D7GC	D7GD	D7GE	D7GF	D7GG	D7GH	D7GI	D7GJ	D7G7
2004 Nov	−0.5	2.2	−5.3	4.9	−0.4	1.5	4.1	−1.9	−0.9	5.0	2.9	3.3	1.5
Dec	−0.1	2.1	−5.4	5.4	0.7	1.9	4.0	−2.2	−0.6	5.0	2.9	3.2	1.7
2005 Jan	0.4	2.5	−5.9	5.8	−0.5	2.4	2.7	−2.3	−0.4	5.0	2.9	3.6	1.6
Feb	0.8	2.9	−5.8	5.9	−1.2	2.7	3.2	−2.7	−0.7	5.0	3.1	3.4	1.7
Mar	1.7	2.2	−5.1	5.8	−	2.6	4.0	−2.9	−0.7	5.0	2.8	3.6	1.9
Apr	1.0	2.0	−5.3	6.5	−1.0	2.7	3.8	−3.2	−0.6	5.0	3.3	4.3	1.9
May	1.4	2.3	−5.5	6.4	−1.0	2.8	3.3	−3.6	−0.5	5.0	3.3	4.3	1.9
Jun	2.2	2.3	−4.8	6.4	−0.6	2.7	3.4	−2.9	−1.2	5.0	3.2	4.6	2.0
Jul	1.7	2.2	−4.8	6.7	0.6	3.4	4.6	−2.5	−1.5	5.0	3.4	5.2	2.3
Aug	2.2	1.8	−4.4	6.3	0.2	3.7	5.4	−2.1	−2.0	5.0	3.5	5.1	2.4
Sep	2.0	1.4	−5.3	6.5	−0.2	3.1	6.0	−1.2	−1.6	4.7	3.7	5.1	2.5
Oct	1.5	1.9	−5.3	6.5	−0.2	3.0	5.8	−1.6	−1.5	4.7	3.7	4.2	2.3
Nov	1.7	2.5	−5.1	6.5	0.1	2.9	4.1	−1.2	−1.5	4.7	3.5	4.3	2.1
Dec	1.7	2.5	−4.2	6.4	−	2.4	2.8	−1.0	−1.7	4.7	3.5	4.2	1.9
2006 Jan	1.2	2.3	−4.7	6.3	−0.8	2.3	5.1	0.5	−2.1	4.7	3.4	3.5	1.9
Feb	1.1	1.6	−4.7	6.4	−0.5	2.3	4.2	0.4	−0.8	4.7	3.5	3.6	2.0
Mar	−0.4	2.5	−4.7	7.0	−0.4	2.1	3.5	0.5	−1.4	4.7	3.6	3.7	1.8
Apr	0.3	2.5	−4.4	7.7	−0.8	2.7	4.4	0.3	−1.6	4.7	3.0	4.0	2.0
May	1.1	2.2	−3.7	9.0	−0.8	2.9	4.0	−0.4	−1.6	4.7	3.2	4.1	2.2
Jun	1.8	3.3	−3.9	9.8	−0.1	2.7	3.9	−0.3	−1.6	4.7	3.2	4.4	2.5
Jul	3.2	2.8	−4.5	10.0	−1.3	2.4	3.3	0.3	−1.4	4.7	3.2	3.6	2.4
Aug	3.4	3.3	−3.9	10.5	−0.5	2.6	2.4	−0.7	−0.9	4.7	3.0	3.9	2.5
Sep	4.0	3.4	−3.5	10.7	0.3	2.8	0.6	−0.2	−1.0	7.1	2.9	3.9	2.4
Oct	4.7	3.2	−3.3	10.8	−0.4	3.1	−0.5	0.9	−1.1	14.0	3.0	3.8	2.4
Nov	5.0	2.7	−3.2	11.1	−0.5	3.1	0.8	0.7	−0.7	14.0	3.2	3.5	2.7
Dec	4.6	2.7	−4.1	11.4	0.6	3.9	2.1	0.5	−0.3	14.0	3.2	3.3	3.0
2007 Jan	3.9	3.5	−4.1	11.2	0.5	3.8	0.9	−1.8	−0.3	14.0	3.3	3.1	2.7
Feb	4.4	4.2	−4.2	11.1	1.2	3.7	1.4	−2.8	−1.0	14.0	3.3	3.6	2.8

1 See chapter text. Prior to 10 December 2003, the consumer prices index (CPI) was published in the UK as the harmonised index of consumer prices (HICP).

Source: Office for National Statistics: 020 7533 5874

17.5 Retail Prices Index[1]
United Kingdom

Indices (13 January 1987=100)

| | All items (RPI) | All items excluding | | | | | Food and catering | Alcohol and tobacco | Housing and household expend-iture | Personal expend-iture | Travel and leisure | Consumer durables | All items excluding mortgage interest payments & indirect taxes (RPIY)[3] |
		mortgage interest payments (RPIX)	mortgage interest payments and depreci-ation	housing	food	seasonal food[2]							
Weights													
	CZGU	CZGY	DOGZ	CZGX	CZGV	CZGW	CBVV	CBVW	CBVX	CBVY	CBVZ	CBWA	
1999	1 000	958	928	807	872	980	179	100	358	95	268	127	
2000	1 000	960	924	805	882	982	170	95	355	101	279	126	
2001	1 000	954	914	795	884	982	169	97	362	96	276	125	
2002	1 000	964	924	801	886	980	166	99	363	94	278	126	
2003	1 000	961	919	797	891	983	160	98	365	92	285	126	
2004	1 000	961	914	791	889	981	160	97	367	93	283	121	
2005	1 000	950	901	776	890	981	159	96	387	89	269	122	
2006	1 000	950	906	778	895	983	155	96	392	90	267	117	
2007	1 000	945	895	762	895	981	152	95	408	83	262	109	
Annual averages													
	CHAW	CHMK	CHON	CHAZ	CHAY	CHAX	CHBS	CHBT	CHBU	CHBV	CHBW	CHBY	CBZW
1998	162.9	160.6	160.3	156.2	166.5	163.8	153.4	192.3	166.2	139.9	162.8	115.9	154.5
1999	165.4	164.3	163.6	158.9	169.4	166.5	155.4	202.6	167.7	139.6	165.6	112.3	157.1
2000	170.3	167.7	166.4	161.3	175.1	171.4	156.7	210.3	176.2	137.2	170.3	108.0	159.9
2001	173.3	171.3	169.5	163.7	178.0	174.3	162.2	216.9	180.0	135.7	172.0	105.0	163.7
2002	176.2	175.1	172.5	166.0	181.1	177.2	164.8	222.3	184.6	133.2	174.2	101.9	167.5
2003	181.3	180.0	176.2	168.9	186.7	182.4	167.9	228.0	194.3	133.2	177.0	99.8	172.0
2004	186.7	184.0	179.1	170.9	192.8	187.9	170.0	233.6	207.4	131.5	178.1	97.7	175.5
2005	192.0	188.2	182.6	173.7	198.7	193.3	172.9	239.8	219.4	131.0	179.2	95.3	179.4
2006	198.1	193.7	187.8	178.3	205.2	199.5	176.9	247.1	231.8	131.7	181.1	94.0	184.8
Monthly figures													
2004 Feb	183.8	182.0	177.7	170.0	189.3	184.9	170.1	230.0	200.0	131.6	177.6	98.0	173.9
Mar	184.6	182.5	178.1	170.4	190.2	185.7	170.2	231.2	201.9	132.1	177.4	98.5	174.3
Apr	185.7	183.6	179.1	170.8	191.6	186.9	170.2	233.4	204.5	132.2	177.8	98.2	174.9
May	186.5	184.3	179.7	171.4	192.4	187.6	170.6	233.8	205.8	132.3	178.5	98.6	175.6
Jun	186.8	184.2	179.5	171.2	193.0	188.1	169.8	234.2	207.4	131.7	178.5	98.5	175.6
Jul	186.8	183.8	178.9	170.5	193.1	188.2	169.2	234.7	208.3	129.0	178.8	95.6	175.1
Aug	187.4	184.3	179.3	170.9	193.8	188.8	169.1	235.2	209.3	130.1	179.1	96.4	175.7
Sep	188.1	184.7	179.4	171.1	194.6	189.5	169.3	235.3	211.3	132.0	178.1	97.7	176.1
Oct	188.6	185.1	179.8	171.3	195.1	189.9	169.9	235.5	212.5	132.2	177.9	97.2	176.6
Nov	189.0	185.4	180.1	171.6	195.5	190.3	170.4	235.0	213.4	132.6	177.9	97.6	176.9
Dec	189.9	186.4	180.9	172.5	196.4	191.2	171.2	234.7	215.6	131.8	178.6	99.1	177.9
2005 Jan	188.9	185.2	179.8	171.2	195.2	190.1	171.6	236.0	214.3	129.4	177.1	94.5	176.7
Feb	189.6	185.9	180.4	171.9	195.9	190.8	172.4	236.9	214.9	130.2	177.6	95.0	177.4
Mar	190.5	186.8	181.4	173.0	196.8	191.6	173.4	236.8	216.3	131.4	178.1	96.7	178.3
Apr	191.6	187.8	182.4	173.3	198.2	192.9	172.7	239.4	218.3	131.4	179.3	95.6	179.0
May	192.0	188.2	182.7	173.7	198.6	193.2	173.7	240.2	219.0	131.4	179.1	95.9	179.4
Jun	192.2	188.3	182.8	173.8	198.8	193.4	173.6	240.5	219.7	131.4	178.9	95.8	179.5
Jul	192.2	188.3	182.7	173.5	199.1	193.7	172.4	241.0	220.2	128.8	180.2	94.0	179.5
Aug	192.6	188.6	183.0	173.8	199.5	194.1	172.7	241.0	220.5	130.3	180.2	94.1	179.8
Sep	193.1	189.3	183.7	174.6	200.0	194.5	172.7	241.1	220.7	131.6	181.0	95.1	180.5
Oct	193.3	189.5	183.8	174.7	200.4	194.8	172.7	241.8	221.4	131.8	180.8	94.7	180.7
Nov	193.6	189.7	184.0	174.9	200.5	195.0	173.4	241.9	222.5	132.2	179.6	95.4	180.9
Dec	194.1	190.2	184.5	175.5	201.0	195.5	174.1	241.6	224.5	131.9	179.0	97.0	181.5
2006 Jan	193.4	189.4	183.7	174.5	200.3	194.8	174.1	242.5	223.0	129.1	179.4	92.4	180.7
Feb	194.2	190.1	184.4	175.2	201.0	195.6	174.9	242.8	224.0	130.0	179.9	93.5	181.4
Mar	195.0	190.8	185.2	176.0	202.0	196.4	174.3	243.8	225.8	131.1	180.0	95.1	182.2
Apr	196.5	192.3	186.7	177.0	203.8	198.0	174.2	245.8	228.3	131.7	181.6	93.6	183.2
May	197.7	193.6	187.8	178.2	204.9	199.1	176.1	246.8	230.0	132.7	182.1	94.3	184.5
Jun	198.5	194.2	188.4	178.9	205.7	199.8	176.8	248.3	231.6	132.6	181.9	94.7	185.2
Jul	198.5	194.2	188.3	178.7	205.6	199.9	177.1	248.3	231.5	129.4	183.3	91.8	185.2
Aug	199.2	194.9	188.9	179.3	206.4	200.7	177.6	249.1	232.6	131.3	183.3	93.0	186.0
Sep	200.1	195.3	189.2	179.6	207.4	201.5	178.1	249.2	235.9	133.0	181.2	94.8	186.4
Oct	200.4	195.5	189.3	179.7	207.5	201.7	179.1	249.7	237.3	133.4	179.6	93.7	186.7
Nov	201.1	196.2	190.0	180.4	208.2	202.4	180.2	249.6	238.7	133.7	179.8	94.5	187.5
Dec	202.7	197.4	191.2	181.7	210.1	204.1	180.6	249.4	242.7	132.9	181.0	96.7	188.6
2007 Jan	201.6	196.1	189.8	180.0	208.9	203.0	180.0	251.3	240.6	130.1	180.8	91.1	187.3
Feb	203.1	197.1	190.7	181.1	210.4	204.4	181.2	252.4	243.0	131.3	181.4	92.1	188.4

1 See chapter text.
2 Seasonal food is defined as items of food the prices of which show significant seasonal variations. These are fresh fruit and vegetables, fresh fish,
eggs and home-killed lamb.

3 There are no weights available for RPIY.

Source: Office for National Statistics: 020 7533 5874

17.6 Tax and Price Index[1]
United Kingdom

Indices and percentages

Tax and Price Index: (January 1988=100)

DQAB

	1992	1993	1994	1995	1996	1997	1998	1999	2000	2001	2002	2003	2004	2005	2006
January	128.1	128.7	132.1	137.2	141.6	143.6	147.1	150.5	152.7	156.7	156.5	161.4	166.9	172.1	175.9
February	128.8	129.6	132.9	138.2	142.3	144.2	147.9	150.8	153.7	157.6	157.0	162.3	167.6	172.8	176.7
March	129.3	130.2	133.4	138.8	143.0	144.6	148.4	151.2	154.6	157.8	157.7	163.0	168.4	173.7	177.4
April	129.6	131.3	135.3	140.3	141.7	143.8	149.7	151.2	155.7	156.3	158.6	164.9	168.9	174.1	178.3
May	130.2	131.8	135.8	141.0	142.0	144.4	150.6	151.7	156.3	157.4	159.1	165.2	169.7	174.5	179.5
June	130.2	131.7	135.8	141.2	142.1	145.0	150.5	151.7	156.7	157.6	159.1	165.0	170.0	174.7	180.3
July	129.6	131.4	135.1	140.4	141.5	145.0	150.1	151.1	156.1	156.5	158.8	165.0	170.0	174.7	180.3
August	129.7	132.1	135.8	141.3	142.2	146.0	150.8	151.5	156.1	157.2	159.3	165.4	170.6	175.1	181.0
September	130.3	132.7	136.1	142.0	143.0	146.9	151.5	152.3	157.3	157.8	160.6	166.3	171.3	175.6	181.9
October	130.8	132.6	136.4	142.1	143.0	147.1	151.6	152.6	157.2	157.5	160.9	166.4	171.8	175.8	182.2
November	130.6	132.4	136.5	141.2	143.1	147.2	151.5	152.8	157.7	156.8	161.2	166.5	172.2	176.1	182.8
December	130.1	132.7	137.2	142.1	143.6	147.6	151.5	153.4	157.8	156.6	161.5	167.3	173.1	176.6	184.4

Retail Prices Index: (January 1988=100)

CHAW

	1992	1993	1994	1995	1996	1997	1998	1999	2000	2001	2002	2003	2004	2005	2006
January	135.6	137.9	141.3	146.0	150.2	154.4	159.5	163.4	166.6	171.1	173.3	178.4	183.1	188.9	193.4
February	136.3	138.8	142.1	146.9	150.9	155.0	160.3	163.7	167.5	172.0	173.8	179.3	183.8	189.6	194.2
March	136.7	139.3	142.5	147.5	151.5	155.4	160.8	164.1	168.4	172.2	174.5	179.9	184.6	190.5	195.0
April	138.8	140.6	144.2	149.0	152.6	156.3	162.6	165.2	170.1	173.1	175.7	181.2	185.7	191.6	196.5
May	139.3	141.1	144.7	149.6	152.9	156.9	163.5	165.6	170.7	174.2	176.2	181.5	186.5	192.0	197.7
June	139.3	141.0	144.7	149.8	153.0	157.5	163.4	165.6	171.1	174.4	176.2	181.3	186.8	192.2	198.5
July	138.8	140.7	144.0	149.1	152.4	157.5	163.0	165.1	170.5	173.3	175.9	181.3	186.8	192.2	198.5
August	138.9	141.3	144.7	149.9	153.1	158.5	163.7	165.5	170.5	174.0	176.4	181.6	187.4	192.6	199.2
September	139.4	141.9	145.0	150.6	153.8	159.3	164.4	166.2	171.7	174.6	177.6	182.5	188.1	193.1	200.1
October	139.9	141.8	145.2	149.8	153.8	159.5	164.5	166.5	171.6	174.3	177.9	182.6	188.6	193.3	200.4
November	139.7	141.6	145.3	149.8	153.9	159.6	164.4	166.7	172.1	173.6	178.2	182.7	189.0	193.6	201.1
December	139.2	141.9	146.0	150.7	154.4	160.0	164.4	167.3	172.2	173.4	178.5	183.5	189.9	194.1	202.7

Percentage changes on one year earlier[1]

	1993	1994	1995	1996	1997	1998	1999	2000	2001	2002	2003	2004	2005	2006
Tax and Price Index[1]														
January	0.5	2.6	3.9	3.2	1.4	2.4	2.3	1.5	2.6	−0.1	3.1	3.4	3.1	2.2
February	0.6	2.5	4.0	3.0	1.3	2.6	2.0	1.9	2.5	−0.4	3.4	3.3	3.1	2.3
March	0.7	2.5	4.0	3.0	1.1	2.6	1.9	2.2	2.1	−0.1	3.4	3.3	3.1	2.1
April	1.3	3.0	3.7	1.0	1.5	4.1	1.0	3.0	0.4	1.5	4.0	2.4	3.1	2.4
May	1.2	3.0	3.8	0.7	1.7	4.3	0.7	3.0	0.7	1.1	3.8	2.7	2.8	2.9
June	1.2	3.1	4.0	0.6	2.0	3.8	0.8	3.3	0.6	1.0	3.7	3.0	2.8	3.2
July	1.4	2.8	3.9	0.8	2.5	3.5	0.7	3.3	0.3	1.5	3.9	3.0	2.8	3.2
August	1.9	2.8	4.1	0.6	2.7	3.3	0.5	3.0	0.7	1.3	3.8	3.1	2.6	3.4
September	1.8	2.6	4.3	0.7	2.7	3.1	0.5	3.3	0.3	1.8	3.5	3.0	2.5	3.6
October	1.4	2.9	3.5	1.3	2.9	3.1	0.7	3.0	0.2	2.2	3.4	3.2	2.3	3.6
November	1.4	3.1	3.4	1.3	2.9	2.9	0.9	3.2	−0.6	2.8	3.3	3.4	2.3	3.8
December	2.0	3.4	3.6	1.1	2.8	2.6	1.3	2.9	−0.8	3.1	3.6	3.5	2.0	4.4
Retail Prices Index														
January	1.7	2.5	3.3	2.9	2.8	3.3	2.4	2.0	2.7	1.3	2.9	2.6	3.2	2.4
February	1.8	2.4	3.4	2.7	2.7	3.4	2.1	2.3	2.7	1.0	3.2	2.5	3.2	2.4
March	1.9	2.3	3.5	2.7	2.6	3.5	2.1	2.6	2.3	1.3	3.1	2.6	3.2	2.4
April	1.3	2.6	3.3	2.4	2.4	4.0	1.6	3.0	1.8	1.5	3.1	2.5	3.2	2.6
May	1.3	2.6	3.4	2.2	2.6	4.2	1.3	3.1	2.1	1.1	3.0	2.8	2.9	3.0
June	1.2	2.6	3.5	2.1	2.9	3.7	1.3	3.3	1.9	1.0	2.9	3.0	2.9	3.3
July	1.4	2.3	3.5	2.2	3.3	3.5	1.3	3.3	1.6	1.5	3.1	3.0	2.9	3.3
August	1.7	2.4	3.6	2.1	3.5	3.3	1.1	3.0	2.1	1.4	2.9	3.2	2.8	3.4
September	1.8	2.2	3.9	2.1	3.6	3.2	1.1	3.3	1.7	1.7	2.8	3.1	2.7	3.6
October	1.4	2.4	3.2	2.7	3.7	3.1	1.2	3.1	1.6	2.1	2.6	3.3	2.5	3.7
November	1.4	2.6	3.1	2.7	3.7	3.0	1.4	3.2	0.9	2.6	2.5	3.4	2.4	3.9
December	1.9	2.9	3.2	2.5	3.6	2.8	1.8	2.9	0.7	2.9	2.8	3.5	2.2	4.4

1 See chapter text.

Source: Office for National Statistics: 020 7533 5874

17.7 Index of purchase prices of the means of agricultural production[1]
United Kingdom
Annual averages

Indices (2000=100)

		Weights	1995	1996	1997	1998	1999	2000	2001	2002	2003	2004	2005
Goods and services currently consumed[2]	C3FU	100	105.7	110.7	105.5	99.5	98.1	100.0	104.3	103.7	106.5	113.7	115.9
Seeds	C3FV	3.3	136.7	136.3	119.2	119.2	109.0	100.0	109.2	105.5	116.0	110.3	108.2
Energy, lubricants	C3FW	8.1	79.7	82.2	82.1	75.1	82.4	100.0	96.7	92.4	100.5	108.8	137.4
Fuels for heating	C3FX	1.0	67.9	81.9	77.3	61.6	66.6	100.0	95.5	87.2	104.5	118.3	158.9
Motor fuel	C3FY	5.1	69.6	71.0	73.1	66.7	77.8	100.0	96.7	91.6	100.7	110.3	143.4
Electricity	C3FZ	1.8	114.1	113.4	109.6	104.8	102.9	100.0	96.9	96.2	96.5	98.9	110.7
Lubricants	C3G2	0.2	84.8	84.9	86.2	88.5	98.1	100.0	101.2	106.2	112.7	113.1	113.1
Fertilisers and soil improvers	C3G3	9.1	103.1	109.5	106.6	95.3	93.3	100.0	115.8	110.3	119.0	130.5	143.3
Straight nitrogen	C3G4	3.9	109.8	121.5	104.4	87.0	82.9	100.0	129.1	120.2	133.1	148.5	168.7
Compound fertilisers	C3G5	4.6	98.0	100.3	109.6	101.9	101.3	100.0	106.7	103.0	109.1	118.4	126.0
Other fertiliser (mainly lime and chalk)	C3G6	0.4	85.2	92.0	93.5	95.9	96.7	100.0	100.5	104.0	103.4	103.8	105.6
Plant protection products	C3G7	7.2	108.8	115.8	116.6	108.2	105.8	100.0	96.8	95.8	95.7	100.6	102.9
Animal feedstuffs	C3G8	26.4	130.6	140.6	125.4	106.5	99.1	100.0	107.4	103.5	104.9	111.6	102.9
Feed wheat	C3G9	2.2	166.2	168.5	133.4	113.6	102.2	100.0	110.8	97.3	107.4	119.3	97.5
Whole barley	C3GA	2.1	161.0	159.5	125.3	108.5	111.5	100.0	101.8	89.5	103.2	112.8	97.8
Whole oats	C3GB	0.2	140.8	153.7	123.3	98.0	104.7	100.0	97.8	90.7	85.1	94.3	94.4
Maize glutten feed	C3GC	0.4	144.3	160.7	117.8	95.3	100.2	100.0	110.0	102.9	122.9	123.8	110.1
Oilcake	C3GD	2.1	109.1	139.8	131.5	91.9	83.5	100.0	109.4	100.4	109.5	112.0	100.0
White fish meal	C3GE	0.4	104.0	133.0	125.3	137.9	93.2	100.0	115.1	134.7	129.1	120.3	126.6
Other straight feedstuffs	C3GF	3.3	133.3	142.6	121.7	98.2	91.8	100.0	114.1	109.3	109.9	115.1	109.1
All straight feedstuffs	C3GG	10.6	141.1	151.5	127.3	104.1	97.1	100.0	109.7	101.3	108.1	114.9	102.7
Feedstuffs non-concentrates	C3GH	0.1	141.1	151.5	127.3	104.1	97.1	100.0	109.7	101.3	108.1	114.9	102.7
Compound feedstuffs for:	C3GI	15.8	123.7	133.3	124.1	108.1	100.4	100.0	105.8	104.9	102.7	109.3	103.1
Cattle and calves	C3GJ	6.2	120.8	130.5	122.0	105.0	99.9	100.0	106.4	105.9	102.5	108.1	103.9
Pigs	C3GK	3.5	132.9	142.0	130.5	112.8	101.9	100.0	105.9	103.3	101.0	107.7	100.2
Poultry	C3GL	5.0	121.7	131.5	121.7	108.7	100.6	100.0	105.9	104.5	104.9	112.8	104.5
Sheep	C3GM	1.1	119.1	129.2	126.5	108.3	98.0	100.0	102.2	106.2	99.4	106.0	101.6
Maintenance and repair of plant	C3GN	7.9	83.4	87.6	91.0	93.4	96.6	100.0	104.3	109.4	116.0	122.5	130.3
Maintenance and repair of buildings	C3GO	3.6	94.8	95.7	97.3	98.5	97.7	100.0	101.9	105.1	108.3	113.4	118.1
Veterinary services	C3GP	3.2	98.1	98.9	100.1	101.1	101.2	100.0	98.6	97.8	101.6	104.6	103.9
Other goods and services	C3GQ	31.2	95.7	98.0	95.6	98.5	99.9	100.0	102.5	105.5	105.2	114.0	114.5
Goods and services contributing to investment in agriculture	C3GR	100	91.9	95.3	98.1	99.8	100.2	100.0	99.0	100.0	101.5	104.4	108.7
Materials	C3GS	71.5	93.5	97.9	100.5	101.6	101.7	100.0	97.3	97.0	97.5	99.4	103.4
Machinery and other equipment	C3GT	28.4	88.3	92.2	95.0	97.7	99.2	100.0	97.4	95.7	95.1	96.1	103.8
Machinery and plant for cultivation	C3GU	8.0	81.5	89.7	93.3	97.7	99.1	100.0	99.6	98.6	98.7	103.8	109.4
Machinery and plant for harvesting	C3GV	14.3	91.1	93.9	96.8	98.4	100.0	100.0	92.3	88.8	88.2	87.3	97.9
Farm machinery and installations	C3GW	6.0	90.4	91.6	93.2	96.1	97.5	100.0	106.3	108.2	106.8	107.0	110.2
Tractors	C3GX	28.6	93.2	98.5	101.0	101.6	102.4	100.0	96.8	98.4	101.4	106.1	110.5
Other vehicles	C3GY	14.5	104.2	107.6	110.0	109.1	105.1	100.0	98.3	96.7	94.4	92.4	88.6
Buildings	C3GZ	19.5	88.6	90.1	93.2	95.6	96.6	100.0	103.3	107.8	112.1	118.1	123.7
Engineering and soil improvement operations	C3H2	9.0	91.2	86.1	89.8	94.8	96.9	100.0	101.4	107.2	110.3	113.3	118.0

1 See chapter text.
2 The sum of the percentages of categories included does not add up to 100% due to the exclusion of some minor categories.

Source: Department for Environment, Food and Rural Affairs: 01904 455249

17.8 Index of producer prices of agricultural products[1]
United Kingdom
Annual averages

Indices (2000=100)

		Weights	1995	1996	1997	1998	1999	2000	2001	2002	2003	2004	2005
All products[2]	C3H6	100	139.2	135.1	117.1	107.0	103.6	100.0	108.3	103.3	110.0	113.4	109.8
All crop products	C3H7	40.2	147.4	130.5	108.9	111.7	109.0	100.0	112.0	104.0	110.7	115.1	108.5
Cereals (including cereal seeds)	C3H8	13.3	166.5	166.2	132.4	113.8	111.0	100.0	107.8	95.0	105.2	114.2	99.1
Wheat for:													
breadmaking	C3H9	1.1	159.8	164.5	139.5	122.8	112.9	100.0	109.6	101.4	110.6	120.8	101.9
other milling	C3HA	1.5	162.8	165.0	133.7	116.0	110.9	100.0	107.5	92.9	104.1	116.8	96.5
feeding	C3HB	6.4	167.0	167.3	135.4	114.0	110.5	100.0	110.5	96.7	105.6	117.7	98.2
Barley for:													
feeding	C3HC	2.5	161.1	157.7	123.9	109.2	112.9	100.0	102.6	89.1	103.7	110.7	98.7
malting	C3HD	1.4	187.3	180.9	128.2	115.1	108.9	100.0	104.8	96.5	107.1	101.6	104.5
Oats for:													
milling	C3HE	0.1	158.5	161.1	128.8	104.9	109.9	100.0	109.8	89.0	90.7	96.3	104.8
feeding	C3HF	0.2	145.0	156.0	119.0	97.0	106.1	100.0	98.5	91.2	86.7	94.4	96.1
Potatoes:	C3HG	4.5	264.6	118.0	63.5	138.8	143.5	100.0	131.0	90.0	105.6	140.3	109.2
early	C3HH	0.4	93.2	68.2	46.3	100.7	51.9	100.0	114.5	73.0	90.0	124.8	98.0
main crop	C3HI	4.1	280.6	121.2	63.4	141.1	151.5	100.0	132.5	90.6	106.0	141.6	109.7
Industrial crops	C3HJ	4.3	147.9	154.4	127.9	118.4	103.4	100.0	111.9	114.4	120.3	121.6	113.9
Oilseed rape (non set-aside)	C3HK	1.2	151.9	164.4	135.6	140.0	102.0	100.0	119.2	121.2	140.3	136.1	112.9
Sugar beet	C3HL	2.2	150.1	152.5	124.9	111.4	108.7	100.0	107.3	114.8	112.1	115.4	116.3
Fresh vegetables	C3HM	7.7	107.5	105.3	97.4	105.2	99.2	100.0	113.6	112.7	125.5	113.7	120.1
Cauliflowers	C3HN	0.4	92.3	89.3	79.1	87.9	82.4	100.0	103.9	117.7	119.8	102.4	125.2
Lettuce	C3HO	0.7	108.7	96.5	114.0	98.6	102.9	100.0	129.2	128.6	151.5	130.2	140.7
Tomatoes	C3HP	0.7	92.9	106.6	86.9	91.8	100.3	100.0	100.1	107.6	135.6	99.8	117.7
Carrots	C3HQ	0.7	142.4	130.9	88.1	125.4	119.3	100.0	166.5	150.4	157.2	144.7	170.5
Cabbage	C3HR	0.4	100.7	104.4	83.2	94.5	94.2	100.0	123.0	109.8	119.7	109.3	122.4
Beans	C3HS	0.2	87.4	88.9	87.3	107.8	102.8	100.0	124.3	118.0	119.1	128.7	127.2
Onions	C3HT	0.5	149.0	107.3	122.8	165.8	104.7	100.0	128.6	126.7	136.1	138.8	112.4
Mushrooms	C3HU	1.3	107.7	110.6	99.1	98.9	98.1	100.0	91.0	95.9	100.6	94.4	83.4
Fresh fruit	C3HV	1.9	101.9	105.5	109.1	105.4	100.0	100.0	99.0	113.9	124.2	112.4	120.1
Dessert apples	C3HW	0.3	120.6	132.7	124.7	110.5	104.3	100.0	109.8	111.3	124.6	120.9	116.5
Dessert pears	C3HX	0.1	121.5	122.7	118.2	110.4	108.7	100.0	128.7	124.8	115.3	114.6	115.0
Cooking apples	C3HY	0.2	105.2	122.9	135.6	150.9	100.7	100.0	105.6	109.4	152.1	142.5	118.8
Strawberries	C3HZ	0.7	100.3	102.6	106.9	93.7	102.4	100.0	94.5	121.7	124.4	97.1	111.8
Raspberries	C3I2	0.2	102.9	92.8	103.3	114.3	104.9	100.0	102.9	128.9	125.7	114.3	152.9
Seeds (excluding cereal seeds)	C3I3	0.5	148.2	155.0	130.9	98.6	97.7	100.0	104.0	95.7	113.6	112.9	114.1
Flowers and plants	C3I4	5.9	99.0	98.3	102.4	103.1	105.3	100.0	105.3	106.8	107.9	105.3	105.6
Other crop products	C3I5	0.7	135.9	139.8	122.2	98.7	97.0	100.0	106.0	98.9	108.6	109.7	110.8
Animals and animal products	C3I6	59.8	133.7	138.3	122.6	103.9	99.9	100.0	105.8	102.7	109.6	112.2	110.8
Animals for slaughter	C3I7	35.3	126.0	132.3	118.0	97.2	95.2	100.0	101.3	103.2	109.5	112.0	110.8
Calves	C3I8	0.1	240.5	218.6	179.3	149.4	115.1	100.0	94.2	120.2	143.9	140.8	106.8
Clean cattle	C3I9	9.7	137.5	117.3	107.1	95.0	101.7	100.0	100.8	103.8	106.7	113.4	114.6
Clean pigs	C3IA	7.0	126.5	146.0	117.5	85.8	83.4	100.0	103.6	98.7	109.0	109.3	109.8
Sows and boars	C3IB	0.2	184.2	201.0	157.1	81.1	81.0	100.0	107.4	94.0	103.2	123.9	124.2
Clean sheep and lambs	C3IC	5.2	120.5	142.7	131.0	97.1	90.2	100.0	101.3	118.5	132.5	131.5	122.9
Ewes and rams	C3ID	0.4	137.0	189.6	198.5	116.3	81.3	100.0	152.4	149.6	188.2	183.5	148.6
All poultry	C3IE	11.5	113.0	126.7	116.8	103.3	99.0	100.0	98.6	97.2	100.0	102.3	102.4
Chickens	C3IF	7.9	120.2	136.3	126.6	105.9	101.3	100.0	100.1	99.5	101.1	104.9	104.6
Turkeys	C3IG	2.9	94.2	102.6	89.5	91.3	90.0	100.0	94.4	89.5	97.8	95.0	93.9
Cows' milk	C3IH	20.1	147.2	147.7	130.6	114.4	108.3	100.0	113.7	101.0	106.4	109.0	109.0
Eggs	C3II	3.2	127.6	142.3	121.1	109.4	98.0	100.0	104.9	109.5	130.7	135.1	121.1
Other animal products:	C3IJ	1.1	146.8	144.7	129.4	108.0	103.0	100.0	107.7	100.0	107.4	110.4	109.3
Wool (clip)	C3IK	0.2	189.0	173.5	150.1	98.6	93.5	100.0	87.0	96.4	108.4	107.3	99.7

1 See chapter text.
2 The sum of the percentages of all the categories does not add up to 100% due to the exclusion of some minor categories.

Source: Department for Environment, Food and Rural Affairs: 01904 455249

17.9 Commodity price trends[1]
United Kingdom

			1996	1997	1998	1999	2000	2001	2002	2003	2004	2005	2006
Wheat £ per tonne	KVAA	Average ex-farm price[2,3]	112.5	91.8	77.8	75.4	68.1	76.9	65.6	77.3	..	..	..
Barley £ per tonne	KVAB	Average ex-farm price[2,3]	103.7	86.3	79.2	74.2	70.1	72.1	64.8	75.5	..	..	..
Oats £ per tonne	KVAC	Average ex-farm price[2,3]	107.4	82.3	66.4	71.1	65.0	67.7	56.6	62.1	..	..	..
Rye £ per tonne	KVAD	Average ex-farm price[2]	113.90	..	..	..	..	78.10	61.40	71.80	86.40	..	..
Hops £ per tonne	KVAE	Average farm-gate price	3 360	3 550	3 500	4 000	4 016	4 081	3 255	3 212	2 496	3 277	3 241
Potatoes £ per tonne	KVAF	Average farm-gate price[4]	100.50	66.10	121.50	119.10	83.30	111.40	81.10	102.80	117.00	98.90	123.70
Sugar beet £ per tonne	KVAG	Producer price[5]	34.40	29.70	29.80	26.40	27.80	30.80	29.60	30.50	30.80	30.90	23.50
Oilseed rape £ per tonne	KVAH	Average market price[6]	186.90	160.20	164.30	112.90	120.40	148.40	148.20	171.60	..	..	..
Apples £ per tonne	KPUE	Dessert average farm-gate price[7]	493.6	525.0	480.3	436.9	357.8	352.2	385.2	460.3	348.9	401.9	607.6
" "	KVAI	Dessert average market price	523.5	462.0	431.5	405.4	408.7	418.2	453.1	551.3	526.1	471.5	..
" "	KVAJ	Culinary average market price	462.8	517.7	575.5	384.1	378.1	422.4	419.4	652.6	592.0	458.7	..
" "	KPUJ	Culinary average farm-gate price	286.8	335.1	341.4	248.9	215.3	175.7	285.7	471.7	259.1	350.8	355.9
Pears £ per tonne	KPUG	Average farm-gate price	445.7	441.9	405.1	426.4	283.3	352.1	402.9	344.0	354.9	341.3	363.7
" "	KVAK	Average market price	461.9	429.5	413.3	396.8	374.0	412.5	463.6	443.0	437.2	426.3	..
Tomatoes £ per tonne	LQMH	Average farm-gate price[7]	742.4	546.9	594.6	576.5	751.6	724.9	793.7	1 042.3	750.0	871.4	993.1
" "	KVAL	Average market price[7]	756.7	549.3	636.0	583.6	629.7	651.3	736.3	824.8	647.2	754.8	..
Cauliflowers £ per tonne	KPUI	Average farm-gate price[7]	270.9	236.8	216.3	211.3	274.1	285.3	329.6	331.7	296.3	344.6	363.1
" "	KVAM	Average market price[7]	363.0	309.8	284.8	242.5	282.9	304.9	365.6	368.2	330.8	408.3	..
Cattle (rearing) £ per head	KVAN	1st quality Hereford/cross bull calves[8,9,10]	131.80	147.00	107.90	88.20	79.50	..	84.90	112.70	113.70	81.53	..
"	KVAO	1st quality beef/ cross yearling steers[9,10]	445.00	427.00	369.00	382.00	400.05	..	403.85	451.54	395.90	429.10	..
Cattle (fat) p per kg liveweight	KVAP	Clean cattle[11]	105.52	96.89	86.10	92.12	89.68	87.53	91.38	95.15	101.18	102.22	..

17.9 Commodity price trends[1]
United Kingdom
continued

			1995	1996	1997	1998	1999	2000	2001	2002	2003	2004	2005
Sheep (store) £ per head	KVAQ	1st quality lambs, hoggets and tegs[8]	44.46	46.83	53.42	31.28	28.62	34.50	..	..	36.03	37.70	30.52
Sheep (fat) p per kg estimated dressed carcase weight	KVAR KVAS	Great Britain[12] Northern Ireland[13]	236.40 214.41	283.13 260.46	239.02 228.23	192.46 179.06	180.27 165.71	196.44 182.67	.. ..	233.40 228.80	271.08 239.91	262.55 227.83	250.10 223.75
Pigs £ per kg deadweight	KVAT	Average price clean pigs	118.80	137.70	110.80	80.60	78.60	95.08	97.75	93.32	102.64	102.85	102.08
Broilers p per kg carcass weight	KVAU	Average producer price	84.0	90.9	86.2	76.7	72.1	70.7	70.6	68.8	68.6	73.6	73.2
Milk p per litre	KVAV	Average net return to producers[14]	24.94	25.02	22.12	19.37	18.35	16.93	19.26	17.10	18.03	18.47	18.47
Eggs p per dozen	KVAW	Average producer price[15]	38.23	45.70	39.33	36.35	34.45	39.28	40.72	42.08	45.95	48.92	45.27
Wool p per kg	KHWQ	Average producer price for clip paid to producers by the British Wool Marketing Board	95.00	86.90	74.90	48.00	46.60	51.30	47.00	50.00	55.70	53.10	50.20

1 This table gives indications of the movement in commodity prices at the first point of sale. The series do not always show total receipts by farmers; for some commodities additional premiums or deficiency payments are made to achieve support price levels.
2 Weighted average ex-farm prices of United Kingdom cereals.
3 Data from 1997 onwards have been revised and are not directly comparable with earlier years.
4 Weighted average price paid to growers for early and main crop potatoes in the United Kingdom (includes all potatoes and a value for sacks).
5 Returns to growers figures since 1986 prices per 'adjusted' tonne at 16% sugar content.
6 Typical contract price adjusted to delivered basis and 40 per cent oil content.
7 Weighted average wholesale prices for England and Wales. Average farm-gate price for England and Wales, crop year (June-May).

8 Average prices at representative markets in England and Wales.
9 Consists of Hereford/cross, Charolais/cross, Limousin/cross, Simmental/cross, Belgian/cross, other continental cross, other beef/dairy cross, other beef/beef cross.
10 From 2002 no differentiation between class 1 and class 2 animals.
11 Based on Meat and Livestock Commission all clean cattle prices.
12 Average of Great Britain weekly market prices as used to determine the level of ewe premium.
13 Average of Northern Ireland weekly market prices used to determine the level of ewe premium.
14 Derived by dividing total value of output by the total quantity of output available for human consumption.
15 Average price of all Class A eggs weighted according to quantity in each grade.

Source: Department for Environment, Food and Rural Affairs: 01904 455332

Government finance

Chapter 18

Government finance

Public sector

(Tables 18.1 to 18.3 and 18.5)

In Table 18.1 the term public sector describes the consolidation of central government, local government and public corporations. General government is the consolidated total of central government and local government. The table shows details of the key public sector finances' indicators, consistent with the European System of Accounts 1995 (ESA95), by sub sector.

The concepts in Table 18.1 are consistent with the format for public finances in the Economic and Fiscal Strategy Report (EFSR), published by HM Treasury 11 June 1998, and The Budget. The public sector current budget is equivalent to net saving in national accounts plus capital tax receipts. Net investment is gross capital formation, plus payments less receipts of investment grants, less depreciation. Net borrowing is net investment less current budget. Net borrowing differs from the net cash requirement (see below) in that it is measured on an accruals basis whereas the net cash requirement is mainly a cash measure which includes some financial transactions. Table 18.2 shows the Public sector key fiscal balances. The table shows the component detail of the public sector key fiscal balance by economic category. The tables are consistent with The Budget.

Table 18.3 shows public sector net debt. Public sector net debt consists of the public sector's financial liabilities at face value minus its liquid assets - mainly foreign currency exchange reserves and bank deposits. General government gross debt (consolidated) in table 18.3 is consistent with the definition of general government gross debt reported to the European Commission under the requirements of the Maastricht Treaty.

More information on the concepts in table 18.1, 18.2 and 18.3 can be found in a guide to monthly public sector finance statistics, GSS Methodology Series No 12, the ONS First Releases Public Sector Finances and Financial Statistics Explanatory Handbook.

Table 18.5 shows the taxes and national insurance contributions paid to central government, local government, and to the institutions of the European Union. The table is the same as table 11.1 of the National Accounts Blue Book. More information on the data and concepts in the table can be found in Chapter 11 of the Blue Book.

Consolidated Fund and National Loans Fund

(Tables 18.4, 18.6 and 18.7)

The central government embraces all bodies for whose activities a Minister of the Crown, or other responsible person, is accountable to Parliament. It includes, in addition to the ordinary government departments, a number of bodies administering public policy but without the substantial degree of financial independence which characterises the public corporations; it also includes certain extra-budgetary funds and accounts controlled by departments.

The government's financial transactions are handled through a number of statutory funds, or accounts. The most important of these is the Consolidated Fund which is the government's main account with the Bank of England. Up to 31 March 1968 the Consolidated Fund was virtually synonymous with the term 'Exchequer' which was then the government's central cash account. From 1 April 1968 the National Loans Fund, with a separate account at the Bank of England, was set up by the National Loans Act, 1968. The general effect of this Act was to remove from the Consolidated Fund most of the government's domestic lending and the whole of the government's borrowing transactions and to provide for them to be brought to account in the National Loans Fund.

Revenue from taxation and miscellaneous receipts, including interest and dividends on loans made from Votes, continue to be paid into the Consolidated Fund.

After meeting the ordinary expenditure on Supply Services and the Consolidated Fund Standing Services, the surplus or deficit of the Consolidated Fund (Table 18.4), is payable into or met by the National Loans Fund. Table 18.4 also provides a summary of the transactions of the National Loans Fund. The service of the National Debt, previously borne by the Consolidated Fund, is now met from the National Loans Fund which receives (a) interest payable on loans to the nationalised industries, local authorities and other bodies, whether the loans were made before or after 1 April 1968 and (b) the profits of the Issue Department of the Bank of England, mainly derived from interest on government securities, which were formerly paid into the Exchange Equalisation Account. The net cost of servicing the National Debt after applying these interest receipts and similar items is a charge on the Consolidated Fund as part of the standing services. Details of National Loans Fund loans outstanding are shown in Table 18.7. Details of borrowing and repayments of debt, other than loans from the National Loans Fund, are shown in Table 18.6.

Income tax

(Table 18.9, 18.10)

Following the introduction of Independent Taxation from 1990-91 the married couple's allowance was introduced. It is payable in addition to the personal allowance and between 1990-91 and 1992-93 went to the husband unless the transfer condition was met. The condition was that the husband was unable to make full use of the allowance himself and in that case he could transfer only part or all of the married couple's allowance to his wife. In 1993-94 all or half of theallowance could be transferred to the wife if the couple had agreed beforehand. The wife has the right to claim half the allowance. The married couple's allowance, and allowances linked to it, were restricted to 20 per cent in 1994-95 and to 15 per cent from 1995-96. From 2000-01 only people born before 6th April 1935 are entitled to married couple's allowance.

The age allowance replaces the single allowance, provided the taxpayer's income is below the limits shown in the table. From 1989-90, for incomes in excess of the limits, the allowance is reduced by £1 for each additional £2 of income until the ordinary limit is reached (before it was £2 for each £3 of additional income). The relief is due where the taxpayer is aged 65 or over in the year of assessment.

The additional personal allowance could be claimed by a single parent (or by a married man if his wife was totally incapacitated) who maintained a resident child at his or her own expense. Widow's bereavement allowance was due to a widow in the year of her husband's death and in the following year provided the widow had not remarried before the beginning of that year. Both the additional personal allowance and the widow's bereavement allowance were abolished from April 2000.

The blind person's allowance may be claimed by blind persons (in England and Wales, registered as blind by a local authority) and surplus blind person's allowance may be transferred to a husband or wife. Relief on life assurance premiums is given by deduction from the premium payable. From 1984-85, it is confined to policies made before 14 March 1984.

From 1993-94 until 1998-99 a number of taxpayers with taxable income in excess of the lower rate limit only paid tax at the lower rate. This was because it was only their dividend income and (from 1996-97) their savings income which took their taxable income above the lower rate limit but below the basic rate limit, and such income was chargeable to tax at the lower rate and not the basic rate.

In 1999-2000 the 10% starting rate replaced the lower rate and taxpayers with savings or dividend income at the basic rate

of tax are taxed at 20% and 10% respectively. Before 1999-2000 these people would have been classified as lower rate taxpayers.

Rateable values

(Table 18.11)

Major changes to local government finance in England and Wales took effect from 1 April 1990. These included the abolition of domestic rating - replaced by the community charge (replaced in 1993 by the council tax), the revaluation of all non-domestic properties, and the introduction of the Uniform Business Rate. Also in 1990, a new classification scheme was introduced which has resulted in differences in coverage. Further differences are caused by legislative changes which have changed the treatment of certain types of property. There was little change in the total rateable value of non-domestic properties when all these properties were revalued in April 1995. Rateable values for offices fell and there was a rise for all other property types shown in the table.

With effect from 1 April 2000 all non-domestic properties were revalued. Overall there was an increase in rateable values of over 25% compared to the last year of the 1995 list. The largest proportionate increase was for offices and cinemas, with all property types given in the table showing rises.

The latest revaluation affecting all non domestic properties took effect from 1 April 2005. In this revaluation the overall increase in rateable values between 1 April of the first year of the new list and the same day on the last year of the 2000 list was 17%. The largest proportionate increase was for theatres and music halls with again, all property types in the table showing rises.

Local authority capital expenditure and receipts

(Table 18.15)

Capital spending by local authorities is mainly for buying, constructing or improving physical assets such as:

buildings - schools, houses, libraries and museums, police and fire stations etc;

land - for development, roads, playing fields; vehicles, plant and machinery – including street lighting, road signs etc.

It also includes grants and advances made to the private sector or the rest of the public sector for capital purposes, such as advances to Registered Social Landlords.

Local authority capital expenditure has risen every year since 2000-01.

Government finance

Spending in 2005-06 increased by 17%, slightly faster growth than in 2004-05.

The forecast for 2006-07 is for much slower growth.

In real terms capital spending increased by 80% between 2000-01 and 2005-06.

New construction and conversion forms the major part of capital spending.

Between 2000-01 and 2005-06 increases in education and transport expenditure have been the main contributors to increases in capital expenditure.

As a result, the education sector's share of capital spending has risen over this period from 19% to 21% and the transport sector's share has risen from 17% to 21%. Housing remains the largest single sector.

Local authority financing for capital expenditure

(Table 18.16)

Authorities finance capital spending in a number of ways including use of their own revenue funds, borrowing or grants and contributions from elsewhere. Up until 31 March 2004 the capital finance system laid down in Part 4 of the Local Government and Housing Act 1989 (the "1989 Act") provided the framework within which authorities were permitted to finance capital spending from sources other than revenue - that is by the use of borrowing, long-term credit or capital receipts.

Up until 31 March 2004, capital spending could be financed by:

revenue resources – either the General Fund Revenue Account, the Housing Revenue Account (HRA) or the Major Repairs Reserve – but an authority could not charge council tenants for spending on general services, or spending on council houses to local taxpayers;

borrowing or long-term credit as authorised by the credit approvals issued by central government. Credit approvals were normally accompanied by an element of Revenue Support Grant (RSG) covering most of the costs of borrowing;

grants received from central government;

contributions or grants from elsewhere – including the National Lottery and NDPBs such as the Sports Council, English Heritage and the Countryside Commission, as well as private sector partners;

capital receipts (that is proceeds from the sale of land, buildings or other fixed assets); sums set aside as Provision for Credit Liabilities (PCL). This required the use of a credit approval, unless the authority was debt-free.

From 1 April 2004, capital spending can be financed in the same ways except that: central government no longer issues credit approvals to allow authorities to finance capital spending by borrowing. However, it continues to provide financial support in the usual way, via RSG or HRA subsidy, towards some capital spending financed by borrowing that is Supported Capital Expenditure (Revenue) - SCE(R); authorities are now free to finance capital spending by self-financed borrowing within limits of affordability set, having regard to the 2003 Act and the CIPFA Prudential Code; the concept of PCL has not been carried forward into the new system, although authorities which were debt-free and had a negative credit ceiling at the end of the old system could still spend amounts of PCL built up under the old rules.

In 2005-06 capital expenditure of almost £2.3 billion was financed by unsupported borrowing, 13% of the total, and more than double the amount financed in 2004-05. Borrowing by the GLA for Transport for London's investment programme and by Birmingham for the refinancing of the National Exhibition Centre account for 33% of the 2005-06 total.

In 2001-02 credit approvals were the principal financing source for capital expenditure, accounting for 25.5% of the total. In 2004-05 Supported Capital Expenditure (Revenue) was the principal financing source, accounting for 25.4% of the total. In 2005-06 central government grants were the principal financing source, accounting for 23.3% of the total.

18.1 Sector analysis of key fiscal balances[1]
United Kingdom
Not seasonally adjusted

£ million[2]

		1995 /96	1996 /97	1997 /98	1998 /99	1999 /00	2000 /01	2001 /02	2002 /03	2003 /04	2004 /05	2005 /06
Surplus on current budget[3]												
Central Government	ANLV	−23 091	−20 475	417	12 302	25 694	27 939	12 998	−8 439	−17 401	−17 437	−14 335
Local government	NMMX	−1 269	−851	−420	−406	−2 179	−1 531	−1 657	−1 270	817	−785	−2 988
General Government	ANLW	−24 360	−21 392	−175	11 086	20 878	21 996	10 861	−11 103	−19 005	−18 489	−18 661
Public corporations	FDDP	−228	−409	−1 046	−1 220	−1 675	−1 828	−631	−2 580	−2 918	−1 741	2 598
Public sector	ANMU	−24 588	−21 735	−1 037	10 607	21 424	23 974	11 061	−11 416	−17 986	−19 485	−16 063
Net investment[4]												
Central government	-ANNS	14 139	9 396	7 844	8 200	9 231	8 076	12 620	16 394	18 582	20 089	18 579
Local government	-ANNT	−1 931	−1 704	−536	−313	−832	−1 882	−1 824	−3 595	−1 001	−230	52
General Government	-ANNV	12 208	7 692	7 403	7 848	6 461	6 574	10 951	12 487	16 371	19 441	18 294
Public corporations	-ANNU	−2 083	−2 257	−2 080	−1 033	−2 944	−2 141	−456	−922	−2 941	−1 287	4 250
Public sector	-ANNW	10 125	5 435	5 250	6 507	5 355	4 072	11 080	13 345	15 499	20 314	22 544
Net borrowing[5]												
Central government	-NMFJ	37 230	29 871	7 427	−4 102	−16 463	−19 863	−378	24 833	35 983	38 252	33 915
Local government	-NMOE	−662	−853	−114	92	1 616	63	62	−3 000	−3 002	187	3 040
General Government	-NNBK	36 568	29 018	7 313	−4 010	−14 847	−19 800	−316	22 387	32 981	38 439	36 955
Public corporations	-CPCM	−1 855	−1 848	−1 026	−90	−1 222	−102	335	2 374	504	1 360	1 652
Public sector	-ANNX	34 713	27 170	6 287	−4 100	−16 069	−19 902	19	24 761	33 485	39 124	37 754
Net cash requirement												
Central government[6]	RUUX	36 153	25 199	2 751	−6 344	−10 664	−37 251	3 366	24 214	42 717	37 455	35 912
Local government	ABEG	−1 139	−843	−820	−404	979	−611	−423	−2 715	−2 712	1 282	4 163
General Government	RUUS	35 014	24 356	1 931	−6 748	−9 685	−37 862	2 943	21 499	40 005	38 737	40 075
Public corporations	ABEM	−3 529	−1 637	−669	699	1 712	1 539	694	3 722	−273	−166	−44
Public sector	RURQ	31 485	22 719	1 262	−6 049	−7 973	−36 323	3 637	25 221	39 732	38 571	40 031
Public sector debt												
Public sector net debt (£ billion)	RUTN	322.1	348.0	352.9	351.6	345.4	312.4	317.6	349.1	384.4	424.1	463.4
Public sector net debt as a percentage of GDP	RUTO	*42.7*	*43.6*	*41.6*	*39.3*	*36.6*	*31.7*	*30.7*	*32.0*	*33.1*	*35.0*	*36.5*

1 National accounts entities as defined under the European System of Accounts 1995 (ESA95) consistent with the latest national accounts. See chapter text.
2 Unless otherwise stated
3 Net saving *plus* capital taxes.
4 Gross capital formation *plus* payments *less* receipts of investment grants *less* depreciation.

5 Net investment *less* surplus on current budget. A version of General government net borrowing is reported to the European Commision under the requirements of the Maastricht Treaty.
6 Central government net cash requirement (own account).

Source: Office for National Statistics: 020 7533 5984

18.2 Public sector transactions and fiscal balances[1]
United Kingdom

£ million

		1995 /96	1996 /97	1997 /98	1998 /99	1999 /00	2000 /01	2001 /02	2002 /03	2003 /04	2004 /05	2005 /06
Current receipts												
Taxes on income and wealth	ANSO	96 465	102 313	114 939	123 875	133 720	144 157	145 122	143 228	145 505	161 116	180 068
Taxes on production	NMYE	95 928	99 599	109 297	115 227	125 099	129 273	133 043	139 827	148 817	154 992	159 546
Other current taxes[2]	MJBC	13 950	15 078	16 223	17 688	18 916	19 698	21 569	23 192	25 748	27 225	28 662
Taxes on capital	NMGI	1 518	1 558	1 684	1 804	2 054	2 236	2 383	2 370	2 521	2 941	3 276
Social contributions	ANBO	45 007	47 219	51 692	54 746	56 935	62 068	63 162	63 529	75 148	80 209	85 404
Gross operating surplus	ANBP	18 130	17 138	16 655	16 755	16 897	16 617	16 861	17 182	18 367	18 418	20 823
Interest and dividends from private sector and Rest of World	ANBQ	4 435	4 369	4 809	5 232	4 307	6 175	4 891	4 541	4 506	5 695	6 552
Rent and other current transfers[3]	ANBS	1 182	1 396	1 084	891	1 037	2 036	2 427	2 474	2 081	2 062	1 973
Total current receipts	ANBT	276 615	288 670	316 383	336 218	358 965	382 260	389 458	396 343	422 693	452 658	486 304
Current expenditure												
Current expenditure on goods and services[4]	GZSN	144 764	148 383	150 967	159 336	172 168	185 763	198 864	217 387	237 126	254 999	275 315
Subsidies	NMRL	5 304	5 496	5 360	4 164	4 215	4 412	4 504	6 043	6 716	6 764	6 404
Social benefits	ANLY	100 473	104 111	105 881	106 585	105 555	108 010	118 269	122 636	130 873	137 492	143 782
Net current grants abroad[5]	GZSI	458	−751	102	−847	−253	−146	−1 861	−626	−995	−579	−305
Other current grants	NNAI	10 325	12 693	13 519	15 199	19 106	21 676	23 932	27 555	31 065	33 719	33 305
Interest and dividends paid to private sector and Rest of World	ANLO	26 766	28 128	29 661	29 364	25 381	26 462	22 565	21 619	22 777	24 601	26 684
Total current expenditure	ANLT	288 090	298 060	305 490	313 801	326 172	346 177	366 273	394 614	427 562	456 996	485 185
Saving, gross plus capital taxes	ANSP	−11 475	−9 390	10 893	22 417	32 793	36 083	23 185	1 729	−4 869	−4 338	1 119
Depreciation	-ANNZ	−13 113	−12 411	−12 320	−12 390	−12 764	−13 092	−13 548	−14 446	−14 996	−16 044	−17 182
Surplus on current budget	ANMU	−24 588	−21 735	−1 037	10 607	21 424	23 974	11 061	−11 416	−17 986	−19 485	−16 063
Net investment												
Gross fixed capital formation[6]	ANSQ	19 138	14 262	13 472	14 055	14 146	13 427	17 307	20 122	21 067	25 672	28 650
Less depreciation	-ANNZ	−13 113	−12 411	−12 320	−12 390	−12 764	−13 092	−13 548	−14 446	−14 996	−16 044	−17 182
Increase in inventories and valuables	ANSR	21	34	139	231	−472	−126	−10	−74	107	−47	−16
Capital grants to private sector and Rest of World	ANSS	4 432	4 032	4 420	4 942	4 304	3 875	7 958	7 564	9 918	10 851	12 626
Capital grants from private sector and Rest of World	-ANST	−353	−482	−516	−367	−427	−756	−989	−1 091	−1 500	−1 211	−1 534
Total net investment	-ANNW	10 125	5 435	5 250	6 507	5 355	4 072	11 080	13 345	15 499	20 314	22 544
Net borrowing[7]	-ANNX	34 713	27 170	6 287	−4 100	−16 069	−19 902	19	24 761	33 485	39 124	37 754
Financial transactions determining net cash requirement												
Net lending to private sector and Rest of World	ANSU	−1 749	−655	−298	237	2 269	3 187	2 473	2 736	2 657	1 046	824
Net acquisition of UK company securities	ANSV	−2 344	−3 942	−1 336	704	−310	949	−350	663	799	430	420
Accounts receivable/payable	ANSW	3 139	−268	−1 167	−299	5 305	−19 685	997	−2 932	5 779	1 121	859
Adjustment for interest on gilts	ANSX	−1 895	−382	−2 349	−2 446	−1 295	−2 630	−361	−1 447	−1 186	−2 304	−2 749
Other financial transcations[8]	ANSY	−379	796	125	−145	2 127	1 758	859	1 440	−1 802	−846	2 923
Public sector net cash requirement	RURQ	31 485	22 719	1 262	−6 049	−7 973	−36 323	3 637	25 221	39 732	38 571	40 031

1 See chapter text.
2 Includes domestic rates, council tax, community charge, motor vehicle duty paid by household and some licence fees.
3 ESA95 transactions D44, D45, D74, D75 and D72-D71: includes rent of land, oil royalties, other property income and fines.
4 Includes non-trading capital consumption.

5 Net of current grants received from abroad.
6 Including net acquisition of land.
7 Net investment *less* surplus on current budget.
8 Includes statistical discrepancy, finance leasing and similar borrowing, insurance technical reserves and some other minor adjustments.

Source: Office for National Statistics: 020 7533 5984

18.3 Public sector net debt[1]
United Kingdom

£ million

		1997 /98	1998 /99	1999 /00	2000 /01	2001 /02	2002 /03	2003 /04	2004 /05	2005 /06
Central government sterling gross debt:										
British government stock										
Conventional gilts	BKPK	232 292	223 105	218 687	204 285	200 833	206 119	232 877	261 373	287 481
Index linked gilts	BKPL	58 729	62 289	65 740	70 316	70 417	75 966	78 982	86 749	98 654
Total	BKPM	291 021	285 394	284 427	274 601	271 250	282 085	311 859	348 122	386 135
Sterling Treasury bills	BKPJ	2 106	4 721	4 453	3 521	9 700	15 000	19 300	20 350	19 100
National savings	ACUA	63 271	64 346	63 331	62 611	62 275	63 087	66 522	68 495	73 346
Tax instruments	ACRV	706	574	535	491	478	376	407	350	308
Other sterling debt[2]	BKSK	25 717	27 347	28 200	29 743	27 770	32 206	34 525	31 760	35 969
Central government sterling gross debt total	BKSL	382 821	382 382	380 946	370 967	371 473	392 754	432 613	469 077	514 858
Central government foreign currency gross debt:										
US$ bonds	BKPG	4 180	4 338	4 388	4 924	2 107	–	1 632	1 587	1 730
ECU bonds	EYSJ	1 606	1 672	1 500	–	–	–	–	–	–
ECU/Euro Treasury notes	EYSV	2 891	3 010	2 701	2 486	1 225	–	–	–	–
ECU/Euro Treasury bills	EYSN	2 249	2 341	–	–	–	–	–	–	–
Other foreign currency debt	BKPH	537	456	364	291	243	172	105	57	1
Central government foreign currency gross debt total	BKPI	11 463	11 816	8 954	7 701	3 575	172	1 738	1 644	1 731
Central government gross debt total	BKPW	394 284	394 198	389 900	378 668	375 048	392 926	434 351	470 721	516 589
Local government gross debt total	EYKP	50 198	51 044	51 707	52 522	52 566	51 353	50 547	53 191	60 024
less										
Central government holdings of local government debt	-EYKZ	–43 172	–45 045	–46 563	–47 789	–47 530	–44 836	–41 540	–42 339	–47 353
Local government holdings of central government debt	-EYLA	–170	–273	–77	–31	–29	–184	–510	–62	–62
General government gross debt (consolidated)	BKPX	401 140	399 924	394 967	383 370	380 055	399 259	442 848	481 511	529 198
Public corporations gross debt	EYYD	15 421	14 344	8 721	9 414	8 859	18 398	12 493	13 607	13 625
less:										
Central government holdings of public corporations debt	-EYXY	–14 590	–10 732	–4 307	–4 714	–4 308	–4 171	–5 188	–5 740	–5 631
Local government holdings of public corporations debt	-EYXZ	–	–4	–123	–124	–122	–121	–120	–121	–112
Public corporations holdings of central government debt	-BKPZ	–7 313	–6 436	–6 126	–5 927	–4 150	–4 441	–4 294	–4 591	–2 347
Public corporations holdings of local government debt	-EYXV	–139	–108	–141	–106	–60	–50	–84	–100	–57
Public sector gross debt (consolidated)	BKQA	394 519	396 988	392 991	381 913	380 274	408 874	445 655	484 566	534 676
Public sector liquid assets:										
Official reserves	AIPD	21 293	22 147	21 498	30 423	28 055	26 387	25 266	25 813	27 835
Central government deposits[3]	BKSM	2 293	1 762	1 879	2 797	2 802	2 900	3 879	3 868	5 212
Other central government	BKSN	–	–	4 756	15 670	10 743	8 141	7 077	3 044	8 498
Local government deposits[3]	BKSO	11 828	12 301	10 221	11 522	11 570	12 535	14 938	17 828	20 085
Other local government short term assets	BKQG	3 693	4 335	5 468	5 719	5 990	6 061	5 599	5 058	5 381
Public corporations deposits[3]	BKSP	1 849	3 520	2 619	2 215	2 336	2 133	2 813	3 411	2 430
Other public corporations short term assets	BKSQ	668	1 300	1 128	1 212	1 180	1 586	1 727	1 463	1 791
Public sector liquid assets total	BKQJ	41 624	45 365	47 569	69 558	62 676	59 743	61 299	60 485	71 232
Public sector net debt	BKQK	352 895	351 623	345 422	312 355	317 598	349 131	384 356	424 081	463 444
as percentage of GDP[4]	RUTO	*41.6*	*39.3*	*36.6*	*31.7*	*30.7*	*32.0*	*33.1*	*35.0*	*36.5*

1 See chapter text.
2 Including overdraft with Bank of England.
3 Bank and building society deposits.
4 Gross domestic product at market prices from 12 months centred on the end of the month.

Source: Office for National Statistics: 020 7533 5984

18.4 Consolidated Fund and National Loans Fund:[1] revenue and expenditure; receipts and payments

United Kingdom, years ending 31 March

£ million

	Consolidated Fund														
	Revenue							Expenditure							Surplus (+) or deficit (-) of Consolidated Fund
		HM Revenue and Customs								Standing services					
	Total	Inland Revenue[1]	Customs and Excise	Vehicle excise duties	National non domestic rates	Interest and dividends	Other receipts	Total	Supply services	Service of national debt[2]	Northern Ireland	European community etc.	Contingencies Fund	Other expenditure[3]	
	1	2	3	4	5	6	7	8	9	10	11	12	13	14	15
	ACAA	EYJN	ACAC	ACAD	RUUD	ACAG	ACBC	ACAI	ACAJ	ACAK	ACAL	ACAM	ACAN	ACAO	ACAP
2002	277 415	146 418	108 026	4 582	10 791	365	7 233	303 480	283 039	14 696	–	6 341	−800	205	−26 067
2003	293 885	144 533	113 520	4 613	19 975	367	10 877	338 191	317 808	14 042	–	7 405	−1 277	211	−44 308
2004	301 011	153 699	119 726	4 816	13 468	516	8 786	345 938	322 672	15 201	–	7 301	501	261	−44 926
2005	329 708	170 130	121 109	4 865	17 326	389	15 889	368 821	342 414	17 654	–	8 910	−500	344	−39 116
2006	359 954	192 715	124 219	5 055	19 597	398	17 970	401 411	373 074	19 263	–	8 858	–	212	−41 456
2001/02	282 174	149 114	104 855	4 402	16 009	361	7 433	292 365	271 998	15 325	–	4 788	–	257	−10 193
2002/03	286 036	145 899	108 721	4 399	17 593	357	9 067	311 296	290 182	14 683	–	6 505	−277	204	−25 262
2003/04	293 052	145 555	115 660	4 712	16 580	352	10 193	335 274	313 072	14 501	–	7 494	1	203	−42 223
2004/05	313 323	158 974	120 924	4 752	15 990	578	12 105	351 237	325 541	16 966	–	8 460	–	267	−37 914
2005/06	336 031	178 707	120 845	5 001	17 762	351	13 365	382 230	355 429	18 323	–	8 139	–	340	−46 200
2002 Q1	82 257	45 878	25 706	1 280	4 032	286	5 075	76 431	75 130	2 111	–	1 933	−2 800	58	5 825
Q2	59 771	31 100	27 482	1 147	–	1	41	72 561	65 455	5 128	–	1 935	–	43	−12 790
Q3	71 182	36 626	26 323	1 147	5 199	64	1 823	71 623	67 345	2 489	–	750	1 000	40	−441
Q4	64 205	32 814	28 515	1 008	1 560	14	294	82 865	75 109	4 968	–	1 723	1 000	64	−18 661
2003 Q1	90 878	45 359	26 401	1 097	10 834	278	6 909	84 247	82 273	2 098	–	2 097	−2 277	57	6 630
Q2	61 171	31 634	28 296	1 191	–	–	50	82 949	75 030	4 760	–	2 102	1 000	56	−21 780
Q3	75 368	37 098	28 474	1 209	6 009	57	2 521	78 159	72 938	3 054	–	2 116	–	51	−2 790
Q4	66 468	30 442	30 349	1 116	3 132	32	1 397	92 836	87 567	4 130	–	1 090	–	47	−26 368
2004 Q1	90 045	46 381	28 541	1 196	7 439	263	6 225	81 330	77 537	2 557	–	2 186	−999	49	8 715
Q2	64 213	32 911	30 061	1 199	–	1	41	83 020	76 032	4 086	–	1 793	1 000	108	−18 808
Q3	72 074	38 847	29 840	1 239	1 316	29	803	87 069	81 009	3 884	–	2 124	–	53	−14 994
Q4	74 679	35 560	31 284	1 182	4 713	223	1 717	94 519	88 094	4 674	–	1 198	500	51	−19 839
2005 Q1	102 357	51 656	29 739	1 132	9 961	325	9 544	86 629	80 406	4 322	–	3 345	−1 500	55	15 727
Q2	67 425	36 762	29 379	1 242	3	39	94 409	86 970	4 426	–	1 883	1 000	132	−26 984
Q3	84 896	43 353	30 516	1 391	5 657	54	3 925	92 502	85 379	4 817	–	2 198	–	106	−7 606
Q4	75 030	38 359	31 475	1 100	1 708	7	2 381	95 281	89 659	4 089	–	1 484	–	51	−20 253
2006 Q1	108 680	60 233	29 475	1 268	10 397	287	7 020	100 038	93 421	4 991	–	2 574	−1 000	51	8 643
Q2	72 430	39 406	30 606	1 284	303	29	802	101 986	94 934	4 382	–	1 612	1 000	58	−29 555
Q3	79 869	47 921	30 571	1 348	–	–	29	99 192	91 420	5 588	–	2 132	–	49	−19 323
Q4	98 975	45 155	33 567	1 155	8 897	82	10 119	100 195	93 299	4 302	–	2 540	–	54	−1 221

18.4
continued

Consolidated Fund and National Loans Fund:[1] revenue and expenditure; receipts and payments

United Kingdom, years ending 31 March

£ million

| | | National Loans Fund | | | | | | | | Other central government funds and accounts | | | |
| | | Receipts | | | Payments | | | | | | | | |
	Surplus (+) or deficit (-) of Consolidated Fund	Total receipts	Interest receipts and profits of note issue[4]	Service of the national debt met from Consolidated Fund	Total payments	Service of national debt	CG Transactions with issue dept for asset revaluation	Net lending[5]	Borrowing required	Surplus (+) or deficit (-) of National Insurance Fund	Departmental balances and miscellaneous	Northern Ireland central government debt[1]	Central government net cash requirement
	16	17	18	19	20	21	22	23	24	25	26	27	28
	ACAP	ACAQ	RUUC	ACAK	ACAU	ACAV	RUUB	ACAW	ACAX	ACAY	ACAZ	ACBA	RUUW
2002	−26 067	21 238	6 544	14 696	19 428	21 237	−1	−1 808	24 255	1 223	5 663	−8	17 361
2003	−44 308	21 043	7 000	14 042	17 012	21 044	3	−4 036	40 276	−238	2 890	−9	37 615
2004	−44 926	22 659	7 455	15 201	23 242	22 658	−1	586	45 510	3 203	−890	−4	43 193
2005	−39 116	23 777	6 123	17 654	26 612	23 991	−	2 619	41 948	4 303	−2 773	−2	40 416
2006	−41 456	24 788	5 524	19 263	27 323	24 708	−	2 616	43 990	7 973	−3 580	3	39 600
2001/02	−10 193	22 596	7 272	15 325	21 822	22 597	13	−785	9 417	3 294	3 342	−10	2 771
2002/03	−25 262	21 724	7 042	14 683	19 186	21 723	−5	−2 532	22 722	2 802	−1 836	−5	21 751
2003/04	−42 223	21 968	7 465	14 501	18 691	21 969	11	−3 289	38 947	2 270	−2 724	−10	39 391
2004/05	−37 914	23 673	6 705	16 966	24 245	23 672	−7	580	38 486	1 436	−1 485	−2	38 533
2005/06	−46 200	24 164	5 842	18 323	29 455	24 379	−	5 075	51 488	7 022	3 650	1	40 817
2002 Q1	5 825	3 749	1 639	2 111	3 156	3 749	2	−595	−6 419	390	104	−5	−6 918
Q2	−12 790	6 783	1 655	5 128	5 634	6 782	−2	−1 147	11 641	1 432	2 804	−1	7 404
Q3	−441	4 049	1 562	2 489	4 724	4 049	−5	680	1 115	225	−1 188	1	2 079
Q4	−18 661	6 657	1 688	4 968	5 914	6 657	4	−746	17 918	−824	3 943	−3	14 796
2003 Q1	6 630	4 235	2 137	2 098	2 914	4 235	−2	−1 319	−7 952	1 969	−7 395	−2	−2 528
Q2	−21 780	6 238	1 477	4 760	5 464	6 238	−	−775	21 005	51	3 572	−3	17 379
Q3	−2 790	4 627	1 573	3 054	3 613	4 628	14	−1 029	1 776	−1 390	−3 196	−3	6 359
Q4	−26 368	5 943	1 813	4 130	5 021	5 943	−9	−913	25 447	−868	9 909	−1	16 405
2004 Q1	8 715	5 160	2 602	2 557	4 593	5 160	6	−572	−9 281	4 477	−13 009	−3	−752
Q2	−18 808	5 637	1 550	4 086	5 464	5 637	−4	−169	18 634	−1 212	6 089	−1	13 756
Q3	−14 994	5 412	1 528	3 884	6 146	5 775	1	371	15 729	2 533	5 892	−	7 304
Q4	−19 839	6 450	1 775	4 674	7 039	6 086	−4	956	20 428	−2 595	138	−	22 885
2005 Q1	15 727	6 174	1 852	4 322	5 596	6 174	−	−578	−16 305	2 710	−13 604	−1	−5 412
Q2	−26 984	5 761	1 336	4 426	8 031	5 761	−	2 268	29 253	1 710	8 516	−	19 027
Q3	−7 606	6 183	1 365	4 817	6 793	6 359	−	434	8 215	532	−381	−1	8 063
Q4	−20 253	5 659	1 570	4 089	6 192	5 697	−	495	20 785	−649	2 696	−	18 738
2006 Q1	8 643	6 561	1 571	4 991	8 439	6 562	−	1 878	−6 765	5 429	−7 181	2	−5 011
Q2	−29 555	5 517	1 134	4 382	5 326	5 384	−	−59	29 364	1 952	4 154	1	23 259
Q3	−19 323	6 827	1 238	5 588	7 688	6 827	−	861	20 184	2 233	10 723	−	7 228
Q4	−1 221	5 883	1 581	4 302	5 870	5 935	−	−64	1 207	−1 641	−11 276	−	14 124

1 See chapter text.
2 Payment to National Loans Fund representing its payments for the service of the National Debt *less its receipts of interest on loans outstanding, etc.*
3 *Includes net issues to Contingencies Fund.*
4 *Prior to 1996-97, receipts from the Bank of England for appreciation of the assets of the Issue Department were included in the total amount for the profits of the issue Department.*
5 *Minus sign indicates a net issue repayment.*

Sources: HM Treasury;
National Statistics 020 7533 5984

18.5 Taxes paid by UK residents to general government and the European Union[1]
Total economy sector S.1

£ million

		1996 /97	1997 /98	1998 /99	1999 /00	2000 /01	2001 /02	2002 /03	2003 /04	2004 /05	2005 /06
Generation of income											
Uses											
Taxes on production and imports											
Taxes on products and imports											
Value added tax (VAT)											
Paid to central government	NZGF	46 649	52 064	53 725	58 676	60 736	64 730	69 081	76 627	79 960	81 547
Paid to the European Union	FJKM	4 661	3 531	4 105	3 451	4 172	3 592	2 518	2 574	1 905	1 964
Total	QYRC	51 310	55 644	58 016	62 350	65 226	68 740	71 920	79 506	82 130	..
Taxes and duties on imports excluding VAT											
Paid to EU: import duties	FJWE	2 290	2 261	2 042	2 049	2 103	2 024	1 893	1 957	2 207	2 264
Taxes on products excluding VAT and import duties											
Paid to central government											
Customs and Excise revenue											
Beer	GTAM	2 631	2 699	2 733	2 848	2 798	2 907	2 952	3 084	3 098	..
Wines, cider, perry & spirits	GTAN	2 999	3 057	3 301	3 652	3 814	4 068	4 430	4 526	4 788	..
Tobacco	GTAO	7 701	7 622	7 551	7 796	7 638	7 639	8 046	8 092	8 113	7 952
Hydrocarbon oils	GTAP	17 171	19 451	21 553	22 510	22 630	21 916	22 147	22 786	23 313	..
Betting, gaming & lottery	CJQY	1 460	1 539	1 527	1 500	1 517	1 317	977	898	876	..
Air passenger duty	CWAA	359	522	845	882	956	802	804	799	874	..
Insurance premium tax	CWAD	685	1 179	1 248	1 511	1 751	1 921	2 189	2 316	2 362	..
Landfill tax	BKOF	218	350	322	456	475	501	545	636	673	756
Other	ACDN	–	–	–	–	–	–	–	–	–	..
Fossil fuel levy	CIQY	880	256	164	84	52	92	9	–	–	–
Gas levy	GTAZ	199	188	–44	–	–	–	–	–	–	–
Stamp duties	GTBC	2 414	3 456	4 623	6 898	8 165	6 983	7 549	7 544	8 932	..
Camelot payments to National Lottery Distribution Fund	LIYH	1 263	1 572	1 665	1 593	1 542	1 520	1 382	1 311	1 354	..
Hydro-benefit	LITN	31	32	32	38	44	44	44	43	40	–
Aggregates Levy	MDUQ	–	–	–	–	–	–	293	341	326	..
Climate change levy	LSNT	–	–	–	–	–	822	813	816	750	738
Renewable energy obligations	EP89	–	–	–	–	–	–	265	375	368	380
Other taxes and levies	GCSP	–	–	–	–	–	–	–	–	–	..
Total paid to central government	NMBV	38 151	42 008	45 569	49 768	51 382	50 551	52 486	53 624	55 965	57 920
Paid to the European Union											
Sugar levy	GTBA	37	72	44	46	43	27	25	19	24	24
European Coal & Steel Community levy	GTBB	–	–	–	–	–	–	–	–	–	–
Total paid to the European Union	FJWG	37	72	44	46	43	27	25	19	24	24
Total taxes on products excluding VAT & import duties	QYRA	37 943	42 009	45 564	49 814	51 425	49 737	51 392	52 395	54 803	..
Total taxes on products and imports	NZGW	91 658	99 826	105 500	113 990	118 436	120 924	126 003	134 801	140 059	143 678
Production taxes other than on products											
Paid to central government											
Consumer Credit Act fees	CUDB	113	168	158	140	150	143	160	146	146	..
National non-domestic rates	CUKY	13 010	13 283	13 764	14 353	15 154	16 252	16 728	16 941	17 382	18 345
Old style non-domestic rates	NSEZ	126	136	130	123	132	131	136	140	146	..
Levies paid to CG levy-funded bodies	LITK	147	162	171	241	207	175	144	150	192	..
Motor vehicle duties paid by businesses	EKED	1 365	1 405	1 503	1 559	1 230	751	736	720	813	..
Regulator fees	GCSQ	54	57	61	69	72	62	60	60	60	..
Total	NMBX	14 815	15 211	15 787	16 511	17 005	17 601	18 084	18 374	18 859	19 855
Paid to local government											
Old style non-domestic rates	NMYH	114	124	131	144	150	161	176	192	208	224
Total production taxes other than on products	NMYD	14 929	15 335	15 918	16 655	17 155	17 762	18 260	18 566	19 067	20 079
Total taxes on production and imports, paid											
Paid to central government	NMBY	99 468	109 120	115 081	124 955	129 123	132 882	139 651	148 625	154 784	159 322
Paid to local government	NMYH	114	124	131	144	150	161	176	192	208	224
Paid to the European Union	FJWB	6 988	5 864	6 191	5 546	6 318	5 643	4 436	4 550	4 136	4 252
Total	NZGX	106 472	115 249	121 540	130 842	135 863	138 998	144 158	153 023	158 789	..

18.5 Taxes paid by UK residents to general government and the European Union[1]
Total economy sector S.1

continued

£ million

		1996 /97	1997 /98	1998 /99	1999 /00	2000 /01	2001 /02	2002 /03	2003 /04	2004 /05	2005 /06
Secondary distribution of income											
Uses											
Current taxes on income, wealth etc											
Taxes on income											
Paid to central government											
Household income taxes	DRWH	75 243	81 901	89 728	96 977	106 866	108 526	110 407	112 356	121 888	130 910
Petroleum revenue tax	DBHA	1 729	963	502	853	1 518	1 310	958	1 179	1 284	2 016
Windfall tax	EYNK	–	2 610	2 614	–	–	–	–	–	–	–
Other corporate taxes	BMNX	25 715	29 844	31 263	36 164	35 878	35 338	31 809	31 918	37 830	..
Total	NMCU	102 687	115 318	124 107	133 994	144 263	145 180	143 238	145 488	160 979	180 293
Other current taxes											
Paid to central government											
Motor vehicle duty paid by households	CDDZ	2 802	3 045	3 116	3 296	3 039	3 540	3 600	3 902	3 935	4 100
Old style domestic rates	NSFA	104	115	114	117	108	109	104	100	94	82
Licences	NSNP	10	11	8	8	2	–	–	–	–	–
National non-domestic rates paid by non-market sectors	BMNY	930	929	971	1 002	997	1 065	1 013	994	995	994
Passport fees	E8A6	–	–	41	89	113	139	153	198	237	277
Television licence fee	DH7A	1 916	2 009	2 179	2 286	2 064	2 183	2 287	2 391	2 508	2 678
Total	NMCV	5 762	6 109	6 429	6 798	6 325	7 036	7 155	7 585	7 770	8 081
Paid to local government											
Old style domestic rates	NMHK	61	64	62	68	76	80	85	92	100	..
Council tax	NMHM	10 059	10 850	12 037	12 918	14 155	15 371	16 809	18 911	20 215	..
Total	NMIS	10 120	10 914	12 099	12 986	14 231	15 451	16 894	19 003	20 290	21 403
Total	NVCM	15 882	17 023	18 528	19 784	20 556	22 487	24 049	26 588	28 060	29 484
Total current taxes on income, wealth etc											
Paid to central government	NMCP	108 449	121 427	130 536	140 792	150 588	152 215	150 445	153 171	168 960	188 374
Paid to local government	NMIS	10 120	10 914	12 099	12 986	14 231	15 451	16 894	19 003	20 290	21 403
Total	NMZL	118 569	132 341	142 635	153 778	164 819	167 666	167 339	172 174	189 250	209 777
Social contributions											
Actual social contributions											
Paid to central government											
(National Insurance Contributions)											
Employers' compulsory contributions	CEAN	25 976	27 761	29 779	31 705	35 212	35 816	35 476	41 459	44 463	47 342
Employees' compulsory contributions	GCSE	19 585	22 073	23 255	23 289	24 772	25 130	25 701	31 013	33 002	35 516
Self- and non-employed persons' compulsory contributions	NMDE	1 658	1 858	1 712	1 941	2 084	2 216	2 352	2 676	2 744	2 852
Total	AIIH	47 219	51 692	54 746	56 935	62 068	63 162	63 529	75 148	80 209	85 404
Capital account											
Changes in liabilities and net worth											
Other capital taxes											
Paid to central government											
Inheritance tax	GILF	1 517	1 649	1 764	2 016	2 181	2 346	2 323	2 486	2 874	..
Tax on other capital transfers	GILG	41	35	41	38	55	37	47	35	48	..
Development land tax and other	GCSV	–	–	–	–	–	–	–	–	–	..
Total	NMGI	1 558	1 684	1 804	2 054	2 236	2 383	2 370	2 521	2 941	3 276
Total taxes and compulsory social contributions											
Paid to central government	GCSS	254 628	282 049	300 096	322 776	342 107	348 656	353 358	376 626	403 760	..
Paid to local government	GCST	10 234	11 038	12 230	13 130	14 381	15 612	17 070	19 195	20 523	..
Paid to the European Union	FJWB	6 988	5 864	6 191	5 546	6 318	5 643	4 436	4 550	4 136	4 252
Total	GCSU	273 933	300 878	320 603	343 412	364 714	371 897	377 501	403 210	431 528	462 255
Total taxes and social contributions as percentage of GDP	GDWM	35.3	36.5	36.7	37.3	37.8	36.9	35.5	35.8	36.2	37.3

1 See chapter text.

Sources: HM Treasury;
Office for National Statistics: 020 7533 5991

18.6 Borrowing and repayment of debt[1]
United Kingdom
Years ending 31 March

£ million

		1996/97	1997/98	1998/99	1999/00	2000/01	2001/02	2002/03	2003/04	2004/05	2005/06
Borrowing											
Government securities: new issues	KQGA	40 800.8	28 484.4	12 048.0	26 426.5	25 789.8	43 433.4	54 068.9	53 220.9	57 290.5	80 668.9
National savings securities:											
National savings certificates	KQGB	3 695.5	4 435.2	3 028.7	1 962.7	3 086.2	2 580.7	2 434.3	1 940.4	1 696.4	1 206.8
Capital bonds	KQGC	450.8	619.0	469.6	35.4	29.0	40.9	107.3	65.0	25.2	34.3
Income bonds	KQGD	1 272.7	1 043.4	1 371.7	653.4	760.5	625.6	484.8	415.3	426.6	567.5
Deposit bonds	KQGE	..	..	..	..	..	..	..	—	..	..
British savings bonds	KQGF	..	..	..	..	..	..	..	..	..	..
Premium savings bonds	KQGG	2 552.5	3 158.8	3 652.8	3 449.4	3 296.0	3 859.6	4 604.5	7 530.1	5 737.8	7 817.5
Save As You Earn	KQGH	34.1	20.7	11.4	5.0	0.3	..	..	—	..	..
Yearly plan	KQGI	..	..	5.2	..	..	..	..	—	..	..
National savings stamps and gift tokens	KQGJ	..	..	..	..	..	..	..	—	..	..
National Savings Bank Investments	KQGK	1 478.7	1 282.3	1 085.0	901.6	955.3	864.9	1 012.4	809.9	817.5	643.6
Children's Bonus Bonds	KGVO	352.4	255.3	205.0	58.5	53.4	45.0	54.0	51.7	66.8	59.5
First Option Bonds	KIAR	1 139.8	1 152.9	1 001.8	34.3	..	..	..	..	..	..
Pensioners Guaranteed Income Bond	KJDW	2 863.8	1 126.9	201.0	590.7	687.2	603.5	662.9	274.2	323.9	142.7
Treasurer's account	KWNF	21.1	39.9	17.1	13.6	12.5	15.2	19.4	13.9	11.1	10.9
Individual Savings Account	ZAFC	..	..	..	257.8	265.9	397.8	405.6	335.4	276.4	261.3
Fixed Rate Savings Bonds	ZAFD	..	..	..	175.9	284.7	192.7	193.0	82.0	86.3	51.2
Guaranteed Equity Bonds	ECPU	..	..	..	..	..	27.2	274.8	227.9	317.1	81.4
Easy Access Savings Account	C3OM	..	..	..	..	..	..	..	126.9	903.5	608.6
Certificate of tax deposit	KQGL	109.4	84.1	66.4	121.4	76.5	77.6	59.6	145.2	114.8	110.6
Nationalised industries', etc temporary deposits	KQGM	53 198.2	46 375.9	39 962.4	40 343.3	56 106.6	62 150.0	55 395.1	47 958.6	25 022.0	22 039.1
Sterling Treasury bills (net receipt)	KQGO	..	..	3 546.2	..	..	..	..	—	..	..
ECU Treasury bills (net receipt)	KQGP	..	..	..	..	..	..	..	—	..	..
ECU Treasury notes (net receipt)	KDZZ	..	..	..	721.1	..	..	..	—	..	..
Ways and means (net receipt)	KQGQ	511.1	..	183.6	5 599.0	12 126.0	12 095.3	3 899.9	22 700.2	..	..
Other debt : payable in sterling :											
Interest free notes	KQGR	99.2	32.4	2 130.9	373.5	972.7	1 427.2	754.0	1 213.2	662.3	1 858.9
Other debt : payable in external currencies	KHCY	2 565.2	..	..	..	..	..	..	1 792.5	..	..
Total receipts	KHCZ	111 145.3	88 111.2	68 986.8	81 723.1	104 502.6	128 436.6	124 430.5	138 903.3	93 778.2	116 162.8
Repayment of debt											
Government securities: redemptions	KQGS	14 488.4	20 678.9	18 575.5	19 815.8	33 722.2	43 642.3	42 109.9	35 087.4	25 130.1	17 456.5
Statutory sinking funds	KQGT	2.2	2.1	2.0	2.0	2.0	1.9	1.9	1.8	1.8	0.4
Terminable annuities:											
National Debt Commissioners	KQGU	..	..	..	..	..	..	..	—	..	..
National savings securities:											
National savings certificates	KQGV	3 263.7	4 058.5	3 449.0	2 405.2	4 546.8	4 177.7	4 146.7	2 769.1	1 979.6	1 107.4
Capital bonds	KQGW	698.3	1 160.5	888.3	324.2	375.0	175.9	155.9	116.9	121.1	159.2
Income bonds	KQGX	1 394.0	1 148.9	880.8	1 686.3	857.0	933.8	1 144.2	977.1	879.5	724.6
Deposit bonds	KQGY	64.8	72.6	84.2	70.2	71.1	45.4	369.9	4.4	..	..
Yearly Plan	KQGZ	96.3	113.2	120.0	141.8	18.4	4.5	3.0	2.0	..	..
British savings bonds	KQHA	..	..	..	..	..	..	..	..	..	..
Premium savings bonds	KQHB	869.3	1 203.1	1 398.4	1 923.8	1 872.6	1 942.9	2 343.3	2 967.4	3 492.4	3 289.2
Save As You Earn	KQHC	70.1	68.2	37.1	34.5	22.9	8.0	3.2	0.5	..	0.5
National savings stamps and gift tokens	KQHD	..	..	..	..	..	..	..	—	1.2	..
National Savings Bank Investments (repayments)	KQHE	1 837.0	2 175.7	2 027.0	1 886.3	1 654.1	1 415.8	1 350.1	1 342.7	1 554.0	1 153.3
Children's Bonus Bonds	KGVQ	257.8	187.9	183.2	69.3	95.0	114.5	92.6	79.8	84.5	95.8
First Option Bonds	KIAS	833.9	1 283.0	1 055.5	298.1	225.2	111.6	77.4	62.2	33.4	36.1
Pensioners Guaranteed Income Bond	KPOB	185.0	318.8	897.8	935.3	2 003.8	1 640.4	703.9	538.5	445.0	428.6
Treasurer's account	KWNG	1.2	11.8	13.7	16.4	13.9	16.5	16.9	14.2	16.2	18.3
Individual Savings Account	ZAFE	..	..	..	12.3	39.9	70.3	105.9	157.6	202.2	194.1
Fixed Rate Savings Bonds	ZAFF	..	..	..	2.8	62.1	110.1	133.6	153.1	92.1	105.0
Guaranteed Equity Bonds	JUWE	..	..	..	..	..	..	3.9	3.3	..	0.2
Easy Access Savings Account	C3ON	..	..	..	..	..	..	..	126.9	189.3	400.6
Certificates of tax deposit	KQHF	478.9	229.0	199.9	159.9	120.1	91.4	161.5	113.1	171.9	152.1
Tax reserve certificates	KQHG	..	..	..	..	..	..	..	—	..	..
Nationalised industries', etc temporary deposits	KQHH	51 979.3	46 835.7	41 776.9	41 089.4	56 004.0	63 127.9	55 695.6	47 757.7	25 949.5	21 943.1
Debt to the Bank of England	KPOC	..	..	..	..	..	..	..	..	..	..
Sterling Treasury bills (net repayment)	KQHJ	4 009.6	1 928.5	..	3 014.8	6 194.2	..	..	—	..	..
ECU Treasury bills (net repayment)	KJEG	..	..	..	2 492.9	..	..	..	—	..	..
ECU Treasury notes (net repayment)	KSPA	318.3	3.3	13.2	..	1 391.9	1 359.6	1 453.1	—	..	..
Ways and means (net repayment)	KQHK	..	5 815.4	..	..	..	..	..	—	9 760.2	36 207.3
Other debt: payable in sterling :											
Interest free notes	KQHL	87.6	1 215.5	850.5	246.4	458.2	1 723.3	1 393.3	990.5	300.4	222.3
Other	KQHM	..	..	..	..	..	..	..	—	..	..
Other debt : payable in external currencies	KQHN	2 661.7	2 082.7	92.0	98.1	1 835.6	2 838.1	1 960.3	47.0	46.5	98.9
Total payments	KQHO	83 597.4	90 593.3	72 545.0	76 725.8	111 586.0	123 551.9	113 426.1	93 313.2	70 450.9	83 793.5
Net borrowing	KQHP	27 547.9	..	..	4 997.3	..	4 884.7	11 004.4	45 590.1	23 327.3	32 369.3
Net repayment	KHDD	..	2 482.1	3 558.2	..	7 083.4	..	..	—	..	..

1 See chapter text.

Source: HM Treasury: 020 7270 4761

18.7 Consolidated Fund and National Loans Fund: assets and liabilities[1]
United Kingdom
At 31 March each year

£ million

		1995	1996	1997	1998	1999	2000	2001	2002	2003
CONSOLIDATED FUND										
Total estimated assets	KQIA	33 992.4	33 809.0	36 177.4	36 061.0	36 148.0	33 932.1	35 967.9	37 458.5	39 694.1
Subscriptions and contributions to international financial organisations	KQIB	5 898.1	6 470.8	6 528.9	6 660.8	7 059.7	6 903.6	7 298.4	7 564.4	8 540.3
International Bank for Reconstruction and Development	KQIC	265.2	271.6	265.0	262.5	266.0	267.1	279.2	279.0	268.2
International Finance Corporation	KQID	62.0	73.1	74.9	72.9	75.6	76.5	85.8	85.7	77.2
International Development Association	KQIE	3 005.5	3 205.8	3 372.7	3 562.2	3 733.3	3 900.0	4 134.0	4 347.8	4 567.5
African Development Bank	KQIF	141.2	148.3	162.9	180.0	199.1	215.7	229.8	259.8	293.9
Asian Development Bank	KQIG	201.5	214.6	240.4	272.5	304.6	339.3	365.5	393.3	420.4
Caribbean Development Bank	KQIH	32.6	34.2	34.1	34.6	36.8	40.7	41.9	44.0	49.1
European Investment Bank	KQII	1 876.4	2 166.6	2 036.5	1 840.7	2 083.1	1 706.6	1 767.3	1 742.1	2 419.2
European Bank for Reconstruction and Development	KPOD	146.3	189.4	175.6	164.2	179.2	170.0	187.4	197.6	239.3
Inter-American Development Bank	KQIJ	107.2	119.6	117.5	219.3	127.8	130.6	145.7	147.3	135.6
International Fund for Agricultural Development	KQIK	42.7	44.2	46.1	48.8	51.0	53.7	56.4	59.1	62.1
Multilateral Investment Guarantee Agency	KQIL	3.2	3.4	3.2	3.1	3.2	3.3	5.4	8.7	7.8
Loans from Votes	KQIP	13 599.7	12 967.0	13 684.7	14 050.0	11 546.3	3 970.3	7 015.3	9 006.1	11 097.1
Issues of public dividend capital:	KQIQ	11 467.0	12 161.1	12 424.8	13 157.1	16 238.5	21 338.3	20 083.6	19 546.2	18 982.3
Army Base Repair Organisation (ABRO)	C3QV	..	..	..	..	..	..	..	..	19.4
Royal Mint	KQIV	7.0	7.0	7.0	7.0	7.0	7.0	7.0	5.5	5.5
Welsh Development Agency	KQIY	10.9	9.8	8.9	8.8	8.6	9.1	9.1	11.0	12.7
British Shipbuilders	KQJA	1 598.3	1 598.3	1 598.5	1 598.3	50.0	21.0	21.0	21.0	21.0
Patent Office	KIAT	6.3	6.3	6.3	6.3	6.3	6.3	6.3	6.3	6.3
NHS Trusts	KIAU	9 603.1	10 173.8	10 349.7	11 078.0	14 158.7	19 216.6	19 539.2	19 184.1	18 600.7
Companies House	KIAV	15.9	15.9	15.9	15.9	15.9	15.9	15.9	15.9	15.9
Central Office of Information	KIAW	0.3	0.3	0.3	0.3	0.3	0.3	0.3	0.3	0.3
Chessington Computer Centre	KPOE	3.5	3.5	..	..	..	..	..	..	..
OGC Buying Solutions[2]	KWNH	0.1	0.4	0.4	0.4	0.4	0.4	0.4	0.4	0.4
Defence Aviation Repair Agency	JRVU	..	..	..	..	..	..	..	50.4	42.3
Defence Evaluation and Research Agency	KWNI	128.8	253.0	274.5	274.5	275.4	275.4	275.4	..	..
Defence Scientific Technology Laboratory	JRVV	..	..	..	..	..	..	..	42.3	50.4
Fire Service College	KWNJ	16.7	16.7	16.7	16.7	16.7	16.7	16.7	16.7	16.7
Forensic Science Service	GPVB	..	..	..	..	–	18.0	18.0	18.0	18.0
Hydrographic Office	GPVC	..	..	..	..	..	13.3	13.3	13.3	13.3
Land Registry	KWNK	55.4	55.4	61.5	61.5	61.5	61.5	61.5	61.5	61.5
Medicines Control Agency	KWNL	1.6	1.6	1.6	1.6	1.6	1.6	1.6	1.6	..
Meteorological Office	KZAZ	..	..	58.9	58.9	58.9	58.9	58.9	58.9	58.9
NHS Estates	GPVD	..	..	..	..	..	0.4	0.4	0.4	0.4
Registers of Scotland	KZBA	..	..	4.3	4.3	4.3	..	..	..	..
Vehicle Inspectorate	KWNM	19.1	19.1	20.3	20.3	20.3	20.3	20.3	20.3	20.3
Driving Standards Agency	LQMI	..	..	..	3.5	3.5	3.5	3.5	3.5	3.5
Ordnance Survey	GPVE	..	..	..	..	..	14.0	14.0	14.0	14.0
Queen Elizabeth II Conference Centre	LQMJ	..	..	..	0.8	0.8	0.8	0.8	0.8	0.8
Contingencies Fund - capital	KQJB	447.0	297.0	977.0	577.0	277.0	277.0	277.0	277.0	..
Balance on revenue accounts	KQJC	1 433.6	1 096.1	954.9	1 546.0	1 026.5	1 442.9	1 293.6	1 064.8	1 074.4
Privatisation receipts	KIAX	1 147.0	817.0	1 607.1	70.1	..	..	..	..	..
Total liabilities	KQJD	..	333 927.9	364 803.0	364 950.8	363 625.5	354 807.7	327 180.6	341 162.2	366 453.7
Liability to balance National Loans Fund	KQJE	286 055.9	331 164.9	362 506.5	362 582.5	361 065.3	351 626.3	324 336.7	338 550.1	362 496.5
Payment from Votes:	KQJF	64.3	63.4	62.4	61.3	60.2	59.0	57.7	56.4	54.9
Married quarters for Armed Forces	KQJG	64.3	63.4	62.4	61.3	60.2	59.0	57.7	56.4	54.9
Liability to Post Office Post-war credits outstanding and interest due - estimated	KQJI	46.0	45.9	45.9	45.9	45.9	45.8	45.8	45.8	45.8
Revenue paid over in advance of collection	KQJJ	37.0	..	28.2	13.8	177.9	259.7	301.7	635.6	1 293.7
Inland Revenue	KQJK	–	–	–	–	177.9	259.7	301.7	635.6	1 293.7
Customs and Excise	KQJL	..	..	28.2	..	..	..	..	..	..
Vehicle Excise Duty	KQJN	37.0	..	..	13.8	..	..	..	..	..
Promissory notes issued by Minister of Overseas Development	KQJQ	996.7	1 005.8	1 021.9	822.1	963.1	783.1	939.9	891.9	954.7
International Development Association	KQJR	656.5	663.2	673.6	484.0	612.3	445.6	553.1	509.7	589.4
African Development Fund	KQJS	93.2	86.2	95.3	95.2	105.6	89.1	141.6	145.5	152.3
Asian Development Bank	KQJT	–	–	–	–	–	1.9	2.5	2.4	2.3
Asian Development Fund	KQJU	140.5	127.6	136.0	120.5	105.4	87.8	78.6	73.2	68.3
Caribbean Development Bank	KQJV	1.3	1.4	1.3	1.3	1.3	1.3	1.5	1.5	1.4
Special Development Fund	KQKC	9.5	10.6	13.2	15.8	16.4	16.9	15.9	13.8	17.3
Inter-American Development Bank	KQJY	1.3	2.0	1.8	1.9	1.0	2.0	1.4	0.7	0.2

18.7

Consolidated Fund and National Loans Fund: assets and liabilities[1]
United Kingdom

At 31 March each year

£ million

		1997	1998	1999	2000	2001	2002	2003	2004	2005
Promissory notes issued by										
Minister of Overseas Development (continued)										
Fund for special operations	KQJZ	8.8	6.3	2.6	2.1	1.1	..	..	..	..
International Fund for Agricultural Development	KQKA	12.3	14.2	16.5	18.4	15.6	12.9	9.9	..	..
International Bank for Reconstruction and Development	KQKB	71.7	81.9	94.3	105.9	112.5	114.6	88.5	..	..
European Bank for Reconstruction and Development	KIAY	6.1	..	7.7	12.1	16.1	17.6	19.8	..	..
United Nations Environment Programme	KJEH	1.8	1.0	..	..	..	..	5.3	..	..
Other contributions and instalments due in respect of international subscriptions, etc	KQYX	1 138.1	1 425.2	1 313.1	1 669.2	1 174.0	955.1	1 608.1	..	..
NATIONAL LOANS FUND[3]										
Total assets	KQKD	419 548.9	418 444.7	421 635.7	426 239.2	425 955.6	434 544.6	448 006.3	..	..
Total National Loans Fund										
loans outstanding	KQKE	46 746.8	46 742.6	48 513.6	49 788.8	51 037.6	50 251.4	47 719.0	44 431.4	45 013.1
Loans to Public Corporations:										
Royal Mail Group plc	KQKF	..	..	..	..	500.0	500.0	550.0	500.0	500.0
Scottish Nuclear Ltd	KQKM	..	..	..	..	..	..	..	..	..
Railtrack	KTCR	..	..	..	..	..	..	..	..	..
European Passenger Services	KTCS	..	..	..	..	..	..	..	..	..
Civil Aviation Authority	KQKQ	447.5	420.9	365.7	342.5	92.5	9.8	8.8	8.2	7.6
British Railways Board	KQKS	601.2	573.7	546.2	518.7	481.3	..	..	..	..
British Waterways Board	KQKU	18.2	18.2	18.2	18.2	16.7	16.3	14.7	14.7	14.7
New Towns - Development Corporations and Commission	KQLD	122.2	36.2	8.0	8.0	8.0	8.0	7.9	7.9	7.9
Scottish Homes	KQLF	392.5	259.8	190.9	179.0	161.6	149.7	138.1	100.6	–
Housing Corporation (England)	KQLH	848.7	4.0	4.0	3.0	3.0	2.0	2.0	1.2	1.4
Housing for Wales	KQLI	..	..	..	..	..	..	..	..	..
Land Authority for Wales	KQLL	1.3	1.3	..	..	..	..	..	..	..
Scottish Enterprise	KQLM	0.5	0.1	..	..	..	..	..	..	..
Welsh Development Agency	KQLN	1.2	1.2	0.9	0.6	0.3	0.2	0.1	..	..
Land Registry Trading Fund	KPOF	..	..	..	..	..	..	..	..	..
Development Board for Rural Wales	KQLO	4.1	4.0	4.0	4.0	4.0	4.0	4.0	4.0	4.0
Royal Mint	KQLP	–	–	–	2.0	5.0	14.8	11.3	15.7	18.1
Crown Agents	KQLS	..	..	..	..	..	..	..	..	..
Her Majesty's Stationery Office	KQLT	..	..	..	..	..	..	..	..	..
Urban Development Corporations	KQLU	..	..	..	..	..	..	..	..	..
Harbour Authorities	KQLV	0.6	0.5	0.4	0.2	0.1	0.1	0.1	0.1	0.1
UK Atomic Energy Authority	KQLX	..	..	..	..	..	..	..	..	..
Ordnance Survey	GPVF	..	..	..	15.5	13.9	12.3	11.0	9.9	8.9
Central Office of Information	KJEI	..	..	..	..	..	..	..	..	..
Registers of Scotland	KZBB	6.4	5.6	5.1	4.5	4.0	3.7	3.6	3.5	3.3
East of Scotland Water Authority	KZBC	163.0	229.0	288.0	283.0	268.0	258.0	248.0	238.0	223.0
North of Scotland Water Authority	KZBD	155.0	189.2	242.0	236.5	236.5	236.5	231.5	231.5	226.5
West of Scotland Water Authority	KZBE	185.0	304.9	425.6	412.4	412.4	412.4	412.4	402.4	402.4
Loans to local authorities	KQLY	42 134.0	42 951.1	44 742.7	46 099.2	47 239.1	47 093.4	44 640.3	41 468.3	42 102.9
Loans to private sector:										
Housing associations	KGVS	0.5	0.5	0.5	0.5	0.5	..	..	..	..
Loans within central government:										
Northern Ireland Exchequer	KGVW	1 602.5	1 681.1	1 611.2	1 602.0	1 533.1	1 473.9	1 380.4	1 372.0	1 440.5
Married quarters for Armed Forces	KGVX	62.4	61.3	60.2	59.0	57.7	56.4	54.9	53.4	51.8
Other assets:										
Exchange Equalisation Account - Advances o/s	KGVZ	650.0	..	..	475.0	5 680.0	831.0	30.0	670.0	910.0
Subscriptions and contributions to international financial organisations:										
International Monetary Fund	KGXE	6 241.2	5 895.6	9 048.1	9 067.4	9 496.6	9 494.5	9 293.8	8 696.8	8 615.9
Gilt-Edged Official Operations Account										
-advances outstanding	KPUF	3 000.0	2 500.0	2 500.0	..	..	..	..	..	..
-surplus not paid to the National Loans Fund	KPUH	..	141.6	190.8	..	..	..	..	..	..
Borrowing included in national debt but not brought to account by 31 March	KGXF	404.7	568.6	317.9	281.6	405.9	417.5	467.1	..	..
Other NLF Assets	GLX9	..	..	..	..	..	..	..	18 545.9	18 792.0
NLF Debtors	GLY2	..	..	..	..	..	..	..	899.0	895.5
Debt Management Account										
-advances outstanding	GPVG	..	..	..	15 000.0	35 000.0	35 000.0	28 000.0	35 000.0	20 000.0
Consolidated Fund liability	KCYI	362 506.2	362 596.4	361 065.3	351 626.3	324 335.5	338 550.2	362 496.5	395 161.4	436 345.0
Total liabilities										
National Loans Fund - Gross liabilities outstanding	KCYJ	419 548.9	418 444.7	421 635.7	426 239.2	425 955.6	434 544.6	448 006.3	503 404.5	530 571.5

1 See Chapter text.
2 Formerly The Buying Agency.
3 From 2003-04 the NLF Account has been prepared on an Accruals basis.
The figures from 2004 onwards reflect this accounting change.

Source: HM Treasury: 020 7270 4761

18.8 British government and government guaranteed marketable securities[1]
Nominal values of official and market holdings by maturity[2,3]

At 31 March each year   £ million

		1996	1997	1998	1999	2000	2001	2002	2003	2004	2005	2006
Total holdings	KQMO	262 262	290 259	297 366	291 788	290 629	285 915	278 808	292 777	321 051	355 553	411 525
Up to 5 years	KQMP	81 122	90 357	86 094	95 112	95 131	92 090	92 780	106 074	88 678	110 477	127 844
Over 5 and up to 15 years	KQMQ	111 510	125 401	131 758	124 603	116 910	120 101	106 044	101 465	131 665	124 754	146 309
Over 15 years (including undated)	KQMR	69 630	74 501	79 515	72 074	78 587	73 724	79 984	85 238	97 500	120 322	137 372
Official holdings:[3]												
Total	HHAW	7 186	6 858	6 345	6 394	6 204	8 210	7 558	10 650	9 118	6 613	21 486
Up to 5 years	HHAY	2 345	2 850	2 499	2 600	2 849	4 652	3 928	4 797	3 321	2 422	7 610
Over 5 and up to 15 years	HHAZ	3 774	3 041	2 726	2 989	2 567	3 009	2 844	4 115	4 015	2 806	6 988
Over 15 years (including undated)	HHBA	1 068	967	1 120	805	788	549	786	1 738	1 540	1 385	6 888
Market holdings:												
Total	HHBB	255 075	283 402	291 021	285 394	284 425	277 705	271 250	282 127	311 933	348 940	390 038
Up to 5 years	HHBD	78 777	87 508	83 595	92 512	92 282	87 438	88 852	101 277	85 357	108 055	120 234
Over 5 and up to 15 years	HHBE	107 736	122 360	129 032	121 614	114 343	117 092	103 200	97 350	127 650	121 948	139 320
Over 15 years (including undated)	HHBF	68 562	73 536	78 395	71 269	77 800	73 175	79 198	83 500	95 960	118 936	130 484

1 The government guaranteed securities of nationalised industries only. A relatively small amount of other government guaranteed securities is excluded.

2 Securities with optional redemption dates are classified according to the final redemption date. The nominal value of index-linked British Government Stock has been raised by the amount of accrued capital uplift.

3 Official holdings were changed following the introduction of the central bank sector in the UK national accounts. These holdings now principally include those of the Debt Management Office and other government departments. The Issue and Banking Departments of the Bank of England are classified within the central bank sector and are therefore part of market holdings.

Source: Office for National Statistics: 020 7533 5984

18.9 Income tax: allowances and reliefs[1]
United Kingdom

£

		1996 /97	1997 /98	1998 /99	1999 /00	2000 /01	2001 /02	2002 /03	2003 /04	2004 /05	2005 /06	2006 /07
Personal allowances												
Personal allowance	KDZP	3 765	4 045	4 195	4 335	4 385	4 535	4 615	4 615	4 745	4 895	5 035
Married couple's (both partners under 65)[2]	KDZR	1 790	1 830	1 900	1 970	..	..	..	..	..	..	..
Age allowance:												
Personal (aged 65-74)	KSOH	4 910	5 220	5 410	5 720	5 790	5 990	6 100	6 610	6 830	7 090	7 280
Personal (aged 75 or over)	KSOI	5 090	5 400	5 600	5 980	6 050	6 260	6 370	6 720	6 950	7 220	7 420
Married couple's (either partner between 65-74 but neither partner 75 or over)[2,3]	KEDI	3 115	3 185	3 305	5 125	5 185	5 365	5 465	5 565	5 725	5 905	6 065
Married couple's (either partner 75 or over)[2]	KEIY	3 155	3 225	3 345	5 195	5 255	5 435	5 535	5 635	5 795	5 975	6 135
Minimum married couple's allowance	C58D	1 790	1 830	1 900	1 970	2 000	2 070	2 110	2 150	2 210	2 280	2 350
Income limit[4]	KEOO	15 200	15 600	16 200	16 800	17 000	17 600	17 900	18 300	18 900	19 500	20 100
Additional personal allowance[2]	KEPG	1 790	1 830	1 900	1 970	..	..	..	..	..	..	..
Widow's bereavement allowance	KEPH	1 790	1 830	1 900	1 970	..	..	..	..	..	..	..
Blind person's allowance												
Single or married (one spouse blind)	KSOJ	1 250	1 280	1 330	1 380	1 400	1 450	1 480	1 510	1 560	1 610	1 660
Married (both spouses blind)	KSOK	2 500	2 560	2 660	2 760	2 800	2 900	2 960	3 020	3 120	3 220	3 320
Life Assurance Relief												
Percentage of gross premium	KFDR	12.5 or Nil	12.5 or Nil	12.5 or Nil	12.5 or Nil	12.5 or Nil	12.5 or Nil	12.5 or Nil	12.5 or Nil	12.5 or Nil	12.5 or Nil	12.5 or Nil

1 See chapter text.
2 The allowance was restricted to 20 per cent in 1994-95, 15 per cent from 1995-96 and 10 per cent from 1999-00.
3 At least one of the partners must be aged 65 before April 2000 to be entitled to the married couple's allowance (MCA). From 2000-01 only people born before 6 April 1935 are entitled to MCA.

4 If the total income, less allowable deductions of a taxpayer aged 65 or over exceeds the limit, the age-related allowances are reduced by £1 for each £2 of income over the aged income level until the basic levels of the personal and married couple's allowances are reached.

Source: HM Revenue & Customs: 020 7147 3082

18.10 Rates of Income tax
United Kingdom

	1997/98		1998/99		1999/00		2000/01		2001/02	
	Bands of taxable income (£)[1]	Rate of tax - Percentages	Bands of taxable income (£)[1]	Rate of tax - Percentages	Bands of taxable income (£)[1]	Rate of tax - Percentages	Bands of taxable income (£)[1]	Rate of tax - Percentages	Bands of taxable income (£)[1]	Rate of tax - Percentages
Lower rate or starting rate[2]	1 - 4 100	20	1 - 4 300	20	1 - 1 500	10[4]	1 - 1 520	10[5]	1 - 1 880	10[5]
Basic rate	4 101 - 26 100	23[4]	4 301 - 27 100	23[4]	1 501 - 28 000	23[6]	1 521 - 28400	22[6]	1 881 - 29 400	22[6]
Higher rate	over 26 100	40	over 27 100	40	over 28 000	40[7]	over 28 400	40[7]	over 29 400	40[7]

	2002/03		2003/04		2004/05		2005/06		2006/07	
	Bands of taxable income (£)[1]	Rate of tax - Percentages	Bands of taxable income (£)[1]	Rate of tax - Percentages	Bands of taxable income (£)[1]	Rate of tax - Percentages	Bands of taxable income (£)[1]	Rate of tax - Percentages	Bands of taxable income (£)[1]	Rate of tax - Percentages
Starting rate	1 - 1 920	10[5]	1 - 1 960	10[5]	1 - 2 020	10[5]	1 - 2 090	10[5]	1 - 2 150	10[5]
Basic rate	1 921 - 29 900	22[6]	1 961 - 30 500	22[6]	2 021 - 31 400	22[6]	2 091 - 32 400	22[6]	2 151 - 33 300	22[6]
Higher rate	over 29 900	40[7]	over 30 500	40[7]	over 31 400	40[7]	over 32 400	40[7]	over 33 300	40[7]

1 Taxable income is defined as gross income for income tax purposes less any allowances and reliefs available at the taxpayer's marginal rate.
2 In 1999/00 the starting rate replaced the lower rate.
3 The basic rate of tax on dividend income is 20%.
4 The basic rate of tax on dividends and savings income is 20%.
5 The starting rate also applies to savings and dividends.
6 The basic rate of tax on dividends is 10% and savings income is 20%
7 The higher rate of tax on dividends is 32.5%.

Source: HM Revenue & Customs: 020 7147 3082

18.11 Rateable values[1]
England and Wales
At 1 April each year

		1996	1997	1998	1999	2000	2001	2002	2003	2004	2005	2006
Number of properties (Thousands)												
Commercial	KMIN	1 228	1 225	1 223	1 219	1 223	1 230	1 234	1 236	1 239	1 234	1 245
Shops and cafes	KMIO	497	491	488	484	478	476	473	469	466	462	459
Offices	KMIP	255	255	257	258	261	269	273	279	284	287	296
Other	KMIQ	476	479	478	477	484	485	487	488	490	485	490
On-licensed premises	KMIR	59	59	59	60	61	61	60	60	60	66	65
Entertainment and recreational:	KMIS	87	87	81	80	79	79	80	80	80	78	79
Cinemas	KMIT	1	1	1	1	1	1	1	1	1	1	1
Theatres and music-halls	KMIU	1	1	1	1	1	1	1	1	1	1	1
Other	KMIV	85	86	80	79	76	76	77	77	78	76	78
Public utility	KMIW	8	8	9	9	8	8	8	8	8	8	8
Educational and cultural	KMIX	41	41	41	41	41	42	42	42	43	45	45
Miscellaneous	KMIY	55	55	56	61	67	70	70	72	74	74	77
Industrial	KMIZ	249	249	250	250	250	251	250	250	250	252	251
Total	KMIH	1 726	1 725	1 719	1 720	1 729	1 740	1 745	1 749	1 754	1 756	1 771
Value of assessments (£ million)												
Commercial	KMHG	19 822	19 859	19 733	19 652	26 320	27 255	27 622	27 713	27 878	33 013	33 548
Shops and cafes	KMHH	6 094	5 959	5 860	5 840	6 801	6 972	6 953	6 863	6 845	8 257	8 311
Offices	KMHI	5 630	5 641	5 624	5 575	8 625	9 191	9 388	9 555	9 591	10 840	11 034
Other	KMHJ	8 098	8 259	8 249	8 237	10 894	11 092	11 281	11 295	11 441	13 916	14 203
On-licensed premises	KMHK	969	970	980	997	1 311	1 347	1 345	1 334	1 320	1 667	1 652
Entertainment and recreational	KMHL	1 018	1 033	1 040	1 045	1 310	1 369	1 430	1 416	1 362	1 467	1 483
Cinemas	KMHM	32	36	39	45	79	92	104	106	96	117	115
Theatres and music-halls	KMHN	21	21	21	20	24	25	26	26	26	34	35
Other	KMHO	965	975	979	980	1 207	1 252	1 300	1 284	1 240	1 316	1 333
Public utility	KMHP	3 469	3 488	3 380	3 361	3 828	3 411	3 460	3 444	3 410	3 680	3 668
Educational and cultural	KMHQ	1 883	1 894	1 773	1 672	1 829	1 872	1 902	1 895	1 904	2 359	2 411
Miscellaneous	KMHR	1 500	1 494	1 464	1 439	2 142	2 172	2 220	2 218	2 022	2 582	2 646
Industrial	KMHS	5 584	5 561	5 540	5 463	6 249	6 202	6 157	6 034	5 935	6 651	6 575
Total	KMHA	34 245	34 299	33 909	33 649	42 985	43 626	44 136	44 053	43 831	51 419	51 983

1 See chapter text.

Source: HM Revenue & Customs: 020 7147 2941

18.12 Local authorities: gross loan debt outstanding[1]
At 31 March each year

£ billion

		2002	2003	2004	2005	2006
United Kingdom						
Total debt	KQBR	52.2	51.2	50.5	52.9	59.7
Public Works Loan Board	KQBS	46.9	44.6	41.3	42.4	47.1
Northern Ireland Consolidated Fund	KQBT	0.3	0.3	0.3	0.3	..
Other debt	KQBU	5.0	6.3	8.8	10.5	..
England						
Total debt	C3OO	38.3	38.2	37.7	40.1	46.1
of which Public Works Loan Board	C3OP	34.4	33.4	31.1	32.2	36.6
Wales						
Total debt	C3OQ	3.6	3.7	3.6	3.7	3.8
of which Public Works Loan Board	C3OR	3.3	3.3	3.1	3.1	3.3
Scotland						
Total debt	KQBX	10.0	8.8	8.8	8.7	9.4
of which Public Works Loan Board	KQBY	*9.3*	*7.9*	*7.1*	*6.8*	*7.2*
Northern Ireland						
Total debt	KQBZ	0.3	0.3	0.3	0.3	0.3
of which						
Northern Ireland Consolidated Fund	KQBT	0.3	0.3	0.3	0.3	..

1 The sums shown exclude inter-authority loans.

Sources: Communities and Local Government: 020 7944 4176;
Public Works Loan Board: 020 7862 6610;
Department of Finance and Personnel for Northern Ireland: 028 9185 8131

18.13 Revenue expenditure of local authorities

£ million

	2003/04 outturn	2004/05 outturn	2005/06 outturn	2006/07 budget
England				
Education[1]	31 293	33 290	36 026	36 994
Transport	4 434	4 673	4 840	5 335
of which:				
Highways	2 004	2 163	2 205	2 158
Public transport	2 430	2 511	2 635	3 177
Social Services[2]	14 870	16 310	17 355	17 761
Housing (excluding HRA)[3]	8 665	13 288	14 068	14 418
Cultural, environmental and planning	7 888	8 519	9 187	9 378
of which:				
Cultural	2 705	2 835	2 965	3 069
Environmental	3 520	3 864	4 246	4 525
Planning and development	1 662	1 822	1 977	1 784
Police	9 076	10 206	10 957	10 828
Fire	1 738	1 925	2 053	2 086
Courts	437	460	58	59
Central services	2 831	2 953	2 415	3 426
Other	120	275	214	248
Net current expenditure	81 353	91 902	97 172	100 534
Capital financing	2 209	2 362	2 455	2 968
Capital Expenditure charged to Revenue Account	936	957	892	819
Interest receipts	-765	-1 125	-1 215	-909
Pension Interest Costs	4 057	3 947	4 785	3 014
Other non-current expenditure[4]	3 038	3 062	3 194	3 234
Specific grants outside Aggregate External Finance (AEF)	-11 897	-17 311	-18 269	-18 219
Revenue expenditure	78 931	83 795	89 012	91 440
Specific and special grants inside AEF	-13 447	-14 090	14 787	39 993
Net revenue expenditure	65 484	69 705	74 226	51 447
Appropriation to/from reserves (excluding pension reserves)	1 266	1 347	810	-572
Appropriation to/from Pension Reserves	-3 687	-4 492	-4 583	-3 449
Other adjustments	-46	2	24	-5
Budget requirement	63 016	66 561	70 477	47 421
SSA reduction grant	-	-	-	-
Police grant	-4 079	-4 168	-4 353	-3 936
Revenue support grant	-24 215	-26 964	-26 663	-3 378
Central Support Protection Grant	-	-	-	-
Council Tax Benefit Subsid Limitation Scheme	-	-	-	-
Redistributed business rates	-15 611	-15 004	-18 004	-17 506
General Greater London Authority Grant	-36	-36	-37	-38
Other items	-130	-90	-104	-111
Council tax requirement	18 946	20 299	21 315	22 453
Scotland				
Net revenue expenditure on general fund	9 283	9 847	10 603	..

18.13 Revenue expenditure of local authorities
continued

£ million

	2003/04 outturn	2004/05 outturn	2005/06 outturn	2006/07 budget
Wales[5]				
Education	1 920.7	2 011.3	2 121.8	2 182.2
Personal social services	987.3	1 069.2	1 164.7	1 221.9
Council fund housing, including housing benefit[6]	371.2	632.4	674.6	692.7
Local environmental services[7]	262.2	289.6	318.9	335.4
Roads and transport	240.8	256.7	270.8	287.2
Libraries, culture, heritage, sport and recreation	217.5	239.4	248.3	250.8
Planning, economic development and community development	86.1	98.6	108.4	107.4
Magistrates', coroners' and other courts[8]	28.8	30.3	3.0	2.9
Council tax benefit and administration and local tax collection[9]	36.0	30.0	31.0	27.7
Debt financing costs: counties	250.8	258.8	272.4	294.7
Central administrative and other revenue expenditure: counties[10,11]	201.7	191.2	203.7	250.9
Total county and county borough council expenditure	4 603.2	5 107.3	5 417.4	5 653.8
Police operational expenditure	485.5	500.7	554.0	
Other police expenditure[10]	24.9	37.5	14.7	
Total police expenditure	510.4	538.2	557.9	572.2
Fire operational expenditure	107.3	117.6	130.9	
Other fire expenditure[10]	8.2	6.9	5.2	
Total fire expenditure	115.5	124.5	135.7	141.0
National park operational expenditure	11.3	13.6	14.8	
Other national park expenditure[10]	2.5	2.1	2.4	
Total national park expenditure	13.8	15.7	17.0	16.8
Gross revenue expenditure	5 242.8	5 785.7	6 128.0	6 383.7
less specific and special government grants (except council tax benefit grant)	-1 004.7	-1 380.8	-1 473.5	-1 356.7
Net revenue expenditure	4 238.2	4 404.9	4 654.5	5 027.0
Putting to (+)/drawing from (-) reserves	23.3	5.7	13.5	-59.7
Budget requirement	4 261.4	4 410.6	4668.0	4 967.3
Plus discretionary non-domestic rate relief	2.2	2.2	2.5	2.6
less revenue support grant	-2 533.4	-2 591.0	-2 751.6	-2 951.8
less police grant	-209.2	-225.8	-235.0	-217.0
less re-distributed non-domestic rates income	-660.0	-672.0	-672.0	-730.0
Council tax requirement	861.0	924.1	1 012.0	1 071.2
of which:				
Paid by council tax benefit grant from the Department for Work and Pensions	133.0	155.0	170.1	167.8
Paid directly by council tax payers	727.9	769.1	841.9	903.4

1 Includes mandatory student awards and inter-authority education recoupment.

2 Includes supported employment.

3 Includes mandatory rent allowances and rent rebates.

4 Includes:
(i) Gross expenditure on council tax benefit.
(ii) Expenditure on council tax reduction scheme.
(iii) Discretionary (non-domestic) rate relief.
(iv) Flood defence payments to the Environment Agency
(v) Bad debt provision.

5 Scotland figures for 2004-05 and 2005-06 are Final Outturn.

6 Service expenditure is shown excluding that financed by sales, fees and charges, but including specific grants.

7 Includes rent rebates granted to HRA tenants for 2004-5 onwards (previously part of the housing revenue account, 100% funded by the Department for Work and Pensions. Includes housing benefit and private sector housing costs such as provision for the homeless. Excludes council owned housing.

8 Includes cemetery and crematoria, community safety, environmental health, food safety and waste collection / disposal.

9 Responsibility for magistrates courts transferred to the Department for Constitutional Affairs on 1 April 2005.

10 Net of council tax benefit grant.

11 Includes central administrative costs of corporate management, democratic representation and certain costs such as those relating to back-year or additional pension contributions which should not be allocated to individual services. The figure also includes capital expenditure charged to the revenue account and is net of any interest expected to accrue on balances.

12 The figure includes agricultural services, central services to the public such as birth registration, coastal and flood defence, community councils and licensing.

Sources: Communities and Local Government: 020 7944 4158; Scottish Executive, Statistical Support for Local Government: 0131 244 7033; National Assembly for Wales: 029 2082 5355

18.14 Financing of revenue expenditure
England and Wales

Years ending 31 March

£ million

		1996/97	1997/98	1998/99	1999/00	2000/01	2001/02	2002/03	2003/04	2004/05	2005[1]/06	2006[1]/07
England[2]												
Revenue expenditure[3]												
Cash £m	KRTN	46 532	47 256	50 189	53 651	57 329	61 952	65 898	75 244	79 303	84 429	87 991
Government grants												
Cash £m	KRTO	23 003	23 840	25 291	26 421	27 809	31 469	32 634	41 777	45 258	45 840	47 345
Percentage of revenue expenditure	KRTP	*49*	*50*	*50*	*49*	*49*	*50*	*50*	*56*	*57*	*54*	*54*
Redistributed business rates[4]												
Cash £m	KRTQ	12 743	12 034	12 531	13 619	15 407	15 144	16 639	15 611	15 004	18 004	17 506
Percentage of revenue expenditure	KRTR	*27*	*25*	*25*	*25*	*27*	*24*	*25*	*21*	*19*	*21*	*20*
Council tax												
Cash £m	KRTS	10 461	11 241	12 332	13 278	14 200	15 246	16 648	18 946	20 299	21 315	22 453
Percentage of revenue expenditure	KRTT	*22*	*24*	*25*	*25*	*25*	*25*	*25*	*25*	*26*	*25*	*26*
Wales[5]												
Gross revenue expenditure	ZBXH	2 990	3 121	3 246	3 424	3 605	4 350	4 709	5 243	5 786	6 128	6 384
General government grants[6]	ZBXI	2 001	1 957	2 009	2 093	2 234	2 345	2 541	2 743	2 817	2 987	3 169
Specific government grants[7]	ZBXG	73	75	84	80	94	601	779	1 005	1 381	1 473	1 357
Share of redistributed business rates	ZBXJ	459	584	612	656	638	697	643	660	672	672	730
Council tax income[8]	ZBXK	449	483	542	596	670	716	776	861	924	1 012	1 071
Other[9]	ZBXL	9	22	..	−1	−31	−10	−30	−25	−8	−16	57

1 Budget estimates.
2 Produced on a non-Financial Reporting Standard 17 (FRS17) basis.
3 The sum of government grants, business rates and local taxes does not normally equal revenue expenditure because of the use of reserves.
4 1993-94 to 2003-04 includes City of London Offset.
5 Gross revenue expenditure is total local authority expenditure on services, plus capital charges, but net of any income from sales, fees, and charges and other non-grant sources. It includes expenditure funded by specific grants. The figures have been adjusted to account for FRS17 pension costs.

6 Includes all unhypothecated grants, namely revenue support grant, police grant, council tax reduction scheme grant, transitional grant and the adjustment to reverse the transfer.
7 Comprises specific and supplementary grants, excluding police grant.
8 This includes community council precepts, and income covered by charge/council tax benefit grant, but excludes council tax reduction scheme
9 This includes use of, or contributors to, local authority reserves and other minor adjustments.

Sources: Communities and Local Government: 020 7944 4158;
National Assembly for Wales: 029 2082 5355

18.15 Local authority capital expenditure and receipts
England
Final outturn: Years ending 31 March

£ million

		2000 /01	2001 /02	2002 /03	2003 /04	2004 /05	2005 /06
Expenditure[1]							
Education	KRUD	1 533	2 064	2 287	2 780	3 087	3 492
Personal Social Services	KRUE	156	158	199	260	285	387
Transport	KRUC	1 410	1 877	2 461	2 552	2 906	3 461
Housing	KRUB	2 779	3 110	3 828	3 485	3 987	4 534
Arts and libraries	GEKZ	194	213	208	196	227	329
Agriculture and fisheries	GELA	45	38	65	72	66	93
Sport and recreation	KRUH	291	314	307	263	305	424
Other[2]	GELB	1 341	1 513	1 631	2 056	2 725	3 218
Fire and civil defence	GELC	46	62	72	68	81	96
Police and probation	GELD	291	359	408	513	561	606
Magistrates courts	GELE	22	33	40	37	46	1
Total	KRUR	8 109	9 741	11 508	12 282	14 276	16 641
Receipts[3]							
Education	KRUT	119	146	233	221	210	217
Personal social services	KRUV	63	71	75	74	75	85
Transport	KRUU	98	138	107	92	101	87
Housing	KRUS	2 441	2 245	3 474	3 622	3 193	2 179
Arts and libraries	GELF	19	19	22	5	10	7
Agriculture and fisheries	GELG	44	42	49	53	45	63
Sport and recreation	KRUX	12	12	21	7	11	48
Other[2]	GELH	600	801	975	1 145	931	987
Fire and civil defence	GELI	8	7	10	18	6	8
Police and probation	GELJ	104	86	70	78	71	96
Magistrates court	GELK	4	12	4	6	8	1
Total	KRVB	3 512	3 579	5 040	5 322	4 661	3 777

1 Includes aquisition of share or loan capital.
2 Environmental services, consumer protection and employment services.
3 Includes disposal of share or loan capital and disposal of other investments.

Source: Communities and Local Government: 020 7944 4076

18.16 Capital expenditure and income
England

£ million

	Expenditure			Income				
	Expenditure on land works, etc	Capital assigned to repayment of debt	All expenditure	Loans	Government grants	Miscellaneous	All income	Gross debt at end of year
Financial year								
	KRVC	KRVD	KRVE	KRVF	KRVG	KRVH	KRVI	KRVJ
1973/74	3 286	225	3 511	2 781	143	619	3 544	18 300
1974/75[1]	3 712	127	3 839	3 209	128	498	3 835	18 884
1975/76	3 917	198	4 115	3 285	177	647	4 109	21 930
1976/77	3 783	312	4 095	3 097	249	803	4 149	24 534
1977/78	3 487	352	3 839	2 677	255	981	3 913	26 282
1978/79	3 621	390	4 011	2 627	351	1 139	4 117	27 103
1979/80	4 249	331	4 580	2 992	385	1 367	4 745	30 187
1980/81	4 476	413	4 889	2 900	492	1 864	5 256	32 076
1981/82	4 061	563	4 623	2 527	470	2 177	5 174	34 069
1982/83	5 090	634	5 724	3 358	416	3 100	6 874	36 231
1983/84	5 890	562	6 452	3 538	379	3 294	7 211	38 698
1984/85	6 352	515	6 867	3 381	327	3 283	6 991	40 554
1985/86	5 748	348	6 096	3 008	360	3 239	6 607	40 138
1986/87	5 899	328	6 227	2 814	388	3 878	7 081	43 033
1987/88	6 091	486	6 577	2 953	297	4 286	7 536	44 904
1988/89	7 166	658	7 824	2 985	270	6 122	9 376	47 295
1989/90	9 590	474	10 064	2 919	440	6 110	9 469	48 695

		Income					Capital receipts set aside[3]	Credit ceiling[4]	Provision for credit liabilities[4]
	Gross capital expenditure	Credit approvals used[2]	Government grants	Capital receipts	Other income	Total income			
Financial year									
At 1 April 1990	-	-	-	-	-	-	4 241	42 167	4 241
	KRVK	KRVL	KRVM	KRVN	KRVO	KRVP	KRVQ	KRVR	KRVS
1990/91	6 869	2 786	907	3 165	542	7 400	2 022	41 125	5 677
1991/92	6 572	3 140	1 041	2 251	674	7 106	1 353	41 234	6 502
1992/93	6 567	3 229	1 210	2 110	619	7 168	908	37 051	6 282
1993/94	7 124	2 948	1 279	3 310	651	8 188	356	37 941	6 041
1994/95	6 950	2 722	1 176	2 458	724	7 080	1 409	37 673	6 921
1995/96	6 910	2 264	1 484	1 966	1 278	6 992	1 160	37 103	7 677
1996/97	6 419	2 120	1 388	2 183	1 132	6 823	1 039	37 261	8 172
1997/98	6 298	2 099	1 262	2 349	1 129	6 839	1 186	36 711	7 540
1998/99	6 630	2 334	1 160	2 662	1 413	7 569	1 130	36 782	7 108
1999/00	6 912	2 301	1 161	3 651	1 487	8 600	1 483	36 364	7 201
2000/01	8 109	3 216	1 298	3 512	2 219	10 245	1 642	36 628	7 231
2001/02	9 741	2 551	2 027	3 579	2 994	11 151	1 403	36 732	7 081
2002/03	11 508	3 216	2 474	5 040	2 858	13 588	1 922	36 608	6 940
2003/04	12 282	3 909	2 642	5 322	3 852	15 725	2 161	37 511	6 774
2004/05	14 276	3 663	3 196	4 661	..	..	..	..	..
2005/06	16 641	3 879	3 909	3 777	..	..	..	..	..

1 Reorganisation of local government in April 1974 transferred responsibility for various services to regional health and water authorities.
2 From 1 April 2004, under the new prudential system, local authorities have not required government approval to borrow, although central government continues to provide some support via Supported Capital Expenditure (Revenue) - SCE(R). It continues to do this by giving annual revenue grants or HRA subsidy to help meet the costs of such borrowing.
3 Excluding Social Housing Grant and European Regional Development Fund (ERDF) grants.
4 At end of year.

Source: Communities and Local Government: 020 7944 4076

18.17 Expenditure of local authorities
Scotland
Year ending 31 March

£ thousand

		1996/97	1997/98	1998/99	1999/00	2000/01	2001/02	2002/03	2003/04	2004/05	2005/06
Out of revenue:[1] Total	KQTA	9 196 125	9 566 936	10 033 985	10 439 999	10 924 634	11 553 927	12 858 533	13 658 834	14 527 867	15 746 429
General Fund Services:	KQTB	7 151 759	6 679 396	7 021 038	7 429 626	7 884 168	8 428 217	9 290 268	10 139 679	10 964 598	12 021 453
Education	KQTC	2 629 961	2 512 725	2 649 170	2 855 945	3 037 780	3 283 827	3 533 853	3 872 786	4 180 675	4 406 876
Libraries, museums and galleries	KQTD	138 483	121 387	124 648	131 696	134 174	138 318	152 308	160 540	161 650	168 953
Social work	KQTE	1 289 928	1 315 387	1 394 142	1 519 191	1 632 843	1 793 732	2 173 752	2 400 652	2 621 134	2 808 040
Law, order and protective services	KQTF	816 315	931 795	952 940	1 006 000	1 047 034	1 088 791	1 130 693	1 226 067	1 306 085	1 501 854
Roads and Transport[2]	KQTG	716 570	440 712	546 945	527 018	564 738	506 326	601 454	611 721	635 329	673 167
Environmental services	KQTH	329 674	343 565	349 413	373 050	393 333	414 975	484 177	525 556	581 220	635 475
Planning	KQTI	210 827	163 380	179 078	198 285	194 771	223 414	265 315	282 572	299 182	351 617
Leisure and recreation	KQTJ	426 422	364 853	368 023	375 579	387 115	401 904	426 495	472 120	494 237	520 612
Other services	KQTL	562 462	456 219	430 790	435 155	465 612	572 136	515 661	585 425	681 288	948 167
Other general fund expenditure[3]	KQTM	31 117	29 373	25 889	7 707	26 768	4 794	6 560	2 240	3 798	6 692
Housing	KQTN	2 000 684	1 658 935	1 754 686	1 821 380	1 886 189	1 954 444	2 224 209	2 295 005	2 459 146	2 609 228
Trading services:	KQTO	74 799	75 976	79 644	87 321	80 355	61 899	74 062	92 782	106 445	103 461
Passenger transport	KQTR	2 849	1 524	121	336	162	343	427	441	282	353
Ferries	KQTS	6 831	7 512	8 930	9 709	10 005	9 650	11 493	11 768	13 759	14 308
Harbours, docks and piers	KQTT	13 482	12 884	15 697	15 923	13 604	10 912	12 222	13 405	12 407	11 995
Road bridges	KQTV	12 759	16 064	16 408	8 231	8 606	6 914	7 267	11 235	13 276	12 366
Slaughterhouses	KQTW	794	850	228	4	..	..	..	..	..	..
Markets	KQTX	14 278	13 479	13 161	14 106	23 844	16 657	17 995	14 824	15 353	17 447
Other trading services	KQTY	23 806	23 663	25 099	39 012	24 134	17 423	24 658	41 109	51 368	46 992
Loan charges:[4] Total	KQTZ	1 121 448	1 126 637	1 152 728	1 109 379	1 100 690	1 114 161	1 269 994	1 131 368	997 678	1 012 287
Allocated to :											
General Fund services	KMHV	639 380	651 982	710 371	701 515	708 822	739 351	738 870	772 852	772 648	792 404
Housing	KMHW	475 507	471 274	438 556	402 936	386 512	369 943	525 201	348 180	212 440	210 856
Trading services	KMHX	6 561	3 381	3 801	4 928	5 356	4 867	5 923	10 336	12 590	9 027
On capital works:[5] Total	KQUA	889 572	813 900	815 981	816 473	802 672	929 631	972 049	1 052 310	1 264 031	1 572 281
General Fund Services:	KQUB	540 127	540 096	541 769	557 119	538 843	610 485	662 869	767 122	1 006 150	1 160 818
Education	KQUC	101 898	112 753	125 341	136 508	127 781	143 268	157 439	172 227	199 387	310 054
Libraries, museums and galleries	KQUD	11 602	9 974	13 231	10 261	5 834	8 683	19 018	12 043	24 796	22 762
Social work	KQUE	20 658	19 660	22 554	22 097	21 539	31 359	30 116	31 966	33 450	37 877
Law, order and protective services	KQUF	41 326	37 701	37 727	37 132	35 761	39 901	53 268	65 477	65 154	51 146
Roads and Transport	KQUG	116 881	108 227	113 954	108 500	117 485	147 975	147 357	200 278	258 071	308 366
Environmental services	KQUH	10 226	21 193	18 397	14 936	17 944	16 396	17 957	20 567	40 773	55 020
Planning	KQUI	51 182	69 648	50 854	52 045	47 684	33 312	40 241	36 496	61 544	76 043
Leisure and recreation	KQUJ	36 232	29 692	40 926	52 365	44 516	39 240	50 558	71 486	74 116	83 681
Administrative buildings and equipment	KQUK	40 014	45 374	35 107	35 824	34 633	53 189	68 438	48 896	64 414	84 569
Other services	KQUL	110 108	85 814	83 678	87 451	85 666	97 162	78 477	107 686	184 445	131 300
Housing	KQUM	345 713	270 005	268 135	255 019	255 189	300 054	284 418	261 715	241 107	382 697
Trading Services:	KQUN	3 732	3 799	6 077	4 335	8 640	19 092	24 762	23 473	16 774	28 766
Ferries	KQUR	521	770	268	1 030	23	467	1	111	608	195
Harbours, docks and piers	KQUS	934	1 175	1 626	1 389	6 192	15 898	20 361	19 503	12 024	12 899
Airports	KQUT	1 149	439	..	..	607	663	1 031	609	572	663
Road bridges	KQUU	277	973	2 791	600	964	882	2 386	2 395	442	12 106
Slaughterhouses	KQUV	112	69	54	12	..	40	116	82	–	–
Other trading services	KMHY	739	373	1 338	1 304	854	1 142	867	773	3 128	2 903

1 Gross expenditure *less* inter-authority and inter-account transfers.
2 Including general fund support for transport (LA and NON-LA).
3 General fund contributions to Housing and Trading services (excluding transport), are also included in the expenditure figures for these services.
4 From 1997/98 loan charges are not included within individual service totals.
5 Expenditure out of loans, government grants and other capital receipts.

Source: Scottish Executive, Statistical Support for Local Government: 0131 244 7033

18.18 Income of local authorities: classified according to source
Scotland
Year ending 31 March

£ thousand

		1995 /96	1996 /97	1997 /98	1998 /99	1999 /00	2000 /01	2001 /02	2002 /03	2003 /04	2004 /05	2005 /06
Revenue account												
Rates[1]	KQXA	1 310 721	1 313 531	1 326 129	1 437 646	1 440 522	1 662 691	1 553 926	1 718 104	1 804 423	1 895 941	1 897 073
Council tax	KPUC	976 465	9 681 531	70 405	1 146 366	1 193 693	1 273 316	1 363 399	1 459 212	1 532 071	1 614 808	1 720 305
Government grants												
Revenue Support Grant	KQXC	3 716 567	3 649 694	3 520 461	3 483 815	3 537 043	3 440 842	3 935 328	4 557 867	5 037 140	5 266 054	5 567 902
Rate rebate grant	KQXG	4 456	496	..	..	..	..	..	..	..	..	..
Council tax												
rebate grants	KPUD	193 937	226 132	260 424	274 940	275 789	279 459	285 131	293 606	307 733	344 899	354 067
Other grants and												
subsidies	KQXI	1 236 160	1 347 706	1 480 890	1 642 045	1 778 216	1 891 839	2 061 297	2 141 543	2 479 311	2 823 820	2 940 137
Sales	KQXJ	64 284	59 059	46 874	39 595	43 660	49 826	..	..	..	..	..
Fees and charges[2]	KQXK	1 528 270	1 539 611	1 625 952	1 668 223	1 682 385	1 776 455	1 789 428	1 954 337	1 785 672	1 845 161	1 951 315
Other income[3]	KQXL	207 005	238 985	290 427	324 932	398 894	453 458	490 574	712 423	515 897	709 226	1 003 925
Capital account												
Sale of fixed assets	KQXM	500 838	499 143	327 569	335 037	303 582	149 504	165 016	207 388	222 844	355 069	366 302
Revenue contributions												
to capital	KQXP	197 606	119 641	149 423	204 982	213 564	210 912	147 760	239 778	212 533	219 593	247 693
Transfer from special												
funds	KMHZ	9 035	2 652	36 929	26 959	125 365	27 317	37 087	39 650	52 619	82 991	72 195
Other receipts[4]	KMGV	29 571	45 067	32 118	45 028	39 014	45 351	90 360	75 846	114 745	130 575	261 872

1 Excluding government grants towards rate rebates and domestic element of revenue support grant (RSG). Including domestic water rate receipts.

2 From 2001-02 onwards, fees & charges incorporates sales.

3 From 1996-97 Other Income includes income from Health Boards and Trusts, Other Public Bodies and Interest on Revenue Balances.

4 Figures include public sector contributions from 2001-02 onwards.

Source: Scottish Executive, Statistical Support for Local Government: 0131 244 7033

18.19 Income of local authorities from government grants[1]
Scotland
Year ending 31 March

£ thousand

		1996 /97	1997 /98	1998 /99	1999 /00	2000 /01	2001 /02	2002 /03	2003 /04	2004 /05	2005 /06
General fund services	KQYA	487 734	557 536	690 569	818 537	935 452	1 032 591	952 692	1 029 338	1 207 912	1 358 190
Education	KQYB	18 324	61 960	92 368	225 668	324 340	380 726	251 333	217 743	287 226	327 905
Libraries, museums and											
galleries	KQYC	137	326	627	507	634	1 137	5 359	1 517	763	818
Social work	KQYD	57 576	59 892	62 167	71 611	78 611	86 533	114 591	205 229	240 665	236 774
Law, order and											
protective services	KQYE	330 767	359 811	366 961	382 246	401 485	423 636	445 275	476 681	512 501	597 322
Roads and Transport[2]	KQYF	403	237	97 649	68 429	57 702	49 900	57 664	27 280	35 038	31 704
Environmental services	KQYG	119	159	89	71	301	2 272	5 407	18 120	39 971	45 338
Planning and											
Economic Development	KQYH	3 337	4 885	2 695	4 311	4 375	20 351	19 434	21 517	20 767	31 293
Leisure and recreation	KQYI	1 509	1 856	1 509	1 491	2 377	3 322	2 968	3 732	5 830	6 256
Other services	KQYK	75 562	68 410	66 504	64 203	65 627	64 714	50 661	57 519	65 151	80 780
Housing	KQYL	856 435	920 700	948 232	959 276	956 239	1 028 529	1 188 626	1 449 616	1 614 976	1 580 504
Trading services	KQYM	..	..	..	403	148	177	225	357	932	1 443
Other trading services	KQYP	..	..	..	403	148	177	225	357	932	1 443
Grants not allocated to											
specific services[3]	KMGY	3 650 190	3 520 461	3 483 815	3 537 043	3 440 842	3 935 328	4 557 867	5 037 140	5 266 054	5 567 902
Total	KMGZ	4 994 362	4 998 697	5 122 616	5 315 259	5 332 681	5 996 625	6 699 410	7 516 451	8 089 874	8 508 039

1 Including grants for capital works.

2 The significant increase in 1998/99 is due to the different reporting of a grant in aid of expenditure on rail passenger services in the Strathclyde Passenger Transport area.

3 Revenue support grant, community charge grant and community charge rebate grants.

Source: Scottish Executive, Statistical Support for Local Government: 0131 244 7033

18.20 Expenditure of local authorities
Northern Ireland
Years ending 31 March

£ thousand

		1994 /95	1995 /96	1996 /97	1997 /98	1998 /99	1999 /00	2000 /01	2001 /02	2002 /03	2003 /04	2004[1] /05
Libraries, museums and art galleries	KQVB	7 214	8 481	10 956	13 928	14 571	19 900	23 097	24 181	32 728	30 062	30 481
Environmental health services:												
Refuse collection and disposal	KQVC	42 109	41 284	52 267	56 246	56 360	62 226	65 289	73 336	90 148	94 715	102 633
Public baths	KQVD	1 648	1 703	1 838	2 585	2 634	1 750	1 724	1 423	..	..	..
Parks, recreation grounds, etc	KQVE	101 319	100 418	111 884	115 302	118 396	158 304	170 999	184 406	194 224	193 617	205 617
Other sanitary services	KQVF	34 582	35 706	39 545	39 682	42 923	44 214	45 552	48 784	52 075	55 349	59 906
Housing (grants and small dwellings acquisition)	KQVG	553	472	489	545	358	37	28	27	12	21	18
Trading services:												
Cemeteries	KQVI	5 984	5 489	5 120	5 626	5 887	5 973	6 151	6 538	7 208	7 980	8 455
Other trading services (including markets, fairs and harbours)	KQVJ	6 587	4 254	8 672	7 016	10 779	9 366	7 209	7 769	18 281	17 489	18 776
Miscellaneous	KQVK	51 741	54 987	63 792	63 375	161 790	86 649	89 881	98 244	79 645	114 971	104 507
Total expenditure	KQVA	251 737	252 794	294 563	304 305	413 698	388 419	409 930	444 708	474 321	490 619	529 036
Total loan charges	KQVL	20 797	21 122	24 363	34 823	26 413	..	..	..	..	..	..

1 Includes estimates for Ballymena Borough council.

Source: Department of the Environment for Northern Ireland: 028 9025 6082

External trade and investment

Chapter 19

External trade and investment

External trade

(Table 19.1 and 19.3 to 19.6)

The statistics in this section are on a Balance of Payments (BoP) basis; compiled from information provided to HM Revenue & Customs by importers and exporters on an Overseas Trade Statistics (OTS) basis, which values exports 'f.o.b.'(free on board) and imports 'c.i.f.' (including insurance and freight). In addition to deducting these freight costs and insurance premiums from the OTS figures, coverage adjustments are made to convert the OTS data to a BoP basis. Adjustments are also made to the level of all exports and EU imports to take account of estimated under-recording. The adjustments are set out and described in the annual ONS 'Pink Book' (United Kingdom Balance of Payments). These adjustments are made to conform to the definitions in the 5th edition of the IMF Balance of Payments Manual.

Aggregate estimates of trade in goods, seasonally adjusted and on a BoP basis are published monthly in the ONS First Release UK Trade. More detailed figures are available from the ONS Databank and are also published in the Monthly Review of External Trade Statistics (Business Monitor MM24). Detailed figures for EU and non-EU trade on an OTS basis are published by The Stationery Office in Overseas Trade Statistics of the United Kingdom.

A fuller description of how trade statistics are compiled can be found in Statistics on Trade in Goods (Government Statistical Service Methodological Series).

Overseas Trade Statistics

HM Revenue & Customs provide accurate and up to date information via the website www.uktradeinfo.com

They also produce publications 'Overseas Trade Statistics'.

Import penetration and export sales ratios

(Table 19.2)

The ratios were first introduced in the August 1977 edition of Economic Trends in an article 'The Home and Export Performance of United Kingdom Industries'. The article described the conceptual and methodological problems involved in measuring such variables as import penetration.

The industries are grouped according to the 1992 Standard Industrial Classification. The four different ratios are defined as follows:

Ratio 1: percentage ratio of imports to home demand

Ratio 2: percentage ratio of imports to (home demand plus exports)

Ratio 3: percentage ratio of exports to total manufacturers' sales

Ratio 4: percentage ratio of exports to (total manufacturers' sales plus imports)

Home demand is defined as total manufacturers' sales plus imports minus exports. This is only an estimate as different sources are used for the total manufacturers' sales and the import and export data. Total manufacturers' sales are determined by the ProdCom inquiry and import and export data are provided by HM Revenue & Customs.

Ratio 1 is commonly used to describe the import penetration of the home market. Allowance is made for the extent of a domestic industry's involvement in export markets by using Ratio 2; this reduces as exports increase.

Similarly Ratio 3 is the measure normally used to relate exports to total sales by UK producers and Ratio 4 makes an allowance for the extent that imports of the same product are coming into the UK.

International trade in services

(Tables 19.7 and 19.8)

These data relate to overseas trade in services and cover both production and non-production industries (excluding the Public Sector). In terms of types of services traded this equates to trade in royalties, various forms of consultancy, computing and telecommunications services, advertising and market research and other business services. A separate inquiry covers the Film and Television industries. The surveys cover receipts from the provision of services to residents of other countries (exports) and payments to residents of other countries for services rendered (imports).

Sources of data

The International Trade in Services (ITIS) surveys (which consist of a quarterly component addressed to the largest businesses and an annual component for the remainder) are based on a sample of companies derived from the Inter-departmental Business register. The companies are asked to show the amounts for their imports and exports against the geographical area to which they were paid or from which they were received - irrespective of where they were first earned.

The purpose of the ITIS survey is to record international transactions which impact on the UK's Balance of Payments, hence companies are asked to exclude from their earnings trade expenses such as the cost of services purchased abroad. Exports and imports of Services are excluded where they are included within an invoice for the import or export of goods; in this case they will already be counted in the estimate for Trade in Goods. However, earnings from third country trade, i.e. from arranging the sale of goods between two countries other than the UK and where the goods never physically enter the UK (known as merchanting), are included. Earnings from commodity trading are also included. Together these two comprise 'Trade Related Services'.

'Royalties' are the largest part of the total trade in services collected in the ITIS survey: these cover transactions for items such as printed matter, sound recordings, performing rights, patents, licences, trademarks, designs, copyrights, manufacturing rights, the use of technical 'know-how' and technical assistance.

Balance of payments

(Tables 19.9 to 19.12)

Tables 19.9 to 19.12 are derived from United Kingdom Balance of Payments - the ONS Pink Book. The following general notes to the tables provide brief definitions and explanations of the figures and terms used. Further notes are included in the Pink Book.

Summary of Balance of Payments

The Balance of Payments consists of the current account, the capital account, the financial account and the International Investment Position. The current account consists of trade in goods and services, income and current transfers. Income consists of investment income and compensation of employees. The capital account mainly consists of capital transfers and the financial account covers financial transactions. The International Investment Position covers balance sheet levels of UK external assets and liabilities. Every credit entry in the balance of payments accounts should, in theory, be matched by a corresponding debit entry so that total current, capital and financial account credits should be equal to, and therefore offset by, total debits. In practice there is a discrepancy termed net errors and omissions.

The Current Account

Trade in goods

The goods account covers exports and imports of goods. Imports of motor cars from Japan, for example, are recorded as debits in the trade in goods account whereas exports of vehicles manufactured in the UK are recorded as credits. Trade in goods forms a component of the expenditure measure of Gross Domestic Product (GDP).

Trade in services

The services account covers exports and imports of services (e. g., civil aviation). Passenger tickets for travel on UK aircraft sold abroad, for example, are recorded as credits in the services account whereas the purchases of airline tickets from foreign airlines by UK passengers are recorded as debits. Trade in services, along with trade in goods, forms a component of the expenditure measure of Gross Domestic Product (GDP).

Income

The income account consists of compensation of employees and investment income and is dominated by the latter. Compensation of employees covers employment income from cross-border and seasonal workers which is less significant in the UK than in other countries. Investment income covers earnings (e.g., profits, dividends and interest payments and receipts) arising from cross-border investment in financial assets and liabilities. For example, earnings on foreign bonds and shares held by financial institutions based in the UK are recorded as credits in the investment income account, whereas earnings on UK company securities held abroad are recorded as investment income debits. Investment income forms a component of Gross National Income (GNI) but not Gross Domestic Product (GDP).

Current transfers

Current transfers are composed of central government transfers (e.g., taxes and payments to, and receipts from, the European Union) and other transfers (e.g., gifts in cash or kind received by private individuals from abroad or receipts from the EU, where the UK government acts as an agent for the ultimate beneficiary of the transfer). Current transfers do not form a component either of Gross Domestic Product (GDP) or of Gross National Income (GNI). For example payments to the UK farming industry under the EU Agricultural Guarantee Fund are recorded as credits in the current transfers account while payments of EU agricultural levies by the UK farming industry are recorded as debits in the current transfers account.

External trade and investment

Capital Account

Capital account transactions involve transfers of ownership of fixed assets, transfers of funds associated with acquisition or disposal of fixed assets and cancellation of liabilities by creditors without any counterparts being received in return. The main components are migrants transfers, EU transfers relating to fixed capital formation (regional development fund and agricultural guidance fund) and debt forgiveness. Funds brought into the UK by new immigrants would, for example, be recorded as credits in the capital account, while funds sent abroad by UK residents emigrating to other countries would be recorded as debits in the capital account. The size of capital account transactions are quite minor compared with the current and financial accounts.

Financial Account

While investment income covers earnings arising from cross-border investments in financial assets and liabilities, the financial account of the balance of payments covers the flows of such investments. Earnings on foreign bonds and shares held by financial institutions based in the UK are, for example, recorded as credits in the investment income account, but the acquisition of such foreign securities by UK based financial institutions are recorded as net debits in the financial account or portfolio investment abroad. Similarly the acquisitions of UK company securities held by foreign residents are recorded in the financial account as net credits or portfolio investment in the UK.

International Investment Position

While the financial account covers the flows of foreign investments and financial assets and liabilities, the International Investment Position records the levels of external assets and liabilities. While the acquisition of foreign securities by UK based financial institutions are recorded in the financial account, as net debits, the total holdings of foreign securities by UK based financial institutions are recorded as levels of UK external assets. Similarly the holdings of UK company securities held by foreign residents are recorded as levels of UK liabilities.

Foreign direct investment

(Tables 19.13 to 19.18)

Direct investment refers to investment that adds to, deducts from or acquires a lasting interest in an enterprise operating in an economy other than that of the investor, the investor's purpose being to have an effective voice in the management of the enterprise. (For the purposes of the statistical inquiry, an effective voice is taken as equivalent to a holding of 10 per cent or more in the foreign enterprise.) Other investments in which the investor does not have an effective voice in the management of the enterprise are mainly portfolio investments and these are not covered here. Cross-border investment by public corporations or in property (which is regarded as direct investment in the national accounts) is not covered here, but is shown in the balance of payments. Similarly foreign direct investment earnings data are shown net of tax in Tables 19.15 and 19.18 but are gross of tax in the balance of payments.

Direct investment is a financial concept and is not the same as capital expenditure on fixed assets. It covers only the money invested in a related concern by the parent company and the concern will then decide how to use the money. A related concern may also raise money locally without reference to the parent company.

The investment figures are published on a net basis, that is, they consist of investments net of disinvestments by a company into its foreign subsidiaries, associate companies and branches.

Definitional changes from 1997

The new European System of Accounts (ESA(95)) definitions were introduced from the 1997 estimates. The changes were as follows:

i)   Previously for the measurement of direct investment, an effective voice in the management of an enterprise was taken as the equivalent of a 20 per cent shareholding. This is now 10 per cent.

ii) The Channel Islands (Jersey, Guernsey etc.) and the Isle of Man have been excluded from the definition of the economic territory of the UK. Prior to 1987 these islands were considered to be part of the United Kingdom.

iii) Interest received or paid was replaced by interest accrued in the figures on earnings from direct investment. There is deemed to be little or no impact arising from this definitional change on the estimates.

New register sources available from 1998 have led to revisions for the figures from that year onwards. These sources gave an improved estimate of the population satisfying the criteria for foreign direct investment.

The definitional changes have been introduced from 1997 and the register changes from 1998. The data prior to these years have not been reworked in Tables 19.13 to 19.18. For clarity, the Offshore Islands are identified separately on the tables. The breaks in the series for the other definitional changes are not quantified but are relatively small. More detailed information on the effect of these changes appears in the business monitor, MA4 – Foreign Direct Investment 2002, which was published in February 2003 and is available on the ONS website.

Sources of data

The figures in Tables 19.13 to 19.18 are based on annual inquiries into foreign direct investment for 2002. These were sample surveys which involved sending around 1250 forms to UK businesses investing abroad and 2250 forms to UK businesses in which foreign parents and associates had invested. The tables also contain some revisions to 2001 as a result of new information coming to light in the course of the latest surveys. Further details from the latest annual surveys, including analyses by industry and by components of direct investment, are available in business monitor MA4. Initial figures were published on the ONS website in a first release, 'Foreign Direct Investment 2002', in December 2003. Data for 2003 will be published in a first release in December 2004, followed by the full business monitor MA4 in February 2005.

Country allocation

The analysis of inward investment is based on the country of ownership of the immediate parent company. Thus, inward investment in a UK company may be attributed to the country of the intervening overseas subsidiary, rather than the country of the ultimate parent. Similarly, the country analysis of outward investment is based on the country of ownership of the immediate subsidiary. As an example, to the extent that overseas investment in the UK is channelled through holding companies in the Netherlands, the underlying flow of investment from this country is overstated and the inflow from originating countries is understated.

Further information

More detailed statistics on foreign direct investment are available on request from Simon Harrington, Office for National Statistics, Financial & Accounting Surveys Division, Room 2.301, Government Buildings, Cardiff Road, Newport, South Wales, United Kingdom, NP10 8XG. Telephone: 01633 813314, Fax: 01633 812855, e-mail simon.harrington@ons.gov.uk.

19.1 Trade in goods[1]
United Kingdom
Balance of payments basis

£ million and indices (2003=100)

		1996	1997	1998	1999	2000	2001	2002	2003	2004	2005	2006
Value (£ million)												
Exports of goods	BOKG	167 196	171 923	164 056	166 166	187 936	189 093	186 524	188 320	190 877	211 616	244 542
Imports of goods	BOKH	180 918	184 265	185 869	195 217	220 912	230 305	234 229	236 927	251 770	280 399	328 233
Balance on trade in goods	BOKI	−13 722	−12 342	−21 813	−29 051	−32 976	−41 212	−47 705	−48 607	−60 893	−68 783	−83 691
Price index numbers												
Exports of goods	BQKR	111.9	106.1	100.9	98.8	99.9	98.3	98.2	100.0	100.3	104.7	107.8
Imports of goods	BQKS	115.6	107.9	102.4	100.8	104.2	103.3	100.7	100.0	99.5	103.7	107.4
Terms of trade[2]	BQKT	96.8	98.3	98.5	98.0	95.9	95.2	97.5	100.0	100.8	101.0	100.4
Volume index numbers												
Exports of goods	BQKU	78.4	84.9	85.8	88.6	99.3	101.5	100.3	100.0	101.5	110.9	127.9
Imports of goods	BQKV	64.1	70.4	76.4	81.5	89.1	93.8	98.2	100.0	106.9	114.8	131.2

1 See chapter text. Statistics of trade in goods on a balance of payments basis are obtained by making certain adjustments in respect of valuation and coverage to the statistics recorded in the *Overseas Trade Statistics.* These adjustments are described in detail in *The Pink Book 2006.*
2 Export price index as a percentage of the import price index.

Source: Office for National Statistics: 020 7533 6064

19.2 Import penetration and export sales ratios for products of manufacturing industry[1,2]

United Kingdom: Standard Industrial Classification 1992

Ratios

			2003	2004	2005
Ratio 1 Imports/Home Demand		SIC Division			
Other mining and quarrying	BBAM	14	177	158	192
Food products and beverages	BBAN	15	26	26	26
Tobacco products	BBAO	16	19	17	17
Textiles	BAZJ	17	75	77	77
Wearing apparel: Dressing and dyeing of fur	BAZK	18	99	100	103
Tanning and dressing of leather: Luggage, handbags, saddlery, harness and footwear	BBAP	19	107	104	108
Wood products of wood and cork (except furniture) articles of straw and plaiting materials	BBAQ	20	38	37	37
Pulp, paper and paper products	BBAR	21	58	42	42
Publishing, printing and reproduction of recorded media	BBAS	22	9	6	6
Chemicals and chemical products	BAZL	24	90	87	92
Rubber and plastic products	BBAT	25	34	35	36
Other non metallic mineral products	BBAU	26	26	25	25
Basic metals	BBAV	27	79	81	87
Fabricated metal products (except machinery and equipment)	BBAW	28	28	25	25
Machinery and equipment not elsewhere classified	BBAX	29	67	65	72
Office machinery and computers	BBAY	30	136	142	159
Electrical machinery not elsewhere classified	BBAZ	31	81	76	73
Radio, television and communication equipment and apparatus	BBBA	32	152	123	262
Medical, precision and optical instruments, watches and clocks	BBBB	33	87	90	93
Motor vehicles, trailers and semi-trailers	BBBC	34	68	69	69
Other transport equipment	BBBD	35	83	75	100
Furniture and manufacturing not elsewhere classified	BBBE	36	64	65	70
Total	BAZY		60	58	62
Ratio 2 Imports/Home Demand plus Exports					
Other mining and quarrying	BBBH	14	54	57	62
Food products and beverages	BBBI	15	23	23	23
Tobacco products	BBBJ	16	11	11	12
Textiles	BAZN	17	54	55	56
Wearing apparel: Dressing and dyeing of fur	BAZO	18	79	80	83
Tanning and dressing of leather: Luggage, handbags, saddlery, harness and footwear	BBBK	19	85	84	86
Wood products of wood and cork (except furniture) articles of straw and plaiting materials	BBBL	20	36	36	35
Pulp, paper and paper products	BBBM	21	48	36	36
Publishing, printing and reproduction of recorded media	BBBN	22	8	5	5
Chemicals and chemical products	BAZP	24	45	45	46
Rubber and plastic products	BBBO	25	27	28	29
Other non metallic mineral products	BBBP	26	22	21	22
Basic metals	BBBQ	27	49	48	49
Fabricated metal products (except machinery and equipment)	BBBR	28	24	21	21
Machinery and equipment not elsewhere classified	BBBS	29	41	40	44
Office machinery and computers	BBBT	30	72	77	79
Electrical machinery not elsewhere classified	BBBU	31	45	46	45
Radio, television and communication equipment and apparatus	BBBV	32	68	69	73
Medical, precision and optical instruments, watches and clocks	BBBW	33	47	49	49
Motor vehicles, trailers and semi-trailers	BBBX	34	48	48	48
Other transport equipment	BBBY	35	43	40	46
Furniture and manufacturing not elsewhere classified	BBBZ	36	50	51	54
Total	BBBF		41	41	42

19.2 Import penetration and export sales ratios for products of manufacturing industry[1,2]

continued United Kingdom: Standard Industrial Classification 1992

Ratios

			2003	2004	2005
Ratio 3 Exports/Sales		SIC Division			
Other mining and quarrying	BBCM	14	151	148	180
Food products and beverages	BBCN	15	15	15	15
Tobacco products	BBCO	16	49	40	35
Textiles	BAZR	17	60	63	62
Wearing apparel: Dressing and dyeing of fur	BAZS	18	96	100	115
Tanning and dressing of leather: Luggage, handbags, saddlery, harness and footwear	BBCP	19	138	122	149
Wood products of wood and cork (except furniture) articles of straw and plaiting materials	BBCQ	20	8	7	7
Pulp, paper and paper products	BBCR	21	34	21	22
Publishing, printing and reproduction of recorded media	BBCS	22	14	9	9
Chemicals and chemical products	BAZT	24	91	88	93
Rubber and plastic products	BBCT	25	27	27	28
Other non metallic mineral products	BBCU	26	18	18	18
Basic metals	BBCV	27	75	79	86
Fabricated metal products (except machinery and equipment)	BBCW	28	21	19	19
Machinery and equipment not elsewhere classified	BBCX	29	67	64	71
Office machinery and computers	BBCY	30	168	201	240
Electrical machinery not elsewhere classified	BBDK	31	80	72	69
Radio, television and communication equipment and apparatus	BBDL	32	172	141	263
Medical, precision and optical instruments, watches and clocks	BBDM	33	87	90	93
Motor vehicles, trailers and semi-trailers	BBDN	34	56	59	59
Other transport equipment	BBDO	35	85	78	100
Furniture and manufacturing not elsewhere classified	BBDP	36	43	43	49
Total	BBCK		53	50	55
Ratio 4 Exports/Sales plus Imports					
Other mining and quarrying	BBDS	14	69	64	68
Food products and beverages	BBDT	15	12	11	12
Tobacco products	BBDU	16	44	36	31
Textiles	BAZV	17	28	28	28
Wearing apparel: Dressing and dyeing of fur	BAZW	18	20	20	19
Tanning and dressing of leather: Luggage, handbags, saddlery, harness and footwear	BBDV	19	21	19	20
Wood products of wood and cork (except furniture) articles of straw and plaiting materials	BBDW	20	5	5	5
Pulp, paper and paper products	BBDX	21	18	13	14
Publishing, printing and reproduction of recorded media	BBDY	22	13	9	8
Chemicals and chemical products	BAZX	24	50	48	50
Rubber and plastic products	BBDZ	25	19	19	20
Other non-metallic mineral products	BBEA	26	14	14	14
Basic metals	BBEB	27	39	40	44
Fabricated metal products (except machinery and equipment)	BBEC	28	16	15	15
Machinery and equipment not elsewhere classified	BBED	29	39	38	40
Office machinery and computers	BBEE	30	47	46	50
Electrical machinery not elsewhere classified	BBEF	31	44	39	37
Radio, television and communication equipment and apparatus	BBEG	32	56	44	72
Medical, precision and optical instruments, watches and clocks	BBEH	33	46	46	47
Motor vehicles, trailers and semi-trailers	BBEI	34	30	30	31
Other transport equipment	BBEJ	35	49	46	54
Furniture and manufacturing not elsewhere classified	BBEK	36	21	21	23
Total	BBDQ		31	29	32

1 See chapter text.
2 Division 13 (Mining of metal ores) has not been published since 1995. Division 23 (Coke, refined petroleum products and nuclear fuel) and SIC 24610 (Manufacture of explosives) are excluded from the analysis. SIC 27100 (Basic iron and steel and ferro-alloys) is not incorporated in PRODCOM and therefore also does not form part of the analysis.

Source: Office for National Statistics: 01633 813065

19.3 United Kingdom exports: by commodity[1,2]
Seasonally adjusted

£ million

		1997	1998	1999	2000	2001	2002	2003	2004	2005	2006
0. Food and live animals	BOGG	6 581	6 286	5 925	5 827	5 491	5 693	6 478	6 462	6 550	6 826
of which:											
01. Meat and meat preparations	BOGS	925	746	657	642	428	516	606	667	729	770
02. Dairy products and eggs	BQMS	745	745	689	660	614	625	760	780	718	722
04 & 08. Cereals and animal feeding stuffs	BQMT	1 800	1 714	1 568	1 604	1 383	1 444	1 681	1 553	1 555	1 606
05. Vegetables and fruit	BQMU	455	408	437	403	401	433	475	508	514	584
1. Beverages and tobacco	BQMZ	4 522	3 930	4 022	4 081	4 139	4 300	4 401	4 116	4 095	4 241
11. Beverages	BQNB	3 305	2 875	3 004	3 065	3 218	3 320	3 478	3 354	3 481	3 728
12. Tobacco	BQOW	1 217	1 055	1 018	1 016	921	980	923	762	614	513
2. Crude materials	BQOX	2 489	2 267	2 087	2 447	2 422	2 645	3 069	3 566	3 745	4 634
of which:											
24. Wood, lumber and cork	BQOY	52	55	66	72	70	81	106	117	131	148
25. Pulp and waste paper	BQOZ	64	47	54	78	81	106	180	244	283	339
26. Textile fibres	BQPA	568	493	447	496	440	472	492	520	516	545
28. Metal ores	BQPB	642	560	518	759	810	928	1 193	1 605	1 713	2 433
3. Fuels	BOPN	11 016	7 513	9 929	17 057	16 386	16 000	16 558	17 885	21 497	25 242
33. Petroleum and petroleum products	ELBL	10 239	7 018	9 123	15 584	14 815	14 321	14 608	16 200	19 795	23 124
32, 34 & 35. Coal, gas and electricity	BOQI	777	495	806	1 473	1 571	1 679	1 950	1 685	1 702	2 118
4. Animal and vegetable oils and fats	BQPI	264	245	197	156	149	210	266	205	235	275
5. Chemicals	ENDG	21 901	22 102	23 071	24 992	27 514	28 386	31 373	32 008	33 389	37 385
of which:											
51. Organic chemicals	BQPJ	4 974	4 914	5 494	5 718	6 090	5 698	6 070	6 040	6 703	8 055
52. Inorganic chemicals	BQPK	1 183	1 153	1 137	1 491	1 636	1 367	1 460	1 543	1 555	2 157
53. Colouring materials	CSCE	1 578	1 542	1 534	1 555	1 521	1 583	1 627	1 630	1 635	1 624
54. Medicinal products	BQPL	5 416	5 850	6 279	7 217	9 067	10 103	11 897	12 326	12 321	13 787
55. Toilet preparations	CSCF	2 569	2 446	2 462	2 597	2 714	2 823	3 122	3 105	3 219	3 481
57 & 58. Plastics	BQQA	3 166	3 194	3 144	3 366	3 416	3 526	3 703	3 846	4 298	4 490
6. Manufactures classified chiefly by material	BQQB	22 675	21 243	20 302	22 673	22 781	21 837	23 119	24 458	26 494	27 789
of which:											
63. Wood and cork manufactures	BQQC	250	253	278	255	261	270	322	291	255	275
64. Paper and paperboard manufactures	BQQD	2 309	2 197	2 020	2 096	2 081	2 019	2 097	1 996	2 044	2 041
65. Textile manufactures	BQQE	3 421	3 259	3 020	3 051	3 022	2 847	2 956	2 846	2 645	2 704
67. Iron and steel	BQQF	3 637	3 321	2 576	2 848	2 879	2 916	3 319	4 245	5 184	5 138
68. Non-ferrous metals	BQQG	2 774	2 433	2 130	3 171	3 033	2 552	2 567	3 229	3 863	4 868
69. Metal manufactures	BQQH	3 368	3 591	3 553	3 595	3 853	3 660	3 766	3 856	4 067	4 549
7. Machinery and transport equipment[3]	BQQI	79 002	78 011	78 875	87 812	87 240	84 395	79 650	78 377	89 382	110 643
71 - 716, 72, 73 & 74. Mechanical machinery	BQQK	22 329	22 695	21 888	22 140	24 244	22 704	24 231	23 810	25 797	28 373
716, 75, 76 & 77. Electrical machinery	BQQL	34 252	34 464	36 012	42 681	41 997	38 706	30 651	28 623	37 120	55 458
78. Road vehicles	BQQM	14 811	14 550	15 077	15 604	13 845	16 316	17 474	18 489	19 440	19 430
79. Other transport equipment	BQQN	7 610	6 302	5 898	7 387	7 154	6 669	7 294	7 455	7 025	7 382
8. Miscellaneous manufactures[3]	BQQO	21 530	20 563	20 263	21 206	21 948	21 985	22 543	22 919	25 108	26 204
of which:											
84. Clothing	CSCN	3 259	2 976	2 804	2 722	2 578	2 507	2 708	2 729	2 712	2 890
85. Footwear	CSCP	605	535	532	514	484	452	426	419	471	522
87 & 88. Scientific and photographic	BQQQ	6 974	6 705	6 732	7 333	7 775	7 212	7 281	7 041	7 245	7 417
9. Other commodities and transactions	BOQL	1 943	1 896	1 495	1 685	1 023	1 073	863	881	1 121	1 303
Total United Kingdom exports	BOKG	171 923	164 056	166 166	187 936	189 093	186 524	188 320	190 877	211 616	244 542

1 See chapter text. The numbers on the left hand side of the table refer to the code numbers of the *Standard International Trade Classification,* Revision 3, which was introduced in January 1988.
2 Balance of payments consistent basis.
3 Sections 7 and 8 are shown by broad economic category in table G2 of the *Monthly Review of External Trade Statistics.*

Source: Office for National Statistics: 020 7533 6064

19.4 United Kingdom imports: by commodity[1,2]
Seasonally adjusted

£ million

		1997	1998	1999	2000	2001	2002	2003	2004	2005	2006
0. Food and live animals	BQQR	13 318	13 223	13 336	13 310	14 269	14 874	16 452	17 208	18 594	19 930
of which:											
01. Meat and meat preparations	BQQS	2 231	2 006	2 144	2 366	2 689	2 793	3 267	3 439	3 618	3 835
02. Dairy products and eggs	BQQT	1 101	1 112	1 167	1 165	1 245	1 291	1 501	1 609	1 700	1 816
04 & 08. Cereals and animal feeding stuffs	BQQU	1 991	1 806	1 719	1 762	1 957	1 985	2 219	2 308	2 364	2 515
05. Vegetables and fruit	BQQV	3 898	4 017	4 040	3 894	4 101	4 374	4 766	4 918	5 447	5 848
1. Beverages and tobacco	BQQW	3 593	4 027	4 451	4 350	4 216	4 501	4 735	4 939	5 102	5 219
11. Beverages	EGAT	2 610	2 881	3 064	2 910	2 854	3 028	3 237	3 474	3 625	3 718
12. Tobacco	EMAI	983	1 146	1 387	1 440	1 362	1 473	1 498	1 465	1 477	1 501
2. Crude materials	ENVB	5 670	5 076	4 861	5 816	5 921	5 420	5 525	5 718	6 128	7 135
of which:											
24. Wood, lumber and cork	ENVC	1 239	1 100	1 088	1 193	1 168	1 236	1 366	1 337	1 357	1 456
25. Pulp and waste paper	EQAH	572	477	510	763	606	488	489	480	477	513
26. Textile fibres	EQAP	590	452	413	412	393	361	337	340	314	299
28. Metal ores	EHAA	1 460	1 314	1 308	1 811	1 997	1 448	1 430	1 648	1 999	2 679
3. Fuels	BQAT	6 824	4 892	5 428	10 016	10 795	10 279	12 311	17 547	25 920	31 727
33. Petroleum and petroleum products	ENXO	5 679	3 976	4 675	9 048	9 525	9 213	11 232	15 307	21 988	26 814
32, 34 & 35. Coal, gas and electricity	BPBI	1 145	916	753	968	1 270	1 066	1 079	2 240	3 932	4 913
4. Animal and vegetable oils and fats	EHAB	603	555	568	491	521	538	614	622	641	785
5. Chemicals	ENGA	17 405	17 379	18 619	20 633	22 745	23 987	26 139	27 927	29 208	31 927
of which:											
51. Organic chemicals	EHAC	4 462	4 508	4 788	5 374	5 529	5 673	6 102	6 801	7 183	7 739
52. Inorganic chemicals	EHAE	1 107	1 015	1 056	1 046	1 171	1 070	1 094	1 366	1 507	2 121
53. Colouring materials	CSCR	975	1 003	956	1 002	975	952	1 003	1 060	1 073	1 122
54. Medicinal products	EHAF	3 100	3 305	4 124	4 714	6 149	7 288	8 189	8 372	8 503	9 210
55. Toilet preparations	CSCS	1 506	1 617	1 774	2 005	2 261	2 499	2 745	2 881	3 035	3 350
57 & 58. Plastics	EHAG	4 168	3 903	3 819	4 144	4 096	4 063	4 403	4 749	5 037	5 439
6. Manufactures classified chiefly by material	EHAH	28 007	27 695	26 930	29 232	30 165	28 735	29 906	32 299	33 469	37 654
of which:											
63. Wood and cork manufactures	EHAI	1 083	1 089	1 145	1 245	1 340	1 436	1 449	1 585	1 506	1 581
64. Paper and paperboard manufactures	EHAJ	4 550	4 504	4 321	4 407	4 864	4 582	4 747	4 841	4 820	5 051
65. Textile manufactures	EHAK	5 003	4 862	4 380	4 365	4 303	4 149	4 089	4 124	3 844	4 043
67. Iron and steel	EHAL	3 337	3 205	2 473	2 731	3 051	3 047	3 237	4 198	4 402	4 957
68. Non-ferrous metals	EHAM	3 625	3 709	2 942	3 711	3 780	3 222	3 320	3 617	3 923	6 193
69. Metal manufactures	EHAN	3 561	3 721	3 789	4 065	4 324	4 501	4 765	4 977	5 355	5 845
7. Machinery and transport equipment[3]	EHAO	80 518	83 300	90 183	102 420	105 386	107 556	101 473	103 883	117 321	146 751
71 - 716, 72, 73 & 74. Mechanical machinery	EHAQ	17 037	17 156	17 313	17 867	18 618	18 901	18 951	19 725	21 851	22 771
716, 75, 76 & 77. Electrical machinery	EHAR	35 792	36 900	42 423	53 631	50 842	49 917	43 656	45 497	55 736	81 701
78. Road vehicles	EHAS	21 704	22 472	24 000	23 117	26 289	28 449	29 921	30 732	31 434	32 955
79. Other transport equipment	EHAT	5 985	6 772	6 447	7 805	9 637	10 289	8 945	7 929	8 300	9 324
8. Miscellaneous manufactures[3]	EHAU	26 568	27 917	29 042	32 798	35 023	36 889	38 168	39 820	42 176	45 079
of which:											
84. Clothing	CSDR	6 630	7 023	7 483	8 495	9 119	9 804	10 323	10 639	11 297	11 856
85. Footwear	CSDS	1 912	1 859	2 041	2 001	2 236	2 365	2 375	2 448	2 563	2 705
87 & 88. Scientific and photographic	EHAW	6 067	6 102	6 170	7 273	7 620	7 044	7 049	7 256	7 415	7 704
9. Other commodities and transactions	BQAW	1 759	1 805	1 799	1 846	1 264	1 450	1 604	1 807	1 840	2 026
Total United Kingdom imports	BOKH	184 265	185 869	195 217	220 912	230 305	234 229	236 927	251 770	280 399	328 233

1 See chapter text. The numbers on the left hand side of the table refer to the code numbers of the *Standard International Trade Classification,* Revision 3, which was introduced in January 1988.
2 Balance of payments consistent basis.
3 Sections 7 and 8 are shown by broad economic category in table G2 of the *Monthly Review of External Trade Statistics.*

Source: Office for National Statistics: 020 7533 6064

19.5 United Kingdom exports: by area[1,2]
Seasonally adjusted

£ million

		1997	1998	1999	2000	2001	2002	2003	2004	2005	2006
European Union:[3]	LGCK	..	99 336	101 537	112 459	114 406	114 737	111 286	111 653	121 494	153 589
EMU members:	QAKW	89 504	89 376	91 911	101 621	103 696	103 408	100 054	100 021	108 918	135 686
Austria	CHMY	1 159	1 190	1 168	1 146	1 224	1 265	1 264	1 094	1 332	1 697
Belgium & Luxembourg	CHNQ	8 451	8 445	9 241	10 322	9 893	10 552	11 374	10 511	11 396	14 885
Finland	CHMZ	1 570	1 434	1 354	1 471	1 611	1 442	1 493	1 362	1 514	1 858
France	ENYL	16 601	16 449	16 907	18 577	19 249	18 757	18 885	18 564	19 933	29 251
Germany	ENYO	20 685	20 590	20 464	22 789	23 655	22 064	20 805	21 671	23 026	27 456
Greece	CHNT	1 047	1 045	1 153	1 229	1 124	1 199	1 252	1 413	1 367	1 494
Irish Republic	CHNS	9 357	9 604	10 783	12 372	13 835	15 422	12 224	14 133	16 297	17 516
Italy	CHNO	8 214	8 608	7 831	8 429	8 404	8 506	8 603	8 401	8 791	9 624
Netherlands	CHNP	13 923	12 983	13 632	15 167	14 599	14 011	13 597	12 030	12 718	16 749
Portugal	CHNU	1 752	1 722	1 712	1 660	1 579	1 518	1 453	1 580	1 697	2 360
Spain	CHNV	6 745	7 171	7 526	8 302	8 363	8 490	8 943	9 100	10 678	12 597
Non-EMU members:[3]	BQIA	..	9 935	9 598	10 800	10 678	11 294	11 198	11 627	12 576	17 903
of which:											
Bulgaria	WYUF	..	81	76	85	122	134	154	155	220	230
Czech Rep	FKML	709	713	733	927	1 075	1 031	1 003	975	1 080	1 581
Denmark	CHNR	2 093	2 057	2 054	2 315	2 267	2 729	2 180	2 042	2 314	3 886
Hungary	QALC	435	498	486	613	612	750	856	933	834	858
Poland	ERDR	1 354	1 213	1 169	1 299	1 297	1 318	1 462	1 413	1 653	2 806
Romania	WMDB	..	235	242	381	341	432	509	610	646	625
Slovakia	BQHB	132	103	114	157	203	201	237	224	259	277
Sweden	CHNA	4 451	4 392	4 035	4 211	3 951	3 873	3 823	4 355	4 586	5 224
Other Western Europe:	HCJD	7 851	7 392	6 244	7 223	6 786	6 334	6 629	7 027	9 730	9 105
of which:											
Iceland	EPLW	157	158	159	193	150	131	141	167	179	188
Norway	EPLX	2 609	2 658	1 999	2 018	1 813	1 696	1 886	1 937	2 211	2 094
Switzerland	EPLV	2 955	2 892	2 768	3 061	3 496	3 080	2 786	2 840	4 985	4 105
Turkey	EOBA	1 734	1 562	1 198	1 800	1 150	1 287	1 638	1 903	2 160	2 423
North America:	HBZQ	23 817	24 091	27 582	33 714	33 408	32 261	32 924	32 750	35 006	36 776
of which:											
Canada	EOBC	2 146	2 147	2 532	3 487	3 203	3 107	3 239	3 339	3 277	3 879
Mexico	EPJX	428	516	577	675	681	704	687	629	638	747
USA	EOBB	20 853	21 082	24 040	29 276	29 244	28 197	28 672	28 576	30 912	31 960
Other OECD countries:	HCII	10 900	6 321	6 728	8 028	7 542	7 469	7 824	8 226	8 577	8 709
of which:											
Australia	EPMA	2 454	2 188	2 155	2 699	2 298	2 114	2 289	2 455	2 580	2 479
Japan	EOBD	4 180	3 127	3 300	3 672	3 673	3 583	3 710	3 862	3 900	4 111
New Zealand	EPMB	409	336	324	305	309	311	348	418	415	373
South Korea	ERDM	1 222	666	949	1 350	1 262	1 461	1 468	1 482	1 677	1 746
Oil exporting countries:	HDII	9 426	7 289	5 524	6 031	6 474	6 229	7 615	7 997	10 850	9 057
of which:											
Brunei	QALF	536	247	124	96	59	61	127	67	43	79
Dubai	QALI	866	830	790	966	1 012	940	1 383	2 019	4 656	2 827
Indonesia	FKMR	674	369	385	404	313	324	452	398	366	312
Kuwait	QATB	481	325	293	338	359	308	373	354	426	438
Nigeria	QATE	410	454	447	524	686	711	738	773	799	820
Saudi Arabia	ERDI	3 656	2 605	1 481	1 557	1 525	1 388	1 819	1 611	1 559	1 644
Rest of the World	HCHW	23 881	19 627	18 551	20 481	20 477	19 494	22 042	23 224	25 959	27 306
of which:											
Brazil	FKMO	1 030	899	739	775	808	880	825	790	836	918
China	ERDN	922	860	1 211	1 468	1 709	1 493	1 924	2 372	2 811	3 268
Egypt	QALL	501	505	539	498	452	463	458	667	543	578
Hong Kong	ERDG	3 215	2 671	2 312	2 673	2 683	2 411	2 481	2 632	3 087	2 863
India	ERDJ	1 576	1 242	1 450	2 058	1 772	1 755	2 284	2 235	2 798	2 696
Israel	ERDL	1 178	1 079	1 295	1 516	1 357	1 428	1 359	1 389	1 352	1 307
Malaysia	ERDK	1 206	677	934	907	1 029	877	1 028	995	1 088	877
Pakistan	FKMU	271	228	221	207	229	240	291	344	461	488
Philippines	FKMX	601	301	239	273	392	352	377	315	279	242
Russia	ERDQ	1 233	929	532	668	893	981	1 420	1 466	1 869	2 051
Singapore	ERDH	2 047	1 598	1 597	1 625	1 592	1 445	1 582	1 710	2 078	2 320
South Africa	EPME	1 646	1 520	1 281	1 413	1 534	1 597	1 766	1 877	2 073	2 182
Taiwan	ERDP	1 036	867	865	1 015	875	848	897	951	939	911
Thailand	ERDO	863	386	463	582	594	529	572	637	638	567

1 See chapter text.
2 Balance of payments consistent basis.
3 Includes Bulgaria and Romania after accession on 1 January 2007.

Source: Office for National Statistics: 020 7533 6064

19.6 United Kingdom imports: by area[1,2]
Seasonally adjusted

£ million

		1997	1998	1999	2000	2001	2002	2003	2004	2005	2006
European Union:[3]	LGDC	..	105 048	109 622	117 644	126 973	136 931	137 404	142 512	158 365	191 175
EMU members	QAKX	93 507	95 528	99 332	105 812	114 337	123 301	122 788	126 403	139 299	163 909
Austria	CHNB	1 393	1 410	1 453	1 410	1 888	2 396	2 776	2 354	2 463	2 912
Belgium & Luxembourg	CHNY	9 390	9 831	10 156	10 927	12 159	13 201	13 205	13 845	15 153	18 858
Finland	CHNC	2 544	2 327	2 365	2 765	2 965	2 791	2 663	2 336	2 432	2 862
France	ENYP	18 020	17 949	18 410	18 644	20 127	20 798	20 389	20 132	22 185	30 535
Germany	ENYS	25 632	25 086	26 812	28 462	30 192	32 442	33 667	35 380	39 171	42 764
Greece	CHOB	396	358	388	451	476	555	613	625	702	756
Irish Republic	CHOA	7 391	7 801	8 705	10 261	12 141	13 176	9 920	10 133	10 410	10 737
Italy	CHNW	9 548	9 739	9 383	9 514	9 860	10 675	11 481	12 186	12 675	13 287
Netherlands	CHNX	12 328	13 404	13 768	15 380	15 395	16 143	16 692	18 195	20 437	23 660
Portugal	CHOC	1 763	1 790	1 822	1 735	1 625	1 761	1 966	1 928	2 018	3 611
Spain	CHOD	5 102	5 732	5 966	6 141	7 360	9 190	9 247	9 120	11 452	13 638
Non-EMU members:[3]	BQIB	..	9 506	10 270	11 824	12 636	13 630	14 616	16 109	19 066	27 266
of which:											
Bulgaria	WYUT	..	76	69	85	101	116	124	150	169	201
Czech Rep	FKMM	450	560	580	802	1 097	1 250	1 412	1 291	1 883	2 575
Denmark	CHNZ	2 316	2 154	2 341	2 630	2 922	3 595	3 399	3 357	4 395	6 247
Hungary	QALD	465	544	668	683	710	846	1 120	1 579	1 859	2 102
Poland	ERED	597	668	676	905	1 166	1 265	1 545	1 834	2 318	4 093
Romania	WMDC	..	228	253	336	448	522	679	786	803	848
Slovakia	BQHC	71	74	102	136	177	211	259	261	369	662
Sweden	CHND	4 693	4 360	4 648	4 951	4 671	4 330	4 568	5 118	5 461	6 340
Other Western Europe:	HBTS	10 755	9 701	10 554	13 040	12 240	12 523	13 331	15 726	20 072	23 419
of which:											
Iceland	EPMW	229	251	282	365	281	289	296	355	346	402
Norway	EPMX	4 666	3 440	3 546	5 563	5 523	5 258	6 423	8 479	12 078	14 440
Switzerland	EPMV	4 636	4 755	5 341	5 485	4 544	4 595	3 759	3 439	3 882	4 380
Turkey	EOBU	990	1 103	1 204	1 450	1 669	2 164	2 619	3 246	3 511	3 952
North America:	HCRB	27 277	27 815	28 035	33 460	34 617	29 811	27 480	27 087	27 128	31 596
of which:											
Canada	EOBW	2 480	2 519	3 026	4 009	3 664	3 563	3 664	4 187	4 155	5 012
Mexico	EPJY	371	366	395	613	680	505	490	411	446	452
USA	EOBV	24 329	24 785	24 360	28 416	29 345	25 149	22 857	22 067	22 184	25 852
Other OECD countries:	HDJQ	14 636	13 205	13 805	15 717	14 154	13 017	12 989	13 641	14 426	13 759
of which:											
Australia	EPNA	1 320	1 363	1 338	1 543	1 776	1 688	1 789	1 868	2 100	2 126
Japan	EOBX	9 031	9 124	9 118	10 214	9 080	8 079	8 085	8 106	8 670	7 932
New Zealand	EPNB	555	517	565	544	542	522	552	584	592	607
South Korea	ERDY	2 147	2 201	2 784	3 416	2 756	2 728	2 563	3 083	3 064	3 094
Oil exporting countries:	HCPC	3 351	3 201	3 228	4 258	3 969	3 780	3 923	4 865	6 017	7 021
of which:											
Brunei	QALG	282	161	66	95	35	33	51	63	25	71
Dubai	QALJ	286	337	433	401	396	499	722	578	643	683
Indonesia	FKMS	862	854	931	1 081	1 128	1 006	875	917	839	960
Kuwait	QATC	168	164	121	314	296	271	313	396	367	746
Nigeria	QATF	100	121	112	89	65	90	83	106	152	206
Saudi Arabia	ERDU	841	791	783	977	933	677	715	1 158	1 714	1 235
Rest of the World	HCIF	27 730	26 899	29 973	36 793	38 352	38 167	41 800	47 939	54 391	61 263
of which:											
Brazil	FKMP	911	883	910	1 114	1 279	1 365	1 477	1 547	1 739	1 904
China	ERDZ	2 379	2 816	3 384	4 826	5 741	6 726	8 342	10 405	12 963	15 330
Egypt	QALM	256	277	255	411	406	416	432	496	350	666
Hong Kong	ERDS	4 146	4 391	4 909	5 917	5 754	5 561	5 500	5 771	6 601	7 384
India	ERDV	1 546	1 382	1 426	1 651	1 816	1 804	2 093	2 290	2 783	3 140
Israel	ERDX	839	875	996	1 025	939	880	861	923	1 002	971
Malaysia	ERDW	1 931	1 892	1 961	2 288	1 939	1 731	1 867	2 024	1 814	1 905
Pakistan	FKMV	362	340	318	363	421	472	519	554	487	515
Philippines	FKMY	726	855	983	1 155	1 155	944	713	657	712	745
Russia	EREC	1 418	1 406	1 324	1 496	2 047	1 950	2 454	3 511	5 009	5 770
Singapore	ERDT	2 585	2 343	2 348	2 395	2 067	1 959	2 672	3 382	3 829	3 781
South Africa	EPNE	1 323	1 351	1 636	2 553	2 841	2 685	2 949	3 277	3 938	3 927
Taiwan	EREB	2 230	2 217	2 626	3 561	2 784	2 385	2 198	2 344	2 225	2 355
Thailand	EREA	1 166	1 264	1 291	1 602	1 607	1 550	1 646	1 762	1 719	1 935

1 See chapter text.
2 Balance of payments consistent basis.
3 Includes Bulgaria and Romania after accession on 1 January 2007.

Source: Office for National Statistics: 020 7533 6064

19.7 Services supplied (exports) and purchased (imports),[1],[2]: 2004

£ million

	Exports	Imports	Net
Business services			
Legal	1 905	415	1 490
Accounting	793	324	470
Management consulting	1 134	708	426
Advertising	1 614	793	821
Market research	352	169	183
Research and development	4 470	1 806	2 664
Insurance: premiums	34	148	-114
claims	47	19	28
Insurance broking	1 320	43	1 276
Financial Services	4 741	1 059	3 682
Property	70	62	9
Management charges	1 729	1 050	679
Procurement	75	149	-75
Publishing services	290	105	185
Recruitment and training	402	502	-100
Other business services	1 738	788	950
Telecommunications services			
Communications	1 739	1 374	365
Computer	4 347	1 516	2 832
Information	1 396	412	984
Technical services			
Architectural	110	11	99
Engineering (consulting, process etc.)	3 621	1 375	2 246
Surveying	136	47	89
Construction	278	142	136
Agriculture and mining	105	38	66
Other technical	2 008	408	1 601
Miscellaneous services			
Operational leasing	328	329	-1
Cultural services			
TV and radio services	253	78	175
Music services (excluding royalties)	33	11	22
Other cultural	276	162	114
Royalties	6 017	4 255	1 762
Trade related services			
Own account earning	511	81	430
Commission	1 522	488	1 033
Commodity trading	84	635	-551
Management services to affiliated companies	2 172	1 197	975
All other services	1 605	897	709
World Total	**47 256**	**21 596**	**25 659**

1 See chapter text.
2 Due to rounding, the sum of constituent items may not always equal the total shown. Data excludes the following industries: Financial, Film and TV, Travel and Transport, Public Sector (including Education) and Law Society members.

Source: Office for National Statistics: 01633 812607

19.8 International trade in services:[1,2] by country, 2004

£ million

	Exports	Imports	Net
European Union			
Austria	547	141	405
Belgium	1 216	503	713
Cyprus	57	66	-9
Czech Republic	100	52	48
Denmark	431	153	278
Estonia	6	19	-13
Finland	432	83	349
France	2 086	2 069	17
Germany	2 919	1 896	1 022
Greece	176	83	93
Hungary	200	38	162
Irish Republic	2 820	894	1 926
Italy	1 284	611	673
Lithuania	11	8	3
Luxembourg	546	165	381
Malta	19	7	12
Netherlands	3 119	1 084	2 034
Poland	111	61	50
Portugal	265	114	151
Slovakia	15	11	4
Slovenia	9	1	7
Spain	755	532	223
Sweden	572	626	-54
Latvia and EU Institutions	24	7	17
EFTA			
Iceland	24	12	12
Liechtenstein	27	5	23
Norway	607	241	365
Switzerland	2 461	669	1 791
Other European countries			
Russia	248	193	54
Channel Islands	364	92	271
Isle of Man	38	20	18
Turkey	91	36	55
Rest of Europe	216	98	119
Europe Unallocated	2 286	872	1 414
Africa			
Nigeria	144	138	7
South Africa	327	110	218
Rest of Africa	467	276	191
Africa Unallocated	144	36	108
America			
Brazil	66	32	33
Canada	395	211	184
Mexico	94	16	78
USA	11 288	5 361	5 927
Rest of America	1 538	325	1 212
America Unallocated	301	75	226

19.8 International trade in services:[1,2] by country, 2004
continued

£ million

	Exports	Imports	Net
Asia			
China	333	63	270
Hong Kong	287	180	107
India	244	236	7
Indonesia	59	29	29
Israel	134	110	23
Japan	1 838	799	1 039
Malaysia	224	21	202
Pakistan	34	47	-13
Phillippines	34	21	14
Saudi Arabia	184	129	56
Singapore	1 413	252	1 161
South Korea	144	38	106
Taiwan	96	36	60
Thailand	72	36	36
Rest of Asia	2 193	1 038	1 155
Asia Unallocated	314	87	227
Australia and Oceania			
Australia	475	183	292
New Zealand	67	54	13
Rest of Australia and Oceania	67	28	39
Oceania Unallocated	11	6	5
Rest of World Unallocated and International orgainisations	190	160	30
World Total	**47 256**	**21 596**	**25 659**
Economic Zones			
OECD	34 571	16 735	17 836
NAFTA	11 254	5 587	5 668
Central and Eastern Europe	573	265	309
OPEC	992	559	433
ASEAN	1 830	368	1 462
CIS	615	391	225
NICs1	1 939	506	1 433
Offshore Financial centres	3 720	887	2 834
ACP	900	611	290

1 See chapter text.
2 Due to rounding, the sum of constituent items may not always equal the total shown. Data excludes the following industries: Financial, Film and TV, Travel and Transport, Public Sector (including Education) and Law Society members.

Source: Office for National Statistics: 01633 812607

19.9 Summary of balance of payments,[1] 2005
United Kingdom

£ million

	Credits	Debits
1. Current account		
A. Goods and services	325 946	370 420
1. Goods	211 616	280 399
2. Services	114 330	90 021
2.1. Transportation	18 167	20 330
2.2. Travel	16 871	32 781
2.3. Communications	3 276	2 931
2.4. Construction	625	570
2.5. Insurance	1 552	891
2.6. Financial	23 333	5 038
2.7. Computer and information	6 026	2 182
2.8. Royalties and licence fees	7 585	5 202
2.9. Other business	32 603	16 769
2.10. Personal, cultural and recreational	2 293	851
2.11. Government	1 999	2 476
B. Income	187 430	160 014
1. Compensation of employees	1 211	1 146
2. Investment income	186 219	158 868
2.1 Direct investment	79 446	35 878
2.2 Portfolio investment	45 066	45 646
2.3 Other investment (including earnings on reserve assets)	61 707	77 344
C. Current transfers	17 279	29 386
1. Central government	4 088	13 537
2. Other sectors	13 191	15 849
Total current account	**530 655**	**559 820**
2. Capital and financial accounts		
A. Capital account	4 310	2 819
1. Capital transfers	3 973	2 224
2. Acquisition/disposal of non-produced, non-financial assets	337	595
B. Financial account	754 174	723 869
1. Direct investment	107 794	50 002
Abroad		50 002
1.1. Equity capital		15 986
1.2. Reinvested earnings		42 236
1.3. Other capital[2]		−8 220
In United Kingdom	107 794	
1.1. Equity capital	84 555	
1.2. Reinvested earnings	10 107	
1.3. Other capital[3]	13 132	
2. Portfolio investment	125 639	166 109
Assets		166 109
2.1. Equity securities		64 827
2.2. Debt securities		101 282
Liabilities	125 639	
2.1. Equity securities	2 671	
2.2. Debt securities	122 968	
3. Financial derivatives (net)		2 451
4. Other investment	520 741	504 651
Assets		504 651
4.1 Trade credits		−1 395
4.2 Loans		134 814
4.3 Currency and deposits		372 082
4.4 Other assets		−850
Liabilities	520 741	
4.1. Trade credits	−	
4.2. Loans	240 176	
4.3. Currency and deposits	279 677	
4.4. Other liabilities	888	
5. Reserve assets		656
5.1. Monetary gold		−
5.2. Special drawing rights		−8
5.3. Reserve position in the IMF		−1 911
5.4. Foreign exchange		2 230
Total capital and financial accounts	**758 484**	**726 688**
Total current, capital and financial accounts	**1 289 139**	**1 286 508**
Net errors and omissions	−2 631	

1 See chapter text.
2 Other capital transaction on direct investment abroad represents claims on
  affiliated enterprises less liabilities to affiliated enterprises
3 Other capital transactions on direct investment in the United Kingdom
  represents liabilities to direct investors less claims on direct investors

Source: Office for National Statistics

19.10 Summary of balance of payments: balances (credits less debits)[1]
United Kingdom

£ million

			Current account									
	Trade in goods	Trade in services	Total goods and services	Compensati-on of employees	Investment income	Total income	Current transfers	Current balance	Current balance as % of GDP[2]	Capital account	Financial account	Net errors & omissions
	LQCT	KTMS	KTMY	KTMP	HMBM	HMBP	KTNF	HBOG	AA6H	FKMJ	HBNT	HHDH
1952	−272	123	−149	−22	231	209	169	229	1.4	−15	−229	15
1953	−244	123	−121	−25	207	182	143	204	1.2	−13	−177	−14
1954	−210	115	−95	−27	227	200	55	160	0.9	−13	−174	27
1955	−315	42	−273	−27	149	122	43	−108	−0.6	−15	34	89
1956	50	26	76	−30	203	173	2	251	1.2	−13	−250	12
1957	−29	121	92	−32	223	191	−5	278	1.3	−13	−313	48
1958	34	119	153	−34	261	227	4	384	1.7	−10	−411	37
1959	−116	118	2	−37	233	196	−	198	0.8	−5	−68	−125
1960	−404	39	−365	−35	201	166	−6	−205	−0.8	−6	−7	218
1961	−144	51	−93	−35	223	188	−9	86	0.3	−12	23	−97
1962	−104	50	−54	−37	301	264	−14	196	0.7	−12	−195	11
1963	−123	4	−119	−38	364	326	−37	170	0.6	−16	−30	−124
1964	−551	−34	−585	−33	365	332	−74	−327	−1.0	−17	392	−48
1965	−263	−66	−329	−34	405	371	−75	−33	−0.1	−18	49	2
1966	−111	44	−67	−39	358	319	−91	161	0.4	−19	22	−164
1967	−601	157	−444	−39	354	315	−118	−247	−0.6	−25	179	93
1968	−708	341	−367	−48	303	255	−119	−231	−0.5	−26	688	−431
1969	−214	392	178	−47	468	421	−109	490	1.0	−23	−794	327
1970	−18	455	437	−56	527	471	−89	819	1.6	−22	−818	21
1971	205	590	795	−63	481	418	−90	1 123	2.0	−23	−1 330	230
1972	−736	665	−71	−52	407	355	−142	142	0.2	−35	477	−584
1973	−2 573	803	−1 770	−68	1 074	1 006	−336	−1 100	−1.5	−39	1 031	108
1974	−5 241	1 118	−4 123	−92	1 184	1 092	−302	−3 333	−4.0	−34	3 185	182
1975	−3 245	1 447	−1 798	−102	518	416	−313	−1 695	−1.6	−36	1 569	162
1976	−3 930	2 532	−1 398	−140	1 100	960	−534	−972	−0.8	−12	507	477
1977	−2 271	3 306	1 035	−152	−280	−432	−889	−286	−0.2	11	−3 286	3 561
1978	−1 534	3 777	2 243	−140	138	−2	−1 420	821	0.5	−79	−2 655	1 913
1979	−3 326	4 076	750	−130	155	25	−1 777	−1 002	−0.5	−103	864	241
1980	1 329	3 829	5 158	−82	−1 683	−1 765	−1 653	1 740	0.8	−4	−2 157	421
1981	3 238	3 951	7 189	−66	−1 058	−1 124	−1 219	4 846	1.9	−79	−5 312	545
1982	1 879	3 198	5 077	−95	−1 273	−1 368	−1 476	2 233	0.8	6	−1 233	−1 006
1983	−1 618	4 076	2 458	−89	280	191	−1 391	1 258	0.4	75	−3 287	1 954
1984	−5 409	4 491	−918	−94	1 284	1 190	−1 566	−1 294	−0.4	107	−7 130	8 317
1985	−3 416	6 767	3 351	−120	−877	−997	−2 924	−570	−0.2	185	−1 657	2 042
1986	−9 617	6 403	−3 214	−156	1 850	1 694	−2 094	−3 614	−0.9	135	−122	3 601
1987	−11 698	6 813	−4 885	−174	1 091	917	−3 570	−7 538	−1.8	333	10 764	−3 559
1988	−21 553	4 450	−17 103	−64	817	753	−3 500	−19 850	−4.2	235	17 201	2 414
1989	−24 724	3 643	−21 081	−138	−654	−792	−4 448	−26 321	−5.1	270	18 001	8 050
1990	−18 707	4 337	−14 370	−110	−2 869	−2 979	−4 932	−22 281	−4.0	497	15 083	6 701
1991	−10 223	4 102	−6 121	−63	−3 244	−3 307	−1 231	−10 659	−1.8	290	5 269	5 100
1992	−13 050	5 602	−7 448	−49	177	128	−5 534	−12 854	−2.1	421	5 090	7 343
1993	−13 066	6 741	−6 325	35	−226	−191	−5 243	−11 759	−1.8	309	11 332	118
1994	−11 126	6 509	−4 617	−170	3 518	3 348	−5 369	−6 638	−1.0	33	2 126	4 479
1995	−12 023	8 957	−3 066	−296	2 460	2 164	−7 574	−8 476	−1.2	533	2 552	5 391
1996	−13 722	11 204	−2 518	93	463	556	−4 755	−6 717	−0.9	1 260	2 811	2 646
1997	−12 342	14 106	1 764	83	3 231	3 314	−5 918	−840	−0.1	958	−8 771	8 653
1998	−21 813	14 672	−7 141	−10	12 330	12 320	−8 374	−3 195	−0.4	489	9 922	−7 216
1999	−29 051	13 597	−15 454	201	1 069	1 270	−7 533	−21 717	−2.4	747	21 416	−446
2000	−32 976	13 615	−19 361	150	4 390	4 540	−10 012	−24 833	−2.6	1 703	12 604	10 526
2001	−41 212	14 423	−26 789	66	11 598	11 664	−6 759	−21 884	−2.2	1 318	17 503	3 063
2002	−47 705	16 830	−30 875	67	23 376	23 443	−9 081	−16 513	−1.6	932	7 202	8 379
2003	−48 607	19 162	−29 445	59	24 587	24 646	−10 122	−14 921	−1.3	1 466	20 507	−7 052
2004	−60 893	25 918	−34 975	71	26 525	26 596	−10 949	−19 328	−1.6	2 063	5 641	11 624
2005	−68 783	24 309	−44 474	65	27 351	27 416	−12 107	−29 165	−2.4	1 491	30 305	−2 631
2006	−83 691	29 605	−54 086	58	22 743	22 801	−12 104	−43 389	−3.4	713	33 726	8 950

1 See chapter text.
2 Using series YBHA: GDP at current market prices.

Source: Office for National Statistics

19.11 Balance of payments:[1] current account
United Kingdom

£ million

		1996	1997	1998	1999	2000	2001	2002	2003	2004	2005	2006
Credits												
Exports of goods and services												
Exports of goods	LQAD	167 196	171 923	164 056	166 166	187 936	189 093	186 524	188 320	190 877	211 616	244 542
Exports of services	KTMQ	57 962	62 096	67 978	73 616	79 666	84 047	89 987	97 077	107 817	114 330	125 561
Total exports of goods and services	KTMW	225 158	234 019	232 034	239 782	267 602	273 140	276 511	285 397	298 694	325 946	370 103
Income												
Compensation of employees	KTMN	911	1 007	840	960	1 032	1 087	1 121	1 116	1 171	1 211	1 249
Investment income	HMBN	91 421	95 435	103 388	101 952	134 114	139 848	123 505	124 881	141 030	186 219	241 564
Total income	HMBQ	92 332	96 442	104 228	102 912	135 146	140 935	124 626	125 997	142 201	187 430	242 813
Current transfers												
Central government	FJUM	2 828	2 173	1 767	3 542	2 465	4 991	3 663	3 968	4 000	4 088	4 047
Other sectors	FJUN	17 201	10 898	10 597	9 678	8 076	9 453	8 572	8 235	8 917	13 191	12 404
Total current transfers	KTND	20 029	13 071	12 364	13 220	10 541	14 444	12 235	12 203	12 917	17 279	16 451
Total	HBOE	337 519	343 532	348 626	355 914	413 289	428 519	413 372	423 597	453 812	530 655	629 367
Debits												
Imports of goods and services												
Imports of goods	LQBL	180 918	184 265	185 869	195 217	220 912	230 305	234 229	236 927	251 770	280 399	328 233
Imports of services	KTMR	46 758	47 990	53 306	60 019	66 051	69 624	73 157	77 915	81 899	90 021	95 956
Total imports of goods and services	KTMX	227 676	232 255	239 175	255 236	286 963	299 929	307 386	314 842	333 669	370 420	424 189
Income												
Compensation of employees	KTMO	818	924	850	759	882	1 021	1 054	1 057	1 100	1 146	1 191
Investment income	HMBO	90 958	92 204	91 058	100 883	129 724	128 250	100 129	100 294	114 505	158 868	218 821
Total income	HMBR	91 776	93 128	91 908	101 642	130 606	129 271	101 183	101 351	115 605	160 014	220 012
Current transfers												
Central government	FJUO	5 297	5 260	6 787	7 482	8 015	7 584	9 296	10 944	12 304	13 537	14 015
Other sectors	FJUP	19 487	13 729	13 951	13 271	12 538	13 619	12 020	11 381	11 562	15 849	14 540
Total current transfers	KTNE	24 784	18 989	20 738	20 753	20 553	21 203	21 316	22 325	23 866	29 386	28 555
Total	HBOF	344 236	344 372	351 821	377 631	438 122	450 403	429 885	438 518	473 140	559 820	672 756
Balances												
Trade in goods and services												
Trade in goods	LQCT	−13 722	−12 342	−21 813	−29 051	−32 976	−41 212	−47 705	−48 607	−60 893	−68 783	−83 691
Trade in services	KTMS	11 204	14 106	14 672	13 597	13 615	14 423	16 830	19 162	25 918	24 309	29 605
Total trade in goods and services	KTMY	−2 518	1 764	−7 141	−15 454	−19 361	−26 789	−30 875	−29 445	−34 975	−44 474	−54 086
Income												
Compensation of employees	KTMP	93	83	−10	201	150	66	67	59	71	65	58
Investment income	HMBM	463	3 231	12 330	1 069	4 390	11 598	23 376	24 587	26 525	27 351	22 743
Total income	HMBP	556	3 314	12 320	1 270	4 540	11 664	23 443	24 646	26 596	27 416	22 801
Current transfers												
Central government	FJUQ	−2 469	−3 087	−5 020	−3 940	−5 550	−2 593	−5 633	−6 976	−8 304	−9 449	−9 968
Other sectors	FJUR	−2 286	−2 831	−3 354	−3 593	−4 462	−4 166	−3 448	−3 146	−2 645	−2 658	−2 136
Total current transfers	KTNF	−4 755	−5 918	−8 374	−7 533	−10 012	−6 759	−9 081	−10 122	−10 949	−12 107	−12 104
Total (Current balance)	HBOG	−6 717	−840	−3 195	−21 717	−24 833	−21 884	−16 513	−14 921	−19 328	−29 165	−43 389

1 See chapter text.

Source: Office for National Statistics

19.12 Balance of payments:[1] summary of international investment position, financial account and investment income

United Kingdom
£ billion

		1996	1997	1998	1999	2000	2001	2002	2003	2004	2005	2006
Investment abroad												
International investment position												
Direct investment	HBWD	211.7	232.4	309.8	438.3	618.8	616.9	637.2	691.1	689.0	752.7	757.5
Portfolio investment	HHZZ	548.3	651.0	703.8	838.3	906.1	937.4	844.0	935.8	1 092.3	1 374.2	1 558.7
Other investment	HLXV	851.7	1 070.4	1 107.7	1 129.7	1 427.5	1 573.1	1 635.8	1 885.1	2 156.2	2 739.1	2 939.8
Reserve assets	LTEB	27.3	22.8	23.3	22.2	28.8	25.6	25.5	23.8	23.3	24.7	22.9
Total	HBQA	1 638.9	1 976.5	2 144.7	2 428.5	2 981.2	3 153.1	3 142.4	3 535.8	3 960.7	4 890.7	5 279.0
Financial account transactions												
Direct investment	-HJYP	23.5	37.3	73.8	125.6	155.6	42.8	35.0	40.9	53.8	50.0	43.2
Portfolio investment	-HHZC	59.8	51.9	32.1	21.4	65.6	86.6	1.0	36.3	140.9	166.1	194.1
Financial derivatives (net)	-ZPNN	-1.0	-1.2	3.0	-2.7	-1.6	-8.4	-1.0	5.4	7.9	2.5	14.3
Other investment	-XBMM	136.7	169.4	14.9	59.6	276.0	174.1	97.2	255.9	325.6	504.7	405.0
Reserve assets	-LTCV	-0.5	-2.4	-0.2	-0.6	3.9	-3.1	-0.5	-1.6	0.2	0.7	-0.4
Total	-HBNR	218.5	255.1	123.6	203.2	499.5	292.0	131.8	336.9	528.3	723.9	656.2
Investment income												
Direct investment	HJYW	28.6	29.5	29.9	33.1	45.0	46.7	51.5	55.1	64.4	79.4	90.4
Portfolio investment	HLYX	20.2	23.8	29.3	25.9	33.0	34.9	32.5	32.5	36.7	45.1	54.9
Other investment	AIOP	41.0	40.8	43.0	41.8	55.1	57.3	38.7	36.4	39.2	61.0	95.6
Reserve assets	HHCB	1.6	1.4	1.1	1.2	1.0	1.0	0.8	0.8	0.7	0.7	0.7
Total	HMBN	91.4	95.4	103.4	102.0	134.1	139.8	123.5	124.9	141.0	186.2	241.6
Investment in the UK												
International investment position												
Direct investment	HBWI	152.6	173.7	213.6	250.2	310.4	363.5	340.6	355.5	384.4	501.2	578.3
Portfolio investment	HLXW	480.0	583.3	692.7	828.8	998.2	958.5	892.3	1 047.3	1 177.8	1 409.7	1 620.1
Other investment	HLYD	1 061.7	1 274.3	1 355.0	1 403.9	1 696.4	1 889.6	1 945.8	2 177.1	2 509.4	3 120.1	3 345.8
Total	HBQB	1 694.4	2 031.3	2 261.4	2 482.9	3 005.0	3 211.5	3 178.7	3 579.9	4 071.6	5 031.0	5 544.2
Financial account transactions												
Direct investment	HJYU	17.6	22.9	45.1	55.1	80.6	37.3	16.8	16.8	42.4	107.8	75.8
Portfolio investment	HHZF	43.0	26.8	20.9	114.1	164.5	48.1	51.0	95.2	87.2	125.6	173.6
Other investment	XBMN	160.7	196.7	67.6	55.5	267.0	224.0	71.2	245.4	404.3	520.7	440.4
Total	HBNS	221.3	246.4	133.5	224.6	512.1	309.5	139.0	357.4	534.0	754.2	689.9
Investment income												
Direct investment	HJYX	16.6	14.9	8.6	17.0	27.4	21.4	16.0	21.9	27.9	35.9	46.9
Portfolio investment	HLZC	23.8	26.5	29.5	31.1	31.0	34.5	32.1	31.6	36.4	45.6	55.5
Other investment	HLZN	50.6	50.8	53.0	52.8	71.3	72.3	52.1	46.8	50.2	77.3	116.4
Total	HMBO	91.0	92.2	91.1	100.9	129.7	128.3	100.1	100.3	114.5	158.9	218.8
Net investment												
International investment position												
Direct investment	HBWQ	59.0	58.6	96.2	188.1	308.4	253.5	296.6	335.6	304.6	251.5	179.2
Portfolio investment	CGNH	68.3	67.7	11.1	9.5	-92.2	-21.1	-48.3	-111.5	-85.5	-35.5	-61.4
Other investment	CGNG	-210.1	-204.0	-247.3	-274.2	-268.9	-316.5	-310.0	-292.0	-353.2	-381.1	-405.9
Reserve assets	LTEB	27.3	22.8	23.3	22.2	28.8	25.6	25.5	23.8	23.3	24.7	22.9
Net investment position	HBQC	-55.5	-54.8	-116.7	-54.4	-23.9	-58.4	-36.3	-44.1	-110.9	-140.4	-265.2
Financial account transactions												
Direct investment	HJYV	-6.0	-14.4	-28.7	-70.5	-75.0	-5.5	-18.3	-24.1	-11.4	57.8	32.7
Portfolio investment	HHZD	-16.8	-25.2	-11.2	92.7	99.0	-38.4	50.0	59.0	-53.6	-40.5	-20.5
Financial derivatives	ZPNN	1.0	1.2	-3.0	2.7	1.6	8.4	1.0	-5.4	-7.9	-2.5	-14.3
Other investment	HHYR	24.1	27.3	52.8	-4.1	-9.0	49.9	-26.0	-10.5	78.7	16.1	35.5
Reserve assets	LTCV	0.5	2.4	0.2	0.6	-3.9	3.1	0.5	1.6	-0.2	-0.7	0.4
Net transactions	HBNT	2.8	-8.8	9.9	21.4	12.6	17.5	7.2	20.5	5.6	30.3	33.7
Investment income												
Direct investment	HJYE	12.0	14.6	21.3	16.1	17.6	25.3	35.5	33.2	36.5	43.6	43.5
Portfolio investment	HLZX	-3.5	-2.7	-0.2	-5.2	2.0	0.4	0.4	0.9	0.3	-0.6	-0.6
Other investment	CGNA	-9.5	-10.0	-10.0	-11.0	-16.2	-15.1	-13.3	-10.3	-11.0	-16.3	-20.8
Reserve assets	HHCB	1.6	1.4	1.1	1.2	1.0	1.0	0.8	0.8	0.7	0.7	0.7
Net earnings	HMBM	0.5	3.2	12.3	1.1	4.4	11.6	23.4	24.6	26.5	27.4	22.7

1 See chapter text.

Source: Office for National Statistics

19.13 Net outward foreign direct investment by United Kingdom companies:[1,2] by area and main country

£ million

		2001	2002	2003	2004	2005
Europe	GQBX	13 743	27 300	16 600	10 814	13 857
EU25	DG7S	12 507	28 865	13 339	11 900	16 931
Austria	CBJD	1 628	797	165	1 322	−395
Belgium	HIIL	103	1 046	−1 241	−544	878
Cyprus	DG8D	−13	−79	−53	18	20
Czech Republic	DG8O	216	49	142	23	8
Denmark	CAUW	−423	543	−53	569	108
Estonia	DG8E	6	5	4	21	6
Finland	CBJE	61	1 124	99	−37	701
France	CAUX	2 794	4 112	6 627	793	3 510
Germany	CAUY	724	8 473	1 552	−366	19
Greece	CAUZ	156	−65	229	−253	52
Hungary	DG8F	746	163	527	336	1 818
Irish Republic	CAVA	2 698	1 674	985	3 325	−363
Italy	CAVB	612	572	500	667	768
Latvia	DG8G	..	1	..	1	−1
Lithuania	DG8H	..	..	..	1	−4
Luxembourg	HIIM	1 019	−2 046	1 313	−1 022	3 425
Malta	DG8I	32	..	58	178	28
Netherlands	CAVC	4 324	13 152	728	4 805	3 058
Poland	DG8J	304	431	4	182	109
Portugal	CAVD	144	88	308	444	248
Slovakia	DG8K	−8	−22	−11	18	19
Slovenia	DG8L	..	..	37	−5	−4
Spain	CAVE	−1 564	288	626	1 131	−43
Sweden	CBJG	−1 134	−35	794	299	2 974
EFTA	CAVG	−1 569	994	2 313	−6 667	75
of which						
Norway	CBJF	508	−329	−274	367	−828
Switzerland	CBJH	−2 077	1 329	2 591	−7 007	856
Other European Countries	DG8M	2 805	−2 559	948	5 582	−3 148
of which						
Russia	GLAA	498	108	2 030	1 831	313
UK offshore islands	GLAC	1 346	−1 249	−1 031	3 528	−3 732
America	GQBZ	23 987	−5 150	15 959	24 321	23 063
of which						
Bermuda	CBKZ	801	−4 371	−2 613	6 242	667
Brazil	CBLA	352	17	786	386	−147
Canada	CAVK	4 142	536	2 521	1 143	3 416
Chile	GQCA	292	1 021	290	675	819
Colombia	GQCB	57	−385	78	225	−715
Mexico	GLAD	−139	939	261	1 386	145
Panama	GLAE	−19	19	58	12	27
USA	CAVJ	15 865	−984	19 300	9 732	17 917
Asia	GQCI	524	5 538	3 601	7 689	4 631
Near and Middle East Countries	CBKF	822	376	82	486	459
of which						
Gulf Arabian countries[3]	GQCC	738	369	−85	293	651
Other Asian Countries	GQCD	−297	5 162	3 518	7 203	4 172
of which						
China	HIIN	662	757	309	539	549
Hong Kong	CAVN	590	1 186	1 285	5 303	1 101
India	GLAF	135	276	193	274	515
Indonesia	GLAG	−31	70	481	−289	−109
Japan	CAVM	−4 219	388	338	37	54
Malaysia	CBKN	−321	334	277	428	243
Singapore	CBKQ	1 681	1 619	−449	−161	−621
South Korea	GLAH	−	174	332	278	2 292
Thailand	GLAI	173	−55	155	181	259
Australasia and Oceania	GQCE	1 478	3 677	−1 524	1 026	−2 289
of which						
Australia	CBJO	1 787	3 322	−492	408	−2 156
New Zealand	CBJP	−323	337	−1 017	258	−169
Africa	GQCF	1 152	2 196	3 454	5 863	6 779
of which						
Kenya	GLAJ	42	32	58	47	71
Nigeria	CBJY	74	220	19	−44	−139
South Africa	CAVO	325	2 265	2 222	3 840	5 716
Zimbabwe	CBKD	40	33	37	91	25
World Total	CDQD	40 884	33 561	38 088	49 713	46 039
OECD	GQCG	28 633	36 096	37 030	18 355	38 628
Central and Eastern Europe[4]	GQCH	1 543	654	156	36	175

1 See chapter text. Net investment includes re-invested earnings.
2 Minus sign indicates net disinvestment abroad.
3 Includes Abu Dhabi, Bahrain, Dubai, Iraq, Kuwait, Oman, Other Gulf States, Qatar, Saudi Arabia and Yemen.

4 From 2003 includes Albania, Bosnia & Herzegovina, Bulgaria, Croatia, FYR of Macedonia, Romiania and Serbia & Montenegro. Prior to 2003 Czech Republic, Estonia, Hungary, Latvia, Lithuania, Poland, Slovakia and Slovenia also included.

Source: ONS FDI Inquiries: 01633 813314; Bank of England

19.14 United Kingdom outward foreign direct international investment position: book value of net assets: by area and main country[1]

At year end   £ million

		2001	2002	2003	2004	2005
Europe	GQCJ	368 465	390 359	408 881	382 104	405 624
EU25	DG8P	330 183	343 931	354 707	348 293	369 252
Austria	CDLZ	2 428	2 679	3 339	4 102	4 137
Belgium	HIIO	6 175	10 364	8 662	7 828	13 322
Cyprus	DG8Q	92	84	80	64	39
Czech Republic	DG8R	858	1 088	954	793	787
Denmark	CDLP	2 607	3 165	3 021	5 256	4 625
Estonia	DG8S	29	29	21	78	14
Finland	CDMA	640	580	588	695	2 454
France	CDLQ	24 683	31 928	31 460	35 313	38 213
Germany	CDLR	13 448	13 924	13 486	12 164	27 184
Greece	CDLS	1 155	498	460	456	605
Hungary	DG8T	1 185	1 403	1 722	1 506	2 568
Irish Republic	CDLT	23 033	29 944	29 989	29 059	27 725
Italy	CDLU	4 267	5 505	10 178	11 322	10 619
Latvia	DG8U	..	51	13	25	22
Lithuania	DG8V	..	24	16	22	16
Luxembourg	HIIP	64 042	62 556	79 208	81 709	87 742
Malta	DG8W	−9	−24	264	1 528	−435
Netherlands	CDLV	164 973	158 478	146 345	131 143	122 017
Poland	DG8X	1 749	2 809	2 900	2 316	1 981
Portugal	CDLW	918	629	973	1 664	1 744
Slovakia	DG8Y	−18	261	332	103	116
Slovenia	DG8Z	89	92	128	54	46
Spain	CDLX	7 091	7 156	9 460	11 318	11 180
Sweden	CDMD	10 747	10 712	11 108	9 776	12 534
EFTA	CDLY	18 931	22 069	27 187	14 468	14 545
of which						
Norway	CDMC	4 340	4 904	4 900	4 934	4 484
Switzerland	CDME	14 584	17 164	21 913	9 104	9 604
Other European Countries	DG92	19 351	24 359	26 987	19 344	21 828
of which						
Russia	GQAA	1 062	744	777	1 627	1 821
UK offshore islands	GQAB	16 579	15 203	22 717	15 678	17 177
America	GQCU	176 685	167 345	178 599	182 091	213 709
of which						
Bermuda	CDOA	6 689	4 929	1 554	7 561	10 603
Brazil	CDOB	2 976	2 050	2 532	3 922	2 942
Canada	CDML	10 328	8 209	8 537	8 922	13 370
Chile	GQCT	1 895	2 036	1 919	2 133	2 798
Colombia	GQCS	1 272	1 752	2 434	1 874	1 097
Mexico	GQAC	887	1 450	1 431	2 461	2 984
Panama	GQAD	204	192	153	132	166
USA	CDMM	143 359	131 800	150 021	140 321	162 883
Asia	GQCL	30 044	28 914	43 118	47 311	57 829
Near and Middle East Countries	CDNH	2 344	1 619	1 559	3 008	3 734
of which						
Gulf Arabian countries[2]	GQCM	1 482	1 027	1 211	2 062	3 033
Other Asian Countries	GQCR	27 700	27 295	41 559	44 303	54 095
of which						
China	HIIQ	2 106	3 212	1 809	1 882	2 713
Hong Kong	CDNN	6 638	5 872	17 221	19 165	23 486
India	GQAE	1 488	1 409	1 555	1 682	2 040
Indonesia	GQAF	1 612	1 014	1 309	1 178	1 202
Japan	CDMP	1 754	1 896	2 361	5 829	6 006
Malaysia	CDNQ	2 390	1 214	1 476	1 592	1 458
Singapore	CDNT	5 947	6 797	9 510	6 610	7 074
South Korea	GQAG	547	927	1 339	1 218	4 597
Thailand	GQAH	831	1 513	1 357	947	1 242
Australasia and Oceania	GQCN	15 487	16 652	17 486	16 888	13 982
of which						
Australia	CDMO	13 700	13 936	16 283	14 586	12 030
New Zealand	CDMQ	1 560	2 524	1 060	1 459	1 060
Africa	GQCQ	8 948	13 516	17 039	17 350	22 210
of which						
Kenya	GQAI	294	278	285	238	291
Nigeria	CDNA	1 044	1 012	1 028	950	902
South Africa	CDMR	4 148	8 765	11 250	10 964	15 634
Zimbabwe	CDNF	166	62	48	103	52
World Total	CDOO	599 628	616 786	665 123	645 744	713 355
OECD	GQCO	522 287	527 681	563 769	537 109	588 116
Central & Eastern Europe[3]	GQCP	4 349	6 449	560	534	652

1 See chapter text.
2 Includes Abu Dhabi, Bahrain, Dubai, Iraq, Kuwait, Oman, Other Gulf States, Qatar, Saudi Arabia and Yemen.
3 From 2003 includes Albania, Bosnia & Herzegovina, Bulgaria, Croatia, FYR of Macedonia, Romiania and Serbia & Montenegro. Prior to 2003 Czech Republic, Estonia, Hungary, Latvia, Lithuania, Poland, Slovakia and Slovenia also included.

Sources: ONS Foreign Direct Investment Inquiries: 01633 813314; Bank of England

19.15 Net earnings from foreign direct investment overseas by United Kingdom companies:[1,2] by area and main country

£ million

		2001	2002	2003	2004	2005
Europe	GQCV	24 719	26 598	26 857	25 782	33 186
EU25	DG93	22 092	23 151	22 972	20 686	26 188
Austria	CBLQ	68	267	317	296	299
Belgium	HIIR	570	545	324	653	818
Cyprus	DG94	26	93	20	22	26
Czech Republic	DG95	132	115	165	110	96
Denmark	CAWI	227	54	197	272	381
Estonia	DG96	2	4	9	3	..
Finland	CBLR	73	95	103	112	105
France	CAWJ	1 610	1 904	1 714	2 107	3 339
Germany	CAWK	679	2 199	1 592	2 328	2 856
Greece	CAWL	95	120	120	102	162
Hungary	DG97	182	232	241	202	281
Irish Republic	CAWM	2 123	1 553	2 197	2 461	2 860
Italy	CAWN	585	517	639	708	581
Latvia	DG98	..	..	−	−	1
Lithuania	DG99	..	..	−	−	..
Luxembourg	HIIS	2 163	1 822	1 500	2 191	2 808
Malta	DG9A	24	36	41	60	26
Netherlands	CAWO	11 465	11 395	11 691	6 651	8 845
Poland	DG9B	194	210	290	218	283
Portugal	CAWP	182	115	175	191	239
Slovakia	DG9C	..	21	..	..	29
Slovenia	DG9D	..	..	..	..	15
Spain	CAWQ	627	672	576	694	737
Sweden	CBLT	970	1 115	959	1 271	1 395
EFTA	CAWS	1 010	1 643	1 761	2 382	3 642
of which						
Norway	CBLS	450	293	319	297	933
Switzerland	CBLU	559	1 349	1 441	2 084	2 708
Other European Countries	DG9E	1 617	1 804	2 124	2 713	3 355
of which						
Russia	GQAJ	297	334	345	841	1 663
UK offshore islands	GQAK	916	1 127	1 332	1 602	1 249
America	GQCX	13 529	14 716	17 586	21 113	25 411
of which						
Bermuda	CBNK	−90	203	1 254	1 629	1 561
Brazil	CBNL	344	378	291	652	701
Canada	CAWW	864	1 015	1 055	1 340	1 827
Chile	GQCY	156	199	273	820	1 141
Colombia	GQCZ	190	200	234	379	411
Mexico	GQAL	−48	295	207	485	452
Panama	GQAM	45	44	55	44	45
USA	CAWV	10 646	11 461	12 723	14 332	17 687
Asia	GQDA	4 356	4 755	5 108	8 001	10 722
Near and Middle East Countries	CBMS	596	398	461	692	1 028
of which						
Gulf Arabian countries[3]	GQDB	420	335	370	549	665
Other Asian Countries	GQDC	3 761	4 357	4 647	7 309	9 695
of which						
China	HIIT	340	255	278	370	571
Hong Kong	CAYB	341	610	1 083	2 541	3 474
India	GQAN	324	496	511	427	534
Indonesia	GQAO	150	132	184	155	208
Japan	CAWY	382	181	332	440	480
Malaysia	CBNA	277	448	477	525	514
Singapore	CBND	1 276	1 053	911	1 651	2 533
South Korea	GQAP	111	233	237	340	587
Thailand	GQAQ	166	162	160	159	221
Australasia and Oceania	GQDD	1 651	2 337	2 022	3 623	3 098
of which						
Australia	CBMB	1 337	1 818	1 518	3 108	2 641
New Zealand	CBMC	304	488	478	279	334
Africa	GQDE	1 849	2 973	2 959	3 958	5 434
of which						
Kenya	GQAR	70	64	81	64	75
Nigeria	CBML	95	282	122	153	192
South Africa	CAWZ	983	1 784	1 693	2 706	3 426
Zimbabwe	CBMQ	61	37	43	87	24
World Total	GLAB	46 103	51 379	54 531	62 476	77 853
OECD	GQDF	36 732	40 229	41 353	43 453	53 919
Central & Eastern Europe[4]	GQDG	791	802	195	74	74

1 See chapter text. A minus sign indicates net losses.
2 Net earnings equal profits of overseas branches plus UK companies' receipts of interest and their share of profits of overseas subsidiaries and associates. Earnings are after deducting provisions for depreciation and withholding tax on profits, dividends and interest.

3 Includes Abu Dhabi, Bahrain, Dubai, Iraq, Kuwait, Oman, Other Gulf States, Qatar, Saudi Arabia and Yemen.
4 From 2003 includes Albania, Bosnia & Herzegovina, Bulgaria, Croatia, FYR of Macedonia, Romiania and Serbia & Montenegro. Prior to 2003 Czech Republic, Estonia, Hungary, Latvia, Lithuania, Poland, Slovakia and Slovenia also included.

Source: ONS FDI Inquiries: 01633 813314; Bank of England

19.16 Net inward foreign direct investment in the United Kingdom:[1,2] by area and main country

£ million

		2001	2002	2003	2004	2005
Europe	GQDH	17 213	15 431	7 013	29 901	81 628
EU25	DG9F	17 509	15 721	5 498	26 412	72 347
Austria	CBOB	−149	..	8	−31	172
Belgium	HIIU	−23	−333	218	1 542	252
Cyprus	DG9G	1	−3	−	−	5
Czech Republic	DG9H	2	..	−	−	−
Denmark	CAYQ	195	114	321	−11	−1 182
Estonia	DG9I	..	..	−	−	−
Finland	CBOC	26	5	26	32	252
France	CAYR	8 779	1 460	414	1 703	9 634
Germany	CAYS	279	11 340	1 437	11 131	6 802
Greece	CAYT	4	7	33	13	13
Hungary	DG9J	1	..	−	..	1
Irish Republic	CAYU	755	210	206	936	1 031
Italy	CAYV	2 848	−208	−468	1 327	−226
Latvia	DG9K	..	..	..	−	..
Lithuania	DG9L	..	..	..	..	1
Luxembourg	HIIV	196	1	−105	−115	142
Malta	DG9M	1	..	−	−	1
Netherlands	CAYW	4 256	1 756	2 452	1 226	51 238
Poland	DG9N	4	1	−	−	1
Portugal	CAYX	7	−18	..	..	−6
Slovakia	DG9O	..	..	..	..	..
Slovenia	DG9P	..	..	..	..	..
Spain	CAYY	224	232	518	..	3 816
Sweden	CBOE	106	493	406	−14	394
EFTA of which	CAZB	−944	−298	1 408	3 016	9 242
Norway	CBOD	−227	−137	−179	−798	962
Switzerland	CBOF	−775	−162	1 411	3 488	7 543
Other European Countries of which	DG9Q	648	9	107	473	39
Russia	GQAS	19	8	..	..	..
UK offshore islands	GQAT	622	−8	32	476	−24
America of which	GQDJ	16 056	−2 051	3 396	−4 792	18 523
Canada	CAZF	−261	562	−325	683	1 593
USA	CAZE	15 025	−2 157	2 676	−5 727	15 565
Asia	GQDK	3 132	2 551	−449	4 081	2 890
Near and Middle East Countries	GQAU	287	−26	−34	384	655
Other Asian Countries of which	GQAV	2 845	2 579	−415	3 697	2 236
Hong Kong	GQAW	70	63	63	..	315
Japan	CAZH	2 572	2 352	−543	817	1 547
Singapore	GQAX	78	157	−76	14	42
South Korea	GQAY	1	−26	−20	193	171
Australasia and Oceania of which	GQDL	92	31	310	1 420	3 429
Australia	CBOJ	112	14	309	1 412	3 429
New Zealand	CBOK	−24	18	2	8	−
Africa of which	GQAZ	63	71	7	−43	60
South Africa	CAZJ	51	63	21	−35	12
World Total	CBDH	36 555	16 033	10 276	30 566	106 531
OECD	GQBA	33 980	16 194	8 984	26 762	103 826
Central & Eastern Europe[3]	GQBB	10	−	4	−32	−

1 See chapter text. Net investment includes reinvested earnings.
2 A minus sign indicates net disinvestment in the UK.
3 From 2003 includes Albania, Bosnia & Herzegovina, Bulgaria, Croatia, FYR of Macedonia, Romiania and Serbia & Montenegro. Prior to 2003 Czech Republic, Estonia, Hungary, Latvia, Lithuania, Poland, Slovakia and Slovenia also included.

Sources: ONS Foreign Direct Investment Inquiries: 01633 813314;
Bank of England

19.17 United Kingdom inward foreign direct international investment position: book value of net liabilities: by area and main country[1]

At year end

£ million

		2001	2002	2003	2004	2005
Europe	GQDM	166 532	157 313	158 903	181 198	270 501
EU25	DG9R	151 245	142 514	142 240	161 327	238 833
Austria	CDPF	385	1 003	349	366	563
Belgium	HIIW	2 208	1 765	1 987	4 338	5 149
Cyprus	DG9S	177	68	67	78	100
Czech Republic	DG9T	14	3	9	6	3
Denmark	CDOV	3 955	2 358	2 086	2 359	1 400
Estonia	DG9U	..	..	–	–	–
Finland	CDPG	1 084	767	946	886	725
France	CDOW	35 213	37 195	36 565	41 100	54 108
Germany	CDOX	29 731	37 737	32 260	39 300	46 170
Greece	CDOY	92	89	86	100	135
Hungary	DG9V	13	8	9	12	12
Irish Republic	CDOZ	4 209	4 544	4 769	5 021	6 990
Italy	CDPA	6 522	5 788	4 580	6 708	5 390
Latvia	DG9W	..	..	..	–	..
Lithuania	DG9X	..	..	..	..	..
Luxembourg	HIIX	2 330	4 985	5 627	5 963	7 794
Malta	DG9Y	24	22	21	5	12
Netherlands	CDPB	60 920	39 512	46 876	47 579	97 851
Poland	DG9Z	19	13	10	7	21
Portugal	CDPC	129	97	115	113	128
Slovakia	DGA2	..	..	..	..	..
Slovenia	DGA3	..	..	..	..	..
Spain	CDPD	606	2 303	3 344	4 536	8 784
Sweden	CDPI	3 613	4 254	2 527	2 849	3 489
EFTA	CDPE	10 465	10 951	13 758	15 752	24 952
of which						
Norway	CDPH	832	1 019	831	242	1 061
Switzerland	CDPJ	9 341	9 717	12 439	14 685	21 568
Other European Countries	DGA4	4 822	3 849	2 906	4 120	6 716
of which						
Russia	GQBC	..	..	..	..	..
UK offshore islands	GQBD	4 366	3 393	2 361	3 500	6 108
America	GQDU	151 338	138 156	145 973	140 090	171 996
of which						
Canada	CDPM	8 693	8 718	11 176	12 108	15 023
USA	CDPN	136 967	124 597	130 512	122 069	149 406
Asia	GQDO	19 388	20 323	19 869	24 800	27 279
Near and Middle East Countries	GQBE	1 788	1 697	1 627	2 765	3 002
Other Asian Countries	GQBF	17 600	18 626	18 242	22 035	24 278
of which						
Hong Kong	GQBG	3 613	2 992	..	..	..
Japan	CDPQ	10 900	11 791	11 949	12 300	13 634
Singapore	GQBH	1 591	1 684	830	925	1 017
South Korea	GQBI	108	448	635	635	641
Australasia and Oceania	GQDP	11 167	8 462	14 336	16 804	12 547
of which						
Australia	CDPP	10 997	8 309	14 160	16 631	12 307
New Zealand	CDPR	149	134	158	153	224
Africa	GQBJ	917	427	560	530	488
of which						
South Africa	CDPS	757	250	387	296	186
World Total	CDPZ	349 342	324 680	339 641	363 422	482 814
OECD	GQBK	329 296	307 395	324 491	340 870	454 826
Central & Eastern Europe[2]	GQBL	84	58	34	..	..

1 See chapter text.
2 From 2003 includes Albania, Bosnia & Herzegovina, Bulgaria, Croatia, FYR of Macedonia, Romiania and Serbia & Montenegro. Prior to 2003 Czech Republic, Estonia, Hungary, Latvia, Lithuania, Poland, Slovakia and Slovenia also included.

Sources: ONS Foreign Direct Investment Inquiries: 01633 813314;
Bank of England

19.18 Net earnings from foreign direct investment in the United Kingdom:[1,2] by area and main country

£ million

		2001	2002	2003	2004	2005
Europe	GQDQ	11 250	5 475	10 158	12 676	17 677
EU25	DGA5	10 086	4 447	9 011	11 329	15 586
Austria	CBOR	93	176	111	61	72
Belgium	HIIY	79	38	165	269	247
Cyprus	DGA6	16	16	24	20	28
Czech Republic	DGA7	1	..	–	–	–
Denmark	CBDL	259	253	305	311	384
Estonia	DGA8	..	..	–	–	–
Finland	CBOS	197	70	36	62	68
France	CBDM	1 632	1 322	2 743	3 842	4 610
Germany	CBDN	−633	−1 109	1 754	2 900	4 278
Greece	CBDO	46	64	4	−4	–
Hungary	DGA9	..	..	–	–	1
Irish Republic	CBDP	426	561	578	471	864
Italy	CBDQ	375	−148	174	408	528
Latvia	DGB2	..	..	..	–	–
Lithuania	DGB3	..	..	–	..	..
Luxembourg	HIIZ	74	87	196	289	224
Malta	DGB4	1	..	–	–	1
Netherlands	CBDR	6 972	2 455	2 405	2 585	2 773
Poland	DGB5	2	1	–	–	1
Portugal	CBDS	6	13	49	47	35
Slovakia	DGB6	..	..	..	..	..
Slovenia	DGB7	..	..	..	..	..
Spain	CBDT	203	52	298	37	1 275
Sweden	CBOU	337	599	167	21	184
EFTA	CBDW	816	735	822	849	1 417
of which						
Norway	CBOT	59	40	–	−20	81
Switzerland	CBOV	749	692	794	819	1 252
Other European Countries	DGB8	348	293	325	499	674
of which						
Russia	GQBM	..	..	..	..	..
UK offshore islands	GQBN	313	267	287	468	642
America	GQDV	7 385	7 314	10 013	12 278	14 253
of which						
Canada	CBEA	147	659	639	1 021	1 373
USA	CBDZ	7 204	6 623	9 054	10 981	12 557
Asia	GQDS	1 099	1 214	−781	168	305
Near and Middle East Countries	GQBO	154	33	114	188	217
Other Asian Countries	GQBP	945	1 182	−895	−19	88
of which						
Hong Kong	GQBQ	11	−52	−456	−474	−704
Japan	CBEC	684	1 022	−538	608	539
Singapore	GQBS	114	100	62	32	87
South Korea	GQBT	3	16	−54	23	79
Australasia and Oceania	GQDT	82	432	835	695	769
of which						
Australia	CBOZ	17	396	802	690	749
New Zealand	CBPA	15	3	4	5	16
Africa	GQBU	154	99	59	59	75
of which						
South Africa	CBED	122	97	50	26	27
World Total	CBEV	19 971	14 534	20 283	25 876	33 079
OECD	GQBV	18 988	13 904	19 715	25 471	32 284
Central & Eastern Europe[3]	GQBW	5	2	1	1	–

1 See chapter text. A minus sign indicates net losses.
2 Net earnings equal profits of UK branches plus overseas investors' receipts of interest and their share of the profits of UK subsidiaries and associates. Earnings are after deducting provisions for depreciation and withholding tax on profits and interest.
3 From 2003 includes Albania, Bosnia & Herzegovina, Bulgaria, Croatia, FYR of Macedonia, Romiania and Serbia & Montenegro. Prior to 2003 Czech Republic, Estonia, Hungary, Latvia, Lithuania, Poland, Slovakia and Slovenia also included.

Sources: ONS Foreign Direct Investment Inquiries: 01633 813314;
Bank of England

Research and development

Chapter 20

Research and development

Research and experimental development (R&D) is defined for statistical purposes as 'creative work undertaken on a systematic basis in order to increase the stock of knowledge, including knowledge of man, culture and society, and the use of this stock of knowledge to devise new applications'.

R&D is financed and carried out mainly by businesses, the Government, and institutions of higher education. A small amount is performed by non-profit-making bodies. Gross Expenditure on R&D (GERD) is an indicator of the total amount of R&D performed within the UK: it has been approximately 2 per cent of GDP in recent years. Detailed figures are reported each year in a First Release published in March and the August edition of the ONS's Economic Trends. Table 20.1 shows the main components of GERD.

The ONS conducts an annual survey of expenditure and employment on R&D performed by Government, and of Government funding of R&D. The survey collects data on outturn and planning years. Until 1993 the detailed results were reported in the Annual Review of Government Funded R&D produced by the Office of Science and Innovation (OSI). From 1997 the results have appeared in OSI's Science, Engineering and Technology Statistics publication. Table 20.2 gives some broad totals for gross expenditure by Government (expenditure before deducting funds received by Government for R&D).

The ONS conducts an annual survey of R&D in business. Table 20.4 gives a summary of the main trends up to 2005.The latest set of results from the survey became available in a First Release dated 24 November 2006 and a Business Monitor (MA14) published on 26 January 2007.

Revisions were made to the Business data for the period 2001 to 2004 and were published at the same time as the 2005 BERD first release on 24th November 2006. The format of this report, similar to MA14, was used as it covers all aspects of the R&D data published by ONS.

Because pre-2001 data have been updated previously, the limited potential for companies to provide accurate data six years and more after the event and resource and system limitations, no revisions were made prior to 2001.

Statistics on expenditure and employment on R&D in Higher Education Institutions (HEIs) are based on information collected by Higher Education Funding Councils and HESA (Higher Education Statistics Agency). In 1994 a new methodology was introduced to estimate expenditure on R&D in HEIs. This is based on the allocation of various Funding Council Grants. Full details of the new methodology are contained in SET Statistics available on the Office of Science and Innovation Web Site at www.dti.gov.uk/science

The most comprehensive international comparisons of resources devoted to R&D appear in Main Science and Technology Indicators published by the organisation for Economic Co-operation and Development (OECD). The Statistical Office of the European Union and the United Nations also compile R&D statistics based on figures supplied by member states.

To make international comparisons more reliable the OECD have published a series of manuals giving guidance on how to measure various components of R&D inputs and outputs. The most important of these is the Frascati Manual, which defines R&D and recommends how resources for R&D should be measured. The UK follows the Frascati Manual as far as possible.

For information on available aggregated data on Research and Development please contact Julie Owens on 01633 812789 (e-mail Julie.Owens@ons.gov.uk).

20.1 Cost of research and development: by sector[1]
United Kingdom

£ million and percentages

	1999		2000		2001		2002		2003		2004		2005	
	£m	%	£m	%	£m	%	£m	%	£m	%	£m	%	£m	%
Sector carrying out the work														
Cash terms (£ million)														
Government	1 464	9	1 593	9	1 160	6	1 053	5	1 243	6	1 240	6	1 247	6
Research councils	622	4	647	4	674	4	713	4	825	4	930	5	1 051	5
Business enterprise	11 302	67	11 510	65	11 978	66	12 469	65	12 677	64	12 816	63	13 410	62
Higher education	3 324	20	3 691	21	4 149	22	4 618	24	4 785	24	5 004	25	5 569	26
Private non-profit	266	2	296	2	325	2	374	2	369	2	406	2	487	2
Total	16 978	100	17 736	100	18 286	100	19 228	100	19 898	100	20 396	100	21 764	100
Sector providing the funds														
Cash terms (£ million)														
Government	2 722	16	2 779	16	2 292	12	2 215	11	2 705	13	2 822	14	2 628	12
Research councils	1 211	7	1 317	8	1 512	8	1 713	9	1 947	10	2 084	10	2 574	12
Higher education funding councils	1 157	7	1 276	7	1 474	8	1 626	8	1 665	8	1 804	9	1 928	9
Higher education	143	1	160	1	184	1	208	1	218	1	229	1	265	1
Business enterprise[2]	8 137	48	8 559	49	8 329	46	8 366	44	8 394	42	8 991	44	9 162	42
Private non-profit	701	4	815	5	888	5	962	5	931	5	960	5	1 022	5
Abroad	2 908	17	2 830	16	3 607	20	4 138	22	4 038	20	3 507	17	4 185	19
Total	16 978	100	17 736	100	18 286	100	19 228	100	19 898	100	20 396	100	21 764	100

1 See chapter text.
2 Including research associations and public corporations.

Source: Office for National Statistics: 01633 812789

20.2 Gross central government expenditure on research and development[1]
United Kingdom

£ million

	1999/00		2000/01		2001/02		2002/03		2003/04		2004/05	
	Intra-mural	Extra-mural[2]	Intra-mural	Extra-mural[2]	Intra-mural	Extra-mural[2]	Intra-mural	Extra-mural[2]	Intra-mural	Extra-mural[2]	Intra-mural	Extra-mural[2]
Defence[3]	798	..	932	..	419	1 685	288	2 502	380	2 364	357	2 283
Research councils	644	894	667	1 024	695	1 244	725	1 457	811	1 643	874	1 752
Higher education institutes	-	1 157	-	1 276	-	1 474	-	1 626	-	1 665	..	1 804
Other programmes	275	810	283	841	282	977	297	1 163	338	1 111	327	870
Total (excluding NHS)	1 717	..	1 882	..	1 396	5 380	1 310	6 748	1 529	6 783	1 558	6 709

1 See chapter text.
2 Extramural Includes work performed overseas and excludes monies spent with other government departments.
3 .. Denotes figures no longer available due to MOD revision between the years 1997 - 2000. The details are outlined in Defence Statistics Bulletin 6, which is available at the following web address: www.dasa.mod.uk

Source: Office for National Statistics: 01633 812789

20.3 Intramural expenditure on Business Enterprise research and development:[1] by industry

United Kingdom: At Current Prices and Constant 2005 Prices

£ million

		Total				Civil				Defence		
		2003	2004	2005		2003	2004	2005		2003	2004	2005
Current Prices												
Chemicals	KDWF	3 750	3 831	3 925	KDWP	..	..	..	KDWZ	..	..	..
Mechanical engineering	KDWG	775	818	802	KDWQ	464	507	520	KDXA	311	311	282
Electrical machinery	KJRT	1 317	1 248	1 277	KJTC	1 059	961	970	KJUL	258	287	308
Aerospace	KDWJ	1 652	2 005	2 197	KDWT	871	943	894	KDXD	781	1 061	1 303
Transport equipment	KDWK	995	934	895	KDWU	..	..	..	KDXE	..	..	..
Other manufacturing	KDWL	1 302	1 237	1 204	KDWV	1 197	1 128	1 127	KDXF	105	108	78
Manufacturing: Total	KDWE	9 791	10 073	10 300	KDWO	8 258	8 194	8 213	KDWY	1 533	1 878	2 087
Services	KDWM	2 643	2 516	2 892	KDWW	..	..	2 737	KDXG	..	..	154
Agriculture, hunting and forestry; fishing	HFRV	136	..	127	HFSA	..	..	127	MKFC	–	–	–
Extractive industries	HFRW	41	36	43	HFSB	41	36	43	MKFD	–	–	–
Electricity, gas and water supply	HFRX	36	21	15	HFSC	36	21	15	MKFE	–	–	–
Construction	HFRY	30	..	33	HFSE	..	..	33	MKFF	..	..	–
Other: Total	HFRU	244	227	217	HFRZ	..	..	217	MKFB	..	..	–
Total	KDWD	12 677	12 816	13 410	KDWN	10 977	10 778	11 168	KDWX	1 700	2 039	2 242
2005 Prices												
Chemicals	HFXA	3 926	3 904	3 925	HFXJ	..	..	..	HFYO	..	..	..
Mechanical engineering	HFXB	811	834	802	HFXK	486	517	520	HFYP	326	317	282
Electrical machinery	HFXC	1 379	1 272	1 277	HFYH	1 109	979	970	HFYQ	270	292	308
Aerospace	HFXD	1 730	2 043	2 197	HFYI	912	961	894	HFYR	818	1 081	1 303
Transport equipment	HFXE	1 042	952	895	HFYJ	..	..	..	HFYS	..	..	..
Other manufacturing	HFXF	1 363	1 260	1 204	HFYK	1 253	1 149	1 127	HFYT	110	110	78
Manufacturing: Total	HFWZ	10 252	10 264	10 300	HFXI	8 647	8 349	8 213	HFYN	1 605	1 914	2 087
Services	HFXG	2 767	2 564	2 892	HFYL	..	..	2 737	HFYU	..	..	154
Agriculture, hunting and forestry: fishing	HFSG	142	..	127	HFSL	..	..	127	MKFH	–	–	–
Extractive industries	HFSH	43	37	43	HFSM	43	37	43	MKFI	–	–	–
Electricity, gas and water supply	HFSI	38	21	15	HFSN	38	21	15	MKFJ	–	–	–
Construction	HFSJ	31	..	33	HFSO	..	..	33	MKFK	..	..	–
Other: Total	HFSF	255	231	217	HFSK	..	..	217	MKFG	..	..	–
Total	HFWY	13 274	13 059	13 410	HFXH	11 494	10 982	11 168	HFYM	1 780	2 078	2 242

1 See chapter text.

Source: Office for National Statistics: 01633 812789

20.4 Sources of funds for research and development within Business Enterprises[1]
United Kingdom

£ million and percentages

		Total				Civil				Defence		
		2003	2004	2005		2003	2004	2005		2003	2004	2005
Cash terms (£ million)												
Government funds	KDYM	1 220	1 335	1 150	KDYU	442	208	210	KDZC	778	1 127	939
Overseas funds	KDYN	3 556	2 993	3 617	KDYV	2 993	2 475	2 690	KDZD	564	518	927
Mainly own funds	KDYO	7 900	8 489	8 643	KDYW	7 542	8 095	8 268	KDZE	358	394	375
Total	KDYL	12 677	12 816	13 410	KDYT	10 977	10 778	11 168	KDZB	1 700	2 039	2 242
Percentages												
Government funds	KDYQ	10	10	9	KDYY	4	2	2	KDZG	46	55	43
Overseas funds	KDYR	28	23	27	KDYZ	27	23	24	KDZH	33	25	41
Mainly own funds	KDYS	62	67	65	KDZA	68	75	74	KDZI	21	19	16
Total	KDYP	100	100	100	KDYX	100	100	100	KDZF	100	100	100

1 See chapter text.

Source: Office for National Statistics: 01633 812789

Agriculture, fisheries and food

Chapter 21

Agriculture, fisheries and food

Output and input

(Tables 21.1 and 21.2)

For both tables, output is a net of VAT collected on the sale of non-edible products. Figures for total output include subsidies on products, but not other subsidies.

Unspecified crops include turf, other minor crops and arable area payments for fodder maize. Eggs include the value of duck eggs and exports of eggs for hatching. Landlords' expenses are included within farm maintenance, miscellaneous expenditure and depreciation of buildings and works. Also included within 'other farming costs' are livestock and crop costs, water costs, insurance premia, bank charges, professional fees, rates, and other farming costs.

Other subsidies

Agri-Environment schemes include Environmentally and Nitrate Sensitive Areas, Countryside Stewardship, Countryside Premium, Tir Cymen, Tir Gofal, Moorland, Habitat, Farm Woodland and Organic Farming Schemes. Included in 'other' subsidies are guidance premium for beef and sheep meat production, Pilot Beef and Sheep Extensification Scheme, non-agricultural horse grazing and farm accounts grant as well as historic data for fertiliser and lime grant and payments to small scale cereal producers.

Compensation of employees and interest charges

Total compensation of employees excludes the value of work done by farm labour on own account capital formation in buildings and work. 'Interest' relates to interest charges on loans for current farming purposes and buildings and less interest on money held on short-term deposit.

Rent

Rent paid (after deductions) is the rent paid on all tenanted land including 'conacre' land in Northern Ireland, *less* landlords' expenses and the benefit value of dwellings on that land. Rent received (after deductions) is the rent received by farming landowners from renting of land to other farmers, *less* landlords' expenses and the benefit value of dwellings on that land. Total net rent is the net rent flowing out of the agricultural sector paid to non-farming landowners, including that part of

tenanted land in Northern Ireland. (Although there has been some updating of the technical procedures for calculating this figure, it corresponds with the previous net rent variable.)

Agricultural censuses and surveys

(Tables 21.3, 21.5 and 21.13)

The coverage for holdings includes all main and minor holdings for each country. Northern Ireland data are now based on all active farm business.

Estimated quantity of crops and grass harvested

(Table 21.4)

The estimated yields of sugar beet and hops are obtained from production figures supplied by British Sugar plc, and the main hop producers in England and Wales. In Great Britain potato yields are estimated in consultation with the British Potato Council.

Forestry

(Table 21.6)

Statistics for state forestry are from Forestry Commission and Forest Service management information systems.

For private forestry in Great Britain, statistics on new planting and restocking are based on records of grant aid and estimates of planting undertaken without grant aid, and timber removals are estimated from a survey of the largest timber harvesting companies.

Average weekly earnings and hours of agricultural and horticultural workers

(Tables 21.11 and 21.12)

Prior to 1998, data were collected from a monthly postal survey, which mainly covered male full-time workers. Between 1998 and 2002 the survey collected information on an annual basis via a telephone survey. The survey was reviewed in 2002 and it was concluded that the frequency of the survey should be increased to four times per year to enable the production of more representative annual estimates. The annual sample size has been retained and has been split between four quarterly telephone surveys.

Results for other quarters can be found on the Department for Environment, Food and Rural Affairs DEFRA (website www,defra.gov.uk).

The survey covers seven main categories of workers and provides data which are used by the Agricultural Wages Board when considering wage claims and by in considering the cost of labour in agriculture and horticulture.

Data on earnings represents the total earnings of regular full-time male workers, aged 20 and over. Figures include all payments-in-kind, valued where applicable in accordance with the Agricultural Wages Order. The earnings and hours of hire farm managers are excluded. Part-time workers are defined as those working less than 39 basic hours per week. Casual workers are those employed on a temporary basis.

Fisheries

(Tables 21.14 and 21.15)

Data relating to the weight and value of landings of fish in the United Kingdom (Table 21.14) is generally obtained from sales notes completed at fish market auctions.

Fishing fleet information (Table 21.15) is obtained from vessel registers maintained by DEFRA in England and Wales and the Scottish Executive Agriculture and Fisheries Department.

Estimated average household food consumption – 'Family Food' Expenditure and Food Survey

(Table 21.16)

The Expenditure and Food Survey replaced both the National Food Survey and the Family Expenditure Survey in April 2001. The new survey is a voluntary sample survey of private households throughout the United Kingdom and the results are produced for the financial year ending 31 March each year. This represents a break in the continuity of the data as results from the National Food Survey were produced for Great Britain and for the calendar year ended 31 December.

The basic unit of the survey is the household which is defined as a group of persons living at the same address and sharing common catering arrangements. Each individual aged 16 or over in the household visited is asked to keep diary records, for a two-week period, of daily expenditure on and weight/volume of food and drink brought into the home and expenditure on food and drink eaten out. Children aged between 7 and 15 are asked to keep simplified diaries.

For the year 2004/05 the sample size includes nearly 7,000 households and over 16,000 persons.

21.1 Production and income account at current prices[1]
United Kingdom

£ million

		1996	1997	1998	1999	2000	2001	2002	2003	2004	2005	2006[2]
Output[3]												
1.Total cereals:	C5X5	2 743.2	2 069.6	1 732.9	1 620.2	1 604.3	1 385.7	1 454.7	1 607.6	1 692.0	1 415.2	1 613.9
Wheat	KFKA	1 808.1	1 357.7	1 186.8	1 105.2	1 119.6	876.6	1 033.5	1 093.8	1 217.2	1 000.9	1 158.0
Rye	VQBG	3.5	3.1	2.8	1.8	1.5	1.8	1.2	1.4	1.6	1.3	1.6
Barley	KFKB	868.9	660.8	504.1	474.6	440.8	465.0	382.0	466.8	424.9	375.0	411.9
Oats and summer cereal mixtures	KFKC	61.8	47.3	38.8	37.9	41.6	41.6	37.2	44.7	47.4	37.0	41.5
Other cereals	VQBH	0.9	0.7	0.5	0.8	0.8	0.6	0.9	1.0	0.9	0.9	0.9
2.Total industrial crops	VQBI	906.6	791.2	848.2	782.9	699.3	773.8	860.0	812.8	798.8	806.7	719.7
Oilseeds	VQBJ	287.1	254.2	282.9	224.6	143.8	177.2	220.4	314.3	266.2	278.7	314.9
Oilseed rape	KFKG	272.6	239.4	262.6	194.4	139.0	171.5	217.4	303.8	256.9	261.7	307.1
Other oil seeds	KIBT	14.5	14.8	20.3	30.1	4.8	5.6	2.9	10.4	9.3	17.0	7.8
Sugar beet	KFKH	358.2	329.1	298.5	279.7	252.1	256.4	282.9	279.7	278.1	268.8	168.2
Other industrial crops	VQBK	261.2	207.9	266.8	278.7	303.4	340.3	356.7	218.9	254.4	259.2	236.6
Fibre plants	VQBL	4.2	3.2	2.6	2.3	1.3	1.7	1.0	1.8	1.3	0.9	1.1
Hops	KFKI	18.4	18.5	13.1	12.1	10.4	9.0	7.2	6.1	5.7	5.4	4.4
Others[4]	VQBM	238.6	186.3	251.1	264.2	291.7	329.6	348.4	211.0	247.5	252.9	231.1
3.Total forage plants	VQBO	96.8	93.4	71.0	75.9	80.9	103.4	90.3	103.7	93.3	94.9	85.1
4.Total vegetables and horticultural products	VQBP	1 747.5	1 621.1	1 627.6	1 667.5	1 561.1	1 612.6	1 591.1	1 672.6	1 611.0	1 681.8	1 730.4
5.Total potatoes (including seeds)	KFKO	636.3	390.0	629.4	749.0	452.9	655.6	480.0	516.9	653.5	502.7	624.5
6.Total fruit	KFKQ	292.0	198.5	258.8	256.9	232.2	238.8	251.2	310.3	315.8	381.5	376.9
7.Other crop products including seeds	VQBQ	38.5	42.3	39.4	42.0	37.7	37.5	25.5	31.6	31.0	31.8	32.8
8.Total crop output (Sum 1 to 7)	VQBR	6 460.8	5 206.1	5 207.2	5 194.4	4 668.4	4 807.5	4 752.8	5 055.5	5 195.5	4 914.7	5 183.3
9.Total livestock production	VQBS	5 749.9	5 555.1	4 693.3	4 326.7	4 361.3	4 263.3	4 567.0	4 834.8	4 831.7	4 878.6	5 244.9
Primarily for meat	KFLA	5 162.3	4 834.5	4 099.8	3 929.3	3 970.1	3 640.9	3 864.7	4 100.6	4 180.9	4 222.7	4 446.7
Cattle	KFKU	1 233.7	1 160.9	1 052.6	1 145.2	1 093.7	955.3	1 145.8	1 227.1	1 277.8	1 388.8	1 567.9
Pigs	KFKW	1 363.2	1 201.5	882.7	784.6	800.4	748.6	686.5	671.5	679.4	677.6	686.7
Sheep	VQBT	890.0	822.4	631.1	574.8	616.8	438.0	613.4	697.7	725.5	683.4	702.1
Poultry	KFXX	1 532.5	1 500.6	1 384.7	1 275.8	1 306.5	1 343.9	1 261.3	1 343.1	1 332.4	1 301.8	1 314.6
Other animals	KFKY	142.8	149.1	148.8	148.9	152.6	154.9	157.7	161.2	165.8	171.0	175.5
Gross fixed capital formation	KFLI	587.6	720.6	593.5	397.4	391.2	622.4	702.3	734.1	650.8	655.9	798.1
Cattle	KUJZ	289.4	378.1	297.1	206.9	189.9	366.5	388.5	444.3	332.8	409.9	526.1
Pigs	LUKB	19.1	15.2	5.6	7.0	6.0	6.1	7.9	7.1	8.0	6.8	8.4
Sheep	LUKA	150.0	196.1	154.0	56.7	63.9	122.5	177.5	154.8	178.0	112.6	138.0
Poultry	LUKC	129.2	131.1	136.8	126.8	131.4	127.4	128.4	127.9	132.0	126.6	125.6
10.Total livestock products	KFLF	3 961.2	3 540.3	3 067.1	2 963.4	2 711.0	3 087.6	2 833.6	3 031.5	3 040.0	2 991.6	2 903.3
Milk	KFLB	3 543.4	3 167.6	2 740.7	2 662.1	2 385.8	2 742.3	2 465.9	2 628.6	2 610.5	2 592.9	2 500.7
Eggs	KFLC	354.1	312.3	281.4	254.2	279.8	306.7	314.1	336.9	380.5	349.6	356.6
Raw wool	KFLD	39.9	35.1	23.9	21.4	22.7	17.3	19.1	20.8	20.2	19.6	16.4
Other animal products	KFLE	23.7	25.3	21.0	25.7	22.6	21.2	34.5	45.1	28.9	29.6	29.6
11.Total livestock output (9+10)	VQBV	9 711.1	9 095.4	7 760.4	7 290.0	7 072.2	7 350.9	7 400.6	7 866.3	7 871.7	7 870.2	8 148.1
12.Total other agricultural activities	LUOS	791.1	722.3	689.2	726.0	638.1	632.2	644.2	650.7	696.8	642.0	670.1
Agricultural services	LUKD	608.0	575.0	570.2	609.5	587.0	604.0	601.4	592.3	636.7	630.7	662.3
Leasing out quota	VQBW	183.1	147.2	119.1	116.5	51.2	28.1	42.8	58.5	60.1	11.3	7.8
13.Total inseparable non-agricultural activities	LUOT	362.1	371.6	421.1	430.4	488.3	624.0	559.8	593.7	636.2	702.8	735.8
14.Gross output at market prices (8+11+12+13)	LUOV	17 325.2	15 395.4	14 077.9	13 640.8	12 867.0	13 414.5	13 357.5	14 166.1	14 400.2	14 129.8	14 737.3
15.Total subsidies (less taxes) on product	LUOU	2 782.1	2 587.8	2 436.1	2 373.2	2 187.0	1 923.3	2 131.3	2 174.2	2 387.3	205.9	84.9
16.Output at basic prices (14+15)	KFLT	20 107.3	17 983.2	16 514.0	16 014.0	15 054.1	15 337.8	15 488.8	16 340.3	16 787.4	14 335.7	14 822.1
of which transactions within the agricultural industry												
Feed wheat	LUNQ	67.0	77.3	78.8	64.4	39.8	43.1	39.0	79.2	103.2	86.5	89.6
Feed barley	LUNR	205.6	192.8	163.6	147.9	136.9	151.9	142.9	159.5	149.1	137.9	167.5
Feed oats	LUNS	16.1	11.8	11.5	14.5	12.6	13.1	10.5	11.1	11.6	9.6	12.3
Seed potatoes	LUNT	33.7	9.2	12.7	28.8	8.5	17.0	14.7	5.9	13.5	11.8	22.6
Straw	LUNU	211.6	160.3	222.1	232.9	258.6	291.2	306.5	177.0	209.0	210.8	188.4
Contract work	LUNV	608.0	575.0	570.2	609.5	587.0	604.0	601.4	592.3	636.7	630.7	662.3
Leasing of quota	LUNW	183.1	147.2	119.1	116.5	51.2	28.1	42.8	58.5	60.1	11.3	7.8
Total capital formation in livestock	LUNX	587.6	720.6	593.5	397.4	391.2	622.4	702.3	734.1	650.8	655.9	798.1

21.1
Production and income account at current prices[1]
United Kingdom
continued

£ million

		1996	1997	1998	1999	2000	2001	2002	2003	2004	2005	2006[2]
Intermediate consumption												
17.Seeds	KFME	380.5	337.2	332.1	327.4	263.6	290.8	275.4	286.6	302.5	309.5	329.3
18.Energy	VQDO	647.4	629.9	598.3	621.9	697.9	683.3	647.0	600.0	669.7	770.6	811.8
Electricity	VQDQ	247.6	232.7	231.0	221.7	230.2	240.1	234.8	204.8	209.8	229.2	246.3
Fuels	VQDV	399.8	397.2	367.3	400.2	467.8	443.2	412.2	395.2	459.9	541.4	565.5
19.Fertilisers	KFMM	1 043.3	1 006.9	831.7	756.0	737.8	755.1	752.2	696.1	776.4	769.0	787.0
20.Pesticides	KFMN	646.9	674.6	653.7	621.0	579.4	526.2	531.2	501.1	576.9	545.8	560.9
21.Veterinary expenses	KCPC	297.7	307.8	288.0	270.0	255.8	241.2	250.1	253.4	279.4	272.8	278.2
22.Animal feed	KFMB	3 185.4	2 804.0	2 444.4	2 260.9	2 139.6	2 367.3	2 223.3	2 371.9	2 517.3	2 391.4	2 422.9
Compounds	LUNY	1 959.5	1 772.2	1 523.5	1 402.4	1 283.3	1 398.2	1 376.9	1 348.1	1 449.6	1 321.3	1 436.0
Straights	LUNZ	937.3	749.9	667.0	631.7	667.0	760.9	654.0	774.0	803.8	836.1	717.4
Feed purchased from other farms	LUOA	288.6	281.9	253.9	226.8	189.3	208.1	192.4	249.8	263.9	234.0	269.4
23.Total maintenance[5]	VQDW	1 109.9	1 090.8	1 024.3	1 016.0	941.4	983.0	960.1	971.0	1 016.8	998.7	1 040.0
Materials	KFMO	745.3	720.9	699.2	698.2	651.2	660.1	636.2	641.9	663.4	654.1	680.1
Buildings	KCPB	364.6	369.9	325.1	317.9	290.2	323.0	323.8	329.1	353.3	344.6	359.9
24.Agricultural services	LUOE	608.0	575.0	570.2	609.5	587.0	604.0	601.4	592.3	636.7	630.7	662.3
25.Other goods and services[5,6]	VQDX	2 277.4	2 314.7	2 300.4	2 323.8	2 151.8	2 104.0	2 097.1	2 186.7	2 399.0	2 321.8	2 349.7
26.Total intermediate consumption (Sum 17 to 25)	KCPM	10 196.6	9 741.0	9 043.0	8 806.4	8 354.4	8 554.9	8 337.7	8 458.9	9 174.6	9 010.3	9 242.0
27.Gross value added at market prices (14-26)	LUOG	7 128.6	5 654.5	5 034.9	4 834.4	4 512.6	4 859.6	5 019.7	5 707.2	5 225.5	5 119.5	5 495.3
28.Total consumption of Fixed Capital	KCPS	2 622.5	2 673.9	2 594.7	2 438.2	2 495.5	2 599.9	2 582.7	2 644.8	2 527.7	2 655.1	2 755.2
Equipment	KCPR	1 295.5	1 322.6	1 329.7	1 317.6	1 267.5	1 263.1	1 262.1	1 206.1	1 194.0	1 207.0	1 201.3
Buildings[5,7]	LUOH	679.2	669.2	681.5	701.3	691.0	685.8	688.3	690.6	671.4	671.0	678.6
Livestock	VQEA	647.8	682.0	583.5	419.3	537.1	651.0	632.3	748.2	662.4	777.1	875.3
Cattle	LUOI	313.5	391.3	314.1	208.2	281.2	348.6	353.2	441.2	361.6	489.7	581.4
Pigs	LUOK	17.4	14.6	8.4	7.7	8.0	6.2	8.0	7.9	8.9	7.5	7.0
Sheep	LUOJ	189.4	155.1	117.6	69.6	120.1	169.5	141.7	173.1	167.8	151.4	161.8
Poultry	LUOL	127.6	120.9	143.4	133.8	127.8	126.8	129.4	126.0	124.1	128.5	125.1
29.Net value added at market prices (27-28)	KCPT	4 506.1	2 980.6	2 440.2	2 396.2	2 017.1	2 259.7	2 437.0	3 062.3	2 697.8	2 464.4	2 740.1
30.Compensation of employees[8]	LUOR	1 880.9	1 929.8	1 975.3	2 029.0	1 900.8	1 950.6	1 966.4	1 916.6	2 008.5	2 177.4	2 160.7
31.Other taxes on production	VQEB	−81.2	−84.5	−88.9	−92.4	−92.2	−77.5	−80.6	−82.8	−96.4	−101.7	−102.9
32.Other subsidies on production	VQEC	243.1	188.9	209.5	318.3	297.0	532.3	565.3	621.7	594.3	2 836.3	2 932.4
Animal disease compensation	LUOM	5.5	15.3	14.3	19.8	29.4	23.2	54.1	60.6	49.4	53.6	..
Set-aside	LUON	159.5	90.2	87.7	170.0	127.3	180.1	142.5	176.7	129.5	–	..
Agri-environment schemes[9]	ZBXC	77.9	83.4	107.5	128.5	140.3	164.1	198.0	224.5	262.0	279.0	..
Other including Single Payment Scheme[10]	VQED	0.2	–	–	–	–	164.9	170.7	159.9	153.4	2 503.7	..
33.Net value added at factor cost	LUOQ	7 450.1	5 672.8	4 996.9	4 995.4	4 409.0	4 637.8	5 053.1	5 775.5	5 583.0	5 404.9	5 654.4
34.Rent	KCPV	228.7	255.8	250.1	239.6	224.5	250.5	255.1	268.6	239.5	215.1	204.6
Paid[11]	ZBXE	302.8	335.8	330.6	322.0	303.3	328.5	341.4	360.5	335.9	309.4	301.7
Received[12]	ZBXF	−74.1	−80.1	−80.5	−82.4	−78.8	−78.1	−86.3	−91.9	−96.4	−94.2	−97.1
35.Interest[13]	KCPU	554.9	622.4	688.6	594.2	628.2	559.6	483.5	450.5	510.5	547.7	571.3
Total income from farming (33-30-34-35)	KCQB	4 785.6	2 864.8	2 082.9	2 132.6	1 655.6	1 877.1	2 348.2	3 139.8	2 824.5	2 464.7	2 717.9

1 See chapter text.
2 Provisional.
3 Output is net of VAT collected on the sale of non-edible products. Figures for total output include subsidies on products, but not other subsidies.
4 Includes straw and minor crops.
5 Landlords' expenses are included within 'Total maintenance', 'Other goods and services' and 'Total consumption of Fixed Capital of buildings'.
6 Includes livestock and crop costs, water costs, insurance premiums, bank charges, professional fees, rates and other farming costs.
7 A more empirically based methodology for calculating landlords' consumption of fixed capital was introduced in 2000. The new series has been linked with the old one using a smoothing procedure for the transition year of 1996.
8 Excludes the value of work done by farm labour on own account capital formation in buildings and works.

9 Includes Environmentally and Nitrate Sensitive Areas, Countryside Stewardship and other management schemes, and Moorland, Habitat, Farm Woodland and Organic Farming Schemes.
10 Land area based schemes which replaced the Hill Livestock Compensatory Allowance Scheme in 2001. These are Tir Mynydd in Wales, Less Favoured Area Compensatory Scheme in Northern Ireland, Less Favoured Areas Support Scheme in Scotland and Hill Farm Allowance in England.
11 Rent paid on all tenanted land (including 'conacre' land in Northern Ireland) less landlords' expenses, landlords' consumption of fixed capital and the benefit value of dwellings on that land.
12 Rent received by farming landowners from renting of land to other farmers less landlords' expenses. This series starts in 1996 following a revision to the methodology of calculating net rent.
13 Interest charges on loans for current farming purposes and buildings and works less interest on money held on short term deposit.

Source: Department for Environment, Food and Rural Affairs: 01904 455080

21.2 Output and input volume indices[1]
United Kingdom

Indices (1995=100)

		1995	1996	1997	1998	1999	2000	2001	2002	2003	2004	2005
Outputs[2]												
1. Total cereals:	VQAN	100.0	111.4	106.2	103.3	100.0	108.6	86.3	104.2	97.7	101.0	96.0
Wheat	LUKH	100.0	112.0	103.9	107.3	103.3	116.1	81.5	111.4	99.8	108.4	103.7
Rye	VQAO	100.0	103.6	103.6	82.1	82.1	78.6	82.1	71.4	67.9	67.9	67.9
Barley	LUKI	100.0	111.3	112.1	95.4	94.2	93.4	95.5	88.1	91.3	83.2	79.6
Oats and summer cereal mixtures	LUKJ	100.0	95.7	93.7	95.0	86.8	103.2	100.1	106.8	116.9	119.7	87.4
Other cereals	VQAP	100.0	79.5	74.7	61.6	95.4	115.9	86.3	126.4	124.3	121.2	121.7
2. Total industrial crops:	VQAQ	100.0	108.3	110.7	112.3	116.3	98.9	92.3	104.5	108.2	104.6	102.6
Oil seeds	VQAR	100.0	114.9	125.7	131.6	150.6	90.3	90.6	112.1	138.5	126.4	151.8
Oilseed rape	VQAS	100.0	115.3	125.4	128.9	137.8	92.8	93.4	118.1	142.8	130.5	153.9
Other oil seeds	LUKN	100.0	107.3	131.7	177.6	374.9	52.9	47.7	22.6	73.1	64.2	110.5
Sugar beet	C5X4	100.0	123.6	131.5	118.6	125.5	107.7	98.9	113.4	108.7	107.2	103.0
Other industrial crops	VQAU	100.0	88.3	78.5	90.0	82.9	87.1	79.4	84.7	80.0	81.1	65.7
Fibre plants	VQAV	100.0	130.4	131.6	107.4	108.4	77.7	53.8	31.3	52.3	37.1	24.4
Hops	LUKP	100.0	126.2	119.6	81.9	69.8	62.1	58.6	58.7	45.0	45.0	38.5
Others[3]	VQAW	100.0	86.0	75.9	90.7	83.8	88.8	81.0	86.8	82.2	83.5	67.6
3.Total forage plants	VQAX	100.0	101.7	115.0	109.4	113.6	117.5	137.4	137.7	135.8	130.8	133.2
4.Total vegetables and horticultural												
Products:	VQAY	100.0	101.4	99.9	97.5	99.4	97.1	94.0	93.3	90.8	92.5	92.2
Fresh vegetables	LUKX	100.0	105.8	100.8	98.8	99.6	93.8	90.6	82.8	82.3	82.6	85.4
Plants and flowers	LUKZ	100.0	94.7	98.0	95.0	98.5	101.0	98.0	107.7	102.3	105.9	101.5
5.Total potatoes (including seeds)	LUKW	100.0	107.7	102.3	90.3	107.1	94.5	100.0	100.8	87.0	95.7	87.1
6.Total fruit	LUKY	100.0	104.1	69.3	88.5	92.1	85.2	90.2	85.0	93.5	108.8	127.4
7.Other crop products including seeds	VQAZ	100.0	89.9	98.6	91.4	101.9	100.1	101.3	69.1	83.0	84.7	81.9
8.Total crop output	VQBA	100.0	107.9	104.6	101.8	104.5	100.0	91.5	98.8	96.1	..	..
9.Total livestock production	VQBB	100.0	89.9	94.8	95.7	92.4	87.7	82.8	85.4	84.1	86.0	86.9
Mainly for meat processing	LULH	100.0	88.9	93.5	94.7	91.9	87.8	80.7	83.7	83.4	85.6	87.2
Cattle	LULC	100.0	69.7	72.6	74.6	76.0	73.8	65.4	75.7	78.1	77.0	83.1
Pigs	LULE	100.0	100.9	110.8	112.2	103.0	86.9	79.7	76.0	67.4	68.0	68.3
Sheep	LULD	100.0	88.7	93.5	99.1	98.9	95.1	68.2	77.7	79.3	84.1	85.1
Poultry	LULF	100.0	103.2	105.6	103.7	98.5	99.3	102.8	98.7	100.3	106.0	103.5
Other animals	LULG	100.0	101.8	102.3	102.3	101.7	101.7	101.4	101.6	101.0	100.9	101.3
Gross fixed capital formation	LULR	100.0	98.3	106.1	104.2	97.4	86.1	99.7	99.8	91.8	92.2	87.8
Cattle	LULN	100.0	99.8	98.4	96.0	96.6	84.3	97.8	93.3	92.2	85.7	87.9
Pigs	LULP	100.0	109.9	115.5	87.1	97.7	66.5	56.2	84.8	67.1	62.9	53.4
Sheep	LULO	100.0	90.8	117.9	122.7	92.4	62.6	97.4	108.7	79.1	93.5	73.4
Poultry	LULQ	100.0	101.8	109.1	102.9	97.3	100.6	96.3	95.9	95.5	98.5	94.5
10.Total livestock products	LULM	100.0	99.5	100.8	99.5	101.6	98.8	100.4	101.7	102.9	100.5	100.0
Milk	LULI	100.0	99.6	100.5	99.0	101.4	98.6	99.8	100.9	102.0	98.9	98.2
Eggs	LULJ	100.0	100.1	104.7	105.7	104.5	103.3	110.8	110.6	108.8	117.8	119.0
Raw wool	LULK	100.0	95.1	97.0	103.3	95.3	91.7	76.2	79.2	77.4	78.6	80.6
Other animal products	LULL	100.0	86.3	90.8	80.8	95.9	80.8	71.3	112.7	140.5	85.1	85.0
11.Total livestock output	VQBC	100.0	93.6	97.2	97.2	96.0	92.0	89.4	91.6	91.1	91.5	91.9
12.Total other agricultural activities	VQBD	100.0	108.7	104.1	103.7	109.0	93.8	92.8	94.5	95.2	99.9	90.2
Agricultural services	VQBE	100.0	107.8	109.4	115.2	123.2	116.3	119.7	119.2	117.3	123.7	120.1
Leasing out quota	VQBF	100.0	111.7	87.1	68.1	65.6	28.0	15.1	22.6	30.0	30.0	5.5
13.Total inseparable non-agricultural												
Activities	LULX	100.0	108.7	108.0	119.0	120.0	131.7	163.9	142.6	146.1	149.5	158.5

21.2 Output and input volume indices[1]
United Kingdom
continued

Indices (1995=100)

		1995	1996	1997	1998	1999	2000	2001	2002	2003	2004	2005
14.Gross output at market prices	VQEG	100.0	99.4	99.9	99.5	100.1	96.5	93.1	96.2	95.0	96.6	96.0
15.Total subsidies (less taxes) on product	VQEE	..	..	..	..	..	..	..	..	..	..	..
16.Output at basic prices	LULY	100.0	99.1	100.5	100.3	101.1	96.9	92.0	96.4	95.4	96.9	96.7
of which transactions within the agricultural industry												
Feed wheat	LULZ	100.0	121.5	176.0	209.9	175.0	120.1	115.1	123.9	196.2	266.3	261.9
Feed barley	LUMA	100.0	105.2	125.8	123.5	113.6	112.2	121.4	128.9	121.4	110.0	114.3
Feed oats	LUMB	100.0	89.2	81.6	100.1	118.2	108.8	112.4	105.6	105.2	102.0	82.2
Seed potatoes	LUMC	100.0	119.1	84.1	82.3	82.1	71.9	78.6	79.6	40.4	55.8	72.3
Straw	LUMD	100.0	84.5	73.3	89.4	81.5	86.8	77.9	83.2	78.1	78.9	61.9
Contract work	LUME	100.0	107.8	109.4	115.2	123.2	116.3	119.7	119.2	117.3	123.7	120.1
Leasing of quota	LUMF	100.0	111.7	87.1	68.1	65.6	28.0	15.1	22.6	30.0	30.0	5.5
Total capital formation in livestock	LUMG	100.0	98.3	106.1	104.2	97.4	86.1	99.7	99.8	91.9	92.3	87.8
Intermediate Consumption												
17.Seeds	LUMO	100.0	102.4	99.2	95.1	95.1	90.6	94.5	89.8	89.6	90.5	91.5
Cereals	LUMM	..	..	..	..	..	..	..	..	..	..	..
Other	LUMN	..	..	..	..	..	..	..	..	..	..	..
18.Energy	VQEH	100.0	106.3	103.3	108.3	101.6	92.8	94.0	93.4	79.4	82.0	76.5
Electricity	VQEI	100.0	99.5	97.4	106.6	101.3	93.7	101.4	103.4	84.0	81.2	80.0
Fuels	VQEJ	100.0	110.9	107.4	109.5	102.0	92.6	90.6	88.7	77.4	82.5	75.2
19.Fertilisers	VQEK	100.0	105.3	114.7	107.5	100.5	88.0	76.9	80.3	68.8	69.9	62.6
20.Pesticides	LUMQ	100.0	103.1	106.7	111.2	108.1	106.7	100.1	102.2	96.5	106.1	98.2
21.Veterinary expenses	LUMW	100.0	102.1	104.1	96.3	90.2	86.5	82.7	86.5	84.4	90.4	90.1
22.Animal feed	LUML	100.0	97.8	94.5	94.7	95.4	91.6	95.1	92.8	96.7	98.4	101.5
Compounds	LUMH	100.0	101.3	97.3	94.9	97.5	89.6	92.3	91.7	91.6	92.6	89.4
Straights	LUMI	100.0	88.7	79.6	83.6	84.0	90.1	94.7	87.1	97.2	99.2	115.1
Feed purchased from other farms	LUMJ	100.0	107.5	133.2	139.8	126.5	113.8	119.7	126.5	136.5	143.1	144.1
23.Total maintenance[4]	VQEL	100.0	97.6	94.7	88.3	86.5	78.2	79.9	75.2	72.4	72.8	67.5
Materials	LUMU	100.0	97.6	93.8	91.1	89.0	81.3	80.1	73.9	70.2	69.5	64.0
Buildings	LUMT	100.0	97.4	96.7	82.7	81.5	72.1	79.6	78.1	77.2	79.9	74.9
24.Agricultural services	VQEM	100.0	107.8	109.4	115.2	123.2	116.3	119.7	119.2	117.3	123.7	120.1
25.Other goods and services[4,5]	VQEO	100.0	104.2	103.7	98.6	95.5	85.7	80.5	79.2	84.8	88.9	81.9
26.Total intermediate consumption	LUNE	100.0	101.7	101.1	99.0	97.2	90.0	88.6	87.4	86.8	89.7	86.0
27.Gross value added at market prices	LUNF	100.0	96.5	98.6	101.2	106.6	110.6	102.9	115.2	112.6	111.5	118.1
28.Total consumption of Fixed Capital	LUNN	100.0	102.7	100.2	99.5	98.1	96.8	95.1	90.9	90.3	89.4	90.4
Equipment	LUNI	100.0	101.3	101.2	99.3	97.3	95.1	93.0	91.4	90.1	89.5	88.1
Buildings[4,6]	LUNG	100.0	105.5	107.3	106.6	103.9	99.6	100.8	102.6	99.8	97.5	93.8
Livestock	VQES	100.0	102.4	91.7	93.2	94.8	100.5	96.5	81.6	83.8	83.7	92.7
Cattle	LUNJ	100.0	105.6	93.2	92.3	94.5	107.2	92.6	81.5	86.8	86.7	98.8
Pigs	LUNL	100.0	92.7	101.0	108.2	97.7	83.2	56.8	82.6	66.1	66.2	57.7
Sheep	LUNK	100.0	96.7	80.6	82.7	92.5	97.3	117.4	76.7	75.9	76.8	84.2
Poultry	LUNM	100.0	103.1	103.6	111.2	105.8	100.8	98.8	99.6	96.9	95.5	98.9
29.Net value added at market prices	LUNO	100.0	93.4	98.9	104.7	118.3	130.0	113.0	151.5	145.8	144.5	160.7

1 See chapter text.
2 Output is net of VAT collected on the sale of non-edible products. Figures for total output include subsidies on products, but not other subsidies.
3 Includes straw and minor crops.
4 Landlords' expenses are included within 'Total maintenance', 'Other goods and services' and 'Total consumption of Fixed Capital of buildings'.

5 Includes livestock and crop costs, water costs, insurance premiums, bank charges, professional fees, rates, and other farming costs.
6 A more empirically based methodology for calculating landlords' depreciation was introduced in 2000. The new series has been linked with the old one using a smoothing procedure for the transition year of 1996.

Source: Department for Environment, Food and Rural Affairs: 01904 455080

21.3 Agriculture land-use
United Kingdom
Area at the June Survey[1]

Thousand hectares

		1996	1997	1998	1999	2000	2001	2002	2003	2004	2005	2006
Total agricultural area	BFAH	18 750	18 653	18 604	18 579	18 311	18 594	18 537	18 464	18 432	18 502	18 713
Crops	BFAA	4 722	4 990	4 971	4 709	4 665	4 493	4 604	4 475	4 589	4 437	4 340
Bare fallow	BFAB	37	29	34	33	37	43	33	29	29	140	150
Total tillage	KIJR	4 759	5 020	5 005	4 742	4 702	4 536	4 636	4 504	4 619	4 577	4 489
All grass under 5 years old	KFEM	1 395	1 405	1 301	1 226	1 226	1 205	1 243	1 200	1 246	1 193	1 137
Total arable land	KFEN	6 154	6 425	6 306	5 968	5 928	5 741	5 879	5 705	5 864	5 770	5 626
All grasses 5 years old and over	KFEO	5 354	5 282	5 364	5 449	5 364	5 584	5 519	5 683	5 620	5 711	5 967
Total tillage and grass	KFEP	11 507	11 706	11 671	11 417	11 292	11 325	11 397	11 388	11 485	11 481	11 594
Sole right rough grazing	BFAD	4 760	4 657	4 621	4 575	4 445	4 435	4 488	4 329	4 326	4 354	4 491
Set aside	DMNF	509	306	313	572	567	800	611	689	559	559	513
All other land on agricultural holdings including woodland	BFAE	751	763	773	789	780	801	802	792	825	872	874
Total land on agricultural holdings	BFAF	17 527	17 432	17 377	17 352	17 083	17 361	17 303	17 227	17 195	17 266	17 472
Common rough grazing (estimated)	BFAG	1 223	1 221	1 227	1 227	1 228	1 232	1 234	1 236	1 237	1 236	1 241
Crops	BFAA	4 722	4 990	4 971	4 709	4 665	4 493	4 604	4 475	4 589	4 437	4 340
Cereals	BFAJ	3 359	3 514	3 418	3 141	3 348	3 014	3 245	3 057	3 130	2 919	2 861
Wheat	BFAK	1 976	2 036	2 045	1 847	2 086	1 635	1 996	1 837	1 990	1 867	1 833
Barley	BFAL	1 269	1 359	1 253	1 179	1 128	1 245	1 101	1 076	1 007	938	881
Oats	BFAM	96	100	98	92	109	112	126	121	108	90	121
Mixed corn	BFAN	3	2	2	2	2	3	4	4	..	..	..
Rye[2]	BFAO	8	9	10	8	7	5	5	4	6	..	..
Triticale[3]	DMNH	7	8	11	13	16	14	14	15	15	13	13
Other arable crops (excluding potatoes)	DMNI	937	1 125	1 210	1 211	979	1 141	1 024	1 098	1 136	1 211	1 172
Oilseed rape	BFAP	356	445	507	417	332	404	357	460	498	519	500
Sugar beet not for stock feeding[2]	BFAQ	199	196	189	183	173	177	169	162	154	148	130
Hops[4]	DMNJ	3	3	3	3	2	2	2	2	2	1	1
Peas for harvesting dry and field beans	DMNK	178	197	213	202	208	276	249	235	242	239	231
Linseed	DMNL	49	73	100	209	71	31	12	32	30	45	33
Other crops	DMNM	204	210	200	197	192	214	204	201	203	252	278
Potatoes	BFAR	178	166	164	178	166	165	158	145	148	137	140
Horticultural	BFAV	189	184	180	179	172	173	176	176	175	170	166
Vegetables grown in the open	DMNN	132	126	125	126	119	120	124	125	125	121	119
Orchard fruit[5]	BFBG	28	30	30	28	28	28	26	25	24	23	23
Soft fruit	DMNO	12	11	10	9	10	9	9	9	9	9	10
Ornamentals	DMNP	14	14	14	13	14	14	15	14	15	14	12
Glasshouse crops	DMNQ	2	2	2	2	2	2	2	2	2	2	2

1 Includes estimates for minor holdings for all countries. See chapter text.
2 Figures are for England and Wales only.
3 Figures for 2004 do not include Wales.
4 Figures are for England only from 2005.
5 Includes non-commercial orchards.

Source: Agricultural Departments: 01904 455332

21.4 Estimated quantity of crops and grass harvested[1]
United Kingdom

Thousand tonnes

		1995	1996	1997	1998	1999	2000	2001	2002	2003	2004	2005
Agricultural crops												
Wheat	BADO	14 310	16 100	15 020	16 449	14 867	16 704	11 580	15 973	14 288	15 473	14 863
Barley (Winter and Spring) .	BADP	6 840	7 790	7 830	6 623	6 581	6 492	6 660	6 126	6 370	5 815	5 495
Oats	BADQ	615	590	575	586	541	640	621	753	749	630	532
Sugar beet[2]	BADR	8 431	10 420	11 084	10 002	10 584	9 079	8 335	9 557	9 168	8 850	8 687
Potatoes	BADS	6 404	7 228	7 128	6 422	7 131	6 636	6 649	6 966	5 918	6 316	5 961

		1995 /96	1996 /97	1997 /98	1998 /99	1999 /00	2000 /01	2001 /02	2002 /03	2003 /04	2004 /05	2005 /06
Horticultural crops												
Field vegetables												
Brussels sprouts	BADT	74.3	82.6	74.2	72.5	78.5	67.3	54.8	42.7	55.8	42.5	48.6
Cabbage (including savoys and spring greens)	BADU	341.5	360.1	309.7	283.6	269.1	254.3	282.1	244.0	229.2	221.9	262.7
Cauliflowers	BADV	247.3	217.1	191.0	191.7	172.4	156.1	107.4	115.8	126.3	168.3	131.9
Carrots	BADW	512.4	624.4	623.1	617.6	673.2	725.8	760.0	718.4	602.4	671.1	718.5
Turnips and swedes	BADX	124.2	135.6	106.9	117.5	123.3	132.1	141.8	104.7	96.5	97.0	114.1
Beetroot	BADY	72.1	72.1	72.4	69.5	63.4	67.1	68.6	56.3	58.8	53.9	51.0
Onions, dry bulb	BADZ	254.3	313.3	329.3	342.0	391.4	392.7	374.9	283.4	373.6	340.9	383.4
Peas, green for market (in pod weight)	BAEA	8.4	6.7	8.2	7.0	7.0	6.7	6.2	7.2	5.9	5.9	5.9
Peas, green for processing (shelled weight)	BAEB	198.0	215.5	167.9	152.0	143.1	184.5	161.0	169.3	167.6	130.3	127.3
Lettuce	BAEC	191.9	187.5	157.7	151.8	155.2	135.8	123.9	109.9	125.6	140.9	131.5
Protected crops												
Tomatoes	BAED	112.8	115.5	114.0	107.6	116.6	113.0	109.1	100.9	75.6	78.1	78.2
Cucumbers	BAEE	88.4	85.6	81.7	83.8	83.8	79.8	71.5	73.6	77.0	61.4	54.5
Lettuce	BAEF	29.7	26.5	24.1	20.6	19.9	18.7	20.9	16.0	16.6	10.8	8.1
Fruit												
Dessert apples	BFCD	138.5	105.4	96.0	97.8	133.9	101.3	104.4	84.0	69.0	91.8	113.1
Cooking apples	BFCE	135.0	118.5	91.1	85.9	112.4	107.5	107.4	95.3	74.9	78.2	100.6
Soft fruit	BFCF	79.2	83.4	60.6	60.8	67.2	65.4	64.6	67.1	79.6	85.9	106.0
Pears	BFBQ	29.7	35.8	33.0	26.3	22.7	26.6	38.5	34.2	29.6	22.7	23.8

1 See chapter text.
2 Figures are adjusted to constant 16% sugar content.

Source: Agricultural Departments: 01904 455332

21.5 Cattle, sheep, pigs and poultry on agricultural holdings[1]
United Kingdom

At June each year   Thousands

		1996	1997	1998	1999	2000	2001	2002	2003	2004	2005	2006
Total cattle and calves	BFCG	12 040	11 637	11 519	11 423	11 135	10 602	10 345	10 508	10 588	10 392	10 270
of which:												
dairy cows	BFCH	2 587	2 478	2 439	2 440	2 336	2 251	2 227	2 191	2 129	2 063	2 066
beef cows	BFCI	1 864	1 862	1 947	1 924	1 842	1 708	1 657	1 698	1 736	1 762	1 733
heifers in calf	BFCJ	818	848	787	763	718	701	728	679	690	638	645
Total sheep and lambs	BFCM	42 086	42 823	44 471	44 656	42 264	36 716	35 834	35 812	35 817	35 416	34 722
of which:												
ewes and shearlings	CKUQ	20 550	20 696	21 260	21 458	20 449	17 921	17 630	17 580	17 630	16 935	16 637
lambs under one year old	BFCP	20 443	21 032	22 138	22 092	20 857	17 769	17 310	17 322	17 238	17 488	17 058
Total pigs	BFCQ	7 590	8 072	8 146	7 284	6 482	5 845	5 588	5 046	5 159	4 862	4 933
of which:												
sows in pig and other sows for breeding	CKUU	649	683	675	603	537	527	483	442	449	403	401
gilts in pig	CKUR	107	116	103	85	73	71	74	73	66	67	67
Total fowls	KPSV	..	..	..	..	..	..	..	178 800	181 759	173 909	173 081
of which:												
table fowls including broilers	CKUT	..	..	98 244	101 625	105 689	112 531	105 137	116 738	119 888	111 475	110 672
laying fowls[2]	CKUV	..	34 286	29 483	29 258	28 687	29 895	28 778	29 274	29 655	29 544	28 632
growing pullets	CKUW	..	11 510	9 860	9 583	9 461	9 367	9 784	8 286	8 156	10 928	9 625

1 Includes estimates for minor holdings for all countries. See chapter text.
2 Excludes fowls laying eggs for hatching.

Sources: Department for Environment, Food and Rural Affairs;
Farming Statistics: 01904 455332

21.6 Forestry[1]
United Kingdom

		1980	1990	2000	2001	2002	2003	2004	2005	2006
Woodland area[2] - (Thousand hectares)										
United Kingdom	C5OF	2 175	2 400	2 793	2 790	2 800	2 807	2 817	2 825	2 829
England[3]	C5OG	948	958	1 103	1 100	1 104	1 110	1 115	1 119	1 121
Wales[3]	C5OI	241	248	289	289	288	285	286	286	285
Scotland[3]	C5OH	920	1 120	1 318	1 317	1 324	1 327	1 330	1 334	1 337
Northern Ireland	C5OJ	67	74	83	83	84	85	86	85	86
Forestry Commission/Forest Service	C5OK	946	956	886	861[4]	855	848	842	838	832
Other[5]	C5OL	1 230	1 443	1 907	1 929	1 945	1 960	1 976	1 987	1 997
Conifer	C5OM	1 372	1 576	1 663	1 660	1 658	1 652	1 651	1 647	1 642
Broadleaved[6]	C5ON	804	824	1 131	1 130	1 143	1 155	1 166	1 178	1 187

		1995 /96	1996 /97	1997 /98	1998 /99	1999 /00	2000 /01	2001 /02	2002 /03	2003 /04	2004 /05	2005 /06
New Planting[7] - (Thousand hectares)												
United Kingdom	C5OO	16.7	17.6	16.9	17.0	17.9	18.7	14.4	13.5	12.4	11.9	8.7
England	C5OP	4.7	4.7	4.4	5.1	5.9	5.9	5.4	5.9	4.6	5.3	3.7
Wales	C5OR	0.4	0.4	0.5	0.6	0.7	0.4	0.3	0.3	0.5	0.5	0.5
Scotland	C5OQ	10.6	11.8	11.4	10.5	10.4	11.7	8.0	6.7	6.8	5.7	4.0
Northern Ireland	C5OS	1.0	0.8	0.6	0.7	0.8	0.7	0.7	0.6	0.5	0.4	0.6
Forestry Commission/Forest Service	C5OT	0.6	0.6	0.2	0.2	0.3	0.3	0.8	0.9	0.3	0.1	0.3
Other[8]	C5OU	16.1	17.0	16.7	16.8	17.6	18.4	13.6	12.6	12.1	11.8	8.4
Conifer	C5OV	7.4	7.7	7.0	6.6	6.5	5.1	3.9	4.0	2.9	2.1	1.1
Broadleaved	C5OW	9.3	9.9	9.9	10.4	11.4	13.6	10.5	9.5	9.5	9.8	7.6
Restocking[7] - (Thousand hectares)												
United Kingdom	C5OX	14.0	15.1	14.2	14.1	15.2	15.3	13.8	14.5	14.9	14.8	14.8
England	C5OY	4.2	4.3	4.4	4.1	3.9	4.0	3.4	3.4	3.2	2.8	3.2
Wales	C5P2	2.3	3.0	2.7	3.0	2.6	2.2	1.9	1.9	1.8	1.6	2.5
Scotland	C5OZ	6.8	7.2	6.3	6.3	8.0	8.0	7.8	8.5	8.9	9.5	8.2
Northern Ireland	C5P3	0.6	0.6	0.7	0.6	0.6	1.1	0.8	0.7	1.0	1.0	0.9
Forestry Commission/Forest Service	C5P4	8.1	8.4	8.5	8.5	8.8	8.9	9.1	9.1	9.9	9.4	9.3
Other[8]	C5P5	5.9	6.7	5.7	5.6	6.4	6.4	4.7	5.3	5.0	5.5	5.5
Conifer	C5P6	10.9	11.6	11.2	11.3	11.9	12.2	11.4	12.0	12.1	12.0	11.6
Broadleaved	C5P7	3.1	3.5	3.0	2.8	3.3	3.0	2.4	2.5	2.8	2.9	3.3

		1997	1998	1999	2000	2001	2002	2003	2004	2005
Wood Production (volume - Thousand green tonnes[9])										
United Kingdom	C5P8	7 610	7 540	7 960	8 090	8 150	8 300	8 970	9 210	9 320
Softwood total	C5PA	6 790	6 830	7 280	7 430	7 500	7 680	8 410	8 700	8 720
Forestry Commission/Forest Service	C5PB	3 950	4 190	4 730	4 850	4 600	4 650	4 820	4 890	4 580
Non-Forestry Commission/Forest Service	C5PC	2 850	2 640	2 550	2 580	2 900	3 030	3 590	3 800	4 140
Hardwood[10]	C5PD	820	720	680	660	640	620	560	510	600

1 See chapter text.
2 Areas as at 31 March.
3 For England, Wales and Scotland, 1980 woodland area figures are the published results from the 1979-1982 Census of Woodlands and Trees and figures for 1990 are adjusted to reflect subsequent changes. From 1998 onwards they are based on results from the 1995-1999 National Inventory of Woodlands and Trees, adjusted to reflect subsequent changes.
4 The apparent fall in woodland cover in 2001 is due to the reclassification of Forestry Commission open land within the forest.
5 Includes private woodland and non-Forestry Commission / Forest Service public woodland.

6 Broadleaved includes coppice. For data based on 1979-82 Census, all scrub and other non-plantation woodland have been assumed to be broadleaved.
7 Figures shown are for the areas of new planting and restocking in the year to 31 March.
8 Includes grant aided planting on non-Forestry Commission/ Forest Service woodland and estimates for areas planted without the aid of grants.
9 Figures have been rounded to the nearest 10 thousand green tonnes.
10 Hardwood is timber from broadleaved species. Most hardwood production comes from non-FC/FS woodland; the figures are estimates based on reported deliveries to wood processing industries.

Sources: Forest Service Agency;
Forestry Commission: 0131 334 0303

21.7 Sales for food of agricultural produce and livestock
United Kingdom

			1995	1996	1997	1998	1999	2000	2001	2002	2003	2004	2005
Cereals:		Thousand											
Wheat[1]	KCQK	tonnes	4 673	4 842	4 737	4 676	4 826	4 707	4 885	4 768	4 825	4 839	4 694
Barley	KCQL	"	3 818	3 734	3 453	3 525	3 454	3 802	2 669	3 018	3 126	2 493	2 415
Oats[2]	KCQM	"	216	235	259	273	270	263	283	311	323	317	347
Potatoes[3]	KCQN	"	5 961	6 146	6 279	5 997	6 210	6 675	6 606	6 892	6 446	6 549	6 087
Milk[4]:													
Utilised for liquid consumption	KCQO	Million litres	6 950	6 866	6 778	6 767	6 889	6 802	6 750	6 824	6 754	6 694	6 655
Utilised for manufacture	KCQP	"	6 890	6 906	7 039	6 806	6 973	6 541	6 751	6 884	7 139	6 725	6 490
Total available for domestic use[5]	KCQQ	"	14 255	14 194	14 258	13 973	14 233	13 738	13 940	14 099	14 292	13 774	13 491
Hen eggs in shell	KCQR	Million dozens	774	775	794	774	738	712	753	746	733	778	772
Animals slaughtered:													
Cattle and calves:													
Cattle	KCQS	Thousands	3 266	2 291	2 264	2 297	2 217	2 275	2 072	2 184	2 188	2 290	2 303
Calves	KCQT	"	26	24	20	32	75	152	92	98	87	103	111
Total	KCQU	"	3 292	2 315	2 284	2 329	2 292	2 427	2 164	2 282	2 275	2 393	2 413
Sheep and lambs	KCQV	"	19 311	18 049	16 660	18 688	19 116	18 442	12 964	14 993	15 095	15 492	16 284
Pigs:													
Clean pigs	MBGD	"	14 021	13 897	15 132	15 872	14 350	12 370	10 446	10 260	9 133	9 150	8 971
Sows and boars	KCQZ	"	355	324	363	415	379	321	180	314	241	240	202
Total	KCRA	"	14 376	14 221	15 496	16 286	14 728	12 692	10 626	10 575	9 374	9 390	9 173
Poultry[6]	KCRB	Millions	783	823	850	857	863	843	866	862	882	882	903

Note: The figures for cereals and for animals slaughtered relate to periods of 52 weeks

1 Flour millers' receipts of home-grown wheat.
2 Oatmeal millers' receipts of home-grown oats.
3 Total sales for human consumption in the UK. Figures for 2004 are provisional.
4 Data to 1994 sourced from the Milk Marketing Boards. Data from 1995 sourced from surveys run by the agricultural departments. 1994 includes two months of data sourced from the surveys run by the agricultural departments.

5 The totals of liquid consumption and milk used for manufacture may not add up to the total available for domestic use because of adjustments for dairy wastage, stock changes and other uses, such as farmhouse consumption, milk fed to stock and on farm waste.
6 Total fowls, ducks, geese and turkeys.

Source: Department for Environment, Food and Rural Affairs: 01904 455332

21.8 Stocks of food and feedingstuffs[1]
United Kingdom

At end December each year
Thousand tonnes

		1995	1996	1997	1998	1999	2000	2001	2002	2003	2004	2005
Wheat and flour (as wheat)	KCRC	1 074	1 031	992	1 000	869	826	719	833	852	761	576
Barley (GB only)	KCRD	1 574	1 534	1 472	1 327	1 404	1 372	1 315	1 300	1 340	1 162	1 179
Maize	KCRE	33	25	45	67	43	37	36	66	52	52	21
Oilcake and meal[2,7]	KCRF	103	89	79	69	72	..	..	..	..	..	..
Oilseeds and nuts (crude oil equivalent)[7]	KCRG	34	28	19	13	20	10	17	10	13	10	..
Vegetable oil (as crude oil)	KCRI	96	101	101	99	98	84	96	89	86	87	..
Marine oil (as crude oil)	KCRJ	17	10	4	..	..	..	..	..	..	..	..
Butter[3]	KCRK	11	14	7	11	22	17	18	19	17	9	3
Meat and offal[4]	KCRL	77	129	162	157	84	54	57	49	47	49	44
Raw coffee[5]	KCRM	11	8	7	8	7	8	13	9	9	11	10
Tea[6]	KCRN	38	39	37	38	38	28	31	29	25	19	19
Sugar	KCRO	766	807	1 003	928	..	..	..	..	..	..	..

1 Recorded stocks, including stocks in bond or held by the main processors.
2 Excluding castor meal, cocoa cake and meal.
3 In addition to stocks in public cold stores surveyed by DEFRA, closing stocks include all intervention stocks in private cold stores.
4 Stocks of imported and home-produced mean and offal held in public cold stores, excluding poultry meat, bacon and ham.
5 Including manufacturers' stocks and additional public warehouses.

6 Covering stocks held by primary wholesalers and held in public/private warehouses.
7 For confidentiality reasons, these data are no longer available for publication.

Source: Department for Environment, Food and Rural Affairs: 01904 455332

21.9 Processed food and animal feedingstuffs: production
United Kingdom

Thousand tonnes

		1995	1996	1997	1998	1999	2000	2001	2002	2003	2004	2005
Flour milling:												
Wheat milling: total	KFTA	5 343	5 501	5 535	5 707	5 668	5 617	5 667	5 616	5 572	5 576	5 611
Home produced	KFTB	4 603	4 772	4 667	4 582	4 701	4 609	4 790	4 648	4 726	4 772	4 596
Imported	KFTC	740	729	868	1 125	966	1 008	877	968	846	804	1 016
Flour produced	KFTD	4 298	4 454	4 439	4 526	4 497	4 486	4 487	4 413	4 370	4 423	4 407
Offals produced	KFTE	1 081	1 111	1 111	1 221	1 181	1 148	1 169	1 179	1 170	1 124	1 159
Oat milling:												
Oats milled by oatmeal millers	KFTF	217	250	259	272	266	261	287	312	322	321	343
Products of oat milling	KFTG	110	123	129	154	157	155	171	186	191	190	204
Seed crushing:												
Oilseeds and nuts processed[1]	KFTH	2 122	2 466	2 587	2 683	2 398	2 380	2 252	2 332	2 210	2 128	..
Crude oil produced, including production of maize oil[1]	KFTI	779	862	909	915	832	820	786	805	769	747	..
Oilcake and meal produced, excluding castor meal, cocoa cake and meal[1]	KFTJ	1 305	1 541	1 614	1 687	1 484	1 475	1 396	1 451	1 361	1 297	..
Production of home-killed meat: total including meat subsequently canned	KFTK	2 383	2 084	2 157	2 273	2 136	2 058	1 757	1 871	1 833	1 869	1 949
Beef	KFTL	973	701	695	704	675	703	649	690	698	717	759
Veal	KFTM	1	1	1	1	2	4	2	3	2	3	3
Mutton and lamb	KFTN	364	345	321	356	361	361	259	300	300	306	331
Pork	KFTO	752	769	871	934	823	721	596	621	578	584	586
Offal[2]	KFTP	293	268	269	278	275	270	250	258	255	260	270
Production of poultry meat[3]	KFTQ	1 427	1 481	1 527	1 548	1 549	1 514	1 566	1 556	1 569	1 564	1 582
Production of bacon and ham, including meat subsequently canned	KFTR	247	243	242	240	243	224	216	215	214	211	214
Production of milk products:												
Butter[4]	KFTS	133	130	139	137	141	132	126	136	131	122	130
Cheese (including farmhouse)	KFTT	363	379	379	367	370	341	395	371	352	359	391
Condensed milk: includes skim concentrate and condensed milk used in manufacture of chocolate crumb	KFTU	181	206	214	192	177	162	161	174	158	161	143
Milk powder: excluding buttermilk and whey powder												
Full cream	KFTV	90	83	96	97	102	105	87	105	102	80	52
Skimmed	KFTW	117	108	108	107	102	83	71	87	115	88	69
Cream, fresh and sterilised; including farm cream[5]	KFTX	238	237	231	237	241	242	307	308	321	325	306
Sugar: production from home-grown sugar-beet (as refined sugar)[6]	KFTY	1 469	1 324	1 524	1 439	1 548	1 325	1 222	1 430	1 368	1 390	1 300
Production of compound fats:												
Margarine and other table spreads	KFTZ	490	491	461	448	421	388	409	415	442	431	..
Solid cooking fats	KFUA	110	123	109	131	125	135	121	114	131	132	..
Production of other processed foods:												
Syrup and treacle[5]	KFUC	48	..	..	..	..	..	..	..	..	..	..
Chocolate confectionery	KSJS	592	608	569	567	553	544	559	584	600	602	515
Sugar confectionery	KSJT	322	351	345	337	317	307	322	338	333	324	277
Cocoa beans excluding re-exports	KFVX	160	189	174	172	168	..	..	..	..	..	..
Breakfast cereals, other than oatmeal and oatmeal flakes	KFUJ	335	343	359	349	354	334	344	343	323	346	375
Glucose	KFUM	607	642	637	644	630	657	701	727	735	737	695
Compound feedingstuffs: total[7]	KFUP	11 609	11 801	11 304	11 206	11 404	10 604	10 888	10 762	10 771	10 904	10 490
Cattle food	KFUQ	4 476	4 430	3 926	3 844	4 264	4 038	4 327	4 212	4 490	4 466	4 263
Calf food	KFUR	307	277	227	198	187	184	180	177	193	200	185
Pig food	KFUS	2 453	2 566	2 659	2 740	2 435	2 082	1 930	1 777	1 536	1 591	1 555
Poultry food	KFUT	3 243	3 280	3 324	3 213	3 139	3 064	3 246	3 458	3 340	3 375	3 269
Other compounds	KFUU	1 130	1 249	1 168	1 210	1 378	1 236	1 204	1 138	1 212	1 272	1 218

Note: The figures relate to periods of 52 weeks (53 weeks in 1998 and 2004) with the following exceptions which are on a calendar year basis: butter, cheese, cream, canned meat, soft drinks, condensed milk and milk powder, canned vegetables, canned and bottled fruit, jam and marmalade, and soups.

1 For confidentiality reasons these data are no longer available for publication.

2 Including poultry offal.
3 Total of fowl, ducks, geese and turkeys (carcase weight).
4 Includes cream from the residual elements of low fat milk production.
5 This survey ceased at the end of 1995.
6 2005 data are provisional.
7 Feed produced for retail sale only.

Source: Department for Environment, Food and Rural Affairs: 01904 455332

21.10 Food and animal feedingstuffs: disposals

Thousand tonnes

		1995	1996	1997	1998	1999	2000	2001	2002	2003	2004	2005
Flour	KFPU	4 297	4 457	4 434	4 529	4 487	4 489	4 481	4 408	4 359	4 426	4 410
Sugar (as refined sugar): total disposals	KFPV	2 177	2 200	2 040	2 143	..	..	..	..	..	..	..
For food in the United Kingdom[1]	KFPW	2 157	2 180	2 007	2 106	..	..	..	..	..	..	..
Syrup and treacle[2]	KFPX	48	..	..	..	..	..	..	..	..	..	..
Meat and fish:												
Fresh and frozen meat and offal, including usage for canning:												
Beef and veal	KFPY	1 206	804	865	872	942	921	907	996	1 001	1 025	1 058
Mutton and lamb	KFPZ	504	501	468	496	497	496	373	423	435	448	460
Pork	KFVA	917	954	1 035	1 092	1 056	990	851	929	991	1 000	1 041
Offal[3]	KFVB	354	312	320	316	324	328	306	318	326	335	343
Poultry meat[4,5]	KFVC	1 511	1 587	1 567	1 651	1 720	1 709	1 717	1 719	1 710	1 797	1 795
Bacon and ham, including usage for canning	KFVD	476	505	481	472	471	492	497	509	514	511	498
Dairy products:												
Butter	KFVI	255	240	256	238	244	255	240	250	251	244	265
Cheese	KFVJ	578	618	616	634	647	597	663	658	672	689	752
Condensed milk[6]	KFVK	195	217	229	205	190	178	172	187	179	186	178
Milk powder, excluding buttermilk and whey powder:												
Full cream	KFVM	97	94	105	106	111	117	92	115	116	98	79
Skimmed	KFVN	138	95	103	91	131	162	86	89	125	169	131
Hen eggs in shell[7]	KFVO	818	833	838	798	780	780	847	858	875	915	895
Oils (as crude oil):												
Vegetable oil	KFVP	1 905	1 960	2 010	1 780	2 449	2 452	2 052	2 036	2 195	..	..
Marine oil for the manufacture of margarine and compound fat	KFVQ	100	52	31	8	8	2	2	2	2	2	2
Potatoes[8]	KFVR	7 055	7 661	7 938	7 626	7 584	8 297	7 793	8 382	7 684	7 825	7 363
Other foods:												
Chocolate confectionery	KFVT	674	698	668	681	681	669	672	668	679	695	646
Sugar confectionery, excluding medicated	KFVU	380	416	410	409	393	393	400	387	387	357	373
Tea excluding re-exports	KFVV	141	148	152	145	133	144	133	136	121	156	120
Raw coffee	KFVW	105	116	118	122	115	109	105	116	109	129	114
Barley:												
For brewing and distilling and for food	KFVY	3 616	3 621	3 481	3 544	3 366	3 694	2 623	2 880	3 077	2 537	2 339
Maize (including maize meal): total disposals	KFVZ	1 411	1 389	1 439	1 448	1 256	1 184	1 243	1 231	1 202	1 212	1 103
Animal feed	KCRT	156	174	184	197	216	232	260	271	297	320	243
Oilcake and meal	KCRQ	4 462	4 429	4 041	3 677	4 035	..	..	..	..	..	..
Wheat milling offals	KCRR	1 132	1 157	1 158	1 273	1 209	1 176	1 205	1 220	1 216	1 163	1 197
Fish and poultry meal for animal feed,[9] (figures relate to sales)	KCRS	378	257	233	216	194	192	180	162	145	136	..

Note: The figures relate to periods of 52 weeks with the following exceptions which are on a calendar year basis: fish and potatoes; condensed milk; milk powder; butter and sugar.
1 Including sugar used in the manufacture of other foods subsequently exported. Excluding sugar in imported manufactured foods.
2 This survey ceased at the end of 1995.
3 Including poultry offal.
4 Carcase weight.

5 Total of fowls, ducks, geese and turkeys.
6 Includes skim concentrate and condensed milk used in the manufacture of chocolate crumb.
7 Million dozen eggs.
8 2005 data are provisional.
9 Before a ban on 29 March 1996 this included poultry meat as well as mammalian meat and bonemeal.

Source: Department for Environment, Food and Rural Affairs: 01904 455332

21.11 Average weekly and hourly earnings and hours of full-time male agricultural workers[1]

England and Wales: At September each year

		2000	2001	2002	2003	2004	2005
Average weekly earnings (£)	LQML	298.24	332.66	366.82	352.88	380.75	422.15
95% confidence interval		(+/-£13.84)	(+/-£15.08)	(+/-£18.88)	(+/-£30.30)	(+/-£28.79)	(+/-£29.39)
Average weekly hours worked	LQMM	49.0	51.9	54.1	51.1	51.0	55.7
95% confidence interval		(+/-1.4)	(+/-1.7)	(+/-2.1)	(+/-3.0)	(+/-2.8)	(+/-3.2)
Average earnings/hours (£)	LQMN	6.09	6.42	6.78	6.91	7.46	7.58
95% confidence interval		(+/-£0.18)	(+/-£0.20)	(+/-£0.19)	(+/-£0.31)	(+/-£0.31)	(+/-£0.26)
Number of workers in the sample		234	251	204	72	94	76

1 See chapter text.
Source: Department for Environment, Food and Rural Affairs: 01904 455332

21.12 Average weekly and hourly earnings and hours of agricultural workers[1] : by type 2005

England and Wales: At September

	Full-time		Part-time		Casual		
	Male	Female	Male	Female	Male	Female	Managers
Average weekly earnings (£)	359.48	279.67	138.56	140.36	197.09	121.80	454.67
95% confidence interval	(+/-£34.99)	(+/-£22.93)	(+/-£18.48)	(+/-£27.55)	(+/-£47.79)	(+/-£33.79)	(+/-£38.73)
Average weekly hours worked	48.0	43.3	21.4	23.0	31.7	21.0	..
95% confidence interval	(+/-3.1)	(+/-3.3)	(+/-2.6)	(+/-4.0)	(+/-7.0)	(+/-5.2)	
Average earnings/hour (£)	7.48	6.45	6.49	6.11	6.22	5.79	..
95% confidence interval	(+/-£0.43)	(+/-£0.45)	(+/-£0.34)	(+/-£0.33)	(+/-£0.40)	(+/-£0.36)	
Number of workers in the sample	50	13	53	22	33	23	36

1 See chapter text.
Source: Department for Environment, Food and Rural Affairs: 01904 455332

21.13 Workers employed in agriculture [1,2]: by type

United Kingdom

At June each year

Thousands

	Regular					Seasonal or casual			All			Salaried managers[3]
	Total	Full - time		Part - time		Total	Male	Female	Total	Male	Female	
		Male	Female	Male	Female							
	BANC	BAMY	BAMZ	BANA	BANB	BANF	BAND	BANE	BANI	BANG	BANH	KAYG
1993	165.3	96.5	13.7	29.8	25.3	85.4	55.0	30.4	250.7	181.3	69.4	7.6
1994	161.0	93.6	13.2	30.0	24.2	82.2	53.9	28.4	243.2	177.5	65.7	7.8
1995	157.4	90.4	13.0	30.0	24.1	83.7	56.5	27.2	241.2	176.8	64.3	7.7
1996	156.4	89.2	12.6	31.2	23.4	81.5	55.6	25.8	237.9	176.0	61.9	7.8
1997	154.4	87.5	12.6	31.2	23.1	80.9	55.3	25.5	235.2	174.0	61.2	7.8
1998[4,5]	155.6	88.0	13.1	29.7	24.7	79.5	55.6	23.8	235.0	172.8	62.2	12.1
1999	144.7	82.7	11.9	27.5	22.6	73.0	51.8	21.2	217.7	162.0	55.6	13.8
2000	128.9	73.4	10.3	24.6	20.6	64.4	45.9	18.5	193.3	143.9	49.4	11.1
2001[6]	120.8	69.0	10.9	22.0	18.9	63.2	44.6	18.6	184.0	135.6	48.5	13.4
	123.5	70.3	11.2	22.5	19.4	64.1	45.4	18.8	187.6	138.2	49.4	14.1
2002	116.3	64.7	11.5	21.7	18.4	64.2	46.2	18.0	180.6	132.6	47.9	13.4
2003	108.4	60.4	10.0	21.0	17.0	62.6	44.8	17.8	170.9	126.2	44.8	12.7
2004 Jun	108.8	58.1	9.8	23.5	17.4	68.3	49.6	18.6	177.0	131.2	45.8	15.2
2005 Jun	109.2	57.2	10.3	24.5	17.2	65.1	46.4	18.7	174.3	128.1	46.2	15.7
2006 Jun	105.4	53.6	10.4	24.3	17.1	64.0	44.4	19.6	169.4	122.3	47.1	14.6

1 See chapter text. Includes estimates for minor holdings for all countries.
2 Figures exclude schoolchildren, farmers, partners, directors and their spouses and most trainees.
3 Great Britain only.
4 Results from 1998 onwards are not comparable with previous years, due to changes in the labour questions on the June Agricultural and Horticultural Census in England, Wales and Scotland.

5 From 1998, all farmers managing holdings for limited companies or other institutions in England and Wales were asked to classify themselves as salaried managers.
6 Due to an English register improvement only the top figure for 2001 is directly comparable with 2000, while the bottom figure for 2001 is only comparable with data from 2002.

Sources: Department for Environment, Food and Rural Affairs;
Farming Statistics: 01904 455332

21.14

Landings of fish by United Kingdom vessels: live weight and value[1]
into United Kingdom

		Quantity (thousand tonnes)						Value (£ million)				
		2001	2002	2003	2004	2005		2001	2002	2003	2004	2005
Total all species	KSJU	458.4	465.6	451.6	461.5	491.7	KSLN	423.7	414.7	396.9	405.6	456.1
Total wet fish	KSJV	322.2	334.9	315.8	335.4	367.2	KSLO	256.3	250.9	218.5	232.5	272.3
Brill	KSJX	0.4	0.4	0.4	0.3	0.3	KSLP	2.0	1.8	1.6	1.4	1.4
Catfish	KSJY	0.7	0.5	0.5	0.4	0.3	KSLQ	0.9	0.7	0.8	0.5	0.6
Cod	KSJZ	28.1	25.7	15.5	15.2	13.8	KSLR	37.4	35.0	22.3	22.7	21.8
Dogfish	KSKA	7.0	5.8	6.7	4.6	2.8	KSLS	6.3	5.4	6.5	4.5	2.5
Haddock	KSKB	42.3	51.9	40.7	45.4	47.6	KSLT	36.3	34.6	27.5	32.7	38.7
Hake	KSKC	2.2	2.1	1.9	2.2	2.6	KSLU	5.3	5.6	4.6	5.3	6.8
Lemon Soles	KSKD	3.6	2.3	2.2	2.1	2.1	KSLV	9.9	7.3	6.7	6.0	6.4
Ling	KSKE	6.9	7.2	4.5	4.3	3.5	KSLW	7.4	7.7	4.6	4.4	3.8
Megrims	KSKF	4.3	4.0	3.6	3.4	3.3	KSLX	7.0	8.0	7.6	7.7	8.3
Monks or Anglers	KSKG	15.1	13.1	10.2	10.8	12.6	KSLY	33.8	27.9	20.9	22.7	30.6
Plaice	KSKH	7.7	5.9	4.4	3.5	3.1	KSLZ	9.0	6.6	5.2	4.3	4.0
Pollack (Lythe)	KSKI	2.6	2.5	2.5	2.1	2.0	KSMA	3.3	3.0	3.6	2.7	2.8
Saithe	KSKJ	9.7	9.9	8.5	9.0	11.4	KSMB	4.3	4.1	3.5	3.8	5.4
Sand Eels	KSKK	1.3	1.2	0.2	0.6	..	KSMC	0.1	0.1	..	..	..
Skates and Rays	KSKL	5.5	5.3	5.8	4.3	3.3	KSMD	5.7	5.3	5.8	4.5	3.9
Soles	KSKM	2.1	2.1	2.3	2.0	1.8	KSME	13.2	12.8	14.3	12.9	12.5
Turbot	KSKN	0.5	0.6	0.5	0.4	0.3	KSMF	3.3	4.2	2.7	2.4	2.5
Whiting	KSKO	15.1	11.4	8.2	7.4	8.9	KSMG	9.9	6.6	5.1	5.0	5.7
Whiting, Blue	KSKP	20.0	8.6	9.7	25.0	28.8	KSMH	0.9	0.6	0.7	1.3	1.4
Witches	KSKQ	2.7	2.2	2.4	2.2	1.6	KSMI	2.7	2.5	3.3	3.7	2.8
Other Demersal[2]	KSKR	17.7	15.1	13.0	10.5	7.7	KSMJ	19.8	18.5	17.6	17.4	12.1
Total Demersal[3]	KSKS	195.5	178.1	143.6	155.8	157.8	KSMK	218.4	198.4	165.1	165.9	174.0
Herring[4]	KSKT	43.8	42.5	55.4	56.2	76.4	KSML	10.4	6.9	7.1	7.6	15.9
Horse Mackerel	KSKU	3.5	1.8	2.0	2.5	4.0	KSMM	0.6	0.4	0.3	0.4	1.3
Mackerel[4]	KSKV	63.9	96.6	106.4	115.3	120.6	KSMN	23.9	42.7	44.3	57.0	78.3
Pilchards	KSKW	6.8	5.8	2.7	1.3	3.6	KSMO	1.7	1.0	0.7	0.6	1.1
Sprats	KSKX	5.1	5.7	5.5	3.9	4.7	KSMP	0.6	0.7	0.8	0.7	1.6
Tuna	KSKY	..	–	..	–	–	KSMQ	..	–	..	–	–
Other Pelagic	KSKZ	3.6	4.4	0.1	0.4	0.1	KSMR	0.8	0.8	0.1	0.2	..
Total Pelagic	KSLA	126.7	156.8	172.2	179.6	209.4	KSMS	37.9	52.5	53.4	66.6	98.3
Cockles	KSLB	19.0	14.3	31.4	12.9	13.2	KSMT	3.8	4.2	19.1	10.1	8.1
Crabs	KSLC	25.0	23.3	25.4	21.7	20.0	KSMU	27.8	26.0	28.1	23.5	23.7
Lobsters	KSLD	1.1	1.2	1.4	1.4	1.4	KSMV	11.4	11.7	13.9	12.6	12.2
Mussels	KSLE	14.9	17.2	3.1	12.1	11.3	KSMW	4.8	4.5	1.7	2.0	1.3
Nephrops	KSLF	28.4	28.4	27.7	30.4	33.8	KSMX	68.4	68.8	64.8	70.3	84.0
Periwinkles	KSLG	0.8	0.2	0.2	0.1	0.1	KSMY	0.8	0.2	0.2	0.1	0.1
Queens	KSLH	8.7	10.8	7.3	5.1	5.5	KSMZ	3.7	4.2	2.9	1.9	2.6
Scallops	KSLI	19.5	18.8	19.3	21.1	20.7	KSNA	29.9	28.0	29.4	31.8	32.7
Shrimps/Prawns	KSLJ	2.6	1.5	0.7	0.5	0.5	KSNB	3.6	2.6	1.1	0.7	0.9
Squid	KSLK	1.4	2.1	3.0	2.9	2.6	KSNC	3.9	4.9	6.8	7.8	6.3
Other shellfish	KSLL	14.9	13.1	16.3	18.0	15.5	KSND	9.2	8.9	10.7	12.4	11.9
Total shellfish	KSLM	136.2	130.7	135.7	126.1	124.5	KSNE	167.3	163.8	178.5	173.1	183.8

1 See chapter text.
2 Includes roes and livers.
3 Includes fish roes.

4 Includes transshipments, i.e. caught by UK boats but not actually landing at UK ports. These quantities are transshipped to foreign vessels in coastal waters and are later recorded as exports.

Source: Fisheries Administrations in the UK: 020 7270 8096

21.15

Fishing fleet[1]
United Kingdom
At 31 December each year

		1995	1996	1997	1998	1999	2000	2001	2002	2003	2004	2005
By size												
10m and under	KSNF	6 320	5 606	5 474	5 487	5 409	5 273	5 227	5 287	5 113	5 092	4 833
10.01 - 12.19m	KSNG	1 016	800	732	628	577	547	536	514	486	465	449
12.20 - 17.00m	KSNH	622	540	523	491	468	467	442	409	405	393	387
17.01 - 18.29m	KSNI	187	164	162	154	154	131	143	129	121	115	112
18.30 - 24.38m	KSNJ	574	509	471	443	414	406	405	322	271	257	253
24.39 - 30.48m	KSNK	212	223	227	226	224	219	218	185	156	147	143
30.49 - 36.58m	KSNL	127	114	104	89	80	77	75	65	63	60	55
over 36.58m	KSNM	117	117	119	121	122	122	123	122	120	112	109
Total over 10m	KSNN	2 855	2 467	2 338	2 152	2 039	1 969	1 942	1 746	1 622	1 549	1 508
Total UK fleet[2]	KSNO	9 174	8 073	7 812	7 639	7 448	7 242	7 169	7 033	6 735	6 641	6 341
By segment												
Pelagic gears	KSNP	67	58	49	50	46	44	47	45	42	31	23
Beam trawl	KSNQ	220	215	153	123	114	111	116	113	162	102	69
Demersal trawls and seines	KXET	..	1 040	..	..	..	..	..	..	..	..	..
Demersal trawls	KSIX	856	..	..	..	..	..	..	..	..	..	..
Nephrop trawls	KSIY	528	411	..	..	..	..	..	..	..	..	..
Seines	KSIZ	165	..	..	..	..	..	..	..	..	..	..
Demersal, Seines and Nephrops	JZCI	..	..	1 428	1 318	1 235	1 208	1 158	969	853	852	799
Lines and Nets	KSNR	267	224	214	187	172	165	146	136	118	123	112
Shellfish: mobile	KSNS	194	265	227	241	243	211	229	228	191	166	153
Shellfish: fixed	KSNT	283	339	352	311	301	297	301	304	307	253	235
Distant water	KSNU	12	15	13	14	12	13	11	10	8	10	10
Under 10m	KSNV	6 757	6 091	6 022	6 027	5 916	5 769	5 713	5 773	5 587	5 395	5 134
Non-active/non-TAC	KSNW	371	–	–	–	–	–	–	–	–	..	..
Other: Mussel Dredgers	JZCJ	..	..	3	2	2	2	7	15	15	13	7
Total UK fleet[3]	KSNX	9 720	8 658	8 461	8 273	8 041	7 820	7 728	7 593	7 283	6 945	6 715

1 See chapter text.
2 Excluding Channel Islands and Isle of Man.
3 Including Channel Islands and Isle of Man.

Source: Department for Environment, Food and Rural Affairs: 01904 455332

21.16 Estimated household food consumption[1]

Grammes per person per week

		Great Britain							United Kingdom				
		1995	1996	1997	1998	1999	2000		2001/02	2002/03	2003/04	2004/05	2005/06
Liquid wholemilk[2] (ml)	KPQM	812	776	712	693	634	664	VQEW	599	555	585	484	460
Fully skimmed (ml)	KZBH	204	137	158	164	167	164	VQEX	160	166	154	158	159
Semi skimmed (ml)	KZBI	899	935	978	945	958	975	VQEZ	931	919	926	975	1 008
Other milk and cream (ml)	KZBJ	255	259	248	243	248	278	VQFA	333	350	358	366	385
Cheese	KPQO	108	111	109	104	104	110	VQFB	112	112	113	110	116
Butter	KPQP	36	39	38	39	37	39	VQFC	42	37	35	35	38
Margarine	KPQQ	41	36	26	26	20	21	VQFD	13	13	12	11	20
Low and reduced fat spreads	KZBK	72	79	77	69	71	68	VQFE	72	70	71	68	55
All other oils and fats (ml for oils)	KPQR	69	71	62	62	58	58	VQFF	70	70	68	68	70
Eggs (number)	KPQS	2	2	2	2	2	2	VQFG	2	2	2	2	2
Preserves and honey	KPQT	39	41	41	38	33	33	VQFH	35	34	33	34	35
Sugar	KPQU	136	144	128	119	107	105	VQFI	112	111	102	99	94
Beef and veal	KPQV	121	101	110	109	110	124	VQFJ	118	118	119	123	120
Mutton and lamb	KPQW	54	66	56	59	57	55	VQFK	51	51	49	50	53
Pork	KPQX	71	73	75	76	69	68	VQFL	61	61	56	56	52
Bacon and ham, uncooked	KPQY	76	77	72	76	68	71	VQFM	68	69	70	70	68
Bacon and ham, cooked (including canned)	KPQZ	39	33	41	40	39	41	VQFN	45	45	47	43	44
Poultry uncooked	JZCH	215	233	221	218	201	214	VQFO	206	199	200	197	212
Cooked poultry (not purchased in cans)	KYBP	22	23	33	33	35	39	VQFQ	43	44	11	10	12
Other cooked and canned meats	KPRB	63	62	52	49	48	51	VQFR	54	59	60	58	56
Offals	KPRC	9	7	7	5	5	5	VQFS	6	6	7	5	5
Sausages, uncooked	KPRD	63	63	63	60	58	60	VQFT	66	66	70	67	64
Other meat products	KPRE	211	207	209	216	221	239	VQFU	313	319	335	330	323
Fish, fresh and processed (including shellfish)	KPRF	68	72	70	70	70	67						
Canned fish	KPRG	29	31	31	29	31	32						
Fish and fish products, frozen	KPRH	46	50	46	46	42	44						
Fish, fresh chilled or frozen								VQAI	51	48	45	42	45
Other fish and fish products								VQAJ	105	106	111	115	122
Potatoes (excluding processed)	KPRI	803	805	745	715	673	707	VQFY	647	617	600	570	587
Fresh green vegetables	KPRJ	225	233	251	246	245	240	VQAK	229	231	228	225	235
Other fresh vegetables	KPRK	470	489	497	486	500	492	VQAL	502	505	505	536	567
Frozen potato products	KYBQ	99	113	106	111	113	120						
Other frozen vegetables	KPRL	101	94	94	88	87	80						
Potato products not frozen	JZCF	89	92	90	89	86	82						
Canned beans	KPRM	117	125	122	118	112	114						
Other canned vegetables (excl. potatoes)	KPRN	110	113	104	99	92	97						
Other processed vegetables (excl. potatoes)	LQZH	48	55	52	54	59	54						
All processed vegetables								VQAM	620	613	611	597	608
Apples	KPRO	183	175	179	181	169	180	VQGN	175	172	171	173	179
Bananas	KPRP	176	185	195	198	202	206	VQGO	203	208	211	217	225
Oranges	KPRQ	66	63	62	63	50	54	VQGP	55	62	64	57	59
All other fresh fruit	KPRR	247	263	276	274	290	304	VQGS	318	351	343	358	392
Canned fruit	KPRS	45	43	44	37	38	38	VQGT	40	39	40	38	36
Dried fruit, nuts and fruit and nut products	KPRT	34	36	35	34	30	35	VQGU	39	41	40	46	51
Fruit juices (ml)	KPRU	244	258	277	304	284	303	VQGX	327	333	322	280	350
Flour	KPRV	57	70	54	55	56	67	VQGY	55	61	52	55	60
Bread	KPRW	756	752	746	742	717	720	VQGZ	769	756	728	695	701
Buns, scones and teacakes	KPRX	36	47	43	41	40	43	VQHA	37	41	44	47	46
Cakes and pastries	KPRY	85	87	93	88	87	89	VQHB	139	122	120	117	122
Biscuits	KPRZ	135	150	138	137	132	141	VQHC	166	174	163	165	165
Breakfast cereals	KPSA	135	140	135	136	134	143	VQHE	133	132	134	131	135
Oatmeal and oat products	KPSB	11	13	16	11	13	15	VQHF	12	13	12	14	19
Other cereals and cereal products	JZCG	251	304	293	270	284	291	VQHG	345	366	360	354	378
Tea	KPSC	39	38	36	35	32	34	VQHK	34	34	31	31	33
Instant coffee	KPSD	12	13	11	12	11	11	VQHL	13	12	13	13	13
Canned soups	KPSE	64	72	70	71	67	71	VQHM	79	80	77	76	82
Pickles and sauces	KPSF	80	84	92	96	91	107	VQHN	121	123	121	120	125

1 See chapter text.
2 Including also school and welfare milk.

Sources: Expenditure and Food Survey;
Department for Environment Food and Rural Affairs: 01904 455067

Production

Chapter 22

Production

Annual Business Inquiry

(Table 22.1)

The Annual Business Inquiry (ABI) estimates cover all UK businesses registered for Value Added Tax (VAT) and/ or Pay As You Earn (PAYE), classified to the 1992 Standard Industrial Classification (SIC(92)) headings listed in the tables. The ABI obtains details on these businesses from the Office for National Statistics (ONS) Inter-Departmental Business Register (IDBR).

As with all its statistical inquiries, ONS is concerned to minimise the form-filling burden of individual contributors and as such the ABI is a sample inquiry. The sample was designed as a stratified random sample of about 77,000 businesses, the inquiry population is stratified by SIC(92) and employment using the information from the register.

The inquiry results are grossed up to the total population, so that they relate to all active UK businesses on the IDBR for the sectors covered.

The results meet a wide range of needs for government, economic analysts and the business community at large. In official statistics the inquiry is an important source for the national accounts and input-output tables, but also provides weights for the indices of production and producer prices. Inquiry results also enable the United Kingdom to meet statistical requirements of the European Union.

Data from 1995 and 1996 were calculated on a different basis from those for 1997 and later years. In order to provide a link between the two data series, the 1995 and 1996 data were subsequently reworked to provide estimates on a consistent basis.

Revised Annual Business Inquiry results down to SIC(92) 4 digit class level for 1995–2005, giving both analysis and tabular detail, are now available free of charge from the National Statistics website at *www.statistics.gov.uk/abi/*, with further extracts and bespoke analyses available on request. This service replaces existing publications.

Manufacturers' sales by industry

(Table 22.2)

This table shows the total manufacturers' sales for products classified to the 1992 Standard Industrial Classification and collected under the PRODCOM (Products of the European Community) Inquiry since its introduction in 1993. Some data are not available for confidentiality reasons or where data have not been published for a given period. Detailed product sales data together with exports and imports data are available in the Product Sales and Trade quarterly and annual reports (PRQ and PRA series).

Number of VAT based local units in manufacturing industries in 2005

(Table 22.3)

The table shows the number of local units (sites) in manufacturing by employment size band. The classification breakdown is at division level (2 digit) as classified to the 2003 Standard Industrial Classification held on the Inter-Departmental Business Register (IDBR). This register became fully operational in 1995 and combines information on VAT traders and PAYE employers in a statistical register comprising 2.1 million enterprises (businesses), representing nearly 99 per cent of economic activity. UK Business: Activity, Size and Location 2006 provides further details and contains detailed information on enterprises and local units in the UK including size, classification and location.

For further information on the IDBR see the National Statistics website at www.statistics.gov.uk/idbr.

Production of primary fuels

(Table 22.4)

This table shows indigenous production of primary fuels. It includes the extraction or capture of primary commodities and the generation or manufacture of secondary commodities. Production is always gross; that is, it includes the quantities used during the extraction or manufacturing process. Primary fuels are coal, natural gas (including colliery methane), oil, primary electricity (i.e. electricity generated by hydro, nuclear, wind and tide stations and also electricity imported from France through the interconnector) and renewables (includes solid renewables such as wood, straw and waste and gaseous renewables such as landfill gas and sewage gas). The figures are presented on a common basis, expressed in million tonnes of oil equivalent. Estimates of the gross calorific values used for converting the statistics for the various fuels to these are given in the *Digest of UK Energy Statistics* (published by The Stationery Office and available on the Department of Trade and Industry (DTI) website at www.dti.gov.uk/energy/inform/statistics/publications). Chapter 1 of the *Digest of UK Energy Statistics* gives more information on these figures.

Total inland energy consumption

(Table 22.5)

This table shows energy consumption by fuel and final energy consumption by fuel and class of consumer. Primary energy consumption covers consumption of all primary fuels (defined above) for energy purposes. This measure of energy consumption includes energy that is lost by converting primary fuels into secondary fuels, i.e. the energy lost burning coal to generate electricity or the energy used by refineries to separate crude oil into fractions, in addition to losses in distribution. The other common way of measuring energy consumption is to measure the energy content of the fuels supplied to consumers. This is called final energy consumption. It is net of fuel used by the energy industries, conversion, transmission and distribution losses. The figures are presented on a common basis, measured as energy supplied and expressed in million tonnes of oil equivalent. Estimates of the gross calorific values used for converting the statistics for the various fuels to these are given in the *Digest of UK Energy Statistics* (published by The Stationery Office and available on the DTI website at www.dti.gov.uk/energy/statistics/publications). So far as practicable the user categories have been grouped on the basis of the SIC(2003) although the methods used by each of the supply industries to identify end users are slightly different. Chapter 1 of the *Digest of UK Energy Statistics* gives more information on these figures.

Coal

(Table 22.6)

Since 1995, aggregate data on coal production have been obtained from the Coal Authority. In addition, main coal producers provide data in response to an annual DTI inquiry which covers production (deepmined and opencast), trade, stocks and disposals. HM Revenue and Customs also provide trade data for solid fuels. The DTI collects information on the use of coal from UK Iron and Steel Statistics Bureau, and consumption of coal for electricity generation is covered by data provided by the electricity generators.

Gas

(Table 22.7)

Production figures, covering the production of gas from the UKCS offshore and onshore gas fields and gas obtained during the production of oil, are obtained from returns made under the DTI's Petroleum Production Reporting System. Additional information is used on imports and exports of gas and details from the operators of gas terminals in the UK to complete the picture.

It is no longer possible to present information on fuels input into the gas industry and gas output and sales in the same format as in previous editions of this table. As such, users are directed to Chapter 4 of the 2006 edition of the *Digest of UK Energy Statistics*, where more detailed information on gas production and consumption in the UK is available.

DTI carry out an annual survey of gas suppliers to obtain details of gas sales to the various categories of consumer. Estimates are included for the suppliers with the smallest market share since the DTI inquiry covers only the largest suppliers (i.e. those more than about 0.5 per cent share of the UK market up to 1997 and those known to supply more than 1,750 GWh per year from 1998 onwards).

Electricity

(Tables 22.8 to 22.10)

The electricity Tables 22.8 to 22.10 cover all generators and suppliers of electricity in the United Kingdom.

The relationship between generation, supply, availability and consumption is as follows:

Electricity generated

less	electricity used on works
equals	electricity supplied (gross)
less	electricity used in pumping at pumped storage stations
equals	electricity supplied (net)
plus	imports (net of exports) of electricity
equals	electricity available
less	losses and statistical differences
equals	electricity consumed.

In Table 22.8 'major power producers' are those generating companies corresponding to the old public sector supply system, i.e. AES Electric Ltd., Baglan Generation Ltd., Barking Power Ltd., BNFL Magnox, British Energy plc., Centrica plc., Coolkeeragh ESB Ltd., Corby Ltd., Coryton Energy Company Ltd., Derwent Cogeneration Ltd., Drax Power Ltd., EDF Energy Plc, E. On UK Plc, Fellside Heat and Power Ltd., Fibrogen Ltd., Fibropower Ltd., Fibrothetford Ltd., First Hydro Company., Immingham CHP., International Power plc., Premier Power Ltd., Rocksavage Power Company Ltd., RWE Npower plc., Scottish Power plc., Scottish and Southern Energy plc., Seabank Power Ltd., SELCHP Ltd. (South East London Combined Heat & Power Ltd.), Teeside Power Ltd., Western Power Generation Ltd.

Production

In Table 22.10 all fuels are converted to the common unit of million tonnes of oil equivalent, i.e. the amounts of oil which would be needed to produce the output of electricity generated from those fuels.

More detailed statistics on energy are given in the *Digest of United Kingdom Energy Statistics* 2006. Readers may wish to note that the production and consumption of fuels are presented using commodity balances. A commodity balance shows the flows of an individual fuel through from production to final consumption, showing its use in transformation and energy industry own use.

Oil and oil products

(Tables 22.11 to 22.13)

The data on the production of crude oil, condensates and natural gases given in Table 22.11 are collected by the DTI direct from the operators of production facilities and terminals situated on UK territory, either onshore or offshore, i.e. on the UK Continental Shelf. Data are also collected from the companies on their trade in oil and oil products. These data are used in preference to the foreign trade as recorded by HM Revenue and Customs in the *Overseas Trade Statistics*.

Data on the internal UK oil industry (i.e. on the supply, refining and distribution of oil and oil products in the UK) are collected by the DTI from the UK Petroleum Industry Association. These data, reported by individual refining companies and wholesalers, and supplemented where necessary by data from other sources, provide the contents of Tables 22.12 and 22.13. The data are presented in terms of deliveries to the inland UK market. This is regarded as an acceptable proxy for actual consumption of products. The main shortcoming is that, whilst changes in stocks held by companies in central storage areas are taken into account, changes in the levels of stocks further down the retail ladder (such as stocks held on petrol station forecourts) are not. This is not thought to result in a significant degree of difference in the data.

Iron and steel

(Tables 22.14 to 22.16)

Iron and steel industry

The general definition of the UK iron and steel industry is based on groups 271 'ECSC iron and steel', 272 'Tubes', and 273 'Primary Transformation' of the UK Standard Industrial Classification (1992), except those parts of groups 272 and 273 which cover cast iron pipes, drawn wire, cold formed sections and Ferro alloys.

The definition excludes certain products which may be made by works within the industry, such as refined iron, finished steel castings, steel tyres, wheels, axles and rolled rings, open and closed die forgings, colliery arches and springs. Iron foundries and steel stockholders are also considered to be outside of the industry.

Statistics

The statistics for the UK iron and steel industry are compiled by the Iron and Steel Statistics Bureau (ISSB Ltd). from data collected from UK steel producing companies with the exception of trade data which is based on HM Customs data.

Crude steel is the total of usable ingots, usable continuously cast semi-finished products and liquid steel for castings.

Production of finished products is the total production at the mill of that product after deduction of any material which is immediately scrapped.

Deliveries are based on invoiced tonnages and will include deliveries made to steel stockholders and service centres by the UK steel industry.

For more detailed information on definitions etc please contact ISSB Ltd. on 020 7343 3900.

Fertilisers

(Table 22.18)

This data set provides an estimate of the quantities of major fertiliser nutrients and compound fertiliser product tonnage delivered to farm in the UK for the fertiliser seasons ending in June of each year. This table has previously included only fertiliser quantities delivered by Members of the Agricultural Industries Confederation (AIC) – Fertiliser sector (previously the Fertiliser Manufacturers Association (FMA). The table has now been fully revised to provide estimates of total UK fertiliser market in order to give more complete data and to eliminate fluctuations which could be caused by any change of membership within the AIC.

This table 22.18 is therefore completely revised from those published in previous editions.

Minerals

(Table 22.19)

Table 22.19 gives, separately for Great Britain and Northern Ireland, the production of minerals extracted from the ground. The figures for chemicals and metals are estimated from the quality of the ore which is extracted. The data come from an annual census of the quarrying industry which, for Great Britain, is conducted by ONS for the Department for Communities and Local Government and the DTI.

Building Materials

(Table 22.20)

Table 22.20 gives the production of a number of building materials which are closely associated with material extracted from the ground. The data come from surveys conducted by ONS on behalf of the DTI.

Construction

(Tables 22.21 to 22.22)

Table 22.21 shows the value of contractors' output in the construction industry in Great Britain. Output is defined as the amount chargeable to customers for building and civil engineering work done in the relevant period plus that done by public sector direct labour. The data come from surveys run by the DTI. As well as being an important input to the National Accounts, it is used by the government and the construction industry in their efforts to fully understand the industry, and also by Eurostat.

Table 22.22 shows the value of new orders in the construction industry; this is also collected by DTI. This information relates to contracts for new construction work awarded to main contractors by clients in both the public and private sectors; it also includes speculative work, undertaken on the initiative of the firm, where no contract is awarded. New orders are used as a good indicator of future output.

Engineering Turnover and Orders

(Tables 22.23 and 22.24)

The figures represent the output of United Kingdom based manufacturers classified to Subsections DK and DL of the Standard Industrial Classification 2003. They are derived from the monthly production inquiry (MPI) and include estimates for non-responders and for establishments which are not sampled. On table 22.24, from December 2006 (reference period October 2006), constant price data are no longer available.

Motor vehicle production

(Table 22.25)

The figures represent the output of United Kingdom based manufacturers classified to Class 34.10 (motor vehicles) of the Standard Industrial Classification 2003. They are derived from the Motor Vehicle Production Inquiry (MVPI).

These figures include vehicles produced in the form of kits for assembly. The value of the kit must be 50 per cent or more of the value of a corresponding complete vehicle.

Drink and tobacco

(Tables 22.26 and 22.27)

Data for these tables are derived by HM Revenue and Customs from the systems for collecting excise duties. Alcoholic drinks and tobacco products become liable to duty when released for consumption in the UK. Figures for releases include both home-produced products and commercial imports. Production figures are also available for potable spirits distilled and beer brewed in the UK.

Alcoholic drink

(Table 22.26)

The figures for Imported and other spirits released for home consumption include gin and other UK produced spirits, for which a breakdown is not available.

Since June 1993 beer duty has been charged when the beer leaves the brewery or other registered premises. Previously duty was chargeable at an earlier stage (the worts stage) in the brewing process, and an allowance was made for wastage. Figures prior to 1994 include adjustments to bring them into line with current data. The change in June 1993 also led to the availability of data on the strength; a series in hectolitres of pure alcohol is shown from 1994.

Made wine with alcoholic strength from 1.2 per cent to 5.5 per cent is termed 'coolers'. Included in coolers are alcoholic lemonade and similar products of appropriate strength. From 28 April 2002, duty on spirit-based 'coolers' (ready to drink products) is charged at the same rate as spirits per litre of alcohol. Made wine coolers include only wine based 'coolers' from this period.

Tobacco Products

(Table 22.27)

Releases of cigarettes and other tobacco products tend to be higher in the period before a Budget. Products may then be stocked, duty paid, before being sold.

22.1 Production and construction:[1] summary table
United Kingdom
Standard Industrial Classfication 1992: Estimates for all firms

£ million

	Total turnover	Gross value added	Stocks and work in progress		Capital expenditure less disposals	Total employment costs
			At end of year	Change during year		

Standard Industrial Classification: Revised 1992

Production and construction
Sections C-F

	ZIYQ	KSCD	KSCE	KSCF	KSCG	AWKC
2000	675 149	228 161	66 571	3 962	27 478	115 943
2001	674 274	229 773	65 831	713	28 823	117 560
2002	669 855	228 613	70 233	520	27 116	119 037
2003	678 072	228 976	67 044	1 845	25 663	118 540
2004	708 164	242 718	68 919	3 936	24 784	120 803

Production industries (Revised definitions)
Sections C-E

	ZIYR	KSCL	KSCM	KSCN	KSCO	AWKH
2000	553 601	185 886	54 945	3 200	25 261	94 209
2001	544 210	182 243	52 732	−824	25 716	93 993
2002	529 380	178 828	50 261	−753	23 182	93 098
2003	527 180	175 826	49 122	−401	22 448	91 317
2004	549 325	186 317	49 139	1 212	21 226	92 453

Mining and quarrying
Section C

	ZIYS	KSCT	KSCU	KSCV	KSCW	AWKI
2000	36 513	22 289	957	−2	2 810	2 669
2001	37 057	22 560	958	64	4 272	2 698
2002	32 950	19 279	882	30	4 813	2 682
2003	32 329	18 173	814	−29	4 420	2 782
2004	34 013	19 407	791	22	3 981	2 758

Mining and quarrying of energy producing materials
Subsection CA

	ZIYT	KSDB	KSDC	KSDD	KSDE	KSDF
2000	31 704	20 489	657	−24	2 572	1 905
2001	32 237	20 765	658	33	4 008	1 945
2002	28 406	17 827	612	7	4 563	1 974
2003	27 506	16 682	506	−47	4 116	1 957
2004	28 852	17 670	484	5	3 665	1 975

Mining and quarrying except energy producing materials
Subsection CB

	ZIYU	KSDJ	KSDK	KSDL	KSDM	KSDN
2000	4 809	1 800	300	21	237	765
2001	4 820	1 795	300	31	264	752
2002	4 544	1 452	271	23	249	708
2003	4 823	1 491	308	18	304	825
2004	5 160	1 737	307	17	317	783

Manufacturing (Revised definition)
Section D

	ZIYV	KSDR	KSDS	KSDT	KSDU	AWKL
2000	469 146	148 793	52 167	3 150	17 004	87 456
2001	461 898	145 230	50 038	−816	16 278	87 574
2002	450 090	144 149	47 669	−667	13 237	86 691
2003	447 637	142 207	46 914	−371	12 677	84 597
2004	463 734	148 991	47 006	911	11 683	85 289

22.1
continued

Production and construction:[1] summary table
United Kingdom
Standard Industrial Classfication 1992: Estimates for all firms

£ million

	Total turnover	Gross value added	Stocks and work in progress		Capital expenditure *less* disposals	Total employment costs
			At end of year	Change during year		

Standard Industrial Classification: Revised 1992

Manufacture of food; beverages and tobacco
Subsection DA

	ZIYW	KSDZ	KSEA	KSEB	KSEC	AWKM
2000	73 872	20 184	7 605	−88	2 271	9 929
2001	74 692	20 324	7 633	87	2 638	10 045
2002	76 764	20 721	7 557	53	2 161	10 416
2003	78 759	21 870	7 677	63	2 364	10 564
2004	83 031	22 734	7 852	161	1 974	10 695

Manufacture of textile and textile products
Subsection DB

	ZIYX	KSEH	KSEI	KSEJ	KSEK	AWKN
2000	14 358	5 506	2 285	−19	275	3 541
2001	13 229	5 051	2 046	41	258	3 096
2002	12 203	4 480	1 881	41	307	2 894
2003	11 396	4 147	1 713	23	234	2 553
2004	10 990	3 858	1 670	19	110	2 384

Manufacture of leather and leather products
Subsection DC

	ZIYY	KSEP	KSEQ	KSER	KSES	AWKO
2000	1 728	676	230	−18	9	330
2001	1 758	595	230	−28	23	320
2002	1 541	571	228	−3	18	275
2003	974	375	145	−1	11	198
2004	940	320	134	−6	19	199

Manufacture of wood and wood products
Subsection DD

	ZIYZ	KSEX	KSEY	KSEZ	KSFA	AWKP
2000	6 186	2 303	610	30	227	1 292
2001	6 571	2 315	585	−17	219	1 374
2002	7 016	2 459	658	37	186	1 626
2003	7 134	2 669	713	49	211	1 444
2004	7 458	2 966	707	8	178	1 671

Manufacture of pulp, paper and paper products; publishing and printing
Subsection DE

	ZIZA	KSFF	KSFG	KSFH	KSFI	AWKQ
2000	45 291	19 492	2 544	125	1 813	10 857
2001	44 922	19 425	2 606	25	1 657	10 856
2002	45 317	19 294	2 651	104	1 477	10 927
2003	44 767	18 684	2 637	78	1 338	11 056
2004	46 039	19 462	2 776	7	1 250	11 077

Manufacture of coke, refined petroleum products and nuclear fuel
Subsection DF

	ZIZB	KSFN	KSFO	KSFP	KSFQ	AWKR
2000	27 855	2 302	1 199	114	623	920
2001	25 369	2 401	1 000	−190	705	898
2002	24 255	2 502	1 287	190	473	1 099
2003	25 348	2 213	1 269	−13	604	1 160
2004	28 000	2 627	1 375	110	500	1 128

22.1
continued

Production and construction:[1] summary table
United Kingdom
Standard Industrial Classfication 1992: Estimates for all firms

£ million

	Total turnover	Gross value added	Stocks and work in progress		Capital expenditure *less* disposals	Total employment costs
			At end of year	Change during year		

Standard Industrial Classification: Revised 1992

Manufacture of chemicals, chemical products and man-made fibres
Subsection DG

	ZIZC	KSFV	KSFW	KSFX	KSFY	AWKS
2000	47 544	15 069	6 249	481	2 729	7 549
2001	48 915	15 821	6 205	−8	2 473	7 959
2002	48 759	15 847	6 208	−14	2 147	8 295
2003	49 779	15 700	6 190	−119	1 926	7 964
2004	50 175	16 060	5 957	−26	1 913	8 219

Manufacture of rubber and plastic products
Subsection DH

	ZIZD	KSGD	KSGE	KSGF	KSGG	AWKT
2000	19 743	7 644	1 824	59	961	4 767
2001	19 869	7 716	1 833	−1	742	4 769
2002	19 637	7 536	1 769	27	690	4 694
2003	19 803	7 533	1 779	78	751	4 762
2004	20 792	7 842	1 880	118	578	4 960

Manufacture of other non-metallic mineral products
Subsection DI

	ZIZE	KSGL	KSGM	KSGN	KSGO	AWKU
2000	12 014	5 154	1 460	94	621	2 821
2001	11 656	4 895	1 332	−4	488	2 828
2002	12 139	5 011	1 354	21	602	2 755
2003	12 573	5 315	1 321	11	579	2 779
2004	13 582	5 811	1 447	89	497	2 998

Manufacture of basic iron and of ferro-alloys
Subsection DJ

	ZIZF	KSGT	KSGU	KSGV	KSGW	AWKV
2000	41 028	15 912	4 063	192	1 334	10 340
2001	40 660	15 316	3 920	−43	1 122	10 098
2002	38 360	14 640	3 626	88	1 179	9 649
2003	38 125	14 623	3 744	216	1 121	9 584
2004	40 921	15 226	4 012	584	1 048	9 514

Manufacture of machinery and equipment not elsewhere specified
Subsection DK

	ZIZG	KSHB	KSHC	KSHD	KSHE	AWKW
2000	33 821	12 286	4 826	−40	872	8 437
2001	32 825	11 770	4 460	−73	792	8 302
2002	32 247	11 841	4 118	−141	673	8 114
2003	32 078	11 785	4 913	134	644	7 914
2004	33 773	12 110	5 028	139	500	8 050

Manufacture of electrical and optical equipment
Subsection DL

	ZIZH	KSHJ	KSHK	KSHL	KSHM	AWKX
2000	69 110	20 504	8 521	1 700	2 331	12 587
2001	63 227	15 813	7 280	−1 130	1 950	12 576
2002	53 048	15 960	6 107	−693	868	11 292
2003	46 638	15 302	5 228	−265	773	10 024
2004	43 319	16 086	5 282	184	718	9 418

22.1

Production and construction:[1] summary table
United Kingdom
Standard Industrial Classfication 1992: Estimates for all firms

£ million

	Total turnover	Gross value added	Stocks and work in progress		Capital expenditure *less* disposals	Total employment costs
			At end of year	Change during year		

Standard Industrial Classification: Revised 1992

Manufacture of transport equipment
Subsection DM

	ZIZI	KSHR	KSHS	KSHT	KSHU	AWKY
2000	60 440	15 553	9 048	454	2 444	10 520
2001	61 366	17 322	9 206	444	2 740	10 740
2002	61 550	16 925	8 581	−473	2 028	10 808
2003	63 338	15 838	7 975	−688	1 659	10 963
2004	66 728	17 164	7 156	−626	1 912	11 264

Manufacture not elsewhere classified
Subsection DN

	ZIZJ	KSHZ	KSIA	KSIB	KSIC	AWKZ
2000	16 156	6 208	1 703	67	496	3 565
2001	16 839	6 468	1 701	81	471	3 714
2002	17 254	6 361	1 643	94	428	3 846
2003	16 923	6 153	1 608	61	463	3 633
2004	17 986	6 725	1 729	151	487	3 711

Electricity, gas and water supply
Section E

	ZIZK	KSIH	KSII	KSIJ	KSIK	AWLA
2000	47 942	14 804	1 821	52	5 448	4 084
2001	45 256	14 453	1 736	−72	5 165	3 721
2002	46 341	15 399	1 709	−116	5 132	3 725
2003	47 214	15 446	1 393	−1	5 351	3 938
2004	51 578	17 918	1 342	279	5 561	4 407

Construction
Section F

	ZIZL	KSIP	KSIQ	KSIR	KSIS	AWLB
2000	121 549	42 275	11 626	762	2 216	21 734
2001	130 064	47 530	13 099	1 537	3 107	23 567
2002	140 475	49 785	19 973	1 272	3 934	25 939
2003	150 892	53 150	17 923	2 246	3 215	27 223
2004	158 839	56 401	19 780	2 724	3 558	28 350

1 See chapter text.

Source: Office for National Statistics: 01633 812435

22.2

Manufacturers' sales: by industry[1]
United Kingdom
Standard Industrial Classification 1992

£ million

Industry		SIC (92)	2002	2003	2004	2005
Other mining and quarrying						
Quarrying of stone for construction	KSPF	14110	..	..	..	..
Quarrying of limestone, gypsum and chalk	KSPG	14120	..	..	..	..
Quarrying of slate	KSPH	14130	..	..	..	..
Operation of gravel and sand pits	KSPJ	14210	..	..	..	..
Mining of clays and kaolin	KSPK	14220	..	..	..	..
Mining of chemical and fertilizer minerals	KSPL	14300	82	..	..	..
Production of salt	KSPM	14400	..	..	..	..
Other mining and quarrying not elsewhere classified	KSPN	14500	57	62	46	47
Manufacture of food products and beverages						
Production and preserving of meat	KSPO	15110	3 373	3 628	3 921	4 117
Production and preserving of poultry meat	KSPP	15120	..	1 930	..	2 131
Bacon and ham production	KSPQ	15131	1 155	1 253	1 331	1 363
Other meat and poultry meat processing	KSPR	15139	3 887	3 977	4 055	4 190
Processing and preserving of fish and fish products	KSPS	15200	1 630	1 706	1 747	1 924
Processing and preserving of potatoes	KSPT	15310	1 224	..	1 284	..
Fruit and vegetable juice	KSPU	15320	..	557	562	561
Processing and preserving of fruit and vegetables not elsewhere classified	KSPV	15330	2 438	2 330	2 458	2 507
Crude oils and fats	KSPW	15410	439	431	402	237
Refined oils and fats	KSPX	15420	518	616	914	889
Margarine and similar edible fats	KSPY	15430	545	471	..	..
Operation of dairies	KTEH	15510	5 207	5 648	5 457	5 704
Ice cream	KSPZ	15520	498	..	..	446
Grain mill products	KSQA	15610	2 748	2 676	2 768	2 500
Starches and starch products	KSQB	15620	397	389	381	429
Prepared feeds for farm animals	KSPI	15710	2 126	2 097	2 405	2 325
Prepared pet foods	KSQC	15720	920	928	972	..
Bread; fresh pastry goods and cakes	KSQD	15810	3 957	4 342	4 410	4 144
Rusks and biscuits; preserved pastry goods and cakes	KSQE	15820	2 889	..	..	3 503
Sugar	KSQF	15830	1 110	1 153	1 133	1 077
Cocoa; chocolate and sugar confectionery	KSQG	15840	3 468	3 532	3 379	3 159
Macaroni, noodles, couscous and similar farinaceous products	KSQH	15850	513	515	..	..
Processing of tea and coffee	KSQI	15860	1 392	..	1 420	1 500
Condiments and seasonings	KSQJ	15870	1 168	1 064	1 205	1 216
Homogenised food preparations and dietetic foods	KSQK	15880	67	67	56	42
Manufacture of other food products not elsewhere classified	KSQL	15890	1 977	1 997	2 158	2 198
Distilled potable alcoholic beverages	KSQM	15910	..	2 123	2 230	..
Production of ethyl alcohol from fermented materials	KSQN	15920	..	..	..	..
Wines	KSQO	15930	24	..	..	58
Cider and other fruit wines	KSQP	15940	440	524	416	454
Other non-distilled fermented beverages	KSQQ	15950	–	–	–	–
Beer	KSQR	15960	3 708	3 769	4 073	3 754
Malt	KSQS	15970	260	253	255	235
Mineral waters and soft drinks	KSQT	15980	..	..	..	3 037
Manufacture of tobacco products						
Tobacco products	KSQU	16000	1 825	1 829	1 838	1 718
Manufacture of textiles						
Preparation and spinning of textile fibres	KSQV	17100	521	438	486	430
Textile weaving	KSQW	17200	678	666	690	593
Finishing of textiles	KSQX	17300	524	409	472	463
Soft furnishings	KSQY	17401	529	592	576	593
Canvas goods, sacks etc	KSQZ	17402	117	113	101	73
Household textiles	KSRA	17403	781	730	654	650
Carpets and rugs	KSRB	17510	841	751	690	720
Cordage, rope, twine and netting	KSRC	17520	86	87	76	82

22.2
continued

Manufacturers' sales: by industry[1]
United Kingdom
Standard Industrial Classification 1992

£ million

Industry	SIC (92)	2002	2003	2004	2005
Manufacture of textiles continued					
Nonwovens and articles made from nonwovens, except apparel	KSRD	17530	167	153	149	162
Lace	KSRE	17541	23	18	16	19
Narrow fabrics	KSRF	17542	187	160	145	136
Other textiles not elsewhere classified	KSRG	17549	438	452	435	455
Knitted and crocheted fabrics	KSRH	17600	244	203	197	..
Knitted and crocheted hosiery	KSRI	17710	..	..	..	..
Knitted and crocheted pullovers, cardigans and similar	KSRJ	17720	351	307	219	199
Manufacture of wearing apparel; dressing and dyeing of fur					
Leather clothes	KSRK	18100	11	9	7	6
Workwear	KSRL	18210	271	287	263	200
Men's outerwear	KSRM	18221	283	292	249	198
Other women's outerwear	KSRN	18222	876	709	792	681
Men's underwear	KSRO	18231	220	195	171	172
Women's underwear	KSRP	18232	553	458	392	334
Hats	KSRQ	18241	45	37	35	31
Other wearing apparel and accessories	KSRR	18249	420	356	315	313
Dressing/dyeing of fur; articles of fur	KSRS	18300	6	4	4	4
Tanning and dressing of leather; manufacture of luggage, handbags, saddlery, harness and footwear					
Tanning and dressing of leather	KSRT	19100	270	..	..	..
Luggage, handbags and the like, saddlery and harness	KSRU	19200	191	167	140	143
Footwear	KSRV	19300	564	292	250	240
Manufacture of wood and of products of wood and cork, except furniture; manufacture of articles of straw and plaiting materials					
Sawmilling and planing of wood, impregnation of wood	KSRW	20100	703	733	745	772
Veneer sheets	KSRX	20200	708	766	808	793
Builders' carpentry and joinery	KSRY	20300	3 001	3 012	3 192	3 152
Wooden containers	KSRZ	20400	399	349	413	404
Other products of wood	KSSA	20510	370	373	391	413
Articles of cork, straw and plaiting materials	KSSB	20520	5	7	6	5
Manufacture of pulp, paper and paper products					
Paper and paperboard	KSSC	21120	3 019	3 103	2 748	2 713
Corrugated paper and paperboard, sacks and bags	KSSD	21211	609	595	550	..
Cartons, boxes, cases and other containers	KSSE	21219	3 073	2 946	3 081	2 859
Household and sanitary goods and toilet requisites	KSSF	21220	..	..	..	..
Paper stationery	KSSG	21230	603	640	606	616
Wallpaper	KSSH	21240	..	188	184	..
Manufacture of printed labels	EQ2T	21251	438	454	462	446
Manufacture of unprinted labels	EQ2U	21252	33	40	45	..
Manufacture of other articles of paper and paperboard not elsewhere classified	EQ2V	21259	328	356	300	290
Publishing, printing and reproduction of recorded media					
Publishing of books	KSSJ	22110	3 206	3 012	3 237	3 081
Publishing of newspapers	KSSK	22120	4 122	4 122	4 320	4 149
Publishing of journals and periodicals	KSSL	22130	6 952	7 115	7 302	7 490
Publishing of sound recordings	KSSM	22140	207	215	..	301
Other publishing	KSSN	22150	505	516	549	629
Printing of newspapers	KSSO	22210	195	205	235	..
Printing not elsewhere classified	KSSP	22220	9 342	9 059	9 190	9 495
Bookbinding and finishing	KSSQ	22230	450	436	409	417
Composition and plate-making	KSSR	22240	412	400	347	..
Other activities related to printing	KSSS	22250	861	669	827	878
Reproduction of sound recording	KSST	22310	..	260	214	270
Reproduction of video recording	KSSU	22320	234	220	248	168
Reproduction of computer media	KSSV	22330	82	..	..	24
Manufacture of chemicals and chemical products					
Industrial gases	KSSW	24110	508	525	528	495
Dyes and pigments	KSSX	24120	713	971	936	878
Other inorganic basic chemicals	KSSY	24130	1 106	1 084	1 090	1 117
Other organic basic chemicals	KSSZ	24140	5 208	4 451	5 825	5 721
Fertilizers and nitrogen compounds	KSTA	24150	699	789	786	801

22.2
continued

Manufacturers' sales: by industry[1]
United Kingdom
Standard Industrial Classification 1992

£ million

Industry	SIC (92)	2002	2003	2004	2005
Manufacture of chemicals and chemical products continued					
Plastics in primary forms	KSTB	24160	2 932	3 394	3 740	3 956
Synthetic rubber in primary forms	KSTC	24170	..	..	..	..
Pesticides and other agro-chemical products	KSTD	24200	427	431	470	434
Paints, varnishes and similar coatings, printing ink and mastic	KSTE	24300	2 726	2 745	2 776	2 648
Basic pharmaceutical products	KSTF	24410	666	740	734	917
Pharmaceutical preparations	KSTG	24420	8 319	9 194	8 761	9 031
Soap and detergents, cleaning and polishing preparations	KSTH	24510	1 871	1 718	1 805	1 632
Perfumes and toilet preparations	KSTI	24520	2 377	2 314	2 171	1 845
Explosives	KSTJ	24610	101	105	110	114
Glues and gelatines	KSTK	24620	358	371	400	425
Essential oils	KSTL	24630	548	..	..	501
Photographic chemical material	KSTM	24640	..	..	250	254
Prepared unrecorded media	KSTN	24650	124	127	..	..
Other chemical products not elsewhere classified	KSTO	24660	1 941	1 766	1 992	1 966
Man-made fibres	KSTP	24700	600	618	587	488
Manufacture of rubber and plastic products					
Rubber tyres and tubes	KSTQ	25110	737	647	569	..
Retreading and rebuilding of rubber tyres	KSTR	25120	..	..	100	..
Other rubber products	KSTS	25130	1 583	1 575	1 614	1 616
Plastic plates, sheets, tubes and profiles	KSTT	25210	3 462	3 560	3 717	4 052
Plastic packing goods	KSTU	25220	..	..	..	2 815
Builders' ware of plastic	KSTV	25230	4 294	4 602	4 450	4 336
Other plastic products	KSTW	25240	3 261	3 418	3 438	3 319
Manufacture of other non-metallic mineral products					
Flat glass	KSTX	26110	260	278	..	271
Shaping and processing of flat glass	KSTY	26120	904	970	1 034	921
Hollow glass	KSTZ	26130	630	627	638	633
Glass fibres	KSUA	26140	325	338	324	336
Manufacturing and processing of other glass including technical glassware	KSUB	26150	248	241	258	188
Ceramic household and ornamental articles	KSUC	26210	462	424	..	..
Ceramic sanitary fixtures	KSUD	26220	..	..	..	181
Ceramic insulators and insulating fittings	KSUE	26230	25	..	..	20
Other technical ceramic products	KSUF	26240	22	22	21	20
Other ceramic products	KSUG	26250	21	19	..	..
Refractory ceramic products	KSUH	26260	374	346	343	339
Ceramic tiles and flags	KSUI	26300	86	92	98	99
Bricks, tiles and construction products in baked clay	KSUJ	26400	..	..	645	646
Cement	KSUK	26510	758	778	763	782
Lime	KSUL	26520	..	61	..	..
Plaster	KSUM	26530	109	123	133	139
Concrete products for construction purposes	KSUN	26610	..	..	2 273	2 285
Plaster products for construction purposes	KSUO	26620	..	..	492	528
Ready mixed concrete	KSUP	26630	960	..	1 017	923
Mortars	KSUQ	26640	119	132	143	141
Fibre cement	KSUR	26650	72	86	97	86
Other articles of concrete, plaster and cement	KSUS	26660	110	105	110	97
Cutting, shaping and finishing of stone	KSUT	26700	..	448	..	..
Abrasive products	KSUU	26810	178	157	167	180
Other non-metallic mineral products not elsewhere classified	KSUV	26820	672	647	716	739
Manufacture of basic metals					
Cast iron tubes	KSUW	27210	..	..	164	187
Steel tubes	KSUX	27220	1 023	928	1 116	1 443
Cold drawing	KSUY	27310	111	113	141	148

22.2

continued

Manufacturers' sales: by industry[1]
United Kingdom
Standard Industrial Classification 1992

£ million

Industry	SIC (92)	2002	2003	2004	2005
Manufacture of basic metals continued					
Cold rolling of narrow strip	KSUZ	27320	76	82	125	108
Cold forming or folding	KSVA	27330	..	113	..	..
Wire drawing	KSVB	27340	237	236	..	223
Precious metals production	KSVD	27410	271	197	253	285
Aluminium production	KSVE	27420	1 968	1 783	1 779	1 814
Lead, zinc and tin production	KSVF	27430	361	258	..	304
Copper production	KSVG	27440	685	625	767	688
Other non-ferrous metal production	KSVH	27450	505	462	641	770
Casting of iron	KSVI	27510	491	440	440	420
Casting of steel	KSVJ	27520	125	107	108	132
Casting of light metals	KSVK	27530	320	309	297	269
Casting of other non-ferrous metals	KSVL	27540	378	369	300	259
Manufacture of fabricated metal products, except machinery and equipment					
Metal structures and parts of structures	KSVM	28110	5 061	4 877	5 609	5 742
Builders' carpentry and joinery of metal	KSVN	28120	1 016	934	981	1 159
Tanks, reservoirs and containers of metal	KSVO	28210	346	288	291	294
Central heating radiators and boilers	KSVP	28220	521	586	661	809
Steam generators, except central heating hot water boilers	KSVQ	28300	539	..	..	..
Forging, pressing, stamping and roll forming of metal	KSVR	28400	1 890	1 829	1 809	1 881
Treatment and coating of metals	KSVS	28510	1 081	1 084	1 157	1 184
General mechanical engineering	KSVT	28520	1 384	2 562	3 030	3 105
Cutlery	KSVU	28610	..	..	25	22
Tools	KSVV	28620	873	822	809	826
Locks and hinges	KSVW	28630	553	573	599	567
Steel drums and similar containers	KSVX	28710	127	113	122	128
Light metal packaging	KSVY	28720	1 156	1 093	1 079	1 099
Wire products	KSVZ	28730	460	482	504	526
Fasteners, screw machine products, chain and spring	KSWA	28740	613	606	612	599
Other fabricated metal products not elsewhere classified	KSWB	28750	1 540	1 637	1 705	1 663
Manufacture of machinery and equipment not elsewhere classified					
Engines and turbines, except aircraft, vehicles and cycle engines	KSWC	29110	2 114	2 092	2 307	2 470
Pumps	KSWD	29121	1 021	1 133	1 157	1 108
Compressors	KSWE	29122	1 087	1 079	1 177	1 197
Taps and valves	KSWF	29130	1 115	1 103	1 164	1 214
Bearings, gears, gearing and driving elements	KSWG	29140	904	837	877	942
Furnaces and furnace burners	KSWH	29210	280	253	267	251
Lifting and handling equipment	KSWI	29220	2 722	2 772	2 960	3 235
Non-domestic cooling and ventilation equipment	KSWJ	29230	..	2 727	2 843	2 808
Other general purpose machinery not elsewhere classified	KSWK	29240	1 945	1 983	1 989	2 106
Agricultural tractors	KSWL	29310	860	765	743	662
Other agricultural and forestry machinery	KSWM	29320	461	474	515	508
Manufacture of portable hand held power tools	EQ2W	29410	309	229	146	145
Manufacture of other metal working machine tools	EQ2X	29420	592	541	537	543
Manufacture of other machine tools n.e.c.	EQ2Y	29430	401	361	336	301
Machinery for metallurgy	KSWO	29510	93	83	73	84
Machinery for mining	KSWP	29521	497	432	525	805
Earth-moving equipment	KSWQ	29522	938	1 016	..	1 230
Equipment for concrete crushing and screening and roadworks	KSWR	29523	527	560	..	..
Machinery for food, beverage and tobacco processing	KSWS	29530	581	609	666	620
Machinery for textile, apparel and leather production	KSWT	29540	136	129	106	97
Machinery for paper and paperboard production	KSWU	29550	213	221	202	158
Other special purpose machinery not elsewhere classified	KSWV	29560	1 726	1 591	1 685	1 623
Weapons and ammunition	KSWW	29600	..	1 638	2 095	77

22.2
continued

Manufacturers' sales: by industry[1]
United Kingdom
Standard Industrial Classification 1992

£ million

Industry	SIC (92)	2002	2003	2004	2005
Manufacture of machinery and equipment not elsewhere classified continued					
Electric domestic appliances	KSYR	29710	1 895	1 986	2 141	1 781
Non-electric domestic appliances	KSWX	29720	517	477	497	453
Manufacture of office machinery and computers					
Office machinery	KSWY	30010	781	..	384	461
Computers and other information processing equipment	KSWZ	30020	5 669	5 238	4 024	3 568
Manufacture of electrical machinery and apparatus not elsewhere classified					
Electric motors, generators and transformers	KSXA	31100	1 964	1 954	2 146	2 335
Electricity, distribution and control apparatus	KSXB	31200	2 279	2 310	2 370	2 467
Insulated wire and cable	KSXC	31300	922	872	985	933
Accumulators, primary cells and batteries	KSXD	31400	376	329	317	263
Lighting equipment and electric lamps	KSXE	31500	1 010	1 034	1 074	1 110
Electrical equipment for engines and vehicles not elsewhere classified	KSXF	31610	..	1 024	878	879
Other electrical equipment not elsewhere classified	KSXG	31620	1 870	1 799	1 739	1 808
Manufacture of radio, television and communication equipment and apparatus					
Electronic valves and tubes and other electronic components	KSXH	32100	3 281	2 946	2 991	2 734
Telegraph and telephone apparatus and equipment	KSXI	32201	1 902	944	931	509
Radio and electronic capital goods	KSXJ	32202	..	..	1 709	..
Television and radio receivers, sound or video recording etc	KSXK	32300	2 562	2 307	2 530	2 086
Manufacture of medical, precision and optical instruments, watches and clocks					
Medical and surgical equipment and orthopaedic appliances	KSXL	33100	2 164	2 072	2 232	2 410
Instruments and appliances for measuring, checking, testing etc	KSXM	33200	5 139	5 072	4 861	4 996
Industrial process control equipment	KSXN	33300	734	652	699	798
Optical instruments and photographic equipment	KSXO	33400	759	810	896	937
Watches and clocks	KSXP	33500	53	50	50	53
Manufacture of motor vehicles, trailers and semi-trailers					
Motor vehicles	KSXQ	34100	20 418	22 466	22 440	23 865
Bodies (coachwork) for motor vehicles (excluding caravans)	KSXR	34201	855	923	844	828
Trailers and semi-trailers	KSXS	34202	858	918	1 053	1 148
Caravans	KSXT	34203	451	..	594	..
Parts and accessories for motor vehicles and their engines	KSXU	34300	8 894	10 022	9 888	9 801
Manufacture of other transport equipment					
Building and repairing of ships	KSXV	35110	1 654	1 421	1 551	466
Building and repairing of pleasure and sporting boats	KSXW	35120	623	602	648	761
Railway and tramway locomotives and rolling stock	KSXX	35200	1 565	1 689	2 099	1 590
Aircraft and spacecraft	KSXY	35300	11 355	11 703	11 837	9 884
Motorcycles	KSXZ	35410	..	..	..	..
Bicycles	KSYA	35420	96	59	55	50
Invalid carriages	KSYB	35430	109	113	..	..
Other transport equipment not elsewhere classified.	KSYC	35500	86	..	83	..
Manufacture of furniture; manufacturing not elsewhere classified					
Chairs and seats	KSYD	36110	2 851	2 923	2 871	2 772
Other office and shop furniture	KSYE	36120	1 114	1 066	1 057	1 105
Other kitchen furniture	KSYF	36130	1 014	960	972	907
Other furniture	KSYG	36140	2 268	2 249	2 004	1 784
Mattresses	KSYH	36150	570	568	593	543
Striking of coins and medals	KSYI	36210	..	..	..	..
Jewellery and related articles not elsewhere classified	KSYJ	36220	369	393	357	309
Musical instruments	KSYK	36300	42	41	43	41
Sports goods	KSYL	36400	313	327	337	333
Games and toys	KSYM	36500	428	364	355	340
Imitation jewellery	KSYN	36610	24	..	28	30
Brooms and brushes	KSYO	36620	150	..	131	..
Miscellaneous stationers' goods	KSYP	36631	194	..	..	..
Other manufacturing not elsewhere classified	KSYQ	36639	434	445	382	419

1 See chapter text. PRODCOM data is published on the ONS website in the PRA and PRQ series of reports.

Source: Office for National Statistics: 01633 812373

22.3 Number of local units in manufacturing industries, March 2006[1]
United Kingdom
Standard Industrial Classification 2003 Division by Employment Sizeband

Numbers

		Employment size									
		0 - 4	5 - 9	10 - 19	20 - 49	50 - 99	100 - 249	250 - 499	500 - 999	1,000+	Total
Division											
15/16	Food products; beverages and tobacco	3 195	1 195	1 345	1 120	540	580	245	140	35	9 195
17	Textiles and textile products	2 390	815	550	455	245	145	25	5	0	4 630
18	Wearing apparel; dressing and dyeing of fur	2 120	725	420	290	85	35	5	0	0	3 685
19	Leather and leather products	340	150	90	70	25	15	5	0	0	690
20	Wood and wood products	4 595	1 670	890	575	170	75	15	5	0	7 990
21	Pulp, paper and paper products	865	330	250	350	175	195	40	5	0	2 205
22	Publishing, printing and reproduction of recorded media	18 080	4 365	2 475	1 545	590	350	120	40	15	27 585
23	Coke, refined petroleum products and nuclear fuel	95	45	15	25	20	10	10	5	5	225
24	Chemicals, chemical products and man-made fibres	1 485	630	505	555	355	275	120	40	15	3 975
25	Rubber and plastic products	2 670	1 430	1 120	1 120	535	365	80	20	5	7 435
26	Other non-metallic mineral products	3 250	1 065	680	600	295	190	45	5	0	6 135
27	Basic metals	685	290	215	285	155	105	35	10	5	1 785
28	Fabricated metal products, except machinery and equipment	14 665	5 280	3 565	2 555	835	325	55	10	0	27 295
29	Machinery and equipment not elsewhere classified	6 145	2 320	1 800	1 450	595	375	120	30	15	12 850
30	Office machinery and computers	505	130	65	90	35	40	10	10	5	890
31	Electrical machinery and apparatus not elsewhere classified	2 445	845	690	625	285	190	70	20	0	5 170
32	Radio, television and communication equipment and apparatus	1 370	350	235	250	120	80	25	20	5	2 455
33	Medical, precision and optical instruments, watches and clocks	1 980	840	600	575	265	135	50	15	5	4 470
34	Motor vehicles, trailers and semi-trailers	1 140	430	330	365	185	185	90	35	25	2 785
35	Other transport equipment	1 245	380	260	200	105	115	40	30	25	2 405
36/37	Manufacturing not elsewhere classified	11 510	3 300	1 605	1 025	340	195	50	20	0	18 045
Total manufacturing (15/37)		80 780	27 375	17 800	14 120	5 955	3 990	1 260	470	155	151 900

1 The data in this table is taken from the NS publication, UK Business: Activity, Size and Location 2006. The count of units refers to local units, i.e. individual sites, rather than whole businesses. All counts have been rounded to avoid disclosure.

Source: Office for National Statistics: 01633 812293

373

22.4 Production of primary fuels[1]
United Kingdom

Million tonnes of oil equivalent

		1995	1996	1997	1998	1999	2000	2001	2002	2003	2004	2005
Coal	HFZQ	32.8	31.1	30.3	25.8	23.2	19.6	20.0	18.8	17.6	15.6	12.7
Petroleum[2]	HGCY	142.7	142.1	140.4	145.3	150.2	138.3	127.8	127.0	116.2	104.5	92.9
Natural Gas[3]	HGDB	70.8	84.2	85.9	90.2	99.1	108.4	105.9	103.6	102.9	96.0	87.6
Primary electricity[4]	HGDN	21.7	22.4	23.5	24.0	22.9	20.2	21.2	20.6	20.4	18.8	19.0
Renewables and waste[5]	HGDO	1.7	1.8	1.9	2.1	2.2	2.3	2.5	2.8	3.0	3.1	3.2
Total Production	HGDP	269.7	281.6	282.1	287.2	297.7	288.7	277.4	272.8	260.2	238.0	215.4

1 See chapter text.
2 Crude oil plus all condensates and petroleum gases extracted at gas separation plants.
3 Includes colliery methane.

4 Includes nuclear, hydro and other non-thermal renewables (wind, tide etc).
5 Includes biofuels and waste, solar heating and photovoltaics, and geothermal aquifers.

Source: Department of Trade and Industry: 020 7215 2710

22.5 Total inland energy consumption
United Kingdom

Heat supplied basis

Million tonnes of oil equivalent

		1995	1996	1997	1998	1999	2000	2001	2002	2003	2004	2005
Inland energy consumption of primary fuels and equivalents[1]	KLWA	218.4	230.1	226.8	230.8	230.4	233.7	236.3	229.9	232.0	233.4	234.3
Coal[2]	KLWB	48.9	45.7	40.8	40.9	36.7	38.6	41.0	37.7	40.5	39.2	40.0
Petroleum[3]	KLWC	75.4	77.8	75.5	76.1	76.0	75.9	75.4	74.0	73.5	75.5	77.3
Primary electricity	KLWD	23.1	23.8	25.0	25.0	24.2	21.4	22.1	21.3	20.6	19.4	19.8
Natural gas	KLWE	69.2	81.0	83.5	86.9	91.4	95.6	95.4	94.2	94.5	96.2	93.4
Renewables and waste	GYUY	1.7	1.8	1.9	2.1	2.2	2.3	2.5	2.8	3.1	3.5	3.9
less Energy used by fuel producers and losses in conversion and distribution	KLWF	68.0	73.0	72.9	75.0	74.2	74.5	75.4	73.2	73.8	73.4	74.7
Total consumption by final users[1]	KLWG	150.4	157.0	153.9	155.8	156.2	159.2	160.9	156.5	158.0	159.9	159.5

Final energy consumption by type of fuel

		1995	1996	1997	1998	1999	2000	2001	2002	2003	2004	2005
Coal (direct use)	KLWH	5.3	4.4	4.3	3.7	3.5	2.7	2.7	2.2	2.1	2.0	1.7
Coke and breeze	KLWI	3.9	1.0	0.8	0.9	0.9	0.8	0.8	0.7	0.7	0.6	0.6
Other solid fuel[4]	KLWJ	0.7	0.8	0.7	0.7	0.6	0.4	0.5	0.5	0.3	0.3	0.4
Coke oven gas	KLWK	0.6	0.4	0.5	0.4	0.2	0.2	0.2	0.1	0.1	0.1	0.1
Natural gas (direct use)	KLWL	50.1	56.5	54.2	55.9	55.1	57.1	57.8	55.2	56.7	56.9	54.8
Electricity	KLWM	25.3	26.5	26.8	27.1	27.8	28.3	28.6	28.7	28.9	29.1	29.7
Petroleum (direct use)[5]	KLWN	63.7	66.1	65.4	66.0	65.7	66.3	67.1	66.1	66.8	68.9	70.4
Renewables	GYVA	1.0	1.0	0.9	0.9	0.7	0.7	0.7	0.7	0.7	0.7	0.6

Final energy consumption by class of consumer

		1995	1996	1997	1998	1999	2000	2001	2002	2003	2004	2005
Agriculture	KLWP	1.3	1.4	1.3	1.4	1.3	1.2	1.3	1.2	1.0	0.9	1.0
Iron and steel industry	KLWQ	6.9	4.2	4.2	4.0	3.8	2.2	2.3	2.0	1.9	1.9	1.8
Other industries	KLWR	29.4	30.3	30.4	30.5	30.9	33.0	33.0	31.3	31.7	31.1	31.3
Railways[6]	KLWS	1.3	1.3	1.2	1.3	1.2	1.5	1.6	1.5	1.5	1.6	1.6
Road transport	KLWT	39.3	40.8	41.3	41.0	41.4	41.1	41.1	41.9	41.8	42.2	42.4
Water transport	KLWU	1.2	1.3	1.3	1.2	1.1	1.0	0.8	0.7	1.2	1.2	1.4
Air transport	KLWV	8.5	8.9	9.3	10.2	11.0	12.0	11.8	11.7	11.9	13.2	13.9
Domestic	KLWW	42.7	48.1	44.8	46.1	46.1	46.9	48.2	47.5	48.2	48.6	47.0
Public administration	KLWX	8.5	8.8	8.4	8.1	8.4	8.1	8.0	7.0	6.7	7.1	7.2
Commercial and other services	KLWY	11.3	11.9	11.7	12.0	11.9	12.2	12.8	11.6	12.0	12.1	12.1

1 Includes heat sold from 1999.
2 Includes net trade and stock change in other solid fuels.
3 Refinery throughput of crude oil, *plus* net foreign trade and stock change in petroleum products. Petroleum products not used as fuels (chemical feedstock, industrial and white spirits, lubricants, bitumen and wax) are excluded.

4 Includes briquettes, ovoids, Phurnacite, Coalite, etc., and wood, waste etc., used for heat generation.
5 Includes manufactured liquid fuels.
6 Includes fuel used at transport premises.

Source: Department of Trade and Industry: 020 7215 2710

22.6 Coal: supply and demand[1]
United Kingdom

Million tonnes

			1994	1995	1996	1997	1998	1999	2000	2001	2002	2003	2004	2005
Supply														
Production of deep-mined coal	KLXA		31.9	35.2	32.2	30.3	25.7	20.9	17.2	17.3	16.4	15.6	12.5	9.6
Production of opencast coal	KLXB		16.8	16.4	16.3	16.7	14.3	15.3	13.4	14.2	13.1	12.1	12.0	10.4
Total	KLXC		48.7	51.5	48.5	47.0	40.0	36.2	30.6	31.5	29.5	27.8	24.5	20.0
Recovered slurry, fines, etc	KLXD		0.1	1.5	1.7	1.5	1.1	0.9	0.6	0.4	0.5	0.5	0.6	0.5
Imports	KLXE		15.1	15.9	17.8	19.8	21.2	20.3	23.4	35.5	28.7	31.9	36.2	44.0
Total	KLXF		64.9	68.9	68.0	68.3	62.4	57.4	54.6	67.5	58.7	60.2	61.3	64.5
Change in colliery stocks	KLXG	KSOL	−4.2	−4.2	−3.0	0.7	−0.2	0.6	−3.5	−0.1	0.9	−0.9	−0.4	−0.1
Change in stocks at opencast sites	KLXH		−0.5											
Total supply	KLXI		69.6	73.1	70.9	67.6	62.7	56.8	58.2	67.5	57.8	61.0	61.7	64.6
Home consumption														
Total home consumption	KLXW		81.7	76.9	71.4	63.1	63.2	55.7	59.9	63.9	58.6	63.0	60.5	61.8
Overseas shipments and bunkers	KLXX		1.2	0.9	1.0	1.1	1.0	0.8	0.7	0.5	0.5	0.5	0.6	0.5
Total consumption and shipments	KLXY		82.9	77.8	72.4	64.2	64.1	56.5	60.6	64.4	59.1	63.6	61.1	62.4
Change in distributed stocks[2]	KLXZ		−13.9	−2.2	−0.9	3.0	−1.2	0.6	−2.3	3.5	−1.4	−2.4	0.5	2.2
Balance[3]	KLYA		0.6	−2.5	−0.6	0.3	−0.3	−0.3	−0.1	−0.3	0.1	−0.2	0.1	−0.1
Stocks at end of year														
Distributed[2]	KLYB		16.0	13.1	12.3	15.3	14.1	14.7	12.3	15.8	14.4	12.0	12.5	14.7
At collieries	KLYC	KSOM	8.5	7.1	4.2	4.8	4.6	5.2	1.6	1.6	2.5	1.6	1.2	1.1
At opencast sites	KLYD		2.8											
Total stocks	KLYE		27.3	20.2	16.4	20.1	18.7	19.8	14.0	17.4	16.9	13.6	13.7	15.8

1 See chapter text. Figures relate to periods of 52 weeks. For 1998, figures relate to 52 weeks estimate for period ended 26 December 1998.
2 Excludes distributed stocks held in merchant yards etc., mainly for the domestic market, and stocks held by the industrial sector.

3 This is the balance between supply and consumption, shipments and changes in known distributed stocks.

Source: Department of Trade and Industry: 020 7215 2717

22.7 Fuel input and gas output: gas sales[1]
United Kingdom

Public supply

Giga-watt hours

		1995	1996	1997	1998	1999	2000	2001	2002	2003	2004	2005
Analysis of gas sales												
Fuel producers												
Power stations[2]	KIKK	145 790	201 929	251 787	267 703	315 400	324 563	312 939	329 847	324 580	341 111	333 834
Coal extraction and manufacture of solid fuels	KIKL	368	344	193	67	14	6	9	–	1	–	–
Coke ovens	KIKM	1	–	–	–	–	–	–	–	–	–	–
Petroleum refineries	KIKN	2 922	2 907	3 002	3 753	4 155	3 641	4 189	3 350	2 773	1 797	1 987
Nuclear fuel production	KIKO	467	874	923	989	1 021	472	1 210	402	369	201	202
Production and distribution of other energy	KIKP	352	437	487	549	629	619	451	709	726	721	715
Total final producers	KIKQ	149 900	206 491	256 392	273 061	321 219	329 301	318 798	334 308	328 448	343 830	336 738
Final users:												
Iron and steel industry	KIKR	19 988	20 940	20 577	20 105	21 622	8 953	8 502	8 791	10 327	9 715	8 410
Other industries	KIKS	150 697	142 820	151 013	155 979	155 193	174 488	171 341	156 375	155 890	143 959	140 271
Domestic	KIKT	326 010	375 841	345 532	355 895	358 066	369 909	379 426	376 372	386 486	396 411	381 879
Public administration	KIKU	46 308	51 411	52 315	51 976	43 253	44 552	46 232	42 998	44 362	50 934	49 385
Agriculture	KIKV	1 210	1 417	1 440	953	1 155	1 522	2 329	2 346	2 324	2 355	2 201
Miscellaneous	KIKW	61 502	65 080	59 022	64 695	62 079	78 978	75 923	66 269	70 068	68 797	64 788
Total final users	KIKX	605 715	657 509	629 899	649 603	641 368	678 402	683 753	653 151	669 457	672 171	646 990
Total sales	KIKY	755 615	864 000	886 291	922 664	962 587	1 007 703	1 002 546	987 459	997 489	1 003 644	983 728

1 See chapter text. The breakdown of consumption by industrial users is made according to the 2003 Standard Industrial Classification.
2 Includes auto-production of electricity.

Source: Department of Trade and Industry: 020 7215 2717

22.8 Electricity: generation, supply and consumption[1]
United Kingdom

Gigawatt-hours

		1995	1996	1997	1998	1999	2000	2001	2002	2003	2004	2005
Electricity generated												
Major power producers: total	KLUA	313 958	326 235	324 133	333 764	336 608	341 783	353 066	353 994	362 600	358 406	362 379
Conventional thermal and other[2]	AWLC	170 056	160 791	133 591	134 009	118 762	131 062	132 744	126 694	139 147	130 882	136 348
Combined cycle gas turbine stations	KJCS	48 720	65 880	86 974	93 832	114 620	117 935	123 846	132 016	128 311	139 405	136 084
Nuclear stations	KLUC	88 964	94 671	98 146	99 486	95 133	85 063	90 093	87 848	88 686	79 999	81 618
Hydro-electric stations:												
Natural flow	KLUE	4 096	2 801	3 337	4 237	4 431	4 331	3 215	3 927	2 568	4 000	3 993
Pumped storage	KLUF	1 552	1 556	1 486	1 624	2 902	2 694	2 422	2 652	2 734	2 649	2 930
Renewables other than hydro	KLUG	570	536	599	576	761	698	738	856	1 154	1 471	1 406
Other generators: total	KLUH	20 084	24 632	26 534	28 938	31 543	35 285	31 721	33 252	35 609	36 900	38 145
Conventional thermal and other[2]	AWLD	15 387	18 334	18 629	19 091	19 419	19 094	16 621	15 788	17 244	15 698	15 550
Combined cycle gas turbine stations	KJCT	2 126	3 535	4 412	5 428	7 141	10 859	8 979	10 577	10 879	11 926	11 836
Hydro-electric stations (natural flow)	KLUK	742	592	832	881	905	755	840	860	660	929	968
Renewables other than hydro	KILA	1 829	2 171	2 661	3 538	4 078	4 577	5 283	6 028	6 825	8 346	9 791
All generating companies: total	KLUL	334 042	350 867	350 667	362 702	368 151	377 068	384 787	387 246	398 209	395 306	400 525
Conventional thermal and other[2]	AWYH	185 443	179 125	152 220	153 100	138 181	150 156	149 365	142 482	156 391	146 580	151 898
Combined cycle gas turbine stations	KJCU	50 846	69 415	91 386	99 260	121 761	128 794	132 825	142 593	139 190	151 331	147 920
Nuclear stations	KLUN	88 964	94 671	98 146	99 486	95 133	85 063	90 093	87 848	88 686	79 999	81 618
Hydro-electric stations:												
Natural flow	KLUP	4 838	3 393	4 169	5 118	5 336	5 086	4 055	4 787	3 228	4 929	4 961
Pumped storage	KLUQ	1 552	1 556	1 486	1 624	2 902	2 694	2 422	2 652	2 734	2 649	2 930
Renewables other than hydro	KLUR	2 399	2 707	3 260	4 114	4 839	5 275	6 021	6 884	7 979	9 817	11 197
Electricity used on works: Total	KLUS	17 411	16 078	16 560	17 408	16 706	16 304	17 394	17 126	18 136	17 081	17 832
Major generating companies	KLUT	16 510	14 967	15 411	16 140	15 461	14 952	16 066	15 746	16 747	15 582	16 266
Other generators	KLUU	901	1 111	1 149	1 268	1 245	1 352	1 328	1 380	1 389	1 499	1 566
Electricity supplied (gross)												
Major power producers: total	KLUV	299 000	311 268	308 722	317 624	321 147	326 831	336 999	338 248	345 854	342 824	346 113
Conventional thermal and other[2]	AWYI	163 818	155 086	127 419	127 788	112 919	124 828	126 434	120 495	132 053	124 052	129 156
Combined cycle gas turbine stations	KJCV	48 525	65 604	86 682	93 005	112 768	116 110	121 344	129 384	125 630	137 170	133 713
Nuclear stations	KLUX	80 598	85 820	89 341	90 590	87 672	78 334	82 985	81 090	81 911	73 682	75 172
Hydro-electric stations:												
Natural flow	KLUZ	4 051	2 763	3 299	4 225	4 409	4 316	3 203	3 914	2 559	3 993	3 987
Pumped storage	KLVA	1 502	1 507	1 439	1 569	2 804	2 603	2 340	2 562	2 641	2 559	2 776
Renewables other than hydro	KLVB	506	488	542	447	574	640	692	802	1 059	1 367	1 309
Other generators: total	KLVC	20 909	23 521	25 385	27 670	30 298	33 933	30 393	31 873	34 220	35 401	36 579
Conventional thermal and other[2]	AWYJ	16 338	17 492	17 815	18 250	18 643	18 499	15 996	15 211	16 711	15 212	15 064
Combined cycle gas turbine stations	KJCW	2 100	3 358	4 192	5 157	6 785	10 318	8 531	10 049	10 336	11 330	11 246
Hydro-electric stations (natural flow)	KLVF	733	584	822	869	894	743	829	849	653	919	952
Renewables other than hydro	KIKZ	1 738	2 085	2 555	3 393	3 977	4 374	5 037	5 764	6 519	7 940	9 317
All generating companies: total	KLVG	319 909	334 789	334 107	345 294	351 445	360 764	367 392	370 121	380 074	378 224	382 692
Conventional thermal and other[2]	AWYK	180 156	172 578	145 234	146 038	131 562	143 327	142 430	135 706	148 764	139 264	144 220
Combined cycle gas turbine stations	KJCX	50 625	68 962	90 874	98 162	119 553	126 428	129 875	139 433	135 966	148 500	144 959
Nuclear stations	KLVI	80 598	85 820	89 341	90 590	87 672	78 334	82 985	81 090	81 911	73 682	75 172
Hydro-electric stations:												
Natural flow	KLVK	4 784	3 347	4 121	5 094	5 303	5 059	4 032	4 763	3 212	4 912	4 938
Pumped storage	KLVL	1 502	1 507	1 439	1 569	2 804	2 603	2 340	2 562	2 641	2 559	2 776
Renewables other than hydro	KLVM	2 244	2 573	3 097	3 840	4 551	5 014	5 729	6 566	7 578	9 307	10 626
Electricity used in pumping												
Major power producers	KLVN	2 282	2 430	2 477	2 594	3 774	3 499	3 210	3 463	3 546	3 497	3 707
Electricity supplied (net): Total	KLVO	317 627	332 359	331 630	342 700	347 671	357 266	364 182	366 657	376 528	374 727	378 985
Major power producers	KLVP	296 718	308 838	306 245	315 030	317 373	323 332	333 789	334 785	342 308	339 327	342 406
Other generators	KLVQ	20 909	23 521	25 385	27 670	30 298	33 933	30 393	31 873	34 220	35 401	36 579
Net imports	KGEZ	16 313	16 755	16 574	12 468	14 244	14 174	10 399	8 414	2 160	7 490	8 321
Electricity available	KGIZ	333 940	349 114	348 203	355 168	361 915	371 440	374 581	375 072	378 687	382 217	387 307
Losses in transmission etc	KGKW	30 020	29 335	27 138	29 818	29 862	31 146	32 077	30 963	32 070	34 083	32 219
Electricity consumption: Total	KGKX	303 920	319 779	321 065	325 350	332 053	340 294	342 504	344 109	346 617	348 134	355 088
Fuel industries	KGKY	8 070	9 211	8 624	8 406	8 037	9 703	8 625	10 060	9 752	8 491	9 162
Final users: total	KGKZ	295 849	310 567	312 441	316 944	324 016	330 593	333 879	334 049	336 865	339 641	345 926
Industrial sector	KGLZ	101 780	107 631	108 102	108 443	112 250	115 286	112 495	113 296	114 006	116 531	119 515
Domestic sector	KGMZ	102 210	107 513	104 455	109 410	110 308	111 842	115 337	114 534	115 761	115 526	116 811
Other sectors	KGNZ	91 860	95 423	99 884	99 091	101 457	103 465	106 047	106 219	107 098	107 584	109 600

1 See chapter text.
2 Includes electricity supplied by gas turbines and oil engines and plants producing electricity from renewable resources other than hydro.

Source: Department of Trade and Industry: 020 7215 5190

22.9 Electricity: plant capacity and demand
United Kingdom
At end of December

Megawatts

		1997	1998	1999	2000	2001	2002	2003	2004	2005
Major power producers:[1]										
Total declared net capability	GUFY	68 140	68 312	70 245	72 193	73 382	70 369	71 465	73 277	74 041
Conventional steam stations	GUFZ	37 395	35 081	35 647	34 835	34 835	30 687	30 327	30 442	30 768
Combined cycle gas turbine stations	GUGA	12 252	14 618	16 110	19 349	20 517	21 800	23 577	25 323	25 897
Nuclear stations[2]	GUGB	12 946	12 956	12 956	12 486	12 486	12 240	11 852	11 852	11 852
Gas turbines and oil engines	GUGC	1 378	1 434	1 301	1 291	1 291	1 433	1 537	1 485	1 346
Hydro-electric stations:										
Natural flow	GUGD	1 311	1 327	1 327	1 327	1 348	1 304	1 267	1 270	1 273
Pumped storage	GUGE	2 788	2 788	2 788	2 788	2 788	2 788	2 788	2 788	2 788
Renewables other than hydro	GUGF	70	108	117	117	117	117	117	117	117
Other generators:										
Total capacity of own generating plant[3]	GUGG	4 625	4 990	5 388	6 258	6 296	6 336	6 829	7 024	7 697
Conventional steam stations[4]	GUGH	3 240	3 248	3 315	3 544	3 464	3 325	3 480	3 416	3 456
Combined cycle gas turbine stations	GUGI	757	1 005	1 243	1 709	1 777	1 854	1 927	2 019	2 164
Hydro-electric stations (natural flow)	GUGJ	145	148	150	158	160	162	165	135	120
Renewables other than hydro	GUGK	483	589	680	847	895	995	1 257	1 454	1 957
All generating companies: Total capacity[3]	GUGL	72 765	73 302	75 633	78 451	79 678	76 705	78 294	80 301	81 738
Conventional steam stations[4]	GUGM	40 635	38 329	38 962	38 379	38 299	34 012	33 807	33 858	34 224
Combined cycle gas turbine stations	GUGN	13 009	15 623	17 353	21 058	22 294	23 654	25 504	27 342	28 061
Nuclear stations	GUGO	12 946	12 956	12 956	12 486	12 486	12 240	11 852	11 852	11 852
Gas turbines and oil engines	GUGP	1 378	1 434	1 301	1 291	1 291	1 433	1 537	1 485	1 346
Hydro-electric stations:										
Natural flow	GUGQ	1 456	1 475	1 477	1 485	1 508	1 466	1 432	1 405	1 393
Pumped storage	GUGR	2 788	2 788	2 788	2 788	2 788	2 788	2 788	2 788	2 788
Renewables other than hydro	GUGS	553	697	797	964	1 012	1 112	1 374	1 571	2 074
Major power producers:[1]										
Simultaneous maximum load met[5]	GUGT	56 965	56 312	57 849	58 452	58 589	61 717	60 501	61 013	61 697
System load factor[6] (percentages)	GUGU	66.0	68.0	67.0	67.0	69.0	65.0	67.0	67.0	67.0

1 See chapter text.
2 Nuclear generators are now included under "major power producers" only.
3 Capacity figures for other generators are as at end-December of the previous year.

4 For other generators, conventional steam stations cover all types of stations not separately listed.
5 Maximum load in year to end of March.
6 The average hourly quantity of electricity available during the year ending March expressed as a percentage of the maximum demand.

Source: Department of Trade and Industry: 020 7215 5190

22.10 Electricity: fuel used in generation
United Kingdom

Million tonnes of oil equivalent

		1995	1996	1997	1998	1999	2000	2001	2002	2003	2004	2005
Major power producers:[1] total all fuels	KGPS	72.70	74.60	71.50	74.90	73.60	74.40	77.38	75.79	77.53	76.83	78.15
Coal	FTAJ	35.02	32.40	27.10	28.70	24.50	27.80	30.60	28.60	31.60	30.40	31.70
Oil[2]	FTAK	3.13	3.00	1.20	0.80	0.80	0.80	0.80	0.70	0.70	0.60	0.80
Gas	KGPT	11.4	15.2	19.3	20.3	24.2	24.4	23.8	25.0	24.5	26.2	25.4
Nuclear[3]	FTAL	21.25	22.20	22.00	23.40	22.20	19.60	20.80	20.10	20.00	18.20	18.40
Hydro (natural flow)	FTAM	0.34	0.20	0.30	0.40	0.40	0.40	0.30	0.30	0.20	0.30	0.30
Other fuels used by UK companies	KGPU	0.1	0.1	0.2	0.2	0.2	0.2	0.3	0.3	0.4	0.5	0.8
Net imports	KGPV	1.4	1.4	1.4	1.1	1.2	1.2	0.9	0.7	0.2	0.6	0.7
Other generators: total all fuels	KGPW	5.8	6.4	6.7	7.1	7.3	8.0	7.6	8.0	8.7	8.7	9.7
Transport undertakings												
Gas	KGPX	0.2	0.2	0.2	0.2	0.2	0.2	0.2	0.2	–	–	–
Undertakings in industrial sector												
Coal	KGPY	1.3	1.2	1.2	1.2	1.0	0.9	1.0	1.0	1.0	0.9	1.0
Oil	KGPZ	1.0	0.9	0.8	0.7	0.7	0.8	0.6	0.6	0.5	0.5	0.5
Gas	KGQM	1.6	1.9	2.2	2.5	2.7	3.3	2.9	3.2	3.4	3.1	3.3
Hydro (natural flow)	KGQO	0.1	0.1	0.1	0.1	0.1	0.1	0.1	0.1	0.1	0.1	0.1
Other fuels	KGQP	1.700	2.037	2.186	2.420	2.640	2.770	2.740	2.968	3.660	3.966	4.851
All generating companies: total fuels	KGQQ	78.60	81.03	78.20	82.00	80.90	82.40	84.90	83.80	86.20	85.50	87.80
Coal	KGQR	36.3	33.6	28.3	29.9	25.5	28.7	31.6	29.6	32.5	31.3	32.6
Oil	KGQS	4.1	4.0	2.0	1.5	1.5	1.5	1.4	1.3	1.2	1.1	1.3
Gas	KGQT	13.3	17.4	21.7	23.0	27.1	27.9	26.9	28.4	27.9	29.3	28.7
Nuclear[3]	KGQU	21.3	22.2	22.0	23.4	22.2	19.6	20.8	20.1	20.0	18.2	18.4
Hydro (natural flow)	KGQV	0.4	0.3	0.4	0.4	0.5	0.4	0.3	0.4	0.3	0.4	0.4
Other fuels used by UK companies[4]	KGQW	1.800	2.183	2.351	2.597	2.863	3.007	2.993	3.242	4.041	4.506	5.669
Net imports	KGQX	1.4	1.4	1.4	1.1	1.2	1.2	0.9	0.7	0.2	0.6	0.7

1 See chapter text.
2 Includes oil used in gas turbine and diesel plant for lighting up coal fired boilers and Orimulsion.

3 Nuclear generators are now included under "major power producers" only.
4 Main fuels included are coke oven gas, blast furnace gas, waste products from chemical processes and sludge gas.

Source: Department of Trade and Industry: 020 7215 5190

22.11 Indigenous petroleum production, refinery receipts, imports and exports of oil[1]

Thousand tonnes

		1995	1996	1997	1998	1999	2000	2001	2002	2003	2004	2005
Total indigenous petroleum production[2]	KMBA	129 894	129 742	128 234	132 633	137 099	126 245	116 678	115 944	106 073	95 374	84 721
Crude petroleum:[3]												
Refinery receipts total	KMBB	92 743	96 660	97 023	93 797	88 286	88 014	83 343	84 784	84 585	89 821	86 135
Foreign trade[4]												
Imports	KMBF	48 749	50 099	49 994	47 958	44 869	54 387	53 551	56 968	54 177	62 516	58 886
Exports	AXRB	84 578	81 563	79 400	84 610	91 797	92 918	86 930	87 144	74 898	64 504	54 098
Net imports	AXRC	−35 829	−31 464	−29 406	−36 652	−46 928	−38 531	−33 378	−30 176	−20 720	−1 988	4 787
Petroleum products												
Foreign trade												
Imports[4]	BHMI	9 878	9 315	8 705	11 418	13 896	14 212	17 234	14 900	16 472	18 545	22 510
Exports[4]	AXRD	21 614	23 681	26 755	24 375	21 730	20 677	19 088	23 444	23 323	30 270	29 722
Net imports[4]	AXRE	−11 736	−14 366	−18 049	−12 957	−7 834	−6 464	−1 854	−8 544	−6 851	−11 725	−7 211
International marine bunkers	BHMK	2 465	2 664	2 961	3 080	2 329	2 079	2 274	1 913	1 764	2 085	2 055

1 See chapter text. The term 'indigenous' is used in this table to cover oil produced on the UK Continental Shelf. This includes small amounts produced onshore.
2 Crude oil *plus* condensates and petroleum gases derived at onshore treatment plants.

3 Includes process (partly refined) oils.
4 Foreign trade as recorded by the petroleum industry and may differ from figures published in *Overseas Trade Statistics*.

Source: Department of Trade and Industry: 020 7215 5184

22.12 Throughput of crude and process oils and output of refined products from refineries[1]

United Kingdom

Thousand tonnes

		1995	1996	1997	1998	1999	2000	2001	2002	2003	2004	2005
Throughput of crude and process oils	KMAU	92 743	96 661	97 024	93 797	88 285	88 014	83 343	84 784	84 585	89 821	86 135
less: Refinery fuel:	KMAA	6 481	6 623	6 572	6 177	5 538	5 252	5 059	5 677	5 528	5 453	5 602
Losses	KMAB	129	152	86	1 005	1 552	1 632	1 233	788	56	−7	132
Total output of refined products	KMAC	86 133	89 885	90 366	86 615	81 195	81 130	77 051	78 319	79 001	84 375	80 402
Gases:												
Butane and propane	KMAE	1 815	1 828	1 950	1 961	1 975	1 917	1 764	2 139	2 281	2 152	2 424
Other petroleum	KMAF	133	144	139	394	361	288	272	537	645	484	427
Naphtha and other feedstock	KMAG	2 711	2 824	2 854	2 316	2 430	3 082	3 428	3 153	3 503	3 168	3 019
Aviation spirit	KMAH	–	–	–	–	16	30	101	28	26	31	32
Motor spirit	KMAJ	27 254	28 046	28 260	27 166	25 230	23 445	21 455	22 944	22 627	24 589	22 620
Industrial and white spirit	KMAK	143	136	128	135	129	122	121	121	104	100	136
Kerosene:												
Aviation turbine fuel	KMAL	7 837	8 305	8 342	7 876	7 249	6 484	5 910	5 365	5 277	5 615	5 167
Burning oil	KMAM	2 924	3 510	3 336	3 442	3 553	3 078	3 088	3 506	3 521	3 613	3 325
Gas/diesel oil	KMAN	27 169	28 903	28 778	27 532	25 750	28 229	26 748	28 343	27 380	28 647	28 486
Fuel oil	KMAO	10 969	11 479	11 747	11 125	10 446	10 296	10 179	8 507	9 495	11 308	10 155
Lubricating oil	KMAP	1 261	1 111	1 231	1 125	907	702	656	509	576	1 136	936
Bitumen	KMAQ	2 459	2 189	2 258	2 172	1 644	1 438	1 707	1 918	1 925	2 196	1 912
Petroleum wax	KMAR	46	41	65	59	261	437	416	430	460	94	98
Petroleum coke	KMAS	759	714	598	678	648	657	513	441	612	633	660
Other products	KMAT	653	655	680	634	596	927	692	378	569	607	1 005

1 See chapter text. Crude and process oils comprise all feedstocks, other than distillation benzines, for treatment at refinery plants. Refinery production does not cover further treatment of finished products for special grades such as in distillation plant for the preparation of industrial spirits.

Source: Department of Trade and Industry: 020 7215 5184

22.13 Deliveries of petroleum products for inland consumption[1]
United Kingdom

Thousand tonnes

		1995	1996	1997	1998	1999	2000	2001	2002	2003	2004	2005
Total (including refinery fuel)	KMCA	80 175	82 013	79 073	78 438	77 976	77 196	76 646	76 603	77 966	80 226	80 977
Total (excluding refinery fuel)	KMCB	73 694	75 390	72 501	72 259	72 438	71 944	71 354	70 556	71 697	73 867	75 375
Butane and propane	ECAQ	2 481	2 439	2 426	2 368	2 249	2 030	2 097	2 553	3 017	3 114	3 554
Other Petroleum Gases (includes Ethane)	ECAR	1 489	1 482	1 561	1 534	1 829	1 886	2 077	2 181	2 043	1 883	2 021
Naphtha	ECAS	2 885	3 010	2 640	2 882	3 100	2 344	1 592	1 592	2 332	2 029	1 916
Aviation spirit	KMCI	29	32	37	36	45	52	59	50	46	49	52
Motor spirit:												
Retail deliveries:												
Leaded Premium / Lead Replacement Petrol	KMCK	7 993	7 043	6 138	4 595	2 629	1 462	838	401	183	74	25
Super Premium Unleaded	KMCL	925	698	506	409	473	403	420	706	861	810	924
Premium Unleaded	KMCM	12 603	14 228	15 188	16 432	18 307	19 008	19 100	19 167	18 291	17 795	16 954
Total Retail Deliveries	ECAT	21 521	21 969	21 832	21 436	21 409	20 873	20 358	20 274	19 335	18 679	17 903
Commercial consumers:												
Leaded Premium / Lead Replacement Petrol	KMCO	149	135	112	91	61	44	34	19	19	14	1
Super Premium Unleaded	KMCP	17	11	9	4	6	6	9	17	22	26	16
Premium Unleaded	KMCQ	285	294	298	318	311	480	538	499	542	765	811
Total Commercial Consumers	ECAU	451	440	419	413	378	530	581	535	583	805	828
Total Motor spirit	BHOD	21 972	22 409	22 251	21 849	21 787	21 403	20 939	20 809	19 918	19 484	18 731
Industrial and white spirits	KMCS	178	184	195	179	174	170	151	157	147	281	284
Kerosene:												
Aviation turbine fuel	BHOE	7 660	8 049	8 411	9 241	9 939	10 806	10 614	10 519	10 765	11 862	12 497
Burning oil	KMCT	2 774	3 336	3 343	3 575	3 633	3 839	4 236	3 578	3 569	3 950	3 869
Gas/diesel oil:												
Derv fuel:												
Retail Deliveries	ECAV	4 814	5 537	6 127	6 602	7 137	7 181	7 846	8 153	9 057	9 517	10 679
Commercial Consumers	ECAW	8 643	8 828	8 849	8 541	8 371	8 451	8 213	8 774	8 655	8 997	8 757
Total Derv fuel	BHOI	13 457	14 365	14 976	15 143	15 508	15 632	16 059	16 927	17 712	18 514	19 436
Other gas/diesel oil (includes Mdf)	ECAX	7 879	8 349	8 053	8 005	7 196	7 528	6 960	6 099	6 326	6 023	6 797
Fuel oil	BHOK	7 975	6 854	3 936	3 105	2 701	2 119	2 587	1 721	1 538	2 063	1 965
Lubricating oils	BHOL	895	864	872	813	790	801	846	829	868	914	750
Bitumen	BHOM	2 420	2 146	2 015	1 967	1 928	1 975	1 935	2 002	1 959	1 991	1 906
Petroleum wax	KMCU	44	44	44	18	37	32	33	51	57	50	72
Petroleum coke	KMCV	1 008	1 210	1 095	887	660	776	702	893	880	1 145	1 042
Miscellaneous products	KMCW	548	617	646	537	719	463	475	596	449	476	484

1 See chapter text.

Source: Department of Trade and Industry: 020 7215 5184

Production

22.14 Iron and steel:[1] summary of steel supplies, deliveries and stocks
United Kingdom

		1995	1996	1997	1998	1999	2000	2001	2002	2003	2004	2005
Supply, disposal and consumption - (Finished product weight - Thousand tonnes)												
UK producers' home deliveries	KLTA	8 257	8 383	8 626	8 260	7 652	7 255	6 762	6 506	6 227	7 083	6 279
Imports excluding steelworks receipts	KLTB	5 384	5 147	5 894	6 466	6 014	6 387	6 978	6 793	6 893	7 272	6 297
Total deliveries to home market (a)	KLTC	13 641	13 530	14 520	14 726	13 666	13 642	13 740	13 299	13 120	14 355	12 576
Total exports (producers, consumers, merchants)	KLTD	8 228	8 917	9 060	8 008	7 623	7 446	6 512	6 320	7 007	7 455	8 408
Exports by UK producers	KLTE	7 828	8 305	8 534	7 876	7 416	7 163	6 182	5 594	6 202	6 275	6 594
Derived consumers' and merchants' exports (b)	KLTF	400	612	526	132	207	283	330	708	806	1 179	1 814
Net home disposals (a)-(b)	KLTG	13 241	12 918	13 994	14 594	13 460	13 359	13 410	12 591	12 314	13 176	10 762
Estimated home consumption	KLTI	13 241	12 918	13 994	14 594	13 460	13 359	13 410	12 591	12 114	13 176	10 762
Stocks - (Finished product weight - Thousand tonnes)												
Producers												
- ingots & semis	KLTJ	1 068	767	946	717	747	727	705	690	706	765	869
- finished steel	KLTK	1 274	1 515	1 358	1 495	1 318	1 039	981	932	917	901	947
Estimated home consumption - (Crude steel equivalent - Million tonnes)												
Crude steel production[2]	KLTN	17.60	17.99	18.50	17.32	16.28	15.15	13.54	11.53	13.13	13.77	13.23
Producers' stock change	KLTO	0.01	−0.07	0.03	−0.11	−0.19	−0.33	−0.14	−0.08	..	..	0.18
Re-usable material	KLTP	0.08	0.07	0.06	0.02	..	..	..	..	..	..	
Total supply from home sources	KLTQ	17.67	18.13	18.53	17.45	16.47	15.48	13.68	11.61	13.13	13.77	13.05
Total imports[3]	KLTR	7.05	7.01	7.49	8.38	7.81	8.43	9.11	9.86	9.32	10.31	9.82
Total exports[3]	KLTS	9.63	10.26	10.43	9.25	8.70	8.61	7.53	7.39	8.65	9.15	8.93
Net home disposals	KLTT	15.09	14.88	15.59	16.58	15.58	15.30	15.26	14.08	13.80	14.86	13.94
Estimated home consumption	KLTV	15.09	14.88	15.59	16.58	15.58	15.30	15.26	14.08	13.80	14.86	13.94

1 See chapter text. The figures relate to periods of 52 weeks.
2 Includes liquid steel for castings only up to 2003.

3 Based on HM Customs Statistics, reflecting total trade rather than producers' trade.

Source: Iron and Steel Statistics Bureau: 020 8686 9050 ext 126

22.15

Iron and steel:[1] **iron ore, manganese ore, pig iron and iron and steel scrap**
United Kingdom

Thousand tonnes

		1995	1996	1997	1998	1999	2000	2001	2002	2003	2004	2005
Iron ore[2]	KLOF	18 670	19 720	20 820	19 532	18 754	16 991	15 113	13 185	15 766	16 013	15 991
Manganese ore[2]	KLOG	32	48	37	22	14	36	4	4	–	6	3
Pig iron (and blast furnace ferro-alloys)												
Average number of furnaces in blast during period	KLOH	8	9	9	9	9	8	7	5	6	6	6
Production Steelmaking iron	KLOI	12 236	12 830	13 054	12 746	12 139	10 890	9 870	8 561	10 228	10 180	10 189
In blast furnaces: total	KLOL	12 236	12 830	13 054	12 746	12 139	10 890	9 870	8 561	10 228	10 180	10 189
In steel works	KLOM	12 121	12 753	13 044	12 746	12 139	10 890	9 870	8 561	10 228	10 180	10 189
Consumption of pig iron: total	KLOO	12 121	12 753	13 044	12 746	12 139	10 890	9 870	8 561	10 228	10 180	10 189
Iron and steel scrap												
Steelworks and steel foundries Circulating scrap	KLOQ	2 390	2 639	2 459	2 380	2 488	2 287	2 019	1 882	1 926	1 787	1 671
Purchased receipts	KLOR	4 688	4 130	5 418	4 045	3 433	3 327	3 001	2 271	2 617	3 371	2 876
Consumption	KLOS	7 012	6 828	7 207	6 408	5 884	5 675	5 006	4 216	4 469	5 123	4 563
Stocks (end of period)	KLOT	319	260	236	253	290	229	224	161	234	242	226

1 See chapter text. The figures relate to periods of 52 weeks.
2 Consumption.

Source: Iron and Steel Statistics Bureau: 020 8686 9050 ext 126

22.16 Iron and steel:[1] furnaces and production of steel
United Kingdom

Number and thousand tonnes

		1995	1996	1997	1998	1999	2000	2001	2002	2003	2004	2005
Steel furnaces (numbers[2])	KLPA	192	192	192	190	181	181	181	173	..	..	..
Oxygen converters	KLPC	11	11	11	11	11	11	11	8	..	..	..
Electric	KLPD	181	181	181	179	170	170	170	165	..	..	..
Production of crude steel	KLPF	17 604	17 992	18 499	17 315	16 284	15 155	13 543	11 667	13 268	13 766	13 234
by process												
Oxygen converters	KLPH	13 082	13 758	13 986	13 426	12 634	11 551	10 271	8 956	10 630	10 667	10 550
Electric	KLPI	4 522	4 234	4 513	3 889	3 650	3 604	3 272	2 711	2 639	3 099	2 685
by cast method												
Cast to ingot	KLPK	2 174	1 892	1 660	784	534	539	369	339	354	383	281
Continuously cast	KLPL	15 250	15 912	16 653	16 346	15 637	14 470	13 024	11 182	12 766	13 383	12 954
Steel for castings	KLPM	180	188	186	185	127	146	150	146	148	..	..
by quality												
Non alloy steel	KLPN	16 243	16 708	17 193	16 145	15 263	14 004	12 482	10 657	12 294	12 809	12 376
Stainless and other alloy steel	KLPO	1 361	1 284	1 306	1 170	1 035	1 151	1 061	1 010	974	957	863
Production of finished steel products (All quantities)[3]												
Rods and bars for reinforcement (in coil and lengths)	KLPP	1 154	1 182	1 118	1 133	893	812	755	487	294	769	730
Wire rods and other rods and bars in coil	KLPQ	1 642	1 536	1 565	1 492	1 407	1 408	1 389	1 394	1 316	1 392	1 035
Hot rolled bars in lengths	KLPR	1 311	1 499	1 716	1 791	1 542	1 545	1 449	1 267	1 107	1 179	1 136
Bright steel bars[4]	KLPS	424	357	385	336	311	337	296	271	273	277	233
Light sections other than rails	KLPT	286	298	302	318	264	183	201	188	116	136	130
Heavy sections	KGQZ	2 549	2 557	2 397	2 346	2 303	1 915	1 931	1 873	1 774	1 694	1 527
Hot rolled plates, sheets and strip in coil and lengths	KLPW	8 077	8 512	8 956	8 454	7 893	7 293	5 841	5 756	6 145	6 437	5 818
Cold rolled plates and sheets in coil and lengths	KLPX	4 100	4 221	4 437	4 288	3 914	3 612	2 944	2 951	2 958	3 001	2 769
Cold rolled strip[4]	KLPZ	267	246	255	259	233	218	201	179	186	156	131
Tinplate	KLQW	791	739	754	772	736	753	602	562	493	507	471
Other coated sheet	KLQX	2 306	2 366	2 534	2 610	2 475	2 471	1 773	1 786	1 811	1 713	1 644
Tubes and pipes[4]	KLQY	1 183	1 317	1 310	1 276	1 100	1 061	1 096	940	1 066	1 076	932
Forged bars[4]	KLQZ	3	3	3	3	2	1	1	1	..	..	..

1 See chapter text. The figures relate to periods of 52 weeks.
2 Includes steel furnaces at steel foundries, only up to 2003.

3 Includes material for conversion into other products listed in the table.
4 Based on producers' deliveries.

Source: Iron and Steel Statistics Bureau: 020 8686 9050 ext 126

22.17 Non-ferrous metals
United Kingdom

		1995	1996	1997	1998	1999	2000	2001	2002	2003	2004	2005
Copper												
Production of refined copper:												
Primary	KLAA	12.0	13.0	9.1	6.4	1.7	–	–	–	–	–	–
Secondary	KLAB	43.0	43.6	51.3	47.4	48.6	–	–	–	–	–	–
Home consumption:												
Refined	KLAC	397.9	396.0	408.3	374.1	305.3	322.7	285.9	260.8	242.2	243.4	165.4
Scrap (metal content)	KLAD	81.0	81.0	69.0	64.6	112.5	132.4	127.0	120.0	120.0	120.0	120.0
Stocks (end of period)[1,2]	KLAE	7.5	6.6	12.8	7.5	7.3	10.4	7.3	..	..	..	..
Analysis of home consumption												
(refined and scrap):[3,4] total	KLAF	493.2	477.3	477.4	438.7	417.8	455.5	212.7	..	..	..	..
Wire[5]	KLAG	321.4	309.4	312.5	287.2	276.1	310.2	151.8	..	..	..	..
Rods, bars and sections	KLAH	59.0	58.3	58.3	53.6	46.9	43.6	21.6	..	..	..	..
Sheet, strip and plate	KLAI	37.1	34.0	36.5	30.5	27.7	32.3	16.9	..	..	..	..
Tubes	KLAJ	75.7	75.6	70.1	67.4	67.1	69.4	22.4	..	..	..	..
Zinc												
Slab zinc:												
Production	KLAL	106.0	96.9	107.7	99.6	132.8	99.6	99.6	99.6	16.6	–	–
Home consumption	KLAM	198.4	195.7	194.8	187.9	198.9	206.5	197.1	202.4	176.2	150.1	161.7
Stocks (end of period)	KLAN	9.8	10.5	10.1	10.6	10.9	10.9	9.5	9.2	8.9	8.9	8.9
Other zinc (metal content):												
Consumption	KLAO	46.8	41.3	41.5	37.3	41.6	46.3	48.2	51.8	52.3	55.4	–
Analysis of home consumption												
(slab and scrap): total	KLAP	245.2	237.1	236.5	221.6	232.1	237.9	226.6	230.4	226.8	232.0	..
Brass	KLAQ	45.2	39.1	41.6	36.6	33.6	34.4	32.2	30.0	30.0	31.2	..
Galvanized products	KLAR	110.7	110.3	108.4	103.8	116.6	120.9	111.8	117.3	113.3	116.2	..
Zinc sheet and strip	KLAS	3.0	3.0	3.3	3.3	3.3	3.3	3.3	3.4	3.3	3.3	..
Zinc alloy die castings	KLAT	46.5	46.5	46.5	46.5	46.5	46.5	46.5	46.5	46.5	46.5	..
Zinc oxide	KLAU	21.6	20.7	20.6	20.4	21.1	21.8	21.8	22.2	22.7	23.8	..
Other products	KLAV	18.2	17.5	16.1	11.0	11.0	11.0	11.0	11.0	11.0	11.0	..
Refined lead												
Production[6,7]	KLAW	320.7	351.4	384.1	349.7	351.0	328.0	366.3	366.3	364.6	245.9	304.3
Home consumption[7,8]												
Refined lead	KLAX	285.4	272.8	270.4	275.5	283.3	294.0	298.3	298.3	314.7	330.3	281.6
Scrap and remelted lead[7]	KLAY	41.6	43.4	39.1	38.4	32.2	39.5	40.6	40.7	34.1	40.8	..
Stocks (end of period)[9]												
Lead bullion	KLAZ	9.5	32.9	15.5	20.9	17.1	10.0	17.2	17.2	24.0	23.0	23.0
Refined soft lead at consumers	KLBA	24.9	28.8	29.1	27.4	25.7	25.8	26.1	26.1	25.3	25.9	25.9
In LME Warehouses (UK)	KLBB	0.4	3.0	2.4	0.1	0.1	0.1	0.1	0.1	0.1	0.1	0.1
Analysis of home consumption												
(refined and scrap): total	KLBC	327.0	316.2	309.5	313.9	315.5	333.5	338.9	339.0	348.8	371.1	281.6
Cables	KLBD	9.8	9.8	9.7	9.7	9.7	9.6	9.6	9.7	9.7	9.7	..
Batteries (excluding oxides)	KLBE	52.7	52.3	54.7	51.6	47.4	50.5	48.2	48.2	51.9	54.1	..
Oxides and compounds:												
Batteries	KLBF	56.2	54.9	56.1	54.4	53.1	55.9	54.7	54.7	55.9	59.0	..
Other uses	KLBG	53.8	56.1	54.5	56.4	57.0	56.8	53.8	53.8	60.6	64.5	..
Sheets and pipes	KLBH	101.2	94.1	91.1	96.1	94.9	102.3	102.3	102.3	109.8	111.4	..
Solder	KLBJ	7.4	7.4	7.4	7.4	7.4	7.4	7.4	7.4	7.2	7.4	..
Alloys	KLBK	15.9	12.1	9.4	9.4	11.9	15.2	24.3	24.3	25.7	33.3	..
Other uses	KLBL	30.0	29.5	26.6	28.9	34.1	35.8	38.6	38.6	28.0	31.7	..

22.17 Non-ferrous metals
United Kingdom
continued

Thousand tonnes

		1995	1996	1997	1998	1999	2000	2001	2002	2003	2004	2005
Tin												
Tin ore (metal content):												
Production	KLBM	2.0	2.1	2.3	0.4	0.4	..	..	1.9	1.9	–	–
Tin metal:[10]												
Production[11]	KLBO	–	–	..	..	..	..	..	1.9	1.9	–	–
Home consumption[11]	VQIX	10.5	10.5	10.4	10.6	9.6	10.0	10.3	6.9	7.1	5.3	3.2
Exports and re-exports[12]	KLBQ	2.7	0.6	0.3	3.4	0.1	0.1	0.4	1.9	1.9	0.6	1.7
Stocks (end of period):												
Consumers	KLBR	1.0	1.0	1.0	1.0	1.0	1.0	1.0	1.0	1.0	1.0	1.0
Analysis of home consumption												
(excluding scrap): total	KLBT	10.6	10.5	10.4	17.5	16.5	17.0	18.8	18.8	1.9	18.4	..
Tinplate	KLBU	3.6	3.6	2.8	2.6	3.0	3.0	3.0	1.9	1.9	3.0	..
Alloys	KLBV	3.4	3.5	3.4	12.1	11.2	11.6	2.6	1.9	1.9	2.6	..
Solder	KLBW	1.1	1.1	1.1	1.1	0.6	0.8	1.5	1.9	1.9	1.5	..
Other uses	KLBX	0.4	0.4	0.4	0.4	0.4	0.4	0.4	1.9	1.9	0.4	..
Aluminium												
Ingot production												
Primary	KLBY	237.9	240.0	247.7	258.4	269.7	305.1	340.8	344.3	342.7	359.6	368.5
Secondary[13]	KLCA	229.7	260.0	242.7	274.8	285.3	237.7	248.6	205.4	205.4	205.4	205.3
Wrought remelt production[14]	C6EW	467.6	500.0	490.4	533.2	555.0	542.8	589.4	549.7	548.1	565.0	573.8
Wrought and cast despatches												
Bar, section and tube[15]	C6EX	142.1	149.6	160.8	168.0	181.7	184.7	177.1	168.3	158.7	157.0	–
Plate, sheet, strip and circles	C6EY	359.2	327.9	350.4	352.5	349.7	419.1	384.8	312.2	274.3	267.3	–
Castings	KLCH	147.0	156.0	152.4	148.0	137.3	134.9	138.2	159.4	127.5	139.7	–
Exports												
Primary ingot	C6EZ	159.4	53.1	219.6	68.7	233.6	347.7	203.4	214.7	244.3	305.1	–
Secondary ingot	KLCC	145.8	152.2	153.3	156.6	143.1	84.2	59.9	35.7	26.9	30.8	–
Extruded products	C6F2	65.8	45.8	56.8	59.7	47.5	25.5	20.7	15.3	14.2	15.8	–
Rolled products	C6F3	185.6	155.5	157.7	160.1	166.6	222.9	198.3	208.8	193.9	192.2	–
Refined nickel												
Production (including ferro-nickel)	KLCM	35.1	38.6	36.1	39.1	39.5	38.0	33.8	33.8	26.8	38.6	37.6

1 Unwrought copper (electrolytic, fire refined and blister).
2 Reported stocks of refined copper held by consumers and those held in London Metal Exchange (LME) warehouses in the United Kingdom.
3 2001 figures only cover the period January to June.
4 Copper content.
5 Consumption for high-conductivity copper and cadmium copper wire represented by consumption of wire rods, production of which for export is also included.
6 Lead reclaimed from secondary and scrap material and lead refined from bullion and domestic ores.

7 Figures for production and consumption of refined lead include antimonial lead, and for scrap and remelted lead, exclude secondary antimonial lead.
8 Including toll transactions involving fabrication.
9 Excluding goverment stocks.
10 Including production from imported scrap and residues refined on toll.
11 Primary and secondary metal.
12 Including re-exports on toll transactions.
13 Predominantly from old scrap.
14 Predominantly using recycled scrap from fabrication.
15 Excluding forging bars

Sources: World Bureau of Metal Statistics: 01920 461274;
Aluminium Federation: 0121 456 1103

22.18 Fertilisers
Years ending 30 June

Thousand tonnes

		1996	1997	1998	1999	2000	2001	2002	2003	2004	2005	2006
Nutrient Content												
Nitrogen (N):												
Straight	KGRM	858	957	912	819	819	714	751	664	662	691	631
Compounds	KGRN	475	483	463	465	449	448	446	467	463	370	372
Phosphate (P_2O_5)	KGRO	394	412	383	347	317	279	283	282	278	259	235
Potash (K_2O)	KGRP	471	501	487	451	409	369	391	375	375	352	325
Compounds - total product	KGRQ	3 115	3 238	3 037	3 013	2 851	2 471	2 511	2 558	2 550	2 221	2 134

Source: Agricultural Industries Confederation: 01733 385230

22.19 Minerals: production[1]
United Kingdom

Thousand tonnes

		1995	1996	1997	1998	1999	2000	2001	2002	2003	2004	2005
Great Britain												
Limestone	KLEA	90 933	82 442	84 252	85 382	82 714	80 810	83 492	88 013	84 445	86 846	81 830
Sandstone	KLEB	15 017	12 581	12 457	13 545	11 870	12 056	11 897	11 788	11 665	11 929	11 609
Igneous rock	KLEC	49 641	43 731	42 370	39 838	45 294	44 633	45 053	44 544	45 305	46 193	45 992
Clay/shale	KLED	13 930	11 804	11 322	12 230	11 355	10 838	10 426	10 306	10 680	11 164	10 898
Industrial sand	KLEE	4 344	4 861	4 704	4 662	4 092	4 095	3 848	3 833	4 073	5 011	4 146
Chalk	KLEF	9 949	9 239	9 550	9 934	9 667	9 213	8 205	8 587	8 066	7 997	7 105
Fireclay	KLEG	708	536	338	577	545	595	459	491	528	402	395
Barium sulphate	KLEH	74	93	57	64	59	54	70	56	..	..	62
Calcium fluoride	KLEI	46	..	58	52	46	21	46	22	..	..	44
Copper	KLEJ	–	–	–	–	–	–	–	–	–	–	–
Lead	KLEK	..	..	..	1	1	..	1	..	..	..	1
Tin	KLEL	2.0	2.1	2.0	–	–	–	–	–	–	–	–
Zinc	KLEM	..	..	..	–	–	–	–	–	–	..	–
Iron ore: crude	KLEN	2	1	2	2	1	1	1	1	–	..	–
Iron ore: iron content	KLEO	1	1	1	1	1	1	..	..	–	..	–
Calcspar	KLEP	..	..	13	15	..	..	12	..	–	..	–
China clay	KLEQ KILC	3 076	2 654	2 798	2 866	2 841	2 779	2 804	2 467	2 378	2 148	1 908
Ball clay	KIMS	..	..	..	..	..	..	..	..	..	..	..
Chert and flint	KLER	..	..	..	..	6	..	2	2	..	2	2
Fuller's earth	KLES	150	183	162	111	83	103	..	33	19	11	–
Lignite	KLET	–	–	–	–	–	–	–	–	–	–	–
Rock salt	KLEU	..	..	..	..	..	..	..	..	..	..	..
Salt from brine	KLEV	..	..	..	..	..	..	..	..	..	..	..
Salt in brine	KLEW	3 548	3 512	3 561	..	..	..	..	..	..	..	..
Anhydrite	KLEX	..	..	..	..	–	–	–	–	–	–	–
Dolomite	KLEY	17 966	16 555	17 282	15 632	13 698	13 069	14 314	12 946	..	..	11 514
Gypsum	KLEZ	..	..	..	..	..	..	..	..	..	1 686	..
Slate[2]	KLFA	275	408	347	425	361	479	551	742	832	901	928
Soapstone and talc	KLFB	4	5	5	5	6	5	5	6	6	4	6
Sand and gravel (land-won)	KLFC	78 031	70 489	74 362	73 016	74 785	74 877	74 599	69 889	68 090	73 061	69 368
Sand and gravel (marine dredged)	KLFD	11 625	11 508	12 004	12 952	13 424	14 356	13 611	12 832	12 131	12 996	13 024
Northern Ireland												
Sand and gravel	KLFG	5 262	7 684	5 138	5 300	5 517	5 073	6 194	5 512	4 894	5 084	5 803
Basalt and igneous rock (other than granite)	KLFH	7 564	6 974	6 286	6 107	7 861	9 480	6 448	6 681	6 051	6 844	7 112
Limestone	KLFI	3 703	4 122	3 500	3 892	4 219	3 538	4 746	4 514	4 887	5 634	5 588
Sandstone[3]	KLFJ	4 779	4 941	6 042	6 584	3 615	2 844	8 070	6 574	6 594	6 915	7 076
Granite	KLFL	..	–	–	–	–	–	–	–	–	..	..
Others[4]	KLFN	812	1 392	625	473	1 579	3 098	753	242	1 055	1 266	2 090

1 See chapter text.
2 Includes waste used for constructional fill, and powder and granules used in manufacturing.

3 Prior to 1993 the 'Sandstone' heading was called 'Grit and conglomerate'. The new heading is all encompassing and was confirmed as correct with the Geological Survey in Northern Ireland.
4 Rock salt, Chalk, Diatomite and Fireclay.

Source: Office for National Statistics: 01633 812082

22.20 Building materials and components: production[1]
Great Britain

			1996	1997	1998	1999	2000	2001	2002	2003	2004	2005	2006
Building bricks[2]	KLGA	Millions	3 046	2 997	3 000	2 939	2 864	2 754	2 750	2 772	2 868	2 748	2 510
Common bricks	GRTD	"	401	422	385	367	342	320	332	315	318	319	304
Facing bricks	GRTE	"	2 430	2 386	2 411	2 369	2 287	2 211	2 209	2 244	2 327	2 202	2 013
Engineering bricks	GRTF	"	216	190	204	204	235	223	210	213	224	227	193
Clay bricks (including sand-lime)	GRTG	"	2 880	2 828	2 830	2 759	2 694	2 595	2 600	2 606	2 707	2 601	2 359
Concrete bricks	GRTH	"	166	169	171	180	170	159	150	167	161	147	150
Cement (grey Portland)[3]	KLGB	Thousand tonnes	12 214	12 638	12 409	12 697	12 452	11 090	11 089	11 215	11 405	11 216	11 460
Sand and gravel	GRTI	"	81 997	86 366	85 968	88 209	89 234	88 210	82 721	80 221	86 057	82 392	77 896
Building sand[4]	KLGC	"	14 655	15 337	13 810	13 941	14 219	13 772	13 221	13 617	13 125	13 730	11 845
Concreting sand	KLGD	"	28 659	30 130	30 244	31 730	31 167	31 656	31 224	31 411	32 529	29 848	29 893
Gravel[5]	KLGE	"	38 683	40 899	41 914	42 538	43 847	42 782	38 276	35 193	40 404	38 814	36 158
Crushed rock	GRTJ	"	132 894	133 787	131 716	132 598	130 307	133 759	126 568	122 885	127 674	121 860	..
Coated roadstone	KLGF	"	26 270	23 906	23 131	22 260	21 785	23 340	23 281	23 139	18 721	20 136	..
Uncoated roadstone	KLGG	"	40 893	40 186	36 816	38 114	36 509	34 638	27 323	28 950	25 260	25 902	..
Fill and ballast	KLGH	"	50 982	51 396	51 623	52 144	53 417	47 225	49 622	42 208	62 460	58 945	..
Concrete aggregate	KLGI	"	14 748	18 300	20 146	20 080	18 595	28 556	26 342	28 588	21 231	16 876	..
Ready mixed concrete[6]	GRXA	Thousand cubic metres	20 892	22 327	22 983	23 550	23 043	23 008	22 597	22 289	22 856	22 432	23 029
Concrete building blocks	GRTK	Thousand square metres	75 866	82 537	84 662	87 767	90 219	87 922	91 474	95 645	96 256	89 997	87 510
Dense aggregate	KLGN	"	34 996	37 250	39 439	38 439	37 629	36 598	35 744	36 745	37 677	36 188	34 956
Lightweight aggregate	KLGO	"	16 316	17 783	19 110	20 830	22 991	22 684	23 478	24 991	25 462	25 561	25 345
Aerated concrete	KLGP	"	24 554	27 505	26 113	28 497	29 599	28 639	32 252	33 909	33 117	28 248	27 209
Concrete roofing tiles	KLGM	"	24 651	24 958	24 981	25 972	26 765	24 825	25 023	21 437	20 739	25 719	23 730
Roofing and architectural slates	GRXB	Tonnes	48 474	44 578	46 159	46 998	41 214	45 604	50 530	50 094	..	..	..
Fibre cement products	KLGK	Thousand tonnes	146.2	163.5	160.9	156.2	..	..	..	..	..	..	..

1 See chapter text.
2 Excluding refractory and glazed bricks.
3 United Kingdom up until 2000. Great Britain for 2001 onwards.
4 Includes sand and gravel used for coating.
5 Includes hoggin.
6 United Kingdom.

Source: Department of Trade & Industry: 020 7215 1555

22.21 Construction: value of output in Great Britain[1]
Standard Industrial Classification 1992

£ million

		1996	1997	1998	1999	2000	2001	2002	2003	2004	2005	2006
All work: total	FGAY	55 243	58 352	62 060	65 704	69 676	74 703	83 592	93 284	102 363	107 006	113 571
New work: total	BLAB	27 926	29 928	32 491	35 587	37 660	39 974	45 370	50 353	57 238	59 412	64 513
New housing: total	KLQA	7 013	7 983	8 430	8 418	9 985	10 234	12 089	15 362	19 447	21 063	23 014
For public sector	BLAC	1 421	1 232	1 069	1 012	1 319	1 437	1 716	2 032	2 628	2 680	3 442
For private sector	BLAD	5 592	6 751	7 361	7 406	8 666	8 797	10 373	13 330	16 818	18 383	19 572
Infrastructure: total	KIAM	6 338	6 311	6 182	6 200	6 453	7 147	8 077	7 363	6 491	6 499	6 533
Other new work: total (excluding infrastructure)	KLQB	14 575	15 635	17 879	20 969	21 222	22 594	25 204	27 628	31 301	31 850	34 966
For public sector	BLAE	4 441	3 756	4 151	4 919	4 854	5 330	6 865	8 875	10 516	10 191	9 939
For private sector	KLQC	10 134	11 879	13 728	16 049	16 369	17 263	18 339	18 753	20 785	21 659	25 026
Private Industrial	BLAF	3 119	3 491	3 810	3 973	3 716	3 702	3 374	3 644	3 978	4 291	4 887
Private Commercial	BLAG	7 015	8 388	9 917	12 076	12 653	13 562	14 965	15 109	16 807	17 369	20 139
Repair and maintenance: total	BLAH	27 317	28 423	29 569	30 117	32 016	34 729	38 222	42 931	45 125	47 594	49 058
Housing: total	KLQD	15 035	15 754	16 202	16 370	16 907	17 626	19 170	21 315	23 229	23 937	24 630
For public sector	BLBK	6 637	6 629	6 506	6 485	6 552	6 632	6 412	7 451	8 302	8 598	8 864
For private sector	BLBL	8 398	9 126	9 696	9 885	10 354	10 994	12 758	13 864	14 927	15 339	15 766
Public other work	BLAJ	5 252	5 079	5 220	5 371	5 685	6 111	6 712	7 930	8 015	8 939	8 779
Private other work	BLAK	7 030	7 590	8 147	8 376	9 424	10 992	12 340	13 686	13 881	14 718	15 648

1 See chapter text. Output by contractors, including unrecorded estimates by small firms and self-employed workers, and output by public sector direct labour departments - classified to construction in the *1992 Standard Industrial Classification*.

Source: Department of Trade and Industry: 020 7215 1953

22.22 Construction: value of new orders obtained by contractors[1]
Great Britain
Standard Industrial Classification 1992

£ million

		1996	1997	1998	1999	2000	2001	2002	2003	2004	2005	2006
New work: total	FHAA	22 834	24 806	27 477	26 079	28 120	29 643	33 411	33 951	39 089	43 932	47 638
Public housing	BLBC	1 073	995	933	969	910	1 084	1 129	1 340	1 697	1 951	2 627
Private housing[2]	BLBD	5 416	6 253	5 997	5 901	6 085	6 525	8 088	9 471	12 153	13 171	13 501
New housing: total	FGAU	6 487	7 248	6 930	6 869	6 995	7 610	9 217	10 812	13 850	15 122	16 129
Infrastructure:												
Water	KIBV	640	733	957	760	1 084	531	936	677	601	1 200	525
Sewerage	KIBW	481	656	737	789	380	540	524	423	393	429	379
Electricity	KIBX	294	382	359	254	244	279	294	255	356	561	620
Roads	KIBY	1 710	928	821	957	1 445	1 572	1 999	1 424	1 092	1 559	1 129
Gas, communications, air	KIBZ	745	693	745	713	1 085	584	485	699	480	694	745
Railways	KIDP	524	416	573	471	539	1 271	1 052	1 189	672	775	636
Harbours	KIDQ	270	182	287	250	215	377	264	228	178	315	243
Total	BAWT	4 664	3 991	4 479	4 195	4 992	5 154	5 555	4 894	3 772	5 532	4 277
of which												
- Public	KIDS	1 671	1 352	1 505	1 495	1 430	2 085	2 491	1 781	1 291	1 949	1 428
- Private	KIDT	2 993	2 639	2 974	2 700	3 562	3 068	3 064	3 113	2 480	3 584	2 849
Other public non-housing:												
Factories	KIDU	91	72	84	72	64	30	65	121	85	48	57
Warehouses	KIDV	14	27	20	24	12	10	11	27	25	26	22
Oil, steel, coal	KIDW	4	4	2	5	1	8	1	4	1	2	1
Schools and colleges	KIDX	707	749	770	791	986	1 498	1 397	1 988	2 586	2 735	2 549
Universities	KIDY	355	273	405	345	329	378	667	760	704	904	636
Health	KIDZ	681	491	769	635	685	813	1 065	1 114	1 378	1 049	936
Offices	KIFP	379	391	292	390	291	395	854	588	785	566	692
Entertainment	KIFQ	259	342	432	435	359	392	400	543	503	668	476
Garages	KIFR	28	34	19	36	44	30	53	34	56	54	55
Shops	KIFS	12	35	35	29	34	38	53	50	60	40	37
Agriculture	KIFT	8	33	17	9	12	46	16	10	4	6	8
Miscellaneous	KIFU	418	441	660	503	999	479	1 328	903	660	595	698
Total	BAWU	2 956	2 894	3 504	3 273	3 815	4 117	5 910	6 142	6 847	6 694	6 169
Private industrial:[2]												
Factories	KIFW	1 603	2 184	1 878	1 698	1 444	1 588	1 341	1 442	1 321	1 753	1 669
Warehouses	KIFX	663	901	1 014	821	1 110	911	866	867	1 158	1 569	1 826
Oil, steel, coal	KIFY	71	64	79	38	34	43	40	74	115	99	105
Total	BAWV	2 337	3 149	2 971	2 558	2 589	2 542	2 247	2 383	2 593	3 421	3 601
Private commercial:[2]												
Schools, universities	KIHP	156	189	351	393	577	702	850	873	744	1 479	1 990
Health	KIHQ	277	356	651	411	455	349	575	744	1 376	1 323	2 786
Offices	KIHR	2 169	2 506	3 472	3 566	4 384	4 748	3 947	3 253	3 555	4 306	5 611
Entertainment	KIHS	1 407	1 847	2 244	2 224	1 873	1 674	1 861	1 521	2 059	2 118	1 913
Garages	KIHT	265	344	315	266	169	190	199	194	272	263	280
Shops	KIHU	1 795	1 937	2 154	1 901	1 889	2 212	2 570	2 675	2 893	3 142	3 870
Agriculture	KIBN	123	148	146	100	77	105	107	158	149	155	172
Miscellaneous	KIBO	198	198	259	321	305	242	374	301	978	377	841
Total	BAWW	6 390	7 525	9 593	9 184	9 729	10 221	10 482	9 721	12 026	13 163	17 462

1 See chapter text. Classified to construction in the *1992 Standard Industrial Classification*.
2 Figures for private sector include work to be carried out by contractors on their own initiative for sale.

Source: Department of Trade and Industry: 020 7215 1953

22.23 Total engineering: total turnover of UK based manufacturers[1]
Standard Industrial Classification 2003

£ million

Activity heading Product group		2001	2002	2003	2004	2005	2006
Class 29: Manufacture of machinery and equipment not elsewhere classified							
2911 Manufacture of engines and turbines except aircraft, vehicle and cycle engines	MXVO	1 911.8	1 823.9	1 716.6	1 631.8	1 847.2	1 951.9
2912 Manufacture of pumps and compressors	MXXO	2 337.4	2 537.3	2 607.7	2 957.1	2 872.2	3 189.3
2913 Manufacture of taps and valves	MXZH	1 358.2	1 330.9	1 281.5	1 205.7	1 230.6	1 194.3
2914 Manufacture of bearings, gears, gearing and driving elements	MYCT	1 227.0	1 004.9	882.4	988.4	947.2	1 037.5
2922 Manufacture of lifting and handling equipment	MYLS	3 348.7	3 080.7	2 991.9	3 141.9	3 541.7	3 916.1
2923 Manufacture of non-domestic cooling and ventilation equipment	MYPT	3 411.9	3 298.7	3 194.3	3 339.7	3 393.0	3 778.2
2924 Manufacture of other general purpose machinery not elsewhere classified	MYRM	2 947.6	2 573.4	2 650.4	2 946.4	3 027.4	2 974.3
2941/3 Manufacture of other machine tools	MYYP	834.3	745.7	842.3	788.5	699.4	766.3
2942 Manufacture of metalworking machine tools	MYWY	912.6	738.6	689.9	603.4	729.6	848.0
2952 Manufacture of machinery for mining, quarrying and construction	MZCE	2 392.4	2 215.9	2 549.2	2 932.8	3 097.9	3 255.3
2953 Manufacture of machinery for food, beverage and tobacco processing	MZFS	629.1	710.8	802.9	949.9	942.1	962.7
2954 Manufacture of machinery for textile, apparel and leather production	MZJP	194.7	158.0	145.9	172.3	122.6	127.6
2956 Manufacture of other special purpose machinery not elsewhere classified	MZQF	2 148.8	2 187.1	2 239.7	2 218.3	2 262.2	2 207.7
2971 Manufacture of electric domestic appliances	MZTZ	2 230.9	2 196.4	2 187.5	2 459.9	2 642.3	2 731.2
Class 30: Manufacture of electrical and optical equipment							
3001 Manufacture of office machinery	MZXQ	1 481.1	1 129.8	919.0	815.2	888.8	1 235.3
3002 Manufacture of computers and other information processing equipment	VBCE	12 086.4	8 915.6	7 533.8	5 014.2	4 233.6	2 994.2
Class 31 : Manufacture of electrical machinery and apparatus not elsewhere classified							
3110 Manufacture of electric motors, generators and transformers	VBEB	3 287.6	2 732.3	2 620.5	2 330.8	2 347.8	2 611.8
3120 Manufacture of electricity distribution and control apparatus	VBFU	4 090.5	3 736.1	3 558.4	3 641.3	3 459.1	3 703.8
3130 Manufacture of insulated wire and cable	VBHW	1 414.7	1 271.6	1 140.0	1 122.9	958.5	1 343.1
3140 Manufacture of accumulators, primary cells and primary batteries	VBJW	493.7	444.6	451.9	460.9	440.0	353.6
3150 Manufacture of lighting equipment and electric lamps	VBLP	1 712.1	1 487.0	1 402.1	1 442.2	1 330.6	1 384.2
3161 Manufacture of other electrical equipment for engines and vehicles not otherwise classified	VBNI	1 034.2	1 042.5	1 037.3	1 006.2	1 003.9	946.5
3162 Manufacture of other electrical equipment not elsewhere classified	VBPK	2 728.1	2 480.9	2 384.4	2 639.0	2 693.6	2 762.6
Class 32: Manufacture of radio, television and communication equipment and apparatus							
3210 Manufacture of electronic valves and tubes and other electronic components	VBRI	4 460.0	4 063.0	4 132.7	4 214.9	3 917.4	3 855.3
3220 Manufacture of television and radio transmitters and apparatus for line telephony and line telegraphy	VBTF	10 527.5	7 112.6	4 088.3	4 170.1	3 610.2	4 074.8
3230 Manufacture of television and radio receivers, sound or video recording or reproducing apparatus and associated goods	VBVJ	4 038.0	3 192.4	3 262.3	3 781.1	3 229.0	3 710.8
Class 33: Manufacture of medical, precision and optical instruments, watches and clocks							
3310 Manufacture of medical and surgical equipment and orthopaedic appliances	VBXH	2 967.5	3 167.7	3 538.6	3 542.5	3 748.6	3 604.1
3320 Manufacture of instruments and appliances for measuring, checking, testing, navigating and other purposes, except industrial process control equipment	VBZF	7 104.8	6 378.5	6 748.6	7 046.2	6 852.9	6 720.9
3340 Manufacture of optical instruments and photographic equipment	VCCV	999.6	1 027.2	1 031.0	1 069.8	1 059.9	1 089.8

1 See chapter text.

Source: Office for National Statistics: 01633 812394

22.24 Volume index numbers of turnover and orders for the engineering industries[1]
United Kingdom
Standard Industrial Classification 1992

Indices (2000=100)

	Total			Home			Export		
	Orders on hand[2]	New orders[3]	Turnover	Orders on hand[2]	New orders[3]	Turnover	Orders on hand[2]	New orders[3]	Turnover
Total Engineering industries *SIC 1992 Division 29, 30, 31, 32 and 33*									
	JIQI	JIQH	JIQJ	JIQC	JIQB	JIQD	JIQF	JIQE	JIQG
1999	93.0	91.8	91.9	93.2	94.1	93.4	92.6	88.6	89.8
2000	104.3	100.0	100.0	105.4	100.0	100.0	102.4	100.0	100.0
2001	95.6	89.6	95.3	105.4	94.5	98.4	79.1	83.0	91.2
2002	92.6	80.8	84.5	104.5	87.9	91.8	72.4	71.2	74.8
2003	92.6	78.9	81.6	108.4	87.9	90.2	65.8	66.8	70.3
2004	88.9	78.3	82.1	102.5	83.9	89.3	65.8	70.8	72.6
2005	92.9	79.3	80.8	103.7	85.8	89.0	74.6	70.5	70.0
Manufacture of Machinery and Equipment *SIC 1992 Division 29*									
	JINX	JINW	JINY	JINR	JINQ	JINS	JINU	JINT	JINV
1999	96.4	99.8	100.4	97.8	105.5	103.6	93.4	89.9	94.7
2000	100.5	100.0	100.0	98.9	100.0	100.0	103.8	100.0	100.0
2001	96.2	97.7	100.8	95.3	101.4	103.3	98.1	91.4	96.4
2002	100.5	95.6	95.4	100.4	98.7	97.2	101.0	90.2	92.3
2003	111.4	99.7	97.2	120.5	105.2	97.6	91.1	90.2	96.4
2004	106.5	99.2	102.5	111.9	96.3	100.2	94.5	104.2	106.7
2005	103.9	102.9	105.6	101.4	96.0	100.9	109.3	114.8	113.8
Manufacture of Electrical and Optical Equipment *SIC 1992 Division 30, 31, 32 and 33*									
	JIPQ	JIPP	JIPR	JIPK	JIPJ	JIPL	JIPN	JIPM	JIPO
1999	90.8	88.2	88.0	89.8	88.2	87.8	92.2	88.2	88.1
2000	106.8	100.0	100.0	110.3	100.0	100.0	101.7	100.0	100.0
2001	95.3	86.0	92.7	113.0	91.0	95.7	69.7	80.0	89.3
2002	87.5	74.2	79.5	107.6	82.4	89.0	58.4	64.4	68.5
2003	80.5	69.6	74.5	99.3	79.0	86.2	53.3	58.4	60.9
2004	77.6	69.0	72.7	95.5	77.5	83.3	51.6	58.8	60.5
2005	85.9	68.7	69.5	105.5	80.5	82.4	57.5	54.6	54.4

1 See chapter text.
2 At end of period, rather than the average value for that period, so the annual value shown for 2000 may not equal 100.
3 Net of cancellations.

Source: Office for National Statistics: 01633 812394

22.25 Motor vehicle production[1]
United Kingdom

Numbers

Motor vehicles		1996	1997	1998	1999	2000	2001	2002	2003	2004	2005	2006
SIC 1992, Class 34-10												
Passenger cars: total	JCYM	1 686 134	1 698 001	1 748 258	1 786 623	1 641 452	1 492 365	1 629 744	1 657 558	1 646 750	1 595 697	1 442 085
1 000 c.c. and under[2]	GKAB	108 645	119 894	112 044	113 204	96 043	93 695	79 545	23 985	15 471	6 111	—
Over 1 000 c.c. but not over 1 600 c.c.	GKAD	845 084	829 079	814 595	776 111	676 438	632 747	711 553	750 840	796 174	854 687	792 187
Over 1 600 c.c. but not over 2 500 c.c.	GKAF	635 861	653 147	720 556	758 478	723 294	634 573	720 067	740 486	690 759	546 744	446 143
Over 2 500 c.c.	GKAH	96 544	95 881	101 063	138 830	145 677	131 350	118 579	142 247	144 346	188 155	203 755
Commercial vehicles: total	JCYG	238 314	237 706	227 379	185 905	172 442	192 873	191 267	188 871	209 293	206 753	207 704
Of which:												
Light commercial vehicles	GKDH	205 372	210 942	203 629	162 176	145 655	169 705	168 311	166 359	178 887	171 866	175 713
Trucks:												
Under 7.5 tonnes	GKDJ	8 913	6 254	5 006	4 107	5 160	5 000	4 600	4 151	4 977	5 533	4 418
Over 7.5 tonnes	GKDL	10 128	7 932	7 002	6 443	6 849	7 359	7 357	7 779	8 537	9 756	11 447
Motive units for articulated vehicles	GKCV	2 631	2 574	2 492	2 739	2 673	2 539	1 795	2 095	2 558	2 755	2 230
Buses, coaches and mini buses	GKDN	11 270	10 004	9 250	10 440	12 105	8 270	9 204	8 487	14 334	16 843	13 896

1 See chapter text. Figures for motor vehicles relate to periods of 52 weeks (53 weeks in 1993).
2 From May 2005 production of 1000 c.c. and under ceased in the UK.

Source: Office for National Statistics: 01633 812394

22.26 Alcoholic drink[1]
United Kingdom

			1996	1997	1998	1999	2000	2001	2002	2003	2004	2005	2006
Spirits[2]		Thousand hectolitres of alcohol											
Production	KMEA	"	4 868	5 297	5 145	4 705	4 210	4 368	4 508	4 553	4 081	4 365	4 485
Released for home consumption													
Home produced whisky	KMEE	"	321	312	289	323	314	321	321	318	319	301	282
Spirit-based Ready-to-drink[3]	SNET	"	..	..	..	..	..	..	105	124	114	84	65
Imported and other	KMEG	"	495	533	505	596	615	647	689	744	792	822	767
Total	KMEH	"	815	845	794	919	929	968	1 115	1 187	1 226	1 207	1 114
Beer		Thousand hectolitres											
Production	BFNK	"	58 072	59 139	56 652	57 854	55 279	56 802	56 672	58 014	57 459	56 255	54 133
Released for home consumption	BAYL	"	59 894	61 114	58 835	58 917	57 007	58 234	59 384	60 301	59 195	57 572	55 735
Production	JYXJ	Thousand hectolitres of pure alcohol	2 360	2 406	2 333	2 364	2 299	2 358	2 352	2 414	2 433	2 338	2 202
Released for home consumption	JYXK		2 448	2 504	2 439	2 428	2 382	2 429	2 473	2 515	2 499	2 398	2 287
Wine of fresh grapes													
Released for home consumption		Thousand hectolitres											
Fortified	KMEM		331	323	370	316	289	287	325	296	298	306	302
Still table	KMEN	"	6 995	7 653	7 979	8 391	8 864	9 534	10 319	10 647	11 768	12 117	11 658
Sparkling	KMEO	"	358	382	416	576	543	515	578	640	676	721	715
Total	KMEP	"	7 684	8 358	8 765	9 284	9 696	10 336	11 222	11 584	12 742	13 143	12 675
Made-wine													
Released for home consumption													
Other than coolers	KMEQ	"	513	485	406	416	431	364	367	339	351	334	317
Coolers[3]	KJDD	"	1 781	1 153	1 244	1 802	2 800	3 712	1 606	423	508	597	528
Cider and perry													
Released for home consumption	KMER	"	5 656	5 513	5 548	6 022	6 006	5 911	5 939	5 876	6 139	6 377	7 523

1 See chapter text.
2 Potable spirits distilled.
3 Made wine with alcoholic strength 1.2% to 5.5%. Includes alcoholic lemonade of appropriate strength and similar products. From 28 April 2002, duty on spirit-based "coolers" is charged at the same rate as spirits per litre of alcohol. Coolers for calendar year 2002 includes only wine based "coolers".

Source: HM Revenue & Customs: 020 7147 0593

22.27 Tobacco products: released for home consumption[1]
United Kingdom

			1996	1997	1998	1999	2000	2001	2002	2003	2004	2005	2006
Cigarettes:		Thousand million											
Home produced	KMFA	"	73.8	71.1	67.8	28.2	49.3	47.7	49.6	49.1	48.2	45.9	44.4
Imported	KMFB	"	9.5	9.9	7.5	6.0	7.3	6.8	6.5	4.9	4.5	4.3	4.6
Total[2]	KMFC	"	83.3	81.0	75.3	34.2	56.6	54.5	56.1	54.0	52.6	50.2	49.0
Cigars:		Million kg											
Home produced	KMFD	"	1.4	1.3	1.2	0.9	1.0	0.9	0.9	0.8	0.7	0.6	0.6
Imported	KMFE	"	0.1	0.1	0.1	0.1	0.1	0.1	0.1	0.1	0.1	0.1	0.1
Total[2]	KMFF	"	1.5	1.4	1.3	1.0	1.1	1.0	1.0	0.9	0.8	0.8	0.7
Hand-rolling tobacco:													
Home produced	KMFG	"	2.1	1.8	1.7	2.0	2.1	2.8	2.8	2.9	3.0	3.2	3.4
Imported	KMFH	"	0.1	0.1	0.1	–	–	–	–	–	–	–	–
Total[2]	KMFI	"	2.3	1.9	1.8	2.0	2.2	2.8	2.8	2.9	3.1	3.2	3.5
Other smoking and chewing tobacco:													
Home produced	KMFJ	"	1.2	1.1	1.0	0.6	0.7	0.7	0.6	0.5	0.5	0.4	0.4
Imported	KMFK	"	0.1	0.1	0.1	0.1	0.1	0.1	0.1	0.1	0.1	0.1	0.1
Total[2]	KMFL	"	1.3	1.2	1.1	0.7	0.8	0.8	0.7	0.6	0.6	0.5	0.5

1 See chapter text.
2 Any apparent discrepency between totals and the sum of the constituents is
  due to rounding.

Source: HM Revenue and Customs: 020 7147 0593

Banking, insurance etc

Chapter 23

Banking, insurance etc

Other banks' balance sheet

(Table 23.3)

The implementation of the review of banking statistics at end-September 1997 has resulted in several changes to this table:

(a)   The table now includes the business of all monthly and quarterly reporting banks in the United Kingdom (UK); it formerly covered only the business of monthly reporting institutions.

(b)   The Channel Islands and Isle of Man are no longer treated as part of the UK for statistical purposes. Banking institutions in the Channel Islands and Isle of Man no longer have the option of being within the UK banking sector and their business, along with the business of offshore island branches of UK mainland banks, is now excluded from the figures within this table. Additionally, the business of the UK banking sector with offshore island residents and entities has been reclassified from UK residents to non-residents.

(c)   The table now contains more comprehensive detail of business with building societies. This business was previously included indistinguishably within the UK private sector elements of the table.

(d)   The aggregate balance sheet of the banking sector has been inflated because it is now reported on an accrual basis rather than a cash basis (accrued amounts payable/receivable are shown under liabilities and assets respectively). Additionally, acceptances have been brought onto the balance sheet and are shown under both liabilities and assets.

With effect from 1998, the balance sheet of the Banking Department of the Bank of England is excluded from this table, and other banks' business with the Issue Department is reclassified from "UK public sector" to "UK banks".

Data for 1999 reflect the acquisition of Birmingham Midshires Building Society by Halifax during that year.

Data for end-2000 reflect the entry of Bradford and Bingley plc to the banking sector during the year. Data for end-2000 also reflect the new reporting during the year of agency business as a result of collateral management via repos and reverse repos.

Bank lending to, and bank deposits from, UK residents

(Tables 23.4 and 23.5)

These are series of statistics based on the Standard Industrial Classification 1992.

Table 23.4 comprises loans, advances (including under reverse repos), finance leasing, acceptances, facilities and holdings of sterling and euro commercial paper. It includes lending under the Department of Trade and Industry special scheme for domestic shipbuilding. Holdings of investments and bills and adjustments for transit items are not included.

Table 23.5 includes borrowing under sale and repurchase agreements (repro). Adjustments for transit items are not included.

Figures for both tables are supplied by monthly reporting banks and grossed to cover quarterly reporters. They exclude lending to building societies and to residents of the Channel Islands and Isle of Man.

Building societies

(Table 23.13)

Building society figures are sourced from societies' annual returns and for each year relate to accounting years ending on dates between 1 February and 31 January of the following year. Figures are society-only as opposed to group consolidated.

Consumer credit

(Table 23.14)

Figures for net lending refer to changes in amounts outstanding adjusted to remove distortions caused by revaluations of debt outstanding, such as write-offs. Class 3 loans are advanced under the terms of the Building Societies' Act 1986.

A high proportion of credit advanced in certain types of agreement, notably on credit cards, is repaid within a month. This reflects use of such agreements as a method of payment rather than a way of obtaining credit. As from December 2006 the Bank of England has ceased to update the separate data on consumer credit provided by other specialist lenders, retailers and insurance companies previously contained in these tables. These categories have been merged into 'other consumer credit lenders'.

23.1 Bank of England Balance Sheet
Liabilities and assets outstanding at end of period

£ million

Consolidated statement

	Liabilities							Assets								
	Notes in circu- lation	Reserve balances	Standing facility deposits	Short term open market operati- ons	Foreign currency public securit- ies issued	Cash ratio deposits	Other liabili- ties	Standing facility assets	Short term open market operati- ons	Of which 1 week sterling reverse repo	of which fine-tr- uning sterling reverse repo	Longer term sterling reverse repo	Ways and Means advances to HMG	Bonds and other securit- ies acqured via market transac- tions	Other assets	Total assets/- liabilit
	B55A	B56A	B57A	B58A	B59A	B62A	B63A	B65A	B66A	B67A	B68A	B69A	B72A	B73A	B74A	B75A
2006	41 366	20 371	–	–	4 758	2 568	15 768	–	36 080	36 080	–	14 900	13 370	7 811	12 671	84 831
2006 Mar	..	..	..	..	..	..	..	..	..	..	..	..	..	..	..	..
Apr	..	..	..	..	..	..	..	..	..	..	..	..	..	..	..	..
May	..	..	..	..	..	..	..	..	..	..	..	..	..	..	..	..
Jun	37 792	21 507	–	–	6 030	2 365	14 461	–	33 370	33 370	–	15 400	13 370	8 176	11 840	82 156
Jul	38 300	19 175	–	–	5 404	2 365	14 640	–	31 820	31 820	–	15 050	13 370	7 968	11 675	79 939
Aug	38 519	18 748	–	–	5 161	2 365	14 721	–	32 230	32 230	–	14 700	13 370	7 953	11 260	79 513
Sep	38 476	18 376	–	–	4 938	2 365	15 438	–	31 110	31 110	–	15 200	13 370	7 846	12 067	79 593
Oct	38 427	17 150	–	–	4 735	2 365	15 507	–	29 900	29 900	–	15 100	13 370	7 850	11 965	78 184
Nov	38 686	19 336	–	–	4 802	2 365	15 181	–	31 560	31 560	–	15 000	13 370	8 236	12 205	80 371
Dec	41 366	20 371	–	–	4 758	2 568	15 768	–	36 080	36 080	–	14 900	13 370	7 811	12 671	84 831
2007 Jan	38 465	18 437	–	–	4 666	2 568	15 703	–	31 110	31 110	–	15 000	13 370	7 073	13 286	79 839
Feb	38 214	17 716	–	–	3 314	2 568	15 180	–	30 110	30 110	–	15 000	13 370	6 727	11 784	76 991

Issue Department

	Liabilities		Assets								
	Notes in circu- lation	Notes in Banking Departemnt	Short term open market operations	Of which 1 week sterling reverse repo	of which fine-tuning sterling reverse repo	Longer term sterling reverse repo	Ways and Means advances to HMG	Bonds and other securities acqured via market transactions	Other assets	Total assets/liabi- lities
	AEFA	AEFB	BL29	BL32	BL33	BL34	B54A	BL35	BL36	BL37
2006	41 366	–	13 044	13 044	..	14 900	13 370	–	52	41 366
2006 Mar	36 988	2	..	..	..	..	..	..	..	..
Apr	38 883	7	..	..	..	..	..	..	..	..
May	37 507	3	..	..	..	..	..	..	..	..
Jun	37 792	8	8 984	8 984	–	15 400	13 370	–	46	37 800
Jul	38 300	10	9 845	9 845	–	15 050	13 370	–	46	38 310
Aug	38 519	–	10 389	10 389	–	14 700	13 370	–	60	38 519
Sep	38 476	–	9 860	9 860	–	15 200	13 370	–	46	38 476
Oct	38 427	–	9 897	9 897	–	15 100	13 370	–	60	38 427
Nov	38 686	–	10 267	10 267	–	15 000	13 370	–	49	38 686
Dec	41 366	–	13 044	13 044	–	14 900	13 370	–	52	41 366
2007 Jan	38 465	–	10 052	10 052	–	15 000	13 370	–	44	38 465
Feb	38 214	–	9 795	9 795	–	15 000	13 370	–	49	38 214

Banking Department

	Liabilities							Assets							
	Reserve balances	Standing facility deposits	Short term open market operatio- ns	Foreign currency public securiti- es issued	Cash ratio deposits	Other liabilit- ies	Standing facility assets	Short term open market operatio- ns	Of which 1 week sterling reverse repo	of which fine-tru- ning sterling reverse repo	Bonds and other securiti- es acqured via market transact- ions	Bank of England notes	Other assets	Total assets/l- iabilitie
	BL38	BL39	BL42	BL43	BL44	BL45	BL47	BL48	BL49	BL52	BL53	BL54	BL55	BL56
2006	20 371	–	–	4 758	2 568	15 820	–	23 036	23 036	–	7 811	–	12 671	43 517
2006 Mar	..	..	..	..	..	..	..	..	..	..	..	..	..	..
Apr	..	..	..	..	..	..	..	..	..	..	..	..	..	..
May	..	..	..	..	..	..	..	..	..	..	..	..	..	..
Jun	21 507	–	–	6 030	2 365	14 508	–	24 386	24 386	–	8 176	8	11 840	44 410
Jul	19 175	–	–	5 404	2 365	14 685	–	21 976	21 976	–	7 968	10	11 675	41 629
Aug	18 748	–	–	5 161	2 365	14 781	–	21 841	21 841	–	7 953	–	11 260	41 055
Sep	18 376	–	–	4 938	2 365	15 484	–	21 250	21 250	–	7 846	–	12 067	41 163
Oct	17 150	–	–	4 735	2 365	15 567	–	20 002	20 002	–	7 850	–	11 965	39 817
Nov	19 336	–	–	4 802	2 365	15 230	–	21 293	21 293	–	8 236	–	12 205	41 734
Dec	20 371	–	–	4 758	2 568	15 820	–	23 036	23 036	–	7 811	–	12 671	43 517
2007 Jan	18 437	–	–	4 666	2 568	15 747	–	21 059	21 059	–	7 073	–	13 286	41 418
Feb	17 716	–	–	3 314	2 568	15 229	–	20 315	20 315	–	6 727	–	11 784	38 826

Source: Bank of England

23.2 Value of inter-bank clearings
United Kingdom

£ billion

		1996	1997	1998	1999	2000	2001	2002	2003	2004	2005	2006
Bulk paper clearings[1]												
Cheque (formerly general)	KCYY	1 161	1 200	1 214	1 226	1 214	1 210	1 178	1 141	1 111	1 062	1 076
Credit	KCYZ	94	94	92	88	82	80	75	69	63	57	56
High-value clearings												
Town	KCZA	–	–	–	–	–	–	–	–	–	–	..
CHAPS Sterling only	KCZB	28 881	36 032	41 501	44 704	49 146	52 913	51 896	51 613	52 348	52 672	59 437
Electronic clearing (BACS)	KCZC	1 250	1 432	1 602	1 761	1 922	2 166	2 382	2 574	2 883	3 150	3 429

1 Excludes inter-branch clearings and clearings in Scotland and Northern Ireland.

Source: APACS - The UK payments association: 020 7711 6323

23.3 Other banks' balance sheet[1]

£ million

		1997[2]	1998[3]	1999[4]	2000[5,6]	2001	2002	2003	2004	2005	2006
Sterling liabilities											
Notes outstanding & cash loaded cards	TBFA	2 832	2 929	3 311	3 359	3 866	3 957	4 207	4 338	4 534	4 987
Sight deposits[7]											
UK banks	TBFB	44 573	37 839	33 463	40 054	59 573	101 905	99 208	109 866	148 202	165 479
UK building societies	TBFC	950	1 277	841	1 168	1 466	2 403	1 736	1 697	2 314	2 277
UK public sector[8]	TBFD	3 781	3 003	3 450	3 403	4 283	3 997	5 679	6 635	7 341	9 046
Other UK residents	TBFE	271 233	295 068	325 392	372 725	415 180	457 077	502 359	566 524	638 684	701 743
Non-residents	TBFF	37 730	43 528	44 581	55 489	55 837	57 218	65 157	72 452	83 608	94 822
Time deposits											
UK banks	TBFG	99 782	111 970	112 530	110 955	125 261	141 401	164 433	230 749	289 656	455 672
UK building societies	TBFH	5 682	4 361	4 253	4 688	4 856	4 487	3 643	4 045	4 098	3 573
UK public sector[8]	TBFI	9 059	9 748	8 064	8 241	8 306	8 936	8 934	10 872	11 378	16 504
Other UK residents	TBFJ	284 629	295 924	282 789	301 007	302 715	306 453	313 244	322 603	353 481	433 436
of which TESSAs	TBFK	20 394	21 568	22 868	24 265	9 752	5 235	1 832	–	–	–
of which SAYE	TBFL	2 254	2 604	2 840	2 726	2 439	2 367	2 226	2 301	2 164	1 900
of which cash ISAs	TFDG	..	..	5 210	13 684	31 298	42 269	52 118	61 033	68 584	..
Non-residents	TBFM	91 040	97 953	116 967	134 844	150 964	151 304	166 449	177 381	203 777	234 754
Acceptances granted	TBFN	19 952	16 658	12 854	10 012	10 627	9 954	2 856	1 446	928	1 105
Liabilities under sale and repurchase agreements											
of which British govt. securities	TBFU	47 297	55 561	56 145	83 819	83 330	78 155	114 468	109 692	180 087	234 606
UK banks[8,9]	TBFP	29 089	43 314	48 213	56 408	60 551	52 079	95 922	86 876	133 938	190 384
UK building societies	TBFQ	20	32	200	36	–	107	170	62	345	–
UK public sector[8,9]	TBFR	6 044	–	–	14 351	5 127	1 402	1 521	113	155	35
Other UK residents	TBFS	18 114	20 918	17 165	22 974	25 732	19 759	19 906	35 038	55 378	58 312
Non-residents	TBFT	5 664	5 469	5 542	9 849	8 643	19 072	18 475	26 669	40 012	54 240
CDs and other short-term paper issued	TBFV	119 266	138 248	158 826	151 153	153 768	157 354	148 606	160 173	165 923	179 554
Total sterling deposits	TBFW	1 046 609	1 125 311	1 175 130	1 297 356	1 392 890	1 494 908	1 618 298	1 813 197	2 139 217	2 600 935
Sterling items in suspense and transmission	TBFX	16 054	15 714	17 307	15 261	16 702	13 318	18 371	17 923	27 479	34 047
Net derivatives	TBFY	8 186	8 342	8 324	10 992	4 029	2 491	−10 672	−15 457	9 894	−33 397
Accrued amounts payable	TBFZ	20 713	24 632	22 122	23 726	22 836	21 541	22 624	26 262	27 108	35 267
Sterling capital and other internal funds	TBGA	103 462	103 868	100 575	133 436	148 294	173 320	204 295	265 344	243 392	299 789
Total sterling liabilities	TBGB	1 197 856	1 280 796	1 326 769	1 484 130	1 588 618	1 709 535	1 857 123	2 111 607	2 451 625	2 941 629
Foreign currency liabilities											
Sight and time deposits											
UK banks[10]	TBGC	90 858	77 128	77 684	99 447	106 368	111 536	139 018	151 946	153 024	184 880
UK building societies	TBGD	1 027	639	681	233	279	373	550	310	615	658
UK public sector[8]	TBGE	226	149	126	1 808	926	833	865	898	1 098	2 279
Other UK residents	TBGF	64 188	60 513	65 203	79 627	95 666	81 590	89 034	111 035	137 651	162 328
Non-residents	TBGG	716 573	766 934	736 792	914 888	1 001 321	997 398	1 055 183	1 185 037	1 427 857	1 552 060
Acceptances granted	TBGH	743	729	619	689	638	754	751	890	846	1 270
Sale and repurchase agreements											
UK banks	TBGJ	21 311	30 669	25 170	38 901	54 499	90 407	224 743	243 933	265 239	259 088
UK building societies	TBGK	–	–	–	–	–	–	–	–	–	–
UK public sector	TBGL	22	–	–	468	1	71	844	858	391	1
Other UK residents	TBGM	25 716	26 742	21 997	35 145	52 438	54 463	73 477	67 544	79 689	83 379
Non-residents	TBGN	100 936	118 909	115 357	139 656	154 976	211 276	289 674	379 695	433 712	419 744
CDs and other short-term paper issued	TBGO	131 620	124 151	151 009	199 510	224 225	234 731	255 590	278 440	341 866	406 487
Total foreign currency deposits	TBGP	1 153 220	1 206 562	1 194 637	1 510 373	1 691 336	1 783 432	2 129 730	2 420 587	2 841 988	3 072 175
Items in suspense and transmission	TBGQ	35 713	25 026	30 548	46 678	47 363	38 355	60 465	92 173	108 217	95 421
Net derivatives	TBGR	8 654	2 656	3 704	−4 472	−3 854	5 816	14 774	22 765	3 347	66 215
Accrued amounts payable	TBGS	21 996	25 184	18 080	18 568	17 756	16 312	15 708	18 214	23 015	36 279
Capital and other internal funds	TBGT	31 676	46 952	69 798	89 359	85 489	87 047	81 778	45 835	93 991	50 591
Total foreign currency liabilities	TBGU	1 251 258	1 306 380	1 316 767	1 660 506	1 838 090	1 930 961	2 302 455	2 599 575	3 070 557	3 320 680
Total liabilities	TBGV	2 449 114	2 587 177	2 643 536	3 144 636	3 426 708	3 640 497	4 159 579	4 711 182	5 522 182	6 262 309

23.3 Other banks' balance sheet[1]

continued

£ million

		1997[2]	1998[3]	1999[4]	2000[5,6]	2001	2002	2003	2004	2005	2006
Sterling assets											
Notes and coins	TBGW	5 225	6 699	9 047	8 007	6 566	6 621	7 464	10 559	9 500	9 279
With UK central bank											
Cash ratio deposits	TBGX	2 566	1 068	1 141	1 275	1 386	1 495	1 609	1 759	1 953	2 271
Other	TBGY	216	383	676	117	143	249	54	100	1 388	17 645
Market loans											
UK banks[7]	TBGZ	139 996	148 138	144 537	149 174	181 350	237 771	263 004	342 699	438 572	618 743
UK bank CDs	TBHB	62 584	65 510	75 071	65 156	68 868	68 728	55 053	59 505	58 780	63 236
UK bank commercial paper	TBHC	29	130	208	8	52	62	5	54	75	410
UK building societies CDs etc and deposits	TBHD	4 242	4 505	5 093	4 748	3 933	4 293	7 200	7 222	5 655	7 481
Non-residents	TBHE	79 368	84 162	74 403	94 381	102 404	89 848	109 665	102 286	128 343	166 599
Acceptances granted											
UK building societies	TBHF	–	–	–	–	–	–	–	–	–	–
UK public sector[8]	TBHG	–	–	–	–	–	–	–	–	–	–
Other UK residents	TBHH	18 573	15 394	11 933	9 496	9 992	9 111	2 777	1 348	817	956
Non-residents	TBHI	1 379	1 264	920	516	635	842	79	99	111	148
Bills											
Treasury bills	TBHJ	554	779	2 749	1 612	8 474	18 752	18 265	14 507	15 707	11 984
UK bank bills	TBHA	18 221	14 110	11 426	7 011	8 098	8 491	1 265	646	24	103
UK building societies	TBHK	–	–	–	–	–	–	–	–	–	375
Other UK	TBHL	1 116	1 221	818	1 202	1 601	485	1 013	955	779	1 636
Non-residents	TBHM	309	207	206	287	744	979	733	702	1 063	1 831
Claims under sale and repurchase agreements											
of which British govt. securities	TBHT	47 158	56 639	64 943	86 362	84 068	77 460	114 091	116 652	187 606	237 177
UK banks	TBHO	27 611	41 969	39 667	46 088	46 585	37 197	77 691	64 353	113 540	160 380
UK building societies	TBHP	345	134	91	116	327	86	114	263	1 048	76
UK public sector	TBHQ	–	–	–	9 067	4 692	5 159	5 231	10 801	11 695	9 168
Other UK residents	TBHR	21 283	23 803	30 338	35 058	36 222	31 363	35 885	50 371	61 311	65 569
Non-residents	TBHS	6 873	5 907	6 310	7 266	7 010	14 271	12 981	20 456	36 261	52 300
Advances											
UK public sector	TBHU	3 872	3 403	2 567	2 746	2 442	3 783	4 414	6 078	6 838	8 092
Other UK residents[11]	TBHV	636 162	672 812	732 649	823 787	891 790	986 835	1 062 650	1 159 833	1 252 836	1 380 079
Non-residents	TBHW	21 102	21 039	23 364	24 494	29 483	31 380	34 603	38 447	49 223	62 314
Banking dept. lending to central govt. (net)	TBNU	–2 741	–	–	–	–	–	–	–	–	..
Investments											
British government stocks	TBHX	23 078	14 714	9 243	2 867	499	–3 545	–8 525	–4 210	–6 203	–11 173
Other public sector	TBHY	283	215	124	88	116	158	385	328	459	569
UK banks[12]	TBHZ	11 922	13 415	13 584	22 935	23 965	23 542	34 971	34 664	36 365	36 655
UK building societies	TBIA	2 875	2 223	2 506	2 251	2 099	1 835	1 702	1 889	2 068	1 891
Other UK residents[13]	TBIB	45 134	48 781	57 391	77 647	82 013	76 773	84 813	100 892	112 593	162 625
Non-residents	TBIC	9 343	11 834	13 775	20 572	23 462	22 821	22 505	26 029	30 487	38 814
Items in suspense and collection	TBID	23 526	23 888	23 441	21 982	24 024	19 577	22 434	22 066	29 714	34 629
Accrued amounts receivable	TBIE	15 003	17 352	15 173	15 919	13 528	15 486	17 204	19 987	19 510	24 909
Other assets	TBIF	12 218	12 593	13 036	12 654	12 876	12 685	11 955	12 875	15 522	14 430
Total sterling assets[14]	TBIG	1 192 264	1 257 652	1 321 486	1 468 527	1 595 380	1 727 136	1 889 200	2 107 562	2 436 032	2 944 021

23.3 Other banks' balance sheet[1]
continued

£ million

		1997[2]	1998[3]	1999[4]	2000[5,6]	2001	2002	2003	2004	2005	2006
Foreign currency assets											
Market loans and advances											
UK banks[10]	TBIH	90 367	72 263	74 250	93 269	104 107	114 809	137 417	149 119	146 316	173 211
UK banks' CDs etc	TBII	13 633	11 065	14 364	13 171	13 298	10 128	13 162	11 026	18 412	13 023
UK building societies CDs etc. and deposits	TBIJ	83	259	451	173	354	357	591	448	411	422
UK public sector[8]	TBIK	25	45	20	30	13	83	91	50	153	105
Other UK residents	TBIL	76 356	83 968	88 847	107 707	118 106	117 669	134 894	153 574	161 488	199 147
Non-residents	TBIM	598 541	616 832	599 146	743 781	783 057	783 168	779 983	839 535	1 013 764	1 104 494
Claims under sale and repurchase agreement											
UK banks	TBIO	24 184	31 900	28 008	41 801	61 188	91 488	225 027	250 209	272 361	257 856
UK building societies	TBIP	–	–	–	–	–	–	–	–	100	67
UK public sector[8]	TBIQ	22	–	–	737	23	486	1 420	1 590	1 125	1
Other UK residents	TBIR	55 945	39 764	33 027	57 876	73 237	86 866	100 817	106 973	135 018	131 709
Non-residents	TBIS	121 101	147 562	146 756	199 990	219 449	256 663	382 672	506 157	612 065	595 615
Acceptances granted	TBIT	743	729	619	689	638	754	751	890	846	1 270
Bills	TBIU	12 728	15 239	19 508	21 878	25 399	20 803	31 429	24 250	24 230	25 917
Investments											
British government stocks	TBIV	3 453	4 755	4 473	3 518	890	226	19	–20	–30	104
Other public sector	TBIW	–	–	–	–	4	18	7	–	–	1
UK banks	TBIX	2 850	4 310	8 607	11 706	10 633	10 298	11 688	13 187	13 176	12 384
UK building societies	TBIY	414	526	631	939	850	1 170	1 570	2 400	2 974	2 683
Other UK residents	TBIZ	4 055	4 584	5 679	12 298	18 129	20 130	21 846	32 882	45 283	60 748
Non-residents	TBJA	186 288	234 563	243 147	297 404	324 073	326 035	334 371	398 040	484 874	563 135
Items in suspense and collection	TBJB	40 175	30 229	29 706	44 885	55 026	44 037	60 804	81 937	112 089	117 498
Accrued amounts receivable	TBJC	23 673	27 821	20 163	21 279	18 969	19 434	18 129	19 561	22 397	32 639
Other assets	TBJD	2 215	3 111	4 648	2 978	3 880	8 735	13 683	11 802	19 089	26 251
Total foreign currency assets[15]	TBJE	1 256 850	1 329 525	1 322 050	1 676 109	1 831 322	1 913 355	2 270 372	2 603 610	3 086 141	3 318 281
Total assets	TBJF	2 449 114	2 587 177	2 643 536	3 144 636	3 426 702	3 640 491	4 159 572	4 711 173	5 522 173	6 262 302
Holdings of own sterling acceptances	TBJG	1 823	2 137	1 725	1 231	916	1 220	411	265	24	19
Holdings of own FC acceptances	TBJH	291	170	150	135	118	58	104	170	222	247
Eligible banks' total sterling acceptances	TBJI	21 366	18 722	14 523	10 597	11 320	10 805	3 035	1 217	152	..
Eligible liabilities	TBJJ	766 683	807 803	849 289	952 062	1 012 194	1 087 877	1 163 917	1 266 726	1 420 348	1 636 053

1 The implementation of the review of banking at end-September 1997 has resulted in several changes to this table. Details are given in the chapter text.

2 Data for 1997 reflect the entry of Northern Rock plc to the banking sector during the year.

3 With effect from 1998 the balance sheet of the Banking Department of the Bank of England is excluded from these data.

4 Data for 1999 reflect the acquisition of Birmingham Midshires Building Society by Halifax during that year.

5 Data for 2000 reflect the entry of Bradford & Bingley plc to the banking sector during the year.

6 Data for 2000 reflect the new reporting during the year of agency business as a result of collateral management via repos and reverse repos.

7 Sterling sight deposits from UK banks and sterling market loans to UK banks in 2003 were depressed by £19 bn following the consolidation of two banks balance sheets.

8 From 2000 the UK public sector series reflects assumption by the Debt Management Office (an executive agency of HM Treasury) of responsibility for government cash management.

9 There is a break in this series in 1998 as a result of the reclassification of the Issue Department of the Bank of England from UK public sector to UK banks.

10 Foreign currency sight and time deposits from UK banks and foreign currency market loans and advances to UK banks in 2001, 2003 and 2004 were each depressed by £14.5 bn, £0.5 bn and £4.7 bn respectively as a result of positions being consolidated out on the merger of two banks.

11 During 2000, 2001, 2002, 2003, 2004 and 2005 sterling advances to other UK residents were reduced by £10.3 bn, £12.9 bn, £16.2 bn, £29.1bn, £30.4bn and £33.6 bn respectively as a result of securitisations and other loan transfers to non-banks or non-residents.

12 Sterling investments in UK banks in 2000 were boosted by Barclay's £5.8 bn investment in Woolwich.

13 Sterling investments in other UK residents in 2000 were boosted by Lloyds TSB's £5.8 bn investment in Scottish Widows Group.

14 Changes in the reporting populations in 1998, 1999, 2000, 2001, 2003 and 2004 account for a net decrease of £7.3 bn, £11.3 bn £0.8 bn, £0.7bn, £0.2 and £4.5 bn respectively in sterling assets outstanding.

15 Changes in the reporting populations in 1998, 1999, 2000, 2001, 2003 and 2004 account for a net decrease of £4.6 bn, £6.6 bn, £0.2 bn, £0.2 bn £0.2 bn and £5.2 bn of foreign currency assets outstanding.

Source: Bank of England: 020 7601 3236

23.4 Industrial analysis of bank lending to UK residents[1]
Not seasonally adjusted

£ million

	UK residents		Agriculture, hunting and forestry	Fishing	Mining & quarrying	Manufacturing			
	Total	of which sterling				Total	Food, beverages & tobacco	Textiles & leather	Pulp, paper, publishing & printing
Amounts outstanding (sterling & other currencies)									
Loans & advances (including under repo & sterling commercial paper)									
	TBOA	TBOB	TBOC	TBOD	TBOE	TBOF	TBOG	TBOH	TBOI
2005	1 632 663	1 333 243	9 363	371	3 262	48 485	11 817	1 641	6 931
2006	1 794 281	1 460 831	9 620	413	4 203	47 467	11 433	1 511	6 404
Acceptances									
	TBQA	TBQB	TBQC	TBQD	TBQE	TBQF	TBQG	TBQH	TBQI
2005	1 015	816	–	1	2	83	7	26	1
2006	1 190	956	–	–	1	104	5	28	1
Total									
	TBSA		TBSC	TBSD	TBSE	TBSF	TBSG	TBSH	TBSI
2005	1 633 678		9 363	371	3 264	48 568	11 824	1 668	6 932
2006	1 795 471		9 620	413	4 205	47 571	11 438	1 539	6 405
of which in sterling									
	TBUA		TBUC	TBUD	TBUE	TBUF	TBUG	TBUH	TBUI
2005	1 334 059		9 218	360	1 352	31 510	9 180	1 100	4 898
2006	1 461 787		9 375	399	1 933	32 388	8 630	1 014	4 915
Facilities granted									
	TCAA		TCAC	TCAD	TCAE	TCAF	TCAG	TCAH	TCAI
2005	1 987 573		11 700	463	11 483	87 320	23 519	2 488	11 885
2006	2 174 837		12 146	504	11 358	88 919	25 048	2 501	11 636
of which in sterling									
	TCCA		TCCC	TCCD	TCCE	TCCF	TCCG	TCCH	TCCI
2005	1 601 306		11 484	452	2 534	52 314	14 792	1 677	7 056
2006	1 743 546		11 834	490	2 586	54 208	15 252	1 689	7 496

	Manufacturing					Electricity, gas and water supply		
	Chemicals, man-made fibres, rubber & plastics	Non-metallic mineral products & metals	Machinery, equipment & transport equipment	Electrical, medical & optical equipment	Other manufacturing	Electricity, gas & heated water	Cold water purification & supply	Construction
Amounts outstanding (sterling & other currencies)								
Loans & advances (including under repo & sterling commercial paper)								
	TBOJ	TBOK	TBOL	TBOM	TBON	TBOO	TBOP	TBOQ
2005	6 253	5 242	7 085	4 267	5 250	4 992	1 163	19 154
2006	5 680	6 121	6 677	3 740	5 902	7 074	4 234	20 657
Acceptances								
	TBQJ	TBQK	TBQL	TBQM	TBQN	TBQO	TBQP	TBQQ
2005	5	9	8	7	19	–	2	2
2006	4	10	8	14	33	–	–	15
Total								
	TBSJ	TBSK	TBSL	TBSM	TBSN	TBSO	TBSP	TBSQ
2005	..	5 251	7 093	..	5 269	4 992	1 165	19 155
2006	..	6 131	6 685	..	5 935	7 074	4 234	20 672
of which in sterling								
	TBUJ	TBUK	TBUL	TBUM	TBUN	TBUO	TBUP	TBUQ
2005	2 933	2 951	3 875	2 468	4 105	4 149	1 130	18 545
2006	2 961	3 762	4 496	2 077	4 533	6 113	3 923	20 127
Facilities granted								
	TCAJ	TCAK	TCAL	TCAM	TCAN	TCAO	TCAP	TCAQ
2005	..	8 896	12 912	7 053	8 107	13 456	6 079	32 720
2006	..	10 193	12 381	6 466	9 810	15 024	11 441	33 381
of which in sterling								
	TCCJ	TCCK	TCCL	TCCM	TCCN	TCCO	TCCP	TCCQ
2005	5 680	5 445	7 749	4 008	5 908	8 576	4 944	29 988
2006	5 360	6 072	8 395	3 508	6 436	10 407	10 110	30 912

23.4 Industrial analysis of bank lending to UK residents[1]

Not seasonally adjusted

continued

£ million

	Wholesale and retail trade						Real estate, renting, computer and other business activities		
Total	Sale & repair of motor vehicles & fuel	Other wholesale trade	Other retail trade & repair	Hotels and restaurants	Transport, storage & communication	Total	Development, buying, selling, renting of real estate	Renting of machinery & equipment

Amounts outstanding (sterling & other currencies)

Loans & advances (including under repo & sterling commercial paper)

	TBOR	TBOS	TBOT	TBOU	TBOV	TBOW	TBOX	TBOY	TBPA
2005	40 548	9 293	13 312	17 943	25 064	20 836	177 152	137 281	6 661
2006	42 358	10 164	14 397	17 797	25 698	26 356	209 857	162 311	6 859

Acceptances

	TBQR	TBQS	TBQT	TBQU	TBQV	TBQW	TBQX	TBQY	TBRA
2005	151	7	120	25	–	–	721	714	–
2006	160	4	99	58	1	1	812	800	–

Total

	TBSR	TBSS	TBST	TBSU	TBSV	TBSW	TBSX	TBSY	TBTA
2005	40 699	9 300	13 431	17 968	25 064	20 837	177 873	137 995	6 662
2006	42 518	10 167	14 496	17 855	25 699	26 356	210 669	163 111	6 860

of which in sterling

	TBUR	TBUS	TBUT	TBUU	TBUV	TBUW	TBUX	TBUY	TBVA
2005	34 325	8 787	9 644	15 894	23 568	16 531	169 826	135 928	6 028
2006	35 826	9 505	10 235	16 086	25 034	21 584	200 935	160 949	5 797

Facilities granted

	TCAR	TCAS	TCAT	TCAU	TCAV	TCAW	TCAX	TCAY	TCBA
2005	64 698	12 315	20 760	31 624	32 991	40 836	231 335	174 199	8 583
2006	68 253	13 960	22 076	32 217	32 487	43 026	272 024	206 171	8 435

of which in sterling

	TCCR	TCCS	TCCT	TCCU	TCCV	TCCW	TCCX	TCCY	TCDA
2005	52 234	11 344	14 861	26 029	29 915	26 062	216 642	169 995	7 529
2006	53 580	12 565	15 465	25 550	30 081	29 409	253 043	200 110	6 660

	Real estate, renting, computer and other business activities				Recreational, personal & community service activities		Financial intermediation (excl. insurance & pension funds)	
Computer & related activities	Legal, accountancy, consultancy & other business activities	Public administration & defence	Education	Health & social work	Recreational, cultural & sporting activities	Personal & community services activities	Total	Financial leasing corporations

Amounts outstanding (sterling & other currencies)

Loans & advances (including under repo & sterling commercial paper)

	TBPB	TBPC	TBPD	TBPE	TBPF	TBPH	TBPG	TBPI	TBPJ
2005	3 752	29 458	19 590	6 317	12 729	10 025	5 304	422 947	36 770
2006	4 409	36 277	17 227	7 498	15 854	12 251	5 591	491 141	41 068

Acceptances

	TBRB	TBRC	TBRD	TBRE	TBRF	TBRH	TBRG	TBRI	TBRJ
2005	–	7	–	–	–	–	4	48	–
2006	–	12	–	–	–	–	5	90	–

Total

	TBTB	TBTC	TBTD	TBTE	TBTF	TBTH	TBTG	TBTI	TBTJ
2005	3 752	29 464	19 590	6 317	12 729	10 025	5 308	422 995	36 770
2006	4 410	36 290	17 227	7 498	15 854	12 251	5 596	491 231	41 068

of which in sterling

	TBVB	TBVC	TBVD	TBVE	TBVF	TBVH	TBVG	TBVI	TBVJ
2005	2 658	25 212	18 266	6 263	12 522	9 073	4 619	206 104	32 472
2006	2 912	31 277	17 120	7 431	15 643	10 891	5 048	246 324	35 832

Facilities granted

	TCBB	TCBC	TCBD	TCBE	TCBF	TCBH	TCBG	TCBI	TCBJ
2005	5 730	42 823	21 857	8 551	15 651	15 786	7 281	473 528	42 091
2006	6 353	51 065	19 587	10 046	19 182	17 402	7 925	547 423	43 617

of which in sterling

	TCDB	TCDC	TCDD	TCDE	TCDF	TCDH	TCDG	TCDI	TCDJ
2005	3 956	35 162	20 426	8 397	15 275	13 148	6 324	235 344	37 390
2006	4 191	42 081	19 479	9 947	18 667	14 454	6 886	275 481	37 890

23.4
continued

Industrial analysis of bank lending to UK residents[1]
Not seasonally adjusted

£ million

Financial intermediation (excl. insurance & pension funds)

	Non-bank credit grantors, excl. credit unions	Credit unions	Factoring corporations	Mortgage & housing credit corporations	Investment & unit trusts excl. money market mutual funds	Money market mutual funds	Bank holding companies	Securities dealers (f)	Other financial intermediaries
Amounts outstanding (sterling & other currencies)									
Loans & advances (including under repo & sterling commercial paper)									
	TBPK	TBPL	TBPM	TBPN	TBPO	TBPP	TBPQ	TBPR	TBPS
2005	17 833	28	4 633	62 869	20 394	1 377	19 707	165 421	93 916
2006	21 495	60	5 593	84 959	20 130	674	17 969	183 572	115 620
Acceptances									
	TBRK	TBRL	TBRM	TBRN	TBRO	TBRP	TBRQ	TBRR	TBRS
2005	15	5	–	–	–	–	–	–	27
2006	15	5	–	–	–	–	–	–	69
Total									
	TBTK	TBTL	TBTM	TBTN	TBTO	TBTP	TBTQ	TBTR	TBTS
2005	17 848	33	4 633	62 869	20 394	1 377	19 707	165 421	93 943
2006	21 511	66	5 593	84 959	20 130	674	17 969	183 572	115 689
of which in sterling									
	TBVK	TBVL	TBVM	TBVN	TBVO	TBVP	TBVQ	TBVR	TBVS
2005	16 512	33	3 914	58 500	5 743	265	13 084	22 558	53 024
2006	20 205	65	4 673	74 403	6 972	91	12 472	25 852	65 759
Facilities granted									
	TCBK	TCBL	TCBM	TCBN	TCBO	TCBP	TCBQ	TCBR	TCBS
2005	20 883	39	4 994	65 575	28 756	1 425	20 534	169 180	120 052
2006	23 625	89	5 916	92 587	33 310	752	18 902	186 684	141 941
of which in sterling									
	TCDK	TCDL	TCDM	TCDN	TCDO	TCDP	TCDQ	TCDR	TCDS
2005	18 998	39	4 235	61 111	12 176	266	13 329	23 822	63 977
2006	21 977	88	4 946	81 888	13 042	106	12 413	26 562	76 568

	Activities auxiliary to financial intermediation			Individuals & individual trusts		
	Insurance companies & pension funds	Fund management activities	Other	Total	Lending secured on dwellings inc. bridging finance	Other loans & advances
Amounts outstanding (sterling & other currencies)						
Loans & advances (including under repo & sterling commercial paper)						
	TBPT	TBPU	TBPV	TBPW	TBPX	TBPY
2005	23 331	26 669	53 903	701 458	558 805	142 653
2006	26 357	33 974	56 171	730 278	587 500	142 778
Acceptances						
	TBRT	TBRU	TBRV			
2005	1	–	–			
2006	1	–	–			
Total						
	TBTT	TBTU	TBTV	TBTW	TBTX	TBTY
2005	23 332	26 669	53 903	701 458	558 805	142 653
2006	26 357	33 974	56 171	730 278	587 500	142 778
of which in sterling						
	TBVT	TBVU	TBVV	TBVW	TBVX	TBVY
2005	21 584	16 520	28 091	700 503	..	141 888
2006	24 374	20 732	27 964	728 623	..	141 549
Facilities granted						
	TCBT	TCBU	TCBV	TCBW	TCBX	TCBY
2005	32 931	30 745	55 894	792 268	605 078	187 190
2006	38 597	37 555	58 236	830 321	640 526	189 795
of which in sterling						
	TCDT	TCDU	TCDV	TCDW	TCDX	TCDY
2005	27 554	19 438	29 203	791 052	604 884	186 168
2006	31 341	22 775	29 474	828 384	640 094	188 290

1 See chapter text.

Source: Bank of England: 020 7601 3236

23.5 Industrial analysis of bank deposits from UK residents[1]

£ million

	Total from UK residents	Agriculture, hunting and forestry	Fishing	Mining & quarrying	Manufacturing			
					Total	Food, beverages & tobacco	Textiles & leather	Pulp, paper, publishing & printing

Amounts outstanding (sterling & other currencies)

Deposit liabilities (including under repos)

	TDAA	TDAB	TDAC	TDAD	TDAE	TDAF	TDAG	TDAH
2005	1 285 158	3 608	192	7 399	38 471	3 272	1 165	4 262
2006	1 467 069	4 147	192	5 692	39 958	3 686	1 175	3 710

of which in sterling

	TDCA	TDCB	TDCC	TDCD	TDCE	TDCF	TDCG	TDCH
2005	1 066 333	3 552	178	3 607	27 337	2 678	983	3 556
2006	1 219 070	4 063	170	3 136	30 063	3 031	957	3 175

	Manufacturing					Electricity, gas and water supply		
	Chemicals, man-made fibres, rubber & plastics	Non-metallic mineral products & metals	Machinery, equipment & transport equipment	Electrical, medical & optical equipment	Other manufacturing	Electricity, gas & heated water	Cold water purification & supply	Construction

Amounts outstanding (sterling & other currencies)

Deposit liabilities (including under repos)

	TDAI	TDAJ	TDAK	TDAL	TDAM	TDAN	TDAO	TDAP
2005	5 332	4 236	9 754	6 637	3 813	4 782	1 843	14 999
2006	4 062	5 612	9 280	6 283	6 150	5 369	3 681	17 520

of which in sterling

	TDCI	TDCJ	TDCK	TDCL	TDCM	TDCN	TDCO	TDCP
2005	3 218	3 556	6 617	3 490	3 239	4 122	1 778	14 697
2006	2 731	4 792	7 511	3 533	4 333	4 564	3 486	17 263

	Wholesale and retail trade				Hotels and restaurants	Transport, storage & communication	Real estate, renting, computer and other business activities		
	Total	Sale & repair of motor vehicles & fuel	Other wholesale trade	Other retail trade & repair			Total	Development, buying, selling, renting of real estate	Renting of machinery & equipment

Amounts outstanding (sterling & other currencies)

Deposit liabilities (including under repos)

	TDAQ	TDAR	TDAS	TDAT	TDAU	TDAV	TDAW	TDAX	TDAY
2005	28 901	3 295	13 338	12 268	5 351	18 275	96 900	28 428	1 366
2006	29 013	3 531	12 952	12 530	5 069	20 352	113 659	33 331	1 568

of which in sterling

	TDCQ	TDCR	TDCS	TDCT	TDCU	TDCV	TDCW	TDCX	TDCY
2005	24 407	3 080	9 952	11 375	5 111	15 038	90 444	27 884	1 294
2006	24 735	3 251	9 819	11 664	4 935	16 440	105 300	32 067	1 448

23.5 Industrial analysis of bank deposits from UK residents[1]

continued

£ million

	Real estate, renting, computer and other business activities					Recreational, personal & community service activities		Financial intermediation (excl. insurance & pension funds)	
	Computer & related activities	Legal, accountancy, consultancy & other business activities	Public administration & defence	Education	Health & social work	Recreational, cultural & sporting activities	Personal & community services activities	Total	Financial leasing corporations

Amounts outstanding (sterling & other currencies)

Deposit liabilities (including under repos)

	TDAZ	TDBA	TDBB	TDBC	TDBD	TDBF	TDBE	TDBG	TDBH
2005	7 348	59 758	17 433	7 137	10 617	12 426	13 123	259 683	4 863
2006	7 969	70 791	22 260	7 800	11 685	14 016	14 068	349 456	5 416

of which in sterling

	TDCZ	TDDA	TDDB	TDDC	TDDD	TDDF	TDDE	TDDG	TDDH
2005	6 240	55 025	16 004	6 827	10 282	11 366	12 696	123 488	3 764
2006	6 795	64 989	21 169	7 479	11 332	13 076	13 637	195 096	3 895

	Financial intermediation (excl. insurance & pension funds)							
	Non-bank credit grantors, excl. credit unions	Credit unions	Factoring corporations	Mortgage & housing credit corporations	Investment & unit trusts excl. money market mutual funds	Money market mutual funds	Bank holding companies	Securities dealers	Other financial intermediaries

Amounts outstanding (sterling & other currencies)

Deposit liabilities (including under repos)

	TDBI	TDBJ	TDBK	TDBL	TDBM	TDBN	TDBO	TDBP	TDBQ
2005	8 120	384	622	9 325	28 754	187	19 853	95 965	91 609
2006	10 433	400	890	13 508	35 090	254	25 720	115 584	142 161

of which in sterling

	TDDI	TDDJ	TDDK	TDDL	TDDM	TDDN	TDDO	TDDP	TDDQ
2005	5 136	383	454	9 047	14 639	106	7 765	22 348	59 847
2006	7 712	399	529	13 239	16 022	236	13 700	34 075	105 289

	Insurance companies & pension funds	Activities auxiliary to financial intermediation		Individuals & individual trusts
		Placed by fund managers	Other	

Amounts outstanding (sterling & other currencies)

Deposit liabilities (including under repos)

	TDBR	TDBS	TDBT	TDBU
2005	66 347	54 237	67 266	556 169
2006	62 562	65 590	71 091	603 891

of which in sterling

	TDDR	TDDS	TDDT	TDDU
2005	58 843	35 676	47 318	553 563
2006	54 396	43 736	44 141	600 854

1 See chapter text.

Source: Bank of England: 020 7601 3236

23.6 Public sector net cash requirement and other counterparts to changes in money stock during the year

Not seasonally adjusted

£ million

		1996	1997	1998	1999	2000	2001	2002	2003	2004	2005	2006
Public sector net cash requirement (surplus)	ABEN	24 701	12 011	−6 622	−1 609	−37 389	−2 750	18 316	38 829	41 366	40 976	32 954
Sales of public sector debt to M4 private sector	KHGZ	−18 972	−16 074	1 603	−1 538	13 536	7 748	−9 193	−32 510	..	..	..
M4 lending[1]	AVBS	59 129	68 186	63 926	78 029	111 202	82 574	107 553	127 820	156 084	158 086	219 309
External and foreign currency finance of the public sector	KHJP	−10 884	−2 453	−4 717	6 198	3 616	3 875	2 486	−13 442	..	..	..
Other external and foreign currency flows[2]	AVBW	18 020	24 565	14 033	−44 911	7 153	−21 607	−25 113	−27 161	4 364	31 304	2 700
Net non-deposit liabilities (increase)	AVBX	−12 652	−5 812	−8 222	−2 936	−31 025	−10 815	−25 149	−20 341	−67 477	−37 567	−31 388
Money stock (M4)	AUZI	59 336	80 339	60 097	33 329	67 198	58 994	68 834	73 271	100 014	150 865	170 027

1 Bank and building society lending, plus holdings of commercial bills by the Issue Department of the Bank of England.

2 Including sterling lending to non-residents sector.

Source: Bank of England: 020 7601 5468

23.7 Money stock and liquidity

£ million

		1996	1997	1998	1999	2000	2001	2002	2003	2004	2005	2006
Amounts outstanding at end-year												
Notes and coin in circulation with the M4 private sector[1]	VQKT	20 642	22 242	23 705	26 269	28 174	30 450	31 889	34 010	36 410	38 508	40 082
UK private sector sterling non-interest bearing sight deposits[2,3]	AUYA	38 447	38 578	36 765	42 130	45 867	50 548	45 594	51 274	50 845	55 208	54 800
Money stock (M2)[3,4]	VQXV	460 108	484 300	514 508	558 334	597 523	649 980	703 920	777 347	845 654	922 687	995 063
Money stock M4[3]	AUYM	682 786	722 133	783 354	816 601	884 873	942 594	1 008 751	1 081 299	1 179 192	1 328 318	1 497 214
Changes during the year[5]												
Notes and coin in circulation with the M4 private sector[1]	VQLU	798	1 609	1 501	2 582	1 957	2 284	1 493	2 189	2 461	2 156	1 596
UK private sector sterling non-interest bearing sight deposits[2,3]	AUZA	3 530	4 399	−754	5 354	3 533	4 914	−6 761	5 321	−227	5 699	−409
Money stock (M2)[3,4]	AUZE	24 358	36 019	30 910	42 397	38 953	51 730	54 704	71 518	..	..	..
Money stock M4[3]	AUZI	59 336	80 339	60 097	33 329	67 198	58 994	68 834	73 271	100 014	150 865	170 027

1 The estimates of levels of coin in circulation include allowance for wastage, hoarding, etc.

2 Non-interest bearing deposits are confined to those with institutions included in the United Kingdom banks sector (See Table 23.3).

3 Revised rules on netting of customers' credit balances against their borrowing increased the UK private sector's outstanding balances of deposits and borrowing by £2.5bn at end-December 1993. Within retail deposit, £1.7bn of the increase was in NIB bank deposits. Re-netting during 1994 amounted to £1.7bn. Changes data have been adjusted to exclude these effects. Building societies' data from 1992 onwards are affected by the revised treatment of building society transit items within M4.

4 M2 comprises the UK non-monetary financial institutions and non-public sector, i.e. M4 private sector's holdings of notes and coin together with its sterling denominated retail deposits with UK monetary financial institutions.

5 As far as possible the changes exclude the effect of changes in the number of contributors to the series, and also of the introduction of new statistical returns. Changes are not seasonally adjusted.

Source: Bank of England: 020 7601 5468

23.8 Selected retail banks' base rate[1]
Operative between dates shown

Percentage rates

Date of change	New rate	Date of change	New rate	Date of change	New rate
1986 Jan 9	12.50	Aug 26	12.00	Jul 10	6.75
Mar 19	11.50	Nov 25	13.00	Aug 7	7.00
Apr 8	11.00-11.50			Nov 6	7.25
Apr 9	11.00	1989 May 24	14.00		
Apr 21	10.50	Oct 5	15.00	1998 Jun 4	7.50
May 23	10.00-10.50			Oct 8	7.25
May 27	10.00	1990 Oct 8	14.00	Nov 5	6.75
Oct 14	10.00-11.00			Dec 10	6.25
Oct 15	11.00	1991 Feb 13	13.50		
		Feb 27	13.00	1999 Jan 7	6.00
1987 Mar 10	10.50	Mar 22	12.50	Feb 4	5.50
Mar 18	10.00-10.50	Apr 12	12.00	Apr 8	5.25
Mar 19	10.00	May 24	11.50	Jun 10	5.00
Apr 28	9.50-10.00	Jul 12	11.00	Sep 8	5.00-5.25
Apr 29	9.50	Sep 4	10.50	Sep 10	5.25
May 11	9.00			Nov 4	5.50
Aug 6	9.00-10.00	1992 May 5	10.00		
Aug 7	10.00	Sep 16[2]	12.00	2000 Jan 13	5.75
Oct 23	9.50-10.00	Sep 17[2]	10.00-12.00	Feb 10	6.00
Oct 29	9.50	Sep 18	10.00		
Nov 4	9.00-9.50	Sep 22	9.00	2001 Feb 8	5.75
Nov 5	9.00	Oct 16	8.00-9.00	Apr 5	5.50
Dec 4	8.50	Oct 19	8.00	May 10	5.25
		Nov 13	7.00	Aug 2	5.00
1988 Feb 2	9.00			Sep 18	4.75
Mar 17	8.50-9.00	1993 Jan 26	6.00	Oct 4	4.50
Mar 18	8.50	Nov 23	5.50	Nov 8	4.00
Apr 11	8.00				
May 17	7.50-8.00	1994 Feb 8	5.25	2003 Feb 6	3.75
May 18	7.50	Sep 12	5.75	Jul 10	3.50
Jun 2	7.50-8.00	Dec 7	6.25	Nov 6	3.75
Jun 3	8.00				
Jun 6	8.00-8.50	1995 Feb 2[2]	6.25-6.75	2004 Feb 5	4.00
Jun 7	8.50	Feb 3	6.75	May 6	4.25
Jun 22	8.50-9.00	Dec 13	6.50	Jun 10	4.50
Jun 23	9.00			Aug 5	4.75
Jun 28	9.00-9.50	1996 Jan 18	6.25		
Jun 29	9.50	Mar 8	6.00	2005 Aug 4	4.50
Jul 4	9.50-10.00	Jun 6	5.75		
Jul 5	10.00	Oct 30	5.75-6.00	2006 Aug 3	4.75
Jul 18	10.00-10.50	Oct 31	6.00	Nov 9	5.00
Jul 19	10.50				
Aug 8	10.50-11.00	1997 May 6	6.25	2007 Jan 11	5.25
Aug 9	11.00	Jun 6	6.25-6.50	May 10	5.50
Aug 25	11.00-12.00	Jun 9	6.50		

1 Data obtained from Barclays Bank, Lloyds/TSB Bank, HSBC Bank and National Westminster Bank whose rates are used to compile this series.
2 Where all the rates did not change on the same day a spread is shown.

Source: Bank of England: 020 7601 3644

23.9 Average three month sterling money market rates[1]

Percentage rates

	1996	1997	1998	1999	2000	2001	2002	2003	2004	2005	2006
Treasury bills:[2] KDMM											
January	6.08	6.01	6.80	5.28	5.72	5.49	3.83	3.80	3.90	4.66	4.39
February	5.94	5.81	6.88	5.04	5.83	5.46	3.87	3.50	3.98	4.69	4.38
March	5.79	5.92	6.95	4.92	5.86	5.23	3.97	3.47	4.10	4.77	4.40
April	5.80	6.09	7.00	4.90	5.92	5.12	3.97	3.45	4.19	4.70	4.42
May	5.82	6.15	7.01	4.93	5.95	4.98	3.95	3.44	4.34	4.66	4.50
June	5.58	6.37	7.29	4.76	5.85	4.99	3.98	3.47	4.58	4.62	4.54
July	5.49	6.63	7.22	4.76	5.83	5.01	3.84	3.31	4.64	4.46	4.53
August	5.54	6.83	7.19	4.85	5.81	4.72	3.77	3.40	4.72	4.41	5.75
September	5.54	6.88	6.94	5.12	5.78	4.43	3.79	3.52	4.69	4.40	4.84
October	5.61	6.94	6.54	5.23	5.75	4.16	3.75	3.65	4.68	4.40	4.94
November	6.05	7.09	6.31	5.20	5.68	3.78	3.80	3.81	4.66	4.42	5.01
December	6.05	7.07	5.72	5.46	5.62	3.83	3.84	3.83	4.68	4.43	5.08
Eligible bill: KDMY[3]											
January	6.18	6.15	7.28	5.63	5.90	5.64	3.91	3.87	3.94	4.75	..
February	6.00	5.99	7.24	5.28	6.01	5.56	3.92	3.65	4.06	4.78	..
March	5.87	6.01	7.25	5.11	5.98	5.37	3.99	3.54	4.19	4.88	..
April	5.83	6.26	7.24	5.02	6.05	5.21	4.04	3.52	4.28	4.84	..
May	5.85	6.31	7.20	5.08	6.09	5.06	4.01	3.52	4.42	4.80	..
June	5.66	6.50	7.42	4.94	6.03	5.08	4.04	3.45	4.68	4.76	..
July	5.57	6.80	7.49	4.89	5.97	5.07	3.94	3.39	4.75	4.57	..
August	5.60	6.95	7.40	4.94	5.97	4.82	3.86	3.42	4.85	4.51	..
September	5.63	7.02	7.20	5.16	5.95	4.57	3.86	3.59	4.83	..	..
October	5.76	7.10	6.91	5.42	5.92	4.26	3.82	3.69	4.79	..	..
November	6.10	7.27	6.52	5.43	5.88	3.85	3.84	3.88	4.78	..	..
December	6.18	7.31	6.05	5.59	5.78	3.88	3.71	3.90	4.77	..	..
Interbank rate: AMIJ											
January	6.36	6.32	7.48	5.80	6.06	5.76	3.98	3.91	3.99	4.80	4.54
February	6.16	6.19	7.46	5.43	6.15	5.69	3.98	3.69	4.10	4.82	4.52
March	6.05	6.20	7.48	5.30	6.15	5.47	4.06	3.58	4.23	4.92	4.53
April	6.00	6.38	7.44	5.23	6.21	5.33	4.11	3.58	4.33	4.88	4.57
May	6.02	6.45	7.41	5.25	6.23	5.17	4.08	3.57	4.46	4.83	4.65
June	5.85	6.66	7.63	5.12	6.14	5.19	4.11	3.57	4.73	4.78	4.69
July	5.73	6.96	7.71	5.07	6.11	5.19	3.99	3.42	4.79	4.59	4.68
August	5.75	7.15	7.66	5.18	6.14	4.93	3.92	3.45	4.89	4.53	4.90
September	5.77	7.21	7.38	5.32	6.12	4.65	3.93	3.63	4.87	4.54	4.98
October	5.94	7.26	7.14	5.94	6.08	4.36	3.90	3.73	4.83	4.53	5.09
November	6.30	7.54	6.89	5.78	6.00	3.93	3.91	3.91	4.82	4.56	5.18
December	6.35	7.62	6.38	5.97	5.89	3.99	3.95	3.95	4.81	4.59	5.25
Certificate of deposits: KOSA											
January	6.31	6.27	7.44	5.74	6.02	5.73	3.96	3.90	3.98	4.80	4.54
February	6.11	6.14	7.42	5.38	6.10	5.66	3.96	3.68	4.09	4.82	4.52
March	6.01	6.15	7.43	5.26	6.09	5.44	4.04	3.57	4.22	4.91	4.53
April	5.96	6.33	7.40	5.19	6.17	5.30	4.08	3.57	4.32	4.86	4.57
May	5.98	6.39	7.37	5.22	6.19	5.15	4.06	3.56	4.45	4.82	4.65
June	5.79	6.62	7.59	5.09	6.10	5.16	4.09	3.56	4.72	4.78	4.69
July	5.69	6.92	7.66	5.03	6.08	5.17	3.97	3.41	4.79	4.60	4.68
August	5.71	7.12	7.61	5.14	6.09	4.90	3.90	3.44	4.89	4.53	4.89
September	5.74	7.17	7.34	5.28	6.08	4.62	3.91	3.62	4.87	4.54	4.98
October	5.89	7.22	7.09	5.86	6.05	4.33	3.88	3.72	4.83	4.53	5.09
November	6.25	7.50	6.82	5.72	5.98	3.91	3.89	3.90	4.81	4.57	5.18
December	6.29	7.57	6.32	5.89	5.85	3.96	3.93	3.94	4.80	4.59	5.24
Local authority deposits: KDPX[4]											
January	6.31	6.27	7.43	5.76	6.03	5.73	3.85	3.87	3.91	..	..
February	6.13	6.15	7.40	5.38	6.09	5.62	3.88	3.61	4.08	..	..
March	6.02	6.14	7.40	5.27	6.08	5.39	4.01	3.55	4.12	..	..
April	5.98	6.33	7.38	5.17	6.12	5.26	4.05	3.54	4.31	..	..
May	6.00	6.38	7.34	5.19	6.14	5.13	4.06	3.54	4.45	..	..
June	5.80	6.57	7.56	5.07	6.09	5.10	4.05	3.57	4.75	..	..
July	5.69	6.90	7.64	5.01	6.04	5.12	3.95	3.39	4.82	..	..
August	5.71	7.11	7.55	5.11	6.06	4.86	3.87	3.43	4.92	..	..
September	5.72	7.19	7.35	5.19	6.05	4.58	3.88	3.61	4.90	..	..
October	5.86	7.21	7.08	5.83	6.03	4.29	3.86	3.71	4.85	..	..
November	6.24	7.49	6.85	5.64	5.96	3.82	3.87	3.90	4.84	..	..
December	6.30	7.56	6.35	5.88	5.80	3.87	3.93	3.92	4.82	..	..

1 A full definition of these series is given in Section 7 of the ONS Financial Statistics Explanatory Handbook.
2 Average rate of discount at weekly (Friday) tender.
3 This series discontinued at end of August 2005.
4 This series discontinued at end of December 2004.

Source: Bank of England: 020 7601 3644

23.10 Average foreign exchange rates[1]

	1996	1997	1998	1999	2000	2001	2002	2003	2004	2005	2006
Sterling exchange rate index (1990 = 100) AGBG											
January	83.2	95.9	104.7	99.6	108.5	104.4	106.9	104.0	102.4	102.1	102.7
February	83.8	97.4	104.7	100.8	108.4	104.1	107.4	102.4	104.8	103.3	102.8
March	83.5	97.4	106.8	102.8	108.4	105.0	106.5	100.6	105.0	103.2	102.1
April	83.8	99.5	107.1	103.4	110.1	105.8	107.1	99.8	105.2	104.4	101.9
May	84.6	99.0	103.4	104.2	108.5	106.6	105.3	97.9	104.6	103.6	104.1
June	86.0	100.4	105.4	104.7	104.6	106.8	103.6	99.6	105.8	104.9	..
July	85.7	104.5	105.3	103.5	105.6	107.2	105.3	99.4	105.9	102.1	..
August	84.7	102.5	104.6	103.3	107.4	105.1	105.4	99.0	105.2	102.8	..
September	86.1	100.4	103.3	104.7	106.2	106.1	106.5	99.2	103.3	103.9	..
October	88.4	101.1	100.7	105.4	109.2	105.8	106.7	99.8	102.2	103.1	..
November	92.0	103.8	100.6	105.7	107.3	106.1	105.9	100.4	101.7	103.2	..
December	93.8	104.4	100.4	106.7	106.4	106.5	105.5	100.3	103.2	103.3	..
Sterling/US Dollar AUSS											
January	1.5306	1.6587	1.6353	1.6509	1.6402	1.4769	1.4323	1.6169	1.8234	1.8764	1.7678
February	1.5364	1.6246	1.6407	1.6276	1.5998	1.4529	1.4231	1.6046	1.8673	1.8871	1.7470
March	1.5271	1.6063	1.6620	1.6220	1.5802	1.4454	1.4225	1.5836	1.8267	1.9078	1.7435
April	1.5145	1.6295	1.6733	1.6105	1.5837	1.4350	1.4434	1.5747	1.8005	1.8960	1.7685
May	1.5152	1.6334	1.6366	1.6154	1.5075	1.4259	1.4593	1.6230	1.7876	1.8538	1.8702
June	1.5418	1.6446	1.6507	1.5950	1.5089	1.4014	1.4863	1.6606	1.8275	1.8179	1.8428
July	1.5539	1.6702	1.6437	1.5747	1.5088	1.4139	1.5546	1.6242	1.8429	1.7509	1.8447
August	1.5502	1.6034	1.6320	1.6073	1.4910	1.4365	1.5377	1.5950	1.8216	1.7943	1.8944
September	1.5597	1.6015	1.6822	1.6243	1.4355	1.4635	1.5561	1.6131	1.7922	1.8081	1.8847
October	1.5862	1.6329	1.6952	1.6572	1.4511	1.4517	1.5574	1.6787	1.8065	1.7640	1.8755
November	1.6626	1.6890	1.6620	1.6214	1.4256	1.4358	1.5723	1.6901	1.8603	1.7341	1.9119
December	1.6647	1.6597	1.6705	1.6132	1.4625	1.4409	1.5863	1.7507	1.9275	1.7462	1.9633
Sterling/Euro THAP											
January	1.1631	1.3559	1.5166	1.4236	1.6201	1.5753	1.6222	1.5222	1.4447	1.4331	1.4582
February	1.1707	1.3906	1.5196	1.4534	1.6266	1.5786	1.6348	1.4893	1.4774	1.4499	1.4637
March	1.1692	1.3944	1.5507	1.4902	1.6377	1.5901	1.6224	1.4649	1.4890	1.4440	1.4500
April	1.1763	1.4243	1.5490	1.5051	1.6730	1.6084	1.6282	1.4505	1.5022	1.4652	1.4402
May	1.1923	1.4217	1.4834	1.5185	1.6655	1.6304	1.5914	1.4030	1.4894	1.4611	1.4637
June	1.2094	1.4499	1.5110	1.5374	1.5882	1.6434	1.5515	1.4234	1.5050	1.4952	1.4560
July	1.2007	1.5247	1.5091	1.5204	1.6052	1.6433	1.5665	1.4277	1.5023	1.4547	1.4540
August	1.1845	1.5043	1.4912	1.5146	1.6478	1.5955	1.5723	1.4286	1.4933	1.4592	1.4785
September	1.2066	1.4591	1.4617	1.5458	1.6471	1.6060	1.5861	1.4338	1.4676	1.4761	1.4811
October	1.2407	1.4623	1.4200	1.5491	1.6994	1.6024	1.5868	1.4334	1.4455	1.4674	1.4869
November	1.2873	1.4914	1.4290	1.5706	1.6664	1.6166	1.5694	1.4426	1.4311	1.4719	1.4834
December	1.3192	1.5053	1.4254	1.5953	1.6302	1.6151	1.5566	1.4246	1.4401	1.4725	1.4860

1 Working day average. A full definition of these series is given in Section 7 of the ONS Explanatory Handbook.

Source: Bank of England: 020 7601 3644

23.11 Average zero coupon yields[1]

Percentage rates

	1996	1997	1998	1999	2000	2001	2002	2003	2004	2005	2006
Nominal Five Year Yield ZBRG											
January	6.85	7.15	6.18	4.30	6.28	5.07	4.90	4.15	4.61	4.43	4.11
February	7.12	6.82	6.10	4.46	6.13	5.04	4.94	3.85	4.63	4.53	4.17
March	7.45	7.07	6.09	4.69	5.89	4.86	5.22	3.93	4.56	4.73	4.33
April	7.52	7.28	5.93	4.66	5.80	4.96	5.21	4.09	4.80	4.54	4.48
May	7.53	6.94	5.95	4.95	5.82	5.14	5.22	3.85	5.01	4.31	4.67
June	7.46	6.96	6.04	5.28	5.61	5.25	5.05	3.72	5.15	4.17	4.69
July	7.30	7.01	6.12	5.49	5.58	5.26	4.88	3.98	5.07	4.16	4.69
August	7.19	6.97	5.80	5.75	5.65	5.03	4.54	4.36	4.96	4.23	4.74
September	7.18	6.72	5.32	6.00	5.65	4.90	4.31	4.46	4.83	4.12	4.67
October	6.97	6.51	4.94	6.25	5.46	4.74	4.36	4.73	4.65	4.26	4.76
November	7.18	6.69	4.92	5.86	5.33	4.55	4.38	4.91	4.58	4.29	4.73
December	7.20	6.46	4.51	5.90	5.14	4.88	4.34	4.71	4.43	4.21	4.80
Nominal Ten Year Yield ZBRH											
January	7.46	7.52	5.96	4.24	5.62	4.75	4.85	4.39	4.76	4.50	4.02
February	7.80	7.15	5.91	4.39	5.44	4.90	4.90	4.22	4.78	4.54	4.10
March	8.08	7.41	5.85	4.60	5.18	4.64	5.18	4.34	4.67	4.74	4.26
April	8.06	7.58	5.69	4.53	5.14	4.90	5.19	4.48	4.92	4.58	4.46
May	8.10	7.08	5.73	4.83	5.23	5.05	5.22	4.23	5.06	4.38	4.58
June	8.09	7.04	5.60	5.07	5.05	5.11	5.05	4.13	5.13	4.25	4.60
July	7.96	6.92	5.65	5.24	5.09	5.10	4.95	4.43	5.04	4.28	4.59
August	7.86	6.97	5.41	5.25	5.18	4.88	4.68	4.59	4.95	4.29	4.58
September	7.86	6.70	5.03	5.51	5.25	4.91	4.47	4.68	4.86	4.17	4.47
October	7.56	6.37	4.93	5.68	5.09	4.77	4.60	4.88	4.72	4.31	4.53
November	7.56	6.46	4.83	5.11	4.98	4.58	4.62	4.87	4.65	4.26	4.45
December	7.52	6.22	4.44	5.19	4.80	4.83	4.55	4.87	4.49	4.17	4.53
Nominal Twenty Year Yield ZBRI											
January	7.89	7.74	5.94	4.36	4.45	4.33	4.69	4.46	4.69	4.45	4.05
February	8.19	7.39	5.88	4.44	4.38	4.42	4.72	4.40	4.72	4.45	4.13
March	8.37	7.59	5.78	4.60	4.25	4.45	4.99	4.56	4.61	4.65	4.29
April	8.30	7.73	5.61	4.53	4.35	4.76	5.02	4.69	4.79	4.53	4.48
May	8.38	7.16	5.67	4.75	4.40	4.87	5.08	4.49	4.89	4.36	4.62
June	8.41	7.08	5.42	4.77	4.37	4.98	4.93	4.44	4.87	4.23	4.64
July	8.34	6.80	5.45	4.67	4.38	4.90	4.82	4.70	4.80	4.24	4.63
August	8.26	6.86	5.30	4.53	4.49	4.69	4.57	4.68	4.69	4.27	4.64
September	8.27	6.64	4.91	4.62	4.63	4.88	4.40	4.74	4.65	4.16	4.54
October	7.98	6.36	4.87	4.56	4.61	4.92	4.54	4.81	4.59	4.30	4.61
November	7.81	6.37	4.73	4.07	4.39	4.53	4.60	4.87	4.50	4.28	4.55
December	7.67	6.17	4.47	4.20	4.30	4.65	4.59	4.76	4.42	4.19	4.62
Real Ten Year Yield ZBRJ											
January	3.42	3.45	3.10	2.00	2.10	2.22	2.52	2.00	1.94	1.75	1.29
February	3.54	3.27	3.06	1.91	2.17	2.27	2.50	1.74	1.96	1.77	1.32
March	3.67	3.43	3.00	1.85	2.05	2.33	2.53	1.79	1.81	1.87	1.41
April	3.63	3.56	2.91	1.70	2.08	2.56	2.43	1.96	1.93	1.76	1.54
May	3.72	3.57	2.92	1.91	2.14	2.58	2.43	1.81	2.05	1.70	1.63
June	3.77	3.66	2.85	1.89	2.12	2.54	2.33	1.67	2.10	1.65	1.68
July	3.70	3.62	2.77	1.90	2.14	2.56	2.42	1.85	2.07	1.65	1.65
August	3.58	3.60	2.65	2.19	2.25	2.42	2.33	1.95	2.03	1.61	1.55
September	3.57	3.52	2.59	2.31	2.28	2.51	2.20	2.05	1.97	1.51	1.49
October	3.41	3.23	2.67	2.26	2.33	2.53	2.36	2.15	1.89	1.57	1.57
November	3.43	3.25	2.40	2.05	2.34	2.39	2.33	2.21	1.88	1.54	1.47
December	3.42	3.11	2.11	1.98	2.23	2.58	2.24	2.03	1.76	1.47	1.56
Real Twenty Year Yield ZBRK											
January	..	3.67	3.06	2.07	2.01	1.88	2.26	2.07	1.96	1.59	0.97
February	3.79	3.49	3.05	1.99	1.95	1.88	2.30	1.98	1.90	1.59	0.99
March	3.81	3.59	2.98	1.93	1.78	1.99	2.32	2.07	1.77	1.72	1.10
April	3.75	3.68	2.85	1.81	1.84	2.25	2.25	2.12	1.85	1.64	1.28
May	3.82	3.66	2.83	1.99	1.91	2.32	2.25	2.03	1.88	1.57	1.33
June	3.86	3.69	2.63	1.97	1.87	2.27	2.17	1.97	1.88	1.53	1.39
July	3.81	3.57	2.58	2.00	1.90	2.24	2.24	2.16	1.87	1.54	1.31
August	3.75	3.57	2.53	2.14	1.96	2.16	2.15	2.14	1.82	1.49	1.21
September	3.76	3.48	2.49	2.26	1.96	2.31	2.06	2.18	1.80	1.40	1.12
October	3.61	3.22	2.59	2.22	1.99	2.32	2.22	2.22	1.76	1.40	1.13
November	3.62	3.18	2.36	1.92	1.94	2.12	2.25	2.21	1.71	1.29	1.03
December	3.62	3.06	2.14	1.87	1.87	2.24	2.21	2.08	1.60	1.20	1.11

1 Working day average. Calculated using the Variable Roughness Penalty (VRP) model.

Source: Bank of England: 020 7601 3644

23.12 Average rates on representative British Government Stocks[1]

Percentage rates

	1996	1997	1998	1999	2000	2001	2002	2003	2004	2005	2006
5 Year Conventional Rate KORP											
January	6.78	7.19	6.33	4.25	6.36	5.17	4.94	4.15	4.59	4.43	4.27
February	7.02	6.86	6.24	4.41	6.23	5.13	4.96	3.88	4.46	4.61	4.34
March	7.56	7.08	6.26	4.65	6.01	4.94	5.23	3.93	4.44	4.77	4.41
April	7.43	7.30	6.11	4.66	5.95	4.97	5.26	4.08	4.66	4.58	4.44
May	7.61	6.98	6.14	4.93	5.97	5.15	5.48	3.83	4.89	4.36	4.44
June	7.52	7.01	6.31	5.27	5.78	5.32	5.10	3.68	5.08	4.24	4.66
July	7.35	7.09	6.14	5.49	5.75	5.34	4.92	3.72	4.98	4.11	4.62
August	7.21	7.02	5.84	5.80	5.81	5.09	4.57	4.30	4.88	4.22	4.84
September	7.20	6.78	5.34	6.04	5.81	4.94	4.25	4.42	4.76	4.18	4.91
October	7.01	6.59	4.88	6.24	5.66	4.78	4.38	4.70	4.57	4.23	5.00
November	7.22	6.79	4.86	5.89	5.50	4.59	4.40	4.88	4.52	4.31	4.39
December	7.26	6.60	4.45	5.91	5.27	4.88	4.34	4.68	4.42	4.27	–
10 year Conventional Rate KORQ											
January	7.42	7.53	6.07	4.16	5.75	4.86	4.84	4.37	4.78	4.51	4.19
February	7.75	7.17	6.02	4.32	5.56	4.88	4.91	4.25	4.75	4.60	4.25
March	8.05	7.41	5.97	4.54	5.29	4.75	5.15	4.51	4.65	4.79	4.39
April	8.05	7.60	5.81	4.48	5.25	4.95	5.23	4.64	4.91	4.60	4.47
May	8.08	7.13	5.85	4.77	5.35	5.13	5.51	4.26	5.07	4.38	4.39
June	8.04	7.10	5.77	5.02	5.15	5.09	5.06	4.38	5.19	4.23	4.74
July	7.91	7.01	5.67	5.20	5.18	5.16	4.94	4.23	5.10	4.20	4.73
August	7.81	7.05	5.56	5.24	5.27	4.92	4.66	4.59	4.99	4.25	4.78
September	7.80	6.77	5.10	5.52	5.32	4.92	4.46	4.69	4.89	4.16	4.74
October	7.51	6.47	4.93	5.70	5.15	4.76	4.57	4.89	4.73	4.31	4.85
November	7.56	6.59	4.87	5.16	5.06	4.58	4.59	5.04	4.66	4.33	4.84
December	7.54	6.34	4.49	5.24	4.88	4.88	4.52	4.94	4.50	4.27	4.93
20 Year Conventional Rate KORR											
January	7.73	7.71	6.04	4.36	4.91	4.52	4.81	4.46	4.73	4.55	4.05
February	8.04	7.35	5.98	4.47	4.80	4.58	4.83	4.37	4.80	4.58	4.13
March	8.28	7.58	5.90	4.64	4.64	4.56	5.12	4.51	4.69	4.79	4.28
April	8.26	7.74	5.73	4.58	4.71	4.84	5.14	4.64	4.91	4.63	4.38
May	8.31	7.21	5.79	4.83	4.77	4.98	5.45	4.44	5.03	4.43	4.59
June	8.31	7.15	5.59	4.92	4.68	5.10	5.03	4.38	5.07	4.30	4.60
July	8.21	6.93	5.63	4.88	4.70	5.05	4.92	4.59	4.99	4.33	4.60
August	8.12	6.98	5.43	4.82	4.79	4.83	4.65	4.67	4.88	4.34	4.58
September	8.11	6.74	5.02	4.97	4.90	4.94	4.46	4.74	4.83	4.24	4.49
October	7.84	6.45	4.92	4.97	4.84	4.80	4.59	4.85	4.73	4.37	4.53
November	7.77	6.50	4.79	4.46	4.64	4.55	4.65	4.93	4.64	4.31	4.48
December	7.67	6.32	4.49	4.56	4.51	4.75	4.61	4.80	4.53	4.22	4.41
10 Year Index-Linked Rate KORS											
January	3.42	3.44	3.01	2.00	2.11	2.21	2.61	2.07	1.88	1.73	1.48
February	3.57	3.23	2.94	1.94	2.16	2.30	2.53	1.81	1.90	1.81	1.54
March	3.70	3.41	2.89	1.90	2.06	2.34	2.55	1.88	1.76	1.99	1.65
April	3.66	3.55	2.80	1.74	2.08	2.55	2.45	1.90	1.94	1.83	1.65
May	3.74	3.52	2.83	1.96	2.15	2.61	2.58	1.74	2.10	1.71	1.96
June	3.80	3.62	2.81	1.93	2.13	2.56	2.35	1.59	2.17	1.67	1.94
July	3.82	3.68	2.67	1.93	2.14	2.57	2.46	1.67	2.12	1.66	1.92
August	3.59	3.59	2.55	2.20	2.25	2.45	2.37	1.89	2.04	1.63	1.80
September	3.57	3.47	2.59	2.32	2.29	2.56	2.24	1.99	1.95	1.49	1.76
October	3.41	3.17	2.66	2.26	2.33	2.55	2.42	2.08	1.83	1.89	1.89
November	3.42	3.23	2.39	2.03	2.32	2.42	2.39	2.16	1.85	1.64	1.87
December	3.41	3.01	2.11	1.99	2.20	2.65	2.30	1.97	1.74	1.27	1.96
20 Year Index-Linked rate KORT											
January	3.58	3.62	3.01	2.06	2.01	1.96	2.35	2.10	1.95	1.68	1.17
February	3.70	3.43	3.01	1.97	1.98	1.99	2.36	1.99	1.94	1.72	1.22
March	3.82	3.55	2.92	1.93	1.83	2.09	2.39	2.07	1.80	1.89	1.34
April	3.77	3.65	2.80	1.81	1.90	2.35	2.32	2.10	1.91	1.77	1.38
May	3.84	3.61	2.79	1.99	1.97	2.41	2.43	2.00	1.99	1.67	1.56
June	3.88	3.65	2.61	1.97	1.94	2.38	2.23	1.93	2.01	1.63	1.61
July	3.72	3.68	2.56	1.97	1.96	2.36	2.30	2.05	1.99	1.63	1.55
August	3.75	3.54	2.51	2.12	2.03	2.25	2.21	2.09	1.93	1.58	1.45
September	3.74	3.43	2.51	2.23	2.04	2.39	2.12	2.13	1.89	1.48	1.37
October	3.60	3.17	2.58	2.18	2.08	2.38	2.29	2.17	1.84	1.51	1.44
November	3.59	3.16	2.35	1.91	2.02	2.19	2.31	2.16	1.80	1.45	1.34
December	3.58	3.02	2.12	1.88	1.94	2.33	2.26	2.04	1.69	1.38	1.43

1 Working day average.

Source: Bank of England: 020 7601 3644

23.13
Building societies[1,2]
United Kingdom

		1996[3]	1997[3]	1998[3]	1999[3]	2000[4]	2001	2002	2003	2004	2005
Number and balance sheets											
Societies on register (numbers)	KRNA	88	82	78	72	68	65	65	63	63	63
Share investors (thousands)	KRNB	37 768	19 234	21 195	21 774	22 237	20 311	20 724	20 901	20 734	22 090
Depositors (thousands)	KRNC	6 718	882	820	642	660	501	440	452	446	370
Borrowers (thousands)	KRND	6 586	2 703	2 934	2 868	2 925	2 579	2 520	2 520	2 570	2 617
Assets and liabilities (£ million)											
Liabilities:											
Shares	KRNE	196 546.4	90 092.8	103 289.8	109 137.7	119 298.5	119 815.2	132 372.9	142 477.1	153 844.0	171 935.0
Deposits and loans	KRNF	73 919.1	31 033.7	33 311.2	34 746.6	44 262.4	37 358.9	37 933.0	49 552.6	64 025.2	70 845.1
Taxation and other	KRNG	3 727.4	1 338.8	1 586.4	1 665.4	1 664.0	1 244.9	1 088.4	1 179.0	1 394.9	2 619.4
General reserves	KRNH	17 940.3	7 331.2	7 926.4	8 301.5	8 987.1	8 511.2	9 043.4	9 489.8	10 123.9	10 677.4
Other Capital	KRNI	4 762.3	1 643.9	1 550.7	1 529.2	1 861.0	1 416.1	1 709.2	2 534.7	3 599.1	4 566.5
Assets:											
Mortgages	KRNK	241 472.9	107 531.5	118 288.4	123 183.4	137 072.3	130 229.6	140 839.7	159 938.2	184 191.0	207 621.4
Investments and cash	KHVZ	51 016.7	21 869.8	27 102.0	29 917.8	36 574.2	35 925.9	38 952.7	43 067.9	46 234.1	49 240.3
Other	KRNN	4 405.9	2 039.1	2 274.1	2 279.2	2 426.6	2 190.7	2 354.4	2 226.9	2 562.0	3 781.7
Total	KRNJ	296 895.5	131 440.4	147 664.5	155 380.4	176 073.0	168 346.2	182 146.8	205 233.1	232 987.1	260 643.3
Current transactions (£ million)											
Mortgage advances	KRNU	38 488.0	28 771.7	21 988.3	23 997.9	28 233.6	29 320.0	33 077.0	43 392.4	51 089.0	50 059.4
Management expenses	KRNX	3 555.3	2 270.5	1 501.7	1 573.8	1 640.7	1 528.0	1 623.6	1 746.4	1 844.2	1 939.9

1 See chapter text.

2 The figures for each year relate to accounting years ending on dates between 1 February of that year and 31 January of the following year.

3 The societies which have converted to the banking sector, namely Cheltenham & Gloucester (August 1995), National & Provincial (August 1996), Alliance & Leicester (April 1997), Halifax (June 1997), Woolwich (July 1997), Bristol & West (July 1997), Northern Rock (October 1997), and Birmingham Midshires (April 1999) have been included in flow figures (using flows up to the date of conversion), but have been excluded from the end of year balances.

4 Bradford & Bingley, which converted to the banking sector in December 2000, is included within flow figures and the end of year balances.

Source: Financial Services Authority: 020 7066 1000

23.14
Consumer credit
United Kingdom

£ million

		1997	1998	1999	2000	2001	2002	2003	2004	2005	2006
Total amount outstanding	VZRD	91 195	106 341	121 547	135 168	150 802	169 209	180 649	198 856	211 037	212 598
Total net lending	VZQC	12 902	15 503	16 133	15 969	19 673	23 443	22 401	25 337	19 666	12 603
of which											
Credit cards	VZQS	3 507	4 858	5 676	6 686	6 229	7 579	8 710	9 998	6 166	2 175
Other	VZQT	9 395	10 647	10 457	9 284	13 445	15 867	13 692	15 340	13 497	10 427
Banks	AIKN	9 050	11 738	11 057	13 217	16 055	17 452	15 269	19 370	11 316	9 325
Building societies' class 3 loans	ALPY	120	–	12	112	63	180	177	172	238	217
Other consumer credit lenders	BM59	3 734	3 764	5 065	2 640	3 554	5 811	6 954	5 796	8 111	3 060
Total gross lending	VZQG	116 998	134 847	148 623	160 744	177 452	196 451	207 255	221 318	217 465	207 627

As from Dec 2006 the Bank of England has ceased to update the separate data on consumer credit provided by other specialist lenders, retailers and insurance companies previously contained in these tables. These categories have been merged into 'other consumer credit lenders'.

Source: Office for National Statistics: 01633 812776

23.15 End-year assets and liabilities of investment trust companies, unit trusts[1] and property unit trusts[2]

United Kingdom

£ million

		1995	1996	1997	1998	1999	2000	2001	2002	2003	2004	2005
Investment trust companies												
Short-term assets and liabilities (net):	CBPL	627	1 076	1 426	2 263	71	423	161	..	73	866	921
Cash and UK bank deposits	AHAG	1 009	1 087	1 577	2 647	1 227	2 202	2 513	1 821	1 346	1 756	1 483
Other short-term assets	CBPN	738	794	1 714	1 734	1 097	1 082	656	805	1 189	1 344	1 549
Short-term liabilities	-CBPS	−1 120	−805	−1 865	−2 118	−2 253	−2 861	−3 008	−2 626	−2 462	−2 234	−2 111
Medium and long-term liabilities and capital:	-CBPO	−43 882	−50 911	−54 821	−49 985	−57 616	−60 412	−54 630	−38 054	−48 076	−48 627	−55 076
Issued share and loan capital	-CBPQ	−13 250	−8 330	−9 350	−8 837	−8 565	−8 934	−8 796	−8 711	−9 873	−8 210	−7 155
Foreign currency borrowing	-CBPR	−1 061	−638	−658	−607	−880	−994	−933	−780	−682	−607	−839
Other borrowing	-CBQA	−622	−823	−1 296	−1 723	−1 716	−2 503	−3 251	−2 246	−2 181	−1 728	−1 420
Reserves and provisions, etc	-AHBC	−28 949	−41 120	−43 517	−38 818	−46 455	−47 981	−41 650	−26 317	−35 340	−38 082	−38 082
Investments:	CBPM	43 410	50 034	51 618	46 575	56 491	59 948	54 822	37 748	48 035	47 212	53 265
British government securities	AHBF	1 194	1 422	1 255	815	1 217	821	645	471	303	466	769
UK company securities:												
Loan capital and preference shares	CBGZ	846	832	1 320	1 359	1 425	1 654	1 516	946	1 079	1 270	673
Ordinary and deferred shares	CBGY	19 384	25 046	27 916	24 729	28 010	33 456	30 338	19 475	23 292	23 941	25 037
Overseas company securities:												
Loan capital and preference shares	CBHA	740	279	1 165	773	979	963	1 143	677	646	682	937
Ordinary and deferred shares	AHCC	19 485	21 047	17 747	17 844	23 330	21 355	19 476	14 453	20 294	18 967	23 065
Other investments	CBPT	1 761	1 408	1 631	1 055	1 530	1 699	1 704	1 945	2 464	1 886	2 784
Unit trusts												
Short-term assets and liabilities:	CBPU	3 116	3 822	4 627	6 883	5 894	8 340	7 979	8 041	10 256	10 229	13 944
Cash and UK bank deposits	AGYE	3 326	3 895	4 731	6 020	4 797	6 969	5 748	5 321	5 243	6 302	7 740
Other short-term assets	CBPW	986	1 201	467	1 343	1 545	2 319	2 763	3 072	5 990	4 930	7 420
Short-term liabilities	-CBPX	−1 196	−1 274	−571	−480	−448	−948	−532	−352	−977	−463	−1 216
Foreign currency borrowing	-AGYK	−1	..	..	..	..	..	..	..	..	−	−
Investments:	CBPZ	104 069	125 841	143 108	163 048	213 553	222 844	204 899	210 002	245 516	269 064	351 645
British government securities	CBHT	1 774	2 716	3 087	3 771	3 627	4 693	4 690	7 077	9 125	9 768	25 181
UK company securities:												
Loan capital and preference shares	CBHU	3 298	5 029	6 494	9 290	13 322	14 654	16 318	21 152	23 972	22 467	29 293
Ordinary and deferred shares	RLIB	59 122	67 509	85 742	93 410	119 496	116 808	103 704	82 851	116 407	130 230	157 149
Overseas company securities:												
Loan capital and preference shares	CBHV	2 145	1 288	1 834	1 801	3 032	3 212	4 046	5 916	9 840	13 673	16 057
Ordinary and deferred shares	RLIC	36 062	47 346	42 898	51 119	70 256	79 601	71 341	63 152	75 074	80 125	105 443
Other assets	CBQE	1 668	1 953	2 593	3 657	3 820	3 876	4 800	9 997	11 098	12 801	18 522
Property unit trusts												
Short-term assets and liabilities (net)	AGVC	186	343	351	254	205	285	247	242	459	466	686
Property	CBQG	1 807	2 582	3 875	2 740	2 722	3 488	2 078	4 026	5 125	5 909	9 623
Other assets	AGVL	11	11	167	197	436	380	151	677	373	1 366	1 864
Long-term borrowing	-AGVM	−131	−45	−246	−106	−75	−391	−90	−75	−76	−63	−250

Note: Assets are shown as positive: liabilities as negative.

1 Including open ended investment companies (OEICs).
2 Investments are at market value.

Source: Office for National Statistics: 01633 812789

23.16 Self-administered pension funds: market value of assets
United Kingdom

End year

£ million

		1994	1995	1996	1997	1998	1999	2000	2001	2002	2003	2004	2005	2006
Total pension funds[1]														
Total net assets	AHVA	443 467	508 581	543 879	656 874	699 191	812 228	765 199	711 572	610 441	692 694	761 066	914 955	..
Short-term assets	RYIQ	22 617	26 114	31 521	35 368	39 005	32 703	36 638	31 337	30 700	46 091	57 476	73 649	..
British government securities	AHVK	41 854	52 659	57 783	80 533	91 084	98 882	92 458	83 754	84 461	88 803	87 579	94 325	102 184
UK local authority long-term debt	AHVO	250	83	89	156	183	133	177	125	42	8	4	4	−3
Overseas government securities	AHVT	11 092	11 721	11 800	13 079	15 493	16 684	19 206	20 383	16 031	16 340	15 075	19 037	19 000
UK company securities														
Ordinary shares	AHVP	219 189	256 625	276 001	339 687	334 648	357 230	299 318	260 696	186 437	186 426	180 561	199 199	207 604
Other	AHVQ	3 935	7 064	6 180	5 618	8 168	9 258	16 978	22 301	30 450	37 082	43 027	48 065	51 083
Overseas company securities														
Ordinary shares	AHVR	74 813	82 164	84 163	104 187	108 884	148 335	135 514	127 893	104 392	125 740	140 282	183 060	200 879
Other	AHVS	3 045	1 184	4 909	3 851	3 842	5 099	12 736	11 781	11 386	12 475	15 996	20 502	23 955
UK loans and mortgages	RLDQ	44	34	83	160	22	14	7	3	−	35	44	6	6
UK land, property and ground rent	AHWA	24 353	21 317	21 637	24 176	24 355	31 107	32 945	30 617	31 658	30 619	30 552	31 613	35 392
Authorised unit trust units	AHVU	13 345	15 212	21 767	21 979	30 596	33 731	34 587	38 083	36 530	62 029	67 482	86 660	100 430
Property unit trusts	AHVW	2 463	2 485	2 666	3 219	3 211	5 498	4 835	5 280	5 869	6 761	10 444	16 687	26 215
Other assets	RKPL	31 318	36 352	30 628	32 978	47 136	82 273	90 841	90 139	82 490	107 229	152 170	..	..
Total liabilities	GQFX	4 852	4 412	5 347	8 118	7 436	8 719	11 041	10 819	10 005	26 944	39 626	..	..

1 These figures cover funded schemes only and therefore exclude the main superannuation arrangements in the central government sector.

Source: Office for National Statistics: 01633 812726

23.17 Insurance companies: balance sheet market values
United Kingdom
End year

£ million

		1996	1997	1998	1999	2000	2001	2002	2003	2004	2005
Long-term insurance companies											
Assets											
Total current assets (gross)	RYEW	31 699	42 795	46 165	56 360	62 937	63 855	58 122	58 518	63 407	72 754
Agents' and reinsurance balances (net)	AHNY	−232	155	1 383	508	384	..	6 373	4 720	..	3 933
Other debtors[1]	RKPN	12 982	15 708	18 210	18 613	21 045	..	34 391	35 414	..	27 591
British government securities	AHNJ	90 996	107 847	127 903	126 223	116 734	119 513	131 305	142 920	157 019	161 906
UK local authority securities etc	AHNN	1 088	914	1 722	1 456	1 170	1 407	1 427	1 547	2 044	1 840
UK company securities[2]	RKPO	304 587	386 734	438 666	539 834	557 293	..	443 535	468 910	..	601 681
Overseas company securities	RKPP	62 378	73 428	82 122	120 665	107 439	..	110 738	110 193	..	165 452
Overseas government securities	AHNS	7 554	8 471	17 515	18 494	18 004	21 285	19 762	20 561	20 161	16 065
Loans and mortgages	RKPQ	6 653	8 271	11 027	10 914	9 687	..	10 994	12 107	..	13 502
UK land, property and ground rent	AHNX	36 209	42 275	45 903	50 387	49 705	53 726	52 658	57 174	60 502	61 037
Overseas land, property and ground rent	RGCP	114	98	252	206	1 975	498	158	184	94	27
Other investments	RKPR	3 886	3 416	5 654	8 334	8 385	..	9 513	17 985	..	18 146
Total	RFXN	557 914	690 112	796 522	951 994	954 760	938 609	878 979	930 233	994 015	1 143 934
Net value of direct investment in:											
Non-insurance subsidiaries and associate companies in the United Kingdom	RYET	3 033	3 426	3 035	3 045	6 133	4 486	4 577	4 191	3 971	8 390
UK associate and subsidiary insurance companies and insurance holding companies	RYEU	575	−239	148	2 245	3 586	4 206	4 569	5 054	3 473	2 528
Overseas subsidiaries and associates	RYEV	986	1 104	1 087	3 638	4 002	5 581	5 463	6 330	2 181	4 455
Total assets	RKBI	562 508	694 403	800 792	960 922	968 481	952 882	893 588	945 808	1 003 640	1 159 307
Liabilities											
Borrowing:											
Borrowing from UK banks	RGDF	2 234	3 027	3 252	6 064	8 272	8 790	4 958	4 164	5 358	5 037
Other UK borrowing	RGDE	1 349	786	1 040	3 070	2 823	5 350	7 406	10 923	8 385	9 036
Borrowing from overseas	RGDD	90	104	148	159	38	81	800	530	793	1 151
Long-term business:											
Funds	RKDC	470 893	581 009	669 301	800 184	838 485	831 051	794 177	824 766	873 071	1 037 658
Claims admitted but not paid	RKBM	1 441	1 436	1 712	2 032	2 249	2 547	3 234	3 699	3 579	3 481
Provision for taxation net of amounts receivable:											
UK authorities	RYPI	2 568	4 207	5 443	6 344	5 381	3 951	2 803	4 055	4 881	8 225
Overseas authorities	RYPJ	9	25	67	314	67	45	−20	2	−13	−2
Provision for recommended dividends	RYPK	276	368	359	201	183	87	32	27	93	22
Other creditors and liabilities	RYPL	6 303	8 083	12 509	17 042	19 031	18 468	23 261	15 870	16 738	16 907
Excess of assets over above liabilities:											
Excess of value of assets over liabilities in respect of long-term funds	RKBR	71 817	89 790	96 456	116 951	79 173	63 337	36 517	62 546	65 641	59 132
Minority interests in UK subsidiary companies	RKTI	–	2	–	25	–	–	–	1	267	–
Shareholders' capital and reserves in respect of general business	RKBS	2 576	3 862	6 299	6 139	10 287	17 044	18 629	15 698	20 719	18 717
Other reserves including profit and loss account balances	RKBT	2 952	1 704	4 206	2 396	2 492	2 130	1 791	3 527	4 129	−57
Total liabilities	RKBI	562 508	694 403	800 792	960 922	968 481	952 882	893 588	945 808	1 003 640	1 159 307

413

23.17

Insurance companies: balance sheet market values
United Kingdom

continued End year

£ million

		1996	1997	1998	1999	2000	2001	2002	2003	2004	2005
Other than long-term insurance companies											
Assets											
Total current assets (gross)	RYME	11 559	12 628	8 524	10 468	8 772	12 264	17 671	20 036	29 258	26 561
Agents' and reinsurance balances (net)	AHMX	11 569	9 405	10 528	12 177	8 362	..	9 492	9 890	..	7 996
Other debtors[1]	RKPS	6 097	5 998	6 277	7 059	7 179	..	14 437	13 255	..	13 310
British government securities	AHMJ	16 893	15 666	16 409	15 938	14 561	15 064	18 390	19 645	19 662	19 818
UK local authority securities etc	AHMN	42	16	14	10	8	6	10	10	49	44
UK company securities[2]	RKPT	17 825	18 845	18 440	18 800	18 585	..	15 362	15 153	..	21 879
Overseas company securities	RKPU	5 072	6 594	8 676	6 284	8 190	..	7 394	7 124	..	12 645
Overseas government securities	AHMS	9 546	8 215	10 459	7 980	6 849	7 134	7 156	5 720	6 662	7 341
Loans and mortgages	RKPV	1 593	1 385	1 335	1 070	1 429	..	1 063	1 400	..	3 040
UK land, property and ground rent	AHMW	2 077	2 842	1 146	1 085	1 069	860	805	859	893	1 470
Overseas land, property and ground rent	RYNK	120	149	107	83	45	4	1	4	5	13
Other investments	RKPW	716	2 465	2 366	2 638	2 294	..	2 182	1 408	..	2 083
Total	RKAL	83 106	84 208	84 281	84 027	77 343	78 789	93 965	94 504	115 356	116 200
Net value of direct investment in:											
Non-insurance subsidiaries and associate companies in the United Kingdom	RYNR	3 195	6 950	5 553	7 074	7 038	10 456	11 706	13 408	19 028	20 530
UK associate and subsidiary insurance companies and insurance holding companies	RYNS	7 170	4 204	6 424	5 617	5 400	8 837	7 190	2 918	2 280	6 071
Overseas subsidiaries and associates	RYNT	14 859	16 402	14 239	17 775	15 993	14 260	9 014	5 718	5 507	6 446
Total assets	RKBY	108 330	111 764	110 497	114 493	105 774	112 342	121 875	116 548	142 171	149 247
Liabilities											
Borrowing:											
Borrowing from UK banks	RYMB	1 524	3 029	1 825	1 392	783	481	1 384	2 046	4 519	893
Other UK borrowing	RYMC	2 536	2 996	1 551	3 186	4 239	10 621	10 472	9 342	10 261	11 080
Borrowing from overseas	RYMD	1 976	1 202	1 600	3 045	1 867	1 964	2 916	2 918	2 476	2 817
General business technical reserves	RKCT	58 618	59 527	60 775	59 455	60 236	60 995	62 776	63 463	67 241	71 710
Long-term business:											
Funds	RKTF	–	–	–	–	–	–	–	–	–	–
Claims admitted but not paid	RKTK	–	–	–	–	–	–	–	–	–	–
Provision for taxation net of amounts receivable:											
UK authorities	RYPO	807	1 253	1 197	939	874	594	941	834	1 094	1 796
Overseas authorities	RYPP	22	7	11	11	11	7	5	84	24	5
Provision for recommended dividends	RYPQ	1 407	2 048	1 318	1 817	2 682	1 957	958	1 082	1 311	5
Other creditors and liabilities	RYPR	3 886	3 873	3 793	4 981	6 293	6 410	8 025	9 567	10 817	10 718
Excess of assets over above liabilities:											
Excess of value of assets over liabilities in respect of long-term funds	RKCG	–	–	–	–	–	–	–	–	–	–
Minority interests in UK subsidiary companies	RKCH	24	60	68	29	33	276	4	6	6	–
Shareholders' capital and reserves in respect of general business	RKCI	35 069	35 172	34 397	35 372	24 699	26 190	31 982	25 153	39 695	43 264
Other reserves including profit and loss account balances	RKCJ	2 461	2 597	4 215	4 265	4 056	2 847	2 411	2 053	4 727	6 959
Total liabilities	RKBY	108 330	111 764	110 497	114 493	105 774	112 342	121 875	116 548	142 171	149 247

1 Including outstanding interest, dividends and rents (net).
2 Including authorised unit trust units.

Source: Office for National Statistics: 01633 812726

23.18 Individual insolvencies
United Kingdom

Numbers

		1996	1997	1998	1999	2000	2001	2002	2003	2004	2005	2006
England and Wales												
Bankruptcies[1]	AIHW	21 803	19 892	19 647	21 611	21 550	23 477	24 292	28 022	35 898	47 291	62 956
Individual voluntary arrangements[2,3]	AIHI	4 468	4 549	4 902	7 195	7 978	6 298	6 295	7 583	10 752	20 293	44 332
Total	AIHK	26 271	24 441	24 549	28 806	29 528	29 775	30 587	35 604	46 650	67 584	107 288
Scotland												
Sequestrations[4]	KRHA	2 503	2 502	3 016	3 195	2 965	3 048	3 215	3 328	3 297	4 965	5 430
Protected Trust Deeds	GJ2I	532	686	1 449	2 144	2 801	3 779	5 174	5 452	6 024	6 881	8 208
Total	GJ2J	3 035	3 188	4 465	5 339	5 766	6 827	8 389	8 780	9 321	11 846	13 638
Northern Ireland												
Bankruptcies[5]	KRHB	415	393	394	401	349	292	334	517	666	821	1 036
Individual voluntary arrangements[3,6]	KJRK	101	84	123	172	267	176	207	318	449	633	774
Total	KRHD	516	477	517	573	616	468	541	835	1 115	1 454	1 810

1 Comprises receiving and administration orders under the Bankruptcy Act 1914 and bankruptcy orders under the Insolvency Act 1986. Orders later consolidated or rescinded are included in these figures.
2 Introduced under the Insolvency Act 1986.
3 For statistical purposes deeds of arrangement are now included with individual voluntary arrangements.
4 Sequestrations awarded but not brought into operation are included in these figures.

5 Comprises bankruptcy adjudication orders, arrangement protection orders and orders for the administration of estates of deceased insolvents. Orders later set aside or dismissed are included in these figures.
6 Introduced under the Insolvency Northern Ireland order 1989.

Source: Insolvency Service: 020 7637 6504/6443

23.19 Company insolvencies
United Kingdom

Numbers

		1996	1997	1998	1999	2000	2001	2002	2003	2004	2005	2006
England and Wales												
Compulsory liquidations	AIHR	5 080	4 735	5 216	5 209	4 925	4 675	6 231	5 234	4 584	5 233	5 418
Creditors' voluntary liquidations	AIHS	8 381	7 875	7 987	9 071	9 392	10 297	10 075	8 950	7 608	7 660	7 719
Total	AIHQ	13 461	12 610	13 203	14 280	14 317	14 972	16 306	14 184	12 192	12 893	13 137
Scotland												
Compulsory liquidations	KRGA	266	254	338	364	344	378	556	436	431	420	416
Creditors' voluntary liquidations	KRGB	175	223	228	208	239	224	232	195	190	149	133
Total	KRGC	441	477	566	572	583	602	788	631	621	569	549
Northern Ireland												
Compulsory liquidations	KRGD	68	60	63	58	83	60	49	95	76	85	78
Creditors' voluntary liquidations	KRGE	54	53	46	45	53	40	53	47	45	53	50
Total	KRGF	122	113	99	103	136	100	102	142	121	138	128

Source: Insolvency Service: 020 7637 6504/6443

23.20 Industry analysis: bankruptcies and deeds of arrangement[1]
England and Wales

Numbers

Industry		1995	1996	1997	1998	1999	2000	2001	2002	2003	2004	2005
Self-employed												
Agriculture and horticulture	KRFY	218	168	155	157	183	173	183	132	151	204	195
Manufacturing:												
Food, drink and tobacco	KRFZ	30	31	18	21	17	18	10	19	14	7	15
Chemicals	KRLA	8	5	5	7	4	2	2	6	2	6	2
Metals and engineering	KRLB	396	411	413	378	385	306	339	257	242	376	228
Textiles and clothing	KRLC	114	91	76	81	87	81	75	33	46	27	28
Timber and furniture	KRLD	158	118	98	96	94	90	88	59	82	65	82
Paper, printing and publishing	KRLE	142	117	104	101	112	80	75	70	58	63	67
Other	KRLF	146	117	116	110	111	84	79	111	100	90	140
Total	KRLG	994	890	830	794	810	661	668	555	544	634	562
Construction and transport:												
Construction	KRLH	2 783	2 713	2 182	1 919	1 911	1 741	1 783	1 637	1 781	1 658	1 976
Transport and communication	KRLI	1 138	1 227	1 162	1 060	1 187	1 120	1 134	1 095	1 116	1 249	1 334
Total	KHGP	3 921	3 940	3 344	2 979	3 098	2 861	2 917	2 732	2 897	2 907	3 310
Wholesaling:												
Food, drink and tobacco	KRLJ	103	77	62	53	45	49	40	48	33	28	29
Motor vehicles	KRLK	33	36	28	20	22	29	20	14	15	13	12
Other	KRLL	122	101	78	92	83	83	61	44	47	40	40
Total	KHGQ	258	214	168	165	150	161	121	106	95	81	81
Retailing:												
Food, drink and tobacco	KRLM	782	662	546	514	438	424	347	311	251	280	256
Motor vehicles and filling stations	KRLN	316	327	276	238	241	237	199	138	128	136	121
Other	KRLO	1 566	1 268	1 048	971	1 032	801	792	680	609	621	772
Total	KHGR	2 664	2 257	1 870	1 723	1 711	1 462	1 338	1 129	988	1 037	1 149
Services:												
Financial institutions	KRLP	185	125	105	79	54	45	39	31	24	28	22
Business services	KRLQ	1 354	1 176	1 117	1 057	1 162	1 127	1 107	1 057	1 023	1 242	1 416
Hotels and catering	KRLR	1 956	1 736	1 603	1 309	1 376	1 263	1 187	1 041	1 038	951	1 125
Total	KHGS	3 495	3 037	2 825	2 445	2 592	2 435	2 333	2 129	2 085	2 221	2 563
Other	KHGT	1 732	2 161	2 077	2 157	2 179	2 199	2 279	2 071	2 379	2 480	2 979
Total	KRLT	13 282	12 667	11 269	10 420	10 723	9 952	9 839	8 854	9 139	9 564	10 839
Other individuals												
Employees	KRLU	1 981	2 471	2 625	3 141	4 357	4 601	5 525	5 900	7 101	9 528	13 626
No occupation and unemployed	KRLV	2 859	3 294	3 051	3 384	4 457	4 856	5 848	6 965	8 978	12 643	17 105
Directors and promoters of companies	KRLW	484	368	310	272	330	296	328	323	420	458	503
Occupation unknown	KRLX	3 327	3 003	2 637	2 430	1 744	1 845	1 937	2 250	2 383	3 705	5 218
Total	KRLY	8 651	9 136	8 623	9 227	10 888	11 598	13 638	15 438	18 882	26 334	36 452
Total bankruptcies	KRLZ	21 933	21 803	19 892	19 647	21 611	21 550	23 477	24 292	28 021	35 898	47 291

1 From January 1991 Industrial Analysis excludes Deeds of Arrangement.

Source: Insolvency Service: 020 7637 6504/6443

23.21 Industry analysis: company insolvencies[1]
England and Wales

Numbers

		1995	1996	1997	1998	1999	2000	2001	2002	2003	2004	2005
Industry												
Agriculture and horticulture	KRMA	99	89	51	65	75	67	90	76	52	35	35
Manufacturing:												
Food, drink and tobacco	KRMB	130	163	93	89	67	104	71	61	69	38	43
Chemicals	KRMC	69	65	31	57	35	61	37	46	30	21	34
Metals and engineering	KRMD	681	658	591	594	698	683	704	739	828	630	591
Textiles and clothing	KRME	567	568	596	526	419	423	320	304	244	168	172
Timber and furniture	KRMF	267	249	181	149	190	187	199	179	92	69	85
Paper, printing and publishing	KRMG	452	438	364	426	387	386	484	545	376	291	253
Other	KRMH	681	599	613	652	780	678	717	768	430	379	441
Total	KRMI	2 847	2 740	2 469	2 493	2 576	2 522	2 532	2 642	2 069	1 596	1 619
Construction and transport:												
Construction	KRMJ	1 844	1 610	1 419	1 325	1 529	1 474	1 509	1 840	1 728	1 653	1 775
Transport and communication	KRMK	706	682	540	504	443	526	481	652	694	596	624
Total	KHGU	2 550	2 292	1 959	1 829	1 972	2 000	1 990	2 492	2 422	2 249	2 399
Wholesaling:												
Food, drink and tobacco	KRML	205	183	158	139	187	150	125	142	108	124	82
Motor vehicles	KRMM	83	95	41	60	38	29	24	64	208	210	198
Other	KRMN	678	429	340	364	394	391	363	512	788	486	487
Total	KHGV	966	707	539	563	619	570	512	718	1 104	820	767
Retailing:												
Food, drink and tobacco	KRMO	246	236	219	186	193	200	114	132	159	121	176
Motor vehicles and filling stations	KRMP	195	227	132	120	142	141	172	174	59	45	59
Other	KRMQ	1 127	956	891	847	919	853	833	902	578	548	626
Total	KHGW	1 568	1 419	1 242	1 153	1 254	1 194	1 119	1 208	796	714	861
Services:												
Financial institutions	KRMR	198	222	111	101	118	57	28	35	48	49	60
Business services	KRMS	1 525	1 500	1 528	1 617	1 831	1 605	1 618	3 215	3 886	3 392	3 462
Hotels and catering	KRMT	692	708	609	626	562	530	538	740	566	511	584
Total	KJRS	2 415	2 430	2 248	2 344	2 511	2 192	2 184	3 990	4 500	3 952	4 106
Other	KHGX	4 091	3 784	4 102	4 756	5 273	5 772	6 545	5 180	3 241	2 826	3 106
Total company insolvencies	KHGY	14 536	13 461	12 610	13 203	14 280	14 317	14 972	16 306	14 184	12 192	12 893

1 Including partnerships.

Source: Insolvency Service: 020 7637 6504/6443

Service industry

Chapter 24

Service industry

Annual Business Inquiry

(Tables 24.1, 24.3 and 24.4)

For details of the Annual Business Inquiry, see the text accompanying Table 22.1.

Retail trade: index numbers of value and volume

(Table 24.2)

The main purpose of the Retail Sales Inquiry (RSI) is to provide up to date information on short period movements in the level of retail sales. In principle, the RSI covers the retail activity of every business classified in the retail sector (Division 52 of the 2003 Standard Industrial Classification) in Great Britain. A business will be classified to the retail sector if its main activity is one of the individual 4 digit SIC categories within Division 52. The retail activity of a business is then defined by its retail turnover, i.e. the sale of all retail goods (note that petrol, for example, is not a retail good).

The RSI is compiled from the information returned to the statutory inquiries into the distribution and services sector. The inquiry is addressed to a stratified sample of 5,000 businesses classified to the retail sector, the stratification being by 'type of store' (the individual 4 digit SIC categories within Division 52) and by size. The sample structure is designed to ensure that the inquiry estimates are as accurate as possible. In terms of the selection, this means that:

> each of the individual 4 digit SIC categories are represented, their coverage depending upon the relative size of the category and the variability of the data;

> within each 4 digit SIC category, the larger retailers tend to be fully enumerated with decreasing proportions of medium and smaller retailers.

The structure of the inquiry is updated periodically, by reference to the more comprehensive results of the Annual Business Inquiry (ABI). The monthly inquiry also incorporates a rotation element for the smallest retailers. This helps to spread the burden more fairly, as well as improving the representativeness between successive benchmarks.

During 2003, the retail sales index was rebased using detailed information from the 2000 annual business inquiry. The reference year is now set at 2000=100.

The latest summary statistics are published each month by First Release. More disaggregated value indices (not seasonally adjusted) are published each month in Business Monitor SDM28, via the National Statistics website: www.statistics.gov.uk/rsi.

24.1 Retail businesses[1]
United Kingdom

£ million and percentages

		2001	2002	2003	2004
Number of businesses	ZABE	210 691	207 513	202 604	200 591
Total turnover[2]	ZABL	251 624	265 577	278 373	289 087
Value Added Tax in total turnover	ZABM	25 249	26 907	28 505	29 458
Retail turnover[2]	ZABN	227 298	238 456	250 849	259 248
Non-retail turnover[2]	ZABO	24 327	27 121	27 524	29 840
Other income					
Value of commercial insurance claims received	ZABP	89	105	65	40
Subsidies received from UK government sources and the EC	ZAEN	24	4	5	10
Employment costs[3]	ZABQ	28 036	29 779	31 367	32 989
Gross wages and salaries	ZABR	25 320	26 933	28 294	29 641
Redundancy and severance payments	ZABS	130	130	134	158
Employers' National Insurance contributions	ZABT	1 733	1 805	1 991	2 166
Contributions to pension funds	ZABU	853	911	948	1 025
Stocks					
Increase during year	ZABV	900	1 284	978	914
Value at end of year	ZABW	21 509	22 400	23 024	23 652
Total turnover[3] divided by end-year stocks (Quotient)	ZABX	10.5	10.7	10.9	11.0
Purchases of goods, materials and services[3]	ZABY	175 593	185 875	194 169	199 948
Goods bought for resale without processing	ZABZ	147 791	155 608	161 304	165 750
Energy and water products for own consumption	ZACA	2 028	1 918	2 048	2 178
Goods and materials	ZACB	3 544	3 845	3 917	4 318
Hiring, leasing or renting of plant, machinery and vehicles	ZACC	788	924	946	822
Commercial insurance premiums	ZACD	688	827	1 001	1 071
Road transport services	ZACE	1 945	2 137	2 545	2 576
Telecommunication services	ZACF	603	561	624	624
Computer and related services	ZACG	581	756	765	919
Advertising and marketing services	ZACH	2 881	3 047	3 378	3 218
Other services	ZACI	14 745	16 252	17 642	18 473
Taxes, duties and levies	ZACJ	4 432	4 576	4 715	4 889
National non-domestic (business) rates	ZACK	3 616	3 726	3 859	3 925
Other amounts paid for taxes, duties and levies	ZACL	816	850	855	964
Capital expenditure					
Cost of acquisitions	ZACM	8 469	9 355	8 776	9 951
Proceeds from disposals	ZACN	1 606	1 240	1 328	1 602
Net capital expenditure	ZACO	6 863	8 115	7 448	8 348
Amount included in acquisitions for assets under finance leasing arrangements	ZACP	474	587	304	327
Work of a capital nature carried out by own staff (included in acquisitions)	ZACQ	144	128	142	148
Gross margin					
Amount	ZACR	78 913	83 708	88 904	94 034
As a percentage of adjusted turnover[4]	ZACS	*34.9*	*34.9*	*35.6*	*36.2*
Approximate gross value added at basic prices	ZACT	51 201	53 545	56 104	59 876

24.1 Retail businesses[1]
United Kingdom
continued

£ million

		2001	2002	2003	2004
Total turnover	ZABL	251 624	265 577	278 373	289 087
Retail turnover	ZABN	227 298	238 456	250 849	259 248
1 Fruit (including fresh, chilled, dried, frozen, canned and processed)	DSSX	4 112	3 997	4 507	4 498
2 Vegetables (including fresh, chilled, dried, frozen, canned and processed)	DSSY	6 662	6 871	8 354	8 475
3 Meat (including fresh, chilled, smoked, frozen, canned and processed)	DSSZ	11 133	11 671	13 505	13 706
4 Fish, crustaceans and molluscs (including fresh, chilled, frozen, canned and processed)	DSTA	2 200	2 299	2 549	2 671
5 Bakery products and cereals (including rice and pasta products)	DSTC	9 424	9 661	12 314	11 850
6 Sugar, jam, honey, chocolate and confectionery (including ice-cream)	DSTD	6 289	6 469	6 446	6 536
7 Alcoholic drink	DSTE	10 625	11 301	12 297	12 993
8 Non-alcoholic beverages (including tea, coffee, fruit drinks and vegetable drinks)	DSTF	5 717	6 476	6 713	7 385
9 Tobacco (excluding smokers requisites, eg pipes, lighters, etc)	DSTG	8 616	9 016	9 204	9 013
10 Milk, cheese and eggs (including yoghurts and cream)	DSTH	7 032	7 233	7 390	7 940
11 Oils and fats (including butter and margarine)	DSTI	1 314	1 222	1 162	1 288
12 Food products not elsewhere classified (including sauces, herbs, spices and soups)	DSTJ	9 986	9 185	4 112	4 399
13 Pharmaceutical products	DSTK	2 744	2 911	2 963	2 980
14 National Health Receipts	DSTL	6 981	7 740	8 647	9 009
15 Other medical products and therapeutic appliances and equipment	DSTN	2 737	2 753	3 122	3 343
16 Other appliances, articles and products for personal care	DSTO	8 543	9 611	10 698	11 114
17 Other articles of clothing, accessories for making clothing	DSTP	1 253	1 293	1 955	2 089
18 Garments	DSTQ	26 777	28 331	29 691	30 395
19 Footwear (excluding sports shoes)	DSTR	4 629	5 270	5 622	5 932
20 Travel goods and other personal effects not elsewhere classified	DSTT	848	1 007	1 175	1 103
21 Household textiles (including furnishing fabrics, curtains, etc)	DSTV	3 568	3 656	3 799	3 978
22 Household and personal appliances whether electric or not	DSUA	6 499	6 580	6 776	6 941
23 Glassware, tableware and household utensils (including non-electric)	DSUB	2 748	2 823	2 843	2 751
24 Furniture and furnishings	DSUC	11 065	12 094	13 285	13 413
25 Audio and visual equipment (including radios, televisions and video recorders)	DSUE	4 500	4 781	4 818	4 999
26 Recording material for pictures and sound (including audio and video tapes, blank and pre-recorded records, etc)	DSUG	3 304	3 591	3 788	4 459
27 Information processing equipment (including printers, software, calculators and typewriters)	DSUL	3 175	3 056	3 077	3 478
28 Decorating and DIY supplies	DSUM	6 279	6 548	6 631	7 417
29 Tools and equipment for house and garden	DSUN	2 669	3 007	3 452	3 243
30 Books	DSUP	2 366	2 752	2 748	2 990
31 Newspapers and periodicals	DSUQ	3 652	3 709	4 067	4 046
32 Stationery and drawing materials and miscellaneous printed matter	DSUW	3 601	3 864	3 824	3 960
33 Carpets and other floor coverings (excluding bathroom mats, rush and door mats)	DSUX	3 182	3 411	3 757	3 354
34 Photographic and cinematographic equipment and optical instruments	DSUZ	1 059	1 402	1 670	1 759
35 Telephone and telefax equipment (including mobile phones)	DSVA	2 398	2 238	2 293	3 010
36 Jewellery, silverware and plate; watches and clocks	DSVB	3 774	4 387	4 312	4 624
37 Works of art and antiques (including furniture, floor coverings and jewellery)	DSVF	1 820	1 509	1 493	1 601
38 Equipment and accessories for sport, camping, recreation and musical instruments	DSVH	3 861	3 624	3 803	3 727
39 Spare part and accessories for all types of vehicle and sales of bicycles	DSVI	752	1 082	572	703
40 Games, toys, hobbies (including video game software, video game computers that plug into the tv, video-games cassettes and CD-ROMs)	DSVM	4 624	5 468	5 962	6 031
41 Other goods not elsewhere classified (including sale of new postage stamps and sales of liquid and solid fuels)	DSVN	3 745	3 359	3 134	3 575
42 Non-durable household goods (including household cleaning, maintenance products) and paper products and other non-durable household goods	DSVO	4 352	4 405	5 017	5 450
43 Natural or artificial plants and flowers	DSVQ	3 028	3 266	3 745	3 094
44 Pets and related products (including pet food)	DSVR	2 724	2 497	2 681	2 999
45 Repair of household and personal items	DSVS	927	1 031	875	924

1 See chapter text.
2 Inclusive of VAT.
3 Exclusive of VAT.
4 Turnover is adjusted to take out VAT.

Source: Office for National Statistics: 01633 812435

24.2

Retail trade: index numbers of value and volume of sales[1]
Great Britain
Not seasonally adjusted

Weekly average (2000=100)

		Sales in 2000 £ million	1996	1997	1998	1999	2000	2001	2002	2003	2004	2005	2006
Value													
All retailing	EAFY	207 149	84.6	89.9	93.4	96.5	100.0	105.9	110.6	113.7	118.8	119.9	123.4
Large	EAFZ	153 022	81	87	92	96	100	107	112	118	124	126	131
Small	EAGA	54 128	97	97	99	98	100	104	106	101	104	103	103
Predominantly food stores	EAFS	89 041	84.6	88.9	93.4	96.6	100.0	106.0	110.4	114.8	119.6	123.6	128.3
Predominantly non-food stores	EAFT	106 359	84.4	90.6	93.2	96.3	100.0	106.8	111.8	114.8	119.9	119.1	121.7
Non specialised predominantly non-food stores	EAGE	18 781	85.7	91.5	92.6	95.2	100.0	105.0	107.4	109.2	111.2	110.8	113.9
Textiles, clothing, footwear and leather	EAFU	27 880	87.0	93.4	93.8	96.0	100.0	108.4	114.9	118.9	124.8	126.7	132.1
Household goods stores	EAFV	27 699	79.2	86.8	91.6	95.7	100.0	107.6	113.1	113.4	117.2	112.8	114.1
Other specialised non-food stores	EAFW	31 999	84.5	89.3	93.1	96.8	100.0	105.7	110.5	115.6	123.0	123.0	123.7
Other retail sale (non-store) and repair	EAFX	11 749	87.6	91.8	97.1	98.8	100.0	97.0	100.5	96.2	102.7	99.1	101.1
Volume													
All retailing	EAHC	207 149	85.4	89.9	92.5	95.7	100.0	106.1	112.2	116.3	123.3	125.8	129.9
Predominantly food stores	EAGW	89 041	89.3	92.9	95.5	97.2	100.0	104.1	108.2	111.9	116.5	119.7	122.7
Predominantly non-food stores	EAGX	106 359	82.1	87.4	89.9	94.3	100.0	108.5	116.2	121.3	129.6	131.9	136.6
Non specialised predominantly non-food stores	EAHI	18 781	86.9	91.5	91.5	94.0	100.0	106.0	110.5	113.8	118.0	119.3	124.0
Textiles,clothing, footwear and leather	EAGY	27 880	82.7	88.1	88.8	92.9	100.0	112.1	123.8	129.6	139.4	144.2	151.3
Household goods stores	EAGZ	27 699	73.2	80.3	85.8	92.6	100.0	109.6	117.8	122.3	130.8	131.1	137.6
Other specialised non-food stores	EAHA	31 999	86.9	90.7	93.6	97.1	100.0	105.9	111.6	117.5	127.0	129.1	130.2
Other retail sale (non-store) and repair	EAHB	11 749	84.6	88.2	93.2	96.2	100.0	99.6	106.5	105.4	117.1	118.0	124.1

1 See chapter text.

Source: Office for National Statistics: 01633 812713

24.3 Motor trades[1]
United Kingdom

£ million and percentages

		Sale, maintenance and repair of motor vehicles and motorcycles; retail sale of automotive fuel (SIC 92 50.00)					Sale of motor vehicles (SIC 92 50.10)			
		2001	2002	2003	2004		2001	2002	2003	2004
Number of businesses	MKEQ	70 942	70 338	70 080	70 260	MKER	26 801	25 856	24 895	24 197
Total turnover	CMRH	136 398	141 867	150 629	154 768	EWRI	92 063	96 968	102 242	104 569
Motor trades turnover	CMRI	131 908	136 346	145 739	148 711	FDFZ	91 015	95 885	101 377	103 582
Retail sales of:										
New cars	CMRJ	28 891	28 433	31 050	30 327	FDGA	27 583	27 065	28 597	27 937
Other new motor vehicles and motorcycles	CMRK	4 011	4 404	4 070	4 775	FDGB	3 514	3 876	3 592	3 923
Sales to other dealers of:										
New cars	CMRL	16 720	20 867	22 855	24 881	FDGC	16 693	20 773	22 336	24 465
Other new motor vehicles and motorcycles	CMRM	3 282	3 703	3 949	4 202	FDGD	2 844	3 085	3 486	3 716
Gross sales of used motor vehicles and motorcycles	CMRN	29 434	27 939	32 050	32 405	FDGE	26 906	26 337	30 106	29 944
Turnover from sales of petrol, diesel, oil and other petroleum products	CMRO	16 750	16 978	17 738	17 785	FDGF	1 087	782	1 184	750
Other motor trades sales and receipts (including parts and accessories, workshop receipts)	CMRP	32 819	14 256	34 027	34 336	FDGG	12 387	4 916	12 076	12 847
Non-motor trades turnover	CMRQ	4 490	5 521	4 890	6 056	FDHJ	1 049	1 083	865	986
Purchases of goods, materials and services										
Total purchases	CMNR	116 458	120 819	127 823	131 754	FDGH	80 657	84 354	89 198	91 517
Energy, water and materials	CMRS	1 441	1 379	1 631	1 740	FDGI	630	542	666	684
Used motor vehicles and motorcycles	COBU	26 166	24 391	27 910	28 680	FDGJ	24 100	22 939	26 239	26 646
Parts used solely in repair and servicing activities	CMRT	5 787	6 397	6 481	7 179	FDGK	2 290	2 616	2 521	2 743
Other goods for resale	CMRU	75 855	80 726	83 396	85 166	FDGL	49 125	53 512	55 108	56 250
Hiring, leasing and renting of plant, machinery and vehicles	CMRV	270	326	349	345	FDGM	62	131	72	81
Commercial insurance premiums	CMRW	435	465	572	555	FDGN	190	198	224	215
Road transport services	CMRX	452	740	778	737	FDGO	268	373	368	408
Telecommunication services	CMRY	274	278	335	299	FDGP	127	129	150	130
Computer and related services	CMRZ	269	306	329	384	FDGQ	162	174	170	188
Advertising and marketing services	CMSA	1 644	1 847	2 076	2 400	FDGR	1 412	1 611	1 742	2 033
Other services	CMSB	3 866	3 964	3 967	4 269	FDGS	2 289	2 130	1 939	2 139
Taxes, duties and levies										
Total taxes and levies	CMSC	936	1 002	1 048	976	FDGT	529	519	520	519
National (non-domestic business) rates	CMSD	586	536	611	600	FDGU	261	245	278	280
Other amounts paid for taxes, duties and levies	CMSE	350	466	437	375	FDGV	268	275	243	238
Capital expenditure										
Cost of acquisitions	CMSF	2 093	2 216	2 290	2 455	FDGW	1 289	1 374	1 380	1 477
Cost of disposals	CMSG	798	846	778	1 009	FDGX	553	593	566	671
Net capital expenditure	CMSH	1 295	1 370	1 512	1 446	FDGY	736	781	813	807
Work of a capital nature carried out by own staff (included in acquisitions)	CMSI	14	12	31	6	FDGZ	9	6	1	5
Stocks										
Increase during year	CMSJ	828	886	1 363	1 294	FDHA	667	661	1 191	1 065
Value at end of year	CMSK	12 155	13 217	14 437	14 920	FDHB	9 005	9 913	10 632	11 071
Total turnover divided by end-year stocks (Quotient)	CMSL	11.2	10.7	10.4	10.4	FDHC	10.2	9.6	9.6	9.4
Employment costs										
Total employment costs	CMSM	9 069	9 400	9 726	10 325	FDHD	4 751	5 024	5 056	5 368
Gross wages and salaries paid	COBP	8 127	8 409	8 669	9 148	FDHE	4 232	4 470	4 487	4 742
National insurance and pension contributions	COBQ	942	991	1 056	1 178	FDHF	520	554	569	626
Gross margin										
Amount	COBR	29 335	31 064	34 080	34 931	FDHG	17 169	18 536	19 556	19 976
As a percentage of adjusted turnover	COBS	*21.5*	*22.0*	*22.6*	*22.6*	FDHH	*18.6*	*19.7*	*19.1*	*19.1*
Approximate gross value added at basic prices	COBT	20 710	21 777	24 072	24 239	FDHI	12 039	13 259	14 242	14 116

24.3

Motor trades[1]
United Kingdom
continued

		Maintenance and repair of motor vehicles (SIC 92 50.20)					Sale of motor vehicle parts and accessories (SIC 92 50.30)			
		2001	2002	2003	2004		2001	2002	2003	2004
Number of businesses	MKES	27 862	28 438	29 188	30 049	MKET	7 800	7 715	7 799	7 950
Total turnover	FDHK	11 890	11 964	12 542	13 419	FDIW	11 752	11 068	13 801	13 483
Motor trades turnover	FDHL	11 493	11 658	12 147	12 857	FDIX	11 557	10 567	13 304	12 363
Retail sales of:										
New cars	FDHM	1 099	1 206	1 081	993	FDIY	22	19	1 168	1 221
Other new motor vehicles and motorcycles	FDHN	..	162	153	345	FDIZ	..	161	..	169
Sales to other dealers of:										
New cars	FDHO	..	4	8	7	FDJA	..	89	509	407
Other new motor vehicles and motorcycles	FDHP	..	–	3	2	FDJB	..	–	..	52
Gross sales of used motor vehicles and motorcycles	FDHQ	1 574	1 079	1 109	1 295	FDJC	173	143	..	367
Turnover from sales of petrol, diesel, oil and other petroleum products	FDHR	371	334	117	193	FDJD	200	85	70	78
Other motor trades sales and receipts (including parts and accessories, workshop receipts)	FDHS	8 424	7 891	9 674	10 022	FDJE	11 096	1 029	11 085	10 068
Non-motor trades turnover	FDHT	397	306	396	562	FDJF	195	501	497	1 120
Purchases of goods, materials and services										
Total purchases	FDHU	7 817	7 806	8 100	8 890	FDJG	9 387	8 611	11 062	10 707
Energy, water and materials	FDHV	367	528	572	636	FDJH	299	171	220	224
Used motor vehicles and motorcycles	FDHW	1 347	892	897	992	FDJI	145	91	..	370
Parts used solely in repair and servicing activities	FDHX	2 734	3 053	3 374	3 846	FDJJ	574	544	410	187
Other goods for resale	FDHY	2 127	2 170	1 774	1 776	FDJK	7 405	6 657	..	8 771
Hiring, leasing and renting of plant, machinery and vehicles	FDHZ	146	75	77	96	FDJL	45	60	151	132
Commercial insurance premiums	FDIA	147	139	204	210	FDJM	64	85	89	78
Road transport services	FDIB	30	13	49	85	FDJN	86	228	267	122
Telecommunication services	FDIC	65	70	97	95	FDJO	60	57	60	44
Computer and related services	FDID	44	34	61	68	FDJP	50	78	75	102
Advertising and marketing services	FDIE	98	109	127	123	FDJQ	76	70	165	204
Other services	FDIF	713	724	868	965	FDJR	581	568	643	473
Taxes, duties and levies										
Total taxes and levies	FDIG	196	194	197	214	FDJS	104	90	102	116
National (non-domestic business) rates	FDIH	146	142	162	151	FDJT	80	74	84	89
Other amounts paid for taxes, duties and levies	FDII	49	52	35	64	FDJU	25	16	19	27
Capital expenditure										
Cost of acquisitions	FDIJ	396	376	433	469	FDJV	207	170	221	196
Cost of disposals	FDIK	89	84	87	116	FDJW	91	106	47	63
Net capital expenditure	FDIL	307	292	346	353	FDJX	115	64	173	133
Work of a capital nature carried out by own staff (included in acquisitions)	FDIM	3	2	1	–	FDJY	2	3	29	–
Stocks										
Increase during year	FDIN	79	51	102	43	FDJZ	43	66	76	79
Value at end of year	FDIO	809	805	881	882	FDKA	1 492	1 498	1 750	1 775
Total turnover divided by end-year stocks (Quotient)	FDIP	14.7	14.6	14.2	15.2	FDKB	7.9	7.8	7.9	7.6
Employment costs										
Total employment costs	FDIQ	2 176	2 298	2 480	2 602	FDKC	1 461	1 348	1 427	1 560
Gross wages and salaries paid	FDIR	1 961	2 075	2 233	2 329	FDKD	1 312	1 209	1 268	1 386
National insurance and pension contributions	FDIS	215	223	247	273	FDKE	149	139	159	174
Gross margin										
Amount	FDIT	5 741	5 878	6 597	6 807	FDKF	3 654	3 833	4 501	4 213
As a percentage of adjusted turnover	FDIU	*48.3*	*49.0*	*52.6*	*50.7*	FDKG	*31.1*	*30.6*	*32.6*	*31.2*
Approximate gross value added at basic prices	FDIV	4 134	4 187	4 552	4 542	FDKH	2 392	2 514	2 831	2 835

24.3 Motor trades[1]
United Kingdom
continued

£ million and percentages

		Sale, maintenance and repair of motorcycles and related parts and accessories (SIC 92 50.40)					Retail sale of automotive fuel (SIC 92 50.50)			
		2001	2002	2003	2004		2001	2002	2003	2004
Number of businesses	MKEU	2 402	2 513	2 710	2 948	MKEV	6 077	5 816	5 488	5 116
Total turnover	FDKI	1 722	1 812	1 955	2 235	FDLV	18 971	20 056	20 089	21 062
Motor trades turnover	FDKJ	1 707	1 737	1 887	2 218	FDLW	16 136	16 500	17 024	17 691
Retail sales of:										
New cars	FDKK	–	–	49	37	FDLX	186	142	154	139
Other new motor vehicles and motorcycles	FDKL	433	194	215	337	FDLY	3	11	19	–
Sales to other dealers of:										
New cars	FDKM	–	–	–	–	FDLZ	–	–	1	2
Other new motor vehicles and motorcycles	FDKN	436	618	419	432	FDMA	1	–	2	–
Gross sales of used motor vehicles and motorcycles	FDKO	329	186	333	481	FDMB	452	193	160	317
Turnover from sales of petrol, diesel, oil and other petroleum products	FDKP	1	–	–	–	FDMC	15 091	15 776	16 367	16 763
Other motor trades sales and receipts (including parts and accessories, workshop receipts)	FDKQ	508	172	872	930	FDMD	404	248	319	469
Non-motor trades turnover	FDKR	15	75	68	18	FDME	2 835	3 556	3 065	3 371
Purchases of goods, materials and services										
Total purchases	FDKT	1 367	1 493	1 512	1 847	FDMF	17 230	18 554	17 951	18 793
Energy, water and materials	FDKU	33	39	59	62	FDMG	112	99	115	136
Used motor vehicles and motorcycles	FDKV	228	142	252	368	FDMH	345	328	140	305
Parts used solely in repair and servicing activities	FDKW	75	112	87	282	FDMI	114	72	90	120
Other goods for resale	FDKX	919	1 049	967	971	FDMJ	16 278	17 338	16 946	17 398
Hiring, leasing and renting of plant, machinery and vehicles	FDKY	4	4	7	1	FDMK	11	56	41	36
Commercial insurance premiums	FDKZ	11	9	23	13	FDML	24	34	32	38
Road transport services	FDLA	4	33	15	34	COBV	64	93	79	88
Telecommunication services	FDLB	6	5	9	16	COBW	16	17	20	16
Computer and related services	FDLC	3	3	4	6	COBX	10	17	18	20
Advertising and marketing services	FDLD	24	35	21	22	COBY	33	22	22	17
Other services	FDLE	60	63	67	73	COBZ	222	479	449	619
Taxes, duties and levies										
Total taxes and levies	FDLF	20	15	29	35	COCA	87	183	200	92
National (non-domestic business) rates	FDLG	15	..	..	12	COCB	84	..	..	69
Other amounts paid for taxes, duties and levies	FDLH	5	..	..	23	COCC	3	..	..	23
Capital expenditure										
Cost of acquisitions	FDLI	25	34	46	53	COCD	176	263	211	260
Cost of disposals	FDLJ	20	5	7	16	COCE	45	58	71	144
Net capital expenditure	FDLK	5	29	39	37	COCF	131	205	140	116
Work of a capital nature carried out by own staff (included in acquisitions)	FDLL	–	1	–	1	COCG	–	–	–	–
Stocks										
Increase during year	FDLM	–11	35	–8	9	COCH	50	72	2	97
Value at end of year	FDLN	378	302	432	393	COCI	471	698	741	800
Total turnover divided by end-year stocks (Quotient)	FDLO	4.6	6.2	4.5	5.7	COCJ	40.3	28.8	27.1	26.3
Employment costs										
Total employment costs	FDLP	132	144	151	153	COCK	548	587	611	643
Gross wages and salaries paid	FDLQ	120	127	136	138	COCL	503	528	545	553
National insurance and pension contributions	FDLR	13	17	15	15	COCM	45	59	66	90
Gross margin										
Amount	FDLS	488	542	630	612	COCN	2 283	2 275	2 796	3 323
As a percentage of adjusted turnover	FDLT	*28.3*	*31.0*	*32.2*	*27.4*	CMQN	*12.0*	*11.4*	*13.9*	*15.8*
Approximate gross value added at basic prices	FDLU	346	353	424	387	CMQO	1 799	1 464	2 022	2 359

1 See chapter text. Figures are exclusive of VAT.

Source: Office for National Statistics: 01633 812435

24.4 Catering and allied trades[1]
United Kingdom

£ million and percentages

		Total catering and allied trades (SIC 92 55.00)					Hotels and motels (SIC 92 55.11 and 55.12)			
		2001	2002	2003	2004		2001	2002	2003	2004
Number of businesses	MKEK	118 988	122 714	123 491	126 696	MKEL	10 890	10 800	10 535	10 416
Total turnover[2]	CMKX	57 738	60 603	63 412	70 216	CMLW	12 047	11 824	12 172	13 009
Taxes and levies[3]										
Total taxes and levies	CMLM	1 505	1 594	1 622	1 789	CMML	371	373	395	427
National (non-domestic business) rates	CMLJ	1 347	1 481	1 495	1 611	CMMI	350	359	380	401
Other amounts paid for taxes, duties and levies	CMLL	158	113	126	178	CMMK	21	14	15	27
Capital expenditure[3]										
Capital acquisitions	CMLP	4 923	4 491	4 068	4 130	CMMO	1 201	1 127	960	938
Capital disposals	CMLQ	520	670	850	615	CMMP	81	225	144	151
Net capital expenditure	CMLK	4 404	3 820	3 217	3 515	CMMJ	1 120	902	815	788
Work of a capital nature carried out by your own staff (included in acquisitions)	CMLR	28	25	31	12	CMMQ	6	13	12	4
Stocks[3]										
Increase during year	CMLN	63	44	42	75	CMMM	–	–12	2	3
Value at end of year	CMLO	1 247	1 132	1 106	1 252	CMMN	207	231	169	168
Purchases of goods and services[3]										
Total purchases	CMLI	26 160	27 408	29 230	31 789	CMMH	4 135	4 327	4 521	4 815
Energy, water and materials	CMKZ	10 938	10 608	12 130	13 354	CMLY	1 766	1 729	2 015	2 042
Goods for resale	CMLA	7 556	8 173	8 851	9 538	CMLZ	469	468	489	560
Hiring, leasing of plant, machinery etc.	CMLB	277	350	275	303	CMMA	50	51	54	66
Commercial insurance premiums	CMLC	374	430	494	540	CMMB	82	106	124	135
Road transport services	CMLD	99	115	96	103	CMMC	19	19	22	8
Telecommunication services	CMLE	235	239	260	265	CMMD	63	61	71	68
Computer and related services	CMLF	130	141	149	169	CMME	31	45	50	45
Advertising and marketing services	CMLG	597	661	686	712	CMMF	177	178	183	203
Other services	CMLH	5 956	6 691	6 289	6 805	CMMG	1 475	1 670	1 513	1 689
Employment costs[3]										
Total employment costs	CMKY	12 965	13 504	14 116	15 296	CMLX	3 005	3 021	3 159	3 269
Gross wages and salaries paid	CMKV	11 971	12 475	12 998	14 084	CMLU	2 755	2 760	2 865	2 992
National insurance and pension contributions	CMKW	994	1 029	1 118	1 212	CMLV	250	260	294	277
Gross margin[4]										
Amount	CMQP	41 918	43 943	45 747	51 079	CMQS	9 825	9 610	9 889	10 548
As a percentage of turnover	CMQQ	*84.5*	*84.2*	*83.7*	*84.2*	CMQT	*95.2*	*95.5*	*95.3*	*94.8*
Value added at basic prices[4]	CMQR	23 466	24 786	25 435	28 872	CMQU	6 191	5 759	5 864	6 294
Accommodation										
Number of establishments	CMLS	23 584	23 559	28 209	28 350	CMMR	12 470	12 874	13 974	14 202
Letting bedplaces	CMLT	1 903 585	2 071 308	2 214 366	2 678 444	CMMS	819 116	1 022 079	1 198 410	965 653

24.4 Catering and allied trades[1]
United Kingdom
continued

£ million and percentages

		Camping sites and other provision of short-stay accommodation (SIC 92 55.21 to 55.23)					Restaurants or cafes, take-away food shops (SIC 92 55.30)			
		2001	2002	2003	2004		2001	2002	2003	2004
Number of businesses	MKEM	3 928	4 175	4 370	4 702	MKEN	52 633	54 340	55 475	57 667
Total turnover[2]	CMMV	2 220	2 631	3 032	3 616	CMNU	18 323	18 843	20 145	21 726
Taxes and levies[3]										
Total taxes and levies	CMNK	77	74	79	90	CMOJ	466	508	515	556
National (non-domestic business) rates	CMNH	74	73	75	81	CMOG	398	468	469	481
Other amounts paid for taxes, duties and levies	CMNJ	3	1	4	8	CMOI	67	40	46	75
Capital expenditure[3]										
Capital acquisitions	CMNN	291	364	345	336	CMOM	1 351	1 222	1 117	1 154
Capital disposals	CMNO	22	38	192	55	CMON	128	112	187	129
Net capital expenditure	CMNI	269	326	153	280	CMOH	1 223	1 110	930	1 025
Work of a capital nature carried out by your own staff (included in acquisitions)	CMNP	7	–	2	–	CMOO	5	4	3	4
Stocks[3]										
Increase during year	CMNL	48	4	2	10	CMOK	14	25	5	13
Value at end of year	CMNM	141	89	102	137	CMOL	298	295	313	326
Purchases of goods and services[3]										
Total purchases	CMNG	1 102	1 184	1 461	1 744	CMOF	8 544	8 637	9 546	10 045
Energy, water and materials	CMMX	233	249	360	449	CMNW	4 231	4 144	4 775	5 053
Goods for resale	CMMY	311	390	411	592	CMNX	2 154	2 067	2 345	2 421
Hiring, leasing of plant, machinery etc.	CMMZ	6	9	8	14	CMNY	42	62	54	48
Commercial insurance premiums	CMNA	32	29	59	59	CMNZ	94	119	117	139
Road transport services	CMNB	4	10	7	11	CMOA	33	38	30	51
Telecommunication services	CMNC	15	12	19	17	CMOB	62	67	71	71
Computer and related services	CMND	20	7	8	13	CMOC	35	28	34	41
Advertising and marketing services	CMNE	78	73	112	111	CMOD	203	248	231	251
Other services	CMNF	402	405	476	480	CMOE	1 689	1 865	1 888	1 969
Employment costs[3]										
Total employment costs	CMMW	428	488	554	578	CMNV	3 790	4 031	4 276	4 638
Gross wages and salaries paid	CMMT	392	450	507	523	CMNS	3 508	3 751	3 971	4 302
National insurance and pension contributions	CMMU	36	38	47	55	CMNT	282	280	305	336
Gross margin[4]										
Amount	CMQV	1 623	1 921	2 260	2 585	CMQY	13 533	14 085	14 936	16 260
As a percentage of turnover	CMQW	*83.8*	*83.2*	*84.7*	*81.4*	CMQZ	*86.0*	*87.6*	*86.3*	*86.8*
Value added at basic prices[4]	CMQX	888	1 128	1 212	1 434	CMRA	7 164	7 544	7 744	8 665
Accommodation										
Number of establishments	CMNQ	4 564	4 247	6 962	6 255	CMOP	1 106	1 809	1 965	1 609
Letting bedplaces	CMRR	940 003	895 191	857 489	1 534 124	CMOQ	55 590	55 406	51 974	42 445

24.4
Catering and allied trades[1]
United Kingdom
continued

		Licensed clubs with entertainment, independent, tenanted, managed public houses or wine bars (SIC 92 55.40)[5]					Canteen operator, catering contractor (SIC 92 55.51 and 55.52)			
		2001	2002	2003	2004		2001	2002	2003	2004
Number of businesses	MKEO	46 320	47 914	47 475	48 146	MKEP	5 217	5 485	5 636	5 765
Total turnover[2]	CMOT	19 163	20 681	21 392	24 481	CMPS	5 985	6 624	6 670	7 382
Taxes and levies[3]										
Total taxes and levies	CMPI	559	611	602	687	CMQH	33	27	31	28
National (non-domestic business) rates	CMPF	497	557	548	628	CMQE	28	24	23	21
Other amounts paid for taxes, duties and levies	CMPH	62	54	53	59	CMQG	4	3	8	8
Capital expenditure[3]										
Capital acquisitions	CMPL	1 895	1 634	1 482	1 490	CMQK	185	144	164	211
Capital disposals	CMPM	273	284	317	262	CMQL	15	12	11	17
Net capital expenditure	CMPG	1 622	1 350	1 166	1 228	CMQF	169	132	153	194
Work of a capital nature carried out by your own staff (included in acquisitions)	CMPN	11	8	13	4	CMQM	–	–	–	–
Stocks[3]										
Increase during year	CMPJ	−11	19	28	40	CMQI	11	8	6	9
Value at end of year	CMPK	486	414	409	511	CMQJ	115	102	112	109
Purchases of goods and services[3]										
Total purchases	CMPE	9 423	10 222	10 675	11 857	CMQD	2 956	3 037	3 028	3 328
Energy, water and materials	CMOV	2 756	2 408	2 959	3 468	CMPU	1 951	2 078	2 022	2 343
Goods for resale	CMOW	4 166	4 836	5 151	5 508	CMPV	455	411	455	457
Hiring, leasing of plant, machinery etc.	CMOX	145	188	116	138	CMPW	34	42	44	38
Commercial insurance premiums	CMOY	141	148	150	177	CMPX	24	27	44	30
Road transport services	CMOZ	16	26	25	17	CMPY	27	23	13	15
Telecommunication services	CMPA	77	79	79	86	CMPZ	17	20	20	23
Computer and related services	CMPB	23	39	33	48	CMQA	20	22	24	22
Advertising and marketing services	CMPC	114	136	127	128	CMQB	25	26	32	19
Other services	CMPD	1 984	2 362	2 036	2 287	CMQC	405	389	374	380
Employment costs[3]										
Total employment costs	CMOU	3 647	3 745	3 834	4 307	CMPT	2 095	2 219	2 293	2 503
Gross wages and salaries paid	CMOR	3 390	3 484	3 566	3 986	CMPQ	1 926	2 029	2 090	2 280
National insurance and pension contributions	CMOS	257	260	268	321	CMPR	169	190	204	222
Gross margin[4]										
Amount	CMRB	12 126	12 819	13 182	15 447	CMRE	4 811	5 508	5 480	6 238
As a percentage of turnover	CMRC	*74.2*	*72.7*	*71.9*	*73.7*	CMRF	*91.3*	*90.9*	*92.3*	*93.2*
Value added at basic prices[4]	CMRD	6 902	7 469	7 708	9 111	CMRG	2 321	2 885	2 907	3 367
Accommodation										
Number of establishments	CMPO	5 445	3 970	5 018	6 047					
Letting bedplaces	CMPP	88 877	71 214	77 371	110 134					

1 See chapter text.
2 Inclusive of VAT.
3 Exclusive of VAT.

4 The total turnover figure used to calculate these data excludes VAT.
5 Includes figures for managed public houses owned by breweries.

Source: Office for National Statistics: 01633 812435

Sources

This index of sources gives the titles of official publications or other sources containing statistics allied to those in the tables of this *Annual Abstract.* These publications provide more detailed analyses than are shown in the *Annual Abstract.* This index includes publications to which reference should be made for short-term (monthly or quarterly) series. Further advice on published statistical sources is available from the National Statistics Customer Contact Centre on the numbers provided on page ii.

Table number and subject in Abstract	Government department or other organisation	Official publication or other source

1. Area

1.1	Ordnance Survey Ordnance Survey of Northern Ireland	
	Office for National Statistics	Regional Trends (annual, Palgrave Macmillan)

2. Parliamentary elections

Elections

2.1	University of Plymouth for the Electoral Commission	British Electoral Facts 1832–1999 (Ashgate) Dod's Parliamentary Companion (annual)

By–elections

2.2	University of Plymouth for the Electoral Commission	Vachers Parliamentary Companion (quarterly) Social Trends (annual, Palgrave Macmillan)

3. International development

3.1, 3.2	Department for International Development	Statistics on International Development 2000/01–2004/05, Tables 1,2 and 12

4. Defence

4.1 – 4.11	Ministry of Defence/DASA	UK Defence Statistics 2003 (The Stationery Office (TSO))

5. Population and vital statistics

Population

		Census

5.1 – 5.3, 5.5	Office for National Statistics	*England and Wales*: Census reports 1911, 1921, 1931, 1951,
		    1961, 1971, 1981 and 1991
		Census 1991, Key Population and Vital Statistics; Great Britain,
		Digest of Welsh Statistics (annual, Welsh Assembly
		    Government)

	General Register Office (Scotland)	*Scotland*: Census reports 1951, 1961, 1971, 1981 and 1991 Census 1991, Key statistics for urban areas: Scotland
	Northern Ireland Statistics and Research Agency	*Northern Ireland:* Census of population 1951, 1961, 1966 and 1971, 1981 and 1991
		Resident population: mid–year estimates
5.1 – 5.3, 5.5	Office for National Statistics	*England and Wales*: Series FM (Family statistics), DH (Deaths), MB (Morbidity), PP (Population estimates and projections), MN (Migration) and VS (Key population and vital statistics) Series PP1, Population estimates: The Registrar General's estimates of the population of regions and local government

430

Table number and subject in Abstract	Government department or other organisation	Official publication or other source
		areas of England and Wales Population Trends (quarterly Palgrave Macmillan) Health Statistics Quarterly (Palgrave Macmillan)
	General Register Office (Scotland)	*Scotland*: Annual report of the Registrar General for Scotland Annual estimate of the population of Scotland
	Northern Ireland Statistics and Research Agency	*Northern Ireland*: Annual report of the Registrar General
5.6	Office for National Statistics	

Projections

5.1 – 5.3	Government Actuary's Department	
	Office for National Statistics: Government Actuary's Department	Series PP2, Population projections – national figures

Migration

5.7, 5.8, 5.9	Office for National Statistics	International Migration – first release of 2005 estimates Series MN (International migration) Population Trends (quarterly, Palgrave Macmillan)
5.10, 5.11	Home Office	Control of immigration statistics United Kingdom (annual) Asylum Statistics United Kingdom (annual)

Vital statistics

5.4, 5.12 – 5.22	Office for National Statistics	*England and Wales*: Series FM (Births, marriages and divorce statistics), DH (Deaths), MB (Morbidity), PP (Population estimates and projections), MN (International migration) and VS (Key population and vital statistics) Population Trends (quarterly, Palgrave Macmillan)
5.4, 5.12 – 5.21	General Register Office (Scotland)	*Scotland*: Annual report of the Registrar General for Scotland Quarterly return of births, deaths and marriages
	Northern Ireland Statistics and Research Agency	*Northern Ireland*: Annual report of the Registrar General Quarterly return of births, deaths and marriages
5.14	Northern Ireland Court Service	Northern Ireland Judicial Statistics (annual)
5.18	Scottish Executive Department of Health	
5.22	Government Actuary's Department	*England and Wales*: Interim Life Table *Scotland*: Interim Life Table *Northern Ireland*: Annual Report of the Registrar General
5.23	Office for National Statistics General Register Office (Scotland)	
	Northern Ireland Statistics and Research Agency	

6. Education

6.1 – 6.11	Department for Education and Skills	Education and Training Statistics for the United Kingdom (annual, TSO)
	Welsh Assembly Government	Digest of Welsh Statistics (annual) Statistics of education and training in Wales (annual and ad–hoc, WAG)
	Scottish Executive	Scottish educational statistics (annual and ad–hoc, SE) Scottish Social Statistics (annual)
	Northern Ireland Department of Education	Annual Abstract of Statistics, Northern Ireland (annual, DENI) Northern Ireland education statistics (annual and ad–hoc, DENI)
	Northern Ireland Department for Employment and Learning	Northern Ireland further and higher education statistics (annual and ad–hoc, DELNI)

Sources

Table number and subject in Abstract	Government department or other organisation	Official publication or other source
7. Labour market		
Labour Force Survey		
7.1 – 7.3, 7.6, 7.10, 7.11, 7.13, 7.16 – 7.18	Office for National Statistics	Labour Market Trends (monthly, Palgrave Macmillan)
7.4, 7.5	Office for National Statistics	
7.7	Cabinet Office	Civil Service Statistics (annual) Monthly Digest of Statistics (Palgrave Macmillan)
7.8	Office for National Statistids	Public Sector Employment
7.9	Office for National Statistics Home Office Scottish Executive	Labour Market Trends (monthly, Palgrave Macmillan)
Claimant count		
7.12, 7.14 7.15	Office for National Statistics	Labour Market Trends (monthly, Palgrave Macmillan)
7.19	Office for National Statistics	Labour Market Trends (monthly, Palgrave Macmillan) Monthly Digest of Statistics (Palgrave Macmillan)
Annual Survey of Hours and Earnings		
7.20, 7.21 7.24, 7.25	Office for National Statistics	Annual Survey of Hours and Earnings (annual, ONS)
Average Earnings Index		
7.22, 7.23	Office for National Statistics	Labour Market Trends (monthly, Palgrave Macmillan) Monthly Digest of Statistics (Palgrave Macmillan)
7.26	Certification Office	
8. Personal income, expenditure and wealth		
8.1	Office for National Statistics	Economic and Labour Market Review, May (monthly, Palgrave Macmillan)
8.2	Board of HM Revenue and Customs	HMRC National Statistics www.hmrc.gov.uk<http://www.hmrc.gov.uk> Economic and Labour Market Review, May (monthly, Palgrave Macmillan)
8.3 – 8.5	Office for National Statistics	Expenditure and Food Survey, annual) (1990 onwards edition- Family Spending) (annual, Palgrave Macmillan)
9. Health		
National Health Service		
9.1	Department of Health service	Appropriation Accounts (annual) Health and Personal Social Services Statistics for England (annual)
	Information Centre for Health and Social Care	Hospital Episode Statistics, England (Annual) General Phamaceutical Services in England and Wales 1996–2006
	Welsh Assembly Government	Health Statistics Wales (annual)
9.2	The Scottish Executive, NHS National Services Scotland	
9.3	Department of Health, Social Services and Public Safety (Northern Ireland)	Summary of Health and Personal Social Services (Northern Ireland) Accounts (annual) Hospital Statistics (annual)
9.4, 9.5	Information Centre for Health and Social Care Welsh Assembly Government Scottish Health Service, NHS National Services Scotland	Health and Personal Social Services Statistics for England (annual) Department of Health, Medical and Dental Workforce Census Health Statistics Wales (annual)

Table number and subject in Abstract	Government department or other organisation	Official publication or other source
Public health		
9.6	Office for National Statistics	Mortality statistics cause series DH2
	General Register Office (Scotland)	Annual Report of the Registrar General for Scotland
	Northern Ireland Statistics and Research Agency	Annual Report of the Registrar General for Northern Ireland
9.7	HPA Centre for Infections	Communicable Disease Statistics Series MB2 (annual)
		Annual Review of Communicable Diseases
	NHS in Scotland	Scottish Health Statistics (annual)
	NHS National Services Scotland	
	Communicable Disease Surveillance Centre (NI)	Annual report of the Registrar General Northern Ireland
		Quarterly return of births, deaths and marriages
9.8 – 9.10	Health and Safety Executive	Health and Safety Statistics (annual)

10. Social protection

Table number and subject in Abstract	Government department or other organisation	Official publication or other source
Social security pensions, benefits and allowances		
10.1	Department for Work and Pensions	National Insurance Fund Account (annual)
	H M Revenue and Customs	
	Department of Health, Social Services and Public Safety (Northern Ireland)	
10.2	Department for Work and Pensions	
10.3	HM Revenue and Customs	
10.4, 10.5	Department for Work and Pensions (Information and Analysis Directorate)	
	Ministry of Defence/DASA (Pay and Pensions)	
	H M Revenue and Customs	
10.6 – 10.8, 10.12 – 10.19	Department for Work and Pensions (Information and Analysis Directorate)	
10.9, 10.11	H M Revenue and Customs	
10.15	Ministry of Defence/DASA (Pay and Pensions)	
Working Family Tax Credit		
10.10	H M Revenue and Customs	Quarterly Enquiry United Kingdom (quarterly)
	Department for Work and Pensions (Information and Analysis Directorate)	
Social services		
10.20, 10.21 – 10.24	Office for National Statistics	Appropriation (annual)
	Department for Education and Skills	Northern Ireland Annual Abstract of Statistics
10.20	HM Treasury	HM Treasury Expenditure Statistical Analyses
Housing and community amenities		
10.25	Office for National Statistics	

Sources

Table number and subject in Abstract	Government department or other organisation	Official publication or other source
11. Crime and justice		
11.1	Home Office	Police Service Strength England and Wales 2002/03 Home Office Statistical Bulletin 11/03
	Scottish Executive Justice Department	Scotland: Report of Her Majesty's Chief Inspector of Constabulary for Scotland (annual)
	The Police Service of Northern Ireland	The Chief Constable's Annual Report
11.2	Home Office	Crime in England and Wales 2003/04 (Home Office Statistical Bulletin 10/04) Crime in England and Wales 2005/06 (Home Office Statistical Bulletin 12/06)
11.3 – 11.9	Home Office	Criminal Statistics, England and Wales (annual) (TSO) Offender Management Caseload Statistics 2003 (annual) Digest of Welsh Statistics (annual, Welsh Office)
11.10 – 11.11	Home Office	Offender Management Caseload Statistics 2005
11.12	Home Office	HM Prison Service Annual Report and Accounts April 2005 – March 2006
11.13	Scottish Executive Justice Analytical Services Division	Recorded Crime in Scotland, 2005/06
11.14 – 11.17	Scottish Executive Justice Analytical Services Division	Criminal Proceedings in Scottish Courts, 2004/05
11.18, 11.19	Scottish Executive Justice Department	Prison Statistics Scotland, 2002 Scottish Prison Service Annual Report and Accounts 2001–03
11.20	The Police Service of Northern Ireland	
11.21 – 11.23	Northern Ireland Office	A Commentary on Northern Ireland Crime Statistics 2003 A Commentary on Northern Ireland Crime Statistics 2004
12. Lifestyles		
12.1	Department for Culture, Media and Sport	Department for Culture, Media and Sport Annual Report 2005
12.2	Department for Culture, Media and Sport	Labour Market Trends (monthly, Palgrave Macmillan)
12.3	Cinema Advertising Association	
12.4	CAA/Gallup/Nielsen EDI	
12.5	UK Film Council	Monthly Digest of Statistics (Palgrave Macmillan)
12.6	VisitBritain Wales Tourist Board VisitScotland Northern Ireland Tourist Board	The UK Tourist: Statistics (annual) www.staruk.org.uk The national tourism statistics website
12.7 – 12.8	Office for National Statistics	Travel Trends (annual, Palgrave Macmillan) Overseas Travel and Tourism First Release Monthly Digest of Statistics (Palgrave Macmillan) International Passenger Survey MQ6 Overseas Travel and Tourism
12.9	Target Group Index, BMRB International	
12.10	Department for Culture, Media and Sport	Camelot – National Lottery Press Releases
	Gaming Board for Great Britain	The Gaming Board for Great Britain Annual Report www.gbgb.org.uk

Table number and subject in Abstract	Government department or other organisation	Official publication or other source

13. Environment

Table number and subject in Abstract	Government department or other organisation	Official publication or other source
13.1, 13.20	Office for National Statistics	Environmental Accounts 2006 autumn edition (biennial) www.nationalstatistics.gov.uk/statbase/Product.asp?vlnk=3698
13.2 – 13.7, 13.9, 13.13, 13.14, 13.16 – 13.18, 13.21	Department for Environment, Food and Rural Affairs	e-Digest of Environmental Statistics (annual) www.defra.gov.uk/environment/statistics/index.htm The Environment in your Pocket (annual)
13.8	Centre for Ecology and Hydrology, Wallingford	www.ceh-nerc.ac.uk/data/NWA.htm
	The Met Office	www.met-office.gov.uk
13.10	Scottish Environmental Protection Agency	www.sepa.org.uk/pdf/data/classification/water_qual_class_2003.pdf
13.11	Centre for Ecology and Hydrology, Wallingford	www.ceh-nerc.ac.uk/data/NWA.htm
	Environment Agency	www.environment-agency.gov.uk
	Water plcs	
13.12	Office of Water	Financial performance and expenditure of the water companies in England and Wales: 2004–2005 & 2005–2006 reports
	Services (OFWAT)	
13.15	Environment Agency	
13.19	The Chartered Institute of Environmental Health The Royal Environmental Health Institute of Scotland	

14. Housing

Table number and subject in Abstract	Government department or other organisation	Official publication or other source
14.1	Communities and Local Government Welsh Assembly Government Scottish Executive Department for Social Development, Northern Ireland	
14.2	Office for National Statistics	General Household Survey
	Northern Ireland Statistics Research Agency	Continuous Household Survey
14.3	Communities and Local Government	
	Welsh Assembly Government	Welsh Housing Statistics (annual, NAfW)
	Scottish Executive	Statistical Bulletins on Housing (SE)
	Department for Social Development, Northern Ireland	Northern Ireland Housing Statistics (annual)
14.4	Communities and Local Government	
14.5	Communities and Local Government Welsh Assembly Government	
14.6	Council of Mortgage Lenders	
14.7	HM Court Service Northern Ireland Court Service	

Sources

Table number and subject in Abstract	Government department or other organisation	Official publication or other source
14.8	Communities and Local Government Welsh Assembly Government Scottish Executive	
14.9	Communities and Local Government	Statutory Homelessness Statistical Release (quarterly) http://www.communities.gov.uk/index.asp?id=1156302

15. Transport and communications

General

15.1, 15.2, 15.4	Department for Transport	
15.3	Office for National Statistics	

Road transport

15.5 – 15.12	Department for Transport	Office for National Statistics (annual, TSO) Vehicle Licensing Statistics (annual, TSO) Monthly Digest of Statistics (Palgrave Macmillan) Road Casualties Great Britain (annual, TSO) Road accidents Wales (annual, National Assembly for Wales) Office for National Statistics: Department for Transport
15.11		Driving Standards Agency
15.13, 15.14	Department for Regional Development, Northern Ireland	Publication: Transport Statistics NI Source: Driver Vehicle Licencing Northern Ireland

Rail transport

15.20, 15.21	Department for Transport	Office for National Statistics (annual, TSO) Health and Safety Executive: Industry and Services (annual) Bulletin of Rail Statistics (quarterly)
15.22, 15.23	Department for Regional Development, Northern Ireland	Translink

Air transport

15.24 – 15.28	Civil Aviation Authority	Monthly Digest of Statistics (Palgrave Macmillan) Civil Aviation Authority; Annual Statements of Movements, Passengers and Cargo Civil Aviation Authority; Monthly Statements of Movements, Passengers and Cargo

Sea transport

15.29, 15.30	Department for Transport	Maritime Statistics (annual, TSO) Monthly Digest of Statistics (Palgrave Macmillan)

Communications

15.31	Royal Mail Parcel Force Capita Business Services Ltd. Post Office Counters Ltd.	Monthly Digest of Statistics (Palgrave Macmillan) Post Office report and accounts (annual)

16. National accounts

16.1 – 16.22	Office for National Statistics	United Kingdom National Accounts (annual, Palgrave Macmillan) Monthly Digest of Statistics (Palgrave Macmillan)

17. Prices

Producer prices

17.1, 17.2	Office for National Statistics	Producer Price Index Press Notice (monthly) Business Monitor MM22, Producer Price Indices Monthly Digest of Statistics (Palgrave Macmillan)

Table number and subject in Abstract	Government department or other organisation	Official publication or other source
Consumer prices		
17.3 – 17.6	Office for National Statistics	Monthly Digest of Statistics (Palgrave Macmillan) Labour Market Trends (monthly, Palgrave Macmillan) Focus on Consumer Price Indices (monthly, ONS)
17.7, 17.8	Department for Environment, Food and Rural Affairs	Agriculture in the UK (annual) Agricultural Price Indices, Statistical notice (monthly) Monthly Digest of Statistics (Palgrave Macmillan)
17.9	Department for Environment, Food and Rural Affairs	Economic and Labour Market Review, May (monthly, Palgrave Macmillan) Agriculture in the UK (annual) UK Economic Accounts (quarterly, Palgrave Macmillan)

18. Government finance

Central government		
18.1 – 18.3	Office for National Statistics	Financial Statistics (monthly, Palgrave Macmillan)
18.4	HM Treasury	Consolidated Fund and National Loans Fund Accounts
	Office for National Statistics	Financial Statistics (monthly, Palgrave Macmillan)
18.5	Office for National Statistics	United Kingdom National Accounts (annual, Palgrave Macmillan)
18.6 – 18.7	HM Treasury	Consolidated Fund and National Loans Fund Accounts
	Office for National Statistics	Financial Statistics (monthly, Palgrave Macmillan)
18.8	Bank of England	
Central government		
18.9, 18.10	HM Revenue & Customs	HM Revenue & Customs website
Rateable values		
18.11	HM Revenue & Customs	HM Revenue & Customs website
Local authorities		
18.12, 18.13	Communities and Local Government	Local government financial statistics (England) (annual)
	Welsh Assembly Government	Welsh local government financial statistics (annual)
	Public Works Loan Board	Annual report of the Public Works Loan Board
	Scottish Executive Statistical Support for Local Government	Local financial returns (Scotland) (annual)
	Department of Finance and Personnel for Northern Ireland	
	Department of the Environment for Northern Ireland	
	Chartered Institute of Public Finance and Accountancy	
18.14	Communities and Local Government	Local government financial statistics (England) (annual)
	Welsh Assembly Government	Welsh local government financial statistics (annual)
18.15, 18.16	Communities and Local Government	Local government financial statistics (England) (annual)
18.17 – 18.19	Scottish Executive, Statistical Support for Local Government	Local financial returns (Scotland) (annual) Capital Returns (Scotland) (annual)
18.20	Department of the Environment for Northern Ireland	District Council – Summary of Statement of Accounts (annual)

Sources

Table number and subject in Abstract	Government department or other organisation	Official publication or other source
19. External trade and investment		
19.1 – 19.8	HM Revenue & Customs	OTS1 – Overseas Trade Statistics – Extra EC, (formerly MM20) (monthly)
		OTS2 – Overseas Trade Statistics – Intra EC and World, (formerly MM20A) (monthly)
		OTSQ – Overseas Trade Statistics – Intra EC, (formerly MQ20) (quarterly)
		OTSA – Overseas Trade Statistics – Extra and Intra EC, (formerly MA20) (annual)
	Office for National Statistics	Business Monitor MM24, Monthly Review of External Trade Statistics (monthly, ONS)
		Overseas Trade Analysed in Terms of Industries MQ10 (quarterly, ONS)
		Monthly Digest of Statistics (monthly, Palgrave Macmillan)
19.9 – 19.18	Office for National Statistics	United Kingdom Balance of Payments (annual, Palgrave Macmillan)
	Bank of England	(quarterly, Palgrave Macmillan) UK Economic Accounts Financial Statistics (monthly, Palgrave Macmillan) Foreign Direct Investment MA4 (annual, National Statistics website)
20. Research and development		
20.1 – 20.4	Office for National Statistics	Business Monitor MA14, Research and Development in UK Business (annual, ONS), (monthly, Palgrave Macmillan),
		Gross Domestic Expenditure on Research and Development (annual, ONS)
21. Agriculture, fisheries and food		
Agriculture		
21.1, 21.2	Department for Environment, Food and Rural Affairs	Agriculture in the United Kingdom (annual)
21.3 – 21.5	Department for Environment, Food and Rural Affairs	Agricultural Statistics; United Kingdom (annual) Scottish Agricultural Economics (annual)
		Welsh Agricultural Statistics (annual, National Assembly for Wales)
21.6	Forestry Commission	Forestry Statistics (annual)
	Department of Agriculture and Rural Development (Northern Ireland)	Northern Ireland Annual Abstract of Statistics
21.7, 21.8	Department for Environment, Food and Rural Affairs	DEFRA Statistical Notice
Food		
21.9 – 21.12	Department for Environment, Food and Rural Affairs	Monthly Digest of Statistics (Palgrave Macmillan)
21.13	Department for Environment, Food and Rural Affairs	Agricultural Statistics, United Kingdom (annual)
Fisheries		
21.14, 21.15	Department of Environment, Food and Rural Affairs	England and Wales: Sea fisheries statistical tables (annual)
	Scottish Executive Agricultural Departments	Scotland: Fisheries of Scotland report (annual) Scottish Sea fisheries statistics (annual, TSO)

Table number and subject in Abstract	Government department or other organisation	Official publication or other source
Family Food		
21.16	Department for Environment, Food and Rural Affairs	Expenditure and Food Survey

22. Production

Table number and subject in Abstract	Government department or other organisation	Official publication or other source
Production and construction		
22.1	Office for National Statistics	Annual Business Inquiry (www.statistics.gov.uk/abi/)
Manufacturers sales		
22.2	Office for National Statistics	ProdCom: Product Sales and Trade Annual Reports – PRA series (annual, ONS)
		Product Sales and Trade Quarterly Reports – PRQ series (quarterly, ONS)
22.3	Office for National Statistics	UK Business: Activity, Size and Location (www.statistics.gov.uk/Ukbusiness)
Energy		
22.4 – 22.13	Department of Trade and Industry (Energy Strategy Unit)	Digest of United Kingdom Energy Statistics (annual) Energy Trends (monthly and quarterly) Annual Business Inquiry (www.statistics.gov.uk/abi/)
Iron and steel		
22.14 – 22.16	Iron and Steel	Iron and steel industry: annual statistics: published by the Iron and Steel Statistics Bureau Corporation Regional Trends (annual, Palgrave Macmillan)
Industrial materials		
22.17	World Bureau of Metal Statistics Aluminium Federation	World Metal Statistics (monthly) Annual Business Inquiry (www.statistics.gov.uk/abi/)
22.18	Agricultural Industries Confederation	Annual Business Inquiry (www.statistics.gov.uk/abi/)
Minerals		
22.19	Department for Communities and Local Government	Minerals (Business Monitor PA 1007) (annual, ONS) Natural Environment Research Council: United Kingdom
	Department of Trade and Industry	Minerals Yearbook
	Department of Economic Development (Northern Ireland)	Northern Ireland Annual Abstract of Statistics
Building Materials		
22.20	Department of Trade and Industry	Monthly Statistics of Building Materials and Components (DTI) Monthly Digest of Statistics (Palgrave Macmillan)
Construction (output)		
22.21	Department of Trade and Industry	Construction Statistics Annual (DTI)
Construction (new orders)		
22.22	Department of Trade and Industry	Construction Statistics Annual (DTI)
Engineering		
22.23, 22.24	Office for National Statistics	Monthly Production Inquiry (ONS)
Motor vehicle production		

Sources

Table number and subject in Abstract	Government department or other organisation	Official publication or other source
22.25	Office for National Statistics	Business Monitor PM 34.10, (monthly, ONS) Sector Review–Motor Trades (formerly Business Monitor SDA27) annual Palgrave Macmillan
Drink and tobacco		
22.26, 22.27	HM Revenue and Customs	Annual report of the Commissioners of HM Revenue and Customs (http//www.hmc.gov.uk/stat/tax_receipt/menu.html http//www.uktradeinfo.com/indexcfm?task=statbulltwo
	Office for National Statistics	Monthly Digest of Statistics (Palgrave Macmillan)

23. Banking, insurance, etc

Banking		
23.1	Bank of England	Bank of England Annual Report and Accounts
23.2	Association for Payment Clearing Services	Yearbook of Payment Statistics
23.3 – 22.5	Bank of England	Bank of England, Statistical Interactive Database
23.6	Bank of England	Bank of England, Statistical Interactive Database
23.7	Bank of England	Bank of England, Statistical Interactive Database
23.8	Bank of England	Bank of England Quarterly Bulletin
23.9 – 23.12	Bank of England	Monthly Digest of Statistics (Palgrave Macmillan) Financial Statistics (monthly, Palgrave Macmillan)
Other financial institutions		
23.13	Financial Services Authority	Building Societies: Statistical Tables www.fsa.gov.uk/pubs/annual/ar03_04/bs_statistics.html
23.14	Office for National Statistics	Business Monitor SDQ7, Assets and Liabilities of Finance Houses and Other Credit Companies (quarterly, ONS)
23.15	Office for National Statistics	Financial Statistics (monthly, Palgrave Macmillan) Monthly Digest of Statistics (Palgrave Macmillan) Business Monitor MQ5, Insurance Companies; Pension Funds and Trusts Investments (quarterly, ONS) First Release
23.16, 23.17	Office for National Statistics	Financial Statistics (monthly, Palgrave Macmillan) Business Monitor MQ5, Insurance Companies; Pension Funds and Insolvency Trusts Investments (quarterly, ONS)
23.18 – 23.21	Department of Trade and Industry	Insolvency Annual Report (DTI) Companies (DTI) Financial Statistics (monthly, Palgrave Macmillan)

24. Service industry

Retail trades		
24.1	Office for National Statistics	Annual Business Inquiry (www.statistics.gov.uk/abi/)
24.2	Office for National Statistics	Business Monitor SDM 28 (www.statistics.gov.uk/rsi)
Motor trades		
24.3	Office for National Statistics	Annual Business Inquiry (www.statistics.gov.uk/abi/)
Catering		
24.4	Office for National Statistics	Annual Business Inquiry (www.statistics.gov.uk/abi/)

Index

Figures indicate table numbers

The Focus On Series
from the Office for National Statistics

The *Focus On* series presents in-depth commentary reports examining different subjects and groups of people in the United Kingdom. Combining data from the 2001 Census of Population and other official sources, the reports provide an up-to-date and comprehensive analysis of their topic area. These reports are aimed at a wide audience including policy makers, researchers, students and members of the general public.

Focus On People and Migration

Focus on People and Migration provides an up-to-date and comprehensive description of the UK population at the start of the Twenty-first century. It includes information on changes in the age structure of the UK, population growth and the role of fertility and migration in driving population change.

DECEMBER 2005
£50.00 ● 1-4039-9327-0 ● 978-1-4039-9327-4

Focus On The Digital Age

This report provides a comprehensive statistical picture of how information and communications technology is impacting on society in the UK.

FEBRUARY 2007
£40.00 ● 1-4039-9326-2 ● 978-1-4039-9326-7

Focus On Ethnicity and Religion

This report illustrates the ethnic and religious diversity of Great Britain and the relationship between these two important aspects of identity. It provides a readable introduction to the subject, presenting information on key demographic, geographic, household and labour market differences between the main ethnic and religious groups. The report also considers the factors that contribute to these differences and illustrates the changes between 1991 and 2001.

OCTOBER 2006
£50.00 ● 1-4039-9328-9 ● 978-1-4039-9328-1

Focus On Older People

Focus On Older People provides a detailed picture of people aged 50 and over in the UK today. It includes information on their characteristics, lifestyles and experiences, placing particular emphasis on changes with age.

NOVEMBER 2005
£40.00 ● 1-4039-9751-9 ● 978-1-4039-9751-7

Keep Up-to-Date with National Statistics from Palgrave Macmillan

Palgrave Macmillan's e-Newsletter brings you the most up-to-date information on publication dates, prices and forthcoming products from the Office for National Statistics.

Register at **www.palgrave.com/ONS/mailinglist** to receive this monthly newsletter.

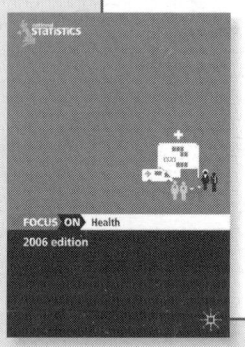

Focus On Health

Combining data from the 2001 Census of Population and other official sources, *Focus On Health* explores topics such as mortality, mental health, sexual health, eating and physical exercise and smoking, as well as public health issues including caring and carers and the use of the health services.

JANUARY 2006
£50.00 ● 1-4039-9325-4 ● 978-1-4039-9325-0

www.palgrave.com/ons

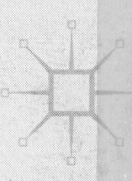